HOME TO WAR

HOME

TO WAR

A History of the
Vietnam Veterans' Movement

GERALD NICOSIA

 CROWN PUBLISHERS • NEW YORK

Excerpts from W. D. Ehrhart's *Passing Time: Memoir of a Vietnam Veteran Against the War* (Amherst, MA: University of Massachusetts Press, 1995), used by permission of author.

Lines from "O! Camil (the Winter Soldier)" are © 1971 Nashnotes, BMI, Inc., and used by permission of Graham Nash.

Lines from "Claymore Polka" are © 1988 James Wachtendonk and used by permission of the author.

Lines from Holly Near's "Hang in There" are © 1973 Holly Near and Hereford Music and used by permission of the author.

Published by Crown Publishers, New York, New York.
Member of the Crown Publishing Group.

Random House, Inc. New York, Toronto, London, Sydney, Auckland
www.randomhouse.com

CROWN is a trademark and the Crown colophon is a registered trademark of Random House, Inc.

Printed in the United States of America

Design by LEONARD W. HENDERSON

Library of Congress Cataloging-in-Publication Data
Nicosia, Gerald.
Home to war: a history of the Vietnam veterans' movement / Gerald Nicosia.
Includes bibliographical references and index.
1. Vietnam Veterans Against the War—History. 2. Vietnamese Conflict,
1961–1975—Protest movements—United States. 3. Veterans—United States—
Political activity—History—20th century. I. Title.

DS559.62.U6 N53 2000
959.704'3373—dc21   00-064417

ISBN 0-8129-9103-6

10 9 8 7 6 5 4 3 2 1

First Edition

This book is dedicated to

Bill Ehrhart, who first showed me the anger,

Bill Trautman, who first told me the stories,

Ron Kovic, who first confronted me with the reality,

Bobby Waddell, who first told me (from his prison cell in Tehachapi) to write it as a book,

Bobby Muller, who gave me a place to stay,

Larry Heinemann, who told me to "shake off the pain,"

Sarah Haley, rest in peace, who gave me my title,

Mary Sue Planck, rest in peace, who reminded me of the unsung heroes, and who was one herself,

Angel Almedina, rest in peace, who kept me laughing,

Jack McCloskey, rest in peace, who offered me help even when his heart was failing,

Max Inglett, rest in peace, who told me to "hang in there . . . a little bit longer,"

Elmo R. Zumwalt Jr., rest in peace, who encouraged and aided me in the last difficult year, and to whom this nation and especially its veterans owe an incalculable debt,

And to

All those on both sides who fought in the Vietnam War,

All those on both sides who refused to fight,

All those who sought to aid their healing.

Contents

Chapter 10
Decade of Betrayal: The Vet Centers in the Eighties

Chapter 11
The Price of War: Settlement of the Class Action Lawsuit and "One Small Step Toward Resolution"

Veterans are the tip of the candle flame.
  —Thich Nhat Hanh

Oh! Camil, tell me why are you in this place?
When you stood up for justice, your country replied
by throwing it back in your face.
  —Graham Nash, "Oh! Camil (the Winter Soldier)"

The casualties of war go far beyond the battlefield.
  —Roger H. C. Donlon, Congressional Medal of Honor,
    Nam Dong, Vietnam, 1964

A whole bunch of people in the world
have no concept of what war is about.
  —James Farley, Marine Medium
    Helicopter Squadron 163,
    Da Nang, Vietnam, 1965

The war is never over in the mind of any veteran.
  —General Hal Moore,
    U.S. commander, Battle of the
    Ia Drang Valley, 1965

Prologue

Along with most of the men and women who served in the Vietnam War, I was a little kid in the fifties and a teenager in the sixties. The young Americans facing the Vietnam War draft had been formed in the late Eisenhower and Kennedy eras, a time of perhaps the greatest overall prosperity and optimism in American history. The Korean War, with its unthinkable battlefield losses to Communism, had dropped quickly into the national unconscious; and the hard-edged anger and paranoia of Cold Warriors like Joe McCarthy and John Foster Dulles were likewise rapidly being worn away, smoothed, and transformed by endless waves of good times and good feelings—delivered especially through the new medium of television.

It is hard now to realize how thoroughly apolitical most of the nation's young were in the early 1960s. Although the New Left, SDS Weathermen, Black Panthers, and the machine gun–toting Symbionese Liberation Army were only a few years away, the sensibility of 1963 was light years from that of, say, 1968. In 1963, the word *revolutionary* still referred to the American War of Independence. Certainly the dark shadows were already starting to fall over the American landscape, even as John Kennedy took the helm of state and uttered those fateful words on January 20, 1961: "Ask not what your country can do for you—ask what you can do for your country." And prophets of the troubled times ahead were making their voices heard. The civil rights movement, which first appeared as a bus boycott in Montgomery, Alabama, in 1955, had begun to shake the hypocritical foundations of American democracy like a mighty earthquake that just kept building.

The greatest spokesman of that movement, Martin Luther King Jr., insisted over and over again that one could not just cull out the wrongs and injustices of a society, keeping them separate from the daily life we hold dear, or file them for future reference—as in some big dead-letter bin of history. "Injustice anywhere is a threat to justice everywhere," he wrote in his "Letter from Birmingham City Jail" in April 1963. In 1967, in the "Declaration of Independence from the War in Vietnam" speech he gave at the Riverside Church in New York, a speech that cost him a great deal of popular and financial support, King made completely clear that he felt all America's ills—militarism, racism, the cruelty and arrogance of the rich toward the poor—were inextricably woven into a single fabric of doom, and that the only answer, the only hope, lay in getting outside the bound-

I

aries of our narrow-minded Americanism and redefining ourselves as "citizens of the world." "Our loyalties must become ecumenical rather than sectional," he concluded. "Every nation must now develop an overriding loyalty to mankind as a whole. . . . If we do not act we shall surely be dragged down the long dark and shameful corridors of time. . . ."

In several places in his Vietnam speech, King referred specifically to the specter of nuclear annihilation, making it clear that "long dark corridors" was not just poetic language, but that the choice for the future had really come down to a universal commitment to "compassion and nonviolence" versus nonexistence for us all. Indeed, "the bomb," as we called it when I was growing up, was the blackest shadow of all, one that none of us could shake, even in our dreams. If TV shows like *Ozzie and Harriet* and *Father Knows Best* made those of us growing up in the fifties know that life could be full of laughter and warm, fuzzy feelings, we also knew that everything could be taken away in the split second it took some politician to push that "little red button." Hiroshima and Nagasaki were but a foretaste, it seemed, of what lay in store for everyone on the planet after 1945.

With all that in view, it is still fair to say that the Vietnam War caught my generation by surprise. Just like the children's war games played by Ron Kovic and his friends on Long Island (which he describes in *Born on the Fourth of July*), my childhood pals and I outside of Chicago—fueled by the same gung-ho Hollywood movies—grew up with arsenals of toy guns and fought hundreds of imaginary battles against the Germans and the "Japs." As far as we knew, even into our teens, the world's bad guys had all been soundly beaten by our fathers' generation.

Part of what was going on, of course, was that our leaders were keeping from us the fact that a war was slowly being ignited in Southeast Asia. With the recent release of hundreds of White House tapes, we have finally gotten a glimpse of the backroom political debate that went on for years concerning the growing American military involvement in Vietnam. Even as Lyndon Johnson was winning the greatest landslide of any American presidential candidate, on November 3, 1964, he called one of his advisors to say, "I'm afraid of Vietnam." Two days after the election, he told Senate Majority Leader Mike Mansfield that he wanted the congressional leaders to be "careful" in plotting a strategy on Vietnam: "Let's look where we're going before we go."

Johnson's Secretary of Defense Robert McNamara told him: "It's a worrisome problem. None of us have a pat answer. . . ." Because they had no answers themselves, our leaders declined to give the "problem" of Vietnam high media visibility. They fumbled with it behind the scenes, in a dark of their own making; and the kid down the block, a kid like me, had no idea that a war was being secretly unleashed until the bombs began to fall right in front of us on our nightly television screens.

When that war was finally revealed, most of us couldn't help but be ambivalent about it. As Kovic and many others have related, we were a generation born and bred on patriotism, on the Pledge of Allegiance every day in school and absolute respect for the American flag, swallowing hard and feeling those little shiver-tingles every time we saw it blowing freely in the breeze. "The land of the free" was not a cliché for us; it was something we were thankful every day for being born into, since everyone from teachers to preachers kept drumming into us how horribly bad all those unfortunate wretches in the rest of the world had it, how glad they were just to get hold of the things we cast off—the used clothes and out-of-date canned food—if they weren't even worse off being tortured in some godawful prison for the rest of their born days just for opening their mouths once too often without thinking first. And as Vietnam veteran Scott Camil said so eloquently: "I believed that the best thing a person could do was give his life for his country." Nonetheless we—I and the young men I hung out with—felt more than a little uneasy about this war, about the way it was being presented to us by our president, with his grave expression and deeply furrowed brow, as one more necessary battle in the endless fight against tyranny. We didn't know any Vietnamese people; we couldn't recall anything they had ever done against us. We naturally wondered—having been brought up to respect and treat other people fairly, which was the "American way"— why we were being asked to go halfway around the world to kill them. For black people, the renowned heavyweight boxer Muhammad Ali expressed his own version of this sentiment: "Ain't no Viet Cong ever called me 'nigger.'"

Of course, we also listened to the rhetoric about "drawing a line against Communism," and so forth; but that argument also seemed pretty lame to many of us, knowing that our nation already had the biggest nuclear arsenal in the world. What use was a "line" when intercontinental ballistic missiles (ICBMs) laden with nuclear warheads could fly right over it—in either direction? And for that matter, why draw the line in some little country that we'd never heard of before, 13,000 miles away?

I was fifteen or sixteen years old when I heard a Catholic priest, in speaking about Vietnam, tell his congregation that it was a "good thing to kill Communists." This claim grated against a number of my ingrained beliefs—even though, like everyone else in my community, I firmly believed that Communism was evil. For one thing, I had been taught that as Americans we must always respect others' political creeds, even if we disagreed with them; and that if people were in the wrong, we must show them what was right. On a far deeper level, I had been taught—by my parents, teachers, and who knows what else, maybe even Andy Griffith's lectures to his television son Opie—to respect the sanctity of all life. *Weren't Communists human beings too, just like I was? So how could it be a good thing to kill them, unless they were actually pointing a rifle at my own head?*

I went out and bought my own Bible, something the priests had advised us against doing, and read in the Gospel according to St. Matthew: "Love your enemies, bless them that curse you, do good to them that hate you, and pray for them which despitefully use you, and persecute you; that ye may be the children of your Father which is in heaven; for he maketh his sun to rise on the evil and on the good, and sendeth rain on the just and on the unjust." When I read Thoreau, at about the same time, I knew that I had a moral duty *not* to fight in Vietnam or in any war I didn't see a clear necessity for.

Not all the potential draft resisters were coming from the kind of religious place I was, however. Some just had practical doubts about the worthiness of waging this particular war. Given the confused goals, the high cost, and the small likelihood of success, it "didn't make sense" to many (a phrase you heard a lot back then). It was only a hair's difference that tipped the scale one way for the young men who went to the war and the other way for those who chose not to. "Two roads diverged in a wood" for all of us, and most of us could just as well have gone either way; there were always pulls in both directions, but the choice we made then, usually out of haste and urgent pressures, has—as in Frost's famous poem—"made all the difference" for us later in life. Long after the war ended, Ron Kovic and I used to read that poem ("The Road Not Taken") aloud to each other, pondering how easily each of us might have taken the other's path.

I remember my father pushing me to enlist and "do your duty to your country." "They won't put you in the front line," he assured me. "You're a college graduate." Of course, they did put college graduates in the infantry, as Phi Beta Kappa and Macalester College student body president Tim O'Brien will attest; but that wasn't the point. It seemed impossible to explain Thoreauvian civil disobedience and passive resistance to my father, a flag-waving Italian-American who had served his country proudly in the Civilian Conservation Corps during the Depression (and then avoided World War II with a heart murmur and an infant son). Like many other young men, I agonized for months.

I was facing the loss of my own draft deferment in the spring of 1971, upon graduation from the University of Illinois in Chicago. I had a draft number low enough to ensure that I would be called up. President Richard Nixon and Vice President Spiro Agnew were both doing their best back then to make the country believe that good boys went to war and only bad boys stayed home. I knew in my bones that that was a phony dichotomy, but I did not have enough self-confidence or enough of a support system around me to make a public protest—as did someone like Stanford's student body president David Harris, who returned his draft card. I also did not think I would survive in a federal penitentiary, which is what Harris chose; but he was a foot taller than I was and guarded, in some sense, by the celebrity of being folksinger Joan Baez's husband.

A good lawyer could probably have found a way out for me; but to most working-class families like mine, hiring a lawyer was about as far-fetched as buying a seat on the stock exchange. Because my draft board was in redneck Berwyn, Illinois, and had reputedly refused conscientious-objector status even to ministers' sons, the only route I could see for myself was an expatriate's life in Canada. "Don't do it," my father told me. "You'll ruin your future." I appreciated the fact that he wasn't condemning me personally, just expressing his love for me in his own way. Still, I remember the immense relief I felt in April 1971, a little over a month before my graduation, upon seeing Vietnam veterans throwing their medals back at the Capitol, which was all over the nightly TV news. The veterans' protest confirmed my long-held suspicion that all of us, vets and nonvets, draft dodgers and "fortunate sons" like Al Gore and George W. Bush, were more alike than different—all of us held hostage to a malevolent stretch of American history, all of us doing our best "to play a bad hand" (in the surprising words of Chicago's hawkish Mayor Richard J. Daley, who had privately warned Lyndon Johnson to get out of Vietnam before his prosecution of the war destroyed the Democratic Party).

The summer of 1971 I went for my draft physical. I also went up to Toronto to check out my prospects for emigration, since my best friend, Larry, and his wife had already situated themselves up there, raving about the "clean, safe, nonviolent city" and the joys of living away from "military-mad America." In fact, I was not at all looking forward to exile, but dreading the isolation and distance from family and home that it portended. I had frequent nightmares of living in strange places, among strange people, and being desperate and yet unable to find my way back to a known world. That June the draft law expired, and for the first time there was significant opposition in Congress to perpetuating the war. Several U.S. senators, led by Mike Gravel of Alaska and Frank Church of Idaho, filibustered the renewal of the Selective Service Act. Without a draft law in place, there could be no actual draft calls; and when the law was finally renewed, at the end of December, the Selective Service decided to call it quits for the year. By then, Nixon had withdrawn a good portion of the American ground troops and switched American involvement largely to an air war over North Vietnam, drastically reducing the need for manpower in the armed forces. Since under the draft-lottery system, you were only vulnerable for one year, I passed beyond the military's clutches as the calendar turned to 1972.

Graduate school awaited me. My own private war was over.

I did not know many Vietnam veterans during those middle years of the 1970s. Nor did I think much about the war, as I struggled to find a job in a depressed and reeling economy—gasoline shortages, soaring inflation—and pursue a writer's life in working-class Chicago. I remember the televised images of the fall of Saigon in 1975, the helicopters airlifting American personnel and fleeing Vietnamese from the roof of the embassy, but it did not have anywhere near the emotional impact of personal crises in my own life at the time. Perhaps the aftermath of the war came home to me most powerfully at that time during the periodic visits I made to see Larry up in Toronto. We had been among the brightest students at a first-rate suburban high school, and both of us had won honors in college—myself in English, he in anthropology. In another era, we might have ended up fellow staff members at a good university, visiting each other's homes on alternate Friday nights and watching our kids grow. But here we were, him divorced and me chronically alone, both of us underemployed, prone to depression, angry at what we called the system, and living largely dysfunctional lives, in two different countries—and somehow the war seemed to have a lot to do with all that.

And then the war, and especially the veterans, came back into sudden focus for me in 1977, when I met Bill Ehrhart. I used to hang around the office of my former writing instructor, poet Michael Anania, at the University of Illinois; one day he asked me along to lunch with one of his poetry students. At this point, having thrown away a four-year fellowship to UCLA, I thought of most graduate students as fatuous and did not relish their company, but this one turned out to be different. He was short, lean, and muscular, and the left side of his jaw and neck were marked by ugly scars. He was by far the most serious and intense young man I had met up till then. Over lunch, after a little preliminary literary chitchat, he related his experiences as a Marine sergeant in the ferocious battle of Hue during the Tet Offensive in 1968. He told us how a North Vietnamese rocket had just nearly missed taking his head off. The explosion, against a wall just behind him, had left him partially deaf for life.

Bill talked of his need to write about Vietnam, but how it was a struggle to concentrate on painful details for more than a few hours, and so he had ended up turning to poetry rather than prose. (No one, perhaps not even Bill, could know then that he would someday become one of the most important poets and prose writers of that war, with seventeen books to his credit by age fifty; but I was certain, even from that first meeting, that he would make some significant contribution with his life.) He also talked at length about the slow, hard process he had gone through of switching from a pro-war to an antiwar point of view; and how that process had been triggered by the things he had seen in Vietnam, which did not jibe with the idealistic beliefs of his youth that had caused him to volunteer for the Marines and for that war. His sentences were sharp-edged, tipped with an anger that cut into any detachment you might have tried to assume. Listening to him talk, in that raspy, chip-on-the-shoulder voice of his, was like watching a man wrestle with his angel—but whether it was a good angel or a bad angel was hard to tell. Through Ehrhart, I began to get my first glimpse—though I could not have articulated it just yet—that the war was still going on for those who had actually fought it.

A few years later, I would see that war being fought again right next to me for several hours inside my car in a driving rainstorm. In the summer of 1982, I was trying to drive nonstop, on too little sleep, the thousand miles from Boulder, Colorado, back to my on-again, off-again home in San Francisco. I didn't like to pick up hitchhikers, but I desperately needed another driver, especially as I headed into a blackening storm. At a little truck stop in Wamsutter, Wyoming, a stringy, clean-shaven guy, of medium height and a few years my senior, offered to drive if I'd get him to Little America, where he could pick up another truck. He was soft-spoken, his clothes were neat, and when he told me he was from Manteno, Illinois, where an old girlfriend of mine had lived, I finally said, "Sure."

For the next hundred miles, Ron Hansen° expertly guided my car through the lashing rain, but I did not get a chance to rest, as I'd hoped; for my driver talked nonstop about Vietnam. Since then, having interviewed nearly 500 Vietnam veterans, I have gotten used to watching those emotional floodgates open. But Hansen's performance, unprodded and totally unexpected, was astonishing to me then; though at that time I hardly knew what to make of it. He'd served in the Army from 1964 to 1970, intending to make the military his career, and had done two tours in Vietnam, the second commencing at the start of the Tet Offensive. The tension ("paranoia," he called it) of never knowing who the enemy was—"Let's have a drink," he'd heard Americans joke with Vietnamese in bars, "tomorrow we'll be shooting at each other"—was driving him crazy, and so was the tension of knowing you were as likely to get killed by misdirected American ordnance as by Viet Cong or North Vietnamese mortars and artillery. Not to mention "the shock to the nervous system of being suddenly flown directly into and out of combat zones." One day he flipped out, threatened to kill his sergeant when the sergeant tried to lead them into an obvious ambush, and they locked him up in a mental ward in-country for a few days.

He served out the remainder of his tour in the bush, and got shot and blown up with a mortar just hours before he was supposed to return to the States. "The luckiest ones were the ones that didn't come back," he said. When I looked puzzled, he added that "nobody's really told the story of Vietnam yet." He explained that he'd been "handled like a piece of meat" in Veterans Administration hospitals, where he saw paralytics waiting hours to be tended. The VA doctors told him he'd never walk again; but he chose to pay for a civilian hospital and got back on his feet defiantly, just in time to go out on the streets of America and hear himself called a killer because he wore the uniform he had expected would bring him a hero's welcome. He moved from city to city, in each one sensing "there were enemies all around," always feeling extremely vulnerable and anxious to protect himself.

°I have used a pseudonym, as I have never seen him again.

For years, he said, he was full of rage and would break out uncontrollably into cold sweats. After the death of his wife, he went off by himself to work, first in the Wyoming oil fields, and then, when those dried up, as a sheep-herder "up on a hill with just a dog and a gun and the coyotes gaining on you all the time." Finally he decided he'd "better get home before he starved to death," and ended up a cross-country trucker based out of Manteno, Illinois. Today I can recognize him as a victim of post-traumatic stress disorder (PTSD), as well as a member of what are loosely called "the tripwire vets"— those veterans whose betrayal runs so deep that they have chosen to turn their backs on the social world for good, even, in some cases, setting up perimeters around their domain to keep out strangers with the threat of violent harm. Certainly Ron Hansen, whose eyes held an extraordinary gentleness, had not been driven quite that far; but just as clearly, he was terribly hurting. "My biggest complaint," he said, "is that nobody ever gave me a debriefing when I left Vietnam." Nobody then or since had made any attempt to help him under-stand his traumatic experience there. "I don't want pity," he said. "I want understanding."

Ron Hansen returned to the anonymity so common to America's war heroes. I went on to minor celebrity as the biographer of Jack Kerouac, and got to meet a lot of people who had before been only names in the media to me. One of those people was Ron Kovic, the highly decorated Marine com-bat veteran whose memoir, *Born on the Fourth of July,* had won a *Playboy* writing award and was already being talked about as the basis for a major motion picture (though the star then being groomed for the role was Al Pacino, not Tom Cruise). The Vietnam War had put Kovic in a wheelchair for the rest of his life, and his mission now was to educate the world about both that war in particular and the true nature of war itself. In many ways Ron Kovic *was* the Vietnam War on wheels, his bushy walrus moustache hiding a complex array of emotions—the proud swagger and angry leer and sardonic smirk—that only occasionally you could catch flashing through his intelligent and not unkind eyes. I will always remember the first time he undressed in front of me, showed me the scar on his back where the AK-47 slug had exited, as well as the "gizmo" hooked to his penis and the urine bag it emptied into, strapped to one of his fragile, pencil-thin legs. I will also never forget those few, emotionally overwhelming times when he let down his dazzling show-man's mask, quit the endless hilarious clowning and occasionally tiresome inspirational cheer, and showed me the mountains of black rage and hatred that he struggled daily to keep in check.

It was through Ron that I met many of the VVAW people whose stories ini-tially inspired me to write this book. From Ron and his friends I learned that the hurt from that war was not over at all; that, quite the contrary, it was deepening every day of their lives and could easily become devastating, even fatal. I watched Bobby Waddell, whose drug problems in the Air Force in Saigon had followed him home in a big way, get sentenced to two years in Tehachapi state prison on a bad rap, most probably because the judge had been influenced by his troubled service record. When I visited Bobby there in March 1987, cooking steaks on a brazier in the snowy prison yard while armed guards looked down on us from above the barbed wire, he told me: "Damn it, you've got to write the story of the veterans. You've got the talent. I'll help you all I can." His words led to my own journey of more than ten years, 50,000 miles, and 600-plus interviews.

The last stop on my journey, appropriately enough, was here where I live in Corte Madera. I sat with the mayor, Phil Gioia, in a gazebo in his backyard, which abuts Corte Madera Lagoon. Inside his house, in the living room, was a special glass case, which held, among a wealth of other Vietnam memorabilia, two Silver Stars, two Bronze Stars with **V** for valor, and two Purple Hearts. Mayor Gioia had drawn my attention because he saw a great deal of action in Vietnam and yet claimed he had "no problems from the war." At fifty-three, Gioia is still trim and athletic and has clearly done well for himself. In addition to serving as mayor of this upscale Marin County village, he is CEO of a computer software company in the East Bay.

Unlike the majority of American soldiers who served in Vietnam, Gioia did not come from the working class. His father, a career Army officer, taught at West Point. Gioia himself graduated from the Virginia Military Institute in 1967, and he grew up in what he calls "the very small world" of the Army elite. The son of General George S. Patton Jr., "Old Blood and Guts," was their next-door neighbor in the fifties at the Academy; George S. Patton III and Gioia's dad were captains together. Among their close friends were some of this nation's most famous soldiers and their wives and children: Joe Love, who had won the Distinguished Service Cross at Pork Chop Hill in the Korean War, General Mark Clark (who had commanded the invasion of Italy in World War II) and his family, and the descendants of General John J. "Black Jack" Pershing, commander in chief of American Expeditionary Forces in World War I. Dick Pershing, the general's grandson, went to ranger school with Gioia, then to Vietnam with the 101st Airborne Division while Gioia went with the equally prestigious 82nd. Like so many of Gioia's friends, Dick Pershing was killed in action in Vietnam.

Starting as a second lieutenant—the enemy's favorite target—Gioia served two tours in Vietnam: the first in 1968, from which he was "medevaced" out; and the second, after returning from nine months in military hospitals, in 1969–1970. On both tours he was almost killed himself. In 1968, he fought in the same terrible battle for Hue that almost killed Bill Ehrhart. In the nearby

A Shau Valley, an NVA rifleman nailed him with two AK-47 rounds, the first through his left wrist, as he held a field telephone to his ear—it felt as if somebody had stepped up and hit him with a baseball bat—and the second through his rucksack. The bullet through his wrist paralyzed his left hand. Either bullet, shifted a few inches in trajectory, would have taken part of his head off. On his second tour, he served with the First Air Cavalry, then with the Fifth Cav in the very hot area called the Parrot's Beak along the Cambodian border. It was there that he was hit a second time, fighting the NVA's 272nd regiment in the Michelin rubber plantation. He came out on the short end of an encounter with a B-40 rocket–propelled grenade, a projectile that is made to take out a tank; but again, the gunner's aim had been off by a few inches, so the shell exploded against a rubber tree instead of his body, leaving only one hunk of steel stuck deep in his stomach muscle. After a subsequent, near-fatal bout of malaria, he returned to combat with the Fifth Special Forces, heading a Special Operations Group (SOG) team that ran secret patrols into Cambodia.

Like his father, Gioia returned from war to teach at West Point. Later, assigned to the staff of the Sixth Army at the Presidio in San Francisco in the mid-1970s, Gioia found the military, especially under President Jimmy Carter, dismal and demoralizing. In 1977, with almost ten years' service under his belt (half the way to retirement), he quit the Army to build a better future for himself in the private sector—beginning anew in the graduate business school at Stanford, where he was elected class president. His academic record was impressive enough for IBM to fly him up to their corporate headquarters in Armonk, New York. But the Wall Street firm of Morgan Stanley made him an even better offer. He launched headlong into an enormously successful business career, which included running the venture-capital group at the Bank of America.

"I really believe in the honor and ethics of soldiering," Gioia solemnly attests. "If the enemy's wounded, you give him medical aid. If the civilians are displaced, you try to help 'em. I really take that stuff seriously." So seriously that when he ran across Lieutenant William Calley, merely under house arrest at Fort Benning after being convicted of the premeditated murder of twenty-two Vietnamese civilians, he was outraged. "This dumpy little fuck was allowed to go to the officers' club and have dinner and have a drink and go home [every night]. I frankly thought they should have taken him out and hanged him."

Gioia makes me understand the mask that it is necessary for professional and/or successful soldiers to wear. The problem—and this has a lot to do with both the genesis and prolongation of PTSD symptoms—is that it is a very hard thing for soldiers to drop that mask, especially after it has been forced upon their psyche as a form of self-protection against the horrors of combat. Gioia insists that true PTSD is a fairly rare occurrence. He tells me the story of two photos. "One photo," he explains, "shows the young cherubic twenty-one-year-old second lieutenant, Fort Bragg, North Carolina, driving a sports car, never heard a shot fired [in anger] in my life." This is the young Lieutenant Gioia prior to going overseas. The second photo shows "a twenty-four-year-old captain, immediately upon coming back from Vietnam, second tour. Thousand-yard kind of stare, you know, no nonsense! It was just a world of difference in those two faces." Gioia says he thanks God that he doesn't look like that anymore. But I look at him, at the way one eye closes more than the other as he squints into the sun, at a certain hardness and resignation in his expression that a decade with the vets has sensitized me to, and I am not so sure he is correct, not so sure he has escaped the dreaded lifelong stigma of the Vietnam veteran— a stigma he would prefer to believe does not really exist.

This is not to suggest that Gioia was being disingenuous with me. I would say rather that he chose not to listen to part of himself—the part that, as he'll readily admit, good soldiers are trained to ignore. In a war, he tells me, "you just do what you have to do." Gioia, in fact, admits that at times he did experience survivor's guilt, especially when he was out of action for nine months in military hospitals while his buddies remained in the line of fire. But the Army psychiatrists "set him straight"; they told him just to concentrate on getting well enough to fight again. "That's how it worked," Gioia explains. Soldiers who survive in wartime have to be "as professional as possible." And a professional soldier does not dwell on losses or the meaning of loss. He learns to see the world "as pretty black and white." He also "doesn't get personally involved with who the enemy is. . . . Real professionals never get psychologically bound up with who's good or bad." In a word, you become *numb* to the niceties of feeling in the civilian world, because it helps you get your job done, and helps you stay alive.

When I ask Gioia if he still thinks about Vietnam every day, he does not hesitate to answer, "Yeah, very definitely." He tells me about the many different unit reunions he's been to (of his Special Forces team, his rifle company, etc.), and how he now uses the Internet to stay in touch with his former military comrades. "It was a big thing, it was a very big thing," he says, "and I think that's why I see the other side of life." In reference to having gone to Vietnam, Gioia uses the phrase coined by American Civil War veterans: "seeing the elephant." To see the elephant, he explains, is to suddenly come to grips with the big issues of life: pain, mortality, and the question: *Why was I spared when others weren't?* "Vietnam was something that was so huge," he continues, "and it was so much bigger than all of us, that it pulled you into this thing where every day you didn't know whether you'd live to see another sunrise. And you'd watch people arbitrarily blown away. I mean, most of the guys were eighteen-, nineteen-, twenty-year-olds. Today, you talk to people who've got kids that are eighteen or nineteen, they haven't figured out what they want to do with their lives yet. By then in Vietnam, these guys were sleeping on the floor of a jungle for weeks at a time, getting rained on, putting up with bugs, wild animals, *the enemy,* fear, homesickness. That's a real challenging thing for a young man, very challenging. You either grow up fast or you can't handle it."

Then, most remarkable of all, Gioia willingly shows me a little chink in his own armor. It appears in the form of a recurrent dream. He's had this same dream for the past ten years or so, and it always leaves him feeling strange. The dream takes place in the present, but there is a kind of dual reality to it. On one level, he knows the war is over; but on the other level, he knows that somehow the war is still going on. This dual reality makes him "edgy." At the start of the dream, he gets a call from someone high up at the Pentagon, who tells him the war is not going well. Gioia narrates:

"So I usually say something like, 'OK, fine, what do you want me to do about it?' And the answer is, 'We need to recall people like you with your specialties.' And I go, 'No, I don't have any desire to go back to Vietnam; I've already done my bit. Plenty of guys never had one tour—so why don't you just look up all those people?' They say, 'Aw, you know, we need people with those specialties.' Then the hook comes—and this is really weird in the dream, when he says, 'You know, Fleener's gone over, we've gotten in touch with him. And Guthrie, we called Guthrie, and he's going, and Rosen's gone.' These are guys I knew, guys I went through ranger school with. And in the dream, you know, you're think-ing, 'God, if those guys have gone back, if Rosen, Fleener, and Guthrie have gone back, I can't let the side down, so I guess I better go back.' *And that's when I realize that they all got killed.* In '69 and '70. And it's a real sick dream. In the dream, I realize, 'Wait a minute. Those guys are all dead. They died a long time ago.' And that's when I wake up."

He dislikes the Vietnam Memorial Wall in Washington, D.C. It's a bit pompous, he thinks, to dwell on 58,000 deaths in Vietnam, when "if you did that for World War II, that wall would be five times longer and five times higher." Yet he too has succumbed to the impulse to look up the names of fel-low soldiers who died. "You remember them as young men," he says wistfully. "They'd be middle-aged like we are today, but you remember them as the young guys they were. They'll never get any older."

Gioia carries his own private Wall with him, wherever he goes. It's in his wal-let: a little photograph of five young Army lieutenants who have just completed jumpmaster school at Fort Bragg, North Carolina, in late January 1968, just before deploying to Vietnam—"just before reality set in with a vengeance." One of them is Gioia himself. Two of the men were wounded in Vietnam; the other three were killed.

"Anytime I hear people pissing on about how tough their life is these days,"

Gioia explains, "I sort of mentally take out that picture. And it is very much with me, and always will be."

There is a pause as what he says sinks in. Then his voice sounds a note of utter certainty: "Always will be."

This book, I hope, will serve as a similar testament, for both the living and the dead.

Vietnam veterans raise the American flag in "distress mode" on a night march to the White House during Operation Dewey Canyon III, April 1971. *Photo © George Butler.*

Coming Up with a Politics: Vietnam Veterans Against the War

1. Six Vets and a Banner

He was twenty-three years old and had not yet taken his pen name of Jan Barry. He was moderately tall, gangly rather than muscular, and with his long nose and lank dark hair looked something like a pensive Henry David Thoreau. He was, in short, nobody out of the ordinary in that crowd of 50,000 antiwar protestors marching through New York City on April 7, 1967. Since he wore a suit and tie and tan raincoat, there was no way to identify him as a Vietnam veteran, except by inference, since he was marching along with a small, ragtag bunch of guys—none of them in uniform—who carried an impromptu painted banner that read VIETNAM VETERANS AGAINST THE WAR! The irony was that at that point there was no such organization—just a hastily improvised slogan that a few guys chose to identify themselves with. But within two months there would be such an organization—Vietnam Veterans Against the War, known more popularly as VVAW—and Jan Barry would be its founder. The organization would put Richard Nixon into a panic, provoke FBI Director J. Edgar Hoover into breaking the law in order to destroy it, precipitate the last major conspiracy trial of the era, and bring to prominence at least one leader of national stature, John Kerry, who would eventually become the junior United States senator from Massachusetts.[1] And the man who had founded it—far from becoming a household name—would be forgotten.

His real name was Jan Barry Crumb, and he had been born and raised in the Finger Lakes region of upstate New York. He had been to Vietnam in 1963 in the U.S. Army's 18th Aviation Company, at a time when the United States was not even supposed to have a military presence in Indochina other than "advisors." Upon his return, he enrolled in West Point. But he was deeply troubled about what he had seen in Vietnam—especially what he perceived as the utter callousness and disdain of the American military toward the human needs of the Vietnamese people. He resigned from the academy in November 1964, feeling completely alone, unable to believe that anyone else felt as he did. To finish out his enlistment he was sent back into the Army, to an installation in Alabama. In spring 1965, the civil rights movement was in full bloom as Martin Luther King Jr. led 50,000 protesters from Montgomery to Selma, and it opened Crumb's eyes a bit further to the injustice in America. That same spring, 22,000 American troops were dispatched to Santo Domingo to save the Dominican Republic from "Communism." Meanwhile, the war in Vietnam took a quantum leap when the Marines landed in Da Nang in March. Jan Crumb did not yet know there was an American peace movement, but when he got out of the military, he went in search of what he called "some other way."

It took him two years to find that other way. He lived in New Jersey for a while, then moved to Manhattan and began working for a newspaper. He left the paper for a job at the New York Public Library, where his coworkers were mostly university students. One day, in March 1967, he heard some of them talking about a big peace demonstration that was scheduled to take place on April 7 outside the United Nations. The day of the demo, he met with a group of friends, planning to attend it in their company. It was a momentous day in his life for more than one reason—he would meet his future wife, Paula, in that group.

Jan Crumb was not the only Vietnam veteran in attendance at what was being called the Fifth Avenue Peace Parade. Prior to the event, a group of less than a dozen vets had gone to the Peace Parade Committee's office to announce that they would like to be featured prominently in the march. When asked their affiliation, they had answered simply that they were "Vietnam veterans against the war." Some worker in the office who had a good sense for publicity immediately made them up a banner with their phrase in bold letters, as if it were a title.[2]

The demonstration was starting off in Central Park, and when Crumb arrived there, he heard someone say, "Vietnam veterans to the front." So Crumb said goodbye to his friends and walked toward a large contingent of older veterans wearing blue overseas caps that read VETERANS FOR PEACE. At the head of that group was a handful of guys his own age, six of whom were in the lead with the long VIETNAM VETERANS AGAINST THE WAR! banner. Behind these Vietnam vets was a scattering of their wives and children.

Crumb did not know any of the Vietnam vets, but he took his place among them, at the very front of the parade. In those days, a lot of people in the country were still furious about antiwar protesters, and Crumb worried that there might be snipers lying in wait for them along the route—or at the very least, counterdemonstrators. Sure enough, as the parade moved along, groups of construction workers began to hurl construction materials at the marchers. They did not throw anything at the veterans, however. He was relieved, but also intrigued by the immunity their military service had apparently earned them.

When the marchers reached the United Nations, the group of Vietnam veterans disbanded. Curious about who their leader was, Crumb inquired among some of the older Veterans for Peace, who led him to a VFP meeting. There, Crumb learned that there was no group called Vietnam Veterans Against the War; that in fact the marchers who carried the banner had hoped that it would draw other Vietnam vets to join them—which, except for the arrival of Crumb and possibly a couple of others, had not happened.

By this time, however, Jan Crumb was convinced that there were a sizable number of Vietnam veterans against the war, and that they should exist as a real organization. He took it upon himself to make that organization a reality.

Crumb began tracking down some of the Vietnam veterans who had marched in the April 7 Peace Parade, or who had come forward later to express their interest, and by Memorial Day he had gathered a group of about ten men. This small group went to Washington for a Memorial Day peace demonstration that had been organized by Veterans for Peace. Two days later, on June 1, 1967, six of those Vietnam veterans met in Crumb's New York apartment at 208 E. 7th Street on the Lower East Side. It was the same day the Six Day War in Israel began.

The meeting took place in Crumb's kitchen, and from the start there was dissension. One vet was Jewish, another had studied Arabic, and a fierce debate began about the merits of each side's cause in the Mideast conflict. Crumb was quick to perceive that they could not, and should not try to, agree on anything except the one issue that had brought them together—the need to end the war in Vietnam.

Most of the six were from the New York area, though there were a couple from out of state who were students at Columbia and NYU. They had gotten together to formulate a statement of purpose, and to elect officers. Jan Barry Crumb was elected president.

The biggest issue to be dealt with was that of creating a separate peace organization solely for Vietnam veterans, as opposed to folding in with the Veterans for Peace. The older organization—composed mainly of World War II vets—really wanted Vietnam Veterans Against the War to join with them, and the prospect of such a union was tempting. Veterans for Peace had attracted a lot of wealthy and influential backers, which enabled them to take out full-page ads in the *New York Times*. But in practical terms, they had had no impact whatsoever on the war, and had apparently been ignored completely by President Lyndon Johnson and the United States Congress.[3] Crumb and his five comrades knew that the particular leverage they had was in speaking as veterans of this very war. People would listen to them about Vietnam *because they had been there.* They agreed that limiting their membership to Vietnam veterans was essential.

This did not mean that Crumb was above learning from those who had gone before him; quite the contrary, he interrogated many of the Veterans for Peace about their history and studied their tactics. It astounded him to learn, for example, that during the Korean War the VFP had gotten a large number of GIs to write their congressmen from Korea, demanding that American troops be pulled out of that conflict. Furthermore, VFP taught him one of his most important lessons in how to deal with warmongering rhetoric—simply turn it back on the warmongers. One of the things that had attracted Crumb to the April 7 demonstration was an ad that VFP had taken out in the *New York Times*, purporting to quote North Vietnam's President Ho Chi Minh: "If you will stop the bombing of North Vietnam, we will promise never to bomb New York." The ad was intended to make people realize that North Vietnam was not bombing the United States—that in fact *we* were bombing them, and that our demand that *they* stop waging war against us was absurd.

Veterans for Peace may have had another appeal for the Vietnam vets, in that its members were committed to end all wars, not just the one in Vietnam. Although many of the Vietnam vets at this point believed their organization would die a natural death when the last American pulled out of Vietnam, there were a few who foresaw that their struggle would continue long after the Vietnam War was won or lost. In fact, for the first few months, Vietnam Veterans Against the War was alternately referred to, even in official correspondence, as Vietnam Veterans for Peace.[4]

Having always been a "very anti-hierarchical person," Crumb considered himself president of Vietnam Veterans Against the War on paper only. They needed to have a certain number of officers for the purpose of filing with the State of New York, but Crumb insisted that all members be treated equally— setting a tone of real democracy that pervaded the organization until its near demise in the mid-seventies.

The organization grew slowly in membership, but its few members had a significant impact from the very start. These were all men who had received the best training in military discipline in American armed forces that had not yet lost their pride, morale, and esprit de corps. Moreover, they were all in their early and mid-twenties, at the peak of their energy, and were fired up with that distinctive driving idealism that seemed to characterize so many of the vets, regardless of whether they had been drafted or volunteered for military service.

In New York City, Crumb and his fellow VVAW members seemed to be everywhere at once. They would spend hours on street corners in Greenwich Village and in Times Square, buttonholing passersby and handing out mimeographed literature against the war. Although within a couple of years their appearance would alter drastically, in the summer of 1967 they all had short hair and dressed like businessmen. As Jan Barry remembers today, they were "convinced that one of the things the peace movement was throwing away was respectability." That conservative image paid off. In the first six months, they were frequently asked to take part in debates and to be interviewed on radio and television talk shows.

Among the early joiners were David Braum, an articulate Columbia University student; two psychiatrists who had served in Vietnam, John Talbott and Art Blank; and a handsome, crew-cut Sp/4 chaplain's assistant named Carl Rogers, who had already become something of a cause celebre in the antiwar movement.

Rogers was one of the many all-American boys who went to Vietnam. Of average height, slender, blue-eyed, fair-haired, and extremely articulate, he had graduated from high school in the small town of Chardon, Ohio, in 1961. Like so many American young men back then, he was extremely patriotic and loved the American flag. In high school, he had driven his own car and worn a closetful of snazzy clothes; not only was he irresistible to girls, but he had been earning an adult's salary since he was fifteen as assistant program director at WNOB in Cleveland, the largest FM radio station in the Midwest. He had even snagged the lead role in his high school's stage production of *Oklahoma!*, and was named the champion square dance caller at the Ohio State Fair. By all rights, he should have had a happy, untroubled future.[5]

In the summer of 1964, however, Rogers got word that he was about to be drafted. Taking his friend's advice, he made plans to enroll in college. Rogers was not so much dodging the draft as he was attempting to preserve a lifestyle that was both pleasing and fulfilling, and which would probably allow him to develop his talents to the fullest. Some might have thought him selfish for not wanting to serve his country as a soldier; but he felt that he was too much of an individual and a "free spirit" for the military to be able to deal with him properly—if they could deal with him at all. He also felt he was so much brighter than the average career noncoms that he could "run rings around them."

Rogers borrowed his first semester's tuition from the Central Presbyterian Church in Manhattan, where he was teaching Sunday School for the summer, and was all set to matriculate at Kent State College in Ohio when he came down with mononucleosis and hepatitis. He was hospitalized and received a temporary medical deferment. After he got better, he discovered that his father had spent his college money. Hence a permanent medical deferment was his only chance of staying out of the military. But at his draft physical in the spring of 1965, as he recalls, an Army doctor jabbed two fingers into his liver; and when Rogers didn't double over in pain, the physician pronounced him fit for service.

After his induction, Rogers was sent to Fort Jackson, South Carolina, where he tried a variety of tricks to get out. Perhaps his most foolish escapade was to imitate a bedwetter who had just been discharged. The guy had been forced to stand with his urine-soaked sheets draped around his neck, while his fellow recruits, acting on the sergeant's order, regaled him with insults. Rogers figured he could handle a little obloquy. *They can do whatever they want,* he thought. *I'll be out of here in two days.* So he deliberately wet his bed one night. Instead of discharging him, however, the Army merely informed him that they didn't have any fresh sheets and he'd have to dry out the ones he'd just peed on, because he'd be sleeping between them for some time to come.

When the Army discovered he could type 75 words a minute with virtually no errors, Rogers was immediately assigned to the company clerk's office. But the company, which had been designated to test out the new (and seriously malfunctioning) M-16 automatic rifle, looked like a potentially dangerous assignment in the middle of a war, so Rogers tricked the clerk into allowing him to transfer to a safer niche—and one that better suited his intellectual temperament—as a chaplain's assistant.

His experience in Vietnam, much to his surprise, was "totally atypical" and, at least for a time, quite enjoyable. He was stationed in Cam Ranh Bay, far from the fighting, and had the chaplain's Jeep for his own use much of the time. He could go into town and dine on lobster at the best restaurants, and he diverted himself by snorkeling off China Beach and mountain climbing when the whim took him. Best of all, he had all the time he wanted to read, and he used that opportunity to study up on the history of Vietnam and its thousand years of armed conflicts. Journalist Bernard Fall opened Rogers' eyes to the problems and political debates within Vietnamese society, and historian Marvin Gettleman showed him the power of the "common man" in affecting a nation's foreign policy—a lesson Rogers hoped to bring home with him to the United States.

The truth is, Rogers could have had a halfway decent life in the military if there wasn't something inside him bugging him to speak up all the time, to object, to question, to buck the system. There were people all his life who thought him "cocky," a natural troublemaker, but that was not the role he really wanted to play. He simply had a conscience with a loud voice, and he decided, as a lot of people do, that in the end it would cost him more to ignore it than to act on its instructions.

While he was still stateside, he'd read a story in *Newsweek* about how much the soldiers at Fort Jackson enjoyed that particular base. He responded with a letter to *Newsweek* reporting that the soldiers at Fort Jackson felt like prisoners and would gladly have been elsewhere if they had had any options. Although the letter was never printed, he circulated it privately at the base. Soon afterward, he got his orders for Vietnam.

Believing it important to document the experience of going to the war, he began taping interviews with other members of his unit bound for Vietnam. That experience soon grew frustrating, however, because out of the first hundred guys he interviewed in Oakland, he could find not one who "really raised questions about the important issues." Shifting gears, Rogers decided that a deeper analysis could be gained by simply interviewing himself over the course of his year in

Vietnam. He did this in hundreds of taped and written letters that he sent to his family and friends, beginning with his arrival in Vietnam in May 1966.

He got in trouble over another letter—one that he sent to his father, who wrote a column for the Chardon *Times-Leader*, in which he printed service-men's letters as a regular feature. The letter, dated December 1, 1966, dealt with the visit of Lyndon Baines Johnson to Cam Ranh Bay. Rogers was upset by the elaborate preparations that were made for Johnson's visit, which included specially painting a Jeep and equipping it with brass bars and a speaker's platform. The visit seemed merely a public relations stunt. By hand-ing out a few Purple Hearts and scribbling "LBJ" on a few fatigue hats, the president could convince the men he was possibly sending to their deaths that he actually cared about them. The waste of time and money that the president's visit entailed seemed to typify the waste and stupidity of the war itself. Moreover, Rogers used the occasion to rail against the injustice of the war as he perceived it.

Rogers' father was incensed by the letter. He severely edited it before he printed it in his column, completely transforming Carl's intent, so that the let-ter came out sounding as if he were gushing about what a memorable experi-ence LBJ's visit had been for the servicemen. Mr. Rogers later wrote Carl that "your tirades have almost caused the banning of my column," and he warned his son that he would never get ahead in life if he kept making himself so "obnoxious."[6]

But Carl had already proved that he could get ahead; he was now going for something a good deal different. A writer who was putting together a book called *Letters from Vietnam,* having heard of Carl's prodigious missives home, requested a contribution from him, and Carl offered him the letter on LBJ's visit. Word of what Carl had done circulated even before the book was pub-lished, and his popularity among the Army brass dropped even lower.

Both he and his chaplain were already marked as agitators. The escalation of the American forces was in full swing, and Cam Ranh Bay was backed up with unloaded cargo ships. The soldiers in the 1st Logistical Command were being worked day and night to get those ships unloaded. The temperature in the holds often reached 130 degrees, and guys were dropping left and right. Many of them complained to the chaplain, who made an official protest on their behalf. Soon afterward, Rogers and his boss were transferred to Phang Rang, a far less secure area, which was the sort of signal the Army often sent to people who stirred up trouble.

At their new station, the two of them were sometimes called to meet with troops in the field. On one such occasion, Rogers got his first sight of a Viet Cong corpse with the ears cut off for GI trophies; he saw a number of such ears being passed around. He photographed the corpse, and made up his mind that day that he was going to spend as much of his life as it took to get this war stopped. It was clear to him that "more bombs, bullets, and lives expended" were not the answer, and that "runways for supersonic jet bombers" were useless in "dealing with an ox-cart economy."

The day he got back to the States in May 1967, he read of the court-martial of Dr. Howard Levy at Fort Jackson. Levy would soon become both a hero and martyr of the growing resistance to the war within the U.S. armed forces, a resistance that was now being organized as the GI movement. Levy alleged, as one of his reasons for refusing to train Green Berets in basic medicine, that the do-goodism of the Special Forces was just a cover for the atrocities committed by the American military in South Vietnam. Rogers figured that his photos of the mutilated Viet Cong corpse were material evidence that could be used in Levy's defense, and he immediately called Levy's lawyer, who offered to fly him down to Fort Jackson. Rogers was never allowed on the witness stand, and Levy was found guilty and sentenced to three years at Fort Leavenworth (a conviction later overturned by the U.S. Court of Appeals). Nevertheless, Rogers' experiences at the trial fortified his determination to continue as an antiwar activist; just as important, he made many valuable contacts there among other peace activists, many of them notables in the movement, like the famous baby doctor, Benjamin Spock.

At Levy's trial, Rogers learned of a group called Negotiation Now!, and he quickly became a member. Negotiation Now! had been founded by a coalition of pacifist-type church folk and a lot of very respectable liberals. Its masthead boasted such big names as Arthur Schlesinger Jr., Dr. Martin Luther King Jr., Norman Cousins, John Kenneth Galbraith, and William Shirer. None of these people could be discredited as radicals or nuts, and their position was only a shade to the left of middle of the road; they accepted the American military presence in South Vietnam as too substantial to be immediately dismantled, and they asked only that the United States make a more serious and visible effort toward a negotiated settlement.

The folly of such an approach was soon uncovered. To begin with, Negotiation Now! spent much of its energy trying to avoid the charge of sympathizing with the Communists. By saying that they did not advocate the United States' withdrawal from South Vietnam, the intellectual strategists of Negotiation Now! tied their own hands in terms of viable options for a lasting peace—which, of course, eventually required American withdrawal. Perhaps most damagingly, the nonpartisan position of Negotiation Now! refused to acknowledge that much of America had good reason to be partisan about this war. Rogers encountered a case in point, when Arthur Schlesinger wrote to American President Lines in San Francisco to ask for a financial contribution. Some naive secretary on the contributions committee, unaware of how much he was revealing, wrote back that they must decline to support NN's campaign, since they primarily handled cargo to and from the Far East, with a number of their ships chartered to the U.S. government. Which was to say that as long as the war continued, they made money, and hence it "would be inappropriate for the company to take a stand in this matter at this time."

Rogers spent only about three months with Negotiation Now!. David Dellinger, who had been a conscientious objector (CO) during World War II, and whose pacifist ideology embraced a broad spectrum of reform movements, told Rogers to "get out" of NN because its stodgy anti-Communist stance seemed more of an obstruction than a help to the peace movement. At about the time when Rogers' doubts about NN were growing strong, he ran across Vietnam Veterans Against the War.[7]

Negotiation Now! had its offices at 156 Fifth Avenue, in the same building that housed the Fifth Avenue Peace Parade Committee. One day Rogers wandered into the Peace Parade office, where he met a guy who was counting VVAW buttons. This button was a pallid thing, a simple helmet in olive drab against a white background, with the words "I support Vietnam Veterans Against the War." Curious, Rogers asked for a phone number, and the guy put him in touch with Jan Crumb. Crumb was just about to call for another meeting at the Peace Parade Committee office (VVAW would soon move into an adjoining office), and he invited Rogers to attend. The two men hit it off immediately, both of them coming from a great depth of conviction, and a powerful alliance was forged, to which Crumb brought his analytical intellect and Rogers his impressive gift for manipulating public opinion. Within a few months, Rogers would be designated vice president of the organization.

Initially it was a hard decision for Rogers to leave Negotiation Now!, which had access to so much more money and influence than the scruffy bunch of guys at VVAW. Rogers' whole style and approach was to make the biggest splash possible, and he enjoyed getting wined and dined by the theological and academic muckymucks at Negotiation Now!, feeling as if he were edging his way toward their eminence and respectability. But he could not deny that politically his heart belonged with the kind of grass-roots activism that the vets represented. The only way to resolve the dilemma, for him, was to give VVAW a higher profile, to make it more of a dynamic presence in mainstream American politics.

Jan Crumb had originally conceived of the organization as more of an educational tool than a political group. For one thing, Crumb was against the wearing of military uniforms to impress the public with the veterans' military service. He saw VVAW as a group of *civilians*, albeit civilians who had gained a vital experience in the war; and he felt they could do the most good on talk shows and in debates with congressmen and State Department people. The trouble with that strategy, though, was that it was too successful. According to Crumb, "at a certain point they didn't want to debate us any longer, because we knew what we were talking about. Not only had we been there, but we'd taken the time and trouble to read the Geneva Accords, and the government officials were constantly lying about what these documents said. So we would quote from the documents, or even have copies of them to hand out. They couldn't stand that situation—that was how shaky the government's position really was."

Rogers was much more attuned to public relations and actual organizing. He designed a number of brochures for VVAW and eagerly stood on street corners handing them out and talking to anyone who would lend him an ear. Early on, he was instrumental in redesigning the VVAW logo. He correctly sensed that the power of VVAW would come from the vets' ability to stand everything military on its head, to use the military's own symbols against it. He wrote to Senator Ernest Gruening of Alaska, the only other senator besides Wayne Morse of Oregon to vote against the Tonkin Gulf Resolution in 1964 (which authorized LBJ's warmaking), for help in getting the official heraldry of the Army's MACV patch.

MACV—Military Assistance Command Vietnam—was the command structure for the first American troops sent to Vietnam in the late 1950s and early 1960s. According to Colonel David Hackworth, a veteran of both Korea and Vietnam, the problem with MACV came with the rapid escalation of in-country American forces during 1965 and 1966, when it was forced to shift "violently . . . from a slow-paced advisory concern to a full-blown war head-quarters." The officers at MACV often seemed out of touch with the realities of combat in the field; even more irritating to the grunts was the fact that the staff at MACV seemed to be living in the lap of luxury—"Fat City," Hackworth called it—while the guys in the field lived on C rations and perpetually lacked even such basic supplies as gun patches and cleaning rods to care for their weapons. No wonder, then, that the average fighting man had little use for the so-called REMF (rear-echelon motherfucker) officers at MACV, who devised missions for them that had little connection to the exigencies of guerrilla war-fare, and which might lead to their being wounded or killed unnecessarily. It was a pleasure for the vets in VVAW to ridicule and subvert the authority of such a group.

The official MACV patch was suitably impressive. In the shape of a shield, it showed two battlements in yellow on a field of red. The gap between the battlements was filled by an upraised white sword. According to the Army's Institute of Heraldry, the red ground alluded to Communist infiltration and aggression from beyond the "embattled wall" (which suggested, along with its yellow color, the boundary of the Chinese nation). Yellow and red, conveniently, were also the Vietnamese national colors. The white sword symbolized American military aid and support, and the fact that the sword was pointed upward and the wall arched indicated an offensive action to push the aggressors back.

To many cynical vets like Carl Rogers, the patch was blatantly racist—the white man saving yellow men from the dirty reds. David Braum was put in charge of designing the new VVAW logo. He too took offense at the confused symbolism of the MACV patch—to reduce thousands of years of Vietnamese nationalism to a conflict between Communism and democracy seemed grossly inaccurate, not to mention placing the Great Wall of China on the Vietnamese border, when in reality it was a thousand miles to the north. The suggestion of "offensive action" seemed a kind of Freudian slip, since the patch was first issued in March 1963 to the 12,000 in-country American "advisors." Worst of all, in Braum's eyes, the sword revealed the fundamental error in American thinking— the refusal "to see that the basic problem in Vietnam is not military—but social, economic, and political." With one brilliant stroke, Braum took the MACV patch and replaced the white sword with an M-16 rifle turned upside down and capped with a helmet: the universally understood symbol of a soldier killed in action—a totem which some say originated in ancient Greece, with a lance in place of the rifle.[8]

The fall of 1967 would see many antiwar demonstrations across the country— most notably, the march on the Pentagon, which was planned for October 21 by the National Mobilization to End the War. The Mobe, as it was familiarly called, boasted a variety of influential leaders and supporters—from old-time pacifists like David Dellinger to young firebrands like Abbie Hoffman and Jerry Rubin, mixed with leftist intellectuals like Norman Mailer. Crumb and Rogers chose "not to participate in or endorse the demonstration as an organization," even though individuals in their group did go there to speak out as Vietnam veterans—and VVAW provided buses expressly for that purpose. This decision, so different from the confrontational VVAW of a few years later, is a measure of how traditional most of these men still were.

While the left-wing radicals attempted to "levitate" the Pentagon, the VVAW contingent lobbied their senators and congressmen. The day after the march on the Pentagon, Rogers and Braum appeared on David Susskind's popular television talk show, successfully debating two right-wing vets and winning Susskind's sympathy for the peace movement, if not the demonstration itself. Then, covering the traditional bases as well, VVAW staged its own Veterans Day memorials, followed by a major ad in the *New York Times* (partly paid for by Veterans for Peace), which was signed by sixty-five vets, calling for immediate withdrawal of all U.S. troops from Vietnam. They had asked the *Times* to run the ad on Veterans Day, but the *Times* refused and ran it on November 19 instead. Jan Crumb had stretched all his resources to come up with those sixty-five signatures, since Vietnam vets were still a long way from flocking to the cause; but the impact of the ad, according to Crumb, was "explosive." The next day it was read into the *Congressional Record* by Senator Gruening. It was republished, with additional signatures, in the *New Republic* and in newspapers in Cleveland, Boston, Detroit, and Los Angeles, where a new chapter of VVAW had just been formed.

In line with Crumb's idea of making VVAW an educational organization, he and his associates set up a separate office to serve as headquarters for a nation-wide speakers bureau, offering "debates with pro-Administration speakers, 35mm color slide programs on Viet-Nam [*sic*], and lecture-discussion pro-grams." Articles about VVAW came out in the *Village Voice,* the *New York Times Magazine,* and *Eye.* As a result of Rogers' appearance on the *David Susskind Show, Redbook* magazine featured a major profile on him. Most significantly, Crumb and his associates had a series of conferences with several senators, where it was suggested that they would be permitted to testify before the Senate Foreign Relations Committee, which Crumb considered "our major project." Referring to this possibility in a letter to VVAW supporters, Crumb emphasized the importance of their simply bearing witness, "since we feel that the majority of the American people have yet to learn of the true nature of the war."[9]

2. Tear Gas, Clubs, and Confetti: The Chicago Blues

Between November 1967 and February 1968 the entire complexion of the Vietnam War changed irrevocably. On November 19, 1967, General William C. Westmoreland, the commander of all American forces in South Vietnam, and Ellsworth Bunker, the United States Ambassador to South Vietnam (the only Vietnam we recognized), appeared together on NBC's Sunday program *Meet the Press* to reassure the American people that American and South Vietnamese forces were "making steady, not spectacular, progress" and "winning a war of attrition"—the only war Westmoreland saw fit to fight. The previous week they had given the same optimistic accounting to Lyndon Johnson and select mem-bers of Congress. Bunker claimed the American forces were ready "to acceler-ate the rate of progress"; and Westmoreland, finding that "an attitude of confidence and growing optimism . . . prevails all over the country," was brash enough to foresee "light at the end of the tunnel."

The only light turned out to be the muzzle flashes from the mouths of tens of thousands of North Vietnamese Army and Viet Cong rifles and artillery pieces at the end of January 1968—the start of the Tet Lunar New Year and what came to be known as the Tet Offensive. Communist forces simultaneously attacked every major city, town, and military base in South Vietnam, and even managed to take over part of the American embassy in Saigon for seven hours. They came close to winning the war in a matter of days. Although they were finally turned back, suffering heavy casualties in every major battle, they won a tremendous strategic victory. They had proved that, far from being on the verge of defeat, they were still a formidable opponent, capable of costing the United States more pain, loss, and death than the American people were prepared to suffer. From that point on, disenchantment with the war would grow steadily throughout the nation. Talk of an American victory changed overnight to the barest hope for some sort of honorable "disengagement."

The peace movement in general had to grapple with its own heavy losses. For while it might have been winning popular sentiment (a majority of the American population had ceased to approve of the war as early as October 1967), it had to face some grim facts: continuing escalation of the American military presence in Vietnam, continuing escalation of the material cost of fighting the war, and, worst of all, a dire increase in the number of corpses on all sides, including several thousand more American boys shipped home in body bags before the year was a quarter gone. It was time for the peace movement to seriously gear up, before there was nothing left to save of Vietnam—not to mention the American military.

Whatever urgency the peace movement felt weighed doubly and trebly on the veterans' movement. The men who were suddenly dying in such large numbers were, after all, their *brothers*. Scarcely a man in VVAW did not know someone who was still over there and in harm's way. The organization no longer had the leisure to be merely an educational tool.

Out of its scant treasury VVAW mustered enough money for a small ad in the *New Republic*, which brought in several new members from the East Coast. From the entire Midwest, however, there came only two applicants, both at Ohio State University in Columbus: Daniel Burdekin, a former Airborne Ranger, and Bill Crandell, an Army second lieutenant who had led a rifle platoon. Burdekin and Crandell were promptly dubbed the "Midwest coordinators."

While the Tet Offensive was bursting across the Vietnamese countryside and across newspaper front pages, an American presidential election was in the making. Those who sought to end the war felt it imperative to unseat Lyndon Baines Johnson. On March 31, 1968, after listening to his closest advisors and State Department pundits tell him for the umpteenth time that the war, *his* war (as just about everyone in the country identified it), was indeed unwinnable, Johnson went on national television to announce that he would not seek reelection to the presidency. The announcement was a tremendous jolt to members of both parties, and threw the presidential race wide open. But back in January and February of 1968, getting rid of Johnson still seemed a monumental task.

The leaders of VVAW saw that they had to get involved in the presidential race. The obvious candidate for them was Eugene McCarthy, the United States senator from Minnesota, a prominent critic of the war, who had announced his candidacy with the specific purpose of promoting a negotiated settlement in Vietnam. In January 1968, however, McCarthy's bid appeared to be just a token gesture; his campaign, according to longtime Kennedy-family advisor Arthur M. Schlesinger Jr., was "desultory and ineffective." But the Tet Offensive was like a mainline shot of adrenaline to his campaign and the man himself. McCarthy, who was known to have fits of mumbling and total withdrawal into himself, was suddenly talking as if he might really become president of the United States.[10]

At this point, Carl Rogers came into his own as de facto leader of VVAW. As another member, Sheldon Ramsdell, later put it, "Carl was the manipulator; Jan was the brains"—but in American politics, manipulation carries the day over brains almost every time, a fact both Carl and Jan were well aware of. As a result of his public appearances, Carl was asked to address the New Democratic Coalition in Miami, Florida, just around the time of Tet. It was at that convention that Rogers met McCarthy; and when McCarthy's workers invited him to come to New Hampshire as a "secondary speaker," Rogers couldn't have been happier to oblige.

On February 3, 1968, Carl issued a "Proposal for the Expansion of the VVAW," in which he envisioned a restructuring of the organization for the express purpose of supporting McCarthy's campaign. "It is clear that there's not much more that can be done in the streets," he wrote, "especially by us, but as an organization we can have an enormous effect—man for man—on the minds of the uncommitted in this election year . . . our abilities and experience can do more than educate. They can motivate!" To begin with, Carl called for opening and staffing a separate office with administrative responsibilities for building a national political program. The chief goal of that program would be to offer "support and endorsement to Senator McCarthy and all candidates against the war."

With lightning speed, Carl used his connections at Clergy and Laity Concerned About Vietnam (CALCAV) to organize 300 New York State veterans, and then managed to transport them to Concord and Manchester to campaign for McCarthy in the New Hampshire primary. Their first objective was to provide testimony disproving the assertion of Johnson supporters that "a vote for McCarthy would bring joy in Hanoi." Among those waving the old flag of the red scare were New Hampshire's Governor John King and Senator Thomas McIntyre. The vets countered by taking out ads in several major New Hampshire newspapers, which read in part: "As veterans of the war in VietNam we are proud to have been among those fighting men for whom you urge support. We do not like being called weak or indecisive. We do not like the implication that we oppose the best interest of our country." The ads were signed by 110 Vietnam veterans, all of whom had "been awarded medals by the United States Government for their service in Vietnam."

One of the issues clouding veterans' support for McCarthy was the question of whether Robert Kennedy, brother of the late president and currently the junior senator from New York, was also going to run. Before heading up to New Hampshire, Rogers and his troupe of 300 antiwar activists went down to

Washington to meet with Kennedy. They packed a church on Capitol Hill, waiting for Kennedy to come and address them, but Kennedy never showed. Instead, he sent his press aide Jeff Greenfield. The vets, according to Sheldon Ramsdell, "nailed Greenfield to the wall. We said, 'Where is Senator Kennedy? We're three hundred or so of his constituents down here, asking, pleading, and begging for a policy on this war.' And Greenfield had all these blabbering excuses—'Well, he had to go to Florida, his father's sick.' So we left Washington, and Bobby went to Chicago that next Thursday and spoke out against the war."

Kennedy's failure to appear before the vets did not hurt him politically, as he was soon to overtake McCarthy in popularity among those who favored a quick end to the war; but it did create a crucial juncture in the veterans' movement, for it sent many of the vets on a wild goose chase, campaigning feverishly for the next six months in behalf of a candidate who was a political dead end, and who would wind up giving virtually no competition at all to Hubert Humphrey, Johnson's surrogate, for his party's nomination in Chicago. Although the vets may have gained no more by supporting Kennedy, since his campaign was cut short by his assassination in Los Angeles in June, the fact that he alienated many of them so early was a case of tragic misunderstanding. In truth, Kennedy supported the American GIs and veterans as much, if not more than, McCarthy.[11]

On February 8, 1968, Kennedy gave one of the most powerful and incisive speeches of his career at a book luncheon in Chicago. He used the occasion to advocate, in the plainest, toughest terms, the complete withdrawal of American forces from Vietnam as rapidly as possible. Most significantly, Kennedy's speech was pro-GI throughout. Rather than condemning the ineffectiveness or immorality of the American fighting man (arguments that were coming from the right and left respectively), Kennedy condemned the men in Washington who had sent them off to a war there was never any chance of winning: "[The failure to secure any area of South Vietnam from attack] has not happened because our men are not brave or effective, because they are. It is because we have misconceived the nature of the war: it is because we have sought to resolve by military might a conflict whose issue depends upon the will and conviction of the South Vietnamese people. It is like sending a lion to halt an epidemic of jungle rot." Over and over again he insisted that one of his chief reasons for speaking out was "to protect the lives of our gallant young men" and "to end casualties." He admonished his fellow congressmen: "We must show as much willingness to risk some of our prestige for peace as to risk the lives of young men in war."

Jan Barry recalls that a group of vets did splinter off to become Vietnam Veterans for Kennedy, and at least one of their press releases survives; but as Carl Rogers saw it, Vietnam Veterans Against the War all but dissolved into Vietnam Veterans for McCarthy (VVFM), and banners and buttons were printed anew to reflect that change. Both men agree that almost all the energy and resources of the organization went into the presidential campaign until the Democratic National Convention in August in Chicago. According to Barry, "VVAW literally had to close up its offices in the late spring of 1968 because there was no more money coming in to support what we were doing."

Not only did the vets go all out for McCarthy, but many of them actively harassed Kennedy. Larry Rottmann, an Army vet who was wounded in Tet and discharged in March 1968, read about Vietnam Veterans for McCarthy as he flew home from Oakland to Springfield, Missouri, and he immediately got in touch with Carl Rogers to assist him in founding a Missouri chapter of VVFM. Once that was done, Rottmann traveled to Wisconsin to assist Rogers in the Democratic primary there. A week later, he went down to Indiana for its primary. Indiana was the first primary Kennedy was eligible to enter, and Rottmann was in charge of a group of vets that followed Kennedy around in order to wave their McCarthy placards in his face every time he spoke to the media.

From Indiana, where Kennedy got 42 percent of the vote compared to McCarthy's 27 percent, Rottmann took his group of vets to the airport in Lincoln, Nebraska, to await Kennedy's arrival for the primary there. Exasperated to see the same guys in his face once again, Kennedy confronted Rottmann and demanded, "Why are you working against me?" Rottmann replied that they weren't working against *him,* but that they were "all liberals or peaceniks on the same road going to Chicago." Furthermore, Rottmann told Kennedy that they simply found McCarthy "more down-to-earth and more sincere, both in his politics and in his lifestyle." Kennedy evidently failed to appreciate Rottmann's point of view; he restated his dismay that Vietnam veterans weren't campaigning on his behalf instead of McCarthy's.[12]

The behavior of the vets toward Kennedy—and the fact that they so readily narrowed their political options—illustrated several aspects of the veterans' movement that would persist for decades. The first was their pride and hardheadedness, their insistence on doing things their own way, and along with that a tendency to overreact when they felt someone was trying to push them too hard in a direction not of their own choosing. Marine hero and wheelchair vet Ron Kovic would later articulate this tendency, saying, "We were determined never to let anyone use us again the way we had been used in that war." Another aspect—a far more positive quality—was the wholehearted commitment these veterans would give to a cause, once they had made up their minds on an issue.

The effects of the veterans' involvement in the McCarthy campaign were swift and dramatic. As soon as they came out with their pro-McCarthy ads, and, in Rogers' words, "had our vets standing on street corners" throughout New Hampshire, the pro-Johnson forces immediately switched their tactics away from identifying McCarthy with the Communist cause, which had been their main weapon against him. On March 12, McCarthy stunned the nation by winning 20 of New Hampshire's 24 convention delegates. When Johnson learned that McCarthy would probably beat him in Wisconsin on April 2 by a two-to-one margin, he made his decision to withdraw from the presidential race—an announcement he made two days before the primary, so that it would not appear as if McCarthy were driving him out. Clearly McCarthy did drive him out, and Vietnam Veterans Against the War—transformed into Vietnam Veterans for McCarthy—deserved a measure of credit for that accomplishment.

McCarthy and Kennedy seesawed in the remaining primaries. Kennedy beat him badly in both Indiana and Nebraska, then McCarthy turned the tables in Oregon (though McCarthy's margin of victory was only 44 percent to 38 percent). California, the big one, bringing with it the largest block of electoral votes, came on June 5, along with the relatively unimportant primary in South Dakota, where because of its proximity to Minnesota, McCarthy and Vice President Hubert Humphrey (now Johnson's surrogate) were expected to triumph. Kennedy won by a small margin in California and an amazingly wide margin in South Dakota. Although Humphrey, collecting all of Johnson's former delegates, was still in a more powerful position than Kennedy, Bobby was headed for Chicago with the full expectation of getting his party's nomination. He had barely left the victory celebration at Los Angeles' Ambassador Hotel when assassin Sirhan Sirhan aimed a pistol at his head, taking him out of politics forever and enshrining him as one more dead American hero.

The Vietnam Veterans for McCarthy, however, were still headed for Chicago with a vengeance. Carl Rogers went to Sarah Kovner, a leader of the New York New Democratic Coalition, out of whose offices he was working, and told her that he needed their help to bring a hundred veterans to Chicago. Since McCarthy was Kovner's choice for president, and since McCarthy had just lost the New York primary, Kovner came up with about $1,500 for Rogers to organize his veterans' crusade to Chicago.[13]

The first thing Rogers did after he got his veterans together was to have a few dozen of them write statements about why they supported McCarthy. The best were then reproduced in large numbers. Some of these letters survive, and they are as affecting today as when they were written, in that time when the country was reeling from the back-to-back assassinations of Martin Luther King Jr. (on April 4) and Kennedy, not to mention the hundreds of young men each month who were still dying in Vietnam.

John Talbott had been a psychiatrist before he was drafted in 1966. He served with the U.S. Army Medical Corps in Long Binh and Saigon from May 1967 to April 1968, returning home with a Bronze Star. He wrote, in a letter that was later reprinted in a newspaper ad for McCarthy: "When I see us heading down the same road to more disasters, more aluminum caskets, more craters in rice-paddies, more murdered leaders, more 'blue-ribbon' commissions on riots, and more dehumanization of us all, I shudder. My vote in the primaries, my time in the campaigns, my money, my heart, my very trust in the system—all, alone, seem worthless. Something must be done, but how? I am only one man. I have only one vote. Because I served my country, because I went to Viet-Nam, because I cared, that doesn't and shouldn't entitle me to more than one vote, one voice, one plea—and this is it, McCARTHY NOW!"

William Rodder Jr., who had been Senior Naval Advisor to the Commanding Officer of a South Vietnamese Navy Coastal Group from May 1965 to May 1966, wrote: "When my Advisory Team first arrived at the Junk Base, the [Vietnamese] Commanding Officer greeted us, 'Why are you here? We don't need you, and we don't want you.' Later he asked, 'Why don't you Americans allow us to determine our own future? Why did you forbid the free, secret elections which the Geneva Accords stated should take place in 1956? Why don't you allow us to evolve our own political-economic system without your interference? Why do you oppose Ho Chi Minh, the father of Vietnam?' . . . I regret that in the United States Overseas Mission Hospital in Danang, I saw scores of Vietnamese hideously burned by American napalm. I realized that the defoliation agents were supplied and sanctioned by Americans to be used against Asians—a fact that no Asian will forget. . . . Finally, after a year's experience in South Vietnam, I concluded that the Vietcong would win the War, because they are closer to the people, more aware of Vietnamese problems, more conscious of national dignity and independence than any of the regimes in Saigon the United States has supported."

Rogers even managed to get letters from active-duty servicemen, such as SK3 Richard T. Roth, who was serving his second tour with the Navy in Vietnamese waters. Wrote Roth: "As an American citizen, and subject to American law, it is my duty to be over here. I am fairly secure behind the steel skin of my ships, but my buddies in the fox-holes are not. Enclosed is a casualty list from *Stars and Stripes*. I think this should be required reading before you cast your ballot."

None of them, however, was as powerful as a letter Rogers had collected earlier in the year, when he was soliciting letters in order to influence Senator William Fulbright to chair a new round of hearings on the war (like those he had chaired in 1966) before the Senate Foreign Relations Committee. Amidst a barrage of what Rogers called impassioned "college rhetoric" came this letter from a nearly illiterate kid from Arkansas, Fulbright's home state, which began: "Senator, it ain't right what's happening in Vietnam." According to Jan Barry, he and Rogers "really found a wide selection of people who had solid things to report," including one guy who had written the early history of the Special Forces in Vietnam. But despite a push from Alaska's Senator Ernest Gruening to introduce such testimony, Fulbright still refused to hold new hearings, later explaining that he felt the veterans would have "gotten blown away by these tough senators." That failure to get results through congressional channels had spurred the vets' quest to bring their message to the presidency.

But as some vets rushed headlong with Rogers toward Chicago, others had already nearly burned out on politics. Jan Barry moved out of New York to do construction work in New Jersey, temporarily abandoning activism because he sensed "Chicago would be a really bad situation and I didn't need it." The irony was that the vets were not going to Chicago to raise hell in the streets, like Abbie Hoffman and his Yippies, but rather to lobby the delegates. According to Jan Barry, they went to the convention "all dressed up in suits and ties, trying to find at least one person from every Congressional district or every state, and they did. They went there and got tear-gassed and beat up on along with everybody else."[14]

Of course no one had any idea what a battlefield Chicago was destined to become that August. Buses filled with billy club–wielding police surrounded the Hilton, and the parks were cleared by National Guardsmen in "Daley dozers"— jeeps specially equipped with barbed-wire cowcatchers, named after "Hizzoner" Mayor Richard J. Daley, Chicago's mayor for life, who was busy inside the Amphitheater like a despot in his bunker, plotting his war against the young, when he wasn't engaged in backroom deals or shaming his city even more by such gaffes as calling Senator Abraham Ribicoff of Connecticut "a Jew son of a bitch" for complaining about the "Gestapo tactics" of Chicago's finest men in blue. The police riots, the violence against the press, and the inane revolutionary camp of the Yippies have all been well described in dozens of books, notably Norman Mailer's *Miami and the Siege of Chicago* and John Schultz's *No One Was Killed.* But nothing short of a twenty-volume oral history could ever hope to record the multiplicity of personal awakenings that the barbarism in Chicago provoked. The vets were no exception. They came away from Chicago with an entirely different mind-set than they had arrived with.

On the way to Chicago, John Talbott issued a press release representing his fellow Vietnam Veterans for McCarthy; it stated in part: "We are not going to Chicago to demonstrate. We are not going to burn flags or draft cards. We are going to inform, to reason, and to implore. We are going to speak out on the most critical issue of this election year." The press release also expressed the hope that the vets could use their political contacts within the Democratic Party, like maverick New York mayoral assistant Paul O'Dwyer, to gain leverage on the floor of the convention. From the moment they arrived in Chicago, however, the vets had neither liberty nor leisure to speak out or to confabulate with Democratic politicos. They were preoccupied with the bloodbath in the streets and had all they could do just to keep from imminent bodily harm.

Talbott and his wife, Susan, were both beaten by police, an experience he claims permanently "radicalized" him. Up to that point he had been convinced that change could come from within the system and still felt committed to preserving the American form of democratic government. Chicago pushed him a good deal farther to the left, to a point where—though not a full-fledged revolutionary—he was ready for more drastic actions.

The guys Larry Rottmann had organized down in Missouri might have passed for Republicans more readily than disciples of Abbie Hoffman and Jerry Rubin. "We had active-duty GIs from Fort Leonard Wood, we had colonels from the National Guard in St. Louis," he enumerates. "We had Vietnam veterans of all stripes and persuasions, who just said 'Yes, we need to get out of the war.'" His chapter of VVFM even had its share of out-and-out right-wingers whose position was: "We can't win this war practically, and so let's cover our bets and get the hell out." Though Rottmann certainly had too fine a moral conscience to subscribe to that brand of military opportunism, he was by no means a radical, much less a revolutionary. "I wasn't into the hippies and Yippies and Black Stone Rangers," he recalls. "I wasn't into trashing anybody. I had seen too much trashing in the war."

Rottmann and several of his Missouri vets drove their cars to the convention. Rottmann himself had a big black '47 Chevy Fleetmaster, with two-foot-tall letters on the side that read: MCCARTHY FOR PRESIDENT. He offered its use to delegates and their families who needed to be shepherded around town, but even on those innocuous errands he got beaten up two or three times, and ended up going to jail twice. On Wednesday August 28, he found himself at Michigan and Balbo, in front of the Hilton, in the midst of the worst of all the police riots. MPs in green uniforms chased him in the Daley dozers and shot tear gas at him. Cops came at him, knocked out his tooth, and broke his arm, all "because I was there to participate in the democratic process!" he exclaims with as much astonishment in retrospect as he felt at the time. Actually the cops did have a specific reason for whacking Rottmann with their nightsticks. He was trying to intervene to keep another cop from beating a thirteen-year-old girl senseless.

Rottmann was wearing his camouflage jacket that day, which was covered with big red-white-and-blue rectangular buttons that said: "Vietnam Veterans for McCarthy." The fact that he was a vet enraged the police more. As they were handcuffing him, kicking him in the balls, and dragging him off to the paddy wagon, they challenged him, "If you are a vet, how could you do that? What, are you a Communist now?" He explained that he was "just here because I want to see how this system works. Don't you see what's going on here? I went and got my ass shot at *for this!*" But the police, convinced that he "had turned somehow," continued to beat him in the paddy wagon on the way to Cook County Jail.

The letters from veterans that Carl Rogers had taken such trouble to select and reproduce never found their way to any of the delegates. The printer was supposed to ship them to the office that Allard Lowenstein, another maverick

Democrat, a representative from Long Island, had set up across from the new Civic Center Plaza (later Daley Plaza). Lowenstein had planned to run his Coalition for an Open Convention from that office, but when he saw what was happening in Chicago, he abandoned not only the effort but also the office. Rogers told him he needed a place for his veterans to congregate, so Lowenstein gave him the key and took off back to his own delegation. Rogers immediately settled in, renaming his group the Vietnam Veterans Committee of the Coalition for an Open Convention. Unfortunately, the letters arrived a day late, and by that time even Rogers couldn't handle the chaos. Because he was working on the McCarthy staff, Rogers was staying at the Hilton, and every night he found himself "getting bashed around by the police" out on the streets; then the next day he and his veteran contingent would regroup over at Civic Center Plaza. The day the cartons of letters arrived, one of the vets asked him, "What do you want to do with these things?" Rogers was so angry and distracted he could only answer facetiously, "I don't give a fuck. Throw them out the window."

A few minutes later Rogers returned from other business to find several veterans throwing thousands of the letters out the front window. The sheets of paper "were blowing in the wind like snow" over the plaza with its gigantic rusted Picasso sculpture, and the droves of people just getting off from work were picking them up to read on their way home. Rogers panicked, told his coworkers to "get the hell out of here," and never came back himself.

In any case, their original plan to greet the buses full of delegates, with cheerful smiles and letters in hand, would have been impossible to carry off in what Rogers now recognized as a "war zone." By the time the letters arrived on Tuesday, McCarthy had already announced—a day before the actual nomination—that he had no chance of gaining his party's endorsement for president of the United States. Some observers felt that he feared an attempt on his life if he began to look like a winner. Whatever his reasons, it was as if he were spitting in the faces of those who had worked so hard for him for the past eight months, telling them their work had been for nothing, that he was giving up before the battle had even been joined.

The most terrible police violence took place in the space of seventeen minutes early Wednesday evening, August 28, but that whole day and night was a blur of pain and madness. Rogers remembers "kids coming into the hotel with cracked heads and lots of blood." Sympathetic delegates and lobbyists, like Rogers, offered their hotel rooms as temporary hospitals. Rogers himself kept running back and forth between the streets and the convention, getting gassed several times, to keep the McCarthy delegates apprised of what was happening. Much later that night, the McCarthy delegates voted to hold a candlelight vigil. They rode their buses back to the Hilton, then joined the kids in Grant

Park, defying the police with their candlelight procession and the singing of old protest songs. Rogers remembers this as perhaps the most dramatic episode of the entire convention.

Recalling Chicago 1968 more than two decades later, Rogers sought to correct the misapprehension that the experience was wholly "traumatic," as so many who were not there and only saw newsreel footage have come to perceive it. He had previously encountered police on horseback using clubs in New York, and a good deal of brutality from the Washington police, also; although he saw a meanness in the Chicago cops that added "a new dimension" and felt that "these guys were having a good time clubbing heads." But for Rogers the essence of the experience "was just one more confirmation of the lies." During the McCarthy campaign, Rogers had drafted an ad with the headline: "Is It in Poor Taste to Call the President a Liar?" At the time, the ad shocked some for its boldness, but it was clear after Chicago—and after the Walker Commission, ordered by the governor of Illinois, exonerated the mayor, the police chief, and individual police officers of any willful wrongdoing—that lying on a big scale had become the American way of life, and that it was just such lying that had kept the war going, and going nowhere, for so many years.

Rogers returned to New York with a strengthened commitment to exposing those lies, and to finding other people, like Jan Barry, who were willing to speak the truth, however ugly and painful, along with him.[15]

3. Changing Directions

Other vets, however, had their lives turned upside down by the McCarthy campaign and its outcome in Chicago. Sheldon Ramsdell had come from a typical Republican family in Ogunquit, Maine, not far from wealthy and prestigious Kennebunkport. Born in 1935, Ramsdell joined the Navy in 1956 for a four-year tour of duty; and though he had been stationed on the USS *Bennington* in the China Sea and the Gulf of Tonkin twice during that period, and planes from his carrier had dropped tons of ordnance including napalm on Indochinese soil, he did not think of himself as a Vietnam veteran until he met Carl Rogers at a draft-card burning in 1967.

By the time he met Rogers, Ramsdell was, at least on the surface, the all-American, midlevel executive—thirty-two years old, just under six feet tall, with a full head of neatly trimmed straight hair, regular features, and businesslike glasses over his big, serious, blue eyes. He had risen quickly in the advertising department of Union Carbide and was a prominent member of the Gotham Young Republican Club. He had even published a how-to book on photography, his avocation (he had been doing highly artistic documentary photography since his stint in the Navy). But under the surface there was a flow of molten lava ready to break through and change his life forever. For one thing, he was gay—at a time when gay almost automatically meant "in the closet"—and therefore hip to the numerous daily hypocrisies that keep the mainstream world running. As a photographer too he knew quite well how images can be cleaned up to look better than the reality they were taken from. But most of all he was getting hit by flashes from his subconscious of something he could not name—something that the vets in VVAW would soon begin to call post-Vietnam syndrome (PVS) or, colloquially, "delayed stress," which would within a few years get its own official psychiatric name: post-traumatic stress disorder (PTSD).

Officially, Ramsdell had never been at war, and even unofficially he had never thought of himself as having been in combat situations—but he had watched men die on his carrier. One of them was his best friend, a dare-devil pilot, who had tried to land his jet one day with extra-special flair and ended up bouncing off the deck in a spectacular fireball captured by Ramsdell in a series of striking photos as it hissed out, along with his life, in the sunny, sparkling China Sea. Not long afterward, Ramsdell was nearby when a crate containing a 100-pound canister of napalm was accidentally dropped down a hatch, burning five sailors to death. At the time he just shrugged off these tragedies, as the young often do; but as the years wore on, he began to think about those losses, and to feel them in the core of his being, and to wonder about the morality of that thing he had been a part of, which more and more he was coming to realize had been a real war effort. Their presence in that place, the dozens of flights every day from his carrier, had been for the purpose of killing human beings—and as that truth sank in, a terror of guilt and uncertainty began to overtake him and led him to look for answers that no government had yet offered him. That same fever of questioning drew him to the draft-card burning at New York's Union Square in the summer of 1967.

Ramsdell admired the guts of the young man who burned his draft card, but he wondered just how far he dared to go himself in opposing his own government. Then he struck up a conversation with Carl Rogers, who not only informed him that he (Ramsdell) could rightfully lay claim to the title of Vietnam veteran, but also solicited him to join VVAW. Ramsdell was incredulous to learn that there existed an organization of Vietnam veterans actively opposing the war. "You're kidding! You'll be killed!" was Ramsdell's first reaction. But, thinking it over for a few seconds, he added in a calmer voice: "But if you manage it, you'll be the most credible dissidents in the nation. The possibilities of this are infinite."

Ramsdell was seduced on the spot by those infinite possibilities. He immediately joined, and within weeks became a key member of VVAW. From the start, he used his photographic talent to document every important activity of the organization. He was with Rogers in February 1968, when Rogers accompanied Martin Luther King Jr. on an antiwar march by Clergy and Laity Concerned to Arlington Cemetery and got King to endorse a statement of VVAW's goals. Ramsdell also became one of the chief veteran press aides in McCarthy's campaign, where, he claims, his paycheck was signed by an official from the Central Intelligence Agency. He suspected there might have been some secret plan by the government to use McCarthy's campaign to "get the youth back into the traditional political swing instead of going off to the left wing"; but such a goal, if it existed, did not seem all that terrible to him at the time—for he was still trying to "get back into the traditional political swing" himself.

Ramsdell had tried to hold down his job and work for VVAW at the same time, but during the McCarthy campaign he simply quit Union Carbide and the straight world for good. It was not just that traveling with McCarthy did not leave him time for a steady job. Working with the other vets, hearing their stories, brought out all the delayed stress he had buried for years. And then the Chicago convention simply tore him up. "I felt betrayed, terribly betrayed!" he says, still choking back tears more than twenty years later. In Chicago he was interviewed by NBC newsman Jack Perkins, who asked him how he felt about the convention as tear gas wafted into the room at the Hilton. Disgusted, Ramsdell answered, "The fat old men with the shiny suits and the big cigars did it their way."

Ramsdell knew that he could no longer be a part of that world. He'd been fed up by the sexism of his Union Carbide colleagues, who would make jokes about the big tits of the waitresses at the Gaslight Club, where they lunched every day. "I gave it up," he recalls. "I said, 'I can't live this way!' And I went out and went crazy! I threw myself into activism like a crazy man." Part of that "craziness" was coming out as a gay man, and another big part of it was working to find solutions "to the social problems at home, in relation to Vietnam, [asking] why are we killing people [in foreign countries] when we haven't even taken care of the needs of our own people?" Ramsdell ended up attacking his own photography book, part of the Dodd, Mead What Do They Do? Series, because of what he felt was its blatant racism—it showed no nonwhite photographers, except for one Japanese. His realization that he had been led to contribute to a "white textbook" had fueled his anger even more, making him feel "I've been used again!"

The transition from successful, conservative young man on the way up to radical left-winger was brutal. "I came out of the service a hero," he explains. "I went into a corporation, *I had it made, and I gave it up!* My family went nuts! They said, 'Jesus! You're set! You can fly anywhere you want. You can afford a wonderful apartment on the East Side.' I had girlfriends, I had enough money and clout and credit cards, and I gave it up. Something said, '*Don't do this! Something is wrong with this!*'" But, by his own admission, he didn't realize what he was getting into, the Pandora's box of his own consciousness that he was throwing open, the pain of so many others that he would experience, as he reexperienced his own long-buried pain—simply by making that commitment to being a full-time activist.[16]

Still other vets came away from Chicago with their lives turned in a happier and more healing direction. Larry Rottmann had felt a deep commitment to education as a means of solving the world's problems even before he went to Vietnam. His father was a professor of economics at the University of Missouri, and his mother worked in the university's public information office. Rottmann had gotten his B.A. in English there and was on his way to a graduate assistant-ship at the University of Melbourne in August 1965 when he learned he was about to be drafted. He enlisted to have "the choice of services and some deter-mination about what direction I might go in." Both his father and his grandfather had been Army vets, and he believed that "this country had been good to me. I did feel I owed something to my country."

After OCS (Officer Candidate School) at Fort Benning, Rottmann served in Vietnam from March 1967 to March 1968, as a liaison officer between the 25th Infantry Division at Cu Chi and the local Vietnamese Special Forces and CIDG (Civilian and Irregular Defense Group). During Tet of 1968, he was wounded in the head by fragments from a 122mm rocket. After he returned from an in-country hospital, he served out his remaining two months as an information officer in Cu Chi, compiling a history of the 25th Infantry Division—the famous "Tropic Lightning" that author James Jones had served with in World War II—later published by McCall.

Rottmann was still no war protester, but "it became pretty clear to me real quick that it [the war] was a bum idea. It was clear to anybody who was look-ing that it was the wrong war at the wrong place at the wrong time against the wrong people for the wrong reasons. It was just a debacle of catastrophic pro-portions." His perception of the "madness" in Vietnam propelled him to join the Vietnam Veterans for McCarthy, but it also had a good deal to do with his beginning graduate studies in education at the Cambridge-Goddard Graduate School Program at about the same time—where, fortuitously, antiwar activist Noam Chomsky was his advisor.

The events in Chicago "pissed [him] off" because he felt Vietnam veterans like himself, the ones who dared to speak out, were under attack. "One of the things that I wanted to do was help legitimize the veterans' point of view," he says, "because I was seeing veterans—antiwar veterans or pro-peace veterans—vilified. . . . [The official attitude was] if you were a veteran then the least you could do would be to keep your mouth shut about the 'bad war.' The worst thing you could do would be to stand up in public and criticize it."

Having been an officer, Rottmann had had the chance to get to know ser-vicemen of all ranks, and he had been deeply impressed by the intelligence and articulateness of people in the military—not, of course, a view shared by many college graduates at the time. "I said to myself, 'These people can be effective,'" he recalls. "Their legitimacy should not be in question. In fact, if anything, their opinions and ideas are more legitimate than those of the administration or the media. There's a story here that needs to be told. So that's kind of how I got into the VVAW business."

Not only did he leave Chicago with a strong commitment to completing his graduate degree, but Rottmann found there a new impetus for an old habit: writing. While he was working in the McCarthy campaign, people had continually asked him, "What's Vietnam like?" He had had difficulty answering them directly, so he would write his responses in private, often in the form of poems, which he would then read to people in answer to their questions. Poetry had the advantage of an economy of words; and the "artistic format," he found, enabled people to "listen better." The other advantage was that the writing enabled Rottmann to distance himself from his subject, "so I would be a little more rational. Instead of screaming, 'You motherfucker, I'll break your head if you call me a Commie again!' I backed off from confrontational politics . . . [and I turned to] the power of the written word."

In Chicago, he and his fellow veterans had been beaten, and he saw firsthand—as he had already seen in Vietnam—that "you don't change anybody from hitting them over the head." The greatest lesson he took away from Chicago was that to change people's minds, you must speak to those minds— either directly, as a teacher, or through the medium of writing.

Following Chicago, Rottmann started speaking at high schools and colleges with Jeremy Rifkin, one of the founders of the Citizens' Commission of Inquiry into U.S. War Crimes (CCI), and later ended up participating in two of the International War Crimes Tribunals in Oslo, Norway. As part of VVAW delegations he traveled to Canada and to Paris to meet with the North Vietnamese and to offer his insights to negotiators on both sides in the Paris Peace Talks. He also made a tour, partly at his own expense, through Italy, Germany, England, France, Norway, Finland, and the Soviet Union, speaking to civic groups, schools, and peace organizations. At various times he spoke and debated alongside major peace movement activists, including Chomsky.

Amid all this frenetic activity, Rottmann found time to continue writing poems, which eventually became a substantial body of work. Even more importantly, in terms of long-term impact, he began to gather, along with Jan Barry, the writings of other Vietnam veterans wherever he found them. He would print some of them in the VVAW newspaper, *First Casualty*, which he later edited; and he would eventually help compile, edit, and publish two collections of Vietnam veteran literature, *Winning Hearts and Minds* and *Free Fire Zone*.

Rottmann, who went on to become one of the foremost educators and writers of the Vietnam generation, was one of the success stories of the first wave of Vietnam veteran activism. But the majority of that group, after the debacle in Chicago, retreated into themselves and away from public confrontation. Jan Barry and Carl Rogers called a meeting of VVAW in New York to regroup, but nobody came. "Everybody was not only discouraged, but just furious," Barry remembers. The big question for all of them was what to do now, after their best efforts had seemingly failed to stir the nation, or to affect the current war policy in any way.[17]

VVAW appeared dead, and it would not be revived till the following year.

4. The GI Movement

The energy of VVAW did not die altogether in the fall of 1968; initially, it began to find its way into other organizations. A shift in orientation, and a definite polarization, was taking place post-Chicago.

In an unpublished piece on his experience there, Carl Rogers described the last day of the convention, Thursday August 29, when a group of delegates, ministers, and protesters led by black comedian Dick Gregory attempted to march to the Chicago Amphitheatre. They were blocked by the National Guard, who initially threatened to arrest them, then gassed them instead with CS, the strongest, most virulent form of tear gas. As he watched the guardsmen putting ammunition clips into their rifles, he suddenly felt great fear of these men he had heretofore identified with because of their familiar uniforms and military bearing. Suddenly soldiers—in so far as they represented the government— were no longer buddies, but the enemy. He cursed at them—calling them "Bastards!"—and no longer sought to defend them to his civilian comrades, which he had been doing up till that moment. He had turned a corner that many other vets would turn in the months and years to come.

That night the McCarthy headquarters was again turned into a makeshift hospital, as Hubert Humphrey, now the recipient of his party's nomination for president, with no commitment at all to ending the war any time soon, went on television to blather about the triumph of his "politics of joy." "At this convention we have recognized the end of an era and the beginning of a new day," said Humphrey. Wrote Rogers in response: "He doesn't know the half of it."

For Rogers, that "new day" meant daring now to challenge the government at every step. Soon after the failed VVAW meeting, Rogers, together with his friend Steve Wilcox and Jan Barry, began to organize LINK—the short name for an operation officially known as the Serviceman's Link to the Peace Movement. It was the first time veterans acted in concert to aid active-duty GIs who were part of the revolt inside the military. Many vets who had been discharged before the American military machine had begun to falter did not know of the existence of the GI movement, and a good part of LINK's job was simply to spread the word, like modern-day Paul Reveres. Recalls Barry: "Suddenly we were discovering this enormous revolt going on within the military that nobody really had any other way of hearing was going on."

LINK not only offered GI rebels the brotherly support of their comrades who were already discharged (and hence able to protest without fear of military punishment); but it also served to connect those GIs (the ones who were in disciplinary trouble and the ones headed for it) with civilian peace activists, to act as the critical "bridge" between the two that until then had been lacking.

From the fall of 1968 through most of 1969, Rogers, Barry, and other vets worked to support and help defend numerous GIs facing court-martial. They became involved in all the famous trials of the time—including those of Navy nurse Susan Schnall, the Presidio 27, and Roger Priest, a seaman at the Pentagon who had begun publishing his own antiwar magazine, *Om*.

VVAW had taken an interest in GI dissenters from its inception. In August 1967, Jan Barry had written to the New York Civil Liberties Union to see if they could help with the case of a seaman who had been sentenced to three months in prison for wearing a peace symbol on his uniform. The ACLU declined to help, for two reasons—since the uniform is a symbol of the military, the seaman's action could not automatically be construed as an exercise of his individual right to free speech, and by the time Barry reached them, the seaman had already served one month of his sentence.

When Barry and Rogers organized LINK, the free speech issue had already become the focus of the growing GI movement. Robert Sherrill, a journalist with whom Rogers worked closely, articulated the problem in an article for the *New York Times Magazine:* "Inevitably, just as a handful of black sit-inners and bus-riders threw the South into such a fit of resistance that a broad civil rights act was forced through Congress, this handful of protesting GIs appear to have pushed the military establishment onto a collision course with the U.S. Constitution . . . either the military will emerge more nearly as 'an enclave beyond the reach of the civilian courts' (the words of Chief Justice Earl Warren, in warning) or the Constitution will be pressed down so heavily on the military system that the old ideal of a 'citizens' army'—complete with all the safeguards of the Bill of Rights—will be considerably closer to achievement."

The GIs that LINK aimed to help were by and large a new breed, a lot more aggressive and defiant, even openly hostile, than that 1967 seaman with his peace symbol. Roger Priest typified this new breed. He was a tall, blond, twenty-five-year-old graduate from the University of Houston, who had originally gone to Europe to avoid the draft, but then changed his mind and decided to return to the States to challenge the whole system. He joined the Navy but was repulsed by the dehumanization of boot camp, and even more offended by the brutality he saw enacted against Marine recruits at a nearby base. When he was transferred to the Pentagon, he got in trouble for refusing extra mailroom duties; his stubbornness should have earned him a simple rebuke, but instead the Navy put Priest through a court-martial, fining him and reducing his rank. Incensed, Priest responded by publishing his antiwar magazine.

When he was brought up for a second court-martial, the government charged Priest with publishing a pamphlet that "contained statements advising and urging insubordination, disloyalty and the refusal of duty by members of the military and naval forces of the United States." But it was clear that the main reason they were angry at him was the way he had bandied about the names of too many sacred cows—Lyndon Johnson, J. Edgar Hoover, Secretary of Defense Melvin Laird, and Chairman of the House Armed Services Committee L. Mendel Rivers (D-S.C.). Priest had a regular vendetta going with Rivers. As a result of scandalous cases like the Presidio 27—where GI prisoners in an Army stockade, after protesting the killing of a mentally disturbed young soldier by a guard, were tried for "mutiny" and sentenced to fifteen years at hard labor—the Army had set new guidelines that gave GIs a great deal more freedom in speaking their own mind. But Chairman Rivers was outraged that General Westmoreland and Secretary of the Army Stanley Resor had apparently caved in to the liberals, and he called them before his committee and dressed them down like schoolboys, forcing them to read aloud the portion of the Constitution that states that the Congress can make laws to regulate the Army. He even told Westmoreland, who came from his home state, "If you have got one drop of South Carolina blood left in your veins, you don't agree with [the new guidelines]." Soon afterward, the Army reverted to cracking down on GI newspapers, coffeehouses, and all forms of organizing. Priest responded by heaping contempt on Rivers in a special court-martial edition of his magazine. When he was charged, redundantly, with "wrongfully and disrespectfully casting contempt" on the Honorable Rivers, Priest quipped that he should have known better—he should have "rightfully and respectfully" cast contempt on the congressman.

Nor was Priest above engaging in outright guerrilla warfare. The stunt that most upset the military was his designation of the War Resisters League as the beneficiary of his GI life insurance policy. He said he hoped to start a trend, so that every time a GI died in Vietnam, the War Resisters League would be ten thousand dollars richer![18]

Carl Rogers became deeply involved in Priest's trial, and when the Navy finally agreed to simply grant Priest an early release from his enlistment, in mid-1969, Rogers brought him on staff in LINK's Washington, D.C., office, where he became a counselor to other GIs who were in trouble for speaking out.

This shift toward confrontational politics did not take place all at once in the veterans' movement—or even among its leaders. In October 1968, Barry and Rogers were still urging whatever members they had left—that is, anyone still on their mailing list—to remain active in the political process, and to continue working for the election of antiwar congressional candidates like Allard Lowenstein and Paul O'Dwyer. They were also attempting to maintain their program of veterans speaking in high schools and colleges—a facet of the veterans' movement that, much to their credit, remained as prominent in the following three decades as it was in the beginning. But there was also a call, for the first time (and quite the opposite of VVAW's hands-off position regarding the March on the Pentagon a year earlier), to get involved in antiwar demonstrations.

The first big demonstration they participated in, after Chicago, was National GI Week, November 1–5, 1968. Sponsored by the National Mobilization Committee to End the War in Vietnam, the goals of National GI Week were to make GIs realize that criticism of the war was not necessarily unpatriotic, to apprise them of their First Amendment rights, and to draw more dissident GIs into speaking out. In all of these tasks, Vietnam veterans played a key role. The strongest proof that antiwar talk was not necessarily un-American or Communist-inspired was to hear it from the mouths of genuine American heroes. So often before, GIs had ignored attacks on the war because they seemed to be attacks on *them*—especially coming from smart-ass kids who were "waiting out the war in college." It was a different matter hearing the same story from guys whose buddies had already died in a war that even the fighters could not see a reason for.

Among the activities planned by the Mobe for National GI Week were visits by civilians and veterans to military bases around the country, including attempts to inspect conditions in stockades, the distribution of antiwar literature, antiwar picnics, "love-ins," and free entertainment—all under the banner of FTA, Free the Army or Fuck the Army, as it was variously interpreted. (Jane Fonda and Donald Sutherland would present virtually the same program, under the same banner, three years later.) But National GI Week also had a political slant. For one thing, its conclusion was timed to fall on Election Day, November 5, when the nation would be offered a selection of three presidential candidates: Hubert Humphrey, George Wallace (of the American Independent Party), and Richard Nixon, all of whom were essentially committed to continuing Johnson's policies in Vietnam—though Nixon, the eventual winner, did claim to have a "secret plan" to end the war, a plan that never really existed. Secondly, truth be told, the Mobe was in many respects a front for the Socialist Workers Party (SWP). Its leaders were already pushing a class-oriented view of American society, which saw the rich as exploiters of the poor both in this country and around the world, and they called attention to the fact that blacks and poor people were doing more than their fair share of the fighting and dying in Vietnam.[19]

The veterans' participation in National GI Week had long-term ramifications. The connection they established with the Mobe would contribute to the rebirth of VVAW a year later, during the period of the Vietnam Moratorium Days. And, for better or worse, the connection with the Mobe continued the pull, begun during the presidential campaign, of the veterans' movement into the scalding vortex of American politics. The vets in VVAW were finding that willy-nilly they had to take sides—for or against the government, for or against various political parties—in order to effect the changes they wanted. Eventually the politicization of VVAW would bring it crashing to earth—in a fall that both disoriented its members and rendered the organization ineffectual for years to follow.

That the veterans' movement began to muddy and bloody itself in politics was due neither to naiveté nor to an abandonment of their identity as American servicemen. Granted, many of them knew little enough about politics at the start, but they had their eyes wide open and were learning fast. Barry and Rogers were insistent that Vietnam Veterans Against the War keep some sort of visible presence, even during what Jan would later call its "latency period." In fact, they turned the organization's management over to a vet named Jim Boggio in Los Angeles, whose enthusiasm had led him to found a recent chapter of VVAW on the West Coast. Boggio's L.A. chapter would become the "national headquarters" for a year—a kind of bluff, which Rogers glossed over by sending out a memo saying it was time New York gave the rest of the country a chance, and that the organization needed "fresh leadership." But there was method to Barry and Rogers' madness, for they were smart enough not to put all their veteran eggs in one basket—especially the basket of some political party, which might not have their best interest at heart. By letting the nation know that Vietnam vets were still organizing, if only far out there in Southern California, they were giving themselves the option of returning to an all-veterans' movement in the future—a move whose wisdom would be borne out soon enough.

The directional changes in the veterans' movement were not merely the result of the whims of its leaders, but direct responses to the situation of the war itself, of the GIs still enmeshed in it, and of the newly created veterans it kept churning out. Before he left office in January 1969, Johnson had halted the bombing of North Vietnam and begun a slight reduction in American troop strength. Soon after President Richard Nixon's inauguration, he began his own slowly paced withdrawal of American forces in what he euphemistically called Vietnamization: the alleged turning over of the conduct of the war to the South Vietnamese—though most of the South Vietnamese leaders, civilian and military, did not want that responsibility, nor did most of them believe they would ever really have to assume it. As for the North Vietnamese, they couldn't have been happier with Vietnamization. As People's Army of Vietnam (PAVN)

General Nguyen Dinh Uoc recalled thirty years later, "[If] side by side with five hundred thousand U.S. troops, the Saigon army had failed, then how could it stand on its feet when the U.S. troops were out?"

Americans continued to die in Vietnam at a frightening rate throughout 1969. And as they died, in what was now most likely a *losing cause,* their fellow troops began to question the worth of risking their own lives for such folly. Disciplinary problems, AWOLs, and outright mutinies suddenly increased all over Vietnam, and the breakdown in morale spread quickly back to the States and other U.S. military bases throughout the world.

A LINK newsletter published in late 1969 let the facts speak for themselves. When the organization had begun in the fall of 1968, the Army prison population stood at about 4,800 and the number of Americans killed in the war totaled 27,509. A year later 37,598 had been killed, and there were 6,400 imprisoned— with the Army in the process of building more and bigger stockades to accommodate the ever-increasing tide of protesters and nonconformists.

The same newsletter, quoting from journalist Robert Sherrill's book *Military Justice Is to Justice, As Military Music Is to Music,* pointed out that during every year since the Vietnam conflict had escalated into a major war, 100,000 Americans in uniform had faced court-martial; and that, contrary to the promises of the Bill of Rights, they were given no possibility of bail, no trial by peers (it was always officers who judged enlisted men), no guarantee of an impartial judge, and no due process. Furthermore, 95 percent of the defendants were convicted. In an article in the *New York Times Magazine,* Sherrill pointed out that a general court-martial (the kind that sits for the most serious offenses) was usually called at the discretion of the commanding officer after he had considered the evidence against the accused. The commanding officer then chose, from among his subordinates, the presiding officer and the panel that sat in judgment, and also named the prosecution and defense attorneys— all of whom already knew which way the wind was blowing, and what sort of verdict they ought to come up with if they wanted to stay in line for their next promotion. As if there weren't already enough bias against the accused built into the system, the commanding officer then got to review the decision. In a system like that, it was no wonder, wrote Sherrill, that three defendants (in the Presidio 27 case) could get sentences of 14, 15, and 16 years at hard labor, respectively, for failure to stop singing "America the Beautiful" on command.

While such travesties were taking place, Richard Nixon somehow found it not contradictory to state his belief that "every man in uniform is a citizen first and a serviceman second, and that we must resist any attempt to isolate or separate the defenders from the defended."[20]

But LINK did not go about its work of exposing such hypocrisies (and distributing tens of thousands of reprinted articles that highlighted them) just for the sake of proving the inanity of the current Administration. The members of

LINK—and to his credit, most especially Carl Rogers—were beginning to recognize a problem for veterans that would soon take on vast proportions: bad-paper discharges. A bad-paper discharge was any discharge that was less than Honorable. Bad-paper discharges could result in anything from the bearer receiving less than standard veterans' benefits to his complete inability to get a decent job or to lead any kind of normal life outside the military. At this time, moreover, all discharges, Honorable or less than Honorable, still came with a set of so-called spin numbers, a form of code that labeled the particular reason for the bearer's separation from the military. Often the spins described a form of maladjustment, which, without the bearer's knowledge, could identify him as anything from a homosexual to an atheist. There were 446 categories listed in the spins, over half of which "ranged from derogatory to damning." Employers, law enforcement officials, VA workers, and others in a position to either reward or punish the freshly discharged GI usually had access to these numbers.

As rebellion in the armed services escalated after the Tet Offensive in 1968, so did the number of bad-paper discharges. Between 1964 and 1973 (the officially designated dates of the Vietnam era), 563,000 vets received less-than-Honorable discharges—7 percent of all men who served during that era. Many of those bad-paper discharges went to the three million men who had served their country under fire in Vietnam, and who had often acted out under pressure and in crazed situations that the six million troops outside of Vietnam were not subjected to. The term post-traumatic stress disorder was not even known when the majority of those discharges were issued.

In the words of Vietnam veteran historian and activist Brian Willson: "Vietnam produced opposition by soldiers and veterans on a scale and a fervor never seen before. . . . Levels of prosecutions for resistance activities dramatically increased during the Vietnam War." Among other evidence, Willson cites such facts as that in 1971 alone, Congress received 250,000 complaints about the treatment of U.S. servicemen by the military—"an unheard of number"—and that in 1972 there were more conscientious objectors than draftees. He also notes that the desertion rate increased nearly 400 percent between 1966 and 1971, and that the Army's prison population tripled during the course of the war, the majority of those prisoners being nonwhite.[21]

5. Enter Al Hubbard

By the fall of 1969, the energy in LINK was beginning to run down. For one thing, the organization had never had more than a hundred members. For another, it began to spread itself too thin, trying to do everything from documenting "the malfunctioning of the UCMJ (Uniform Code of Military Justice)" to publishing a "Congressional directory for GIs (with views on how to register opinions with legislators)"—in addition to its mainline work of funding and supporting GI defendants like Roger Priest, attempting to reverse their convictions when they occurred, and lobbying Congress to show more concern over the continuing miscarriages of military justice. As if all that weren't enough, Rogers and Wilcox had plans to extend the movement overseas, to connect with malcontent GIs through coffeehouses and R & R (Rest and Recreation) centers throughout the world, and to start their own GI antiwar coffeehouses in Hong Kong, Tokyo, Sidney, and Bangkok. Rogers admits that partly they "wanted to do a little world traveling," but they were also seeking new ways to be "a thorn in the side of the military." But the whole plan fell through because they just couldn't get the money for it.

Before it went out of business, LINK accomplished some astounding feats, perhaps most remarkably, the sending to tens of thousands of GIs in Vietnam a flyer asking them to take part in a referendum on the question: "Should the United States bring its soldiers home from Vietnam?" Many of the flyers were returned—with, as might be expected, a high percentage of soldiers voting to send themselves back to the States—but by that point LINK was incapable of making effective political use of its findings.

By the fall of 1969, the civilian peace movement was building again, in a bigger and more dramatic way than ever before, and it was drawing attention, energy, and money from every available countercultural source. The biggest recipient of all these goodies was a coalition of the National Mobilization to End the War, which had recently been reborn as the New Mobilization Committee, and a significantly younger, more mainstream group called the Vietnam Moratorium Committee. These groups worked together in an unusual harmony to plan a series of monthly Vietnam Moratorium Days, beginning October 15.

The demonstrations on October 15 took a variety of quiet but impressive forms, everything from students wearing peace armbands to speeches and readings of the names of the war dead on village greens throughout the nation. In many large cities there were completely nonviolent rallies of tens of thousands of people, who came simply to show their support for an immediate end to the war. Some observers estimated that as many as ten million people took part in that first Vietnam Moratorium Day.

Building on that energy, the second Moratorium Day resulted in the largest single political demonstration in the history of the United States, on November 15, 1969. Somewhere between half and three-quarters of a million people pressed together into the forty-one acres around the Washington Monument to hear daylong speeches against the war—while inside the White House, the chief executive, who had previously stated his determination not to be affected by any show of opposition to the war, amused himself by watching college football.

The third Moratorium Day, which would have fallen on December 15, never happened—by then, the peace movement had once again begun to unravel into myriad different ideological strands. But the demonstrators had been more successful than they realized, pushing Nixon and his national security advisor Henry Kissinger away from plans to greatly escalate the war, possibly even to the point of using nuclear weapons, and back toward their "Vietnamization" strategy of propping up the Saigon regime with money and materiel in preference to American bodies.[22]

Among the accomplishments of the Moratorium Days, though no one knew it at the time, was the revival of the Vietnam veterans' movement.

Because of his visibility in LINK, Carl Rogers had been asked to serve on the steering committee of the last major antiwar conference, at Case Western Reserve University in Cleveland on July 4 and 5, 1969—the conference where the National Mobilization Committee, demoralized by its failure to produce a significant "counterinaugural" demonstration in January, underwent its transformation into the New Mobilization Committee. The fact that the New Mobe had moved at least a few notches to the right, away from radical extremism and toward Middle America, doubtless made it more congenial to Vietnam veterans. At the same time, the Vietnam Moratorium Committee was forming, and its leaders—David Hawk, David Mixner, Marge Sklencar, and Sam Brown—were all people Rogers was intimately connected with from what he called the "children's crusade" for the McCarthy campaign. Soon LINK, the New Mobe, and the Moratorium Committee were all working out of the same Washington headquarters at 1029 Vermont Avenue NW.

VVAW had become merely a mailing list after the Democratic convention in Chicago, and Rogers controlled that list. One day Sheldon Ramsdell asked to use the list to get together a New York veterans' group in support of the Moratorium. Ramsdell had spent the past year working for the New York Press Service and hanging out in the thick of Democratic Party politics, and he had made some powerful connections. Through Congresswoman Bella Abzug he had met wealthy New England Brahmin Peggy Kerry, who worked for Robert Morgenthau, the attorney general of New York. Peggy was the sister of Silver Star recipient Lieutenant (j.g.) John Forbes Kerry, who would soon join the reborn VVAW as its star member. Ramsdell had also become close with Adam Walinsky, formerly a junior attorney under Bobby Kennedy at the Justice Department and later a member of Kennedy's Senate staff. It was Walinsky who had called Ramsdell and asked him to get the veterans involved in the Moratorium.

Jan Barry, who'd been doing a lot of writing and introspecting, as well as working with LINK, suddenly felt the call to get on board as a veteran activist again, and he and Ramsdell worked hand in hand to put out the call to veterans. According to Barry, the New York office of the Moratorium "provided us an umbrella from which we reconstituted the organization, and a whole new wave of people came in."

Within a few months, VVAW had several hundred new members. Many of them came directly out of VA hospitals, bringing with them word of the terrible conditions that Vietnam veterans were experiencing in those places. At the same time, the story of the slaughter of some 500 Vietnamese civilians at My Lai was just breaking, and a number of people began to call for veterans to testify about the atrocities they had witnessed in the war. Barry's first response to these demands, especially the ones that came from the media, was: "This is crazy. We're not coming forward just to titillate you with atrocities; it's [to say] that they're part and parcel of the official policy there, whether it's written down or not to do this." But, according to Barry, "they didn't want to hear this." Nevertheless, he got involved with a number of groups that were focusing on the war crimes issue, including Tod Ensign and Jeremy Rifkin's CCI (Citizens' Commission of Inquiry) and a church-based organization called the Committee to Investigate United States' War Crimes. Although veterans were being recruited independently by many of these groups, a number of them, once they got active, filtered into VVAW.[23]

The most important new member to enter VVAW that fall (1969) was a black man named Al Hubbard, an Air Force veteran of both Korea and Vietnam. In fact, he claimed to have been on American air transports bringing supplies to the beleaguered French during their war with the Viet Minh, the forerunners of the present Viet Cong. Al was older by at least a decade than most of the other vets in VVAW, and he was already highly politicized. He was a tall, lean, light-skinned black man and wore a militant Afro hairstyle, a goatee, and talked in the lingo of the Black Panthers, to whom he had strong connections, though more as a sympathizer than a member. In Sheldon Ramsdell's view, Al had "a good healthy attitude [on the subject of racism]. We needed him badly. We had to get people of color [into VVAW]."

Hubbard was by all accounts a character, what in certain places like Greenwich Village in the fifties would have been called a hipster. He even wrote his own brand of poetry. He had injured his back in a military plane crash, lived on a service pension, and took a large quantity of prescription drugs for back pain. He was always ready to have a good time; and by all accounts, he had a great affinity for the opposite sex. The other vets found him attractive as a leader for a variety of reasons. He had been a sergeant in the Air Force and had the tough discipline of a noncom who's used to getting things done quickly and efficiently. He also had an angry edge that gave teeth to his social conscience, so that he did not fight from the head only, but also from the heart. In the words of Sheldon Ramsdell, "Al had a bit of a complex" over the inferior roles he'd had to play in life—a black man in a white man's world, a sergeant doing the work of officers, always making others look good, and helping white men fight two wars against people he considered his dark-skinned brothers. Like a lot of younger blacks in that period, Hubbard felt impelled to stand up to authority and to get some of life's good things for himself.

He started the process by telling people he had been a captain, not a sergeant—a deception that later almost cost VVAW its credibility in the media and before the American people. But from the moment Al came into VVAW he began to make friends and acquire followers, not least of all because of his fierce enthusiasm for reform. "I used to get a kick out of him," Ramsdell recalls, "because he was actually having a good time with all of this [organizational work of VVAW]."

Hubbard had grown up in Brooklyn and gone into the Air Force planning to make it his career. But he had been in only twelve years when the plane crash forced him to take a medical retirement. After leaving the service, he went to the University of Washington, where he earned an undergraduate degree and began his career as an activist. According to Mike Oliver, a VVAW national officer who later lived with Hubbard, Al "had real feelings for the Vietnamese and what it meant to grow up black in America," believing that as a black man he could understand the oppression of third world peoples everywhere. In addition, Hubbard had evidently studied American history in depth, since he could discourse knowledgeably about it. When Oliver came into the organization in 1970, he found that "his [Hubbard's] mind was the most forceful one there."

Hubbard began to act as a leader from the day he joined VVAW. "He was an out-and-out leader, there was no doubt about it," says Oliver, who recalls Al's dynamic manner and strong speaking voice. "The guys respected him, and he was absolutely crucial. VVAW was a defunct organization that had one aim, just to bring the troops home. In 1969 that started to change, and then in 1970 we came up with a politics." The new, reconstituted VVAW had a definite set of political beliefs, and it was around those beliefs that the members organized. According to Oliver, Al Hubbard had a lot to do with that change: "He was more grass-roots oriented, and he had a much better comprehension [than other VVAW members] of how racism permeates this society, and how it really holds this country back. He knew that if we were unified it would be a great America, a good America, but . . . that there is not one America, there are two Americas."[24]

Jan Barry was still president of VVAW, but the actual leadership roles were fairly fluid, and often posts were created specifically to utilize individuals' talents. Hubbard quickly became the organization's executive secretary. One of his first acts was to sketch out a plan for making VVAW a service organization for Vietnam veterans, as well as an instrument for social change. Like a lot of Vietnam veterans, Hubbard was repelled by the blind patriotism of the VFW and the American Legion, which he blamed "for the military attitudes in this country through their unlimited lobbying." Both the VFW and the American Legion were having a hard time recruiting the younger veterans, many of whom had returned from Vietnam with a permanent distrust toward all organizations. It did not help that members of the older veterans' organizations often looked askance at Vietnam vets as losers, druggies, and misfits. "These younger veterans are not content with a para-military, pro-war organization representing them," wrote Hubbard in a VVAW policy paper. "We are their answer."

Hubbard felt there would be a great attraction in a veterans organization that held "a view toward world peace rather than world domination," especially if it also offered the perks that veterans had previously looked to the older organizations for. He suggested VVAW offer its members brochures of veterans' benefits, service officers trained in social work and medical disability benefits, and the chance to purchase health and life insurance at group rates; in addition, he suggested the organization lobby on behalf of veterans' benefits as well as "for social programs which will enable our polarized society to relate to each other and each other's problems." He also made an attempt to comply with the requirements for VVAW's recognition and accreditation as a Veterans Administration–approved service organization.[25]

Obviously Hubbard did not accomplish his whole program overnight, but the changes he laid out contributed to the tide of new members that poured into VVAW in 1970. That tide also swelled in response to Richard Nixon's escalation of the war into Cambodia in April and the subsequent killing of four students at Kent State University during a protest demonstration on May 4. Until that point—when Americans began to kill Americans over the war—many Vietnam veterans, however bitter, had accepted the war as a tragic necessity. But Kent State served as a watershed for thousands of veterans, pushing them to voice their opinions for the first time. Bill Ehrhart, who had won a Purple Heart as a Marine infantryman, and who was beginning to forge his new identity as the poet W. D. Ehrhart, would later describe his radicalization after Kent State in terms that echoed the feelings of countless others:

> It isn't enough to send us halfway around the world to die, I thought. It isn't enough to turn us loose on Asians. Now you are turning the soldiers loose on your own children. Now you are killing your own children in the streets of America. My throat constricted into a tight knot. I could hardly breathe. . . .
>
> I cried until there was nothing left inside and my mind was more lucid than it had ever been before.
>
> And then I knew. It was time—long past time—to put aside excuses and pride and vain illusions. Time to forget all that was irretrievably lost. Time to face up to the hard, cold, utterly bitter truth I'd tried to avoid for nearly three years. The war was a horrible mistake, and my beloved country was dying because of it. America was bleeding to death in the ricefields and jungles of Vietnam, and now the blood flowed in our own streets.

I did not want my country to die. I had to do something.
It was time to stop the war.[26]

It would take another year after Kent State before Ehrhart would be able to shed enough of his own warrior identity to feel comfortable about joining VVAW, but many veterans joined within days or weeks of that shattering event. In April 1970, VVAW had a membership of about 600; five months later, there would be over 2,000 names on its rolls, with members in almost every state and more than a dozen chapters around the country. The highest concentrations of members were in New York, Ohio, Pennsylvania, New Jersey, Washington, D.C., and Wisconsin.

One of Hubbard's first moves was to send members out to organize chapters on campuses. Although GI educational benefits weren't nearly as good in the sixties as after World War II, many Vietnam vets had gone to college, usually to the cheaper state schools—if only to lose themselves for a few years in an atmosphere of good times, rock music, and the type of learning that did not involve large daily doses of death and destruction. Hubbard sensed that however much these vets might want to forget Vietnam, they had plenty of suppressed emotions that would eventually need an escape valve. His instinct proved right on the mark. From 1970 until late in the war, VVAW groups continued to spring up on campuses throughout the country, and often existing veterans' groups of the drink-and-party variety would convert into chapters of VVAW. It did not take long for college veterans to realize the power, as well as the catharsis, that came from sharing their war experiences with one another. The campus chapters of VVAW would become one of the organization's strongest bases of support in the years to come.

Two other major areas where VVAW recruited were the VA hospitals and black political groups, especially the Black Panthers. Although the visits to VA hospitals brought in many new members, the reason for them was largely humanitarian; the vets in VVAW were devastated to learn how poorly their injured and disabled peers were being cared for. "Everybody was in this thing together for a good purpose," attests Sheldon Ramsdell, "and the purposes weren't just the war." Ramsdell, who visited Bethesda Naval Hospital and several others, found that "the guys [there] loved us. The policy of the war wasn't always an issue with them; they just liked the idea that the people who had been over there had come back to find out what their problems were." According to Ramsdell, it was by visiting vets in the hospitals that VVAW first learned of the magnitude of the drug problem among guys returning from Vietnam. Similarly, when Hubbard took other veterans to Panther meetings with him, it wasn't simply to recruit new members; although that did happen, since a lot of Panthers, just like other young black men, had gone into the service either via the draft or economic necessity. In fact, Hubbard even managed to organize a

Black Panther chapter of VVAW in Harlem. But Hubbard's main purpose was to raise the collective consciousness of VVAW to the issue of racism, both in the war and at home. Bringing VVAW into contact with Black Power organizations had a lot to do with its rapid transformation, in Ramsdell's words, from "a slick PR operation" into a "real radical movement." Hubbard was one of the first people in VVAW to suggest—as Martin Luther King Jr. had suggested in his "Declaration of Independence from the War in Vietnam" speech—that American violence abroad stemmed from the precedent of repressing people's freedom at home.

Still another part of Hubbard's program was to get VVAW involved in the congressional elections of 1970. He felt that VVAW could be crucial in helping to form "a Congress that will be responsive to the needs of the people . . . we will be searching out candidates from a cross-section of political ideologies who our membership believes will best represent sensible Vietnam and post-Vietnam policy, and moreover, a reasonable military and foreign posture. We will encourage support of peace candidates throughout the country. . . ."[27]

Thanks to all these new activities, as well as the ongoing lectures at high schools and colleges, VVAW took on a far higher profile in 1970 than it ever had before. Small donations were pouring in by mail from all over the country. Such was their newfound cachet that they even received a one-hundred-dollar donation from former Undersecretary of State George Ball.

On a one-to-one, human level, VVAW was also having a good measure of success. Ramsdell took part in VVAW excursions to draft boards in Brooklyn, where the vets would storm in and literally chase out droves of teenagers (many black) who had come to register or enlist. "Go home! You've got no business here!" the vets would yell at the kids who seemed all too willing to go where they had been. "You've got a drug problem? Wait till you come home!" Though technically encouraging draft evasion, none of the vets were ever charged with that crime. What most impressed Ramsdell was the sympathy the vets found among the workers in such places. VVAW, he asserts, was continually "helped a little along the way from a lot of dissidents inside government," people with caring hearts who did not want the "grinding up of our people, our minorities," to continue.

But VVAW still had one conspicuous failure. The media, by and large, were ignoring the organization. Time and again VVAW would send out press releases for one of its events, only to have not a single reporter, not a single news camera show up. There seemed to be no explanation for why the media would not cover people who apparently had all the credibility in the world, unless it was as an act of political censorship. According to Ramsdell, the leaders of VVAW felt that "those in high places" did not want us to be out telling these war stories, and how we felt about the war, because we were just devastating. When people heard us, we converted them in five minutes!" Finally, in frustration,

Ramsdell went to the LaGuardia Center at New York University and got them to donate a half-inch video camera, with which Ramsdell set about to document VVAW's activities himself so that the historical record would be complete, even if daily journalism remained oblivious.

One of the first big events VVAW set up under Hubbard's influence, in early 1970, was an afternoon of hearings on the drug problems of GIs in Vietnam and returning veterans. They got permission to use a high school auditorium one Saturday afternoon, and brought down a number of black and Hispanic vets to testify about their experiences. Most of them had been in trouble with the law as youths, and had been given the routine choice offered by judges of that time—jail or Vietnam. All of them had had drug problems before they went to Vietnam, and all of them had come home even more severely addicted.

VVAW sent out a flood of press releases, but very few kids showed up. None of those present was even able to find Vietnam on the big Southeast Asia map the vets had put up. The afternoon was a bust, although it was preserved on videotape by Ramsdell's camera.

The irony was that a few reporters had finally shown up. But their attitude was less than enthusiastic. Ramsdell recalls one turning to the other and asking, "How did you get stuck with this fucking assignment, anyway?"

"I don't know," the other replied. "I think I'm being punished."[28]

Obviously, VVAW would have to find a more forceful way to deliver its message, or it was going to have even less impact than the mainline peace movement, which had already fragmented in the period between the Moratoriums and Kent State. Despite a fresh burst of campus protests and peace demos following the invasion of Cambodia and the shooting of four students in Ohio, the "make love not war" generation was already threatening to vanish—along with the music and mud of Woodstock, and the glamour of a bevy of dying or already dead rock stars—into myth and memory. Even many arch peaceniks realized that the veterans had a greater staying power because they had the greatest personal stake in seeing the war end. They were the last best hope to keep the country from an endlessly protracted "Vietnamization," which would mean the continuation of a world of hurt for people both here and in Southeast Asia, not to mention the daily pain that was felt by so many who truly wanted peace.

Shared Nightmares: From Operation RAW to the Winter Soldier Investigation

1. On the Road to Valley Forge

Over Labor Day weekend 1970, the United States witnessed one of the most shocking episodes of the entire Vietnam War, and it took place on American soil. Over two hundred American veterans of the Vietnam War "staged a successful search and destroy mission, clearing the road from Morristown, New Jersey, to Valley Forge, Pennsylvania, of enemy forces along the route"—or so stated a press release issued by VVAW after the event. In reality, it was a performance of guerrilla theater on a stage nearly 100 miles long. The mission was code-named Operation RAW, an acronym for Rapid American Withdrawal, whose letters spelled *war* backwards. Operation RAW was "designed to dramatize the war by simulating actual combat conditions" where ordinary Americans could experience them—on their own streets, in the places where they shopped and did business every day. And the "enemy" was not armed men—neither Vietnamese nor American soldiers—but simply the "ignorance" that kept politicians and everyday citizens supporting a war that could not, at least in the eyes of many of its veterans, ever be won.[29]

Operation RAW was the brainchild of Al Hubbard, who was helped along in its conception by two of his friends, Michael Oliver and Craig Scott Moore.

Mike Oliver was born to Irish parents in England during the "little blitz" of 1944, came to America in 1958 and, since he was a United States citizen because of his father's earlier naturalization, got drafted in 1964. He went over to Vietnam with the 101st Airborne in April 1965, and wound up with the 1st Air Cavalry Division after participating in the battle of the Ia Drang Valley. The Ia Drang was where he saw some of the bloodiest fighting of the entire war. The American military called it a victory, but it was a debacle of the first order for the men who fought it. The American command had attempted to fight a set-piece battle against main force North Vietnamese Army regulars, and in so doing had airlifted raw American soldiers into ideal ambush sites prepared by the NVA. Using the hit-and-run guerrilla tactics they had developed against the French a decade before, the North Vietnamese had decimated several U.S. companies, virtually smashing Charlie Company of the 1st Battalion, 7th Cavalry, out of existence.

But it wasn't just the blundering military strategy that had turned Oliver against the war. He had been raised to be tolerant of other races and ideologies—his postman in England was a Communist, and about as decent a fellow as he ever knew—and he had a hard time with the "rednecks and racism" in the U.S. military. It was clear to him, from the moment he saw Vietnamese digging out the remains of their ancestors from a local graveyard to keep them from being desecrated by an American base that was being built there, that America was in the process of devastating an ancient culture, a place where it had no right to meddle at all. Equally disconcerting to Oliver was the rapidity with which the Vietnamese were being corrupted by American wealth. One day he observed an old man, a "papasan" (village elder), hitting his own grandchild to make the toddler cry, so that he could beg money or food from the American soldiers. "From that moment on," asserts Oliver, "I knew, there's something wrong here."

Scott Moore was the tall, blond, good-looking scion of a rich industrialist family from New York. He had commanded an Army platoon in Vietnam and had the grace and easygoing likability of a natural leader. Unlike many of the vets (including Oliver) who could never talk to their families about Vietnam, Moore's mother and father supported his antiwar activism, and his mother Madeleine even served as the office secretary of VVAW in their new head-quarters at 156 Fifth Avenue. Moore was also atypical in that as a privileged kid going to the American College in Switzerland he could easily have avoided the war altogether. Most of his classmates, including Sylvester Stallone—later beloved as the most famous celluloid Vietnam warrior of all, Rambo—never saw military service. But Moore was "pro U.S. policy" and wanted to help the war effort; in fact, after he enlisted and successfully negotiated Officer Candidate School, he had a notion to make the Army his career. But it took him only a few weeks in Vietnam to change his mind. He was sent to replace a first lieutenant who had been killed, in a platoon that had already been badly mauled; and from the time he got there, in May 1968 when the "mini-Tet" uprising was occurring, his platoon sustained fresh casualties every third or fourth day. The last straw was when the brass sent him into an area where they assured him there were no Viet Cong, and his platoon walked right into a deadly ambush. Scott couldn't help feeling "they were killing a lot of kids for no god-damn reason. It had to stop."

Oliver had come into VVAW by reading one of the organization's ads while working his way through the University of Pennsylvania in Philadelphia. When he called New York, Al Hubbard immediately asked him to come up and work in the national office. Oliver was a kind of titan, both in physical build (about six feet four in height) and in terms of energy and commitment; and in no time Hubbard made him a national vice president of the organization. Scott Moore ran across Hubbard and Jan Barry when he returned to New York from Germany with his family after getting discharged. Because of their prominent position in society, the Moores had substantial contacts in government, and Hubbard doubtless saw Moore as an asset in terms of increasing the organization's political clout. He immediately designated Moore as national treasurer of VVAW.[30]

The planning for Operation RAW began when Hubbard and others in the national office came to the conclusion that local leafleting, lectures, and protests were not going to do the trick of getting American soldiers out of Indochina. They were also spurred by the ongoing investigation of Lieutenant William Calley concerning the massacre of 500 civilians in the village of My Lai, which had occurred on March 16, 1968, but did not begin to break in the press till Seymour Hersh leaked it in the fall of 1969. The accounts and vivid photos of the slaughter of hundreds of women and children by American soldiers had shocked the nation, and people were questioning how such atrocities could have been committed by a civilized people. Many officers were implicated in the policies that had led to My Lai, but the Army had chosen to scapegoat Calley, who had been the closest to the actual killing, and to treat the incident as a freak occurrence. Others in America, while continuing to support the war, simply imagined that some of the boys were going crazy over there. But the members of VVAW wanted to show the American public that it was the very conditions of fighting that guerrilla war that resulted in the de facto genocide of the Vietnamese people.

It really seemed that the American public could not fathom what was happening in Vietnam—that the predigested slices they were getting in the newspapers or on TV had merely served to numb their palate to the actual taste of daily horror that every man over there knew but had so much trouble articulating. In plain terms, the vets began to think that the only way to wake up the American public was to make them *live* the war themselves. Recalls Moore: "I felt that Operation RAW was the only way for the veterans who were against the war to really show what was happening. It was a little melodramatic, maybe, in some ways, but there was no focus on what we had seen, and this was a way of getting that focus. . . . We were pretty freaked out about doing it, about re-creating that experience."

Indeed Moore had good reason to be worried. He had seen guys literally cracking up on the floor of the VVAW office, moved for the first time to relive their war experiences in the presence of other angry and radicalized vets.

A number of guys who had recently joined were, in Moore's words, "off the edge." At one point, Moore even suggested to Hubbard that they should forget about Operation RAW. He told Al, "It's too heavy—people won't understand, or they'll think we're just crazy." But Hubbard reminded him that many of the guys *were* a little crazy from the war, and that the best therapy for them was to open up about their pain and what had caused it.

In fact, VVAW was just beginning to initiate the "rap groups," which were groups of veterans sitting around in a room and confiding to one another the most troubling aspects of both their military service and their experiences in coming home from the war. Toward the end of 1970, Al Hubbard would bring in two psychiatrists, Chaim Shatan and Robert Jay Lifton, to guide the discussions. It is possible to see Operation RAW as a kind of extension of these early rap groups into the public at large. Moore, for one, would later observe "a lot of hate and aggression" pouring out of his comrades during the march.

Word of the imminence of Operation RAW began to spread, but the reactions among Vietnam veterans were mixed. The action drew a whole new crowd of vets into VVAW, but it also antagonized many. Moore recalls a couple of guys from his platoon coming up to see him at the VVAW office, angry at his position against the war and unable to fathom why he would march against his own government on the streets of America. He felt embarrassed, and he worried about whether he had made the right decision. The tension of veterans disagreeing with veterans was already threatening to shatter their fledgling movement.

Hubbard's response was to try to develop a number of dedicated leaders besides himself. One such vet was ex-Marine Joe Urgo. Urgo had been hanging around the VVAW office for several days when Hubbard put him in charge of the mailing list, and eventually he became the organization's highly efficient membership secretary. According to Urgo, Hubbard was always trying to maintain an equilibrium between "the anger and the political consciousness" of VVAW's members, and he tried to emphasize the bond between them based on the fact that "we were all Vietnam vets . . . held together with a real center of understanding that we were doing something that needed to be done." It was Hubbard, together with Scott Moore, who saw that to undertake the "serious task" of ending the war they would have to go beyond the earlier intellectual level of the organization and actually utilize their "experience of the military"— to back up their determination with a "methodical" show of force.[31]

One of the first "methodical" steps Hubbard took was to incorporate the organization. Urgo recalls him grabbing any available vets in the office one day to sign the certificate of incorporation. On July 29, 1970, Vietnam Veterans Against the War submitted its application as a membership corporation, and two weeks later it was approved by New York's Commissioner of Education. By stressing that the organization aimed "to collect and disseminate information to the public," with regard both to ending the war and promoting veterans' rights, VVAW gained the right to raise funds and acquire property in a nonprofit manner. That legal status as a 501(c)(3) corporation, though technically it should have kept the organization from endorsing partisan political positions, allowed VVAW to receive critical donations, which funded a variety of actions (like Operation RAW) that openly challenged the foreign policy of the United States government.

Like the government that was waging the war, VVAW began to operate on money it didn't actually have. With five thousand dollars in its treasury, it ended up spending twenty thousand dollars to make RAW happen. Deficit spending would be necessary to carry VVAW through the next two major demonstrations as well—the Winter Soldier Investigation and Dewey Canyon III. Each time, VVAW trusted that the publicity and contacts generated by the demo would bring in enough money to pay the bills, and most of the time it worked; they were able to rely on pledges of future support to keep their creditors at bay.

VVAW rented buses to take vets from several locations in New York City across to Morristown, New Jersey. It was Hubbard's idea to begin the march in the black ghetto there. They would travel 86 miles to Valley Forge, following the exact route that had been taken by George Washington's Continental Army on the way to their encampment there during the "Winter of Despair" in 1777–1778. The vets were instructed to wear their combat fatigues and pistol belts, and the 110 who had Purple Hearts were to wear gauze armbands stained red. VVAW supplied each of them with a toy M-16 rifle, and actors from the Philadelphia Guerrilla Theater came along to pose as their victims. The vets planned to march about 25 miles a day—hardly a leisurely stroll, especially since they were carrying their bedrolls and other camping equipment—and would stop three times along the way, camping on the land of friendly farmers. No vehicles were allowed on the march, other than those designated to carry food, body bags and other props for their guerrilla theater, and emergency supplies. The vets were not allowed to bring their wives or girlfriends with them, though a special contingent of Nurses for Peace accompanied the march to provide medical aid.

Hubbard and the executive committee of VVAW carefully screened applicants for the march—first, to make sure they were genuine Vietnam veterans, and second, to find out why they wanted to take part in the operation. No one was turned away for ideological reasons, but it was important for the leaders of VVAW to find out just where their constituency stood on major issues. There were many goals to Operation RAW besides attempting to show Middle America what the war really looked like, and one of those goals was to bring the organization together into a more cohesive whole.

VVAW worked overtime getting out publicity releases to the media. A few days before the march began, Scott Moore and a friend drove the entire route, talking to police in each town to let them know that they would carry no real weapons, and that they would merely be simulating acts of violence as part of their guerrilla theater.

VVAW intended to harm no one during Operation RAW, but they certainly wanted to provoke strong reactions. Many of the handouts they printed up for the march were just short of incendiary. One of them equated the American citizens who did nothing while their boys died in Vietnam with the Vietnamese civilians who failed to speak out to prevent our troops from walking into an ambush. The flyer went on to explain that soldiers usually got back at such treacherous villagers by killing them. "Many of you have known that Vietnam is a trap, an ambush for American GIs, and you have said nothing to prevent our buddies (your sons) from going into it," the flyer concluded. "WHAT SHOULD WE DO ABOUT *YOU?*" Less antagonistically, the flyer also noted the plain hard fact that "today (if today is average) about 32 of our buddies in Vietnam will be killed and about 140 will be seriously wounded."

Another flyer, meant to be handed out after the performances of guerrilla theatre, read:

> *A U.S. infantry company just came through here*
> *If you had been Vietnamese—*
> *We might have burned your house*
> *We might have shot your dog*
> *We might have shot you . . .*
> *We might have raped your wife and daughter*
> *We might have turned you over to your government for torture*
> *We might have taken souvenirs from your property*
> *We might have shot things up a bit . . .*
> *We might have done ALL these things to you and your whole TOWN!*
>
> *If it doesn't bother you that American soldiers do these things every day to the Vietnamese simply because they are "Gooks," THEN picture YOURSELF as one of the silent VICTIMS.*
>
> *HELP US TO END THE WAR*
> *BEFORE THEY TURN **YOUR** SON INTO A BUTCHER . . .*
> *or a corpse.*[32]

The majority of the vets on the march came from the New York area, although there were representatives from VVAW chapters as far away as Kansas City, Missouri. VVAW encouraged veterans to join the march along the route, and over fifty eventually did. The march was scheduled to leave Morristown at 7 A.M. on Friday, September 4, 1970, and to arrive in Valley Forge around noon of Labor Day, Monday, September 7. VVAW called for a major peace rally to take place in Valley Forge when the vets arrived, and asked peace groups of every persuasion to take part. They hoped to attract a crowd of ten thousand. There were active-duty GIs who planned to march on RAW, and Hubbard saw this as a chance to expand VVAW into "a national coalition of Veterans, National Guard and Reservists, and active duty servicemen for peace, so that the men having firsthand knowledge of the military and the Indochina War can effectively voice their opinions."

Within the organization, Hubbard circulated a written list of several such goals. The marchers would "demand that the military recognize its complicity in America's domestic and international racism and fight against being used for this end as vigorously as it fought to eliminate discrimination within its ranks." He referred to the fact that the U.S. military had only integrated its fighting units some twenty years earlier.

Hubbard also looked to the future, to the time when the war itself would no longer be an issue. With great foresight, he sought to open up the horizon for a Vietnam veterans' movement to continue as long as any of the vets were left alive. The marchers, he wrote, must also "demand an immediate increase in Veterans Administration funds to correct the deplorable inhumane conditions that prevail in VA hospitals, and to facilitate the initiation of rehabilitative programs responsive to the needs of wounded Vietnam Veterans." Not only had many members of VVAW observed the VA hospital situation firsthand, on their regular visits to wounded veterans, but *Life* magazine had done an exposé in May 1970 called "Our Forgotten Wounded" that rocked the nation. The article, illustrated with painfully graphic photos of neglected veteran patients, asserted that "one out of every six men wounded in Vietnam ends up in an understaffed, overcrowded VA hospital," and it quoted exceedingly damaging testimony from a former Marine named Marke Dumpert, who had been paralyzed from the neck down by a rocket blast at Khe Sanh. Dumpert said of the infamously bad Bronx VA that "it's like you've been put in jail or been punished for something."

Hubbard's final goal was to have RAW prepare the nation for war crimes hearings. This goal derived from the Citizens' Commission of Inquiry into War Crimes in Indochina (CCI), a group to which VVAW had become closely connected through attorney Mark Lane and his activist companion, actress Jane Fonda. CCI had been holding small war crimes hearings throughout the United States and Canada for the past year, collecting more and more veterans who were willing to speak out about the violations of international law and the Geneva Accords that they had committed themselves, or seen committed, in Vietnam. Many of these vets had been located by Lane, who was concentrating on atrocities testimony in his latest book, *Conversations with Americans*. CCI was planning a major war crimes tribunal to be held in Washington, D.C., in December 1970, with dozens of vets testifying in the spotlight of the national media, in an attempt to fix responsibility for atrocities like My Lai higher up the chain of command than the mere lieutenants like Calley, who had simply broken under the relentless frustrations of guerrilla warfare. The leaders of VVAW saw Operation RAW as a chance to support the efforts of CCI in showing "that the true blame lies at this time with President Nixon, the Joint Chiefs, Melvin Laird [then Secretary of Defense], high-ranking military officers, and those who remain silent or profit from the war." Most significantly for the future of VVAW, Operation RAW would also announce the intention of VVAW to hold its own war crimes hearings, which had been given the name of the Winter Soldier Investigation.[33]

There were already sufficient vets to form up a company-size unit, composed of three platoons, two squads to a platoon. The line of march would be accompanied by four vehicles—one for medical supplies, one for chow, one for water, and one for communications. The search-and-destroy routines were rehearsed with the actors from the Philadelphia Guerrilla Theater troupe, composed mostly of Quakers. It was impressed on all the vets that no flags or posters of any kind were to be carried on the march—they were to attempt, as much as possible, to look like soldiers, not antiwar demonstrators or hippie peaceniks, though many, unavoidably, had already joined the counterculture in appearance as well as sentiment.

The hundred and fifty men who showed up at the "soldiers' huts" above Wick House in the Morristown National Historic Park, or were bused over from the Washington Square Methodist Church in Greenwich Village, where they'd slept the night before, looked like soldiers all right, but not the proud troops they'd been in Vietnam. There were representatives of every branch of the service—Army, Navy, Marines, and Air Force—and they all wore their military uniforms, mostly combat fatigues, many sporting an assortment of medals and ribbons in juxtaposition to their VVAW buttons and peace symbols. Most wore the soft, floppy "bush hats" they had worn in the jungle not so long before. There was a dazzling array of red armbands, signaling the vets with Purple Hearts. They all carried their canteens, ponchos, and sleeping rolls, as well as their dummy weapons. But their hair often flowed in tangles over their shoulders, there were many beards and moustaches, and their clothing had a decidedly ragtag quality—shirts were unbuttoned and hung out at the waist, pants were rumpled and tattered, and there wasn't a spit-shined boot in the crowd. One journalist commented that they looked like George Washington's motley, bedraggled Army for sure.

Their honorary commander, however, was none other than General Hugh B. Hester, U.S. Army (Retired). Hester had been speaking out for years against what he perceived as "a war of aggression, naked and raw," initiated by the U.S. government against the people of Indochina, as well as deploring the senseless waste of American military strength in the Vietnam War. And he was not the only public servant supporting Operation RAW. Senators George McGovern and Edmund Muskie and Congressmen John Conyers Jr., Paul O'Dwyer, and Allard Lowenstein had all endorsed the action. But the biggest coup of all was getting Jane Fonda to agree to address the rally in Valley Forge.

A number of VVAW leaders had command authority on the march, but everyone knew that the real commander was Al Hubbard. Over and over again he had stressed in his memos the need to maintain order and discipline. "If we don't," he had written, "the whole thing could turn into a circus which obviously will be detrimental to the cause. We must impress upon the American public that we are serious in our efforts. Our buddies are still getting zapped and maimed every day." Because the Ohio contingent—known as Buckeye Recon—was the best-organized unit, they were asked to lead the march and to initiate the episodes of guerrilla theater. As the point team, Buckeye Recon was also charged with fending off potential violence, which threatened to break out twice along the way—once, when a seventeen-year-old kid pointed a real rifle at them, and again, when an angry citizen came at them with a baseball bat.

Outreach to the black community was evident in all facets of the march; it began with a distribution of VVAW leaflets in the black ghetto in Morristown. Two dozen blacks were scattered throughout the column—not nearly as many, percentage-wise, as in the front lines in Vietnam, but certainly an improvement over the all-white organization of a few years earlier.

Along the way, guys kept showing up with cameras. Almost all were police officers and government agents, who were already preparing dossiers on almost every active member of the organization—a file that would eventually stand about ten feet high. There was even surveillance from the sky as police helicopters periodically passed over the line of march. By and large, the organization was not yet concerned about infiltration by government "plants," so it was some months before Ohio coordinator Bill Crandell learned that one of the sixteen men in Buckeye Recon was working for Army intelligence.[34]

There were also many confrontations along the way with World War II vets. "They don't like this?" sniped one middle-aged guy holding up an American flag. "Why don't they go back to Hanoi?" The scariest moments, however, occurred when the vets began to believe their own simulations of "harassment and interrogation" patrols in Vietnam. It happened just as Scott Moore had feared it would; the line between guerrilla theater and genuine brutality began to fade as months of violence-charged experience boiled to the surface in the hallucinatory atmosphere of men in green uniforms wielding automatic rifles against helpless civilians.

Moore would direct the vets and actors beforehand almost like a football coach calling his plays—drawing arrows with his finger in the dirt to show who was to come from where and do what. The problem started with vets shoving the actors a little harder than they needed to. They trussed them up with their hands behind their backs, just as they had done to Viet Cong suspects, often tying a line of prisoners together so that they could drive them in a herd like captured animals. But it was not a classroom demonstration; it was street theater all the way. The vets began to shout at the actors, demanding information about their "units" or political affiliation that the actors could not give any more than most Vietnamese civilians had been able to. Each time an actor failed to answer a question, he was knocked to the ground or yanked to his feet again, only to be knocked back down as his own confusion and his interrogator's rage fed off each other, just as they had in the war.

The fury of such scenes—coming from a real place of pain and horror deep inside the veterans—was contagious. They would all start yelling at once: "Kill him!" "Cut his belly open!" "Kill him! We don't want him! He's a drag on us!" "We ain't got no time—rip him off!" Vets seemed almost gleeful as they blindfolded both men and women and swung their boots toward the soft lower bellies of their victims; then they bounced actors against brick walls, and pressed knife blades right against their throats. It started to get really out of hand when they began stringing the prisoners up from tree branches—a common torture in the war. The agony of a man hauled into the air by his bound wrists, winched over a tree branch, is not something you have to fake. The actors were suddenly hurting for real; and like sharks smelling blood, some of the badly stressed-out vets went after them viciously.

"If you're lyin' you're gonna die, papa-san!" threatened one wild-eyed ex-Marine as he dangled a frightened actor from a hangman's branch. Everyone froze as they realized that what they were watching was no longer a simulated drama but a tragedy about to happen. The vet pressed his knife against the actor's throat, and for half a second it looked like it was about to sink into the actor's jugular. Time stood still as the vet lifted up his victim's shirt and traced some awful remembered vengeance on the actor's naked chest—just shy of actually drawing blood. "How many VC? Beaucoup VC?" the vet taunted fiercely, murder in his eyes, completely lost in the blur of past and present so that he could have killed without even knowing he was doing it. Then he slammed the actor against the tree trunk, and other vets began yelling, "Untie him!" and they rushed in and quickly took the shaken actor down.

Tragedy was averted, but already the question was being raised—at least quietly, in some of the veterans' minds—what price, activism? What price, speaking out? Were too many ghosts being awakened; or, more pertinently, were the results worth the memories these actions stirred? Most of the vets, according to Bill Crandell, "revisited Vietnam at some point during Operation RAW." But it was doubtful that the spectators felt anywhere near as much horror as the vets themselves were reliving. After each segment of guerrilla theater, Hubbard would explain to the public that the scenes they had just witnessed were "something the Vietnamese experience every day—absolute repression, an infringement on all civil liberties—and it's done in your name. They're murdered and butchered by guys like us, who are carrying out the policy of this government, that you are allowing to continue. If you continue to remain silent, *you* are responsible."

That was hardly the message most people got, however. A documentary movie crew (from Bowling Green Films) who followed the march went about interviewing spectators, and most of the reactions were discouraging. One woman said the vets could do whatever they liked as long as they didn't "obstruct property, personal lives," but personally she advised them to look for peace "in your home, with God." Another woman suggested that "if they want to protest, they could look a little bit nicer." Still another woman, who at least showed by her embarrassed laughter that she had been affected, said that she had gotten scared by the guns, since she wasn't used to seeing them; and when prodded to think what the "point" might be, she answered intelligently, if a bit unsure of herself: "To shock people into [realizing] what could happen in a small town like this—right?"

By and large, the men interviewed had had stronger reactions than the women, but most of them seemed to be missing the intended message even more blatantly. Asked if he thought the guerrilla theater was effective, one guy in a camouflage cap—possibly a peacetime veteran, since he looked ten years older than the guys on the march—mocked, "Effective in doing what? Helping the enemy or us?" "Stopping the war in Vietnam," the interviewer clarified. The guy in the cap responded that "Victory would stop the war in from six to eight weeks. If you'd have done it seven years ago, probably not even half the casualties would be in existence now."

Another guy, even more skeptical, jeered: "If they're foolish enough to want to walk to Timbuktu and eat C rations, man, I tell you, I think they're sick in the head!"

Still, the veterans found evidence of sympathy everywhere they went—from people waving or making peace signs from passing cars, to signs on mailboxes with legends like "Anti–Vietnam War vets welcome to stop for water." In the little town of Sergeantsville, New Jersey, people had food set out on tables for them. Yet the vets had no illusions about the difficulty they were facing. After the march was over, Hubbard was notably modest in summing up what he felt they had accomplished: "I think we've raised some questions. I don't think we've converted anyone. I think we've caused them to think a bit, and I think that's all we set out to do, is to make them think."

Perhaps even more to the point, in explaining what Operation RAW was all about, were the words of Bill Crandell to a middle-aged man, who failed to understand the veterans' motives. "We don't want our boys to be butchers and murderers, and we don't think the parents want that either," said Crandell, "because they're gonna come home to you and they're gonna be a little bit different than when they went. It's not gonna be the same son you sent to Vietnam."[35]

There was more foresight in Crandell's words than even he probably realized, for the force that would propel the veterans' movement for decades to come was the lifelong struggle of men and women to come to terms with the irreversible change within themselves that had been wrought by the war.

The veterans' movement, in some sort of poetic justice, or perhaps simply by Emerson's famous law of compensation, was destined to leave its own permanent changes on America, but for the moment those changes were painfully slow in coming. There was a fair amount of local news coverage of the march, but few national stories. On the sheer level of spectacle, however, Operation RAW could not have been more successful. In shifting their emphasis from political argument to scripted drama, the vets had finally succeeded in making themselves visible to a nation that had thus far been virtually blind to their existence. With a few more slight adjustments, they would find the perfect vehicle for baring their collective soul in all its power and complexity.

2. A Spokesman Emerges: "Lincoln and Kennedy Combined"

One of Hubbard's coups was to have the veterans link up, on the third day, with the Family of Man, an all-black organization led by ministers like James Farmer, the former director of CORE during the period of the "freedom rides." Several hundred members of the Family of Man, many of them quite young, were on a march from Washington, D.C., to New York; their next stop was Philadelphia, to denounce racism from the cradle of American liberty. The veterans and the Family of Man made camp together somewhere out in eastern Pennsylvania, and Mike Oliver remembers them having "beautiful" discussions together till late in the night.

Many of the discussions were politically charged. Hubbard discoursed on the theories of Karl Marx, and Urgo recalls that it was the first time he heard capitalism and imperialism discussed as major topics within the organization. But like a lot of the vets, Urgo still balked at designating his country "an imperialist aggressor." Most of them, he recalls, were extremely hesitant to jump on another political bandwagon so soon after getting rudely tossed from the military juggernaut and its tainted crusade to liberate Vietnam. As he listened to the debates, he relates, he kept thinking, *I've gotta learn. I've gotta figure this out.*

The vets showed none of that indecision to the world at large as they arrived at Valley Forge on the morning of September 7. The conclusion to Operation RAW was their greatest piece of theater to date. A skirmish line of 200 vets, rifles at the ready, swept across the Grand Parade Grounds shouting, "Peace . . . now!" over and over. They were met by a crowd of over 1,000 civilians—friends, wives, supporters of all sorts, including many children—and another group of vets, many disabled and in wheelchairs, who had been unable to make the march. (The oldest vet there was 78-year-old William G. Briggs, who had fought with the 80th Infantry Division in the Argonne Forest during World War I; he told a reporter, "I tried to serve my country then and I'm trying to serve it now.") There was a joyous reunion, with shouts and wild embraces—the vets in effect getting the welcome home they had never received when they got back from Vietnam.

A different sort of greeting awaited them from members of the Douglas A. MacArthur post of the Veterans of Foreign Wars. The VFW was staging their own counterdemonstration, replete with "In God We Trust" and "Why Lose?" signs and both American and Confederate flags.

David McQueen, a national aide for the VFW, explained their presence: "This ground has been desecrated by these people [the Vietnam veterans], and we wanted to make sure a few good Americans stood on it today."

"Why don't you go to Hanoi? They need boys like you!" said one VFW member.

"We won our war. You see, these fellas didn't," explained another VFW member to the Bowling Green Films crew. "And from the looks of it, they couldn't win."

Quite to the contrary, most of the vets on Operation RAW felt that the war was being lost not by the cowardice of American soldiers but by the spiritual bankruptcy of smug businessmen and so-called solid citizens just like those VFW members, who for close to a decade had sent boys to be killed and maimed without ever asking any thoughtful questions about either the morality of the undertaking or even whether the war was winnable. More to the heart of the matter, the vets, unlike the bulk of middle-class America, which was content to sit on the sidelines and root for their favorite team, wanted to take an active role in the carrying out of democracy; and they felt that to begin the process of reclaiming their government, they needed, in Hubbard's words, to "fix the blame" not only for a botched war, but for such crimes as "international racism," where it belonged: "on the Johnsons, Nixons, Westmorelands, Abrams [the current commander in Vietnam], etc."[36]

Author Mark Lane, in his typically overblown fashion, warned the VFW members that they wouldn't "stand a chance" trying to stop the demonstration; and that if they persisted, "they [the Vietnam veterans] will kill you." The VFW guys silently retreated to the George Washington Memorial Chapel, though a few of them were later observed listening to the antiwar speeches.

Jane Fonda stood on the bed of an old green pickup truck to address the assembly at Valley Forge. In place of the usual political bunting, the vets had hung black zippered canvas bags, which resembled body bags, over the edge of the makeshift speakers' platform; on each of the bags was stenciled the words: "YOUR SON?" To great cheers—more than she would ever hear from

American veterans again—she began: "This is not my country right or wrong. It's my country, but what is wrong must be changed. I can't escape the belief that My Lai was not an isolated incident but rather a way of life for many of our military."

She also told them, "One thing Nixon can't ignore is the sound of his own troops marching against his own policies. . . . The rest of us can be accused of being reds, hippies, unpatriotic, what-have-you, but the guys who have been there can't be ignored." She declared her belief that the GI protesters were "the cutting edge of the peace movement." The vets gave her a standing ovation.

Fonda had already become the American Brigitte Bardot—a bona fide sex symbol, whether steaming up the screen with her robotically perfect body in *Barbarella* or lilting little girl–like in the cozy love nest of *Barefoot in the Park*. But a journalist at Valley Forge that day, observing Fonda looking a bit wan without her makeup, quipped that she looked more like "the next Susan B. Anthony"—an up-to-date suffragette, to be sure, in bell-bottoms, beads, and orange shirt. But Fonda was no schoolgirl; at thirty-three, she'd lived six years in Europe, where she'd "learned how much people hate us." She'd spent the past couple of years getting an intense political education from the likes of Mark Lane, a Kennedy assassination conspiracy theorist, and Huey P. Newton, one of the most dynamic and brilliant leaders of the Black Panthers. Echoing Newton, she told reporters at Valley Forge that "any black militant in this country who isn't armed is a fool" and that she doubted "if change can be non-violent."

Lane told the vets, "We built this country man-by-man, and we can tear it down man-by-man," and it was clear that Fonda had brought a similar agenda to the veterans' movement, seeing herself as a kind of political lifesaver in a sea of murder and treachery. "People lose their lives for their beliefs," she warned a circle of vets. "I've always hated the war. But it was the Indians . . . I read a story in *Ramparts* magazine. And I began to see how the Indians are systemically oppressed. The jails are full of political prisoners. So I'm committed to change—even women's liberation is part of it, because we're going to free you guys too."

A vet named Bob Hoffman objected to Fonda's prescription for overthrowing the establishment, telling her he'd seen all the violence he cared to see in Vietnam, and that he planned to go to law school so that he could help to reform the country "from the inside." It was a prescient exchange, for as the heady drug of revolution began to spread throughout the veterans' movement in the next couple of years, the vets themselves would have trouble disentangling their own feelings from desires foisted on them by those in the peace movement, who were often intoxicated by the vicarious violence of radical rhetoric.

Actor Donald Sutherland, Fonda's companion from the FTA show, gave an affecting reading of the last thirty or so pages of Dalton Trumbo's antiwar classic, *Johnny Got His Gun*. Then, after the celebrities, the vets listened dutifully to a spectrum of political commentators. Representative Allard Lowenstein, the maverick Democrat who had led the movement to "dump Johnson" in 1968, pointed out that Nixon's policy of "lose and stay in" (that is, withdrawing American troops at a slow enough pace to keep the South Vietnamese government alive for a few more years) was more absurd than that of the hawks, who, however inhumane, were at least logical in calling for a quick and brutal victory. Lowenstein, a small, unprepossessing man in glasses, was a charismatic speaker, and he aimed his wry humor at the many middle-aged and middle-class folks in the crowd. By contrast, the Reverend James Bevel of the Southern Christian Leadership Conference was clearly issuing a challenge to the radicals when he asked people to join him on a march to the United Nations, to present the secretary general with a petition charging the United States with genocide in Southeast Asia.[37] But by all accounts, the man who most stirred the vets was one of their own, Lieutenant (j.g.) John Forbes Kerry, a Silver Star winner who had gotten an early discharge to run for Congress from his native Fourth District in Massachusetts.

Kerry had had an action-filled tour as a swift-boat commander in Vietnam, where he was severely wounded in an ambush, gaining three Purple Hearts and a Bronze Star, in addition to the Silver Star, which by all rights should have been a Navy Cross. But Admiral Elmo "Bud" Zumwalt Jr. had intercepted the paperwork for Kerry's Navy Cross and changed it to a lesser award so that he could approve it himself (the Navy Cross requires congressional approval) and pin it on Kerry a few days later, as an "impact award," to boost morale.

Kerry could not help but sense the irony of his being a war hero, since he had not wanted to fight in the war at all. Before Vietnam, he had led a life of privilege. His father, a lawyer, had worked in the foreign service, and John had been schooled at St. Paul's and Yale, with summers in Europe. Exceedingly tall and rangy, Kerry was a good athlete, and at Yale he had distinguished himself as an orator; in fact, he delivered the senior oration at his graduation in 1966, criticizing the draft and the war. He had been planning to pursue his graduate studies abroad when he received a notice from his draft board that he would soon be called. Though he questioned the policy behind the war, he did not see either jail or exile as a reasonable alternative for himself; besides, he says he "believed very strongly in the code of service to one's country." So he enlisted in the Navy, to see for himself what was going on and at the same time to stay out of combat. To that end, he volunteered for assignment on one of the swift boats—short, fast aluminum craft that were used for patrol duty off the Vietnam coast. Two weeks before he arrived in Vietnam, the Navy began changing the deployment of the boats, sending them up the rivers instead to ferret out pockets of Viet Cong that were guarding the waterways for their own use. Still, Kerry shrugs off the attribution of heroism. In the action of February 1969 for which he was awarded the Silver Star, he maintains that he simply got tired of being ambushed. "The riverbank just erupted with small weapons fire," he recalls. "We were caught in it. So I turned all the boats right into it, and we charged the riverbank—beached right in the positions, ran ashore, and ran right over the ambush. Then I took one boat upstream with me, and we took [were hit by] a B-40 rocket on the boat, and I guess I just got pissed off again, and I went straight into the rocket position. I wanted to see some of the enemy and fight 'em. So we did, and we beat the hell out of 'em. We went into this village and captured a lot of weapons and people and VC flags."

Stationed in New York a few months later, in the spring of 1969, Kerry, showing the same gumption, went directly to Admiral Walter F. Schlech Jr. to request the early discharge. Before he had gone to Vietnam, he had spent hours debating the value of the war and the help we were allegedly giving the Vietnamese people, but once in combat "the answers hit [him] pretty hard, right in the face." He was appalled by "the lack of strategy, the stupidity of many of the missions, the apparent lack of political will by this country to pursue [the war], the lack of a commitment to the men who were fighting in the field, [and] the absurdity of some of the losses that we were incurring," as well as "the corruption within the [South Vietnamese] government." "Everything added up," he says in hindsight, explaining how "this kid coming back, from nowhere," who "wasn't known from Adam," suddenly found it in his heart to run for Congress in order "to make an antiwar statement." Schlech, who disagreed with Kerry's position on the war, agreed to set him free from the Navy. "To his enormous credit," remembers Kerry, "he understood where I was coming from, and he said, 'That's a fair request. You've served honorably, and you've done your duty, and I think you have a right to exercise your judgment.'" Kerry's discharge came through on January 1, 1970.

Kerry never did run for Congress that fall, but it wasn't because he got cold feet. His immediate target was the incumbent Democrat from the Fourth District, Philip Philbin, who had been consistently hawkish about the war. Kerry had felt that a highly decorated Vietnam vet such as himself running against Philbin would "make clear the need to take action . . . lend to the debate and help in the process of ending the war." But a coalition of antiwar forces had already come up with a redoubtable opponent to defeat Philbin in the Democratic primary, Father Robert F. Drinan, S.J., the dean of Boston College Law School and a widely known critic of the war. Kerry immediately pulled out of the race to make way for Drinan, and eventually became chairman of Drinan's campaign.

While working for Drinan, Kerry, who was still "so anxious to tell the story . . . just burning with this anger" to make the public aware of "what was going on," began speaking about his war experiences to various civic groups. At one of these groups Jan Barry heard him speak, and introduced himself to

Kerry afterward. Shortly thereafter, Kerry appeared on the *Dick Cavett Show,* and spoke so eloquently against the war that several other members of VVAW were impressed with his power and presence. Kerry did some work for the Moratorium Committee, and soon made contact with a number of VVAW leaders, including Al Hubbard and Skip Roberts from the New York office, and three energetic and politically active antiwar vets from Massachusetts: Bestor Cram, Lenny Rotman, and Chris Gregory. At that point Kerry "didn't think of it [VVAW] as much of an organization," but he was "amazed that there were some other vets who felt the same way" and was eager to link with their cause.[38]

Kerry joined VVAW in the spring of 1970, but his existence was still a fairly well-kept secret until he stepped onto the back of the pickup truck at the Valley Forge Parade Grounds and began orating from the jury-rigged microphone. Suddenly everyone was riveted by his statesmanlike figure. Kerry stood about six feet six in his immaculate fatigues; and his thick, dark hair, only a tad long and definitely well trimmed, swooped forward over his angular, clean-shaven face. Sheldon Ramsdell remarked to Kerry's sister Peggy, whom he already knew, that John "has got looks like Lincoln, and sounds like a Kennedy. Whoa, Peggy! Where have you been hiding this guy?—Get him on the road!" VVAW would soon do just that, and as Ramsdell recalls, Kerry became "the greatest spokesperson we could possibly have."

That day at Valley Forge, Kerry told the cheering crowd: "We are here because we above all others have earned the right to criticize the war on Southeast Asia. We are here to say that it is not patriotism to ask Americans to die for a mistake, and that it is not patriotic to allow a president to talk about not being the first president to lose a war, and using us as pawns in that game."

Less than a year later, Kerry would get rid of a few of the extra words, and turn that speech into the most famous one he ever delivered.

The finale came at three in the afternoon, and it was hands down the most dramatic flourish of the whole operation. To start, down the slope of the meadow came seven guys from the Valley Forge veterans' hospital, all of them in wheelchairs or on crutches, to join the VVAW troops. A couple of them were amputees, another had had his leg shattered by a .30-caliber bullet, and their brothers-in-arms helped carry them to the front of the rally, where a new battle line was forming. Once more they all grabbed their plastic rifles. Hubbard yelled, "Company, atten-shun! Present arms!"

The rifles were lifted up. Then a new command was issued: "Break arms!" With a single will, the two hundred men each raised their knee and cracked their toy rifle in half. Then they threw the pieces to the ground and stomped them into the dirt. A great cheer went up, as they made the V symbol for peace with index and middle fingers, or held aloft the clenched fist of militant revolution. Once again they began chanting, "Peace . . . now!" Then the celebrities made their exits, and buses took the vets home. An hour later, as one journalist observed, the meadow at Valley Forge was quiet except for the sound of children flying kites and a few "strange echoes."

Those strange echoes of Operation RAW would reverberate for more than two decades, while its first significant impact would be felt just a day later. Tuesday night, congressional candidate Karen Burstein hosted a fund-raiser for VVAW at her home in Lawrence, New York. Hubbard and twenty other vets, who had been putting cornstarch in their boots for their sore feet the past four days, and who were still nursing hoarse voices from all the yelling and chanting, suddenly found themselves beneath the neatly trimmed cedars and willows on a lush suburban lawn, amid two hundred well-to-do Long Islanders, having their glasses filled with champagne punch by servants, and listening to the trendy blare of protest music while people made small talk and the ice cubes clinked like the sound of money. Hubbard spoke movingly, telling this upper-middle-class audience (few of whom probably had sons in Vietnam) that "the best way to keep faith with our fighting men is to bring them back alive—now!" Jane Fonda, having been given the title of "honorary national coordinator," spoke as well. At the end of the evening, VVAW was $1,320 richer.

The real success of Operation RAW for the men involved, however, could not be measured in dollars or prestige. Among Michael Oliver's most valued possessions is an eight-by-ten photograph of fifty young men sitting naked around a campsite in eastern Pennsylvania, blacks and whites mixed together—all of them having just come from skinny-dipping in the Delaware River. It was taken on that magical night when VVAW and the Family of Man came together. "I had been home for four years," Oliver recalls, "and it was the first time I didn't feel estranged. I was with a bunch of people I could just relax with. It was a very moving moment for me. I felt like I was a part of the pack. I felt that my nightmares were their nightmares, and that we were all suffering the same thing."[39]

3. War Crimes Testimony:
Fonda, Lane, and "Brands of Swiss Cheese"

Of all the many accomplishments of VVAW over more than three decades, none demanded so much individual courage, none brought down so much condemnation, and none is likely to have such a lasting impact, as the Winter Soldier Investigation, which was held at the Howard Johnson's Motor Lodge in Detroit, January 31 through February 2, 1971.

The first seeds of Winter Soldier (as it came to be known) were sown when the American press picked up Seymour Hersh's revelations about the My Lai (or Son My) massacre, which had taken place on March 16, 1968. Hersh's reports were first printed in November 1969, and they provoked great anger in the Nixon administration. There was undeniable evidence that over 500 Vietnamese civilians had been wantonly killed by a platoon from the U.S. Army's Americal Division, led by a somewhat unbalanced young lieutenant named William Calley. Nixon raged to his staff that it was "those dirty rotten Jews from New York" who were behind the adverse publicity on My Lai (Hersh was Jewish but actually from Chicago). In typical Nixon fashion, he retaliated by continuing to fund the controversial Provincial Reconnaissance Units, which were CIA-controlled American hit squads in South Vietnam, telling his staff, "We've got to have more of this. Assassinations. Killings." Nixon also ordered official surveillance of both Ronald Ridenhour, the GI who first reported the massacre, and Hersh.

Unable to refute the testimony about My Lai, the Nixon administration, according to Hersh, sought to "soft-pedal it." They tried to preserve the good image of the American military by insisting that My Lai was "an isolated incident." According to Jan Barry, such statements "infuriated" a number of Vietnam veterans in VVAW, who considered them more "official lies." These veterans responded by making plans "to bring to light enough other first-hand accounts of American atrocities to demonstrate beyond doubt that Mylai [sic] was neither 'isolated' nor an 'incident.'"

VVAW in the fall of 1969 was in no way large or wealthy enough to stage its own war crimes trials; but its leaders, including Jan Barry and Al Hubbard, began to look to other peace groups—"clergy, law, Quaker, and college committees"—for help in putting together an investigation. The result was the formation, in January 1970, of the Citizens Commission of Inquiry into U.S. War Crimes in Indochina (CCI).

There were several key nonveteran members of this coalition. One was the Reverend Richard Fernandez, a minister of the United Church of Christ, who had been a chief organizer of the Vietnam Moratorium Days. Fernandez was also a leader of Clergy and Laity Concerned (CALC) and had access to fairly large amounts of money that had been earmarked by church donors for ending the war. Even more critical to the formation of CCI were an odd couple of activists named Tod Ensign and Jeremy Rifkin. Ensign was a fairly strait-laced young lawyer from Battle Creek, Michigan, whose passion for justice had led him to the New Mobilization Committee, into and out of the Office of Economic Opportunity, and on to work for a Black Panther support group called the National Committee to Combat Fascism. It was while working with the Panthers that Ensign met his future partner, Jeremy Rifkin, an investigative journalist from New York and also something of a quirky New Age crusader. Rifkin was later to become a kind of modern prophet of ecological doom with his sensational exposes of subjects ranging from biotechnology ("giant killer tomatoes" and biological warfare) to the beef industry, but at that point he was simply a gadfly to the establishment, having recently been "kicked out of VISTA [Volunteers in Service to America] for being too left-wing." Moreover, he had an ax to grind regarding war crimes, since he had Jewish relatives who had been victims of the Holocaust.[40]

Both Ensign and Rifkin were political activists with clear-cut agendas of reform, and they inevitably approached the issue of war crimes testimony as crusaders bent on returning sanity to what they considered a government gone out of control. The very genesis of CCI had its roots deep in left-wing politics both in America and abroad. Ensign and Rifkin were first struck by the idea of a war crimes investigation when they read a newspaper ad placed by Ralph Schoenman, secretary to Lord Bertrand Russell. Schoenman had recently come to America after serving as secretary general of the International War Crimes Tribunals, which Russell had sponsored in Stockholm and Copenhagen to expose what he saw as the criminality of America's involvement in Vietnam.

The International War Crimes Tribunals had gotten a lot of press in Europe, though they were mostly blacked out in the United States, despite the publication of much of the testimony in a credible book, *Against the Crime of Silence,* financed by the Bertrand Russell Peace Foundation. Russell had probably hindered the dissemination of the findings of his tribunals by prefacing them with a letter to President Johnson declaring that "within living memory only the Nazis could be said to have exceeded in brutality the war waged by your administration against the people in Vietnam . . . this war is loathed and condemned by the vast majority of mankind. . . ." But the Russell Tribunal had another major flaw besides its founder's sometimes intemperate rhetoric. Although it had more than its share of esteemed scholars, authors, and professors—who had investigated everything from the history of American intervention in Indochina to the fundamentals of aerospace weapons systems—as well as political activists, like Carl Oglesby, former president of the radical antiwar and pro–civil rights organization Students for a Democratic Society (SDS), it lacked veterans. To date, only a handful of Vietnam veterans had testified at the hearings—among them, the now famous recanting Green Beret, Don Duncan, who had trashed the Vietnam War in *Ramparts* magazine. There was certainly room to question whether what they had reported had anything to do with the daily experience of the majority of veterans.

Ralph Schoenman aimed to set up a war crimes tribunal in the United States. Rifkin and Ensign offered Schoenman their services, and together they organized a meeting to discuss My Lai at Town Hall in New York. Appearing were a number of excellent speakers, including Jonathan Schell, who had written *The Village of Ben Suc* (about a Vietnamese village that was completely razed in an American effort to "save" it); and Noam Chomsky, the brilliant linguistic theorist from MIT, who told the audience that "once you create a free fire zone [areas designated by the U.S. military where any Vietnamese might be killed], that is ipso facto a genocidal plan." Two or three hundred people attended, but once again the forum was weakened by the absence of authoritative veteran voices relating their own experiences in support of the historians and political theorists.

In working to create an American version of Russell's war crimes tribunals, Ensign and Rifkin made two important innovations. The first was their decision not to call it a *tribunal*, which implies a body that sits in judgment and has the power to dispose of criminal cases, but rather an *investigation*. Hence they came up with the name, Citizens Commission of Inquiry into U.S. War Crimes in Indochina. The second change was to include, from the start, as many Vietnam veterans as possible.

Both Rifkin and Ensign had been involved with the peace movement for years, and they had their office in the so-called movement building at 156 Fifth Avenue, which housed a variety of left-wing organizations, including the ACLU and the American Servicemen's Union. VVAW at the time had its office in the sister building across the street, which housed the New Mobilization Committee. Rifkin and Ensign went over to the VVAW office to ask Jan Barry for help in getting "veterans to document the war crimes policies, and show that the Calley thing is just a scapegoat." Ensign believed that My Lai "was the logical consequence of the types of policies which were employed in Vietnam," a point of view that Barry wholeheartedly endorsed.

Rifkin and Ensign were lucky if they had $200 between them. Barry had no money to offer but gave them what he could—the VVAW mailing list, which contained a little under a thousand names. Ensign did not find it as useful as he had hoped, however, because most of the vets he called in different parts of the country weren't organized into chapters and "had very little recognition of themselves as an entity, and the whole idea of the war crimes revelations was pretty novel, and to a lot of them it was frightening." One guy named Chris, whom Barry introduced them to, put up a screen and began showing them color slides of GIs posing with severed Vietnamese heads. According to Ensign, Chris was one of the GIs in the photos, "and he was obviously very ambivalent about this whole issue and how he should respond politically," and he refused to testify.

That same month, January 1970, a small group of congressmen—including William Fitts Ryan (D-N.Y.), Abner Mikva (D-Ill.), and Robert Kastenmeier (D-Wis.)—convened an ad hoc panel to examine the issue of war crimes in Vietnam. Although it was a completely unofficial hearing, they did bring in experts like psychiatrist Robert Jay Lifton. They also heard the testimony of one veteran, Peter Martinson, who had been a witness at one of Russell's war crimes tribunals. Ensign and Rifkin attended, and through Martinson they met another vet named Robert Johnson, a West Point graduate who was totally revulsed by what he had seen in the war. Johnson, who was still on active duty at Fort Meade, Maryland, became one of CCI's principal organizers—though the organization itself had been named and its goals set chiefly by Ensign and Rifkin. Johnson even went up to Canada and found deserters up there who were willing to talk.

CCI worked fast. The first war crimes hearings took place in Toronto, Canada, in February 1970, kicking off a series of hearings in thirteen more cities throughout the year. At first there was so much reluctance among veterans in the States to testify that Ensign and Rifkin figured it would serve as a "pump-priming" to start with witnesses in Canada, where they could speak outside the shadow of the American government's intimidation. There may also have been some trepidation among veterans early on that they would be liable to prosecution by the military for the crimes they confessed to, but Ensign quickly ascertained that the U.S. military could not recall a veteran to active duty solely for the purpose of court-martialing him. Veterans therefore had a de facto immunity, no matter how heinous the acts they admitted taking part in.

In Toronto, Ensign and Rifkin had put together a "deserters' committee" of veterans with the help of an old Communist Party member named Phil Spiro— who hated the fact that all of them, including Ensign, had long hair—and a Quaker family named Poteet. The Poteets had Vietnamese deserters (former South Vietnamese officers) in their home as well, who added their own perspective to the discussions. They rented space in a posh hotel and staged the first hearings as a press conference. Much of the Canadian press turned out for it, but only a smattering of American newsmen.

Ensign was aware of the fact that Senator Fulbright had held congressional hearings three years earlier, which, dealing with the strategy of saturation bombings and search-and-destroy missions, had touched on the matter of criminal policy—or at least the potential violation of the Hague and Geneva Conventions. But Fulbright's major omission, as Ensign saw it, was that he "didn't get down to field-level, command-level stuff, like what happened at such-and-such a period—like the Cedar Falls Operation, which involved thirty thousand troops. No one said, 'Oh, General, can you tell us why are you using Rome plows [large plows that were used to raze entire villages]? . . . My God, you're destroying the material basis of people's livelihoods—that's a war crime.'"

Ensign and Rifkin structured that first press conference so that it concentrated not on the testimony of academic experts, like the Russell War Crimes Tribunals, but on the recollections of the veterans. At the same time, they sought to highlight the connection between what the United States was doing in Vietnam and previous, well-recognized war crimes such as the Nazi devastation of the Polish countryside in World War II. "I realized right away," recalls Ensign, "that we had a tiger by the tail, that this was really dynamite. I don't mean in some glitzy, media-mongering sense. I mean that this was something that really threatened to tear the whole goddamned fabric of the military machine. Because we weren't just buying their idea that Calley and the others should be pilloried, but we were saying: 'Let's look at the policies. If we're going to assign criminal responsibility, let's start at the top—as we did at Nuremberg—not at the bottom."[41]

The first American hearings were held that same month, February, in Annapolis, Maryland. CCI's next inquiry, held in April in Springfield, Massachusetts, featured a guy named David, who had been involved in what he called a "turkey shoot" where over fifty civilians had been encircled and "mowed down," and who had participated in the taking of noses and ears for souvenirs. According to Ensign, David was very withdrawn, "carrying this [memory of the atrocities] around with him like a big lump [in his chest]." He found it a great relief when Ensign and Rifkin turned on their tape recorder, and his story "just came pouring out [with] tears and anguish." Ensign and Rifkin, by contrast, could barely stand to hear his tale and were "devastated" afterward—Rifkin even more traumatized than Ensign, because of the Holocaust connection in his family. Their perseverance paid off, however, since, largely as a result of David's story, the *New York Times* came out for the first time to cover the hearings.

By August, CCI had staged six more sets of hearings around the country, financed largely out of the pockets of the coordinators, as Ensign and Rifkin dubbed themselves and their newest confrere, Michael Uhl, a Vietnam veteran who had served as a platoon leader in Vietnam with the 11th Infantry. A momentum was building. One of the witnesses at the Boston hearings was Larry Rottmann, who had worked at the command level in the 25th Infantry and was thus able to implicate a fair number of higher-ups concerning their knowledge of war crimes in the 25th's area of operations. The hearings in Buffalo were even more exciting to Ensign because, in his words, "until then it was more us, the progenitors of this event [who were in charge]. In Buffalo it began to take on the form of the veterans themselves doing it." The Buffalo hearings and press conference were followed by a large evening meeting on the campus of the State University of New York, where they filled a hall with 400 people, including New York Senator Charles Goodell. It was at the time of the Kent State shootings, and the whole campus had erupted, with veterans leading many of the demonstrations. Goodell, according to Ensign, "thought he was coming to another antiwar protest," but left tremendously impressed by the power of the confessions he heard.

CCI's goal was to cap the series of hearings with a grand finale, the National Veterans' Inquiry, which they planned to hold in Washington, D.C., in early December 1970. The idea was to distill the best testimony from the previous hearings into a single national forum. But even as their grass-roots work paid off in the growing number of veterans who were coming forth to testify, their financial means were diminishing. By August, they were ready to make common cause with VVAW, which via Al Hubbard and other new leaders was moving toward its own series of war crimes hearings. For the first time, VVAW had the resources to make such hearings a reality, and those resources came in the person of multimillionaire actress and celebrity Jane Fonda.

When Fonda attached herself to the VVAW she was, according to Ensign, "in her revolutionary mode—red stars, Mao jackets, raised fists, all that kind of stuff." She was living in an elegant townhouse on East 70th Street in New York, in the process of filming *Klute,* and holding court amidst quite a radical entourage, which included a number of males she was, or at least was rumored to be, romantically involved with—among them, her costar and fellow antiwar activist Donald Sutherland. But the key to her involvement with the vets was the gadfly journalist Mark Lane, who was often at her side and for a time even lived in her townhouse.

Lane's book *Conversations with Americans,* an exposé of alleged crimes, was scheduled for publication in December 1970. But the book was marred by a lack of documentation. He chose to use fictitious names for his interviewees, allegedly to protect these men from "the anger of an outraged society." An even more questionable decision was Lane's omitting to verify the military records of his witnesses. When, after his book was published, Lane was asked by *New York Times* journalist Neil Sheehan why he didn't cross-check any of his interviewees' stories with military records, Lane replied, "Because I believe the most unreliable source regarding the verification of atrocities is the Defense Department." As the war crimes issue heated up, Lane doubtless knew that his book would be challenged as to its authenticity and accuracy; and so it was in his interest, both literary and commercial, to have a group of certified veterans corroborate his stories. At Lane's urging, Fonda began using her name to do some heavy-duty fund-raising for the VVAW war crimes hearings.[42]

VVAW decided to call its planned event the Winter Soldier Investigation, taking the title from the metaphor used by Revolutionary War propagandist Thomas Paine: "These are the times that try men's souls. The summer soldier and the sunshine patriot will in this crisis shrink from the service of his country, but he that stands it now deserves the love and thanks of man and woman." Paine was referring to Washington's troops who stayed on past their original enlistment, during that bleak winter of 1777–1778 at Valley Forge. Similarly, the Vietnam Veterans Against the War saw themselves as soldiers who continued to serve their country when they were most needed. They also knew that they were likely to suffer more than a few fresh casualties in shouldering the burden of— in their own words—"our responsibilities to our fellow Americans." According to Bill Crandell: "The identification with Paine's pamphlet marked the beginning of VVAW's self-awareness that ours was a revolutionary role, and it noted our embracing of the American tradition of revolution rather than aping Lenin's, Mao's, or Castro's ways."

There was certainly a good measure of resistance to the Winter Soldier Investigation even within VVAW. According to Scott Moore, "A lot of people were real afraid of doing that. A lot of veterans, including myself, felt we were betraying some sort of trust. Telling something secret that was gonna help the enemy. You know, we were still at war. But I went ahead with it. I still felt it was necessary to tell this story because we were throwing away lives for no reason. We were just sacrificing a lot of kids, mostly working-class kids, who had no choice."

Moore recalls that his two uncles who had fought in the Korean War also tried to dissuade him from going public, telling him that they had "seen that same shit in Korea"—that such horror stories were a part of all war. Moore also knew, from firsthand experience, that most GIs in combat are not particularly upset to learn that the enemy is being bombed—even if it means that some enemy civilians are getting killed. The guys in his unit would applaud the huge craters left by American B-52s during the saturation bombing of large, often populated areas of the countryside, because "it was real basic. The more of those [500-pound bombs] that dropped, the more chance we had of getting out of there." But the decision to go ahead with the Winter Soldier Investigation really came from the same sort of apolitical motive: the veterans' belief that the more they talked about the war, the sooner it would be over for all of them, and especially for the innocent kids who were still getting killed.

There was still a lot of denial going on with the American public about the nature of the war. Moore admits that the way they lined up the veterans to testify about atrocities might have been "a little bit mechanical," since it did not give the vets a chance to say much about the mitigating circumstances of what it was like to be a soldier under the pressures of guerrilla warfare in a jungle setting, and other pertinent contexts. But since "the American public rejected the whole concept" of atrocities, it seemed necessary to make their point with a sort of battering ram. Moore's wife, Chris, who helped set up the hearings, remembers that "there were a lot of people who were calling the veterans' movement liars. They said it [the illegal conduct of the war] didn't happen. So it seemed very important at the time to absolutely say, without a doubt, in sworn testimony, 'Yes, it did. It really did.'"

It was Jane Fonda's decision to hold the Winter Soldier Investigation— which now coincided with the National Veterans' Inquiry, taking Ensign's original projected date of early December—not in Washington, D.C., but in Detroit, because Detroit was closer to "working-class America." Ensign thought her plan to reach the "proletarian mass" in Detroit a "cockamamie idea," but he went along with it, because by this time Fonda pretty much had control of the purse strings. Since VVAW had a growing membership in Ohio and other states to the west, Detroit would also prove easier for many of the witnesses to reach.

Still, Ensign worried about the lack of network news correspondents in Detroit and figured they'd have to work that much harder to get the worldwide attention they wanted. One advantage Detroit did have, however, was its proximity to Canada—to the large community of both United States and Vietnamese military deserters who had gone into exile there. Ensign came up with the idea of establishing a hookup between the Veterans Memorial Building, which sits right on the river in Detroit, and a hotel on the other side of the river in Windsor, Canada. According to Ensign's plan, veterans in Detroit would literally be able to look across the river to their comrades in Canada, and to those Vietnamese veterans who wished to testify as well; the exiles could then participate in the Winter Soldier proceedings by means of a two-way radio. The plan was foiled when someone in one of the veterans' groups Ensign had met with alerted the police to his potentially criminal use of the Memorial Building.

Ensign would eventually learn that they were under surveillance by the State of Michigan's Red Squad. "Red squads," many of them officially labeled as "civil disobedience units," were operating under the auspices of local law enforcement agencies across the nation. Supposedly aimed at stemming the violence of antiwar protests, many of them had attained the anti-Communist witch-hunting fervor of the early 1950s McCarthyites. CCI had drawn red squad attention probably because of Fonda's high profile as a dissident. She had only recently returned from a trip to Hanoi, where she'd been photographed, much to her subsequent chagrin, sitting proudly in a North Vietnamese antiaircraft gunner's seat, thereby garnering the nickname, which has clung to her ever since, of "Hanoi Jane." But even more of a liability to CCI than Fonda's un-American image, her petulant manner, and her stubbornness about where and how to hold the hearings was her unswerving devotion to Mark Lane. At her insistence, Lane had been put on the steering committee of the Winter Soldier Investigation, along with herself, Don Duncan, Al Hubbard, the Reverend Richard Fernandez—dubbed by Ensign "a big money man in the churches"—and the leaders of CCI.[43]

One day Ensign got a call from the eminent psychiatrist and author Robert Jay Lifton, who was scheduled to speak at the hearing. By this time, there had been a large amount of scuttlebutt about Lane's forthcoming book. Most of the talk concerned the unsubstantiated nature of the charges he was printing, and the fact that, in Ensign's words, "he [Lane] went in for the cheap thrill kind of stuff"—the most sensationalistic, bizarre, and sadomasochistic type of behavior, women with their vaginas split open or sewed up with wire, heads lopped off with sabers, etc.—rather than exploring the more ordinary but equally devastating abuses that our military inflicted on a daily basis upon the Vietnamese people: the burning of their "hooches" (homes), killing of their livestock, and so forth. Lifton warned Ensign that the Winter Soldier Investigation would be severely compromised if they kept Lane onboard. "I don't think you realize what a terrible reputation this man has," Lifton informed Ensign, telling him that Lane's research on earlier books had been impugned for its sloppiness, that his research methods were often unethical, and that he (Lifton) was reluctant to keep working on the same team with this man. He referred to Lane as a "muckraking merchant" and in other equally strong language.

Lifton's call was particularly disturbing, since CCI was relying on Lifton not only for his own testimony but also to bring in other credible psychologists and authorities. Lifton was close to such luminaries as Richard Falk, the professor of international law at Princeton who had edited a pioneer study of war crimes, and Peter Weiss, an attorney from the Center for Constitutional Rights, which was on the cutting edge of challenging the legality of the war in Vietnam. Weiss in turn was married to cosmetics heiress Cora Weiss, who had founded Women Strike for Peace and singlehandedly financed a whole array of antiwar activities.

Ensign did not want to get into a turf struggle with Lane, but he agreed completely with Lifton that the power of the war crimes testimony depended on its absolute truthfulness, and that it would be harmful to "muck it up" with stories that had great shock value but dubious credibility. In addition, Lane's bossy manner had already begun to grate on the leaders of CCI. But the final straw was their discovery that Lane intended to set himself up as the "interrogator" at Winter Soldier.

In September, there was a new series of war crimes hearings in Sweden staged by a Communist Party–influenced coalition called the Stockholm Peace Committee. Ensign sent a couple of his veteran witnesses over to Stockholm, one of whom was his fellow CCI coordinator Michael Uhl. Uhl had been in Calley's brigade in the American Division, but his testimony was, in Ensign's words, "not the absolutely electrifying, knock-your-socks-off-type testimony" that My Lai had produced. Mark Lane went along to observe the proceedings; and when they returned, Lane complained bitterly that CCI's witnesses didn't have an adequate number of atrocities to report. Ensign felt that Lane was talking about veterans who had committed war crimes as if they were "brands of Swiss cheese," which they were trying to market, rather than seriously traumatized human beings who needed to be handled with great compassion and sensitivity. It especially disturbed Ensign to see Uhl being "pilloried" by Lane for the insane reason that he hadn't killed enough Vietnamese to be a first-rate witness.

The thing that most upset Uhl was that in Stockholm Lane had played the role of "prosecutor" and castigated Uhl and his fellow veteran for the terrible things they had done. Lane's accusatory tone was the exact opposite of what was called for. The point of the hearings was not to blame individual veterans for the criminal acts they had been encouraged—and sometimes actually ordered or coerced—to commit; it was to call into question the entire American warmaking policy in Southeast Asia and to put in perspective the awful dilemma that American ground troops faced in fighting a guerrilla war and taking part in an internecine conflict among different factions of a single Asian nation.

After the October meeting of the joint CCI/VVAW steering committee at which Lane attacked Uhl, the CCI trio told Al Hubbard that they "could not work with this guy" (Lane) any longer, and Hubbard agreed that Lane's badgering had become intolerable. At the next meeting, the CCI group confronted the others with an ultimatum—they had to dump Lane, or CCI would cease working on the Winter Soldier Investigation. Fonda told them, "No, *we're* not out—*you're* out!" Hubbard, well aware of who was paying his bills, hastily agreed with her.[44] The split between VVAW and CCI was complete.

Almost. For though the two groups never officially worked together again, CCI still had the support of numerous individual veterans. Most of the veterans simply wanted to tell their story; they didn't care about the infighting among leaders of the peace movement, so long as they were given opportunities to speak out. Hence many of the Vietnam Veterans Against the War agreed to testify at CCI's National Veterans' Inquiry, which, cut loose from the Winter Soldier Investigation, was held in Washington, D.C., December 1–3, 1970, at the Dupont Plaza Hotel. Because VVAW needed time to regroup, its own hearings were moved up to the end of January 1971, which gave many veterans the opportunity to testify twice at a national forum. Attendance at the National Veterans' Inquiry was disappointing, however—never more than a hundred people at one time, and almost all college students. Not much of what was said there made it into the newspapers anywhere in the country, and certainly not onto the front pages.

The veterans' movement now had to acknowledge that it was ass-deep in so-called movement politics, a quagmire worse than any monsoon mud they may have encountered in Vietnam. Just as the peace movement now had to listen to the harsh wisdom of veterans, vets had to listen to the sometimes inane rhetoric of professional radicals and apparatchiks. For better or worse, those who did not carefully listen to their opposition were likely to end up out of the game.

Another consequence of the split—one whose impact cannot be underestimated in terms of how the veterans viewed the long-term course of their activism—was that the ball of change was thrown squarely into the veterans' court. From the point when Fonda and Lane began drawing boundary lines over the various veterans' groups—one hesitates to say, like victors dividing the spoils of war, but the metaphor is irresistible—the veterans saw that they had no one to depend upon for their salvation but themselves, a situation they had known all too well the first time around, in Vietnam itself. This recognition, which could have been demoralizing, galvanized the veterans to take the reins into their own hands. A group of veterans who had testified for CCI in Washington, D.C.—including Mike McCusker of Oregon, and Ken Campbell, John Beitzel, and Nathan Hale from Philadelphia—went to Al Hubbard and put Al's leadership on the line. They told him that they would not stand for any more interference from the likes of Lane and Fonda, and that they intended to make the Winter Soldier Investigation a Vietnam veterans' production from start to finish.

In the end, Winter Soldier would be just that. CCI would have its victory, though history for the most part overlooked it. As Ensign says, with just pride: "We began that process [of holding hearings based on the testimony of veterans]. It was a bottom-up force. It didn't need so-called experts or pseudo-*Star-Trekker* type guys. We had the line: 'You don't give speeches, you're not telling people what it means, you're putting it out as testimony, you're letting it be pristine and clean.' And those kind of things were more or less followed [at the Winter Soldier Investigation]."[45]

4. Breaking Down in Detroit: "I Didn't Know What Was Going On"

Perhaps the most revealing moment about the whole Winter Soldier Investigation came when Jane Fonda attended a private screening of the film *Winter Soldier* made by fifteen peace activists called the Winterfilm Collective. The screening took place at Francis Ford Coppola's Zoetrope office in San Francisco, with Mike Oliver, who was by then a national officer of VVAW, coming down to show the film to Fonda, Graham Nash, and several other major financial sponsors of the hearings.

The film is an unembellished, hard-hitting, black-and-white record of many of the more dramatic witnesses at the investigation. In many ways, it is a more powerful statement than any of the printed versions of the testimony, because on film you can hear the anger and sorrow in the voices of these unlikely participants in a thousand forms of human brutality, everything from torture to genocide, and at times you can see them fighting back tears, or even breaking down—despite their having been trained to suppress emotion—from the depths of their torment.

Oliver was in the projectionist's booth, putting the second reel on the projector, when Fonda burst in on him, in his words "crying her eyes out." Oliver's first thought was that he was the "bad guy" again. As one of the chief planners of Winter Soldier, he had fought constantly and bitterly with both Fonda and Mark Lane. For starters, they had wanted the keynote speaker to be antiwar activist and professor Sidney Peck, but Oliver had finally convinced them to accept a less political choice, Robert Jay Lifton—ironically, the very man who had told Tod Ensign he did not want to be associated with any event of which Mark Lane was a sponsor.

Oliver also remembered one day during the investigation when he had been called to deal with a veteran who was showing off a Viet Cong ear on his key chain. Oliver, knowing how the sight of the ear might freak out many of the veterans who were about to testify, quickly confiscated it and gave it to a Buddhist friend for safekeeping. Mark Lane was incensed when he heard what Oliver had done. Lane claimed that Oliver had blown their chance to call a press conference and drop the ear in front of the media.

Over a year later, in April 1972, in the Zoetrope screening room, Fonda, rather than attacking Oliver again, now confessed: "I just never knew. I had no idea. I just didn't understand." She pleaded for him to forgive her, saying that until she saw the first reel of *Winter Soldier* she hadn't realized what the veterans who had come to Detroit were trying to do. It had finally dawned on her that the Winter Soldier gathering was primarily about the veterans' need to heal.

This apology, from a woman who had already spent two years in the antiwar movement, a good deal of that time with both active-duty servicemen and Vietnam veterans, might seem incredible, except for the fact that those who had been to that war lived in a world to themselves and often found it impossible to communicate with anyone who had not been there.

Fonda and Lane had assumed that the point of the veterans' testimony lay in its political implications, as a condemnation of American imperialism. By contrast, Oliver, like Tod Ensign, had known that the most forceful thing the vets could do in Detroit was to tell in straightforward detail what their daily experience in Vietnam was like. The politics, he felt, could be read into that. But for him, as for many other veterans, the politics was secondary to the personal catharsis the veterans obtained by sharing their plight with one another and with anyone who would sincerely listen.[46]

Tom Hayden, cofounder of SDS and still a leader of the New Left, passed through Detroit during the Winter Soldier Investigation (in fact, he first met Fonda, his future wife, there). He claims that until he listened to veterans speaking about their war experiences, it had never occurred to him that the United States might lose the war. In other words, before Winter Soldier, the war for him was chiefly a foreign policy issue. Afterward, at least in part because of what the vets said in Detroit, he began to see more clearly that "losing a war is a state of mind." The major loss for individual soldiers, he learned, was not of the territory they were holding, but a loss of their own mental peace: "It's loneliness; it's seeing your buddies die without believing that they died for anything worthwhile; it's marking your time, hoping that you don't get killed for nothing; it's indulging in mindless, nihilistic behavior. There's nothing good about it, and it goes on for twenty-four hours a day for most of a year of a young man's life, until they get out. And so it's personally felt in all kinds of ways in your head and in your gut."

Scott Camil, formerly a gung-ho Marine, now looking Christ-like with long hair and beard and chiseled Semitic features, was one of the most dramatic witnesses at Winter Soldier. Camil testified about slitting old men's throats and the abominable sexual torture and murder of a female Viet Cong suspect. He stated that he had always believed in the rightness of his actions and in his nation's urgent need for him to perform these terrible tasks. It amazed him, therefore, to see a band of American neo-Nazis marching through the snow and bitter cold outside the motor inn, carrying banners that read: "HOWARD JOHNSON'S HARBORS REDS" and "JANE FONDA IS A COMMUNIST."

Becoming a Communist was the furthest thing from Camil's mind. He came to Winter Soldier because he was "very angry and pissed" at having been misled by his government. Oddly, he found himself laughing a lot there, which he attributed to his having been brought up all his life not to show pain—a lesson the Marines had merely reinforced. There's a moment near the start of the film *Winter Soldier* that shows what the occasion meant to Camil. He bumps into veteran Ken Campbell, who had been a forward observer in the same company as Camil, just after Camil had returned to the States. Having heard of each other, they compare notes about famous battles and fellow Marines. One can almost read the relief on their faces, to have found another who would surely understand, because he had been to the same place. Winter Soldier for Camil and so many others was just this chance to connect again with their fellow men, and with the America they had once loved enough to risk their lives for.

There was an innocence among these veterans that was almost childlike, and totally incongruous with the hell of experience they had just come from. They could not imagine that anyone would think they were lying, or that they had some ulterior motive in bringing forward such gruesome testimony. They came, for the most part, without political motivation, nor did they expect to be categorized politically for their action. They assumed it would be obvious, as Joe Urgo puts it, that "they had every reason to expose the truth and get this stuff off their chest." Moreover, many of them believed that Winter Soldier, rather than continuing to politicize the war, would in fact put an end to their nation's political agony. "Our naive belief," wrote Bill Crandell, "was that the testimony of 125 American combat veterans on the criminal nature of the Vietnam War would simply end it, that an America already shocked by war crime and already turning toward calls for peace would simply demand an end to the slaughter of innocents and the waste of our brothers."

Yet the depth of the testimony, both very personal and very comprehensive, generated its own political impact, because it was not just the portrait of a war that was being painted, it was the portrait of a whole society. Urgo recalls being struck as if by a revelation when he heard one vet testify, "They've been getting us ready for Vietnam since grade school." Suddenly he found himself listening with new ears to testimony about racism in schools and sexism in the culture and the role of churches in supporting the military—for confessions that began with traumatic war stories often ended with vets reflecting on how they'd ended up in such an unlikely, down-and-dirty fight so far from home. The witnesses at Winter Soldier "were exposing every aspect of the superstructure," Urgo recalls. "They were showing that all of education, all of religion, all of the laws—everything was leading us toward having to defend this empire in a certain way. . . . It was completely overwhelming, because I'd never realized the extent of the crime that we'd committed. And so it made me more serious. And I think it made me more angry, more determined to stop the war."[47]

Still, what was going down at Winter Soldier was not for the most part an intellectually apprehended experience. It was deeply felt, as evidenced by the many vets, both among the witnesses and in the audience, who broke into tears over and over again.

In contrast to the relative austerity of the National Veterans' Inquiry, Winter Soldier was a mob scene. There was never a time when the main hall of the Howard Johnson's wasn't packed with people—sitting on the floor, lining the aisles, even listening out in the hallways. A little over 100 veterans testified, but another 500 to 700 veterans from all over the continental United States came to listen and share.

Those who wanted to testify were carefully screened by Oliver, Hubbard, Scott Moore, and other officers of VVAW, as well as by Fonda and her associates, to make sure that they were who they said they were, that they had served where they said they did, and that only the strongest testimony went before the microphones. All veterans participating in Winter Soldier were required to bring their discharge papers (DD-214s). Moreover, Oliver and Moore had fashioned a special "atrocity room" in a nearby house, with hundreds of papers taped to the walls—lists of troop movements and unit assignments which they correlated with the individual claims of war crimes that were being brought before them every day. Despite this meticulous documentation, many of the Midwest papers, such as the *Detroit News,* tried to discredit the hearings by questioning the authenticity of the veterans who testified; with all their digging, not one fraudulent veteran was discovered. The East Coast papers avoided the whole issue of credibility—and kept from looking foolish—by simply refusing to cover the hearings. The local stringer for the *New York Times* explained that he found nothing newsworthy to report because "this stuff happens in all wars."

There were a smattering of articles sympathetic to the veterans in the underground press; and Pacifica Radio, with major channels on both coasts, devoted to a pacifist, left-wing perspective on current events, gave them excellent coverage. The CBS television crew that showed up were themselves deeply impressed, but none of their footage made it to the nightly news.

The vets still showed inexperience when handling the press, but overall Winter Soldier was stunningly well organized for such a mammoth event. The testimony was so thorough because Mike Oliver, Jeremy Rifkin, and Bill Crandell had spent months crisscrossing the country in search of a representative sampling of veteran witnesses. Not the least benefit to the organization of this diligent search was the fact that new VVAW chapters got set up in many of the places they stopped. The workload was lightened, too, by the growing number of nonveterans who were lending a hand. Two Catholic antiwar activists provided the house that the VVAW steering committee used as their base in Detroit; and five clergymen of different denominations, including the director of missions for the Detroit Metropolitan Council of Churches, offered safe housing for the witnesses.

The testimony was presented by unit. Sunday, January 31, there were speakers from the First Marine Division, Third Marine Division, and First Air Cavalry Division; Monday, February 1, from the 101st Airborne Brigade and Fifth Special Forces; and Tuesday, February 2, from the 25th Infantry Division, First Infantry Division, Fourth Infantry Division, Ninth Infantry Division, and Lieutenant Calley's Americal Division. In the evenings, and between panels, the veterans held talks on such subjects as "What We Are Doing to Vietnam," "What We Are Doing to Ourselves," violations of international law (including outlawed weapons), POWs, racism in the military, and press censorship. A special panel of psychiatrists, several of whom had served in Vietnam, discussed the impact of the war on American society. The first public testimony about the potential toxicity of Agent Orange was given by Dr. Bert Pfeiffer of the University of Montana.

As riveting as the atrocities testimony was, some of the insights given by veterans into the clandestine workings of American foreign policy—illuminating for the first time what would come to be known in future Watergate and Iran-Contra investigations as the secret or "shadow" government of the United States—had even greater national impact. Perhaps the most startling news to come out of Winter Soldier was the revelation of the U.S. invasion of Laos in February 1969, code-named Operation Dewey Canyon I. Five veterans described their role in the invasion, claiming that an entire regiment of the Third Marines had penetrated several miles into that neutral nation, conducting combat maneuvers along Highway 922 and beyond, and suffering dozens of casualties in fierce fighting. They further charged that the U.S. military had refused to medevac out (evacuate by air) the wounded and dead, to prevent press discovery. Their exposé made front-page headlines in Detroit and Chicago, and a follow-up investigation by the *Detroit Free Press* uncovered other veterans throughout the country who testified to having taken part in the operation. The testimony was explosive because the Pentagon had issued a blanket denial only days before, declaring, "We have never had ground troops in Laos."[48]

The revelation of Operation Dewey Canyon was followed for days and months by other news stories in which American military personnel testified to systematic fighting in Laos. In late 1972, the *St. Louis Post-Dispatch* and the

Boston Globe ran credible stories asserting that the United States had regularly transported combat troops into Laos over a sixteen-month period that extended to the end of 1971. The witnesses were helicopter pilots from the 101st Airborne who had participated in the top-secret program code-named Command and Control North. Although the missions, consisting usually of mercenaries commanded by Army Special Forces, were primarily intended to gather intelligence, these troops had been involved in combat and several had been killed. Such missions were in violation of the Cooper-Church amendment, passed in 1970, which prohibited the use of American ground troops in Cambodia and Laos. But even before Cooper-Church was passed, it would have been a violation of international law for the United States to launch combat troops against a neutral nation. Even as these missions were occurring, the Pentagon was issuing statements denying that American combat forces were operating in Laos, and asserting that all Special Forces had already been withdrawn from Vietnam.

Clearly, Winter Soldier drove a heavy wedge into the American government's credibility, creating a crack that kept widening all the way through the Nixon administration's Watergate fiasco in 1973 and 1974. The American military's credibility had already been severely damaged by the 1968 Tet Offensive and the perennial failure of Vietnamization, but Winter Soldier took that challenge a quantum leap further, questioning the morality of America's superpower status and habitual interventionist politics. One of the points brought out at Winter Soldier, and verified in subsequent news stories, was that servicemen participating in these illegal missions were often required to sign papers in which they promised never to tell the true location and nature of their activities. When they went out on the missions, they wore uniforms stripped of all American insignia and personal identification tags, and if caught in Laos they were under no circumstances to reveal their true identity; but even if they did, the United States would not acknowledge them as its soldiers. On certain missions the Americans even dressed in North Vietnamese Army uniforms and carried the Russian weapons commonly used by the NVA. In effect, the American government was attempting to turn a generation of young men into liars in order to cover up its own misconduct—or, to put it more charitably, to hide the gap between its stated foreign policy goals and the realpolitik it practiced.

One reason Winter Soldier came off as such a professional and convincing presentation was that for once the vets were not limited by a bare-bones budget. The total spent on the affair was estimated at between fifty and seventy-five thousand dollars. In addition to Fonda and Lane, there were donations from a wide spectrum of individuals and organizations—among them the United Auto Workers' Emil Mazey, Michigan Secretary of State Richard Austin, and the Business Executives Move for Peace. Legendary rockers Graham Nash and David Crosby (who were contacted by Jane Fonda) and folksinger Phil Ochs gave benefit concerts before and during the hearings. Still, as with Operation RAW, VVAW went into the red before it was over, but they counted on the book contract they had with Beacon Press (to publish excerpts of the testimony), the forthcoming films of both RAW and Winter Soldier, and other revenue-bearing projects to bail them out.

Winter Soldier heralded a significant change of opinion in the American public toward the Vietnam veterans—not only in terms of a new willingness to hear their side of things, but also in the amount of respect and credibility they were accorded. Over a dozen members of Congress endorsed the hearings. South Dakota Senator George S. McGovern, who would challenge Richard Nixon in the 1972 presidential race, and Congressman John Conyers Jr. of Michigan called for full congressional investigations into charges leveled by the veterans at Winter Soldier; and Berkeley's radical black Congressman Ronald Dellums offered the veterans office space in Washington, where they could repeat their charges within a stone's throw of the House Armed Services Committee and Foreign Relations Committee.

Perhaps most striking about Winter Soldier was the great humility of all involved. These men, who deserved to be honored for the courage it took to bare their pain and to assume responsibility for actions their country had asked them to perform—even as they had already been honored (at least minimally, with medals and citations) for risking their lives in the performance of those deeds—now came before the world in an attitude of profound apology. On the last night of Winter Soldier, several carloads of veterans drove across the border to Windsor, Canada, to meet with a delegation of Vietnamese students in exile, who had been denied visas by the Canadian government to come to Detroit for the hearings. These American veterans signed their own symbolic "people's peace treaty" with the Vietnamese. As Jan Barry recalls, the gesture was intended as a means of embracing the people they had harmed, of asking forgiveness for those they had killed.

Despite the leftist orientation of many of its sponsors, Winter Soldier did not come off as an attack on the United States. What the veterans insisted over and over was that *America knew better* than to do the things it was doing in Vietnam. They pointed out that search-and-destroy missions, free-fire zones, the relocation of people into strategic hamlets (which were enclosed by barbed-wire, and hardly more congenial than a concentration camp), defoliation of agricultural land, and B-52 pattern-bombing raids against undefended villages and populated areas (which refused to distinguish between combatants and civilians) *were all in violation of codes and treaties the United States had previously signed or accepted:* the Rules of Land Warfare, the Geneva Conventions and Accords, and the Nuremberg Charter. In effect, the veterans were asking America to listen to its own much-touted morality and to begin to practice what it had spent two centuries preaching. At the same time, though, the veterans were careful to point out that the war crimes the United States was committing in Vietnam did not stem from the misconduct of individual soldiers—which the government had tried to establish by scapegoating Calley and a handful of his fellow officers—but rather resulted, according to an official VVAW statement, "from conscious military policies . . . designed by the military brass, National Security Council, and major universities and corporate institutions, and passed down through the chain of command for conversion into Standard Operational Procedures (SOPs) in the field."

The Winter Soldier Investigation had more than a few echoes of what had taken place at Nuremberg a quarter century before, when Nazi officers and administrators were held to account, and sometimes asked to pay with their lives, for war crimes committed by their nation, National Socialist Germany. Not the least of these echoes was the shock engendered in good men upon learning how far other good men would go in violation of their own conscience when called to serve their country. John Kerry was one of these good men, who found himself extremely uncomfortable at Winter Soldier. "There was a lot of stuff that I hadn't heard," he recalls. "There was a lot of rough stuff out there, and it blew some of my images. I mean, it shattered some of my conceptions. It educated me to a degree about certain aspects of the thing, and it was hard to understand what was believable and what wasn't. Was it all real? Or wasn't it? It was shattering stuff, it really was, to sit there and listen to these guys talk about things that they personally said they did. And there were enough bona fides in many of these people—you saw their DD-214s, you knew where they'd served, you could talk to them and see the anguish—you could cut through what was bull and what wasn't. And it was a very, very heavy, difficult kind of thing to listen to. And it was painful."

Nevertheless, the veterans were always quick to point out the humanity of so-called war criminals, and to suggest that Americans needed to learn a new way of thinking more than they needed to be put on trial. Bill Crandell stated that it was unfair to blame atrocities on individual soldiers. "We spent our whole lives being trained to obey orders," Crandell explained.

It is a measure of how *pro*-veteran Winter Soldier was that it brought hundreds of new veterans into VVAW, many of them signing up right at the Howard Johnson's. Earlier that month, the February *Playboy* had hit the stands, and it contained a full-page ad for the organization donated by Hugh Hefner. The ad had been designed by Hicks and Greist, a major New York advertising agency, at a nominal charge. The layout could not have been more striking: a flag-draped casket spotlighted against a stark black background, with a caption underneath that read: "In the last ten years, over 335,000 of our buddies have been killed or wounded in Vietnam. And more are being killed and wounded every day. We don't think it's worth it." Next to a short text that told what VVAW stood for, there was a clip-out coupon, which enabled any veteran to join simply by filling it out—no dues required up front, though later a $5 per year membership fee would be assessed. Between the influx of vets at Winter Soldier and the large number who responded to the *Playboy* ad, the membership of VVAW rose to more than 5,000 by mid-February, with hundreds more pouring in every week.

One of the significant effects of the *Playboy* ad was that the organization suddenly gained a thousand members who were GIs still on active duty in Vietnam. VVAW claimed that "the Nam members are from every service and every job classification, from Grunt to Doctor, from Battery Commander to Nurse, from IV Corps to I Corps, from Laos to Cambodia to Thailand to the South China Sea." Having such a wealth of members still in the war zone not only gave the organization additional credibility (and concomitantly, made it seem a bigger threat to the government's current policy), it also gave VVAW a built-in intelligence network, providing up-to-the-minute information on troop movements and strategic aims.[49]

Among Winter Soldier's many accomplishments was to give the veterans a means of articulating their actual experience and the insights they had gained from it. What they did in Detroit went far beyond confession; they were, in the classic Quaker phrase, "speaking truth to power." As just one example of their new fearlessness, they staged a demonstration right in the middle of Winter Soldier, protesting the ongoing bombing of Cambodia. There was also talk among some of the vets about going to Washington and shooting the president, although Ken Cloke, the GI movement attorney who worked with the steering committee of Winter Soldier, believes it was the government's own undercover agents who fomented such seditious plans. In any case, Cloke and the other organizers of VVAW worked quickly to "cool all that stuff down."

Cloke had been enlisted into the Winter Soldier Investigation to check out the legal situation of all those who testified, to make sure that none of the witnesses would be liable to prosecution; and if by chance they were prosecuted, to help prepare their defense. But it soon became apparent that what the vets needed at Winter Soldier was less a legal defense team than a battery of psychologists and counselors to help them get through the deep trauma that was being opened in each one of them and submitted to public view. According to Cloke, "what happened was unbelievable. The whole concept of war crimes was transformed as a result of this experience—panels going for an hour or two hours, twelve people on some of the panels—and it was a ritual expurgation of guilt." While there is good reason to believe that some of the incitements to violence at Winter Soldier came from the government itself or veterans who were working for the government, it may well be that other veterans were driven to the edge of irrational behavior by the enormous surge of delayed stress the hearings released.

One of the aspects of the Vietnam experience that was clearly revealed at Winter Soldier was how much the soldiers had had to block out at the time to get their job done. Veterans talked about using marijuana and hashish while out in the field to blunt the terror of ambushes and booby traps, and some admitted calling in air strikes "for the hell of it" while under the influence of drugs. The need for oblivion extended all the way back to the rear echelons, as evinced by the testimony of an Air Force enlisted man, who said that he refused to think about where the bombs he was onloading might end up, because it was too difficult to admit that he was really helping kill people. Another thing that was often being blocked, of course, was survivor guilt. One black veteran talked of how traumatic it was for him to be spared when the rest of his squad was massacred—the Viet Cong thereby sending him a message that they sympathized with him because of his skin color. Unable to accept his own salvation at such a price, he had deserted to Japan. In the words of Ken Cloke, all these stories came from a deep psychic level "that you don't get reached at unless you're confronting death." There was a direct correlation between the amount of feeling the veterans had suppressed during the war and the amount of delayed stress that lay somewhere in their cortex ticking like a time bomb, waiting to wreak havoc not only on their own psyches but on all those around them. At least, for the ones whose brains began to "go off" at Winter Soldier, there was a massive support group, in the form of fellow veterans and psychological experts, to help them get through the initial terrifying stages of what Lifton called their "authentic descent into hell."

It may well be that the heavy emotion at Winter Soldier actually obscured the impact of some of the testimony. Some members of the audience, like Scott Moore's parents, were "blown away" hearing what these once clean-cut young men had done to the Vietnamese people; others were swept up in the political and historical drama of the event, like Fonda, and missed hearing the personal tragedy in each man's confession. As Oliver describes it, "The entire thing did not have an effect on her [Fonda] until she saw the movie." When, detached from the intense atmosphere of that conference room in Detroit, she finally perceived why these men needed so badly to speak out, she was so shaken that Oliver had to hold her a while, just to calm her. As he explains it: "What I got from that [her crying in the projection room] was that she really had a feeling now, after watching the first reel, of just what it was like for the guys to be there, and what they were doing. I think she finally got an inkling of what really was happening in Vietnam. Not just that, but what was happening with us internally and what was happening at Winter Soldier. I interpreted it as kind of a confession, you know, '*I just went through this with my eyes closed, and I did all these things, and I didn't know what was going on, and now I know what's going on, and wow!*'"[50]

5. The World Begins to Listen

Shortly after his return from Detroit, Graham Nash wrote a song called "Oh! Camil (the Winter Soldier)." Nash, who was riding a wave of success, money, and adulation as the rock group Crosby, Stills, Nash and Young hit their peak of popularity that year, had come to the event high on drugs and looking for a good time as much as to do a good deed, but he was instantly sobered by his contact with the veterans. He was struck by the fact that, with their long hair and ratty togs, "these guys looked like normal people of the generation, but you scratched the surface only a short way down, and there was this tremendous, tremendous anger. It was *right* below the surface." Something in their anger touched a long-buried anger in him, dating back perhaps to his being a child of the London blitz, with its frightening blackouts and the pain of an absent father in the military. He was astonished to learn that some soldiers, such as Camil, had actually sent photographs of dead enemy bodies to their families.

Furious that the war had become "a giant joke," that horror had become so commonplace, trivialized to the level of a postcard home, he wrote the song in a matter of minutes, "just vomiting on the paper," and then raced down to the recording studio to immediately put it on tape. "Oh! Camil" served not only as a catharsis for Nash, but as a validation to the veterans that their recollections could touch others who had not been to the war; it moved Camil so much that he made a special trip to San Francisco to thank Nash, not for the celebrity the song gave him, but for helping to publicize things that he still found difficult to talk about. Nash frequently performed the song in concert, and he included it on his *Wild Tales* album. Although not the hit that some of his other counter-cultural songs were (such as "Teach Your Children" and "Marrakesh Express"), it brought a powerful witness of the war to many people who had never been to that far-off, much-battered country, and who had not made it to Detroit to hear the veterans themselves:

> *Oh! Camil, tell me what did your mother say*
> *when you left those people out in the fields*
> *rotting along with the hay?*
> *Did you show her your medals?*
> *Did you show her your guns?*
> *Did you show her the ears that you wore?*
> *Did you show her a picture of the people you killed*
> *not for God, but for country and war?*
>
> *Oh! Camil, tell me why are you in this place?*
> *When you stood up for justice, your country replied*
> *by throwing it back in your face.*
> *When you tell me your story,*
> *are you making amends*
> *for all of the hatred you saw?*
> *Will you tell all the people about the people that cry*
> *out for God, not for country or war?*

The experience Nash had in Detroit made the war a personal issue for him, deepened his "sense of intense injustice" and pushed him to get a lot more serious about working for peace. The same effect was repeated again and again when other people—through his song, through the documentary film, through articles, or just by word of mouth—encountered the testimony of Winter Soldier.[51]

Despite the "official censorship blackout," as VVAW's follow-up report called it—one story in the *New York Times* a week later, three minutes on CBS "mostly irrelevant to the subject" by VVAW's reckoning, and wire stories that were uniformly buried—word of the hearings did get out to people who counted. In addition to Emil Mazey of the United Auto Workers and Michigan Secretary of State Richard Austin, other prominent figures, such as black comedian-activist Dick Gregory and the Reverend Ralph Abernathy of the Southern Christian Leadership Conference, expressed their support. Even more significantly, South Dakota Senator George McGovern publicly called for a full congressional investigation into the charges raised at Winter Soldier and suggested that the Vietnam veterans in Detroit be brought en masse to Washington to testify. Several congresspeople got behind the idea—including John Conyers Jr. (D-Mich.), Ron Dellums (D-Cal.), Bella Abzug (D-N.Y.), Michael Harrington (D-Mass.), Robert Drinan (D-Mass.), Charles Rangel (D-N.Y.), William Fitts Ryan (D-N.Y.), Shirley Chisholm (D-N.Y.), and half a dozen others. In effect, the VVAW were being invited to come to Washington by the Congress of the United States—a concept that had seemed utopian when Jan Barry first broached it four years earlier.

In the following months, several other VVAW-sponsored Winter Soldier investigations were held locally around the country, and excerpts from the one in New Jersey were aired as a 90-minute special on Channel 13 (WNET) on the anniversary of My Lai. NBC followed with its own one-hour special, "The Vietnam Veteran," focusing on VVAW. *Time, Newsweek,* and CBS's *60 Minutes* eventually sent out their own reporters to prepare stories.

The fallout from Winter Soldier was so diverse that much of it went unnoticed at first, but almost all of it tended to strengthen the organization. In Minneapolis, a local church foundation funded the opening of a halfway house for vets in trouble. In Boston, money was raised for a VVAW bus to tour New England campuses. In Wisconsin and Massachusetts, bills were introduced to keep draftees out of the war. In Detroit, VVAW members worked with the League of Revolutionary Black Workers to redress the inhumane conditions at the Wayne County Jail. In Chicago, draft-counseling and GI organizing, centered around the Chicago Area Military Project (CAMP), received a boost in terms of additional volunteers and new funding sources. In New Mexico, a group was formed to deal with the problems of Chicano veterans.

The course of the war itself was affected, since even as the Winter Soldier Investigation was taking place, the Pentagon was planning to launch a second invasion of Laos, code-named Dewey Canyon II. When the cover was blown on Dewey Canyon I at Winter Soldier, the Pentagon was forced to change the code name of the operation to Lam Son 719, and, with greater consequence, to shift the burden of the fight to the South Vietnamese troops, severely limiting American participation.[52]

There were other less dramatic but equally important results. Winter Soldier succeeded in bringing various sixties protest movements together with the cause of veterans. One such group that was deeply affected by Winter Soldier was the emerging feminist movement. On the last day of the investigation in Detroit, folk singer and feminist Barbara Dane read a statement relating the response of women activists to the lessons taught by these recanting male warriors:

> We, meaning all the women, all the men, everyone here, every American, we are all veterans over in Southeast Asia. Some of us . . . have spent years during the escalation of the war responding . . . with long, tedious hours and weeks of organizing, education and mobilizing our fellow Americans to protest what we saw as a steadily unfolding drama of criminal acts being perpetrated in our names. The system of sexism and racism in America in which we, as women, have been forced to participate both as indoctrinators (sometimes called mothers and teachers) and as victims (sometimes known as chicks and broads) has also created its counterpart of resistance and protest. . . . We recognize and firmly object to the separations between nations and peoples and particularly women and men, produced by the military system; we recognize also that any successful struggle against these separations from which wars result, must involve a confrontation within ourselves and among ourselves, but will finally be won through the unity of all of us. Sexism and racism will fall away only through a united struggle. We admire the courage of the veterans who testified here. We wanted especially to find a way to voice our opinions and to build a common language between us. . . .

It would take a long time for that common language to begin to emerge, and for the male bonding among veterans to break down sufficiently to allow true collaboration with the women's movement. But a significant start was made in that direction at Winter Soldier.

Winter Soldier was a small stone thrown hard and far out into a large pond—America's perennially overconfident, jingoist consciousness—and it would take a long time for all the ripples to reach shore. The delayed effects of Winter Soldier forced the veterans to an even bolder action, Dewey Canyon III, which would finally penetrate the national headlines. It was the perception that Winter Soldier was failing, even as it occurred, that led several of the leaders to caucus during their stay at the Howard Johnson's in Detroit, and to plan their next action for that coming April in the nation's capital—taking the name of their mission from the secret incursion by the American military into Laos they had just uncovered, and adding the "III" when the second Dewey Canyon mission came to light later in February. Certainly the unqualified success of Dewey Canyon III would give even more credit to what happened at Winter Soldier.

Another victory, in its own way, was the fact that a complete transcript of the Winter Soldier testimony was sent to the Pentagon, and the military never refuted a word of it. Senator Mark Hatfield of Oregon subsequently read large segments of it into the *Congressional Record*.

In the final analysis, perhaps the greatest success of Winter Soldier was that such a thing happened at all in the still war-mobilized America of early 1971. As Mike Oliver later pointed out: "You've got the war going on, and you got guys who were there coming back telling you what it was like. That's never ever happened before, to my knowledge. . . . We [the activist vets] were a minority, because the majority of vets came back to this country and just shut down all of their memories. They got back on the escalator and lived a civilian's life. But I absolutely believe that the goals of VVAW were goals that a good portion of Vietnam veterans would say, 'Yeah, that's right,' from their own experience. Pete Lemmon was a guy from National City, Michigan, who was a Congressional Medal of Honor winner. He was at the Winter Soldier Investigation. Who's gonna say he wasn't a Vietnam vet? I don't know who we represented. We fuckin' represented ourselves, and if people believed what we were saying, fine. If they didn't believe what we were saying, fine. We just had something to say, and we said it."[53]

3

A Limited Incursion into the Country of Congress: Dewey Canyon III

1. Preparing for the Assault

Tod Ensign had foreseen that the veterans would be making a big mistake by not going directly to Washington, but it was only after Winter Soldier failed to attract more than a modicum of media attention that the leaders of VVAW reached the same conclusion. At that point, John Kerry was assuming a major leadership role in the organization, and it was clear to him that Winter Soldier had been more like a fumble on the one-yard line than a touchdown.

"Dewey Canyon III, in Washington, was basically my concept," Kerry recalls. "It grew out of the frustration of what I saw in the Winter Soldier effort. Winter Soldier didn't break through. Here was this group out in Detroit, and I went out to it, but I was struck by the lack of interest. America was asleep, and people didn't care. I think we got one small piece in the *New York Times,* if I recall correctly. It was just marginal. There was a little coverage out there in the papers—Detroit and Chicago. So out of that came a sense of, 'Hey! We gotta somehow reach America on this subject.' So I suggested a march on Washington, which we began to conceptualize right there that weekend. In fact, we had a steering committee meeting right in the hotel and decided on it at the end of the weekend."

Mike Oliver, however, claims that the idea for an action like Dewey Canyon III had been growing in all their minds for months: "The demonstration in Washington was the next logical step for VVAW. After RAW, we knew we were gonna have a big demonstration in the spring in Washington—we just didn't know the details." Every spring for the past several years there had been major peace actions in Washington. According to Oliver, Winter Soldier was simply the place where Dewey Canyon III was officially announced and the dates set: Sunday April 18 through Friday April 23, 1971. The name Dewey Canyon III was also arrived at by consensus. Parodying the military's euphemistic style of dealing with death and destruction, the vets quipped that they would be making their own "limited incursion into the country of Congress."

Far from John Kerry being the father of Dewey Canyon III, Oliver sees the situation as the other way around. He speculates that "the only reason John joined VVAW was for Dewey Canyon. He was appointed by Al Hubbard to the executive committee. There was never a vote on John; all the rest of us went through elections. He was appointed for the specific reason of Dewey Canyon . . . because of his contacts—with the Democratic National Committee, with Ted Kennedy's office. His contacts were invaluable."

The dates for Dewey Canyon III were chosen purposefully. The civilian peace movement was planning two weeks of major demonstrations beginning on Saturday April 24. The first action, a massive rally, would take place that Saturday under the auspices of the National Peace Action Coalition, a Trotskyist descendant of the Moratorium committee. NPAC was planning completely legal, nonthreatening actions, but close on their heels would come the People's Coalition for Peace and Justice (PCPJ) and the so-called May Day Tribe, both of which had a far more radical agenda. Led by Chicago Seven defendant Rennie Davis, PCPJ had descended from the various Mobilization committees, but it was staffed by far more hard-line socialists (of the SWP variety) than NPAC. PCPJ and its running dog, the wild-eyed youth of the May Day Tribe, were talking of blocking highways and a variety of other guerrilla actions to shut down the entire government. Word had it that hundreds of thousands of hippie protesters were headed for Washington at the end of the month. Davis and his followers planned to cause continuous chaos in the capital until the government met their wholly unrealistic ultimatum: approving the People's Peace Treaty, which had been drawn up and adopted by both American and North Vietnamese students the year before. The veterans wanted to be done with their own mission before any such madness or manic acting out began. It was essential that their statement be perceived as originating solely with Vietnam veterans and not confused with the plethora of peace rhetoric that had been dulling the nation's ears for years.[54]

The first step in making Dewey Canyon a reality was for Mike Oliver to move to Washington. He rented a house, from which he handled organizing, fundraising, and logistics. For a few weeks Oliver himself "was the national office in Washington," but he eventually hooked up with two other capable organizers, Michael Phelan and "Captain Jack" Mallory. Meantime, John Kerry hit the road, beginning a series of speaking gigs to raise money for the demonstration. The leaders of VVAW knew that to make a bigger impact than Winter Soldier, they would need to mobilize thousands, not hundreds, of veterans this time, and bringing such an army of men to Washington was an expensive proposition.

The planners of Dewey Canyon could not agree as to tactics. Some wanted it to be an orderly march, culminating in the traditional sort of lobbying of Congress that veterans' groups had been doing for decades. Others felt there should be a return to the use of guerrilla theater, which had proved so effective on Operation RAW. In the end, both approaches would be carried out, sometimes by radically different factions within VVAW. But almost all the members agreed on one form that the protest should take—it should provide a means for veterans who wished to return their medals, as a sign of their opposition to the war, to do so in a way that would generate the maximum impact on a national level. The original plan was for the veterans to place all of their medals in a simulated body bag or to pin them on a plastic dummy, which would then be delivered to Congress, the Pentagon, or the White House. Some of the angriest vets were even talking about dropping them into "shitcans filled with blood." John Kerry objected, however, that such street theater would probably terrify onlookers more than it would move them, and he suggested that they ought to turn in their medals at a special joint session of Congress; or, if that were not possible, they might place a table out in front of the Capitol instead, on which the men could simply lay down their medals after reading a brief statement of their reasons for doing so.

Oliver knew that one of the keys to a successful demonstration in Washington would be to win the support of the Washington police. What they had going for them was the fact that there were many Vietnam veterans already on the police force (since vets could get an early discharge if they became law enforcement officers). Consequently, Oliver prepared a leaflet addressed to "our brothers in blue," which spelled out the reasons that VVAW was coming to Washington. According to Oliver, the gist of the letter was that as veterans "we know all about paranoia, and we're not going to cause any. We're going to be lawful; we'll cooperate in any way, shape, or form we can." The leaflets were distributed to all the police stations in D.C., and soon they started showing up on the bulletin boards inside.

One of the things that Winter Soldier had accomplished was to publicize the existence of VVAW to numerous small Vietnam veterans' groups that had recently formed around the country. Many of these groups had sent representatives to Detroit to check out this organization that was purporting to speak for all Vietnam veterans. Some, like Sam Schorr, the leader of the fledgling California Veterans' Movement in Los Angeles, became convinced that they should incorporate their groups as chapters of VVAW. As a result, many of these smaller veterans' groups pledged to send delegations to Washington for Dewey Canyon. Some, from the larger cities like Philadelphia and Baltimore, promised to deliver veterans by the busload. Oliver confidently expected a turnout of ten thousand or more.

A note of reality was sounded, however, by some of the veterans' groups that sent requests to VVAW for financial aid in getting their members to

Washington. Many of these vets, only recently discharged, were filled with enthusiasm but still jobless and virtually broke. The VVAW treasury was simply not rich enough to allow for subsidizing travel even for all the actual VVAW members, of which there were now about 12,000 around the country. Most of those veterans had joined the organization following the *Playboy* ad, and few could afford to make voluntary donations.[55]

As the enormous logistical preparations for Dewey Canyon commenced, the Nixon administration began to challenge the military credentials of VVAW members. Nixon never came out and directly called the VVAW impostors, but spokesmen for the president would drop not-so-subtle hints, like repeatedly using the adjective *alleged* in front of the word *veterans* whenever they referred to VVAW—a habit the press had picked up. Another form of counterattack by the Republicans was to sponsor the formation of a pro-war group called Vietnam Veterans for a Just and Lasting Peace (VVJLP)—an organization that, in the assessment of VVAW's leaders, had scarcely more than half a dozen members. In response, VVAW encouraged all veterans taking part in Dewey Canyon to come in their uniforms, wearing whatever medals they might have, and to bring along their DD-214s (discharge forms) for additional proof of their authenticity.

It was during the preparation for Dewey Canyon III that news began to break of the disastrous South Vietnamese invasion of Laos, code-named Lam Son 719, which had commenced on February 8, 1971. American units had gone into Laos with the Army of the Republic of Vietnam (ARVN), essentially in a support role, under the code name of Dewey Canyon II. At this point in the Vietnamization process, the Pentagon expected the South Vietnamese to begin winning victories with their own combat units, but American officers in the field still had grave doubts about the ability of the ARVN to even hold its own against equal-sized NVA units. Despite mounting American casualties, Secretary of Defense Melvin Laird insisted that the invasion of Laos was going according to plan. By late March, in the words of historian Gloria Emerson, "Lam Son 719 was crumpling. Three battalions of South Vietnamese troops— anywhere from one thousand to one thousand five hundred men—had been lifted out of Laos on March 18 by American helicopters in a rout denied by both Saigon and Washington."

Despite the American press's attempts to play down the South Vietnamese defeat, the vets in VVAW, who had their own hotline to the war, knew quite well that the American commanders and their Vietnamese counterparts had screwed up, and that American lives were again needlessly being lost. The fresh accumulation of casualties—one hundred Americans dead and eight hundred wounded—spurred the VVAW to put everything they had into their own Dewey Canyon campaign, "to search out and destroy," in John Kerry's words, "the last vestige of this barbaric war."[56]

The vets planned to assemble at their chosen campsite on Sunday April 18. They were angling for use of the campus at either Georgetown or American University, but permission was slow in coming. On Monday April 19 there would be a march from the campsite to Arlington Cemetery, led by a contingent of Gold Star Mothers and other parents of veterans and GIs. From the cemetery the vets would march to the Capitol, where they would present their demands to Congress, which included the convening of a special joint session to hear the testimony of veterans. Tuesday April 20 would be another day of lobbying, interspersed with episodes of guerrilla theater. A delegation would also be sent to the White House to present a similar list of demands.

Wednesday April 21 would see a continuation of the lobbying and guerrilla theater. Additional delegations would be sent to the Supreme Court and to the Pentagon. Thursday April 22 lobbying would conclude, and the vets would stage a day-long Winter Soldier Investigation in front of the Capitol. At midnight there would commence a candlelight vigil with the reading of the names of the dead. Friday April 23, if no joint session of Congress had been granted (the vets did not expect it would be), they would hold their own symbolic session outside the Capitol with all the pro-peace congressmen and senators they could muster. The finale would be the returning of medals, followed by a march back to the campsite.

A late addition to the schedule was the formation of a delegation to the national headquarters of the Veterans Administration to discuss the need for better benefits, especially jobs programs and medical care. While the most urgent work for VVAW was to keep more vets from being killed or wounded in Vietnam—literally "a matter of life and death," in the words of Sam Schorr—it was becoming increasingly clear that the vets who made it home were getting hit hard in a different way. Recent studies showed that the jobless rate for veterans between the ages of 20 and 29 was 10.2 percent, compared with a 6.8 percent rate for nonveterans—and the figures for disabled, black, and Hispanic vets, and vets 24 or younger, were even more discouraging. Among just-discharged vets, the unemployment rate ranged as high as 22 percent. Closely tied to the problem of veteran unemployment were the use of drugs, depression, and attempted suicide. Getting the VA to initiate a comprehensive drug rehabilitation program was another major goal of Dewey Canyon. As ever, there was foresight among the VVAW leadership that veterans' problems would not disappear when the war ended, and that a veterans' movement might well be needed for years to come.

In contrast to past actions, more attention would be paid to disseminating information to the press in advance. A press office was created, not only to reach the national media, but also to notify the participants' hometown newspapers, as well as underground and GI papers. One of the techniques, engineered by Jan Barry, was to approach newspapers that had slighted Winter

Soldier and to demand they make up for their oversight by giving better coverage to future activities of the veterans' movement. The ploy worked quite well; not only did *Time* and *Newsweek* take the bait, but smaller papers out in Middle America began to pay attention too. In late February and early March, the *Madison Capital-Times* (Wisconsin) ran a nine-part series on the actions of VVAW and the problems of vets in general.

A major coup was the national press conference VVAW staged in Washington on March 16. The date marked the third anniversary of the massacre at My Lai. Congressman Michael J. Harrington (D-Mass.) lent them his office in the Cannon House Office Building for the occasion, and reporters came from a number of top papers, including the *New York Times*, the New York *Daily News*, and the *Washington Post*. General David M. Shoup, retired commandant of the Marine Corps and a Medal of Honor winner, came in person to announce his "wholehearted support" for the upcoming action; moreover, he backed the VVAW completely in their demand that Congress set a date for a complete United States pullout from Vietnam. Another highly decorated officer, retired Army Brigadier General Hugh B. Hester, a veteran of both world wars, sent his full support in absentia, along with a scathing indictment of the war and of the Nixon administration for continuing to wage it. In his statement he charged that the Vietnam War was "a genocidal war," and he opined (in a passage none of the papers cared or dared to quote) that the use of "indiscriminate bombing and shelling . . . especially with white phosphorous, napalm and personnel cluster bombs" was "as evil as Hitler's crematories."

Even as Shoup was speaking, VVAW had two representatives in Paris—including Native American veteran Mike Hunter, a former airborne ranger with a Silver Star—offering their apologies to the North Vietnamese for the genocide that had occurred at My Lai and elsewhere in Vietnam. Unfortunately, that private peace offering never made the papers.

At the press conference in Washington, VVAW, like a tout trotting out a prize racehorse for a few minutes to stir interest, gave John Kerry an opportunity to speak following Shoup. Flashing his Silver Star, Bronze Star, and three Purple Hearts, Kerry spoke confidently of five thousand veterans marching on the capital, and he made clear that they would be calling not only for an end to the war, but for a whole array of veterans' benefits, including a substantial increase in employment and counseling services. Then, unleashing a quick burst of his silver-tongued wrath, Kerry spoke of the Vietnam War as a kind of cruel prank played on the youth of America, who were being "given the chance to die for the biggest nothing in history."

The press conference brought interest from a variety of places, including *60 Minutes,* and the snowballing publicity led to a whole new spate of local Winter Soldier hearings around the country. The leaders of VVAW began to worry that Dewey Canyon itself could leap out of their control—especially with the increasing presence of agents provocateurs in their midst. Special care was taken to record in advance the names of all veterans who would be returning their medals. Although the leaders of VVAW were still not in agreement as to how this activity should be staged, they all concurred that the ceremony must proceed with dignity and a sense of order.[57]

Care was also taken to see that a congressional delegation would be waiting to greet the veterans when they reached the Capitol after their march from Arlington Cemetery. By this time the vets knew the importance of tailoring the image they cast in the media; and whether or not those in power—specifically, Richard Nixon and the Republican Party—decided to pay them much attention, they knew it must *look* like they were making an impact on the American government.

This time VVAW was going for the heartstrings of America. VVAW representatives were sent round to various VA hospitals to bring as many wounded vets down to the demo as possible. And with so much attention being paid to prisoners of war in the media—encouraged by Nixon and his own press corps, who were using the plight of POWs as a rationale for continuing the war— VVAW decided to co-opt the issue. Their march to Arlington Cemetery would feature a special contingent of POW families, and POW armbands would be worn throughout the week. Some vets even painted "POW" on the back of their jackets—which could be read symbolically in a variety of ways, meaning perhaps that they were prisoners in their own country, or prisoners of their memories of the war. An appeal to join VVAW would also be made to the vast number of jobless veterans, so that their urgent needs could be made visible to the American public. Although the organization already had a genuine interest in improving veterans' services, the leaders of VVAW were not above a mild opportunism; they were savvy enough to know that many vets would come to Washington because they didn't have a job rather than to end the war. Looking to the downtrodden to swell their army of sympathizers, VVAW even appointed a coordinator to deal with the third world population in Washington.

To avoid any possible glitches with the authorities, Mike Phelan sought to obtain permits for every major event. The authorities, however, were slow to respond, and by the start of Dewey Canyon the vets were still lacking several permits. No permit was issued even for an event as theoretically noncontroversial as the wreath-laying at Arlington Cemetery.

Even worse, the week before Dewey Canyon was to start, there was not a cent left in the VVAW treasury. John Kerry was certainly doing yeoman's service at fund-raising. He had given up his book contract with Random House in order to travel and speak throughout the country on behalf of VVAW: organizing, bringing in veterans, asking for donations—working sometimes twenty hours a day. But when Phelan had trouble with the park permits, Kerry had to return to Washington to marshal a group of lawyers, and in the end Kerry negotiated many of the permits personally. This accomplished, he returned to the VVAW office, only to receive a phone call telling him that five thousand vets were waiting for their bus tickets to D.C., but no one knew where the money to purchase them would come from.

Kerry immediately got on the phone to some of the biggest Democratic Party fund-raisers in New York and set up a meeting. When it broke up, VVAW was $75,000 in the black, and busfare for at least a few hundred out-of-towners was assured. In some cases, however, other veterans' groups were reduced to sending token representation; out of three hundred vets in Southern California who wanted to come, only seventeen were able to make the trip. Many guys were forced to hitchhike or to travel on their own grubstake.

As April 18 approached, two major problems manifested. The government, in fear of the great peace tribe that was preparing to descend on Washington for the May Day actions, erected a high wood-and-wire fence around the Capitol, supposedly to protect Congress from violent agitators—but, in effect, cutting legislators off from the people they were supposed to represent. The fence put a crimp in the vets' plan to hand their medals over to a congressional delegation at the end of the week. The second problem, a good deal more serious, was that the vets had not been able to arrange for a legal campsite in the Washington area.[58]

2. Shut Out at Arlington: The Crazy and the Dead

The vets had, in effect, been too successful with their initial publicity campaign. Every article and press release on Dewey Canyon III was being scrutinized at the highest levels of the Justice Department and, quite possibly, by Richard Nixon himself. The Justice Department would later reveal that they fully expected five thousand vets to show up in Washington, and that they also expected "an equal number of radical street people, sympathizers and other hangers-on." Moreover, it may be that the vets' use of guerrilla theater had shaken up the government more than they intended, suggesting how easy it would be for a well-trained army—America's own Army!—to sweep into the nation's capital and seize control. Although spokesmen for VVAW always insisted on the organization's adherence to nonviolence, the image of these former troops—rangy, grim- or poker-faced young *killers*, savagely bearded and long-haired, carrying guns (even if they were almost always toy guns)—could not have been comforting to those at the seat of government, who knew themselves to be the target of every angry thought this group held. Then, too, there was just enough ambiguity in statements by the leaders of VVAW to suggest that a change of tactics might be in the wind. In her March 26 column, which she devoted entirely to VVAW and its upcoming Dewey Canyon action, Mary

McGrory quoted John Kerry (out of context) as saying, "You just have to slam people over the head."

The other thing that roused the Justice Department was knowing that hundreds of thousands of hippie protesters would be following in the veterans' wake just a day later. While VVAW was asking to camp on the Mall, the People's Coalition for Peace and Justice (PCPJ) was asking to camp in Rock Creek Park, only a few miles away. With antiwar protesters in both locations, the White House would be virtually encircled by hostile forces. Suppose the vets stayed on in Washington past the twenty-third and became the shock troops in a mass insurrection—could real revolution be far behind? (It didn't help that the vets had chosen to begin their actions, symbolically, on April 19, the anniversary of "the shot heard 'round the world," which began the American Revolution.) In any case, the Justice Department later confessed that they "prepared for the worst." In practical terms, this meant they determined to keep the vets from establishing a campsite anywhere on government property.

The Justice Department, working with the Secretary of the Interior, sought an injunction in U.S. District Court to keep the veterans from camping on the Mall. The vets argued that precedents had already been set for such an encampment, since the government had already permitted both the Boy Scouts and, on a separate occasion, a poor people's coalition to camp in the very same spot. On Friday April 16, Judge George L. Hart ruled in the government's favor. The vets, who had spent a year or more in Vietnam being told they were not wanted there, were now being told they were not wanted in their own country, either; and that if they chose to sleep on capital ground, they would be outlaws. Through their attorney, former Attorney General Ramsey Clark (who had repented of his hawkish views while working for LBJ), the vets immediately appealed Judge Hart's ruling. But since no decision on the appeal could be expected till the following week, the vets would either have to postpone Dewey Canyon III—a near impossibility—or go ahead and forage for a place to sleep. Since many of them had had to do as much in Vietnam during weeks in the field, it seemed no big deal to do so on American soil, which was, at least theoretically, a less violent environment, and where the enemy was certainly more clearly defined.

Although Washington, D.C., had already suffered one major invasion—by the British in 1812—and every manner of political demonstration, violent and non-, the city was shaken to its roots by what began to happen there on April 18, 1971. Not since the Bonus March of 1932 had the city seen such a fiercely determined, actual army of men, military veterans, come before the nation's government with so earnest a cause. That day, well over a thousand men in their service uniforms, bedecked with their nation's highest honors, bore down on the Capitol. Their hairstyles had changed a lot since they had fought an unseen enemy in places like Tay Ninh and Dong Ha, but they were still for the most part trim and powerful, in the prime of their youth, their eyes betraying what they had only recently come from—either glazed with the "thousand-meter stare," with which a man learns to look beyond an endless field of hurt, or flashing angrily at the continuum of injustice that seemed to carry across from Vietnam to the runway where they had deplaned into a completely foreign America, a country more deeply troubled and unsure of itself than they could ever have imagined when they left it to defend its standard of freedom halfway round the world. There were those who scoffed at their scruffy, shaggy appearance, who claimed that real veterans would not wear peace symbols on their sleeves or carry the American flag upside down (which was meant, actually, only as a signal of distress). But their memories were as real as their DD-214s, and they no longer felt they had to prove anything to anybody, although many bore a visible proof in the cane they walked with, or a missing limb, or a paralyzed body, or simply in the friends who could no longer walk beside them, the ones in whose behalf they came now to speak, the ones they had seen shipped home in body bags or could not even bury, blown to stardust in a plane crash or melted into fertilizer in some godforsaken jungle in Vietnam.

They had no place to camp, and so they ended up in West Potomac Park, beside the Lincoln Memorial, and on the Mall, that rectangular strip of green several blocks long between the Washington Monument and the Capitol— ironically, within a stone's throw of the future site of the Vietnam Veterans Memorial Wall. Bedrolls were laid down, flags planted or—still upside down— wrapped around tree trunks, and gear stowed, as the vets made ready to paint a picture for the nation of what the Vietnam War was really all about. They presented quite a picture themselves. While some were in crisp dress uniforms with freshly pressed overseas caps, most wore the wrinkled camouflage fatigues and floppy bush hats favored by jungle warriors. From their chests hung a glamorous array of medals signifying valor (though some preferred to pin them to their hippie headbands or the legs of their trousers); and on their hats, sleeves, and lapels they sported the insignias of some of their nation's most prestigious and storied fighting units: the Big Red One (the First Infantry Division), which had been the first American unit to land in France in World War I; the Black Horse Regiment (11th Armored Cavalry) that had invaded Mexico in 1915; the "Fighting Fourth" Infantry Division, which had led the assault on Utah Beach on D-Day, led the way to Paris, and pushed back the Nazis in the Battle of the Bulge; the First Marine Division that had liberated Guadalcanal and the Third and Fifth Marine Divisions that had fought side by side on Iwo Jima; Tropic Lightning (James Jones' 25th Infantry); the Screaming Eagles (the 101st Airborne); and the First Air Cav (including the Seventh Cavalry, descendants of Custer's troop). There were even some older guys in World War II uniforms, like Scott Moore's father, Craig, in his pilot's jumpsuit. But almost all shared one insignia: the red, yellow, and white VVAW button or patch.

A couple of the more erudite journalists saw history repeating itself in yet another way. They compared the motley VVAW army, bringing home its message of lost confidence, to the Union Army of the Potomac as it traipsed brokenly over the same ground on its retreat from the unexpected defeat at the second battle of Bull Run.

The number of veterans who showed up was a lot smaller than VVAW had anticipated. During the week the ranks of protesters crested at about 2,000, a figure that included Gold Star mothers, girlfriends, and at least some civilian sympathizers. The vets even suspected that the government had infiltrated their ranks with civilian agitators for the purpose of discrediting them. The daily count of veterans remained fairly constant at around 1,200, but that figure is also deceptive in that many veterans, because of the need to return to jobs and families, only stayed a day or two; yet their absence was not noticed since new veterans were showing up all the time to replace those who had just left. (The count at the campsite on the Mall was closer to a thousand, but that was because there were a fair number of vets who either lived nearby or else managed to find lodging with friends or sympathetic peace movement people.) In addition, many vets came to watch, dressed in their civilian clothes, often choosing not to identify themselves as fellow soldiers but offering silent sympathy. An accurate count is also complicated by the fact that other veterans' peace groups—notably the Concerned Officers Movement (COM), and the remnants of Tod Ensign's and Mark Lane's witness groups—were in Washington at the same time, and veterans sometimes slipped back and forth between their actions and those of VVAW. The total number of vets who came through D.C. during those five days to observe or participate in actions to end the war may well have exceeded three thousand.

One thing was certain: this time the media was paying attention. There were front-page stories and editorial columns about the veteran invasion in almost every major newspaper in the country, and the vets dominated the Washington papers all week long. Every afternoon VVAW spokesmen would hold their own news briefing, which they dubbed "the five o'clock follies," the name mockingly given to the military's daily (and often deceptive) briefings to newsmen in Vietnam. Afterward, the peace army would gather in local bars to check out how much coverage they had gotten on the evening news.

Sunday morning the media blitz had been kicked off by the appearance of John Kerry and Al Hubbard on the national television program *Meet the Press*. The two of them made an exceptionally impressive and articulate team speaking as two former officers, of the Navy and Air Force respectively, who had served in Vietnam. The only problem was that "Captain Al Hubbard," as he was introduced, had in fact held no higher rank than sergeant; and the extent of his service in Vietnam was also a matter of question.

The Nixon administration responded quickly on several fronts. One tactic was to continue trying to discredit the veterans as veterans. Hubbard's actual service record was brought before the press with lightning speed. When it became apparent to the White House that Kerry and most, if not all, of the other veterans could prove their authenticity, Nixon's strategy shifted toward minimizing their impact, while at the same time arranging ways to oust them from Washington should that need become critical. If the criminal justice system failed to keep the vets at bay, Nixon and his staff were quite prepared to implement a military solution. The 82nd Airborne was put on standby.

At 10 A.M. on Monday morning, April 19, about 1,100 vets began crossing the Arlington Memorial Bridge to Arlington Cemetery, with a contingent of five Gold Star mothers leading the procession. At the front of the march, just behind the two vets who carried the large VVAW banner, were the guys in wheelchairs and on crutches, which had become a VVAW tradition. Two of the guys in wheelchairs, James Dehlin and Bill Wyman, had lost both their legs when they stepped on mines; both were only twenty years old. There were also a couple of blind vets tapping their way along with white canes.

The march snarled traffic, but many of the motorists showed sympathy with the vets, returning the marchers' two-finger V peace signs. Motorcycle police rode alongside the marchers, but kept a respectful distance.

Just outside the cemetery, at the horseshoe base near John F. Kennedy's grave, a ceremony for the war dead—American and Vietnamese—was conducted by Reverend Jackson Day, a chaplain who had resigned from the military a few days before. Then a delegation of two veterans and two Gold Star mothers attempted to enter the cemetery, in order to lay two large memorial wreaths at the Tomb of the Unknown Soldier, to honor the dead from both the U.S. and Vietnam.

As the delegation approached the entrance, two grave diggers accompanied by a park police captain shoved the towering black gates closed in their face. The superintendent of the cemetery had ordered the cemetery closed to the veterans on the basis of a rule that prohibited political demonstrations inside. John Kerry, trying hard to keep his dignity, spoke to the park police: "These guys risked their lives to go out and pick up those bodies and put them in body bags so they could be shipped home. You can't bar these men from paying honor to their friends." Still, the gates remained shut.

Many of the vets began to get very angry. One of them hurled his toy M-16 at the closed gates; it shattered, shards of plastic barely missing the police captain. Another threw his Army mess kit, whose contents clattered to the ground.

One of the Gold Star mothers, Mrs. Marcella Kink, burst into tears, pleading "No" to the violence, and several women in the crowd began to weep with her. TV cameras moved in for a close-up of Mrs. Kink sobbing—a bit of publicity that would cost the government dearly—as she told newsmen: "My boy was killed in Vietnam. I didn't speak out then. It's my fault." Gesturing to the marchers, she added: "They're all my boys now."

There was talk of storming the gates, but when John Kerry asked them to leave peacefully, most of the vets quickly calmed down. Most of them had had their fill of violence in Vietnam, they explained later, and were anxious to avoid getting into any more.[59]

In the words of veteran Jack Smith: "We weren't going to fight back; we were nonviolent. We didn't want to be seen as a bunch of rowdy veterans who were coming back from Nam to now fight the country. We were people who had learned hard lessons, and we wanted to share those lessons with the country."

The wreaths were reluctantly laid at the gate to Arlington; then the marchers reassembled and began heading back toward the Capitol. Still shocked, the vets wondered aloud about how the government could treat them so callously. One young man silenced those around him by saying, "You got to go back to Nam and die there, man, to get in there [Arlington]."

As they marched, they called cadence, just as they had learned to do on parade in boot camp so many months before, to keep the pace. Only this time the cadences had quite a different content. Typical military cadence calls were full of macho boasting and sexist imagery—for example: "I don't know but I've been told / Eskimo pussy is mighty cold!" This time the vets called out lines like: "Heighdy, heighdy, heighdy ho! / Richard Nixon's gotta go!" or "Been to Vietnam you know / This fucking war has gotta go!" According to Sam Schorr, it was very effective, because they were "still giving the same picture out"—sharply trained, highly disciplined soldiers acting in unison—but this time the message was not intimidation (how easily they could kill an enemy in their path), but rather a show of collective conscience (how wrong it was that their strength and dedication had been misused). Schorr also felt that the calling of antiwar cadence strengthened their solidarity as a group, made them feel more significant than the many crowds of people who had gathered there in the past demanding an end to the war.

Along the way they were joined by Congressman Paul McCloskey, a liberal Republican from California who was suggesting that Nixon ought to be impeached for having exceeded his constitutional powers, an idea that had gotten started soon after the invasion of Cambodia in May 1970. McCloskey was himself a Marine veteran of the Korean War.

An Air Force bus passed the marchers, and the recruits inside cheered and stuck their hands out the windows making the V for peace.

Ironically, the Daughters of the American Revolution were holding their convention in Washington that same week, at Constitution Hall. They had gone to Arlington to lay wreaths the day before and had been given a friendly welcome. As the vets marched past a group of them, they changed their chant to: "One, two, three, four / We don't want your fucking war!" Some of the DAR ladies smiled; another complained, "It's obscene." One of them, with an obvious look of displeasure, caught the eye of a marcher and told him: "Son, I don't think what you're doing is good for the troops." He replied, "Lady, we are the troops." As journalist Mary McGrory pointed out in her column a few days later, these Vietnam veterans were probably "as spirited and ragged as the ancestors they [the DAR] worship—and whose rebelliousness they have so firmly forgotten."

As the vets wound around the back lawn of the White House, the presidential helicopter was landing. Many of the vets raised their fists, chanting "Bring our brothers home, bring 'em home—now!" but Nixon was not onboard yet. He was about to fly to Virginia for a speech, after which he would return to speak to the DAR that evening. He planned to ask the DAR to join him in "a new American revolution." To the vets he presented only his notorious "stone wall" of calculated indifference.

As the vets passed the Justice Department they gave the Nazi arm salute, shouting "Sieg Heil!" A worker on a balcony flashed them the peace sign, and the vets cheered in appreciation.

On the steps at the west front of the Capitol, the veterans were met by several more dissident congresspeople, including Bella Abzug, the outspoken, flamboyant feminist (D-N.Y.), Donald Edwards, a Democrat from California who had served as chairman of the liberal Americans for Democratic Action (ADA), Thomas M. Rees (D-Calif.), and Ogden Reid. To get a better view, some of the vets climbed up into a dry fountain, and others mounted a nearby statue, ignoring Kerry's pleas for them to come down. Police watched, chagrined, as the vets seemed to treat the Capitol area as if it were occupied territory, but none attempted to remove them.

Representing the executive committee of VVAW, Jan Barry presented the congressional delegation with a list of sixteen demands. Among the most important were: legislation for "immediate, unilateral, unconditional withdrawal" of all U.S. military and intelligence forces from Indochina; amnesty for all Americans who had refused to serve in the Indochina war; formal inquiry into alleged war crimes in Indochina; and improved veterans' benefits, including vocational training, psychological counseling, and drug rehabilitation. Then the vets were subjected to the usual congressional speechmaking; but when Abzug, and later McCloskey, called for withdrawing all American troops by the end of the year, many vets booed loudly, yelling, "We want the end now!"[60]

Before the start of lobbying, the veterans moved their campsite closer to the Capitol, onto the small quadrangle of the Mall between Third and Fourth streets.

The veterans approached lobbying in an extremely systematic way. Members of each regional chapter targeted their own congresspeople, and careful notes were kept on each congressperson's responses. Later, back at the campsite, the vets filled out large posterboard charts that showed both the previous voting record of each congressperson on relevant bills—such as the Indochina

Disengagement Act, which had been defeated in December—and where they now stood on issues like cutting off funds for the war and amnesty for war resisters.

The veterans had come to Washington wide-eyed and idealistic. It may seem strange to think of men who had seen such brutal combat as innocent, but in fact their political naiveté was still boundless. Most of them genuinely believed that all they had to do was *show up* in Washington, and that once the nation saw that its veterans opposed the war, the war would be brought to a swift conclusion. Congress would respond immediately to the will of the people. It was probably the veterans' frustration with the unresponsiveness of Congress, more than anything else that week, that gave birth to an increasingly cynical and aggressive veterans' movement after Dewey Canyon.

Often the vets found that congresspeople known for their hawkish views were "out" when they came calling. But when they did get in to meet their representatives, they mostly got the traditional congressional runaround. Even some who had begun to oppose the war, like Republican senator from Illinois Charles Percy, insisted that the vets listen to their views first, rather than deferring to the testimony of men who had actually been to Vietnam.

The experience had by Marine Sergeant Jack Smith with his congressmen was typical of scores of other sessions going on all over Capitol Hill. Smith had nearly finished his undergraduate degree at the University of Connecticut when, no longer able to support himself as a carpenter, he had enlisted in the Marines. He had served in Vietnam in 1967 and again in 1969, had witnessed a fair share of atrocities, and when he came home, had put together a grisly slide show featuring mutilated Vietnamese bodies to show his family and friends what the war was really like. The slide show, and Smith's articulate presentation of it, had come to the attention of Robert Jay Lifton, who referred to it in his book *Home from the War.* Ending the war had become a fierce cause with Smith, and had virtually taken over his life. He had already planned and executed a number of daring actions in Connecticut, sometimes in connection with Reverend William Sloane Coffin at Yale, and he had come to Detroit to testify at Winter Soldier. At Dewey Canyon, Smith met with William Cotter, his congressman from Hartford.

Smith is an imposing presence—six feet six, broad-shouldered, with a wide brow and strong chin. He looked like a linebacker; but when he opened his mouth, the gush of sharp-tongued New England intelligence made him sound like future town-father material. Not unreasonably, Smith expected that "when I let him [Cotter] know what's going on as someone who's been there, then he's going to say, 'My God, we need to have hearings, and to make some important policy decisions about whether we want to continue fighting the war in the way we're doing it.'" Instead, Cotter explained that he was simply voting the way his constituents wanted him to vote. Cotter represented a largely working-class district, whose voters basically supported the war and had no use for longhairs or hippies. What Smith deduced was that congressmen could not be looked to for leadership in bringing about change.

Smith also went along with some of the vets who were lobbying Senator Abraham Ribicoff of Connecticut, a notorious liberal who had challenged Chicago's Mayor Daley for using "Gestapo tactics" at the Democratic National Convention in 1968. Smith was shocked to find that Ribicoff didn't want anything to do with the veterans. "We had fought the war, so we weren't clean," Smith explains. "He wanted clean antiwar people, in the sense of unsullied by actual experience." Ironically, Smith got much the same reception from Senator Tom Dodd, who was solidly pro-war; and though he could not have expected Dodd to be moved by arguments for peace, he was stung by the fact that Dodd would reject him now, when Dodd had sent him the American flag that Smith had carried all over Vietnam during his two tours of duty there.

The congressman they hoped most to get to—the big cheese of the war industry—was Senator Strom Thurmond (R-S.C.), who was a senior member of both the Armed Services and Veterans' Affairs committees. Thurmond, a thirty-nine-year-old reserve officer when war was declared against Germany, had volunteered for active duty, and had subsequently taken part in the invasion of Normandy as a member of the 82nd Airborne, winning eighteen decorations before the war was over. He was a darling of veterans' organizations, and had won (or would soon win) service awards from all of them—the DAV, the American Legion, the VFW, the Military Order of the Purple Heart, the AMVETS, and dozens more. It would be safe to say that there was no one in the country who had better qualifications as a patriot than Strom Thurmond, and Strom Thurmond was behind the Vietnam War one hundred percent.

Thurmond refused to meet with the VVAW. Many of the VVAW members were already taking matters into their own hands, however, and they figured it was time that the distinguished senator from South Carolina show a little of the same courage in confronting the no longer armed men he had sent to war as he had expected of them on the battlefield with armed North Vietnamese. A group of vets, including Jack Smith, cornered Thurmond in one of the little electric cars in the congressional subway, the network of underground passageways through which congressmen are transported between the congressional office buildings and the Capitol.

The vets tried to talk Thurmond into sponsoring a full investigation of the war—not just Winter Soldier–like hearings on war crimes, but a real review of the whole history and policy behind the present conflict. They tried to appeal to his sense of honor, but Thurmond paid no attention, choosing to lecture them on their own duty to support their country. Sam Schorr and a couple of his friends from the California Veterans' Movement could no longer contain their anger and decided to do a bit of guerrilla theater right there in the congressional subway. They pointed their toy M-16s at Thurmond and "nailed him." Recalls Schorr: "We told him he was a goddamn gook VC and blew his ass away. And he was furious, just foaming. It was great." Thurmond responded with "every cliché he could think of about the antiwar movement . . . 'Commie asshole pinko bastards get a job' shit . . . He was just going off his nut." A friend of Schorr's who had been having a hard time since Dewey Canyon began—having flashbacks and taking mescaline to try to cool down—pulled his Bronze Star off his uniform and shoved it in Thurmond's face, saying, "That's your goddamn antiwar movement, sucker!" Then he put the medal back on, and they let Thurmond go. The vets took over the electric cart and began pursuing other congressmen, until the police chased them off.

Were some of the vets truly crazed victims of delayed stress, acting out their flashbacks for the nation, or were they being pushed toward violence by an unbelievably insensitive government? Arguments could be made in support of both views, but Smith, one of the more level-headed observers, saw enough tortuous evasion on the part of congressmen to provoke even the mildest of protesters. More and more of the vets were being driven to fight against the war in the public eye, rather than through the maddening equivocation of the established legal channels.

There were still two strong arguments for working within the system. One came from the ascendancy of John Kerry within the organization. Kerry had made it clear, in every speech he gave, that he was against both outright revolutionary violence and even the kind of disruptive public-circus tactics of Abbie Hoffman and his Yippies. When questioned by an audience about whether he believed in civil disobedience, Kerry would answer, "No, I absolutely don't." His advice to people who wanted to join the ranks of protesters was: "I think you ought to go out and vote." He still believed that the United States had the best form of government in the world, and that the way to effect change in this country was simply "to communicate—to go out and organize." Years later, in summing up his memories of VVAW, he recalled: "People were sort of doing that [working within the system], but not recognizing the value of it, in some respects, and talking this crazy kind of stuff, and I just had no room for that."[61]

One of the people Kerry felt was "talking this crazy kind of stuff" was Al Hubbard. The dynamic between the two men was unusually difficult, because both were obviously operating from sincere beliefs, yet each had a great deal of scorn for the other's goals—Kerry wanting nothing to do with Al's "confrontational politics," and Al having little respect for the American legal apparatus that John wanted so much to belong to, an apparatus that had been used for so many years to hold down people of color. In Mike Oliver's words: "Al knew that John was using VVAW—and John knew that Al knew it—and then this thing [the *Meet the Press* scandal] came down, and it was just two rams butting heads."

There was already a lot of friction going on between Kerry and Hubbard, not the least of which was the class difference: Ivy League versus black ghetto. On top of which Kerry had been an officer, and Al, despite his claims to the contrary, an enlisted man. Within VVAW, officers versus grunts was already becoming a major issue, especially since the organization had a strongly democratic bias; reacting against the rigidly hierarchical world they had just come out of, a majority of the vets were insisting that no one man's voice should carry more weight within the organization than any other man's. But beyond all of that personal rivalry, Kerry and Hubbard were also opposed on the matter of goals. In Kerry's words, Hubbard and the group of vets allied with him were "highly motivated into a higher social agenda," while Kerry felt that "it was a mistake for Vietnam veterans to get involved in a broader agenda than just ending the war and dealing with Vietnam veteran issues."

Hubbard felt that it was meaningless to talk about the wrongness of the war in Vietnam without putting it in the larger context of class and race warfare. As he was later to write in *The New Soldier*, the casebook on Dewey Canyon assembled by VVAW and published by Collier, a black man could not help wondering about the many paradoxes of the war: "hearing a Vietnamese invite *you* to live in *his* home, after the war, and an American explain why *you* can't live in his block, after the war" and "feeling happy to be leaving a country in which *you* do not belong and sad to be returning to a country in which *you* are not allowed to belong."

Kerry "didn't feel it was inappropriate for people to feel something about it [racism and inequality]. Obviously we all commented on it as individuals, and should have," he says, "but to take the organization into those things [civil rights projects, for example], I thought, weakened our ability to remain this sort of singular special spokesperson on the issue of the war. . . . Our mission was a special mission that came out of our special credibility, and our special credibility was that we were the troops, we were the guys who had been there. And with the strength that came out of our wearing the uniform came the ability to reach America. We did not need to get into the demonstrative actions of people who didn't have that credibility . . . And tactically it was my belief that wherever we could reach Middle America, that was our audience, and that was what we should be trying to do—not trying to tackle a larger agenda that was simply gonna confuse the communication, and frankly turn a lot of people off and make it harder to get through."

Because Kerry held such importance for VVAW—as speaker, as fund-raiser, as political liaison—it was natural for the organization to begin leaning toward the sort of conservative, orderly approach that he represented. If nothing else, Kerry's presence guaranteed that the veterans would not give up on Congress quite yet.

The second force in that direction was the apparent willingness of the system itself to acknowledge the veterans' right to address their government. The most encouraging event of that Monday was the decision by the Washington District Court of Appeals to lift the injunction barring veterans from camping on the Mall. A panel of three appellate judges declared that the veterans should be accorded the same privilege given to the Boy Scouts for their Jamboree and to the poor people who had established their Resurrection City on that very piece of ground. The judges asked simply that the veterans provide their own sanitary facilities and clean-up team, that they pitch tents only for medical aid, and that they refrain from breaking ground or building fires. For the moment, at least, the system seemed to be working in the veterans' behalf, although there was still concern over the fact that Nixon's lawyers planned to appeal the Washington District Court's decision directly to the Supreme Court.

Monday night, as if in further confirmation of the nation's respect for them, CBS anchorman Walter Cronkite (who by this time almost spoke as a kind of national conscience) did a short but sympathetic piece on the veterans' presence in Washington. It was clear to the leaders of VVAW that "the Nixon administration was really feeling this incredible pressure and were liable to make irrational decisions." The initial quiet from the White House after the lifting of the injunction worried the vets a good deal, especially as it was one of Nixon's aides who had said, in a different context, "You never let your enemies know what you're doing." They felt as if perhaps they were sitting in the eye of a hurricane that would soon blow them away.

Because the Nixon administration literally had its back to the wall—with a battalion of combat-seasoned veterans, many of whom would not have been too reluctant, given the chance, to wring Richard Nixon's neck, camped a mile from the White House—the leaders of VVAW knew that it was essential to orchestrate and control the amount of confrontation taking place between themselves and the government. According to Jack Smith, the Bonus March of 1932 was much on their minds. Terrified of a revolution in his backyard, Herbert Hoover had called out the federal troops, under General Douglas MacArthur, to disperse the thousands of unemployed World War I vets who had marched on Washington to demand their long-deferred service bonuses. MacArthur's troops had opened fire on the veterans, killing several. If anything, Nixon and his advisors—many of whom would later be sent to prison for criminal acts relating to a betrayal of the public trust during the Watergate affair—seemed even more paranoid and closer to the edge than Hoover (who had to deal with the near collapse of the country during the Great Depression). According to Smith, "We could see in their eyes that these guys were really getting crazy, that these people were not in control of the government, not in control of what they were doing." As a result, the leaders of VVAW argued among themselves as to how far they could go without seriously risking their followers' lives.

The way things were looking, the vets knew they might be in line to receive an enormous outpouring of sympathy when they returned their medals. If that happened, there would be no way that Nixon could turn Dewey Canyon into a replay of the Democratic National Convention in 1968. A large part of Middle America had rejoiced to see hippies getting their heads bashed in Chicago; but the veterans, longhaired and shabby as many of them were, touched the heartstrings of America in a way the hippies never had. That these men had the guts to speak out about what they had seen earned them even more approval from the general public. What it all added up to was that the veterans' movement had the potential to start a revolution in America, but its leaders could not decide whether that was really what they wanted to do. Those who felt that the problem of the war stemmed from fundamental problems in the government of the United States—and that consequently that government had to be changed at all cost—welcomed the prospect of a battle on the barricades, much like the student revolt in Paris in 1968. But there were others in VVAW, like John Kerry, who felt that the American government was amenable to reasonable argument, that wrongful policies could be amended with a bit of skillful advocacy, and that if the vets pushed their demonstrations too far, precipitating riots, the whole process could be blown apart.[62]

As Dewey Canyon began to roll forward with an irresistible momentum, the interior debates within VVAW were complicated by the presence of a goodly number of what Jack Smith affectionately called "the crazies." These were vets who had seen too much combat, witnessed the mutilation of too many human bodies, and "taken too much incoming"—in that succinct phrase the war bequeathed us for what it means to cower in your bunker hour after hour as your brains are rattled by the impact of high explosives through a couple of feet of earth above your head. In short, they were the classic victims of post-traumatic stress disorder (PTSD), or delayed stress.

Almost all the vets appreciated the urgency that the crazies felt to make their story known. Almost all of them had experienced the same wall of silence when they came home from Vietnam, had seen the way strangers, friends, even family would change the subject when they tried to bring up the war. Those who had been in combat were forced to live with a thousand horrors bottled up inside them, and the only escape—for those who weren't lucky enough to find one of the early rap groups—was through drink, drugs, or manic activity. The crazies were looking for confrontation, looking to precipitate arrest and jail as a way of dealing with the insanity they had witnessed in Vietnam. But the crazies, however sympathetically they might be looked on by their fellow veterans, were a problem for the organization—because they would not take orders, because they were ruled by emotion and not reason, (in Smith's words) "wanting to be on the go all the time, and not being able to do anything focused," and because they were capable of any sort of action at any time, maybe even a reenactment of the violence that had set them off in the first place.

Sam Schorr, who was labeled (at least by some) as one of the crazies, saw the two factions in VVAW in a more political light. "There was a radical faction, and a general antiwar faction that was very single-issue oriented and did not want confrontational politics. That was basically John Kerry's people. Barry [Romo] and I led a group that we called the anti-imperialists' coalition. We formed up with the Ohio contingent, the Florida contingent, and the Idaho contingent. Basically we agitated for a little bit more radical situation. . . .

"There were a lot of things that happened that weren't organized by the New York center. The essence of Dewey Canyon for those guys [from New York] was the symbol of vets going to the Capitol to lobby against the war. Basically keep it at that level, and not get into any confrontations with anybody. The guerrilla theater that they planned was very tame stuff. What we wanted to do was go out and take it right against the American people, so to speak, put it right in their laps."

Monday night, with history-in-the-making swirling all around them like a bonfire, the vets tried to forget their worries by dancing and drinking and toking on the occasional shared joint, as a local rock band played John Lennon's "Give Peace a Chance" and other countercultural anthems on a flatbed truck pulled up against the encampment. In a way it looked like some odd parody of a political convention, with vets clustered around posters that marked their home states, and just as at a convention, they argued late into the night, over everything from violence versus nonviolence to whether their medals should be returned to Congress or tossed on the White House lawn. At the same time there were echoes of Woodstock, which most of the vets had missed the first time around: the music punctuated by announcements about some girl looking for "John from New Jersey" or calling for someone from Wisconsin to come and get their comrade who had passed out.

The biggest cheer, however, was given to a four-year-old boy, who went up on the stage to tell the crowd: "My daddy's in Vietnam, and I'm not for it!" That really said it all. This encampment was not about politics so much as it was about families, and keeping people alive and together. When the band finished, the vets curled up in their bags and ponchos for the most peaceful sleep they would get all week.[63]

3. Outlaws on the Mall

Within a few months of Dewey Canyon III, the two divergent movements in VVAW—the confrontational or revolutionary faction and the orderly reform faction—would begin to part company almost completely. But the interesting thing at Dewey Canyon was how well they worked together, complementing each other, playing off each other for maximum effect.

Tuesday April 20 was a perfect example of this kind of synergy. The confrontational vets had decided that they could not overlook the affront given them the day before at Arlington Cemetery. Two hundred vets marched back in single file across the Arlington Memorial Bridge, and this time Al Hubbard went head to head with the superintendent himself, who stood in front of the closed gates, with a line of park police just behind him. "This is not a demonstration. This is a memorial service," Hubbard declared. Acting as if yesterday's insult were merely someone else's lame joke, the superintendent proceeded to welcome them into the cemetery.

Once inside, the vets marched up a hill, where a Gold Star mother and a veteran together placed two wreaths—one marked "Allied" and the other "Indochina"—under a crab apple tree. A double file of vets then knelt down before a plot of tombstones, and many raised their fists in the air to signify their determination to keep any more of their brothers from dying. From somewhere down below, at the site of a fresh burial, there came the sound of rifles firing in salute, followed by a bugler playing taps.

Later that day, guerrilla theater was performed on the steps of the Capitol. For several minutes it seemed as if the nation's capital were under attack, with helmeted soldiers rushing about, yelling, grabbing civilians, and firing their realistic (though smaller than actual size) model M-16s. Three girls wearing straw coolie hats attempted to flee from the infantrymen and were cut down with a simulated burst of automatic rifle fire; as they collapsed, they clutched their stomachs, bursting balloons filled with red paint, which splattered over the steps. "Waste 'em! Get the body count!" shouted the soldiers. One middle-aged woman turned away, pronouncing the drama "disgusting." Afterward, several of the veterans smashed their toy weapons against the steps, angry that some people did not believe they were really veterans. Nixon had leaked a rumor that two-thirds of the VVAW were impostors.

A more instructive episode of guerrilla theater took place at the Old Senate Office Building, where a platoon led by Bill Crandell pinned their victims to the ground and demanded identification papers. "Why are *you* here? This is our home," the "Vietnamese" responded, as the soldiers roughed them up. Then Crandell proceeded to explain to viewers, "If they don't have IDs, therefore they are Viet Cong. So we take them in and torture them. . . . You have to get the sense of how much GIs are encouraged to hate the Vietnamese. That's why we're against the war."

Some of the mock warriors added a striking innovation; they had their faces painted in skull-like masks of white and black greasepaint, which the vets called "death face," while others had "P.O.W." written on their foreheads. It was almost as if the ghosts of the men and women who had been killed or lost in Vietnam had come to point the finger at their true assassins and captors: the war makers in the government of the United States.

Two of the guys who started the use of death face had served in graves registration in Vietnam. The graves registration guys were among the severest psychiatric casualties from the war. Not only were they forced on a daily basis to put together mangled heaps of body parts into some semblance of corpses that could be shipped home to loved ones and honorably buried; but they were usually outcasts among their fellow troops, hated by the buddies of every man whose body they handled, for no matter how well they did their job, they would be attacked for not being compassionate enough (usually they did everything they could, including lots of drugs, in order not to feel) and for not paying the proper respect (but it was hard to pay respect to a collection of stumps and bloody hunks of flesh without going even crazier than they had already gone). These two men were both tremendously stressed out, suffering from nightmares almost every night, which they tried to shut off with a surfeit of drugs, psychedelic and otherwise. Both naturally gravitated toward the crazies. Though they were hardly effective proselytizers, they acted out their roles in the guerrilla theater with an intensity, heightened by the greasepaint, that sent shudders through the crowd.

Strong as these images were, they did not satisfy the revolutionary vets like Sam Schorr and Barry Romo. Schorr's radicalization had begun after his return from the war, when he joined a chapter of SDS along with several other Vietnam veterans at Valley Junior College in Van Nuys, California. All of them quickly adopted the anti-imperialist banner. He describes his group of vets as "raving lunatics and rowdies" and claims they were "probably the crazier segment of the SDS chapter." Explains Schorr: "They kept talking about war and making revolution, and we said, 'We know how to do that.'" Soon after SDS split up, leading to the random street violence of the so-called Days of Rage, Schorr went through a heavy period of what he calls PVS (post-Vietnam syndrome) and expatriated himself in Europe. But the invasion of Cambodia, followed by Kent State and the subsequent killing of black students at Jackson State, brought him back to America "to do something about it." Returning to Southern California, he hooked up with a revolutionary group in Venice—composed of everyone from followers of Che Guevara and old Communist Party people to members of the American Friends Service Committee—and as he began to organize other vets to join this loose circle of activists, the California Veterans' Movement (CVM) was born.

A child of the Mexican-American working class, Barry Romo, by contrast, had held right-wing Republican views for most of his life. He had wanted to be a priest and had gone to Vietnam as a young lieutenant convinced that it was both his patriotic and religious duty to stop Communism. He was an exemplary soldier there, winning the Bronze Star for single-handedly rescuing a trapped squad that was under heavy enemy fire. The bulk of his radicalization had come not from leftist ideology but from the killing and maiming he had witnessed in

Vietnam—the sergeant in his platoon who had had his balls blown off by a "Bouncing Betty" mine on Romo's last day in Vietnam, and the nephew (who was Barry's age) who had been killed the day before on the DMZ, whose body Barry was asked to escort back to the States, so that death would literally follow him even in his homecoming. "I went to college and tried to forget the war," he recalled years later in a speech to another peace movement aimed at Central America. "Although I'd seen people die, and I'd seen the uselessness of the war in Vietnam, it didn't bring me some kind of instant consciousness, that made me understand that my friends that had died and lost their limbs had done so for nothing. But friends at college didn't spit on me, they argued with me. And the things I'd grown up with, the things I had been taught, which I was trying to hold on to as an excuse for not being politically involved, crumbled. And like tens of thousands of other Vietnam vets, I became politically active." Unlike Schorr, Romo eased his way, a step at a time, into the peace movement—at first simply making speeches at peace demos about his day-to-day experiences in Vietnam, much like Green Beret Don Duncan and others before him had done. But once he got involved with Schorr, the California Veterans' Movement (CVM), and then VVAW at Winter Soldier, what he heard from other veterans triggered all of Romo's own delayed stress, and he plunged into antiwar and anti-imperialist activism with a fervor that few of any political stripe could match.

Jack Smith recalls Romo running about with his rebel's headband on, a leader of the crazies: "He wanted to have a demonstration on every corner, in terms of sitting down and blocking traffic, doing anything to disrupt. If the cops were nasty, he wanted to fight 'em back . . . rather than going about the hard work of organizing, being disciplined and creating a certain image." Short, slender, with muttonchop sideburns, a receding hairline, and intensely flashing dark eyes, Romo made an improbable pair with Schorr, who was much larger and slower moving, and had a gigantic mop of frizzy hair and thick glasses. In Schorr's words: "Barry was a real motor, and I was basically an organizer type." But what they shared was an attitude of defiance and a belief in the power of spontaneity. "The New York people were very much into letting the government know [what they were doing] and getting permission," Schorr explains. "We [the West Coast vets] were into 'Fuck them, let's go do it!'"

Schorr and Romo felt that the guerrilla theater outside the Capitol, which was being filmed by numerous cameras almost as if it were a movie set, was no longer immediate or scary enough to jar passersby from their fog of complacency. So they led a sortie of about twenty-five vets into the Capitol Rotunda, breaking through into the roped-off area where dead Presidents had lain in state. One of the guys lay down, and they draped an American flag over him; then they proceeded to hold a full military service for their "dead" comrade. The Capitol police grew extremely agitated and started to move in on them, but the tourists began cheering for the vets and telling the police to back off.

Sheldon Ramsdell recalls that at some of these unplanned guerrilla theater episodes, the tricolor National Liberation Front (NLF) or Viet Cong flag began appearing. The use of the enemy's flag at peace demonstrations in the United States was a highly provocative gesture, and it had become one of the most controversial tactics of the movement, generating a good deal of internal debate as to whether it actually turned off more people than it spurred to positive action. It was especially upsetting to some people to see veterans waving the flag of the army that had killed many of their fellows, and the sight perhaps cast additional doubt on whether they really were veterans. Ramsdell suspected it was one or two government agents provocateurs who started the use of the NLF flag, but he concedes that once the flag had been introduced, there were more than enough genuine crazies to rally around it.[64]

•   •   •

Inside the Capitol chambers, while the march to Arlington and the various guerrilla actions were taking place, another two hundred vets attended hearings by the Senate Foreign Relations Committee about proposed ways of ending the war. That was not a very exciting or satisfying experience, for the vets really wanted to participate in such hearings themselves. But they were up against their own wall, since the congresspeople who took their side were not, for the most part, in power positions on the key congressional committees.

They had been granted audiences with both Senator William Fulbright (D-Ark.), chairman of the Senate Foreign Relations Committee, and with Stuart Symington (D-Mo.), a member of the committee. Fulbright, who had been prevailed upon by President Johnson in 1964 to help get the Tonkin Gulf Resolution through the Senate (the bill that essentially gave LBJ his vast war-making powers in Southeast Asia), had spent the past several years atoning for his sins, so to speak, by forcing Congress to listen to the antiwar point of view. Though he was often looked to as a figurehead of dissent, he had not been able to change Congress's commitment to prosecute the war. Likewise Fulbright had not been able to effectively utilize the dissent of veterans, though he had been presented with offers of testimony since Jan Barry Crumb first contacted him in 1967. Symington, who had less of a debilitating reputation as a bleeding-heart liberal, seemed a more promising liaison with the power brokers of the Senate. He had agreed to meet with the veterans because they came with letters of introduction (procured through Jack Smith and his connections at Yale) from some of the biggest-name old-money liberals in northwestern Connecticut.

The pitch they gave Symington, though, was far from genteel. A Missouri vet named John Upton, a former Navy corpsman with the Marines, who had seen some very brutal firefights, modeled a government-issue T-shirt for the senator. It had a skull and crossbones on the front and was labeled "Charlie's

Hunting Club" on the back; it was given out in his unit as a reward for killing Vietnamese. Symington said he was shocked and felt the matter needed looking into. But Symington, even with Fulbright's cooperation and the friendly ear of another dove on the Senate Foreign Relations Committee, Frank Church (D-Idaho), was not able to budge the rest of the committee to agree to hearings involving the veterans. Although Symington argued that "these guys [at Dewey Canyon] are legitimate American heroes," a majority of the committee still regarded them "as a small splinter group that represented nothing."

Nevertheless, the fact that Fulbright had gotten these "how to end the war" hearings scheduled was a victory in itself; and the crowd of vets in the gallery lent a sense of reality and urgency to war talk that for too many years had sounded as airy as abstract mathematics. The Foreign Relations Committee was considering six bills that had been introduced in the Senate having to do with ending the war—the two most important being the McGovern-Hatfield amendment to cut off funding for the war by the end of the year (1971); and a resolution by Vance Hartke (D-Ind.) calling for immediate withdrawal of all troops from Vietnam. The McGovern-Hatfield amendment had been kicking around for over a year; but when it had been defeated the previous September, it had garnered 39 votes of support (out of the 51 needed)—a good indication that it might well pass this time around. Nixon, of course, was opposed to all of the bills and continued to assert that a withdrawal deadline would undermine the Paris peace negotiations, endanger the withdrawal, and fail to secure the return of prisoners—even though the North Vietnamese had repeatedly offered to talk about releasing the prisoners as soon as the United States set such a deadline.

VVAW was determined to chart its own course, though there were other military groups attempting to open their own channels to Congress. Mark Lane was back on the scene, having hooked up with the Concerned Officers Movement (COM). COM was still a very small organization, composed of mostly white, university-educated, and what Jack Smith called "Waspy" types, most of them active-duty officers, who were almost too legitimate for VVAW to swallow. Congressmen Ron Dellums (D-Calif.) and John Conyers Jr. (D-Mich.) assembled an ad hoc panel before which COM members and a few vets could testify. The panel was scheduled to meet for four days, beginning Monday April 26, in the House Caucus Room of the Cannon Office Building. An immediate fear arose among the VVAW leadership that if they let themselves be associated with these ad hoc hearings, they would again share the discredit Mark Lane brought with him. The Dellums Committee Hearings seemed more likely to blunt than enhance the impact of Dewey Canyon. The muddying of congressional waters with these other soldiers' groups made it seem all the more urgent to the VVAW to get one of their own people, the most impressive and articulate combat veteran they could find, to address the Foreign Relations Committee.

They had just the man, of course, in John Kerry. In an organization that agreed on very little, there was almost unanimous assent to the proposition that Kerry should be their national spokesman, but putting him in front of a congressional microphone seemed all but impossible.

And then the miracle happened, in a way no one could have predicted. Senators Claiborne Pell (D-R.I.) and Philip Hart (D-Mich.) hosted a fund-raising party for the veterans. Since the Democratic Convention in 1968, Pell had consistently tried to keep his party from tying its future to the government of South Vietnam, and he had doggedly emphasized the moral issues of the war as well. Hart's credentials with the antiwar movement were just as strong, since his own wife had been arrested in a peace demonstration at the Pentagon and had refused to pay income taxes in protest against Nixon's air war. In fact, it was Jane Briggs Hart who had come up with the idea of the party, which was held at the Harts' home on Tuesday night. Fulbright and several other congressmen showed up; and Kerry, who had never dreamed of making a speech there, suddenly found himself talking to the assembled group about "what was in my heart and in my gut and on my mind." Fulbright was so impressed that he told Kerry he wanted him to speak before the Foreign Relations Committee, and he promised to redouble his efforts to persuade his colleagues the next day. Kerry was stunned. He went back to where he was staying that night (he was not sleeping on the Mall) and immediately began trying to assemble the various drafts of fund-raising speeches he had been using for the past few months into a single powerful narrative of what it felt like to be a Vietnam veteran come home.[65]

Before the party broke up, however, there came word—like the crack of doom—of a Supreme Court decision that would change the course of Dewey Canyon III. The Nixon Justice Department had submitted an emergency petition to Chief Justice Warren Burger that morning, asking that Burger, in his capacity as judge for the District of Columbia, overturn the verdict of the Court of Appeals, which had decided in favor of allowing the veterans to camp on the Mall. A few hours later—allegedly the speediest decision on record—Chief Justice Burger reversed the ruling of the Court of Appeals. The injunction was reinstated "with full force and effect," and the veterans were given till 4:30 P.M. on Wednesday to vacate their campsite.

To the vets, the debate seemed crystal clear. Should the constitutional right to assemble peacefully take precedence over National Park Service regulations about how the Mall could be used? But Nixon's lawyers had confused the issue, claiming that to allow the veterans use of the Mall would set a precedent that could be cited by the People's Coalition for Peace and Justice (PCPJ), which planned to use government property as a base for their avowedly nonpeaceful protests the following week. Burger's ruling was heavily influenced by the Justice Department's contention that government security was dependent on getting rid of the vets.

The truth is, it was not government security so much as Nixon's own security that was at stake. The president was growing desperate to get the veterans out of the public eye. Tuesday night Walter Cronkite had again focused on the presence of VVAW in Washington, this time showing their banner on the national news. But in seeking to evict them from the Mall, Nixon made a critical mistake. The Supreme Court ruling had two major effects. It pushed more of the veterans in the direction of the revolutionaries and crazies, stiffening their will to resist a government that had now added insult to injury. The second effect—a result, ironically, that Nixon had wanted to avoid at all cost—was that it focused attention on the campsite itself. A nation that for almost a decade had felt itself beleaguered by a war it could not win, and ostracized by much of the world community for its actions in South Vietnam, now found itself identifying with those weary-looking veterans, who apparently had no home except that pitiful cluster of pup tents, bedrolls, and lean-tos outside the Capitol, and whose own government had now raised its hand against them.

Former Attorney General Ramsey Clark tried hard to achieve a legal solution. He began, Wednesday morning, by asking that the full Supreme Court be polled on the issue of upholding Judge Hart's original ruling to ban the encampment. Despite Clark's eloquent argument against "government by injunction," all of the justices concurred with Burger's decision, except for William O. Douglas, who abstained. (Douglas had also been the only justice to urge that the Supreme Court rule on the constitutionality of the war, which he had called the "most important issue of the sixties to reach the Court.")

While the justices were meeting, Clark went into conference with Justice Department lawyers to try to strike a compromise. The Justice Department itself was unsure about how or when the injunction would be enforced. It would become clear later that the government attorneys had been pressured into taking immediate action against the vets even though their better judgment had been to wait and see what developed. Hence the Justice Department was looking for its own way out of the looming catastrophe. Deputy Attorney General Richard Kleindienst offered the vets two alternate campsites and free transportation from either site to the Capitol. But the locations he chose—Robert F. Kennedy Stadium and Bolling Air Force Base—were not acceptable to the VVAW leadership. Both seemed more like detention centers than campsites. The vets had no taste for either a return to military discipline or for being corralled in a sports stadium, the way many dissenters had been rounded up in the totalitarian states of Latin America.

Nixon, meanwhile, was attempting to wash his hands of the affair. His press secretary Ronald Ziegler told newsmen that the president "was taking no part in handling the situation" and that he was leaving the fate of the veterans to "appropriate agencies."

Support for the vets was beginning to grow in Congress, however. Senator

Edward M. Kennedy, who had until then been quietly sympathetic to the vets, now chose to come to their campsite and speak publicly in their behalf. "You have served your country well abroad and will serve it even better here in Washington," Kennedy told the edgy crowd on Wednesday morning. "If the country can find a place for you to stay in Vietnam, they can find a place for you to stay here." The vets appreciated the courage it took for Kennedy to join their ranks, remembering that it was one of his brothers who had begun our serious military involvement in Vietnam, and another who had died in a presidential run based chiefly on ending it.

Nor was Kennedy alone in feeling that the establishment had a duty to care for, not arrest, its veterans. Sixteen House members offered their Capitol Hill offices as a place to sleep, should the vets be evicted from the Mall—the group included seven Democrats from New York: Bella Abzug, Shirley Chisholm, John Dow, Ed Koch, Bertram Podell, William Fitts Ryan, and James Scheuer. Senator Philip Hart introduced a sense-of-the-Senate resolution supporting the veterans' right to camp on the Mall, but it was immediately stalled by opposition from Strom Thurmond. In the House, friendly representatives tried without success to get Speaker Carl Albert (D-Okla.) to rule in favor of the vets remaining on Capitol grounds.

The friendly members of government were still a minority, and, as far as the vets could see, the full power of the law was about to descend on them like a division of General Giap's NVA regulars. Nor could they look to the fact of being veterans as a shield, especially since both the Veterans of Foreign Wars and the American Legion had issued statements asserting that the men in Washington did not represent the views of most veterans of the "Vietnam conflict" (the older vets being still unwilling to recognize Vietnam as a real "war"). By the same token, the AMVETS had closed the door of their regular luncheon meeting to VVAW members. Although the vets took some consolation in hearing that 26 Marines at Quantico had refused to participate in riot control against them, and that 400 of the 500 military guards at Arlington Cemetery had said the same, they knew that the government still had more than enough manpower to remove them by force.[66]

4. Democracy in Action: Playing It for the Media

If the government wanted trouble, some of the vets were ready to give it to them. Schorr, Romo, and their fellow firebrands saw their opportunity. On Wednesday April 21 they led a march of about seventy-five veterans to the Pentagon for the purpose of turning themselves in as war criminals. It was another march in perfect formation, with the men calling out their favorite antiwar cadences. Their esprit was not dampened when the huge doors to the

Pentagon's mall entrance were locked in their faces; they could afford to wait, knowing that the Pentagon was under more pressure than they were. They clapped and stomped their feet, waving their upside-down American flag and showing pure defiance, especially since they had already caught flak from their own leaders. Most of VVAW's top guns, including Kerry, Hubbard, Mike Oliver, and Mike McCusker (a firebrand in his own right from Oregon), opposed the march to the Pentagon. They thought that Schorr and his followers would probably be arrested, detracting from the positive image that VVAW had created up to that point.

Less than a month before, Lieutenant William Calley Jr. had been sentenced to life imprisonment for the murder of twenty-two Vietnamese civilians at the village of My Lai—although Nixon, responding to the storm of protest that arose throughout the nation, later ordered Calley released from the Fort Benning stockade, pending Nixon's own review of the verdict. Schorr felt that if his seventy-five vets "joined Calley in the brig," it would underscore the fact that the real problem was not what was going on in the hamlets of Vietnam, but the kind of decision making that was going on inside the Pentagon.

Schorr thought the points they could score were worth the risk. He recalls: "The press was eating it up. We really hit the nerve on that one. The Pentagon finally said, 'All right, we'll let representatives come in.' At first we refused that, saying, 'We all go in or nobody goes in.' Then we talked about it some more and took a vote. So three of us went in—Biff, whose head was messed up; John McDonald, who could only speak three words in a row before he quit; and myself. The press came in with us, which the Pentagon didn't want. So General [Daniel] 'Chappie' James, the first black general, comes up. They thought this was a great move on their part. He says, 'What do you want?' We said, 'We want to turn ourselves in, we're war criminals.' [He said,] 'We don't accept war criminals here, that's a police matter.' I said, 'What do you mean? You've got Calley in jail.' So at that point he says, 'Let's go to my office.' As we were going down the hall, the press were going, 'Keep working him! Keep working him!' So we got in there and James says, 'Well, we can't accept you as war criminals.' I said, 'Who can accept us?' He says, 'If you really think you committed a crime, you should turn yourselves in to the police.' I said, 'Do you have any representatives of the Hague Court here? Maybe an international court will accept us.' He goes, 'We don't commit war crimes.' I said, 'Well, you better let Calley go then.' He said, 'We can't do that because he's under military criminal law.' And I said, 'You're just full of shit, you know that? We're getting out of here. We're gonna go talk to people who make sense.' So we got up and left."

Wednesday, as the day before, different groups of vets pursued their varying strategies around the capital. Guerrilla theater was performed in front of the Justice Department, while lobbying continued all day long on Capitol Hill. Visitors of all stripes pilgrimaged to the campsite, but none made more of an impression than Thich Nhat Hanh, a South Vietnamese Buddhist monk, who told the vets, "Every one of us is responsible for the suffering in Vietnam . . . but I admire you very much for breaking through the curtain of misinformation and finding the truth."

The eyes of the nation were on the veterans' encampment on the Mall, as though the vets and the government were two strong men with a grudge against each other, and the question was were they going to settle it peaceably or come to blows, and if they came to blows, just how rough would it get? People of all sorts were drawn to the encampment to talk with the vets, but most often it was active-duty GIs or young men facing the draft who showed up full of questions. Even some West Point cadets came over to discuss the success of various military tactics. To many of the vets, the camaraderie they shared with these people, and the chance they had, by communicating their experiences in Vietnam, to keep others from making the wrong decision, were more important reasons for being in Washington than to cry out to the deaf ears of Congress. Schorr recalls some really compelling exchanges, including one episode later that night when two men who had pretended to be ex–National Guardsmen finally broke down and confessed that they had served in Vietnam. Up till that point, because of the negative stereotypes, they had not wanted to identify themselves as Vietnam veterans.[67]

*   *   *

Just when it seemed the tension could get no greater, another bombshell was dropped in the veterans' midst. John Kerry got a call from Lawrence Spivak, the longtime host of *Meet the Press,* informing him that Al Hubbard had lied to the American public about his rank, and probably about where he had served as well. Spivak demanded to know if VVAW had known in advance of Al's deception. Kerry swore that they had all taken Al's word on faith, but Spivak remained agitated, arguing that the integrity of the show had been compromised. The fact that Hubbard had been a sergeant, not a captain, though it had little bearing on what he had witnessed (especially since the government could not definitively say he had never been in Vietnam), nevertheless cast doubt on the credibility of every member of VVAW. It thrust the whole organization into a defensive posture.

Kerry attacked Hubbard mercilessly in front of the other leaders of the organization. According to Mike Oliver, Kerry was deeply embarrassed, feeling that Hubbard had discredited everything they had said to the American people on *Meet the Press,* which had been such a tremendous opportunity to publicize their cause. Of course, as Oliver also notes, Kerry "had all these political aspirations" and going on national television had been "a big, big step" toward getting himself elected to public office. The last thing Kerry had wanted was to appear to the American people as a fraud, even if only by association.

Perhaps the greatest irony was that Kerry actually liked Hubbard and respected the work he had done for VVAW. Kerry argued against drumming Al out of the organization, and in public he defended him unequivocally. But there is no doubt that this press debacle impelled Kerry even more strongly to identify himself with the system, and to shy as far as possible from any taint of lawbreaking or unseemly conduct.

At 4:30 Wednesday afternoon, an alarm clock rang over the public address system at the campsite. There were no police anywhere around. The vets all crowded around the speakers' platform—many of them perched, for a better view, atop the nearby Ryder and U-haul trucks—to hear the latest about their legal situation. Word came down that the Supreme Court was still in special session. An hour later, Ramsey Clark appeared in person to give them the news, both good and bad.

First, the bad: the Supreme Court had voted against them. The vets began chanting, as draft resisters had been doing for years: "Hell, no! We won't go!" Then Clark explained that they had won an important concession. The Justice Department had agreed to let the vets stay on the Mall *so long as they didn't sleep there.* Justice had weakened its stance against the vets in part because it had been forced to compromise with the People's Coalition for Peace and Justice, offering PCPJ the use of West Potomac Park rather than Rock Creek Park, where the militant protesters would be less easy to control. Hence Justice was now in the bind of appearing to offer an unruly mob of radicals virtually the same piece of land that it had been trying so hard to wrest from American combat veterans. As a result, Justice was prepared to let the vets do pretty much what they wanted on the Mall—even play rock music throughout the night— just so they did not attempt to sleep there. However absurd that position, the Justice Department signaled its intention to enforce the court order. If the veterans defied it, Clark warned, they would be subject to arrest. Clark told them: "I would like you to comply with it."

The little VVAW army was thrown into pandemonium. John Kerry spoke in favor of abiding by the Supreme Court's decree, and he advised the vets that if they did resist, they should try to be "totally nonviolent, nonprovocative." Kerry knew that they were skating on thin ice. Earlier in the day, Mark Lane had taken a small group of protesters to the Supreme Court and gotten eleven people, including himself and three women, arrested for trying to force their way into the Justices' chambers. The worst of it was, Lane had told the papers that his gutsy bunch was "associated with the veterans' protest." If VVAW's own members reinforced this militant image, they might bring the heel of repression down so hard that everything they had already gained, including the goodwill of the nation, would be lost.

When Al Hubbard took the microphone, the crowd, not yet knowing that he had been shamed as an impostor, expected a more aggressive response. They began cheering, "Right on!" and "We won't go!" But Hubbard, who was still on the defensive, meekly suggested that they accept their limited victory. He agreed with Kerry that the vets had no alternative but to leave for the night, and then he suggested alternate places to stay.

The courtyard of Washington National Cathedral had been offered to them, and there were some smaller churches available too. Also, the mayor of D.C. was willing to designate a city park as an alternate campsite. Congressman Donald Riegle Jr. (D-Mich.), one of the sponsors of the upcoming Dellums Committee Hearings, had already opened his office to vets as a dormitory, and several more congresspeople, including Dellums himself and Don Edwards of California, were about to do the same. In a way, it seemed as if it might be an even bigger propaganda victory if the vets were turned out of the Mall by Nixon and then offered refuge in the halls of Congress. But Mike Oliver, for one, saw things quite differently.[68]

Oliver got up in front of the confused crowd of vets and roused them to anger in his stentorian voice. "Fuck that!" he responded to the advice of the previous speakers. "We're gonna sleep on this Mall tonight, and we're gonna see what happens. We ain't gonna take one step backwards; we'll take two forward." Oliver explains that he was thinking like an infantryman: "You never split your forces in half—you always keep your forces together. And it was my opinion that if we left these tents here, and just guarded them, and slept someplace else, we were copping out. When you've got them [the vets] all here, I don't care if they're drugged or drunk, they're under your control. You have people sleeping all over the city, you're not gonna have a good directed demonstration. You'd lose it." John Kerry accused him, in a friendly way, of "formulating confrontational tactics"; and Oliver replied, "Well, so be it."

Oliver, however, was simply a dissenting voice from the national office. The various delegations of veterans had not yet been heard from, and the leadership of VVAW was doing its best to keep chapter representatives from coming up on the platform to express their views. Sam Schorr and his radical coterie had been going for two and a half days straight and were dead on their feet. He had met with the leaders of his "anti-imperialist coalition," including Romo of California, Scott Camil of Florida, and Gary Steiger of Ohio, and they agreed it was time that the vets in their chapters were allowed to voice a counterproposal. When some of the leaders of VVAW tried to stop Schorr from grabbing the mike, he threatened, "If you don't allow us to have our say, we're gonna break from this demonstration." So Schorr was finally allowed to speak.

He recalls: "I was absolutely hoarse, I had no voice left, 'cause we'd been singing, chanting, agitating, for two and a half days. And I got up there and laid out the proposal. Basically our position was very emotional: we fought, we died, we got maimed, our brains are scrambled, fighting for this goddamn piece of dirt. If there's anybody who has a right to sleep on it, it's us. We're gonna sleep, goddamn it. Fuck *them,* we're cool."

Faced with having the organization torn apart before their eyes, the national leadership fell back on VVAW's democratic tenets. They offered to put the matter to a vote among the entire membership (at least those who were then present on the Mall), and all factions agreed to abide by the will of the majority.

Oliver expected that the radicals would be outvoted. But there were others high up in the organization, like Scott Moore, who had foreseen that the vets might eventually be forced to break the law. Moore knew that it was essential for VVAW to stand behind all of its members. If vets were arrested, VVAW would have to bail them out—otherwise it would lose credibility. The question was, where would bail money come from? Moore's mother, Madeleine, was working in the temporary national office on 14th Street, in what she refers to as a "red-light district." Earlier that day, she had phoned a personal friend in Indiana, a member of the family that owned Eli Lilly, the huge drug manufacturer. Her friend offered to provide blankets and camping supplies, but she told him that what they needed instead was $10,000 to keep the vets out of jail, should arrests be made. Her friend wired the money immediately.

The less than 900 vets then on the Mall went into state caucuses to vote, either by voice or a show of hands. The California delegation was the first to arrive at a result: 32 to 1 in favor of sleeping. The California vets celebrated their decision by breaking out a huge bag of marijuana and rolling joints for all their neighbors.

For a while it looked as if the vote might go either way, until the entire Pennsylvania delegation—comprising 94 members, and rivaling New York in influence—voted to sleep. A Pennsylvania vet who was suffering from chloracne and nervous disorders related to Agent Orange poisoning supposedly hefted his bottle of Boone's Farm wine and gulped down a few tranquilizers, declaring that he would be the first one to sleep there that day. According to Jim "Thor" Halassa of Philadelphia, the rest of the delegation immediately lay down by his side and pledged to sleep with him.

The final vote was 480 to 400 in favor of sleeping on the Mall. Once it was clear that a majority were willing to risk arrest, a motion was passed to declare the vote unanimous. Then a public announcement was made, for the benefit of any authorities who might be listening, that if faced with arrest, the vets would submit peaceably and "march off as prisoners of war." They planned to be arrested by states, clasping their hands over their heads and singing the national anthem as they went.[69]

Almost from the moment that the decision was made, congresspeople began filtering down to the campsite to offer their support and a kind of token protection—almost as if to challenge the police: if you arrest the vets, you arrest Congress too. There was never any real danger of that happening, however, since from the start of the "sleep-in" the park police stated their intention of letting the vets be.

The company of congresspeople, if not essential, was nonetheless heartening. Shirley Chisholm and Bella Abzug acted almost as den mothers to the group. No one kept track of all the faces that passed through, but none could miss the arrival of Ted Kennedy around midnight. Kennedy sat on the ground amid a veritable throng of admirers. The senator from Massachusetts talked and sang, and reputedly even shared a joint, with the veterans.

I. F. Stone, publisher of the influential leftist paper *I. F. Stone's Weekly,* addressed the group, recalling how as a young Washington reporter in 1932 he had witnessed MacArthur's troops burning down the tents of the Bonus Marchers. Stone predicted that if Nixon attempted to use troops to drive out the Vietnam vets, it would be "the biggest mistake [he] . . . ever made." That evening many of the vets hurried across the street to nearby bars to watch their momentous decision replay on both local and national news broadcasts. Cronkite, most important of all, gave them significantly more time than in the past two days.

It started to drizzle early in the evening, and vets crawled under ponchos and makeshift shelters, or pitched tents wherever they felt like. The lights from the Capitol dome and from a nearby construction site began to glitter through the raindrops and shine from every slick surface, giving the campsite a magical look, almost as if it were the set of a movie. There was a darker overtone, too, as more than one press person observed that the gathering of rain-slick ponchos looked an awful lot like a collection of rubberized body bags awaiting shipment home. A perimeter was set up, just as at a firebase in Nam, and many vets lay awake, expecting arrest at any moment and not wanting to be caught off guard; but more often than not the surprises were pleasant ones. At 10 P.M. they heard a radio newscast that police planned to make no arrests that night; and at 11:30, the cast of the antiwar musical *Hair* showed up to regale the vets with song and dance.

Whatever Nixon may have thought of them, the mood of the veterans was more weariness than defiance. Lieutenant William Kinsey of the park police perhaps sensed that, for he told the press, "We are not going in there at one in the morning and pick up some wounded veteran and throw him into the street. We don't treat people like that. There will be nothing before morning." Indeed there was only a token police force observing the campsite throughout the night.

Reporters roamed the camp all night with pad and tape recorder, and what they heard sounded a lot more like Will Rogers' cracker-barrel wisdom than Communist revolution. A twenty-seven-year-old vet named John Mitchell, solemn and full-bearded, told the *Washington Post:* "It's against my grain to take part in something like this, but the morality of this week of protest overpowered my reservations. . . . This legal thing about not being able to sleep on the Mall was invoked as a way to shut us up, to get rid of us. It may be illegal to spend the night here. But it's a lot more illegal to continue the war in Vietnam, to commit the atrocities we've committed."[70]

Vietnam veterans, trained by their country to be among the most efficient killers in the world but totally unprepared to deal with such matters of conscience, were groping that night for ways to express a truth they felt in their bones. A couple, in imitation of the draft resisters, burned their discharge papers. Others, in what one journalist termed "an Aquarian version of the American Legion," linked arms with the troupe of *Hair* to sing "Give Peace a Chance," followed by a chant of "Power to the People."

But the most effective articulation of that truth was being prepared a short distance from the Mall, by a young man named John Kerry, who had just received the most important phone call of his life. William Fulbright had phoned to tell him that he was slated to speak before the Senate Foreign Relations Committee Thursday morning. A majority of senators on the committee had come round to accepting the legitimacy of the veterans' views, including George Aiken, a staunch Republican from Vermont. Known as "Old Granitehead," Aiken believed as deeply as Nixon in America's need to show strength throughout the world, but unlike Nixon he felt that America's continuing presence in Vietnam was draining that strength at a dangerously rapid rate.

Kerry worked frantically throughout the night fleshing out his speech, expanding the opening and conclusion, till he had some three thousand words. The key to piecing it together was Kerry's own sense of wastefulness; specifically, he tried to imagine what it would have meant if he had died in Vietnam, and he could not picture anyone saying that he had "died for something good." If there was really nothing worth dying for in Vietnam, then sending even one more young man to his death there was unconscionable. To think of paying with his life to bolster somebody else's self-image literally made him sick. "I felt it," he recalls, "and it just came out." He only hoped that he could make the Congress of the United States feel it too.[71]

5. The Return of Medals:
Forgiving the Living and Making Peace with the Dead

Thursday morning, April 22, 1971, the *Washington Daily News* ran the front-page headline: VETS OVERRULE SUPREME COURT. The veterans' defiance of their own government got front-page, usually sympathetic coverage in most of the major papers in the country. Overnight, the balance of power had shifted from

Richard Nixon to that little ragtag army on the Capitol doorstep. It was, as they say, a whole new ball game.

The Justice Department had been severely compromised, and Justice's attorneys desperately sought for ways to save face. They even tried offering the vets new alternate campsites—a gesture as futile as offering to step out of the way after a steamroller has finished flattening you. The park police were already making a joke out of the order to evict the vets. One policeman, staring at the field of tents, told the press that he had observed no evidence of vets camping. Asked why he was taking no action, Park Police Captain Archie Finagin replied, "To my knowledge as of this moment there are 250 persons talking and chatting and drinking coffee just like any other group of visitors."

No one was more upset than Judge Hart, who had been urged by Justice to issue the original injunction prohibiting the veterans from sleeping on the Mall. Judge Hart summoned the Justice attorneys to come before him to explain why the injunction was not being enforced. President Nixon met immediately with Attorney General John Mitchell, Deputy Attorney General Richard Kleindienst, and the chief of Justice's Civil Division, L. Patrick Gray. As a result, Gray went before Judge Hart and, acknowledging that the Vietnam veterans had turned out to be "peaceable," asked him to dissolve the injunction. Hart did so at once, but he was outraged that the White House had attempted to manipulate the federal court system in such a "degrading" manner. He pointed out to Gray that if Justice did not intend to enforce the 4:30 P.M. deadline on Wednesday, it should have come before him at that time to request that the injunction be dissolved.

"This court feels that one equal, coordinate branch of government, the judiciary, has been dangerously and improperly used by another equal, coordinate branch of government, the executive," Hart reprimanded Gray (and by extension, Nixon). "You have put the Vietnam veterans in a situation of openly defying the law of this country and openly defying the courts of this country. This is a position this country cannot tolerate and live with."[72]

While the legal drama was unraveling at the Justice Department and the U.S. District Court, the veterans directed new offensives against both Congress and the Supreme Court. Wanting as much of a spotlight on Kerry as possible, the national leadership of VVAW did not authorize any demonstrations that morning, but Sam Schorr and Barry Romo decided it was time for another guerrilla action. According to Schorr, word came to the campsite that a couple of vets had gotten tossed out of the Supreme Court building for demanding that the court rule on the constitutionality of the war (it may simply have been a delayed report of the arrest of Mark Lane and his band the day before). In any case, several of the vets began getting excited, yelling, "Yeah yeah yeah—firefight at the Supreme Court!" Schorr and Romo led a group of about 150 vets on the run, past the Capitol, to the Supreme Court building, where, just as at the Pentagon, they found the doors locked.

The vets remained standing on the steps of the court, but they formed an aisle to let people pass through, so that the police would have no legal basis for arresting them. They began singing "All we are saying / Is rule on the war" to the tune of "Give Peace a Chance." Then someone led the group in singing "America the Beautiful" and "God Bless America"—a scene that would be echoed a few years later in the powerful conclusion of Michael Cimino's film *The Deerhunter.* They also recited the Pledge of Allegiance. After a group of 4-H Club youths filed past the court, the vets switched to chanting: "One, two, three, four / We don't want your fucking war!"

To show solidarity, the vets began putting their arms around one another's shoulders and waists; then, as they chanted, "Stop the war—now!", someone got the idea to kick out his leg to emphasize the *now!* Almost immediately, the whole line of vets fell into step, kicking out their legs simultaneously in a bizarre cancan, while photographers snapped pictures that went a few steps beyond the surreal. Schorr claims the cancan originated in the "sense of exhilaration we were feeling about the power we felt we had . . . because we were the people they'd sent to fight the war. If there was anybody who had the right to be at the Supreme Court to say this thing was wrong, it was us. And we were exercising it regardless of any other considerations. We had nothing to lose, everything to gain. They had everything to lose, nothing to gain."

The Supreme Court police were finally pushed beyond their limit. They ordered the vets to leave, and when the vets sat down on the steps, they called for the city police, who began making arrests. The charge was obstructing the administration of justice—a federal offense. Most of the vets clasped their hands behind their heads and marched quietly into the waiting police buses; though a few of the vets forced the police to carry them off, and one even smashed his toy M-16 rifle on the court steps. When Metropolitan Police Chief Jerry Wilson arrived on the scene, he was impressed at what "a very coopera-tive group" the vets were, but it certainly helped that the police were acting with extraordinary gentleness themselves, even addressing the vets as "sir" when they asked them to come away. Wilson ordered his men not to arrest sev-eral disabled vets who were present, including two legless vets in wheelchairs, Bill Henschel and Bill Wyman. Both men complained angrily about this "dis-crimination," saying they wanted to be arrested with their "brothers," but Wilson simply would not take them.

Out of nowhere Mark Lane appeared, attempting to offer the vets legal advice, but he was ignored by most.

One hundred and eight vets were arrested at the Supreme Court. The national leaders of VVAW, standing across the street, tried desperately to con-vince these men not to defy the law, since bail on a charge of obstructing jus-tice was $500. John Kerry, on his way to speak in Congress, told the men on the police buses that their arrest would "defeat the purpose" of VVAW's presence in Washington and weaken their overall strength by "splitting up" the camp. But Schorr, Romo, and their followers did not flinch, even at the prospect of a $5,000 fine and/or a year in prison if convicted. Schorr felt the arrest would be "very invigorating" because it would give the rest of the encampment "something to focus on." It certainly gave the photographers some of their best shots of the week: uniformed, bemedaled military veterans marching off prisoner-of-war fashion, escorted by uniformed police, with the pillars of the Supreme Court and numerous American flags flying in the background. It also produced one of the most pithy quotes. While he was being booked, John Hamill of New York City told the *Washington Post:* "All we want the Chief Justice to do is rule on the constitutionality of the war, and all he's done this week is tell us we can't sleep on the Mall."[73]

Richard Nixon evidently felt the same way about the arrests as Sam Schorr, since the Justice Department intervened with the District of Columbia to have the charges against the vets reduced to the minor accusation of disorderly conduct. The vets were all freed a few hours later on $10 bond each. As if to get the incident out of the public eye as quickly as possible, the Justice Department further agreed to a test trial of four of the defendants the following day, to obviate all 108 having to come before the court.

Kerry was right about one thing—when the vets broke the law, Nixon could make them play by his rules; but when they operated within the system, the system was forced to take notice. The two hours John Kerry spent in front of the Senate Foreign Relations Committee Thursday morning had more impact on the fate of men still fighting in Vietnam than anything else the veterans did in Washington that week—with the possible exception of the return of their medals. Moreover, in terms of beginning the long process of establishing a respectable image for Vietnam veterans, Dewey Canyon III triumphed principally because of what the nation heard him say there that day.

Wearing his fatigue uniform, T-shirt showing at the neck and his longish hair swiped just out of his eyes, Kerry sat facing a row of dark-suited senators a generation or more older than himself. The gallery behind him was crowded with fellow veterans, who gave him what moral support they could; but with the television camera lights in his eyes, and his mind fuddled by lack of sleep, he was clearly on his own, forced to rely on the same sharp survival instincts that had kept him alive in Vietnam. In fact, he apologized to the committee for not having organized his presentation more carefully, but there was something so heartfelt about everything he said that it transcended the boundaries of an ordinary speech, political or otherwise. From the standpoint of articulating the mind-set of Vietnam veterans, his speech was a near work of genius; but its historical importance came not so much from its clever turns of phrase as from the power it generated simply by stating so many plainly true facts that no one within the U.S. government had yet dared to speak or even face. John Kerry's testimony was nothing less than a shockingly real tale of "The Emperor's New Clothes"—and the character whose naked body he held up to ridicule was not so much Lyndon Johnson or Richard Nixon as America itself, with its perennial, fatuous belief that it could do no wrong.

Kerry told the committee that the United States had "created a monster" in Vietnam. He described some of the atrocities that had been recounted at the Winter Soldier Investigation, which he reminded the senators were in addition to "the normal ravage of war, and the normal and very particular ravaging which is done by applied bombing power of this country." America was not threatened by reds, Kerry asserted, but rather by its own crimes both against the Vietnamese and against the "millions of men who have been taught to deal and to trade in violence, and who are given the chance to die for the biggest nothing in history." These young men, who returned to America "with a sense of anger and a sense of betrayal which no one has yet grasped," knew that their country had lied to them, knew that they had not been "preserving freedom" (in Vice President Agnew's phrase), knew that their nation was speaking and acting with the height of hypocrisy, and that their bodies and their lives were being spent to perpetuate that hypocrisy. Such men would bring back to their native land feelings of hatred and shame that would only continue to tear the country apart. Not only that, but they would themselves be a living war wound, which might take the country decades to heal.

Kerry pointed out that America had scarcely begun to deal with the needs of the men it had sent to "fight Communism" on a foreign shore. While the president apparently still worried that men were not free in Vietnam, he seemed untroubled that "the largest corps of unemployed in this country are veterans of this war." Nor did he seem troubled that "the [VA] hospitals across the country won't or can't meet their demands." Nor had he given a thought to the astounding fact that 57 percent of all those entering the VA hospitals talked of suicide, and 27 percent admitted having tried. Vietnam veterans were killing themselves in record numbers, Kerry explained, because "they come back to this country and they have to face what they did in Vietnam, and then they come back and find the indifference of a country that doesn't really care," a country that simply "shrugged off" hundreds of thousands of deaths because it lacked the "moral indignation" to say no to the callous waste of human life.

He reminded the senators that it was real people we were killing "by remote control" in our massive bombing of the Plain of Jars in Laos, and real people who were being murdered in the "free-fire zones" in Vietnam—real people who "only wanted to work in rice paddies without helicopters strafing them and bombs with napalm burning their villages and tearing their country apart . . . [who] wanted everything having to do with the war, particularly with the foreign presence of the United States of America, to leave them alone in peace. . . ." They were, moreover, people with an ancient culture and traditions, who did not want to be "molded after our own image" and who had to be coerced "to take up the fight against the threat we were supposedly saving them from."

Over and over again Kerry used the word *mistake* to refer to the deployment of American military forces in Vietnam. While that perception may seem tame after decades of hindsight, at that moment in April 1971 it was tantamount to political heresy and could have spelled ruination for the young man's future political career. Kerry went beyond attacking some of the fundamental assumptions of American foreign policy; he attacked high-placed persons in both political parties and accused them of the gravest crimes: "We are here to ask where [Robert] McNamara, [Walt Whitman] Rostow, [McGeorge] Bundy, [Roswell] Gilpatric and so many others, where are they now that we, the men whom they sent off to a war, have returned? These are commanders who have deserted their troops, and there is no more serious crime in the law of war. . . . These men have left all the casualties and retreated behind a pious shield of public rectitude. . . .

"Finally, this administration has done us the ultimate dishonor. They have attempted to disown us and the sacrifices we made for this country. In their blindness and fear they have tried to deny that we are veterans or that we served in Nam. We do not need their testimony. Our own scars and stumps of limbs are witness enough for others and for ourselves."

Kerry not only had the guts to say what he believed, but he had the force of personality to make those beliefs credible. Hardly a person in that congressional chamber was not shaken when he asked, "How do you ask a man to be the last man to die in Vietnam? How do you ask a man to be the last man to die for a mistake?" But the clincher—the thing that guaranteed that Kerry would not be forgotten as just one more naysaying prophet of doom—was that he refused to end his speech on a note of bitterness or despair. After all he had been through—his own personal wounding, the loss of many of his friends—he insisted that he and his fellow Vietnam veterans would continue the struggle "to pacify our own hearts, to conquer the hate and the fear that have driven this country these last ten years and more."

In enunciating their goals, he gave validation to the work of every member of Vietnam Veterans Against the War. If they were successful, he promised, then "in thirty years from now when our brothers go down the street without a leg, without an arm, or a face, and small boys ask why, we will be able to say 'Vietnam' and not mean a desert, not a filthy obscene memory, but mean instead the place where America finally turned and where soldiers like us helped in the turning."

Although earlier, on the Senate floor, a Republican senator had accused the VVAW of inviting "a devastating Communist attack on rearguard American troops heading for home," now in the Foreign Relations Committee chamber all the senators were deeply respectful in their follow-up questions to Kerry.

The questioning lasted over an hour, and it ended with a flourish as Senator Stuart Symington (D-Mo.) asked Kerry to move his microphone so that the senators could have a clear view of the medals on Kerry's chest.

"That's a Silver Star?"

"Yes, sir."

"And that is a Purple Heart?"

"Yes."

"With three clusters on it. You have been wounded three times?"

"Yes."

"I have no further questions," said Symington, and the room erupted in applause. The senators later declared Kerry's testimony one of the most eloquent pleas for disengagement from Vietnam they had heard.[74]

Though the vets had apparently won the ear of Congress, there was still no response from the nation's chief executive. That night VVAW staged a candlelight march to the White House, and it was the best-attended event of the week. Part of the jubilation of the march came from the vets hearing, just beforehand, the announcement of Judge Hart's dissolution of the injunction against them. "You may camp in peace," a lawyer told the assembled marchers, eliciting a welter of cheers and clenched fists. Candles were then passed out and lighted one from another. Two thousand demonstrators—veterans, many with "P.O.W." still scrawled on their jackets in anticipation of arrest the night before, their wives and girlfriends, parents who had lost sons in the war—marched up Pennsylvania Avenue behind a Marine veteran named Mike Milligan. Milligan carried an upside-down American flag tied to a tree branch. The flag had covered the coffin of his best friend, John "Bo" Bloschichak, who had been killed in Vietnam two months short of his nineteenth birthday. It was Milligan's way of saying what they all felt—that it was "a march for the guys that will never march again."

The onlookers, including the intermission crowd of *Hair*, were mostly sympathetic, often flashing the peace sign, while passing cars honked their horns at the ten-block-long procession; but though the lights remained on in the White House, President Nixon gave no sign to acknowledge that he had even seen the marchers.

Afterward, back at the campsite, the veterans and their friends once again sang "Give Peace a Chance." Then a veteran with two artificial legs, named Philip Lavoie, was hoisted with his steel crutches to the stage. Lavoie told the crowd that he would continue to love America, even though he would be reminded of the war every single day for the rest of his life. "America is beautiful," he asserted. "We're just trying to get this country straight."

Many of the vets then went over to Washington National Cathedral, to join in another candlelight ceremony that was being sponsored by the Concerned Officers Movement (COM), which included a reading of the names of the dead. The Reverend William Sloane Coffin gave a short talk first, crediting the nation's veterans with proving that "the war is a lie." Many of the officers in COM were still on active duty, and they had been warned that to show up in uniform could result in their being court-martialed. Coffin was thus astounded, and deeply moved, to find himself preaching to a sea of four hundred dress uniforms (out of a total attendance of over 3,000). After Coffin's sermon, several Gold Star mothers spoke, including Louise Ransom, whose oldest son, Robert, a second lieutenant with the Americal Division, had died on Mother's Day 1968, after stepping on a mine a few days before. Ransom was becoming an important activist—standing up, among other causes, for unconditional amnesty for deserters and draft resisters, and for an effective rehabilitation program for the many Vietnam veterans who ended up in prison.

With the service at the Washington Cathedral, the mission of the veterans in Washington was beginning to turn from advocacy to elegy. Almost all their actions up to that point had been geared toward affecting the United States government and the American public. But the return of their medals the following day, Friday April 23, was something the veterans chose to do mostly for themselves. It was the personal catharsis many of them needed to regain their own sanity. And yet it created images, disseminated around the globe by the media, that spoke about the war in a way that no photographs had yet done.

There had already been powerful photos of the damage and cruelty of the war that had been dramatically exploited by the antiwar movement—the naked little Vietnamese girl running down a road, her face twisted in agony as her skin melts from her bones after being burned by napalm; or the police chief of Saigon assassinating a prisoner by firing a bullet into his temple. But those were photos that spoke only of a kind of unredeemable blackness at the heart of modern warfare. The photos of vets throwing back their medals, though often just as painful, touched people in a different way. One of the most famous photos, of Marine Captain Rusty Sachs, showed this burly former helicopter pilot bawling like a baby as he prepared to fling his deceased comrade Roger P. Harrell's Silver Star over the wire fence—after having dedicated his return of medals to both Harrell and another lost comrade, Robert Cramer, whose needless death he was symbolically laying at the feet of the U.S. government. But even this photo, one of the hardest to look at because of the absolutely raw human emotion it portrays, speaks of a kind of hope also. If warriors themselves could renounce war, these photos seemed to say, then perhaps war was not a scourge the human race would have to bear forever. And perhaps, just perhaps, this seemingly interminable war would someday actually end.

The return of the medals was the most disciplined action of the entire week. Whereas on other days, at other demonstrations, there had been wrangling over tactics and the splintering off of radical groups, the tone of this final action was utterly solemn and respectful. Some vets chose not to participate, but those who did formed a long, orderly line leading up to a table and microphone in front of the six-foot-high fence at the foot of the Capitol steps. As the process began, something like eight hundred vets stood patiently awaiting their turn to give back their medals, though some could not keep from sobbing loudly as they inched along.

One of the reasons—beyond the sacredness of the affair—for the care with which the event was orchestrated was that it was technically illegal. Vice President Spiro T. Agnew, who in a couple of years would resign his office under threat of impeachment on charges of accepting bribes, had refused to grant a permit to VVAW to use the Capitol grounds. Ironically enough, he had already granted a permit to the Communist-supported People's Coalition for Peace and Justice to use those same grounds the following day. Fortunately, Capitol Police Chief James Powell decided to ignore Agnew just as the park police had ignored Nixon and Judge Hart; Powell declared that "unless these people become violent or disrupt the Congress, it doesn't warrant prosecution."

As for the president himself, he had evidently washed his hands of the whole affair. Nixon was spending the day with his daughter Julie in Virginia and planned to stay out of town for the duration of the remaining protests.[75]

As each veteran came forward, Jack Smith checked his credentials. Smith, who was the first to return his medals, set the precedent by identifying himself and making a brief statement at the microphone. Smith declared the medals "a symbol of dishonor, shame, and inhumanity"; and like many who followed, he offered their return as a kind of apology to the Vietnamese people, "whose hearts were broken, not won" by acts of "genocide, racism, and atrocity." Some men were crying so hard that when they got to the microphone they could not speak at all. In Smith's view, "the tears were mostly for the internal anguish that people were feeling. . . . From our point of view, it wasn't what the government did to us, it's what we had done together, the government and us as individuals. And we wanted to come to terms with that, take our part of it, and the government in the healing had to take its part of it—to say, 'Here's how we screwed up.' And then we could heal. There were some people who wanted to translate that into, 'Let's get the government,' or, 'It's all their fault'. . . . We wanted to rip the mask of hypocrisy off of what was going on and deal with it, so that we could all get back as a country to the values that we had grown up on, and that we felt we stood for."

Many vets dedicated the return of their medals to fallen comrades; and for some, like Ron Ferrizzi, this act was also a ritual purge of guilt. Ferrizzi prefaced his story by saying he had chosen to return his medals even though his wife planned to leave him if he went through with it. He then told how he had been on a recon mission when the lead helicopter was downed by antiaircraft fire. His chopper had landed nearby, and he had rushed into the burning craft, futilely trying to save the men trapped inside—an act of heroism that won him the Silver Star, along with a Purple Heart and a handful of other medals. Before hurling them all at the bronze statue of Chief Justice John Marshall, Ferrizzi named those who had died virtually in his arms: "This is for Specialist 4 Bob Smeal, and for Sergeant Johns, and for Lieutenant Panamaroff, who were killed in behalf of their country." Ferrizzi then fell crying into the arms of Rusty Sachs, who had just made a similar dedication.

Ferrizzi explained to a *Washington Post* reporter: "So many people are dead, like they don't exist anymore, and they give me a fucking medal. That's supposed to make everything okay again." Neither the medal nor the act of throwing it away could bring those people back, but for Ferrizzi, as for so many others that day, the return of their medals was an act of making peace—or at least beginning to make peace—with the terrible knowledge that they had survived at the cost of others' lives. Far beyond any condemnation of their own or their government's conduct, that simple act, that simple motion of the arm (whether in fierce anger, as some did it, as if they were tossing a grenade, or with gentle care, simply laying them down on the steps), was a statement that they still cared enough about human life to speak up in its behalf, and to sacrifice something they valued in order to honor its preciousness. "I feel strange," Ferrizzi told the *Post* reporter, still reeling from the rapid barrage of conflicting emotions he had just undergone. "I feel fantastic. I feel like I'm clean, that I'm completely cleansed."

Still others pledged some future work of restitution to continue that cleansing. One vet expressed his hope "that someday I can return to Vietnam and help build that country that we tore apart."[76]

Sometimes relatives would come up, with or without medals to present. The sister of a soldier missing in action (MIA) accused President Nixon of taking her brother's life. A fifty-six-year-old World War II vet, Gail Olson, too overcome to speak, played a faltering taps on his bugle; then explained that he wished to honor all who had died in Vietnam, including his son William. He tried to say something in behalf of the children of Vietnam, but could not continue, and ended by saying that he prayed for peace. He had put tears in the eyes of some of the fiercest-looking vets. Two Gold Star mothers came up next. "I am here to join all of these men," said one of them. "In each one of them I see my son." The publisher I. F. Stone began to weep.

Even the angriest vets were allowed to say whatever they were feeling, and some scorched the air with their curses. One hurled away what he called his "merit badges for murder"; another called them "garbage." One vet called for "death to the fascist pigs" who held power in America; another, disposing of the Purple Heart he had won in Vietnam, said, "I hope I get another one fighting these fuckers."

Some of the reporters and television crew members, along with a few of the spectators, had gotten behind the fence, and they found out just how angry the vets could get when they began to scavenge through the pile of decorations for souvenirs. Several vets immediately scaled the fence and chased after those ghouls who had taken for trinkets things that had been consecrated to the dead. According to Jack Smith, the vets "were ready to tear these reporters limb from limb." The souvenir hunters quickly returned their booty, but as soon as the vets retreated, new scavengers dove into the growing pile, and more chases ensued— with the vets growing ever more frustrated that, short of murder, there was no way to keep the media and the public from trivializing their memorial by treating it like a common trash heap.

Certainly many soldiers and veterans who witnessed the return of medals did not understand and did not approve. Some, like career Army officer Philip Gioia, who had two Silver Stars himself and was still serving, felt "very uncomfortable to watch people degrading the military, especially those who had served honorably." But Larry Rottmann contended that they were actually honoring the military by proving that soldiers are people of conscience. Moreover, Jack Smith felt the return of their medals was the strongest warning they could give other young men not to follow in their footsteps. "The medals meant so much to the guys," Smith explains. "They stood for things that they had risked their lives for. Throwing these things was like wrenching a part of yourself and giving it back. But you had to make the statement, because the country wasn't willing to listen. . . . Guys who were following after us were still dying in Vietnam."

For many of the vets, the decision to return their medals was one of the hardest choices they ever made. It was especially hard for the ones like John Kerry who still loved and believed in the nation they had risked their life for. Kerry recalls that he "was in this dilemma between what everybody wanted to do and what I felt." Since he was a leader of the organization, he also worried "what would the perceptions be if I didn't, so it was just a very difficult moment for me. And I did what I thought was right, and I'm very proud of what I did— I threw back my ribbons." But Kerry waited almost till the very end to do so, and like many of the other veterans who were still torn by ambivalence, he did not throw back the medals themselves, but only the colored cloth that rides above them. Even more significantly, perhaps, he did not throw what was his until he had first thrown back the medals that had been entrusted to him by two veterans who could not be there—one of whom was a Marine still mending in a New York VA hospital. It was almost as if he had to convince himself that he should do this thing because he was "duty bound" to do so—just as he had gone to the war itself against his own judgment because he had felt the call to serve others.

After the first hour, the line of vets waiting to throw their medals back was still huge, so the ground rules had to be changed. Vets were permitted to simply walk up to the fence and throw them over whenever they wished, and only those vets who felt they had something important to say were handed the microphone. The process speeded up, and by the end of the second hour, most of the vets present had gotten a chance to make their personal statement, whether by gesture, words, or both.[77]

For all the trauma involved in returning those medals, and dredging up the memories of the terrible scenes in which they had been earned, most of the vets came away from this final event with a strongly positive feeling. John Good, a lieutenant who had earned five medals in seven months of combat, told the press, "I didn't feel much about them when I got them—this [the day he returned them] is the first time I have been proud to have them." His sentiments were echoed by many others. Even Rusty Sachs, who had resigned his commission in the Marines a few months before because of his "contempt" for the way the executive branch was running the war, and who had cried for two hours straight after returning his medals, later told a *Washington Post* reporter that his action that day "was the absolute top of the mountain" for him.

After returning to the campsite to begin their final cleanup, many of the vets participated in the planting of a fifteen-foot American elm purchased from the National Park Service. It was the same type of tree under which George Washington had taken command of the Continental Army. They planted it in the southwest corner of their campsite, but did not mark it in any way, and a few years later none of them would be able to say which one it was. But the anonymity in the planting of that tree typified all that they had done that week. The names of only a few of those several thousand men even made it into the newspapers; and with the exception of John Kerry, none was committed to the permanent rolls of American history. As they had served namelessly and self-lessly in Vietnam, they now completed their weeklong service in Washington, wishing to be remembered not for their individual heroism but for their collective "symbolic plea for the preservation of all life and the environment."[78]

6. Aftershocks

There were many veterans who were at Dewey Canyon and yet weren't officially there, meaning they watched, they sympathized, they occasionally took part, but they didn't wear a button or a patch or carry a VVAW membership card—and if you asked them, they would vehemently deny belonging to the organization. An even larger group—many of whom could not get to Washington for lack of money or a job or family commitment—intently followed the actions of Dewey Canyon III in the media or by phoning friends in Washington. Among this latter group was a former Marine lieutenant named Robert O. Muller, known to his friends as Bobby. During Dewey Canyon, Muller recalls that he was stuck in New York doing "political gigs," although Al Hubbard swears he saw Muller show up on the last day. Even then, according to Hubbard, Muller kept somewhat apart. Other veterans also recall seeing Muller in Washington during the operation. One thing is certain. Of all those veterans who were affected by Dewey Canyon, none, not even John Kerry, would prove more important to the future of the Vietnam veterans' movement than this man, who observed, listened, and took notes all week from the private box seat of his wheelchair.

Bobby Muller had been shot through both lungs and through his spinal cord while leading a charge up a hill in I Corps (northernmost South Vietnam). The hill was not heavily fortified; it was being held by a suicide squad of only about fifteen NVA soldiers. Muller, by contrast, had a reinforced battalion of about 600 South Vietnamese soldiers (ARVN) under his command, as well as ten Marine tanks backing him up. Before assaulting the hill, he was able to call in airstrikes by four jet fighter-bombers, as well as an hour and a half of "prep fire" from heavy artillery, 155mm howitzers and eight-inch guns. The tanks further "softened up" the enemy by expending half their ammunition on the hill. But even with all that assistance, the ARVN troops repeatedly failed to drive the enemy out. They would advance a few meters, take sporadic fire, and immediately fall back. Fiercely angry at their cowardice, Muller vowed to lead them up the hill himself, using three tanks to spearhead the advance. But as soon as a few enemy shots rang out, the ARVNs fled, leaving Muller and the Marine tankers completely vulnerable. That was when Bobby got hit, and his life changed forever.

Unlike in previous wars, the lives of men with spinal-cord injury were usually preserved because of the quick medical evacuation by helicopter (medevac) available from most battlefields in Vietnam. Muller was taken first to a hospital ship anchored off Vietnam and later flown back to a military hospital in the States. Not long after he regained consciousness, he was told that he would be a paraplegic for the rest of his life, that he would never again feel anything from his stomach down, never be able to move his legs or to beget children. But Muller never once, at that time or in the years to follow, felt sorry for himself. "I couldn't have cared less [about being paralyzed]. The only thing that mattered was that I was alive," he recalled. "The sorrow in being told that I was in that condition was so lost in the overwhelming joy of seeing that doctor come down and tell me, 'You're going to make it.'"[79]

Muller was wounded in April 1969, and a year later found himself on the paraplegic ward of the infamously bad Bronx VA Hospital. He was one of the veterans interviewed by TV news after *Life* magazine ran its brutal exposé of the hospital—the rats, the filth, the lack of care—in May 1970. Muller, who had gone to Vietnam a bright-eyed college graduate with a strong sense of duty to his country, had found much there to make him question the validity of American involvement. Not only had he seen ARVN troops repeatedly refuse to fight side by side with the Americans who were supposedly there to help them defend their country, but often enough those ARVN would cross over to join the Viet Cong the minute they were given the chance. One day Bobby had gotten a real insight into what was going on. He went outside the perimeter of his firebase to dump a couple of cans of garbage, and he had no sooner emptied them on a refuse heap than the entire population of a nearby refugee village swarmed in, kicking aside a dozen decomposing dead rats to grab up such treasures as tattered cigarette butts and rancid pieces of meat. It dawned on Bobby—as it never would on generals like Westmoreland or his recent replacement, Creighton Abrams, or even on Nixon's chief negotiator to the Paris peace talks, Henry Cabot Lodge—that these people did not enjoy what the Americans were doing to them, that they were not grateful for the chance to eat garbage. He realized then that America was destined to lose in Vietnam, since the military itself had taught him "the number one rule in guerrilla warfare— that you cannot win a guerrilla war unless you have the popular support of the people."

But what happened in the Bronx VA was more than an illumination; it was a complete conversion. In Vietnam, Muller had grown frustrated with stupid orders and self-defeating strategy, but in the Bronx VA he began to feel the need for what he later called "social revolution." It was in the Bronx that Muller came to believe that the government he had put his faith in had willfully betrayed him, had lied to him in order to use him "as a pawn in a game." From the moment that TV crew stuck a microphone under his nose, he discovered that he had a gift for articulating what was on his mind. Although many people would later credit him with being one of the most persuasive speakers of his generation, Muller felt he was only doing what he had to: "If you got conviction and you know what it is you feel strongly about, you can say what you really believe in whether there are 10,000 people in front of you or just one. If you believe in it, it's easy, even for somebody who wasn't a speaker, like me." He was soon speaking all over the place—at high schools, colleges, and on a variety of television shows, where he was interviewed by the likes of Dick Cavett and David Susskind. And always his message was the same: "The tragedy in my life is not that I'm a paraplegic, because I'm a lot better man today than I ever was before. The tragedy in my life is that I was, as so many Americans still are, so totally naive and so trusting. . . . I was an idiot because I never asked the question 'Why?' And that is my greatest tragedy—one which was shared by all too many Americans."

Muller was credited with being one of the founders of the first Long Island VVAW chapter, in Nassau County, and he readily admits that "to all intents and purposes I was one of the leading national spokesmen for VVAW. There weren't a lot of guys back in those days that had more visibility than me. I'd go to a demonstration or we'd do a march—who do you think would wind up on the front page? The guys in a wheelchair like me." Moreover, whenever Muller would appear on a TV talk show, they'd always put a label under him on the screen: "Bobby Muller, VVAW." Yet Muller would invariably deny to the interviewer that he was a member of VVAW. Such disclaimers were not an act of subterfuge—though in Muller's later political career, just as in John Kerry's, the specter of membership in VVAW would be conjured whenever it was useful to portray him as subversive or un-American. What Muller would say was "I support the organization in what it is trying to do, but I'm not joining anything."

Muller explains further: "It was just my personal thing, but it was a view that was shared by a lot of the guys. It continues to this day! That was part of what consistently had to be recognized and addressed in efforts to galvanize Vietnam veterans—that a lot of guys just like me very, very strongly felt the need to keep a distance. We didn't want to join anything! Even an organization that I was so strongly affiliated with, on a national basis, and did a whole lot of speaking for. There was a lot of intensity to feelings. [We felt] 'Fuck you, fuck everybody.'"

Muller's version is that he *was* moved by Dewey Canyon III, but only at a distance. Hubbard claims he was present at least part of the time but chose to keep on the sidelines, and that Muller told him his role at DCIII would be as an "investigative reporter." Hubbard supposedly replied, "Okay, Bobby, I think you're on the right track. This is what you want to do, go ahead and do it." The atmosphere of the organization at that point was very loose, almost anarchistic, and to belong to VVAW did not mean one had to perform any particular actions or even follow any party line.[80]

One of Bobby's closest friends in the organization, in fact, was another Long Islander named Ron Podlaski, a big, bearlike man who was as uninhibitedly demonstrative as Muller was guarded and cautious. Podlaski had been in and out of jail and lived a hard life on the streets, seeing his friends cut down one after another by the lure of drugs and crime, before he had volunteered for Army Airborne. He had gone to Vietnam never having heard of that country, but believing that America "stood on the side of what was right and good," and had gone the full nine yards as a Green Beret ranger attached to MACV/SOG (Special Operations Group), participating in the Phoenix Program (targeting enemy leaders for assassination) and other secret missions in Cambodia and Laos. The experience left him "feeling very, very discouraged." "No one was interested in saving the Vietnamese," he would recall later. "We were interested in saving our own asses and getting home safe." The irony was that he got home fairly intact (other than a few shrapnel wounds) but had become a speed freak because of the pills he was given to keep awake on long-range reconnaissance patrols; and it was not long before he got into heroin as well.

Podlaski had nowhere near the intellectual and academic background of Muller, but like a lot of working-class vets, he could muster a good deal of moral force when it came to doing his duty; and almost as soon as he got back, he felt that call of duty once again, this time in the service of telling people "how much the Vietnamese wanted us out of their country." He had organized an unusually powerful series of Winter Soldier hearings at the Garden City Hotel on Long Island, which had impressed Muller a good deal. They began going around Long Island together, speaking out against the war, and, according to Podlaski, together they would "supply a one-two knockout punch that was unbeatable." At that time, Muller's anger was still "unfocused"; according to Podlaski, Muller "wasn't sure whether he didn't like the Vietnamese or the Americans."

Watching Podlaski throw back his medals at Dewey Canyon (or, in the alternative, hearing Podlaski tell him about it) may have helped Muller focus that anger. Muller, who had begun to study law, was already being courted by the Democratic Party on Long Island as a possible congressional candidate; in all likelihood, he was still struggling with the question of how far he wanted to go in antagonizing a government that might one day employ him again. As he would point out much later in his career, when he had already crossed the Rubicon in terms of choosing to work outside rather than inside the system, it would have been the easiest thing in the world for him to accept the role of loyal patriot/public hero, and to spend the rest of his life garnering praise and rewards from those whose consciences needed buttering up, who liked to hear a guy in a wheelchair say how much he believed in the American way of life. Instead, Muller chose to spend his life debunking mindless Americanism, and to act as a big thorn in the side of every proponent of such Americanism, including dozens of the toughest congressional policymakers and several successive presidents of the United States. DCIII moved Muller significantly closer to making that choice. Al Hubbard says he watched Muller join the other vets who were throwing their medals back at the fence on the final day.

Among the wheelchair veterans at DCIII was Bill Wyman, the legless vet from Boston who had led the original march on Arlington, then tried and failed to get arrested at the Supreme Court on Thursday. Wyman, still recovering from the mine he had stepped on in Vietnam not long before, threw back his medals without a word; but he too was evolving toward a greater radicalism. A year down the line, Muller and Wyman, side by side with another wheelchair vet, who was currently cooling his heels at a poolside in California, would shout down Richard Nixon himself.

Muller ended up accepting several speaking engagements that weekend, including gigs with Congresswomen Bella Abzug and Karen Burstein. Perhaps even more significant, he agreed to contribute an autobiographical essay to the book on Dewey Canyon that John Kerry and his friends were assembling, which was published later that year by Collier under the title *The New Soldier*. Muller's piece ended up being one of the strongest in the book, forever cementing his connection with VVAW—a connection that would cause him a good deal of embarrassment over the years, as he tried to build a broad-based veterans' constituency, and which he would often try to play down.[81]

*   *   *

A true Vietnam veterans' movement was born at Dewey Canyon—no longer just an antiwar mouthpiece or a cheerleading club for world peace. And though many of the participants, including VVAW's founder Jan Barry, had been striving to create such a movement for several years, that movement, when it finally burst forth, was something far grander, more complex, more tenacious, and more unmanageable than any of them could ever have imagined. It was now a being with a life of its own, and it would resist attempt after attempt to kill it, even when those who sought to quash it were among those who had assisted at its birth.

Moreover, the Vietnam veterans' movement that came out of Dewey Canyon would defy anyone's construing it as right wing or left wing, Republican or Democrat, American or Communist. It would fit no one's preconceived structure; it would be tamed into no group's political corral. What it was was a path that had been opened, with the utmost dedication, at great cost, for millions of men and women to travel on. Some who would use it were still in hiding, nursing their wounds; some who were on it now (like Ron Podlaski, shortly to leave for the Maine woods and several years of working out his war stress in natural peace, away from people) would go off it, then return; others would leave it for good; and still others had thousands of miles to travel before it would be of use to them. But the point was that it was there, now, and would remain so probably till the last Vietnam veteran was laid to rest.

In any case, the challenge to find out how far that path led would occupy a good many people, both men and women, for several decades to come.

*   *   *

Although the big event of Friday April 23 was the return of medals, there were other significant activities. At the Superior Court, four of the veterans arrested on the steps of the Supreme Court were tried as a test case, to see whether the other 104 arrestees should continue to be prosecuted. The trial turned into a farce, in which the prosecutor's principal concern seemed to be whether a group of 4-H Club youths had heard the veterans chanting: "One, two, three, four / We don't want your fucking war." One vet opined that "the only obscene thing I used was the word *war*." Judge William Stewart, finding "no evidence of any violent act," found the defendants not guilty. Acknowledging that the veterans may have "inconvenienced some," Stewart reminded the prosecutor that "inconvenience alone doesn't warrant a criminal prosecution." The remaining 104 vets were thus cleared of all charges.

In Congress, the veterans achieved yet another victory. In the House of

Representatives, Jonathan Bingham (D-N.Y.) and Paul Findley (R-Ill.), both World War II vets, held hearings with former intelligence and public information officers to explore the distortion of news about the Vietnam War. In the Senate, George McGovern and Philip Hart held hearings on atrocities committed by U.S. forces in Vietnam. At the Senate hearings, Scott Camil testified that "seventy percent of the people my unit killed were women and children. It was like a big hunting trip. . . . We burned down villages. We killed everybody." Although the room erupted in controversy when another vet, former Navy Lieutenant Melvin Stephens, contended that he had seen schoolchildren murdered by the Viet Cong too, what mattered was that Congress was finally discussing and debating matters that should have been dealt with at least half a decade earlier.

The plan had been for the vets to clear out before the swarms of hippies, Yippies, and various civilian peace movement people began arriving on Saturday. The vets' impact had been so striking that VVAW leaders feared diluting it by mixing in with the protests of the National Peace Action Coalition (NPAC) and the People's Coalition for Peace and Justice (PCPJ). Already conservative congressmen like John Ashbrook (R-Ohio) and Richard Ichord (D-Mo.), chair of the House Committee on Internal Security, were warning that the coming NPAC and PCPJ demonstrations would be "under substantial Communist influence"—a taint that the vets could scarcely afford to share. Yet the vets were also young men, caught up in the excitement of a countercultural revolution and the headiness of feeling their own personal power to alter history—not to mention the pull of their male hormones toward the flock of miniskirted and bluejeaned radical young women who were headed for Washington with more than political adventures on their mind ("Girls Say Yes to Boys Who Say No" was the slogan of a provocative antiwar poster of the era). So with only a slight shift of gears, several hundred vets stayed on for the wild and frenzied May Day demonstrations.

During the week following Dewey Canyon, many of the more radical vets, like Hubbard and Romo, performed a number of their own outrageous stunts, like pelting the doors of the Pentagon with sacks of chickenshit. There was already growing within the organization a lot of resistance to the kind of street theater typified by the Chickenshit Brigade—and not just from straight-arrow types like John Kerry. Skip Roberts, a Marine vet who had organized for McCarthy in 1968, thought VVAW could generate a huge populist groundswell if tens of thousands of veterans were to speak in unison. Having run the Washington office of VVAW during Dewey Canyon, Roberts went to Hubbard afterward to suggest that they should immediately begin working toward a similar action for the following year, 1972. Roberts envisioned this action, "Dewey Canyon IV," taking place over Easter school break, or else during the summer, perhaps around Labor Day. His idea was to re-create Dewey Canyon III on a much grander scale, something like a hundred thousand vets descending on the capital just in time to influence the upcoming presidential election. Roberts felt the key would be to go after the large number of vets now on campus, and to set a date for the demonstration when veteran college students would be free to attend.

The interaction that followed between Hubbard and Roberts had a profound effect on the future of the Vietnam veterans' movement. Hubbard absolutely opposed any new attempt to build a broad base of support for VVAW. Hubbard told Roberts, "We're not going to get bigger. We're going to get smaller and purer." The irony of Hubbard's suddenly putting a damper on the organization's growth—and thereby halting an expansion that he himself had fostered—was not lost on Roberts, who felt that Hubbard must be acting as a government agent and should no longer be trusted. But Hubbard felt that his actions were consistent with the VVAW charter, which he had helped frame; specifically, it was Hubbard who had included a "dissolution clause" in that charter, which obligated them to disband the organization as soon as the war ended. Hubbard explains his position: "One of the things I was very, very adamant about was that I didn't want VVAW to become another professional veterans' organization—I wanted that kind of mentality to wither on the vine." He claims that he dreaded the prospect of VVAW members someday coming together to celebrate the founding of their organization, in the manner of the VFW or American Legion. "I'm ashamed that VVAW had to be founded," he says today. "I'm ashamed for this country—not for the people who were a part of it, but for this country creating an environment in which something like that had to come into being."

Roberts, however, held a distinctly different view of what was going on. He recalls Hubbard talking about the concept of "weather vets"—alluding to the small, extremist, ultra-militant faction known as the Weathermen or Weather Underground, which had splintered off from SDS—and his intention of forming a "cadre" of dedicated revolutionaries to direct the organization. A committed trade unionist whose grandfather had organized the steelworkers in Bethlehem, Pennsylvania, Roberts was not opposed to violent confrontation when necessary, but he felt that such tactics could be successful only when large numbers of people combined to voice their desire for change—the most basic tenet of collective bargaining. Roberts therefore felt that Hubbard in his quest to "purify" the organization would surely take it down the road to ruin. Moreover, Roberts felt the impetus to reduce VVAW's membership, and to undermine its democratic approach, was coming from those who were attempting to foment an armed rebellion in the United States. That revolutionary movement itself, he believed, was as much a product of government provocateurs as of hard-core Communists and "authentic crazies," whether drugged-out hippies or stressed-out vets. Roberts could not make out for sure what category Hubbard fell into, but he was convinced that Hubbard "was there as the key person that was trying to destroy what was going on," and as such, Roberts felt the need "to take Hubbard out" before they could get on with the business of ending the war.

VVAW was about to embark on a tumultuous two-year ride, the stresses of which would end up tearing the organization apart, but not before a great deal of healing was accomplished—including the end to American involvement in the Vietnam War. One of the big problems for the organization immediately after Dewey Canyon—and one of the reasons Roberts found so little support for his project to bring 100,000 vets to Washington—was that many VVAW members were convinced they had already won their battle with the government. As Jan Barry told *Ramparts* magazine, "Some of them [the vets at Dewey Canyon] actually thought the war would end after we had been here a few days. . . . They thought that Congress would be grateful to them."[82]

Certainly the victory of Dewey Canyon III was substantial, and though the war did not end overnight, the impact of those veterans who came to Washington would be felt in more ways than anyone had originally imagined. The old draft law was about to expire in June, and, quite unexpectedly, opponents of the war like Senator Frank Church (D-Idaho) and Senator Mike Gravel (D-Alaska) found enough support to keep a filibuster going till the very end of the year, so that it could not be renewed. Unable to call up any more young men until a new draft was in place, the military was severely limited in terms of how much manpower it could allot to Vietnam; and as a result of the military's dwindling replacements, President Nixon was pressured to increase the pace of troop withdrawals.

In June 1971, almost seven years after it had passed the Tonkin Gulf Resolution giving President Johnson carte blanche to begin the Vietnam War, the United States Senate (although it had repealed Tonkin Gulf a few months earlier) passed the first resolution indicating that America should "terminate [the war] at the earliest possible date." The resolution, sponsored by Majority Leader Mike Mansfield, merely represented the "sense of the Senate" and was completely nonbinding. It was the weakest sort of statement that Congress could make in terms of saying that the war was wrong, but the fact that it was made at all probably owed a great deal to VVAW's presence in Washington. Of course the May Day demonstrations, taxing the Washington law enforcement agencies to the limit, may have shaken up the congresspeople as well; and one cannot discount the impression that was being created on Capitol Hill by a civilian peace movement whose perseverance had weathered every obstacle for almost a decade. But the fact is that until the vets lent their voice to the cause, the mainline peace movement had made no substantial impact on either the United States government's policy in Vietnam or on the way the media was portraying the war. After Dewey Canyon, such changes began to rain fast and hard.

On June 13, 1971, the *New York Times* began publishing excerpts from the forty-seven-volume secret history of the Vietnam War, prepared by thirty-six top government and military analysts at the behest of former Defense Secretary Robert McNamara, which had been surreptitiously copied and carried out of the Rand Corporation by Daniel Ellsberg and Tony Russo, both of whom had served as advisors in Vietnam and both of whom had been motivated by their consciences to let the American public in on the truth of the war. This extraordinary history, which came to be known as the Pentagon Papers, proved, in the words of Senator Mike Gravel (who went to great lengths to read portions of it into the *Congressional Record*), that "from the beginning, the war has been an American war, serving only to perpetuate American military power in Asia. . . ." The Nixon administration did everything in its power to keep the Pentagon Papers from being made public, including filing an injunction against the *Times* and the other papers that had begun to publish them (an injunction that was swiftly lifted by the Supreme Court). For months Ellsberg and Russo had been trying fruitlessly to get someone to print these documents; and that the *Times* finally agreed to do so less than two months after Dewey Canyon and the May Day demonstrations can hardly be a coincidence.

Moreover, the Winter Soldier testimony, which had been under wraps for so long, was now spread across the pages of *Life* magazine in the July 9, 1971, issue. *Life,* sold in drugstores and supermarkets across America, pulled no punches in quoting some of the most hair-raising stories that had come out of the VVAW hearings—the stoning of a three-year-old Vietnamese child, farmers shot in their rice paddies for target practice, prisoners routinely tortured with electrical wires, bayoneted, and thrown out of helicopters. *Life,* perused not by scholars but by housewives between chores, by their kids when homework was done, and by workingmen with their feet up after dinner, was now informing Norman Rockwell's America that "the massacre at Mylai [*sic*] emerges not as an isolated aberration but as an extension of all that had gone before and was going on at the time, different in only two respects: the large number of civilians killed, and the fact that men were caught and brought to trial." This kind of coverage was unthinkable even a year before. The last paragraph of the article specifically alluded to the vets who came to Washington, and the very last sentence was a summary that came from Dewey Canyon itself: "And at a microphone in front of the Capitol, one [vet] said it for all of them: 'I have only one thing to say to the Vietnamese people,' he cried. 'Oh, God, God, I'm sorry.'"

Like a massive B-52 raid out of hell, Dewey Canyon shook the ground under veterans and active-duty GIs alike. On May 15, Armed Forces Day became "Armed Farces Day" as antiwar demonstrations occurred at nineteen bases across the nation, rocking every branch of the military. The protests continued through Memorial Day. On Monday May 31, three hundred Air Force personnel presented an antiwar petition to the U.S. embassy in London; they represented hundreds of other disaffected airmen at all eight Air Force bases in England, who had grouped together under the banner of People Emerging Against Corrupt Establishment (PEACE). The military, reeling under this incredible barrage of dissent from within—including ten admitted major incidents of mutiny, and doubtless many more "minor" ones that went unrecorded—virtually gave up prosecuting the dissenters. In the case of the antiwar petition in London, only one man, a Vietnam vet who served as the group's legal counsel, was court-martialed.[83]

7. Nixon Hits Back, and the POW Movement Is Born

Even with all these achievements, Dewey Canyon III was not the unmitigated success many of the vets at first imagined. Robert J. Lifton, who was working with many of the DCIII vets in so-called rap groups at this time, found that the adrenaline high of taking over Washington and defying the Supreme Court was soon followed by a drastic letdown when the evidence of their "real failure" began to sink in. Many became angry when they realized their "inability to get senators or congressmen to commit themselves firmly, or take political risks of any kind, to end the war." Others were disenchanted by the "star system" that had emerged at Dewey Canyon, feeling that the kind of elitism that had turned them against the war (a few generals and diplomats on high pretending to know what was best for soldiers and country folk whose daily life they were mostly ignorant of) was being repeated now in the leadership of VVAW. The fact that the press had rushed to listen to a former officer like John Kerry with his lofty, Yale-accented political dialogue, and had by and large ignored the humble concerns of the enlisted men—working-class vets who, among other things, were often out of work and couldn't afford decent schooling on the meager GI Bill—seemed to confirm to some in Lifton's group that the things they opposed in the military were just as evident "in society in general." Rather than giving these vets hope, then, Dewey Canyon actually abetted their hopelessness.[84]

Ironically, one of the biggest losses of Dewey Canyon resulted from Richard Nixon's perception that VVAW had beaten him in Washington. Nixon, never a cheerful loser, was determined to get back at the Vietnam veterans in every way he could. This was the same period when Nixon asked his aide John Ehrlichman to form an independent investigating team to stop leaks of damaging information to the press—a group that came to be known as "the Plumbers." Two members of that team, E. Howard Hunt and G. Gordon Liddy, would soon be catapulted into national notoriety when it was discovered that, among other illegal acts, they had burglarized the office of Daniel Ellsberg's psychiatrist, and a few months later, directed the break-in of Democratic National Committee headquarters at the Watergate Hotel. History may never fully document the vast range of "dirty tricks" Nixon began to implement against those he imagined his enemies—former Attorney General John Mitchell would eventually refer to "White House horrors" that included illegal wiretapping, hush money, even planned arson to recover embarrassing documents—but there is no doubt that the Vietnam veterans' movement was one of his prime targets.

Nixon directed his special counsel Charles Colson to inquire about the possibility of getting the IRS to revoke VVAW's tax-exempt status. But his efforts to get back at VVAW went well beyond official governmental channels. John Kerry's brother-in-law David Thorne and his friend George Butler had documented (with tape recorder and camera respectively) the entire Dewey Canyon III operation as Thorne's senior project at the Columbia School of Journalism. Because veterans were "hot" just then, Collier offered them a book contract—but only provided John Kerry's name was on the book jacket—and the book, called *The New Soldier,* was rushed into print within a few months. The initial print run was 35,000 copies—quite impressive for that day. The advance was also sizable (most of it was donated to VVAW). Thorne was thus puzzled to find the book available in few bookstores. The next thing he knew, the editor who had commissioned the book was fired. On the grapevine, Thorne heard that "the White House really put the kibosh on it [*The New Soldier*]." He was told that "Nixon was freaked out by the book—he was really worried that the veterans' movement was going to make the antiwar movement legit."

What Nixon never seemed to understand was that most of the veterans were not out to get him per se, but were acting from a genuine concern for the well-being of their brothers. Forrest "Rusty" Lindley Jr., a former Green Beret captain who had participated in Dewey Canyon, spoke extensively to the press not as a supporter of any radical movement but strictly as a proponent of keeping both ARVN soldiers and American GIs from "dying for something they didn't believe in, namely the Ky-Thieu government." Lindley would eventually become a tenacious veterans' advocate in Washington, a diligent researcher of Vietnam veteran social history, and a noteworthy columnist for the only veterans' national newspaper, *The Stars and Stripes—The National Tribune.* The tragedy, Lindley asserts, was that the VA had been on the verge of developing a program to deal with delayed stress in returning veterans when Dewey Canyon put the Vietnam vets on Nixon's hit list. Two early bills to fund some form of stress-treatment centers had already been introduced. Now, with pressure mounting from the White House, both the VA and Congress would resolutely deny medical and psychological help, even the most basic sort of readjustment counseling, to the many Vietnam veterans who suffered from exposure to the traumas of modern guerrilla warfare. Their decisions would not be reversed for almost a decade.[85]

Meanwhile, having found that he could not look to Vietnam veterans or active-duty servicemen to corroborate his views on how the war might still be won, Richard Nixon turned to his last best hope: the prisoners of war (POWs) and the missing in action (MIAs). If the Vietnam veterans did not wish to be honored by their President's continuing to wage war, and if the servicemen in Vietnam did not feel particularly "supported" when he subjected them to the risk of grave wounding or premature death as "pawns for foreign policy" (as they were viewed by his Secretary of State Henry Kissinger), then Richard Nixon would rely on his ace in the hole. For the past two years, Nixon had been exploiting the heart-tugging potential of the POWs and MIAs as a rationale for prolonging the war.

To begin with, Nixon had quite uncustomarily combined the POW and MIA numbers, claiming there were "1,600 Americans in North Vietnam jails under very difficult circumstances," when in truth many of those 1,600 were MIAs already presumed dead—a category that is technically referred to as KIA/BNR: Killed in Action/Body Not Recovered. Then he had roused the anger of the American public against the North Vietnamese for their cruelty in not returning the prisoners immediately, even though warring nations normally don't return prisoners until after hostilities cease. The plight of these men was repeatedly thrust before the public eye—with POW/MIA bumper stickers and wrist bracelets, with a "go public" campaign that called for media attention to the inhumane treatment of American prisoners by the North Vietnamese, and with sentimental and spectacular public events, like the National Day of Prayer for U.S. Prisoners of War in Vietnam (November 9, 1969) and the Constitution Hall "extravaganza" (May 1, 1970) at which Senator Robert Dole hosted some 1,000 POW/MIA family members. Thus when Americans contemplated the suffering wrought by the war, they began to think more of white men (mostly Air Force officers) in cages than of the grunts of all colors slogging through the jungle or of Asians being blown to kingdom come by earth-shattering B-52 raids.

Even as the VVAW were moving from Winter Soldier to Dewey Canyon, Nixon was honing his new strategy like a knife blade that would hamstring the peace movement. On March 9, 1971, he told the press: "As long as there are American POWs in North Vietnam we will have to maintain a residual force in South Vietnam." At another news conference, on April 16, he stated categorically that he would keep U.S. ground and air forces in Vietnam "as long as there is one American prisoner being held prisoner by North Vietnam." Nixon's circular reasoning was neatly summarized by historian H. Bruce Franklin, who wrote, "Since North Vietnam was making the release of the prisoners contingent on a U.S. withdrawal . . . the war could literally go on forever."

For Nixon, the key difference between the vets and GIs, on the one hand, and the POW/MIAs, on the other, was that the latter group were not in a position, at least for the time being, to gainsay the president's use of them as an excuse to prosecute the war.

After Dewey Canyon, Nixon turned his back on the veterans almost com-pletely. Until the Paris Peace Accords were signed in January 1973, Nixon would act as if the only players that mattered in the whole Indochina conflict, the only ones he was duty-bound to serve, were the silent figures behind the barbed wire—the "daddies" who wanted to come home "safe, sound and soon"—the American POW/MIAs.[86]

4

Invisible Wounds: Post-Traumatic Stress Disorder

1. The Rap Groups: An Intuitive Sort of Trust

In November 1970, Dr. Robert Jay Lifton received a letter from Jan Barry, still nominally the president of Vietnam Veterans Against the War, but just another troubled Vietnam vet as far as Lifton knew. Lifton was already one of the most famous psychiatrists in the United States. A research professor of psychiatry at Yale, Lifton had won the National Book Award for his study *Death in Life: Survivors of Hiroshima* and had written extensively about other victims of man-made disasters, including the Holocaust and the My Lai massacre. Lifton had hardly begun his career as a political activist; but, as a Jew investigating the horrors perpetrated upon the Jewish people in Nazi concentration camps, he could not help feeling outrage, and he found a similar outrage overtaking his scholarly detachment as the casualties of the Vietnam War began to skyrocket in the late 1960s.

Lifton's sensibility, moreover, was that of an independent radical. He had served as a psychiatrist in the Korean War and traveled the world extensively afterward, making two independent trips to Vietnam with his wife, in 1954 and 1967, to get a firsthand sense of what was going on there. So Lifton's gradual affiliation with the Vietnam antiwar movement, just as he had already become a key thinker in the movement to abolish nuclear arms, was not done on a whim or because it had become a popular intellectual trend. Lifton was genuinely concerned with "the larger problem of human survival." As he relates: "Just announcement of My Lai [in late 1969] made a very profound impression on me. I responded to reading about it with feelings of rage and anger and a sort of guilt that this was being done by my country. It changed my sense of myself in American society, in the direction of having to do more to combat that war. So I involved myself more in war crimes issues."

In 1970, Lifton helped to create the Education/Action Conference on U.S. Crimes of War in Vietnam, and edited a book called *Crimes of War*—"a legal, political, and psychological inquiry"—for Random House. Such work brought him to the attention of California Senator Alan Cranston, who was chairing a Veterans' Affairs subcommittee that had begun hearings in the wake of the My Lai revelations. A liberal Democrat and World War II veteran, Cranston had a particular interest in the special needs of Vietnam veterans and the psychological injuries they might incur from the ordeal of an unpopular and morally questionable war. Lifton testified before Cranston's subcommittee in November and December 1969, and in January 1970. He talked about the sort of environment that can lead to the commission of war crimes, and the psychological disturbances that occur in soldiers who are led to commit, or even simply witness, such atrocities. In Lifton's view, the Vietnam War, with its "permanent free-fire zones," technological overkill, and daily "body count," was the very sort of matrix of "disorder and absurdity" from which evil is born: "My Lai illuminates, as nothing else has, the essential nature of America's war in Vietnam. The elements of this atrocity-producing situation include an advanced industrial nation engaged in a counterinsurgency action in an underdeveloped area, against guerrillas who merge with the people—precisely the elements which Jean-Paul Sartre has described as inevitably genocidal. In the starkness of its murders and the extreme dehumanization experienced by victimizers and imposed on victims, My Lai reveals to us how far America has gone along the path of deadly illusion."[87]

Lifton repeated his "psychohistorical analysis" of the Vietnam War at a Congressional Conference on War and National Responsibility, which had been initiated by several concerned congressmen, including Abner Mikva (D-Ill.) and Robert Kastenmeier (D-Wis.). In his congressional testimony, Lifton used a phrase that at the time was virtually meaningless to the American psychological and psychiatric professions, but which would soon set fire to the imagination of a generation of researchers: post-Vietnam syndrome (PVS). Lifton later claimed that the term had actually been coined by VA psychiatrists. Although in these early talks he was already predicting "psychological effects specific to the Vietnam War," he felt (or so he wrote a few years later) that the word *syndrome* could be used to denigrate such appropriate and healthy responses to the war as rage, guilt, and protest. In any case, Lifton was in the process of conceptualizing the components of what came to be known as PVS, until a new term replaced it later in the 1970s: post-traumatic stress disorder (PTSD).

Lifton's theorizing in this regard was vastly aided by the stories he listened to from the veterans themselves. Call it PVS, shell shock, nerves, battle fatigue, soldier's heart, combat exhaustion, or (according to a lot of military psychiatrists) just plain malingering, Lifton knew it when he heard it. And he knew he was hearing it, for example, at a December session of the Cranston hearings in the testimony of former Army Captain Max Cleland, who had lost both legs and an arm to an exploding grenade in Vietnam. Cleland (who was destined to become a United States senator from Georgia) explained: "To the devastating psychological effect of getting maimed, paralyzed, or in some way unable to reenter American life as you left it, is the added psychological weight that it may not have been worth it; that the war may have been a cruel hoax, an American tragedy, that left a small minority of young American males holding the bag."

It was Lifton's high visibility as an opponent of the Vietnam War, as well as his willingness to acknowledge post-Vietnam syndrome, that led Jan Barry, Al Hubbard, and a few VVAW comrades to attend one of his lectures on Hiroshima survivors, which was sponsored by the Post-Doctoral Psychoanalytic Training Clinic at New York University in May 1970. At that time the NYU clinic had become deeply involved both in antiwar politics and in treating the psychological maladies of Vietnam veterans, chiefly through the round-the-clock activities of its tireless codirector, Dr. Chaim F. Shatan. Besides practicing psychotherapy and writing numerous articles, Shatan, a Jewish Canadian transplant, found time to join peace protests on the street, to work with the Central Committee for Conscientious Objectors and the GI coffeehouse movement, and to arrange for low-cost or free psychotherapy for indigent veterans, not to mention raising four children of his own.

Through his work with veterans at the NYU clinic, Shatan had gotten connected with Tod Ensign and CCI, and was instrumental in helping plan the National Veterans' Inquiry in Washington, D.C. But his interest in veterans went as far back as the stories written by his father, who was a veteran of the czarist wars in Russia; and after getting his medical degree in Montreal, Shatan had worked with World War II vets at a Canadian veterans' hospital. In 1956, he had been asked to investigate the so-called Parris Island death march, where a Marine drill sergeant had punished his rebellious recruits by taking them on a night march through the swamps, which ended with the drowning of six young men. (Shatan's subsequent article about it, "Bogus Manhood, Bogus Honor: Surrender and Transfiguration in the United States Marine Corps," was killed for being "too political" by *Dissent* magazine, which had commissioned it, and not published till 1978.) More recently, Shatan had become educated about the matter of American combat atrocities in Vietnam through his acquaintance with child psychiatrist Gordon Livingston, a former regimental surgeon under the command of Colonel George S. Patton III. Dr. Livingston had been kicked out of Patton's unit for protesting things like the use of prayers to incite troops to "pile on the bastards," the posting of signs such as "Four More Killing Days Till Christmas," and the mailing out of regimental Christmas cards that featured a color photo of Vietnamese bodies stacked like cordwood outside Patton's command tent.

Shatan, who knew Robert Lifton through various peace committees, used the occasion of Lifton's National Book Award for *Death in Life: Survivors of Hiroshima* to invite him to NYU. Although Lifton had originally been slated to speak about his work in Japan, that same week the four students were killed at Kent State by National Guard troops, who had been called out to suppress anti-war protests; and Lifton immediately changed his topic to "My Lai and Kent State," which was advertised on posters all over Greenwich Village and drew a large crowd, including many Vietnam veterans. After the lecture, some of the vets met privately with Shatan and Lifton. But both Barry and Hubbard were too busy at that point, preparing for Operation RAW and the Winter Soldier Investigation, to ask Lifton about giving psychiatric help to Vietnam veterans.

Even when Barry finally wrote to Lifton in November, he had only a general idea of where Lifton might take them. According to Lifton, "He said two things in the letter: 'Guys are hurting. They're opposed to the war, and they want to deal with their hurt, and they don't want to go to the VA. They also want to make known to the world what the war is like. Can you help us in some way?'"[88]

By the time Lifton got Barry's letter, he had already interviewed a number of Vietnam veterans, including participants in the My Lai massacre, for material for his congressional lectures and the several magazine pieces he had already published on the psychic costs of the war, as well as his contributions to *Crimes of War*. It is to Lifton's credit that he took the step no one had yet ventured, wading hip deep into the mental and spiritual wreckage of the war to begin a systematic effort to patch up the survivors.

Barry explained to Lifton that VVAW sought a way of healing "the severe psychological problems of many Vietnam veterans" and at the same time altering the political policy that kept the war going. In other words, Barry and the other VVAW leaders felt that if they could find and stanch the source of what they considered a criminal war, they could also put an end to veterans' nightmares and other nervous disorders; but as of yet the connection between physical harm and emotional pain still eluded them. Lifton readily accepted Barry's invitation to speak at the Winter Soldier Investigation in Detroit at the end of January, but he was less sure how to develop a therapeutic procedure for dealing with "death immersion, psychic numbing, [and] residual guilt," which veterans of modern war, victims of "technological atrocities" (such as Hiroshima), and other trauma survivors all experienced.

Lifton, the premier theorist, turned to Chaim Shatan, who was actively working as a therapist and had many friends with clinical experience. His choice of a teammate could not have been better, for besides the practical knowledge Shatan brought to the endeavor, "Hy" had the kind of sunny personality that can establish an instant rapport with almost anyone. There was a pronounced difference in appearance and demeanor between the two men. Lifton was tall, stiff, slow, and somber in his movements and speech; Shatan was short, voluble, and animated, a kind of streetwise pixie who looked more fun-loving than Freudian.

Lifton, Shatan, Barry, and several VVAW members met for a preliminary dis-

cussion, and the veterans explained that they had learned of one another's problems during the intense conversations they would have in the VVAW office, the
memories and revelations of one man sparking the memories and insights of
another, often into the wee hours of the morning. They "rapped," they said,
about the war, American society, and their own lives, and the key to the openness that evolved among them was that they could trust one another completely. It was an intuitive sort of trust they could never feel toward someone
who had not experienced Vietnam—kind of like they were the only people who
got the same jokes, black as that humor might be. Sometimes when they
rapped, however, one vet would get too angry and crazy or maybe actually flip
out, think he was back in the Nam; or sometimes another vet might fall in love
with the sound of his own words, inventing as he went along, and end up wasting everyone's time with a lot of bullshit. But when they shared honestly and
equally with one another, their group talks left them feeling less burdened and
alone, more in touch with themselves, and better able to connect with the outside world. What they needed in these sessions was someone with greater psychological knowledge who could guide their talk toward coherent conclusions
and help resolve the dilemmas that were keeping them from functioning normally in society.

Taking his cue from the veterans themselves, Lifton suggested they form
regular "rap groups," which would meet once a week for two hours in the
VVAW office. Only within the protective walls of VVAW could the vets feel safe
enough to continue to speak whatever was on their mind, especially now that
each group would contain three or four outsiders, male and female facilitators,
who called themselves "professionals" rather than therapists, and whom the
vets called "shrinks." Both the professionals and the vets made a point of not
referring to these volunteers as "leaders," since the word *leader* had acquired
such odium for almost anyone who had been to Vietnam. These professionals,
about forty altogether, were actually top-notch clinicians from a wide range of
post-doctoral programs and psychoanalytic institutes in New York.

The first rap group was held on Saturday, December 12, 1970, in VVAW's
seventh-floor headquarters at 156 Fifth Avenue. The vets immediately inducted
the professionals into the group on an absolutely equal footing with themselves,
calling them by their first names and "jarring" them (as Lifton put it) with challenges about the way they lived and with the very same questions the vets put
to one another. Any posture of superiority in the professionals was deeply
resented by the vets, and even Lifton's note-taking quickly became a bone of
contention. After a veteran complained that Lifton could not truly be part of the
group and write about it at the same time, Lifton stopped taking notes altogether. Although his colleagues had mixed opinions on his acquiescence, Lifton
claimed "what had been at issue was the veterans' pride and emerging confidence in shaping their own group pattern."

From the beginning, Lifton and Shatan had a sense that they were pioneering "a new group form," and they attempted to hold back as much as possible from any preconceptions about how the rap groups should develop. Lifton tried to keep in mind only three major guiding principles. He wanted the rap groups to proceed from "affinity": "the coming together of people who share a particular (in this case overwhelming) historical or personal experience." He wanted the professionals, besides empathizing with the vets, to manifest at all times a "presence": "a kind of being-there or full engagement and openness to mutual impact—no one ever being simply a therapist against whom things are rebounding." And he wanted the vets to assume the responsibility of "self-generation": "to initiate their own process and conduct it largely on their own terms . . . even when calling in others with expert knowledge."

Although Lifton had suggested they begin with two rap groups, the veterans, many of whom had already bonded deeply with one another, did not want to be broken apart; and so for the first month all the interested veterans (about twenty) showed up at the same Saturday meeting. It rapidly turned into a "zoo," according to one vet, with some vets inviting journalist friends and other folks turning up just to watch the show. The first few meetings were nearly blown apart by the explosive rage and pain of men who were often for the first time letting out just a fraction of the hell that they had been forced to hold inside. The emotional charge was also powerfully heightened by the fact that the war itself was still going on—the invasion of Cambodia had taken place only a few months earlier—and men were still getting wounded and killed with no end in sight. Usually the meetings rolled on unstoppably, with men "going off" like the successive concussions of a munitions dump on fire, for four, six, or even eight hours.

When the first rap group became too unwieldy, its members decided that it must break into two smaller groups, but no agreement could be reached as to how it should be divided. The "old-timers" wanted to stick together; the newcomers feared rejection; and many from both camps, feeling that their tentative attempt to regain some human intimacy had once again been betrayed, just wanted to walk off for good. Luckily one of the professionals made the kind of split-second, instinctual decision that can sometimes save a battle from being lost: he announced that the people on his left constituted one group, and those on his right constituted the other group. From that point on, there were two successfully functioning rap groups. One disbanded eight months later, shortly after it moved out of the VVAW office; and the other, which remained at the VVAW office, continued for over two years.

Lifton worked with the group that stayed at the VVAW office, and found that of the dozen vets who showed up each week there were usually one or two new faces and one or two who had dropped out. In two years, something like 115 vets (still all male) passed through that group. The vets insisted on an "open door policy" which admitted anyone willing to confess his feelings and concerns like a "brother"—even veterans and active-duty servicemen who had never been to Vietnam. The flux within the group was further increased by the fact that many of its members had to travel around the country—and even to Paris and Russia on occasion—to carry out their political activities. In addition, many of the vets were looking for work, and others found themselves unable to stay put or to commit to any activity or relationship for more than a few weeks simply from a profound and inexplicable restlessness. Their own instability, Lifton reported, was "a constant subject of discussion."

About a dozen veterans participated in Lifton's group for at least a year, and one became a highly responsible "veteran-coordinator"; the other group developed a similar core of highly motivated subjects, many of whom were becoming "students" as well—in the sense that the drive to heal themselves soon spilled over into an ardent need to learn more about their unknown but obviously common malady, so that they could begin to help others. Among two of the most promising student-subjects in Lifton's group were Army Intelligence Sergeant Arthur Egendorf and Marine Sergeant Jack Smith, who had done two combat tours in Vietnam.

Smith, a huge man and one of the most radical of the antiwar veterans, appeared out of the blue in Lifton's rap group one day with a color slide show he had prepared of his tour in Vietnam as a "form of penance." It contained such images as dead Vietnamese impaled on barbwire to a soundtrack of Woodstock rock songs. One vet was so spooked by Smith's show that he ran from the room, complaining that it would give him nightmares. The other vets watched it "transfixed" (according to Lifton), unable to speak but deeply affected. The slide show, which Smith had shown in a number of cities, had reputedly converted several veterans to the VVAW cause. It had also drawn forth a lot of latent racism. At a VFW hall, one older vet declared: "I just don't care. I am a white, red-headed Irishman, and I care most about other white, red-headed Irishmen like myself. I can't worry too much about blacks or gooks." Smith was so furious at this rebuff to the humanity he was trying to reclaim in both himself and those he proselytized that he began screaming that "the revolution" would have its revenge on the bigoted Irishman, and even contemplated bombing the VFW hall. In the rap group, Smith confessed that his experience with such brutishness and insensitivity—such denial of the truths he himself had been forced to confront—"reverted" him to the kind of primal, violent behavior he had learned in Vietnam, and which he was desperately trying to escape.

Smith's slide show and accompanying stories helped Lifton crystallize several concepts about the nature of post-Vietnam syndrome (PVS). Lifton believed that Smith had gotten so angry at the crass VFW guy because the encounter had been "a rejection of his survivor mission and a threat to his overall personal transformation."[89] Those phrases—*survivor mission* and *personal transformation*—became central to Lifton's understanding both of the pain the vets were experiencing and of the critical choice they were facing: the forked road, one way leading to an increasingly deadened response to life itself, a devalued existence and a fast or slow ride out of this world; the other way a conscious effort to "animate" their guilt and to connect their actions and feelings with the rest of the world, to know themselves and their fellow men in both their best and worst aspects, and thus to create a human topography on which the possibility of change could be mapped, pursued, and perhaps eventually attained. In numbing themselves there was temporary reduction of pain and the safety of known terrain; in reaching out to others there was an enormous vulnerability that required a courage even greater than they had had to summon under fire in Vietnam; but most of the vets, including Smith (who would overcome the VFW rebuff and many others to become a world expert on PTSD), saw the path of vulnerability as the only way out of Vietnam, the only possible route home, back to an identity that at least somewhat resembled the one they had lost in the war and one they could feel comfortable living with for the rest of their life.

Arthur Egendorf, the other group member who took a strong interest in the dynamics of the rap sessions and how to make them more effective, was a Harvard graduate whose sense of estrangement or being "uprooted by the war" was quite different from Smith's and the majority of working-class vets'. Before the war, Egendorf had planned to become a lawyer and then an international economist. He had grown up in Philadelphia among well-educated and privileged people, who were more concerned with taste and manners than with social conscience, who were interested in other countries as places for tourism or postgraduate study, and who read the newspaper for the sports or securities statistics, and not to know how much suffering in other countries might coexist with American prosperity. Before he enlisted (to keep from being drafted), he had soaked in a year's worth of culture in France and Germany. Indochina seemed like a big bore; and even after he was sent to intelligence school, the "eighth-grade level" of classroom work made the military seem like a big joke.

Vietnam changed everything for him. As a "spy handler," he did not see face-to-face combat with the enemy, but he discovered something equally fearful: that the enemy was all around him, unseen but no less deadly. On the walk to his hotel or villa he might encounter sniper fire, and one night he was literally blown out of his bed by an exploding rocket. But what truly disquieted him was his sense that the war was completely built on lies. It was far more than just the fact that as a secret agent, going under the name of "Artie Levy," his whole identity was a sham, and even his commonplace speech to people on the street full of carefully contrived deceptions. As he talked to these ordinary people, including some of the leftover French colonists from an earlier imperialist foray that had failed, it began to dawn on him that he and his fellow American soldiers were the ones who were being duped worst of all. One such Frenchman told him: "Given the people you've put in power and the way you're bombing and burning to try keeping them there, the insurgents will keep looking like the true patriots to the people in the countryside." Egendorf felt as if his eyes were suddenly opened, and what he saw was that "the war was already lost."

Egendorf had been proud of having adapted well to espionage, keeping his feelings far from the surface and cultivating an aloof facade that made it all but impossible for anyone to "get to" him. The only ones to begin to break through his smug reticence were the lovely Vietnamese whores on Tu Do Street; and the night it all changed for him, his vulnerability to women (like Smith's vulnerability with the VFW) helped punch the hole in his psyche that let all the new things enter. For he had been on the roof of his hotel in Saigon one hot night, getting some air while several career sergeants stood gawking and cheering at a display of American firepower, helicopter gunships fusillading an area of ramshackle huts less than a mile away, when his eyes chanced to stray downward to the roof of the building next door, where there were several beautiful Vietnamese girls, prostitutes, dressed in graceful silk *ao dais* with their waist-length black hair waving in the breeze. Just at that moment one of the sergeants yelled: "Goddamn, that's a gorgeous sight!" But he wasn't talking about the women; he was talking about the sight of Vietnamese homes bursting into flames as tons of red-hot metal and explosive ordnance rained down upon them. "In a flash I saw beyond the flames, to the people being incinerated like trash," wrote Egendorf years later, in his autobiography *Healing from the War*. "I knew then that something had touched me, and that I'd never be the same."

When Egendorf returned to the States in April 1969, he still had a year to serve on active duty in Washington, D.C. Already he was having adjustment problems. Overseeing international spy assignments—like the retired Army officer who had been recruited to seduce a Japanese secretary in the hopes that she might copy some agricultural documents from Communist China—left him feeling sick at the callous manipulation of human lives that often passed for, in the words of John F. Kennedy, "assuring the survival and success of liberty." He grew so angry watching Nixon lie about having destroyed "the central headquarters" of the North Vietnamese Army in Cambodia that he almost destroyed the television set. But the worst problems he had were in his most intimate relationships. He began growing his hair longer, wearing countercultural clothes, and going to political demonstrations, and found that he could no longer talk to his former best friend, Spee, an Army engineer who was sitting out the war at the Pentagon, or his former girlfriend Linda, who turned a deaf ear to his endless monologues about the war and what they could do to stop it. His parents, who wanted most to help him readjust, drew the brunt of his ire.

He demanded they sell the family business, a cemetery for blacks, sobbing that they were guilty of earning their money from "black people's deaths" and that the advantage they had bestowed on him was "now tainted with the blood of the guys who died on our side, and the many others who died on theirs."

Once Egendorf was discharged into civilian society, things only got worse. Recalling that period, there was still anguish in his voice decades later: "So where was I going to go, and who was I going to meet? I had no real communion with anybody. Not that I was terribly close to anybody before the war, but somehow I felt an intensity that I didn't know where to put. In the initial months that I was out of the Army, this was a constant source of pain and discomfort to me. I really couldn't talk to anybody. . . . There were some women when I started to audit psychology courses at Columbia. I could find maybe a sensitive woman who would sit [with me]. But even then, I could tell that I was being heard as a phenomenon, rather than as a person."

When Egendorf recalls that period of his life, the word that seems to come to him most readily is *intensity.* "I felt intensely about something that I had no way to communicate," he says, recounting his "bizarre behavior." While still in the military, he would send off angry letters to Vice President Spiro Agnew (who had made a career of denouncing the antiwar protesters until forced to resign in 1973 for bribe-taking), covering them with "Top Secret" stamps and "all the trappings that would show that they were written from the inner sanctum." Later, out of the military, he would at one point go so far as to explore the possibility of bombing the Pentagon "as a display that the people on the inside were not going to stand for this [continuation of the war]." The liberal Ivy Leaguer of a few years earlier could scarcely have comprehended such behavior in others, let alone himself.

Also, he was crying all the time, often on the slightest provocation—seeing the Capitol rotunda lit whitely at night, or a newspaper photo of Vietnamese women weeping over their dead. His interest in economics dissolved entirely while he was in Vietnam; upon his return, he began to develop a passionate interest in psychology, as well as in counseling others who were deeply hurt or who had confronted death, as he had. He tried calling the Philadelphia VA hospital to tell them he wanted to "work with vets," but nobody there knew what he was talking about. The summer of 1970, after his discharge, he worked in New York as a YMCA counselor, almost craving the full dose of social misery he encountered there, till he was laid off by a budget cut. But even this was not what he really wanted. Over dinner one night he told a friend, "I have something to say. I want a fucking soapbox." Years later, Egendorf explained what he meant: "If he had asked me, 'Well, what do you have to say?' I'm not sure I could have articulated it simply. But it certainly had to do with the war. It certainly had to do about human horror. It certainly had to do with the complacency that I felt in the midst of. In New York, life went on as usual, and I knew people were bleeding and dying halfway around the world, and people back here were not terribly concerned. So all that churned in me."

When he learned that B-52 bombing missions had resumed over North Vietnam, he called Dial-A-Demonstration in New York, and rushed down to the nearest Vietnam War protest at Columbus Circle. Garbed in fatigues and combat boots, he was "ready for war," but he found a bunch of laid-back hippies smoking dope—a sight more like a picnic than a revolution. A few weeks later, he read in the *New York Times* about Vietnam Veterans Against the War and Operation RAW, and he promised himself that once he'd been accepted into graduate school he would make an effort to connect with them.

When Egendorf came down to the VVAW office in December, he told Joe Urgo that he was a counselor and that he had read some of Robert Jay Lifton's pieces on veterans. Urgo told him to come by the following Saturday and he could see Lifton in person, and so Egendorf showed up at the second meeting of the first VVAW rap group, literally burning with enthusiasm and anticipation.

He wasn't disappointed, for he met both Lifton and Chaim Shatan, as well as a dozen fellow vets that he knew instantly he belonged with. As he described them in *Healing from the War*, they were "in fatigue shirts, with beards, unkempt hair, and heavy looks." Most importantly, they were *antiwar*, not in the impassive way of the Columbus Circle hippies or the jaded, fashion-conscious way of the grad students he'd met at Columbia; but "they had intensity," he recalled, "and they had a similar feeling to mine, which was that it is appropriate for us to express our views at a national level. . . . It was as if—for those of us who had been touched deeply, and felt that we were not turning away from what touched us—we had inherited some kind of legitimacy. It was as if we had gone through a peacetime OCS [Officer Candidate School]. We had become catapulted to some leadership position. We were not going to keep silent." In the cramped, always buzzing three rooms of the VVAW office, among the scruffy guys who looked and cared like he did, Egendorf sighed with relief, knowing that he had found both a home and a vehicle for what he wanted to become.

He had wanted to be with other vets so that he "could do something for and with the guys," but the rap groups also showed him that he "had some capacity to respond to them," opening the war-sealed well of his own humanness, so that he need no longer be the bitter outcast making caustic remarks at Georgetown cocktail parties, or the angry, misunderstood son throwing away his education and bringing only shame to his family. The rap groups gave him the sense that he was doing what he was supposed to be doing with his life. And a big part of that coming to terms with his new identity grew from his relationship with both doctors, Chaim Shatan and Robert Jay Lifton, who became his mentors. Becoming a psychologist was now Egendorf's dream; and these two men, especially, showed him that one could act positively within the "psychological crucible" that he had chosen as his way to develop. Lifton and Shatan "did something that was in my heart to do that I couldn't *not* do," Egendorf explains. "When I found myself sitting in a rap group with fellow veterans—and my veteran-ness, and my understanding of this, and my going through the same business *and* my interest in being a therapist all were there and available—it was like, 'Thank you.' I didn't know to pray or say something like that, but it was like an inner relief: *Ah! This is like heaven-sent!*"[90]

2. A Crisis of Identity: Lifton and Shatan "Join the Veterans' Club"

To understand the conclusions Robert Jay Lifton came to about the nature of post-Vietnam syndrome (PVS), one needs to know a little about the work of Lifton's own mentor, the award-winning psychologist and writer Erik Erikson. A student of Freud's daughter Anna, Erikson had fled the Nazis in the 1930s and emigrated to America, where he pondered the problem of *historical* (in addition to simply social and familial) influences on the human psyche. Erikson reasoned that since wars change the face of the earth, they also change the men and women who live through them. In his study of the mind's collision with history and culture (or more aptly, to borrow a seventies term, *culture shock*), Erikson worked for several years with a group of American World War II veterans.

Even before World War II ended, Erikson foresaw that the survivors were going to have a large task ahead of them, creating new identities to fit a world they had never experienced before—because it did not exist yet. As he worked with the war veterans, he found that they were indeed undergoing a crisis in which their previous beliefs about an all-powerful, forever-beneficent America were smashing against the unforeseen reefs of a profound disillusionment, and they themselves were growing ever more depressed and bewildered as they forged on, at an ever greater cost to their energy and spirit, in a losing race with change. Erikson saw this ethical and ideological buffeting, which the veterans were forced to endure, as much like the crisis of faith that Luther and other great spiritual leaders had suffered when the cultural and historical currents of their time swept the known world out from under them.

Erikson's conclusions about the abrasive relationship between person, time, and place were not all doomsaying, however. He saw that out of the "developmental crises" that occur for all of us, in good times or in war, we are able to shape our long-term commitments, and hence our identity; and that identity, tested in fire, becomes a gift both to ourselves and to the new world we inhabit. People who have created such identities are less vulnerable to future change, better able to handle those matters which extend beyond their immediate existence and to prepare for the coming turns in the road before they and the rest of mankind actually get to them.

Even prior to working with the VVAW rap groups, Lifton had a firm understanding, perhaps from his grounding in Erikson and from his study of the aftermath of Hiroshima, that the Vietnam veterans would be preoccupied with "finding their survivor significance." That is to say, he knew that those who were not numbed into total incapacity would be engaged in trying to make sense of their past, to learn the truth of what they had experienced, and to find purpose in the life that lay ahead. To the Cranston Veterans' Affairs subcommittee in January 1970, he described the returning Vietnam veteran in a way that the rap groups would absolutely confirm: "His overall psychological task is that of finding meaning and justification in having survived, and in having fought and killed. That is, as a survivor he must, consciously or unconsciously, give some form to the extreme experience of war, in order to be able to find meaning in all else he does afterward in civilian life."

What did come out of the psychologists participating in the rap groups was a more specific profile of how Vietnam veterans had been spiritually wounded and of what their special requirements for healing might be. In the *New York Times,* Saturday, May 6, 1972, Chaim Shatan published an op-ed article called "The Grief of Soldiers," which came to be a landmark in the literature of post-Vietnam syndrome, and later post-traumatic stress disorder. Shatan had delivered the article, a solicited piece, to the *Times* almost a year earlier, and he had been told several times that they were "ambivalent about it." When it finally appeared, the *Times* "expurgated" (as Shatan called it) several crucial passages, including a reference to "the death and evil which surrounded" our troops in Vietnam, and a paragraph challenging the Nixon administration's claim that there were "fewer psychiatric casualties" in Vietnam than in any other U.S. war.

In the article, which ran under the title (not Shatan's) "Post-Vietnam Syndrome," Shatan picked out six characteristics that seemed to be shared by most of the vets he had worked with. The first was a persistent guilt that could not be "turned off"—guilt at having outlived their fallen comrades, and guilt over those who had been maimed and killed *on both sides.* This guilt led both to a desire to atone and, failing that, to reckless forms of self-punishment, such as substance abuse, one-car accidents, etc., that were often just a shade less determined than actual suicide. The second was a feeling of being scapegoated, used, and betrayed; and the third, a concomitant, was rage at society in general, as well as any particular individuals they believed had duped and/or manipulated them. The fourth was "combat brutalization" (what Lifton called "psychic numbing"), a result of the military training that aimed to make soldiers effective at the job of fighting and killing, where feeling could only get in the way. That intentional loss of touch with their feelings led to the fifth characteristic: alienation from their own humanity and other human beings; and alienation led irresistibly to the most devastating attribute of all: an inability to love, to trust, to accept affection, or to be intimate on any deep level with other people.

What made Shatan's opinion piece so controversial, as well as so seminal, was that he insisted these characteristics were not random or accidental but key pieces of a not-yet-quite-assembled puzzle. "Clinicians will recognize them," he wrote, "as hallmarks of frustrated mourning, or submerged grief." In a very prescient concluding passage that the *Times* also edited out, Shatan wrote that "the Vietnam returnee is unheralded, unwanted and all but unemployable," and he suggested that "his failure to mourn" could only be healed by society's "moral acceptance" and an embracing of each veteran's physical and emotional needs—as if he foresaw the importance of the Welcome Home parades that would only begin to come a decade later.

Shatan's claim that not only was post-Vietnam syndrome a real, qualifiable condition, but that it was a form of "impacted grief" which the U.S. government had contributed to by teaching soldiers to dehumanize the enemy and to deny their own compassion and sensitivity, seemed to point a finger of responsibility at actual villains; and it was not long, predictably, before he found himself under attack. When he read an expanded version of the same report (under his original title, "The Grief of Soldiers") at the 1972 annual meeting of the American Orthopsychiatric Association (AOA) in Detroit, a VA hospital chief stood up to accuse Shatan of trying to "lynch" the VA, which had refused to recognize any form of post-Vietnam syndrome, and of presenting a whitewash of veterans who were in reality "adolescent, poisoned before they come to us, and possessed of unpalatable personalities."[91]

An even more controversial finding of both Shatan and Lifton was that healing from post-Vietnam syndrome seemed to require, or at least be strongly aided by, some form of political or moral activism—some involvement in righting the wrongs and ending the unjust conditions that had led to the veterans' distress. In his book *Home from the War,* Lifton wrote: "For a number of them [Vietnam veterans], and at varying intervals, political activities become inseparable from psychological need. Telling their story to American society has been both a political act and a means of psychologically confronting an inauthentic experience and moving beyond it toward authenticity. For such people not only is protest necessary to psychological help—it *is* psychological help." In his AOA paper "The Grief of Soldiers," Chaim Shatan went even further in validating the radical political demonstrations of VVAW as healing activities:

> To men who have been steeped in death and evil beyond imagination, a "talking cure" alone is worthless. And merely sharing their grief and outrage with comrades in the same dilemma is similarly unsatisfying. Active participation in the public arena, active opposition to the very war policies they helped carry out, was essential. By throwing onto the steps

of Congress the medals with which they were rewarded for murder in a war they had come to abhor, the veterans symbolically shed some of their guilt. In addition to their dramatic political impact, these demonstrations have profound therapeutic meaning. Instead of acting under orders, the vets originated actions on their own behalf to regain control over events—over their lives—that was wrested from them in Vietnam.

As much as Erikson's work had legitimized the introduction of a wider, historical and cultural context in the practice of psychological healing, what Shatan and Lifton (and soon many other psychologists) were saying about the need for hurting veterans to confront and challenge not only the people, but the very assumptions, that had sent them to Vietnam seemed to many more orthodox folks like a kind of quackery, verging on religious heresy and political treason. The government and its FBI guard dogs, for one, did not take kindly to shrinks meddling in foreign policy, especially when their advice impinged on matters of national security and the so-called Communist threat. The same government surveillance and intimidation that had been used by the Nixon administration against VVAW was brought to bear upon the psychologists who chose to work with disturbed Vietnam veterans. Chaim Shatan reported that almost from the day he began participating in rap groups, much of his mail would arrive already opened and resealed with sticky paper, usually bearing a stamp that read: "Received Damaged at Post Office," or "Damaged in Handling at U.S. Post Office." Letters Shatan sent to other psychologists who worked with veterans were also opened and resealed in the same way. One of the psychologists on the same 1972 Orthopsychiatric Association panel about Vietnam was accosted by an Army colonel who wanted to know the details of his association with Dr. Shatan; and another panel member, who had gone on TV to talk about the mental problems of veterans, was warned by a high federal official not to make further such appearances.

At the time of their initial studies, the psychologists were as caught up as the veterans in the "life or death" situation that Sam Schorr spoke of. It was natural, then, for them to speak with perhaps excessive emphasis and urgency of a healing process that began with the realization that this war was wrong, that the U.S. government had misled its citizens and, most especially, the young men who had risked their lives in the service of a false cause. Yet even thirty years later, most of these psychologists have retreated only slightly, if at all, from their early position.

"For the healing process to take place, they [the veterans] needed to confront what they had been part of," Lifton commented on his past views. "That's almost beyond politics, though inevitably it gets to the question of: *Should we have been there?* Or: *Why was I sent there?*

"Certainly, in that early work with veterans, politics was very actively involved in the whole process, and I tried to be very open and honest about it. There are always moral questions, which are inseparable from political questions, that are at issue. I think some psychologists may make the mistake of imagining that it's all a technical matter.

"If you studied Nazi doctors or Hiroshima or, I'd have to say Vietnam—it's of a piece—there would be something absurd about not considering moral dimensions as integral to the psychological issues. Now, I don't think that's only true in extreme situations. It's true *all* the time, except the issue is more nuanced and more hidden. I believe that psychological work *is* a moral enterprise, and there are always moral issues actively involved. But you have to be very careful about not insisting that a particular political view is the only moral one.

"If you're working with antiwar Vietnam veterans, politics is at the heart of it. And it tended to be antiwar people who came into those orbits for simultaneously psychological and, broadly speaking, political and ethical purposes. It didn't mean that a person who didn't have a clear antiwar perspective couldn't in some way heal. I would never make that statement. But the antiwar perspective tended to be associated with the kind of confrontation I was talking about—confrontation in the sense of looking at your own experience, what it was really like. If one felt the need to defend the ostensible justice of the war, that was generally accompanied by a playing down of the destructive things that one did or that others in one's group did, and less of a confrontation with the full experience. Such people may tend to come out more with greater degrees of numbing and something like suppression of experience, and perhaps a point of view that 'we could have won the war and probably should have gone all out,' which is a point of view one hears these days.

"You don't want to throw around the word *sickness* too easily, even though it can be tempting. What one wants to say is that if you glorify the war, there's likely to be some numbing and suppression involved in that, or repression. And that, in my view, is because of the nature of the war."

It is important to realize that when Lifton, Shatan, and their confreres talk about the need for veteran activism or "confrontation with evil" they are not necessarily talking about political demonstrations, though of course those played a central role in veteran healing while the war itself was still going on. While some vets, like Jack Smith, were impelled to make broad, dramatic gestures with their protest actions, hovering close to the edge of violent revolution, others like Arthur Egendorf followed their natural bent toward a quieter, perhaps more scholarly, but no less dedicated pursuit of social change. Egendorf too marched on occasion, but he preferred to let the "militants" like Al Hubbard and Joe Urgo mount the demonstrations. As a result, Hubbard and Urgo would continually harass Egendorf for being insufficiently political, accusing him of being (as Egendorf put it) "into a personalist ego trip." The irony is that without the support of its nonpartisan and more traditionally oriented members the entire movement to achieve veteran healing would have had a lot less credibility; and yet both sides were desperately needed to break through the stone wall of public indifference. Nevertheless, the war at home between militant advocacy and working within the system (as John Kerry stood for) could not help extending even into the study and treatment of veterans' psychological disorders; and like the Vietnam War itself, that war at home would drag on for decades without resolution.

According to Robert Lifton, there was a separate war among the shrinks. As the rap groups progressed, a number of the professionals found themselves growing very uneasy with the kind of parity between doctors and "patients" that the veterans were demanding. On a couple of occasions, the professionals met to discuss their own disagreements and doubts about the direction the groups were taking. The professionals fell into two camps, Lifton asserted: "one who wanted to see the rap groups as group therapy, and one who wanted to see them as a social experiment of an egalitarian nature, in which it was better to continue to call them rap groups and of which the political elements were a [necessary] part." Lifton himself was "always enthusiastic and very intense" about maintaining the unorthodox status of the groups, and refusing to view them as group therapy. Shatan, at least in Lifton's memory, tended to be one of the shrinks with qualms, though Lifton was ultimately able to get Hy to follow his lead, "but maybe a little more slowly." As for the professionals with the most misgivings, Lifton recalls that they "tended to leave rather early in the experience."

Shatan claims that he was actually quite ready to cross that previously sacrosanct boundary between therapist and comrade, or simply friend. For one thing, he was aware that "people had tried to get group meetings of Vietnam vets going before that [the rap groups], but what was wrong about them is that they tried to get them going in doctors' offices or in hospitals, and the last place that vets wanted to be at that time was in any setting that represented any kind of authority. They wouldn't even go to the offices of psychiatrists who were themselves Vietnam veterans." Certainly by the time Shatan read his paper "The Grief of Soldiers" at the American Orthopsychiatric Association (AOA) convention in early 1972, he had already established a "kinship with the veterans," and was championing the cause of "moving beyond therapy alone, and toward advocacy." In fact, Shatan acknowledged that in the course of providing therapy for the vets he had enlisted in a public crusade. "Our goal is to give the widest publicity to the unique emotional experiences of these men," he told the 1972 AOA audience. "To do so, we go—together with the veterans—wherever we will be heard: conventions, war crimes hearings, churches, Congress, even abroad."

Fact of the matter was, the shrinks had very little choice about what role they would play, for the veterans themselves were calling the shots; in effect, they were forcing the shrinks to surrender their time-honored stance of detachment for the privilege of being allowed in to treat them—that was the deal, and the shrinks could take it or leave it. Shatan recalls them repeatedly asking of him and the other professionals: "What is your stake in this? Are you just here to hear war stories, or are you one of us?" There was certainly a sizable peril for the shrinks in crossing that line, for no one joined the veterans' club without paying dues in blood, or something just as precious.

Shatan recalls how involvement in war traumas turned his whole life topsy-turvy: "One thing that happened to me, and it happened to a lot of us, is that the first six months in the rap groups were very, very heavy. Everything you heard was completely unvarnished; it was very disturbing, very upsetting. And after most of the rap groups I attended during the first six months, I had a lot of trouble sleeping. Sometimes I had combat nightmares. Of course, I had never been anywhere near combat. I missed all the wars. And I couldn't go back to sleep when I woke up from a combat nightmare. I seriously considered stopping to go to the rap groups, because it was too hard on me; and in fact, a number of volunteers dropped out, although other ones came along. We kept on looking for them." Shatan finally solved his own problem when he hit upon the idea of dictating his thoughts and impressions after each rap group into a tape recorder, and then mailing each week's cassette to his friend and "confessor," the antiwar priest Robert Drinan, who had recently been elected to Congress.

Lifton's personal experience in the groups seems to have been less torturous and debilitating than Shatan's, at least partly because he had already learned how "you can subsume stress to your professional function" while working with the Hiroshima survivors—a trip through the Valley of Death that for a brief time had nearly put him out of commission. With the Vietnam veterans, he encountered "plenty of stress, but it was good stress." He "experienced lots of pain, anxiety, some nightmares," but also "found it compelling, moving, liberating." From his four years in the groups, he chooses to remember "the enormous satisfaction feeling yourself functioning without leaving out anything in yourself, so to speak." Although after publication of *Home from the War* he did seek to withdraw somewhat, he adds: "I would emphasize satisfaction more than the stress."[92]

3. Sarah Haley Starts a Revolution in Boston: "When the Patient Reports Atrocities"

One reason it was such an uphill battle for the rap group shrinks to convince people of the abundance of veterans' mental problems was that, throughout the war and for several years afterward, the Pentagon and the VA virtually denied the existence of any such problems. In the late 1960s, the Pentagon claimed that the Vietnam War had actually produced fewer "psychiatric casualties" than any other U.S. war. This claim was based presumably on the numbers of veterans who turned themselves in for psychiatric observation, as well as those who were declared permanently unfit for duty because of psychological disorders. It did not take into account the fact that many veterans did not manifest any emotional disturbance until some time after their discharge.

However unjust and myopic, the Pentagon's insistence on the mental well-being of Vietnam veterans killed their chance of getting psychological help at the majority of VA hospitals and clinics. The VA historically had given precedence to treating injuries and illnesses that could be proven to be "service connected," that is, caused by or incurred during a soldier's tour of duty. Since the VA had no reason to suspect that the large number of maladjusted Vietnam veterans showing up on its doorstep could trace any of their behavioral problems to the war, its hospitals and clinics generally refused to treat them.

If Vietnam vets were seen at all, it was usually to provide them with the "quick cure" of a bag full of pills. Whether a vet was depressed, suicidal, chronically drunk, beating his wife, suffering from severe headaches, insomnia, nightmares, night sweats, and attacks of paranoia, or simply unable to hold down a job or to care about the physical circumstances of his life, he was handed a junkie's fortune in tranquilizers, with plenty of renewals. He might even be given several knockout drugs together. Vietnam veteran and writer Larry Heinemann, who would years later receive disability compensation for PTSD, recalls being sent home from Chicago's Hines VA in 1969 with both Valium and Librium—a potentially dangerous combination—which kept him "stoned on the couch" for four months. According to Heinemann, the attitude of the VA doctor who saw him was, "You're wonnathem stone-fucking CRAZY Veetnam vet'rans, pal." The only alternative to drug therapy, the doctor said, was for Heinemann to "sign himself into the nut ward." Heinemann told her, "I just got out of one fucked-up institution. What makes you think I want back into another?"

The military shrinks, "psych officers," who routinely issued a clean bill of health on every screwed-up GI head that came their way, were compromised from the start by the orders they were under to keep the war machine functioning. In this respect, the psych officers were under the same compulsion as every other medical unit in the American military: "to preserve the fighting strength." What this meant was that doctors and shrinks alike were to fix hurt soldiers in such a way as to get them back to their stations as quickly as possible—and not to concern themselves much, if at all, with the need for long-term recuperation or treatments that yielded benefits only months or years later.

General Westmoreland himself had recommended that military psychiatrists assume "a personnel management consultation type role." Hence combat psychiatrists in Vietnam, according to two of them who wrote about it in the *American Journal of Psychiatry*, were forced to let their commanders "work out solutions" to the soldiers' problems. The mind doctors confined themselves to helping both officers and enlisted men "see where their feelings might be interfering with their use of . . . skills." That is to say, they were to teach the troops not to let feelings get in their way, whether they were fighting in the field or merely working in an office. The confessions of such shrinks made it clear to Robert Lifton and others that psychiatry in the military was an arm of command, and thereto gave its allegiance—rather than to the troubled men who came seeking help.

In *Home from the War*, Robert Lifton took a closer look at the Army's psychiatric statistics that had been presented by H. Spencer Bloch in the *American Journal of Psychiatry* in 1969. At that time, the Army was claiming return-to-duty rates of 56 percent for psychosis, 85 percent for psychoneurosis, 90 percent for alcohol and drug problems, and 100 percent for combat exhaustion. Lifton acknowledged that combat psychiatry as it was then practiced did indeed work—that is, it alleviated men's symptoms sufficiently so that they could again adequately perform their job. The problem, according to Lifton, was that there was "neither medical-psychiatric follow-up nor concern with other forms of destructive or self-destructive behavior that might replace the original symptoms." In other words, the Army did not care to find out whether a soldier who was treated and discharged for anxiety, say, over killing a Vietnamese villager might later be recklessly exposing himself to mines and enemy fire, or abusing alcohol and other drugs, or, safely back in the States, committing violent crimes that could land him in jail or the morgue—despite the fact that instances of such "delayed psychiatric casualties" were being observed daily.

Lifton went on to denounce the Army's use of "ostensibly brilliant psychiatric statistics" as a form of "psychiatric technicism," the professional equivalent of "body count." By measuring their success in terms of the number of bodies they could keep out of hospital beds, or move from hospital beds back to the barracks, these psych officers, alleged Lifton, were attempting to sever prevention and treatment from the larger ethical issues. In the pursuit of such goals, Lifton charged, the military psychiatrist "falsifies the effects of the war and further corrupts the profession." From his contact with former combat shrinks, including several who had joined VVAW, Lifton observed that "they find it no easier to come to terms with their immersion in the counterfeit universe than does the average GI. They too feel themselves deeply compromised. They seem to require a year or more for them to begin to confront the inner contradictions they experienced."

Chaim Shatan pointed out a similar flaw in military psychiatry in one of his NYU "memos to the psychiatric community." Shatan quoted a letter from Captain B. C. Ewing in Qui Nhon, Vietnam, which had been printed in the *New York Times,* January 18, 1971. In his letter, Captain Ewing told of the horrors he witnessed daily: an old Vietnamese killed by an American Jeep, a boy killing his friend by tossing a supposedly disarmed grenade, a squad ambushed by part of its own platoon, and GIs addicted to heroin, which had become the second most frequently reported "disease" in Vietnam. Captain Ewing concluded his letter: "We are tragically destroying ourselves. . . . Your sons are being physically and morally corrupted by your war." In his memo, Shatan underlined the dilemma: "'Moral Corruption' is *not* in the Standard Classified Nomenclature of diseases. . . . They [veterans] can expect little help from the VA without proof that their affliction is 'service connected' and can be diagnosed according to the revised APA classification (*DSM II*)."

APA and *DSM II* were two sets of initials that would bedevil Vietnam veterans for almost the entire decade of the seventies. APA stood for American Psychiatric Association, the bastion of conservative psychiatric thought, far larger and far more resistant to the winds of change than the American Orthopsychiatric Association (AOA), which was in the vanguard of developing new clinical techniques for the Age of Aquarius. *DSM II* was the APA's secret weapon, and no psychologist or psychiatrist dared go against it without risking the entire future of his professional career. *DSM II* was the *Diagnostic and Statistical Manual, Second Edition;* and as far as the APA was concerned, if a mental disorder did not merit a listing somewhere in there—like they say about the Yellow Pages—then it just plain didn't exist. In 1971, you could search the *DSM II* till your eyes hurt, but you would never find post-Vietnam syndrome, post-traumatic stress disorder, or anything remotely like it.

For three years in a row (1971, 1972, and 1973), the American Orthopsychiatric Association held panels on the psychological damage inflicted by the Vietnam War, involving people such as Shatan, Lifton, Egendorf, and others who were in the forefront of studying the problem. But when Chaim Shatan tried to get the APA to sponsor such a panel, they turned a deaf ear. Then, when the APA did hold its own panel on Vietnam veterans, in Dallas in May 1972, it was only to discuss the alleged success of the military's new program for rehabilitating active-duty drug users. The panel was stacked with psychological professionals who were connected with either the military or the VA, including Dr. Jerome Jaffe, the man President Nixon had claimed would "solve" heroin addiction in America.

When Dr. Jaffe presented his argument—replete with slides and statistical charts—that the military in Vietnam had virtually wiped out its drug problem, he was challenged by another psychiatrist on the panel, Dr. A. Carl Siegel. Siegel had resigned his officer's commission to protest the way drug-using troops were being ramrodded through a week-long "cure," which was no more than a brutal incarceration with no access to drugs. He was less concerned with Jaffe's statistics than with the long-term effects on the troops thus "treated" and sent home, often with a dishonorable discharge. But the most powerful criticism of Jaffe's claims came from a psychiatrist and Vietnam veteran in the audience, Dr. Gordon Livingston. Livingston was the regimental surgeon who had gotten under Colonel George S. Patton III's skin in an enterprising number of ways—including the dissemination of an Easter prayer, parodying Mark Twain's famous "War Prayer," in which God was invoked to help "thy son, George Patton" bring death and destruction even to "the least of thy children as they hide from us in the jungle." Livingston, who clearly had a way with words, stood up at the APA forum to denounce the government's "deceptions" regarding the alleged health of Vietnam veterans. "Official statistics about drugs," he declared, "are just like the body count—all lies." Robert Jay Lifton, also on the panel, agreed that the government had manipulated its statistics concerning both killing and healing "to distract everyone from the absurd evil of the war," and that these phony numbers—the official equivalent of "out of sight, out of mind"—were "the ultimate epitomization of that very evil."[93]

Many of those who were grappling with this paradox—of the officially invisible and yet obviously real psychological wounding of Vietnam veterans—began to think that money was one of its primary roots. Just as it saved the military millions of dollars to dump drug users back into civilian society, so would it save the VA many more millions to limit its mandated services to the *physical* wounds of combat. The first *Diagnostic and Statistical Manual (DSM I)* was published in 1950, and it had been heavily influenced by military psychiatrists who had served in World War II, including Carl and William Menninger. Moreover, according to Chaim Shatan, "at that time the VA was in the forefront of psychiatric treatment," so that "the best [psychiatrists] wanted to work for the VA." As a result, *DSM I*, which held sway from 1950 to 1968, had a four-page section on "gross stress reactions," which were attributed either to civilian catastrophe or military combat. *DSM I* did not deal with delayed stress as such, and it suggested that if the patient continued to suffer from stress symptoms for over a year, another explanation should be found. But at least the existence of a category of illness attributable to combat gave the VA license to treat disturbed veterans, who were far more numerous following the Second World War than is widely known.

Some of those World War II vets were still occupying VA mental wards when *DSM II* was readied for publication in March 1968—a month after the Tet Offensive had begun—with all reference to war neuroses eliminated. Many professionals dealing with delayed stress in Vietnam veterans, including Dr. Shatan, would later postulate a "definite connection" between the increasing casualties in Vietnam and the disappearance of combat stress disorders from the *Diagnostic and Statistical Manual.* Shatan noted that in the preface to the 1950 edition there had been special mention of the value of the stress definitions to military psychiatrists, psychiatrists working with veterans, and insurance companies; while in the 1968 edition, all reference to such groups had been dropped.

Most of the psychiatrists working with the vets in the early 1970s were not aware of the erasure of stress reactions from the *DSM*, nor did they immediately realize, as Shatan later put it, that *"combat* was a dirty word." Projects and events having to do with the study and treatment of veterans' stress reactions were springing up all over the United States and even in Canada, despite the U.S. government's refusal to recognize that a combatant's subsequent bizarre or atypical behavior could have anything to do with war stress. The first Marine POW to return to the States, James Johnson Sweeney, for example, was court-martialed for having made a few radio broadcasts sympathetic to the North Vietnamese; and despite his many characteristic PVS symptoms, Shatan and fellow psychiatrist Peter Bourne (a founding member of VVAW) could only get him off by concocting a diagnosis of temporary psychosis.

Shatan had helped spark the now raging wildfire of this psychiatric revolution with his *New York Times* editorial and "Grief of Soldiers" article, which had been widely reprinted. He had also been instrumental in seeing that the VVAW rap groups got exposure in a variety of major media, including an article in *The New Yorker* and a segment on NBC news. Shatan became a kind of delayed stress gadfly, traveling all over the country, mostly on his own money, to bring the concept to professional conventions and veterans' groups wherever he could find them. Within months of the founding of the New York rap groups, similar informal groups of veterans and psychiatric personnel had begun meeting in numerous cities, including San Francisco, Urbana, Detroit, Montreal, Atlanta, Philadelphia, and Boston. One group that especially interested Shatan was in Vermont. Called the Champlain Valley Employment Project, it was formed originally to scare up employment for the legion of jobless vets on both sides of Lake Champlain (in both Vermont and New York), but the group had moved gradually toward examining veterans' psychological problems, which were often at the root of their inability to work.

Research was sparked as well. In March 1973, Shatan took part in a symposium on Vietnam in Detroit that was sponsored by the Michigan Psychiatric Society. Shatan had been invited by a Holocaust survivor named Emmanuel Tanay, who had actually been sent to Vietnam by Richard Nixon in 1968 to investigate Vietnam veterans' psychological problems. When Tanay returned, he informed Nixon that guerrilla warfare was extremely dangerous to soldiers' mental as well as physical health; that these young men were in no way prepared for it, and that if the government insisted on sending them to engage in it, the least it could do would be to give them a thorough debriefing and plenty of counseling when they got back. Naturally, Nixon had rejected Tanay's findings. Now, in a friendlier atmosphere, Tanay was able to invite many Vietnam veterans from nearby Macomb County Community College to the conference. Tanay had begun to develop special family counseling for these vets at the college, and with Shatan's encouragement he would soon begin making noncommercial videotapes about how the Vietnam experience was affecting the veterans' intimate relationships. Shatan recalls many of the vets coming up to him afterward and asking him: "How do you know this stuff? How do you understand it? You seem to feel just what we felt." The symposium not only stimulated much greater participation by veterans in the therapeutic programs at Macomb College, but it opened Shatan's eyes to the "commonality" among trauma survivors, which would eventually become one of the major breakthrough areas of post-traumatic stress theory.

The Macomb College vets began sending Shatan enormous piles of poetry and personal recollections, which illuminated emotions he had felt in his own nightmares, and cemented the bond he had now come to feel with all types of trauma survivors. Such bonds were developing throughout the stress-research community. In Detroit, another Holocaust survivor named Henry Krystal began working with Tanay; and in New York, clinical psychologist Florence Pincus began enlarging the scope of the VVAW rap groups with her own insights as woman, Jew, and survivor of the influenza epidemic of 1918, which had left millions dead worldwide. One of the vets in her group, Al Singerman, the son of Holocaust survivors, soon began organizing his own rap groups for Holocaust survivors and their children.[94]

It was another woman, a psychiatric social worker named Sarah Haley, in the big VA outpatient clinic in Boston, whose research into veterans' stress disorders literally blew the existing psychiatric definitions to pieces and began to put a whole new definition on the map. A slightly pudgy woman with a pleasant oval face and extra congenial smile, Sarah Haley seemed the least likely person in the world to make waves, although she had been an antiwar protester during the sixties. In 1969, she had a "glamorous" job teaching at a prestigious university hospital but wasn't making enough money to live on, and so she went to work for the VA solely because it would allow her to pay her bills. Her friends all warned her that the VA's psychiatry program was "fifth-rate," that she would find herself treating "chronic schizophrenics and passive-dependent men with bleeding ulcers," and that her career would surely go down the tubes. But despite the fact that she entered upon her new VA job with the meagerest of expectations, she couldn't help being "shocked at the low caliber of the general run-of-the-mill health person there." As she recalls: "These were not mental health people that you would want anybody in your family to get near."

Her first week at the VA, she worked on an intake team. It was her job to see patients newly brought into the clinic; then they would go on to see a psychiatrist, and at the end of the day she and the other professionals would meet to discuss all the cases and make dispositions. One day, a young man in a highly agitated state was brought into the clinic by his parents. He had only been home from Vietnam for three days, and his parents had no idea what to do with him. He was having total body tremors and exhibiting "startle response" every few minutes. If a car backfired or a door slammed, he would dive under the nearest table. After much rambling, the young man told her he had been at a place called My Lai, that terrible things had happened there, but that it was difficult for him to piece it together. He was confused and experiencing a lot of amnesia, but he did remember seeing the bodies of women and children and vomiting into the bushes. He also remembered that he could not shoot anybody himself, that he had thrown his gun down. The American soldiers who did the killing had sought to intimidate him and the others who didn't shoot: "If you ever tell anybody, we'll come get you. Or we may come get you anyway."

The story of the My Lai massacre had not yet broken in the press, and Haley was dumbstruck by what she heard. Yet she tried to respond sympathetically, since the young man confessed that he had felt he could not tell his story to anyone; he was certain people would either disbelieve him or, if they did believe him, would think that Vietnam veterans were all drug-crazed maniacs. He also feared for his life, knowing that once the story got out he might be tracked down by vengeful guys from his unit. Indeed any other intake worker might have dismissed him as delusional, but Haley had reason to believe him. Her father had been on special operations with the OSS in North Africa during World War II, a self-admitted "assassin for his government." He had told her about seeing a truckload of German prisoners who were led out and made to kneel in front of a ditch, where an American officer shot each one of them methodically in the back of the head. Then the Americans dumped their bodies in the ditch and shoveled it over. Thus Haley, as she puts it, had "no illusions about war."

Haley took the young vet to see the psychiatrist on duty that day, a Japanese woman who would eventually have a nervous breakdown from hearing so many white and black Americans talk about killing yellow people. At the end of the day, Haley walked into the intake room, eager to talk with the others about this young man's case in particular. What she found was that they had already filled in all his blanks in the intake log. Across from his name, the *presenting problem* was listed as "severe agitation and anxiety"; his *diagnosis* was "paranoid schizophrenia"; and the *recommendation* was "5 mg. Stelazine [a powerful tranquilizer] daily. Return in one month." Flustered, Haley insisted that the young man was telling the truth; her righteous indignation infuriated the others so much, she says, that they nearly locked her out of the room. The whole team of psychiatrists, psychologists, and social workers ganged up on her to pound a single lesson into her obviously green head: "Sarah, you don't know the system."

Haley had nothing to go on but a big hunch, but she decided to follow it. It seemed to her that a lot of mental health professionals—especially these ones at the Boston VA clinic—had great difficulty in listening to the recital of trauma; as a defense, they either disbelieved it off the bat, turning it into the less threatening notion of "delusion," or else withdrew from the patient as quickly as possible so as not to have to hear more about it. The other horn of this troubling dilemma was that the traumatized person, especially if he was a Vietnam veteran, would almost never come in and spill his guts to a perfect stranger. Trauma patients need to establish trust with a therapist, and the Vietnam veterans coming into the VA clinic were never being given the chance to do this. It was by the merest lucky chance that the My Lai veteran had seen something in Sarah Haley that made him believe he could confide in her, thereby opening the door not only to his own dark secrets but to possible help for a whole generation of trauma victims.

Haley perceived, correctly, that the reason the My Lai vet could not remember all the details of his trauma was that much of the most painful material had been repressed. In the coming years, she would encounter the same phenomenon in hundreds of Vietnam veterans, some of whom could only recall five or six months of their 12- or 13-month tour of duty. Therefore taking a history of the patient's overseas experience was one of the first steps she undertook with any new Vietnam veteran patient. She further realized that in a successful treatment the stuff that was eating away at them would have to be brought slowly and steadily to the surface—that there were no quick fixes, like "5 mg. Stelazine daily." Equally ineffective, she would soon discover, was "the sort of non-authentic treatment" where the professional would talk about family issues or other daily matters that were troubling the patient, but never bother asking about the existence of trauma in his past; for if the professional didn't ask, the trauma victim would seldom bring it up on his own. Haley was aghast to learn, for example, that an analyst friend of hers had "successfully" treated a Vietnam veteran solely on the basis of working through his rivalry with his father and had never even asked the veteran about his missing foot!

The day she met the My Lai vet, Sarah asked in her sweetest manner, "Would anybody mind, even if he's schizophrenic, if I call this fellow up and offer him an appointment weekly for support?" The others indulged her. That was just the beginning of her quest. She began "scrounging the halls" of the VA clinic for Vietnam veterans. They were easy to find, she recalls, not just because they were younger than the Korean and World War II vets, but she could immediately spot their "thousand-yard stare"—that steely, slightly narrowed, untouchable Clint Eastwood gaze—and fierce, bristly attitude. "Some of them," she recalls, "were presenting themselves in a demanding kind of behavior that was guaranteed to alienate people. I used to say to Vietnam veterans who did that, who would go to a contact officer or some bureaucrat in the VA and pitch a fit and be obnoxious, that 'You're really letting them off the hook. You then say, "Well, fuck you, man, you make me wait half a day, I'm leaving!" You leave, and they're terrifically relieved, because they don't have to deal with you. If you could be a little more cool, they would *have* to deal with you. But they don't *want* to deal with you, and they're eager for an opportunity to have you exit.'"

Most of the Vietnam veterans Haley found were coming in to see a VA psychiatrist merely so that they could get their next month's supply of Valium. Haley would go to the psychiatrists and inquire whether they had ever asked these veterans about their Vietnam experience; the usual reply from the shrinks was that they had stopped asking because the veterans didn't want to talk about it. Haley was flabbergasted that none of the VA psychiatrists—with the exception of two notable women, Lillian Rodriguez and Constance Hartwell—evinced any interest in learning the cause of the tremendous anxiety for which they were blithely prescribing shelves of medications. Haley would ask the shrinks if she could treat their patients; and when this was no longer possible, because her own caseload had gotten too large, she would try to direct the stressed-out vets to either Rodriguez or Hartwell.

During the next five years, Haley put immense effort into doing outreach into the larger Boston community. Aware that many Vietnam veterans were staying away from the VA completely, because of their hatred of authority and red tape, she made contact with as many veterans' groups as she could find, and soon she was sitting in on rap groups at the VVAW office on Harvard Square. She even helped arrange for VVAW to get a desk in the Boston VA hospital, so that veterans who already knew the system could counsel other veterans who were just coming into it.

VVAW in turn began to refer troubled vets to Haley at the outpatient clinic. Even more significantly, Haley began to develop close relationships with several of the VVAW leaders in Boston, such as Lenny Rotman and Dennis O'Brien. She referred to them as the "bad actors," the guys who would appear at the VA hospital and outpatient clinic almost every day to give a hard time to the doctors and psychiatric workers who were shirking their jobs. They would often gang up on the most notoriously incompetent employees. One doctor became their special target; hoping to get him fired or else force him to resign, they would leave him poison-pen letters, steal medicines from his bag, and once even hit him. Within a short time, the VVAW hospital desk was removed.

Although Haley admired the gutsiness of these confrontational vets, she felt they and their friends would actually get more service out of the VA if they simply learned to play by the rules in a more crafty manner. Hence she drew them private, coded schedules, letting them know what days and times to come in so that they would encounter a more empathetic intake team. She knew that her strategy was working when, later in the year, one of the VA workers asked rhetorically: "Why is it that all the Vietnam veterans come in Monday morning?"

During those first few years at the VA, Haley encountered a great many vets who talked about participation in atrocities. She found most of them to be "terribly guilty, feeling unclean, not worthy to be back in the world." For Haley, it created a fearsome struggle in her own mind, as she asked herself over and over: *What do I do with this material?* She would often hear a story such as some young guy having killed a whole Vietnamese family simply because he was overcome by anger and frustration. It troubled her that perhaps it was not in the realm of psychotherapy to be helping somebody sort through such a thing, that perhaps she should be directing them to a clergyman instead.

To contain her anxiety, Haley felt she had to write down what she was experiencing. At the time she started to write her now famous paper, there were only two other papers available on the psychiatric problems of Vietnam veterans, Shatan's "The Grief of Soldiers" and Peter Bourne's "The Vietnam Veteran" in *Psychiatry in Medicine.* A heavy responsibility was thus placed on Haley to make an impact with her own statement. She began by mulling over what is considered the cornerstone of every medical record, the "chief complaint," known in the jargon as the "CC." In psychology as well as medicine, the first question always to the patient is: "What's wrong?" But instead of hearing, "Doc, I have a bellyache," or "Doc, I'm seeing visions," or "Doc, I'm terribly depressed," what Haley would hear time after time was, "Doc, I think I'm a murderer . . . I slaughtered innocent civilians."

Working with these men and the material they brought up was so painful that it took Haley two years to complete her article. Called "When the Patient Reports Atrocities," it was published in the *Archives of General Psychiatry* in 1974 and was immediately recognized as a landmark work. By precise delineation of the symptoms of several veterans she had treated, Haley established that the Vietnam veteran who had witnessed or taken part in atrocities could not be handled merely as a traditional case of traumatic war neurosis, but presented a completely new challenge to psychotherapy.

According to Haley, soldiers in earlier wars had passed through traumatic experiences with the assurance that the horror of killing and wounding was necessary, that whatever harm they caused or received was "in the line of duty." Following both World War II and the Korean War, the psychiatric literature contained numerous accounts of veterans who were troubled by feelings of guilt, depression, anxiety, and/or suppressive symptoms. The psychiatric explanation was that combat experiences had "stirred up unacceptable, unconscious wishes and fantasies." The standard method of treatment was "to alleviate the guilt and thereby aid repression by taking the responsibility from the individual and placing it on a higher authority (one was following orders)." In addition, the therapist was urged to treat the "consecutive depressions" of the veteran, which presumably occurred because of the successive separations he had endured, beginning with leaving his family to go to war, and ending with losing his beloved comrades either through death or simply discharge. In exploring these depressions, the therapist was advised to examine the veteran's "unconscious wishes and fantasies."

Haley put a swath of 50-caliber holes through the classical treatment model with the case histories of two veterans she called John and Bob. A bright, college-bound young man, John had volunteered for the Marines after his brother had been killed in Vietnam; once he got there, unable to see the Vietnamese as people, he killed both prisoners and civilians upon the least provocation. Before leaving Vietnam, he finally got to know some high-ranking Viet Cong prisoners, and they shared food, cigarettes, and family snapshots. When he was ordered to kill them, he couldn't, though the job was done anyhow right in front of him by the commanding officer and other American soldiers. When John got home, he could not get interested in anything, whether girlfriends or college studies; and when Haley met him, he was on the verge of flunking out. He was deeply depressed and abusing drugs to numb his painful memories. He told her that he was guilty of war crimes and that he should be tried for his crimes: "No one can forgive me—I don't deserve to live." After showing up only sporadically for treatment, he attempted suicide while on LSD, then abruptly broke off the therapeutic relationship by saying that "talking couldn't help."

What Haley did not realize was that John had come to her initially because he had been told she was trustworthy by his friend Mike, whom she had treated previously. A year later, John showed up in her office again under the pretext of bringing Mike back for further counseling. At this time, John confessed to her that "he had needed to believe that just one person cared, that one person could be trusted to know what he had done and not reject him." He seemed much stronger and less guilt-ridden than he had a year earlier; and when she commented about his improvement, he explained that he had spent the past year working against the war. He said that he could now live with himself because he was paying his dues by "telling other people about the war and helping other veterans," though he still doubted he would ever be able to love a woman in more than a superficial way.[95]

The case of Bob seemed even more incomprehensible in terms of classical war neurosis. Bob had joined the Marines from a large, working-class family and had already gotten into trouble as a gang member and "tough guy" before going to Vietnam; when he got home, he could not hold down a steady job, "felt angry and sad all the time," and was referred to psychiatric treatment at the VA after threatening to kill his wife, who had been unfaithful to him and now wanted an abortion. Haley learned that Bob had often brutalized Vietnamese prisoners and civilians, that he had enjoyed killing the enemy, and one time participated in "blowing away" a whole group of villagers that he believed had set booby traps for his men; he had also been involved in the fragging murder of an inexperienced American officer who had ordered him and his men on a suicidal assault against a well-entrenched Viet Cong position.

Although Bob admitted a murderous rage toward an assortment of people, including his wife, his mother, and "peace nuts," he could not commit himself to a regular course of therapy; after a few sessions, he stopped coming in except to pick up medicine. Like John, he expressed his belief to Haley that "talking doesn't help." But quite unlike John, Bob claimed that he felt no guilt over anything that had happened in Vietnam, and felt that all the killing he had done had been justified by the threat to his own and his men's survival. At the same time, Bob knew that something had gone terribly wrong with his life, that Vietnam "had done a job on his head"—though he couldn't say exactly what. "I'm not the same," he told Haley hopelessly.

What was revolutionary about Haley's conclusions was her insistence that, above and beyond all other means of treatment, the therapist must establish a bond of trust with the patient: "Establishment of a therapeutic alliance for this group of patients *is* the treatment rather than the facilitator of treatment. It is critical that in every sense the therapist be 'for real': a 'real person' more so than a transference figure, and a 'real person' respectful of the veteran's strengths and concerned about but not 'put off' by their psychopathology . . . and it is the constancy of the 'person' of the therapist that enables these patients to confide in another person rather than act on their fears and projections." To prove her point, Haley cited a Vietnam veteran who had seen her on a "drop-in" basis for three years before he was able to relate the combat experience that had been plaguing him ever since he returned home.

Another major requisite of the treatment Haley proposed was the therapist's ability to identify with the veteran who had participated in atrocities: "The therapist must be able to envision the possibility that under extreme physical and psychic stress, or in an atmosphere of overt license and encouragement, he/she, too, might very well murder. Without this effort by the therapist, treatment is between the 'good' therapist and the 'bad,' out-of-control patient, and . . . the patient may correctly assume he is being 'cleaned up' or 'white-washed' in order for the therapist to tolerate him." Hence, with these men, the therapist must learn "to hear horrifying realities, and . . . tolerate natural feelings of revulsion, yet resist an equally natural tendency to punish." Haley admitted that such tolerance well might strain "the therapist's judgmental tolerance to its limit."

As if Haley hadn't already done enough to demolish the traditional approach to war neurosis, she suggested that even the diligent process of working through the patient's grief and guilt might not be sufficient, and that patients might also have "to establish an individualized pattern of treatment" that involved "paying their dues" to society for the crimes they believed they had committed. (Or, in the case of those like Bob who felt that nothing in Vietnam was criminal as long as it kept them alive, it was still vital to encourage them to find productive, rather than self-destructive, ways to mourn their loss and to reestablish the boundaries of moral behavior.) Like a glove thrown down before all those APA shrinks who had refused to see soldiering as the path to psychic disaster, Haley concluded with the warning: "Combat vets may play down or embellish their 'war stories,' but initially their reports should be taken at face value. The only report that should not be accepted at face value, although one may choose not to challenge it initially, is the patient's report that combat in Vietnam had no effect on him."

When Haley's article was published, it galvanized a whole generation of therapists, some of whom had been sitting on the fence and some who, because of their own Vietnam experience, had been afraid to speak up for fear of unleashing their own repressed horrors. Art Blank, who had been chief psychiatrist with the 93rd Evacuation Hospital at Bien Hoa in 1965–1966, had been a founding member of VVAW, and his remarks condemning the hypocrisy of President Lyndon Johnson had been read into the *Congressional Record* in January 1968. At that time, post-Vietnam syndrome was still unknown, at least in name, but in his statement that was read to Congress Blank had suggested the severe stress that soldiers in Vietnam were subjected to while fighting an unpopular war. Said Blank: "At least one-fourth to one-third of the American soldiers in Vietnam are 'very much opposed.' They do not believe 'in the righteousness of our cause,' and therefore feel that the war is unjustified . . . however, the soldiers are driven by a sense of duty to do what the U.S. government orders them to do and by their wish to avoid punishment. . . ."

But Blank, who had become a professor at the Yale Psychiatric Institute, cited the "enormous pressures of work" as a reason for not wanting to make public his own war-related traumas. Yet he often involuntarily relived the worst one—the time an active-duty GI had come to see him in Saigon and tried to kill both of them with a grenade (Blank had barely gotten out the door before the grenade detonated). He told Haley years later that her article had moved him to learn that "somebody was out there doing something," but what affected him even more powerfully was the knowledge "that he was finally going to have to confront and deal with and sort out his own Vietnam experience." Blank would eventually come to head the VA's Vet Center Program, the first major governmental effort to treat PTSD nationwide, for over a decade.[96]

Haley's paper became an indispensable part of the engine that in time succeeded in revamping the definition and therapeutic approach to stress in the forthcoming *DSM III*. But even as she worked on it, a network of delayed-stress activists was forming across the United States—a network she would soon plug into as a key figure herself.

4. A Community of Healing Forms:
The First National Conference in St. Louis, 1973

While Haley and a few sympathetic VA coworkers were forging a New England limb of the PTSD research body that had begun to grow in New York with the work of Shatan, Lifton, Egendorf, Smith, and their cohorts, another far-flung limb of this still barely visible skeleton appeared in the unlikely milieu of West Los Angeles.

In the late 1960s and early 1970s, L.A. was still America's dreamland. The sun shone every day (at least it was supposed to), and the smog wasn't yet completely stifling, especially on the west side, where the soft Pacific Ocean breeze kept life fresh and expansive. The west side was the anything-goes boardwalk at Venice, obscenely healthy bodybuilders and sexy roller-skaters in bikinis that would shock your midwestern aunt; it was the sunnyside-up optimism of affluent Santa Monica, the movie star psyche of tony Brentwood, and the perennial tan of Westwood with its incomparably glamorous campus, UCLA. Even the west side VA, situated in a mile-long belt of lush greenery in Brentwood, was more like a country club than the usual piss-and-vinegar dungeons that passed for veterans' hospitals in most of America.

However improbable, L.A.'s west side was suddenly exploding with delayed stress because its cheap, nook-and-cranny oceanfront apartments were filled to busting with Vietnam vets. No one could have designed a more perfect draw for the lovelorn, pain-weary guys just back from that flesh-tormenting hellhole in Southeast Asia. Here were legions of available, fun-loving girls, year-round outdoor living, cheap colleges, and plenty of things that eased the mortal burden, like swimming pools and rock concerts. It would take a bit of time before this Shangri-La revealed itself to be nine-tenths mirage, and by that time thousands of vets would be living homeless on the streets or in the boarded-up concessions on the old, condemned Venice pier, thousands more in prisons for drugs or trying to make their boss or girlfriend listen to their woes at the point of a knife, some gone stark crazy to live as "tripwire vets" in commando posts up in the canyons, or others still, dead by their own device, driving off some ocean cliff in their car or dining on a whole bottleful of downers.

By the early 1970s, the casualties of this new war of attrition here at home began showing up in alarming numbers at the West Los Angeles VA in Brentwood. Fortunately, two extraordinary individuals on staff there picked up immediately on what was happening: a former psych officer in Vietnam who had a steel plate in his head from when he had nearly been blown away in a chopper crash, Floyd G. "Shad" Meshad, and a top-notch adolescent psychiatrist named Leonard Neff. Well ahead of his time, Neff ran a ward just for Vietnam veterans at the Wadsworth VA Hospital in Brentwood, and Meshad was the social worker on the ward.

Neff was immensely helpful to all those psychologists who were trying to figure out, in Haley's words, "what's going on with these guys?" Adolescent psychology is considered one of the most difficult specialties, because adolescents are often impossibly mercurial: outrageously rude one day and remarkably sensitive the next. Cognizant that the average age of ground troops arriving in

Vietnam was nineteen (still three or four years from a fully gelled identity), Neff began by asking: what happens to these fluid states when an adolescent is put in a life-and-death situation? His answer was that all the unresolved questions of identity simply froze, ossified. Other psychologists, building on Neff's conception, would soon begin using the term "foreclosed childhood" to describe a variety of individuals who had been cheated of normal psychic development, from Vietnam veterans to incest survivors and children of alcoholics.

Neff would become one of the most brilliant theoreticians in the field of PTSD study before his untimely death of cancer; and his gift for pithy phrasing would yield easily graspable handles for his often complex typology, as when he referred to Vietnam vets as "invisible patients with an invisible illness." Meshad, by contrast, was a hands-on psychic repairman—with the charisma and fast rap of a brother-love preacher and the guts and grit of an inner-city paramedic. A Lebanese Catholic, Meshad had been raised in the Deep South, in a "macho world of football and strength." He had proved that he could play football with the toughest competitors, though he was only five foot seven, because, in his words, he was "strong-willed, success-oriented, with lots of drive." That same kind of fearless determination to meet life's hardest blows and come back smiling was what had pushed him to volunteer for Vietnam.

As an undergraduate Meshad had studied theology and philosophy with the Jesuits, while also completing an ROTC program. Upon graduation, he received a second lieutenant's commission and trained with the 82nd Airborne, then got a deferment for graduate school so that he could pursue his real interests in the fields of mental health and criminology. After he got his master's degree in psychiatric social work, he went back on active duty and was sent to the mental hygiene clinic at Fort Leavenworth, Kansas, where he got his baptism of fire working with "the incorrigibles at the bottom of the prison." Meshad ran a group at the clinic, and a lot of the guys he saw "had been in some heavy situations in Vietnam and were real angry about it"; moreover, being among their fellow combat vets, and insulated from the outside world by their often steep sentences, they were willing to open up completely about the injustices they felt had landed them in prison.

After a year of "beating the system," earning plaudits and promotions while managing to keep out of the war, Meshad decided it was time for him to see for himself what these less lucky fellows had gone through; he volunteered, and was sent to Vietnam as a psych officer in January 1970. What he found there, up near the DMZ, appalled him. His job was to support a single psychiatrist who was supposed to be handling the mental problems of Army, Navy, and Marines in most of I Corps, the upper fourth of South Vietnam, and arguably the most brutal combat area. The whole of Vietnam at that time, he estimates, had about twenty-five mental health professionals handling close to half a million troops. They assigned him a helicopter, in which he flew around the whole

DMZ area for several months, talking with troops and taking down their stories, and in the process earning himself a Bronze Star.

Then came a change of command at his M.A.S.H. unit. The new commander hated all of the psychiatric personnel, as well as anything or anybody who was "unclean," including (in his view) black people. The new commander took one look at Meshad's bristly Mideastern black combat moustache and said either he or the moustache would have to go; when neither went, Meshad was told he would be fined ten thousand dollars. As a captain, a company-grade officer, Meshad demanded a general court-martial, risking imprisonment in order "to stand up to this absurdity," which he now saw as the entire massive "rip-off—of the grunts, of the Vietnamese, of the American people." He won, but "got spanked" by the Army anyway by being transferred to an extremely hot area in the south. On his new assignment as "flying psych officer" he was shot at every day, and in no time his chopper was shot down. The pilots were killed, but Meshad got off easy—in his own eyes—with just a fractured neck and back and a "torn-up" head.

By the time he got through months of convalescence, partly in Vietnam and partly at a VA hospital in the States, he had lost fifty pounds and did not want to hear any more about the war. In May 1971 he and his girl got in a camper and headed for California, where he expected "to just gain weight and eat health food and lay out on the beach." But the day after he arrived, his friend Frazier, a former sergeant on his psych team, with whom he was staying, took him over to a graduate school reception at the University of Southern California. Frazier introduced Meshad to Dr. Phil May, an English psychiatrist who was currently running the Brentwood psychiatric hospital in the Wadsworth VA complex.

Meshad recalls: "I just got real sarcastic. I'd had a few drinks; I'd been on a morphine synthetic for pain all the way out of Alabama cross-country. I've still got severe fractures and compressions, and my head's just totally bald with road tracks all over it. And I was always wearing a cap—just pissed off, nobody to talk to. There were no counselors or Vet Centers. I was pretty angry. So I just ate him up all night. He said, 'I really want to know. I really care about you. And I really want to help.' And he says, 'We have quite a few Vietnam vets that are brought in by police and emergencies into the hospital. I'm really disturbed because a lot of my staff are diagnosing them as schizophrenic.' He had a major international reputation on the clinical treatment of schizophrenia. And he said, 'Vietnam vets are not schizophrenic, but I'm not really sure what it is.'"

May told Meshad that there were really no diagnostic slots for troubled Vietnam vets besides schizophrenia or character disorders (which cover, in Meshad's colorful phrasing, "people who are just born an asshole or who like to be nasty all the time"). What made the situation all the more urgent was that Brentwood had the largest psychiatric facility for veterans in America, handling about sixteen hundred inpatients each day and about fifteen thousand outpatients yearly. Still angry, Meshad bitched that at least part of the reason for the vets' ongoing psychiatric problems was that he and his GI coworkers had never been able to give anything other than "Band-Aid therapy" in Vietnam. Out of the blue, May offered Meshad the opportunity to come work at the Brentwood psychiatric hospital, to evaluate the VA's treatment of Vietnam veterans and to educate his staff about their "condition." "What 'condition'?" Meshad asked. "I just know I'm pissed off." "You need to deal with that too, you know," May replied.

But Meshad was having none of it. Like most vets, he still distrusted the VA completely and "hadn't separated it from the military." The following weekend, Meshad drove his girlfriend and all their belongings up to San Francisco with the vague idea of working in a free clinic, but he merely holed up with some old friends and "sat vegetating" for three weeks. Somehow Dr. May got his number and began calling him twice a week, making every effort to get him to come back down to L.A. and take the job he'd offered him at the Brentwood VA. May pleaded with him that he and his staff really needed to know what Meshad had to teach; and he cajoled him with the fact that Southern California had the largest Vietnam veteran population in America, promising, "You can go out there and just take care of the world."

Meshad was unconvinced, but his life was falling apart—twenty-six, jobless, his gorgeous teenage girlfriend looking to him for direction, and him crying every day, feeling inadequate, not wanting to return to his folks in Alabama a failure. Nothing Dr. May said moved him so much as the fact that the psychiatrist seemed truly concerned about him and what he was going to do with his Vietnam experience. Gradually Meshad found himself looking forward to May's calls, if only to have someone to argue with; and the next thing he knew, he and his girlfriend were in their truck rattling back to L.A., back to living in someone's attic, just as antsy and uncomfortable as before, but feeling a little less ridiculous for having at last some small sense of purpose.

All of which was almost whacked out of him the next day when he went for his meeting with the Brentwood VA psychiatric staff. He walked into a room filled with bookcases and dark wood, which made him think, strangely enough, of Hugh Hefner's Playboy Mansion. There he sat, surrounded by stiff-looking men and women in long white coats and name tags, and himself in Navy bell-bottoms and a Venice Beach tank top, his hair growing every which way in orange and other abnormal colors (it had changed from jet black after he'd gotten "scalped" in the helicopter crash in Vietnam), looking about as funky as funky comes. Dr. May in his very British accent began introducing all the other psychiatrists, who sat staring at Meshad in undisguised astonishment that "this was the guy he'd been talking about!" Finally Meshad burst out laughing, and try as he might, he couldn't stop, till Dr. May began to laugh too, but the others just sat there grimly, afraid to say a word—as if Meshad were an IRS auditor who'd come to uncover their participation in the biggest scam of all time.

Dr. May's clout, as both chief of psychiatry and director of the hospital, carried the day; and like him or not, the staff approved Meshad's appointment. Meshad was astonished to find himself suddenly a part of the hated VA, but he felt like he "had to belong to something"; at least he liked Dr. May, and the job gave him "a chance to take a shot at an institution that sucked." The next day, having deduced that he wasn't as a big a threat as they imagined, the staff started coming to him with their various problems with Vietnam vets, and Meshad suddenly felt like he was "back in Nam," helping people "team up" on difficult individuals. A few hours later, all hell broke loose, and Meshad's life changed forever.

Dr. May came to Meshad and said that the day before one of their psychiatrists had made "a major mistake." The psychiatrist, a German woman, had been offended by the crude antics of a couple of Vietnam vets and had kicked them off the ward. The vets had then gone to join a bunch of their comrades under the Venice Beach pier, and they had phoned *Time, Look*, and *Life* magazines, all of which were just spoiling for stories that would tear into the VA— especially after the succès de scandale of *Life*'s story on "Our Forgotten Wounded," which had run a year earlier, in May 1970. So the VA was counting on Meshad to do damage control, and a meeting was set up between one of the two angry vets and Meshad outside the VA hospital.

The kicked-out vet was prepared to go at it with Meshad too, but Shad appeared in his usual funky dress, looking "weird" (by his own account); and when one of the hospital administrators announced that "Shad's also a Vietnamese vet," both young men cracked up. It was so pitifully typical of the VA's ignorance at that time, according to Meshad, that "they didn't even know how to say 'Vietnam vet,'" and the kind of jaundiced, black humor that all combat vets share broke the ice between social worker Meshad and his new patient. The vet told Meshad about his buddy who "was dying under the Venice pier," that if the guy died he was prepared to shoot the German doctor, and that in any case he was going to smear them up and down by going ahead with the news stories. Meshad told him he didn't care about the stories, he just wanted to go down to the pier and talk to the vet's buddy; and so they hopped in Meshad's old truck and did just that.

It was at Pacific Ocean Park, site of the old Venice pier (which eventually washed out), that Meshad's education started. Almost nine hundred homeless people were living on or under the pier, and over three hundred of them were Vietnam vets. Meshad remembers "hundreds of Vietnam vets just cruising. It was like Saigon or Da Nang. It just blew me out." On the pier he found vets who had thrown their sleeping bags into little niches carved out of the now defunct amusement rides. There he met the first vet's friend Larry, who related immediately to Shad as a fellow veteran and agreed to come back to the hospital with him.

The next day, with the help of psychiatrist Leonard Neff, Meshad set up a special psychiatric ward just for Vietnam vets. Larry and his friend were assigned doctors to deal with their psychiatric problems, but Meshad would also be on hand for them to talk things out. Then each day for months afterward, Meshad went back down to POP (as the park was called) to "work the pier" and the area behind it, meeting and ferreting out lost and despondent and potentially explosive Vietnam vets. Without knowing about Lifton and Shatan in New York, Meshad got many of these vets to come to a rap group at the hospital, and that group quickly overflowed into a second; for those still leery of the VA, he started another rap group at the Venice Legal Aid Clinic up over a health food store just off the beach. One of the black vets led Meshad down to Watts, where he got yet a fourth group going at a place called Central City Bricks. Then a psychiatric intern from East L.A., Armand Morales, induced Meshad to set up a fifth group in his barrio, and that was the last, since Meshad was now leading groups every night of the week.

One day, in his search for troubled vets, Meshad went to a community hall in Venice where the California Veterans' Movement (soon to become VVAW) was holding a meeting. He had already gone to the rallies of similar "anger groups," and always he would listen quietly to their tales of rage and frustration, trying to keep his own head cool. "Everybody at that time was twenty, twenty-one years old," he recalls. "There was so much anger, you walk in there you couldn't cut it with a machete it was so thick." This particular time, there was a wild-eyed vet in a wheelchair haranguing about forty or fifty other vets; at times, as his raving reached a frenzied pitch, he would lift himself straight up with his arms so that it looked like he was going to walk right out of his chair. After the meeting, Meshad hesitated to introduce himself to the speaker, but the guy wheeled right over and shook Meshad's hand, saying that he had heard all about his counseling work and that he wanted to come to his rap group over the health food store.

The wheelchair vet came to about six of the rap group meetings, and his anger was incandescent. A former Marine sergeant, he had been shot through the spine while leading an assault against a Vietnamese village. He now repented of his heroism. He said that the American government had robbed him of his ability to fuck, and when they enabled him to fuck again that was when he would stop being angry. The guy seemed potentially self-destructive and Meshad worried about him when he stopped coming to the meetings, though already Meshad knew that Vietnam vets were all terribly restless and it was almost impossible to get them to commit to anything, even a program of healing, for more than a few weeks. But the guy was showing up at more and more rallies and beginning to lead major protests, and Meshad figured that as long as he could vent his anger in words he'd be safe from doing himself any real harm — that, after all, was the secret principle that made the rap groups so successful.

The wheelchair vet did not self-destruct; instead, he spent the next twenty years continuing to talk out his anger. His name was Ron Kovic, and at times he would act as Shad's friend, at other times his deadly enemy. But that was part of what PTSD was all about too.[97]

*   *   *

By early 1973, the country-wide stress network was so well defined, and so much information was accumulating in its various nodes, that Shatan and some of the other research pioneers decided it was time for all of them to sit down together and pick each other's brains. The First National Conference on Emotional Problems of Vietnam Veterans was held at Concordia Seminary in St. Louis for three days in April 1973, hosted and funded by the Missouri Synod of the Lutheran Church. Jack Smith had been working at the National Council of Churches in the tall building known as the "God Box" on Riverside Drive in upper Manhattan, and he had managed to interest a Presbyterian minister named Mark Hanson in the cause of veterans' recovery and readjustment. As though he had been touched by the spirit, Hanson became a veritable fire-brand, organizing veterans' self-help projects and setting up rap groups all over the country, and he also became one of the most impassioned veterans' advocates in front of Congress. It was Hanson who did most of the organizing for the St. Louis meeting, which comprised about 90 vets, 60 shrinks, 30 chaplains, and 10 VA people who were piggybacked on at the last minute.

Besides the New York heavyweights, there were Meshad and Kovic from L.A., a former military chaplain from San Diego named Bill Mahedy who had been running his own rap groups, and two major players from San Francisco, both Vietnam combat vets: former Marine corpsman Jack McCloskey and a black vet, Harold "Light Bulb" Bryant, who together had founded an impressively effective group called Twice Born Men, in which ex-prisoners and Vietnam veterans (and sometimes men who were both) helped sort out one another's problems. According to Shatan, the conference "generated a tremendous esprit de corps. We really felt glued together as an operation that was working for the same purposes."

Shatan and his contingent conducted workshops on rap groups. What he found was that many people who were just getting their feet wet in stress treatment wanted to approach rap groups as standard psychotherapy, and he had to keep explaining that the standard talking cure was not what veterans generally needed; what they did need was "to feel empowered to take charge of their own lives as part of the treatment, they had to do the treatment on their own turf, and it had to feel self-generated, they had to run it." Another important achievement of this first national conference was the establishment of various committees: one to sponsor the passage of new legislation pertaining to mental health care for Vietnam veterans, one to organize political and social action, and one to provide journalists with material for accurate media stories on delayed stress. They also established a coordinating council, composed of half veterans and half psychiatric professionals, which would keep rap groups around the country in touch with one another and be able to mobilize them for political action or call upon selected individuals to appear before Congress or professional conventions and on radio or television.

The ethic that emerged from the 1973 St. Louis conference was, in Shatan's words, "no leaders and no followers—we were all in there as peers on an equal footing." But there was plenty of friction nonetheless, and the grumblings were just beginning. The coordinating council had three codirectors, all of them Vietnam veterans, two white and one black, and they fought almost immediately about priorities, with the black vet emphasizing political and employment issues while the white vets stressed the urgent need for psychological help. Shatan recalls that a lot of time and energy was consumed in that first year in conference calls between the professionals on the coordinating council and the co-directors, "trying to troubleshoot the personality problems."

Indeed personality conflicts were threatening to undo the harmony of the entire occasion—a development that might seem strange at a gathering of psychiatric professionals until one realizes that those who help the psychically distressed cannot help absorbing some of the burnout themselves. The most tragic rift, one that would not be healed for a couple of decades, was between Lifton and Shatan. Shatan was on the committee that organized the election of the coordinating council, and so he had agreed not to run himself. Lifton, naturally, *was* nominated to serve on the coordinating council. But just as Shatan was about to get up to announce the slate of fifteen candidates, Lifton leaned over and whispered to him: "Hy, I want you to let them know that even though I'm not going to be on the council, I'm with them just as much as I've ever been all along." Shatan was shocked that Lifton had chosen such a moment to reveal that he was "starting to pull out"; and fearing that such an announcement would throw the conference into chaos, he refused to make it. A month later, that rift grew even bigger when the publication party was held for Lifton's book *Home from the War* and neither Shatan nor any of the other rap group shrinks or vets was invited, which Shatan interpreted as a denial of the "equal basis" all of them were supposed to be on. Not only that, but, as Shatan remembers, "right after the book was published, Lifton phoned me, and he said, 'Hy, I'm not gonna be able to come to the rap group meetings anymore, and I'd like you to tell the vets that." Once again Shatan refused to collaborate in what he saw as "leaving the vets with their guts out on the shelf to dry"—as so many journalists had already done to them—and he warned Lifton that the removal of his presence was "going to be extremely harmful to the whole self-help movement with which your name has been so strongly identified." Though they did continue to work together with the VVAW rap groups for another two years, a lot of the trust between them was permanently lost.

The most acerbic conflict, however, came predictably between the professionals who were doing rap groups and the members of the VA's medical and psychiatric staff. Explains Shatan, "The VA guys wanted to pooh-pooh the whole thing; and even if it was so [i.e., if war caused some stress disorders], hardly anybody was suffering [according to them]." During the St. Louis conference, Shatan and Lifton gave an interview to the *Chicago Tribune* in which they claimed that 20 percent of Vietnam veterans were affected by delayed stress; the VA shrinks countered in the same article that at most 5 percent were affected, and that obviously Shatan and Lifton had become obsessed by the war. Shatan felt most affronted by the assertion of Dr. Jerome Jaffe, then Chief of Medicine in the VA, that it was the things Shatan and Lifton said (rather than episodes from the war) that were troubling Vietnam veterans. Moreover, Dr. Jaffe regarded the work of both Shatan and Lifton as "an insult to brave men." Shatan replied that it was a good thing, then, if they were only insulting 5 percent instead of 20 percent, since "5 percent would have meant 200,000 instead of almost a million"—an apparently insignificant figure in Dr. Jaffe's eyes.

The miracle of the St. Louis conference in 1973 was that, despite all these political agendas, there emerged in the workshops a harmonious rapport and a genuine willingness to cooperate in making further breakthroughs. Shad Meshad regarded the conference as "the pivotal turn in American history for mental health on PTSD." Little Shad roomed with six-foot-six Jack Smith, whom he regarded as "a walking Ron Kovic. He was just as angry as Ron all the time, and this guy was walking—he was even more dangerous!" In addition, he says, all the vets "would try to eat my ass as soon as the fact came up that I was working for the VA." Nevertheless, the conference was powerfully healing for Meshad himself: "It was so exciting for me because I *never* thought I'd have a forum; I thought I was going to be doing this alone the rest of my life. And I would have. I just thought that's the way it was, no one cared, no one; I'm the only one doing this. Everybody thought that. Of course, Shatan and Lifton had the power of the university [behind them]. I was dealing with crisis after crisis. And so we got there and realized that we have a post-traumatic condition here, and we need to work on it."

Meshad had written a special paper for the conference, titled "New Needs Require New Services," which he had circulated in-house at the VA. He and the others exchanged their writings, and then got together the following afternoon to "kick around" the various ideas that were just surfacing. The intensity of their discussion reminded Meshad of his sessions with the vets at Venice Beach, but now instead of feeling drained he felt supported. If it hadn't been for St. Louis, he later realized, he would have "just burned like a candle, just *twooh!* eventually."

Another remarkable thing was that—outside of the hard-core VA conservatives—there was no conflict in styles of treatment, nobody telling anybody else, "No, wait, you've got to do it this way. . . ." Their approaches did indeed vary a good deal—from Shatan's and Lifton's focus on grief and guilt, to Meshad's "action-junkie" manner of letting a group run until the guys tired of "punching themselves out," to the more inhibited stance of one volunteer rap group facilitator from the William Alanson White Institute, who was reluctant to even offer vets a ride in his car for fear of becoming more peer than therapist. Yet, according to Shatan, what they were startled by "was not so much the differences as similarities." Chief among their agreements was that the treatment had to emerge from a "community of consent," where those who came to be healed created their own format and no single person or elite group of professionals was running the show. As Meshad put it, the process depended on following one's "instincts," as well as the Golden Rule of "what felt good for me probably felt good for you; what hurt you could hurt me." For Shatan, the key to the "esprit de corps and sense of cohesiveness" came precisely from that sense of bonding between healer and veteran that some of the therapists were still fighting shy of.

"In fifteen minutes or less you could tell where a person was coming from," Shatan explained, "because you had already been there, and having been there you could dovetail right into the experience. You wouldn't take words out of other people's mouths, but you knew what they were gonna come up with, and the result was that people would open up in a way that was extraordinary. By the end of [my first] hour and a half with a group of guys, I felt as if I'd been meeting with them for months."[98]

5. Turning the Psychiatric Guns Around:
Post-Traumatic Stress Disorder Gets Recognized

The first congressional bill calling for the government to provide psychological help for Vietnam veterans was introduced by the Jesuit priest Robert F. Drinan, formerly the dean of Boston College's law school, shortly after his election as a representative from Massachusetts' Fourth Congressional District in November 1970. Drinan, an uncompromising dove who had published a book in 1966 attacking the rationale for the war, had been aided in his campaign by John Kerry of VVAW, and through VVAW he had met Chaim Shatan. After Shatan began sending him taped monologues about his experiences in the VVAW rap groups, Drinan quickly drafted a bill authorizing the government to determine and meet the mental health needs of Vietnam veterans. But Drinan was considered a bit of a dreamy radical even by many New Left Democrats, and his Vietnam veterans' readjustment bill met the same fate as his other drastic legislation, such as his resolution to impeach Nixon for war crimes in Cambodia—it was largely ignored.

By that time, however, the Vietnam veterans had already gained a more powerful ally in Congress. In 1969, Senator Alan Cranston (D-Calif.) had become chairman of the Labor and Public Welfare Subcommittee on Veterans' Affairs, and he immediately initiated oversight hearings on the health care being offered to returning Vietnam veterans. These hearings revealed the grossly understaffed and overcrowded conditions in VA hospitals—as well as shocking facts, such as that during the entire Vietnam War only 10 percent of the VA hospital beds were actually occupied by Vietnam vets (most were occupied by older, indigent veterans with non-service-connected illnesses). The testimony at the Cranston hearings had sparked *Life*'s scathing indictment, "Our Forgotten Wounded." After they closed the medical hearings, Cranston's subcommittee then began a very extensive series of hearings on the psychological problems of Vietnam veterans. It was at Cranston's second set of oversight hearings that Robert Jay Lifton had presented his observations on the psychological struggle of Vietnam veterans "to find meaning and justification in having survived" a brutal guerrilla war; and it was at the Cranston readjustment hearings that triple amputee Max Cleland, who would later head the VA under President Carter, had spoken eloquently of "the inevitable psychological depression after injury."

Based on what was revealed at those hearings, Cranston introduced a number of bills to improve the lot of Vietnam veterans, including a better GI Bill and a veterans' employment act. In conjunction with John Pastori, chairman of the Appropriations Subcommittee, Cranston requested tens of millions of dollars for the upgrading of VA medical facilities and the hiring of thousands of new hospital workers. Despite the protests of Nixon's VA chief Donald Johnson that his facilities were already quite adequate, Cranston's requests were almost all eventually approved over the course of the 1970s; although, according to one observer, Forrest Rusty Lindley, "it was too late for most Vietnam veterans. The damage had been done, long before the additional staff and better facilities arrived."

Actually, a Senate reorganization in early 1971 promised to give Cranston an extraordinary opportunity to help Vietnam veterans. Previously, veterans' issues had been handled by subcommittees of two different committees: Labor and Public Welfare handled health care, education, and employment, while the Finance Committee handled compensation and pensions. In 1971, the two disparate subcommittees merged into the new Veterans' Affairs Committee, and Alan Cranston was appointed chairman of its Subcommittee on Health Care. Cranston lost no time in introducing a bill, S2091, aimed directly at providing readjustment counseling for Vietnam veterans, as well as alcohol and drug rehabilitation. Unfortunately, the bill's timing could not have been worse. It came before Congress in June 1971, at a point when Nixon was still reeling from the assaults on his Vietnam policy by John Kerry and the other veterans at Dewey Canyon III.

According to Vietnam veteran and historian Rusty Lindley, Dewey Canyon III had had a "profound effect on the Nixon White House and its policies toward Vietnam veterans. Nixon and White House hatchet man Charles Colson became obsessed with the VVAW and its impact on public opinion. The White House launched a concerted effort to discredit not only VVAW, but also the problems the war was creating among returning soldiers. Their position was that 'the Vietnam veteran was too busy in school or on the job to have any read-justment problems'. . . . The Nixon administration was adamantly opposed to the provision of any assistance that would indicate that the war was adversely affecting veterans."[99]

Nixon's personal opposition helped kill Cranston's bill for an "outreach pro-gram" to promote the readjustment of Vietnam veterans. Once it had been shot down, the outreach bill acquired a loser's stigma that was hard to shake. For the remainder of the decade, the bill would be reintroduced every year, passing the Senate five times, only to be defeated again and again in the House. But Cranston's bill would at least give the PTSD community of veterans and ther-apists a focus for their lobbying in Washington. Shatan, for one, remembers the dozens of hours he spent advocating its passage in congressional offices, and how hard it was to win over those on both sides, the staunch conservatives as well as the brashest critics of the war. As for the pro-war congressmen, "they listened very respectfully, they gave you all the time in the world," but, claims Shatan, "they didn't respond very much." Doves, like Oregon's Republican Senator Mark Hatfield, usually let their younger "Vietnam generation" aides lis-ten to Shatan's pitch, and occasionally, as in Hatfield's case, the young aides finally "swung him round" to the veterans' cause.

The introduction of readjustment bills in Congress also forced the VA to begin commissioning its own studies of the situation. The first such study was conducted in August 1971 by Louis Harris and Associates. Unfortunately, Harris's "Study of the Problems Facing Vietnam Era Veterans: Their Readjustment to Civilian Life" presented more paradoxes than answers, per-haps reflecting society's still raw confusion over the war. For example, 62 per-cent of Americans identified Vietnam veterans with "a war that went bad"; and almost half those interviewed believed Vietnam veterans were "suckers," hav-ing been led "to risk their lives in the wrong war in the wrong place at the wrong time"; while "overwhelmingly, veterans felt that family and friends were doing all they could to make them feel at home," even though 58 percent of the vets also agreed that "people at home just didn't understand" what they'd been through. While the pollsters could only play with numbers, the rap group shrinks and psychiatric professionals had a much clearer picture of the dimen-sions of the catastrophe because they had opened the door into the often hell-ish personal lives of many Vietnam veterans. One of the areas that Sarah Haley began to explore was the problems Vietnam veterans were having with their

wives and children. What she found was that many veterans were having difficulty with intimacy, or with a wife's pregnancy, or especially with the vulnerability of a newborn baby. In 1975, she authored a paper called "The Vietnam
Veteran and the Preschool Child," in which she talked about the powerful associations that could be triggered in a veteran by a baby's crying or by the sight
of a small child's spontaneous cruelty.

Much of Haley's insight had come from a veteran with two preschool sons.
One day this veteran had come home to find one of his little boys twirling their
kitten around by its hind leg, preparing to throw it against a wall. The veteran
had gone into a frenzy, hitting his child, and later spending all night shaking in
bed. In therapy, he told Haley that he felt his Vietnam experience had contaminated his child, that the child was on the verge of becoming a "murderer,"
which was how he sometimes viewed himself. Haley explained to him that it is
normal for very young children to act sadistically and to feel gleeful at their own
apparently "omnipotent" capacity to hurt or kill other creatures; that parents
need to intervene, but that such behavior "won't last very long in the real world.
It catches up with them soon enough."

What happens with soldiers in combat, Haley posited, is that they "have to
slide down the developmental ladder. They have to slide back to kill or be
killed." At that point, they begin to feel the same "rush" of heady omnipotence
that the "terrible two"-year-old feels when he torments the household pet. The
problem is that the two-year-old child is developmentally in the right place; the
soldier is not, since he has already learned a variety of moral and ethical behav-
iors that later tell him he has done bad things, things to hate himself for. As she
explained this to her veteran patient, it hit him like a bolt from the blue that he
and his GI comrades used to hold Viet Cong prisoners out the door of a helicopter by one foot—just as his son had held the cat—and if the prisoner didn't
give the desired information, they would just as gleefully let him go. He had
repressed that memory until that moment in therapy.

Haley concluded in her paper that to witness naked aggression anywhere—
even in their own children—couldn't help reminding veterans of the naked
aggression they had witnessed in Vietnam. As a result, Vietnam veteran fathers
needed a lot of reassurance that what their kids were going through was nor-
mative, and they needed to be shown how to avoid the trap of going to one of
two extremes: either withdrawing from their children completely to avoid such
painful feelings, or overcontrolling their children, demanding that they never
show any of the aggressive or destructive behavior which their fathers practiced
in Vietnam.

Haley's paper was published in the *Journal of Contemporary Psychotherapy*
in the spring of 1974, and soon thereafter she was interviewed for a story on
veterans by the *Boston Phoenix,* a progressive underground paper. The writer
went on to interview Chaim Shatan as well, and he told Shatan that he really

must meet "this lady from Boston." Having already read "When the Patient Reports Atrocities," Shatan immediately contacted Haley and invited her to be part of a symposium he was organizing at the next convention of the American Orthopsychiatric Association (AOA) in March 1975 in Washington, D.C. Called "War Babies," the symposium would examine the effect of trauma on children— ranging from children who were experiencing the terrorist violence in Northern Ireland to children who were simply forced to relocate unexpectedly, as, for example, if their house had burned down. Shatan would also discuss the children who were reared with absent fathers, specifically, fathers serving in the military during wartime, and how the anxiety and depression of the remaining parent, the mother, was communicated to the children and resurfaced in them as behavioral patterns in later life—a situation Haley knew firsthand, since her father had been gone for several years during World War II.

For Haley, meeting Shatan was like getting caught up in a whirlwind. He put her in touch with Leonard Neff at the Brentwood VA, and Neff immediately invited her to come to the next annual meeting of the American Psychiatric Association (APA), which was going to be held in Anaheim, California, in May 1975, two months after the AOA meeting. Neff was organizing an APA panel on Vietnam veterans that included Shatan and Peter Bourne, and he wanted her to read her new paper on Vietnam veterans and their children there. Neff's panel was only going to be a sideshow, however. The big bombshell at the APA's 1975 convention would be the preliminary discussions concerning the preparation of a new *Diagnostic and Statistical Manual, DSM III*, which, unbelievably, were not slated to touch upon Vietnam veterans at all.

Dr. Shatan, like most other psychiatrists, knew that the APA had recently formed a committee to consider the need for revisions in *DSM II*, but he had not paid much attention to the lack of stress disorder classifications in *DSM II* because for the first three years he had been preoccupied with the inadequacy of the *military* psychiatric manuals. But in 1974 he got a call from a public defender in Asbury Park, New Jersey, who was trying to plead a veteran innocent on charges of breaking and entering by using the grounds of war neurosis. The judge had thrown out his defense, citing the lack of any such category of illness in *DSM II*, and someone had recommended the P.D. call Dr. Shatan. Shatan immediately perused his copy of the manual and was aghast at how much it had omitted to say. Although Shatan had alluded to the inadequacy of *DSM II* as early as February 1971, when his first memo to professional colleagues had complained of its lack of anything like a "moral corruption" category, he had never before realized fully what a limb he had climbed out on. Now, like a lightbulb flashing on, he saw that there was absolutely no underpinning of authority for the work he and Lifton and the others were doing with veterans—a potentially disastrous situation, since the issue was sure to keep getting raised in legal cases, VA claims, and so forth.

Shatan told the Asbury Park public defender to call Dr. Robert Spitzer at the Psychiatric Institute in New York. Shatan felt sure that Spitzer, who was heading the APA's "task force" on *DSM III,* would have some good words to impart about the inclusion of combat stress reactions in the new manual. Instead, the P.D. called Shatan back and told him that, according to Spitzer, there would be nothing about war neurosis or gross stress reactions in *DSM III.* Profoundly disturbed, Shatan phoned Spitzer himself, and Spitzer confirmed that he did not want to see any kind of "post-combat reactions" included in the revision. Then Shatan, knowing that Spitzer had been a consultant to the committee that had produced *DSM II,* asked how it had come about that the whole section on combat stress reactions, based on the work of the Menningers, had been removed from the first *DSM.* Spitzer claimed he had no knowledge of that matter, but from his antagonism toward restoring that section, Shatan began to suspect that a secret agenda was already in place—a suspicion that would be greatly reinforced a few months later at the APA convention in Anaheim.[100]

While the doctors argued, history itself was conspiring to bring delayed stress into the open as an important psychological issue. In 1972, in the Buffalo Creek Valley of West Virginia, several mining communities had been wiped out by a flood caused by the collapse of three earthen dams owned by the local coal company. Two years after the disaster, more than 90 percent of all those exposed to the death and damage—even those who had not experienced the actual flood—were exhibiting "disabling psychiatric symptoms," everything from depression and anxiety to psychosomatic symptoms and even apparent psychosis. The ACLU helped the residents of Buffalo Creek bring a lawsuit against the coal company, which was settled out of court for $14 million. Thoroughly convinced that these people had suffered psychologically in a very grievous way, the judge was outraged that the psychiatric profession could not assist him with a useful diagnosis, that he, a nonmedical person, had to assign a phrase to cover their psychological damage because of the inadequacy of the "reactive" diagnoses ("anxiety reaction," "depressive reaction," etc.) officially available to him. The judge therefore took the occasion of ruling on the settlement to chastise the APA for not having any form of stress definitions in the *DSM II.*

The APA was of course embarrassed by the judicial censure and concomitant bad publicity it received from the Buffalo Creek disaster, and its position on stress was under attack from other directions too. The Nazi concentration camp survivors were demanding reparations for the decades of post-traumatic stress they had endured; and survivors of other civilian disasters—earthquake and tornado victims, for example—were testifying to similar long-term patterns of behavioral change and life disruption. So the APA announced that it would hold a special daylong symposium at its 1975 convention in Anaheim to allow the psychiatric team from Cincinnati that had evaluated the Buffalo Creek survivors to present their findings.

Chaim Shatan meanwhile lost no time in organizing a Vietnam Veterans' Working Group (VVWG) to assemble data on delayed stress that could be submitted to the APA convention. The Working Group brought together the most progressive people treating stress disorders in Vietnam veterans from around the country—forty-five professionals from New York, Massachusetts, Michigan, California, and elsewhere. With Jack Smith as his research assistant, Shatan prepared an analysis of the differences between *DSM I* and *DSM II;* and the Working Group sent out this analysis, followed by regular updates on their research, to possible funding sources. Small grants from the American Orthopsychiatric Association (AOA) and the Presbyterian Church helped them early on.

In May, the post-traumatic stress advocates descended eagerly on Anaheim, but it did not take long for them to realize that they were entering "very surreal" territory; and most of them would come away having had, as Sarah Haley described it, "the most demoralizing experience of my life."

The symposium on Buffalo Creek was promising, and so were the words of APA president Leo Rangell, who stood up afterward to announce the imminent launch of *DSM III.* "I guarantee you," Sarah Haley remembered him saying, "there will be a stress disorder diagnosis [included in the new volume]." There was only a bit of qualmish curiosity among Haley and her friends, wondering why Rangell had referred to the concentration camp and civilian disaster survivors but had not mentioned anything about veterans, combat, or Vietnam.

Shatan recalled that most of the shrinks were far more interested in getting their picture taken with Minnie Mouse and Pluto than in talking about veterans; and it was only by accident, at a party thrown by Dr. Robert Spitzer to celebrate the commencement of work on *DSM III,* that Shatan learned that Spitzer himself was involved in the committee that would be working on a stress definition. When Shatan expressed his surprise, having just recently heard Spitzer voice opposition to putting in a stress definition (at least one related to combat), Spitzer laughed, "Oh yeah, I'm the Czar of Nosology," as if it were the latest in-joke. Shatan, however, seeing how ominous the situation looked for delayed-stress advocates, immediately asked for a meeting between his own Vietnam Veterans' Working Group and the stress-definition committee.

For the remainder of her life, long after *DSM III* had taken its place on every therapist's desk, Sarah Haley could still get herself "into a very bad funk" thinking about that meeting. She recalled: "The meeting took place in a conference room at the Disneyland Hotel. We were all sitting around a big table, and there were Mickey Mouse rides swinging around right outside the window. What we didn't understand was that other people had asked to have a hearing, if you will, to put forth their thoughts about Vietnam veterans and a stress disorder diagnosis. So what happened in this meeting was that Hy and myself and others presented our stuff, and these other people, the most notable of whom was a psychologist named Lee Robbins from the Midwest, presented theirs. Lee Robbins had done a study of returned Vietnam veterans and the incidence of drug abuse, and essentially said, 'These guys are all character disorders. They came from rotten backgrounds. They were going to be malcontents and dysfunctional anyway. Vietnam just probably made them worse, but Vietnam is not the cause of their problems. They're alcoholics and drug addicts.' The government loved her. For years, whenever they wanted to make a point, they would call her in."

Robert Spitzer was clearly on Lee Robbins' side. He reportedly told Shatan's group of delayed-stress advocates: "You don't have any evidence. You don't have any figures. You don't have any research." Haley recalls that "Spitzer and I started out hating each other and seeing each other as the enemy." Haley was even more upset by the implication Spitzer seemed to be making that if they included combat as the cause of a particular stress disorder, then everyone who had been in combat would claim to be disordered and the government would go broke trying to take care of them. According to Haley, Spitzer tried to sell them on the idea of keeping the status quo: "If you have long-standing problems about some combat you were in, let's look underneath for the real reason why—your early childhood neurosis."

Robbins had in fact conceded that there was more depression in Vietnam veterans than in college students their age, but she even used that fact to push the anticombat viewpoint. Since the received thought was that depression doesn't usually occur in people unless they've already been predisposed to it, Robbins reasoned that troubled Vietnam veterans must have gone to war with a predisposition to depression. The task force shrinks were also pushing the idea of normal stages of development—such as infancy, childhood, adolescence, and adulthood—and the theory that each time one passed to a new stage there were normal "adjustment reactions." Thus, in their view, combat was a normal fact of adulthood, and it was to be expected that some veterans might have more difficulty than others in making the transition to war from civilian life, just as some people had more trouble adjusting to parenthood and other adult responsibilities. If your transition was difficult enough, you then developed an "adjustment disorder."

Shatan perceived the task force's hidden agenda when he learned that *DSM III* was really being done under the influence of the Department of Psychiatry of Washington University in St. Louis, several of whose professors had been mentors of Bob Spitzer. Those professors were all very biologically oriented. "Biologically oriented," Shatan explains, "means that they were reluctant to accept the idea that social, psychological, political, and economic factors could have an influence on psychiatric symptoms in people." According to Shatan, the "St. Louis group" felt that Vietnam veterans, just like any other psychiatric patients they treated, were suffering from "medical disorders."[101]

Shatan, Smith, Haley, and their confreres were not deterred, and kept push-ing till Spitzer at least granted them a fair hearing. Among the concessions Spitzer made was to allow certain members of the Vietnam Veterans' Working Group to join the Reactive Disorders Subcommittee of the *DSM III* task force; and even those who were not placed on the subcommittee formally, such as Sarah Haley, were allowed to attend its meetings as "informal members." Spitzer also agreed to let them present a panel on Vietnam veteran research at every annual meeting of the APA for the next five years—until the new *Diagnostic and Statistical Manual* officially went into effect, as planned, in 1980. At the same time, however, he stacked the cards against them by appoint-ing a psychiatrist named Nancy Andreasen from the University of Iowa as head of the subcommittee dealing with stress disorders. Andreasen worked mostly with burn victims, especially children, and her initial reaction seemed to be totally against those who were investing their time in research with Vietnam veterans. Moreover, her traditional psychiatric outlook appeared so rigid that some members of Shatan's working group thought of her as "the Ice Princess."

For the next several months, the Vietnam Veterans' Working Group went into high gear, sending out questionnaires and compiling records and tables on 724 veterans. Sarah Haley, lacking training in statistics, tried a very simple tac-tic at the Boston VA outpatient clinic: she would stay at the VA after it was closed for the day, going through every folder of every Vietnam veteran that had been seen in the clinic for the past year. She focused on those vets who had been in-country, and among these she tried to isolate veterans who had actu-ally seen combat. She then went over the log sheets to compile a list of all the diagnoses that had been assigned Vietnam combat veterans. What she discov-ered was astounding. Ninety percent of the combat vets had been stuffed into an official, APA-sanctioned category such as "depressive reaction," "anxiety reaction," or some other reactive diagnosis. But following the official diagnosis, the VA psychiatrists would add their own working diagnosis in parentheses, and what they almost always wrote in the parentheses was "TWN"—an abbrevia-tion for the old World War II term of "traumatic war neurosis." Only a small handful of these vets had actually developed a major psychiatric disorder such as manic-depression or schizophrenia. "But mostly they were not psychotic," Haley explains. "They were just hurting."

In March 1976, Haley and other members of the Vietnam Veterans' Working Group presented their findings to the American Orthopsychiatric Association's convention in Atlanta, Georgia. Nancy Andreasen was in the audience, to rep-resent the hierarchy of the *DSM III* task force and to play devil's advocate. Her official role was to hear and evaluate whether the delayed-stress advocates had made a successful case for combat as a cause of illness. But Haley and others got the distinct feeling that Andreasen wanted to say, "There, there. Just go away quietly."

In fact, Andreasen turned out to be a good deal more vocal in refuting the conclusions of Shatan's group. Far from an intellectual slouch, Andreasen "bombarded them with methodology," Haley recalled, scarcely concealing her hostility as she made them all look like a bunch of inept fools. Haley claims she and her friends "went away from that meeting feeling really depressed." It seemed a strong possibility that the APA would reinstitute a stress diagnosis without including combat as one of the stressors—a Pyrrhic victory that would be nothing to celebrate, that would for all practical purposes put them back to exactly where they had started, with no useful diagnosis for their thousands of Vietnam veteran patients.

Even were the Reactive Disorders Subcommittee to restore the definition of gross stress reaction from *DSM I*, it would hardly be a help to those working with veterans, because gross stress reaction as it applied to soldiers was little short of damning. In *DSM II*, gross stress reaction had been transmuted to "adjustment reaction," and the one example relevant to the military had been of a soldier who panics, throws down his rifle, and runs trembling from the battlefield. The implication was that people who displayed any sort of stress reactions during combat were defective and unmanly, weaklings who failed to pass adulthood's sternest test: "the demands of war." "As a consequence," explains Jack Smith, "those men who did not recover quickly and had persistent reactions were suspected of and scrutinized for predisposing factors. . . . These persistent reactions were clearly . . . an automatic indication of underlying personality disorder." Embedded even in *DSM I*, according to Smith, was the assertion that "healthy individuals snap back or recover quickly."

Two months later, when Sarah Haley arrived at the APA's 1976 convention in Miami, she heard a voice behind her calling, "Sarah, wait up!" It was Nancy Andreasen. The unbelievable had happened. Andreasen had begun to observe delayed-stress symptoms in the burn victims she was treating, and the symptoms of her burn victims greatly resembled the problems she had been hearing of in Vietnam veterans. Though still not completely won over, a turning point had been reached in her thought, and enough of Andreasen's "ice" had begun to melt so that she and Sarah actually became friends; in effect, she soon became the Working Group's secret advocate on the Reactive Disorders Subcommittee. She confessed that she was now leaning toward including combat as a stressor, and she encouraged Haley and her group to keep strengthening their case.

Andreasen's goodwill made it possible for the Vietnam Veterans' Working Group to present a whole series of detailed tables as well as a major paper at the 1977 APA convention in Toronto. That convention was the true turning point for delayed stress's reentry into American psychiatric practice. After the Working Group's presentation, Spitzer called for a powwow of the Reactive Disorders Subcommittee, with Shatan, Lifton, Jack Smith, Nancy Andreasen, and a pioneering family therapist from Syracuse named Lymon C. Wynne, who had recently begun to be swayed by Shatan's and Smith's logic. No longer able to stem the tide, Spitzer agreed that a stress definition including combat factors would be put into *DSM III*, and he charged Andreasen with writing the definition. But Spitzer made it clear that they were not going to call it "post-combat stress" or "post-catastrophe stress"; it would be known as "post-traumatic stress disorder."

What occurred next was on the order of a major miracle. Andreasen, rather than writing the definition herself, invited Shatan, Smith, Haley, and the other leading combat stress agitators to write whole sections for her, and agreed merely to "edit" their work. Shatan recalls that they were "practically dictating" the new definition of post-traumatic stress disorder into the *DSM III*. A little over a year earlier, the delayed-stress advocates had been fighting for their professional life; now, in one coup, the challengers had stormed the fortress and turned the guns around. At least for the moment, they had triumphed. Combat became the paradigm for the whole category of post-traumatic stress.

Spitzer, understandably, was not pleased with the result. What Shatan called the St. Louis group fought very hard to include preexisting disorders as a factor in some cases of post-traumatic stress (i.e., war made some people sick because they were disturbed before they even got there); they fought equally hard to keep out the notion of delayed stress, which posited that a vet could return home seemingly well adjusted and then manifest war-caused behavioral problems months or years later. Spitzer's group won on preexisting conditions; Shatan's group won on delayed stress, which became part of the *DSM III* definition of PTSD. But the subtle change which made post-traumatic stress a "disorder" rather than a "reaction" was also a loss, as far as Shatan was concerned, because *reaction* would at least imply that soldiers were *reacting* to what had happened to them in combat; whereas *disorder* sounded like something one was born with, with the implication that the sufferers were defective since birth. Moreover, according to Shatan, the official definition was significantly "depoliticized" before it went into the manual.

The original definition that Shatan's group wrote included references to Vietnam as an unpopular war, and also talked about Korean War veterans and World War II veterans who did not break down until decades later—material that was expunged from the preliminary draft, which was published in 1978. Nevertheless, publication of that initial draft was a victory of proportions that could not even have been imagined when the rap groups were first organized. A few of the places where veterans were seen, including the Boston VA hospital, began implementing the new diagnosis and the proposed treatment almost immediately. That initial draft also spurred psychiatric professionals across the country to radically change the way they dealt with Vietnam veteran patients, and it led to a host of further innovations in treatment. And its political impact was immense. The fact that combat stress was once again officially recognized by the APA enabled those lobbying for the passage of Senator Cranston's outreach bill to gain a majority in both houses of Congress in less than two years. It had everything in the world to do with the passage in 1979 (a few months before the definition became official) of the bill that funded the first readjustment program for Vietnam veterans: the Vet Centers.

But in a very real sense the battle was just starting, and those who were most deeply involved in the treatment of Vietnam veteran stress problems began to gird themselves for the long haul. As Chaim Shatan recalls: "We were happier with the new definition than with what had preceded it. It made a lot of things possible that weren't possible before. We weren't happy with the way it was watered down; and we weren't happy with the fact that as soon as it went in, a movement to revise it began immediately."[102]

5

Trampling on the Bill of Rights:
The Gainesville Conspiracy

1. Winning Battles and Losing the War:
From Operation Heart of America to Operation Peace on Earth

In some sense, the Vietnam veterans had won their victories at home too quickly. By late spring 1971, riding the crest of international media attention both from Dewey Canyon III and from the success of the initial rap groups, and with VVAW's ranks swelling (at least on paper) to 25,000, the radical veteran leaders realized they had a tiger by the tail. The tiger was a grass-roots political movement that seemingly had the power to affect the American government's world-policy decisions, as well as momentous domestic issues, everything from unemployment and medical care to the very root evils of racism, poverty, and the alienation of the disenfranchised and down-and-out. Suddenly there were unexpectedly urgent questions in the minds of these veteran leaders—questions they hadn't expected to encounter after leaving the regimented world of military ranks, casting off all that "Mickey Mouse" hierarchy with one big hawk of disgust. The questions, now glaringly obvious, were: who was going to ride this tiger and point its direction? And, even more disturbing, what was the tiger's final destination going to be? Hopefully neither a public zoo nor a private museum—where, rendered harmless as a quaint artifact of late sixties–early seventies history, it would pose not the least threat to a room full of kindergartners come to view its once fierce silhouette.

As the political repercussions of Dewey Canyon and the ensuing tumult of the May Day demonstrations ushered America into the unquiet summer of 1971, a few of the more perceptive veteran leaders saw something even more startling: that the whole veterans' movement was there for the taking; and that just a few people, by calling themselves leaders, might end up representing the entire community of Vietnam veterans. What was more, the farthest-sighted amongst them realized that what hung in the balance was not just the fate of those several million men and women touched by the fire of our most recent foreign policy debacle—vets who ranged from the bearded, grungy, and disgruntled grunts of Dewey Canyon III to the decorated officers bucking for their chance to climb the command ladder, the Oliver Norths and Bud McFarlanes and Colin Powells and Norman Schwartzkopfs who came to prominence in the next several decades. What hung there, big and bright as a golden piñata, but somehow still invisible to most, was the future role of the soldier in contemporary society.

In the summer of 1971, however, no one had the leisure for thinking much about possible prizes. The big change—the end of the war—had not yet arrived, but even the fiercest hawks had to see that the wind was shifting. Following the publication of the Pentagon Papers in early June, a Gallup Poll showed that 61 percent of the American public favored complete withdrawal from Vietnam. And finally, on June 22, the antiwar movement won its first major congressional victory when the Senate passed the Mansfield Resolution, nonbinding but still as jolting as a left hook to Nixon's jaw, calling for termination "at the earliest possible date" of American participation in the Vietnam War.

In St. Louis in July, two months after Dewey Canyon III, VVAW held its most turbulent national meeting to date. Many remember it as the meeting where John Kerry and Al Hubbard went head to head. Kerry made a long speech punctuated at frequent intervals by the demand: "Who is Al Hubbard?" Voicing his opposition to Hubbard's various political and social agendas, Kerry even challenged Hubbard to prove he was a Vietnam veteran. Feeling supplanted, and weakened politically by the impending resignation of arch supporter Mike Oliver (who was about to leave for California as a field organizer), Hubbard "freaked out," screaming insults at Kerry from the opposite end of the hall. Each time Kerry would denounce his authenticity, Hubbard would bounce up out of his chair, holding his back and grimacing, as if in great pain, and at one point he even pulled up his shirt to exhibit his scar.

For a minute it seemed as if Hubbard might have to be restrained to keep from coming to blows with Kerry, but then Kerry played his trump card: he resigned from the executive committee himself. Most of the other coordinators were flabbergasted, though many had seen it coming, suspecting that once John's political career had gotten in gear he would move on to bigger and better things. In Oliver's words, Kerry "came, he saw, he conquered, and he split!" Kerry's resignation made room for Hubbard to stay on as a national coordinator; but Al's credibility was by now so badly damaged that he could no longer provide the strong leadership the organization needed in this pivotal time. Moreover, Hubbard suffered an attack of stomach ulcers shortly after the meeting.[103]

The fight between Kerry and Hubbard demoralized the whole organization. Oliver recalls that "things got rocky" in the national office from that time onward. Many of the brightest guiding lights, like Scott Moore, felt disappointed that Hubbard had lied to them; and others felt disappointed by Kerry's untimely exit. One of the results of this infighting, and the subsequent removal of those two strong personalities from leadership, was that the power of the executive committee became diluted as the coordinators from the twenty-four regions sought more participation in planning the organization's activities. A whole new dialectic entered the organization, which had nothing to do with ending the war per se, but had to do instead with whether they would build a "mass space" for VVAW and turn out 100,000 vets for the next big Washington demo—as national coordinator Skip Roberts envisioned—and implement a broad-based, responsible power structure; or whether they would push the hard line of an armed revolutionary movement—which was the goal that Hubbard, Joe Urgo, and some of the other intransigent radicals were now insisting on.

Labor Day—which had been Skip Roberts' target date for a second, far more massive Dewey Canyon event—came and went with nary a veteran protester showing up in Washington. Many of VVAW's regional leaders had argued that future Dewey Canyons would simply happen spontaneously when vets felt the need. In September 1971, the prison riot at Attica filled the news; and for four days the nation watched mesmerized as hundreds of armed prisoners held forty guards hostage, demanding everything from more humane treatment to wholly unrealistic, adrenaline-pumped fantasies such as "safe transportation out of confinement, to a non-imperialistic country." The whole drama exploded in one bloody Shakespearean death scene when Governor Rockefeller ordered the New York State Police to move in and terminate the rebellion in a massive display of firepower—leaving 29 inmates and 10 hostages shot to death by government bullets. Radicals of every persuasion had been watching Attica with riveted attention as a litmus test of what to expect from the government in the coming decade. In Roberts' view, Attica pushed VVAW further into the camp of those who wanted to turn it into an underground organization, a collection of "revolutionary cells." Roberts missed a lot of the national office arguments that summer because he had opted to travel cross-country with Jane Fonda and Donald Sutherland on their FTA tour of military bases. Returning to New York after one of his trips, Roberts discovered the notes of the last executive committee meeting dominated by a discussion of whether VVAW ought to adopt a policy of violence. Margaret, their Quaker bookkeeper, approached him, deeply troubled, because she felt they would no longer want a nonviolent person on their staff.

By the conclusion of the next national coordinators' meeting, in Kansas City, November 12–15, 1971, all such questions had become hypothetical, since the disintegration of the national office was virtually complete. "There was no one

V VAW activities in 1967–1968, presented in a photo collage by Sheldon Ramsdell. *Left to right, across top:* David Braum, Jan Barry Crumb, and Dan Weiss at a debate in Valley Stream, New York, on January 28, 1968; a crowd at an antiwar rally in Union Square, New York City, on Veterans Day, 1967; David Braum speaking at a Veterans Day rally, 1967. *Across middle:* Stephen Greene at the Union Square rally; Carl Rogers, David Susskind, and David Braum on Susskind's television show, October 22, 1967; *(below Susskind photo)* Senator Ernest Gruening, one of the first congressional doves, with Carl Rogers; Francis Rocks and Stephen Greene at Union Square. *Across bottom:* Jan Barry Crumb speaking at the debate in Valley Stream; students at the debate; Carl Rogers seeking endorsement of V VAW positions from the Reverend Martin Luther King Jr. *Photos by Sheldon Ramsdell.*

Vietnam veterans march in the April 15, 1967, Fifth Avenue Peace Parade to the United Nations building. This is the banner that launched VVAW. *Photo by Ted Reich, courtesy of Jan Barry.*

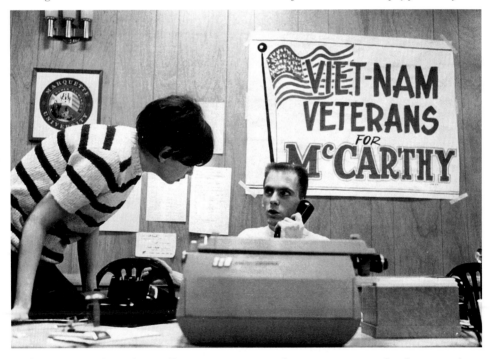

Carl Rogers consults with a staffer in Eugene McCarthy's Wisconsin state headquarters about recruiting Vietnam veterans to support the senator's presidential campaign, Madison, Wisconsin, spring 1968. *Photo by Sheldon Ramsdell.*

Al Hubbard talks with the press at the Winter Soldier Investigation in Detroit, January 1971. *Photo courtesy of the VVAW Archive.*

The Ohio contingent of VVAW formed the lead platoon in Operation RAW, the 86-mile march from Morristown, New Jersey, to Valley Forge, Pennsylvania. Infantry platoon leader (both on the protest march and in Vietnam) Bill Crandell, squatting at far right, stated that one member of the platoon later revealed himself as an undercover agent for Army intelligence. *Photo by Mary Webster.*

In the last ten years, over 335,000 of our buddies have been killed or wounded in Vietnam. And more are being killed and wounded every day. We don't think it's worth it.

We are veterans of the Vietnam War. We have fought and bled from the swamps and hills of Vietnam to the plains of Cambodia. We have seen our buddies die there. And we can no longer remain silent.

We have seen the Vietnam War for ourselves. And from what we have seen, we believe that it is wrong, unjustifiable and contrary to the principle of self-determination on which our nation was founded.

We believe that the Vietnam War is a civil war—a war in which the United States has no right or obligation to intervene. We believe that the Saigon Government must stand or fall on its own. And we have seen the type of government it really is. A military dictatorship in which there are no free elections and some 40,000 people are held as political prisoners. We don't think that is the kind of government worth fighting for.

We have seen what the war is doing to Vietnam. The country is being physically destroyed by bombing, defoliation, and the killing of its civilian population. (Civilians in Vietnam are being killed and wounded at the rate of 200,000 a year, 60% of them children. And 80% of them as a result of American firepower.) And we don't think that that's worth it.

We have seen what the war is doing to our own country. We are being torn apart. Our young people are being alienated. Our most pressing domestic problems are being neglected for lack of funds while the war which has already cost us $130 billion goes on at $800 a second...$48,000 a minute...$2,880,000 an hour. Meanwhile the value of our dollar is being destroyed by inflation. And we don't think that that's worth it.

We have seen what the war is doing to our buddies and their families. Over 43,000 have already been killed and another 292,000 wounded—many of us maimed for the rest of our lives. And more are being killed and wounded every day. And we don't think that that's worth it.

We believe that the basic problems of Vietnam are not military but social, economic, and political. We believe that there is no military solution to the war. We believe that, in any case, we cannot win a land war in Asia. And we believe that in this nuclear age our national security does not require us to win it.

Therefore, we believe that the best way to support our buddies in Vietnam is to ask that they be brought home, now, before anyone else dies in a war that the American people do not understand, did not vote for, and do not want. And we think that that's worth fighting for.

If you're a Vietnam veteran and feel the same way we do we ask you to join us. If you're a concerned citizen we ask you to support us by filling out the coupon below. But we ask you to please do it now. The lives of a great many of our friends depend on it.

*Casualties as of November, 1970.

P

65

The VVAW ad, donated by Hugh Hefner and photographer Leonard Nones, which ran in *Playboy* in February 1971 and eventually brought more than 10,000 new members into the organization.

Two thousand active-duty GIs take part in the anti–Vietnam War "Armed Farces Day" march outside Fort Hood in Killeen Texas, on May 15, 1971. *Photo courtesy of Dave Cline.*

Marine combat veteran and VVAW ambassador Tom Zangrilli stands to address representatives of the Communist National Liberation Front in Paris, 1971. *Photo courtesy of the VVAW Archive.*

Joe Urgo, wearing a VVAW button, embraces his former enemy, now a guide at the War Museum in Hanoi, August 1971. *Photo by David McReynolds.*

Vietnam veteran Barry Romo (later national coordinator for VVAW) testifies at the local Winter Soldier investigation in Los Angeles, 1971, sponsored by KPFK-FM radio and the Pacifica Foundation. *Photo © Jeffrey Blankfort.*

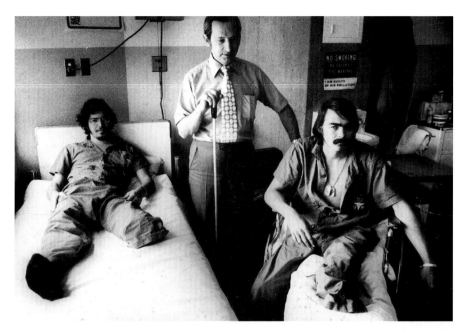

Many early leaders of the movement, like double-amputee Bill Wyman (*left*), came out of the overcrowded and poorly maintained VA hospitals of the late 1960s; he's shown here with Al Caracciolo (*center*) and John Diakoyani at the Manhattan VA, circa 1971. *Photo © Fred W. McDarrah.*

Senator Ted Kennedy and John Kerry discuss the Supreme Court injunction against Vietnam veterans sleeping on the Mall and whether the vets ought to risk violating it, Washington, D.C., April 21, 1971. *Photo by Sheldon Ramsdell.*

Marine captain Rusty Sachs (*light hair*) hugs First Air Cavalry crew chief Ron Ferrizzi at Dewey Canyon III. Both veterans had just finished dedicating the return of their medals to dead comrades. *Photo © Fred W. McDarrah.*

to keep feeding information to the 102 storefronts [individual chapters]," Roberts encapsulates the situation. "The bad guys won."

Between July and November 1971, VVAW staged a large number of actions, both local and global, but there was no overriding theme or direction. Yet the range of its activities and the forceful displays of its presence indicated an organization still alive and well. Moreover, despite Roberts' fears, every last action was completely peaceful, even if some were outrageously provocative. While an all-veteran trip was being planned to meet with North Vietnamese negotiators in Hanoi, Joe Urgo became the first Vietnam vet allowed into Hanoi on a three-person delegation cosponsored by the War Resisters League and the People's Coalition for Peace and Justice (PCPJ) in August. Urgo's first stop had been in Japan to attend the eighteenth international conference to end the use of nuclear weapons; he toured Hiroshima and Nagasaki, where he met with the North Vietnamese delegates, who encouraged him to return with them.

In Hanoi, Urgo was well received everywhere he went, which included meeting with youth groups and civilian survivors of a My Lai–type massacre and taking a tour of the War Museum, which focused on American "war crimes." At the end of the tour, Urgo and the tour guide spontaneously embraced—it turned out the man, only a few years older than Joe, was a veteran of the North Vietnamese Army. Two months earlier, a delegation of VVAW members, including Ken Campbell and Larry Rottmann, had taken part in the second International War Crimes Tribunal in Oslo, Norway; and on their way there and back had stopped in Moscow, where they had similarly met with former Vietnamese and Laotian enemies and made overtures of friendship.

Just as VVAW had already taken on longer-term veterans' concerns, such as bringing media attention to the inadequate care in VA hospitals, in mid-August the organization made a decisive turn toward involvement in pressing social causes quite outside the veteran realm. The action was termed, with wonderful double entendre, Operation Heart of America. Four caravans of trucks—from New York, California, Florida, and Kansas City—loaded with medical supplies, food, and clothing, and driven by Vietnam veterans, converged on St. Louis, joined up there to form a military-style convoy of about fifteen vehicles, and proceeded on to Cairo, Illinois. There, they came to the aid of a poor black community, which was under perpetual economic oppression and violent harassment from a deadly alliance of racist police, the local White Citizens Council, the Ku Klux Klan, paramilitary vigilante groups, and a viciously bigoted and well-armed citizenry. Al Hubbard was later to call the mission's successful conclusion one of VVAW's "two crowning moments."

"I did recognize early on that there was no way we could function in a vacuum and that we couldn't wear blinders," he recalls. "Cairo had to do with people and the dignity of your existence as a person. Social concerns like Cairo were part and parcel of the politics, the mind-set, and the atmosphere of the time. I saw what this country was doing in Vietnam was ridding itself of all of those things that they perceived to be drains on their ability to control and to prosper. Support poor people? 'Fuck that! Send 'em to war and let 'em be killed, and then we don't have to spend any money on welfare!' This is the kind of connections that I made with Cairo."[104]

The Kansas City VVAW, pushed by the concern of Randy Barnes, actually mustered several smaller convoys to Cairo over the next two years, some of which were shot at but still got through.

Coming into the November national coordinators' meeting in Kansas City, VVAW had certainly racked up some impressive accomplishments. Besides the relentless schedule of actions—which included surprise greetings to Nixon when he arrived to speak or fund-raise at places like New York's Waldorf-Astoria or the Conrad Hilton in Chicago, free "teach-in" concerts with the likes of Peter Yarrow (of Peter, Paul and Mary), Country Joe McDonald, and John Prine at Columbia University and Tompkins Square Park, lectures at colleges and universities nationwide, and gate-crashing a number of traditional Veterans Day parades—VVAW had managed to begin publishing its own newspaper, *First Casualty,* and (sparked by the literary interest of Jan Barry) to assemble poetry and fiction manuscripts by veterans, which would soon be published in a series of books by the First Casualty Press. In addition, VVAW had continued to extend its connection with other liberal activists and movements, powwow-ing with the Business Executives Move for Peace in Chicago, for example, and sponsoring support groups such as the Attica Brothers Defense Committee. Few members could therefore see that the organization was veering toward imminent disaster.

What happened in Kansas City at the national coordinators' convention in November was an avalanche of resignations. One of the most critical was that of Scott Moore. Besides wealthy and powerful connections, Moore had brought VVAW his nonpartisan level-headedness. He had just completed a month-long tour of chapters all over the country, and his report to the executive committee was heavily pessimistic. Future convoys like the one to Cairo, he warned, were "too much for the organization to handle." Coordinators in many areas felt that the focus on Cairo had deprived them of attention to their own problems. Many of these coordinators—especially those in very right-wing areas like Oklahoma and Alabama—were encountering enormous hostility and having a hard time just keeping their storefronts open. The effort to get a veteran drug clinic going had been stymied by lack of money and a likely location, and several promises of help had already fallen through. Other coordinators, such as Brian Adams in Denver, told Moore that their members were "apathetic and generally relate only to large actions"; without another Dewey Canyon–like event, Adams felt, they would soon vanish for good. Large numbers of vets were going back to school or trying to get their lives in gear with a good-paying career, and many were content to let Nixon wind down the war at his own pace, however slow.

"It is my feeling that VVAW is basically a paper organization with a few hard-core leaders who are keeping it alive," Moore concluded. "People don't know and generally don't really care what is happening."

Moore could offer only two possible solutions: go back to the doors of Congress, using mass civil disobedience if necessary to grab national attention; or else "bring together the hard-core leadership of VVAW to start a new party." But that he felt no real enthusiasm for the project of reorganizing VVAW slipped out in one of his final remarks, before tendering his resignation: "My personal politics are not in accord with the men and women I am supposedly representing."

In a memo written shortly after the Kansas City convention, Mike Oliver let the cat out of the bag: "Various political factions . . . are trying to make inroads within the VVAW. Just for your information they are . . . Progressive Labor Party [the Maoists, who would soon manifest in force in VVAW as members of Bob Avakian's Revolutionary Union], Socialist Workers Party (NPAC [National Peace Action Coalition, created by the SWP and some labor groups], YSA [Young Socialist Alliance], SMC [Student Mobilization Committee, heavily influenced by the Trotskyists], etc.), Republican Party, Democratic Party, and other dehumanizing organizations." Although Oliver doubtless included "Republican Party" and "Democratic Party" in his enumeration of pernicious forces so as not to trample on anyone's political toes, he was pointing out a real threat: the far-left organizations, especially the Socialists and Maoists, had begun waging serious battle for the hearts and minds of VVAW. Combat veterans meant credibility; and at this stage in the antiwar movement, the far left was hardly credible even to itself anymore.

By September 1971, the New York "staff meeting minutes" were filled, as Skip Roberts pointed out, with allusions to the revolutionary rhetoric of firebrands like the black French writer Frantz Fanon and martyred black prisoner George Jackson, a Communist-inspired organizer who had been shot to death by guards in San Quentin the previous month. Moreover, the executive committee, under the influence of secretary Joe Urgo, was issuing directives "to develop a reading list and have discussions among staff about what we read. . . . We have to understand Marx and Lenin and pull out the parts of their writings that are relevant and provide hope for mankind." Whereas under Moore's guidance VVAW had once sought donations from big business, the current New York State regional coordinator Ed Damato—who would soon come under Avakian's Revolutionary Union (RU) sway along with Urgo—was now issuing memos to his "brothers" to "confront these war profiteers." Damato was instrumental in planning what he saw as a moral crusade to "talk to the heads of corporations that profit from the war. We will ask them why they support a war that has given them profit at the expense of the Vietnamese and the millions of Americans who served there. Sperry Rand, AMF, Pan Am, General Motors . . ." Significantly, Damato noted that his corporate confrontations to date had been "attended by a minority of the membership."[105]

Skip Roberts was acting from a similar perception—that VVAW was rapidly narrowing rather than building its constituency—when he fought to dump Al Hubbard from the executive committee at the Kansas City convention in November 1971. Realizing that Hubbard still had too large a following to get him expelled or force him to resign, Roberts conceived a plan to "take Hubbard out" along with himself by calling for the resignation of all the old officers. Roberts had pretty much burned out on veteran organizing, figuring that they had lost the battle anyway, and he was ready to move on to more conventional labor union work. His motion to replace all of VVAW's former officers lost by two votes. He resigned from the executive board anyway, and watched grimly as a new coalition swung into power. It consisted, he recalls, of "government agents, liberals who could be guilt-tripped, and our authentic crazies."

Roberts' loss was no victory for Hubbard either. Although he remained on the executive board, Al's moment in the sun had passed; the organization's creative energy began to bubble from new and wilder sources, whether government agents, "authentic crazies," or committed revolutionists—and sometimes it was hard to tell those three categories apart; sometimes, it seemed, they might even unite in the same person. In any case, though Hubbard's lean jaw, knowing eyes, and proud afro would be seen at VVAW demos for the next couple of years, he was like an enfeebled, white-haired statesman trotted out at party fund-raisers—a venerable fixture, but a leader no more.

The practical result of this energy shift was that large numbers of vets began to drop out of VVAW, or to remain only (as Moore foretold) as a paper membership. To put it quite simply, the mass of Vietnam veterans were not going to buy into violent revolution, or even violent self-defense. In December 1971, VVAW began a whole series of new actions to capture the public's attention— the most dramatic of which were takeovers of the Lincoln Memorial in Washington, D.C., the Betsy Ross House in Philadelphia, and the Statue of Liberty in New York Harbor—the latter two directed from a secret winter encampment at Valley Forge. But with a significance no one really understood till much later, they were all undertaken at the local level. The die had been cast in Kansas City in November, when another major Washington, D.C., action had been definitively ruled out, and the delegates had voted to limit the powers of the national office, decreeing that no new national actions could be initiated without first winning a two-thirds vote of support from the regional coordinators. In effect, they had handed over the power to formulate actions to twenty-four different boards—turning the national office into hardly more than spectators at a series of regional football games, each one played by different rules.

The Statue of Liberty takeover on December 26, dubbed Operation Peace on Earth, made it onto the front page of newspapers around the world, including the *Stars and Stripes*, the military's own paper, thus reaching the very troops in Vietnam whose lives VVAW wanted to save. The Statue of Liberty takeover, in Al Hubbard's eyes, was VVAW's other "crowning moment"—preserved for history in photographs of an upside-down American flag hanging from Liberty's face like a red-white-and-blue teardrop. But even with the dozens of other nationwide actions VVAW staged that Christmas week, very little change was actually effected. Some vets declared their own victory, having proved, in the words of one of the Lincoln Memorial arrestees, John Kyper, that "patriotism is not solely the property of the powerful." But the problem, as always, was that the message received depended on who was hearing it.

The tough thing for a lot of VVAW people to accept was that there were plenty of other Americans who did not agree with anything they said, who felt, in fact, that they were "selling out to the Communists." Hardest of all was to realize—but realize it they did—that even a lot of their fellow Vietnam vets felt this way. "Exhausted and somewhat dispirited," according to John Kyper, the guys at Valley Forge broke camp on December 30, a day earlier than planned. Beside the general exasperations and hurt feelings that always occurred when such strong-willed, proud, impassioned, opinionated, and distrustful people tried to work together, there were the latest casualty figures to deal with. The count for 1971 was another 1,381 Americans killed, and 8,936 wounded, in action in Vietnam. 156,800 American military personnel remained there—in the killing zone.

No one was even keeping track of the Vietnamese.

And the peace talks were still stalled, as the United States had just rejected North Vietnamese negotiator Madame Binh's latest proposal. Although American troop withdrawals continued, Nixon had simply switched his military focus to the air war over North Vietnam. In a series of missions known as Operation Proud Deep Alpha, some 1,000 sorties were flown against North Vietnamese military targets from the 26th through the 30th of December—Nixon's first so-called "Christmas bombings."

None of them felt like celebrating the New Year. Anxious to get in one last protest on New Year's Eve, 100 vets rushed down to Times Square for a midnight "counter-rally" to try to confront their foolishly reveling fellow citizens with the stark facts of what was still going on in the world—most of them feeling, as New York VVAW leader Ed Damato put it, that the civilians who hadn't been to war all looked like a "bunch of clowns."[106]

Then, like everybody else, they waited for the ball to come down.

2. Caught Between the Maoists and the Police: The Winter Soldier Organization

Despite the apparent stasis, year by year things *were* changing, and nowhere so visibly as in the American military itself—once the nation's strongest bastion of conservatism. The year 1971 had seen the rise of large-scale mutinies among enlisted men. In October, almost the whole of Bravo Company, First Cav, at Firebase Pace on the Cambodian border, had refused to continue night patrols. Several senators and congressmen had called for an investigation, but the infantrymen refused to budge. There were also stunning denunciations and resignations from some of the highest brass.

Lt. Col. Anthony Herbert, prolifically decorated in both the Korean and Vietnam wars, had charged two of his superiors with covering up war crimes; and, after praising VVAW's Winter Soldier Investigation, was pressured by the Army to resign his commission. West Point graduate Major Joseph Westbrook, who had earned three Silver Stars in Vietnam, was so revolted by the conduct of the war that he claimed conscientious objector status as an exit from his second tour there. But the most shocking revelations came from a most unlikely renegade, Army Colonel David Hackworth. Hackworth, who would go on to become one of the most perspicacious critics of the American military, was originally denounced by the Army as "insubordinate and treacherous" for his appearance on ABC television's *Issues and Answers,* where he "disclosed the bankruptcy of American training and tactics and the incapacity of the [South] Vietnamese Army, identified the lies and some of the liars who kept it afloat, and all but declared the war a lost cause, unwinnable." A full-bird colonel with a sack of medals (110, to be precise) and five years' service in Vietnam, Hackworth had once been called "the best battalion commander . . . in the United States Army" by no less than Creighton Abrams, four-star general and commander of MACV. After he had taped the interview for *Issues and Answers,* Hackworth felt he had no choice but to apply for retirement and continue his work to end the war "outside the institution." After the interview aired on June 27, 1971, General Abrams immediately put him under a rule of silence. Were he to have remained in the Army, he wrote in his memoir *About Face,* "no stone would go unturned in an effort to make my life as unpleasant as possible."

The problem, as journalist Richard Boyle wrote in his book *Flower of the Dragon,* was not that the military lacked eyes and ears and brains, but that the men in power in America were refusing to listen to the truth. This willful rejection of reason by a whole society had not been unknown in the twentieth century—how else explain the rise to power of a Hitler or a Stalin? A similar, if less extreme, national madness would provoke some of the more bizarre political twists in the United States in the early seventies. In 1972, the stone wall of denial erected by the politicians and policymakers would lead to a drastic change in leadership in VVAW, and to the emergence of two new leaders— Scott Camil and Barry Romo—both of whom were acting (in very different ways) from the best of intentions, and both of whom would help to preside over the eventual demise of the organization.

Scott Camil had begun to loom as a force within VVAW from the time of Winter Soldier, when his atrocity testimony managed to shake up a room full of people who already thought they had heard the worst that human could do to human. Like a lot of vets who had seen too big a share of blood and brutality, ex–Marine Sergeant Camil could be described as on fire most of his waking hours. He always moved and talked rapidly, as if a nearly limitless supply of energy were coiled just under his taut swarthy skin, pressing to burst free, and his dark-brown eyes burned with a menacing intensity. But there was an extra edge to Scott that made even other vets react to him in a stronger than average way—so that they might either love him or despise him right off. Most, though, would agree that he was "totally committed," and "a good person to have covering your backside."

To appreciate why Camil became a natural leader you almost had to see him in action. Although not classically handsome, he was over six feet tall with a strong, slim, wiry frame and a patriarch's bushy black beard; and his long, wavy black hair was bound back with a defiant leather headband. He had the kind of innate self-assurance—"a guy who could handle himself," as they say in American bars—that is as appealing to other men as it is sexy to most women. Moreover, though his formal education had been spotty at best, he was extremely articulate and had a born teacher's sense of how to use emphasis to get a point across. Mike Oliver, who remained one of Camil's strongest supporters when most of VVAW had turned its back on him, admitted that Camil "was a little too headstrong," and that he "wasn't very political—he didn't have a real understanding of why we were doing what we were doing." But Camil had the simple virtue of always knowing what he believed in; and once he got a goal in his sights, he would pursue it as single-mindedly as when he had killed VC in his role of "Camil the Assassin," as he was known in Vietnam. According to Oliver, from the time he joined VVAW Camil had one huge idea looming in his mind: "He was just against the war."

One could guess that at least some of Camil's fury came from a desire to make good on the load of bad karma that had been dumped on him through no fault of his own, merely through his desire to be a good American man, a Communist fighter—as he had been taught growing up with a tough cop for a stepfather in redneck Hialeah, Florida. When he got to Vietnam, he had found that his fellow Marines were being killed by "gooks" of all size, gender, and political persuasion, and so he had done his best to kill as many Vietnamese as he could—men, women, and children. It wasn't till he got back home and read the Pentagon Papers that he realized that what he had done was wrong—that he "had been tricked"—and that his conduct was not so distant from that of the good German boys of the thirties who had followed orders and exterminated Jews (whose blood he shared) because they had been told it would serve the ultimate good of their country.

Following his participation in Dewey Canyon III, Camil, made southern coordinator, had personally set up more than a dozen Florida, Georgia, and Alabama VVAW chapters and built them into a well-disciplined and cohesive organization. The southern group's strong showing in the Cairo convoy had only added to Camil's reputation, but it was in Kansas City in November 1971 that he left a truly indelible mark in every VVAW member's mind. Camil came to Kansas City with an armful of proposals—some of them amazingly apt and far-sighted.

Seeing that Nixon had turned the POW/MIA issue into "the single most explosive issue of the war," Camil proposed going directly to the POW/MIA families to gain their support in pressuring Nixon for total withdrawal. The existing leadership of VVAW, already sliding over to the Communist side, replied that the Democratic Republic of Vietnam (North Vietnamese) and the Provisional Revolutionary Government (Viet Cong) had more important concerns than American POW's; and besides, the POW/MIA families seemed far too right-wing to give ear to the wishes of VVAW. Camil had already received permission to organize an embassy of six veterans to Hanoi for the purpose of creating a liaison between the North and South Vietnamese governments, to expedite peace negotiations, and he came up with the additional plan of offering Hanoi the chance to trade one POW for three VVAW members, who would remain in Hanoi till the war ended. Unfortunately there were no volunteers to play hostage, other than Camil himself. Camil further expressed his concern that the trip be arranged as "an all-American project"—that they fly only on American-owned airlines, for instance, instead of taking the usual route on Aeroflot (the Russian airline) through Moscow. He sensed, rightfully, that many vets in VVAW were disgusted by the growing Communist affiliation—or even the appearance of such an affiliation—within the organization (just as John Kerry had lambasted Al Hubbard for going to Moscow to receive an award from the Russians). The VVAW leadership replied that "there are no scheduled U.S. passenger flights to Hanoi, only scheduled bombing runs." The proposal where Camil ran into the most resistance, however, was one that, at least on the surface, seemed eminently reasonable.

Camil proposed VVAW return in force to Washington, D.C., and there apply pressure in every conceivable way to the legislators who were still voting to fund the war. After the assembly of coordinators defeated the plan, he was told it was "a closed issue at this point." Camil replied that such a tactic was "never a closed issue." He then made known an even more radical proposal, which he intended to submit to the coordinators for their approval. If undertaken, he claimed, it would guarantee the end of congressional support for the war. It was this proposal that nearly blew the Kansas City convention wide open, and which branded Camil as both dangerous and crazy for the remainder of his time in the organization.

What Camil sketched was so explosive that the coordinators feared lest government agents even hear of it. So they decamped to a church on the outskirts of town, with the intention of debating the plan in complete privacy. When they got to the church, however, they found that the government was already on to them; their "debugging expert" uncovered microphones hidden all over the place. An instantaneous decision was made to move again—to Common Ground, a Mennonite hall used by homeless vets as a "crash pad," on 77th Terrace. This time a vote was taken to exclude anyone but regional coordinators and members of the national office. The rest of the members, even trusted leaders such as Randy Barnes and John Upton (who had earned their credibility in the mud and tears of Dewey Canyon III), were forced to wait outside on the grass, where messengers brought frequent word of what was going on inside. According to Barnes, everybody knew that the discussion in that hall "was grounds for criminal indictment of conspiracy."

Discussion was not exactly the word for it. John Upton recalls it being "a knock-down-drag-out [fight] at times." Randy Barnes remembers "people standing up on the tables yelling and screaming at one another." The proposal that fired so much anger was called the "Phoenix plan," in mockery of the U.S. government's similar program in Vietnam. There was, in fact, good evidence that the United States Studies and Observation Group (SOG)—known to those inside it as the Special Operations Group—had used its own Special Forces, those of South Vietnam, and even South Vietnamese mercenaries to murder various Communist and Communist-sympathizing village chiefs, political leaders, and other influential citizens in South Vietnam. Some say as many as 10,000 were assassinated, in order (theoretically) to rebuild a more democratic infrastructure in the south. Hence the name "Phoenix": a better, stronger Vietnam was supposed to rise from the ashes of the Communist-tainted one. Similarly, Camil now proposed the assassination of the most hard-core conservative members of Congress, as well as any other powerful, intractable opponents of the antiwar movement—the ones who would rather die than see America suffer a military defeat in Vietnam. Fine, let them die, suggested Camil—in fact, help them along in that direction—and once they were cleared out of the way, a truly democratic America could arise, one that would choose to be at peace with the rest of the world.

When the Phoenix plan first came before the steering committee meeting, John Upton had been standing almost next to Camil, and he recalls that "at first it was laughed off. Then he [Camil] became really irate, and some other people that were supporting that got really irate, and it got down to a really hard discussion about it. There was a time, I'm not kidding you, I was almost one of them. Especially when we moved over to 77th Terrace, a lot of people were convinced that *this was the way to do it.* I thought it was a novel idea, but it was not something I would support. I looked on it as doing just what we were fighting against. It was killing people for no [good] reason. I remember saying this, and somebody stood up and called me a 'moderate'! If I went an inch more crazier than I was, I could have endorsed it one hundred percent. Scott was pissed off just like I was. He was one of those people I really identified with— with the anger I saw there. My whole instinct here was, 'Let's demonstrate and do these things against the fucking war, to get the word out. Let's talk in high schools. But let's do things legal. Let's get the right permits.' The Phoenix plan was like, that's what needs to be done, but, God, we can't really do that."

The Phoenix plan, like the rest of Camil's proposals, was voted down in Kansas City, but its specter had only begun to haunt the organization; and, ironically enough, among those whose imaginations it enflamed were those very agents who had been charged with finding a way to destroy VVAW.[107]

It also immediately made Camil himself a government target, perhaps for the very sort of elimination he had envisioned for some of the diehard supporters of the war. On December 22, 1971, FBI Director J. Edgar Hoover sent a classified memo to the director of the Jacksonville office, dealing specifically with Camil. It read in part: "Information developed to date regarding subject [Camil] indicates clearly subject is extremely dangerous and unstable individual whose activities must be neutralized at earliest possible time." Several other memos that followed used that same word, *neutralize,* in an even less ambiguous context, such as: "Jacksonville continue to press vigorously to insure that all necessary action taken to completely neutralize subject without delay." As Camil later explained: "When you pin the government down, they'll say, 'Well, "neutralize" just means to render useless.' But if you talk to guys in the field, they say it means to kill."

When Camil returned to Florida from Kansas City, despite his failure to get any of his programs adopted, he took with him a goodly measure of respect from many coordinators and much of the membership. That seeming paradox made perfect sense to Randy Barnes: "There was a lot of resentment about the national office being 'movement-heavy.' We had people in the steering committee that belonged to Trotskyist organizations, Maoists, Leninists. . . . There was a lot of resentment from those of us out here in the field who were having demonstrations and doing the work." According to Barnes, these plain, apolitical, hardworking combat veterans were filled with a great idealism and a euphoria at having survived one of the bloodiest wars in history. Their attitude was: "We've done it! There's nothing we can't do." They were quite aware of the fact that with Dewey Canyon III they had almost single-handedly resurrected the dying peace movement. They felt certain they did not need—nor did they want the interference of—doctrinaire left-wing sects, not so different in their narrow-minded fanaticism from the anti-Communist flag wavers who had sent them off to the war in the first place. And here was Scott Camil telling them they could still get through this thing on their own, by virtue of the same inner strength that had brought them home alive from the killing fields of Vietnam. No politicians had helped them then, and they didn't need any goddamn politicians now—that was Camil's message. In their heart of hearts few veterans could disagree, and many of them were willing to cut Scott Camil plenty of slack for his guts to say it.[108]

•   •   ◉

Early 1972 was a dismal time both for the antiwar movement in general and for VVAW. The rivalry between the two main leadership groups, the Trotskyist-affiliated National Peace Action Coalition (NPAC) and the Communist Party–affiliated People's Coalition for Peace and Justice (PCPJ), had grown fiercer and ever more self-defeating, even as the number of protesters that either side could marshal dwindled to a few thousand, and sometimes only a few hundred, at any given demonstration. Though the government was winning few of its numerous trials against antiwar activists, it was breaking their morale and their bank accounts through months of costly and time-consuming legal defense. On April 5, Father Philip F. Berrigan, Sister Elizabeth McAlister, and the rest of the Harrisburg 7 won a mistrial in the Pennsylvania court where they were charged with conspiracy—in an alleged plot to kidnap Secretary of State Henry Kissinger, blow up generators in the heating tunnels under Congress, and vandalize draft boards. But in the process of fighting the government's bizarre (not to say fantastic) charges, the Catholic left—of which the Berrigan brothers, Philip and Daniel, were the most charismatic leaders—got caught in a crossfire of political agendas, which ended with former friends hating one another. The financial burden of the trial had been well over half a million dollars.

Though VVAW had not yet endured a legal war of that magnitude, the national office sent out a plea for contributions in late January, noting that the arrest of over 500 members in the past four months, and the frequent imposition of unreasonable bails and fines, had virtually emptied the organization's treasury. Then there was the cost of an endless succession of overseas trips, like Hubbard's trip to Hanoi with folksinger Pete Seeger, which donations from celebrities like Jane Fonda only partly defrayed.

On March 31, 1972, the North Vietnamese Army had come pouring across the DMZ to initiate a major offensive in the south, and Nixon had responded on April 6 by once again ordering massive airstrikes against North Vietnam; then, on April 15, he extended the bombing to include the cities of Haiphong and Hanoi. The North Vietnamese claimed that the Americans had begun to bomb civilian targets, including hospitals and their extensive network of dikes, which kept seawater out of thousands of rice farmers' fields. At Nuremberg, after World War II, similar actions by the Nazis against the dikes in Holland were deemed war crimes worthy of punishment by death.

This time around, VVAW, paralyzed by lack of money and effective leadership, let the rest of the antiwar movement take the lead in protesting the bombing of Hanoi and Haiphong. Only a few hours after the start of attacks on those cities, nearly a thousand peace people massed in Lafayette Park across from the White House (and hundreds were arrested), while so many Quakers assembled for a vigil outside the White House that the Quaker president inside was forced to order police to disperse them (without arrests). Two days later, the National Student Association called for a strike on its 515 affiliated campuses; the strike, scheduled for April 21, was endorsed by all eight Ivy League schools. But even before the campus strike, which would be nearly as widespread (if not quite as violent or long-lasting) as the one following the killings at Kent State almost two years earlier, the nation was rocked by large-scale, angry demonstrations coast to coast—from Harvard students taking over and setting fire to the Center for International Studies, to Columbia students blocking traffic on Broadway, to 1,500 demonstrators in San Francisco surrounding the Federal Building.

What finally pushed VVAW fully back into the fray was Nixon's decision on May 8, 1972, to mine all North Vietnamese ports and to bomb the North Vietnamese rail lines leading into China. These actions were seen by even those who had previously supported the war as unconscionably reckless and likely to ignite a global conflict, especially since ships of many nations, including the Soviet Union, unloaded their cargoes in Haiphong Harbor. According to triple–Purple Heart Vietnam veteran Danny Friedman, many vets in VVAW saw the mining of Haiphong Harbor as evidence that "the United States government had gone insane" and had therefore "lost its right to act" in international affairs. Now more than ever it seemed—especially to the activist New York–New Jersey crew—that the only solution was to get the United Nations to take the United States into custodianship until all U.S. forces could be withdrawn from Vietnam.

U.N. Secretary-General U Thant and the U.S. ambassador to the United Nations, George Bush, had both steadfastly ignored the petitions and requests for meetings that VVAW had been submitting since the previous December. Guerrilla-theater mania was still afoot in the organization, and so 300-plus-pound Danny Friedman, fellow gridiron heavyweight Brian Mattarese, and Al Hubbard talked a few other vets into creating an "assault team" that would scale the fence around the U.N., enter the side of the building, and make their way quickly to the roof, where they would chain themselves to the railing. Having underestimated the weight of the chains and locks, however, they barely made it over the fence, and were out of steam before they had run halfway up the steep ramp on the side of the building. A group of painters and groundskeepers tackled them and kept them cornered with their tools till the police arrived. The vets chained themselves to the nearest steel post, but the cops quickly cut them loose and gave them the bum's rush off the property.

The next day, Friedman was severely beaten by police when he attempted to aid fellow VVAW members who had taken over the U.N. chapel. Burning for a payback, he went to see VVAW's newest national coordinator, a soft-spoken, deceptively easygoing, six-foot-four vet from Louisiana named Pete Mahoney. Mahoney, originally from Brooklyn and a "compromise candidate" between North, South, East Coast, and West Coast factions at the most recent national steering committee meeting in Houston, had his own grudges to settle. As a nineteen-year-old Army second lieutenant, he had won both the Bronze Star and the Vietnamese Cross of Gallantry, but his quest to help the South Vietnamese preserve their independence had seemed "totally futile," and he ended up feeling as if he had participated in "a waste of resources and lives." His return to the United States had been even more bitter and disturbing. His first Veterans Day back from Vietnam, in the fall of 1971, Mahoney was arrested for trying to march in the New Orleans Veterans Day Parade. In fact, everyone in his Louisiana State University campus chapter of VVAW was arrested—a "welcome home" that had been ordered by no less than Congressman F. Edward Ebert, chairman of the House Armed Services Committee.

Someone had tipped off Mahoney that George Bush was scheduled to speak that evening at a United Nations Day dinner at the chichi Riverdale School in the Bronx. Not only had Bush refused to meet with VVAW, but as U.N. ambassador he had rejected all proposals that had to do with the rights of the Vietnamese people to reunify their own country. Friedman and Mahoney led a small group, including nonveteran VVAW nurse Anne Hirschman, down to the local blood bank to pick up some of the old blood that is routinely discarded each day. They then added a few quarts of water and red food coloring to bulk it up, and packaged it in lightweight plastic bags and balloons.

At the Riverdale School, Friedman, Mahoney, Hirschman, Mattarese, and another VVAW member mingled with the students and tried to remain inconspicuous until dinner was served. Then they burst in upon Bush and his tablemates, Danny demanding: "Will you talk to us?" Bush immediately called for security to arrest the motley VVAW gang, whereupon Friedman yelled, "Then the blood of the Vietnamese people be on your head!" Sending his blood bag in a well-executed spiral pass toward the wooden beam over Bush's head, Friedman managed to douse the future forty-first United States president with a little of the same fluid whose spilling had come to be deemed so inconsequential on Asian soil.

The five of them made a Mack Sennett–style escape with the entire Secret Service and local police contingents on their tail. As they drove off in their well-hidden getaway car, they exulted in the success of their mission, but within hours undercover agents and informants had fingered all of them for the FBI. In Peter Mahoney's FBI file, the incident would be mentioned as evidence that he was indeed "a dangerous man."[109]

Down in Gainesville, another VVAW leader was catching more FBI attention. Ironically, Scott Camil, now a student at the University of Florida, had begun leading student protests, even though he felt student protests usually made no dent at all in government policy. But Camil was desperate, because he felt Nixon was on the verge of co-opting their issues. In the first four months of 1972, Nixon had withdrawn another 70,000 troops from Vietnam, leaving only 65,000 Americans in-country, most of them Air Force personnel; he promised to get all troops out of the field by August. As for his stepped-up air war against North Vietnam, Laos, and Cambodia, he had assured the American public that these thousands of new bombing missions were merely "protective-reaction air strikes," intended to keep the enemy from harming Americans on their way out and to preclude further Communist aggression against South Vietnam. In addition, his highly praised and well-televised friendship missions to Peking in February, and to Moscow in May, had greatly enhanced his image as peacemaker—putting Jerry Rubin, Abbie Hoffman, their Youth International Party (Yippies), and the rest of the peace movement's media performers in a distant backseat. On May 14, 1972, the latest Harris poll showed that 59 percent of the American people felt their president was taking the proper actions to end the war and achieve "peace with honor."[110]

*   *   *

Pending before Congress were two new bills that would require the president to end all American involvement in Vietnam within thirty days. While Camil turned his energies to getting those bills passed, speaking out to the press and at numerous demonstrations, the VVAW coordinator in Colorado, Brian Adams, came up with a far more comprehensive plan for rechanneling veterans' activism. In the spring of 1972, Adams authored a proposal for the transformation of Vietnam Veterans Against the War into what he called the Winter Soldier Organization (WSO). It would be a year before VVAW officially became

VVAW-WSO, during which time Adams' initial idea would undergo numerous revisions and refinements. But the initial concept was already being kicked around in early 1972, and at its core was the creation of a nonexclusive mass organization that could go on working for social change long after the end of the Vietnam War.

On the surface there were many good reasons for opening the doors to anyone who, in Adams' words, "fully accept[ed] those basic principles defining the organization." Later he would add that members must also accept "a *minimum program* directed towards a common goal"—the goal being a more just and less violent United States. VVAW desperately needed money (read: membership dues), helping hands, and better turnouts at actions, and the number of returning veterans would soon drop drastically as Nixon completed his "Vietnamization" of the war. In this respect, the Winter Soldier Organization was not that different a development than the tack SDS cofounder and Chicago Seven conspiracy defendant Tom Hayden took when, with his future wife Jane Fonda and other civilian peace activists, he formed the Indochina Peace Campaign (IPC) that same spring.

The idea of the IPC, Hayden claimed, was "to go mainstream based on an analysis that the system had partially opened up, we had a much wider audience now, that now it was possible to pressure Congress." Rather than marginalizing themselves "by being anticountry, antiflag, antieverything," Hayden felt the time had come for the dissidents to build a grass-roots power base through old-fashioned "community organizing," that is, welcoming everybody to join and speaking a language that everyone understood. The difference— a big one—was that Hayden now spoke solely of working within the system, just as John Kerry had done from the start, whereas the incipient WSO was already veering toward "confronting the oppression" of any government where the haves still ruled over the have-nots. No small factor in this difference was the powerful pull being exerted on VVAW by the Maoist Revolutionary Union (RU).

This far-left radical group, formed in California in 1968 from splinters of both the Communist Party USA and SDS, had organized rapidly in many working-class pockets throughout the country. Wherever possible, the RU sent its veteran members to join VVAW, and some of these RU plants (most of them no doubt completely sincere in their antiwar stance) had already attained important leadership positions in VVAW. Often, too, existing VVAW leaders had simply been recruited into the RU because their enormous anger was pitched to a similar frequency as the RU's raging frenzy against the capitalist system. The danger was that every member of the RU was pledged to carry out the will of its monomaniacal chairman, former Berkeley activist Bob Avakian, and Avakian meant not only to confront the system of oppression but (if his fiery speeches and tracts were to be taken literally) to tear it down wholesale.

Adams would at some point join the RU himself, but in his early arguments aimed at expanding VVAW he stuck to more mundane concerns. He pointed out that the organization was already being run in large part through the grunt work of many women. Some were the veterans' "old ladies"; and others, like nurse Anne Hirschman, had come over to VVAW because it seemed a lot more genuine and full of warmth and good cheer than the rest of the peace movement. The organization had already voted to accept nonveteran women (and men) into its ranks in the fall of 1971, though there was still a debate as to whether they were full or only associate members. It was not fair, wrote Adams, to treat these women as "a VVAW women's auxiliary" any more than they should treat men without service discharges who joined their cause as "a VVAW nonveterans auxiliary." To remain an exclusive organization, opined Adams, would "glorify . . . the status of being a veteran"—just as the American Legion and the VFW already did—and thus play into the whole macho military myth that had led to wars like Vietnam and to generations of traumatized veterans like themselves.

In part the movement toward the Winter Soldier Organization had come straight from Hubbard's perception that there would be no end of Vietnam Wars so long as American society was riven by fundamental problems such as racism, poverty, and so forth; and according to Joe Urgo, the debate was still "hot and heavy" that spring in VVAW as to whether theirs was a narrow struggle of veterans against a wrongful, imperialist war or whether their mission was to "keep moving things forward, keep organizing" in the whole society. But Urgo also saw a greater, and to him more exciting, change taking place in the organization—a "deepening" in the sense of veterans beginning to get a political philosophy. It was inevitable, he felt, because the radical left was already forcing them to define their positions—did they support a North Vietnamese victory, for example, or did they merely want to see American troops out of the fighting? Because of the "muddled" thinking of the mainstream vets, the radicals were taking over. "Every time I turned around," Urgo recalls, "I had to deal with some kind of political question, so the choice kept getting put to me to 'figure this out.' How do you 'figure it out'? . . . You have to have a philosophy that supports the politics."

As the organization turned more and more to leftist radicals for such support, especially to the Maoist RU, the U.S. government saw VVAW as an ever greater threat to its national security, and thus began to step up its attacks on the organization. "They decided to go against our weaknesses," Urgo explains. He saw these weaknesses as "the individualism, the machoism, the lack of deep political understanding on a broader level among the guys on the bottom" that kept them from fighting back in more sophisticated ways against the government's lies and sophistry. Their "inability to struggle politically . . . allowed an open door for a lot of these police agents to come in and sound like they were saying the same thing as us." And so the RU came into the organization from one side, the police agents from the other, and together they formed a volatile mix that could not help but "confuse and demoralize" everyone, as Urgo says, and lead VVAW into its ultimate spiral toward destruction.[111]

3. The Government Indicts the Veterans' Movement

As summer 1972 approached, all factions of the peace movement, as well as the groups within VVAW, turned their eyes toward the national nominating conventions of the Republican and Democratic parties. There was no doubt whatsoever that the Republicans would renominate Richard Nixon, one of their most popular presidents since Abraham Lincoln, but the Democratic presidential primaries had been more of a horse race.

At first, the outstanding Democratic contender had been Senator Edmund Muskie of Maine, a big, ruggedly handsome, gravel-voiced liberal who had been pushing for complete withdrawal from Vietnam for the past two years, but Muskie fell quickly to one of the "dirty tricks" that had become the stock in trade of Tricky Dick (as both admirers and opponents had come to call him). During the New Hampshire primary, Nixon's henchmen—officially, operatives of CREEP, the Committee to Re-Elect the President—had planted stories in the press that Muskie was anti-"Canuck" (the derogatory name for French-Canadians, a major constituency in New England) and that his wife's intelligence was several notches below Jackie Kennedy's. Standing on the back of a flatbed truck outside the office of the *Manchester Union Leader*, Muskie had denounced such dishonest and vindictive journalism, but as he spoke tears came to his eyes. Rumors later circulated that some creep from CREEP had dosed him with a hallucinogen beforehand.

America was not yet ready to elect a "weeping" candidate. Overnight, Muskie's popularity among voters dropped sharply. Hubert Humphrey, forever a presidential hopeful, could not shed the taint of having served as LBJ's vice president during the time of the war's greatest escalation, nor did he help matters by always seeming to speak out of both sides of his mouth on every issue. With a few unseen boosts from the Republican Party, South Dakota Senator George McGovern quickly emerged as the Democratic front-runner. Nixon could not have been happier to have McGovern as his chief opponent, since he could portray McGovern as a loony radical, a loose cannon for sure, who consorted with the same anti-American, Communist-sympathizing "thugs and hoodlums" Nixon had been denouncing with so much success since he first ran for public office.

The Democratic National Convention was scheduled to take place in July in Miami Beach, but it was not expected to elicit any fiery antiwar protests, since even Yippie leaders such as Rubin and Hoffman had publicly endorsed McGovern (much to Nixon's delight). The Republican National Convention had originally been slated for San Diego, a bastion of Nixon's staunchly right-wing supporters, but Nixon's advisors soon saw the folly of this decision. California was also home to whole tribes of peace-loving hippie freaks and droves of young people whose only vocation seemed to be marching, chanting, and waving picket signs. Moreover, within the past couple of years, San Diego, with its huge Naval base, had witnessed some of the most stunning demonstrations and mobilizations of the GI movement. On one occasion, 10,000 service-age folk, many in uniform, staged an antiwar picnic in one of the city's parks. Sailors on several of the aircraft carriers stationed there—including the *Kitty Hawk,* the *Ticonderoga,* and the showpiece nuclear carrier *Enterprise*—had attempted to hinder them from sailing to Vietnam, often with threats of sabotage or mutiny.

Leaning that his security would be in jeopardy in San Diego, Nixon contemplated interning antiwar protesters in the sort of camps that had been used for the Japanese in World War II. An even more bizarre plan was concocted by Watergate burglar G. Gordon Liddy, whereby the leaders of the peace movement would be abducted and detained in Mexico until after the convention had ended. Finally coming back to reality, Nixon simply ordered his party to move the national convention to another conservative mecca, Miami Beach, home turf of Nixon's drinking buddy and confidant, real estate tycoon Bebe Rebozo. Nixon's shoo-in nomination and attendant ceremonies—what the Zippies, a new countercultural group, were calling his "coronation"—would take place there August 21–24, little more than a month after the Democrats left town.

VVAW planned to attend both conventions, but their presence at the Democratic Convention would consist of only a small group of lobbyists. To talk to McGovern's staff about ending the war would be preaching to the choir, but VVAW's national steering committee had decided that veterans could play a useful role in pushing various urgent domestic concerns on the Democratic Platform Committee. Taking up their new role as spokesmen for the poor and down-and-out, VVAW would try, and fail, to get the Democrats to adopt a guaranteed minimum income of $6,500 for every American family. Nevertheless, the convention as a whole was so sympathetic to them that on the final evening (July 13) the delegates passed a resolution condemning the Nixon administration for trying to "intimidate and discredit" VVAW.

The Republican National Convention was a different matter altogether. Although making Nixon listen to reason seemed a lost cause, many veterans felt they could impress the Republican delegates by the authority and sincerity of their presence—just as they had impressed at least some of the congressmen at Dewey Canyon III. The message they had for the Republicans was simple and clear: it was time to get their leader to accept the Provisional Revolutionary

Government's (Viet Cong's) seven-point peace proposal, for that alone was going to end a war that was critically dividing the American nation, not to mention bankrupting its most vital social programs. After gaining the Republicans' attention, the next move was for VVAW to lend its voice to a chorus of other national organizations with the same message, including the United Farm Workers, the National Welfare Rights League, the Southern Christian Leadership Conference, the National Tenants Organization, and the big peace coalitions.

For some odd reason, it seemed to be mostly the RU vets, the committed revolutionaries, who favored trying to sway the Republican delegates. Other vets, who were close to the burnout point in regard to political activism, agreed with the logic of Al Hubbard. Speaking through a bullhorn to a Miami crowd, Hubbard explained: "VVAW came to Miami *not* to try to influence the Republican Convention, because we know that scenario was written four years ago, and that there is no means of influencing them, but what we came here for was to expose it, and to ask a few basic questions of the American people." Barry Romo, the newest national coordinator now working out of Chicago (where the national office had moved), seemed to be walking a fine line between the groups. Romo defined VVAW's role at the GOP convention as "public opposition."

Either way, whether the intended audience was the Republican delegates or the whole nation, the vets knew they could take center stage as no other challenger or lobbying group could, and that was the major contribution they hoped to make in Miami. To this end, they devised a plan they were sure would jolt the nation: Phase 1, Operation Junction City II; followed by Phase II, Operation County Fair I. Together the two operations would come to be known informally to the vets who participated in them as "The Last Patrol."

Junction City II was a spinoff from the highly successful Cairo convoys. The VVAW leadership envisioned convoys of protesters leaving from San Francisco, Los Angeles, Chicago, New England, and New York—with veterans leading the way, followed by thousands of other pissed-off citizens—and all of them converging around Jacksonville, Florida, for the final ride down to Miami Beach. Their dream was to pick up vehicles in every town and city along the way, creating a convoy perhaps four hundred miles long! County Fair I, scheduled to begin on August 21, would be split into four separate actions: Assault Day, where the vets made "a simulated land, sea, and air assault on Miami Beach," a sort of collective muscle-flexing; Peace Day, where they marched and spoke in support of the seven-point peace proposal; Liberation Day, where they attempted to win over (through persuasive argument, not force) various corporations, civic groups, and individuals who still backed the war; and Unemployment Day, where they would again march and rally, this time "to demonstrate the need for action by the government on the employment problem."[112]

Junction City II and County Fair I might easily have gone the way of other best-laid plans simply from the immense apathy—and often enough real despair, not so far beneath that apathetic surface—in seventies America, not to mention the now hopeless discord in the peace movement itself. But the United States government nearly stopped the whole show with a move none of the vets had expected: a big legal bomb, exploding right in the heart of VVAW, as if the government had now turned to fragging (at least figuratively) its own former troops.

On July 3, 1972, FBI agents served subpoenas on 22 men and 1 woman, all members of VVAW, demanding that they appear before a grand jury in Tallahassee, Florida, at 9 A.M. on Monday, July 10, 1972, the very day the Democratic National Convention would open in Miami. The 23 people subpoenaed represented almost all the leaders of the organization who had helped plan actions for both the Democratic and Republican conventions, including national coordinators Barry Romo and Pete (blood on Bush) Mahoney and southern regional coordinator Scott Camil. Other regional coordinators and almost all the Florida chapter coordinators were among those summoned to the Tallahassee courthouse, at the very northern end of Florida (over 400 miles from Miami, where many of them had planned to meet with Democratic Party leaders).

Since VVAW actually had little to contribute to McGovern's nomination, there was some question as to what the government intended to accomplish by keeping these leaders away from the Democratic Convention. One plausible explanation was that Nixon's gang of tricksters had hoped to spark a protest riot in Miami that would bring shame on the Democrats similar to the grisly scenes in Chicago four years earlier, which had helped defeat Hubert Humphrey. VVAW took the subpoenas very seriously, however, and sought to augment the individual veterans' lawyers with representation from the Center for Constitutional Rights (CCR) in New York, which had extensive experience with grand jury litigation. Although at first CCR sent down only a few of its lower-level staff attorneys, the decision to involve them in the case would eventually prove crucial.

After pumping the VVAW leaders for information about their lifestyles, friendships, finances, and recent travel, the Justice Department's special prosecutor Guy Goodwin dismissed all save four of them at 4:30 P.M. on Thursday July 13. The day before, the *Atlanta Constitution* had run a puzzling story under the headline "BOMB PLOT AT GOP CONVENTION PROBED!" Thursday evening, Stan Michelsen, Florida VVAW's assistant state coordinator and one of the subpoenaed twenty-three, received a phone call from someone who claimed to be a government agent, warning of a plot to murder Scott Camil under the pretext of preventing his "escape." Michelsen got in his car and headed off Camil, who was on his way back from the airport after picking up

Mike Oliver. Michelsen persuaded Camil not to return to VVAW's defense headquarters in Tallahassee, where he had been staying. Later that night, forty heavily armed policemen blocked off both ends of the street, then burst in on the VVAW house, shotguns in hand, ripping the place apart in search of Camil.

After spending the night at a friend's, Camil met with his lawyers and a group of reporters, who accompanied him to the courthouse to witness his surrender. That same morning, the Justice Department issued indictments against 6 of the 23: Camil, Don Perdue, and Alton Foss of Florida VVAW; Bill Patterson and John Kniffin of Texas VVAW; and Pete Mahoney of the national office. (In October, Stan Michelsen and nonveteran hippie entrepreneur John Briggs, who sold Camil a crate of wrist rocket slingshots, would be added to this select list to create the "Gainesville Eight.") The principal charge against them was "conspiring to promote, incite and participate in a riot" at the forthcoming Republican National Convention in Miami.

Although the vets in VVAW were too well disciplined to be thrown into complete chaos, the federal grand jury indictments certainly knocked the whole organization off balance. Arguments broke out immediately as to who was to blame—and should Camil and his pals be dumped as liabilities to the organization, or should the organization support them and pay for their defense even if they were guilty, etc. In fact, national coordinator Barry Romo believed they *were* guilty, and he determined to stay out of Florida (except for a brief visit during the Republican convention) lest he have to make this admission before the grand jury.

Clearly, the organization that had boasted only months earlier of its ability to lead a 400-mile-long convoy of protesters to Nixon's doorstep had just acquired a lot more weight to carry—not that they hadn't learned to carry a lot of added weight before, in even more deadly surroundings. In fact, the government that now saw these men as enemies would soon get a chance to witness just how effective military training could be.[113]

4. Kovic Confronts the Florida National Guard: A Call to Revolution

It was something of a miracle that the Last Patrol came off as well as it did. Convoys left on schedule from five locations: New York, Detroit, Chicago, Salt Lake City, and California State University at Northridge, in the San Fernando Valley. Altogether they comprised over 200 cars, vans, trucks, and motorcycles, and carried about 1,200 vets and their girlfriends, while another 100 or so veterans came down on foot from northern Florida in the so-called "March Against Murder." It was not the 25,000–100,000 people they had aimed for, but a respectable showing nonetheless.

The spike in this potent VVAW motor cocktail was unquestionably the convoy that left from Cal State Northridge. To begin with, it had pooled the considerable store of brigands, madmen, rabble-rousers, Communists, and roaring radicals in both the San Francisco and Los Angeles chapters; then it had dipped down to pick up some of San Diego's hardened GI movement fighters, then headed straight across the Southwest on Route 10 for San Antonio and Houston, to gather in the Texas crew, who had been known to talk of guns and revolution with an earnestness that might have given pause even to Chairman Avakian. But there were no guns, no drugs, not even a bottle of beer allowed on this convoy, or any of the others. The vets were going to play this one completely by the book.

Though they might look like the "hirsute vagabonds" the government had portrayed them as—with wild masses of black and blond hair (not yet a gray strand to be seen) bursting out from under their floppy boonie hats, and beards halfway down their chests, as though they had just done two years before the mast—they were careful to abide by every law, including traffic laws, between San Diego and Miami. A good thing, too, since by the time it reached Austin, the southern convoy was under constant surveillance by the Secret Service, the FBI, state police, and local police—an escort of half a dozen unmarked cars just before and just behind them. The FBI was keeping such an accurate record of their movements that when a vet living ahead of the convoy wanted to find out where to join them, he simply called the FBI, and was told of a nearby town they were due to pass through in forty minutes.

The southern convoy would have a special place in history for yet another reason. A former Army artilleryman named Frank Cavestani, having migrated from New York to L.A. with his eyes on a movie career, had swung a deal with French photographer Catherine Leroy to make a documentary about the Last Patrol. He decided to focus his film on three vets in the southern convoy: Tom Zangrilli, Jack McCloskey, and Ron Kovic.

Zangrilli was a tall, well-built guy from the ultra-conservative, working-class city of Berwyn, Illinois, just outside Chicago. A clean-cut kid, he had joined the Marines, like many of his friends, to "do our jobs," and had twice extended his combat tour in Vietnam, participating in numerous firefights as well as the weeks-long battle of Hue, for which he was awarded the Navy Cross, two Bronze Stars, and two Purple Hearts. Only after he came back in 1969 and started reading books about Vietnam and its thousand-year struggle for independence did a sense of betrayal set in, a feeling that the politicians had used them as pawns since "they were not fighting to win [the war]." Now a militant revolutionary, Tom Zangrilli wore his bush hat at a rakish tilt, with the brims folded to a point in front like one of the Yankee Doodle heroes of '76, but somehow the long straight tresses hanging down beneath it (and tucked neatly behind his ears) didn't seem to fit with his chiseled, manly features, nor did the Abraham Lincoln chin beard look quite right either—as if they were only stage hair he could just pull off, and at any moment he might head back to Berwyn and go to work for a steel mill or open a bar (all of which he did eventually do). Ron Kovic, Zangrilli's best friend and fellow Marine, had come from a similar background— a patriotic, working-class Catholic family in Massapequa, Long Island. Like Zangrilli, Kovic had voluntarily returned for a second year in Vietnam; and also like Tom, the former straight-arrow high school wrestler and gymnast (Kovic) had tried to cool his anger against the government by growing his hair long and [adopting the co]unterculture of the West Coast. One big difference, [Kovic ha]d a lot more to be angry about. Just before the 1968 [election, a b]ullet had severed his spinal cord, paralyzing him for [life and removing] any sensation from his midchest down.

[McCloskey, curious]ly, bore some physical resemblance to Kovic. Both [were of medium height w]ith dark hair and Gaelic faces (Kovic was Irish on his [mother's side]), small, upturned noses, soulful, penetrating brown [ey]es that partly hid their expression. A Navy corpsman [who had seen c]ombat with the Marines, McCloskey had been seri-[ously wounded, earn]ing a Silver Star and a Bronze Star, but he had man-[aged to finish his ful]l tour and come home on his feet. Kovic was the [younger man] and certainly had an edge on charisma, though [McCloskey was the] better organizer.

Having come from Philadelphia, McCloskey had moved west after the war and almost single-handedly put together the formidable San Francisco VVAW. Moreover, McCloskey had started veterans' rap groups in San Francisco and then connected them with rap groups for former prisoners, forming an organization called Twice Born Men, helping to pioneer theories of readjustment that went well beyond the Vietnam experience.

There was an intense rivalry between Kovic and McCloskey, but no rivalry at all between Kovic and Zangrilli. Zangrilli saw Kovic as a "wild man" and an "individualist" but "not a leader by any stretch of the imagination . . . he couldn't lead a hungry man to hunt a chicken." What made Kovic notable, according to Zangrilli, was just one thing: "he was an unstoppable speaker—he had more energy to do that than anybody."

Frank Cavestani recorded some memorable footage of McCloskey reminiscing about his return from Vietnam with fifty-six morphine syrettes taped to his leg, having become a junkie to obliterate the guilt from all the men, women, and children whose lives he had failed to save; and McCloskey confessing that he had cried for so many dead men in Vietnam that it had robbed him of the ability to cry. But there was a cerebral, philosophical quality about McCloskey that didn't project dynamically onto celluloid. Zangrilli, whom Cavestani had originally planned to build his film around, came off even worse. He proved stiff on camera, and had trouble finding more to say than: "We just wanna let the world know that people who fought the war . . . think it's wrong too." Kovic, by contrast, could not be shut up; his words flowed naturally and built beautifully to emotional crescendos that carried his listeners with him as if on a powerful torrent. He was dogged at it too, speaking to any pair of ears or camera lens that crossed his path; and refusing to rest, so that Anne Hirschman, the VVAW medical director in Miami, feared for his health, since his paralysis affected his breathing and at some points it seemed as if he was just barely getting his breath. But that too was part of Kovic's magic on screen: he put every facet of the war's wounding out front for the world to see. By the time they reached Miami, Cavestani knew he had his star.

On Saturday morning, August 19, the caravans converged in their descent on Miami. Thirteen miles outside the city, one group of vets left their vehicles to march into the city, carrying upside-down flags as their guidons and counting cadence with antiwar chants—"Ho! Ho! Ho Chi Minh! Ho Chi Minh is gonna win!"—or whistling tunes such as "When Johnny Comes Marching Home." The rest of the vets simply drove on into the sprawling countercultural encampment at Flamingo Park. As the long line of VVAW vehicles cruised slowly through the swarms of protesters—in their T-shirts, shorts, and lots of exposed tan skin looking not much different than the typical campus crowd on Easter break—there was much cheering, blowing of horns, and tossing of flower bouquets, as though the vets were some long-awaited army of liberation.

In "People's Park," the vets mingled with the newest more-radical-than-thou antiwar faction called the Zippies, led by *High Times* publisher Tom Forcade. The Zippies characterized themselves as serious working-class rebels (hippies they saw as mostly spoiled rich kids). They opposed voting, calling it a "means of preserving privilege," and were also, in Zippie Steven Conliff's words, "intensely anti-Christian and militantly unpatriotic." Their credo was that "wars would end only when the old farts who declared them had to fight them," and to this end they would give as good as they got in any physical tussle. Zippies justified their belligerence by viewing themselves as the new vanguard of American social reform, and many of their ideas were actually quite useful and salutary. For example, they denounced the mindless consumption of drugs— which they felt were coming mostly from government agents—especially downers, such as the quaaludes that were currently inundating the scene. They blamed the widespread use of downers for the fact that many would-be revolutionary leaders like Abbie Hoffman were now tranquilized, if not actually zonked-out in dreamland, most of the time (Forcade himself would commit suicide with downers a few years later, and Abbie too would go out on them in 1988). On the other hand, there was the same silly—and in some sense self-defeating—side to Zippie as there was to hippie and Yippie, like the "Zippie Free Women" who claimed to battle sexism by appearing topless in Flamingo Park and at many of the protest actions.

The vets were so disturbed by the endless rock and roll and pot parties that they soon moved to a separate section of the park, to indicate that they were not just another act in the general circus of good-times seekers. They wanted to show they were "here for a purpose," said veteran Lynn Witt, who couldn't dance if he wanted to, since his right leg, shattered in Khe Sanh, was held together by a steel brace.

Into this hodgepodge of causes and strategies came the equally sober-minded Avakianist Communists of the Revolutionary Union, who were most influential, according to Steven Conliff, in the Attica Brigade—"Attica Means Fight Back!" they chanted—and (clandestinely) in VVAW. The debates in Flamingo Park ran all night long, and about the only thing everyone there could agree on was their hatred of Richard Nixon. VVAW came out on the peaceful side of every argument—partly from practical considerations. With a near-bankrupt treasury, even civil disobedience seemed foolhardy, especially since the Miami courts were hitting CD demonstrators with $50 fines instead of the usual $10. A weightier consideration was that the eyes of the judicial system were now on VVAW. After the Gainesville indictments, VVAW's lawyers had warned the indictees to stay away from the Republican Convention. Once out on bond they were legally entitled to travel anywhere, but should they go to Miami and should violent acts occur there, their very presence (whether or not they participated in the violence) could be cited as one of the "overt acts" necessary for a court to convict on conspiracy; moreover, the alleged conspirators could then be held responsible for any other criminal actions, including riots and killings, that might take place there. Though both Mahoney and Camil showed up in Miami anyway, they kept a much lower profile than usual.

In fact, VVAW ended up as a kind of peacekeeping force in Miami. On the last day of the convention, when the Zippies' Godzilla Brigade attacked several busloads of Republican delegates—roughing up and spitting on even the likes of South Carolina Senator (and war horse) Strom Thurmond and New York Senator James Buckley (brother of right-wing ideologue William F.), and "tearing the gladrags" and "destroying the hairdos" of their wives—VVAW marshals rushed in to break up the melee, and reputedly saved the lives of those South Carolina delegates still inside a bus that the Zippies were about to set afire.[114]

The most important factor in VVAW's decision to be peaceful, however, may simply have been their own awareness of how powerful their very existence had become, how deeply their images had already become seared into the war-guilty American psyche. They were clearly soldiers, and it wasn't just the fatigues, the helmets, the combat boots, or the occasional plastic M-16s they carried. Their faces, and sometimes their bodies, showed that they had been there, to that place that was still just a disquieting word to most Americans (like *AIDS* would become a decade later), or at best a blurry, loud, horror-filled image on their television screens. These men spoke with the voice of experience, and their chants erupted from somewhere deep in their guts, with an irrefutable conviction: "One, two, three, four! / We don't want your fuckin' war!" (that one repeated now for the ten thousandth time); or, "Bring our brothers home / NOW!"; or, "Babies keep on dyin'! / And nobody seems to care!" (the latest one, a response to the escalated air war). And at the front of each procession were the three wheelchair vets who had earned their place as leaders: Bill Wyman, Bobby Muller, and in the middle Ron Kovic, looking utterly exhausted and occasionally throwing his head back to ease his breath, but his hands reaching out firmly to the arms of Bill's and Bobby's chairs on either side of him, holding fast to them as they were pushed along, as if those brother vets were his life-raft.

In his own way, Kovic was as hotheaded a revolutionary as Scott Camil (who came to Miami in defiance of the Gainesville indictment, carrying plans to jam the Miami airport's radar with a thousand metal-foil balloons). In fact, a short time after Miami, Camil found Kovic carrying a gold-plated, sawed-off carbine under his lap blanket, and the bond between the two men was cemented. And in his unpublished memoirs, Kovic would recount a serious plan he had concocted to storm the White House with a few trusted companions and a trunk full of machine guns he had purchased at Big 5 Sporting Goods. The plan was only thwarted, he contended, by a government agent dressed as a Hindu, who drove off with the car and the machine guns after Kovic had left it unattended, motor still running, in a no-parking zone in San Francisco.

Although Zangrilli thought it hopeless to try to coach or discipline Kovic, there was one man on the Last Patrol who had Ron's full attention: war correspondent and political journalist Richard Boyle. Boyle's book *Flower of the Dragon* about "the breakdown of the U.S. army in Vietnam," recently published by Ramparts Press, had made a pretty big splash, at least in the antiwar community. Kovic was immediately drawn to him by his prowess with women, and Boyle could hold his own against Kovic's fast-rattling wit better than anyone Ron had ever met. Boyle knew that Kovic was unpopular with many of the vets because of his "grandstanding," but he foresaw that Kovic might become "the best speaker of the veterans' movement." Boyle was intrigued with the possibility that Kovic's "masterful ability to whip up a crowd" could lead to the toppling of what they both called "the gangster government of the United States."

Three thousand Florida National Guard troops had been summoned to Miami and were being housed in high school gymnasiums, while 2,000 members of the 82nd Airborne Division and 500 Marines were stationed at nearby Homestead Air Force Base. To surround the demonstrators with so much firepower before any substantial violence had occurred seemed blatant intimidation. To undermine this military threat, VVAW sent organizers over the fence at Homestead, and leafleted both the GIs and the Guard. But VVAW was very careful not to advocate desertion, mutiny, or any other actions that might lead to charges of treason. The official VVAW line to the troops was: "They're bringing you out to fight your brothers; *you've* got to make that decision [to do so, or to refuse]."

Boyle and Kovic, however, had other plans. On Monday August 21, they joined a VVAW march to one of the high schools where the National Guard was bivouacked. Kovic had not been authorized to speak there, but Boyle told Kovic that, with the right sort of persuasion, they "could really put it together and bring about an insurrection, a popular revolution scenario." Once Kovic saw the orgiastic red light of the television cameras, there was no stopping him. Boyle narrates: "Ron delivered a speech to the Guard, something to the effect: 'They sent us to Vietnam to fight against the people. We found we were on the wrong side. And if they ever make us fight again, we'll fight with the people, and it will be the people's army.' One of the National Guardsman, a black, put his rifle down and raised his fist: 'Yeah, man!' It was electric. You could feel in the Guard that the thing was starting to turn, that they were about to go over. So the officers pushed the Guard back into the high school and locked the door so they couldn't continue to hear Ron speak. I said, 'Ron, this is great.' Afterwards, we went to a bar with a couple of other vets. I said, 'I bet you'll be on the evening news.' He didn't believe it. Well, that night it was the lead story on Walter Cronkite's evening national news.

"That was an incredible political event. It was an incident in history, like in 1917 when the Czarist troops refused to fire on the crowd. After that, it went very quickly. Once the troops refuse to fire on the crowd, or even worse for the government, their fellow soldiers, if one unit joins the revolution, then the next unit joins, and it goes very quickly. Then you're down to the palace guard. That's why coups often happen in a matter of hours. So undoubtedly the government was freaking out. When the National Guard, in effect, were ready to join, were sympathetic to the vets, that's what made them go 'tilt.' The Nixon administration was terrified. They were monitoring hourly what the vets were doing."

By the time VVAW had gotten to Miami, their elaborate four-part plan, Operation County Fair I, had gone completely by the board. With Kerry long gone, Camil discredited, Pete Mahoney hors de combat as one of the eight Gainesville indictees, and Hubbard relegated to being mostly an onlooker, the de facto leadership of the organization had devolved upon the newly promoted Californian Barry Romo. At Dewey Canyon III, Romo had led some of the wildest, in-your-face actions, including the cancan on the steps of the Supreme Court, but in Miami it was clear he had undergone a sea change. He had grown quiet, sober, serious, with his once fierce emotions reined tightly under control, though the tension of inner explosions could still sometimes be heard quavering in his voice. Some people, including Tom Forcade, claimed the change had come from Romo's having joined the Avakianists, and that he was no longer his own man but only a puppet of the RU. That Romo had earlier formed an alliance with a Florida VVAW member named Jerry Rudolff, who was exposed during Democratic Convention week as an undercover agent of the Dade County police, cast further suspicion upon his striking transformation. In any case, Romo's head was now as clear and decisive as a four-star general's, and he had put out a standing order for all vets to cooperate with the authorities. He was "absolutely against violence," he said, because it was "counterproductive."[115]

5. The Battle of Miami Beach

The showpiece of VVAW protests was timed to coincide with Nixon's arrival at Republican headquarters in the Fontainebleau Hotel. Just after noon on Tuesday August 22, as Nixon's plane was touching down at Miami International Airport, the entire Last Patrol began their silent march to the Fontainebleau. Sunday night SDS had made a similar march, with only half as many people, to intercept guests arriving for the pre-convention dinner, but discipline had broken down just as they reached the hotel and the scene had degenerated into rock- bottle- and egg-throwing, with no significant political confrontation at all. Tuesday morning the Yippies and Zippies had attempted a similar uncoordinated assault on the Fontainebleau and been repulsed just as quickly by delegate jeers and police threats. In fact, the whole smorgasbord of protests thus far had been marked by a rejection of leadership, as well as what might be termed revolution by whim. VVAW's silent march to the Fontainebleau was intended, among other things, as a corrective to such anarchy.

By all accounts, the silent march Tuesday afternoon was the most striking protest in Miami—perhaps in the whole course of the antiwar movement. The vets were divided up into platoons according to states, each group being led by its disabled members, as they passed through five miles of central Miami. According to Barry Romo, many of the younger policemen watching from police vans parked along the route began to cry; he assumed they were fellow Vietnam veterans. The "eerie procession" of 1,200 battle-clad vets and their women partners "moving up Collins Avenue in dead silence" stopped journalist Hunter Thompson in his tracks. Wrote Thompson: "Nobody spoke; all the 'stop, start,' 'fast, slow,' 'left, right' commands came from 'platoon leaders' walking off to the side of the main column and using hand signals . . . that was not the kind of procession you just walked up and 'joined.' Not without paying some very heavy dues. . . . The silence of the march was contagious, almost threatening. There were hundreds of spectators, but nobody said a word. I walked up beside the column for ten blocks, and the only sounds I remember hearing were the soft thump of boot leather on hot asphalt and the occasional rattling of an open canteen top."

At the gate to the Fontainebleau, the veterans' column came up against perhaps a thousand heavily armed Florida state troopers. Hunter Thompson felt that the police were nervous, intimidated, and "clearly off balance," and part of the reason that the vets inspired such fear was the incorrect advance intelligence provided by the FBI. The Bureau, now headed by Acting Director L. Patrick Grey (an upstart anxious to prove himself as tough as his late famed predecessor, J. Edgar Hoover), had warned Florida law enforcement agencies that "VVAW [was] the most potentially violent organization traveling to the conventions." In fact, the FBI rank and file were so convinced of this claim that many individual agents considered the assignment to work undercover in VVAW extremely dangerous. Even when undercover agents who had ridden with the convoy got to Miami and told their comrades of VVAW's nonviolent policy, the other agents refused to believe them. Till the very end of the convention, the watchword at the FBI was "that if any group had the knowledge, training, resources, and motivation to employ violence, it was the VVAW."

For a full five minutes the vets and the cops faced off, eyeball to eyeball, nothing being said. Then one of the vet leaders got on a bullhorn and announced: "We want to come inside." Thompson described a shudder going through the crowd of onlookers, and he himself was so sure of an impending battle that he stuffed his notebook and his watch in his pants. "There was no mistaking the potential for real violence," he wrote. "And it was easy enough to see, by scanning the faces behind those clear plastic riot masks, that the cream of the Florida State Highway Patrol had no appetite at all for a public crunch with twelve hundred angry Vietnam Veterans." As Thompson astutely perceived, the police were in a no-win situation; either they got mauled by the veterans, or, if they managed to beat the vets back with their superior weaponry, they would have the whole world watching on that night's national news as they bashed and maybe killed the nation's war heroes, all of them unarmed, and a significant portion even disabled. What was more, Thompson sensed the situation being drawn as if in a swift vortex toward that very conclusion. "All it would take," he thought, "would be for one or two Vets to lose control of themselves and try to crash through the police line; just enough violence to make *one* cop use his riot stick. The rest would take care of itself."

Richard Boyle, who was there on the sidelines with Thompson, likewise recalled, "This was one of those times in history where you feel it's about to happen . . . Miami could have gone that way very easily. If those Highway Patrol, for example, had started firing at the vets, it would have been the beginning of a civil war. Because you had in those vets there the makings of an officer corps of a rebel army. And they were not kids like in SDS. You club them over the head, and they freak out. These guys, you club them on the head, you're gonna get killed. You had expert weapons people. A lot of them were former officers. These were not people to fuck with."

The vets then proceeded to sit down in a large semicircle across all three northbound lanes of Collins Avenue, totally blocking traffic coming into Miami Beach. For several minutes the police demanded that they move, and the vets refused, daring them: "Bust us!" With the situation nearly at flash point, Ron Kovic suddenly erupted into one of the most fiery speeches of his career. As Thompson described it, Kovic's words "lashed the crowd like a wire whip." Ironically, as Kovic spoke, a military helicopter hovered overhead, as if he were the next Viet Cong target to be blown away, but Thompson marveled that Kovic's words even overrode the noise of the chopper blades. When just about everyone had given up hope of averting a bloody catastrophe, Republican Congressman Paul McCloskey arrived like a deus ex machina. McCloskey, who had consistently opposed Nixon on his Vietnam policy, had absolute credibility with all the antiwar people, including the vets. Moreover, McCloskey had his own grudge to settle with Nixon. The tall, personable, Kennedy-haired California Republican had run against Nixon in the New Hampshire primary, but Nixon refused to allow any of McCloskey's delegates to nominate him for the presidency or even to speak from the floor of the convention. In effect, McCloskey was being gagged from speaking out against the war. He now saw his chance to get back at Nixon and to facilitate the veterans' cause in one stroke. So he talked the state troopers (who were only too eager to compromise) into allowing three disabled vets to enter the hotel and to wait there for Nixon's arrival. In exchange, the vets would pull back from the Fontainebleau and reopen Collins Avenue.

McCloskey knew Boyle from Boyle's political work in San Francisco, and so it was no surprise that three wheelchair vets were chosen to go in, and that they happened to be Bill Wyman, Bobby Muller, and Ron Kovic. This was just the chance Kovic had been waiting for, and he and Boyle had already worked out a scenario for just such an occasion. When Nixon tried to shake Kovic's hand, all three vets would fall out of their wheelchairs; and Kovic, who had the shoulders and forearms of a bodybuilder, would seize hold of Nixon's arm or leg and refuse to let go until Nixon agreed to listen to the full range of the veterans' grievances, including their need for jobs and better medical care. Boyle imagined it would be "an incredible confrontation on national television, with a thousand vets outside waiting to find out Nixon's answer to their demands for justice in coming home."

As Kovic, Wyman, and Muller prepared to move through the police lines into the Fontainebleau, Barry Romo lifted his bullhorn and announced that they would follow their original plan for the action, which was to continue making their speeches and then return to camp, having shown the world that Nixon would not meet with them. Recalls Boyle: "I went, 'What the fuck!' I mean, it's like the Super Bowl, and we're at their opposing one-yard line with ten seconds to go and it's fourth and one, and we got 'the Refrigerator' [Chicago Bears 350-

pound lineman William Perry] ready to take the ball across. And the coach says, 'No, we're going to quit the game and concede.' It just didn't make any sense. But it happened so fast and so surprisingly that nobody grabbed the bullhorn. We probably should have grabbed the bullhorn from him and slugged him with it and continued. But we did have a military discipline, and when the commander says we go back, we do. Anyway, the momentum of the demonstration was broken."

Boyle put out word that Romo had killed their chance to meet Nixon because he was actually a paid agent of the government. Mike Oliver was also upset with Romo, feeling that when he had helped get Romo appointed to the national office it was "one of the worst mistakes" he'd ever made. Oliver figured Romo was listening not to the dictates of the FBI but to "the little clique of vets around him" who were mouthing "a typical, radical Communist viewpoint of anti-imperialist [propaganda] . . . boring as shit" (he did not yet know that Romo was rubbing shoulders with the RU). But Romo, who served in VVAW for decades afterward, maintains that his motivation was to keep the demonstration intact, and that it was his job as "tactical leader" to judge "how far we could push the situation." In this case, he judged that more good would be achieved by remaining on the street than by falling for an obvious government ploy. "They [the three wheelchair vets] weren't gonna meet with Nixon. You can bet on that," Romo asserts. "If Boyle thinks Richard Nixon was meeting with Ron Kovic, give him something else to smoke. . . . I loved Ron, but he was a man in a wheelchair, not a wheelchair with a man sitting on it; he still had to subscribe to the discipline and democracy of the organization. . . . And the context was, when we did stuff, we did stuff as groups. What we said was, 'We all stay together. We ain't gonna move off the street in exchange for people walking into a hotel where they're not gonna meet anybody.' It was all or nothing."

Wednesday August 23 was the day Richard Nixon would finally appear inside the cyclone fence and barbed wire–enclosed Miami Convention Center to accept his party's nomination for a second term as president of the United States. Like the past two days, the heat was scorching, and tensions were short, especially among the police, who had already suffered plenty of humiliation from the Yippies and Zippies at the Democratic Convention a month earlier. The police had been held on a short tether for two months, partly because Police Chief Rocky Pomerance had wanted as much as anyone to keep the peace that summer and protect Miami Beach's (and his own) good name. For both police and demonstrators, there were by now a whole heap of grudges to settle, and only a few hours left to settle them.

No one could say exactly who or what provoked it, but about two o'clock that afternoon, without warning, the police began shooting volleys of tear gas canisters into the crowd of demonstrators advancing toward the convention center.

They were using CS gas, the most virulent form available; it caused terrible burning in the skin followed by nausea, and would cling like syrup to clothing, so that the victim carried it with him wherever he ran. In strong enough doses it could cause blindness, especially if the victim wore contact lenses that trapped it against the eyeballs, and in those who had respiratory problems or were otherwise debilitated (such as the elderly) it could cause death. Even the healthiest young people found that "it makes you sick as hell." No sooner had the demonstrators been stunned and stricken by the gas than phalanxes of police in gas masks and riot gear descended upon them from several directions, clubbing indiscriminately with their nightsticks as they came, to drive them in a rout toward the waiting police wagons and a whole fleet of rental trucks brought just for the occasion.

Thus began "the Battle of Miami Beach," which some participants felt was bloodier and more brutal even than Chicago '68. In fact, there would be over 1,000 arrests that night, easily twice the number that had been made on the final night of the Chicago convention. The main difference was that this time—by deliberate decision to avoid the "overplay" they had been charged with after their coverage of the Chicago riots—the media mainly kept their cameras trained inside the convention hall, allowing the fighting on both sides to get about as dirty as any uncontrolled street brawl gets. The battle went on for more than seven hours, with demonstrators escaping down side streets only to return minutes later to wreak revenge on isolated cops or to gang up on helpless, middle-aged Republican delegates, whose buses the Zippie saboteurs had skillfully disabled several blocks from the convention center. On the protester side, there were instances of lead pipes used against police and of frail delegates shoved, punched, kicked, and spat upon; on the police side, there were savage, unwarranted beatings of protesters who had surrendered peacefully, like undercover FBI agent Cril Payne. Looking like any other hippie "freak" and devoid of IDs, Payne had no way of proving to the police who arrested him that he was a government agent. In his memoir *Deep Cover,* he recalled in excruciating detail how, after they had handcuffed him, they beat his shoulders, arms, legs, and feet with their sticks nearly to the point of crippling him, and then held him bent over while the worst of the lot shoved a nightstick partway up his anus.

In the picture Payne gave of the riot, Miami Beach began to look a lot like Vietnam. He wrote of "Huey Cobras [helicopter gunships] . . . screaming across the sky, darting between the luxurious high-rise hotels along the beachfront, hovering over crowds of demonstrators, then swooping down over Collins Avenue with a deafening roar. You could actually see the crew in their helmets and flight suits. One crew member was standing in the open doorway as if he were sighting his fifty-caliber machine gun in the Mekong Delta. There was a continuous wail of sirens. Clouds of tear gas floated up in every direction. On virtually every side street, some type of police skirmish was in progress."[116]

Some of the vets had started out toward the convention center with pacifist Dave Dellinger's group, intending to take part in civil disobedience there, and they were caught in the middle of the burgeoning riot. Hearing that their brothers were in trouble, the rest of the vets rushed out to help them, but the madness quickly became so overwhelming that VVAW was incapable of any concerted action, and by nightfall the Last Patrol was splayed all over the city. In his documentary film Frank Cavestani captured scenes of vets in front of the convention center, wearing their black-and-white "death face" makeup, shouting "Murder! Murder!" or "Liars! Liars! Liars! Liars!" at the incoming Republican delegates; vets with fists raised confronting lines of helmeted police with visors down, sticks in hand; vets wetting down bandannas to put over their noses as protection against the horrible billowing tear gas; the wounded being dragged off and policemen guarding captured prisoners with their hands tied behind their backs, all of it in the hazy glare of spotlights through tear gas vapor and punctuated by the loud explosions of the canister-launchers—a real-life combat flashback, as underscored by the comment of one vet: "It was sheer hell."

Cut loose by the utter chaos, Ron Kovic once again made his own move. As his final act of revenge against Nixon, Congressman Paul McCloskey had given Kovic two delegate's passes to the convention. Passing right through the riot, Boyle wheeled Kovic up to the convention center entrance, where they met Cavestani, who was about to go in himself; in the confusion, Cavestani was able to get Kovic in with his press pass, and Ron left his delegate's passes with Boyle to give to Bobby Muller and Bill Wyman. By moving slowly and speaking politely Kovic was able to get halfway down to the delegates' area just below the podium, but he was stopped there by security. Since he threatened to make a scene, the guards let him stay put, but warned him to *shut up*—two words that were not in Kovic's vocabulary. In his "sweat-soaked marine utility jacket covered with medals," with a sergeant's three chevrons on the sleeve, he tried connecting with the elegantly dressed members of the American ruling class, for whose privileged lifestyle he had sacrificed even the small comforts of peeing and shitting freely, without the aid of catheter and rubber gloves. While these fine folks tried to avoid eye contact with him, not wanting to have their evening spoiled, Kovic demanded: "Do you hear me, people? Can I break through your complacency? Do you hear me when I say this war's a crime? . . . I ask you to join me in my protest, come over this line and sit with me if you feel this war in Vietnam is a crime." His offer found no takers, not even among the younger people, to whom most particularly he addressed his words. But when the guards again returned to silence him, the commotion he caused managed to attract the attention of CBS correspondent Roger Mudd, who interviewed him live for two minutes on the national news broadcast.

The security men were set to remove him again, but by this time he had learned that Muller and Wyman were in the hall, positioned strategically in the center aisle, two hundred feet from the podium at which Nixon would soon make his acceptance speech. Kovic pacified the guards by agreeing to move farther back, then seized the chance to maneuver over next to Muller and Wyman. They handed Kovic a STOP THE WAR sign, but it was rapidly torn out of his grasp. Wisely, they kept another such sign in reserve for the thunderous moment (the whole hall shaking with the sustained applause and shouts of "Four more years!") when Nixon appeared on stage.

In Kovic's memoir, *Born on the Fourth of July,* he describes the moment when Nixon began to speak: "and all three of us took a deep breath and shouted at the top of our lungs, 'Stop the bombing, stop the war,' as loud and as hard as we could, looking directly at Nixon. . . . We continued shouting, interrupting Nixon again and again, until Secret Service agents grabbed our chairs from behind and began pulling us backward as fast as they could out of the convention hall." In Oliver Stone's film based on Kovic's book, the same scene is portrayed with actor Tom Cruise dynamically cursing down Nixon with his own voice alone. The actual scene, as recorded in Cavestani's movie *The Last Patrol,* shows something quite different from both those versions. In blurry black-and-white, a very fragile and Christ-like Kovic, long straight hair draped on either side of his tired, agonized face (his moustache and goatee virtually lifted line for line from the iconic images every Catholic has seen from childhood on), just barely manages to gasp out the words: "Stop the bombing! Stop the bombing!" and as he pauses for breath the other two come in with their unsynchronized, and not much more strongly vocalized: "Stop killing women and children!"

Actually it was not surprising that the three of them should have been at the end of their strength after a week on the road and camped in Flamingo Park, sleeping on air mattresses the whole way, taking part in numerous actions and the endless conferences before and after each one—and in Cavestani's film it is easy to see that Muller and Wyman are even thinner, and a good deal less physically robust, than Kovic. What is surprising, even astonishing, is the access of adrenaline-fueled anger in which Kovic rebounds to fully-amped sound and fury once he and his friends have been dragged outside the hall, the doors locked and chained behind them, and he can witness firsthand what kind of damage is being inflicted on his fellow vets—indeed on anyone who still has the gall and guts to venture into the streets at all.

"They kill you in Vietnam, or they kill you back home in the streets—you can't win as a Vietnam veteran in this country!" Kovic spews forth venomously, his California tan deeply flushed in the movie lamps. His hands jab the air as if in search of a lethal weapon with which to get even. "We saw it in Vietnam, and we see it here in the streets right now—crimes! Our brothers are being brutalized and broken in the streets and they're being killed in Vietnam right now and that man in there is crazy! . . . I gave three-quarters of my body in Vietnam so that my brother doesn't have to get knocked down into the street, to get. . . ." And then his words trail off.

Cavestani wisely ended his film not with Kovic at white heat, with reason beginning to sink (even for one as logical as "the Sarge") into uncontrollable rage; but rather with the long passage through the hall as Kovic is forcibly removed. With Nixon having just finished his speech—which included the words, "Let's give those who have served in Vietnam the honor and the respect that they deserve and that they've earned"—Cavestani records as voice-over to Kovic's disappearance in the crowd the opening line of the following speaker, who is clearly anxious that some of Nixon's belovedness rub off on him.

"He has spoken for those who love their God, their families, and their country," the new speaker sums it all up—as if Richard Nixon had a monopoly on those things. The irony was clear, and the people getting clubbed that night knew it best of all. There *were* some Americans who could speak for themselves about their love for God, family, and country, and a good many of them were Vietnam veterans.

The actual end of the film, though, was even more dramatic. Filming stopped when a tear gas canister slammed into Cavestani's camera.

He even had the presence of mind to yell: "Cut!"[117]

6. One Stressed-Out Agent Provocateur and a Roomful of Macho Vets

Back in Los Angeles, Ron Kovic was censured by his own VVAW chapter for refusing to take orders and acting like a media star in Miami. The whole organization, in fact, was suffering from what Kovic termed "vicious" feuds. Kovic and Boyle were pissed off mightily at Barry Romo; and Romo, furious with Scott Camil, was only inches away from throwing Camil to the government sharks. The organization that returned from Miami was dangerously weakened and in no condition at all to fight the toughest battle yet for its collective survival.

From the time Nixon took office, over twenty grand juries had been convened to investigate the antiwar movement, and hundreds of indictments had been brought against its participants, but the strangest indictments by far were those of the Gainesville Eight. In a document that well might have been penned by science-fiction wizard Isaac Asimov, it was alleged that Vietnam veterans, led by Scott Camil and his cohorts, had planned to disrupt the Republican Convention by a series of coordinated attacks on Miami Beach police stations, police cars, retail stores, and "communications systems." Organized into "fire teams" and guided by a spotter plane (the spotter plane was mentioned to the grand jury but unaccountably left out of the indictment), they would make their assaults with a variety of weapons, ranging from the mundane "automatic weapons . . . and incendiary devices" to crossbows, "wrist rocket slingshots," ball bearings, lead weights, cherry bombs, smoke bombs, and fried marbles.

In May 1972, shortly after Barry Romo was elected to the national office, he went down to Miami to organize full-time in preparation for the conventions At his first meeting with the Florida VVAW in Hialeah, Romo smelled trouble. In the room were about twenty vets (many of whom he knew nothing about), along with members of the Miami Conventions Coalition, Maoists from the Progressive Labor Party (PL), two Zippies, and two allegedly pro-Castro Cubans. Scott Camil stood up and explained that if they were attacked by police or government troops, they could fight back with a number of inexpensive weapons—among them, wrist rockets and fried marbles. Then Camil passed out maps of Miami with all the police stations circled in yellow. Romo felt as if he were living his worst nightmare, and he took Camil aside and told him that he was inviting arrest. Not only was such talk extremely dangerous, but Romo felt it was superfluous as well, since it seemed obvious to him that Vietnam vets would know how to protect themselves if rioting did break out. He told Camil to put away his sample weapons and to collect all the maps that had been passed around, but when the maps came back, the count was one short. It later turned out at least two of the men in that room were narcotics agents of the Dade County police—called "Salt" and "Pepper" because one was white, the other black: Jerry Rudolff and Harrison Crenshaw. The map, purportedly "designating locations for firebombings," did indeed show up in the grand jury's indictments.

Romo also was disturbed to learn that Camil was dealing drugs; and even after he was indicted by the grand jury, Camil reputedly had hundreds of pounds of marijuana drying on the roof of his house out in the Everglades. Romo figured he had to be a cop or, at the very least, a police informer to get away with such capers.

The situation, however, was a lot more complex than Romo realized. Camil, like a lot of Vietnam vets and ex-Marines, liked to have guns at hand. His mother had once given him a present of three M-1 rifles for target shooting; and since her ex-husband and another son worked for the police, she thought it nothing unusual. Also, like so many of his combat buddies (especially the stressed-out variety), he was obsessed with self-defense and in a constant state of hypervigilance. Moreover, Camil had received secret training from the Jewish Defense League (JDL), a group that believed in the militant defense of the Jewish race. Having had relatives exterminated by Adolph Hitler, Camil was convinced that pacifism merely led to full occupancy in the death camps.

This was the era when rumors were rampant about the government's plan to kidnap and/or intern members of the antiwar movement. Considering the forces arrayed against them, Pete Mahoney, who attended all of the Florida planning meetings where Camil held sway, was surprised that there was actually *so little* talk of violence. The conspiracy indictments all focused on one particular meeting that had been held in Gainesville in late May. Mahoney remembers that "eighty percent of the meeting dealt with the normal logistical kind of things for organizing a demonstration—parade permits, where were we gonna camp, portable shitters, all that kind of stuff." In fact, the meeting was all but over, with most of the guys starting to get drunk or high from too much beer and too many hits of pot, when a veteran named Bill Lemmer—a burly, rough, crazy sort of guy (no dearth of them in the vets' movement)— announced that he had some vital information to impart, that they had all better listen up because it might save their lives.

Lemmer, the Arkansas-Oklahoma regional coordinator, claimed he had just learned of the Miami Beach police receiving a large shipment of M-16 automatic rifles—the standard-issue killing weapon in Vietnam. He also claimed that a whole contingent of angry, racist black cops—all of them over six feet tall!—were being sent to Miami from Washington, D.C., "to beat the shit out of people." Miami Beach was an especially vulnerable place for demonstrators to get trapped, because it was an island separated from the mainland by a two-and-a-half-mile-wide inlet of the ocean called Biscayne Bay, which could only be crossed on narrow causeways, whose access was controlled by five drawbridges. Lemmer began a game of "what if." For example, he postulated, *What if the police shut off all the causeways to Miami? What if they raise the drawbridges and start shooting the demonstrators?* Lemmer quickly answered his own questions. The government planned to kill a few members of the New Left, he said. They would blame the deaths on the demonstrators, then declare martial law and either wipe out or round up everyone who had protested the war. The presidential elections would be suspended indefinitely, and Nixon would become the United States' first full-fledged dictator.

The best thing for them to do, Lemmer claimed, was to shoot first, ambush the police before the cops could surround them. That would provoke a riot, and in the confusion most of the demonstrators would get away. A "mass crackdown" was sure to follow, but the vets could evade the government by breaking up into well-armed "cells" and going underground, whence they could serve to spearhead a nationwide resistance movement.

Camil thought it was a "weird idea," and most of the vets there did not take Lemmer seriously. He was known to be the "most militant" VVAW member at the University of Arkansas, where he had already hatched a number of goofy plans; in one case, he had talked a teenage student into attempting to bomb a university building. He had even been offered a psychiatric discharge by the Army before being sent to Vietnam. But as Mahoney recalled, many of the intoxicated veterans were "feeling somewhat macho" and got into the act of bragging about things they could do to derail Miami law enforcement. Lemmer kept egging them on, saying things like, "It's time we got weapons and started the revolution," and suggesting that they could disassemble some automatic weapons, strap the parts to their bodies, and sneak them into the Republican Convention for the purpose of blowing away pro-Nixon delegates. Camil, who must have heard an echo of his long-buried Phoenix plan in Lemmer's strident rhetoric, said something like, "Yeah, we're gonna give 'em their own medicine back."

Though far from imagining himself a revolutionary, Camil began to think that Lemmer had raised a serious issue: the subject of self-defense. Should the demonstrators be attacked by police, it would be better, Camil proposed, for the veterans to create a number of diversionary actions throughout Miami. His plan was, first, to blow up the lifting mechanisms on the five drawbridges, to keep them permanently down; then, second, to pull the cops off the civilian peace people and pit them against the vets, who were better able to meet force with force. The vets would bring no weapons into Miami Beach, where they could be accused of provoking violence. Instead, should a police attack begin, the vets would wreak havoc in the outlying areas, targeting government buildings— police stations, post offices, recruiting stations, etc.—but not individuals. While the police struggled to restore order and to capture the vets, Miami Beach could be safely evacuated.

In the match of male egos that followed, Mahoney recalls that a rivalry developed between Camil and his Florida friends, on one side, and John Kniffin and his Texas bunch on the other. Kniffin had somehow acquired a workable medieval crossbow, and he demonstrated its efficaciousness by putting an arrow through the living room door. Camil then brought out his box of toys. He produced a wrist rocket—a slingshot with a special wrist brace that allows the user to draw back the sling with many times the force one could normally endure— supposedly able to fire a missile 225 yards. He then explained that if you took ordinary marbles—which would just bounce off a target—and fried them ahead of time, they would acquire many cracks, so that when they struck an object they would shatter, turning into shrapnel. During the May protests against the mining of Haiphong harbor, when the Sheriff's Police and Highway Patrol had been called in to beat demonstrators who were blocking a street in Gainesville, Camil and 70 other vets had made effective use of these hunting slingshots, defending themselves with a fusillade of ball bearings and fried marbles that had put 18 policemen in the hospital and sent 54 more scurrying for medical attention. They had managed to escape before the police could regroup.

Camil also told of dousing police with ammonia-filled balloons to force them to take off their face masks. Finally, he got out some ordinary potassium permanganate, a disinfectant they had used in Vietnam to treat athlete's foot. By mixing it with glycerin, another household item, he showed them how to produce a minor explosive—something that could be used to set police cars on fire. According to Mahoney, "Everybody considered that we were talking extreme scenarios"; it was by no means a plan "to storm the Republican Convention," as later portrayed.

Most of the vets stayed on for another day or two. At some point, while Lemmer was still there, Camil got a call from Martin Jordan, the former Arkansas coordinator whom Lemmer had replaced. Jordan had become suspicious of Lemmer when, despite the apparent financial destitution of his family, Lemmer began coming up with airline tickets to demonstrations all over the country. Then Jordan discovered that of 36 demonstrators arrested for trespassing at Tinker Air Force Base in the spring, Lemmer alone had been released on his own recognizance. When Camil confronted Lemmer with these inconsistencies, Lemmer suddenly confessed to working as an agent for the FBI. He claimed he had had to become an informer to keep from going to jail on a marijuana bust, and that the FBI had offered him protection from military intelligence, which was hounding him for his antiwar activities. Apparently repentant, Lemmer offered to become a "double agent" for VVAW if they wanted him to do so.

From that one meeting, based on the testimony of FBI informer (and, it would seem, agent provocateur) William W. Lemmer, came 90 percent of the material later fashioned into the Gainesville indictments. Before leaving for Florida, Lemmer had even admitted to a friend, Boston graduate student Barbara Stocking, that he was part of an FBI plot to arrest or "take out of circulation" all the leaders of VVAW.

From the very beginning, there were serious questions about the validity of the indictments. For one thing, Scott Camil had in his possession no automatic weapons. He did own the semiautomatic M-1 carbines his mother had bought him, but they were the one-shot-at-a-time American military rifles that had been outmoded since the Korean War. M-1s can be converted to full automatic by a sharp gun hobbyist, but so can most modern rifles. Nor did he possess any grenades, though he had been offered several crates of them, along with mortars, bazookas, submachine guns, and other explosives, by a guy named Pablo Fernandez and some of his fellow right-wing, anti-Castro Cubans. Fernandez later turned out to be on the payroll of the Dade County narcotics squad, the Miami police, and the FBI, as well as to have close connections with Nixon's Watergate conspirators. For another thing, it appeared that Camil had been the subject of a previous government entrapment effort only a few months earlier, when he had been charged with kidnapping after trying peaceably to collect $100 for some friends who'd been burned on a drug deal. Before that case was dropped for lack of evidence, he was arrested twice more, on equally bogus charges, including a claim that he had cheated the IRS of eleven dollars. He was also hassled by Naval Intelligence and spied on by the Gainesville police, the Alachua County Sheriff's Department, and the Florida Region II narcotics squad. Within a six-month period, he had eighteen charges brought against him—not one of which he was ever convicted of.

Not that Camil wasn't reckless. When asked, long afterward, whether Lemmer was crazy, Camil responded: "We were all nuts! One minute it was peace and love, and the next minute it was get guns and kill the motherfuckers!" Camil did many things that almost seemed calculated to bring the government's wrath down on him. But Camil reasoned that he was merely confirming his own effectiveness as an agitator. "I felt that they wouldn't be fucking with me if I wasn't irritating them," he said. "So their fucking with me became my positive reinforcement. The more they fucked with me, the more I knew I was on the right track."[118]

Camil wasn't the only one who felt that way. Many newspaper articles and editorials relating to the Gainesville indictments made the same point—that the Nixon administration, through its twisted use of grand juries and the new anti-riot and conspiracy statutes (which had only come into being in 1969), was making criminals out of honest citizens and thus turning the government into the biggest criminal of all. The *St. Petersburg Times* editorialized: "To silence the critics, the government accuses them of crimes they have not committed . . . the Nixon Justice Department has developed a sorry record of politically motivated prosecutions based upon the amateurish pursuit of nebulous plots at which any first-year law student would scoff. . . . The suppression of legitimate dissent creates disrespect for laws which are abused and for the government which immorally exercises this power." An editorial in the *Charlotte Observer* asked pertinently: "If there was a conspiracy, how much of the planning came from the FBI's own informer? Would there have been a plot without him?"

Lucian Truscott IV, a third-generation West Point graduate who had resigned his commission to protest the war (and who later became the best-selling author of *Dress Grey*), wrote in the *Village Voice:* "The VVAW have long been the focus of Nixon administration efforts to discredit veterans who returned from Vietnam disillusioned with a war they had fought but not believed in. There are reports now that Charles Colson, the special assistant to the President who was identified by the *Wall Street Journal* two years ago as 'Nixon's hatchet man,' had the VVAW infiltrated soon after Nixon took office in 1969. . . . The Nixon administration has been willing to go to any length to prevent this organization of angry veterans from picking up the kind of credibility which is enjoyed by other veterans groups."

Many newspeople were quick to detect the similarities between the Gainesville conspiracy case and several other such cases that Nixon's attorneys had brought against antiwar protesters and other critics of his administration—

among them, the Boston 5 (including Dr. Benjamin Spock and Reverend William Sloane Coffin), the Chicago 7, Bobby Seale and the Panther 8, the Panther 21, Daniel Ellsberg and Anthony Russo, the Harrisburg 7 and their fellow Catholic radicals, and the Camden 28 (who had raided draft board, FBI, and Army intelligence records in one fell swoop)—none of which had resulted in a single sustained conviction. The Gainesville case seemed almost a carbon copy of the failed Harrisburg prosecution, in which the government had sought to prove that Father Philip Berrigan and six other leaders of the Catholic left had conspired to kidnap Henry Kissinger and demand as ransom the release of all political prisoners in the United States. Not only was "the idea of a bunch of priests and nuns zipping off with Henry Kissinger" patently absurd, as one of the jurors later commented, but the whole case had been based on the testimony of a government informer even less credible than William Lemmer. The chief witness against the Harrisburg 7 had been an ex-convict named Boyd Douglas, who admitted to being a compulsive liar and often contradicted himself on the witness stand.

Even before the Gainesville indictments were handed down, Lemmer's credibility had all but evaporated. In early June, Lemmer's wife, in the course of separating from him, had sworn out a warrant for his arrest and petitioned the court to have him committed as mentally insane; she had later withdrawn the petition only because she feared for her life, since Lemmer had threatened her with an assortment of loaded firearms, and had even attempted to stab her. Meantime, a University of Arkansas doctor, after examining Lemmer, recommended he receive psychiatric treatment. The most damaging evidence, however, came from a tape-recorded, eight-hours-long interrogation of Lemmer conducted by former VVAW coordinator Martin Jordan and veteran Donald Donner after Lemmer had returned to Arkansas.

A lawyer independent of the case who listened to Lemmer's taped confession described it as "hair-raising." Lemmer spoke of wanting vengeance against various members of VVAW, whom he blamed for his wife's decision to leave him. In letters to her, which she turned over to the VVAW, Lemmer even detailed plans to use his airborne ranger training to strangle some of them with piano wire. But rather than coming across as a misfit or monster, Lemmer actually sounded halfway sympathetic. Neither Judas nor executioner, he was clearly a victim himself—one more severely traumatized combat vet. Well aware of his own unbalance, he had scrawled on his wall: "PVS kills." In the interview, he said he had been sincerely antiwar ever since returning from Vietnam, and that his protest activities while living off base at Fort Benning had led the military to "persecute" him in various ways, including shooting into his trailer and setting him up for drug arrests. The persecution followed him back to his home state, where he and his wife had extreme financial difficulties as he struggled to continue his studies at the University of Arkansas.

The FBI had evidently made a devil's deal with him. Not only would they keep military intelligence and other police from hassling him, they would also pay him a princely salary (first thing he did with the money was buy a Toyota sports car), in exchange for which he need only report on what he saw and heard at VVAW and other peace-movement meetings and plant a few ideas (dreamed up at FBI headquarters) in his fellow protesters' minds. Lemmer somehow felt he was actually "cover[ing] a lot of people, myself included," by his cooperation with the government; that the protection from arrest granted to him would naturally extend to the other vets with whom he protested the war. He managed to rationalize his promotion of violent actions through his belief that some kind of violent rebellion was about to happen anyway, and he might as well get some connections on the inside of the power perimeter while he could—perhaps to hedge his own revolutionary bets, perhaps in the hope of protecting his friends, perhaps both. Camil saw Lemmer as a fellow Vietnam vet, "a brother," who was deeply afflicted with post-Vietnam syndrome (PVS) just as he himself was. Camil maintains that he argued with the defense lawyers throughout the trial to "make them go easy on this guy." "We don't want to fuck him up," he would tell them. "It's not his fault he's like that—it's the government's fault."

On November 7, 1972, in the federal court in Gainesville, the eight conspiracy defendants pleaded innocent to all of the government's charges. The seven veterans all declared themselves guilty, however, of something they had not been charged with: "crimes against the people of Indochina." John Briggs, the twenty-year-old nonveteran who had procured some of the wrist-rocket slingshots for Camil, confessed that he was also guilty of allowing his government to wage an illegal war—an act of solidarity that won him the epithet of "VVAW sympathizer," which evidently sounded to the authorities close enough to the McCarthyite term "Communist sympathizer" to be useful in establishing his guilt. Judge David Middlebrooks set bond for each of them at $10,000; and when the lead defense attorney, Morton Stavis of the Center for Constitutional Rights (CCR) in New York, asked that they be allowed to post only 10 percent of that amount, the judge told him, "If you argue further with me about the bonds, I am going to refuse to allow you to practice law in the Northern District of Florida"—setting the tone for a trial whose whole modus operandi would be the suppression of the defendants' free speech and right to challenge the court.[119]

7. Peace with Honor; Heroes Dishonored

In the fall of 1972 there was scant public attention to the Gainesville conspiracy case, chiefly because the war itself, like a long-lingering critical illness, had finally entered its acute phase. The result for the antiwar movement was the most dismal period in its almost decade-long existence.

McGovern's presidential campaign ran into trouble before it was even out the starting gate. His vice presidential running mate, Thomas Eagleton, made the disastrous admission that he had been given electroshock treatment for mental disorders; and even more corrosive to McGovern's image was his indecisiveness about how to handle the scandal, though he eventually dumped Eagleton in favor of Sargent Shriver, the late President Kennedy's brother-in-law. The main problem, though, was that McGovern was a one-issue candidate, and Nixon knew just how to steal his thunder on the subject of the Vietnam War. As Hunter Thompson observed, Nixon demonstrated that he did indeed have a "secret plan" to end the war, just as he'd promised in 1968: "The plan was to end the war just in time to get himself re-elected in 1972." On October 26, less than two weeks before the election, Nixon's chief foreign policy aide, Henry Kissinger, announced the successful conclusion of his secret negotiations with North Vietnam. "Peace is at hand," declared Kissinger with his elitist, smirky Harvard smile that left much of America in awe of him, and in so doing virtually guaranteed Nixon the landslide of electoral votes he got on November 7 (521 to McGovern's 17, from lone Democratic holdout Massachusetts).

By the end of 1972, the nation was deadened with war weariness, and Kissinger's peace agreement—like the fabled Grecian gift-horse—seemed safer left unexamined. Kissinger's announcement of a breakthrough was, in fact, based mainly on one concession from the North Vietnamese: Hanoi had at last agreed to a peace agreement that left South Vietnamese President Nguyen Van Thieu (temporarily) in power. What Kissinger did not reveal was that he himself had yielded on several points that virtually guaranteed the eventual overthrow of the Thieu government and the destruction of South Vietnam as a sovereign country. Kissinger had agreed to leave all North Vietnamese troops in place in South Vietnam after the cease-fire. He had agreed to an "election commission" comprising both Thieu's government and the Communist Provisional Revolutionary Government (PRG). What Thieu saw correctly was that he was having a coalition government forced down his throat—a coalition that included, and recognized the legal status of, his dreaded and deadly enemy: the Viet Cong.

Kissinger had also backed off from earlier U.S. and South Vietnamese demands that a cease-fire include Laos and Cambodia. Finally, he had ensured his "formula for defeat" (as one State Department official called it, off the record) by leaving the Communists in control of both sides of the demilitarized zone (DMZ). Though the military resupply of both armies was to be on a strict one-to-one basis, there was no real means for policing the cease-fire, especially since the Communists alone monitored traffic across the DMZ.

The agreement, which had actually been reached on October 8, was not signed before the election, chiefly because Kissinger had neglected to get Thieu's approval before shouting it from the rooftops. Of course, Kissinger had failed to consult Thieu because he knew in advance what Thieu's reaction would be. Once he heard of it, Thieu denounced the agreement, privately, as a complete betrayal of his nation by the United States. But in public, Nixon, Kissinger, and Thieu continued to make a show of working in concert, and the American people were duped into keeping Nixon as their president under the assumption that just a few minor details needed to be worked out before his having achieved—miracle of miracles—"peace with honor." The American press fell all over itself to describe Kissinger's "dramatic negotiating break-through," when what he had really accomplished, as Seymour Hersh put it, was a "negotiating breakdown."

Sliding back into office with almost 61 percent of the popular vote—close to LBJ's huge margin in 1964 in his crushing victory over Barry Goldwater—Nixon had a mandate to do just about anything he wanted anywhere on the globe (Bob Hope joked on his annual Christmas show that Nixon was seen in New York "picking out a crown"). But Nixon was actually in a tight spot, since his reelection had not engendered any political coattails, and he would have to deal with Democratic Party majorities in both the Senate and the House. The next Congress was sure to vote an end to spending on the Vietnam War as soon as it came into session on January 2, 1973. Faced with Thieu's refusal to sign the peace agreement, Nixon attempted to save face by demanding changes on Thieu's behalf that he knew the North Vietnamese would likewise refuse; and once the North Vietnamese, tired of Nixon's bad faith, broke off negotiations on December 14, Nixon had the excuse he needed to resume massive bombing of North Vietnam.

Nixon would later take credit for bombing the North Vietnamese back to the negotiating table; but it was not American bombs, which had never forced their submission to anything, that brought them back, it was simply his own dilatory acceptance of the October 8 agreement. Nixon knew that he could not claim "peace with honor" while his South Vietnamese allies were screaming "betrayal," and so the unprecedented "carpet bombing" of North Vietnam he ordered in the waning days of his first presidential term was aimed chiefly at reassuring Nguyen Van Thieu that America would always intervene to keep the Communists from taking over his country.

In the twelve days from December 17 to 28, the American military bludgeoned Hanoi, Haiphong, and other highly developed areas of North Vietnam with the most concentrated aerial bombardment ever used against any human population. Air Force B-52 Stratofortresses plastered densely inhabited areas with their "arc-light" strikes of crater-making 2,000-pound bombs in half-mile-wide swaths. Together with the smaller F-4 Phantom and F-111 fighter-bombers, they dropped in the first five days alone 100,000 tons of explosives, the equivalent of five early atomic bombs. At the end of twelve days, American planes had dropped on North Vietnam the destructive equivalent of all the bombs dropped on Japan during the entire Second World War.

Throughout the world there was strong condemnation of this second round of "Christmas bombings," even from many of America's allies (Swedish Premier Olof Palme compared them to Nazi atrocities in Guernica, Lidice, and Treblinka); and within the country a voice of conscience was raised against them not just by the usual antiwar organizations but also by nearly the entire religious community.

As it happened, Barry Romo had arrived in Hanoi just three days before the start of the Christmas bombings. Sponsored by VVAW, he had made the trip with a delegation that included folksinger Joan Baez, retired Brigadier General Telford Taylor, who had served as U.S. chief counsel at Nuremberg, and a Yale minister named Michael Allen. Having intended a peaceful stay delivering Christmas presents to POWs, they instead spent most of their trip alternately huddling in bomb shelters by night—where Baez sang Christmas carols and "Kumbaya" to calm everyone's fears—and by day roaming the city as an ad hoc witness team to inspect the damages. What they saw horrified even Taylor, who had come as a believer in the virtuousness of the American military. America's supposed "pinpoint bombing," they found, had destroyed Bach Mai Hospital—a 900-bed facility, the largest in North Vietnam—killing twenty-five doctors and nurses and countless patients, some of whom had been buried alive in the rubble. It had also wrecked the terminal of Gialam International Airport, and leveled a village filled with old men, women, and children that they had passed through only a few days before.

Taylor had already written a book called *Nuremberg and Vietnam: An American Tragedy,* in which he had insisted that senior American officers must take responsibility for the atrocities carried out by their subordinates—just as America and her allies had held German senior officers responsible for Nazi atrocities. Still, he evidently had a hard time believing that his own government could have deliberately authored a catastrophe of the magnitude he observed in Hanoi. He offended both Romo and Baez by announcing that the worst thing he'd seen in North Vietnam was the failure of the North Vietnamese to provide bomb shelters for the American POWs who were endangered by off-target American bombs. But Romo eventually forgave him, believing that Taylor "had one of the worst problems of delayed stress that I've ever seen" because he had been unable to integrate his long life of service as a political officer and, later, a professor of international law at Columbia University with the wanton carnage wrought by American military might he'd witnessed in Hanoi. The most he could bring himself to say in behalf of the North Vietnamese, after he got back, was that they were totally independent, totally dedicated, and hence unbeatable by any outside army, which Romo considered "a very loving statement."

Romo himself recalls having a near breakdown at a banquet in Hanoi in honor of the peace mission. In the midst of "toasting to the reunification of Vietnam" and to "Uncle Ho, a nationalist and the George Washington of his country," Romo suddenly found himself hit with the vision of "my nephew dying—the people I had killed . . . my life passed before me." He began crying inconsolably, until a Communist diplomat, Mr. Quat, took him aside and told him: "You can't work off guilt. Guilt has no place to go except self-destruction. And you can't work off hate, because hate is self-destruction. You love the Vietnamese. That's something you can grow on. . . . When the war ends, you'll be the only American to have fought in the South and to live under the bombings in the North. When this victory is won, it's gonna be your victory too. And you can have the same happiness that all the Vietnamese have."

That prophecy would, unfortunately, be a long time in coming true for Romo and most other veterans; and "meanwhile," as Jan Barry wrote to the *New York Times,* "it's been a black Christmas . . . and not the last, I'm afraid, of this war." Peace agreement or no peace agreement, Vietnam vets still faced a long-term weariness that was well expressed by Gainesville "conspirator" William Patterson: "The war goes on in our heads every day," he told an interviewer, "and it's not about to end."[120]

. . .

On August 14, 1972, several days before the Last Patrol even reached Miami, journalist John Kifner had published a long piece in the *New York Times* citing William Lemmer as the "key" to the Gainesville conspiracy case and examining the many contradictions and loose ends in his testimony. But the veterans waited in vain for the other shoe to drop. Months passed with no follow-up article, no attempt by the press to go beyond Lemmer's pathetic psychopathology and to dig up the bigger conspiracy, the one formed within the U.S. government to discredit and undermine VVAW—the conspiracy in which Lemmer, far from being the key, was merely a pawn. As Jan Barry explained to *New York Times* editorial director Herbert Mitgang, the lack of such investigative reporting had allowed the government to keep the public deceived with its own sinister mixture of disinformation, innuendo, and rumor: "One of the defendants, Pete Mahoney, in fact has found that in speaking around the country, even sympathetic audiences have the misimpression that the indictments were brought *after* the Republican Convention, and in response to some action the VVAW must have done there."

Public speaking by the defendants was therefore one of the chief ways to get the truth out. It would take tens of thousands of dollars to keep them traveling around the country for an entire year, and such a project could not be done without the full support of the VVAW national office in Chicago—both in fund-raising and in coordinating the defense effort. By the end of summer, Barry Romo had made the fateful decision: VVAW would back the Gainesville defen-dants all the way. It "killed" them do so, he recollects, but they knew "that if there was a conviction of these guys for a violent attack on the Republican Convention it was the end of VVAW." In fact, not only did VVAW national throw its weight behind the defendants, but regional chapters all over the coun-try got involved in leafleting, soliciting donations, holding rallies and sponsor-ing appearances by the eight, and sometimes joining forces with local ACLU groups to publicly endorse the merits of their case.

Despite the harmonious front, however, bitter squabbling occurred from the very beginning, making deep cracks in the unity of the organization. A lot of this internal dissension came from the usual questions of who was getting the money that was raised and what it was actually being used for. If the defendants were sometimes the loudest complainers, this too was understandable. The government itself was feeding their discontent—referring to them in press statements as the "bad apples" in an otherwise okay veterans' organization: the old strategy of "divide and conquer." Moreover, there was the obvious discon-tent of five to twenty years in a federal penitentiary hanging over these eight young men, all in their early or mid-twenties, as well as the considerable trauma of having, as Pete Mahoney put it, to "spend one year being a professional defendant."

Two things rapidly emerged in their favor. First, and foremost, was simply who they were. It turned out most of them were actually quite sympathetic, even admirable, individuals, and newspapers around the country reveled in printing their profiles, so rich in irony at a time when Nixon himself was prais-ing the virtues of Vietnam veterans and when his own administration was begin-ning to look less and less virtuous under the growing dark cloud of the Watergate burglaries and such questionable command decisions as his order to repeat the Christmas bombings.

The core of the Gainesville Eight were seven young men who, between them, had spent a total of 111 months in Vietnam, received 57 medals and cita-tions, and were all honorably discharged. Even Scott Camil, the most contro-versial of the defendants, was praised in the *Miami Herald* by no less an authority figure than Gainesville Mayor Richard Jones. Recalling how Camil had helped calm people during the May riots, Jones called him "a likable, intel-ligent and well-motivated young man with strong convictions." In the same arti-cle, Alachua County Sheriff Joe Crevasse was quoted as saying, "We've never had any trouble with Scott or the VVAW." It was also noted in several articles that most of Camil's family were involved in public service, and that his own ambition upon leaving the Marines—before the government sullied him with an array of criminal charges—had been to run for Congress.

Pete Mahoney rated a whole article by *New York Post* columnist James A. Wechsler. Up till then, Mahoney, tall, quiet, and self-contained, clean-shaven but with incongruous shoulder-length wavy hippie hair, had been something of a mystery figure. Wechsler revealed that he had gone to St. Pius X Seminary to prepare for the priesthood, but had dropped out of college just after the 1968 Tet Offensive to join the Army, from a sense of duty to his country. His bright mind made Officer Candidate School (OCS) a breeze, and by March 1970 he was already a first lieutenant in Vietnam. What had opened his eyes was being assigned to train People's Self-Defense Forces during Nixon's Vietnamization program. Within weeks after his first class of South Vietnamese trainees had "graduated," they had all marched off to join the Viet Cong. "That's when I started to realize they must really believe in something," Mahoney told Wechsler, "and that I as an American shouldn't be telling them they had no right to believe in it." Wechsler made no bones about his bias. He concluded his piece: "Mahoney deserves better of his countrymen than the tainted prosecution initiated by the heirs of [former Attorney General] John Mitchell." Anyone reading that column would have had a hard time disagreeing with him.

Bill Patterson was as much of a war hero as Camil. As an Army helicopter door gunner, he insisted on returning to the same battle from which he had just been brought back to base after being shot through the arm. For this valorous devotion to his comrades he had been awarded the Distinguished Flying Cross. But in his heart Patterson carried far more guilt than glory, a lot of it having to do with having killed 13 unarmed Vietnamese civilians with the .50 caliber on his cruising death ship. When he learned of the courtmartial of Army Lieutenant William Calley for the murder of civilians at My Lai, Patterson turned himself in to the authorities at Fort Bliss, asking to be tried for the same crimes as Calley, but the Army brushed him off. (Interestingly, Tom Zangrilli had reacted with a similar outrage when he heard of Calley's trial; he thought "they must be joking," since his Marine outfit had killed civilians on a routine basis, and would scarcely bat an eyelash unless perhaps it were a baby that got killed.) Having moved to Texas from New Jersey to study political science, Patterson went on to organize the El Paso VVAW, attracting the attention of the FBI as another potentially dangerous revolutionary. When his bail was set in the Gainesville case, it was originally $25,000, as high as Camil's; and the government cited his Distinguished Flying Cross—given only to exceptionally fearless soldiers—as evidence of why it was safer to keep him in prison.

Patterson was a poor fit as revolutionary, but if anyone could fill the bill, besides Camil, it might have been John Kniffin. A native of Texas, Kniffin had volunteered for the Marine Corps in 1965. After serving 32 months in Vietnam as a tank commander in the Third Marine Division, Kniffin was honorably discharged as a staff sergeant. With the long straight hair of an Apache brave and the mean profile of tough-guy actor Charles Bronson, Kniffin told stories of having participated regularly in "a hunting game to see how many people you could kill so you could go on R and R to China Beach or Saigon." He had become, he said, one of America's "mercenaries . . . killing to get a trip to Kuala Lumpur." One could easily imagine Kniffin bursting into the Oval Office in his cowboy boots, tanker's cap, khaki shirt with the triple chevrons on each sleeve, and crossbow in hand, ready to count some serious coup. In reality, he was a thoughtful man, who told political historian Fred Cook that "it takes you six months to two years [after returning stateside] to find out why your head is so messed up." Kniffin had joined VVAW as a way of helping to heal his own self-acknowledged post-Vietnam syndrome.

Far more tragic than any of them, though, was ex–Navy corpsman Alton Foss. A native Floridian, Foss was only seventeen and a popular high school athlete when he enlisted in the Navy, in 1964; a year later, he found himself tending casualties with the Ninth Marines south of Da Nang. In May 1966 he himself was wounded in an ambush, shot twice in the left leg. Both bones in his lower leg were shattered, leading to osteomyelitis, and the nerve to his foot was destroyed. He had been in and out of the VA on a regular basis since 1967, and by the time of the Gainesville trial, in July 1973, he had had ten operations. VA doctors had actually worsened his condition by severing his Achilles tendon when they put him in traction. As a result, he had great difficulty walking and often used a wheelchair, but his greatest debility from the war was psychological. For months after his wounding, he had been treated with morphine and Demerol, and had soon acquired a severe addiction. He also suffered from delayed stress and "anxiety problems about being a cripple," which manifested in terrible outbursts of temper—one of which got him fired from his delivery job with Miami's Hatton Drug Company. Foss had gotten back at them by stealing one of their trucks loaded with hospital drugs; he had been caught, and sent into a drug rehabilitation program rather than prison, but his dependency was only temporarily cured. At the time that he was indicted for conspiracy, his mother and father had both recently died, and his wife had left him, taking their two young sons with her back to New Jersey.

Foss's life was as shattered as his lower left leg bones when, as Miami VVAW coordinator, he was visited in his Hialeah home by Pablo Fernandez, the right-wing Cuban who was busy collecting three different government paychecks. The occasion was a planning meeting for the Democratic National Convention, and it was attended by, among others, Bob Davis of Miami's Metro Community Relations Board, who later reported to the press what was said there. At the meeting, Fernandez had tried to frighten Foss with a tale that Abdala, the most militant Cuban exile organization, planned to blow up the Center for Dialogue, an antiestablishment meeting place often used by VVAW. Fernandez offered to sell Foss fifty submachine guns to protect the meeting place; but Foss, on edge as he was, had declined.

Not satisfied with the point it had proved, the government—or whoever was really in charge—then sent the two Dade County undercover cops Salt and Pepper (Jerry Rudolff and Harry Crenshaw) to coax Foss to meet with Fernandez again regarding the purchase of the submachine guns. Foss declined to go to the meeting they had set up. Rudolff and Crenshaw came after Foss a third time, just before the Democratic Convention, allegedly bought three tabs of LSD from him for $2.50 each, and then had him busted on a narcotics charge—the arrest that led to their being unmasked as VVAW infiltrators. Foss's version of the event was that the two agents summoned him to a midnight meeting in the Orange Bowl's parking lot, threatened to bust him unless he finked on his VVAW friends; and when he refused, they invented the LSD transaction. However strange his tale, it was not nearly as preposterous as the syndicated AP story about him that ran a few days after the grand jury indictments were issued; according to that story, Dade County's Public Safety Department (a front for its narcotics squad) claimed that it had gone after Foss to prove that "the VVAW was supported by narcotics sales"!

What government agents did after Foss's arrest exposed their true motives. They took his shoes—including the orthopedic shoe for his left foot he had been given at the hospital, with an ankle brace built in—and threw him in a cell at the Dade County jail. Foss protested that he could not walk without the special shoe, and they told him to "hop or crawl" instead. Then they took him aside, and offered him the chance to avoid being indicted by the grand jury in Tallahassee if he cooperated with them in helping to convict the other leaders of VVAW. Foss was eventually released from jail; but even then, he was taken to a motel and sequestered there with his girlfriend. Camil claims the government provided him with drugs to bend him to their will. In any case, Foss agreed to let the FBI tape-record his telephone conversations with Scott Camil.

Hearing that Foss was ready to sign a "confession" that the police had gotten him to dictate, Camil, Perdue, and Mike Oliver snatched him out of the motel and took him to a secret VVAW hideout, where they forced him to get off drugs cold turkey. Foss was so desperate for his painkillers that he tried various ruses to get himself hospitalized, even swallowing rubbing alcohol and pulling a steel pin out of his foot; but the vets refused to let him fall back into the government's clutches until the trial actually began.

Still, Foss's life would be a long downhill slide from the time the government singled him out for indictment.[121]

8. "Innuendo and Supposition," and FBI Agents with Earphones

The Nixon administration was not impervious to the kind of persecution it practiced against the Vietnam veterans, however; and the second boon they received was the start of the president's fall toward threatened impeachment and forced resignation—a sudden turning of the tables, a reversal of hunter and hunted, that could not have been foreseen only a few months earlier, when Nixon's law-and-order legions had carried on their war against dissent with seeming impunity, gassing and bashing whatever stood in his path to an absolute, and ultimately Pyrrhic, victory.

When the six veterans were indicted for conspiracy, the late May and early June break-ins at Democratic National Committee (DNC) headquarters in the Watergate Hotel were still seen as just a low-grade burglary; but by the time Michelsen and Briggs were added to make the Gainesville Eight, in late October, the president's crooked pot had begun to simmer. One of the burglars caught rifling DNC files and installing a bug in Democratic Party chairman Lawrence O'Brien's telephone was James W. McCord, a former CIA agent currently working for CREEP, Nixon's reelection campaign organization. Another was Bernard Barker, an occasional sidekick of Pablo Fernandez, the Cuban submachine gun and grenade salesman. Barker had also taken part in the break-in of Daniel Ellsberg's psychiatrist's office the previous September. McCord and Barker were being supervised by E. Howard Hunt and G. Gordon Liddy, and both Hunt and Liddy had had dealings with John Ehrlichman and Charles Colson, two of Richard Nixon's closest advisors. It would take two years for the nearly full unraveling of the story, but with each step the trail got closer to the Oval Office and the chief executive's big, self-bugged desk.

On September 15, 1972, a Washington, D.C., federal grand jury indicted the five Watergate burglars and their two bosses, Hunt and Liddy; meanwhile Nixon and two other close assistants, H. R. "Bob" Haldeman and John Dean, had worked all summer to make sure that the investigation did not get any nearer to the White House. But on October 15, the *Washington Post* reported that Nixon's plan for political sabotage against his opponents was connected to the Watergate burglary through Haldeman and his close aide, Dwight Chapin, who had both passed along instructions to the chief saboteur, Donald Segretti. Even more damaging, on October 25, the *Post* revealed that Haldeman controlled the slush fund that had paid for both the political sabotage and the Watergate break-ins.

By now, the *Post*'s investigative team of Bob Woodward and Carl Bernstein were determined to keep chasing the story of their career, and the only thing still keeping Nixon at arm's length from their snapping jaws was the reluctance of the rest of the American press to join in the hunt—that is, to take their charges seriously. An October 1972 poll showed that half the nation still had no notion what "Watergate" even referred to.

One of the people who was keeping close watch on the story, however, was attorney Morton Stavis, cofounder of the Center for Constitutional Rights (CCR) in New York.

Several lawyers had come to the aid of the Gainesville Eight, including Camil's friends Larry Turner and Carol Scott, and two Texas attorneys representing Kniffin and Patterson: Cam Cunningham and Brady Coleman. But the wisest move the defense committee made was to bring in CCR's "Morty" Stavis as the lead attorney on their case. Stavis was a stocky, feisty, take-no-shit-from-anyone labor lawyer and general crusader for justice, who had won many civil rights cases in the South during the early sixties. He had already seen the government manufacture evidence and trample all over the Bill of Rights during the legal odyssey of the Chicago Seven, since another CCR cofounder, William Kunstler, had been lead attorney for that conspiracy trial and Stavis had been principal attorney for the ensuing contempt case. Stavis smelled government treachery from the day he came onboard in the Gainesville case, and he was to be proved right again and again.

It was Stavis who first spotted the possible connection between the Watergate burglary and the Gainesville conspiracy indictments. To begin with, there was the proximity in time. McCord, Barker, and their three Cuban accomplices were caught in DNC headquarters at 2 A.M. on June 17; the conspiracy subpoenas were served on VVAW members on July 1. What clinched the connection, though, was the testimony of James McCord during his trial in January 1973. McCord tried to defend the break-in by stating that the Internal Security Division of the Justice Department—i.e., prosecutor Guy Goodwin's employer—had suspected the Democratic Party of consorting with violent radical groups. The only such "violent radical group" McCord mentioned by name was Vietnam Veterans Against the War. His argument, in a nutshell, was that the government had found it necessary, for its own protection as well as the public safety, to learn if the Democratic Party might be conspiring to overthrow the American system of two-party constitutional government. VVAW was thus the government's alibi. No one in their right mind would buy a scenario of potbellied liberal politicians bearing arms against their own government, but a sizable number of citizens still bought the stereotype of the crazed Vietnam veteran as someone to fear.

After McCord and Liddy were convicted by a jury (and the other five burglars having pleaded guilty), the United States Senate voted unanimously on February 7, 1973, to establish a select committee to investigate "Watergate"—the single word that had come to stand for the whole tangle of secret government crimes and quasi-legal intelligence operations just now coming to light. In sworn testimony before the Watergate Committee, McCord several times repeated his assertion that the DNC break-in had been justified by the plausible threat of collusion between the Democratic Party and VVAW in a plot to violently obstruct the reelection of Richard Nixon. But anyone with half a legal mind could see that this flimsy excuse would have seemed virtually ludicrous without the Gainesville indictments to back it up. Hence Stavis proposed—and it became one of the main thrusts of his defense—that Nixon's guilt-ridden

Justice Department and his complicitous advisors had hastily concocted "the Gainesville conspiracy," perhaps in some White House conference room, as a means of deflecting the Watergate investigation that was sure to follow. One figure who linked the two cases was former Assistant Attorney General Robert Mardian, who had left his job as head of the Internal Security Division to work for the Committee to Re-Elect the President (CREEP); in Miami, Mardian's job had been to oversee security for the Republican Convention. Mardian was thus able to provide material from the surveillance of "radical" groups such as the VVAW for political use by Nixon's campaign committee. In this murky atmosphere, where politics merged with justice, Gainesville could easily have served as part of the greater Watergate cover-up.

Stavis wanted to use the Gainesville trial to reveal not only how the Justice Department had set out to get VVAW, but how American justice itself had been perverted to serve the cause of continuing the war. One of the worst symptoms of this perversion, Stavis felt, was the transformation of the grand jury system into "a Star Chamber procedure." Instituted in fifteenth-century England, in the time of all-powerful kings, the grand jury was devised as a means to protect against just such harsh and arbitrary prosecution as was practiced in the infamous, juryless Star Chamber. According to Stavis, the serious abuse of the grand jury system began in the 1950s, during Senator Joseph McCarthy's campaign to ferret Communists out of government and other influential places. At least if people were summoned to testify before the House Un-American Activities Committee (HUAC), where many of McCarthy's charges were being investigated, they could bring along a lawyer to warn them when possible self-incrimination or other legal pitfalls loomed near. But people called to testify before an American grand jury were not permitted to have counsel present and could be jailed for refusing to answer questions.

Under Richard Nixon, the Justice Department began to use the grand jury system primarily in an attempt to defeat—or at the very least, frustrate—the antiwar movement. In fact, Stavis and many others felt the whole Internal Security Division was established chiefly to tie up the peace movement with an endless proliferation of indictments. As head of the Internal Security Division, Robert Mardian had personally supervised many of the antiwar conspiracy trials that had been prosecuted by his right-hand man Guy Goodwin; and Mardian's and Goodwin's conduct in these cases was, to quote Stavis, "not governed by the Marquis of Queensberry's rules." Mardian, whose politics were considerably to the right of Nixon's, never hesitated to authorize wiretapping and other questionable means of surveillance; and in March 1974, Mardian himself would face indictment for conspiracy to obstruct justice by the grand jury investigating Watergate. Looking back years later, Stavis declared that "under Robert Mardian, and implemented and detailed by Guy Goodwin, there was probably the worst use of the grand jury that we've ever experienced.

Even in the worst days of the anti-Communist crusade, grand juries were not used in this fashion."

One thing seemed certain: even if the Gainesville conspiracy had not been conceived specifically as a way to explain the Watergate break-ins, the same contempt for constitutional rights and safeguards, and the same sleazy, hoodlumish tactics, were employed by the government in both instances.

The earliest indications of government foul play, besides the revelation of Lemmer's role as provocateur, were a series of burglaries committed against the Gainesville defendants and their attorneys. On Thanksgiving Day 1971, Camil's house (and Florida VVAW headquarters) had been broken into; the only things taken were VVAW membership lists and pages of testimony from veterans about their experiences in Vietnam. A month later, his house was hit again, and this time four rifles were taken. While both robberies took place before the Gainesville case had materialized, Nixon's "dirty tricks" teams, the so-called Plumbers, were already in full operation. In September 1971, Bernard Barker and his Cuban break-in team, under the direction of Hunt and Liddy (in a preview of their Watergate operation), burglarized the office of Daniel Ellsberg's psychiatrist. It had been almost a year before that, in late 1970, that Nixon had established the Intelligence Evaluation Committee (IEC), headed by none other than "Grand Jury Bob" Mardian, to facilitate illegal surveillance of the antiwar movement. According to agent Claude Meadow of the FBI's Gainesville office, orders had gone out at that time to "nail the leaders" of VVAW.

Any likelihood that it was just veteran paranoia making these sort of connections was dispelled in July 1972 when the office of Camil's attorney Carol Scott was broken into just two days before he was scheduled to appear in front of the grand jury; the burglars left her petty cash, electric typewriter, and other valuable articles, but took her entire file on just one client: the ex-Marine VVAW leader. Moreover, there was evidence of an attempt to bug her telephone. Several months later, when Camil's other attorney, Larry Turner, was flying back to Gainesville from New York, where he had been preparing legal briefs with the CCR attorneys, he was asked to check his briefcase; upon arrival in Gainesville, he found that the briefcase had somehow disappeared. When it was returned to him a day later, it was obvious that someone had rummaged through the papers inside. Strangest of all, in early July 1973, just a few weeks before the start of the Gainesville Eight trial, an FBI agent turned over a copy of the *Winter Soldier* film to the Jacksonville sheriff's office. The film had been stolen from the home of a VVAW member by two FBI informants, who had evidently not known that the film could be procured commercially from a distributor of documentaries; or perhaps things had gotten to a point where it seemed easier to get evidence by stealing it than, as John Houseman might say, in "the old-fashioned way."

Almost every week that spring and summer, there were startling revelations from the Senate Watergate Committee about the extent of illegal wiretapping and other electronic surveillance that the Nixon administration had authorized against its perceived "enemies." For five days on national television, Nixon aide John Dean (now a witness against his former boss) described what came to be called "the White House horrors"—one of which was Nixon's attempt in June 1970 to gain FBI approval for the "Huston Plan." Dreamed up by another Nixon aide, Tom Charles Huston, as a response to the continuing large-scale campus protests against the war, especially the riots that followed the Kent State shootings, the Huston Plan had called for a wide range of wiretaps, break-ins, "black bag" jobs, tamperings with the U.S. mail, and other illegal forms of harassment and interference in the lives of private citizens who happened to disagree with their government—all to be authorized by just one man: Richard Nixon. The Huston Plan was killed immediately by J. Edgar Hoover—some think because it removed too much of *his* power to authorize such surveillance—but Dean's and others' Watergate testimony gave every indication that Nixon had gone ahead and implemented the plan on his own, with the collusion of many lesser FBI officials. There was thus ample cause for the Gainesville defense team to file several pretrial motions requesting that the government reveal what if any spying had been done on the eight defendants.

One revelation the defense lawyers focused on was made by Watergate burglar James McCord in his testimony before the Senate Select Committee. McCord claimed that, prior to the Gainesville indictments, he had received reports on VVAW from the Internal Security Division (ISD), and that at least some of the material he read on the veterans' activities had been derived from bugging. The defense team asked for the right to question ISD Special Prosecutor Guy Goodwin about McCord's testimony; the request was summarily denied by federal district court judge Winston Arnow.

By late April 1973, the concentric circles of Watergate guilt had already reached Nixon's innermost group of associates, including John Ehrlichman, H. R. Haldeman, and John Mitchell. The government's sweeping denials of any link between its espionage and sabotage tactics in Watergate and its conduct of the Gainesville case lost credibility when Pablo Fernandez was shown to have connections with Watergate burglar Bernard Barker. The link between Watergate and Gainesville was reinforced still further when another associate of Barker's, Vincent Hanard, told of being offered money to infiltrate the VVAW by convicted Watergate conspirator E. Howard Hunt. And so Judge Arnow was forced—despite his repeated claim that "the government is not on trial in this case"—to allow the defense to subpoena one government witness who had been implicated in the Watergate affair: John Mitchell.

The former attorney general appeared in Arnow's courtroom in Pensacola, where the pretrial hearings took place, on April 25, 1973. Although Mitchell told the press, upon arrival, that he "was not even sure who the Gainesville Eight are," he managed to testify on the witness stand, somewhat perplexingly, that he had "no recollection of any electronic surveillance" relating to these people he could not identify. Each time Stavis tried to get Mitchell to be more specific about what he did know of the Gainesville indictments, the government objected, and Arnow sustained every objection. Stavis recalls that Arnow "tried desperately to stop me from interrogating Mitchell," to the point of fining Stavis $25 for each unacceptable question that he asked. Arnow absolutely refused to let Stavis question Mitchell about Watergate; and when Stavis went on anyway to ask whether Mitchell knew about the crimes committed by G. Gordon Liddy's spy squad, the judge himself objected: "That's completely irrelevant. . . . One more question, and if it's no better than the rest, you are finished." So Stavis gambled all on that last question, but before he could finish asking Mitchell, "Do you know *who knows* all the surveillance activities . . . ?" Goodwin objected again, and for the thirtieth time Arnow sustained his objection. Then, after Mitchell had been on the stand only one hour, Arnow announced: "This hearing is concluded."[122]

Arnow went so far as to complain to the bar association in New Jersey (where Stavis had his practice) about Stavis's "disrespectful" behavior.

Ironically, the defense team had asked the original grand jury judge, David Middlebrooks, to recuse himself, since (among other things) he had appeared openly hostile to the vets who had refused to testify. Comparing the recalcitrant veterans to the defendants in the Chicago 8 trial, Middlebrooks had remarked that Chicago judge Julius Hoffman—famous for having had defendant Bobby Seale carried bound and gagged into his courtroom—hadn't gone "far enough." Middlebrooks had even kept four VVAW members locked in jail until Supreme Court Justice William O. Douglas intervened to order their release; but Winston Arnow, the judge they got in place of Middlebrooks, made even less pretense of being unbiased. In Stavis' words, Arnow "wanted a conviction so bad he could taste it."

Arnow had just begun his war against the defendants. Incensed that the defense attorneys, prevented from bringing up Watergate in the courtroom, were spreading their theories about government conspiracy throughout the national press—and that the defendants were doing much the same thing on their cross-country speaking tours—Arnow threatened to impose a "gag order" on the entire defense camp. For starters, he banned the sketching of courtroom activity by media artists and confiscated any sketches that had already been made. A CBS artist then made a sketch from memory of one of the pretrial hearings; and after it was broadcast on the television news, Arnow fined the network $500 for contempt of court. The *Gainesville Sun* editorialized that Arnow was "way off-base" in attacking the press, and that he was infringing not only on the First Amendment right to free speech but also on the Sixth Amendment guarantee of a public trial. Despite the fact that the contempt citation was quickly overturned on appeal, Arnow went on to issue his gag rule more than two weeks before the trial began. According to the gag rule, the eight on trial, their attorneys, and anyone involved in their cause were all prohibited from making public statements concerning the case. In effect, the entire VVAW had been muzzled, and the defendants and their supporters were put on notice that it would now be a crime (in the judge's words) to try "educating the jury and the people through the media that the trial is a farce, a political repression and a political trial."

CCR attorney Nancy Stearns felt that "there was a much larger question involved than merely what was going on in that courtroom. We thought it was tremendously important that we should be able to speak to the nation about what was happening." The trial itself did not last long enough for the gag rule to be overturned, but many VVAW members chose to defy it, including a small army of veterans and their supporters who came to Gainesville several weeks before the trial to form a protest encampment in one of the parks. In response to Arnow's initial warning, in fact, VVAW founder Jan Barry had called a news conference on the steps of the Federal District Courthouse in Washington, D.C., demanding that "the President's intelligence-gathering agencies, Mitchell's Justice Department, Gray's FBI and various individuals associated with those organizations" come clean about their conspiracy to deprive VVAW and its membership of their civil liberties.

Arnow refused to acknowledge that such allegations had anything to do with the trial in his courtroom. He routinely denied a host of defense motions, ranging from challenges to the conspiracy statute and Goodwin's use of the grand jury to requests for dismissal of charges based on lack of evidence (the only "weapons" thus far shown to the court were a single carton of slingshots). Most of all Arnow stood as an impenetrable wall against any defense motions that sought to determine "whether and to what extent employees and agents . . . of the government participated in espionage, infiltration, sabotage, provocateurism, and electronic surveillance of the defendants or the Vietnam Veterans Against the War." At one point, reprimanding Stavis for his persistence in this direction, Arnow declared: "There is nothing before this court but innuendo and supposition that does not even suggest government misconduct, much less prove it." It almost sounded as if he were talking about the government's own case.

Trying to silence Stavis once and for all, Arnow produced a statement by FBI Agent Robert L. Pence: "I have caused inquiry to be conducted and as a result thereof have determined that no information in this case was derived from acts of espionage, infiltration, sabotage, provocateurism or electronic surveillance." The FBI claimed that the tape of a phone call between Camil and Foss, which had come to light earlier, had been legally recorded. But other recordings kept surfacing faster than the government could explain them, including a tape produced by Miami police officer Ralph Aguirre of Camil talking on the phone with Pablo Fernandez.

Among the individuals the defense wished to question on the subject of electronic surveillance were Richard Nixon, John Mitchell's assistant Robert Mardian, and prosecutor Guy Goodwin himself. Arnow steadfastly refused their requests, offering them instead a succession of affidavits, in which many of these individuals avowed that such surveillance had never occurred. The defense argued that the government had been caught lying on such issues before—most notably, in the case of the illegal wiretaps used against Daniel Ellsberg—and that it was therefore essential that they be allowed to question government representatives directly.

Arnow eventually granted a hearing on the issue of illegal electronic surveillance, from which many interesting facts emerged. *Miami Herald* staff writer Rob Elder had conducted his own thorough investigation (which resulted in an explosive article in *Ramparts* magazine called "Dirty Tricks on Trial"), from which it was learned that Cuban double agent Pablo Fernandez had worn a bug when he offered to sell Camil and Mahoney submachine guns and explosives. The FBI claimed that no tape existed from the encounter, however, since the bug had allegedly failed. Fernandez also admitted to Elder that he had acted as an agent provocateur—after which, according to journalist Fred Cook, he became "an acute embarrassment" to the government. Guy Goodwin successfully kept Fernandez from being subpoenaed for questioning by the defense lawyers, even after Fernandez's associate Angelica Rohan testified that Fernandez had used electronic surveillance against the VVAW several times— an assertion Goodwin objected to as hearsay. Once again, Judge Arnow sided with Goodwin, and he resumed his routine of fining attorney Morton Stavis $25 each time he persisted with more questions about the electronic eavesdropping activities of the absent Fernandez.

The issue was apparently resolved—at least to Arnow's satisfaction—when Guy Goodwin swore to the court, despite a mountain of contradictory evidence, that "there has been no electronic overhearings of any kind . . . of the said defendants at any location."

Not long afterward, on the day jury selection began, Pete Mahoney and members of the defense team had retired to their assigned conference room in the courthouse, when Mahoney noticed moving shadows behind the air vent down near the floor. As he bent down to peer through the vent, Mahoney spotted a couple of men working at a large electronic panel in a closetlike space; they were systematically moving a wire from their own machine down and up rows of telephone jacks—as if they were seeking just the right connection. The defense lawyers immediately got a couple of sympathetic young marshals to open the door to the "closet" next door, which turned out to be the telephone terminal room, and the guys inside turned out to be FBI agents, with their pockets full of electronic gear, including amplifiers, transmitters, and earphones.

Attorney Nancy Stearns, though she had assumed some form of illegal, unconstitutional surveillance might be conducted during the trial, thought "it was just beyond the pale to find the FBI men on the other side of the wall from you with your client." Fortunately *New York Times* correspondent John Kifner had been there to witness the incident. The defense lawyers went straight to Judge Arnow, who, knowing he was under the scrutiny of the media, agreed to hold an informal hearing on the matter the next morning. In the privacy of his chambers, the judge listened to an expert explain how by connecting the phone terminal from the defense office with the phone terminal from the FBI office in the same building, the FBI would be able to listen to every phone call the defense made. The FBI agents responded that they had gone to the terminal room for quite an opposite reason: to check out a rumor that the defense was bugging them! Their excuse, in Stearns' eyes, was "just hooey," but the judge blocked the defense from cross-examining the agents, and he rejected every defense motion for a mistrial or, at the very least, a full evidentiary hearing. There had been too many delays already, the judge said, and the defense was "making mountains out of molehills." Then, throwing down his pencil, the judge ended the discussion by declaring, "Somebody has to believe somebody."

Stearns felt that at least the judge had given them "a very good appeal point," since the privilege of lawyer-client conversations had been compromised. Mahoney felt the FBI had been "just flat-out dumb," for, innocent or not, their gaffe focused a lot of national media on the trial, including a piece by Kifner in the *New York Times*. "Bugging, Watergate, vets—it all came together," Mahoney recalls.[123]

9. "Is Perjury Part of a Prosecutor's Duty?"

What in retrospect looks like recklessness and arrant stupidity by the government has to be understood in the political climate of the time. Richard Nixon, by doling out hundreds of thousands of dollars in hush money, still fully expected to be shielded from investigation in the Watergate scandal. Moreover, Nixon was still riding high as the hero who had ended the Vietnam War. On January 27, 1973, the peace agreement between the United States and North Vietnam, negotiated by Kissinger and finally having been approved by South Vietnamese President Nguyen Van Thieu, was formally signed in Paris. The terms Nixon had gotten had been no better than what the North Vietnamese had been offering several years (and tens of thousands of human lives) earlier. His "peace with honor" was no more than a cease-fire in place; and though the agreement officially acknowledged the Provisional Revolutionary Government (PRG) as a political authority in the south, neither Thieu nor Nixon meant to treat the Communists as such. Astonishingly enough, four days earlier, just after the treaty was initialed, Nixon declared on television (as oblivious as Walt Whitman to self-contradiction) that "the United States will continue to recognize the Government of the Republic of Vietnam [Thieu] as the sole legitimate government of South Vietnam." Such double-talk, according to Seymour Hersh, made it "inevitable that war would continue."

In fact, the war never stopped. On Sunday January 28, the day after "peace was declared in Vietnam," American television viewers were shown scenes of Richard Nixon attending a special church service, where the minister praised Nixon's courage in not flinching from the years of "armed conflict" necessary to bring about a treaty that was fair and just to all sides. A few minutes later, on the same news broadcast, viewers were shown Viet Cong rockets being fired at an American air base, as well as Viet Cong attacks on the city of Tay Ninh, which, only 65 miles northwest of Saigon, was still under siege by Communist forces. On February 8, Thieu announced that his government would continue removing civilians from contested areas and confining them in "strategic hamlets," and that Communist sympathizers would still be subject to arrest. During the first ten days after the agreement took effect, the South Vietnamese Army initiated hundreds of infantry and armor assaults, air attacks, and shellings of PRG-controlled areas. Even George Orwell might have had a hard time calling this a "peace."

Skepticism concerning the negotiations had led to a massive "counterinaugural" demonstration in Washington on January 20, three days before Nixon's appearance on television announcing the treaty's acceptance. Eighty thousand demonstrators—most from the two major coalitions, NPAC and PCPJ, but a fair showing from VVAW as well—had gathered in the capital to announce the founding of a "national emergency network," which would continue pressuring Nixon to sign the agreement, and then make sure that he did not turn around and violate it. The VVAW contingent staged their own mock signing of the earlier Nine-Point Peace Treaty; but they warned, presciently, that "it is not enough to sign a piece of paper . . . the war continues until the treaty is implemented."

Most of the country, however, was amply willing to buy Nixon's and Kissinger's ultimate snow job; and then, to soothe everyone's nerves in the following months, there was the real joy and satisfaction of seeing almost 600 POWs returning flight by flight, as well as the withdrawal of the last 23,000 American fighting men (though still not all the technicians and advisors). In the Nixon administration there was a euphoria that made Watergate seem like a blemish that would soon fade, and that promoted an attitude of "You can get away with anything if you're tough enough." While high school and college graduates, no longer worried about the draft (which ended officially with the war), scrambled for jobs in a slow economy, and the nation drifted lethargically toward the middle of a decade that would be remembered chiefly for gasoline shortages, cocaine's ascendance over marijuana, and a new generation of rebels without a cause—kids with funny haircuts, tattoos, and metal rings in their skin, who called themselves punks—the body politic moved inexorably to the right and the veterans' movement ran aground on the shoals of a dozen different, ever more angry causes.

In April 1973, VVAW officially added the hyphenated suffix WSO—for Winter Soldier Organization—to its name and added the Revolutionary War flag with the motto "Don't Tread on Me" to its logo. A sampling of the pages of that month's issue of the VVAW-WSO newspaper *Winter Soldier* reveals Vietnam veterans intensely engaged in supporting a wide range of radical causes: the independence struggle in Guinea-Bissau; the legal defense efforts for Pat Chenoweth, a sailor accused of sabotaging the USS *Ranger* to keep it from sailing to Vietnam, and for Gary Lawton, a black ex-Marine community activist being railroaded through a second two-million-dollar murder trial, pertaining to the ambush of two white police officers in Riverside, California; and Operation County Fair, the establishment of a free medical clinic for poor, rural blacks in the Klan-ruled territory of Bogue Chitto, Alabama. The month before, a Midwest veterans' support convoy had been organized to aid the hundreds of Native Americans, members of the American Indian Movement (AIM), who were under siege by the federal government at Wounded Knee, South Dakota; and a few months later, the veterans would jump into the issue of prison reform, beginning with the creation of the Leavenworth Brothers Offense/Defense Committee by Randy Barnes and Kansas City VVAW—which raised over $100,000 for the legal defense of several prisoners, many of them veterans, on trial for their role in a prison riot, and published a newsletter exposing the terrible prison conditions that had led to the riot.

In America that spring of 1973, political tension escalated toward some unknown flash point that some thought might even be actual revolution. "The whole thing is up for grabs," Richard Boyle told Ron Kovic at one point, and there were some who honestly believed Nixon would call in the 82nd Airborne to take over Congress and stop the Watergate hearings before they could uncover his own role in the conspiracy.

There was every reason to think that way, since the government was pushing repression far beyond every constitutional safeguard, and the veterans' movement, along with black and Native American activists, were currently taking the brunt of it. In Los Angeles, vets leaving the VVAW office were routinely pulled over by police, handcuffed, searched, and held for a warrant check; Tom Zangrilli received such treatment ten times in a month. Fifteen policemen without a warrant broke into a VVAW house and ransacked the place, then

arrested everyone present on the ground that they had found "traces" of marijuana. A group of VVAW members who had gone to a black church in L.A. to
help protest a policeman's fatally shooting an unarmed black youth found themselves beaten by seven carloads of sheriffs, then locked in a jail cell where they
were again beaten and forced to breathe tear gas for hours. In several cities
government-authored letters and leaflets were circulated among VVAW members that accused certain individuals of stealing money from the organization,
being flunkies of the Progressive Labor Party (PL, another Maoist group), or
any other divisive charge that could be thought up. In Reading, Pennsylvania,
an old industrial city where the RU had already made deep inroads into the
VVAW membership, veteran Dennis Boyer recalls that "literally every morning
I could look out my window and see people with telephoto lenses and people
in unmarked sedans circling the block all the time with binoculars."

Even in such lopsided combat, however, the underdogs have their own
weapons. "Silence, exile, and cunning," had been the choice of Ireland's foremost literary rebel James Joyce, but in the United States under Nixon the path
to legal victory for the counterculture had been forged by, among others, attorney Charles R. Garry, who was very much a model for the Gainesville defense
team. After winning dismissal of the murder and kidnapping charges against
Black Panther Bobby Seale in New Haven, Garry had explained his modus
operandi: "When the fix is equal, justice prevails." One of Garry's strategies to
even the fix was to challenge the assumption that the average, mostly white,
largely male jury was actually a "jury of one's peers" for every defendant. In the
New Haven trial he and the other defense counsel spent eighteen weeks sifting through 1,500 veniremen—at enormous cost to the court—before they
agreed upon the twelve jurors who would hold life-or-death power over Seale
and his codefendant Ericka Huggins. In large part, it was the younger, blacker,
predominantly female jury that had forced the resulting mistrial; and so, in
Gainesville, Stavis and his team set about with similar determination to achieve
the most sympathetic possible jury. Stavis hired a psychologist named Jay
Schulman, who had pioneered an analytical technique for jury selection that
had been used successfully in the trials of Philip Berrigan and black militant
professor Angela Davis. The jury they got was a Schulman triumph: average age
31; 7 women; 3 blacks; 1 Vietnam vet; a professor's wife; a health food devotee.

By all accounts, the trial was extremely orderly, with none of the rollicking
countercultural antics of the Chicago 8 trial four years earlier. Still, the defendants never once let the court, or the public, forget that they were veterans. All
except Perdue and Michelsen wore fatigues or khakis much of the time; and
even Briggs, the "sympathizer," wore a VVAW T-shirt under his denims. There
were the more somber reminders, too: Foss in his wheelchair; Foss and some
of the others setting off the court's metal detector every day because of all the
shrapnel (and in Foss' case, steel pins) embedded in their flesh. The only sig-

nificant rebellious act they performed was deeply connected with their own military service. August 15 was the official date set by Congress to cut off all funding for Nixon's illegal bombing of Cambodia. The night before, a vote was taken in the defense camp as to whether they should mark the occasion in some manner in court that day. The lawyers were against it, but the defendants were for it; and, as in most other matters, the lawyers chose to let the defendants determine their own strategy.

On the morning of the fifteenth, one of the defendants stood up, in the presence of the jury, and requested that everyone stand for a minute of silence in commemoration of the Cambodian dead and wounded. Judge Arnow flew into a fury. He snapped, "You can't do that!" and then, as all the defendants, their attorneys, and some others in the courtroom stood in silent meditation, he blustered on and on about all the rules they were breaking. Finally Arnow, realizing that everyone had retaken their seats and ended their silence, ordered the jury out of the room, and then announced that he was citing all the defendants and their attorneys for contempt of court. Stavis marched up to the bench and asked if the judge had made a record of all the offenders, but Arnow had made no such record and couldn't even say for sure who had been standing and who hadn't. Stavis pointed out that if Arnow tried to issue contempt citations with nothing in the court record to justify them, he himself would be subject to legal sanction. Stifling his rage, Arnow backed down. It was clear to everyone in the court at that moment that Stavis knew more about the law than the judge did.

Arnow tried to get his revenge for the minute of silence by filing charges against all the defense attorneys with their respective bar associations, but the charges were so poorly written they were immediately thrown out. The defense learned that he was a yokel whose biggest case concerned the tax problems of a small gas station, and he had won a federal judgeship merely by never stepping on anyone's toes. He was in way over his head with the Gainesville conspiracy case, but tragically never seemed to realize it, and so came off more and more looking like a fool. At one point Richard Boyle's hearing aid began to squeal, and the judge demanded that he identify himself. Boyle replied, "I'm from *Rolling Stone*." The judge asked if that was a town in Kansas, and the whole courtroom cracked up.

Guy Goodwin, whose Internal Security Division was currently under investigation by the Senate Watergate committee, chose not to prosecute the case himself, but turned it over to local prosecutors Jack Carrouth and William Stafford. Goodwin's dandyish figure was frequently seen "slipping in and out of the FBI offices," according to *The Nation*, "but never in court."[124]

The government's principal witness, as expected, was William Lemmer. Lemmer repeated his earlier charges against Camil and the VVAW and even added a few more not mentioned in the original indictments. He accused Camil of organizing "political assassination squads" (O how that half-baked Kansas

City "Phoenix plan" was now coming back to haunt him!), and he claimed Camil had overseen "rifle, pistol, and mortar practice" for his rebel soldiers far out in the swamps, as if Camil were the Jewish Che Guevara of rural Florida. Lemmer also talked of Camil's hidden derringer (now the fantasy had shifted to Camil as riverboat gambler, it would seem), and of Camil offering him a "contract" to kill a political enemy (Camil as gangster). On a melodramatic roll, Lemmer recalled veterans with "fishline bolos" for tripping police horses, homemade grenades, and the targeting of particular policemen for assassination.

That Camil was obsessed with guns and self-defense was a self-evident truth; and a number of VVAW coordinators, including Barry Romo and Randy Barnes, felt that Camil was probably guilty of at least some of the criminal intentions attributed to him. But then a lot of angry Vietnam veterans entertained violent fantasies, including Ron Kovic, who had gone so far as to buy a trunkload of automatic rifles with which to storm the White House. Such fantasies might even have been part of their PTSD symptomatology. In actual fact, even the angriest vets like Camil and Kovic rarely ever used any kind of violence against their opponents or enemies. In the end, the sense of being able to protect themselves was what these vets really needed to achieve; and for most of them, actually hurting other people was anathema, the last thing they ever wanted to do again.

In the next three weeks, the government trotted out another two dozen undercover agents and informants, but none of them could match Lemmer's spectacular inculpation; in fact, most of them admitted finding VVAW members unexpectedly well behaved, nice, peaceful people. Though little, if any, proof was given of VVAW's violent intentions, many curious facts emerged from this long parade of spying witnesses. For Richard Boyle, the most interesting revelation was how badly the government must have wanted to nail VVAW, for the FBI does not readily expose two dozen experienced undercover agents simply to win a conviction. One shocking disclosure was that at a VVAW meeting attended by Mahoney in New Orleans, the other seven members present were all government agents! It turned out that government agents made up fully half of the VVAW membership in Louisiana. Another disclosure, even more startling, was that one of the government agents called to the witness stand in Gainesville, a Vietnam veteran with the unlikely name of Emerson Poe, had attended a defense strategy meeting only the day before. "It was [out of] Kafka," said Richard Boyle, "but Kafka wouldn't even believe that trial."

Poe's testimony, in some respects, spelled the downfall of Goodwin's case against the Gainesville Eight. His very presence as a witness was a symptom of the blatant overreaching that had brought the case to trial in the first place. As VVAW's Florida state coordinator and assistant coordinator for the southern region, Poe had been one of the VVAW members subpoenaed to appear before the Tallahassee grand jury in July. At that time, Stavis had forced all the veterans who wanted Center for Constitutional Rights (CCR) representation to sign a statement attesting to the fact that they were not a government agent. Most of those subpoenaed had signed, including Poe. Stavis had also sought to compel Goodwin to reveal whether or not he had any agents in the defense camp. Under oath, Goodwin had testified before Judge Middlebrooks that none of Stavis's clients was a government agent.

The defense camp was thus caught way off base the day Poe took the stand in Gainesville. But none were more surprised than Scott Camil, who, acting as his own defense attorney, got the chance to question Poe directly. Camil had regarded Poe as one of his close friends—an illusion that Poe now did his best, though never very convincingly, to dispel. Camil asked Poe: "Isn't it true you gave a surprise birthday party for my girlfriend Nancy?" Poe had to answer yes. Wasn't it true that Scott and Nancy had helped Emerson and his wife decorate their Christmas tree? Yes again. Wasn't it true they had baby-sat for the Poes? Yes. Wasn't it true that Scott and Nancy had taken care of their child while Mrs. Poe was having a miscarriage? Poe could not deny that either, though he claimed he couldn't remember if Scott and Nancy had consoled them afterward. But when Camil asked him point-blank, "Poe, are we friends or not?" Scott's former right-hand man somehow managed to answer: "No."

It turned out that for months Poe had been copying the Florida VVAW newsletter on an FBI Xerox machine. But the testimony the government counted upon to condemn the Gainesville Eight actually came very near exonerating them. Although the newsletter did offer VVAW members the opportunity to order wrist-rocket slingshots, and though it did recommend that they lay in a goodly supply of projectiles such as ball bearings and fried marbles, it also stressed that demonstrations should be peaceful if possible, and that weapons such as the wrist rockets were only to be used in self-defense. On cross-examination, Poe was forced to admit that he had no knowledge of VVAW's planned use of weapons other than what he had put into the newsletter.

The real shame now began to fall onto Goodwin and the prosecution, for it soon came out that Poe was one of *three government agents* who had been planted in the defense camp. Another was Art Franz, a member of the Louisiana VVAW, who had also signed one of Stavis's affidavits declaring himself not an agent. Goodwin had thus perjured himself regarding Franz too. Franz was less of an issue, since he never testified at the trial, whereas Poe had met regularly with the defense lawyers at strategy meetings, and had even helped them select the jury. Moreover, he held a key to the defense lawyers' mailbox and regularly picked up their mail.

Stavis, in his own words, "raised holy hell" about the special prosecutor's betrayal, but the government was not about to prosecute Goodwin for perjury. The only recourse left to Stavis was to file a civil suit against Goodwin for prosecutorial misconduct—a case that went all the way to the Supreme Court in the early 1980s. Stavis won the case in the District of Columbia's Court of Appeals, but within a matter of days the Supreme Court decided another case to the effect that a police officer could lie with "absolute privilege" and not be sued civilly for doing so. Goodwin then petitioned the appellate court for a rehearing; and the appellate court, taking its cue from the new Supreme Court decision, decided that a prosecutor too had absolute immunity from civil suits concerning any misconduct done "in the performance of his duty"—even lying on the witness stand! The big, still unanswered question, as Mahoney put it, was: "Is perjury part of the performance of a prosecutor's duty?" The Supreme Court refused to hear the case, and the appellate court's final verdict, in Goodwin's favor, stood—a decision that left Stavis shuddering in horror. Again to quote Mahoney, what that decision meant was that "prosecutors can essentially do anything they want. They can put you in jail for years, they can send you to your death—and there's no way you can get back at them if they use illegal or underhanded means to prosecute you."

Mahoney did a good deal of shuddering himself during the Gainesville trial, for the third agent who surfaced inside the defense camp was Carl Becker, the man he considered his best friend. Becker had come from Louisiana with Franz, ostensibly to lend Mahoney moral support. A nonvet who had long been active against the war, Becker had replaced Mahoney as Louisiana state coordinator after Mahoney had been elected to the VVAW national office, and Becker had even assisted Mahoney in his move to New York. Then, as in his relocation to Gainesville for the trial, Mahoney was "just glad to have a homeboy come with me." After Franz and Becker stopped showing up at the defense meetings, the other defendants were convinced they were both informers, but Mahoney defended Becker until the moment the government called him to the witness stand.

Then it became apparent at once that Becker was (in Mahoney's words) "the worst of the informers, the prosecution's garbage man." There were still big holes in the prosecution's case, many parts of the indictment that had never been substantiated with an ounce of evidence, and Becker did his best to fill those holes by inventing conversations with the defendants that proved their guilt. Most of the informers, according to Mahoney, "essentially told the truth; they started with reality and then shaded it a little to make it sound worse than it was. Becker out-and-out lied: he just testified to things that flat never happened." It was Becker who implicated John Briggs in the conspiracy, since there was no other evidence against him, while in reality Becker had never even met with Briggs. And it was Becker who alleged that he had heard Mahoney declare his belief in violence as the only means of ending the war.[125]

10. Winners with a Broken Back

During the trial, the government made a great deal of the fact that some of the defendants, including Camil and Kniffin, owned guns. Their "weapons" were always mentioned in conjunction with that other favorite expression of the prosecution's: "fire teams"—but such scare tactics did not play well to a rural southern jury. This was territory where working-class folk generally kept a rifle in the back of their pickup truck, and where it was no big thing to take children along to target practice. After the Gainesville trial ended, one of the jurors stopped by Stan Michelsen's house and, after shaking hands with a few vets, went on to show them the pistol he kept in his glove compartment.

Nevertheless, Stavis saw the case as "very complicated and very difficult," and neither he, Nancy Stearns, nor any of the other attorneys were certain of winning an acquittal. "There were two things against us," Stavis recalled. "One was the prejudice of the judge, and the other was . . . I use the word *craziness*. But I don't mean that they [the defendants] were crazy people, but sort of nonsensical . . . a ridiculousness that came out of that whole Vietnam syndrome. I mean, suddenly you took a bunch of people, and all they were doing was carrying guns and killing people. I will never forget Patterson talking to me about how it felt to be up there in a helicopter with a machine gun, machine-gunning peasants who were running away. What did you do to young men? Perfectly decent young men, and the last thing in the world they'd normally be thinking of is killing, and suddenly that became their whole raison d'être, their whole purpose in life. And they come back, and they change their perspective. So what happens? They think of crazy and silly things, talking about guns and slingshots—utter nonsense. You've got to put yourself in that time frame. All these people were veterans of the Vietnam War, and they were upset. We're now beginning to find out a little more as to what happened to these young men— what happened to their psyche. What we were seeing were some of the first evidences of it, at that particular time. That's a lot of what this case was about."

As early as October of 1972, Stavis and his colleagues had come up with the idea of a defense based on post-Vietnam syndrome. They had called up Dr. Chaim Shatan, who had recently published his seminal piece "The Grief of Soldiers" in the *New York Times,* and Shatan organized the Gainesville Defense Mental Health Committee, which comprised about eight of the leading delayed stress theorists, including himself, Dr. Robert J. Lifton, Arthur Egendorf, Jack Smith, Florence Pincus, and Dr. Jon Bjornson, who had served as a psychiatrist in Vietnam and later became very active in VVAW. That fall, all the defendants were brought up to New York for two weeks, and those on the Mental Health Committee took psychiatric depositions from them. What they found was that many of them were indeed suffering from post-Vietnam stress. Among the startling revelations was the fact that for years Alton Foss had had great difficulty eating, a condition he had suffered from since his first day in combat in 1966. After working for hours to save the life of a critically wounded Marine, he had come back to camp, where the commander had congratulated him and offered him a hot meal; but as he had started to eat, he had smelled the wounded man's blood on his hands and vomited, and ever afterward the connection between food and death had been fixed in his mind.

The Mental Health Committee also helped the lawyers to understand their clients. Not only were the veterans far more politically unsophisticated than CCR's previous antiwar clients, they suffered from physical and psychological wounds, and experienced an intensely visceral anger, that had initially been difficult for their defenders to comprehend. The second thing the Mental Health Committee accomplished was, in Shatan's words, "a sort of therapeutic preparation for the trial." For the act of being tried on major felony charges, having their freedom—not to say their whole future—thrown in jeopardy, was triggering massive delayed stress attacks in many of them. The defendants were suffering from insomnia, nightmares, and flashbacks, losing their jobs and relationships, and fighting savagely among themselves—hardly the ideal conditions for constructing a viable defense.

Shatan claims the Mental Health Committee succeeded in sending the defendants back to Gainesville in much better shape for the trial, even though Stavis ultimately chose to drop the PVS defense. Stavis reasoned that it was better to present the defendants as "decent, honorable young men who were sound people. . . . We just thought, instead of portraying them as being crazy, that we'd portray the *prosecution* as being crazy." Ironically, while the vets got better, the shrinks found their own lives coming under attack for the help they gave. Not only did government surveillance of them increase markedly after their involvement in the trial, but at one point Shatan received a letter from one of the vets in his rap group explaining how vulnerable the Pentagon was to being bombed. The letter also included a blueprint of a federal munitions warehouse, which the vet said he thought Shatan might be interested in helping blow up. To avoid entrapment, Shatan carefully sealed up the material and hand-delivered it to the Gainesville defense team.

When it came time for Stavis to mount his defense, he chose to make none at all. It was the same strategy that Charles Garry had used in Bobby Seale's murder trial in New Haven, implying to the jury that the government's charges were so unfounded and preposterous that they did not deserve to be dignified with a formal answer—and it had worked. In the Gainesville trial, the government's case had already been thoroughly demolished, thanks especially to a brilliant cross-examination of Lemmer by Camil's attorney Larry Turner, which left the chief prosecution witness looking like a violence-obsessed, confused, and irrational psychopath.

Equally harmful to the government's credibility was the ever-growing Watergate scandal, whose corrupt tentacles seemed to reach in every direction, just as the defense had claimed. By August 31, 1973, when the Gainesville jury was sent out to deliberate on a verdict, President Nixon was already deeply embattled with the Watergate Special Prosecutor, Archibald Cox, and with United States District Court Judge "Maximum John" Sirica, in a losing struggle to keep from surrendering the tapes of his private meetings with the

Watergate conspirators; and talk of impeachment was all over the media, as well as the dominant topic in Congress.

Stavis put only one witness in front of the jury—a chemical expert who explained that Camil's so-called bomb, the mixture of glycerin and potassium permanganate, would never have worked as an incendiary device to detonate police-car gasoline tanks.

The jury were out for only three and a half hours, most of which they spent having lunch, while several of the defendants were photographed by the press playing Frisbee on the courthouse lawn. When the jurors returned, they had big smiles on their faces. The verdict was acquittal for all the defendants, on all counts.

That night, Friday, there began a victory party that continued for the rest of the Labor Day weekend. Lawyers, veterans, and well-wishers gathered at the defense headquarters, and even John Kifner of the *New York Times* and a few of the former jurors came by to offer congratulations and to share in the euphoria.

Bill Lemmer was not celebrating, however. A year later, an Associated Press story would quote him as saying that he had been "used as a decoy by the prosecution and then dropped." Remarried and about to become a father, he was broke and out of work, and had no friends to turn to. Sadly, he had found that his former FBI handler, Dick O'Connell, the one man he had always counted upon for protection and solace, wouldn't even return his Christmas card.

None of the defendants left that trial without their own scars; and for some, the wounds took years to even begin to heal. Pete Mahoney was one of the hardest hit. Already burdened by the guilt from all the South Vietnamese troops he had been forced to order to their death, he now had reason to distrust everyone, friends and authority figures alike.

"Probably the greatest single thing was simply the betrayal," Mahoney says. "Even to this day, my immediate reaction to a stranger who's nice to me is, 'What does this guy want from me?'" The rest of the 1970s would become a "lost period" for him—dropping out of school, drifting, using drugs, working at the "totally innocuous" job of cashier at an off-track betting establishment, where he'd sit in a glass cage for eight hours a day and talk to no one. "My life was a series of short bursts," he recalls, the pain still in his voice two decades later. "I didn't stay with anything very long. I'd go for a little while with something and then totally change directions. I didn't have any real close friends, my marriage broke up very quickly. It was just a total time for me of floating through life. I couldn't focus myself in any real, meaningful way over any long period of time. Any time any situation I was in would get to a stressful point, then I would just run away from it."

Eventually, in the 1990s, Mahoney became a permanent expatriate in Russia.

None of the seven veterans returned to their activist work in VVAW. Having spent $1.5 million on the prosecution, Nixon's Justice Department had emptied

VVAW's treasury and forced the national office into debt to cover the $189,000 in defense costs (a figure that would have been considerably higher if Morton Stavis, Jay Schulman, and others on the defense team had not worked at reduced rates and donated much of their time). The government, in Richard Boyle's words, had "broken the back of the organization." It was doubtful whether many other vets who had not yet "come out" to talk about and deal with their Vietnam experience would even consider taking part in activist causes now, after the sordid notoriety of the Gainesville trial.[126]

A far more profound question, though, was what right the government had to exercise such a destructive influence over the lives of its innocent citizens, and over those who had risked their own lives to defend the basis of its virtually limitless power.

6

Unfinished Business: The War Against the VA

1. John Musgrave and the Walking Dead, USMC

At VVAW headquarters in Chicago on the night of April 30, 1975, there was a celebration bordering on manic frenzy. The half-dozen national coordinators, including Barry Romo, Ed Damato, Brian Adams, and Sam Schorr, and one staff person, Marla Watson (soon to be Schorr's wife), all lived together in a little north side apartment at 827 West Newport; and they had spent the whole day with the radio and TV going, intently following the blow-by-blow account of the Communist advance toward Saigon, almost as if they were tuned in to a World Series baseball game. It was suppertime in Chicago when news came that the North Vietnamese Army had entered the capital. Marla Schorr recalls that a steady stream of "political people" began ringing their doorbell, wanting to talk with those the war had affected most deeply and, in some cases, figuring there would be a party. The coordinators hadn't planned one; but before anybody had a chance to think about it, music was blaring, the booze was broken out, and a huge crowd of revelers was dancing and doing the cancan to celebrate the collapse of South Vietnam and the end of the Vietnam War.

The evening, she says, got "really crazy," but the dominant emotion she felt was "elation." Looking back, she found many reasons for it. One was the fact that people had come from every part of the city to congratulate them for what had been years of essentially lonely, unappreciated work. Besides that refurbished sense of importance, which had been dwindling ever since Dewey Canyon III, they felt like *they* had won, because, at least in the Chicago office, "there was so much support and identification with the [Communist] Vietnamese." Also, there was finally some kind of "definitive resolution to the war," which the ambiguous 1973 peace treaty had not provided. But fueling some of that frenzy was also an undercurrent of desperation and uncertainty about their own futures. She and the coordinators in that apartment, and a few more staff members who lived close by, regarded themselves as a family; and working against the war in their "collective," she says, was more than a full-time job, it was "all you lived, breathed, ate, and slept for your time there." In one sense, the end of the war meant joy and freedom for them—the sudden thought that they could "all go home and go back to another part of real life and get on with it." But for such committed revolutionaries, it also meant the very scary thought, she remembers, of "trying to figure out what the fuck to do with ourselves now."

In the midst of that slightly off-kilter celebration (for Vietnam's "liberation" also spelled America's defeat), Watson felt an urge to call the guy who had unwittingly recruited her into VVAW, John Musgrave, down in the little town of Baldwin City, Kansas. In May 1970, Watson had been finishing her freshman year at the University of Kansas in Lawrence, and was on the steering committee for the campus antiwar organization. When her campus, like others nationwide, erupted in chaotic anger over the shootings at Kent State, VVAW sent Musgrave to speak there.

Even for an antiwar veteran, Musgrave was a pretty shocking sight. His fatigue-clad body fit the part of a war hero—tall, lean, and muscular—but one couldn't see much more of his angularly handsome face than two piercing eyes glaring from a giant globe of curly hair and beard. Watson was skeptical of the notion that a veteran could be antiwar, and she scoffed at the idea that peace people and vets could ever be on the same political side; but from the moment Musgrave opened his mouth, she was riveted by the authority of his words. It wasn't just the array of medals he'd earned, including three Purple Hearts, or the fact that he was clearly still suffering from war wounds—he walked with a limp, and his left arm could move only slightly—or even his clear, calm voice touched by a southern twang. What struck her most powerfully was that his experience of the war had given him "a more legitimate right to speak" against it than she or her friends could ever have, even with their far more detailed, academic knowledge of the war and Vietnamese history.

Almost immediately, Watson switched to working with VVAW in Lawrence, then got involved in the chapters in Emporia and Kansas City too. The original challenge for her was to avoid being treated like a groupie, but once she proved her seriousness she was allowed to contribute her substantial organizational skills to some of VVAW's most significant national actions, including the convoys to Cairo, Illinois. Despite the natural sexism of male veterans—"What's a nice girl like you doing in a place like this?" Scott Camil asked her at a national steering committee meeting—she became more and more indispensable to operations in the Midwest region, and began to have a voice in national policy decisions. After the transformation of VVAW into the Winter Soldier Organization, with its insistence on equality for veteran and nonveteran members, she became the most influential woman in the organization. To her parents' utter horror, when she graduated from college in the spring of 1973, she accepted an invitation to work full-time in the national office in Chicago. To keep her from going to live with "six crazed veterans," they offered to pay her way through graduate school, with a trip to Europe thrown in; but Marla knew where she was needed, and went to live in that communal "fishbowl" of an apartment on West Newport for almost three years.

The call she made to Musgrave, on the night that Saigon fell, did not alter her commitment to the veterans' movement; but it was a bucket of cold water on her ideology, and opened her eyes to needs in the veteran community, and a possible new direction for veteran activism, that had not seemed so obvious before.[127]

John Musgrave wanted no part of celebrating South Vietnam's downfall. He didn't see anything to celebrate; in fact, he was crying as they spoke. "All I could see," he recalls, sobbing again at the memory, "were dead Marines . . . who fought to their last breath, who died so horribly . . . trying to make this fuckin' country proud." Images of American embassy officials clambering onto helicopters with "the family silver stuffed into pillowcases" had enraged him. America's panicked departure, he says, "just made a mockery of all that sacrifice. Not that the war was ending. It had to end. But that we could just run out like that. That we didn't have the courage to settle it, to negotiate a settlement when we knew we didn't have the guts to win it, if it ever deserved to be won in the first place. And if it didn't, then we should have known enough to get out. And to leave behind thousands of Vietnamese who had believed in us, as much as those children that carried the rifles for us. . . . It just broke my heart. It was more than a defeat, it was shameful."

Loss certainly weighed heavily on Musgrave that terrible night; but the heaviest weight was neither the loss of a quasi-democratic government in South Vietnam nor the damage to his body: being deprived of the use of his left arm and forced to live in constant pain. It was the loss of innocence. He felt he and his fellow veterans had been profoundly used. "They used the most precious commodity we had," he explains, "that love of country. I did *anything* they told me to do. And even if there was a hint that they wanted something done, I was willing to do it. My job wasn't that much different than those poor bastards at the Pusan perimeter, at the Chosin Reservoir in Korea, or in Tarawa or Guadalcanal or Bataan or Normandy or the Argonne, Belleau Wood, any of those places, any of the wars of the twentieth century. I was in the infantry. You hunt people down and you kill them. The job never changes. The horror is always the same. . . . And then to turn around and be used by some other political jerks on the other end of the spectrum. I just wasn't buying it. I'd been fucked enough, thank you very much."

To understand what happened to a guy like John Musgrave is to understand why the Vietnam War did not end with the surrender at Saigon's Presidential Palace. Musgrave was as American as Kansas corn, as Eisenhower and Harry

Truman and generations of naive midwestern and southern true-believers. He grew up in redneck, working-class places in Missouri, Virginia, and Florida, before his family settled in Baldwin City. As a kid, he was steeped in local history—the Santa Fe Trail, John Brown, "Bloody Kansas" and the Missouri-Kansas Border Wars, Quantrill's Raiders, Jennison's Jayhawkers and the Red-legs. The chivalrous codes and virtues of the Old South were always in his voice and close to his heart (in Vietnam he carried a Confederate flag folded up inside the webbing of his helmet liner, as well as a rebel flag decal on the stock of his M-16). Where he grew up, there were two things you gave without thinking: service to others, and unswerving loyalty to the land of your birth.

In 1966, at the age of seventeen, he talked his parents into letting him enlist in the Marines "for adventure and a shortcut to manhood." His country was at war, a call to duty he had been taught to jump at; moreover, it didn't look like it would last long, so he wanted to get in on it before it ended. "I was eager to prove that I loved my country as much as any old man that sets on his ass and swills beer in a VFW," he recollects. "I was tired of being considered a punk by everybody, and I was under the impression that I would gain some respect by serving my country." Once in, he volunteered for infantry and then for Vietnam. The Marines, he says, decided they had "a live one."

Musgrave loved the Marine Corps; he was, in the most old-fashioned sense, proud to be a Marine, proud to have that responsibility and identity. In no time, he was thinking of it as a permanent career. His gung-ho, lifer's attitude earned him the nickname "Gunny"—short for gunnery sergeant, a choice slot in the Marine Corps just under first sergeant, which it takes a decade or more to attain—and he remains "Gunny" to his friends to this day.

Gunny Musgrave went to Vietnam not to free it from Communism but because they told him that if the Commies weren't stopped in Southeast Asia, we'd have to fight them in California; and he believed them. After he got there, he says, "the way the war was being handled, even to an eighteen-year-old butt-plate grunt, looked just stupid." As a Marine rifleman, they had taught him that "war is a real estate business"—that you seize the enemy's land and then deny him the use of its resources. But in Vietnam they were forever fighting in the same places—gaining a piece of property one day, giving it back the next, then shedding fresh blood to take it all over again. "Countin' meat," he recalls bit-terly, "was the yardstick for victory. We just didn't understand why we were being held back and why we didn't go up north." Instead, they endlessly hunted the enemy, while the enemy just as efficiently hunted them, in the rugged ter-rain near the Demilitarized Zone—the DMZ, which came to stand for "Dead Marine Zone" to them, because they lost so many people there.

He learned to kill Vietnamese and to burn their villages without feeling bad at all. A dead Vietnamese was just a "dead gook," but a dead or wounded Marine "tore out his guts." "While I was there," he confesses, "if you'd've given me the option of having one Marine in my squad killed or kill every Vietnamese in that whole damn country, I'd've said, 'Kill 'em all!' Because that one man out of my squad was more important to me than every Vietnamese, regardless of age or sex or philosophical background."

Musgrave identified completely with his unit: Delta Company, First Battalion, Ninth Marines. The First Battalion was originally known as "Walking Death," because it had killed so many NVA. Delta Company was the "Death Dealers," and his unit patch showed a monsterlike Marine beating a tiny Vietnamese to death. While he was there, the names became horribly ironic, as the First Battalion suffered heavier casualties than almost any American unit in Vietnam. The nicknames were changed to "the Walking Dead" and, for his company, "Dying Delta." He still refers to the men in his unit as "some of the finest human beings that have ever walked the face of this earth or been produced by this country," and credits whatever courage he displayed in battle to the fact that he was more afraid of shaming himself in front of them than of being killed. White and black, they loved and fought for one another; and when he lay critically wounded, one of the men who tried to carry him back to safety was an especially courageous black Marine from Louisiana, who was himself killed in the process. That black man knew Musgrave's Confederate flags were not a symbol of racist hate; they just "meant home," a place few of them ever got back to.

A lot of Delta Company died fighting again on ground they'd already fought for, in Operation Hickory I and later in Operation Buffalo—both occasions when his unit "got hurt real bad." From the American side, Operation Buffalo was the third bloodiest battle of the war. July 4, 1967, two days after Buffalo began, was the second worst day of Musgrave's life. The temperature was over 120 degrees, and his company was fighting for its life on a trace—a firebreak road that was rigged with electronic fences, part of "McNamara's line," which was supposed to keep out the North Vietnamese—northeast of Con Thien and just south of the DMZ. In fact, three NVA regiments, at least 2,000 troops, "some of the finest light infantry in the world" by Musgrave's account, came pouring across McNamara's line and completely overran First Battalion's Bravo Company in the first two hours. There was no cover for them, since all the vegetation had been plowed down. Delta Company, badly under strength at only 100 men, fought for seven days just to get back all of Bravo's dead. On that broiling Fourth of July, the bodies decomposed so rapidly they couldn't tell the corpses apart except by their equipment; and the only way to get them out was to stack them like cordwood on the backs of tanks, the smell of blood mingling forever in his memory with that of diesel fuel.

Twice during that murderous summer Musgrave was wounded seriously by shrapnel, medevaced out, and then brought back to fight again. Many of the men in his unit had been wounded three or more times, though three Purple

Hearts was supposed to be the limit for a soldier to remain in combat. He did not get hit again till early January 1968, just before the start of the Tet Offensive. His platoon, the "Foul Dudes" ("Never have so few been so fouled by so many") walked into a horseshoe-shaped ambush, once again near the DMZ, in northern Quang Tri Province. In less than a minute ten Marines were shot, both corpsmen killed instantly. Musgrave spotted the NVA soldier who was ripping them up with an RPD, a Soviet light machine gun that fired AK-47 rifle rounds. He aimed to kill the NVA gunner, but his opponent shot him instead— ending Musgrave's tour in Vietnam, his military career, and very nearly his life as well.

Three 7.62mm rounds struck him, one in the jaw and two in the left side of his chest. Only one stayed in him, lodging against his spine; the most damaging one tore a hole through his chest and out his back "big enough to stick your fist through." "I knew I was dead," he recounts without bravado, "because I saw a lot of men wounded like I was wounded." His buddies knew he was a goner too, but in true Marine tradition they refused to let his body fall into enemy hands. More than one Marine was killed trying to get him out, but at last a couple of them succeeded.

He never knew how or why he survived. His jaw was broken, a good part of one trapezius muscle was gone, nerves were cut, ribs shattered, and a lung pierced. At "Delta Med," the field hospital at Dong Ha, he was triaged with the mortally wounded, pushed in a corner to die. When he kept breathing, they shipped him to the surgical intensive care unit at Alpha Med in Phu Bai, where he set a record for hanging on the edge of death for seven days. They rushed his medals ceremony so that he would still be alive to receive them. His arms and legs tied down in racks, IVs in both wrists and elbows, two chest tubes draining bloody fluid, his jaw wired shut, and his brain woozed out on morphine, Musgrave had his "brief moment in the sun" as the commanding general of the Third Marine Division and the commanding general of the Eleventh Vietnamese Division came to his bedside to present him with his third Purple Heart and a handful of other medals and ribbons, including two Vietnamese Crosses for Gallantry in Action, with bronze palm and with gold star—the two highest awards for a foreign soldier from the South Vietnamese government. Musgrave remembers thinking: "Gosh, I hope I live so I can tell Mom and Dad about this."

He spent the next seventeen months in Naval hospitals. The first one was Great Lakes in North Chicago, where he got excellent care but was treated like a "class project" for Navy corpsmen in training. Also, the crowding there during the Tet Offensive meant he was continually getting switched from cot to cot (from which he caught crabs) and sometimes being left for hours on a gurney out in the hall. Things got a lot better five months later when he transferred to Quantico Naval Hospital, a smaller facility, in Virginia. He was treated with great respect there, and singled out by an old physical therapist, a woman "built like a fireplug," Lt. Commander Stankovitch, who foresaw that he could regain at least some of the use of his left arm if he just forced himself to push beyond the pain. Half of each day he spent with a weapons training battalion, helping young officers learn the tools of their trade, and the other half with Lt. Commander Stankovitch, learning from her the will and determination to get back more muscular control than the doctors thought him physically capable of. Through her help, more than any doctor's, he beat every expectation they had held for his recovery.

Musgrave still felt a lover's devotion to the Marine Corps, and he gladly agreed to a Marine recruiter's request that he speak in schools and at public forums about the war. But everywhere he went, people asked him questions that he couldn't answer, and he didn't like the tone of the questions. Something sinister had happened to the nation's patriotism. Having loads of idle time as he completed his recuperation in the hospital, he determined to read everything about Vietnam he could get his hands on, so he could argue more effectively with the critics of the military.

He began with Bernard Fall's *Hell in a Very Small Place, Street Without Joy, The Two Vietnams,* and *Last Reflections on a War.* Dr. Fall was a French journalist who had fought with the French Resistance in World War II, then gone to Indochina in 1953 to gather firsthand material for a doctoral thesis on the crumbling of French colonial power there. A decade later, he was regarded as the foremost Western authority on Southeast Asian political unrest, guerrilla warfare, and national liberation movements. He had earned his bona fides in Musgrave's eyes, however, when he had walked point with Musgrave's own Marine unit, during Operation Chinook, seeking material for a sequel to his earlier books, one that would document the Americans' tragic attempt to follow in France's footsteps. Unfortunately, that literary endeavor remained as fragmentary as America's political influence in Vietnam, when a "Bouncing Betty" land mine cut short the life of Fall and his gunnery sergeant escort.

From Fall's chronicles, Musgrave proceeded to Senator William Fulbright's *The Arrogance of Power* and *Vietnam Hearings,* eventually working his way through dozens of writers and historians who had done research on the roots of the current conflict, regardless of whether they were antiwar or not—even Graham Greene's seminal novel, *The Quiet American.* The more he read, however, the worse he felt. This was still two or more years before the revelations of the Pentagon Papers, but there were enough troubling facts in the literature then available to make him feel he should simply go back to being a soldier, and let the politicians worry about questions of right and wrong. So he quit reading.

He volunteered several times to return to Vietnam, but his commanders would not hear of it. He wanted desperately to remain in the Marine Corps, where his awards got him immediate respect and where he was "treated like a man," where he had responsibilities and a profession. He was terrified of returning to civilian life as a "crippled punk," certain to be taunted as "a killer . . . the guy that ate the bowls of babies for breakfast." As much as he feared combat, it made more sense and seemed less cruel to him than some of the malicious lies of the peace movement. Such was the turmoil inside him, and such the turmoil in his country, that "going back into hell" in Vietnam, where he could easily be killed or suffer even more grievous injuries, looked like a desirable thing to do— the only solution to his many quandaries.

Three Purple Hearts would normally have bought him a ticket out of combat zones, but he was even willing to sign a waiver of that privilege. The choice was not his, however, because he couldn't get past the Physical Evaluation Boards. At the age of twenty and still a corporal, he was given a full medical retirement by the Marine Corps and sent home as a disabled veteran. He still couldn't vote or legally "buy a fuckin' beer in this country," he recalls bitterly.

A little of the edge was taken off his bitterness by the terrific welcome home he got back in Kansas. He had returned early on a convalescent leave; and since he was the first native son to be so highly decorated and still alive, they made a big fuss over him, including a front-page article with photos in the local paper. One of his childhood friends, hearing that he might die of his wounds, had quit high school, enlisted in the Marines, and volunteered for Vietnam, just to "avenge" his hurt. This kid himself got wounded twice and would return disabled not much after Gunny.

Musgrave found that the war had gone through his community "like a friggin' vacuum cleaner"—almost every young man had joined up or been drafted, and many were now fighting in his place in Vietnam. That was the main reason he did not immediately speak out against the war. Thanks to the reading he'd done, he was already convinced, not only that the war was being poorly run, but that it was "just flat-ass wrong." Nevertheless, he bore a Marine Corps tattoo on his arm, and was imbued to his core with the loyalty every Marine feels toward every other Marine, living or dead—a family (unlike their real one) that they can never lose or be expelled from. There was nothing he could do but keep his mouth shut and, since no one had a job for him, go to college.

The VA did not help him to find a job, and it would scarcely have helped him with college either if he had not been declared 100 percent disabled. The GI Bill at that time offered veterans who were less than 35 percent disabled a mere $135 per month for everything—an amount that would have covered tuition, books, and supplies at the cheapest state school, leaving almost nothing for living expenses. As a 100 percent disabled vet, however, he was eligible to have his entire educational costs paid as "vocational rehabilitation," plus a living allowance on top of his disability pension. Though going to college had never been one of his dreams, he deliberately chose the two most expensive private schools in the state, Baker University and Ottawa University, since he would never have had the chance otherwise, and partly for the satisfaction of knowing the VA would "shit BBs" when they saw how much money they were going to have to dole out.

Musgrave's bad attitude was growing by leaps and bounds. He remembers hanging out on his old block and being offended to hear his former friends and neighbors "talking the same old shit about 'goddamn niggers.'" It dawned on him, quite painfully, that if the black Marine who had tried to save his life (now dead) had moved in with him there, they would both have been run out of town or killed: "And he'd done more for his country in a couple of months than they would ever do in their whole lives." His college campus was not much more tolerant. To avoid making waves, he knew he should play down the fact that he was a vet; he wore Banlon shirts, plaid slacks, and wing-tip shoes. But evidently his jarhead past was still showing through (his crewcut didn't help), because a couple of other vets took him aside to give him some friendly advice about pledging fraternities. They told him it was time to grow his hair long and to dress a little funkier. "Whatever you do," they warned him, "don't talk about Vietnam, and don't wear anything related to the military."

Furious, he rushed back to his room, where he had a stash of military gear that he sometimes used for hiding out in the woods for a few days. This time, however, he pulled on his blue jeans, jungle boots, and what he promptly dubbed his "fuck you" field jacket (since it bore all his Marine unit mottos and insignias), and strode defiantly across campus, muttering to himself: "If you don't like me, take me out!"

These were rough times for him. His delayed stress was kicking in hard. Plagued by nightmares filled with blood and death and hospital wards, he would drink all day and all night till he collapsed. Then he'd wake up screaming, which happened so many times the kid he roomed with finally moved out. He was ready to take on anyone at the slightest provocation, and actually did get in a couple of fights, till he learned how difficult it was to win with only one good arm; after that, he put on a "crazy" act much of the time, to scare people off. His body was subjected to operation after operation (till after number 17 they finally gave up trying to fix him), and he was in pain every day. Whenever he went to the VA hospital, they sent him home with a bag full of Talwin, a synthetic morphine that is a heavy-duty painkiller but also one of the most abused drugs on the street because of the extreme euphoria it produces, especially combined with antihistamines. Fifty milligrams of Talwin would trick him into feeling he was on top of the world—"like a pimp," he says, who will one day start "kicking the shit out of you" for no reason, and yet you can't help coming back for more. The more he took, the foggier his head became, making it harder and harder to deal wisely with his problems, to get his life back on track.

What finally helped him do that was "coming out of the closet" about his feelings against the war, which was one of the hardest things he ever did, and took years to fully accomplish. The process began at the first national Vietnam Moratorium on October 15, 1969. When Musgrave walked into the auditorium where they were demonstrating at Baker University—wearing his usual "fuck you" jacket and carrying a pennant that said, "I Support the Boys in Vietnam"— the leader of the campus antiwar movement anticipated trouble. They had already disagreed publicly on most issues about the war, so in a gesture of conciliation he offered Gunny the chance to speak against the Moratorium. But by this time, Musgrave had secretly come to feel more comfortable with people in the peace group—who acted on their beliefs and took real risks—than with those barstool Walter Mittys who slapped his back and congratulated him on killing Communists. When he got up on stage, he said he did not oppose the Moratorium; in fact, he told them, he had fought in Vietnam to protect their right "to say no to the government when you think something is wrong." He even claimed that saying no to injustice was not just a right in America, it was a "duty." What he did ask was that people in the peace movement stop giving America's soldiers the impression "that you don't give a damn about them . . . that you only care about the enemy." He suggested every person there take the time to write a caring letter to a serviceman in Vietnam. The audience gave him a standing ovation.

It took a lot of hammer blows to break through the granite wall of his refusal (out of loyalty to the Corps) to speak about his own experience in Vietnam. One blow, a big one, was President Nixon's announcement on November 3, 1969, in his famous "silent majority" speech, that he was about to begin withdrawing American troops from Vietnam in order to turn the war over to the South Vietnamese—a withdrawal he projected taking years to complete. Musgrave's response—much like John Kerry's before the U.S. Senate a couple of years later, if slightly less eloquent—was: "Look, if it ain't worth winning, it ain't worth dying for." His first public end-the-war (rather than antiwar) speeches were "strictly for the American fighting man," he says, and harped on one theme only: the need to get our soldiers out of Vietnam as quickly as possible.

People kept asking him to give talks, and he accepted every offer, no longer hesitant to side against his own government. But it took two more huge jolts before he was willing to reveal everything he knew about the war, and to condemn the way it was being fought. Kent State pushed him quite a bit closer— the sight of government soldiers "killing our own children." *God, now the war's come home!* he thought. *We've brought it home, and that's madness.* It was just after Kent State that he finally began to let his hair grow long. What finally changed his mind about shielding the military, though, was the trial of Lieutenant Calley for the murder of hundreds of Vietnamese civilians at My Lai. It seemed to Musgrave like the ultimate betrayal for the government to send its young men on a mission to kill and then to put them in jail for doing it a little too well. "We didn't kill because we liked it," he explains his change of heart. "We didn't go to Vietnam because we just couldn't wait to kill somebody. We went because they told us we had to go. They needed us. We did *the job* that they laid out for us. We did what they asked us to. And a lot of times, we did more than they asked us to because we knew that's what they *really wanted*. And if they couldn't be any more loyal to us than that, then they didn't deserve our loyalty."[128]

2. The Men Who Got Left Behind

In December 1970, Musgrave joined VVAW in Lawrence. Having just given up drinking, he eschewed the vets who were there just to party, and soon shifted to the more serious group in Kansas City. By the time they got to Washington, D.C., for Dewey Canyon III in April 1971, his energy and articulateness had marked him as a leader. Still, he agonized over the decision to give back his medals, since radical acts ran contrary to his nature. Those medals represented something very special to him—neither the status symbols of manhood they were to him as an awestruck kid, nor the "merit badges of murder" some of the vets were now calling them. They were metallic and cloth symbols worth exactly what they had cost in blood and suffering; and his own had been purchased at an exceedingly high price, both to himself and the men who had gotten hit trying to save him. Throwing them over that wire fence was one of the toughest acts he ever performed. But he felt the government had pushed him to it—radicalizing him more than he had ever believed possible—when it denied him and his buddies access to Arlington Cemetery, to pay tribute to their dead comrades. After that, it became a point of honor to prove he could not be intimidated by the U.S. government any more than he had been by the NVA. His handful of medals went over with a special barb for Nixon—a note attached which read: "To the American people, the silent and ungrateful." Standing at the microphone, he pointed at the Capitol building and said, "The main thing that I wish I could return are the lives I took in their name."

Because he was not the typical antiwar activist, not even the typical antiwar vet, UPI put out a story about him, which his parents heard while on vacation in Colorado, not even knowing he had left Kansas. His hometown paper then did another front-page story, this time playing up his remarkable transformation into war protester, as if it had happened overnight from something bad he'd eaten. When he returned to Baldwin City, he faced shock, dismay, and anger in everyone he knew, everyone who mistakenly thought they knew him.

His PTSD only got worse. There was virtually no understanding for him anywhere, not even in VVAW, where many of the vets were suspicious of his outspoken conservatism and continued allegiance to the Marine Corps. Most of them were put off by his patriotic mannerisms, like the heartfelt *"Semper fi!"* with which he'd greet fellow Marines. "I didn't want the war to be wrong," he says, his voice still suffused with angst two decades later. "I wanted to wake up and be proven wrong. I didn't want to have to admit I killed people *for nothin'*. I didn't want to have to admit that people I loved had died *for nothin'*. That I had been crippled *for nothin'*. I was begging for somebody to please show me we need to be there [in Vietnam]. Please, don't make this experience in my life be just a waste. Let me salvage something. One of the poems I wrote about the war, the last line was: 'It would have been nice if it all could have meant something.' I wanted so desperately for some president to make it all right. But they couldn't, because there wasn't nothing to make it right with."

Musgrave took on some of the most dangerous assignments in VVAW. As Kansas coordinator (and later as head of the whole Midwest region), he led several convoys to the embattled black community in Cairo, Illinois—a social justice issue he was behind one hundred percent. *What am I doing fighting for the rights of man in the jungles of Indochina*, he thought, *if I can't make them a reality in the United States?* He also took a supply convoy to the Sioux Indians of the American Indian Movement (AIM) who were under siege by federal agents at Wounded Knee, South Dakota, though he felt a lot more ambivalence about that mission, since he learned too late that there was a contingent of vets with rifles along who intended to serve as "shooters" to help protect the Indians' perimeter. He also knew that by crossing state lines with a rented truck to aid fugitives from the FBI, he was laying himself wide open to a conspiracy indictment. That situation got even more out of control when Musgrave and a group of Indian college students he'd brought up from Kansas were taken hostage by members of AIM—a near catastrophe he barely talked his way out of.

Though he was troubled by the moral implications of working with a violent movement like AIM, Musgrave never showed any concern for his own person— though he admits he had plenty of fears, which he forced himself to overcome. He became as dedicated to ending the war as he had been to fighting it while he was there; and once he started speaking out against it, he did so without reservation, to the furthest possible limits, and there was absolutely no stopping him. Having missed Winter Soldier in Detroit, he held his own Winter Soldier hearings at Ottawa University and in Kansas City. His educational speaking tours took him all over the country, through most of the colleges in the Shenandoah Valley in Virginia, up to Canada, and even to Rome, where he testified before the 1972 War Crimes Tribunal that was part of Bertrand Russell's series of socalled "Stockholm Conferences." Nothing could shut him up—not death threats from the Ku Klux Klan (he met them at his door with an M-1 carbine, while his roommate handled the sawed-off .12-gauge automatic shotgun), not the FBI's attempts to get him in front of a grand jury, not even the gag rule imposed by Judge Arnow at the trial of the Gainesville Eight. After the judge had issued a warrant for his arrest, for violation of the gag rule, Musgrave, keeping a few steps ahead of the police, went ahead and called yet another press conference, announcing to the world his intention of continuing to violate it—impressing even the jaded national press with his guts.

He only quit speaking when he felt VVAW itself had let him down—when he realized the organization he was talking about (the only one, beside the Marine Corps, that had ever given him a modicum of pride, comfort, and hope) didn't exist anymore. It was December 1973, and almost all his trusted Kansas friends had already dropped out. The idea of belonging to an "anti-imperialist organization" did not play too well in the Plains states; and Musgrave's rank and file, most of them from small towns just like Baldwin City, couldn't care less about the fine distinctions between the various brands of Communism. All they knew, they told him, was that the national office in Chicago was starting to sound just like the people they'd fought in Vietnam.

Musgrave's friends warned him that he'd better get out too, that the organization was being run by the RU—rabid, suicidal Maoists—but he resisted believing them as long as he could. It was hard for him to withdraw, having already invested so much energy—so much of his adult life—in VVAW. But the new national officers shoved an unpleasant reality in his face when they made him the target of an inquisition concerning his political views. He was accused not only of being "naive," but also called a "reactionary" and a "revisionist," and subjected to a litany of reprimands, he says, "that often comes out of the mouths of ideologues when you don't agree with them." At the same time, he realized they wanted to keep him in VVAW mainly because they still needed a few vets around to legitimize the organization, since the membership roster was becoming top-heavy with activist women and nonvets, most of whom were extreme leftists and professional politicos. These were people he did not like at all, and he saw no reason to stick around just to help *them* out.

Musgrave's resignation from VVAW was exceedingly painful and acrimonious. One of the financial patrons of the organization, disturbed that he'd quit, asked him why; and he told this person in plain terms. The patron immediately stopped funding the organization, and two national officers promptly came down from Chicago to chew out Musgrave for betraying his fellow vets. What they said hurt him even more deeply because these two people had formerly been his good friends. They told him to stick his anti-Communist paranoia up his ass. He was later quoted by an interviewer as saying that "VVAW turned into a bunch of fucking Commies." It took years on both sides before the resulting hard feelings even began to heal.

Meanwhile, PTSD was eating him up. He still woke up screaming almost every night, a burden his wife learned to live with. The one vent for his tensions was skydiving—using equipment specially modified for his disability—but there were times between surgeries when he couldn't jump, and then he'd want to climb outside of his own skin, feeling like his body didn't belong to him anymore. The pain never stopped, it just got quieted a little by the drugs from the VA: morphine, Demerol, Dilaudid, and the round white Percocet tablets he ate like candy, which did not screw up his brain as badly as Talwin had. His tolerance for painkillers had grown so high that it was useless to try aspirin or even codeine No. 4. There were times when it seemed the only positive step he could take, he says, would be to "cancel my own ticket." He seriously considered killing himself, and it was a miracle that he didn't, in view of the lifetime of pain in his body he knew lay ahead, as well as the endless war in his mind.

The only thing that kept him going was his sense of mission, and that mission remained basically the same from the time he came home until well into his forties. It was to heal himself; to keep other GIs from being needlessly hurt, as he had been; and to help those who had been hurt to heal too. When VVAW became a front for the Revolutionary Union, and later the Revolutionary Communist Party, he felt the same sense of betrayal he had when he discovered his own government's culpability in sacrificing his youth and health (and nearly his life) for a lost war and a wrong cause. But he was also aware that the government itself had let him down again after the war, because there was no one in the Veterans Administration—which had been created expressly "to care for him who shall have borne the battle"—who showed the least little bit of concern about his healing. A million pills could not substitute for one Lt. Commander Stankovitch, and he found no Stankovitches in the VA.

Musgrave felt as warm and grateful toward the Disabled American Veterans (DAV) as he did distrustful and angry toward the VA. In 1976, the National Adjutant of the DAV, Dale Adams, had commissioned a study of the psychological needs of Vietnam veterans by Dr. John Wilson of Cleveland State University. A disciple of Erik Erikson, Wilson would eventually come to be regarded as one of the dozen top theorists on PTSD in the world. He hooked up with the DAV after Cleveland State refused to continue funding his own innovative study of Vietnam veterans on campus, called "The Forgotten Warrior Project." Dale Adams offered Wilson $45,000 to extend his original study to 400 Vietnam veterans in the Cleveland area; and the resulting two-volume report, *Identity, Ideology and Crisis in the Vietnam Veteran in Transition,* became a landmark in PTSD literature. More than that, it became the basis for the DAV's development of the first major counseling service for Vietnam veterans. In 1977, based on Wilson's recommendations, the DAV began establishing a network of seventy storefront "outreach" clinics nationwide—neighborhood places where Vietnam veterans could just "drop in" for advice, rap groups, and sometimes professional therapy—most of which it kept open well into the 1980s. Adams, a World War II vet, knew that the future life of the DAV depended upon its ability to attract the fresh blood of this new young generation of veterans; and he also knew that the VA, with its miserably dirty and understaffed hospitals and its terminally bad attitude, was alienating Vietnam veterans in droves.

Musgrave worked as a DAV outreach program counselor in Lawrence for three years. He was also on call for years as a veterans' crisis-intervention counselor for a group called Headquarters, Incorporated. Working for those groups, he saw and personally helped hundreds of Vietnam vets who had slipped through the Grand Canyon–sized cracks in the VA. His philosophy of counseling was to completely eliminate the "professional distance" between himself and other troubled veterans—the very opposite of the VA's stilted, bureaucratic, red tape–belabored approach. A lot of times he was able to assist vets simply by *knowing* them, he says, meaning something a lot deeper than a wave or a handshake: "You get to know 'em, you *listen* to 'em, you *care* about 'em." In one case, at least, knowing and caring about someone meant that Musgrave drove to the house of a vet who had barricaded himself inside with a bunch of weapons, and who was threatening to kill anyone who came in to get him, including his wife and minister. The cops were afraid to get near him, but Musgrave—who knew the guy as a counselee (and recognized that he was just one more vet with the Vietnam War still being fought inside him)—walked right in and simply told him what he needed to do. To everyone's amazement, the two of them came out together, no guns in sight, and the guy let Musgrave drive him to a hospital in Topeka. According to Musgrave, the guy knew he needed professional help, but couldn't get up the courage to ask for it; and what he needed to break through that inertia was for "*somebody else* to tell him that it would be best for him."

Musgrave admits that he too had trouble coming up with that "private courage" to get help for himself. Like so many other professional warriors, trained to fight the strong and to assist the weak, he could not accept the fact that he was incapable of healing himself. The VA only compounded the problem of a warrior's pride, because they made it so hard for a vet with readjustment problems to get help. One of the biggest drawbacks, before the VA's own Vietnam Veterans' Outreach Program was inaugurated in 1979, was that a troubled veteran had to get a medical diagnosis from a VA doctor before any such services could be provided; this usually meant a psychiatric diagnosis, which would likely be stigmatizing for the rest of his or her life. Moreover, veterans were only eligible for counseling and readjustment services if they were patients in a VA hospital—a requirement that kept away all but the most abysmally desperate. In 1980, when the first Vet Center opened in Kansas City—modeled, as all the VA's new counseling centers were, on the storefront operations that had been pioneered by John Wilson and the DAV, and even earlier by Shad Meshad with his rap groups by the Venice Pier—one of its first customers was John "Gunny" Musgrave.

Musgrave walked in with an attitude of total skepticism—reluctant to believe anything good could come from the VA—and he immediately jumped down the throat of his black peer counselor, Bill Covington. "You weren't even in Vietnam, how the fuck you gonna help me?" Musgrave demanded. "What do you know?" "I know as much as you'll *let* me know," Covington responded, looking him in the eye. "And I can help you as much as you'll *let* me help you." "Oh," said Musgrave, almost choking on the word. For the first time since he landed in Vietnam, thirteen years earlier, he dropped his "bad-assed grunt attitude"—no longer feeling it necessary to hide behind it—and began to let his real feelings show. And thus began his first real healing, strangely enough under the big round seal of the Veterans Administration he so detested.

But Musgrave never lost his bitterness toward that institution for the way it had abandoned him and his fellow veterans to their own misery and suffering for so many years, left many of them to die alone and forgotten—so different from the way those men had learned to care for each other in Vietnam. When Musgrave came upon the unsettling evidence of live American POWs who had been left behind in Indochina, that issue became more than just a political lobbying point for him. It came to symbolize a much larger issue: the American government's repudiation of a whole generation of its war veterans.

"America's honor is at stake," he relates passionately. "When men are abandoned . . . you have sacrificed all honor. *All honor.* The Marine Corps has a code. It's been carved in stone and written in blood for well over two hundred years. And that is: 'You don't leave your dead, and you *never* leave your wounded.' And I'm living proof of that. Men didn't leave me, even though they knew I was going to die and even though I was begging them to leave me . . . [Just like taking care of PTSD and Agent Orange–related problems], bringing the POWs home is living up to an obligation, it's unfinished business. How many veterans out there, part of their PTSD is that sense of betrayal, the sense of a country that didn't care about them when they were there and doesn't care about them when they're home? And how much does the POW symbolize that sense of betrayal? Hey, pardner, if they'll walk away from an Air Force colonel who got shot down driving one of the most sophisticated aircraft in the world, and an Academy graduate, they'll walk away from some dirt-ball retired corporal from the Marine Corps that gets in trouble in Baldwin City, Kansas.

"The most important issue to me, is if they left those men there then, they'll leave my sons next time. One day they're going to ask for my children, two boys. How am I supposed to feel, when I know that the war I fought in isn't over yet? How can I have pride in my country and trust in my government? I don't trust my government. I haven't trusted my government since I came home. The legacy of Vietnam isn't in how *we* feel, it's in how we feel when they come for our kids. And how our kids are going to feel from listening to us talk. I don't think my children are going to feel the same way about going to serve that I felt. And that is a casualty for this country of that war."

But when the VA used to hear Vietnam veterans talking like this, Musgrave scoffs, they claimed it was because the vets "had problems with potty training." By contrast, Musgrave "never had any gripe against the Marine Corps." "The Marine Corps gave me exactly what I begged them to give me," he explains. "I was in a little over three years, and they retired me like I'd been in for twenty years. They take better care of you than the VA. The VA's the enemy of the veteran, not the friend."[129]

3. "Bad Paper" and "A Friend in the White House"

After the Gainesville acquittal, VVAW struggled to regain the lost momentum of its campaign to reform the VA. That campaign had been kicked off promisingly in 1971, when Skip Roberts had engineered the first VA "hospital zaps," inviting reporters, network cameramen, and local congresspeople to join him on surprise visits to the filthiest, most trashed-out and overcrowded wards, usually while the hospital administrators were out to lunch. Almost every issue of *Winter Soldier* (the monthly newspaper published by VVAW-WSO) from October 1973 through the time of VVAW's last major national action, Dewey Canyon IV, in July 1974, contained articles dealing with the inadequacy of the VA. The articles, representing the focus of the organization itself, dealt with four major issues. These were: 1) the large number of vets who were blocked from using the VA by less than Honorable discharges; 2) the fact that the national director of the VA, Donald Johnson, consistently sided with the Nixon administration in downplaying the needs of Vietnam veterans; 3) the continuing cutbacks in the VA's budget; 4) the serious shortfall of the current GI Bill.

The first issue, "bad paper," was one that VVAW had taken the lead in publicizing from the late 1960s on. As the war progressed—after the Tet Offensive—toward obvious defeat, and as troops in Vietnam began to see themselves as sacrifices to a lost cause, morale in the ranks dropped steeply; insubordination and mutinies increased; and the attitudes and habits of the counterculture, including long hair, drug use, and an aversion to authority, were adopted by large numbers of enlisted men. Troop discipline was vanishing so fast that the Pentagon feared its entire military machine would soon be rendered ineffective, its carefully arranged caste structure simply collapse. To salvage America's armed forces, commanders were authorized to get rid of—i.e., discharge—any real or potential troublemakers as quickly as possible. The decision that a soldier was unfit for duty, if it was couched as a General or Undesirable discharge, could be made by a junior officer, even a first sergeant. Such discharges, called "administrative," did not require a court-martial, and thus could be handed out rapidly and with little cost to the military.

By 1974, at least 560,000 veterans had received less than Honorable discharges. Of these, 300,000 were General discharges, which meant the bearer was still eligible for VA benefits, though many employers refused to hire veterans so designated, and there were other adverse impacts as well. The remaining 260,000 vets with "bad paper" were simply cut off from any government help at all, and not even eligible for a civil service job. GIs were often harassed into accepting a bad discharge, or coaxed by the promise of some superior that such discharges were "automatically upgraded"—a plain lie. There was not much of a choice in any case, since a GI who chose to fight an administrative discharge was barred from cross-examining witnesses, challenging affidavits, and appealing the decision in a military court. Once the discharge had been given, it usually took a year or more before a veteran could get his case heard at the Discharge Review Board for his branch of the service, in Washington, D.C., and the veteran had to pay for all costs, including transportation of himself, his counsel, and witnesses. Even then, only 15 percent of those who applied for discharge upgrading won their appeal.

The chief tragedy of all those bad discharges was that many of them went to blacks, Hispanics, poor whites, and other underprivileged—read: economically handicapped—young men, who were in need of society's compassion, not one more kick in the pants. Many of them should not have been in the military in the first place. Back in 1966, when Lyndon Johnson refused to call up the military reserve units, for fear of antagonizing the middle classes, his Secretary of Defense, Robert McNamara, devised a solution to the acute manpower shortage called Project 100,000. The target was the large pool of poorly educated and sometimes mentally deficient youths who roamed the streets of America's urban ghettos or were tucked away in the poverty belt of Appalachia or other backwaters of rural America, especially in the Deep South. Such youths were usually kept out of the military by their low score on the battery of Armed Forces Qualification Tests (AFQT), which draftees and volunteers alike were subjected to. Normally the military rejected all candidates who scored below the 10th percentile on the AFQT, and took as few as possible from those whose scores fell between the 10th and 30th percentiles, a so-called "marginal group" denoted as "Category IV." A wizard with numbers, McNamara saw that by finagling the standards a few notches here and there, he could draw from this group an extra hundred thousand kids a year; and the middle class would have no further worries about the need to mobilize their sons who were dodging the war in the reserves.

The gag, as Larry Heinemann says, was that military service would be a great boon to these marginal kids. "Disadvantaged" not only by poverty but, in many cases, by an IQ in the lower 60s and a fourth-grade reading level, McNamara's 100,000 were supposed to have their lives turned around in the military as part of what Johnson's Labor Secretary Willard Wirtz called a "human salvage program." It was claimed they would receive remedial education and special occupational training certain to land them a lucrative job upon discharge. No less a personage than Daniel Patrick Moynihan, cabinet or subcabinet officer to every U.S. president from Kennedy through Ford, and later U.S. senator from New York, approved of Project 100,000 as "a socializing experience for the poor—particularly the Southern poor."

Between 1966 and 1972, when it was terminated, Project 100,000 pulled in over 400,000 substandard recruits. Even more Category IV individuals were admitted as volunteers, though not officially part of Project 100,000, thanks to the lowered AFQT score requirements. Eighty percent of this whole group were high school dropouts, and some were even mentally retarded. Forty-one percent were black—a significant fact, considering that during the Vietnam era black GIs were twice as likely as whites to receive a less than Honorable discharge. Far from learning useful vocational skills, 40 percent of them were slated for combat assignments; and 50 percent of those in the Army and Marines were sent to Vietnam, where they served as cannon fodder, as unskilled men always had.

Fulfilling the dire predictions of many career officers, "McNamara's boys" proved to be among the worst disciplined soldiers wherever they served, and many never got past boot camp, where three times as many went AWOL as their "average soldier" counterparts. Eighty thousand went home with Undesirable, Bad Conduct, or Dishonorable discharges, and another 100,000 scraped through with General discharges, giving them the dubious benefit of using a VA that had little to offer to even those far more qualified, while saddling them for life with a "less-than-Honorable" label. Most returned to civilian society with more problems than they had left with. A study two decades later showed that the Project 100,000 vets were doing worse than their nonveteran peers in every major category of achievement.[130]

A separate issue from bad discharges, but one that definitely influenced how the VA dealt with particular veterans (just as it influenced many potential employers) was the military's use of a Separation Program Number—colloquially called a "spin number"—on every veteran's DD-214. There were over 500 different entries in the government's lexicon of reasons for discharging a soldier, each one indicated by a different three-digit number that could be tacked on to the start of a much longer separation number on his discharge form. Anyone with the code book could look at a vet's DD-214 and learn his secret, real or imagined character flaw, for few of the spin numbers spoke of virtues. There were numbers that signified—among a host of other more or less subjective categories—"apathy," "unsatisfactory handling of personal affairs," "unsanitary habits," "sexual deviate (aberrant tendencies)," "antisocial character," "inadequate personality," "pathological lying," and "habitual shirker."

While the spin-code manual was supposed to be classified, a study revealed that 20 percent of the nation's 100 largest corporations admitted having copies and using them when they came to hire employees. Moreover, they were routinely issued to VA facilities, where the staff used them in deciding veterans' benefit claims. One particular spin-code horror story concerned a veteran named Sal Horley, who had volunteered for two tours in Vietnam, was wounded in combat, and received an Honorable discharge. When he went to the VA to get treatment for his leg wounds, the doctors repeatedly refused to help him; it turned out they had assumed he merely wanted painkillers for getting high, since his spin code identified him as a drug abuser. The catch-22 of the crusade to end spin codes was that even after the Pentagon agreed in May 1974 to stop putting them on discharge forms and to issue veterans new "spin-free" certificates upon request, thousands of Vietnam veterans had already placed their old forms on file with the VA, unemployment offices, job agencies, and so forth—and no law ever required that they be shredded, along with the damning manuals. In many cases, as a *Winter Soldier* article warned, spin codes had left veterans "branded like cattle" for life.

A lot of the credit for the Pentagon's capitulation on the spin-code issue belonged to VVAW-WSO. From late 1973 through the spring of 1974, they had built up an enormous pressure on the Nixon administration through community organizing, letter writing, and networking, to raise the national consciousness about the desperate plight of many Vietnam veterans. What helped make VVAW's campaign so effective was that this was a bad time for almost all Americans, who had become sensitized to the fact that government was doing a poor job of watching out for their welfare. Inflation and recession were hitting the country hard at the same time—a phenomenon that had rarely been seen before. Record numbers were unemployed, but the prices of food and gasoline kept skyrocketing; on top of which, there was a drastic (and some say artificially contrived) shortage of gasoline, which left panicked motorists inching for hours toward their local filling station in lines that literally wrapped around the block.

Richard Nixon could not help but respond to the barrage of public complaints, especially since he was coming under the increasingly heavy fire of the Senate Watergate Committee. Besides, his own stunt of trying to make political capital off the fact that he had brought the POWs home had completely backfired. On May 24, 1973, Nixon had thrown a lavish dinner to honor their return, with the largest guest list in White House history, which included all 591 POWs, their families, numerous political figures who wanted to bask in their glory, and a platoon of Hollywood celebrities led by *Sands of Iwo Jima's* come-back-to-life Sergeant Striker, John "Duke" Wayne himself. At the same time as the POWs were banqueting with the president, however, Congress—at Nixon's clear behest—was getting set to slash the VA's health care budget by $65 million. The year before, Nixon had pocket-vetoed a bill that would have appropriated an additional $113 million for veterans' medical services.

He had also tried (and failed) to reduce compensation to disabled vets by $160 million, had opposed GI educational increases as "excessive and inflationary," had impounded funds already appropriated to help colleges enroll vets, had cut funding from a job-listing program to give vets priority for over a million jobs, and had vetoed special burial and health benefits for veterans. A political cartoon shortly after the feting of the POWs showed two men peering in through the spiked fence around the White House, watching the homecoming celebration. One of them says to the other: "Gee, it must be nice to be a hero and have a friend in the White House." One is a young black man wearing a battle jacket with one sleeve tied off; the other is a young white man using a crutch to replace his missing leg.

Vietnam veterans, and VVAW-WSO in particular, rallied the media to challenge Nixon for his hypocrisy in welcoming back a few planeloads of POWs from Hanoi while ignoring their three million comrades, who'd come home a little earlier to the spiritual prison of the nation's vast indifference. Nixon took the bait by declaring March 29, 1974, as Vietnam Veterans Day. It was the first anniversary of the withdrawal of the last American troops from Vietnam, a poor enough cause for celebration considering that South Vietnamese forces were already beginning to crumble; but even more insulting, Nixon once again placed the spotlight on himself—on his own actions that had "ended" the war—rather than the veterans he was supposed to honor. Vietnam Veterans Day thus became just the national platform VVAW-WSO wanted.

They planned to demonstrate at VA hospitals and offices across the country on that day. When VA chief Donald Johnson got wind of what was going on, he sent out an urgent message on the hotline to all his regional directors, warning them to prepare for the onslaught of protesters and urging them to keep mum and avoid confrontation whenever possible. Doing just as their boss told them, the VA administrators either passed the buck, advising the veteran delegations to look to Washington for answers ("I'm only one of 260,000 employees of the VA!" pleaded the New York regional director to a roomful of angry vets); refused VVAW-WSO demonstrators entrance to VA buildings (which happened in Denver); or, like the two-faced bureaucrats at the Santa Barbara VA hospital, extended a welcome to the protesters but closed their offices for the day before the marchers arrived![131]

4. Vietnam Veterans Day Without the Veterans, and a VA Chief Too Busy for His Clients

Paranoia was Nixon's Achilles' heel, and this time it foiled him completely. Aiming to lay low on Vietnam Veterans Day, he scheduled no formal ceremony, and appeared only briefly to give one of his all-purpose, patriotic speeches at

Fort McNair's National War College. "The American effort [in Vietnam] . . . was in good conscience," Nixon told a few hundred Army officers, airmen, wives, and government officials, "honorably undertaken and honorably ended." He encouraged Vietnam veterans to feel pride in having served a "good cause," which had increased the chances of future world peace. He also promised to look into the questions that had been raised about POWs abandoned in Southeast Asia; and he reiterated his opposition to any form of amnesty for draft resisters, saying, "It sometimes seems that more attention is directed to those who deserted America than those who chose to serve America." The Marines Corps' Drum and Bugle Corps played, but the audience waited in vain for a fly-over of Air Force fighter jets, because the drizzling sky refused to clear. Also conspicuously absent were Vietnam veterans themselves, except for a handful of disabled vets, who had been brought over from a nearby VA hospital.

That public relations tactic backfired too, as the disabled vet who was chosen to represent the Marine Corps, Randy Taylor—a highly decorated former sergeant who had served nearly five years on combat duty—originally refused the president's invitation, in order to protest "the indifferent attitude of his government" toward the readjustment problems of Vietnam veterans. Taylor finally agreed to sit in the reviewing stand, but only—as he told the *Washington Star-News*—because his parents in Covington, Virginia, had asked him to. Taylor's full tragedy would take another decade to unravel, as his life would alternate between bouts of severe depression and intense veteran activism, leading to a forty-day hunger strike in San Francisco in 1984, whose aim was to force the Democratic National Convention there to adopt a platform pledging greater assistance to troubled and homeless Vietnam vets. The national news covered the efforts of fellow veteran Ron Kovic to coax him to end his hunger strike, which he did just before the convention began, but almost no one covered his suicide a year later.

Without ever having doffed his raincoat, Nixon hurried back to the White House to catch a helicopter to Andrews Air Force Base, then a jet to his weekend retreat in sunny Key Biscayne.

The national press, goaded by the fierce rhetoric of veteran activists, lambasted Nixon again for this further hypocritical slap-in-the-face to vets. The *New York Times'* coverage of Vietnam Veterans Day focused on the several hundred veterans who had marched down Pennsylvania Avenue and jammed into a hearing of the Senate's Veterans' Affairs Committee, to press their demand for better benefits. The *Times*, perhaps emboldened by the now-thick blood scent of Watergate, described in detail how the vets booed the VA officials who testified, especially when they mentioned Nixon's name, and shouted, "Lies! Lies! Lies!" every time some senator spoke of his alleged concern for their welfare.

The toughest shots at Nixon, however, came from *Washington Post* journalist William Greider, who had been hammering at the president's shabby record on helping veterans—and at his boondoggling VA—in a relentless series of columns and articles dating back to 1969. In his March 29 piece, Greider questioned whether a "one-time non-holiday" could really compensate millions of Vietnam veterans for having been "virtually ignored" for years; and he quoted one veteran activist who called it a "farce." "It's not parades or proclamations, but jobs and hard cash for college that they're after," Greider explained. Then he proceeded (in that article, and its follow-up on March 30) to take the lid off what was really going down in the nation's capital concerning veterans' rights.

While Nixon and his new vice president, Gerald Ford, were offering Vietnam veterans "salutatory remarks" and watered-down "emotional fanfare," Greider reported, Nixon's personal representative was down at the Capitol telling congressmen that Vietnam veterans were "better off than World War II veterans"—that they were already getting too much money for college and thereby unfairly pushing up the cost of living in America. Five years after Gunny Musgrave had scoffed at the notion of going to college on $135 a month, the GI Bill had inched up to $220—an amount that was still supposed to cover everything from tuition and books to transportation and living expenses. In that same period, rents had easily doubled, and gasoline had gone from 35 cents a gallon to well over a dollar. By 1974, so many veterans' groups were lobbying for an increase in educational benefits—most notably, the National Association of Collegiate (later Concerned) Veterans (NACV) led by legless veteran Jim Mayer—that the House passed a bill upping the single veteran's monthly college allowance by $30. Senator Vance Hartke (D-Ind.), who chaired the Senate Veterans' Affairs Committee, was trying to push the increase up to $50. Meantime, four senators who had never before been on the same side of any fence announced that a $50 boost was still far too low, and they proceeded to introduce their own bill, the Comprehensive Vietnam Era Veterans Education Benefit Act, which would provide Vietnam veterans who were enrolled in college with tuition vouchers worth up to $600 per month.

The four senators were the Senate's premier liberal, George McGovern (D-S.Dak.); one of its premier hawks, former chairman of the Republican National Committee, and usually a Nixon defender, Robert Dole (R-Kans.); a critic of Nixon's from within his own party, Charles Mathias (R-Md.); and a conservative Democrat who had usually sided with the president, Daniel Inouye (D-Hawaii). What all four had in common was that they had benefited from the generous GI Bill after World War II. Inouye, who had enlisted in the famed 442nd Regiment of Japanese-Americans that had fought so valiantly in Europe during World War II, and who had lost an arm in combat, recalled how when he and his comrades came home, people were "falling all over themselves to give the returning [vets] horses, free cars, typewriters, parades and keys to the city." "But for the Vietnam veteran," he said with great insight, "there is no one to greet him, and usually someone to curse him." He also offered his own bridge of sympathy to the Vietnam vets, saying that "the caliber of the bullets [in Guadalcanal, Germany, Inchon, and Vietnam] may have been different but the pain was just about the same." Open-minded even to the issue of amnesty for both draft dodgers and military deserters—a concept that Dole still found distasteful—Inouye suggested that a nation that honored Russian dissidents like Alexander Solzhenitsyn should also be "big enough" to forgive its own rebels and nonconformists, including many of those more than half million young veterans shackled for life with "bad paper."

Normally one would have expected the administrator of the VA—as the chief veterans' advocate in the country—to be pushing Congress to authorize the biggest possible package of veterans' benefits. But Donald Johnson, a former national commander of the American Legion, had instead asked Congress to *cut* veterans' benefits. Nor did he even bother showing up for the congressional hearings on a new GI Bill. He had a more pressing engagement, he said—a call to speak at the American Legion Hall in Waukegan, Illinois. In his place, Johnson sent his chief benefits director, Odell W. Vaughan, to argue strenuously with the Veterans' Affairs Committees in both the House and Senate that any increase in educational benefits in excess of 8 percent (about $18 a month) would be "inflationary." Vaughan also relayed his boss's adamant opposition to paying veterans' tuition costs, as opposed to a simple monthly stipend.

In Greider's two Vietnam Veterans Day pieces, he gave damning evidence that Nixon had turned the VA into his personal factotum. It could ably pare down educational benefits that would not fit in Nixon's budget, but it couldn't seem to manage to get veterans their checks on time (which also benefited the government by keeping veterans' money in the federal treasury for sometimes six or eight months longer than it should have been there). The long delay in receiving benefits checks, skimpy as they were, had already forced many vets to drop out of school and left others deeply in debt. Hearing from friends about the bureaucratic nightmare that lay in store for them, a lot of Vietnam vets had never even bothered applying for college aid under the GI Bill, saving the government still more money.

The irony of Vietnam Veterans Day, wrote Greider, had left vets "choking on their bitterness," and had "evoked, not so much glory, but the grief that still lingers. . . ." What Greider did not spell out (and perhaps was dissuaded from mentioning) in his *Post* pieces was the main reason Nixon needed to shortchange Vietnam veterans. Nixon had just managed to swing an emergency appropriation of $600 million to prop up the faltering economy of South Vietnam, and he was trying to convince Congress to come up with another $2.7 billion for his friend Nguyen Van Thieu. By canning the McGovern-Dole bill, the VA could save the government at least $250 million, to help defray those hefty foreign aid bequests. As Mary McGrory said it flat out in the less circumspect *Washington Star-News:* "Although war spending was never considered inflationary, veterans benefits are."

American politics in the spring of 1974 was doing a tumbling act. As Nixon teetered closer to his eventual Humpty-Dumpty crash, the existing VA began to get pulled off balance as well. Gods were falling daily, the unthinkable was suddenly commonplace, and Vietnam veterans were beginning to knock substantial holes in what had for years seemed an impenetrable stone wall of separation from the American community. Vietnam Veterans Day had hit that wall like a B-52 Arc-Light bombing mission, and the fresh air and sunshine were starting to pour in on veterans across the country, but things were happening almost too fast for veterans to enjoy the changes. With so many voices speaking, a confusion began to set in as to who the "real" spokesmen for Vietnam veterans actually were—a confusion that would persist and hinder Vietnam veteran causes for decades to come.

April that year was certainly "the cruelest month" for Donald Johnson and a host of bureaucrats at the VA who depended on him for their jobs. Scandals broke one after the next. It came out that Johnson had stacked the VA's key positions with former American Legion cronies as well as Nixon campaign workers. He had used VA money to make a promotional film, which starred himself holding forth on a bench in Lafayette Park across from the White House. Also on the VA's tab were his limousine, his bodyguard, his staff luncheons at fancy hotels outside Washington, and even a $2,000 vacation to Florida. Among the more serious charges against him was his decision to pay a construction company's $10.3 million cost-overrun claim against the VA without a federal audit— a payment Congress felt should not have exceeded $6 million. Hints of conflict of interest began to leak out when it was learned that the president of the construction company, John Donovan, had employed two close associates of President Nixon—one of whom happened also to be the general counsel for the Republican National Committee—to present his claim.

Then more skeletons tumbled out of Johnson's closet—including a series of lucrative, no-bid contracts he had awarded to his neighbors and personal friends. He had even made one of his neighbors VA comptroller, in charge of the VA's $13 billion yearly budget—the third biggest of any federal agency. The straw that broke the camel's back—and it was no small straw—was the resignation of the VA's chief medical director, Dr. Marc Musser, on April 15. Musser specifically blamed Johnson for interfering with Musser's work, hiring a nonphysician (for the first time in history) to head the VA's Department of Medicine and Surgery, and then forbidding Musser to complain to Congress about the problems this had created.

Scarcely two weeks after Vietnam Veterans Day, a whole chorus—including the Government Accounting Office (GAO)—was screaming bloody murder over

Johnson's unseemly ways of doing business. The groups calling for his resignation ranged from the VFW, the DAV, and the Paralyzed Veterans of America (PVA) down to little-known but influential lobbying groups like the National Association of Collegiate Veterans (NACV), as well as VVAW and its small, cocky offshoot: Ron Kovic's American Veterans Movement (AVM), which had come to national prominence after Kovic and a small band of mostly wheelchair vets had gone on a seventeen-day hunger strike in Senator Cranston's California office in February, then staged a spectacular takeover of the Washington Monument on March 28. Nixon, ever the prudent (and loyal) politician, answered the public outcry by ordering the VA to assemble an investigative team charged with untangling its various messes. When it was learned that Johnson planned to head the team himself—i.e., to investigate his own conduct—protest thundered even from Congress. Senator Alan Cranston (D-Calif.), a liberal who had defended Vietnam veterans almost since the first few Kennedy-era advisors rotated stateside, charged that Nixon had "put Dracula in charge of a blood bank." And Olin "Tiger" Teague (D-Tex.), former head of the House Veterans' Affairs Committee and far to the right of Cranston, echoed the Californian by suggesting Nixon had "put a fox in charge of a hen house."

Once "Tiger" Teague jumped into the fray, Johnson was doomed. Teague, whose cutting Texas drawl silenced all but the boldest opponents, was the most highly decorated World War II vet in Congress (he sometimes wore his Medal of Honor around his neck for effect), and he had chaired the Veterans' Affairs Committee from 1955 to 1973. Nobody could accuse Teague of being a soft touch for needy veterans, as he had chastised an overgenerous VA back in 1950 for letting colleges squeeze too much money out of the GI Bill. But this time, an outraged Teague decried the fact that for four years in a row he "had found it necessary to add substantially to the budget proposed for the Veterans Administration." Not only had the VA's administrator scanted medical services for veterans, Teague revealed, he had also pushed his underpaid workers to the brink of striking in several cities, including Boston, Portland, and Miami. Moreover, Teague charged that Johnson had filled the VA's most important, high-salaried positions with "incompetent . . . unqualified . . . inexperienced" individuals, and had "completely wrecked the leadership of the Department of Medicine and Surgery" through his continual harassment of staff. The congressman found Nixon's promise to improve the VA with a special White House "Domestic Veterans Council"—again to be headed by Johnson!—as ridiculous as Johnson's own self-investigation committee. Nothing short of Johnson's resignation, Teague concluded, could save the VA.

On April 19, 1974, Johnson told the press he confidently expected to remain head of the VA for 33 more months—the rest of Nixon's elected term, which neither he nor Nixon would see. But a few days later, a disgruntled VA subordinate of Johnson's, who had been demoted to a National Cemetery job for criticizing his boss, began to spill the beans about more of Johnson's shady deals. Deciding it was time to cut loose from his clumsy Iowa farmboy, who couldn't seem to keep his feet out of the manure, Nixon quietly asked for Johnson's resignation. The night of April 22, Johnson announced that he was quitting—"with great pride in my record," he said—but he refused to give the press a definite date. In fact, he planned to remain on the job till June, so that he could qualify for his federal pension.[132]

Had the Vietnam veterans' movement been able to offer a united front when Johnson was toppled, a whole new era in just benefits and care might have begun. But VVAW-WSO, which deserved more credit than any other single group for exposing the VA as the naked emperor—or perhaps more aptly, big-bellied, unproductive family mooch—that it was, was itself in disarray, torn between the conflicting ambitions of a veterans' self-help group and a revolutionary cadre. By May 1, 1974, not only had spin codes and Donald Johnson been dumped, but VVAW-WSO was making significant inroads in discharge-upgrading as well. They had set up two flourishing discharge-upgrade centers in San Francisco and in Oakland, which served as models for similar operations that were springing up—with and without VVAW-WSO affiliation—all over the country.

Each VVAW-WSO discharge-upgrade office comprised a mixture of staff workers and law students. They provided well-documented applications to an ace lawyer in Washington, D.C., who was winning an unprecedented 80 percent of his cases. Still, the Discharge Review Boards in Washington were overloaded with cases—they had heard only 36,379 appeals in the past seven years—and it was clear that most of the half a million remaining cases could not get heard in time to make a difference in those veterans' lives, if indeed the majority of cases would ever be heard at all. The only real solution, according to VVAW-WSO—and it was a brilliant idea—was for the military henceforth to issue a single-type discharge to all departing personnel. This single-type discharge—which did not attempt to categorize or label a veteran's character in any way—could be issued retroactively to all veterans who requested it.

It would have taken an enormous effort to lobby for a single-type discharge, but VVAW-WSO decided to stretch its limited resources even further by pushing at the same time for complete amnesty for draft resisters too. In fact, the organization's revolutionary rhetoric often made it seem as if helping vets with discharge upgrades was subsidiary to a general amnesty; and since its positions were often dictated by the largely nonveteran RU, it was no surprise that VVAW-WSO sometimes sounded almost apologetic about including vets in the amnesty package. "Because the war was wrong, resistance is right," argued an article in *Winter Soldier*, as if struggling to explain itself. "Just as we are now raising a demand for amnesty for those who resisted the war by going into exile, underground or prison, so we are raising the same demand for GIs who resisted the war and the military."

VVAW-WSO's list of social justice causes during the mid-1970s was disconcertingly broad—reflecting, to some degree, the megalomania of the RU and its successor, the Revolutionary Communist Party, which with a membership of less than seven hundred claimed it would overthrow capitalism and install Maoist governments in the United States and Western Europe. Comrade Avakian, the leader of the RCP, was a classic victim of self-delusion; but in the fervent crusading of VVAW-WSO one senses rather the deep-felt, wounded idealism of so many Vietnam veterans, who were not yet ready—especially after witnessing and experiencing such terrible human loss—to let the dream of a better world die.

Certainly VVAW (which dropped the WSO after another internal split in November 1975, and which still exists, doing effective work in places like Chicago, New York, and New Jersey, now in the 21st century) has reason to be proud of its record of accomplishments. These included the defense of prisoners' rights in Attica and Fort Leavenworth, the successful operation of a medical clinic in Bogue Chitto, Alabama (treating hundreds of rural blacks, whom white doctors there would not touch), coast-to-coast demonstrations against apartheid in South Africa, and support work for dozens of workers' strikes, from the Chrysler plant in Detroit to the coal mines of Harlan, Kentucky, to the grape fields of Southern California. But one cannot escape the conclusion that back in that volatile spring of 1974, when the doors of change were swinging wide, when even the *Washington Post* editorialized that a far more responsive VA might result from Johnson's downfall, VVAW took a critically wrong turn. The consequences of that wrong turn were painfully evident in the last major national action VVAW would ever stage, Dewey Canyon IV, which was a debacle from start to finish. Ironically, DC IV snuffed out the organization's potential for mainstream political leadership far more effectively than Al Hubbard's attempt to dissolve VVAW the following year, with a little ceremony at the Fourth Street Methodist Church in New York City—which the RCP folk, still soaring on their self-deluded radical rhetoric, treated as a bad joke.[133]

5. Dewey Canyon IV: Defeat in Washington

Dewey Canyon IV was scheduled to take place in Washington, D.C., July 1–4, 1974, near the start of a planned summerlong campaign of protests by seventeen peace groups against Nixon's continuing covert war in Southeast Asia. The main issue that summer for the antiwar movement—now much shrunken and virtually impotent—was that neither the U.S. nor South Vietnam was living up to the Paris Peace Agreement signed in January 1973. The truth was that Nixon and Kissinger had never intended to see it carried out, because they were both irrevocably committed to perpetuating two separate Vietnams, one Communist and one "free," and maintaining a puppet government in South Vietnam that would always yield to U.S. interests. The peace accords, by contrast, called for South Vietnam to cease hostilities against all Communists inside its boundaries and to allow complete freedom of speech and of the press; for the U.S. to stop building up the military capability of South Vietnam and to stop intervening in its internal affairs; and for North and South Vietnam to cooperate in holding a general election in South Vietnam, with the possibility that Vietnam might be reunited under one government if the people so chose. In reality, however, Thieu's government continued killing and imprisoning Communists wherever it could find them, and it refused to release 200,000 Communist political prisoners, which it was bound to do within 90 days of the signing of the peace agreement. Meantime, the United States, far from keeping its hands out of South Vietnam, continued sending Thieu military equipment—including 150 F-5E fighter jets—and was still funding 86 percent of the Saigon government's national budget. Nixon even wanted Congress to give Thieu another $2.5 billion, essentially so that South Vietnam could sustain its military campaign to drive the Communists out.

VVAW-WSO decided it would come to Washington with five demands: 1) universal unconditional amnesty for all draft resisters and vets with bad paper; 2) adequate benefits for all vets; 3) a single-type discharge for all vets; 4) an end to all aid to Thieu and also to Lon Nol, the anti-Communist puppet ruler of Cambodia; 5) the resignation of Richard Nixon. On the surface, their agenda sounded innocuous enough, and the first three demands went right to the heart of the war against the VA. But the last two were political and partisan in a way that VVAW had striven hard to avoid during the great triumph of Dewey Canyon III. One could perhaps have argued for the right of veterans to defend the peace agreement, though their military experience no longer had the same urgent relevance to American policymaking in Southeast Asia. And calling for Nixon's resignation could have been construed as an act of patriotism, except for the way that they were doing it. Rather than condemning Nixon for his lies and deceptions concerning the Watergate burglary, and the shame he had brought to the presidency, they attacked him for "representing all the exploitation and repression of the American people by the profit-seeking corporations that really run this country." The RU faction in VVAW even fought against using the slogan "Impeach Nixon," claiming it fostered the "bourgeois, liberal delusion" that American government actually worked. They preferred to hint at an armed uprising with the phrase: "Throw the bum out!" For the most part, VVAW was now allowing the RU to make the rules for the entire organization.

That was just the beginning of their bad judgment, not to say madness. They got a permit to camp on the Mall; but just as in 1971, the government forbade them to actually sleep there. They counted on the goodwill of the police to overlook infractions of that rule, as in 1971, only this time the cops were less inclined to be forgiving. With the president facing impeachment, the whole capital was tense, people were worried about their jobs, and one of the deepest recessions in history made government workers even more edgy about being fired. Still, the police might have felt some goodwill toward the vets had they played up their service to America, as they did in 1971. Instead, they bedecked their campsite and portable stage with Communist flags—honoring North Vietnam, the Viet Cong, the Pathet Lao, and the Cambodian United Front—and went around chanting, "Kick Nixon in the ass, for the crimes of his class!" Moreover, though VVAW-WSO managed to turn out a couple of thousand people, as VVAW had in 1971, this time their ranks were swelled with the mostly nonvet members of ultra-leftist groups like the RU, the Revolutionary Student Brigade, and the Indochina Solidarity Committee. According to journalist Gloria Emerson, less than a dozen of the original veteran participants of Dewey Canyon III made it back to Washington for DC IV.

The first night, pissed-off park policemen came walking and riding horses through their campsite, shoving sleepers awake and forcing them to move on. The protesters sometimes pushed back, lack of sleep feeding their irritability, and tempers flared on both sides. The next night, VVAW strung ropes from tree to tree at the height of horseback riders. But as the morning mist began to fade at sunrise, they faced a line of mounted police itching for vengeance. Former Army intelligence captain Dave Curry says they felt like "Native Americans [who] woke up and saw the cavalry there."

There was a lot going on behind the scenes as well. In June 1974 the FBI had obtained a document from the Wisconsin RU called "District Bulletin on Veterans' Work," in which RU leadership declared that "veterans are an extremely important potential revolutionary force" and advised its cadre "to link up with veterans" in the "fights . . . against the Veterans Administration for benefits." This same document focused on the need for RU members to participate in VVAW-WSO's "upcoming demonstration in Washington . . . [which] will have a significant effect in determining the direction of the vets' movement." Even more explicitly, the document concluded: "By helping to build a Washington demonstration . . . we can begin to realize our goal of linking the veterans' struggle with the overall anti-imperialist movement."

A few months later, VVAW-WSO only poured more gasoline on what the FBI saw as a dangerous Communist bonfire, when at its fourteenth National Steering Committee meeting in St. Louis the delegates voted—after a tempestuous debate—to officially affiliate VVAW-WSO with the RU. Then in July 1975, at the fifteenth National Steering Committee meeting in Milwaukee, according to the detailed notes taken by an FBI agent, the delegates voted "to openly support the RU and its programs and activities, as well as its political line" and to "purge all local chapters that disagreed with the unification with the RU." While things had not gone quite that far at Dewey Canyon IV, the reckless embrace of a deranged extremist faction—"in order to prevent the VVAW-WSO's collapse," as one veteran leader rationalized—was well in progress.

On Tuesday morning, July 2, the demonstrators marched to the VA, and twenty of them simply stormed into the building, demanding to see the new VA head. In fact, Nixon had not yet found anyone who wanted the job. Even Admiral Elmo Zumwalt Jr., who had commanded the in-country Naval forces in Vietnam in the late sixties, had turned down the post. Although he felt Vietnam veterans had been treated poorly by the VA and that "much improvement in their benefits" was required, he "did not see any possibility of getting those changes made." When a lesser VA official came to meet with the demonstrators, a few hotheads yelled something about "the system" being "incapable of dealing with the needs of this country's people," and that any further talk would be "a useless waste of time"—so they all turned around and left.[134]

That afternoon, there was a demo at the Court of Military Appeals, which could have led to some promising discussion, but instead the demonstrators taunted police with fists raised, chanted "Fight back!" and made speeches about giving Nixon a Dishonorable discharge. The park police retaliated by driving everyone out of the campsite at 3 A.M., and threatening to arrest anyone who remained. Most of them ended up in the basement of a church; and when they returned to the Mall on Wednesday morning, battle lines were sharply drawn. The park police talked of stopping any further actions. As a group of demonstrators approached the campsite, a police car drove up on the sidewalk to block their way, smashing into several people, one of whom, a black vet, was badly hurt. The demonstrators surrounded the car and beat on it, forcing the cops inside to flee for their lives.

Later Wednesday morning, at the Justice Department, the demonstrators were angry and even more daring in their provocations, stenciling "Universal Unconditional Amnesty" slogans on the walls with spray paint, pounding on the locked doors, and cheering obscenities. This time the government had readied an equally provocative response. The doors of the Justice Department swung open, and several SWAT teams came running out, swinging their clubs at the crowd. The demonstrators backed off, and the SWAT teams went back inside. The demonstrators "were feeling really good," according to Danny Friedman, the big ex-linebacker and cofounder of Brooklyn VVAW, who was among them. The D.C. police even seemed amiable as they escorted them back to the Mall. But their mood of victory shattered quickly once they started settling back into their campsite only to have the park police kick them out again.

It was late afternoon, burning hot and sticky humid; everyone was dog-tired, and nerves were badly frayed. Though it was already rush hour, the VVAW-WSO mob began pouring down the streets leading to the Capitol. They were determined to denounce imperialism on the steps of Congress, where some of them had made such a dramatic impact throwing back their medals three years earlier. But this time there had been no preparatory congressional lobbying, and no eloquent, dignified John Kerry spellbinding the entire Foreign Relations Committee. The demonstrators did not give a damn that they were completely stalling the heavy traffic. They were ready to return violence for violence, to mete out a little of the same might-makes-right medicine they had spent all week cursing imperialism for ramming down the throats of the poor and oppressed. The cops, seeing a fight coming, decided to make the first move, and to head them off before they ever reached the Capitol.

When they reached Pennsylvania Avenue, some of Nixon's own White House police—real storm troopers, according to Friedman—blocked their way, along with park police on motor scooters, ordering the demonstrators to get back on the sidewalks. Sick of being harassed, the demonstrators refused to be slowed to a single file and kept on down the middle of the street. They let the disabled vets lead the way. The police started driving their scooters right into people, and a fracas soon developed. The VVAW-WSO mob knocked over several of the scooters, and were then met by a line of helmeted police with shields and clubs, who waded into the marchers, knocking the disabled vets out of their way. Dave Curry tried to shield a blind black vet from getting hit, and got his own head bashed open instead.

Danny Friedman, wearing a portable amplifier across his broad shoulders, spoke into a megaphone to try to restore order to their formation. Some cop tried to grab it away from him, and they played tug of war with a canvas strap, till the cop figured he couldn't outmuscle a 300-pound vet, so he just started jabbing Friedman with his nightstick. Friedman, who never liked being bullied, laid the cop out with one swipe of the portable PA system. Seeing a dozen cops zeroing in on him, the big man tried to escape back to the park by backflipping over a parked car; but he backed into a van, and the next thing he knew half the police force was vying for the chance to whack his big, round head and even bigger, rounder stomach with a nightstick.

Somehow or other, part of the VVAW-WSO troop broke through to the Capitol, where they congratulated themselves as two ex-POWs, John Young and Alfonso Riate, denounced the war in Indochina, and Riate sang antiwar songs in Vietnamese; but unfortunately, this time the rest of the country wasn't listening or watching. That night, they defiantly slept on the Mall again, but the police no longer seemed to care. And the next day, July 4, Danny Friedman, wearing his bloodied shirt, a bloodied bandage around his head, and walking slowly because of several broken ribs—looking like a somewhat better-fed version of the wounded patriot in Archibald Willard's famous Revolutionary War painting—led the march of several thousand people down Constitution Avenue to the Ellipse (past the site, unbeknownst to everyone, of the future Vietnam Veterans Memorial Wall). There, a huge rally was held with music and entertainment, and many more excoriations of capitalist imperialism and "corporate big daddies" were pronounced.

The following issue of *Winter Soldier* put the best possible face on a disaster, claiming that Dewey Canyon IV had sent its thousands of participants back to their hometowns across the country filled with a "determination . . . to build both the veterans' movement, and its larger anti-imperialist movement." They also claimed they had proved that "the people united can never be defeated." But in truth, many of them did feel defeated, or, like Friedman, "really messed up." Friedman recalls that he "slowed down a lot" as an activist after DC IV, and so did many other of the original VVAW founders who had held on till that point. It wasn't just that their bodies were weary of being beaten, or that their heads had been opened up too many times. VVAW-WSO—and with it for now, the whole Vietnam veterans' movement—had lost the moral high ground, and it would take years to regain it.[135]

6. Kovic Meets Unger: The Patients'/Workers' Rights Committee in Long Beach

Apart from all the political machinations, there was an indomitable spirit of self-help that had driven VVAW's dynamos from the very beginning. That spirit was not owned by any particular group or clique of veterans, any more than it could be claimed by or tied to just one organization. And just as VVAW was in its death throes, at the start of 1974, a savvy former member in Los Angeles, who had already been censured and then expelled from an RU-dominated chapter, grabbed hold of the continuing momentum of that self-help wheel to start his own organization, which narrowly missed bringing down the whole VA. He was one of a class of vets who were forced to deal with the VA almost every day of their lives because of the nature of their injury—paralysis following trauma to the spinal cord. Not knowing who he was, the country had already begun to hear his insistent voice two years earlier at the Republican National Convention in Miami. His name, which was about to lose its anonymity forever, was Ron Kovic.

After returning from Miami in August 1972, Kovic was repeatedly reprimanded by Sam Schorr for chasing Hollywood celebrities and promoting himself in the liberal media as VVAW's "political star"; and eventually he had been forbidden to ever speak again in the name of the organization. Unfazed, Kovic merely switched to the VVAW group in Orange County, where he formed a close friendship with the chapter coordinator, ex-Marine Bill Unger. Unger's father had been a lieutenant colonel in the Marine Corps; and when all Bill's youthful rebellions (like trying to be a pool hustler) had failed, and he came home jobless, penniless, and badly beaten, his dad hustled him off to Marine boot camp. Six months later, in December 1967, Unger found himself in Vietnam, a replacement in Hotel Two One, the Marine company that had nearly been obliterated two months before in Operation Medina (the same suicide mission Scott Camil got wounded on). Unger had a lacerating tour of duty himself. His first wounding occurred on Operation Pegasus, when his unit was sent from Con Thien on the DMZ (no picnic ground) to help lift the siege of Khe Sanh. At Khe Sanh, a mortar round that exploded on top of his bunker flipped him against a wall, giving him a concussion wound that caused scar tissue to form in his left temporal lobe. Since the damage was not immediately visible, he was not medevaced; but soon afterward, he started having serious memory and hearing problems.

Unger was relatively happy during the next few months in a Combined Action Group (CAG), which did humanitarian work with civilians in the villages (and gave him a chance to drink and "hang with women"). But he continued to see heavy action and to get "banged up a bunch of times." In December 1968, though he'd come to hate the war, he extended for six months, for no more reasons than that he'd been "raised in the Marine Corps" and that the CAG was "almost a human situation," where it was possible to show some compassion for the Vietnamese as human beings. Then, in Phuc Tien, a "little nowhere town" 35 miles from Chu Lai, his compound was attacked by VC. As he fired from a crouch, several mortars exploded around him and a bullet blasted through his right knee. When he tried to stand, he found the knee was locked in a bent position. Medevaced to Camp Drake in Japan, he could no longer contain his anger. As soon as his leg got better, he went AWOL, and was then transferred to the Marines' Devil's Island for "shitbirds": Guantanamo Naval Base in Cuba. His body had become emaciated from recurring bouts of malaria, and his hearing problems got worse. There were constant brawls between the Navy guys and the Marines, and Unger got his head knocked around some more, as well as getting his rank busted and ten major charges (inciting a riot, etc.) brought against him.

The charges were dropped, and Unger was sent to Camp Lejeune, North Carolina, for discharge as a PFC. A couple of bus rides brought him to Orange Coast College in Costa Mesa, California, where he let his blond hair grow long and tried to hide the fact that he'd been a Marine. Then Kent State happened, and at Orange Coast he heard a brilliant speaker named Richard Robertson from the Radical Professors Union explain the Vietnam War. "Five minutes later," he says, he was a "revolutionary." When Kovic met him at a draft-board demo in Orange County in 1971, Unger's straight yellow hair was down to his ass, his untucked dress-blue shirt carried a huge assortment of war medals and peace buttons, his face sported a three-day growth of beard, and he was carrying a National Liberation Front (Viet Cong) flag. His eyes flashing with humor and reckless intensity, he looked like a California "pretty boy" who'd just surfed the River Styx. When they were arrested together that day, Bill took extraordinary care to see that Ron was protected from harm in jail. In the following years, Bill's household on Charle Street in Costa Mesa, which included his beautiful wife, Trisha, and often an assortment of her equally pretty and equally radical girlfriends, became a haven of warmth and acceptance for Kovic during his many periods of loneliness and depression.

Early 1973 was one of those especially bad times for Kovic. He had just been jilted by the (reputedly) most beautiful woman in VVAW, a strong-minded feminist lawyer named Joan Anderson, and the pain was worsened by the rumor that she had thrown him over for his former friend and now nemesis, Tom Zangrilli. One day Kovic slipped in the bathtub, and a sore developed on his bottom. Every paraplegic knows that a bedsore has to be taken care of immediately; he has to "go down," which means to spend many hours a day out of his chair, on his stomach, to allow it to heal. A bedsore that gets big enough can lead to death from septic shock. Kovic neglected the sore until it grew to the size of a quarter, and then he was forced to hospitalize himself at the Long Beach VA.

He spent ninety-three days in the hospital, much of the time on his stomach, strapped to a gurney, which he was able to move up and down the halls only with great effort, poling himself along with two canes. Those were three of the hardest months he ever lived through. Even though he'd survived the unspeakable Bronx VA, he was shocked by the conditions at the Long Beach hospital. Partly it was that he'd naively expected the VA to have fixed its problems by now, especially after that devastating exposé in *Life*. But he found that "the conditions and treatment [in Long Beach] were just as bad, if not worse," as when he had come home from the war in 1968.

The hospital seemed to him like a zoo where every human horror and infirmity was on display: "the drugs men took to hide their pain, the awful bedsores that never seemed to go away, the hideous place, the depressing and sickening green walls, the windows that were always locked, the putrid, stifling air that always hung like death, the stink of that place always in your nostrils, in your clothing, your oversize shirts with the government label that always reminded you of Auschwitz, the constant crying and screaming, the absurdity of the bingo games in the midst of so much suffering and misery and pain."

He was on Spinal Cord Ward C-1, where the patients' urine bags, including his own, were not emptied often enough, and frequently spilled over on the floors. He recalls how he usually left a trail of urine as he poled himself along on his gurney. Not only were patients left lying for hours in their own excrement, but no one intervened to stop the open use of every sort of drug. Both acid and heroin were readily available on the paraplegic ward, and one night Kovic even watched a black vet from Vegas freebasing cocaine there! The drug use was but a secondary symptom, however, of the even deadlier despair that hung like a poisonous cloud over that ward, and to some degree over the entire hospital.

It was clear to the paraplegics on Ward C-1 that most of them were there not to get well but to die. They were not getting the care they needed, and most of them were sliding down month by month, year by year, toward an end that was only too easy to see. Marty Swanson stood out as a fearsome example of what Kovic did not want to become. Marty had been a high school football star, and he once showed Ron a picture of what he'd looked like when he was in the Airborne. He was tall, strongly built, and looked extremely sure of himself. Now he was emaciated, his arms and legs withered, and he lay drunk in bed all day, sometimes crying out in a weak, whining voice. His bedsores had gotten so bad that his bones were actually starting to pop out through his skin, and it was obvious they were never going to heal—at least with the sort of "treatment," i.e., neglect, he was getting at the VA. When he was finally off the gurney, Kovic bought Marty a bottle of Wild Turkey whiskey at a nearby liquor store and smuggled it in to him in a brown bag, but Ron assiduously avoided using booze or hard drugs himself, having seen too many wheelchair vets go to an early death that way. In fact, Marty's time would soon be up. He checked out of the hospital and into a motel, but he wasn't bothering to wash, and his sores festered worse than ever. His room smelled so bad that friends stopped coming to see him, and his girlfriend ran off with his disability check. Eventually they found him dead—like so many others who passed through that ward.

Each time he learned of another friend gone, Kovic said, it was like having one more chunk gouged out of his own flesh. His great fear was always that he would be the next to die. "I didn't want it to happen to me," he recalls. "I wanted to do anything to stay in this world, even with all I had to endure each day." What made these 93 days on the gurney even harder was the fact that none of his erstwhile VVAW friends bothered to come down to visit him—including his former lover Joan.[136]

Kovic decided to fight back against the world's indifference, and to keep alive his own activist spirit, by organizing a Patients'/Workers' Rights Committee. Partly he was influenced by Joan Baez's ex-husband, David Harris, whom he had met and heard speak a few times at antiwar rallies. Having gone to federal prison for resisting the draft, Harris had organized strikes among the other prisoners to improve their living conditions and also just "to make it difficult for them [the prison authorities] to carry on with business as usual." But an even bigger influence was Bill Unger, who showed up at the Long Beach VA hospital not long after Kovic got there.

Unger had been badly beaten at a demonstration in Watts; and before he was released from the "Glass House" (the LAPD lockup downtown), he was worked over again, this time by a police judo expert twice his size, who shoved his head against the cement floor. The beatings exacerbated Unger's concussion wound from Khe Sanh, and he began having epileptic seizures, as well as increased hearing and memory loss. The cops had reinjured his shattered knee too, which required a brace. He went to the Long Beach VA hospital for treatment; and while he was there, they offered him a job as a management analyst. The job gave him access to all wards of the hospital, and in no time he ran across Kovic. Together they planned and then made the Patients'/Workers' Rights Committee a reality. Unger had already gotten to know many of the vets there during his years of volunteer work as a veterans' rights counselor. His primary job would be to recruit members to the group; but since as management analyst he was privy to the hospital's confidential files and financial records, he could also supply facts and statistics to back up their charges of VA incompetence. Kovic, who was great at speaking off the cuff, would lead the discussions every Thursday evening. Kovic also made use of his proclivity for rapping with strangers to roll all over the hospital with a tape recorder hidden under his pillow, interviewing every patient he met about their experiences there.

Besides the usual tales of piss-bags overflowing and call buttons unanswered for hours, Kovic's tape captured some truly shocking stories. He learned that vets who had dared to complain about poor conditions or inhumane treatment were routinely "punished" by being given Thorazine and other heavy-duty tranquilizers. If they persisted in their protests, they were often threatened with being put in a straitjacket, sent to the psychiatric ward, or even lobotomized. Kovic's friend, journalist Richard Boyle, who came down to the hospital to research a series of articles for the *L.A. Free Press,* claimed to have found evidence that several otherwise normal vets had been locked in the psych ward, and at least one vet had actually been given a lobotomy to stop him from mouthing off against the VA. Boyle's article succeeded in triggering a congressional investigation into the drugging of veterans against their will.

In the meantime, the Patients'/Workers' Rights Committee began meeting once a week at 6 P.M. in the little grassy area behind the paraplegic ward. Within a few weeks, they were attracting a crowd of over one hundred people, including many paraplegics and quadriplegics and even some doctors and nurses, to talk about problems and air grievances. According to Kovic, there were also a goodly number of patients from the psych ward, their minds blanked out on Thorazine, staggering about and muttering to themselves or screaming obscenities. Bottles of wine in paper bags went round the group, loosening tongues and fueling the often heated debate. The hospital administration quickly perceived them as a threat. After a month or so, an unmarked van would circle past each of their meetings, with the driver holding a walkie-talkie and guys leaning out the windows photographing them with high-powered lenses. It was later confirmed by Boyle that they were agents of the FBI. Kovic also began to receive anonymous death threats on the telephone.

Despite the harassment and intimidation, the group's numbers increased week to week, and a sense of solidarity continued to grow. Besides Kovic and Unger, a number of strong-minded individuals—potential leaders—came to the fore. One was an Air Force veteran, Stan Price, who had survived a year in Vietnam unscathed, only to break his neck in a surfing accident the first week after his discharge. Price was the highest-level quadriplegic (a break a quarter inch higher would have stopped his heart), unable to move his arms at all, but still completely fearless. Another key figure was little Michael "Max" Inglett, a lower-level quad, who had some use of his arms. Inglett had served a full tour as a combat medic in Vietnam, winning a Purple Heart and Bronze Star; but when he came home, still on active duty, he began having blackouts and psychotic breaks, and one night tried to hold up a liquor store with an unloaded derringer. The store owner had shot him through the spine, paralyzing him for life. A small-time performer and comic before enlisting in the Army, Inglett was gutsy and feisty, and had developed a ventriloquist's act in his wheelchair. But his career broke down on the rocky road of his continuing mental problems, which included frequent flashbacks, a tendency to manic-depression, and occasional bouts of schizophrenia. Nevertheless, Max's nature remained exceedingly gentle and caring; and when he was feeling good, he could catch everyone up in his own infectious enthusiasm. Still "Doc" in his mind, he would breeze around the hospital, trying to solve everybody else's problems—one more giving vet who had been drilled too well in how to ignore his own personal needs.

Having done extensive work with the GI movement, Unger had gotten to know Jane Fonda during her FTA and Indochina Peace Campaign (IPC) tours. One day in the spring of 1973, Unger got word that Fonda was going to be speaking at California State College at Long Beach, just across the way from the VA hospital. Kovic called her office, asking that she come to the hospital after her speech and attend a special meeting of the Patients'/Worker's Rights Committee. When she agreed, Kovic and Unger knew they had a publicity gimmick of major proportions.

They printed up leaflets with Fonda's picture, announcing her imminent visit to the Long Beach VA, and passed out hundreds of them to patients; the rest they taped to walls in every ward. As the time of her arrival neared, the entire hospital buzzed with gossip and arguments about her, and many vets were very angry. The World War II vets seemed to hate her most of all, having been outraged by her unauthorized trip to Hanoi and especially by her posing for photos in an NVA gunner's seat, pretending to shoot down American planes. Every time Kovic rolled past them, the World War II guys would shout "Traitor!" and "Communist!" The death threats against him came more often, and he even heard from fellow patients that there was talk of poisoning his water or hiring some hit man to come into the unlocked ward at night and shoot him as he slept. For safety, Unger began sleeping next to him.

Fonda's visit was a huge success. She arrived at noon, and the lawn behind Ward C-1 quickly filled up with a couple of hundred people, including the usual contingent of guys from the psych ward raving incoherently. The World War II vets and their wives immediately staged a counterdemonstration, shouting denunciations and singing "God Bless America!" in an attempt to drown her out. But most of the vets were impressed with her sincere concern; and even more significantly, she was deeply affected by them. Kovic recalls that she looked "stunned," as if "she had walked into hell," and that it was obvious she had never witnessed anything like this before. Indeed the seed was planted for one of her greatest movies. A few days later, she sent her partner Bruce Gilbert and scriptwriter Nancy Dowd down to the hospital to meet Kovic and Unger and begin research for a screenplay, which became the basis for the film *Coming Home.*

Kovic followed up on her visit by calling a huge press conference right in the paraplegic ward. He played his tapes for the newspeople, then led them through some of the other wards. The camera crews followed him, recording the appalling sights for the evening news, and many vets were courageous enough to give interviews. It became very hot for Kovic after that—he was known not only as a "Communist" but, perhaps worse, as "a friend of Jane Fonda"—and he did not improve relations with the World War II vets by putting up a poster of Mao next to his bed. Unger thought he must have "balls of lead" to perform such provocative acts; but the truth was, Kovic would often push himself too far, then crack from his own nightmare fears and paranoia— products of his delayed stress. And that was just what happened now. As soon as his bedsore healed, in early July, he asked Unger to help him flee on a plane to San Francisco.

Kovic cooled out for a week or so at Richard Boyle's place in Mill Valley, watching the Watergate hearings on TV, and then Boyle talked him into going down to Florida to observe the Gainesville conspiracy trial. There, Kovic pissed off VVAW again by speaking freely to the press, even though Judge Arnow had already issued his gag order against the organization, and VVAW had decided that only one spokesman should violate it: John Musgrave. Even more aggravating to them, Kovic said almost nothing in defense of the Gainesville Eight, but instead talked of his own disillusion with America and harped on the "sickening hospital conditions" in Long Beach! The July 19, 1973, issue of *Rolling Stone* gave the "mass movement" VVAW vets even more cause to revile Kovic. It contained a lengthy profile of him by fellow activist David Harris, whose tone bordered on worshipful, as he portrayed Ron as the chief hero of the veterans' movement. There was even a huge centerfold photo of Kovic, in full color, by noted photographer Annie Leibovitz. Wearing a fatigue jacket, he sat in the middle of a flooded parking lot in Venice, California, staring fiercely at the camera, with—irony of ironies for all those RU folks who detested him as "reactionary"—a National Liberation Front flag pasted over the Everest and Jennings logo on the side of his wheelchair. Being Ron, he couldn't help trumpeting his newfound celebrity to all his friends by singing the current hit song "On the Cover of the *Rolling Stone.*"[137]

After a few months with his parents in Massapequa, Long Island, Ron returned to California and moved into a little apartment just off the beach in Marina Del Rey, next to artsy, beatnik-populated Venice. He planned to start writing his autobiography there, at 24½ Hurricane Street, but the name of the street proved only too apt, as Kovic soon found himself at the center of an even greater storm of veterans' activism.

It began in Long Beach late that fall (1973) with what proved to be the final meeting of the now-combined L.A.–Orange County VVAW. Several under-cover government agents in the organization had already been exposed, and everyone was on edge. Further tension was created by the split between RU and non-RU vets; and there was still a lot of hostility against Kovic for having talked out of turn in Gainesville, though Ron felt it was mostly sour grapes because he wasn't parroting the RU party line that "Whizzo" (as he mockingly called WSO) wanted him to. One of Unger's friends, a hefty, half-crazed Puerto Rican vet named Alfredo Cabrera (with six years in the Marines, two tours in Vietnam, and three gunshot wounds), stood up and said out of the blue: "I think there's two agents in this room, and one of them is either Ron Kovic or Tom Zangrilli!" Zangrilli, the secretary, threw a handful of papers in the air and resigned. Next, the black Vietnam veteran Gary Lawton walked out. An ex-Panther, he'd been set up for murdering two police officers in Riverside, and it would take three trials before he was acquitted (with massive support of all kinds from VVAW and other leftist groups). As he left, Lawton said, "I've seen this shit in the Panthers—it's gonna destroy your organization." Kovic then turned on Cabrera's friend Bill Hager, who had already gone over to the pro-gressive WSO side, and charged that Hager had never repaid him $300. At that point, recalls Kovic's new friend Bob Waddell, "All hell broke loose. It was hor-rible. Suddenly, VVAW women were just bawling their brains out. Even the guys were crying. Everybody walked out of there, pissed off, swearing."

The new year of 1974 looked dismal for Kovic. He was making scant progress on his book, and he felt painfully isolated. After he'd withdrawn his tremendous energy, the Patients'/Workers' Rights Committee had quickly fallen apart. Political activism had always proved the best cure for his loneliness, but there was no group left that he could feel comfortable with. In desperation, he drove up to the People's Union co-op onion farm outside Fresno, which Joan Baez and David Harris had bought as a haven for peace movement people, ex-convicts, and Vietnam vets. He spent a few days hanging out with Harris, ask-ing him about the hunger and work strikes he'd organized in prison.[138]

7. The American Veterans Movement

One night after he got back to Hurricane Street, Kovic sat at his new rolltop desk and began typing the words: "ARM—American Revolutionary Movement."

A couple of ideas stood out in his head. Thinking about the unfortunate rift that had developed between Vietnam vets and World War II vets at the VA hospital, Kovic recalled that his own father had served in the Navy in World War II, and he felt that any new veterans' movement should be open to vets from all wars. He also felt that the United States government needed a revolutionary change, and that a new veterans' movement should help foment that change. But as he mulled over the prospects for creating such an organization, and even toyed with writing slogans and bylaws for it, he began to think that using the word *revolutionary* would only make it easier for the government to discredit and perhaps even destroy the group before they could establish a national presence. So with one twitch of his forefinger, Kovic changed ARM to AVM, and the American Veterans Movement was born.

The next day, Kovic cashed his disability check and drove to the U.S. Flag and Banner Shop in downtown Los Angeles, where he ordered up a thousand dollars' worth of red-white-and-blue flags, banners, posters (that bore his own picture from the centerfold of *Rolling Stone*), buttons, and membership cards emblazoned with the letters AVM. On the front of the membership card was the slogan: "We Will Fight / We Will Win," and on the back was an outline of the United States with the AVM initials stretching from coast to coast, as if they had already organized throughout the nation. Kovic listed his own address on Hurricane Street as the "National Office."

He let all the merchandise sit in his trunk for a week before showing it to Unger, whom he tantalized on the phone with hints about a "really important surprise." It was a kick for Kovic to go out every day and look at the stuff, and a kind of secret power trip too, to imagine that he held a whole veterans' organization in the trunk of his car, when he himself was still the only member. Unger, however, gave him just the enthusiastic response he was hoping for. For years, Kovic had been coming up with wild ideas that went nowhere, but this one, Unger felt, "was ripe." They had both recently lost close friends from the paraplegic ward; and the Long Beach hospital—the largest general medical and surgical facility for veterans in the nation—was as overcrowded, under-staffed, drug-ridden, and dreary as ever. Unger referred to it as the "San Quentin" of the VA's 170-hospital system. That same day, after driving down to the hospital for Kovic to get a checkup, they began organizing for AVM together. Many of their friends from the Patients'/Workers' Rights Committee, like Stan Price and Max Inglett, joined immediately.

One of the first people to jump on board AVM was Bob Waddell. Waddell had gotten hooked on pure heroin while working in the Air Force mail depot in Saigon. Having won an Honorable discharge through Nixon's "drug amnesty" program (which did nothing to curb his substance abuse, however), Waddell had spent a couple of years working with VVAW in Indiana, then hitchhiked to California with his new bride, an Irish beauty named Shannon. Just before they left Indianapolis, Shannon had handed him the *Rolling Stone* with David Harris's article about Kovic. Bob had gotten so excited he'd clipped the whole thing out and stuffed it in his backpack, and he'd been carrying it around ever since. In Long Beach, where his brother lived, he began going to classes at the VA hospital to learn how to care for paraplegics and quadriplegics, since the VA had a program where it would pay qualified people to care for paralyzed veterans in their own home—and that was the kind of meaningful, people-serving job that appealed to Bob.

Eventually Waddell worked inside the VA as well, giving physical therapy in the spinal cord–injury unit. He quickly became a kind of legend there himself. He was as handsome as a young Robert Redford, powerfully built, and had an enormous crop of curly, flaming red hair and beard. His energy was unbelievable, and even more striking were his endless patience and limitless generosity. He seemed incapable of hating anyone, and had the gift of turning anger into laughter in a matter of seconds. One day on the paraplegic ward, he heard a voice ask, "Who's that guy?" and someone answered, "Bob Waddell." Bob turned round to see the guy from the *Rolling Stone* centerfold smiling and sticking out his hand: "I'm Ron Kovic. I've heard a lot about you." "I've heard a lot about *you* too!" Bob shouted, hugging Kovic and practically lifting him out of his chair. They spent the next couple of hours telling each other their life stories, and from that day on remained bosom friends.

Waddell proved invaluable as an organizer for AVM. By early February 1974, they had close to 100 members, mostly from the hospital, and were already beginning to attract the wrath of VVAW leaders like Bill Hager, who felt AVM was drawing away what little lifeblood was left in the original organization. That AVM invited VVAW to its meetings was only salt in the wound, as was the fact that most of the AVM members continued to wear their VVAW buttons too. Unger told Kovic it was time to get serious about their goals and strategies. Kovic's original posters listed three demands: 1) Impeach Nixon; 2) Increase rights for all veterans; 3) Improve disgraceful conditions in the VA hospitals. Unger convinced Kovic that they should drop the "impeach Nixon," and that they needed to remain completely nonpolitical, both to build a national membership and to differentiate themselves from the strident partisanship that was killing VVAW. Unger, who was an excellent writer, sent out letters explaining the goals of AVM to hundreds of congresspeople, and many wrote back expressing their support.

For Kovic, however, things were moving far too slowly, and he was anxious to make use of his tremendous media contacts, from which VVAW had temporarily cut him off. He knew that the news people, who loved his articulateness and flair for drama, had actually been pleading with VVAW to get interviews with *him* again instead of the dull, doctrinaire spokesmen they were sending in his place. He hatched a plan to take over some important politician's office and hold it till Donald Johnson, the hated head of the VA, agreed to meet with them in person. The only AVM members he shared the plan with were Unger, Waddell, and Max Inglett, who all pledged that they would stick with him no matter how rough the situation got. According to Unger, the choice of politician was easy. Senator Alan Cranston, chairman of the Senate Subcommittee on Veterans' Health and Hospitals, had an office in the new Federal Building in Westwood, some twenty miles from Long Beach, and right across from the West Los Angeles VA. Cranston was scheduled to return to California on February 13 to chair a special hearing on conditions at the Long Beach VA—a hearing that had originated in part as a response to the scandalous material submitted to Congress by the Patients'/Workers' Rights Committee almost a year earlier. The circle had been completed, so it was the perfect time and place to put the spotlight on Cranston. Moreover, he was one of the few congresspeople they could count on not to throw them out.

Kovic put out word to all his members that they had a scheduled meeting with Senator Cranston in Westwood at 2 P.M. on Tuesday, February 12— Lincoln's Birthday. He said he wanted as many of them as possible to come along, to tell the senator about conditions at the hospital, and that they would only have to be away from their ward for a few hours. It was all made up; and, as Kovic well knew, Cranston would still be in Washington on that day. But his lie succeeded in producing a magnificent convoy of two dozen cars driving slowly up the 405 freeway, their headlights on and their windows and bumpers decorated with AVM stickers. At Wilshire they exited and filed into the Federal Building's parking lot.

Both Unger and Kovic were suddenly impressed by their own creation: over a dozen vets transferring into their wheelchairs—paraplegics, quads, amputees—and another dozen or so from the neurology and psych wards, whose faraway eyes and wasted expressions made them look as if they were clearly losing the war at home. Most had shaggy hair and beards; some wore their utility jackets covered with ribbons and medals; others still wore their blue hospital clothing with "Property of U.S. Government" stamped in big black letters on the front, as well as their ID wristbands; Max and Bill were in their full dress uniforms, with Trish looking beautiful and equally elegant beside them; all wore their AVM and VVAW buttons. Still unbeknownst to the majority, Kovic and Inglett also carried AVM flags and banners folded under their chair cushions. According to Kovic, it was the greatest feeling in the world to finally be "taking charge"—asserting their humanity, and voicing opposition to the system that had discarded them. He felt happier and stronger than he had in years.

Kovic had called the press ahead of time, and there was a crowd of news people awaiting them in Cranston's office. Cranston's poor office workers had no idea what was happening. They tried to ask the vets to leave, but could scarcely get a word in edgewise. Kovic was talking nonstop—a slick jive that discombobulated the workers even more—while Unger, Waddell, Waddell's brother Mike, and a couple of Unger's ambulatory friends from Movement for a Democratic Military (MDM) moved chairs in front of doors and took over the telephones. When the workers started to panic, Unger calmly explained that they simply wanted to speak with Senator Cranston and Donald Johnson about conditions at the Long Beach VA. Meanwhile, Kovic made a slew of long-distance calls to Washington; and each time some worker protested, Ron would wave them off, saying, "Just one more call—it's to my mother."

The press was eating it up, eager to see what would develop. Cranston was unavailable, but they talked to his right-hand man, Lou Haas, who assured Unger that Government Service Agency (GSA) police would not be sent to remove the disabled vets. "We believe in the right of protest," Haas asserted. Johnson was also unavailable, though his office claimed he would "be in touch." At that point, a lot of the vets decided they had made their statement, and left. Fifteen vets remained—eleven of them disabled, six in wheelchairs—along with Trish Unger and Shannon Waddell, who was several months pregnant. They evicted the workers from one room in the office, barricaded themselves in, and announced that they were staying until both Cranston and Johnson arrived.[139]

Support for the vets materialized almost immediately. Leonard Weinglass, the Chicago Seven Conspiracy attorney, came by to offer his services. Both the Red Cross and the Beverly Hills chapter of Another Mother for Peace brought them food. That first night, Max Inglett recalls looking down from Cranston's thirteenth-story windows at a candlelight vigil, the well-wishers arranging themselves in a peace symbol in front of the Federal Building.

Late Tuesday evening, Cranston called to relay an official statement from Johnson, who said he could not meet with them for at least thirty days. That night, several more vets left, feeling they had done all they could. According to Waddell, Kovic was literally in tears, pleading with the rest not to leave him. They held a meeting, and Kovic announced: "We've got to intensify it. We're going to have to escalate our tactics." As if by telepathy, two or three people spoke the words "hunger strike" at the same time. Because of the precarious health of several of the vets, including quads such as Stan Price and Max Inglett, it was originally decided that Kovic, Unger, and Waddell should be the only hunger strikers; but Inglett swore he would fast along with them, and eventually a couple of others insisted on joining too. Both Unger and Waddell remember the strikers making a solemn vow among themselves—that they would sooner die of hunger than let one another down, and that they were ready to accept death if that were the price of winning help for their fellow veterans.

The next morning, Wednesday February 13, Cranston finally showed up, and the hearing on conditions at the Long Beach VA commenced on the eighth floor of the Federal Building. Unger, Inglett, and a wheelchair vet named John Adams came down for a few hours to testify before the Senate subcommittee, and to present Bob Waddell's suggestion that the VA create a national network of "halfway houses" for disabled vets as an alternative to hospitalization in the VA. Though a great deal of damning testimony was heard—including instances when VA patients were used as "guinea pigs" for the medical students at UC Irvine, with which the Long Beach VA was affiliated—VA officials did little more than praise their own drug education program and offer platitudes about "strengthening the staff and communication." The vets were even miffed at Cranston, who tried to claim that he could have fixed some of the problems at Long Beach if the vets had spoken up earlier. "We've been sending things like this to you for four years, Senator!" shouted a cane-carrying vet in the audience.

As far as Kovic and Unger were concerned, the oversight hearing was a bust. Calling their takeover an "encampment," they announced that their AVM members would neither leave Cranston's office nor eat solid food till the head of the VA deigned to come to California and speak with them. In a bit of guerrilla warfare, they deliberately changed the director's name from Donald E. to Donald M. Johnson, to imply that he was just a pawn of Richard M. Nixon—and Johnson would spend the next several months correcting the dozens of news people who kept getting his middle initial wrong. His middle initial, in fact, seemed to mean more to him than the hunger-striking vets, even though Unger warned the press: "If Johnson doesn't come to meet with us, then he's going to have some dead vets on his hands."

It turned out the windows of the Federal Building were sealed shut, so they were unable to hang out their AVM flags and banners. But the world did not fail to take note of them. Their biggest break was a major story on the strike, along with an exposé of the Long Beach VA hospital, on *Channel 4 News* by reporter Don Edwards (who later died tragically at the hands of suicide guru Jim Jones' followers in Guiana). Soon their story was making headlines nationally, and each day a growing stream of people—veterans, journalists, Hollywood celebrities—came to visit them and pay their respects. By the second day of the hunger strike, even Cranston's staff had been won over by their sincerity and dedication, and they presented the vets with several heart-shaped boxes of Valentine's chocolates (which the strikers wouldn't touch, of course). When the government retaliated by locking out further visitors, a support group formed every day at the foot of the Federal Building, carrying AVM flags, singing and chanting, and waving up to the vets. Each morning, the strikers chalked the number of fast days in reverse image (so that it could be read by those outside) on the window with a bar of soap. Folksinger and peace activist Holly Near was kept from meeting with them, but she inspired them nonetheless by belting out her pro-NLF song

"Hang In There" from below, while the vets listened with their ears pressed against their thirteenth-story windows:

> You gotta hang in there a little bit longer
> Though I know it's been too long
> For twenty-seven years you have been fighting
> Twenty-seven years you have been strong . . .

The vets also had a television set with which to follow news coverage of the strike; and for several days Cranston refused to allow any of the five phones to be shut off, so that the vets literally had unlimited calling privileges round the world on the government's tab (though later the government would pass along a $10,000 phone bill to AVM, which AVM never paid). Kovic even made several calls to Richard Boyle in Vietnam, trying to get Boyle to organize a similar strike of disabled Vietnamese veterans, but Boyle demurred, since he was barely keeping a step ahead of Thieu's secret police himself.

As the strike built momentum, their biggest worry was not the government but dissension in their own ranks. From the start of AVM, the VVAW people had been warning Unger that Kovic was a monstrous egotist and that there was no way to control him. They told him that once the cameras and news people arrived, AVM would instantly become RKO (punning on the name of an early Hollywood studio)—the "Ron Kovic Organization." That was the main reason Unger had kept Alfredo Cabrera out of the Cranston takeover. Even though Unger admired Cabrera's revolutionary zeal, he knew Cabrera's scornful opinion of Kovic: that Ron was incapable of talking about anything but himself, and that he used the antiwar movement as a "tool" to perpetuate his own glory. What Kovic wanted, Unger felt, were uncritical, adulatory followers like Bob Waddell, who would do his bidding without hesitation. In fact, the presence of Waddell as a yes-man for Kovic was causing Unger some serious problems—though there was also doubtless a measure of personal jealousy involved, since Waddell had come to supplant Unger as Kovic's best friend in the movement.

Unger tried hard to keep the hunger strikers focused on realistic goals; he believed "you don't fight unless you're going to win." But as the strikers became international heroes, Kovic's self-aggrandizement began to peak off the chart. He told Unger they should stay in Cranston's office till Nixon resigned, and Unger told him, "That's just an absurdity—you might as well shoot yourself in the head." To avert the falling out between them that was rapidly approaching, Unger called a meeting on the third night, which he got Stan Price to chair. Unger announced that with the hunger strike becoming such big news, they needed a third AVM coordinator, and he nominated Max Inglett for the position. In truth, what Unger needed was a veto over Kovic, and he knew that Inglett could be counted on to take his (Bill's) side. As the strikers voted overwhelmingly for Inglett, Ron sat fuming, but he did not try to stop the proceeding. Later Kovic took Unger aside and said, "I know what you did." "Of course you know," Unger replied. Ron nodded at Unger's cool savvy, and there was no further hostility as the three coordinators divided up responsibilities for the remainder of the strike.

During the second week, Inglett became very ill. He said he wanted to die for the cause, but the others insisted he be hospitalized. Even his evacuation became grist for their media mill, as they sent him off draped in an American flag. But once he got to the hospital, Inglett continued to refuse food. After they'd done all they could to boost his health, the doctors released him, and the hunger strikers agreed to let him return to Cranston's office, where he continued to fast with the others. Several other vets ended up being taken to the nearby Wadsworth VA Hospital, including Unger, who had suffered an epileptic seizure. Their health was further imperiled when the GSA police (on the pretext of observing "fire regulations") made a middle-of-the-night raid on Cranston's office, removing the vets' medical supplies stored in the hall outside their room.

News that some of the strikers might be nearing death galvanized even more support for them. There was now a 24-hour vigil outside the Federal Building, and the vigilers demanded to meet with the vets, to assess their condition. On Saturday morning, February 23, the police told the strikers they would be allowed to go outside for a brief time and then return to Cranston's office. Unger was against going out, but Kovic persuaded everyone to do it. No sooner had Unger begun to address the support group with a bullhorn than—from the sides of his eyes—he saw a police SWAT team taking up positions around the building. Unger immediately led the vets in a mad dash back to the doors, but they were locked. It looked like the government had trumped them, ending the takeover. As Waddell and Kovic screamed at the cops, Unger began bashing the glass door with his cane—mostly in protest, since he figured it was bullet-proof. But suddenly the glass gave way, and one of the SWAT officers threw open the door, lunging to grab Unger. But Inglett shoved his wheelchair between them, and Unger rushed inside pushing Max's chair, while the other vets followed right behind. The whole SWAT team began to converge on them, then halted, as if unsure what to do. One of the officers, who wore a flak jacket and carried a high-powered rifle, turned to his comrades and said in astonishment: "These are fucking *patients!* What the hell are we here for?" Then the vets called for an elevator, and the SWAT team made no effort to stop them from riding back up to the thirteenth floor.

The strikers had their first victory, and it brought them together in absolute solidarity, the way men who have been in combat together become brothers for life. "On that day we became unbeatable," Unger asserts. Moreover, the media were uniformly scathing in their denunciation of the government for its attack on the vets. The *Los Angeles Times* ran a front-page story, in which they defended Unger's action in breaking down the door by suggesting that he had suffered an epileptic seizure and needed to go back inside to get his medicine. The starving vets became the third hottest story in the country, just under Watergate and the kidnapping of heiress Patty Hearst by the Symbionese Liberation Army (SLA). The post office began delivering huge bundles of fan mail to them, and even senators and congresspeople were writing and phoning to pledge their assistance in keeping the vets from being prosecuted.

It became de rigueur for politicians who were running for office to stop by the Federal Building with photographers and often a TV crew, so that they could be seen shaking hands with the hunger strikers. Gradually the police became more lax about guarding the door, and all sorts of visitors routinely paraded through again, including Richard Boyle and his buddy Tim Page, the daredevil Englishman who'd almost been killed taking prize-winning photographs of the Vietnam War. Doctors and nurses came to volunteer their services. A high school class came to hear Kovic talk about his life in a wheelchair. Some of the vets who had left on the first and second days returned to join in the hunger strike, and new vets that they had never seen before also showed up—at least three of whom, Unger believes, were police agents. A supposedly paralyzed World War II vet, "Bernard," appeared with what he claimed was a bag of his own skin, which had fallen off because of poor treatment at the VA; but one day Unger caught him walking into the bathroom. The FBI even set up an office on the floor just above them.[140]

It seemed they had everyone in the world looking in on them but the very man they were clamoring for: Donald M. Johnson. The VA's official position was that AVM was no more than "a splinter group of the militant Vietnam Veterans Against the War, and without a national base"—hence not worthy of the director's personal attention. The break the vets needed came on Monday February 25 during a nationally televised news conference with President Nixon. A notoriously provocative reporter named Sarah McClendon refused to accept Nixon's claim that Johnson had already solved all the VA's problems. She accused Johnson of having lied to Nixon, and then asked, "Why isn't he meeting with those vets out in California?" Deeply embarrassed, Nixon immediately ordered Johnson to fly to Los Angeles and put an end to the hunger strike.

Johnson arrived at the Federal Building in Westwood on Thursday morning, February 28; but instead of going directly to Cranston's office on the thirteenth floor, he ensconced himself in the VA's regional office on the seventh floor. Though the vets, now in the fifteenth day of their hunger strike, were extremely weak, Johnson demanded that they come *to him.* He claimed there was a VA regulation that stipulated veterans' cases could only be discussed in private— i.e., on VA turf—and that the press would have to be barred from their meeting. The hunger strikers replied that they were willing to waive their right of privacy, for they had no intention of leaving their "barricades" until they saw Johnson face to face. Johnson waited an hour in the seventh-floor office, then took a limo back to the airport and returned to Washington.

According to Unger, the news people finally had the sort of story they wait years for, an occasion "when they can make a difference." "The warmth for us was past belief," he says. "We had all become monks [in the eyes of the media]—we were living our religion. We're sitting up there [on the thirteenth floor] not even sure if Johnson is still here. We were all dead by then; we were crap, man. Paralyzed guys sleeping on mats, dirty, no showers. Our bodies were falling apart. 'Nerve lines' were coming down my face, stretching into my neck; they looked like someone had taken knives. My eyes were becoming sockets. Twenty news people come swarming in, and these guys are dying to tell us how they crucified Donald Johnson down below. Every single one of them was saying, 'And I told him, why don't you go up? These guys can't walk'—and all this stuff. They were writing their stories as they were talking to us, they were so excited. It had turned over. We were the twenty-first century. The media was us. Our essence had flowed into everyone around us."

Johnson was slammed in virtually every major paper in the country. Even the *New York Times* reporter seemed aghast that Johnson, after traveling 3,000 miles, had refused to take a 30-second elevator ride from the seventh to the thirteenth floor of the Federal Building—especially when he was being asked to meet with "wounded veterans in wheelchairs." His insistence on remaining in the VA office was described as "a smoke screen . . . to keep the issues from the public." Kovic lost no time in waxing eloquent in the press, charging that Johnson's snub was simply further evidence that "this administration has lost contact with the people, with the vets of this country; it has lost contact with humanity, lost compassion for the suffering of the people." On Friday, March 1, Senator Cranston's office in Washington received hundreds of phone calls demanding that Johnson capitulate and meet with the veterans on their own terms. Evidently the White House received a similar barrage of calls, because on Friday afternoon Johnson announced that he would make a second trip to California.

On Saturday, March 2, Johnson finally arrived at Cranston's office in Westwood, accompanied by two security men, as though he feared for his life. This time he faced the international media, including news teams from France and Japan. There were so many supporters in the small room where the vets had been cloistered—attorney Leonard Weinglass, congresspeople, representatives of peace groups like Women Strike for Peace—that the army of reporters had to take turns going in and out, and some of the fifteen vets present voluntarily gave their place to the press. While Kovic, Waddell, Inglett, Stan Price, and John Adams blasted Johnson before the cameras inside Cranston's office, Unger and other vets gave interviews to reporters out in the hall. Johnson had no answers for any of the vets' questions—including Adams' dead-serious taunt: "If the government can allocate 85 billion dollars for bombs, why can't it allocate more than 2.5 billion dollars for men's bodies busted up by bombs?"—and he seemed nonplussed when several of the vets refused to shake his hand. The vets tried to wrest some promise of reform from him; specifically, they asked for three things: 1) a task force to review and update VA standards; 2) the establishment of disabled veterans' centers; and 3) a national veterans' hotline. Johnson told them he would look into their charges and proposals and meet with them again in a few weeks.

There was no question who had won the match. The seventeen-day hunger strike was now officially over; and as soon as that news hit the airwaves, congratulatory telegrams poured in from around the country—many from veterans' groups. The following day, Sunday, the *Los Angeles Times* ran a photo of Kovic being pushed out of the Federal Building by Bob Waddell, Bob's fist and Ron's two spread fingers raised in the warm sunshine. The caption read simply: "Victory!"

Johnson and the vets faced off again on Monday, March 25, at the Wadsworth VA Hospital, a few blocks from the site of the hunger strike. In the interim, Kovic burned like a roman candle, flying all over the country to drum up support for AVM. In Palo Alto, he got a pledge of financial assistance from Joan Baez (who was initially suspicious, then smitten by his charisma); in New York City, he fought for the reinstatement of Veterans Commissioner Carl McCardin, a black Vietnam veteran, who in turn threw his support behind Kovic; and in Washington, D.C., he discussed joining forces with the Veterans Office of the influential National Puerto Rican Forum.

Johnson came to the March 25 meeting with a nine-page report, but Kovic came even better prepared, with an armful of endorsements from the likes of Edward Kennedy and soon-to-be governor of California Jerry Brown, as well as a battery of prestigious witnesses. Under the bright spotlights of network television, Kovic suddenly looked like a statesman himself, wearing a dress shirt and colorful tie, with his beard shaved and his unruly tresses trimmed to just below the ear. His eyes still ablaze with anger, he attacked Johnson for failing to let him see the report before the start of the meeting, then introduced his prestigious cast of supporters, which included a vice commander of the Jewish War Veterans, representatives of the Order of the Purple Heart and the ACLU, Dr. Marc Stretton from the American Federation of Federal Employees (representing VA hospital workers), and Congressman Jerome Waldie. Johnson refused to answer any questions from the press. Where Kovic was fiery and suave, the pudgy, red-faced Johnson looked stiff and defensive, and especially foolish for having brought along three bodyguards this time. Pointing them out, Congressman Waldie asked: "Does the VA chief view vets as his enemy?" Kovic made a similar point, recounting how when he was at the VA in Washington recently, two of Johnson's security guards had kept him from using the elevator to get to the administrator's office.

The most powerful indictments, though, came from some of the other vets, who recounted their horror stories of insensitive treatment in the VA hospitals. Quadriplegic Stan Price told of being dropped on the floor at the San Diego VA, and then struck on the chest by an aide who claimed Price (without use of arms or legs) was trying to "hurt" him. Max Inglett told of having to lie "in my own human waste" for hours in Long Beach, while the nurses kept turning off his call light. Inglett recited the tale of a nurse who had emptied his urine bag and then, with urine still on her hands, tried to stick a thermometer in his mouth. "Would you mind washing your hands?" he asked, and she responded: "What difference does it make? It's *your* urine."

Johnson was quick to point out that neither Price nor Inglett had received their spinal-cord injury in the war; and he specifically tried to demean Inglett by revealing that he had been wounded in a liquor-store holdup. The roomful of people were shocked into silence, wondering how Inglett would respond to such an audacious challenge, but the reply came from a completely unexpected quarter. A slight, middle-aged man—with the tan, sunglasses, and poise of a professional performer—stood up and introduced himself to Johnson. He was Tony Diamond, executive director of BRAVO, considered one of the most right-wing of veterans' organizations. A Korean War vet, he had done four "tours" entertaining American troops in Southeast Asia. No one could wave the flag harder or higher than Tony Diamond; no one was ever more vociferous about "prolonging the American Dream" and "preserving our liberty-loving doctrines."

"I've known Max Inglett since 1969," Diamond began. "He drove my Jeep for a week when I was in Vietnam with the USO, doing shows with the First Cav." Diamond declared that Johnson ought to show respect to Inglett as a man who had "worn the uniform, come hell and high water." Then Diamond rummaged in his briefcase, pulled out a piece of paper, and read aloud the citation for Inglett's Bronze Star.

Johnson was on the ropes, and all the figures with which he tried to salvage the VA's image ("medical care budget up 115 percent, staffing up 38 percent") were shot down by Kovic's rejoinder: "The reality of the situation is unrelated to the statistics." Desperate to make some points with the audience, Johnson said he would be willing to consider a more detailed proposal for disabled veterans' centers. But Waddell, who had first suggested them, rebuffed him, saying that since Johnson apparently dismissed everything else they had to say, there would be little use in trying to work with him on the housing project. "Forget it!" Waddell concluded. "We want your resignation now!"

Kovic and several other vets also called for his resignation; then Kovic dropped his bombshell. "Mr. Johnson, you have not begun to respond to the national crisis of veterans," he began to read from a prepared statement. "By your inaction we must now escalate our tactics—in a peaceful manner, of course, because we are non-violent—to reach out to more and more people in this country. You may look down from your window one day, Mr. Johnson, and see tents going up in Lafayette Park, and you'll know that the veterans from all over the country have come to tell you of their grievances. Remember the 1932 Bonus March? We don't want to do this, but we may have a second 1932 Bonus March if there is no more response than this."

Johnson abruptly got up. He said he had another meeting to go to, and he regretted that AVM had rejected his "considerations." "The VA is moving forward!" he declared, provoking the vets to chorus, "Liar! . . . Coward! . . . Corruption!" Then Kovic jumped in again, astounding even his own AVM coordinators by promising that "a nationwide protest encampment movement will start in Southern California in about two weeks!"[141]

8. Two "Motherfuckers," Two "Godfathers," and the Dream of "A Fair Shake" for Veterans

In fact, Kovic waited scarcely two days to start his new series of "encampments." On Wednesday, March 27, 1974, he and six other AVM leaders—including Unger, Inglett, and Waddell—flew to Washington, D.C., to demand a meeting with Richard Nixon the next day, the eve of Vietnam Veterans Day. Nixon's office did not even bother responding to them. Typically impulsive, Kovic led his group to the White House anyway, where they joined one of the visitors' tours. His idea was to scout out a room that it would be possible for them to take over. But the security agents spotted them immediately and cut them off from the other tourists, then gave them the bum's rush out.

Outside, they met the woman from *Rolling Stone* who had been waiting to report the story of their takeover. She looked deeply disappointed, but Kovic simply pointed to the 555-foot white marble needle of the Washington Monument and said, "We're going to do it there instead."

Once again, they entered with the tourists. At the top, they confiscated the elevator key and told the tourists they would have to leave by walking down. Then, after barricading the doors and hanging AVM and American flags out of the windows, the vets called police on the elevator phone, once again demanding to meet with Nixon. Two hours later, one of the doors was battered open by a gigantic park policeman, who had sprinted up the entire 898 stairs. "What the hell's going on here?" he demanded; but before anyone could answer, he picked up the metal elevator chair and smashed it into Unger's head, knocking him clear across the room. Then he rushed toward Stan Price, who pleaded that he couldn't use his arms. When Kovic started to say something, the burly cop lifted

Kovic's chair by one of the metal bars, using only one arm, and shoved Kovic out so violently that the metal plate in Ron's leg rang like a bell when he hit the marble floor. The other cops who came in on the first one's heels helped him finish the job. One of them threw the elevator stool at John Adams, severely bruising his frail paraplegic's leg; another one knocked Inglett out of his chair and kicked him in the back, injuring his kidneys.

The cops then herded the vets into the elevator and stopped it halfway down, threatening to punch them out again. Unger and Waddell both warned that they had their badge numbers (the cops had taken off their name tags but left their numbers on) and would file assault charges if the cops hurt them any more—just in time to make the headlines for Vietnam Veterans Day. Looking worried, the cops took them down to the lobby. As soon as they came out of the elevator, they were besieged by news people, and photographed by both the police and the press. Beyond the police line was a sea of ordinary people, applauding the vets.

Unger started screaming at the police captain in charge that he'd better not try to make any arrests, when all of a sudden he went into a grand mal epileptic seizure. At that point, the captain decided it made more sense to call for ambulances than to haul the vets off to jail.

Outside the monument, photographers snapped photos of Kovic and Inglett in their wheelchairs, American flags on their laps, holding up their hands with the two-finger V victory sign. Those images literally went round the world, and had a good deal to do with the debunking of Vietnam Veterans Day in the American media. They were also more nails in the career coffin of Donald Johnson, who resigned a little over three weeks later. The day after the takeover, even Richard Nixon was forced to extend them credibility. A far cry from the days when he was dragged forcibly out of the Republican National Convention, Kovic and his AVM leadership were granted an audience with James Cavanaugh, Nixon's Presidential Assistant for Domestic Affairs, who promised them a presidential inquiry into what they were now calling "the national veterans' crisis."

Back in California, Kovic's Second American Veterans' Bonus March began to look like a real possibility. Hundreds of calls, telegrams, and letters of support came in every day. Some were from celebrities like Steve Allen and Jerry Lewis, containing vague promises of "assistance," but many more were from veterans who claimed to be organizing an AVM chapter in their own town or city. There was even a chapter of active-duty Navy personnel at Point Mugu south of Santa Barbara. If all the letters were truthful, Unger figured they must have 10,000 supporters nationwide; though Kovic began claiming 100,000, and Inglett a million. Clearly, AVM had struck a chord that resonated deep in the American psyche, and there was a chance that it could achieve something great. Just as clearly, Kovic and Unger could see how tenuous their gains really were. They felt like movie stars who had to stuff their fan mail in boxes because they had no time to read it all; and they lacked even the simple office staff that most movie stars had for answering such mail. They were incapable of responding to all their supporters, let alone trying to connect everyone in a smoothly functioning organization.

Because AVM had no apparatus for coordinating activities at a national level, it could only publicize its vision and hope that individual veterans around the country would of their own initiative work to implement it. Kovic's vision was both simple and striking enough to catch people's imagination. His father had told him of the 1932 Bonus Army, when 15,000 World War I vets who'd lost their jobs in the Depression marched on Washington (some of them bumming their way 3,000 miles) to demand that the government redeem their military bonus certificates in hard cash. When the Senate voted down their proposal for an early payoff (which had been passed in the House), President Hoover sent troops—led by Douglas MacArthur—to force them out of Washington at gunpoint. To Hoover's lasting shame, several veterans were killed in the process. Though they had failed in their quest, those World War I vets had left an indelible impression of the American citizens' right to talk back to their government and—when it malfunctioned—to apply a little muscle to correct it.

Kovic felt that if the AVM could bring 100,000 vets to Washington—their tents pitched all over Lafayette Park and the Mall, this time dubbed "Nixonville" rather than "Hooverville," and their massive picket lines surrounding the White House—the government could no longer ignore their demand for decent benefits. Harking back to the Last Patrol to Miami, he called for car and truck caravans to "trek across and through our country, acquiring other caravans as they wend their way to Washington"—starting on Flag Day, June 14, 1974, and arriving in time for a big march to the White House on July 4, the nation's birthday and, coincidentally, his own as well. However attractive, the idea was also a huge gamble, especially since they had no lines of communication to let them know what their 10,000 "members" were really thinking. But for Kovic and AVM, it wasn't so much a case of putting all their eggs in one basket, as that the Bonus March was the only basket they had.

There were many practical problems that undermined AVM. For one, it was not tax exempt and had no efficient means of raising money. But an even bigger liability was the growing split between its two main coordinators, Kovic and Unger. Unger tried to focus on issues that would pull other veterans' organizations into coalition with them. He cited an array of distressing facts, many from a recent, well-funded study by Daniel Yankelovich: 50 percent less GI Bill participation among minority veterans and among educationally disadvantaged veterans, 250 percent less GI Bill participation among veterans with dependents, 33 percent of all Vietnam veterans unemployed, 54 percent unable to meet their financial obligations, 45 percent seriously dependent on alcohol, and 17 percent hooked on illegal drugs (roughly double the percentages of their nonveteran peers in almost every category of problem). Kovic, however, was dreaming up ways for his Second Bonus Army to provoke a confrontation with "the young boys from the 82nd Airborne with fixed bayonets" at the gates to the White House. He pictured himself at the head of the insurgent mob, challenging the soldiers to shoot. If Vietnam veterans were killed, he imagined it would have the same effect as when the czar's soldiers shot down Bolshevik demonstrators in Red Square at the start of the Russian Revolution—precipitating "the overthrow of the entire United States Government." If, on the other hand, American troops refused to shoot American veterans, he believed that would also trigger a revolution: a shift in power more profound than any since the defiance of British rule nearly two hundred years earlier. Either way, he figured, he and AVM would win.

Unger and Kovic spent long nights arguing out their differences. Kovic felt that their image in the media was most important, and Unger recalls that Ron would sometimes even pose in front of a mirror and practice crossing his legs by using his hands to lift one on top of the other—to create a graphic exhibition of his own disability, and by extension, the physical devastation of war. Unger would quote David Harris back to him: "Don't ever allow your front to be bigger than your back." He warned that unless they could deliver at least ten thousand vets in Washington on the Fourth of July, they would look like frauds, and all their media hype become a weapon against them.

The two of them traveled together and met with numerous veterans' groups. Unger worked hard to be the diplomat, always open to new suggestions, always ready to change his mind if it were expedient to do so; but Kovic took a "maniacal" stance (according to Unger) that alienated a lot of potential supporters. More and more, Unger tried to handle AVM's public relations by himself, and he began dealing on his own with some groups—especially VVAW, which Kovic now hated. From a conversation with Barry Romo, Unger first learned of VVAW's plan for their Dewey Canyon IV demonstration on July 4, which Kovic had neglected to mention to him. "Ron, you son of a bitch!" Unger accosted him, accusing Kovic of having planned the Second Bonus March as a ruse to get back at his old rivals. "I didn't know," Kovic said. When Unger kept calling him a "son of a bitch," Kovic said in a softer tone, "If I knew, I forgot." All their literature had already been put out, and there was no going back, but the last thing in the world Unger wanted was a confrontation with VVAW.

Unger decided it was time to take seriously all those warnings he'd received about keeping an eye on Kovic. And since he couldn't do it himself, he brought in some watchdogs. He invited Alfredro Cabrera into AVM, and assigned another good friend, Jerry Latsko, a very big and very bright guy, to tail Ron on his cross-country speaking tour. Kovic's charisma, however, was well-nigh irresistible. The next thing Unger knew, he was getting long-distance collect calls from Kovic, who would immediately put Latsko on the phone, and Latsko would start raving about how "people go rabid when they listen to Ron!" Kovic and Latsko claimed they had already met hundreds of vets who were organizing caravans to Washington for the Bonus March.[142]

One person who had quickly cooled toward Kovic was Joan Baez. Kovic claims she had tried to seduce him, then was disappointed in his performance in bed; but Baez had a reputation for getting involved with veterans, and the situation was complicated by the fact that Unger had started dating her as well. Another concern for Baez regarding her support of Kovic was her well-established connection with VVAW. Whatever her motives, she paid two of the sharpest San Francisco VVAW honchos, Jack McCloskey and Lee Thorn—both of whom had their own beefs with Kovic—to take part in the Bonus March and keep Ron from sabotaging Dewey Canyon IV. "Everyone was scared shitless of Ron Kovic," says Unger, who had come to realize that assuming the role of Kovic's manager was like "thinking that the casing on an atom bomb will keep it inside."

By the time Kovic and Latsko reached Washington, D.C.—on their final swing of coalition building—Kovic calculated he had well over 10,000 vets lined up for the Bonus March. Angel Almedina, head of the Veterans Office of the National Puerto Rican Forum, saw it quite differently. Even after weeks of barnstorming, Kovic and AVM "didn't have a goddamn thing going for them," Almedina recalls. "But they played a good game. I dug it. Ron would say, 'Yeah, a hundred thousand vets coming to DC.' I'd say, 'Man, there's two motherfuckers over there.' 'Two hundred thousand, yeah, right.' But that was cool. I just went along with it at that point, but I realize now how great that was."

Almedina saw a lot to admire in Kovic even then, for he was a consummate hustler himself. A Puerto Rican scarcely five feet tall, Almedina had grown up on 113th Street and Third Avenue, in the middle of the East Harlem barrio. Like most of the kids raised there, he lived his life within a few square blocks until he was eighteen—and what he knew of the outside world was only what he saw on his family's TV screen. Then at eighteen, like almost every other undeformed young male in the barrio, he was drafted into the Army infantry. The draft, he says, "was the big business in our community." When Almedina came home, that Puerto Rican military brotherhood became a double-edged sword. On the one hand, it meant he had literally hundreds of guys with whom he could talk about the war; and the families of those guys, unlike so many white middle-class families, treated veterans as if they "had done good" by serving in the military. He had a ready-made support group, but the catch was that to be admitted he had to suppress his true feelings. "All my people wanted to talk about war and mayhem," he recalls, still anguished. " 'How many did you kill?' I'd say, 'I killed them all!' because my people wanted to hear that. What am I supposed to tell them? 'I was scared—I'd shit a brick'? Hey, no! 'Any motherfucker that came up to me, I'd shoot them!' I played it like that for years, 'cause you're more macho when you kill the motherfucker, than when you shit in your pants."

Hiding his pain took a tremendous toll on him. Almedina "lived in bars," became a huge boozer and pill popper, chased whores, and watched helplessly as his marriage fell apart and his wife skipped out with their infant son. Though he had no money or means for seeking out formal therapy, he found a place to air his problems in the many community meetings that were happening in Spanish Harlem at that time. Unemployment, drug addiction, and general lack of self-esteem had trapped Puerto Ricans in an endless cycle of poverty and degradation. The Department of Labor was starting to pour big money into the National Puerto Rican Forum, and there was a lot of talk about creating housing and jobs. Suddenly here was this little, fast-talking guy standing up at every meeting offering to organize an army of Vietnam veterans to rebuild their community.

"I got live bodies that want to do something!" he pleaded, and the National Puerto Rican Forum hired him as director of its new Veterans Office. At his request, they sent him down to Washington, D.C., because he figured he could work more deals being next door to the VA Central Office, because there was "mucho nice suburban money" in nearby Maryland and Virginia, and because Capitol Hill was "where they cut the pie, and you ain't there, you got shit." It was also the best place for "busting [congressmen's] balls," which he frequently did in collaboration with Harlem's half-black, half-Spanish congressman, Charles Rangel, himself a Korean War veteran and recipient of the Bronze Star.

It wasn't just Almedina's big-heartedness that made him respond favorably to Kovic and Latsko, though they seemed pathetic enough trying to organize a veterans' movement from someone's borrowed bedroom. A born networker, Almedina saw that the American Veterans Movement could be good for all veterans, and would certainly move his own projects further along. There had never yet been a truly multiracial coalition of American veterans—meaning one that dealt with multiracial issues, not just possessed of a multiracial membership—and he decided to push AVM in that direction. Kovic and Unger, on their side, were glad to get support wherever they might find it.

Kovic lacked the patience to be a good organizer, however, and so it was Unger who came east to work with Almedina on putting together the coalition. Both of them born go-getters with a bit of flimflam in their soul, they instantly disliked each other. Unger took one look at Almedina with his six-foot bodyguard, a gorillalike ex-Marine called "Gungie," and decided he was a "snake." Almedina, for his part, regarded Unger, as he did all of Kovic's friends, as a "slimeball." Yet they were forced to depend on each other if the coalition was to survive. According to Unger, they were both "calling in all their favors," feeling that it was "make it or break it." They knew how many people were watching and just waiting for them to make a misstep—most especially, the leadership of VVAW, with whom it was apparent they were "on a real bad collision course."

Almedina brought Unger to meetings with some of the top leaders, as well as the top financial backers, of both the National Puerto Rican Forum and the even more powerful National American GI Forum: an organization of Mexican-American veterans, which had been created to oppose discrimination against them after World War II. Latino vets, Almedina knew, were concerned with the kind of social justice and bread-and-butter issues—"three square meals a day, a roof over their head"—that AVM seemed to be emphasizing. Despite having already cut deals with everybody from Black Panthers to John Birchers, Unger was shocked at some of the places Almedina led him to. In one backroom sat two guys, one Mexican and the other Puerto Rican, both over two hundred pounds, both wearing what today would be $1,500 suits, $5,000 watches, and lots of diamond jewelry. They were both surrounded by bruisers who were clearly their "security." Angel whispered in Bill's ear: "The god-fathers." It turned out one was a rum-runner, the other a dope-runner, and they had both played essential roles in providing money and manpower to build the Hispanic veterans' movement. These men broke the law for a living, but they were deeply patriotic and devoted to their respective communities.

Luckily Unger had stopped taking all the drugs the VA had put him on, because these "godfathers" expected him to drink for hours with them before they got down to deal-making. In the end, the two mobsters were surprisingly friendly, because the Hispanic veterans' organizations they championed were hurting, just like every other veterans' group, from Nixon's budget cuts. Complaining that Nixon had "slashed all their throats," one of them told Unger he could get out a thousand people for the Bonus March, if Unger didn't mind guys who looked a little rough-edged. Unger diplomatically declined, saying they had to keep their image clean in the press. But the connection was made and sealed, and suddenly AVM had more resources than it had manpower to utilize.

The National American GI Forum gave AVM use of its office on Vermont, and began printing up and distributing flyers for the Bonus March. Together with the National Puerto Rican Forum, they arranged for several Hispanic churches in Washington to provide space for the marchers to sleep, since the U.S. Park Service had denied AVM a permit for camping in either Lafayette Park or the Mall. The Puerto Rican Forum also offered a large, ramshackle house for AVM's leaders to use as a command post.

The coalition grew daily. Unger managed to find common ground with the Jewish War Veterans, the Black Servicemen's Caucus, the AFL-CIO, Cesar Chavez's United Farm Workers, a Republican Party veterans' club, a group of Panthers from Washington's black ghetto, and even, according to Almedina, a black gang from North Carolina "with rifles and shit." Unger was crossing so many boundaries so quickly that the Justice Department's Office of Civil Rights decided to intervene. They sent over a couple of field agents to see what was going on—under the pretext, says Almedina, of making sure that if anyone got killed, it wasn't "a white killing a black or Spanish guy," or vice versa, "but just strictly a killing." Privately, one of their top agents, a Puerto Rican from new York, told Almedina that Nixon and his "boys" were scared to death that the Puerto Ricans were coming to get them.

"You're Puerto Rican and you're bringing Puerto Ricans from New York and around the country into D.C.," the agent explained. "The last time the Puerto Ricans came here to do anything, it was in 1954, when Lolita Lebron and three other Puerto Rican nationalists shot up Congress. The time before that, two Puerto Ricans tried to assassinate Truman, only they hit a couple of Secret Service men instead." Unger gladly let an undercover Justice Department agent "infiltrate" his meetings, since he had nothing to hide, and since he could count on no one else killing him while the agent was around. At one point, the D.C. police—possibly as an act of harassment—towed away Almedina's and Unger's cars, but the Justice Department agent saw to it that they were returned in half an hour, so that surveillance of the veterans' coalition would not be interrupted.[143]

On June 14, 1974, the "lead group" of the Second Bonus March left Los Angeles as planned. It consisted of Max Inglett, Alfredo Cabrera, and four other vets in a van, a couple of vets in cars, and a flatbed truck carrying food and supplies. Their vehicles broke down several times on the way to Las Vegas, where they were greatly aided by a legally blind Vietnam-era vet named Rick Kuhlmey. Although Kuhlmey's AVM chapter boasted over a hundred members, only two veterans actually joined the caravan.

From Las Vegas, things quickly went downhill. There were more mechanical breakdowns, some of the disabled vets became ill, and they ran into fierce midwestern rainstorms. It took them a full week to reach St. Louis, then several more days to make Indianapolis, where at least they were greeted by a CBS camera crew. But even coverage on the five o'clock news did little to convince veterans to dump their plans for a big Fourth of July weekend in favor of charging off to a questionable reception in Washington, D.C., in the gloomy final days of Watergate. Jack McCloskey, who in his capacity as "observer" had unexpectedly developed some friendly feelings toward AVM, felt that Kovic's ideas were "very good" but that Ron had needlessly rushed to put them into practice. In vain he tried to persuade the AVM leadership to postpone the Second Bonus March for another six months, during which time the necessary grass-roots organizing could take place. As it turned out, the "lead group" ended up being the only caravan to reach Washington, with something like a dozen vehicles and no more than thirty vets. None of the other groups of interested veterans had actually hit the road—for a variety of reasons: no money, no coordinating instructions from "AVM headquarters"

(Kovic's apartment), and no further communication from their "leader": Ron Kovic.

Not to say that the effort was a total loss, since in many ways it was highly satisfying for the vets who made the pilgrimage; and even more importantly, it showed the great potential for organizing a Vietnam veterans' movement with a far broader base than VVAW's. That potential was visible in the universally friendly reception they got from Middle America. Alfredo Cabrera, who had more than once experienced the hostility of police to VVAW (and had the bumps on his head to prove it), was amazed by the cross-section of people who welcomed the little AVM convoy.

"We could pull into almost any town, U.S.A., the most right-wing little communities," Cabrera recalls, "and immediately have people buy us food, just sit and talk, give us directions, help us out, take us to a restaurant. AVM was trying to remain neutral politically, to attack the problems of the veteran, and it worked real well. Anywhere America that we pulled in, we were greeted. Never a hostile anything from anyone. They might not have liked the way we looked, because we were still longhaired hippies, with beards down to here, but they knew we were veterans and what we were talking was something they could relate to. We weren't attacking God and country and the government. All we were saying was, 'Hey, veterans deserve a fair shake.'

"Until AVM, there was no organization that had that fine point in the middle. I was really impressed by the support. Old redneck cops coming over and telling me, 'You're doing a great job. Hang in there.' And buying me lunch. I was flabbergasted."

That lesson was not lost on another wheelchair vet, Bobby Muller, who had once shared the same ghastly Bronx VA ward with Kovic, and in 1972 had shouted down Nixon by Kovic's side. Since then, Muller had begun studying for his law degree at Hofstra University and was getting his feet wet in Washington politics through his work with the Paralyzed Veterans of America (PVA). In late June 1974, Muller was invited to a reception for Vietnam veterans staged by that venerable right-wing warhorse from South Carolina, Strom Thurmond. Unger, Almedina, and a few of Angel's "Mexican mafia" people crashed it, figuring to spread the gospel of AVM deep in the sanctuaries of the Republican Party. Thurmond was too busy promoting the B-1 bomber and AWACS aircraft to talk about Vietnam veterans' issues, however, and so Unger and Muller went off to talk by themselves. Muller put his hand on Unger's shoulder, looked intensely right in his eyes, and said, "Bill, I want you to tell me honestly—Ron tells me that there are thousands of veterans on their way across the country right now to participate in this Bonus March. Is that true?" Unger, feeling a little like Lyndon Johnson promising military victory in Vietnam, said, "I believe it is." Although Unger lost all credibility in Muller's eyes a few days later, a seed was planted of what might have been, and what might still be if it were put together by someone with a steadier commitment than Kovic.[144]

9. The Second American Veterans' Bonus March

Unger's meetings with Barry Romo and the leaders of VVAW were far less friendly. As July 4 approached, and publicity for the Bonus March began to eclipse the preparations for Dewey Canyon IV, Romo and his Washington crew were livid. They decried AVM's attempt "to channel the vets' movement into a meaningless and harmless scrabbling for a few bennies here and there from the VA." Their stomach was turned particularly by "AVM's repeated boasts of its red, white and blue 'patriotism.'" "When AVM speaks of 'giving veterans the rights they fought to protect' and how they must do honor to the 'flag we fought for,' it is in fact saying that the war in Indochina was right," editorialized VVAW's paper *Winter Soldier*.

Seeing the fancy digs the AVM leaders enjoyed—for Kovic had taken to renting his own expensive hotel rooms—as well as the vast amount of publicity they were putting out, VVAW staff worker Bill Branson was convinced AVM was on the government's payroll. How else, wondered Branson, could Kovic attract so much media attention when his entire organization was smaller than VVAW's Washington office? Unger's answer was that to a large extent "Kovic and [Scott] Camil *were* the veterans' movement." Both Unger's heroes were anathema to Romo, and Cabrera recalls Romo excommunicating Unger from VVAW with the words: "Don't call me 'comrade'! I've sweated too long and hard and shed too much blood."

The problem for Unger was that VVAW's watchdogs, McCloskey and Thorn, were still participating in all their meetings, and couldn't be tossed out without alienating Baez. Thorn especially became the unforgivable "thorn in Unger's side." If Romo was paranoid about Kovic and Unger, Thorn was Unger's worst paranoid fantasy come true: Mephistopheles in the flesh. An exceedingly tall, angular man with hawklike features, a dangerously analytical intellect, and a sharp, opinionated way of speaking, Thorn would continually cut into Unger's organizing and fund-raising speeches, destroying every pro-AVM argument Unger made. "I didn't know if he was in the FBI, the CIA, or the RU," Unger recalls. "I just knew that guy was bad news." Unger and McCloskey had previously gotten along well, but now suddenly McCloskey was parroting Thorn's attacks on Kovic and AVM. The next thing Unger knew, Thorn was encouraging a mutiny among some of AVM's core members, especially those who were already dubious about Kovic's leadership, like Alfredo Cabrera.

Whatever slim chance AVM might have had to pull off the miracle of the

Second Bonus March was sabotaged by Thorn's painting Kovic—and it wasn't hard to do—as a monumental liar. Worse, he told everyone that AVM was "a fucking joke—there is no AVM." Thorn's broadcast of the fact that there were no more caravans bound for Washington naturally had a snowball effect, and most of the veterans' groups who were considering participation in the march quickly backed off. To be fair to Thorn, he had his own principled view of the war between VVAW and AVM. "You don't fight sectarianism with egoism," he said.

Besides, Thorn was mostly just pointing out weaknesses that already existed in AVM. AVM had come up with some tremendously catchy slogans—"Broken Bodies, Broken Hearts, Broken Promises" was one that journalist Robert Klein would use (slightly altered) for the title of his shocking VA exposé half a decade later—but in many ways AVM was more slogan than substance. An editorial in the *Gainesville Sun,* a liberal, pro-veteran paper, gently nudged AVM to consider that phrases like "ending the national veterans' crisis" and "increasing rights for all veterans" needed "much shaping before [they] enter the black and white of the statute books." Indeed, a couple of weeks after the Bonus March, Unger would sit down and write a three-page, single-spaced position paper filled with facts and figures from recent Defense Department studies and private surveys—detailing the problems with the VA and suggesting a number of specific solutions, all in a voice that rang with authority. But by then, as Unger admits, he "knew AVM was gone," and he was simply thinking, *What can I salvage?*

AVM had hoped to reach Nixon with "the whiff of campfires" from Lafayette Park; but not only did no Bonus Army of vets materialize to pitch camp there, the park itself was put off-limits to them by the Park Service. In a desperate act of grandiosity, Unger and Kovic hand-delivered a petition to the Supreme Court on July 1, claiming the Park Service had overstepped its authority and demanding that the Bonus March Coalition be given use of the park "until . . . they feel that the administration of Richard M. Nixon is making a serious attempt at ending the National Veterans' Crisis." The Supreme Court never answered.

One of the few bright spots was a benefit concert by Joan Baez at the Washington Coliseum. She had also made a special record for them, "Where's My Apple Pie?", which she offered them a percentage of. From the concert and the record, they netted a few thousand dollars, with which they planned to bring marchers to Washington. But whom to get? Almedina told them he had hundreds of vets in Harlem just waiting for a bus ticket down, so they turned the money over to him. Almedina hired about four buses, but what he filled them with were teenagers and their families from the Puerto Rican barrio, whom he promised "a picnic" in the nation's capital!

The morning of July 4, Kovic led about fifty vets in a silent procession to the

Tomb of the Unknown Soldier, where they laid a silk rose and played taps on a harmonica. The media loved it; and much to VVAW's chagrin, the little ceremony was featured prominently on the TV news, while their own huge rally was virtually ignored. An even bigger horror to VVAW were the hundreds of American flags AVM passed out to the marchers as they assembled in Meridian Hill Park (also known as Malcolm X Park) on 16th Street NW—though some of the vets did carry them upside down in the VVAW tradition, against Kovic's wishes. With the three busloads of Puerto Ricans (one bus was hijacked by a group who wanted to go sightseeing), there were a little over three hundred people gathered for the 2.2-mile march to the White House. The route was all downhill, to accommodate the many disabled vets. At the head of the parade was Connie Panzarino, a friend of Kovic's from high school and a near quadriplegic since childhood (whom Kovic described to everyone as "a nurse who had been blown up in Vietnam"). Kovic followed just behind, holding on to the back of her electric wheelchair.

The march began in a black ghetto. Almedina recalls that the atmosphere was more than festive. "We were all blitzed," he says. "There was cocaine and heroin and all that. Downers, uppers, in-betweeners, booze, bags full of shit [medications] from the VA." Almedina claims that in part they were just reacting to "the pressures from the man"—the FBI surveillance that was everywhere, including in helicopters flying overhead. Unger was a nervous wreck, gobbling down Valiums and phenobarbitals to keep from having another seizure. Everyone was waiting for Kovic's "hundred thousand vets" to show up. Pacifica Radio was covering the march live, and there was an array of foreign media. When reporters politely mentioned that there seemed to be less than one hundred actual vets present, Kovic would reply, "These are the point men! The rest are coming soon." Since the march had already begun, the reporters asked when the rest would appear. Never missing a beat, Kovic kept up his jive: "They're coming. They're going to be parachuting in."

According to Almedina, the cops hassled some of the Puerto Ricans, and even arrested his younger brother for jaywalking, but they kept a good distance from most of the veterans, especially that black "gang" from North Carolina, who were packing rifles in their duffel bags. When they got to the White House, Bob Waddell was waiting for them across the street in Lafayette Park, with a "Woodstock kind of sound system," which some rich woman had put up thousands of dollars for. Unger took the microphone to address the crowd, but by this time most of the Puerto Ricans had drifted away to enjoy the sandwiches and drinks Almedina had bought for them, and Unger's voice blared into the faces of sixty or seventy vets. He told them that they were "the first group like this ever": "Who cares about the numbers of people? Look who you represent!" But he was "really chilled" by the ugly looks Thorn and McCloskey were giving him and everyone else, and he hastily concluded his speech, just in time to see them walking away. Calling it the "Boner March," even loyal Waddell stalked off in disgust, and the next day caught a flight back to California.

Despite the fact that they had no permits, the vets put up a few lean-tos in the park; and the cops—seeing that there was no longer a threat of violence— left them alone. They proceeded to get even "blitzier"—to use Almedina's word—and stayed till nightfall. For the rest of his life, Inglett would remember lying on the grass, exhausted, watching the Fourth of July fireworks blaze and die away in the darkness—as AVM itself had.

A few days later, Unger led a coup to expel Kovic from AVM; then he used his own and Inglett's proxy vote to dissolve the organization. Devastated, Kovic fled to Paris, intending to go into exile.[145]

Many people blamed Kovic's ego for the demise of AVM; but as Unger pointed out, none of those critics (except perhaps for McCloskey) had made any real effort to help tone him down. There had only been the all-out, frontal assault of Lee Thorn. Still, Unger blamed himself for assuming that he could single-handedly contain Kovic's ambition. The tragedy of AVM, however, arose from more than just the flaws in Ron Kovic's personality. As the years rolled on—and a decade later, for example, Bobby Muller got booted from a leadership role in his own organization, just as Kovic had been—it became clear that what had happened to AVM was a paradigm of the repeated collapses within the Vietnam veterans' movement. VVAW was undergoing a similar collapse, though more people were involved, and hence it would take longer to fall apart completely.

Some saw Kovic as a lunatic, others as a genius, but in the end he had touched the nation's conscience chiefly as a wounded veteran, better able than most to articulate the abuses he and thousands of others like him had had to endure—not from the Vietnamese, but from the U.S. government. The main reason his movement had fallen apart was because its members had not been able to trust one another sufficiently to continue working together. It also seemed that Vietnam vets had a generic aversion to leaders, especially those from within their own ranks. For years to come, that kind of antagonism and suspicion would recur like a perennial plague to decimate Vietnam veteran organizations of every size, shape, and ideological color—often before they grew past infancy.

The real question, though, for those who hoped to keep alive the movement— and the ongoing process of readjustment it represented—was whether that fatal mistrust grew from some spiritual disease whose virus had been planted in veterans during the war itself, or whether outside pressures were to blame. Certainly the stress had only increased for veterans who had decided to become active politically or even just to voice their personal grievances. On leaders like Kovic, Scott Camil, Bill Unger, and others, that stress had increased enormously— largely from the fierce opposition of the U.S. government. Hence the most pertinent question—but also the hardest to answer, because so many people did not want it answered—was how much did the government itself have to do with the fragmentation of the Vietnam veterans' movement?

10. A Tutorial in the VA Administrator's Office— Complete with Hammer and Nails

After vowing to the last minute that he would go down fighting, even if it meant an impeachment trial in the Senate, Richard Nixon went on television on the evening of August 8, 1974, to announce his resignation from the presidency. On August 5, he had been forced to release transcripts of three taped conversations from June 23, 1972. The transcripts showed that Nixon and Haldeman had formulated a plan to obstruct the FBI's investigation of the Watergate break-in. They were incontrovertible evidence of Nixon's complicity in the Watergate cover-up—complicity that he had been denying to the American public for the past two years.

On August 9, 1974, Nixon's hand-picked successor, former Michigan congressman and House minority leader Gerald R. Ford, was sworn in as 38th President of the United States. A former college football player, tall and fair-complected, Ford had an easygoing manner and plain-spoken midwestern drawl that put him in sharp contrast to Nixon's sweaty, manic intensity and sometimes thoughtless verbal outbursts. In the best of times, Ford might have been a harmless place-holder; but thrust at the helm of a nation still reeling from a constitutional crisis, a nation beset by runaway inflation and double-digit unemployment, he proved woefully inadequate.

Ford was a good horse trader and deal maker, but social progress was not in his vocabulary. He opposed forced integration of schools, tax breaks for the poor, and the creation of public works jobs. His greatest virtue seemed to be his unwavering party loyalty. Just as he had staunchly defended Nixon's innocence until the release of the incriminating transcripts, Ford issued Nixon a blanket presidential pardon only a few weeks after taking office, to protect him from any kind of federal prosecution—outraging many people who felt no president should be above the law. That decision came under even heavier criticism when Ford followed it a few days later with only a limited pardon or "clemency" for Vietnam war resisters and military deserters—all of whom were required to pay a "penalty" of public service before being accepted back into American society. Under Ford's program, fugitives from the military who turned themselves in and performed two years of alternate service would be given a "clemency discharge," which was still less than Honorable and conferred no veterans' benefits. Needless to say, few young men jumped at his offer.

One of Ford's first acts as president—even before his controversial pardons—was to appoint a new head of the VA. His choice was no surprise: his old pal "Rowdy," former Indiana congressman and national commander of the VFW, Richard L. Roudebush. A Republican, Roudebush was further to the right than Nixon. Fervently anti-Communist, he had opposed Nixon's phased-withdrawal from Vietnam because he still believed in going for "total victory" over Hanoi, and he felt the best way to deal with Russia and the Communist bloc in Eastern Europe was to sever all diplomatic and economic relations with them. In 1970, Roudebush had answered Nixon's call to run against incumbent Indiana Senator Vance Hartke, a Democrat who had consistently challenged Nixon's Vietnam policy. Roudebush had lost by a fraction of a percentage point, but he was rewarded for his effort by a patronage job in the administrative offices of the VA. By the time of Donald Johnson's resignation, Roudebush had worked his way to the number two spot as deputy administrator.

Roudebush's appointment as VA administrator was quickly approved by Congress. Rowdy was a big, fat, jovial man, a farmer and livestock broker, whose chief passions seemed to be football and the American flag. Moreover, he seemed to have a genuine concern with helping veterans "readjust to civilian life"—he had been severely wounded himself in Italy during World War II—and he also seemed genuinely determined to keep the VA independent from "other levels of government." The initial reaction from most veterans' groups was favorable, though a note of warning was sounded by activist Rusty Lindley, a former Green Beret captain who was now the one-man gang keeping alive Washington's privately funded Vietnam Veterans Center.

Lindley had been trying to forget his two combat tours by living out John Denver fantasies in Colorado, but he couldn't keep from coming down to Washington for Dewey Canyon III, just to see what was going on. He ended up staying on as VVAW's legislative director for a year, then worked as a writer and consultant for George McGovern for a couple of years, then created his own job at the Vietnam Veterans Center. For two decades he would get by on such makeshift employment, while helping to write and talk through Congress some of the most important Vietnam veteran legislation of that period, as well as advising the top Vietnam veteran leaders—and always get lost in the shuffle when credit was doled out.

Lindley felt the change from Johnson to Roudebush was mainly cosmetic, and warned that Roudebush's "very association with an established veterans' organization, the VFW, makes him unsuitable to head the VA." The problem, according to Lindley, was that the two biggest veterans' groups, the American Legion and the VFW, consistently opposed bills and programs that benefited Vietnam veterans, because they wanted as much of the VA pie as possible to go to their own constituency, which comprised mainly World War II vets—men twenty to thirty years older, with distinctly different needs.

By the time Roudebush took over, in mid-October 1974, several Vietnam veterans' self-help centers had sprung up around the country: Flower of the Dragon in Santa Rosa, California; Swords to Ploughshares in San Francisco; and a nationwide collection of storefronts called VETS (Veterans Education and Training Services) projects, funded by the National League of Cities and U.S. Conference of Mayors, among the more notable of which were the Seattle Veterans Action Center (SEAVAC) and the Veterans Service Center in East St. Louis. Roudebush made an effort to visit a sampling of these centers, and he made a good impression on even hard-core veteran activists like Jack Smith, who had been continuously promoting Vietnam veteran causes since his entry into one of Lifton's VVAW rap groups four years earlier.

Currently an undergraduate psych major at Columbia, Smith was on his way to becoming one of the world's leading authorities on PTSD himself. With the support of the National Council of Churches (NCC), he had put together a group of about a dozen psychologists and sociologists to conduct a major study of the impact of the Vietnam War on the entire generation that came of age in the sixties. They intended to place a special focus on the readjustment problems of Vietnam veterans as compared with their nonveteran peers. Led by sociologist Robert S. Laufer from Brooklyn College, and guided by pioneer PTSD researchers like Robert J. Lifton, John Talbott, and Arthur Egendorf, who had just earned his Ph.D. from Yeshiva University, they had organized under the umbrella of the National Veterans' Resource Project (NVRP), a networking group that had been born at the St. Louis conference on veterans' emotional problems sponsored by the NCC in 1973. In 1974, they began research, including many field interviews, for what was originally called the Cross Generational Study of the Impact of the Vietnam War. The title was soon shortened to the Vietnam Generation Project, then changed again to the Legacies of Vietnam, or just the Legacies Study.

The Legacies Study was urgently needed because the majority of congressmen refused to believe that Vietnam veterans had special readjustment problems, and hence they consistently voted down legislation authorizing the VA to develop programs to treat those problems. A Vietnam veteran readjustment bill had been introduced yearly in the Senate since 1971 by Alan Cranston, and in the House by Bella Abzug in 1973. Opponents always objected on the same grounds: mainstream psychiatric literature denied war as a cause of veterans' psychological difficulties. The Legacies Study could help in two ways—by directly educating the legislators, who doled out the money needed for healing, and by influencing the psychiatric profession, on whom the legislators relied for advice.

A whiz at fund-raising, Smith had gotten the Legacies Study off the ground with a $40,000 grant from the Hazen Foundation and another $5,000 from the Russell Sage Foundation. Smith then met with Burt Brown, director of the

National Institute of Mental Health (NIMH), who agreed to fund the project to conclusion, at an estimated cost of a quarter million dollars. But the Office of Management and Budget (OMB)—presumably under pressure from Richard Nixon—forbade Brown to use NIMH money to fund any study related to Vietnam while the war was still going on. When Smith began looking for further money to keep the Legacy project alive, he ran into a double bind. Even though Smith's contacts got him in the door at some of the richest funding groups—including the Ford Foundation, the Field Foundation, the New York Foundation, the Carnegie Corporation, and the Whitney Foundation (where he met with John Hay Whitney himself)—they all expressed the same reservation about financing such a large-scale project with private money. According to Smith, "They all said to me, 'Look, this is a federal problem, and the VA ought to be dealing with it. Your job is to convince the VA to deal with it.' And the VA was saying there's no problem." In fact, when the Legacies Study was offered to the National Institute of Mental Health a second time, Roudebush opposed it along with OMB.

APA honcho Robert Spitzer tipped the VA's hand (and his own as well) when Smith and Chaim Shatan met with him at Columbia in 1974 to discuss their Vietnam Veterans' Working Group on "post-combat disorder." At one point, according to Smith, Spitzer told them, "I don't care if it exists. If we recognize this disorder, do you realize what it's going to cost the federal government in terms of compensation?" But if the color of the government's thinking was green, it wasn't just the shade of money—it was olive drab, too. As Smith eventually came to realize: "Post-traumatic stress disorder at its basic level is an undermining of the morale, the willingness to fight. If you give it legitimacy, you're basically telling people that it's okay to have questions about war. The military has a vested interest in not recognizing these kinds of psychological difficulties, because it presents all kinds of problems for them in the conduct of wars. It's far easier [for the military] if you say, 'Real men don't get it.' PTSD and the recognition of it is profoundly political."

*   *   *

The downing of the Legacies Study was only one of the things that quickly soured Vietnam veteran activists on Roudebush. He had talked a good fight about helping Vietnam veterans to enroll in school and addressing the mammoth problem of bad discharges. And he instituted a few useful changes—a corps of 1,300 "vet reps" on college campuses to make sure vets were getting their GI Bill checks on time and to give personal aid and counseling; and an ambitious program to contact all 7.5 million Vietnam-era veterans, by telephone or letter, to inform them of their various benefits. He even published the phone number of his personal assistant, inviting veterans to call him with their problems. But at a basic level, nothing at all had changed. Reporter Sarah McClendon, herself a World War II veteran of the WAC, wrote an article in early 1975 for the new *Penthouse* magazine series on "the Vietnam veteran's dilemma," in which she damned Roudebush as a slightly touched-up carbon copy of his predecessor. In fact, she pointed out, Roudebush had kept on most of Donald Johnson's staff, many of whom had been hired solely on their political credentials, and he even seemed to be taking advice from Johnson on a daily basis.

Johnson, it turned out, had remained in his VA office for almost five months after his resignation, even after Roudebush had been appointed administrator in his place. Nixon had promised Johnson a new job, then had gotten too bogged down in Watergate to follow through; but Johnson had determined to stick around until Nixon's successor finally made good on the deal. No one could get Johnson out of the VA until President Ford appointed him Deputy Assistant Secretary of Commerce at a salary (then quite respectable) of $36,000 a year. Though Roudebush himself did not participate in this unconscionable cronyism, he was implicated in the message it gave out of "business as usual" at the VA—especially when he made no effort to contradict Ford's absurd declaration on Veterans Day 1974 that "VA medicine is first-rate." Even worse, Roudebush failed to correct many of the urgent practical problems that belied that label of "first-rate." Funding was being cut yet again from essential services—prosthetics centers and speech clinics, for example. Most VA hospitals were still badly understaffed. Vets were still having a hard time proving eligibility for service-connected compensation (a process that sometimes took nine months or more); even those certified as eligible found that the VA often delayed in purchasing needed equipment, such as a wheelchair, when VA accounts bulged with money that had been allocated for that very purpose. And despite Roudebush's special phone line, most veterans' phone calls went unanswered, same as before.

Jack Smith's eyes were opened when he read a story in the *New York Times* about Roudebush dedicating a new VA hospital in Indiana. Roudebush was quoted as saying Vietnam veterans were "crybabies" whose problems all stemmed from losing their war. To Smith, the interview revealed that Roudebush "was lying through his teeth—he was just trying to placate us." After talking with his own NVRP staff, he phoned up some of the most energetic Vietnam veteran leaders he knew—Jack McCloskey, Harold "Light Bulb" Bryant, a black vet who ran the Veterans Service Center in East St. Louis, and another black vet, Jim Credle, who was doing everything from amnesty work to prison outreach programs from his base at Rutgers—to decide what course of action to take. The consensus among them was that Roudebush simply wasn't hearing what they had to say and that "something critical" had to be done to wake him up and finally shake up the VA for real.[146]

Smith, a professional carpenter, got the idea of nailing Roudebush into his office with a group of Vietnam vets. He fashioned several two-by-fours with a hinged joint in the middle that could be folded to fit into a briefcase; then when needed, they could be unfolded to their full length and bolted solid. There were not many volunteers for the mission, however. He ended up going down to Washington with Jack McCloskey, Art Egendorf, a vet on his staff named Gonzalo Orrego, and his secretary Ellen Hawkins, daughter of a black minister from Harlem. They all stayed at the house of Corinne Browne, a freelance writer in Washington who had also written on veterans for *Penthouse,* and had begun work on a book about wounded Vietnam vets at Letterman Hospital in San Francisco called *Body Shop.*

Dressed for business, Hawkins went to the VA central office at 810 Vermont NW and "cased" the administrator's office on the tenth floor. She returned with a floor plan, and reported that there were three big, thick doors, all solid mahogany, which would be easy to nail shut. Roudebush was scheduled to be in the next day at 9 A.M. So at 9:15 A.M., they all showed up in three-piece suits, with their briefcases filled with literature on delayed stress, C rations, changes of clothes, plastic baggies for a latrine, as well as the special two-by-fours, hammers, and 16-penny framing nails. McCloskey and Browne waited in the lobby with bundles of leaflets. Egendorf was poised to call the press. Smith, Orrego, and Hawkins rode Roudebush's private elevator to the tenth floor and told his secretary they had an appointment with the administrator.

Flustered, she told Roudebush, "These people are here from the National Resource Project, and I don't have them on the calendar." Roudebush said he had just finished a meeting and would be glad to see them for a minute. It dawned on them that he was not in the right office. He had gone back to his old deputy administrator's office because the administrator's office was being redecorated for him that day (Johnson having just moved out). The three made an on-the-spot decision to go ahead with their plan anyway. They went in, shook Roudebush's hand, and then rushed to close the doors. Each person pulled out and bolted open a pair of two-by-fours, and proceeded to nail one across the top and one across the bottom of each door. The trouble was, the deputy administrator's office had cheap, hollow-core doors, which couldn't be nailed into. They fastened the two-by-fours to the sides of the door-frame, but they knew it would still be easy for someone to punch right through those hollow-core doors.

Roudebush was at his wit's end, not sure whether he should be terrified or not. Orrego, once a Young Lords gang member and later a combat infantryman, looked menacing enough. But Smith was even more fearsome. With his hulking six-foot-six frame, he still looked as if he'd missed his calling in pro football, and his voice when under pressure got louder and passionately intense, his words accelerating in staccato bursts like a machine gun. He was clearly very angry, but Roudebush realized he was not talking violence, he was saying serious things, making sense.

"You've been listening to everybody and talking out of both sides of your mouth," Smith began, "and you said that people are 'crybabies.' We've got a bunch of data here, and we're going to sit and go over it with you . . . and we ain't gonna fuck around with you anymore and have you talking about what you're gonna do. . . . Double-talk is over. Now is the time for action! And it ain't going to be you. It's going to be the president."

They handed Roudebush one of the flyers that McCloskey and Browne were busily handing out downstairs. It read: "The Veterans Administrator has been sequestered and will not be released until a Presidential commission on Vietnam veterans is appointed." Then they pointed out the window to the White House, and told Roudebush they'd let him go when the White House signaled agreement to the presidential commission by raising a special flag. In the meantime, they were camped out with a week's worth of food, and the tutorial began.

While they'd been hammering the doors shut, however, Roudebush had managed to call one of the GSA guards for help, and by now a crowd of them were swarming outside the office, waiting for the order to move in. Fortunately it took the government a while to ascertain that the three "sequesterers" meant Roudebush no harm, and in that time they actually got him to listen to quite a bit of material concerning the readjustment problems of Vietnam veterans. After four hours, Smith recalls seeing a glimmer of respect starting to show in Roudebush's face. Their session was ended abruptly by GSA policemen bashing down the doors with a steel coat-tree. Entering with guns drawn, they handcuffed Smith, Orrego, and Hawkins, and led them off to the D.C. city jail.

Roudebush refused to say he had been kidnapped, assaulted, or even threatened with harm, and so the police were forced to charge them only with a misdemeanor: destruction of government property. From the start, there was huge support for them from the veterans' community, and the police were so scared of a big demonstration outside the jail that they quickly moved them to an outlying station. David Addlestone, who had been defending servicemen since his days as an Air Force judge advocate, and who had afterward run the Lawyers' Military Defense Committee in Saigon, came to bail them out. To forestall publicity, they were brought to trial quickly; and in any case, with the country gearing down to survive a major economic crisis, it was impossible to generate any enthusiasm in the media over a crusade for veterans' rights. The Republican judge, after playing it safe by letting the black woman off, threw the book at Orrego and Smith.

He chastised Orrego for his drug convictions and furiously harangued Smith for what he claimed was an unheard-of criminal record of 86 arrests. The truth was, they had all been for civil disobedience related to protesting the Vietnam War, though several of his actions had pissed off the government in a big way— like blockading the Connecticut Turnpike, shutting down the nuclear submarine base at Groton, and mining the Naval harbor at New London with balloons. It also didn't help that Smith had an FBI file of 15,000 pages and a permanent, government-authorized phone tap. The judge told him, "You've been toying with this government, and it's about time somebody taught you a lesson." "I learned my lesson when I was in Vietnam," Smith replied. "Well, you're about to learn another one," said the judge. He fined them both several thousand dollars to replace the doors the GSA police had destroyed—"I'm a carpenter," Smith objected, "I can fix them for about $6.98 apiece"—sentenced Orrego to three months, and gave Smith the maximum: a year in the federal penitentiary at Lorton, Virginia.

Smith and Orrego were initially taken back to the D.C. city jail, where the tide began to turn for them. It seemed every veteran in the jail (and there were plenty) had heard their story and regarded them as celebrities. Large groups of veterans began gathering in the hall outside their cell, asking Smith and Orrego to help them get their discharges upgraded or to file appeals for denied benefits. There were not enough guards to stop the ruckus, and it only got worse when several vets asked Smith and Orrego to lead a daily rap group "inside the joint."

The warden let Orrego go after five days and even tried putting Smith in irons, but it soon became apparent that the only way to quench the growing revolt was to get rid of Smith. Lorton, however, having heard tales of this veteran rabble-rouser, wanted nothing to do with him. After a week and a half, the D.C. warden called Smith into his office at ten o'clock on Saturday night and told him, "You're just too much of a pain in the ass." They were kicking him out of jail. At five on Sunday morning, in the pitch black, he was tossed out with only the clothes on his back. He walked over to a friend's house, then hooked up with his lawyers, who lent him busfare back to New York.[147]

The National Veterans' Resource Project was out of money and dead in the water. Smith, while continuing his studies, wangled grants for himself and Chaim Shatan from the Presbyterian Church and the American Orthopsychiatric Association to research the history of combat stress disorders; and eventually both of them got onboard the committee of the *DSM III* task force, charged with writing the official definition of post-traumatic stress disorder. Although a proposed definition was submitted and tentatively approved in 1976, there would be a four-year period of "field testing" before it was finally included in the new manual, published in 1980.

During all these years, the VA did little for Vietnam vets with readjustment problems, other than sedate them with heavy-duty tranquilizers. Guy McMichael III, who worked as the general counsel on the Senate Veterans' Affairs Committee from 1971 through 1976, admits that "readjustment counseling was certainly on the back boiler," but he claims that was largely because it was a low priority for the vets themselves. "What they were concerned about were GI Bill benefits, compensation programs, the quality of medical care in VA hospitals, and bad paper discharges," he recalls. "So it was those kind of very concrete issues that occupied our attention. Some people felt that even to concentrate your energies on something like readjustment counseling was simply a cop-out, a way of ignoring the more immediate and expensive programs of 'Give us some decent GI Bill benefits. We need jobs . . . drug treatment centers . . . educational benefits.'"

Although McMichael, later the general counsel for the VA itself during Jimmy Carter's presidency, is admittedly a bit defensive on the subject, he also makes the valid point that the VA was incapable of dealing with an undefined psychiatric problem: "People [working at the VA] say, 'How are we going to determine who gets help and who doesn't? What's it going to cost? How many people are we talking about?' Those are very natural concerns."

The only recourse for troubled Vietnam vets in that slow-moving decade — the ones who weren't lucky enough to have access to a Jack Smith or Chaim Shatan or Sarah Haley or Shad Meshad—was to act out. There were several incidents that shook the nation. In 1974, a vet named John Debone escaped from the Wadsworth VA Hospital in Los Angeles, got hold of a gun, and took some policemen hostage in Griffith Park. He was talked into surrendering peacefully by Wadsworth VA psychologist Leonard Neff, who spoke to Debone as his "captain" in military lingo. Another notorious case involved a vet named Mark Williams who held up a 7-11 store in Dallas, shot the phone off the wall, then waited for the police to come, requesting that they kill him. The police, many of whom were Vietnam veterans, refused to shoot, and he too surrendered without a fight.

Unfortunately, almost every TV police drama and quite a few movie thrillers picked up on the juicy character of the "crazed Vietnam vet," the "walking time bomb," and a stereotype was born that is still called upon occasionally, a quarter century later. It may have been good entertainment, but it did not help the cause of more humane treatment for Vietnam vets, especially when that involved reaching deeper into the public's pockets. Roudebush, though, came through better than anyone had expected. Moved by his encounter with Smith (who would in time become his good friend), he attempted to do right by Vietnam vets. Besides coaxing well over half of them to use their educational benefits, he also fought for an increased budget to guarantee some 800,000 home loans. Under Roudebush, the VA opened several new hospitals and nursing homes, and two special centers for the rehabilitation and job training of paraplegics. And on October 15, 1976, at Roudebush's urging, President Ford signed a law extending the maximum period of veterans' educational assistance from 36 to 45 months, and making vets eligible for such assistance for a period of ten (rather than just eight) years after discharge. Roudebush's accomplishments were all the more remarkable considering the financial constraints imposed upon him by the Ford administration. Ford's response to an economic slump and galloping inflation was a replication of Nixon's—keep military spending up, and drastically cut back government social programs, including aid to veterans, the poor, and the unemployed.

In sporadic pockets around the country, most notably in Milwaukee, Madison, and Chicago, VVAW-WSO still kept up its pressure on local VA hospitals and offices, calling out the troops for a sit-in or occasional takeover whenever some new VA policy redounded to the harm of veterans. One such stunt involved a 12 percent increase in disability compensation, which the VA attempted to offset by reducing disability ratings for as many veterans as possible. Nationwide protests led by VVAW-WSO caused the VA to reverse its decision in many individual cases, reinstating a veteran's original percentage of disability. There was even a second takeover of the Statue of Liberty, on the Bicentennial Fourth of July weekend (1976), in which one of the banners hung over Liberty's (shamed?) face read: "Extend & Expand the G.I. Bill."[148]

11. Universal and Hypocritical Amnesty

Overall, the two years of the Ford presidency were not a good time for Vietnam veterans. Silence still blanketed the war's aftermath in the media, books, and movies. The movement for recognition of PTSD had barely toddled its first few steps, and already there was growing dissension even among the professionals who championed it. One major dissenter was Charles Figley, a psychologist at Purdue who founded the Consortium on Veteran Studies in 1975—a competitor in the quest for moral authority with Smith's and Shatan's Vietnam Veterans' Working Group. Figley, who had fought with the Third Marine Amphibious Force in Vietnam in 1965–1966, worried that the public would begin to see all Vietnam veterans as deranged by post-Vietnam syndrome.

One of the goals of Figley's consortium was to "depoliticize the debate over the mental health of Vietnam veterans"—and one of the first steps in that direction, he believed, was to make clear that most Vietnam veterans were emotionally stable and that only a "small but significant minority of *combat* veterans are suffering from the frightening and debilitating aftershock of Vietnam." Figley also opposed any sort of government compensation for combat stress disorders. He felt that a veteran could successfully overcome most of the ill effects of PTSD if he were enabled by a therapist to examine his combat experiences "in a systematic and objective way." By the same token, he warned: "If they're compensated for the symptoms, there's no incentive whatever for them to work through the experience. If they work it through, if they're successful, they won't get paid anymore."

On top of everything, a country that began to look on its involvement and subsequent defeat in Vietnam as the cause of everything bad, from gasoline shortages to rampant drug abuse to a general psychic malaise or "soul sickness," started for the first time to see the war's protesters as somewhat admirable, if not actual heroes. While the move to forgive, accept, and properly value war resisters was a major step forward in the nation's gradual healing process, it was also, in some ways, a diversion from meeting the needs of the warriors themselves, who for the most part had had their lives damaged far more severely than those who had fought their battles in the counterculture. The great Vietnam movement of the years 1974–1976 was only tangentially related to veterans. It was the crusade for Universal and Unconditional Amnesty, which embraced draft dodgers, deserters, and all those who had been tagged for life with bad paper as a result of their military service—a large number of veterans, to be sure, but less than a tenth of all who had served during that period. Moreover, it was a movement doomed to fail because of the vastly differing needs of its constituency, and in its failure it brought down the hope of most of those veterans it sought to embrace.

There were two major poles to the amnesty movement. One pole was the Americans in exile for desertion or draft evasion—most in Canada, and a lesser number in Sweden, France, and England. The exile contingent was spearheaded by AMEX/Canada, a political organization built around an exiles' magazine in Toronto. Its leader was Jack Colhoun, former all-American boy and gung-ho patriot (star athlete, honor student, senior class president, ROTC cadet), who began his seven-year exile in Canada after deserting the Army in 1970, because he could not in good conscience fight in Vietnam. After helping found *AMEX* magazine as an organ of the Union of American Exiles, Colhoun became a tireless activist for unconditional amnesty, organizing dozens of conferences in the United States, Canada, and abroad, and even arranging highly dangerous speaking tours of draft dodgers and deserters on what he called "guerrilla-like sweeps" through the United States. The other pole of the amnesty movement was the coalition of peace and religious activists (who opposed the war or championed the right of conscience, or both) in the United States. The peace/church contingent was led by Americans For Amnesty, a group formed by many high-profile activists, such as former U.S. Attorney General Ramsey Clark, Women Strike for Peace leader Cora Weiss, and Gold Star Mother Louise Ransom. Ransom, Colhoun's stateside equivalent in terms of marathon energy, had dedicated her life to redeeming her son Lieutenant Robert Ransom Jr.'s death (from a mine blast near Quang Ngai, on Mother's Day 1968), by "insuring that never again will there be another Vietnam" and also by "making amends to the living" who had suffered from the war.

The two poles came together in the early 1970s to form the National Council for Universal and Unconditional Amnesty (NCUUA), which eventually drew in nearly a hundred different peace, church, and social justice groups—ranging from the American Civil Liberties Union to the American Friends Service Committee, from the Black Economic Development Conference to the Committee for a Sane Nuclear Policy. Both Colhoun and Ransom never varied from their demand that any amnesty had to include not only draft evaders and deserters, but also all the GIs who had been given less than Honorable discharges—792,000, by NCUUA's estimate (based on Defense Department figures revised in 1975). NCUUA's position was that amnesty should also include the million-plus young men who broke the law by failing to register for the draft, as well as a variety of civilian resisters.

NCUUA faced many problems in pushing such a manifold amnesty. To begin with, despite its pro-veteran rhetoric, the coalition was heavily weighted in favor of peace and social justice groups. Then there was the rub that the public only cares about people who catch its imagination, and exiles (especially well-to-do kids who threw away their pampered life for a life of altruistic poverty) were inherently more glamorous than some working-class slob who couldn't get a decent job because he got drafted and rebelled against military discipline. Only about 25,000 draft resisters had fled the country. But in the words of Lawrence Baskir and William Strauss, two senior officials on President Ford's Clemency Board: "The exiles captured the attention of the public and the press. Over time, they became the stuff of political mythology."

Social class, and its concomitant political clout, also worked against the veteran side of the amnesty crusade. Green Beret deserter Gerry Condon, who returned from Sweden to support NCUUA, recalls that "we had to fight for that [the inclusion of veterans with less than Honorable discharges] because the amnesty coalition in the U.S. was based in the church and the civil liberty groups that were primarily interested in the white, middle-class draft resisters, sons of their own. They didn't care too much about some black vet who might have got a bad discharge because he was resisting racism, or the war, in the military. That was a big battle in the amnesty movement." Congressman Robert Kastenmeier (D-Wis.) had tried introducing broad amnesty legislation in the House. Ford promised to veto it, but never got the chance, because there were not enough sympathetic congressmen even to vote it out of committee. As black Congressman Ron Dellums from Oakland explained: "The people who need amnesty have few votes and little influence. Nothing much politically will happen to members of Congress who make these powerless ones their enemies." President Ford, of course, had issued his own Clemency Proclamation in September 1975; but as a result of its stringent demands (up to 24 months of alternative service plus "acts of contrition," etc.), only 19,000 Vietnam veterans with bad paper and 2,600 civilian offenders applied. Of those, a mere 11,000 veterans and 1,800 civilians received relief.

With 1976 an election year, NCUUA put all its eggs in the basket of electing a pro-amnesty candidate. In February it declared a National Amnesty

Week, which garnered a great deal of local support (dozens of big-city mayors marked the occasion with proclamations) and national media attention. But all the presidential candidates still tiptoed around the issue. On the Republican side, Ford claimed he had already done enough, and Ronald Reagan thought he had done too much. Flag-waving American Independent George Wallace refused to talk about it. Far-left Democrat Jerry Brown, who had held three draft deferments (as Jesuit seminarian, Berkeley undergraduate, and Yale law student), said he needed more time to develop a position. Moderate Democrat Henry "Scoop" Jackson of Washington and liberal Democrat Morris Udall of Arizona spoke, respectively, of "bringing the boys home" and "expanded clemency"—without specifics. The two front-running Democrats, middle-of-the-roaders Hubert Humphrey of Minnesota and Jimmy Carter of Georgia, offered scarcely more encouragement. Humphrey talked of rehashing Ford's program with another opportunity for dodgers and deserters to perform "alternative civilian or humanitarian service." Carter, the most promising of the lot, declared his intention to "pardon" those in exile—a pardon, he pointed out, only "says you are forgiven," whereas "amnesty says what you did was right"—and to "treat deserters on a case by case basis."

The Democratic National Convention was held in mid-July 1976 in New York City. NCUUA used its many contacts in the Democratic Party, especially longtime antiwar activist Sam Brown, to get a plank added to the Democratic platform that promised "a full and complete pardon for all those who are in financial or legal jeopardy as a result of their opposition [to the war]." Such action, if carried through, would mean a fresh start for everyone from bad paper vets to civilians who had refused to pay taxes that funded the war. But nominee Carter, whose folksy grin masked one of the canniest politicians ever to mount the hustings, quickly distanced himself from such extreme portions of his own party's platform, announcing that he retained his own position on amnesty and that he did not feel bound by the amnesty plank "either as a campaign statement" or as a program "to implement as president." Championing deserters or guys with bad military records was nobody's idea of a surefire vote-getter.

NCUUA decided its only hope was to twist Carter's arm by making amnesty a highly visible issue at the convention. Their strategy hinged on nominating a draft resister, Fritz Efaw, for vice president. Efaw, who had spent seven years in England, where he'd organized the Union of American Exiles, returned to the United States as a convention delegate representing Americans abroad, for the sole purpose of promoting amnesty. In fact, he risked arrest just to help others, since in a few months—if Carter were elected—he would be able to return legally, as one of the few covered by Carter's limited pardon. Efaw was nominated by Louise Ransom, and his nomination was seconded by Ron Kovic. Altogether, the three speeches gave NCUUA about fifteen minutes of prime-time, round-the-world television coverage. In their speeches, both Ransom and

Efaw lobbied for "total amnesty for over a million Americans," and Efaw specifically mentioned including vets with less than Honorable discharges. He also attacked Carter's plan for a "case by case review" of the near half-million war-era deserters as totally impracticable. Of the three speeches, Kovic's was the most riveting, but half of it was about the poor conditions in the VA hospitals and the other half about his own suffering; he never once mentioned the word *amnesty*.[149]

In November 1976, Carter narrowly won election to the presidency over Ford, the first president to be turned out of office in an election since Herbert Hoover half a century earlier. Sensitive to his shaky position without a strong electoral base of support, Carter was still a man of his word, but not more than that. He announced his intention to pardon the draft resisters in exile—and no one else—on the day after his inauguration. For two and a half months, NCUAA representatives beat on his door, insisting that his pardon would be "flatly discriminatory on the basis of race and class." They reminded him of his own sympathetic campaign statements about "the poor and black Georgians who didn't have the money to hide out in college, who opposed the war but went anyway." Many of those "poor and black Georgians," they told him, "ended up as deserters or vets with less-than-Honorable discharges." But come January 21, Carter granted his pardon to only some forty thousand men, leaving at least ten times as many in limbo, subject to the recommendations of a Pentagon study.

In April, the second step of Carter's program was announced. Deserters and bad paper vets—if they had the time and money to present their case—would be given six months to come before a special review board. Deserters, if they could prove their desertion was due to their opposition to the war, and so long as they did not desert while stationed in Southeast Asia, would receive no punishment and be free to reenter American society; but their criminal record would not be erased, and they would receive a less than Honorable discharge. Bad paper vets who had completed their tour in Vietnam or two years of good service, and who had not actually been court-martialed, would be granted an automatic upgrade to General discharge, but not Honorable; others would have to meet the same stringent criteria as before. The real catch was that the Department of Defense was given no money to advertise the program, so that most vets, if they heard of it at all, heard secondhand; and fearing that it was just a reprise of Ford's alternate-service amnesty, or worse, a ploy to put them in jail, most stayed away.

Of the roughly 500,000 Vietnam-era deserters, only 4,200 were eligible for a General discharge, and only 885 actually made it through Carter's program. Of the more than three-quarter-million bad paper vets, only 33,308 were considered eligible for a discharge upgrade, and only about 16,000 received one. Sadly, by this point the media had lost all interest in the issue, and the amnesty advocates were themselves burned out. As Jack Colhoun wrote, it was time "to pay some attention to our personal lives, neglected for nearly a decade."

The work of discharge upgrading, undertaken by dedicated veterans' self-help groups, would proceed slow as molasses for the next several decades. In the meantime, a final, disgraceful footnote was added to Carter's halfhearted pardon. Congressmen anxious to prove themselves more patriotic than Carter, led by Strom Thurmond and, surprisingly, Alan Cranston, passed a bill—"particularly vindictive," Baskir and Strauss called it—to prohibit most of the vets with newly upgraded discharges from ever receiving veterans' benefits. After ten days of hemming and hawing and worrying about the political repercussions of a veto, Carter, much to the chagrin of his pro-veteran supporters, signed it into law.[150]

7

Too Little Too Late: Operation Outreach

▬▬▬▬▬▬▬▬▬▬▬▬▬▬▬▬▬▬▬▬

1. Two New Champions Enter the Fray:
Max Cleland and Stuart Feldman

For years, Vietnam veteran activists had been crying for the need to get "the class of '46" out of the VA—referring to the many World War II vets who had moved into key positions there. Most especially they wanted to see the VA headed by a Vietnam veteran. Jimmy Carter's first official act, a few hours after he had been sworn in as 39th president of the United States, was to appoint a new administrator of the VA. At 4 P.M. on January 20, 1977, a heavy-set thirty-four-year-old man, sandy-haired and boyish-looking, rolled into the Oval Office to accept the position—the youngest ever to hold it. He was Max Cleland, a former Army infantry captain, whose two legs and right arm had been blown off by a grenade in Vietnam.

Carter knew Cleland from Georgia politics. Cleland had supported Carter in his successful run for governor in 1970, and had himself won two terms as a Georgia state senator. But Carter's selection of him had little to do with either Cleland's ambition and drive (sizable though they were) or with Deep South kinship. To begin with, Cleland had experienced the callous and often out-of-date treatment in VA hospitals firsthand. And he had been one of the first to speak up about the special psychological needs of Vietnam veterans, when he testified before Senator Alan Cranston's subcommittee hearings on Vietnam veteran health care, in December 1969. In Georgia in 1972, after Carter had appointed him to head a commission examining the needs of Vietnam veterans, he pushed through a bill giving veterans special preference for educational loans and grants. Then, after losing his bid for a third term in the Georgia Senate, he went to California to work in Cranston's reelection campaign. Cranston claims he "fell in love with Max" the first day he heard him testify in the Senate.

In March 1975, Cranston rewarded Cleland with a staff position on the

Senate Veterans' Affairs Committee, where Cleland's reformist zeal smashed headlong into decades of VA inertia—"this vast, government agency," he described it, "with its 230,000 employees serving more than 500 different facilities including 172 hospitals, 58 regional offices, 44 clinics, 88 nursing homes and 107 national cemeteries." In his nearly two years serving the Senate Veterans' Affairs Committee, Cleland honed his negotiating skill to such a degree that Cranston told Carter he'd be a fool not to let Max head the VA. Indeed, Cleland would become the most successful VA administrator since General Omar Bradley rolled out the red carpet for returning World War II vets. That same skill would also bring Cleland a lot more condemnation and contempt than he could have imagined, and certainly more than he deserved; for he'd learned how to get things done in Washington, which is to say: the art of compromise.

Part of the problem was the huge euphoria among Vietnam veterans that followed Cleland's appointment. According to Guy McMichael III, whom he appointed as his general counsel, "People had these kind of wild-eyed notions that he was going to walk in and fire everybody and restart the agency, which he couldn't have done had he wanted to." Actually Cleland did act fairly quickly to bring a new face to the VA. He surrounded himself with men his own age—many of them Vietnam vets—or only a few years older. More importantly, they comprised many of the best minds dealing with veterans' issues in the country.

One of Cleland's sharpest "special assistants" was a veteran named Dean Phillips, who had earned a Silver Star and two Bronze Stars with the 101st Airborne in Vietnam; and then, at home, while fighting a battle with cancer, had worked almost full-time for veterans' benefits while simultaneously earning several college degrees, including a doctorate of law. Phillips combined intellectual brilliance with extraordinary compassion, and many felt he would become *the* veterans' leader of his generation—until cancer (probably Agent Orange–induced) claimed his life in the early 1980s. As vice chairman of the Colorado Board of Veterans' Affairs, Phillips had drafted legislation giving tax credits to blind and paraplegic veterans and waiving their tuition at state schools, and had fought to retain veterans' preference programs and to expand veterans' employment rights. He had been involved in several lawsuits against the federal government for its failure to implement veterans' programs, and in Washington he championed the need for judicial review of the Veterans Administration and its all-powerful decisions over veterans' lives—something the government had resisted since the Civil War.

Another key appointment Cleland made was of Dr. Jack Ewalt as chief psychiatrist. Although an older man who had counseled World War II vets, Ewalt had a great sympathy for the stress problems of Vietnam veterans, having run across many World War II vets who had been similarly traumatized by their part in the killing of civilians and other unheroic, brutal acts. Perhaps Cleland's most crucial appointment was of Guy McMichael III as his general counsel, the man whose job it was to see that needed legislation got passed. McMichael was a veteran of the peacetime Army (1962–1964), a political idealist who had worked in Bobby Kennedy's 1968 presidential campaign and helped Indiana's liberal senator Vance Hartke get reelected in 1970. When Hartke was made chairman of the newly formed Senate Veterans' Affairs Committee, he summoned McMichael to Washington as an associate counsel, and within a year McMichael had become the committee's general counsel. For five years, McMichael used that position to fight hard for a better GI Bill. He was driven by a real sense of "calling" to "do good" for Vietnam veterans, whom he felt had "gotten the shaft" by their own government's attempt to "fight a war on the cheap." "One of the ways of doing that [cutting war costs]," he explains, "was slighting benefits for veterans."

McMichael had a hand in every major achievement of Cleland's tenure as VA administrator—the opening of still more hospitals and clinics; the creation of a nationwide toll-free telephone system to allow calls from anywhere in the country to a VA benefits counselor; the boosting of GI Bill educational benefits yet again, including an extension in eligibility for veterans who were delayed in applying because of medical or psychological problems, which increased the rate of participation to 65 percent, the highest for any program since the VA came into being in 1930; the development of a work-study program for vets who could not afford college on the GI Bill alone, and the Predischarge Education Program aimed at the educationally disadvantaged; and Cleland's crowning achievement: the implementation of the Vietnam Veterans' Outreach Program, which saw the opening of nearly a hundred storefront Vet Centers across the country.

McMichael was not an unmixed blessing, however, and to understand some of his failings is to understand a lot of what soured Vietnam veterans' honeymoon with the VA under Cleland. The relationship between Cleland and McMichael was problematic from day one, since during the two years Cleland had worked as a staff lawyer on the Senate Veterans' Affairs Committee, McMichael had been *his* boss. McMichael never quite adapted to the tables being turned, and preferred to see himself as Max's surrogate rather than his employee—a dynamic Cleland regrettably encouraged. Cleland liked to brag about how he had once talked a disturbed vet out of killing a VA doctor, but the truth was he often used tough negotiators like McMichael to insulate himself from the anger of the veterans' community as well as the backroom haggling and bullying on Capitol Hill. As Rusty Lindley liked to say, infuriating Cleland no end, smiling Max in his wheelchair with his well-draped stumps "was entirely symbolic . . . Max was to the Veterans Administration as the poster child is to the Easter Seal Campaign."

In some ways, Cleland did represent a quantum leap forward in terms of the

VA's responsiveness to the needs of Vietnam veterans. He arranged for Carter to sponsor a Presidential Review Memorandum on the Status of Vietnam Veterans—the first such fact-filled study to come from the executive branch since the war began, and the first White House document to endorse a readjustment program for Vietnam vets. Its release on October 10, 1978, marked a turning point for many legislators, who were cornered into admitting the substantial needs of Vietnam veterans and no longer dared vote against measures to help them—as they had for a decade—simply because they would "cost a lot" (never mind that few had worried about the cost of the war itself). Late in 1977, Cleland also managed to secure funding for the long-deferred Legacies Study, though its scope was significantly reduced. Conducted by five investigators— only two of whom, Laufer and Egendorf, were in on the project's design—it became primarily just a study of veterans' readjustment rather than the whole Vietnam generation. The projected analysis of resisters and deserters was entirely cut out, according to Jack Smith, because Cleland did not dare request such funding. With a budget drastically cut, and not enough researchers, the study was not completed till 1981, when Carter (and with him, Cleland) were already out of office and the new Republican Congress had virtually no interest in its results.[151]

What happened with the Legacies Study typified the unfair burden of past neglect placed on Cleland's shoulders. No matter what he did, it was not going to be enough; and yet there were still plenty of people in government who thought veterans were already getting too much. Private deals within the so-called "Iron Triangle"—the VA, the House Veterans' Affairs Committee, and the traditional veterans' organizations such as the American Legion and the VFW—still determined the parceling out of veterans' benefits. Although the VA was now officially (if not totally) sympathetic to Vietnam veterans' demands, the other two corners of the triangle were still dead-set against them. Certainly cracks had started to appear in the old alliances. The Disabled American Veterans, composed solely of vets with service-connected disabilities (and perhaps with an eye to expanding their own membership base), had early on recognized the readjustment problems of Vietnam vets, and spent significant chunks of money to deal with them. More and more, the DAV was distancing itself from the "we won the good war" attitude of the American Legion and VFW. And with the ascendancy of the Senate Veterans' Affairs Committee— especially once Alan Cranston took over as its chairman in 1977—the saber-rattling good old boys on the House committee, like Tiger Teague and Ray Roberts of Texas and Sonny Montgomery of Mississippi, were being forced to share what had once been their absolute authority.

Still, there were pitfalls aplenty for Cleland's wheelchair to drop into—not the least of which were the fierce rivalries among many of the veterans' advocates. Cranston's former chief counsel Jonathan Steinberg had recently been promoted to general counsel of the Senate Veterans' Affairs Committee—the job McMichael had just vacated. Steinberg was already beginning to flex his political muscle by sometimes even chairing committee meetings himself, in Cranston's absence. Add to this mixture the outspoken and uncompromising Bobby Muller, leader of the newly formed Council of Vietnam Veterans (soon to become Vietnam Veterans of America), as well as the vociferous legion of delayed-stress partisans like Smith, McCloskey, and Meshad, and you had the recipe for an ego shootout of ghastly proportions.

What staved it off, temporarily, was Cleland's incredible tenacity and grace under pressure. Within a month of his nomination, he went to Capitol Hill to testify in support of a readjustment counseling program for Vietnam veterans— the first time any presidential representative had done such a thing. And when congressmen demanded facts and figures and a concrete proposal, Cleland coolly promised to come up with them as soon as possible. At the end of October 1977, Cleland assembled in the Washington Central Office a group that would never before have fit under one roof without killing one another: skeptical representatives of the old VA; the chief counsel, Guy McMichael; new, Vietnam-era VA spokesmen like Dean Phillips and Tim Craig, formerly president of NACV; firebrands like Shad Meshad and Bill Mahedy, a radical ex-Army chaplain and Vietnam veteran whose job with the Los Angeles VA was to go out into the streets and deal with vets considered too dangerous or crazy to be handled as inpatients; and the conservative, research-oriented, delayed-stress theorist Charles Figley from Purdue. Black Vietnam veteran Bill Lawson, NACV's Vice President for Minority Affairs, who was also part of the group, called it Carter and Cleland's "Vietnam veteran brain trust."

Their first meeting, appropriately, was on Halloween. For several hours they talked about what the VA wanted and what the vets thought was needed. Figley provided the statistics that gave "a theoretical basis" to the proposed readjust-ment program. Meshad and Mahedy described a working model, which they called a "storefront center." McMichael, taking his cue from Cleland, told them: "It sounds good. We like it. Write it up."

That night, Meshad and Mahedy secluded themselves in an upper-floor office at 810 Vermont NW, bouncing ideas off each other, taking copious notes, and drawing a diagram of their prototype. Near morning, Mahedy typed up a five-page proposal for the program. It was, Mahedy recalls, based on two main components. The first was their experience of storefront operations in the Los Angeles area. These included a center for job, benefits, and stress counseling run by a vet named Ken Brooks in a tough black neighborhood off of Western Avenue in south-central Los Angeles, and a discharge-upgrade organization called the Center for Veterans' Rights, run by another vet, Pat Wood, out of St. John's Episcopal Church. Of course they also had in mind Meshad's own rap groups in the basement of the Brentwood VA Hospital, which he had dubbed the Vietnam Veterans' Resocialization Unit (VVRU). The second component was what Meshad called "the circle of treatment," born of his theory that you could not completely heal the wounds of war on an intrapsychic basis, but that you had to facilitate social readjustment as well through employment counseling, relationship counseling, and so forth.

The next day, which Pastor Mahedy knew as the Feast of All Saints, they handed the proposal to McMichael, and were bowled over by his seemingly miraculous response: "It looks good. We'll take it." What McMichael didn't tell them was that he had a lot of work even within the VA to convince doctors and administrators that such a program was necessary or even desirable—for, as he recalls, many of them were uneasy about any form of off-site treatment that was "not under their control." And there was still zero support for it in the House Veterans' Affairs Committee, although Meshad stayed on in Washington for several weeks, going head-to-head with Tiger Teague and other committee members in a futile attempt to convince them of its merits.

McMichael and a committee headed by Dr. Jack Ewalt would spend the next couple of years doctoring up Meshad and Mahedy's original plan with the work of a number of more traditional, theoretical psychologists. They also removed components like the job placement service, which seemed to many of the older congressmen like a special favor to Vietnam vets. Despite their kowtowing to the House committee in every possible way, the measure failed yet again to make it to the floor. But Cleland, to his everlasting credit, kept on plugging for it, though there were precious few other voices in government backing him up.

McMichael berated Vietnam veterans for their attitude of "We're entitled to these benefits as a matter of right, so why should we bother to go out and ask for them?" "In terms of actual interest-group pressure on the Hill," he asserts, "there wasn't a lot from Vietnam veterans." Although his attitude might have been a tad more understanding, McMichael identified a real problem. When VVAW's latter-day revolutionaries came to testify, he pointed out, they alienated as many people as they won over. The National Association of Concerned Veterans (NACV) was the most visible presence before Congress, but they had little funding and depended almost exclusively on volunteers. The effectiveness of Vietnam veteran lobbying was undermined even further by the continual warring between NACV and the readjustment advocates. NACV, whose membership comprised mainly vets on campus or recent graduates, wanted a better GI Bill, as well as more employment programs. According to NACV president Tim Craig, its "top priority was not the psychological needs of Vietnam veterans"; it was "getting them enough money to go back to school, getting them health care benefits." The members of the Vietnam Veterans' Working Group, and their most obsessed champion on the Hill, Rusty Lindley, argued just the opposite—that until vets got psychological counseling, nothing else was going to go right in their lives.[152]

McMichael was not the only government official to comment on the lack of a Vietnam veterans' lobby, but only a few who saw the problem ever attempted to solve it. Of those inside the system, the most successful attention-getter, partly because of his bulldog determination and partly because he was a genius at working the media, was a slight, unassuming lawyer in his late thirties named Stuart Feldman. Feldman had bounced around the Kennedy, Johnson, Nixon, and Ford administrations, as well as working for the Rockefeller and Ford foundations and the Urban Coalition, before he found a congenial niche at the National League of Cities and U.S. Conference of Mayors. During all this time, one great quest occupied almost his every waking hour: to make the U.S. government act justly toward its Vietnam veterans.

Like a lot of government workers in the sixties, Feldman met regularly with a small group of his colleagues to discuss what to do about the ongoing tragedy of the Vietnam War. But while most people had their eyes focused on the histrionic protesters, Feldman was looking at the vets. So many of them were working class, so many high school dropouts, so many black or from other ethnic minorities. If the GI Bill could lift all these people up, it would serve a multitude of purposes. It would help to break the poverty cycle in various ghetto communities; it would facilitate the integration of many lily-white American universities; and it would doubtless help to end the war more quickly, for those who had experienced the results of a wrongheaded policy would be catapulted via higher education into positions of influence and authority. All that had to be done, he figured, "was run a raid on the federal treasury for scholarships for poor kids," just as the World War II GI Bill had done.

Looking into current GI benefits, Feldman quickly realized that $100 a month was hardly going to send many ghetto youths to the Ivy League. In fact, because tuition costs varied so much from state to state, Vietnam vets could not even afford public education in half the states, especially those in the East and Midwest. The average tuition at a state college in Pennsylvania, for example, cost three to four times what a California vet would have to pay for the same education. As a result, a much higher percentage of vets in the so-called Sun Belt states were going to school on the GI Bill than elsewhere in the country.

Even disregarding the inequity of tuition costs, there was the curious fact that the 1966 GI Bill actually paid Vietnam vets $10 a month less than Korean vets were getting thirteen years earlier. What Feldman discovered was that Lyndon Johnson had threatened to veto any more generous bill for purely political reasons. A big GI Bill would have forced him to acknowledge that a major war was in progress, which he was trying to play down; and it would have added substantially to the cost of a war that was already beginning to bankrupt his

Great Society. The problem Johnson created for veterans was never overcome, for their benefits began from such a small base that even what the VA considered "large increases" meant little, and failed to catch them up to World War II levels. While Nixon made sweeping promises to the million vets who returned from the war during his presidency, he held GI Bill increases to a minimum in an attempt to fight inflation, which ironically had been caused in large part by the war. Unemployment soared under Nixon; by the time his successor Ford left office, there were 600,000 Vietnam-era vets out of work. Twenty-one percent of all vets aged 20 to 24, and 36 percent of black vets that age, had no job and little means of studying or training for one. Even the 65 percent Vietnam veteran "participation rate" for educational benefits was deceptive, because it only recorded how many vets had started schooling, not how many had *completed* their curriculum. Because of the shortfall of living allowance, the dropout rate for Vietnam vets was significantly higher than for their World War II peers.

Starting in 1965, America's black ghettoes exploded in riots summer after summer, culminating in the fierce racial violence—including widespread burning and looting of white stores in black neighborhoods—after the assassination of Martin Luther King Jr. in April 1968. In Washington, D.C., federal troops were called out to protect the government offices and the white neighborhoods, as smoke from burning buildings blackened the skies over much of the capital. At that point, some people in government began paying serious attention to Feldman's proposal to use the GI Bill to enrich the black community, to give blacks a bigger slice of the economy and a bigger stake in keeping the peace.

Feldman even heard that LBJ had gotten interested in his idea and had "sent it to the appropriate people for their reaction." Thus Feldman began a decade of watching his hopes for helping Vietnam vets ricochet like pinballs throughout the American government—racking up some major accomplishments, and a great deal more frustration. What he found was that, without sufficient follow-up (in terms of people going over to encourage and direct their activities), government workers generally passed the idea—and the buck—on to someone further down the line. It turned out Johnson had given the ball to the Assistant Secretary of Defense for Manpower, who'd passed it to the VA and the Department of Health Education and Welfare (HEW), who in turn had bounced it back to the colleges and universities, telling them it was their responsibility to get more minority students enrolled. Angered by such a farce, Feldman had then given his friend Jay Rockefeller (later to become the Democratic senator from West Virginia) a detailed plan of how the VA could be made to work for blacks and other low-income Americans. First, according to Feldman, they had to get the White House's backing; second, stimulate colleges and technical schools to increase their remedial and motivational courses;

third, work with the military to set up a recruiting system before GIs were discharged; and fourth, put together a financial aid package that took into account variations in tuition cost and that included part-time jobs.

The Rockefeller Foundation declared the plan "too political" because it "involved lobbying," and they refused to get involved. At that point, Feldman decided to become a one-man lobby for Vietnam veterans himself. He went directly to Daniel Patrick Moynihan. A liberal Democrat who had served in Lyndon Johnson's Department of Labor, Moynihan had engineered much of LBJ's antipoverty program; and then, called to serve in Nixon's Department of Housing and Urban Development (HUD), he had managed to convince Nixon to keep many of his predecessor's Great Society programs, which the Republicans hated, such as Model Cities and the Job Corps. For a brief time in 1969, Nixon agreed to almost everything Moynihan proposed, and Moynihan sold him Feldman's idea as a study for HEW called "the President's Commission on the Vietnam Veteran."

From there, Feldman rock-'n'-rolled for the next eight years. He got into the confidence of William Jennings Bryan Dorn, the number two man on the House Veterans' Affairs Committee, while simultaneously working with Jonathan Steinberg on Cranston's Veterans' Subcommittee, then later the Senate Veterans' Affairs Committee. In 1970, he went to work for the National League of Cities and U.S. Conference of Mayors, and a year later coaxed the million-dollar grant out of the Office of Economic Opportunity (OEO) that allowed them to create their Veterans Education and Training Services (VETS) program in ten cities across the country. It was that OEO money, funneled through the NLC/USCM's VETS committee, that created landmark Vietnam veterans' self-help groups such as SEAVAC in Seattle and the Veterans Service Center in East St. Louis. Like a charmed man, Feldman got the grant renewed from various government discretionary funds for the next five years.

During that period, with the aid of Congressman Silvio Conte (R-Mass.) and Senator Warren Magnuson (D-Wash.), he also talked the government into coughing up $6 million for a special Upward Bound program of remedial and motivational courses for veterans, based on a model course at UCLA Extension School, and $25 million for a Veterans Cost of Instruction Program (VCIP), which paid colleges a bonus of several hundred dollars for each veteran they enrolled. Much of the money paid out by VCIP was used—as the law stipulated—to open some 1,000 veterans' offices on college and junior college campuses across the country, staffed mostly by Vietnam veterans. Then Feldman reached into the two-billion-dollar Emergency Assistance Act to create the "split-job program," which allowed two vets to share a full-time, $5,000-a-year public job while continuing to study and collect their GI Bill checks. Under Carter, he continued to obtain funding for the split-job program through the Comprehensive Employment and Training Act (CETA). At one point, when he returned yet again to testify before the House Veterans Affairs' Committee, a staff member grimaced and complained: "The last time you were here, you cost us a billion dollars." "Actually, it was several billions," Feldman corrected.[153]

2. A New GI Bill over Danishes and Coffee, and Muller and Kovic Part Company

By the time Carter came in, Feldman was worn down as a lobbyist. He had tried to turn some of the VETS city projects into veterans' lobby groups, but they had too many problems of their own; and besides, as Feldman well knew, a successful lobbyist has to be based in Washington. In early 1976, Feldman created the Committee for Public Advocacy, whose principal goal was to stimulate and guide the organization of a lobby for Vietnam veterans. But what really convinced Feldman that it was time to end his career as Lone Ranger, and to turn the job over to professional advocates, was the abysmal failure (in his eyes) of the Carter administration to meet the basic needs of so many hard-put Vietnam veterans—all the more stinging in view of Carter's promise to pay "a special debt of gratitude to those young men and women who served in Vietnam."

The fact that Carter had abandoned the deserters and bad paper vets was just the beginning of his betrayal, as Feldman saw it. At the end of Carter's first year in office, Vietnam veteran unemployment had actually risen almost 10 percent, with blacks, younger vets, and combat vets being hardest hit. (One particularly disturbing study in Cleveland showed over 40 percent of combat vets out of work.) The biggest disappointment was Carter's HIRE (Help through Industry Retraining and Employment) program. Even before his inauguration, Carter had announced his intention to help veterans find jobs, but only a small fraction of the $140 million appropriated to help private industry create training programs for Vietnam veterans (the heart of HIRE's mission) was ever spent. The program had been saddled with ridiculous demands—for example, an employer could only apply for federal reimbursement of training costs if he hired at least 100 veterans at one time, a condition even the biggest companies had trouble meeting. It hadn't helped, either, that Congress had taken almost five months to get the legislation passed, which some critics attributed to Carter and Cleland not pushing hard enough in its behalf. Another problem was that the program had not kept its focus on veterans, but had been expanded to include the long-term unemployed and the unemployed young. By March of 1978, HIRE, whose goal was to put 200,000 veterans to work, had produced jobs for only 200 of them, and was conceded by most of the Department of Labor officials who administered it to be a "dismal failure."

Carter and Cleland had blundered in the area of veterans' education too. In

October 1977, the Senate passed the GI Bill Improvement Act, which attempted to remedy many of the inadequacies and inequities people like Feldman had been pointing out for years. In addition to an across-the-board increase of 6.6 percent in educational benefits, it included an accelerated payment plan, so that a veteran could use his benefits at a faster rate at schools with a high tuition cost, and it extended benefits for an additional two years for veterans whose eligibility had begun in 1967, when payments were still only $100 a month. The most controversial part of the measure directly addressed the fact that (as Senator Cranston expressed it) "equal dollars do not constitute equal educational opportunity, particularly in high-cost states." It provided for the federal government to pay $66\frac{2}{3}$ percent of a veteran's yearly tuition fee in excess of $700—the kind of direct cash payment that had enabled thousands of World War II vets to go to Harvard and Yale (while only a few dozen Vietnam vets attempted either school on their total current monthly benefit of $292).

Tiger Teague and Chairman Ray Roberts of the House Veterans' Affairs Committee could not stomach the bill. Veterans could go to "virtually any state school" with "money left over," Teague said (ignoring sheaves of contradictory statistics). They felt that those who chose a high-cost school should foot the bills themselves (ignoring the fact that vets in some areas had no choice but an expensive college or technical school). Moreover, Teague viewed the bill as an insult to his two sons, both Vietnam vets, who (he claimed) felt sufficiently appreciated already and had no need for special favors. When Teague and Roberts announced their intention to rewrite the bill, there was an uproar among many congressmen, including some members of the Veterans' Affairs Committee, who thought the proper thing was for Roberts to convene an open-to-the-public conference committee, which would reconcile the differences between the Senate and House versions of the bill. Teague replied: "It's just quicker and easier without a whole lot of people." So he and Roberts got together with a few Senate and House staff members around a dining table— as Teague later reported to the *Dallas Morning News*—and stayed up all night working out their version of a compromise. At 4 A.M., over Danishes and coffee, they wrapped up a GI Bill that satisfied *them,* and later that morning turned it over to Congressman Robert Edgar (D-Penn.), who was incensed that a law that might affect the lives of millions of Vietnam-era veterans had been drafted "in the dark."

As Teague and Roberts changed it, the federal government would only pitch in $33\frac{1}{3}$ percent of tuition costs over $700 if the states offered a matching contribution. If the states failed to pay a third, the federal government would offer to *loan* the veteran two-thirds of his excess cost—the amount Cranston, Edgar, and other congressmen had wanted to give him outright. The loan would be forgiven only if the veteran successfully completed a four-year course of instruction, which did not allow for various emergency interruptions—like rais-

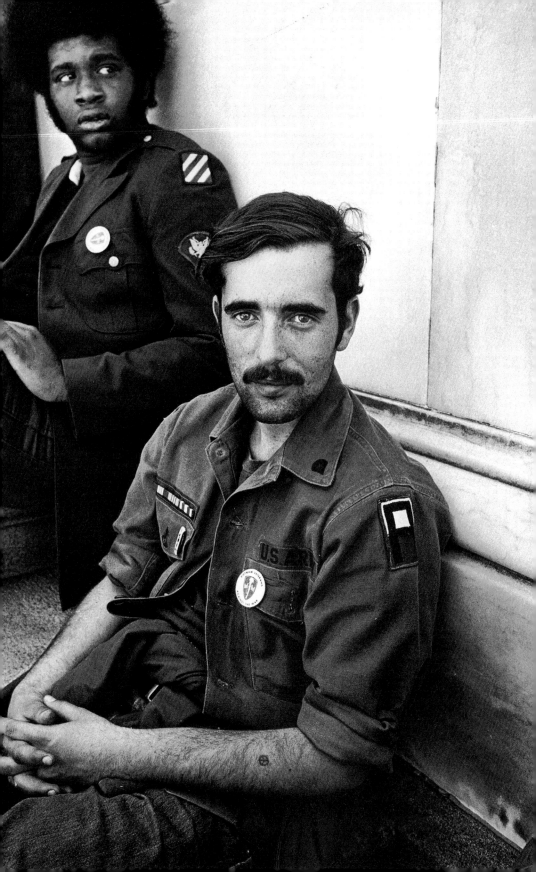

Vietnam veterans hurl their medals over a wire mesh fence protecting the Capitol at the climax of Operation Dewey Canyon III, Washington, D.C., April 23, 1971. *Photos © Fred W. McDarrah.*

Preceding page: Two Vietnam veterans wait to be admitted to their congressman's office to lobby for peace during Operation Dewey Canyon III, April 1971. *Photo © George Butler.*

Dr. Chaim Shatan, pioneer psychiatrist in creating the "rap group" style of therapy for post-traumatic stress disorder in Vietnam veterans. He's shown here in his Manhattan office, voicing his opposition to U.S. military involvement in Central America, 1988. *Photo by Gerald Nicosia.*

Sharing their wisdom at a Vet Center regional training session in Las Vegas, February 1985, are (*from left*) Army nurse Janet Ott, a therapist at the Seattle Vet Center; Air Force nurse Joan Craigwell, team leader of the San Diego Vet Center; Army nurse Lynda Van Devanter, cofounder of VVA and author of the first memoir of a Vietnam nurse, *Home Before Morning;* Army nurse Rose Sandecki, the first woman team leader of a Vet Center (in Concord, California); and Chris Noel, whose Armed Forces Radio Network show "A Date with Chris" was heard by GIs in Vietnam from 1966–1970. *Photo courtesy of Shad Meshad.*

Sarah Haley, a PTSD research pioneer, who wrote her seminal piece, "When the Patient Reports Atrocities," while working as a psychiatric social worker at the Boston VA Hospital. *Photo by Gerald Nicosia.*

Above: Shad Meshad (*right*) counsels a Hispanic Vietnam vet in his East Los Angeles veterans' rap group, 1973. *Photo courtesy of Shad Meshad.*

Jack McCloskey (*left*) attends a symposium on Agent Orange in Sacramento in March 1984, only days after being forced to step down as team leader of the Waller Street Vet Center. Beside him is fellow Vietnam veteran medic and activist Ron Perez. *Photo by Jackie Murphy.*

Staff and Vietnam vets unite to shut down the Waller Street Vet Center in a strike, protesting the dismissal of team leader Jack McCloskey and other vet-friendly employees, San Francisco, 1984. *Photo courtesy of Eric Schwartz.*

The California convoy (part of the Last Patrol), sporting VVAW logos and National Liberation Front flags, rolls into Miami Beach for the Republican National Convention, August 1972. *Photo courtesy of the VVAW Archive.*

Vietnam Veterans Against the War block Collins Avenue in Miami Beach during the Republican National Convention, August 1972, demanding a meeting with Richard Nixon. *Photo by Per-Olof Odman.*

Wheelchair vets (*from left*) Bobby Muller, Bill Wyman, and Ron Kovic return dejected from the Fontainebleau Hotel in Miami Beach with their fellow VVAW members, after failing to obtain a meeting with President Richard Nixon during the Republican National Convention in August 1972. *Photo by Per-Olof Odman.*

The Gainesville Eight, posing for a press-packet photo before the trial, spring 1973. *Top row, left to right:* John Briggs, Peter Mahoney, Stanley Michelson, William Patterson, Don Perdue. *Bottom row, left to right:* Scott Camil, Alton Foss, John Kniffin. *Photo courtesy of Morton Stavis.*

Defense lawyers meet with the prosecutors to examine the evidence—a single crate of "wrist rocket" slingshots—in the Gainesville Conspiracy trial, summer 1973. *From left:* Scott Camil's attorney Larry Turner; prosecutor Jack Carrouth; Miami police undercover agent Gerald Rudolff (known as "Salt"), who deliberately obscures his face; an FBI agent named Frank; and defense counsel Nancy Stearns from the Center for Constitutional Rights. *Photo courtesy of Scott Camil.*

VVAW does a demonstration in Gainesville, Florida, August 1973, to protest Judge Arnow's gag order. *Photo courtesy of the VVAW Archive.*

VVAW National Steering Committee Meeting, Boulder, Colorado, February 1972. At least two undercover government agents are present: William Lemmer (*front row center, with beard, holding large book*) and Emerson Poe (*second row, second in from right, with fedora hat and sunglasses*). Also present are Gunny Musgrave (*back row, fifth from the right*), Scott Camil (*next to Gunny, wearing headband*), Pete Mahoney (*second row, left of middle, with white shirt and white name tag*), and Jack McCloskey (*third row, second from left, with white sweater next to tall man raising his fist*). *Photo courtesy of Scott Camil.*

ing a family—that might occur in the meantime. Since few states had funds available to play the matching-grant game, Teague and Roberts had done little more than create a loan program for veterans through the VA that duplicated loans already available through other federal agencies.

The outraged senators and congressmen threatened to mutiny against Teague's "iron control." Daniel Moynihan, newly elected the Democratic senator from New York, and ever a friend to both veterans and the poor, complained that the GI Bill Improvement Act had been "quietly emasculated in private discussions." If ever the moment had come for Carter and Cleland to intervene, to use the substantial force of the executive branch to do a little congressional arm-twisting, it was now. Major newspapers, including both the *Washington Post* and the *Boston Globe,* cried out for the White House to do just that, to "act decisively" and "stand with Vietnam-era veterans." Carter was called on specifically "to put this year's presidential influence behind last year's campaign rhetoric." But both Carter and Cleland gave tacit consent as Carter signed the emasculated bill into law, "merely extending the inequities," according to Congressman William Ford (D-Mich.), and "buying a new package of trouble to replace the old package of trouble."

Several weeks before Carter's inauguration, partly out of distrust of the president-elect, Feldman had gone to two of his best press contacts at the *Washington Post*, Philip Geyelin, editor of the editorial page, and Colman McCarthy, an editorial writer, to convince them that it was up to the press "to keep the issue of fair treatment for veterans alive." The result was an unprecedented series of some forty editorials and articles, running from January 9, 1977, through July 27, 1978, which dealt with the needs of Vietnam veterans as "this important piece of the unfinished business of the Vietnam War." Often they were accompanied by the wonderfully sardonic pro-veteran cartoons of Pat Oliphant. Most of the pieces were written by McCarthy, but occasionally other heavy-hitting veterans' advocates stepped to the plate, including William Greider, Don Winter, and even Feldman himself. The series, besides its role as surrogate lobbyist, also served to introduce the public to some of the most important present and future leaders of the Vietnam veterans' movement. Bobby Muller, Max Cleland, and the coming champion of the Vietnam Veterans Memorial Wall, Jan Scruggs, were among those profiled in feature pieces.

The *Washington Post* series commenced in a tone that was friendly and supportive toward Carter and Cleland, merely nudging them in the direction of "making good" on their promises to help Vietnam veterans. As Representative Dave Bonior (D-Mich.) wrote, looking back: "The Carter administration seemed to hold the promise of one last chance [for Vietnam veterans to get the benefits they deserved]." By the end of the series, however, the tone had shifted to sharply critical, even at times openly hostile. Carter was accused of having made chiefly "symbolic gestures," and both he and Cleland were rebuked for their tendency "to underestimate the problems facing many Vietnam veterans." The *Post* even insinuated that Cleland was still covering up his own problems from the war: "Cleland seems too sunny to be real, too ebullient, inwardly too unscarred . . . for someone who carries such visible wounds." Other papers, like the *Boston Globe,* followed the same progression, eventually coming to lament Carter's lack of sympathy toward those he claimed to honor, and his administration's continued dodges "to avoid facing the fundamental inequities in the nation's veterans-benefits program."

Carter's treatment of Vietnam veterans was only a small part of the nation's growing disenchantment with his presidency. His "man from Plains" and "man of the people" persona quickly wore thin, especially since he seemed to be bungling the economy worse than Ford had. The inflation rate, 6 percent in 1976, had galloped to 12 percent by 1980, unemployment remained high, and the interest rate climbed to a staggering 20 percent. After a mob of fundamentalist Iranian students stormed the U.S. embassy in Teheran on November 4, 1979, taking 63 Americans hostage, Carter's repeated failures to free them—both through negotiation and military maneuver—made him seem totally inept, incapable of taking care of his people at home or abroad.

Carter's biographer, Douglas Brinkley, has explored some of his ambivalence toward Vietnam veterans. Carter, an Annapolis graduate, served in the military longer than any president except Eisenhower, and he had planned to make the Navy his lifetime career till his father's death brought him home to run the family peanut farm. As governor of Georgia, he had called for a Lieutenant Calley Day, to show support for Georgia's most infamous Vietnam serviceman; but when he ran for president, he downplayed his ties to the military. "A lot of what Carter was trying to do," Brinkley says, "was put Vietnam behind and move on." Having inched out Gerald Ford by one percent of the popular vote, his purchase on the presidency was far from secure, and he worried about identifying himself with special interest groups like Vietnam veterans. In that respect, says Brinkley, "he didn't have a broader vision," and so he was "negligent towards veterans' issues" mostly from "a huge naiveté"—a belief that he could best win support by creating a bland image of himself for public consumption.[154]

The anger vets felt toward Cleland's VA, however, was not just a reflection of their loss of respect for his boss. At the end of 1977, Don Winter did a detailed and less than flattering portrait of Cleland in the *National Journal.* His title, "Cleland—The Vietnam Vet in the World War II Vet Mold," encapsulated much of the problem. Together, World War II and Korean War vets outnumbered Vietnam-era vets more than two to one, and they had built an effective power base through the traditional veterans' organizations. Thus it was not surprising to find Cleland leaning in their direction. "They've got the money, the numbers, a lot of the votes in Congress and the kind of programs they support appeals to Cleland," Winter wrote.

According to Winter, Cleland had become "a run-of-the-mill guardian of his political turf." Cleland talked glowingly of new hospital construction, of the VA doubling its inpatient load and tripling its outpatient load, and of increasing hospital staffing by 38 percent. But as Ron Kovic had pointed out, statistics do not necessarily correlate to quality of life; and Winter suggested rather damningly that Cleland's "constant round of public appearances, congressional testimony, interviews, staff consultations and visits to VA installations" had become "an escape" from dealing with a thousand different voices demanding not only improved service and benefits but a complete transformation of the VA.

One of the loudest of those voices was the National Research Council of the National Academy of Sciences (NAS), which had been asked by Congress to conduct a three-year study of the VA health care system. Its report, released in June 1977, concluded that far too much of the VA's money and resources were consumed in caring for aging veterans with nonservice-connected ailments. In 1977, the average World War II vet was fifty-six years old; and even if he had come home perfectly healthy from the war, chances were he now had more than a few geriatric complaints. If general medical patients were sent to civilian hospitals, it would free up VA facilities and personnel to deal with many more service-connected illnesses and disabilities (those that were traceable to military service), a much higher percentage of which belonged to the veterans of Vietnam. The National Academy of Sciences went so far as to recommend that VA hospitals "ultimately be phased into the general delivery of health services in communities across the country." That is to say, they felt the VA should get to work on putting itself—or at least, a good part of its health care system—out of business. The study so angered some of the congressmen who had commissioned it that they tried to withhold the final payment of $6 million to the NAS.

Cleland not only had no use for the National Academy's study—and no intention of surrendering a significant portion of his budget to some form of national health care program, which would provide for all citizens equally—but he railed against it, claiming it had "seriously disturbed veterans of this country." For Cleland to argue in favor of VA health care "as an exercise in privilege for Americans who happen to have been discharged from the armed forces under honorable conditions" was sure to win him lots of points with the VFW and the American Legion. But, as Winter made clear, what it meant in practical terms was that a lot of battlefield-injured Vietnam vets would have to go without treatment in order for that "breaking wave" of older vets (as Cleland called them) to keep their traditional "entitlements."

While Cleland was enjoying what he admitted was the "luxury" of being the first VA star, the Vietnam chickens were coming home to roost in sky-darkening flocks—far more inexorably than ever they had for Richard Roudebush or even Donald Johnson. Carter and Cleland were both playing the game of symbols over substance—a dangerous game to play with angry Vietnam veterans, who had already been waiting almost a decade for decent treatment. Carter created a new position at the Department of Labor (DOL) specifically to placate the outcry over the half a million unemployed Vietnam vets: the Deputy Assistant Secretary for Veterans' Employment. And he hired the most politically correct person he could find for the job: Roland Mora, a disabled Marine captain, a Vietnam veteran with Native American blood, and a Cranston nominee from California, who had been active with the United Farm Workers. The trouble was, Mora had no gift for administration. In Tim Craig's opinion, "He shot himself in the foot. It was the first time we had had a veterans' contingent at the Department of Labor, but he picked some really bad people [to work for him], which helped his downfall."

Jan Scruggs, a mildly disabled Army vet who had gotten his master's degree in psychology from American University and was still unemployed two years later, published a denunciation of the DOL's failures in the *Washington Post*. He pointed out that the purported ten-point preference for disabled vets in civil service hiring had become a "joke . . . generally not enforced" and sometimes "intentionally circumvented by federal agencies." Even more disgracefully, the DOL, which was supposedly enforcing (through Mora's new office) affirmative-action programs for hiring Vietnam-era veterans, had filled less than 1 percent of its own jobs with such veterans, making it almost the worst federal agency for a young vet to seek a job in. The DOL, Scruggs wrote, was setting "a miserable example for private industry."

It fell to Washington correspondent Frank Greve in a syndicated piece called "A Legacy of 'Lost' Veterans" to nail the lid on the coffin of Mora's, DOL's, and Carter's veterans' policy. Although Greve quoted Mora at length in the article, showing his intelligence, Mora sounded more like a doomsayer than a leader with viable solutions. Mora predicted, "As time goes on, we'll see more and more psychological warfare between the vets and the civilians they fought for," and he seemed to pass the buck to employers and society in general, blaming them for "discrimination against veterans." "They [employers] want to forget the war," he told Greve, "so they forget the vet." However accurate his remarks, they sounded far too hopeless, and lacked the hint of any plan to turn the situation around. Greve then reinforced the gloom by juxtaposing Mora's comments with several alarming statistics. Beside the 511,000 unemployed, he tallied 50,000 homeless Vietnam-era veterans and 500,000 in criminal justice custody—125,000 in jails and prisons, and the rest on parole, probation, or pretrial release—with black vets seven times as likely to be incarcerated as white vets.

The most devastating part of Greve's piece, however, was the way he bracketed the interview with a sketch of a dozen homeless Vietnam veterans camped out on Dupont Circle. All the statistics in the world could never have the impact of those graphic images: "a dozen ragged men nodding in the sun"; "one of them flips an empty bottle that once held cheap wine . . . another passes around a shoplifted can of Vienna sausage"; "mostly, they do nothing"; "they talk about . . . sleeping in a laundromat, a basement, or an apartment hall." The piece was drenched in painful irony, like the local "cons" (ex-convicts) scorning the vets as "nothin' but hired killer Toms." But the sharpest irony was Greve's ending the piece with, first, a VA spokesman claiming "these guys are no different from other groups of vets," and, second, a vet named Sam praising the virtues of Wild Irish Rose whiskey and Gilbey's vodka, which, he affirmed, helped put them to sleep. The implication was that even cheap booze was helping Vietnam vets more than the VA and the DOL.

A few months later, Mora was canned, the first of several Carter scapegoats.

By the end of 1977, Stuart Feldman, like a lot of other Vietnam veteran advocates, had had his fill of Carter and Cleland's claims of having initiated a "recovery period" for Vietnam veterans. When people like Guy McMichael talked about the VA's success in "making educational benefits as widely available as possible" or "reinvigorating the agency," Feldman's response was: "Horseshit!" Across the country, more and more Vietnam vets were beginning to truly fear (according to the *Post*) "that as time wears on they will increasingly be forgotten and that administrative or legislative solutions to their problems will not be forthcoming." An ABC special, "The Class That Went to War," which aired on December 1, dared to tell the country that "the end of the war was only the beginning of [the veterans'] problems," and quoted the fulminatory Ron Kovic: "We definitely felt betrayed by the government, and lied to and manipulated and angry, and absolutely fed up."

Other vets were beginning to think along the lines of Feldman, that the answer was not further outpourings of rage but rather "an independent advocacy voice to raise, and then sustain, the needed pressure for change." Curiously, the biggest supporter of creating a Vietnam veterans' lobby was Kovic's old wardmate at the Bronx VA, his longtime political and social rival: Bobby Muller. Kovic liked to say that the feud between them stemmed from Ron's having "dated all the pretty girls Bobby wanted"; but Muller, who'd coaxed the nervous Kovic into his first speaking gig at a Long Island high school, felt genuinely horrified by the direction Kovic's career had taken, and eventually came to believe that he had "created a monster . . . a fucking maniac." What worried Muller most was "the self-pitying nature of his rap—his consistent, 'Look at me, I can't fuck, I can't walk, I lost my legs, I lost this, I lost that.'" Muller felt that Kovic had "muddied up the waters" with his emotional rhetoric, and that he had been "counterproductive" in terms of advancing veterans' causes, because "the intensity of his extreme passion" had "burned bridges with people that could have been helpful for a whole lot of different things."

While Kovic took to the streets, Muller got his law degree and went the suit-and-tie route—trying to *build* bridges, to change the system from within. ("Bobby's just trying to pretend he's not in a chair," Kovic would retort when people questioned their different approaches.) By 1977, Muller had worked his way up to legislative director of the Eastern chapter of the Paralyzed Veterans of America (PVA). But Muller, who in his own way had as much extreme passion as Kovic, was chafing at the bit, forced by the neutrality of his small organization "to get along with congressional committees and VA officials" and yet wanting desperately to "challenge the policies set by those committees and officials." What really pushed him to break with PVA was reading the National Academy of Sciences' report on VA hospitals. It suddenly became clear to him that the reason he and his friends had received such horrendously inadequate care was that special interest groups had laid claim to VA dollars before American troops ever got to Vietnam. Half the men on his original Bronx VA ward were already dead, but the money that could help the living was still being siphoned off. The VFW and American Legion were already lobbying for—and Congress was looking favorably upon—a bill called the Veterans and Survivors Pension Improvement Act, which offered financial security to all veterans who became disabled in later life. By the terms of the bill, any veteran over the age of sixty-five was ipso facto presumed "totally and permanently disabled"—a judgment that seemed to make a mockery of the sacrifice under fire of those like Bobby Muller.[155]

3. Fighting Back: Muller Takes On the Whole Government, and Dave Christian Takes On Jimmy Carter

From the time Stuart Feldman had met Muller, in 1973, he had considered Muller "the most articulate guy" working full-time on veterans' issues. But they had had little contact again until 1976 and 1977, when they both got heavily engaged in the fight to revamp the GI Bill. Grateful for Feldman's work, Muller managed to get him some money from the Paralyzed Veterans of America to enable him to lobby full-time. Then one day they went down to the Hays-Adams Hotel for lunch and irrevocably changed the history of the Vietnam veterans' movement. Feldman spoke of his insurmountable struggles as a lone lobbyist. Muller said that more and more Vietnam veterans were now willing to come forward and talk about what the war had done to them—that they now realized "that unless they organize themselves they cannot expect someone else to care." At some point, the two of them began talking about the possibility of raising money to build a real Vietnam veterans' organization; and Feldman, by his account, "chose" Muller to be its leader.

They incorporated their organization as the Vietnam Veterans Coalition. The initials, VVC, reminded a lot of Muller's comrades of the Viet Cong, so they quickly changed it to the Council of Vietnam Veterans (CVV). Because he had seen how the leadership of VVAW had repeatedly been attacked, Muller decided the Council would not be a membership organization, but strictly an advocacy group, and that there would be no attempt to make it democratic. Policy decisions would be made dictatorially by Muller and Feldman. That limitation may have been why all of the funding sources Feldman originally planned to tap, like his Rockefeller connections, originally gave them the cold shoulder.

Nevertheless, the Council of Vietnam Veterans was off and running like some Kentucky Derby long shot primed with amphetamine. The PVA, perhaps from guilt at having restrained Muller for so long, gave him a good-bye gift of $41,000 as a starting grant for the Council. But the real edge Muller had was Feldman's media contacts, especially Colman McCarthy at the *Post*. On February 10, 1978, McCarthy did a feature story on Muller and the birth of the Council, which caught the eye of a young Democratic congressman from Michigan named Dave Bonior.

Bonior, an Air Force staff sergeant who had served stateside during the Vietnam War, was disturbed about how few Vietnam-era vets had ended up in Congress, compared to the hundreds of vets who had been elected to national office in the years immediately following World War II. He was also concerned with the fact that even though there were a couple of dozen Vietnam-era vets in Congress, only one served on a Veterans' Affairs committee (in the House), and none seemed actively involved in promoting Vietnam veteran causes. When Bonior read the *Post* story about Muller and the Council, he immediately called their office and offered to help. What he proposed was to bring together members of Congress who were Vietnam-era veterans "as an active caucus working on Vietnam veterans' issues." Muller loved the idea; and Bonior, who was nearly as wired as Bobby, took only a few weeks—aided by Congressman John Murtha (D-Pa.)—to assemble a group of ten representatives and one senator called the Vietnam Veterans in Congress (VVIC).

Muller's Council and Bonior's VVIC quickly joined forces to pressure the Carter administration to support the Vietnam Veterans' Outreach Program bill (the authorization for storefront counseling centers), and to oppose the Veterans and Survivors Pension Improvement Act. When Congress passed the old-age pension bill, whose chief beneficiaries were World War II vets, at a cost of $930 million for just the first year, and then turned down the Vet Center bill aimed at helping Vietnam veterans, at a cost of only $12 million, Muller felt it was "a slap in the face" to his own constituency. The battle lines were sharply drawn, and what Muller found most disheartening was that arrayed among his staunchest opponents were the supposed "friends" of Vietnam veterans, such as Cranston, Cleland, Steinberg, and McMichael.

At one point, McMichael took Muller aside to explain to him why the Carter administration, as well as Cranston's Senate Veterans' Affairs Committee, supported the Pension Improvement Act. According to Muller, McMichael told him that Strom Thurmond had frustrated Carter's attempts to revive LBJ's War on Poverty. So Carter felt the Pension Act was the next best thing, because it would bring the families of 30 million veterans (40 to 45 percent of the population) "under the protective umbrella of at least some form of guaranteed annual income assistance." Muller exploded.

He recalls: "I argued that pensions, going back to the Bradley Commission Report, the President's Commission Report [under Eisenhower], would be lowest priority of all the veterans' benefits programs, for the obvious reason that here you had a very costly benefit program that had nothing to do with military service—absolutely fucking nothing! So why should the VA be paying out all these sums of money? And I argued that that should be a social welfare decision for Americans and not simply for that special class of citizens known as veterans. I said, 'Guy, what you're doing is you're trying to effect national welfare policy by subterfuge. Instead of taking the issue of "Should Americans have a minimum level of annual support so as not to live in the degradation of poverty?" and debate that as an issue for the American people collectively to decide, yes or no, you're using veterans' benefits as the sugar on the pill to bring it into reality.'"

Muller, as much a whirlwind in a wheelchair as Kovic when his ire was roused, became a formidable enemy of the White House, the Veterans' Affairs committees, and the VA. He went after Cranston and Steinberg, who were, he says, "collecting accolades and plaques" from the traditional organizations so that Cranston would have a "patriotic cover for his leftist and progressive issues." In California, Cranston's home state, he blasted the senator for posing as a "veterans' hero" when he had actually done "diddly squat" for Vietnam veterans. And he blasted him for "abdicating the responsibility of the Senate chair" by letting a staff person, Jonathan Steinberg, make critical decisions that affected millions of veterans' lives. In a similarly ruthless fashion, Muller took on McMichael and Cleland. McMichael Muller chastised for encouraging the "generational conflict" between World War II and Vietnam vets as a means of enhancing his own control of veteran politics, and for only responding (like Steinberg) to the needs of veterans who had "the political strength to force accountability." Both McMichael and Steinberg, Muller scoffed, had left Vietnam veterans "whacking it against the wall." For Cleland, Muller had even more scorn than for the absentee, Cranston. While Steinberg and McMichael were second-string veterans' power brokers, Cleland, Muller said, had become merely "their puppet."

To be fair to Cleland, if he hadn't gotten shell shock in Vietnam, he should have gotten it in the VA administrator's office. By 1978, his second year on the job, he was being hit by a thousand different demands and criticisms—which, though few realized it at the time, was actually a sign of the growing strength of the Vietnam veterans' movement and of the growing recognition of the unique and in many respects precious identity of Vietnam veterans. Books like Kovic's *Born on the Fourth of July,* Michael Herr's *Dispatches,* and Philip Caputo's *A Rumor of War,* feature films such as *Coming Home* and *The Deerhunter,* and a spate of respectful documentaries and made-for-TV movies all contributed to the self-esteem and ego strength of Cleland's constituency. But that insight, even had it been articulated, could have brought little consolation to the VA boss, who was as badgered for the right things he hadn't done as for the wrong things he supposedly had.

The VA appeals system was as archaic as ever. A veteran challenging the VA's assessment of his eligibility for benefits was not permitted to pay more than *ten dollars* for an attorney's services—by a law that dated back to the Civil War and was supposedly enacted to protect veterans from shyster lawyers. Worse, a veteran was prevented by law from taking his case to court once the VA's own Board of Veterans Appeals (BVA) had turned him down. In response to Dean Phillips' eloquent pleas, the Senate had enacted a bill providing for judicial review of the VA's administrative decisions and allowing vets to pay reasonable attorneys' fees, but once again the House killed such progressive veterans' legislation. Much of the opposition came from the VFW, which felt its turf was being invaded, since VFW volunteers had traditionally represented vets for free before the BVA.

In the area of health care, a fresh series of VA hospital scandals was making headlines, this time in the Southwest. In 1978–1979, an award-winning investigative reporter and former VA psychology intern named Robert Klein published a series of 89 articles for the *Albuquerque News,* all of them filled with horror stories gleaned from patients and staff of the Albuquerque, Houston, and other major VA hospitals and "soldiers' homes." His indictment of VA malpractice ranged from patients' routinely incomplete and often lost medical records to psychosomatic diagnoses for patients with real physical wounds (like a body filled with shrapnel), medical school students being allowed to experiment on VA patients, veterans drugged into long-term depression and even pushed to suicide by the wrong medications, and veterans being fed on prisoner rations and sometimes actually held against their will in VA hospitals and domiciliaries. Some of Klein's revelations received national exposure in a *20/20* television program based on his work, which followed a similar *60 Minutes* special. After beefing up his journalism with a couple of years of intensive research, Klein published his even more damaging findings in a book called *Wounded Men, Broken Promises.* By then, 1981, two of his major targets, Carter and Cleland, had already been bounced from office.

One of the things Klein's book showed, sadly enough, was that Max Cleland got blamed for all the VA's failings, and he got blamed by everyone, from ex-grunts whose claims had been denied to his own high-ranking VA employees. Letters to *DAV* magazine called for "Little Max" (who had been six feet two before his wounding) to resign, and a DAV service officer claimed Cleland had "sold them down the river" by being "nothing but a yes man for the president." The cruelest attack on Cleland was the suggestion that he had been "fragged" (deliberately blown up by his own men)—a widespread rumor Klein claimed was given credence by a number of important Vietnam veteran leaders, including Rusty Lindley. Cleland told Klein he had simply picked up a grenade that had armed itself by falling off his jacket, but Klein quoted an Army weapons expert stating that "those things just don't happen like that." Robert Klein pushed the fragging theory mercilessly. Whether or not his own men had actually tried to kill him, Klein wrote, sinking his claws in, "the fact that suspicions have been raised at all speaks volumes about the way a man is seen by the men and women he expects to lead."[156]

*　　*　　*

In some respects, what had happened was that the nation, and Vietnam vets in particular, had come to expect too much of the government and the VA in regard to healing from the war. In 1978, for the first time, a few articles were printed and a few voices raised to suggest that the issues involved were vaster than any congressional bill or any government agency alone could tackle.

One of the most prescient of those pieces was "After Vietnam: In Pursuit of Scapegoats" by therapist Jeffrey Jay, published in *Harper's* in July 1978, at a time when almost every new Vietnam veterans' program had either been stalled in Congress or failed of its objective. Warned Jay: "Both psychiatrists and the lay public are quick to see the ruined marriages, unemployment, and drug abuse among the 3 million Vietnam veterans as symptoms of psychiatric damage, warranting compensation or medical attention. My own talks with veterans convince me that their problems are not so simple, nor so easily addressed. The veteran's conflicts are not his alone, but are bound to the trauma and guilt of the nation. And our failure to deal with our guilt renders the veteran the symptom-carrier for society and increases his moral and emotional burden." The answer, or the beginnings of one, Jay suggested, lay in each American's assumption of personal responsibility for the war, so that the veterans would no longer be singled out as the "losers." If the veterans were suffering from a loss of meaning in their lives, it was not the war so much as American society that had denied it to them. It was *we,* he wrote, referring to America's citizens individually and collectively, who had "squandered the idealism and commitment of these men," and hence only *we* could give meaning to their sacrifices by "seeing value in their service." Above all, he counseled, we could honor them by acknowledging our own ethical confusion and trying to restore a sense of fairness and humanity to American life.

What Jay asked for was not so different, if a bit more sophisticated, than the national apology for the war that Ron Kovic kept asking for.

Another voice crying in that post-Vietnam moral wilderness was that of Jan Scruggs. Like a young Henry Ford or Orville Wright, he was still a small-town nobody with a great idea. The idea had come from a number of places—most prominently, from a father, Dr. Victor Westphall, who in 1971 had built a memorial chapel in Angel Fire, New Mexico, to his son David killed in Vietnam; and from an interview William Greider had done for the *Washington Post* in January 1977 with a Mexican-American Vietnam veteran named Gino Pacheco, who had spoken of the need for "a monument or . . . some gesture of respect" in response to his own bitter homecoming and the cold shoulder of Carter's recent "pardon." But Scruggs had hustled that idea all over the Washington, D.C., area, handing out questionnaires to 600 Vietnam veterans at local universities, to conduct his own private and very ambitious study of what he called "the psychological aftermath of that peculiar war." The D.C. community of politicized Vietnam vets was still a small and tight-knit group, and it did not take long for him to be noticed by *Post* writer Greider, who described Scruggs' study in one of his veterans' stories, which led to the *Post* commissioning an op-ed piece from him in May 1977. Scruggs used the piece to present the dismal results of his study—eleven times as many combat vets still plagued by nightmares as vets from units that had taken no casualties, 50 percent of all Vietnam vets (by their own assessment) psychologically damaged by the war, nearly 100 percent of black combat vets psychologically damaged— but he also bootlegged in his personal views near the end. Declaring that "this country has never before given veterans the shoddy treatment that has been bestowed upon those who served in Vietnam," Scruggs ventured that "America's final recovery" from the war depended upon "a national reconciliation." And though he was not the first to call for such a thing, he asserted with greater clarity than anyone else yet had that "a national monument is in order to remind an ungrateful nation of what it has done to its sons."

Congressman Dave Bonior, who would soon work with Scruggs to help make that monument a reality, was saying many of the same things, though he eventually grew cynical about the possibility of veterans and nonveterans ever meeting on equal ground. "Benefits alone will not give dignity to each Vietnam veteran's long years of waiting," Bonior wrote afterward, expressing the philosophy that propelled him through those difficult years. "It falls to Vietnam veterans to move ahead despite the nation. . . . They cannot let the nation's errors dominate their lives. . . . If Vietnam veterans must make a private peace, then those who make that peace will be the stronger because the job was the harder."

The lessons were already clear, and the teachers and prophets were already advising vets against a full-scale assault on their own government—which could only turn out as futile and ultimately traumatic as their assault on that will-o'-the-wisp, "evil" Communist government in Vietnam. They advised vets and nonvets alike to turn inward for the "reconciliation" Scruggs wished to promote.

But in 1979 few vets and fewer nonvets were listening. The passions were running too high, and healing for many was still a life-or-death issue. And so the crash of hope came hard and quickly, as the sandcastle of Carter and Cleland's wishful "recovery period" washed out with the tide of political reality.

That disastrous year started out with a bang, as Carter made the colossal error of firing a Vietnam veteran hero, Dave Christian, from his "special assistant" job under Roland Mora at the Department of Labor. A Green Beret captain who had done two tours of duty in Vietnam, Christian claimed to be the most highly decorated Vietnam veteran. That claim was occasionally disputed, but no one could deny he was at least in the running with seven Purple Hearts, two Bronze Stars, two Silver Stars, the Distinguished Service Cross, and two Vietnam Crosses for Gallantry. His left hand was permanently crippled from a stab wound, and his back was a mass of scars from being shot and burned with napalm. After returning to the States, he'd spent seven years in and out of military and VA hospitals. Like most vets so severely injured, he'd had many run-ins with callous government doctors; but Christian, who'd grown up on welfare in a blue-collar neighborhood in Levittown, Pennsylvania, and then gone to live on his own in Brooklyn at age thirteen, feared no one and fought back. He was almost thrown out of the Valley Forge Army Hospital for bringing an NBC film crew in to do a documentary on amputees and plastic-surgery cases.

What Christian discovered was that once a wounded soldier got discharged from the military, and put out of a military hospital, there would be a lapse of six or seven months before he was eligible to enter a VA hospital. For men like himself who needed nearly continuous care, such a hiatus was life-threatening. As soon as he was well enough, he went to Capitol Hill to argue against such "gross inequities" and to accuse the government of "fighting the injured fighting man." Thus he began a thirty-year career in Vietnam veterans' activism. In Washington, he met Bobby Muller and the equally young ex–Green Beret captain, Rusty Lindley; and for three years he shuttled back and forth to Rutgers Law School in Camden, with the intention of becoming a veterans' lawyer or lobbyist, much like they were. The need to support his growing family kept him from getting his law degree, but he remained an exceedingly loud voice in the capital, pushing the government "to honor Vietnam veterans for their service in order to end the 'stigma' and 'shame' of having served in Vietnam." When Mora needed a Department of Labor liaison to the VA for the HIRE program, he chose Christian for the job; just as Muller called on him when he needed an initial slate of members for the Council.

The trouble between Christian and Carter actually began on Veterans Day 1978. In the summer and fall of that year, there was considerable pressure being put on Congress, especially by the National Organization of Women (NOW), to end veterans' preference in civil service hiring. When Carter announced that he supported ending veterans' preference, in an attempt to placate those who were lobbying for an equal-employment policy, many of the veterans in his administration were furious—especially Dean Phillips, who had opposed a similar campaign against veterans' preference by the women's movement in Colorado; Rusty Lindley, who'd spent most of his post-military life unemployed (or at least unsalaried); and Dave Christian. When Christian was picked to deliver the keynote address at the dedication of the first Vietnam Veterans Memorial Plaque, at the Washington Amphitheater on Veterans Day, he planned to speak up for those half-million unemployed men for whom veterans' preference was at least a small life-jacket in a sea of indifference.

He got a chance to speak about it sooner than he thought. The White House asked him to go down to Oklahoma to support the Democratic candidate for governor; and while Christian was in Oklahoma City, some reporter asked him what he thought of Carter's plan to cut veterans' preference. Christian answered that it would make his own job (of putting vets back to work) "tougher." The next day, several of the local papers ran banner headlines such as "Executive Disagrees With Boss," and the story got picked up nationally.

At the last minute, Christian was told he could not speak at the dedication of the memorial plaque, but instead would be allowed to lead the crowd in the Pledge of Allegiance. Rusty Lindley wanted Christian to spit some chewing-tobacco juice in Carter's eye, but Christian had a great sense of the dignity of the occasion and felt he had to live up to the expectations of the thousands of older vets present, including many World War I vets. He remembers looking out over the crowd, the hundreds of blowing flags, the yellow autumn leaves in the distance, and being "very upset," knowing that if he opened with the word *I*, the whole crowd would automatically begin to recite, "I pledge allegiance, to the flag, of the United States of America. . . ." Carter was standing expectantly, hand over heart, eyes on Old Glory. "*It* gives me great pleasure to be here today," Christian began. "Let me tell you about the plight of our nation's veterans. . . ."

While Carter stared fixedly at the flag, looking more and more vexed, Christian spoke for about four minutes about the country's neglect of Vietnam veterans and the terrible results: unemployment, homelessness, lack of self-esteem, high suicide rate, and continuing casualties from exposure to the defoliant Agent Orange. He also mentioned what he felt was the national disgrace of no Tomb of the Unknown Soldier for the Vietnam War, and even worse, no Vietnam veterans' memorial. Very consciously he never mentioned Carter's name. When he'd finished, he turned to Carter and invited the audience to "join our president in saluting the greatest flag in the greatest nation in the world." After the Pledge, Christian offered his hand to Carter. Shaking it, Carter looked him in the eye and said, "Son, you are going somewhere someday."

What Carter had in mind was the unemployment line. In January, Christian went the way of Roland Mora. He was told that his appointment as senior staff officer at the DOL would not be renewed, even though he had been lured from his home in Bucks County, Pennsylvania, with the promise of a secure position. They gave him four days to pack up and get out. Quicker than that he went to his friends in the press, like Bernard Weinraub of the *New York Times* and syndicated columnist Mary McGrory. Weinraub did a front-page story in the *Times*, painting Christian as a kind of noble, Jimmy Stewart character who'd been kicked out for being "too visible" and too successful in getting vets "to organize politically" for their rights. McGrory's piece, titled "No Heroes Need Apply," took even harder shots at Carter's administration. In it, she quoted Christian's pointed question: "If the Department of Labor Veterans Employment Service can't find me a job, what are they doing to the guys who have trouble filling out the forms?"

Christian's firing was just the story the press had been looking for to crack Jimmy Carter's nice-guy image. Jessica Savitch interviewed Christian for national news, and Tom Brokaw sought him for *The Today Show;* then he was grabbed by their competitor, *Good Morning America.* Carter frantically called his labor secretary, Ray Marshall, to do damage control, and the DOL had to eat humble pie by putting Christian back to work—though it was at a lesser job, and in the Philadelphia office, out of Carter's hair and no longer in the national spotlight. The affair hardened Carter's belief that Vietnam veterans were bad news for him at a time when they needed his sympathy more than ever.[157]

4. Frank McCarthy Springs a Series of Ambushes, and Another Vietnam Veteran Leader Goes Down

Not only was the Outreach Program a long way from House approval, but a new issue with the gravest implications for Vietnam veterans' well-being—indeed for their very *survival*—had just appeared on the congressional horizon. It came with the menacing name of Agent Orange.

In March 1978, a popular Chicago TV news commentator, Bill Kurtis, had narrated an hour-long documentary called *Agent Orange, the Deadly Fog.* It was based on the work of a Chicago VA benefits counselor named Maude DeVictor. As a nurse in the Navy she had been exposed to radioactive materials, which she believed had caused her later breast cancer; she had also spent years studying sociology and law. In June 1977, the wife of a career Air Force vet had called her, saying her husband was dying of cancer because he had been sprayed with defoliant in Vietnam. He had, in fact, suspected he would die that way from the time the clouds of Agent Orange mist rolled over him, denser, he said, than the worst Los Angeles smog. Volunteering at the Chicago VA hospital, DeVictor had interviewed a great many Vietnam vets, especially those listed "DU"—Diagnosis Undetermined—which often turned out to be cancer cases.

She found that many of these vets had been in areas where defoliants were used extensively, and that many of them also had female partners who had miscarried or borne children with significant birth defects.

Agent Orange was by far the most popular defoliant used in Vietnam. It was a clear liquid, stored in drums with orange bands around the outside. Between 1961 and 1970, some 12 million gallons of it were sprayed on jungle areas throughout Vietnam, to deprive the enemy of the lush tropical plant growth, which was used so successfully to stage ambushes and to cover troop movements. Agent Orange was a mixture of two chemicals, 2,4-D and 2,4,5-T, both of which had been used extensively inside the United States to control weed growth in rural areas. Already in the 1960s there was concern about the possible health risks posed by the spraying of these defoliants, especially 2,4,5-T, which was known to contain trace amounts of a dioxin called TCDD. The dioxins were generally considered the most highly toxic group of chemicals ever created by man. In 1979, the Environmental Protection Agency would ban the use of 2,4,5-T domestically, except for range lands and rice fields. It was health concerns that motivated the military to terminate the use of Agent Orange in Vietnam in 1970.

After Kurtis's program aired on WBBM (a CBS affiliate), the Chicago VA was deluged by Vietnam veterans claiming defoliant-related illnesses; and as the story spread across the nation, so did the claims, which soon totaled in the thousands. The VA's initial response, according to veterans' advocate Ron Bitzer, who visited the VA's Central Office at that time, was to dismiss the whole affair as nonsense. Some VA officials even scoffed that CBS had been duped into broadcasting "the propaganda of North Vietnam." Maude DeVictor meanwhile continued submitting a series of papers to the VA, filled with statistics that seemed to show a correlation between Agent Orange exposure and certain diseases, especially cancers, in Vietnam veterans. The VA not only dismissed her assessments as meaningless, they grew increasingly hostile toward her investigative work; they harassed her, moved her to jobs she didn't want, and eventually forced her to resign.

Stories questioning the toxicity of Agent Orange were rampant in the media throughout the rest of 1978; and despite the VA's best efforts to stop it, a movement was born. It did not take long for the other shoe to fall, and it did so with a loud clunk in Norwalk, Connecticut. There are some meetings in the Vietnam veterans' movement—as throughout history—that seem fated: Ron Kovic meeting Bobby Muller, Muller meeting Stuart Feldman. In Norwalk Hospital on June 14, 1978, two Vietnam combat vets shook hands for the first time. They were Paul Reutershan and Frank McCarthy; and not only would their names be forever after linked together, but their combined force would shake to its foundations the United States Veterans Administration and just miss bankrupting some of the richest chemical companies in the world.

A member of the Big Red One (First Infantry Division), McCarthy had been badly wounded by shrapnel when his truck convoy had been ambushed, but he had kept firing his machine gun at the enemy till the convoy was out of danger—for which he'd been awarded the Bronze Star. In the mid-1970s he had given up a career in sculpture and filmmaking to found the Vietnam Veterans Unifying Group (VVUG), a nonprofit organization geared to helping disabled veterans and children whose fathers had been killed in action during the Vietnam War. A story in a New York paper about Vietnam vets dying of cancer had led McCarthy to Reutershan's hospital bed. He came simply to help, but Reutershan sent him on what would become a lifelong crusade.

Reutershan, who neither smoked nor drank and had taken perfect care of his health, was dying of stomach and liver cancer. A newspaper story about Maude DeVictor had triggered his own memories of flying through clouds of Agent Orange as a helicopter crew chief in Vietnam. No longer able to pay his medical bills, he'd written to President Carter for help in getting admitted to a VA hospital. The answer from a White House aide conveyed Carter's "thanks," and assured Reutershan that "careful consideration is given to all suggestions from those who share his [Carter's] concern for the well-being of the nation." He was now planning to sue Dow and two other major chemical manufacturers of Agent Orange, using a lawyer from his railroad conductors' union.

Even flat on his back in a hospital gown, Reutershan was the most dynamic and charismatic individual McCarthy had ever met. Mainly by telephone and mail, he had already put together a nationwide network of doctors, scientists, researchers, and over 1,000 veterans, which he had incorporated as Agent Orange Victims International (AOVI). McCarthy recalls that the phone never stopped ringing as they talked. But as incredibly strong as Reutershan seemed, McCarthy sensed that "this man was handling way too much." On the spot, McCarthy offered to turn over all the VVUG's assets to Reutershan's group, and to work in partnership with him to win treatment and compensation for all Agent Orange victims, especially the children.

In retrospect, the fact that the VA turned a deaf ear to so many credible claims seems almost incomprehensible. But Max Cleland was blindsided by Agent Orange. For two years he had been fighting a pitched battle to get delayed stress recognized and to get Congress to foot the bill for at least some form of treatment. All the experts had told him it was delayed stress that was killing vets and wrecking their lives, driving them to drugs and booze and keeping them from being productive members of society. Now all of a sudden here were another group of screaming "crazies," only they were saying that nine-tenths of the problems with Vietnam vets—even things like lack of sex drive and kids with learning problems—were due to getting too many whiffs of a common weed spray. Cleland felt he had to draw the line somewhere, and draw the line he did. And like a lot of people pushed to the brink of desperation, he drew it way too hard and way too absolutely.

As soon as the issue began to get a high profile, Cleland held a series of secret meetings with chemical industry representatives at the VA. Excluding veterans, doctors, and the general public, these meetings were in violation of the open-meeting provision of the Federal Advisory Act; and eventually NACV, with the aid of the National Veterans Law Center (NVLC) at the Washington College of Law, sued the VA and compelled them to open the doors to their rule-making process. In the meantime, the secret meetings resulted in the VA establishing its official position on Agent Orange of "no health effects."

VA doctors were informed that it was VA policy to initially deny all Agent Orange disability claims and then to forward them to the Central Office for review. There were several deadly catches built into this system. The first was that headquarters could not approve an Agent Orange claim unless the veteran's service record verified herbicide exposure. The VA set this requirement knowing full well that almost no veterans (except for those few actually engaged in spraying the stuff) had "herbicide exposure" in their service records. The second catch was a memo from Cleland instructing his workers that there could be no certainty about Agent Orange's harmful effects for "another decade"— even though the government, thanks to several EPA studies, already knew quite a bit about the carcinogenic, teratogenic, and fetotoxic qualities of dioxin, which was a contaminant in Agent Orange. Reutershan's and McCarthy's letters asking the VA to conduct its own epidemiological study were politely ignored, as was a request by the National Veterans Law Center (NVLC).

When McCarthy met with Cleland to push the idea of a VA study, Max told him: "No. Forget it. No way. We've got more important things. There's post-traumatic stress to deal with." In a similar vein, Cleland rejected the prospect of an outreach program to locate veterans who were experiencing unusual health problems—another proposal of the NVLC—with the curious logic that such an outreach program would only cause Vietnam vets "needless anxiety."

The last, and worst, catch was a seeming compromise with Agent Orange claimants. Cleland encouraged all veterans with unexplained health problems to visit outpatient clinics for a medical evaluation. But at the same time, the VA issued a series of memos to the examining doctors informing them that "the likelihood of herbicide poisoning is virtually zero," and instructing them to offer troubled vets "simple reassurance"! Even more treacherously, the VA warned its staff not to make any entries in the patient's medical record concerning Agent Orange–related complaints "unless unequivocal confirmation of such a connection has been established." And the VA, of course, had already set up guidelines that made it all but impossible for an "unequivocal confirmation" to be established.[158]

As soon as the VVIC caucus was established in 1978, Dave Bonior and his fellow congressmen pushed for President Carter to honor Vietnam veterans with a special proclamation, but Carter was silent on the subject. Cleland favored the idea; and when the Congress enacted its own joint resolution, declaring May 28 (Memorial Day) through June 3, 1979, as Vietnam Veterans Week, Cleland went ahead and proclaimed it himself. Backed into a corner, Carter still refused to offer Vietnam vets a White House dinner, but he reluctantly acceded to an afternoon reception in the East Room on Wednesday, May 30. At the same time, a commemorative postage stamp was being designed, which showed the Vietnam Campaign ribbon, and Carter agreed to present the stamp that day.

Stuart Feldman was overjoyed, and worked furiously with the U.S. Conference of Mayors to arrange parallel events all over the country. The media jumped in enthusiastically too, and CBS offered to reshow the highly praised episode of their *Lou Grant* show called "Vet," which had first aired on January 12 of that year. Because of Carter's ambivalence, however, many Vietnam veteran leaders, including Bonior and Bobby Muller, gave only halfhearted support to Vietnam Veterans Week, feeling "there would be time enough for symbols after basic benefits had been won."

Five hundred Vietnam veterans were hand-picked for Carter's reception. Those who seemed too dangerously hotheaded, like angry Sicilian Frank McCarthy (whose birth name was DiMarini), were carefully excluded. Carter came in looking nervous and quickly leaped onto the stage, hugging Cleland for reassurance. The front row was a line of wheelchair vets, including Ron Kovic (who had mellowed considerably after the publication of his autobiography, *Born on the Fourth of July*, and his recognition at the Democratic National Convention in 1976) and Bobby Muller. Carter seemed deeply moved; and his eyes, lowered to those wheelchairs, filled with tears. He threw away his prepared speech and spoke from his heart. In a voice that quivered and sometimes broke, he told them: "The nation has not done enough to respect, to honor, to recognize, and reward the special heroism [of the Vietnam veteran]." He acknowledged that many people regarded them as "unfortunate reminders of the war that was different," but declared that their service in an unsupported war required "an extra measure of patriotism and sacrifice." After reading from Philip Caputo's *A Rumor of War*, he ended with a paraphrase of Caputo: "We love you for what you were and what you stood for and we love you for what you are and what you stand for."

Then Carter unveiled the stamp and turned to Cleland, who was seated beside him, to say that Max deserved a lot of credit for the fact that Vietnam veterans were now being honored and for the respectful treatment they were finally getting at the VA. There was applause and then "a pregnant pause." Suddenly Frank McCarthy (who'd gotten in with a friend's ticket) stood up and, as he says, "ambushed" the President. As TV cameras from every major network swiveled toward him, McCarthy demanded: "What about Agent Orange victims, Mr. President? Thousands of our men are dying because of it! We need a study!" According to McCarthy: "He'd like to die. He couldn't even speak to me. He just looked up from the microphone in horror. And I just kept speaking." UPI's version was: "Carter, looking grim, heard McCarthy out. . . ." McCarthy began yelling: "Dow Chemical lied! . . . Vietnam veterans are dying at twice the rate here in the States as they were in actual combat!" As he went on, *Washington Star* reporter Fred Barnes saw "sweat spread over his [Carter's] face." Over and over McCarthy demanded a study, till Carter was forced to say: "Max and I agree."

Shortly thereafter, a White House Task Force on Agent Orange, as well as an Inter-Agency Working Group (which included the VA), were created; and Carter authorized the first VA study of Agent Orange, called the Ranch Hand Study, because it tried to evaluate the health effects on the pilots who sprayed Agent Orange—whose missions were code-named Operation Ranch Hand. But even though preliminary results from the Ranch Hand Study in December 1979 revealed that dioxin could be stored in body fat for long periods—thus explaining why vets might come down with an Agent Orange–related illness years after exposure—none of these new committees moved an inch toward remedying any of the veterans' health problems or even toward allaying their anxiety.

Part of what was going on was a splaying of attention over too many different concerns—some of which had been postponed, some of which had just come to light, but all of which had fallen together on a VA that was just getting its second wind after the sorry performance of the past three administrations. But there was also no doubt a continued hardening of feeling against Vietnam veteran activists, who, Cleland gibed, were "in the business of advocating." This hard line was again apparent at the first congressional hearings on Agent Orange, which opened on June 26, 1979. Despite extremely moving testimony by veterans, especially those who had had children with dozens of severe birth defects (like Michael Ryan, whose daughter Kerry had been born with double reproductive organs, a hole in her heart, and a left hand attached to her elbow), the VA spokesmen persisted in claiming Agent Orange was no more harmful than aspirin, and that "birth defects can only be caused by exposure of the pregnant female." The impact of the hearings was further vitiated by fierce wrangling between Vietnam veteran leaders—in particular, the feud between Bobby Muller and Frank McCarthy. In the beginning, Muller felt that Agent Orange was a potentially fatal distraction for the veterans' movement, while McCarthy felt that all other veterans' issues should be shelved until the full extent of Agent Orange damage was known, and until help was forthcoming for all the victims, especially the children.[159]

The Vietnam veteran activists were not helping the VA with its attitude problem. When the Vet Center Bill was finally passed and signed into law on July 13, 1979, they jeered at the paltriness of its $12 million appropriation—about one-twentieth of 1 percent of the whole VA budget. Some vets pointed out that all 92 vets centers cost the government about as much as *one* new tank, and Stuart Feldman noted that in a few months of lobbying back in the fall of 1971 he had gotten Congress to come up with over twice that amount just for the Veterans Cost of Instruction Program. Feldman also complained that "during the two years Cleland took to get the psychological counseling program passed, the spending for the GI Bill declined about $2 billion, a net loss to the Vietnam veterans of $1,988,000,000." The first Vet Centers had hardly opened their doors when organizations like the Center for Veterans' Rights were already denouncing them as "too little too late." Leaders like Rusty Lindley ridiculed Cleland for having taken two years "to get the House to buy off on a piddly $12 million pilot project."

As Cranston and Cleland prepared to come to California to dedicate the state's first Vet Center in Van Nuys, they were scathed by the local Vietnam veterans' organizations. One group put out a flyer denouncing Cranston as a "do nothing," and President Carter as a "know nothing" whose "ignorance is virtually destroying us." But their worst venom was saved for Cleland, "the man with no credentials . . . a token stooge . . . an 'is nothing' overseeing as important an agency as the Veterans Administration." "Instead of correcting the mistreatment, which he also had the privilege to once taste," they charged, "he turned his back and sold us out at every opportunity."

Cranston, who was up for reelection that year, was mortified by the threat of public protest at the dedication of the VA Outreach center. He quickly struck a deal with local veteran leaders; he would hold hearings on the continuing readjustment problems of Vietnam veterans, including "government mistreatment of Agent Orange victims and disabled veterans," in exchange for their promise not to picket the dedication ceremony. The dedication was scheduled for Saturday morning, January 26, 1980, and the hearings would commence that Saturday afternoon at Patriotic Hall in downtown Los Angeles. But no leaders could speak for every Vietnam veteran; and when Cranston and Cleland showed up at the Van Nuys Vet Center, they were accosted by about fifty angry vets wearing orange T-shirts, waving signs that said "Agent Orange Victim" and screaming insults at the two dignitaries into the bank of television cameras.

For Cleland that mild Southern California winter day, it was a particularly bitter blast of man's ingratitude. He had spent years, as he relates, trying to talk the nation's power brokers into underwriting the Vet Centers; and now that he finally had "a tangible product" to offer his constituency, they were pissing on it, and pissing on him too. Of course the Agent Orange controversy had grown a lot hotter since the filing of hundreds of lawsuits against Dow Chemical and the other major manufacturers of the herbicide—the latest one brought in Los Angeles on November 27, 1979—and the consolidation of the many cases into a major class-action lawsuit under federal jurisdiction. Cleland, unfortunately, was the man in the hot seat, being asked to take sides on an issue he knew next to nothing about, but that was as urgent and passion provoking to many veterans as their own life or death, and the life or death of their children.

What passed for a "hearing" at Patriotic Hall was in fact a no-holds-barred assault on the man in the wheelchair—living symbol of the entire VA to many embittered vets. "Did you lose your balls in Vietnam, too?" one vet taunted him, when Cleland declared that he would not cooperate with the plaintiffs in the Agent Orange lawsuit, which he saw as "nothing more than a publicity stunt." Others, enraged by his seeming indifference, tried to push him out a fourth-floor window, and one even took a swing at him. Frank McCarthy was one of the vets who had come out from New York with the specific intention of harassing the VA chief, and January 26 was merely the start of his relentless crusade devoted to making 1980 the worst year of Cleland's life.

Cleland had a full schedule of Vet Center openings that year; and wherever he traveled, a contingent of Agent Orange Victims International (AOVI) was waiting to abuse and harangue him. He was haunted by a legion of men dying of cancer and of severe neurological disorders, as well as men whose children had been born with catastrophic birth defects. Finally, at a NACV convention in Kansas City, he threw everyone except McCarthy out of his hotel room. As McCarthy relates: "He said, 'The only thing I can get you is the Vet Centers. Won't that help you?' And I said, 'No, it won't do a goddamn thing for me, Max. *Nothing!*' He sat down, and he cried. Max wanted to help. He cared, but he couldn't [help]. The power lay in the hands of the Congress."

In November 1980, Jimmy Carter was crushed in the presidential race by the incredibly popular former governor of California (and ex–Grade B movie star), Ronald Reagan. Although the wrath of Vietnam veterans probably had only minimal effect on Reagan's electoral sweep, Carter's defeat ended yet another tragic chapter (and far from the last) in the history of the Vietnam veterans' movement. Certainly it was a personal tragedy for Max Cleland, who had poured his heart, what was left of his body, and his soul into his job. But it was also a tragedy for all Vietnam veterans, including those who had worked so furiously to bring about his downfall.

It was his brother Vietnam vets who—if they did not literally turn him out of office—had nailed Cleland to a cross of contempt, and made such a sorry spectacle of him that it would be many years before another Vietnam veteran was placed in the position of VA administrator. Perhaps even sadder, Vietnam veterans had permanently silenced one of the best advocates in government they had yet had—maybe the best they would ever have—for Cleland in his subsequent political career has avoided as much as possible talking about veterans' issues.

That silence cannot, however, obscure his remarkable legacy. He never flinched from criticism, but did his best to respond to every complaint that reached him, no matter how lowly the source. He instituted much-needed reforms in medical services, expanding the VA's drug- and alcohol-treatment facilities and reversing its poor retention rate for physicians. He appointed a Vietnam veteran as head of the Rehabilitation Medical Service, a post he created, and created other needed positions like a Chief of Physical Therapy. He tried to match people with jobs—like the blind Korean War vet he chose to run the blind rehab units. He inaugurated a storefront counseling program that, despite endless political assaults, has endured now for more than two decades. And perhaps most amazingly for any government official, he had the guts to speak his mind. On Memorial Day 1979, marking the start of Vietnam Veterans Week by placing a red, white, and blue wreath at the Tomb of the Unknown Soldier, Cleland refrained from the usual platitudes that get men reelected and reappointed to office. He told how the service of Vietnam veterans had been ignored, scorned, and resented. He told how such treatment had hurt them more than their physical wounds. And, in some sense mocking the very week of honor he had worked so hard to bring about, he declared: "All soldiers who fought in Vietnam are unknown."[160]

No matter who was to blame in bringing such a good man down, this time the Vietnam vets had done a number on themselves. The war had truly come home.

8

An Indictment of the System: The Wadsworth Strike

1. The Hostages Are Welcomed Back, and Ronald Reagan Takes Aim at the Vet Centers

On January 20, 1981, only hours before Jimmy Carter turned the presidency over to Ronald Reagan, he finally struck a deal for the release of the 52 American hostages still being held by the Islamic fundamentalist followers of the Ayatollah Khomeini, leader of the revolutionary government of Iran. They had been held captive for 444 days, and during the latter part of 1980 millions of Americans had become fixated on the national humiliation they represented, as well as the patriotic challenge to bring them home. Carter's image was hopelessly tarnished by a botched commando raid on April 25, 1979, in which an American helicopter and cargo plane collided in the Iranian desert, and eight American servicemen were killed. Feeling as if they could make up in morale for what their commander-in-chief lacked in brains and gumption, many disenchanted citizens responded to the so-called "hostage crisis" by displaying yellow ribbons outside their homes and workplaces—to symbolize an attitude of national loyalty and patient remembrance (based on the scenario of a prisoner coming home after three years, in a currently popular song entitled "Tie a Yellow Ribbon 'Round the Old Oak Tree").

Ronald Reagan, who knew the value of good theatrics, brought the 52 hostages home on his own presidential jet, *Freedom One,* arranged for them to recuperate at West Point, and then offered them a lavish homecoming reception in the White House Rose Garden. Individuals and corporations showered the hostages with money and gifts—from champagne and chocolates to free cars, luxurious hotel rooms, and lifetime passes to sporting events. In Washington, D.C., a half-million people turned out to greet them, and in New York two million took part in a ticker-tape parade more festive than anything since the end of World War II. Congress offered them each a gold medal and financial compensation—on top of their regular salaries—of $200 for each day they had spent in captivity.

Veterans all over the country were outraged. Most of the Iranian hostages were State Department employees, who had taken a high-risk assignment for the pay, prestige, and possible advancement it brought; whereas most veterans had laid their life on the line solely from a sense of duty, with little money and less glamour, and sometimes not even a "thank you," to reward them for it. In Denver, a World War II vet who had been held by the Japanese for over three years in a camp in Manchuria—at times kept naked in below-zero temperatures and subjected to other gruesome tortures—wrote the *Denver Post* to say that when he got back the government had paid him $1.50 a day for his ordeal and hadn't even bought him a train ticket home. But by far the angriest were the Vietnam vets. "Like a dam breaking," according to Ron Kovic, they suddenly began speaking out and making their presence known in a flood of letters to the editor in virtually every newspaper, including the *New York Times*. Incredibly for such a divisive lot, their thousands of letters read almost as if they had all been authored by the same person. Over and over again, they said they did not resent the "ballyhoo" or the "public gesture of thanks" given the hostages, but they couldn't help wondering (as *Time* magazine summed up their collective complaints): *"Where the hell is my parade?"*

In Pasadena, Ron Kovic was still recuperating from a serious back injury, and he watched the hostages' return on TV from his sickbed. He was living with Ron Bitzer, an Army vet who had cofounded the Center for Veterans' Rights (CVR) in Los Angeles. He and Bitzer had met in New York in 1976, when Bitzer was working with the amnesty movement, and they had subsequently become good friends. They shared a wacky sense of humor; and, as Bitzer explains, they made "a good team." Kovic spoke with the emotion and authority of a combat vet; while Bitzer, who'd spent his tour of duty in Taiwan, provided the credibility and composure of someone who had gotten his degree in political science at Johns Hopkins, training for a career in the State Department that had never materialized. After hearing about the planned ticker-tape parade for the hostages, Kovic recalls that he grew increasingly "uncomfortable and anxious."

Kovic told Bitzer that they had to stage a press conference at Patriotic Hall in Los Angeles at the exact hour of the ticker-tape parade in New York. Bitzer, who had replaced his friend Pat Wood as director of the Center for Veterans' Rights, was in the perfect position to orchestrate such a press conference. "In 1970, hundreds of guys with Purple Hearts [in VVAW] were saying what was needed for them to come home," Bitzer explains. "Nothing had changed ten years later. How could you not believe these guys? They were saying what was true. The country was not ready to hear it. The politicians were not ready to act on it. But it was clear to me: I had my marching orders. This is what the guys said they needed, and all I was out there trying to do was stimulate more of a forum for listening to their message. And I wasn't the one to deliver it. I didn't have a Purple Heart; I wasn't even in Vietnam."

There was no one better to make that pitch than Kovic. Sitting out in front of Patriotic Hall in his wheelchair, in a cheap checkered shirt and sleeveless sweater, at the center of a racially mixed group of earnest-looking, working-class vets with protest placards, his own brow furrowed as if deeply troubled, he provided the perfect picture to be counterposed with the ticker-tape parade in New York. The media ate it up; and the best part was, as Bitzer said, that everything he was saying was true. Kovic spoke eloquently about the "cold shoulder" Vietnam vets had been given when they returned from the war, and suggested that "Americans should widen their perspective from those fifty-two to the millions who have problems today because they didn't get that kind of reception." He said he had been disturbed by "something missing" in all the celebrations of the hostages' freedom, and that "something" was any indication that the nation remembered the existence of its several millions of Vietnam veterans, "who deserve to be welcomed and to be treated with the same respect as the Iran hostages." "We all belong to this country too," Kovic declared, adding that though many of them had become "lost" and no longer had "a vote or a voice," they still needed to be recognized and appreciated. "We're all still here," he concluded. "We know who we are, and we're determined not to be forgotten. Please don't forget us."

On Ted Koppel's *Nightline* the following night, February 3, Kovic read a five-minute speech that avoided his usual weakness of talking about himself, and instead focused on hard facts. Most explosively, he revealed Reagan's plan to close the 91 Outreach centers within the next six months. That news hit the Vietnam veterans' community like a bombshell. Reagan had taken office mouthing lots of clichés about his commitment to veterans, but now the cat was out of the bag about his secret talks with his young budget director, David Stockman. One of the worst problems Reagan had inherited from Carter was runaway inflation; and Reagan's solution, like that of Nixon and Ford before him, was to severely curb federal spending. It was Stockman's "brilliant" idea that $900 million could easily be cut from what seemed to him the VA's bloated budget. And it was not just do-nothing bureaucrats who would get the ax. Stockman proposed eliminating 20,000 employees from the VA's Department of Medicine and Surgery, and 3,200 from the Department of Veterans' Benefits. He also sought to eliminate the Veterans Cost of Instruction Program, the Targeted Technical Assistance Program (which funded the development of vocational rehabilitation programs for disabled and Vietnam-era veterans), the Disabled Veterans Outreach Program, the Incarcerated Veterans Project, the Legal Services Corporation (which helped indigent and rural veterans to apply for discharge review), Special Programs (which included kidney dialysis services), most of the VA medical research programs, and unemployment compensation for veterans who declined to reenlist.

The hardest cut for Vietnam vets to swallow, however, was the measly $32 million budgeted to fund the existing 91 Vet Centers and to add about 40 more during the next two fiscal years. With one stroke of his pen, Stockman aimed to wipe out the entire readjustment counseling program, in effect thumbing his nose at eight years of research, lobbying, and protest by thousands of individuals to get it enacted into law, and thumbing his nose at the 39,000 vets who had already obtained help there, as well as the million more (by some estimates) who needed it.

Ironically, just as Reagan prepared to shut down the Vet Centers, most of them recorded a dramatic increase (often 50 percent or more) in the number of vets coming in for their first visit. News reports and television programs about the hostages publicized the existence of the Outreach centers to vets and their families who had not yet known of them, so that in one week the Vet Centers received millions of dollars' worth of free advertising. The hostages' homecoming had triggered delayed-stress reactions in thousands of vets, including many who had never acted out or sought help before. According to a story in *Time,* hundreds of relatives of Vietnam veterans were calling centers about vets who had literally spent years holed up in their own homes ("hostages to the war"); many showed up at the centers seeking counseling or simply looking for a way out of their intolerable non-lives—or to keep from exploding like the alienated vet in Rochester, New York, who killed his mother and went berserk in a bank. In fact, the sensitive handling of troubled vets by Vet Center personnel during this period did a great deal to defuse what could have been a nationwide outbreak of violent rage.

Alan Cranston, usually cautious in criticizing his political opponents, was moved to say publicly that "to eliminate the single most visible program for Vietnam veterans" was "enormously insensitive and ill-advised"—especially when the Reagan administration was preparing to double the Defense Department's budget over the next five years and send $90 million (three times what the Vet Centers needed) in military and economic aid to the dictatorship in El Salvador. The commander in chief, so eager to push America to the brink of military intervention in Central America, was the same man who, when running for the governorship of California in 1966, had said: "Once you ask the men of this nation to go into combat, you owe an obligation to those men." But neither Reagan nor Stockman showed the least compunction about their action. Stockman referred to the Vet Centers as "dispensable expenditures"—a phrase that sounded a lot like "protective reaction strikes"—and Vietnam veterans as a "noisy interest group."

As Myra MacPherson noted, Stockman seemed incapable of enunciating the phrase "rap groups" without a disdainful curl of his Ivy League lips. Appearing totally ignorant of why the centers had been created in the first place, he claimed Vietnam veterans could get all the counseling they needed "within the VA system." As for the numerous other veterans' services he was killing, he cited President Reagan's plan (an early version of Newt Gingrich's "Contract with America") "to get the federal government off the backs of the taxpayers by returning many responsibilities to state and local control"—as if state governments, presupposing they had the will to help, actually had any money to create a gamut of veterans' programs. Such a posture also managed to obscure the fact, as Cranston pointed out, that "our obligation to veterans is fundamentally a national responsibility" and that "veterans programs are an inseparable cost of national defense." At the same time as he attempted to gut the VA, Stockman hit vets with the double whammy of shutting off the Comprehensive Employment and Training Act (CETA) funds, which kept afloat most private veterans' self-help groups, including the Center for Veterans' Rights (CVR). Stockman's apparent assault on veterans had an especially ironic sting in light of the fact that he had spent the war years dodging the draft with a Harvard Divinity School deferment.[161]

Ron Bitzer believed the government had hidden motives for trying to do away with the Vet Centers and self-help groups, which had become "a bone in their throat." The counselors in Vet Centers, he theorized, were far more committed to helping Vietnam veterans than the average VA worker, and were more likely to try to organize Vietnam veterans to fight politically for their causes. He cited some interesting statistics from one of the program's own surveys: 78 percent of Vet Center counselors worked more than 40 hours a week; 86 percent of them worked evenings, 33 percent on weekends; 75 percent went on their own time to visit vets in institutions, and 57 percent had visited vets in their own homes. Bitzer felt the VA bureaucracy was threatened by such a potential hotbed of veterans' activism, especially since the Vet Centers were increasingly being drawn into the Agent Orange controversy. He scoffed at the VA's recent complaint that Vet Centers no longer gave "most bang for the buck" because they now dealt largely with "repeaters." As Bitzer pointed out, Vet Center counselors encountered serious readjustment problems in over a dozen different areas nearly every day—unemployment, lack of adequate housing, psychological difficulties, VA benefits problems, marital problems, alcohol and drug abuse, financial need, criminal charges, and Agent Orange complaints, to name a few. When veteran clients came back for further help, Bitzer said, it was simply evidence that "the Vet Centers are beginning to do their job."

For Bitzer, it was really an issue of control. Most Vet Center employees were themselves Vietnam veterans, and the government "could manipulate them" more effectively if they had to work inside VA facilities and not in fairly autonomous storefronts. According to Bitzer, even a supposed Vietnam veterans' advocate such as Jonathan Steinberg wanted to maintain that kind of control, and that was why Steinberg had lobbied to cut out a portion of the original Vet Center legislation that would have offered government funding to private organizations, like the CVR, which were doing comparable counseling work.

Steinberg, he says, wanted to keep veteran firebrands like Shad Meshad tied to a government payroll, and to force upcoming firebrands like Bitzer to accept a government paycheck if they wanted to keep doing veterans' work.

Reagan's contempt for Vietnam veterans showed again as he groped for nine months for a suitable head of the VA. At first he put forward William Ayers, a sixty-seven-year-old former Ohio congressman and World War II patriot in the mold of Johnson and Roudebush, but with even less experience in handling veterans' affairs. When Ayers' nomination didn't fly, he looked to thirty-two-year-old Dave Christian, who had worked in Reagan's election campaign, and whose credentials as both a war hero and a veterans' advocate were unimpeachable. But Christian, who had a lot more integrity than Reagan gave him credit for, refused to run a VA whose best programs had been hatcheted by David Stockman under the guise of "cutting the fat." He sent Reagan a personal appeal, printed in a number of newspapers, asking the president not to "block out" Vietnam veterans' problems because it was politically expedient, and warning that veterans expected more of him than the "shattered dreams" they had been handed by previous administrations. When Reagan failed to respond, Christian angrily announced that he would not be "a male whore," and promptly withdrew his name from consideration.

Perhaps hoping for the publicity value of a Cleland clone, Reagan then turned to two wheelchair-bound Vietnam vets, John Behan, a New York state assemblyman, and Vincent Rios, a California leader of the newly incorporated Vietnam Veterans of America (VVA), as possible nominees. Behan wanted the job so badly he went straight to Washington to canvass for it, happily pledging "to eliminate unnecessary bureaucracy in the agency." When those nominations found no congressional favor, Reagan fell back on a Republican Party hack, Robert P. Nimmo, a World War II vet whose chief recommendation was his friendship with Reagan's own loyal crony, Edwin Meese III.

Meese was one of the president's most trusted counselors, and in Reagan's second term he would get the job of attorney general. But being friends with him was not a testimonial to virtue. In the coming years, Meese would become the subject of eleven separate ethics investigations, and he was also implicated in the Iran-Contra cover-up. While not in Meese's league, Nimmo got caught up in scandals from almost the day he took office in July. Despite Stockman's decree of austerity for the VA, Nimmo spent $54,000 refurbishing his office, and sent the old furniture to his daughter's office; he also spent $6,441 for a chauffeur he was not entitled to, until public outcry forced him to pay the money back. When he needed to fly from Reno to Washington, the former bomber pilot chartered an Air Force plane at a cost of $5,600, rather than flying first class in a commercial airliner at a tenth the cost. His chief interest was golfing, but he also showed talent for saving money at veterans' expense, like managing to stall a congressionally mandated Agent Orange study for the entire time he was in office. He felt the agency should stop "coddling Vietnam vets"; and even before he had started his new job, he went on the *Today* show to debunk the notion of serious long-term health problems associated with Agent Orange exposure.

For the first six months of Reagan's presidency there was actually no one running the VA, though there were two acting administrators, Rufus Wilson and the chief medical director, Dr. Donald Custis—neither one of whom took responsibility for what was going on there, which made it all the easier for Reagan to bend the agency to his will. After announcing that October 1, 1981, would be the final day of operation for all Vet Centers, Reagan had Stockman impound money that had already been allocated for VA health care hiring, thereby instituting a personnel freeze for the readjustment counseling program. Both the comptroller general and the VA's general counsel deemed that action illegal; and Senators Alan Cranston and Lawton Chiles (D-Fla.) introduced a resolution in the Senate that condemned Stockman for usurping congressional authority. Cranston also sued Stockman in Federal District Court to force him to release the VA's funds. The suit, litigated for free by the counsel for Vietnam Veterans of America, Joseph Zengerle, was successful.[162]

From 1976 through 1980, it seemed the only in-depth writing about Vietnam veterans' readjustment problems—outside of Gloria Emerson's National Book Award–winning work *Winners and Losers* and the *Washington Post*'s editorial series—was being done in *Penthouse* magazine's monthly feature, "The Vietnam Veterans Advisor," authored by Bill Corson. Corson, who went from a seventeen-year-old Marine recruit assaulting Japanese emplacements on Tarawa to distinguished service in both the Korean and Vietnam wars, was virtually a lone voice in those years, condemning the government's negligence while at the same time inspiring Vietnam veterans toward self-reliance. He is another of the movement's unsung heroes, whose words changed thousands of lives and probably saved quite a few; and yet his columns always managed to credit others, even Max Cleland and the DOL's unpopular Deputy for Veterans' Employment Roland Mora, when he felt they deserved it. But by early 1981, after a hiatus of half a decade, "the floodgates were open" (as Kovic puts it) as far as mentioning Vietnam again in the American press. Many factors contributed: a spate of excellent Vietnam movies in the late 1970s like *The Deerhunter* and *Apocalypse Now;* the rapid expansion of Vietnam Veterans of America (which was basically Muller's Council transformed into a membership organization); the return of the Iran hostages; the fight to save the Vet Centers; the release of the five-volume *Legacies of Vietnam* study in March 1981; but perhaps most of all a sufficient lapse of time for the nation to begin examining its own dark and painful deeds relative to that tiny Southeast Asian country, which like it or not had grown to become a touchstone of the American conscience.

That spring, *Time* and *Newsweek* did major pieces on the readjustment struggle of Vietnam veterans. Both magazines had covered the Vietnam War extensively, almost week to week, but had then gone years without touching the issue of the veterans' war at home—"an absolute scandal," according to Ron Bitzer. Finally, on July 13, 1981, *Time* put Vietnam vets on their cover, with a story called "Fighting for Their Rights: The Forgotten Warriors," which set the Vietnam veterans' movement squarely in the nation's view, and a major turn in national consciousness was achieved. Bitzer and his cohort Kovic had a lot to do with making that cover story happen, but no one had more to do with it than an ex-Marine private named James Roger Hopkins, who'd lost most of his hearing and a lot of other things in Vietnam, and who was two months dead when the July 13 issue hit the stands.[163]

2. Jim Hopkins: A Marine Twice Betrayed

In Atlanta, Georgia, writer Bob Klein had recently interviewed an angry two-tour combat veteran named Ken Baker, who had been refused VA treatment for the ringing in his ears, which he believed had come from the firing of 106mm recoilless rifles. Baker felt like he wanted to explode, to take out twenty or thirty of the bureaucrats who had frustrated him, but he knew that wasn't the answer. "The problem," he told Klein, "is how do you shoot the VA?" Clear across the continent, cruising up the San Diego Freeway through Westwood in his red 1946 Willys Jeep, looking out at the malignant white hulk of the Wadsworth VA Hospital, Jim Hopkins figured he had found the answer.

The next day, Saturday, March 14, 1981, Hopkins woke up hungover in his Jeep in the hospital parking lot. He was surrounded by a sizable arsenal: three handguns, a Ruger .357 magnum, a .38 Smith & Wesson, and a .45 Colt automatic; a Ruger mini-14 semiautomatic rifle; and a Remington pump-action 12-gauge shotgun. He was still wearing his combat boots and camouflage fatigues from the day before, when he'd gone out to a place called Texas Canyon near Newhall, where he and a bunch of other survivalist Vietnam vets often let off steam shooting up tin cans and sagebrush. After smearing lampblack under his eyes to cut down on the sun's glare, and loading 100 rounds into his ammo belt, Hopkins maneuvered his Jeep into position, threw it into reverse, and, after making sure there were no pedestrians in his path, drove pedal-to-the-floor through two sets of glass doors. His Jeep came to rest in the Wadsworth Hospital lobby, in the midst of a diamond field of broken glass, only yards from where Ronald Reagan's representative had told the assembled press on December 10, 1980, that there would be no reduction in medical care for veterans.

Hopkins yelled for everyone to clear out of the lobby, took careful aim with his Ruger mini-14 rifle, and fired several bullets into the official portraits of Ronald Reagan and Jimmy Carter hanging on the wall. For good measure, he fired a few shots into the ceiling with his .45 and shotgun. Then, putting the weapons down, he grabbed a nearby flagpole and leaned it so the flag fell over the hood of his Jeep. After a final swig of Jack Daniels, he settled back into the Jeep, shouting that he'd been poisoned by Agent Orange and that he wanted his veterans' benefits.

Hopkins was arrested without a struggle and arraigned two days later, with bail set at $25,000. Since he was nearly broke, it looked like he would have to stay in L.A. county jail till his trial. But Ron Bitzer and his CVR coworker Michael McCarthy immediately took up his cause. They held a press conference at the VA on Monday morning and got Leonard Weinglass to serve as his attorney; and after his arraignment, they talked the Brentwood Hospital into admitting him to the psychiatric ward, even though VA regulations stipulated that anyone under criminal indictment could not receive treatment.

Hopkins turned out to be a very bright man, and to have some legitimate beefs with the VA. A high school dropout from a broken home in a blue-collar suburb of St. Louis, he had joined the Marines at age seventeen, influenced both by war comics and the heroic tales of his grandfather, who had fought in World War I. Hopkins was especially proud that he was born on the Marine Corps's 173rd birthday, November 10, 1948. Sent to I Corps, near the DMZ, in August 1967, he had lost his notions of glory in his first firefight, when a mortar blast flung a comrade's leg nearly on top of him. He returned claiming three Purple Hearts and a Bronze Star, serious wounds to his knee, head, and chest, as well as growing deafness from the "stick grenade" that had sent shrapnel into his face and skull. In addition, he was beset by a plethora of physical and nervous problems: diarrhea, swollen joints, numbness in his extremities, fatigue, night sweats and shiverings, nightmares, flashbacks, suicidal depressions, and uncontrollable rages, which often led to violence.

When he read about the thousands of veterans who were claiming neurological disorders due to Agent Orange exposure (he could hardly have missed the *Los Angeles Reader*'s cover story on that subject three weeks earlier), Hopkins was sure that he too was a victim of the toxic herbicide. But the VA repeatedly refused to give him treatment for any of his complaints, and several times they declared they could not give him service-connected status because his military records had been lost. The latter statement was not implausible, since a major fire at the Defense Department's National Personnel Records Center in St. Louis in 1973 had consumed thousands of veterans' DD-214s, as well as their subsequent medical histories. His eligibility for treatment was also in doubt because of his General discharge, which he had received because of his numerous punishments for offenses such as drunkenness, going AWOL, and striking an officer.

Hopkins' latest conflict with the VA bureaucracy had resulted from its refusal to certify his deafness, so that he could get a typewriter telephone (a device for taking and sending messages over the phone lines in the days before e-mail) from the telephone company. Two days before he shot up the lobby, he had spent all day at the Wadsworth Hospital's ENT clinic undergoing a full workup, and had consequently missed his appointment for discharge upgrading before the traveling panel of the Board of Veterans Appeals, which wouldn't be back in L.A. for another year. At the end of that long day of tests, the doctors still refused to sign the document saying that his hearing was impaired.

What interested Bitzer and McCarthy so much in Hopkins' case was Hopkins' awareness of the links between his military experience and the downward spiral his life had taken, and also Hopkins' willingness to let his own life stand as an example, and if necessary a sacrifice, to those who did not believe Vietnam veterans needed special care. Hopkins did not languish in the Brentwood Psychiatric Facility, but spent his time writing down much of his personal history, as well as issuing political statements to bolster the cause of veterans' rights. One such statement, dated March 19, 1981, exudes a haunting sincerity as well as simple eloquence. "Perhaps my actions were a little dramatic," he wrote, "but then our needs (Vietnam Veterans) are very dramatic. If only one person has or will be helped, then I have achieved my goal. It is important to remember that my actions were taken out of extreme frustration, and that my intentions were NEVER to hurt or kill anyone." He also appealed to an altruism that went far beyond his own needs: "It is high time that the Veterans Administration and various government agencies be shaken from their lethargy toward ALL veterans, not just Vietnam Era vets. . . . I call on President Reagan to stop spending millions of dollars on Inaugural balls, and utilize the money for what the defenders of this fine country are entitled to."

Hopkins did not fit the stereotype of the Vietnam vet as walking time bomb or crazed loner. A big, burly, good-looking guy, he liked playing the macho Marine—he'd even killed a man in a barroom fight, which had been judged an act of self-defense—but he was also trying to overcome the many strikes against him. He was patriotic to a fault (his favorite song was "The Marines' Hymn"), liked to read military history, and said he'd reenlist right away if they'd let him; he almost always held a good-paying job; he was a loving father to his ten-year-old son Chris from a previous marriage; and he inspired complete devotion in his current wife, Suzanne, a gorgeous blonde as bright and articulate as he. Like a lot of Vietnam veterans, he had a bad substance abuse problem, especially with alcohol. Suzanne had forgiven him the times he'd beaten her in a drunken rage—believing herself just another victim of his delayed stress—and she immediately joined the veteran activists who were pleading for him to be given medical attention and not a long prison sentence. Suzanne became one of the biggest assets to Hopkins' case, as she embarked on an intensive campaign of speaking and giving interviews. Perhaps better than any-one else, she understood the meaning of her husband's action: "He made a bold enough statement that even the Veterans Administration understood: I need help!" she wrote in one of her press releases. "It's really quite shameful that such a dramatic act was necessary to bring attention to the thousands of vets who often receive less than adequate care, if any, at Federal facilities."

The government responded by attacking Hopkins' credibility. They claimed he had been merely a supply clerk, had won no medals, and had served in Vietnam only five and a half months before his bad conduct got him transferred to Okinawa. Hopkins' supporters countered by producing a letter he had writ-ten to his brother Joseph from Vietnam, describing his experience on a truck convoy, where the driver, sitting beside him, was shot through the head by a sniper. After interviewing him, as he had interviewed hundreds of vets, McCarthy felt Hopkins' war exploits had the ring of truth. And Ron Bitzer thought there was a strong possibility that the government had deliberately altered Hopkins' military record "to defuse the Vietnam veterans' rights issue."

At the Brentwood Hospital, the doctors claimed they could find no evidence that Hopkins suffered from either PTSD or any Agent Orange–related disor-ders, and that his principal problem was alcoholism. But as Bitzer pointed out to the VA's acting administrator Dr. Custis, and later in a telegram to Ronald Reagan, 40,000 other Vietnam vets had already showed up at the VA claiming Agent Orange disabilities, and had been turned away because the VA lacked "a protocol for the diagnosis" of such illnesses or even a standard Agent Orange screening examination. As for the VA's record of diagnosing and treating PTSD, it was almost as slipshod. At the Brentwood Hospital, Bitzer discovered, the doctors were using a complicated set of criteria to establish PTSD, which entailed a far longer list of symptoms than was required by either the American Psychiatric Association or the VA's own Department of Medicine and Surgery. Two PTSD experts, Dr. Chaim Shatan and one of his protégés, Dr. Yael Margolin, who was then working at the Montrose VA Hospital in New York, attest that in 1981 most VA psychiatrists still did not bother taking a veteran's military history before completing a psychological assessment. In fact, two years after the Vet Centers had opened, the VA still had no standard protocol for diagnosing PTSD either; and the tendency of most VA doctors, according to Shatan and Margolin, was to ignore its existence whenever possible. Veterans evincing psychological problems were still questioned chiefly about their child-hood; or else, like veteran Tom Bodensick, who suffered from chronic insom-nia and unpredictable outbursts of temper, they were reprimanded for "the inability to adjust to adult life."

For Bitzer, the issue went far beyond proving that Hopkins had a real dis-ease, or that he was innocent of a crime against the federal government. As Bitzer wrote in an open letter to Dr. Custis on March 16, Hopkins was the bearer of a message the VA could no longer afford to ignore: "All Vietnam veterans must know . . . what the intent of the Veterans Administration is concerning improvement of health care, especially for possible victims of Agent Orange poisoning." The VA, however, went ahead and kicked Hopkins out of the Brentwood Hospital, dumping him back into the criminal justice system.

In mid April, the Brentwood Hospital remanded Hopkins to federal custody. By this time, however, Bitzer and McCarthy had raised enough money through hundreds of small donations, as well as a benefit performance of the Vietnam War play *Tracers*, to bail him out. Hopkins returned to living with Suzanne in their two-story "barn" in Calabasas, near the Pacific Ocean. His trial on charges of destruction of federal property was scheduled for July. Already his case had become a cause celebre to the Vietnam veterans' movement, and he was invited to speak to many veterans groups, especially those who were demanding the VA open its doors to Agent Orange victims. Veterans in Austin brought him in to address a huge Vietnam Veterans Day rally at the State House on May 8, and Hopkins' speech received a standing ovation. Drawing on his knowledge of history, he told them how the Mexican General Antonio Lopez de Santa Anna, laying siege to Texan revolutionaries at the Alamo, had sounded the *Deguello*, which meant: "Show no mercy—slaughter them all." "Now the Veterans Administration has sounded the *Deguello* for us," Hopkins warned the crowd. He was followed by a veteran's nine-year-old son, whose left arm and hand had been deformed since birth. "If the government doesn't start helping us soon," the boy said, "there won't be anyone alive left to study."

For a few hours, Hopkins was the toast of Austin, and he even received an offer from billionaire H. Ross Perot to pay for the medical tests necessary to prove he had been poisoned by Agent Orange. Hopkins told Suzanne he wanted to move to Austin once the law got done with him in California. But there was evidence that the strain of being a veterans' hero was taking its toll. On the march to the State House he had suffered a flashback, screaming to Suzanne to watch out for "mines on the trail." When he got back to Los Angeles two days later, he found that veterans' protests there were heating up considerably. On Friday May 15, inspired partly by Hopkins' daring, two patients at the Brentwood Psychiatric Facility went on a juice fast to protest the fact that neither of them had seen his psychiatrist in two weeks. Hopkins was roiled by the constant reminder of tragedies from the war, and for several nights his sleep was fractured by endless nightmares, so that he awoke each morning exhausted and drained.

Still, Hopkins remained confident that he would win in court. He also talked of how much it meant to him to be reunited with Suzanne, after being able to see her only two hours a day while in the hospital. They spent most of Sunday morning, May 17, in bed, "fucking and reading," she says. He was in good spirits when she left him, around one o'clock, to drive into Malibu for food, beer, and cigarettes. But when she got back, a couple of hours later, she found the door locked with the dead bolt, which Jim never used when at home. She called, but got no answer. Inside, she found him propped up on their bed, blue eyes wide open, dead, with a bottle of Jack Daniels, a shot glass, and an empty vial of sleeping pills on the nightstand. There was, however, no whiskey on his breath (she tried giving him mouth-to-mouth resuscitation), the nightstand was not within his reach from where he lay, and she was also puzzled to find two photographs beside him, of his son and of her, which he had never liked much. Moreover, as long as she had known him, he had never drunk out of a shot glass. Other things were missing or suspiciously out of place. There was no suicide note, though Jim had written her lovingly every day when he'd been locked up in the Brentwood VA.

Sheriff's investigators did not think Hopkins had committed suicide. They suggested that he had died from an "accidental overdose" or "natural causes, such as a seizure." Suzanne strongly suspected he had been murdered by the government to keep him from leading a nationwide rebellion against the VA, and a lot of vets believed the same—though McCarthy and Kovic, who had both talked with him on the phone that week, had heard unmistakable depression in his voice. He and Suzanne were both out of work, and the bills were mounting. His last writings showed a growing cynicism. "I feel that I and my fellow Marines who served our country have been betrayed not once, but twice," he wrote in his journal. "Once by not intending to win [the war] and twice by having our rights and needs as veterans repeatedly ignored. . . . [I feel] sorrow for the over 57,000 who died for nothing." In any case, many of his fellow vets were determined to see that Jim Hopkins had died *for something*.[164]

Los Angeles coroner Thomas Noguchi agreed to do an autopsy on Hopkins' body, and "to try to determine if Hopkins was suffering from Agent Orange effects"—a hopeless quest, since the amount of dioxin required to do damage (a few parts per trillion) was virtually undetectable at that time; and dioxin-related abnormalities (except for the very distinctive chloracne) generally mimicked a variety of other diseases. Unwilling to wait for Noguchi's dubious results, vets who knew or had heard of Hopkins began showing up at the Wadsworth Hospital and the Center for Veterans' Rights on the Monday after his death. Ron Bitzer worked with a group of them to draft a telegram to President Reagan, which was sent on Wednesday, May 20. Reagan, they knew, planned to spend the upcoming Memorial Day weekend at his mountain ranch near Santa Barbara.

The telegram, sprinkled with Hopkins' own statements as well as excerpts from the absurd clean bill of health given him by the VA, requested first off that Reagan come down to Los Angeles to meet with a delegation of concerned veterans. Four more demands followed: 1) that the president "order an immediate investigation into the failures of Wadsworth and Brentwood VA Hospitals to provide evaluation and treatment" to Hopkins; 2) that Reagan "order a national investigation into the Veterans Administration programs of psychological counseling for Vietnam veterans by a team of non-VA experts in the field of delayed stress"; 3) that he order the VA to develop as soon as possible a screening examination for veterans claiming injury from Agent Orange, and to cooperate with groups like the Center for Veterans' Rights "for the purpose of outreach to veterans concerning the Agent Orange services" of the VA; and 4) that he "appoint an expert panel of non-VA individuals to evaluate the need for a national delayed re-entry program for all 4.2 million Vietnam veterans."

The telegram was sent mostly for its publicity value. Bitzer hardly expected a reply, since he had not yet received an answer from Dr. Custis, whom he'd written over two months earlier. But a group of six angry vets decided they really did have a right to meet with Reagan, and—following Hopkins' lead—they came up with a strategy to force his hand. They walked into the lobby of the Wadsworth Hospital that Wednesday afternoon, set up a card table and a coffeepot over on the west end, and said they would stay until their demands were met. At the same time, the two Vietnam veteran hunger strikers at the Brentwood Hospital, John Keaveny and Marlin Adkins, were kicked off their ward, and they came over to the Wadsworth Hospital to continue their strike on the front lawn. Almost immediately five other vets joined their hunger strike, and a couple of tents were pitched to house them all.

Once the media reported the protests, Vietnam veterans began streaming to the Wadsworth VA as if drawn by a magnet. Within a couple of days, there were dozens in the lobby and hundreds milling on the lawn outside. Twenty tents had sprung up, and there were American flags, posters, and homemade banners hung everywhere—with slogans such as "Don't Forget James Hopkins" and "Let's Finally Bring the Vietnam Veteran Home," and provocative questions like: "Who Said Vietnam Is Over?" Dozens of bags of groceries had been donated to the vets in the lobby, and someone had even set up a television for them. There was also a tiny black cardboard casket surrounded by funeral wreaths, with a small slot on top and the words "James Hopkins Memorial Fund." The lobby pay phones were manned by vets, who would answer with the words: "Inside Six!"—which had become their official title, to distinguish them from the hunger strikers outside. Both inside and outside, the protesters identified themselves by wearing a black armband in memory of their martyred hero.

Soon it was not just local vets showing up but also guys from distant states who had quit their job and taken an indefinite leave from wife and children to "be with their brothers." One homeless vet, a former Green Beret whose leg had been shredded by a land mine, brought his whole family to live in the lobby, and said it was a lot more comfortable than the car they'd been living in for weeks. Black comedian Dick Gregory, a veteran of numerous civil rights hunger strikes, arrived to coach the hunger strikers on the lawn, a group that had quickly grown to twelve, including former AVM leader Max Inglett. A hemiplegic veteran of the 101st Airborne, Richy Goldstein, flew in at his own expense from New Zealand to support them. There was also (according to disabled First Infantry veteran Steve Androff) "a whole cast of characters coming down out of the mountains—burly 'Namers with beards and camouflage." Most pleasing to Bitzer and McCarthy was the appearance of a number of World War II and Korean War vets, who showed solidarity with the Vietnam vets by offering their own testimony against the VA. And Ron Kovic, the father of all Vietnam veteran hunger strikers, was finally coaxed out of hiding in his favorite little hotel in San Francisco to come join them. Hardly shy of cameras, Kovic had nonetheless been extremely reluctant to get involved in the Wadsworth protest. Not only was he feeling his own need to heal, and to steer clear of the "dark dreams" of vets like Hopkins; but he sensed that—unlike his neatly orchestrated and tightly managed hunger strike at Cranston's office—this one would be a tremendous convulsion of anger and hostility, beyond everyone's control, and almost certain to lead to violence.

By the weekend, the L.A. papers were clogged with stories about the Wadsworth occupation, and the mistreatment of American veterans had become an international scandal. The lobby was lit by klieg lights all day long, and cameramen roamed the lawn finding an endless supply of veterans who wanted to be interviewed. The VA was not pleased, to say the least, but they also refrained from acting hastily, fearing to make yet another blunder. For the first time in years, the vets were being dealt nothing but high cards, and Bitzer and McCarthy aimed to play their hand for all it was worth. When they learned that Hopkins' body was scheduled to be returned from the L.A. county morgue in a day or two, they planned a military funeral for him at the Westwood Veterans Cemetery, just across Wilshire from the Wadsworth Hospital, on Monday May 25—Memorial Day.

That weekend, the vets were incensed by Reagan's continuing silence. Then on Monday, Memorial Day, they were further stirred by a statement from White House spokesman Larry Speakes in Santa Barbara. Reagan, back in the saddle at his vacation ranch, was "aware of the hunger strike," Speakes announced at a press conference, "but he had no reaction" and "no plans to contact the veterans." The president's snub and the military funeral for Hopkins staged by Vietnam veteran director John DiFusco, together with the carloads of media people who kept arriving, served to galvanize the whole hospital and even much of the Westwood neighborhood. "Mourners" appeared from everywhere, including a local motorcycle gang, dying men from the Wadsworth cancer ward, and droves of psychiatric patients from the nearby Brentwood facility, who had apparently been loosed especially for the occasion.[165]

3. From Protest to Circus: Meshad and Muller Battle Kovic and Bitzer

That week, the emotional intensity at Wadsworth erupted into every sort of madness. Partly it was because the stakes had now truly become life or death.

Infuriated by Reagan's lack of response, most of the hunger strikers took a public vow to starve themselves to death, if need be, to wake up the president and the rest of the government too. Kovic immediately dropped out of the hunger strike, saying he was no longer angry enough to want to die changing the system. Other strikers were getting sick, and a couple had to be hospitalized inside the Wadsworth VA. But new strikers always appeared to replace the lost ones, and sometimes they were vets from the psych ward who had been taking Thorazine only the day before.

Even more dangerous, guns began showing up all over the encampment, despite Bitzer and McCarthy having decreed no booze, drugs, or weapons anywhere near the protest. What made the situation still more dicey was the blurring of the veterans' demands. Sometimes a new GI Bill was included, sometimes an audit of the entire VA. Other vets felt they were fighting to preserve the Vet Centers, to force the VA to award disability compensation for PTSD (still almost impossible to get), or to restore the full VA budget. Fortunately, there was still a core of goals that both the inside and outside groups seemed to agree on, even if, as Kovic told Bitzer, "Gandhi must be rolling over in his grave" to see half-crazed, armed veterans trying to pull off nonviolent civil disobedience. Those core goals, the gravity that still held them all together, however tenuously, comprised: 1) a meeting with Reagan; 2) an independent investigation into Hopkins' death and into VA health care generally; 3) an independent investigation into the long-term health problems caused by exposure to Agent Orange; and 4) some form of delayed reentry program, including a complete medical and psychological exam for all Vietnam vets, help with discharge upgrading, and outreach to veterans with PTSD and dioxin-related illnesses.

The government's solution, as it had been for over a decade, was to try to split the unity of the veterans' movement. Although Shad Meshad's radical activism had never endeared him to the VA bureaucracy, the big guns at Central Office announced that they would send a delegation to Westwood to negotiate *with Meshad,* who was conveniently still on a government payroll, as if Washington had the right to designate a leader for the hundreds of protesting vets in California. Meshad eagerly jumped at the chance to cut the Gordian knot of the Wadsworth strike, and thus to become a major veterans' leader. To be fair to him, he felt he knew what was really going on a lot better than Bitzer and Kovic. He had actually worked with Hopkins in therapy groups after some of Hopkins' earlier suicide attempts, and he was convinced that Hopkins' claims of having been in combat were completely bogus, that he was a deeply frustrated guy who was trying to act out some John Wayne or Sergeant York fantasy to give himself importance. Meshad felt that by pushing him to center stage, Bitzer and Kovic were "making a patron saint of a guy who's not a real Vietnam vet." Meshad also suspected that many nonvets had recently joined the encampment, telling wild war stories just to get the attention of the media. Bitzer and Kovic privately acknowledged that some of their "troops" were pretenders; and Meshad felt if they weren't constantly "running on emotion" they'd know it was time to throw in the towel, before they destroyed the credibility of the whole crusade for veterans' rights.

Meshad, in what seemed criminal audacity to Bitzer and Kovic, went on dozens of radio shows, and was even flown to New York to appear on *Good Morning America,* to discredit the Wadsworth protest, and to push his own cause, which was the preservation of the Vet Centers. Having gone from being "the golden boy for Carter" to number one on Reagan's VA hit list, subject to all sorts of harassment (including phone taps and death threats), Meshad felt like he had reached his "last stand, Custer against the Indians." Unless the public's attention was diverted away from what he saw as the Wadsworth circus, and back to the vital need for more Vet Centers to deal with the real, daily crisis in many veterans' lives, Meshad believed his entire life's work since returning from the war was down the drain. Above and beyond the politics, he claimed there were two overriding reasons that impelled him to try to end the protest. First, he did not want to see any Vietnam veterans starve to death—no matter how good the cause, and with a cause like Hopkins he felt they would be dying "for nothing." Second, he knew that with so many armed vets on one side, and so many police, SWAT teams, L.A. County Special Sheriff's Force deputies, and FBI agents "just waiting to shoot somebody" on the other, the situation was ripe for a bloodbath—and he was sure the vets would get the worst of it.

Meshad thus proceeded to negotiate with the VA for the entire duration of the strike. But Bitzer and McCarthy managed to "ace him out" (in Bitzer's words) by getting all the vets both inside and outside to repudiate Meshad's leadership. As far as Bitzer was concerned, someone working for the VA was simply not qualified to be negotiating with the government on behalf of a hostile constituency like Vietnam veterans. Bitzer still respected Meshad as "a very dedicated person," but Kovic was convinced he had become a traitor; and it infuriated Kovic to see Shad's face peering out of the fourth-floor office of the hospital administrator, where he imagined Meshad spilling all of the veterans' secrets to "the enemy." A rift opened between Kovic and Meshad, his former counselor, during that period that never fully healed.

The government also courted Bobby Muller, leader of the fledgling Vietnam Veterans of America. Though VVA still had less than 5,000 members—less than one-tenth of 1 percent of Vietnam-era veterans—Muller's presence was already strongly felt in Washington. Moreover, Muller was such an articulate and colorful speaker that the press relished going to him for quotes and commentary; and unlike Kovic, Muller, with the disciplined mind of a lawyer, always backed up his arguments with a wealth of statistics. At the time of the hostages' homecoming, Muller had declared that Vietnam veterans ought to join in the celebration, not throw a wet blanket on it, as Kovic and Bitzer had done at Patriotic Hall. Now Muller again jumped in on the government's side, claiming to represent a voice of reason in the Vietnam veteran community, in contrast to the dope-smoking, gun-toting radicals at the Wadsworth encampment.

Indeed, the government had stooped to using smear tactics against the entire protest and its leaders. According to Kovic, VA spokesmen repeatedly told the media it was just "a bad element" who were taking part in the sit-in and the strike, and that the whole rebellion had been "fomented by outside agitators"—meaning Kovic, Bitzer, and McCarthy. Moreover, the government portrayed them all as gangsters, who were trying to extort benefits they didn't deserve through threats and intimidation. Hence Kovic was aghast to see his old comrade-in-arms Muller, who had fought by his side against Richard Nixon at the Republican National Convention, also denouncing the Wadsworth protest as irresponsible and not the proper way to bring about change. After Muller attacked the protest in the *New York Times*, claiming that it did not represent the position of the majority of Vietnam vets, Cable News Network asked him to debate Kovic and Bitzer on national television.

Muller, still in D.C., appeared in front of Kovic and Bitzer on a big TV screen in CNN's L.A. studio. Kovic recalls that he felt sad seeing Muller in his three-piece suit and tie, his formerly long wavy hair cut short and going prematurely gray; it was clear he was "cultivating a new, mainstream image." Still, Kovic thought perhaps Muller had a right to appear as a kind of "elder statesman," and he wanted to yell, "Hey, Bobby, how ya doin'?" But Muller right away commenced "poking and prodding" at the two of them in a "caustic" manner, trying to "assert his dominance" in a way that reminded Kovic more of ruthless Teamster boss Jimmy Hoffa than of the fierce, defiant young paraplegic in the Bronx VA hospital that he remembered, determined to walk in braces if it killed him, or the friend who had coaxed him to speak that first time at Levittown High School. Kovic and Bitzer argued that the struggles and sacrifices of the vets at Wadsworth were admirable; that they were locked in a life-or-death battle, and needed everyone's support. Muller, however, looking hard as "granite," refused to show sympathy for any of them. Addressing himself to "Mr. Bitzer" and "Mr. Kovic," Muller contended that the confrontational approach no longer worked; and sounding a lot like John Kerry ten years earlier, he instructed them that the only hope for veterans was to work within the system, and specifically, to work through his organization, VVA. Kovic was especially piqued by Muller's statement that the Wadsworth protest was "of no consequence in the greater scheme of things."

It was Bitzer who lashed out hardest at Muller. He told him that the guys at Wadsworth had been disenfranchised a long time ago, that this was the only forum they had for their complaints, and he taunted: "We're not about to end this hunger strike for you, Mr. Muller." As Muller prepared to respond, the sound went out on his part of the broadcast; the show ended with an unusually mute Bobby Muller, clearly furious and staring "steely-eyed" at his opponents.

"Who does he think he is—God?" Kovic said afterward. He was convinced that a lot of Muller's condemnation came simply from his instinct to compete— they had both been pole vaulters in high school—and that Muller was jealous of all the media attention the California vets were getting. For Kovic, that was no excuse to undermine hundreds of vets who were going through "agony" to make a better world for their brothers, and he swore that day that he would never forgive Bobby Muller, no matter how long he lived.

Even Shad Meshad believed Muller opposed the Wadsworth protest because he "hated Ron Kovic." Muller admits that his suspicions were raised as soon as he saw that Kovic was involved. But in his own eyes he was fighting to save the veterans' movement by trying to end the protest, even as Kovic and Bitzer felt they were fighting for the same cause by keeping it alive. To this day, Muller has no regrets about his role in helping shut down the demonstration.[166]

By late May 1981, Robert Nimmo had already been nominated as the next VA administrator, though he was not yet confirmed by Congress. Nimmo's pick for deputy administrator, Nick Longworth, as well as the VA's acting general counsel, Robert Coy, were both men that Muller had "gone around the track with" for many years working on veterans' issues, and they all shared a "common agenda." Longworth told Muller that Nimmo would be happy to help Muller win congressional commitment to keep the Vet Centers, and that Nimmo much preferred to have Muller representing Vietnam veterans than Dave Christian, who, even though he was a Republican, seemed too much of a "wheeler-dealer" (as Muller recollects the conversation). Longworth then told Muller that once Nimmo took office, the VA would move in many of the directions Muller wanted. There was, however, a quid pro quo. Longworth said the Wadsworth protest was endangering support for Vietnam veteran programs both in Congress and within the VA. "What I need is your help," Muller recalls him saying. "Help me defuse this situation. It's counterproductive. It's raising the hackles of the people that I'm trying to get to cooperate with us, to make happen what we need to have happen."

Muller also talked with Coy, who assured him that Hopkins was a fraud, that he had only been in Vietnam "a day or so," and that his wife had concocted the whole story of his PTSD. Figuring that "this thing was a scam which was playing into the hands of the people that were trying to knock out the Vet Centers and PTSD," Muller felt he had to expose it as a "bullshit issue" before the scrutiny of the press did so, and "tarnished" all of them with his lies. It had taken many years just to convince a majority of congressmen and VA bureaucrats that PTSD was *real* and deserved a special program, and Muller feared that one "phony" like Hopkins could bring the vets right back to where they started, with those in authority looking askance at every PTSD claim. Moreover, "grabbing" this particular "engaging banner," which was destined to "dissolve," would "make it that much harder to get people to rally behind [their] next banner," no matter how credible the cause. "Hopkins was not where we wanted to draw the line," Muller asserts. "If you're not right in what you're saying, you lose the only thing you can really sell, which is integrity and reputation. What they [the Wadsworth protesters] did was emotionally appealing, but emotions won't carry the game. If we are not truthful, we got nothin'."

Finally, Muller felt that even if Jim Hopkins' cause were real, continuing to demonstrate in support of it would likely damage "the advocacy of the [PTSD] issue." No matter what programs were legislated to help veterans, Muller knew, "the agency [the VA] can frustrate the expressed intent of the Congress in innumerable ways." In other words, you don't bite the hand that feeds you; and if you're a veteran, you try not to piss off (or on) the VA.

Ron Bitzer could not have disagreed more. "I always felt that the VA was the logical target for a protest," he says. "It was beautiful to see vets encamped right at the VA hospital in tents. I thought, *What an embarrassment to the government to have disabled vets come right up to the steps of the VA and not go in! What an indictment of the system!*"

The growing divisiveness within the veterans' community, though, was ugly and frightening. People on all sides were receiving death threats. Vets were continually attacking other vets with vicious words and character assassinations. It was as if they all hated the mirror image of themselves, Kovic said, as if every time someone rose up and became a strong leader, other veterans had to tear him down. It was hard to tell how much of the feuding and the madness was real, and how much was due to undercover agents and provocateurs sent by the government. Fistfights broke out daily, and a veteran tried to rape a nurse (who was there to support the protest) in a phone booth. Some of the vets attacked Kovic for continuing to act as spokesman when he was no longer on the hunger strike. One of the hunger strikers, Clarence Stickler, a Marine vet whose head had been split open by a grenade in Vietnam but whom the VA had denied disability compensation, threatened to punch Kovic out if he didn't stop hogging the limelight. One night Kovic was awakened in the tent where he was sleeping with his friend Pat Marinello, and a vet from the psych ward pointed a loaded pistol in his face. The vet told Kovic he was going to pull the trigger, and Kovic fully expected to die. Then the vet walked away, and was immediately grabbed by hospital security.

Guys in hospital pajamas roamed the encampment. Some who were on Thorazine stood frozen in strange positions, like mannequins. So many physical and psychic casualties in one place made Kovic think of the movie *Night of the Living Dead*, as if he were finally witnessing the full "scrap heap" from the Vietnam War, and he could no longer stand being there for more than a few hours at a time. As the hunger strike moved into its second week, several vets began suffering major health problems, but the VA's Nick Longworth refused to authorize the daily physical examinations for them that Bitzer requested. A diabetic named Alejandro Lopez, a former Marine infantryman, grew dizzy and nauseous and had to be taken into the Wadsworth emergency room; he was coaxed to quit the strike by his wife and children, who were told he might die if he did not eat soon. Most of the other strikers were now taking juice to keep their strength up, but they renewed their pledge to let the government "keep seeing funerals" till it met their demands.

While Ronald Reagan refused to be inconvenienced by a visit to the Wadsworth vets, he found time to address the Army cadets at West Point on "defense issues." Following up on an earlier speech in which he had called the Vietnam War a "noble cause," Reagan told the cadets that "in much of the '70s there was a widespread lack of respect for the uniform, born perhaps of what has been called the Vietnam syndrome." But he assured them that "the era of self-doubt is over," and that contempt for the military had been a "temporary aberration." An editorial in the *Charlotte Observer* suggested the president should listen to the pleas of the "bearded veterans collapsing during the hunger strike" at Wadsworth before he pronounced the nation completely healed; and rather than offering the nation more of his cheery rhetoric, it opined, "he should do more for the veterans of that divisive war." Likewise, Senator Alan Cranston sent Reagan a telegram, advising him that "the problems of these veterans are continuing symptoms of the terrible heritage of the Vietnam War," and urging the president to "reply to the Vietnam veterans who have contacted you in order that your Administration may open a meaningful dialogue with them." The striking vets were even becoming part of popular culture. A Paul Conrad cartoon in the *L.A. Times* showed the Wadsworth Hospital with the caption: "No parade was scheduled again today for Vietnam veterans."

Throughout society in general, there was widespread support for the protest. The vets were visited by delegations and representatives from such groups as the Southern California Council of Churches, the L.A. County Federation of Labor, the L.A. County Board of Supervisors, and the Alliance for Survival (an antinuclear group), as well as a car caravan of Irishmen who were picketing the British consulate. Most passionate, and most heartwarming, was the support from the veterans' community. Letters and telegrams poured in from around the country—some from individual vets, some from groups like the Texas Brotherhood of Vietnam Veterans, and some even from government entities, like the City of Oakland's Vietnam-era Veterans Program. Sometimes they were sent formally to the Center for Veterans' Rights; more often they had an address like "Inside 6 / Wadsworth Lobby / Brentwood VA Hospital / Los Angeles CA," or even just "Ron Kovac [*sic*] / Wadsworth Medical Center / Los Angeles"—and, as Rebecca says in *Our Town*, "the postman brought them just the same." There were long personal sagas of difficult recoveries from the war.

There was pithy praise, such as: "YOUR FRONT LINE STAND IS IN THE TRADITION OF THE VIETNAM VETERAN"; and succinct advice, such as "HANG TOUGH." But few were more to the point than the solecistic question which Robert L. Dupee of San Bernardino hoped the veterans would pass along to the president: "IF YOU WILL NOT HELP THE VIET NAM VETS THEN HOW CAN YOU EXPECT AMERICANS TO FIGHT FOR THEIR COUNTRY AND IT'S IDEALS IN THE FUTURE?"

What really scared the government was the fact that vets at other VA hospitals were talking of organizing similar protests. Vets in Santa Rosa, California, even took over the post office there to show support. After the first "sit-in in sympathy" with the Wadsworth vets began at the Elsmere VA in Wilmington, Delaware, on May 29, the reaction to the whole affair at Central Office (according to Nick Longworth) was "consternation." A reporter from the Washington-based veterans' newspaper *Stars and Stripes* told Bitzer the government was "scared stiff" of a national veterans' strike against the VA. Determined to stifle the first rumblings of discontent, the VA put its GSA police on alert at every VA hospital. Not that the VA was any less worried when it learned of another group that planned to stage a "Welcome Home, Vietnam Vets" rally for the hunger strikers and the rest of the Wadsworth encampment: the unofficial brotherhood of California motorcycle clubs, a large proportion of whose members were vets themselves.[167]

The VA's first move was to try to sweep the whole mess under a legalese carpet of evasive promises. On Thursday, May 28, 1981, at the request of the president, Dr. Donald Custis responded to the May 20 telegram from Ron Bitzer (he had never bothered replying to Bitzer's March 16 letter). Custis's letter, like those of Bitzer, was widely circulated to the press. Custis informed Bitzer, first, that "the President had decided to continue the ongoing work of the Interagency Work Group" that was studying the health effects of Agent Orange, and that in 1982 the IAG would have nearly $10 million for research, three times what it had in 1981. Custis affirmed that such research would be "a major priority of this Administration." Second, Custis pointed out that Reagan's latest budget gave the VA $1.3 billion more than it had been given the previous fiscal year, and that Reagan was no longer advocating reductions in personnel in the Department of Medicine and Surgery or the elimination of any veterans' services. Third, concerning the Outreach Program, Custis directed Bitzer to study the Reagan Bipartisan Budget Resolution, which had been sent to Congress on April 28. That resolution allowed for spending up to $26 million to fund the Vet Centers for fiscal year 1982, *if Congress chose to extend the program.* Almost as an afterthought, Custis noted (in what was really the most substantial policy statement in the entire letter): "The President wants you to know that he is specifically committed to keeping the Outreach Centers funded and open. . . ."

Custis's letter hit the volatile Wadsworth encampment like a bombshell.

Suzanne Hopkins, who had become something of a loose cannon, immediately held a press conference declaring victory. Five of the hunger-striking vets celebrated by dining at a restaurant on Sunset Boulevard. Their spokesman said Reagan's response "was a lot more than we thought we were going to get." Bob Muller immediately sent out his own letter to Bitzer and Kovic, with copies to everyone from Ronald Reagan down to the director of the Wadsworth Medical Center, stating that VVA believed Reagan had met the protesters' "most significant goals" in a "commendable manner" and that, in the case of the Vet Centers, "a major breakthrough" had been made. According to Muller, "to continue protesting in light of the very significant commitments the hunger strikers were given is unwarranted" and would constitute bad faith. Moreover, he warned Bitzer and Kovic that "any continued action" now would cause "serious and irrepairable [sic] damage to the Vietnam Veterans community." In conversations with the media, Muller stated his case even more strongly. He said that "the deal was cut," that he had a "memo" from Nick Longworth "pledging" that all the claims and commitments enumerated by Custis would be carried out; that, in short, to keep bitching now made Vietnam veterans look like "unreasonable" troublemakers.

Muller's letter effectively shut off support to the Wadsworth vets from the thousands of vets now affiliated with VVA. It also convinced the moderate protesters to quit, pulling out the segment in the middle that Bitzer and McCarthy had been best able to manage, and leaving the extremes: the weirdos, psychos, and "living dead," on one end, and the fire-breathing radicals on the other. Bitzer had wanted to low-key the hunger strike, feeling that it tended to draw attention off the main issues and also to escalate hostile feelings on both sides. He also sensed that the hunger strikers were reluctant to "join forces with the main effort" toward VA reform; that their action was fueled mainly by raging ego. Because Vietnam veterans had suddenly become a hot topic, a young advertising agent, a nonvet, saw his chance to make a big splash and put a couple of the strikers on *Good Morning America;* and after that, so many vets (usually of the crazier, attention-starved variety) jumped onboard the hunger strike that Bitzer had to create a daily scorecard to keep track of them. A disciple of Gandhi, Bitzer had also wanted to keep the inside protest completely peaceful and minimally disruptive; but more and more, the unruly mob in the Wadsworth lobby—dozens of whom sported orange T-shirts that said "Inside Six" or just "JH"—interfered with the normal functioning of the hospital.

Bitzer was torn after receiving Custis's letter. There were clearly some victories in it—not the least of which was the fact that it had been sent at all. They had also won, without seeking it, he says, "the first formal support of the White House for the Vet Center program." But overall it was "a bitter disappointment." It offered "no new proposed changes in the Veterans Administration," and much of what Custis took credit for had been achieved by Congress, not

Reagan or the VA. The $10 million for Agent Orange research, which Custis had attributed to Reagan's goodwill, had already been mandated by Public Law 96-151. Likewise, it was Congress that had voted—against the president's stated wishes—to appropriate $26 million for Operation Outreach in Fiscal Year 1982. The Reagan Bipartisan Budget Resolution that Custis ballyhooed failed to guarantee that money would be spent on any specific items in the VA budget. Moreover, there were glaring omissions in Custis's response. He made no mention of their demands for a delayed reentry program and a meeting with Reagan, and he likewise ignored their call for an investigation into Jim Hopkins' death.

But the failure that most bothered Bitzer was Custis's refusal to address the matter of a nationwide evaluation of VA hospitals by non-VA investigators. The issue was a sore spot with Bitzer because he had been stymied on it several times before. After dealing with hundreds of complaints from the Long Beach VA Hospital in the late 1970s, Bitzer had gone to Washington and researched many little-known VA regulations. One of them specified that each VA hospital must perform quality-assurance studies, which they called "physician peer review." On a hunch that the VA wasn't even attempting to fulfill that obligation, Bitzer filed a Freedom of Information Act request for all the peer review documents for a specific period of time from the Long Beach hospital. When the Legal Aid Foundation went to bat for him, the VA realized it had a major problem on its hands—mostly, Bitzer suspected, because they had no such documents to show him. The government's response was to rush a bill through Congress making it illegal for the VA to release peer review documents to the public. Hence Custis's silence on this topic seemed to Bitzer just further evidence that "the Veterans Administration may be *incapable* of responding honestly to Vietnam veterans in 1981 or ever."

It was not really a question of calling off the protest, which now had a wild momentum not subject to any one person's will, but whether or not Bitzer should remain its representative. He chose to see it through to the end, knowing that his education credentials (which included graduate school at Columbia University and academic publication of his veterans' research) compelled the VA officials to respect him more than they did any of the other leaders. Kovic was also pushing to keep the protest alive, figuring they should hold out till Reagan came—just as the hunger strikers had won in 1974 by forcing Donald Johnson to meet with them. There were still many people behind them, many things in their favor. They received donations of juice, computer time, and medical attention from non-VA doctors and nurses. A "People's Vet Center" was set up in the lobby to calm vets who might be going over the edge. Support on the East Coast seemed to be growing as well. They got a favorable mention on the national TV news magazine *20/20,* and a couple of Philadelphia radio stations gave them daily coverage.[168]

4. Tents in Lafayette Park: The Hunger Strike Moves to Washington

At the end of the second week, the VA sent a four-man negotiating team to Wadsworth, led by Robert Coy. They insisted on meeting with Bitzer alone, which made him feel vulnerable, especially since Coy spent much of the time on the phone with his bosses in Washington, being coached on matters that Bitzer could scarcely keep track of. According to one of Meshad's assistants, Ray Scurfield, Coy was "a very conservative Republican, a straight Central Office character," whose mission was to scuttle the protest, rather than to respond sympathetically. Bitzer's failure to quickly gain concessions from the VA made a number of the vets turn against him, and one of them even pulled a knife on him. Bitzer then let McCarthy take over the negotiating for a while, which Coy crowed about to the press, claiming "the spokesmen with whom he dealt changed almost every day."

The VA was feeling the heat as much as Bitzer, however. Stressed-out vets were coming out of the woodwork, and the encampment continued to grow. The *L.A. Times* coverage became increasingly sympathetic. One highlight was an op-ed piece called " 'Crybabies' No More—Except in Mourning" by UCLA lecturer and Vietnam vet Frank McAdams. A former Marine lieutenant, McAdams asserted that the only crying he'd done was for the seven men in his platoon who "joined the select group that ended its pain forever over there." He lambasted Reagan for the "bloody hypocrisy" of his posturing as a "gung-ho patriot," and suggested that many of the peace movement people "have shown more sympathy, understanding and support for Vietnam veterans" than the majority of politicians and generals, whose sons "received special draft-board consideration" while "the 'peace people' were being clubbed by police in Chicago" trying to end the war. McAdams said he was sick of hearing well-off, middle-class Americans, including American Legion members of Reagan's generation, asking: *"What do you Vietnam people want?"* McAdams replied with his own question: "What is the matter with the U.S. government that it is so reluctant to help a group of people—Vietnam veterans—who fought the most unpopular and longest war in our history?"

On Friday, June 5, Custis sent a second letter to Bitzer. This time he promised the VA would perform "an in-depth review of the health-care delivery" at the Wadsworth and Brentwood hospitals "with specific reference to the Hopkins case." He also acceded to Bitzer's request to have "an independent review of these same areas," including "the adequacy of medical evaluations relating to disability claims associated with post-traumatic stress disorders" and "the adequacy of Agent Orange screening examinations." He promised that he would act "as soon as possible" on Bitzer's request that the VA appoint patient representatives at its medical centers, and he offered to have an expert in the toxic effects of herbicide exposure conduct a briefing for vets in the Los Angeles area. Finally, he offered to sponsor a meeting in Washington, D.C., for representatives from the various Vietnam veteran organizations, at which all issues and proposals would be open to discussion, including a delayed reentry program, the extension of eligibility for GI benefits, and disability compensation for post-traumatic stress disorder.

Bitzer was elated both with Custis's promises and with his new supplicatory attitude, as the medical chief expressed hope that they could work together "to improve the quality of life of all veterans." Yet the *L.A. Times* reported on Saturday morning, June 6, that "'serious, delicate' negotiations" were continuing with "no end in sight." Part of the problem was that hunger strikes have a life of their own—as Bitzer had feared early on. During that third week, two more strikers had collapsed, Charles Bass and Max Inglett, and both had been hospitalized inside the Wadsworth facility, Inglett with a serious kidney infection. Heady with a sense of having the government "on the run," many of the protesters also felt a need to avenge their fallen comrades by winning every last concession before quitting the field. And so they were still calling for Reagan to leave his ivory tower; though some vets argued for accepting a "scaled down" surrender, such as formal White House approval of the latest VA agreements, while others required a meeting with at least a White House representative. Coy, on his side, was adamant that the government had reached its limit of giving; and he commented snidely that "if the president sent a telegram every time Ron Kovic broke the law, Western Union would make a lot of money." Then he added a menacing fillip, saying that for the first time the hospital was seriously "considering the alternative" of eviction.

Meanwhile, on Sunday, word was out that 1,000 bikers from all over California were converging on the Wadsworth VA. Panicking, federal authorities asked the governor of California to mobilize the National Guard. As the Harleys began thundering into the hospital parking lot around noon, ridden by massive, muscled homeboys with military medals pinned to their club jackets and cutoff vests, several National Guard helicopter troopships hovered expectantly overhead. But only about 150 motorcyclists showed up, and they spent the day quietly mingling with the protesters, drinking juice out of paper cups, and giving interviews to the media. The helicopters circled a few times, then left, taking the guardsmen back to a nearby base for what the government called "routine maneuvers."

That Sunday afternoon, another hunger striker went down, former Marine Richard Ogden, who had gone nine days on distilled water; he was later revived by a nurse. The bikers were visibly moved. One of their leaders, "Laco Bob," vowed that they would get every vet in California who could ride to come down the following Sunday, to show support for the strike and, if necessary, to replace any strikers whose health was jeopardized. The government took his promise seriously, since the motorcycle clubs had mustered 30,000 members to support a toys-for-children event at the Rose Bowl.

By Sunday evening, Coy told the press that talks between veterans and the VA had reached "an impasse." The White House, he said, had "refused to become involved in the negotiations," and Coy had no authority to speak for the president. He warned that the protesters faced expulsion or arrest if they did not leave voluntarily—but he avoided giving them a deadline. The vets were nonetheless already planning the next phase of the battle. "If they eject us from here," McCarthy told reporters, "we will simply go to Washington and make another effort to see the president." On Monday June 8, Coy met once more with McCarthy, but only to reiterate the VA's demand that the protesters clear out. On the lawn, Ogden collapsed again and this time had to be hospitalized; and another striker, Robert Ware, who'd gone thirteen days on just liquids, was too sick to continue. Other vets immediately replaced them.

The VA had all its excuses lined up. Many of the vets occupying the lobby supposedly were not vets but "bums," and no one could argue that many of them (even those who *were* vets) looked the part. Moreover, the inside/outside distinction had blurred, as vets on the lawn regularly came in to use the washrooms, and many roamed the hospital halls all day to proselytize the patients or just as a form of diversion. VA counsel Robert Coy said they were keeping Wadsworth from providing its usual "type of quality care." At 6 A.M. on Tuesday June 9, having given warning a few hours earlier, the VA moved to end the protest, which was beginning its twenty-first day.

Facing a wall of forty-eight GSA police, with a substantial force of FBI agents behind them, the campers outside rapidly packed up their tents and belongings and left without resistance. A small group stayed behind to clean the trash and cigarette butts from the lawn and to sweep up the lobby. According to Steve Androff, who was in his fourteenth day of fasting, the hunger strikers wanted to show themselves as law abiding. The only one to remain was Max Inglett, who now lay in critical condition inside the hospital, having refused to accept anything but water for seventeen days. Seven of the inside protesters, who chose to practice passive resistance, were carried out by guards and later fined $10 each for trespassing.

Robert Coy gloried in his apparent victory. The protest "didn't have to happen," he told the press. "I think we're a nation of laws and there's a legal way you can communicate with your representatives and those involved." Unable to resist throwing yet another of his barbs, he professed that the Wadsworth demonstration had "built barriers rather than bridges." To show his magnanimity, he offered the protesters his private telephone number at the hospital, in case they wanted to keep talking.

Meanwhile, a fleet of trucks, followed by a media caravan, was taking the protesters to St. John's Church on Adams Boulevard near Watts, home of the

Center for Veterans' Rights. Bitzer's idea was that they should all go into retreat there for a few days, to cool their emotions and reconnoiter. He felt they were "on the cusp of something big," but that the way to make it happen was "to follow up on the headway they were making locally." The hunger strikers, however, had already made up their minds and were gleefully shouting, "On to Washington!" They set up an empty five-gallon Arrowhead water jug and began asking for contributions to cover the cost of travel. The celebrities who had been supporting the strike—like Mike Farrell, star of TV's *M*A*S*H,* and Robert Walden of *Lou Grant*—stuffed in wads of cash; and in the coming days, the jug filled to the very top with hundreds of smaller donations.

Soon after their arrival at St. John's, Ron Kovic was sitting in the parking lot talking to some TV people, telling them that he planned to go along to Washington for a stepped-up confrontation with the government. Suddenly Clarence Stickler walked up and punched Kovic in the mouth. Stickler had been on the hunger strike for eighteen days, but no one was paying him any attention. It came out later that Stickler had already been diagnosed with both epilepsy and paranoid schizophrenia, but had repeatedly been refused treatment by the VA. Stunned, Kovic began screaming for help, and several vets pulled Stickler away from him. But Kovic remained deeply shaken, and immediately retreated to Bitzer's house in Pasadena with Pat Marinello, who advised him to get out of town before someone actually killed him. The next day, Kovic flew back to his hideout, the York Hotel, in San Francisco; and three months later he took the Concorde to Paris, intending yet again to go into permanent exile from America.[169]

Bitzer too found himself repudiated, if not quite so violently, by the hunger strikers. (And he too would soon abandon the veterans' movement for an extended stay in India.) Bitzer's counsel to turn to meditation and prayer vigils had little appeal to guys who were adrenaline-driven and manic from having pushed their bodies to the limit. Besides, as Steve Androff recalls, they were all getting "fuzzy" and "paranoid" from lack of food. On the one side, the government was pushing their buttons—telling them, for example, that after a month they still couldn't figure out what had killed Jim Hopkins—and on the other, rabble-rousers were playing on their desperation, egging them on to raise the stakes, even to the point of instigating nationwide riots. Comedian Dick Gregory told them that if they pressed on as the civil rights protesters had, they would surely "win a great victory for the people." So the next day, Wednesday June 10, they all decamped from St. John's and moved to TV evangelist Gene Scott's Faith Center Church in suburban Glendale, to prepare for their grand assault on Washington. Scott, whose money-raising techniques had been under investigation by various government agencies for several years, supported the kind of aggressive tactics that Bitzer had studiously avoided—to the point of letting Hell's Angels park their Harleys on his church lawn. As Allan Parachini wrote in the *L.A. Times*, the focus of the protest had changed, and the protest-ers were now talking with radical zest—as Kovic had years before—of "pitch-ing tents on the White House lawn."

Yet, despite the omens of approaching disaster, something magical had hap-pened; some little angel, as in a Jimmy Stewart movie, had tipped the balance in favor of the veterans. The *L.A. Times* reported the end of the Wadsworth demonstration in a front-page story that seemed openly biased toward the vets, painting them as decent joes waging war against insensitive and out-of-touch bureaucrats. Two days later, the *Times* ran a powerful editorial cartoon by Paul Conrad, showing the rows of white tombstones in a veterans' cemetery, with one tombstone saying, "Let's declare this a lie-in in sympathy with the VA sit-ins!" and its neighbor replying, "We can't. This is Government property!" Parachini's piece on the Glendale encampment, which followed on June 18, contained extensive interviews with many of the protesters, letting them tell their own heartbreaking stories—like former Army engineer James Doran, who'd been traumatized by seeing ARVN troops dismember Viet Cong bodies. Doran had lost his VA educational entitlement during a lengthy recovery from a motorcycle accident; then, when he protested, was told (like Jim Hopkins) that his records had been lost. His life had taken a steep slide into depression and helplessness; he hadn't worked in two years, had been supported by his sis-ter for the past year, and told Parachini that unless the VA gave him a "fair shake," he'd probably remain in "never-never land" till he died.

The first of the Wadsworth protesters, led by Michael McCarthy, arrived in Washington the week of June 14, 1981. Calling themselves the Veterans Coalition, they announced plans for a massive mobilization of Vietnam veter-ans in the nation's capital on July 4. Response from the government was almost instantaneous. On Tuesday, June 16, the U.S. Senate voted 98–0 for a bill that authorized the VA to treat Vietnam veterans whose ailments were attributable to Agent Orange. While the bill did not specify how a vet was to prove his sick-ness came from herbicide exposure, it was still a major breakthrough. Praising the measure's passage, the *L.A. Times* declared that "at least the principle of helping Agent Orange victims has been established."

During the rest of June 1981, Congress passed several more bills to benefit Vietnam-era veterans. The House unanimously approved an extension of the Vet Center counseling program for three years (later reduced in compromise to two years). Both the Senate and the House voted to give Vietnam veterans two more years to use many of the provisions of the GI Bill. The House also enacted a law making Vietnam veterans eligible for low-cost Small Business Administration loans of up to $200,000. At the very end of the month, the House unanimously passed H.R. 3499, its own version of the earlier Senate bill "providing [for] expeditious health care for veterans suffering from Agent Orange and expanding the scope of the Agent Orange study mandated by

Congress in 1979." The hunger strikers showed their gratitude on June 30 by voluntarily reducing their number from twelve to nine.

In Los Angeles, Bitzer, despite having become a leader without an army, kept up pressure on the VA. On June 17, he requested a meeting with the "outside team" of two physicians, who had supposedly just completed their "independent evaluation" of the Wadsworth and Brentwood hospitals. What he learned was that the two doctors had spent three days at the Westwood VA complex, but they had mostly looked into the mishandling of Hopkins' case—apparently with a view to doing damage control for the VA. Ironically, they hadn't even called Hopkins' widow. Nevertheless, one of them, Dr. Robert Wallerstein, was brave enough to say that "many of the complaints of the protesting veterans were valid." This was still a far cry from the full-scale investigation the protesting veterans had demanded, and Bitzer did his best to raise a fuss with press conferences claiming they had been shortchanged and calling for a more extensive follow-up.

The VA quickly fought back. They released to Ronald Soble, a friendly contact at the *L.A. Times,* an allegedly complete set of Hopkins' military and medical records. Soble promptly used this material to publish a three-page article in the *Times,* entitled "Viet Veterans' Martyr—A Fantasy Hero?" Soble claimed Hopkins had never been wounded in Vietnam and had received no medals. His MOS (military assignment), wrote Soble, was not infantryman but "supply clerk." He portrayed Hopkins as a dreamer with a weakness for booze, who was "simply trying to con the VA into giving him a monthly benefit check." The Wadsworth vets, he concluded, had "picked the wrong individual to rally around." Even these supposedly damning records, however, established that Hopkins had spent his five and a half months in Vietnam in some pretty dangerous places. For three and a half months he had been stationed near the DMZ, and had made helicopter runs to Con Thien, one of the most heavily besieged pieces of South Vietnamese terrain in the entire war—ironically, the very place where Hopkins' detractor Bobby Muller had himself been wounded. Hopkins' last two months in-country had been spent with an infantry unit guarding Quang Tri Air Base, which was subject to continual enemy mortar and sniper fire.

Bitzer knew the story would be "extremely damaging" to their cause, and he protested that the VA had no right to release records that were usually considered confidential. The VA replied that since Bitzer had already released records of Hopkins' inadequate treatment at the Brentwood Facility (which had been smuggled out Pentagon Papers–style), the seal of confidentiality had already been broken. Bitzer pointed out that he had had the permission of Hopkins' widow to publicize those documents, but the VA did not back down from its campaign to discredit Hopkins, nor did they apologize to his family.

In Washington, the Veterans Coalition worked originally out of St. Stephen's Church of the Incarnation on 16th Street, which had once served as a base for

Martin Luther King Jr. But in a matter of days, Michael McCarthy triumphed in obtaining permits to assemble and camp, first, in Lafayette Park, and then in Constitution Gardens, where the Vietnam Veterans Memorial Wall would soon be built. Dozens of military tents went up right across from the White House—as Ron Kovic had once envisioned—and the twelve hunger strikers kept a round-the-clock vigil. Steve Androff recalls that they were still getting a huge amount of media attention, both international and domestic. "You turned on the TV, and every channel, it's on there," he says. "They're talking about the spraying and what it is and who's the victims. And they've got all these vets they're interviewing, and they're pulling up their shirts: 'This is what it looks like.' You've got these guys saying, 'Oh, I've got that too.' There were a lot of guys walking around that didn't know that they were poisoned. They knew something was wrong. This brought the whole thing about PTSD out in the open, too, at the same time. And they got a lot of the prison programs together because of this. In the long run, history will probably prove that this was the best thing that happened for the Vietnam vet."

According to Androff, they set up petitions to Congress for the vets who visited their campsite to sign; and in the four weeks they were in Washington, they gathered several thousand signatures. By now, there were thirty-one members of the Vietnam Veterans in Congress (VVIC) caucus. The sponsorship of the VVIC—led now by Representative Tom Daschle from South Dakota—gave the encampment legitimacy and ensured that they would get a hearing on Capitol Hill. The Agent Orange bill passed by the House was weaker than the one passed by the Senate, and neither one addressed the full range of issues raised by the strikers. House Veterans' Affairs Committee chairman Sonny Montgomery (D-Miss.) still displayed some skepticism toward Vietnam veterans' special needs; and there was fear that when the House and Senate got together in a conference committee to reconcile the two bills, the Senate version would be drastically watered down. McCarthy argued with wavering congressmen that *both* bills needed toughening. Building on Bitzer's work, he suggested the new law compel the VA to establish medical protocols for dealing with both PTSD and phenoxy herbicide poisoning, and that it require the protocols to be designed by "a committee of Vietnam veterans and non-VA experts in concert with the VA."

Even legislation would mean nothing, McCarthy pointed out, if the VA was incapable of interpreting it. Currently the VA employed not even one expert in toxic herbicides, and its one "environmental physician" happened to be a thoracic surgeon. He also argued that the proposed VA epidemiology study include "the detection and treatment of psychological effects of exposure to Agent Orange"—thus probing for the "missing link" many vets suspected between Agent Orange and PTSD. The hunger strikers announced that they would continue their strike on a full diet of juice until an acceptable compromise bill was signed into law, and until other major issues were discussed by Congress, such as a delayed reentry program. They were heartened by news that a group of Vietnam vets in prison had begun fasting in sympathy with them.

Although the hunger strikers were discussed every day in congressional hearings, the president continued to turn a deaf ear, as well as a blind eye to the tents in Lafayette Park and the vets marching every day with a garrison flag past the White House gates. When Reagan was caught by a reporter who asked him point-blank about his views of the strike, he quickly parroted the standard line that most of the protesting vets had already been satisfied, and that the VA was "handling the situation" regarding the rest. During the first week of July, several more strikers were winnowed out by health problems. Of those who remained, all claimed to have fasted over a month, and most counted more than forty days. Dick Gregory had quit as their advisor, however, because of his concern that at least some of them were not rigidly adhering to the fast—a concern shared by Bitzer, who had heard tales of nightly parties with both food and girls.

What kept the protest working was a sense of cooperation on issues larger than any individual. Like the AVM seven years before, they embraced "the broad spectrum of the American Nation," but they did so with the sort of cheery good-heartedness that AVM had desperately lacked. "We have come here on a mission of life, not death," read one of the hunger strikers' official statements. "We are working . . . to hopefully celebrate with the American people . . . the beginning of the end of the Vietnam War at home." Thus nobody could fault them for grooving with the Beach Boys and boogieing to Richie Havens at their big Fourth of July rally in Constitution Gardens—attended by thousands of people, both vets and nonvets. And when they announced the start of "Vietnam Summer," it was somehow a thing of friendship, goodwill, and, as they said, "good faith" in their government—unlike the season of antiwar anguish and frenzied protests that was given the same name by SDS back in 1967.

On Monday, July 6, 1981, the hunger strikers testified before members of both the House and Senate Veterans' Affairs committees. They were heard with great respect; and thanks to the behind-the-scenes work of researchers like Bitzer, they had a thick sheaf of facts to present in support of their arguments: a post-Vietnam death rate twice as frequent as during the war, with 57,000 vets dead between 1973 and 1979 from suicide, cancer, and "death under mysterious circumstances"; a divorce rate double the national average; an unemployment rate still double the national average, and one out of four vets earning less than $7,000 a year; one-third of the adult-male prison population composed of Vietnam veterans; and an estimated half-million Vietnam vets manifesting "a severe inability to assimilate back into American Society"—among others.

Several more meetings and discussions with congressmen were held during the next ten days, and three more strikers dropped out as "a gift to the public" for their show of support. *Time* magazine's cover story "Viet Nam Vets: Fighting for Their Rights" appeared the second week of July, as Congress continued to wrestle over a final version of the Agent Orange bill and several new Vietnam veteran measures were introduced. H.R. 3971, submitted by VVIC member Leon Panetta (D-Calif.), required the VA "to establish patient ombudsmen" at its medical facilities—whose lack had long been decried by Bitzer. There were now only three hunger strikers left—Steve Androff and John Avalos, who had begun their fast on May 27, and Tom Paster who had joined them on May 31. Congress, at least, showed increasing concern that they might die, and even Sonny Montgomery began to soften toward them. On Tuesday July 14, Panetta brokered a meeting between the protesters and several key congressmen, at which the hunger strikers were offered, as a concession for their agreement to end the strike, one last, all-embracing hearing before a select subcommittee of the House Veterans' Affairs Committee.[170]

5. The Cost of a 10-Second Jeep Ride: "This Protest Isn't Over"

At the final congressional hearing in 334 Cannon, all three hunger strikers were invited to speak, and they proudly arrived "all dressed down" in starched fatigues and spit-shined boots. Besides the VVIC and Veterans' Affairs committee members, many notable congresspeople were present, including Senator Edward Kennedy and Representative Shirley Chisholm, as well as representatives from VVA and the VFW—not to mention about twenty cameramen. During the testimony, Androff felt someone nudging him to make room at his table. It was Max Inglett, back from the grave, with a big smile on his face. He had started for Washington with a couple of other strikers on the Fourth of July, in a motor home painted red, white, and blue and dubbed the "Freedom Express." After falling sick again in Salt Lake City, he had flown on to D.C., arriving just in time to testify himself. Telling of the difficult choice he had had to make—whether he could help veterans more as a dead martyr or a live activist—he upstaged even the "heavy-duty confrontation" of Tom Daschle and Sonny Montgomery with the spokesmen from the VA. The congressmen and the VA chiefs were wrangling over who was better qualified to decide the best interest of Vietnam veterans; but this day, at least, thanks to the guts of those like Max, the Vietnam veterans got to speak for themselves, and the American people heard them loud and clear.

After the conclusion of the hearing, Congressman Panetta addressed the full House to announce that the last three Vietnam veteran hunger strikers would end their strike on Thursday July 18. Panetta used the occasion to read a lengthy statement into the *Congressional Record*. "It is truly unfortunate that these veterans felt they had to resort to a hunger strike to gain the attention of the administration and the Congress," he chided his colleagues. He also read from a written "Response" that the VVIC members had given the protesters, filled with promises and commitments regarding Agent Orange, PTSD, and other veteran needs. The twenty-one members of Congress who signed the "Response" declared, among other things, that they found the veterans' "complaints about inadequate medical treatment justified and their overall proposals for redress quite reasonable." They also—a first in the history of American government—applauded the action of the protesters, and lightly slapped the president's wrist for failing to do so: "We strongly support the right of all Americans to petition the government for redress of grievances. While we cannot speak for the Administration or the President concerning the coalition's desire to meet with President Reagan, we will endeavor to establish, at the earliest possible date, a panel of interested Members of Congress to hear the concerns of Vietnam Veterans."

The congressmen pledged speedy action in almost every area of veterans' concerns, with the exception of a delayed reentry program, which they deemed "not feasible at this time" because of its expense. The cost of screening the slightly less than 3 million men who had served in Vietnam was estimated at $270 million—the price of two MX missiles, as Ron Bitzer pointed out. The VVIC did add apologetically: "In no way do we imply that our work on behalf of Vietnam veterans is complete. Much remains to be done." A few days later, an editorial in the *Christian Science Monitor* said much the same thing, warning "Mr. Reagan" that he could not afford to remain aloof from the problems of Vietnam veterans: "Until their wounds are healed, the nation's wounds will not be healed."

After fifty-three days without solid food, Steve Androff broke his fast, along with his two remaining comrades, and was briefly hospitalized for swelling in his legs and feet. He and his "big burrito brother" John Avalos had both lost over forty pounds. They returned to Los Angeles as heroes, and for months nearly every veteran they met would offer them a free steak dinner. But Androff always reminded people that "the whole thing started out with Jim Hopkins trying to get treated for Agent Orange"—that Hopkins was the real hero. Androff remembered Hopkins as "just another guy" who used to stop in the gas station where he worked in Pacific Palisades, near the Vet Center. Androff had suffered for years from a skin rash that the doctors were unable to diagnose, and he and Hopkins talked about having many of the same physical and nervous ailments, and about their mutual problems in getting help from the VA. Androff knew him merely as "Jim"; but when he saw a picture of that 1946 Willys Jeep in the newspaper, he "put two and two together."

Two days after the end of the hunger strike, newly sworn-in VA administrator Robert P. Nimmo announced that the Outreach Program would add 42 Vet Centers nationwide during the next three to four months, and that the program's budget for the next fiscal year was being increased to $29.6 million.

Hopkins' ten-second Jeep ride was about to benefit hundreds of thousands of Vietnam veterans, to the tune of hundreds of millions of dollars. For all the rhetoric that had been expended for a decade and a half, urging Vietnam veterans to work for change *through the system,* the truth was that more had been gained for them when Hopkins crashed through those double glass doors of the Wadsworth Hospital, and from the two-month-long protest that followed—with all its violence, threatened violence, and coercive tactics—than had been won in fifteen years of peaceful lobbying.

In the end, even Bobby Muller, though he never outright approved, backed off from his attacks on the hunger strike, seeming to tacitly acknowledge (in the words of Steve Androff) "that this was maybe the only way to expose the VA for what they really were." It was clear from the start that Robert P. Nimmo had been dragged kicking and screaming to the aid of Vietnam veterans. On July 15, 1981, the day Nimmo moved into 810 Vermont NW, he was quoted in the *New York Times* as saying that Vietnam vets "had not been shortchanged by the Government." According to the *Times,* he also "disputed charges by some that Vietnam veterans had been treated with 'less sensitivity' than other veterans." Ron Bitzer was one of the first to smell a rat, and he immediately wrote to Nimmo demanding a detailed explanation of how the VA planned to implement all the promises made by Dr. Donald Custis in his June 5 letter. Specifically, he complained that the brief visit of three physicians to the Brentwood and Wadsworth hospitals was hardly an "in-depth review" by anyone's standards; and he asked why even the limited findings of those three doctors had not yet been released. But though Bitzer ended his letter by pleading that "an urgent need exists for Vietnam veterans and the government to communicate," he did not hear directly from Nimmo until two months later.

In the meantime, Nimmo and a couple of VA medical directors came to Los Angeles to conduct a "briefing" at the Brentwood Psychiatric Facility on the health effects of Agent Orange exposure. The catch was that neither Ron Bitzer nor any other local Vietnam veteran activists were invited or even notified in advance. Learning of the briefing at the last minute, Bitzer did his best to get the word out to the veterans' community; but the CVR was out of money and running solely on volunteer energy, and he and an assistant only managed to round up a small crew to confront Nimmo and his entourage on August 17. They were allowed in to the briefing, but only as spectators. Afterward, Nimmo held a press conference at the VA regional office in the Federal Building, where he tried to explain the VA's foot-dragging on Agent Orange and other issues raised by the Wadsworth protest by saying that other veterans' groups had urged him "not to go too far" in changing established VA procedures and policies. Bitzer and his group held their own press conference outside the building, protesting Nimmo's secret maneuvers and their exclusion from the Agent Orange discussion.

Bitzer tried writing to the hospital administrators of Wadsworth and Brentwood, and got no answer. In September, Nimmo finally sent him copies of the three reports by the independent investigators, after Bitzer had forced his hand with a Freedom of Information Act request for them. And though Nimmo finally ordered the Long Beach VA hospital to appoint a patient representative (a year and a half after Custis had promised to create such a position), Bitzer felt he and his fellow activists were now being treated as "has-beens" by the VA. The government people's strategy, he believed, had been "to try to mollify" the protesters while they worked "to get the media on their side again." Certainly Nimmo's letter to Bitzer on September 10 had a softer tone than one might have expected after Bitzer's public denunciation of him, with Nimmo pledging: "We are sincerely interested in the well being of all veterans, including those who served in Vietnam, and we are committed to carrying out our responsibilities in an appropriate and understanding manner."

That, however, was the last communication Bitzer ever received from him. Nimmo kept one of the lowest profiles of any VA administrator, in a field of eleven mostly undistinguished names. His short tenure was marked chiefly by benign neglect, though he did seem to have a grudge against Agent Orange disability claimants, exclaiming at one point that they had no cause to grumble about something as inconsequential as "teenage acne." More typical was the sighting of Nimmo at a Washington golf course during the groundbreaking for the Vietnam Veterans Memorial Wall. Nimmo's ouster came just about the time of the Wall's dedication in November 1982, when Reagan got sick of all the bad publicity he'd generated—friend of Meese or no.

For the VA, the Wadsworth protest had been a bureaucratic wrinkle to be smoothed, but for the vets involved—and especially for those who needed help—it was harder to forget. A lot of powerful bonding went on there, but eventually people had to return to their own far less glamorous lives. "There's a letdown," Bitzer observed. "One day you're on national media, the next day you're cold potatoes. And so a lot of these guys went through withdrawal."[171]

One guy who had gone by the wayside amidst all the powerbrokering was Clarence Stickler, the brain-damaged vet who had literally knocked Ron Kovic out of the veterans' movement. Having traveled to Washington with the other protesters, he had continued his hunger strike for forty days, using his own money to buy juice for those who were broke. John Avalos, president of the Veterans Coalition, would later say that it was Stickler who had pulled them through the toughest time, before Congress threw open its doors. Avalos also said they all "really respected him." On July 2, Stickler had collapsed, and soon afterward had gone home to his mother in Port Hueneme, California. Both his head and body were out of kilter from the fast, and his schizophrenia was exacerbated by the crazy fragmentation his life had fallen into. A thirty-five-year-old man with no job, he was treated with contempt on the street, and even by his ex-wife, who kept him from seeing his two children; but he was still getting asked to give interviews on radio talk shows. Knowing he needed help, he tried to check himself into the Sepulveda VA on July 22. At first, the intake workers told him he was not sick enough for hospital admission. When he dropped one of their IBM typewriters on the floor—"to show them how easy it was to destroy something," he told his mother—they changed their mind.

Not only had his head been smashed against a tree by a grenade explosion in Vietnam, which led to frequent epileptic seizures, but he also suffered from severe delayed stress. He told his friend Steve Androff that it was due to more than just the usual "pressures of being under fire." Androff recalled that he "had been troubled for years by what he had seen and done in Vietnam." Stickler claimed he had been ordered to kill entire Viet Cong families—men, women, and children—and that as a good Marine he had not questioned his commanders. After he got home, he said, he "used to cry like a baby" every time the memories flashed before him. He was also tormented by survivor guilt because he had gone on leave in Bangkok the week that most of his squad had been killed in action.

The Sepulveda VA initially admitted Stickler to their PTSD program. But hearing him quote from the Bible and describe visions of perpetual-motion machines, the doctors were convinced he was just an ordinary loony. They also believed he was making up the story about being blown into a tree, because his combat records did not mention a head wound, and so they refused to certify his illnesses as service connected. Moreover, they felt he was too "antisocial" to benefit from group therapy with other vets. They reluctantly kept him hospitalized there through August, letting him out on weekends to spend time with his family. On Saturday August 22, while out on pass, he got into a brawl with his brother, another troubled vet, and bashed him with a board. Arrested for assault, he was sent back to the VA hospital on August 26. This time they stuck him in the general psychiatric ward. Stickler was extremely hostile, fought with other patients and refused to take the tranquilizers they gave him. They discharged him for noncooperation on September 1, 1981.

Stickler was deeply depressed. He told people that he had been fighting for three years to get help at the VA, and that, judging by the guys he'd met on the strike, he probably had to "look forward to" ten or fifteen more years of rejection and humiliation before the government admitted his claims. Besides, he was nearly broke and had no place to sleep. Two days later, his mother paid a week's rent for him at the Milner, a cheap hotel on South Flower Street in downtown Los Angeles. He talked to both Androff and Avalos, seemed very moody, and bitched a lot about the VA. "They'd send me to the detox ward and then say there that I'm too crazy for this ward," he told them. "Then they would send me to the crazy ward, and they would say I'm an alcoholic." At times he did sound a little crazy, especially when he spoke on and on about his plans to live in luxury with the rich people at the Hilton. At night, in the hotel bar, nursing the few beers he could afford, he sounded even crazier talking about all the people he wanted to kill and the things God had told him and the angels he was seeing everywhere. It was time for him to come to heaven, he said. He usually ended up starting a fight and getting tossed out.

His mother paid for his room at the Milner for another week. On Sunday night, September 13, he called her to say he'd just watched a TV movie called *High Ice*, and that he needed to know the name of the highest mountain in the world so that he could go and climb it. She told him he didn't know anything about mountain climbing, but he told her, "Mom, I'm going to try." After he hung up, he set fire to his bed, then ran downstairs to confess that he'd tried to commit suicide. While the hotel staff put out the fire, Stickler disappeared. Early the next morning, he called his mother again, begging her to come down from Port Hueneme, fifty miles away, and pick him up; but she told him to go back to his hotel. He did, at 7:30 P.M. Monday night, wearing two huge black eyes. The hotel manager told him to get lost, and refused to return the two small suitcases that contained all his earthly belongings: clothes; girlie magazines; a Bible marked at the Book of Job; and clippings, papers, and a flag from the VA protest.

Half an hour later, Stickler walked into the nearby Los Angeles Hilton and took the elevator to the eleventh floor. People heard a tremendous crash as Stickler's body plunged through a window and hurtled in a shower of broken glass toward a roof ledge eight floors below.

Spokesmen for the VA said they "had no reason to believe that he was going to do this [commit suicide]" when they discharged him, and that they had deemed him "no threat to himself or society." Fellow hunger striker Bill Rigole said that, on the contrary, Stickler had often spoken of committing suicide if the VA failed him. Another fellow hunger striker, Gene Dorr, said he had repeatedly warned the VA staff handling Stickler's case "about the likelihood of Clarence committing suicide if he didn't receive help from them." Rigole, Dorr, and several other angry vets assembled on the Wadsworth lawn to accuse the VA of "criminal negligence" in Stickler's death. A different VA spokesman responded: "They seem to imply the VA is obligated to keep patients from committing suicide, and if they commit suicide, it's the VA's fault, and that isn't quite the system."

The Sunday after Stickler's death, many of his fellow protesters held a candlelight vigil for him in front of the Wadsworth Hospital. A year later, in June 1982, they presented plaques to the VA in honor of both Stickler and Hopkins (whose death had at long last been adjudged a suicide achieved by an overdose of two drugs, chloral hydrate and methaqualone, neither of which had been in his possession when he died).

The tributes were satisfying but, in a way, superfluous. Both men had spoken eloquently for themselves, without words. Hopkins had forced open a discussion that the highest figures in the U.S. government had spent years trying to stifle. Stickler's suicide was another wedge in the door. His most fitting epitaph came from John Avalos: "This was his way of saying, 'Hey man, this protest isn't over.'"[172]

9

The Specter of Chemical Warfare: Agent Orange

1. Victor Yannacone Takes On "A Walking Wounded, Sick, and Dying Army"

Paul Reutershan died of abdominal cancer on December 14, 1978, having lived longer than any of his doctors had predicted. The previous July, he had gone to the Islip, Long Island, law firm of O'Hagen, Reilly and Gorman, which handled claims for his railroad employees' union. Reutershan's medical bills were already astronomical, and he felt his family should not have to pay them. But even more importantly, he wanted to leave a legal mark against those who had poisoned him and his fellow Vietnam veterans, so that he would not have "died for absolutely nothing." Personal injury attorney Edward Gorman took the case, at least partly out of sympathy, since he himself was a veteran of many bloody South Pacific battles in World War II, including Guadalcanal. In September 1978, he filed a $10 million damage suit in U.S. district court against Dow Chemical and two other manufacturers of Agent Orange.

Gorman had, in fact, thought the case hopeless until he had met with a self-styled "country lawyer" from nearby Patchogue, Long Island: Victor Yannacone. On Sunday morning, August 6, 1978, he called Yannacone to invite him to lunch at the Oconee Diner in East Islip, to discuss Reutershan's suit. Yannacone had planned to spend the day fishing or playing golf with his father, but "propitious circumstances," he says, lured him to the lunch. That morning, he had been cleaning out his always voluminous files; and when Gorman called, he had been on his way to the Dumpster with "a cubic foot of Air Force material on dioxin and its environmental impact."

There was good reason for Gorman to go to Yannacone. Victor John Yannacone Jr. was one of those rare lawyers for whom the public welfare was virtually his sole reason for being. He had been raised on Long Island to fill the footsteps of his father, an equally feisty Italian-American legal advocate in the field of workmen's compensation and personal injury. But Yannacone had gone his father one better. In 1969, at the age of thirty-three, he had become the father of environmental law. Not only had he named the field, he'd written a two-volume book on it, *Environmental Rights and Remedies* (The Lawyers Cooperative, 1971).

In college, Yannacone's interests had lain in medicine, biochemistry, mathematics, and philosophy. But duty and his father had called all too clearly. He had bounced around among half a dozen schools, finally getting his law degree from New York Law School with (he claims) "the lowest average" in his class. Tall but not prepossessing—with thick glasses, receding, unruly hair, large nose, big jowls, and double chin—Yannacone might well have never gotten far beyond his little office on Rose Street except for two things. One was a tremendous flair for drama and a sense of his own self-importance on the world's stage. The other, even more significant, was hitting his professional stride at just that point when the crucial legal battles in American society were moving from civil rights to environmental protection. Having served as an attorney for the NAACP, Yannacone took the idealism of the early civil rights movement—the belief that society has a legal responsibility to protect the well-being of each of its members—and applied it to the earth itself and the corporations that were permanently altering it, destroying its habitability. The result was a legal revolution that, as Yannacone liked to boast, may well have taken sixties' New Age radicalism off the streets and into the courtroom, where it would prove to have a far more lasting impact.

The early environmental movement in America, kickstarted by Rachel Carson's book *Silent Spring* (1962), a fierce indictment of the entire range of agricultural chemicals as poison rather than panacea, met with a massive discrediting from both the chemical industry and those who viewed progress as bigger profit margins. Carson herself, dying of cancer when the book came out, was subjected to vicious attacks. By 1966, conservationists (as the environmentalists were originally called) were in full retreat, going out of their way to keep from seeming too aggressive or disruptive of the American way of mass consumption. As far as Yannacone was concerned, the soft voice of gentle admonition—letters to editors, appeals to government agencies—was utterly useless when human greed was in the picture. "Yannacone's law," he said, was: "When someone shoves, shove back harder"; and he claims to have coined the phrase: "Sue the bastards!"

He got his first chance in 1966, when the Suffolk County Mosquito Control Commission dumped 5,000 gallons of DDT into a lake near his home, where many people—hundreds of children, even his own wife—often went swimming. The lake was soon awash in dead fish; and Yannacone began to worry that the ongoing summer spraying of DDT might have a similar, although longer-term, effect on human beings. Yannacone filed a suit against the county executive in behalf of his wife, Carol, and "all the people of Suffolk County," including "those children yet unborn," asking the court to restrain the mosquito commission from further use of DDT.

Yannacone did not yet have either a legal strategy or sufficient evidence to win; but his suit was more than the crackpot effort the chemical companies at first thought it. In fact, it was the bold, if unsupported, opening shot in what later came to be known as the "DDT wars." Lacking testimony from scientific experts that could prove "serious, permanent, and irreparable damage," Yannacone relied on "Neanderthal" tactics like holding up a bottle of DDT to exhibit the skull-and-crossbones logo on the label, as proof of its toxicity. He planned to rely on ruthless cross-examination—of which he was a master—to show that the mosquito commissioner was completely ignorant of the health risks from the pesticides he so freely used. On August 15, 1966, Yannacone won an injunction—the first of its kind anywhere—against continued use of DDT by Suffolk County. Another major part of what Yannacone considered his victory was the founding of the Environmental Defense Fund (EDF) during the trial—a nonprofit organization that would promote similar litigation wherever feasible.

The most important achievement of the case, however, was Yannacone's creation of at least a tentative constitutional argument in support of "the right of all Americans of this generation and of those generations yet unborn to a healthful environment." The argument, which he would strengthen in subsequent cases, was based on the Fifth, Fourteenth, and especially the Ninth Amendments. The Fifth guarantees that no one shall be harmed without "due process" of law. The Fourteenth guarantees "equal protection" to every citizen, born or naturalized. And the Ninth opens the door wide to a host of other possible rights: "The enumeration in the Constitution, of certain rights, shall not be construed to deny or disparage others retained by the people." Through that door Yannacone introduced successive litigations intended to bring the chemical industry to its knees. The thrust of each suit was that "large corporations, especially chemical companies, in the U.S. today, because of their technological knowledge and economic power, are really fiduciaries of the public health, safety, and welfare," and that they have "a duty to warn consumers about any potentially dangerous effects."

During the late sixties, Yannacone was like an attack dog on a rampage against DDT and related insecticides. In the end, he succeeded in getting a judge in Wisconsin to declare DDT a "pollutant" under the water-quality provisions of state law. The public, educated to the harmful effects of the so-called chlorinated hydrocarbons, began to demand action; and city after city in the Midwest soon ceased using both DDT and a chemically similar, even more powerful poison called dieldrin. For his work, Yannacone received high praise from the National Wildlife Federation, which declared: "Most of the initiative for the conservation law movement can be attributed to Victor John Yannacone Jr."

During the following decade, Yannacone remained at the forefront of shaping environmental law. And so it was that in 1974 he was presented by the Air Force with the foot-high stack of documents on Agent Orange and dioxin. By that time, all of the military's unused Agent Orange had been moved from Vietnam and from a collection facility in Mobile, Alabama, to permanent storage on Johnson Island in the South Pacific. The barrels had started leaking, and the Navy brass in that area were terrified, according to Yannacone, that "if this herbicide really got into the Pacific Ocean, it could wreak havoc with the phytoplankton and protozoa and perhaps produce a worldwide eco-catastrophe." The Air Force, which maintained ownership of the herbicide, sought to burn all of it on a Dutch incinerator ship called the *Vulcanus,* but to do so they first had to file an environmental impact statement. It was for help in drafting this statement that they had sought out Yannacone.[173]

Hence when Yannacone met with Ed Gorman and his partner Pete Reilly, he had a whole box of evidence to offer them that the military regarded Agent Orange as a very toxic substance. Gorman and Reilly felt they were out of their depth in the scientific end of the case, however, and they offered to pay Yannacone to join them as chief litigator. Yannacone, surprisingly, refused. Although he felt Reutershan might well be correct about the cause of his illness, he also knew that no legal cause and effect had ever been established in a cancer case. Trying to prove a causal link between Reutershan's exposure to Agent Orange in 1968 and his cancer in 1977 was a bigger job than even Yannacone cared to undertake.

A few months later, when Reutershan died, Gorman realized the case would die too unless it were broadened to a class-action suit—an area in which he had little expertise. Once again, he phoned up Victor Yannacone, and once again Yannacone declined to get involved. A day later, a furious Vietnam vet parked his truck in Yannacone's driveway and vowed to remain until Yannacone agreed to take over the case. He said he had made a deathbed promise to Reutershan to continue the lawsuit in behalf of all Agent Orange victims, in order to "alleviate the suffering" caused by sickness and birth defects and to compensate the families of those who had died. It was Frank McCarthy, and he used all his Sicilian power of persuasion on his fellow *paisan.*

McCarthy told Yannacone he had been treated like a "moron" and an "insane person" by all the previous lawyers he had talked to for thinking he could sue a cluster of *Fortune* 500 chemical companies and probably the U.S. government too without putting up even a small retainer. He said he knew Yannacone wasn't interested in making money, that he was "totally fearless, one of the most articulate spokesmen in the world," and probably "the only man who had the balls and tenacity" to take on such a case. When Yannacone still refused, McCarthy switched from flattery to an appeal to Yannacone's patriotism. Like a lot of Italian-Americans, Yannacone was a staunch flag-waver, with an almost blind devotion to the country that had lifted his forebears from a land of chronic poverty.

McCarthy warned him that "the best and bravest of a generation, our Vietnam combat veterans," would lose their faith in "this great nation" if it seemed the legal system cared as little about them as the Department of Defense apparently had during the war, and as the VA quite clearly had afterward.

Yannacone replied that he was "burned out from the DDT wars." He told McCarthy that the environmental suits had cost him hundreds of thousands of dollars that he had never recouped. The vets had no chance of winning, he said; and besides, in the end the government might be to blame. There was always the chance they had given the chemical companies a "hold harmless" agreement when they'd purchased Agent Orange—which would mean the government had assumed all liability for potential injury from its use. He was now forty-three years old, tired of crusading, and "felt like a washed-out heavyweight" whom McCarthy was asking "to go out and do it one more time." Again Yannacone said no.

McCarthy went home, but he called Yannacone several times in the next 24 hours. Yannacone kept reminding him that there was no "strategy set in place, no case drawn up, no lawyers, no money, no nothing." McCarthy replied that no one had known how to take on "the legislative powers" and the president, either, but he'd already made Carter and Cleland sweat over the issue and was currently lobbying the House to begin holding hearings. "We'll go to any length," McCarthy told him. "We have an army. That's what we have. We have a walking wounded, sick and dying army."

Finally Yannacone said, "We can't win." McCarthy exulted to hear him use the first person plural: "Yeah, I know—so what?" "Well, we'll do it anyway," Yannacone sighed, and invited McCarthy back to his office to discuss the case. It was December 22, the day before his wedding anniversary, which always made him feel good (since his wife Carol was both his devoted coworker and best friend), and he was filled with the Christmas spirit. Later, recalling why he took the case, Yannacone explained that when hurting people came to him, he felt "trapped in this duty idea" that he had to "fix them." He had also kept hearing his father's voice, telling him that "litigation is the essence of civilization, it *is* civilization"—the best means man had devised "to leave the world a better place than we found it."

When they got back together, Yannacone told McCarthy he could not proceed until he knew what the goals of the case were to be. McCarthy laid out three: "find out what was killing these young men; punish the son of a bitch that was doing it; and restore the dignity of the Vietnam combat veteran as an American soldier." Yannacone immediately smoothed them out into legal language. The first became a quest "to obtain information about the health effects and risks associated with exposure to Agent Orange contaminated with 2,3,7,8-tetrachlorodibenzo-para-dioxin (TCDD), to which Vietnam veterans were exposed during military service in Southeast Asia." The second became: "to obtain compensation for disability and death from disease attributable to service in Southeast Asia." The third: "to obtain vindication of their rights as veterans entitled to at least the same rights and honor as American veterans of any other declared or undeclared war involving the United States."

McCarthy and Yannacone agreed that the bulk of monetary damages that might be won from the case should not be paid to individual veterans, but should go to establish a foundation and a trust fund. The chief reason was that McCarthy had already estimated—based on Reutershan's extensive networking—that there were probably at least 150,000 vets eligible to make Agent Orange claims. Therefore a settlement of even several hundred million dollars would be broken down to "chump change," Yannacone figured, when divided among so many people. The foundation would create and oversee, among other things, a legal assistance program for Vietnam veterans and a Vietnam veterans' casualty commission, which would compile and make publicly available demographic and medical information on all Vietnam veterans. The trust fund would reimburse the U.S. government for money it paid Vietnam veterans in Title 38 (service-connected) VA disability benefits and Social Security compensation due to Agent Orange–related illness. The trust fund would also be used to provide corrective surgery, mechanical aids, and other benefits to the children of Vietnam veterans who had been born with "catastrophic polygenetic birth defects." One of the goals of the suit, in fact, was to see that such children were "recognized for what they are—disabled American veterans of the war in Vietnam."

As Yannacone drafted his 186-page complaint, he once again put forward his notion that the American chemical industry "acted as a trustee of the public health, safety, and welfare." Admitting that such concepts "are alien to modern jurisprudence," he tried to push American law toward the "mainstream of jurisprudence . . . Roman law and the Talmud and a number of other good-quality sources." As in the past, Yannacone's erudition, eloquence, and wit threatened to undo him. His acrimonious break with the Environmental Defense Fund in the early seventies came largely from EDF board members' perception of him as an overly flamboyant and self-aggrandizing "showman," whose elaborate arguments were sometimes mostly hot air.[174]

His learnedness, however, had produced one theory worth following up. It was a theory he planned to unveil like the centerpiece diamond in a well-wrought monstrance once the case actually came to trial—when he got the chemical company executives square in the sights of his mercilessly analytical intellect. Yannacone had evidence that the granddaddy of all chemical companies, the German mega-firm I.G. Farben Werks, "knew all about the toxicity of dioxin" (even before the chemical had a name) as far back as 1888. They had already found that chlorinated hydrocarbons could be produced more efficiently at higher temperatures; but they soon discovered that the more efficient the process, the more it yielded a pernicious by-product, a chemical they called a "chloracnegen" because of its ability to cause a severe, persistent acne in those exposed to it. This "chloracnegen" was the very same substance that a few decades later would be described by the Environmental Protection Agency as "the most toxic small molecule known to man" and by Harvard biochemistry professor Matthew Meselson as "the most powerful carcinogen known": dioxin.

In 1914, according to Yannacone, the six major German chemical companies in the I.G. Farben combine created a business alliance with six American chemical companies, in order to make sure they survived the coming world war. In 1937, with the Second World War in sight, another deal was cut, formalizing the arrangement. Dow's sister company was C.H. Boehringer; Monsanto's was Bayer; Hercules' was Badischer Anilin. For Yannacone, this private history was vital to the Agent Orange case because of what he called "the 33,000 pieces of silver letter." In 1960, many of Dow's workers in the plant that produced 2,4,5-T (one of two major herbicides that would later make up Agent Orange) were falling ill. Monsanto had been having a similar problem with its 2,4,5-T workers since 1947. In 1949, there had been an explosion in Monsanto's 2,4,5-T plant in Nitro, West Virginia, which had contaminated more than 100 workers, many of whom became seriously ill and later died. Hence by 1960, the chemical companies understood that they had a problem with some highly toxic contaminant in 2,4,5-T. Dow wrote to its German sister company C.H. Boehringer for help. In response, Boehringer explained about the poisonous "chloracnegen" (dioxin) they had found in their own 2,4,5-T, and offered to sell Dow a recipe for greatly reducing the amount of that contaminant in future batches of the herbicide. Dow readily agreed to pay $33,000 for the information, but as part of the deal Dow had to pledge not to disclose the change in their process or any information about their workers' chloracnegen-related illnesses for a period of ten years.

The trick, it turned out, was simply to cook the mixture at a lower temperature. The new process somewhat decreased the yield of 2,4,5-T, but it also eliminated the massive workers' compensation problem that Dow had been facing; and so Dow quickly adopted it.

For the sake of protecting a trade secret, however, both Boehringer and Dow committed themselves to hiding facts about the dangerous and potentially deadly side effects of their herbicide. This was one very important part of the Agent Orange story that Yannacone was itching to bring out during an actual trial. It was why his second promise to the veterans—after pledging to vindicate them as soldiers—was to give them a "day in court." If he could prove that the chemical companies had lied to the government, it would not only let the American people see what kind of greed had been masking as patriotism for too long, it would also probably put the environmental movement back into high gear—and thereby give additional value to the sacrifice of so many veterans and their families.

Yannacone began with the premise that the veterans wanted truth more than financial gain. As he told *Barrister* magazine shortly after taking the case: "The veterans just don't care about money. They care about having something done, that this should never happen again. The hundreds of veterans whose claims are now being pressed and the children of those veterans, who must finish their lives lacking eyes and ears and with other defects and deformities, are eloquent testimony to a danger that can only be ignored to the peril of all of us so unfortunate as to be still at risk from exposure to contaminated herbicides." Speaking for all the vets he met through his Los Angeles storefront, Ron Bitzer stated the same position even more strongly: "Vietnam veterans knew [from the start] that a whole lot of money wasn't gonna come down, but they would very much have been helped by the truth on Agent Orange."

Another decision that was made within days of his taking the case was that Yannacone would not sue the federal government. In theory, the government was immune from having to pay damages to sick or injured servicemen, under the so-called *Feres* Doctrine, promulgated by the Supreme Court in a 1950 decision. In *Feres v. United States*, the court reaffirmed the concept of "sovereign immunity"—which dated back to the all-powerful kings of the Middle Ages—in order to protect the government from liability for torts committed against soldiers, which could have amounted to many billions of dollars after World War II. But Yannacone knew that many attorneys *had* filed tort suits against the government. Such action was not only an effective way to embarrass the government, but it could also have remunerative results. In an asbestos case brought by shipyard workers in Tyler, Texas, the government had paid $4 million in damages simply for the case's "nuisance value," even though no liability could be established. "Every lawyer worth a damn," Yannacone claims, "felt that they could shake the government down for money [in the Agent Orange case]." McCarthy, however, stressed to Yannacone that he and the majority of veterans he knew—ranging from career soldiers to draftees—did not want to embarrass the U.S. government with a lawsuit. According to Yannacone, "They could not believe that their government and their leaders and their officers would have ever deliberately poisoned anybody, least of all their own troops. No one heard anything in the course of their training that would have led them to believe that."

The issue of whether to sue the U.S. government was also a highly emotional one, as legal historian Peter Schuck pointed out in his book *Agent Orange on Trial*; it turned on one's interpretation of patriotism, and whether patriotism precluded ever attacking one's own country. McCarthy and Yannacone both took the position of "my country right or wrong." McCarthy felt he would betray the ideals Vietnam vets had fought and died for if he charged his own government with such high crimes. Yannacone claimed he "felt morally obligated not to sue the government."

Yannacone wanted to highlight the unswerving devotion to duty he had observed in many vets, even those who had been blatantly mistreated or gravely injured by their own government. His favorite metaphor was to equate the Vietnam combat vets with the Roman centurions, who supposedly did not leave their posts at Pompeii even in the face of burning lava from Mount Vesuvius. By focusing on "the dignity of the American fighting man" he hoped to avoid what he called "the politicization of the litigation," but in fact he just hastened it. From the moment that he filed his case, reporters began asking him: "Why don't you sue the government?" Yannacone explained that he "would not touch the politics of the war," and that he "didn't want to get into the morality of the war," because what concerned him was that "our troops went when our country called them." "They were entitled to be better served by the American chemical industry," he went on, and the fact that "the I.G. Farben successors here [Dow, Monsanto, et al.]" treated them in such an "amoral" manner "was enough moral outrage for this particular lawsuit."[175]

2. "Breaking Balloons": The Filing of the Class Action Lawsuit and the Birth of "The Cause"

The second presiding judge, Jack Weinstein, would later complain that litigating the Agent Orange case without the federal government was "like playing *Hamlet* without the Prince of Denmark." The left wing of the veterans' movement—the reconstituted VVAW (purged of the RCP) and Tod Ensign's Citizen Soldier (an updated version of the Citizens' Commission of Inquiry), for example—were quick to challenge what looked like Yannacone's cover-up of the strongest evidence yet of the war's inherent evil. Ensign and his partner, Vietnam veteran Michael Uhl, published a book called *GI Guinea Pigs* (Playboy Press, 1980), which used examples of both the so-called atomic vets (those consciously exposed by the Pentagon to nuclear radiation) and Agent Orange victims to try to prove once again that the United States was guilty of barbaric war crimes. "Once a nation's military command throws its own soldiers into the path of its weapons of destruction," they wrote, "has it not already forfeited the support of its own people as well as its capacity for defense?"

But even those less inclined to make political capital out of the Agent Orange tragedy wondered if there weren't some essential truths about the Vietnam War that needed to be examined during the course of the suit. Old-fashioned liberal Democrat Ron Bitzer, of the Center for Veterans' Rights, felt that justice— especially in terms of compensation—would not come to the Agent Orange victims until Americans were willing to admit the fundamental wrongness of the war. Every time the nation heard some new piece of Vietnam horror, Bitzer speculated, "it freaked the country out." And "once you turn this country upside down on something as basic as war and peace," he theorized, "you've gotta expect that the dust is gonna have to settle before they start listening to other concerns that you might have." For Bitzer, the Agent Orange lawsuit and its public trial could have been a means of settling some of that dust, and reestablishing a consensus concerning why America goes to war and how those who suffer from it should be treated.

Yannacone, however, insisted that if there were anything wrong with the war, it was the fault of the elected representatives who allowed three different presidents to make foreign policy, stripping them of their constitutional powers. Regarding Agent Orange, the only person in government Yannacone blamed was Secretary of Defense Robert McNamara. McNamara, according to Yannacone, had "stupidly" ignored the studies of his subordinates showing that the Vietnamese could not be starved out by herbicides, and that herbicide use would only serve to antagonize those farmers and villagers whose sympathy we were trying to win. McNamara's "war crime," in his eyes, was not poisoning both Americans and Vietnamese, but simply his "classical hubris" and "the bungling ineptitude of his management team at the Pentagon." To look further than that, he felt, "wouldn't do a damn thing for the veterans except dishonor them." As for the big questions—"who started the war, whether it should have been continued, whether we should have nuked Hanoi"—he considered them all meaningless from a legal point of view. They were "the kind of stuff that's best left for philosophers and historians."

His approach to Agent Orange victims was not to see them as the casualties of an unjust war or of a political mistake. He believed that "wars are never right or wrong, wars are only expedient"; and the Vietnam War in his eyes "was inexpedient. It did not solve any problems." The thrust of his lawsuit was in quite a different direction. It was "to graft into soulless corporate entities [the multinational chemical corporations] a moral standard and a conscience."

At 11 A.M. on Monday, January 8, 1979, Yannacone filed his 186-page complaint in the United States District Court for the Southern District of New York, in Manhattan. It was, as he describes it, a "white paper structured by the need for public information and education." He boasts that it "contained everything that was known in the world at that time about the use of phenoxy herbicides in Vietnam and the toxicity of dioxin." It also contained the corporate histories of the five named defendants: Dow, Monsanto, Hercules, Diamond Shamrock, and Thompson Hayward. Gorman's firm was no longer listed as attorney for plaintiffs; it was Yannacone & Yannacone, the little Patchogue firm of Victor and his father, purporting to represent the entire class of injured Vietnam veterans. By the time Yannacone stepped off the Long Island railroad at 2:30 that afternoon, his office had already received hundreds of phone calls from media sources all over the world. By his recollection, he spent the next twelve hours with a telephone stuck in his ear, "until three A.M., when Australia signed off."

The Agent Orange lawsuit, for better or worse, would bring Vietnam veterans more publicity than any event since the fall of Saigon. Because it "came out of nowhere," as Ron Bitzer put it, it rocked a nation that was finally certain it had laid Vietnam to rest forever. It was also, Bitzer claims, "blown out of proportion because some bright attorneys knew they were working in a vacuum." For years, many veterans' advocates would rue the day Agent Orange came to public notice—not because those many thousands of vets and their children who were affected did not genuinely need help, but because the issue often distracted attention from other less dramatic problems, such as PTSD and unemployment, which afflicted far greater numbers of Vietnam veterans.

Other veterans' advocates decried Yannacone's swift plunge into litigation for a different reason. Attorney Tod Ensign, practicing military law from his office at Citizen Soldier, was approached for help by Reutershan and Gorman even before they contacted Yannacone. "Just overwhelmed with the idea of what it would mean," Ensign had turned them down flat. His instinct was "that it was a massive undertaking, and that anyone who would even have the chutzpah to take it on should do so with a real sense of modesty and careful planning and the desire to mobilize as many resources as possible." Yannacone's daring had guaranteed that he would be designated lead attorney, but in Ensign's eyes he "was totally unqualified to handle the case," since he had never before tried a product liability case. But Ensign blames the ensuing "disaster" as much on himself and his fellow attorneys as on Yannacone. They were all passively saying, "Oh my God! This thing is beyond our ken!" he explains, when they should have "gone around the country and mobilized a really effective committee of lawyers who had the experience Yannacone lacked, and then presented him and others with a fait accompli." Yannacone would then have been forced to integrate his efforts with theirs. Instead, everyone, including VVA, "let a situation grow that was very inimical to seeing justice done." Because of the nature of class action, all subsequent attorneys representing Agent Orange victims— which included Ensign—were tied to the same case, and the Multi-District Litigation Act imposed the same rules on all of them. Hence they were all "stuck with Yannacone's leadership, which was," in Ensign's view, "by and large nonleadership."[176]

Yannacone very much wanted the cooperation of Vietnam Veterans of America (VVA), and for a few months he received limited help from them. A great deal of Bobby Muller's lobbying strategy was currently being developed by a brilliant, nonveteran Yale Divinity School graduate named Steve Champlin, who served as director of VVA's Washington office. He was, in Yannacone's view, "the power behind the throne." As soon as Yannacone filed his suit, Champlin offered to trade data with him. Yannacone had a great deal of material on Agent Orange, other herbicides, and dioxin, including Air Force records and other military information, that Champlin wanted; and in return, Champlin offered an equally large body of confidential information from Capitol Hill, concerning the points of view of various legislators whose support Yannacone sought. In March 1979, a few months before both the House and the Senate held groundbreaking hearings on Agent Orange, Yannacone met with Muller and Champlin at the Holiday Inn on Nesconset Highway, near Muller's home.

Muller had painted himself into a corner regarding Agent Orange, and he was looking for a graceful way to get out of it. Frank McCarthy, who had supported Muller in creating the Council of Vietnam Veterans, had gone to speak with Muller as soon as Reutershan clued him into the Agent Orange issue. Muller did not want to hear about it, and he and McCarthy had many bitter fights on the subject. Muller thought the big Vietnam veteran issue of the eighties was going to be dapsone, an antimalarial drug routinely given to GIs in Vietnam, which had turned out to be carcinogenic. "He saw the emotion [in the Agent Orange issue]," Steve Champlin recalls. "He could go to a room with twenty vets and get the guys standing up and banging the table [at the mention of Agent Orange]. But he couldn't figure out how Vietnam vets could argue [causation]." According to Champlin, Muller was especially leery of the Agent Orange issue because the VA and almost all its medical directors maintained that it was completely harmless, that "you could drink it for breakfast." Since Muller had to fight the VA on so many other issues—especially ones that were already well established, like PTSD—he felt that if he cried out about Agent Orange, they would just have something else to use against him. In Champlin's view, Muller feared that if he advocated for the Agent Orange issue and it proved bogus, he would be stereotyped for the rest of his life as just another "longhaired, idiot veteran yelling at the VA."

In addition, Muller, who had already aroused the suspicion of right-wing vets because of his VVAW background, may have sensed that he could not afford to take on the conservative wing of the veterans' movement over such an apparently shaky issue. Many Vietnam veterans who still saw the war as a worthy cause had reacted instinctively against the appearance of the Agent Orange issue, imagining that it was just one more left-wing ploy to discredit their military service and—to use the phrase coined later by B. G. "Jug" Burkett—to "steal their valor." Indeed, this position seemed to make sense at the time, and was voiced by a lot of heavyweights on the right end of the veterans' political spectrum. One such heavyweight was James Webb, a former Marine captain and combat veteran, who had won the Navy Cross, Silver Star, two Bronze Stars, and two Purple Hearts. Having gotten his law degree after the war, Webb became the first Vietnam veteran to work on a Veterans' Committee in Congress, serving as Minority Counsel in the House in the late 1970s. While managing during the same time to become a best-selling novelist (*Fields of Fire*), Webb provided legal counsel at numerous PTSD hearings and every Agent Orange hearing, save one.

According to Webb, "Agent Orange is the classic example [of veterans' issues being manipulated by nonveterans to justify their own actions] . . . The Agent Orange issue came out right about the same time the 'boat people' [refugees from Communist Vietnam] started showing up. And you had a lot of people, the Mary McGrorys of the world, who felt very comfortable just sort of damning the entire war experience, all of a sudden confronted with people who were jumping into the sea [to avoid torture in forced-labor camps], and not being able to flippantly say that this was an immoral, genocidal war [anymore], and yet at the same time not wanting to have to extend legitimacy to what the people [veterans] did there. And so what they did was they fell back on issues like Agent Orange, as a way to be able to extend some sort of a warm feeling toward a veteran without having to respect what he did."

When Webb became Secretary of the Navy under President Reagan, his fellow Annapolis graduate, Admiral Elmo Zumwalt Jr., would ask him why he took no interest in the Agent Orange issue. Webb replied, "I was there and I didn't get cancer, so I'm not worried about it."

Muller was savvy enough to know he didn't need enemies like Jim Webb.

McCarthy says that for months he "shoved Agent Orange down Bobby's throat till he could not turn away from it." But Muller was as stubborn as McCarthy and as little likely to be forced into a position not of his own choosing. What turned Muller around on Agent Orange, according to Champlin, was the Environmental Protection Agency's emergency suspension order against all domestic use of 2,4,5-T except on rice fields and rangelands. The ban on general use and sale of the herbicide went into effect on March 1, 1979. It was immediately appealed by Dow Chemical Company, still one of the major manufacturers of 2,4,5-T. But on April 12, 1979, Michigan Federal District Court Judge James Harvey ruled against Dow, upholding the suspension order and affirming that the EPA had good reason to judge the herbicide a health hazard.

The EPA had reached its decision on the basis of three impressive recent studies. One confirmed the claim that women in Alsea, Oregon, whose hills were heavily sprayed with 2,4,5-T, suffered almost three times as many miscarriages as women in herbicide-free cities such as Eugene and Corvallis. Moreover, miscarriages in Alsea peaked in June, eight to twelve weeks after the annual spring spraying of timberland. The other two studies were conducted in Sweden, and showed a strong correlation between exposure to 2,4,5-T and soft-tissue cancers. Although the Office of Technology Assessment and the Interagency Working Group on Agent Orange concurred that these studies were more credible than much of the previous evidence against the herbicide, there was a whole list of at least partly credible 2,4,5-T/dioxin horror stories in the few decades since the herbicide had been created near the end of World War II.

Besides the explosion at the Monsanto plant in 1949, there were similar disastrous health results from explosions at the Badischer Anilin & Soda-Fabrik

(B.A.S.F.) plant in West Germany in 1953 and the ICMESA chemical plant in Seveso, Italy, in 1976. In the aftermath of the latter contamination of 700 densely populated acres with trichlorophenol (a close chemical relative of 2,4,5-T), the pope even granted rare permission for certain women to have an abortion to prevent their giving birth to "monster" children. Even scarier was the revelation in the late 1970s that the whole neighborhood of Love Canal, New York, built on a toxic waste dump containing 140 pounds of dioxin, was awash with cancers, birth defects, and immunodeficiency illnesses of every variety.

In April 1970, the U.S. Surgeon General had issued a warning about the toxicity of 2,4,5-T, which had put an immediate stop to the Pentagon's defoliation program in Vietnam. The Departments of Agriculture and of Health, Education, and Welfare had also moved quickly to restrict domestic use of 2,4,5-T at that time. That unprecedented, near-panicked government response had been precipitated by the testimony of a biochemist, Dr. Jacqueline Verrett of the Food and Drug Administration, before a Senate subcommittee. Dr. Verrett asserted that dioxin was "100,000 to a million times more potent than thalidomide [a sedative given to pregnant women in the 1960s with terrifying results] as a cause of birth defects in some species." Her opinions were backed up by other experts, such as Dr. John Bederka at the University of Illinois in Chicago, who estimated dioxin to be "100,000 times more toxic than cyanide." "But cyanide is lethal with a single dose," Bederka cautioned, "whereas we don't know how dioxin is most toxic. Ten molecules a day for a year may be more toxic than a one-time exposure."

Yannacone would later claim to have evidence that dioxin is physiologically active even at the single-molecule level. As the Agent Orange case proceeded, he elaborated his "single hit theory," which presupposed that a molecule of dioxin could scramble the DNA in a cell's nucleus much like a quantum of ionizing radiation. Thus one molecule of dioxin striking an egg or a sperm cell like a well-aimed bullet could produce devastating birth defects if that egg or sperm developed into an embryo. Similarly, Yannacone hypothesized, on the basis of work by an endocrinologist from the University of Wisconsin named Ted Goodfriend, that a single molecule of dioxin might also damage one of the so-called stem cells in the human immune system. A limited number of stem cells produce all of the lymphocytes (B cells and T cells) that are necessary to prevent a bacterial or viral infection or to keep cancerous tumors from developing. Knocking out even a small number of stem cells, Yannacone argued, would be "akin to breaching a wall around a castle." Dioxin might thus lead to a person's death, not by direct action, but by making the body vulnerable to various invaders or renegade cells. This theory, said Yannacone, would account for the fact that so many veterans in their thirties were suffering from cancers and other diseases usually seen only in men of quite advanced age, when the immune system normally begins to fail.[177]

Yannacone discussed much of this scientific evidence with Muller and Champlin when they met for a long breakfast on Long Island. According to Champlin, Muller now felt he had a "green light" to speak out on the Agent Orange issue using the public platform of VVA. More than that, he felt that he had made a "strategic" goof in waiting so long and that VVA needed to "move in" on the issue in a big way. Without slighting Muller's genuine concern for the victims of Agent Orange, Champlin admits that Muller also saw the issue as an important "trick" that he could use in promoting the cause of a national membership organization for Vietnam veterans. Muller's main job at that time, says Champlin, was "getting people excited," and he knew that Agent Orange as a tactic worked well to that end.

Muller's response disappointed Yannacone greatly. The self-appointed president of VVA absolutely refused to get involved in the litigation, saying he had "bigger fish to fry"—by which he meant the building up of a mass base for his organization. According to Yannacone, Muller said he wouldn't do anything to hurt the Agent Orange victims' case so long as Yannacone "stayed away from fund-raising or tapping any of his financial sources." That settled, Muller then offered "to do anything he could" for Yannacone "without interfering with his own efforts." Yannacone had the strong feeling that Champlin was behind Muller's decision to stay out of the lawsuit, that he was a kind of "Rasputin" pushing Muller to politicize the organization for the sake of his own "hidden agenda." In Yannacone's view, "sick vets" were less important to both of them than the political revolution Agent Orange could help them to accomplish.

West Pointer Joseph Zengerle, who would later be appointed Assistant Secretary of the Air Force by Ronald Reagan, was already having arguments with Muller about VVA's growing political (and usually antigovernment) thrust. Zengerle would serve as VVA's counsel till 1982, but his own politics were decidedly "centrist"—certainly a lot closer to Yannacone's than Muller's were. According to Zengerle, "Muller wanted to throw a hand grenade at the VA system, to blow it up and start all over again." Agent Orange became a symbol to him, and another example of the hospital and benefit system that he "hated." Says Zengerle: "The whole thing had to be thrown out and redone. He wanted a new Bradley Commission [a government commission created by the Eisenhower Administration to examine the VA's failings]. Many people viewed that as throwing the baby out with the bath." It was difficult for Muller to see Agent Orange as anything less than another weapon in that political struggle.

Zengerle did not approve of the way Muller seized upon issues like Agent Orange to get attention. It was a question, he says, of "using the provocative credential of Vietnam veterans"—like "breaking a lot of balloons"—to make people sit up and listen. In the case of Agent Orange, the irony was that Muller remained "a little uncomfortable with the issue" itself—never quite sure of its validity—and at times saw it as a distraction from the causes he really wanted to pursue. Zengerle, however, took it upon himself to help Yannacone directly, pro bono.

Soon after Yannacone filed the class-action lawsuit, the chemical companies asked the court to issue a gag order, to keep Yannacone and his supporters—notably, Frank McCarthy—from traveling around the country to talk to Vietnam veterans' groups. Ostensibly, Yannacone and McCarthy sought to educate vets about Agent Orange and the nature of the lawsuit, but it was also clear that they were soliciting potential plaintiffs as well. As VVA's counsel, Zengerle (with Muller's tacit consent) filed an amicus curiae brief in defense of Yannacone's right to speak, on First Amendment grounds. The judge ruled against the gag order, freeing up dialogue on the Agent Orange issue—which was perhaps the one point on which all Vietnam veterans, including Muller, could agree.

That was, in fact, the last help Yannacone would ever see from VVA. In 1981, Muller led an official veterans' peacemaking delegation to Hanoi, which nearly destroyed VVA, as well as precipitating Zengerle's definitive break from the organization. John Catterson subsequently took over as chief counsel. A disabled Marine combat veteran who'd renounced his former hawkish views, Catterson eventually became an outspoken activist much in Muller's own mold. He had as little use for Yannacone as Muller, and steered clear of the lawsuit until just before the settlement.

In yet another ironic twist, it was Muller's apparent switch to Agent Orange crusader that led to open war between him and Frank McCarthy. Yannacone had guessed right about Champlin's "hidden agenda," at least insofar as Champlin had devised a three-part strategy for the "breakthrough" of VVA into national prominence. The three areas Champlin felt VVA needed to develop were 1) a strong media presence; 2) a sophisticated legislative strategy; and 3) a solid financial base, from both membership dues and mainstream grants. Muller's articulate, charismatic spokesmanship guaranteed media attention, and Champlin single-handedly engineered much of VVA's legislative strategy. But getting money was the nut they hadn't yet cracked, till Agent Orange came along.

McCarthy recalls Muller telling him, shortly after his meeting with Yannacone: "Now I know the vehicle that we're gonna be able to raise money with. This is *the cause.*" Indeed, VVA soon obtained a Ford Foundation grant to set up an Agent Orange hotline, which was publicized on hundreds of radio stations throughout the country. The hotline simply offered vets a means of obtaining information on Agent Orange–related illnesses, and most of the vets who called were mailed a standard packet, which included a VVA membership application. The hotline brought in 50,000 calls the first year, from which VVA was able to recruit nearly 10,000 new members.

It was over the hotline that McCarthy and Muller had their first fierce arguments. McCarthy had been hired to train the telephone operators manning the hotline, and it soon began to bother him that vets with serious problems were being grabbed up by VVA for their dues, dispatched a few pieces of paper, and then forgotten. He told Muller that VVA needed to develop programs and services for Agent Orange victims, which would include supplying referrals to doctors and medical centers. Muller was adamantly opposed to such forms of assistance—seeing them, apparently, as both a distraction and a financial drain. McCarthy was supported by a VVA staff worker named Joan McCarthy (no relation), who actually attempted to do some crisis counseling on the hotline. But Joan McCarthy left VVA within a few months, according to McCarthy, because of the resistance she encountered from Muller and other officers. Frank McCarthy quit right after she did, protesting that Muller was using Agent Orange as "the heartthrob that would bring the bucks," and that vets who contributed to VVA had been led to think their money was helping victims. He claimed VVA would even send media people to film seriously ill veterans, to "show that they were doing good work."

What finalized the split between Muller and McCarthy was VVA's first newsletter, which came out that spring (1979), just after McCarthy left VVA. The newsletter focused almost exclusively on Agent Orange, and it featured a story about Paul Reutershan, including an interview with him. McCarthy was enraged that Muller was now posing as the champion of his dead friend. According to Champlin: "Frank went ape-shit because [he felt] Reutershan was his private property. Bobby shouldn't quote him. In some ways, it *was* his private property, because Frank paid the dues and so he had a moral claim. But, on the other hand, it wasn't his private property; it was a movement."

On top of everything, McCarthy learned that Muller had arranged—and that VVA was taking credit for—new Agent Orange hearings before the House, which were to start on June 21, 1979. After the House Veterans' Affairs Committee had held a two-hour hearing on Agent Orange the previous October—a hearing stacked with "nonbelievers" from the VA, the Air Force, and the VFW—it had stonewalled requests for further hearings. Muller had gone to his friend, Congressman Albert Gore (D-Tenn.), a member of the Vietnam Veterans in Congress (VVIC), who had asked his friend, Congressman Robert Eckhardt (D-Tex.), to stage the hearings before the House Committee on Interstate and Foreign Commerce, which Eckhardt chaired. Gore (later vice president of the United States under Bill Clinton) was the perfect person to direct meaningful Agent Orange hearings, since he had spent several years dealing with environmental health issues and overseeing various toxic cleanups, including Love Canal. Yannacone had helped considerably by allowing Champlin to interview many of his clients and to select the most dramatic cases to bring before the committee.

McCarthy suddenly felt like the issue he had spent a year fighting so hard for, with virtually no money and no media, had been ripped off by (in

Champlin's words) "the Vietnam veterans' equivalent of a Wall Street investment bankers firm." Champlin explains: "Frank had been doing a terrific job when nobody else would. From his perspective, we [VVA] didn't do it as well as he did because Frank was one of those guys that'd be on the phone till midnight with you, if you had a crisis. But he didn't have the kind of money to advance a congressional hearing, which Bobby could do. Frank hardly had the ability to fly in and stay at a hotel. So Frank gets blown away, basically, and has bad feelings about it. And he has a right to have bad feelings, because as a result of VVA's moving in on his issue, the role he played kind of got forgotten. And when VVA started to make money, Frank was upset, because he felt that was his money."[178]

3. An Eight-Year-Old Stick of Dynamite Cracks the Government's Armor

There are several versions of what happened when Frank McCarthy confronted Bobby Muller in Congress on June 21, 1979. By all accounts, there was a good deal of screaming. Some say that McCarthy attempted to punch Muller. McCarthy claims he simply warned Muller that if he kept using Reutershan's story to promote VVA, he would sue him. Muller's response, he says, was to wheel into him and smack him in the balls, an area that was still excruciatingly tender because of unremoved shrapnel from a VC mortar. Tempted to hit back, McCarthy caught himself and dodged away, figuring Muller would love to give him the bad publicity of having "attacked" a man in a wheelchair. Several people sicked the federal police on him anyway. Though McCarthy was quickly released, he never forgave Muller for what he considered the ultimate betrayal of their friendship. McCarthy claims Muller could never look him in the eye again, that McCarthy had become "his fuckin' ghost . . . his conscience."

Champlin had a more pragmatic view of the incident. Muller, he explains, played for keeps; and once McCarthy chose not to work with VVA, "he paid a price for that decision." It was, in fact, both Muller's strength and his limitation that he saw people as either allies or enemies. McCarthy, for better or worse, had crossed the line into the wrong camp. "It's hard, because Bobby's just not gonna be intimidated," Champlin says, "and he's just gonna come back at you hard, and you're not gonna win 'cause he's in the wheelchair, so you're gonna have to give up."

Though both McCarthy and Yannacone testified at Eckhardt's hearings, it was Muller along with eight-year-old Kerry Ryan who became the stars—"two gimps in wheelchairs," recalls Champlin, "who brought the house down." The media could not resist photographing them together. In one famous photograph, their wheelchairs drawn up side by side, their heads bent together, they even looked strangely alike. Kerry's hair was cut into a boyish bob, and Muller with his perennially slim frame looked as fragile as she did. Most strange of all, Muller's right elbow was bent and his right hand cocked spastically in the photo, matching almost exactly the bend of Kerry's right elbow where her deformed, four-fingered hand jutted out. Yannacone recalls how another wheelchair vet had come racing down the hall to hand Bobby some papers, and in the course of his maneuvers had "popped a wheelie," which Kerry had never seen done before. Kerry leaned over, grabbed Muller's sleeve, and asked him: "You going to teach me how to do that?" An NBC camera caught it for the world. Says Yannacone: "There wasn't a dry eye in the place, mine included."

Muller led off the hearings by calling for the VA to establish a presumption of service connection for cancer and liver disorders in Vietnam veterans. It was a bold demand. Muller let the government know that "complacency" and "lethargy" would no longer be tolerated, that not only its decisions against Vietnam veterans, but even its logic, would be challenged again and again. Muller pointed out that if the EPA said 2,4,5-T was dangerous, and the VA said it was not, then one of them had to be proved wrong. And he used the brilliant tactic—like Shylock asking, "If you prick us, do we not bleed?"—of asking how Vietnam vets could be immune to a poison that did such terrible things to "the rest of the human race."

Kerry's parents, Michael and Maureen Ryan, both told their story. Raised in a patriotic Irish-American family in Brooklyn, Michael had gotten drafted, then married a few months later, at age twenty. Sent to Vietnam with the Eleventh Armored Cavalry in August 1966, he'd helped build the base camp at Long Binh—an area that was heavily sprayed with Agent Orange. Like every other GI in Vietnam, he was told that Agent Orange was "nontoxic to man or animals." He often drank rainwater that was likely contaminated with the herbicide. Within weeks, he became ill, but no one could pinpoint the cause. He was constantly exhausted, his body was covered with pus-filled sores, he suffered excruciating headaches, nausea, chest pains, shortness of breath, and drastic weight loss. Eventually the doctors called it "walking pneumonia."

Ryan later took part in Operation Cedar Falls, saw guys he knew get killed and had a close call himself with a VC mortar that flung him off the ground; but he returned home in September 1966 relatively unscathed. Over the next four years, he worked for IBM, then switched to a police job in Brooklyn, eventually transferring to the police force in Suffolk County, Long Island. During those years, he suffered numerous health problems, including wildly fluctuating weight, liver trouble, migraine headaches, rashes and boils, hearing loss, and chronic nervousness. He never connected any of it to Vietnam, however. He saved enough money to buy a modern, three-bedroom split-level house in picturesque Stony Brook, and looked forward to starting a family. On January 23, 1971, his first child, a daughter they named Kerry, was born with eighteen obvious major birth defects; and it would take numerous operations over the next several years just to keep her alive and to give her even the semblance of a human life.

Maureen Ryan learned about Agent Orange and dioxin through various news articles in the late 1970s, but it was Jimmy Breslin's article about the death of Paul Reutershan and the Agent Orange lawsuit that got her to take action. She contacted Victor Yannacone, and Yannacone quickly convinced them to become his clients. As Peter Schuck put it, Yannacone now "had the articulate, photogenic, all-American parents" and the "tragically damaged child" he needed to capture the nation's attention as his lead plaintiffs. But he also got something more: people who were clearly so honest, unselfish, and giving that no one could possibly accuse them of having joined the lawsuit and turned against their own government for money or other base motives.

Champlin recalls that when the Ryans came before the Commerce Committee, their tremendous sincerity—their ability to "be themselves"—overwhelmed everyone, and made even Chairman Eckhardt cry. Michael Ryan seemed perplexed about why his government had lied to him. "We were told the enemy was in the bush and he wore black sandals," he said. "We never suspected the enemy could be in the air around us." He said he still loved the United States and would serve again if called, but that he wanted "this country to get back the way it was," before it had callously used him and his fellow veterans as "human guinea pigs." He also wanted it to provide the necessary medical treatment for all the victims, including his daughter. Maureen talked about how much bitterness came with the realization that her daughter's misery and humiliation (she'd be in diapers for the rest of her life) was not due to an act of God but to the reckless use of toxic chemicals by her own government. "Now I realize Kerry had every right to be on a bicycle instead of in a wheelchair," she said.

A month later, before the Senate Veterans' Affairs Committee, Maureen Ryan expressed her family's sense of horror and betrayal even more directly: "Just as truly as the bullets and bombs killed on the battlefields in Vietnam, maiming thousands of our men, Agent Orange has come home from those battlefields with our men. It has come home to maim and kill additional thousands of men who naively thought they made it home safely. . . . But what the United States and what our Vietnam veterans did not know was that they carried home a tremendous legacy with them. They did not know that genetically on those battlefields were their children."

Most impressive of all was Kerry herself. "Right then she was trust and innocence, *love*, which is what people with developmental disabilities have during those years if they have a good family," Champlin remembers. "She was just love." Her image, and excerpts from the hearings, ran on prime-time TV, and she was featured in major stories in the *Washington Post* and the *New York Times*. If Yannacone lit the fuse with his class-action lawsuit, the Commerce

Committee hearings, and Kerry herself, were the dynamite. "It exploded, it exploded," recalled Champlin, in wonderment even a decade later that such fierce government resistance had been overcome.

Not about to surrender without a fight, the government presented its own testimony at the hearings as to the difficulty of documenting exposure to Agent Orange, and then of establishing exposure as the unequivocal cause of a particular disease. According to VVA's legislative director John Terzano, there was also a good deal of unofficial government scoffing, away from the microphones, that Muller and the other veterans were "off their rockers" in trying to prove that anyone had gotten sick from Agent Orange. Subsequent to the hearings, two VVIC congressmen, Thomas Daschle (D-S.Dak.) and David Bonior (D-Mich.), introduced the first bill requiring the VA to address Agent Orange–related health concerns and to compensate several categories of victims. Another VVIC member, John Heinz (D-Penn.), managed to get the bill passed in the Senate, but in the House it was killed immediately by the Veterans' Affairs Committee. The VA, meanwhile, asked Vietnam veterans to refrain from filing claims until it received the results of the Air Force's Ranch Hand study (an epidemiological study focusing on the personnel who actually conducted the spraying missions in Vietnam)—which was expected to be completed in six more years, and is, in fact, still being carried out now in the twenty-first century.[179]

The fact that Agent Orange legislation was even getting serious consideration, however, was a formidable chink in the government's armor. In the coming years, VVA and the VVIC together would keep poking bigger and bigger holes, till real help finally began to pour through. VVA now had carved out its niche in the Agent Orange affair; again and again, every year for well over a decade, its representatives would supply the congressional testimony aimed at changing the laws to favor compensation for Agent Orange victims. Just what that compensation would consist of was of course a more difficult thing to decide. As Ron Bitzer asked, a bit tauntingly, in testimony before the California State Assembly: "How does one compensate a family for the loss of a child or the birth of a deformed person? How does one compensate a sterile man?" The tentative grasp of legislators in this area, not to say their often outright confusion, made it inevitable that some sort of definitive ruling would have to come from the courts.

In a little over a year since Maude DeVictor's initial data had been broadcast on WBBM-TV in Chicago, and since Reutershan had founded Agent Orange Victims International (AOVI), an immense jump had been made in national awareness concerning the toxicity of Agent Orange; and thousands of veterans were spreading the word to thousands more every day. But anytime a new idea moves into the public forum that quickly, there is always a backlash of resistance to it. It threatens the status quo, and even more disturbingly, it threatens people whose careers were built on the old system that the new idea is capable of shattering. In the case of Agent Orange, the government backlash was enormous and longer-lasting than almost anyone could have imagined.

Rushing the issue into the media's spotlight also accelerated the political divisions in the veterans' community. Bobby Muller, for all his powerful advocacy in Congress, remained deeply conflicted about Agent Orange. As late as 1981, he told Australia's Minister for Veterans Affairs, Tony Messner, that (in Messner's words) "this wasn't the issue . . . this wasn't the key factor." According to Messner, who was concerned about his own veterans who had been in Vietnam, Muller insisted that it was "the war experience" itself that caused most of their health problems, not herbicide exposure. Frank McCarthy remained convinced that Muller had taken up the Agent Orange cause only because of his political ambitions, and because (in McCarthy's words) "he hates this country, and every minute he's in that wheelchair he blames this government for it."

McCarthy, in turn, was attacked, labeled a junkie, and at one point even kidnapped by other veterans who imagined he was trying to profit financially from AOVI. Tod Ensign and Michael Uhl at Citizen Soldier also received death threats for their purported mercenary interest in the issue. In addition, the latter two had their lives threatened for supposedly using their Agent Orange crusade "to radicalize this country," and for having "stabbed American veterans in the back by testifying about alleged war crimes." "It was the most vituperative kind of fifties-style, McCarthyite stuff," recalls Ensign, who still has a desk full of recordings made from such phone calls. "The Agent Orange case played out a lot of the same red-baiting and radical-baiting that we saw in other parts of the veterans' movement."

Divisiveness bred destructive paranoia. Frank McCarthy keeps a list of AOVI donors who were killed in car accidents or by apparent drug overdoses just before or after making a large donation. His favorite story is of Dr. Wilbur McNulty, the scientist at the Oregon Regional Primate Research Center in Portland, who demonstrated the toxic effect of dioxin on rhesus monkeys and their unborn offspring. Although Dr. McNulty's experiments were carefully checked and double-checked, and his results expressed quite cautiously, the chemical companies attempted to discredit his decades of work based on one incident where he allegedly misappropriated a little over $100 in government funds. Yannacone too suffered his share of discrediting accusations, including the frequent charge that he had taken the veterans' case with his eye on the main chance. Yannacone, in turn, would eventually accuse McCarthy of "being in the lawyers' pockets."

Agent Orange, says McCarthy, became "a battle between the political left and the political right in this country, and it's still being fought over the same philosophical and political convictions that the Vietnam War was fought over." He might have added that it was also fought in the same no-holds-barred, internecine style of that war. It was, in any event, the worst possible climate for the complex, legally difficult Agent Orange lawsuit to get an impartial hearing in.[180]

4. The VA's Agent Orange Exam and Other Smoke Screens

The largest mass toxic tort case in history, *In re Agent Orange Product Liability Litigation,* was played out against a backdrop even more sinister than the political infighting of Vietnam veterans. Always just offstage was the austere presence of that mammoth federal agency known as the Veterans Administration, which billed itself as the "true advocate of the veteran," and which posed before every governmental hearing as the ultimate authority on veterans' affairs. The VA would spend more than a decade—till well after the lawsuit had fizzled into the history books—denying, or trying to deny, every Agent Orange disability claim that came across its desk.

The VA's blanket opposition to Agent Orange claims was all the more insidious because of the agency's public stance of sympathy and support for those veterans concerned with possible chemical injury during their Vietnam service. In 1978, the VA, according to its own later press release, "took immediate steps in what has become a continuing search for answers." The agency claimed that it made "an extensive effort to gather authoritative information on Agent Orange and other known phenoxy herbicides from scientific literature and other sources." A private research firm had supposedly been hired to produce "an in-depth critical analysis and a summary of conclusions" from "the entire body of knowledge" on the subject. The VA also claimed a special role in the Interagency Working Group (IWG) established by President Carter, for the dissemination of Agent Orange information and the development of government policy regarding "the possible long-term health effects of phenoxy herbicides and contaminants."

The VA was proudest of its Agent Orange Registry, established in August 1978, to enable Vietnam veterans to report illnesses or disabilities which might be dioxin-related. There were two ostensible reasons for the Registry: first, "to evaluate the magnitude of the problem"; and second, to identify the complete group of potential claimants, so that when proof of causation was established for their health problems, the VA could the more readily find, treat, and compensate them. Three years after beginning to compile this roster, the VA had 60,000 names of ex-servicemen—not one of whom had received, or had any prospect of receiving, a dollar in disability compensation.

According to VA policy, every veteran who expressed concern about herbicide poisoning was supposed to receive a "comprehensive VA physical examination" under the guidance of one of the VA's 180 "environmental physicians," stationed throughout the VA medical center system. Each veteran would also be asked to complete a questionnaire "about his Agent Orange–related experiences in Vietnam." By August 1981, according to Dr. Barclay Shepard, director of the VA's Office of Environmental Medicine, over half of these questionnaires had been transferred to a "special computer data bank."

To hear the VA doctors tell it, they were anxiously awaiting the results of three major Agent Orange studies, in order "to resolve the Agent Orange issue . . . with sound scientific principles." The "answers" which would help them provide the correct medical diagnosis and treatment of Vietnam veterans were expected from three sources. The first was the Air Force's Ranch Hand study, begun in 1978. It compared the mortality and morbidity rates of the 1,278 veterans who took part in Operation Ranch Hand (the aerial spraying missions) with a control group of Air Force personnel who flew the same planes but did not spray Agent Orange. The second was a long-range epidemiological study of possible Agent Orange–related health effects among all Vietnam veterans, which had been mandated by the U.S. Congress in early 1979, under Public Law 96-151. That study had been awarded (over two years later) to UCLA. The third was a study by the Centers for Disease Control (CDC) of the correlation between Agent Orange exposure and veterans whose children had birth defects.

The VA, it seemed, had the situation well in hand. Until all the facts were known, the agency urged Vietnam veterans "to keep abreast of developments" and "to maintain a life style conducive to good health." It also promised that "no eligible veteran will be denied medical care and treatment."[181]

The reality was somewhat different.

In July 1980, when the House Veterans' Affairs Committee at last held its own exploratory hearings on Agent Orange, Bobby Muller had a chilling story to tell of a Vietnam veteran who went to the VA seeking "medical care and treatment." The vet had the rashes, headaches, chest pains, and respiratory problems associated with dioxin poisoning. But the VA doctors, ignoring his protestations about herbicide exposure in Vietnam, locked him in the psych ward for three weeks, then sent him home with a bagful of Valium, Librium, and sleeping pills. After his family left for the weekend, the veteran (in Muller's words) "put the VA prescribed pills to their final use."

Depression and its final payoff, suicide, were also known to be effects produced by dioxin—a fact apparently missed by the VA's information gatherers and analyzers. The suicide rate in Love Canal, for example, was eight times the national average.

By mid-1981, 45,000 vets had passed through the VA's Agent Orange screening program; but though many of them had suspicious rashes, neither the environmental physicians nor the Chloracne Task Force managed to detect a single case of chloracne. Dr. Shepard stated that of these 45,000, *just five* claims of "skin conditions" were service-connected "on the presumption that they were due to exposure to Agent Orange." But even in the five skin disorder cases that won service connection, the VA refused to issue a diagnosis of chloracne, which would have been prima facie evidence of dioxin poisoning. Thanks to media queries following James Hopkins' attack on the Wadsworth Medical Center, it came out that the Chloracne Task Force was still "in the process of refining diagnostic procedures." Like the child pointing out the emperor's nakedness, Ron Bitzer asked simply: "If the VA is not finding chloracne among Vietnam veterans, could it be that its physicians are not really looking?" Bitzer suggested that the only fair thing for the VA to do was to repeat those 45,000 examinations after it had finally instructed its physicians how to recognize chloracne— a suggestion that met with complete silence.

The VA had learned to "talk the talk" on Agent Orange, just as it had on PTSD; but at ground zero, where troubled veteran met VA employee, it was still a long way from "walking the walk" with victims of either affliction. With all the theories and statistics and legal precedents bouncing through the air, overworked hospital staffs sometimes failed to see that there were real, suffering human beings inside the often angry Vietnam veterans and their families who came to them for help. Typical of a thousand others was the story of Alan Wynn, once a tall and handsome young man from Camarillo, California. While serving as an artilleryman with the First Air Cavalry in Vietnam, Wynn had lost a lot of friends to bullets, booby traps, and mortars, and had come home with a fair amount of enemy metal in his own body. He had paid no attention to the thick fog of defoliant they were always spraying to clear base areas for the Cav. He never connected it to the blisters he started getting two weeks after he landed in Vietnam. They clustered around his eyes and in his mouth, bursting into open sores and spewing pus. When he returned from Vietnam, the blisters kept coming, worse than ever. They prevented him from working or going to school and, he claims, ruined his marriage. Eventually doctors controlled his skin outbreaks with cortisone, a drug that left him enervated and constantly vulnerable to colds and other infections.

When Wynn heard about Agent Orange, he felt he had found the cause of his problems, and he expected the VA to help. After a quick examination, some VA doctor decided "there were no indications" his blisters could be traced to exposure to Agent Orange. No one at the VA would believe he had lost jobs and friends because of his festering skin. "If you can't eat and you've got to eat baby food through a straw," he asked them, "do you think *your* personality would change?" His request for disability compensation was turned down. He ended up, at thirty-one, unemployed and living with his mother.

The VA's fear, Wynn learned, was that the yearly cost of paying all the Agent Orange disability claims would amount to several billion dollars. Far from keeping those budgetary worries secret, VA administrator Robert Nimmo expressed doubt that the VA could afford to pay such claims, which would likely extend well past the year 2000. Not surprisingly, the VA remained steadfast in its refusal to implement a compensation program until there was "absolute proof" that Agent Orange caused human health problems. Like thousands of others, Wynn's appeal to the Board of Veterans Appeals (BVA) went nowhere. He pinned all his hopes on the class-action lawsuit, which he joined as a plaintiff and tried to get other veterans to join.

In fact, the VA was guilty of out-and-out fraud. The DAV discovered that much of the time the VA's supposedly expert "Agent Orange examination" consisted of only a urinalysis and a simple blood test—when according to procedural rules set by the VA Central Office, concerned veterans were also supposed to be getting a full blood workup, chest X-ray, liver and renal function profiles, sperm count, and referral to a dermatologist. It also came out that after a veteran underwent an Agent Orange exam, the VA often did not even stamp "Possible Herbicides" in his chart. In the words of the DAV, what was needed was a wealth of "additional data" from "exams in their fullest," while the VA was trying to get away with "providing minimal service."[182]

5. The California State Hearings: The Politics of Science and the Manipulation of Certainty

In September 1981 the Defense Department released documents showing that "the number of people exposed to Agent Orange was substantially larger than originally thought." Two months earlier, the California State Assembly held its own Agent Orange hearings, which came to the same conclusion.

John G. Cano served in Vietnam with the 25th Infantry Division in 1968–1969, extending his tour to become the division's combat artist. He recalled frequent exposure to Agent Orange both in jungle areas and on base-camp perimeters. The troops were always told it was for "their benefit" and "not harmful to their health." Home from the war, he fathered two daughters with birth defects. His daughter from before the war was in perfect health. Throughout the 1970s he suffered from a "skin irritation," depression, anxiety, and a variety of health problems, culminating in acute liver damage. He had been wounded three times in Vietnam, but because of poor treatment in military hospitals he refused to seek help at the VA. Besides, there seemed no point in doing so, when the VA was telling vets like him: "The best available scientific evidence fails to indicate that exposure to Agent Orange or other herbicides used in Vietnam has caused any long-term problems for veterans or their children."

The VA also urged veterans not to refrain from having children just because they feared the possibility of birth defects. But as Cano stated to the California State Assembly: "This [awareness of the long-range after effects of Agent

Orange exposure] makes me wonder what hereditary effects from Agent Orange are yet to come upon my children's children, and their children's children." It was "far beyond the call of duty," he said, to demand that his descendants and the descendants of other veterans "physically pay for a *mistake* made by the government during the Vietnam War. . . . I made the choice of serving the country. Now, my children have no such say."

While the government played its game of "absolute proof," men, women, and children went down under an invisible fire, no less lethal than the one that took people down in Vietnam. New York fireman and former Marine helicopter crewman Tom Devitt, unable to live with a growing list of complaints—weight loss, insomnia, lethargy, endless infections, etc.—blew his brains out with a shotgun on Christmas morning 1979, in front of his wife, Patricia, and their six-year-old son. "We thought that my husband was a survivor of the Vietnam War," she wrote Senator Cranston afterward, "but was he really?"

There *were* people in government who were beginning to look and to care, even if most of them weren't in the VA. In Texas, State Representative Larry Don Shaw introduced House Bill 2129, to create the first state Agent Orange Assistance Program. He had been impressed not only by the 1,500 Vietnam vets who had expressed their concern about unexplained illnesses and children with birth defects, but also with alarming statistics, many of them from DAV studies: Vietnam vets dying at the rate of 1,000 a month; more vets dead since the war than during it; and Vietnam vets committing suicide at a rate 33 percent higher than the national average. There were already enough studies to convince him of the toxicity of Agent Orange, with its load of dioxin nearly 1,000 times more concentrated than in the 2,4,5-T sprayed domestically as weed-killer (according to western regional coordinator of the Agent Orange lawsuit, Dorothy Thompson, who based her estimate on the Air Force's own studies). There was a New Zealand study, which showed significantly higher numbers of congenital birth defects in the offspring of people exposed to aerial spraying of 2,4,5-T. There was a Swedish study, which showed a significantly higher incidence of soft-tissue carcinoma in factory workers exposed to dioxin. There was a Czech study, which showed significant neurological damage in factory workers exposed to dioxin. There was the much higher than normal rate of chromosome damage in people living in Love Canal. And there was the powerful evidence of studies conducted at the University of Texas by Dr. Jack Killian, who had directed medical research at Dow for thirty years. Dr. Killian's experiments with rats and mice had shown that dioxin not only produced birth defects, cancer, and neurological damage, but that it severely damaged the thymus gland, which plays a role in sustaining the immune system.

"We in Texas are tired of the Veterans Administration, their bureaucracy, and their run-around," Shaw told the California State Assembly. "And we have chosen to take the issue away from the federal government and act upon it ourselves as a state."

The two-year Texas screening and counseling program had a half-million-dollar price tag. It was passed unanimously by both chambers of the Texas legislature in 1981, and signed into law without a quibble by a Republican governor who, it was said, "made Ronald Reagan seem like a flaming liberal." In the next few years, several other states—most notably, Massachusetts and New Jersey—followed Texas's example to create their own high-caliber state Agent Orange commissions.[183]

The House Subcommittee on Oversight and Investigations in Washington produced a report that denounced the presidency, the VA, the Department of Defense, and Dow Chemical Company for failing to examine honestly and fully the health issues raised by Agent Orange. The report, which was quashed by the Reagan administration, was leaked to the *New York Times* in March 1981. It accused the VA of basing its denial of Agent Orange claims on "inaccurate and incomplete information." It also charged that "VA personnel, in many cases, did not even know what Agent Orange was" and that they "were often hostile" to Vietnam veterans seeking help. Most damningly, it exposed the double bind in which the VA had placed Vietnam veterans who thought they had been poisoned by Agent Orange. Such vets were told they had to "demonstrate beyond doubt" that Agent Orange had injured them, while at the same time the VA "declined to specify what level of scientific certainty will be required to establish the connection between Agent Orange exposure and ill health effects." In other words, the VA had put these already sick and stressed-out vets on a treadmill, and no matter how hard they tried to prove their case, the VA could always refute their efforts as inadequate.

The VA claimed never to have seen the silenced report, but said that even if accurate, it also proved the agency had managed to focus "more research energy" on Agent Orange than "any other issue in the last fifteen years." Such was the VA's astonishing ability to have its cake and eat it too. Under the direction of soon-to-be-confirmed Robert Nimmo, the VA's Lewis Carroll–like paradoxes would continue, with Nimmo offering to help Vietnam veterans by "putting the [Agent Orange] issue to rest."

The report also slammed the Pentagon for refusing "in the face of verified scientific data, to acknowledge that there could be a problem with Agent Orange" and for taking "no precautions to prevent exposure of servicemen." "Despite a White House directive to phase out defoliant operations," said the report, the Pentagon had continued to spray Agent Orange on and around its own troops in an amount fourteen times greater (per unit of area) than herbicide applied domestically. The Defense Department, like the VA, claimed ignorance of the documents in question, especially the alleged White House directive regarding elimination of the Ranch Hand program.

The report found Dow also deeply at fault for failing to notify the Pentagon of an outbreak of chloracne at one of its Agent Orange–producing plants in 1964.

In the face of such governmental and corporate bungling, the report declared it "insupportable" for the VA to continue denying Agent Orange claims. VVA came to the same conclusion after conducting an informal poll of its 10,000 members. Muller's feisty new assistant, a partially paralyzed Army veteran named Ken Berez, announced at a press conference that "these [Agent Orange] examinations are a joke." The VA's success in sweeping such untoward appraisals under the rug led Senator John Heinz (R-Penn.) to request the General Accounting Office (GAO) do its own oversight study of the VA's Agent Orange policies and programs.

The GAO's report, released in October 1982, was devastatingly critical of almost everything the VA had done to date. It concluded that the VA had failed to provide thorough or timely exams for the majority of Vietnam vets who had come to them worried about herbicide exposure. It described the VA's $1 million-a-year computer file based on those examinations as "inaccurate and unreliable" and recommended that it be scrapped. Heinz said the report proved that the VA was still ignoring both the physical and psychological needs of Vietnam veterans. Representative Thomas Downey (D-N.Y.), who co-commissioned the study, told the press: "The lack of concern, the callous attitude and the negligence on behalf of the Veterans Administration [that was documented in the GAO report] is inexcusable." Among other things, the report found that the VA had taken complete medical histories from only 10 percent of the 90,000 vets who had come to them with Agent Orange claims, that only 36 percent of those vets had received complete physicals, and even then, the examining doctors— supposed to be "experts in environmental medicine"—had often known little or nothing about dioxin and its toxic effects.

Even before the release of the GAO report, the VA's usually sanguine Dr. Barclay Shepard was forced to admit that the VA's Agent Orange program was "inadequate." He also (quite uncharacteristically) contradicted his boss, VA administrator Robert Nimmo, who had pronounced the VA's tissue-sampling program a "major effort" to find out if Vietnam vets were falling ill in disproportionate numbers because of exposure to Agent Orange. For the past three years, doctors in all 172 VA hospitals were required to send body-tissue samples taken from Vietnam vets undergoing surgery to the Armed Forces Institute of Pathology in Washington for analysis. While Nimmo bragged that the program would soon yield a "complete sampling . . . of the current medical problems of Vietnam veterans," Shepard revealed that only a few hundred out of many thousand eligible Vietnam veterans had actually been biopsied. Under oath before the Senate Veterans' Affairs Committee, Shepard admitted: "It appears to be a flagrant disregard of a VA regulation."

"It sounds like a good program," quipped a representative of Texas's Brotherhood of Vietnam Veterans, "too bad no one told the doctors about it."

Shepard declared that the VA needed to educate its physicians about the symptoms of chemical poisoning, to offer families genetic counseling, and "to establish better communication with Vietnam veterans' groups." Nimmo, his chief counsel Robert Coy, and chief medical director Dr. Donald Custis apparently disagreed. They distributed an Accuracy in Media (AIM) report that exonerated both Agent Orange and dioxin to VA medical personnel across the nation, along with a cover letter that referred to the majority of Agent Orange complaints as "emotional allegations" and encouraged VA personnel to downplay the dangers of herbicide exposure in order to reduce veterans' "anxiety levels."

Two leaders of the Vietnam Veterans in Congress, Tom Daschle (D-S.Dak.) and Leon Panetta (D-Calif.), were furious that the VA should "disseminate material which so blatantly ignores many of the facts" on Agent Orange, especially since the AIM report was "obviously not representative of a scientific or medical organization." AIM's media watchdogs could hardly claim "knowledge on issues concerning toxic chemicals, public health, or the environment." At the same time, the VA had chosen *not* to distribute five major European epidemiological studies, as well as a study by the National Institute for Occupational Safety and Health, that all pointed to dioxin as a likely cause of soft-tissue sarcomas and/or birth defects. The information on Agent Orange that the VA chose to give its medical workers seemed a clear indication that the agency was "eagerly seeking to discredit" the issue.

Daschle and Panetta enjoined the VA to "improve on the quality of information provided your field personnel." But such an approach, however well intentioned, begged the question of what was "good information" concerning Agent Orange, and whom to rely on as a source of it. More and more, people on all sides of the issue pinned their hopes for resolution on the three American studies in progress—the Air Force's Ranch Hand study, the birth defects study by the CDC, and the full-scale epidemiological study that Congress had ordered the VA to perform, and which the VA in turn had contracted out to UCLA. Yet there were serious pitfalls in thinking that either scientists or statisticians could unravel the Agent Orange controversy. Even riskier was the attempt to tie adequate medical treatment for Vietnam veterans and their families to such studies.

Ron Bitzer, in testimony before the California State Assembly in July 1981, pointed out that "the impact of environmental pollution on our health, whether it be cotton dust at the factory, benzene at the work place, herbicides used to fight the Vietnamese or the fruit fly, all of this has become a political as well as a scientific controversy." The political controversy, said Bitzer, could not help "impairing the ability of science to resolve the question" of Agent Orange's toxicity. The medical profession, far from being an impregnable fortress of objective truth, was vulnerable both to the winds of public opinion and, especially in the research department, to the influence of government and industry purse strings. Bitzer went so far as to suggest that "the medical profession represents a serious obstacle to Vietnam veterans" seeking answers to their health problems.

No better example of what he was talking about could have been staged than the actual appearance, following Bitzer, of Dr. Gary Spivey, associate professor of epidemiology at UCLA, before the California Assembly. The Assembly was holding hearings on AB 14, a "dishwater bill," according to its sponsor, Veterans' Affairs Committee Chairman Richard E. Floyd. AB 14 called only for California's Department of Veterans' Affairs to provide the state's Vietnam veteran population with information concerning the likelihood of their having been exposed to Agent Orange, as well as a list of diseases and symptoms connected with dioxin poisoning, and to create a register of those veterans who suspected they had herbicide-related health problems. Unlike Larry Don Shaw's Texas legislation, it had no provisions for outreach or for assisting veterans in filing VA claims. Dr. Spivey's testimony was much anticipated by Vietnam veteran activists across the country, since UCLA had appointed him the "principal investigator" in designing the Agent Orange epidemiological study requested by the VA.

Dr. Spivey's bias against self-proclaimed Agent Orange victims was evident from his first words. Although dioxin "has the reputation of being the most toxic synthetic chemical known to man," he said, that reputation was based mostly on "animal studies." As far as he was concerned, there was "to date little evidence for any specific human health effects" from it other than chloracne. Then Dr. Spivey set the chamber in an uproar by declaring that "Agent Orange was used primarily in areas where few or no troops were located." In that room were many Vietnam veterans ready to testify that Agent Orange had been sprayed right on top of them. The Department of Health and Human Services would actually back up those veterans' claims with a public announcement a couple of months later. HHS Secretary Richard Schweiker had uncovered some shocking data concerning aborted spraying missions. Defense Department records showed that on at least 90 occasions, Ranch Hand aircraft were forced to turn back because of enemy fire or engine failure; and in 41 instances, those aircraft simply dumped their cargo of Agent Orange onto the friendly (usually American) troops below.

Dr. Spivey's next assertion was one that the chemical companies were now trumpeting to the media in their massive damage-control campaign. "Dioxin," he said, "under most conditions, is very unstable and is usually degraded within a week." Sunlight, heat, and humidity (a summary of the climate in Vietnam) were supposed to "enhance the degradation." Once again, he failed to mention the wealth of contradictory evidence. In Seveso, Italy, for example, where sunlight, heat, and humidity are also in plentiful supply, children who returned to supposedly detoxified areas *five years after the ICMESA plant exploded* were still developing chloracne.

As if bent on refuting the many veterans who had already testified of strange physical illnesses visited on themselves and their families, Dr. Spivey claimed that "the most serious consequence of the use of Agent Orange" was in all likelihood "the fear which is generated by the current publicity." Confused,

Assemblywoman Cathie Wright asked Dr. Spivey how all "these aches and pains and certain other symptoms" she'd just heard about from veterans could have been caused by fear alone. Dr. Spivey replied that "the bad reception that the veterans have received since they returned home" created stress, and that "the types of symptoms that are being reported are common symptoms in people who are under stress."

Dr. Spivey even defended the VA's lapse in failing to treat chloracne, saying it was "a very difficult condition to diagnose . . . very hard to distinguish from ordinary acne." But still, no one in that chamber expected to hear the man in charge of designing the nation's only full-scale epidemiological study of veterans exposed to Agent Orange come out against AB 14, a bill intended merely to educate concerned vets and to reassure them, according to Assemblyman Floyd, that "you're one of ours . . . let's get it listed, let's get you into some kind of screening." Spivey stunned everyone not only by stating, "I recommend against adoption," but by his several reasons for such categorical opposition. Going his earlier statement one better, he now claimed "there is no evidence, at this point, of any major health effect from exposure to this substance." He asserted that a California Agent Orange Commission would only be "scaring people over things that we don't understand," and that the "engendered fear" would be "damaging to the health of the veterans." And, lastly, he worried that the bill would cause the State of California to waste money duplicating programs that had already been created by the VA—ignoring the fact that California was considering such a commission precisely because the VA had failed to do its job.

On the heels of disbelief came outrage. Some of the vets were a hair's-breadth from leaping up and throttling him. One vet, a pugnacious little Armenian named Tim Boyajian who had studied under Spivey, later did assault the doctor and was arrested. He claimed Spivey had said, "It's going to be hard to do an unbiased study on a bunch of dope fiends." Even Chairman Floyd, a Korean War veteran, could not keep from lashing out at Spivey in a stuttering, profane outburst: "If a man is suffering from stress . . . hell, maybe he isn't suffering from the effects of Agent Orange. But he thinks he is. Hell, isn't that as dangerous for this man who is operating within our society—isn't the fear of transmitting something to an unborn child—isn't that as evil a thing to sleep with as . . . maybe you're going to prove it isn't, but the veteran is not a scientist . . . if he feels isolated, feels that he is actually ill from something, wouldn't it be more important for us to publicize the facts? . . . I think there's more fear out there with the fact that nobody is saying anything to the veterans."

Floyd also slammed Spivey, recipient of a state paycheck, for advocating that the state not waste its money on a program to help Vietnam veterans. In an excess of righteous indignation, Floyd recommended the epidemiological study be canned, rather than let Spivey foist his prejudices on it: "I would object to this, as a study. I would rather see this money go down into a human study on what is happening to a man who did his number in Vietnam, now—not on rats and mice . . . but the individuals . . . [like] a man here who had lesions—who has lesions today, after ten years. I want to study that man—that man's whole being, not only his physical being but mental being. . . . I think that's less a waste of money than a study which is predicated on a myth."[184]

In less than an hour, Spivey had managed to torpedo his own epidemiological study. A year later, it would be taken from UCLA and the VA, largely as a result of the controversy caused by his undiplomatic remarks, but also because it appeared he was never actually going to finish even the design. The study was given to the Centers for Disease Control (CDC), which, three years after the congressional mandate, had to start again from scratch. Spivey's timetable had projected the design phase of the study to be completed by July 1982, and a "preliminary study" to yield results "a year or two" after that. After the preliminary study, he envisioned "a major follow-up study," which would take from three to five years to produce "more definitive results." By his calculation, this meant that no answers worth taking seriously could be had, probably, until 1989! But when asked how long before vets could expect to have "definitive proof" that they were poisoned by Agent Orange, Dr. Spivey suggested the answer might range from five years to "never." Thus the vets were being asked to wait one year, then two years, then five more years, to find out that they might be finding out nothing. But at least that was some kind of time frame. Once the study moved to the CDC, all bets were off as to a completion date.

The fact that studies could be endlessly delayed was one of the main arguments against relying on them, especially when that reliance involved the fragile health of human beings. Many congressmen, including, surprisingly enough, Alan Cranston, were arguing that the VA needed "to protect the integrity of the service-connected disabled program by delaying any action on disability claims" until the scientific studies were done. But as Ron Bitzer pointed out, while the VA sat on its high horse, the suffering and dying continued. Marine combat veteran Jess Godoy, who fathered two sons with birth defects after his return from Vietnam, testified to the Assembly following Dr. Spivey: "All I ever seem to hear is talk. I don't see anybody doing anything about it [the health effects of Agent Orange]. Me, myself, I'm concerned about my children now. . . . I was really taken advantage of . . . but that's in the past, you know, I accepted that. But now when you're starting to mess with my children, the war continues . . . how much time do you need? I think it's time that they started looking at the children . . . talking about budgets is fine, but I'd like to see some results."

As it turned out, the time concern of veterans like Bitzer and Godoy was justified. It was not till 1996 that the first American study, performed by the Institute of Medicine, "tentatively linked" at least one form of birth defect to Agent Orange exposure. By that time, many disabled children of Vietnam veterans were in their mid- to late twenties, and others were already dead.

There were even more basic problems with the studies. Bitzer told the story of how Dow Chemical once fired a researcher studying chromosome damage from benzene because his results were not what they wanted to hear. Besides the fact that studies could always be manipulated by those with money and power, they were also subject to faulty design. The Air Force's Ranch Hand study, which was surrounded by controversy from start to finish, was a perfect example of how a study might look impressive but in reality be meaningless. The Surgeon General had developed the protocol for the Ranch Hand study under the premise that the airmen who sprayed Agent Orange would most dramatically manifest the health effects, if any, from exposure. But the National Research Council later questioned this premise. It was quite possible, for example, that helicopter crews flying through clouds of Agent Orange were far more exposed to the chemical than the men in the enclosed cockpits of the C-123s that had actually sprayed it. Representative Larry Don Shaw warned as early as 1981 that the results of the Ranch Hand study would probably be disappointing, and that the study itself might end up being used against Vietnam veterans. "Mark my words," he told the California Assembly, "we'll see it come, that they have done this long-term exclusive study and there are no negative effects of Agent Orange, when they should be testing those people, the grunts, that were down in the jungle that had it dripping all over them, or were walking through the wet jungle."

The bottom line was that no study in the world could provide absolute certainty of anything. As long as the VA demanded "definitive proof," the Vietnam veterans (said claimant and activist Steve Androff) "were fucked." Putting it more euphemistically for the California Assembly, Ron Bitzer explained: "As long as the VA can rely on the argument for the need for additional research, there will be a delay on a comprehensive policy for disabled Vietnam veterans, and the VA will be able to successfully avoid change." Bob Muller, from whom one might have expected caution, was right in the government's face on that point, in his testimony before a House Veterans' Affairs subcommittee in July 1980. Since the VA was demanding specific data from the veterans, Muller demanded the VA get specific too. He challenged its representatives "to stop saying, vacuously, that we need more evidence; and to start asking the serious questions: precisely how much evidence, and precisely what type of evidence, do we need? The VA's answer is . . . they are waiting for something like absolute certainty. But what is this 'certainty'? What does it require? More importantly, is the VA's 'certainty' achievable at all?"[185]

6. The Ranch Hand Study and the Work of Dr. Ton That Tung

As *New York Times* journalist Richard Severo and National Veterans Law Center attorney Lewis Milford would later reveal in their book *The Wages of*

War, the top members of the Reagan administration had agreed that "Vietnam veterans claiming sickness from Agent Orange should not be paid." Historian Wilbur Scott would also come up with evidence that the White House Agent Orange Working Group (formerly Carter's Interagency Working Group, now reconstituted with Reagan appointees) did its best to derail compensation for Agent Orange victims. According to Scott, when the preliminary morbidity results of the Ranch Hand study became available in 1984, the Air Force submitted its original report to the Agent Orange Working Group (AOWG) for review, as demanded by the chair of the AOWG's Domestic Council, Under Secretary of Health and Human Services Donald Newman. When the report was finally released to the media, significant portions had actually been (in Scott's phrase) "tampered with." Where the original report had said that dioxin could not be ruled out as a cause of illness in Ranch Hand personnel, the expurgated and rewritten version claimed the study tended to confirm the harmlessness of the herbicide.

In 1988, when the Air Force released an updated report, it became clear that the Ranch Hand study actually pointed an incriminating finger at Agent Orange. The Ranch Handers, it showed, had significant physiological differences from the control group of veterans (those not exposed to Agent Orange) in six of the eleven areas investigated. The Reagan administration was not happy with the update, to say the least, and Donald Newman sent a memo to all federally funded Agent Orange researchers bemoaning the "serious breach" of etiquette by the Air Force in going directly to the press with their findings. Perhaps to make up for the gaffe, the Air Force insisted once again that the Ranch Hand study proved the innocuousness of Agent Orange. Declared retired Air Force Major Jack Spey, president of the Ranch Hand Association, in testimony to Congress, May 3, 1988: "Thus far the conclusions of this ongoing study show no significant differences between Ranch Hand personnel and the matched comparison group. Did the mission of Operation Ranch Hand do harm to the health of those performing that mission . . . [or] those combatants or noncombatants who may have been on the ground? When the facts and science are weighed carefully, unemotionally, and in total—the answer remains no."

It also came out years later that the government began to worry, once the epidemiological study went from UCLA to the CDC, that the CDC would successfully establish the link between herbicide exposure and veterans' illnesses. For one thing, the man in charge of the CDC study, Dr. Vernon Houk, seemed as sympathetic to the veterans' claims as Dr. Spivey had been disdainful. When Dr. Houk testified to a House Veterans' Affairs subcommittee in 1983 that he gave credence to the suspected link between dioxin and soft-tissue sarcoma, the VA's ever-loyal Dr. Barclay Shepard was heard to say: "Somebody's gonna have to take him on."

Ailing Vietnam veterans, in the early 1980s, did not yet know that they were playing for their lives with a stacked deck, but they saw that their options for redress were quickly vanishing. One of those options that had absorbed a lot of their early effort was legislation. There was, in fact, initial euphoria when Tom Daschle's Agent Orange compensation bill, H.R. 1961, was approved by a House Veterans' Affairs subcommittee in mid-1983. The bill called for the temporary presumption of service connection (a preliminary for paying claims) for chloracne and porphyria cutanea tarda, a liver disease, if symptoms had manifested within one year after a veteran left Southeast Asia. More generously, it provided for temporary service connection for soft-tissue sarcomas if they had originated within twenty years after a veteran's overseas tour. Daschle even put an escape clause into the bill, specifying that the VA could terminate compensation if the major studies showed no correlation between these diseases and herbicide exposure.

H.R. 1961 had faced stiff opposition from the time of its introduction, in October 1982. The new VA administrator, Harry Walters, had testified against it, warning that the presumption of service connection for these three diseases would "jeopardize the viability of [the VA's] compensation program." Walters' benefits director, Dorothy Starbuck, then assured the House committee that money had nothing to do with her boss's views. Sonny Montgomery and Alan Cranston (the respective House and Senate Veterans' Affairs chairmen), however, made no secret of the need they felt to "hold the line" against a tide of Agent Orange compensation demands.

What changed a lot of congressional minds was a little town in Missouri called Times Beach. Back in 1971, the EPA had banned the manufacture of hexachlorophene, a chemical that had acquired a brief vogue in toothpastes, soap, and skin-care products. The problem with hexachlorophene was the same as with its close chemical relative, 2,4,5-T: it could not be manufactured without creating the by-product of dioxin. One of the major manufacturers of hexachlorophene had been Northeastern Pharmaceutical and Chemical Company (NEPACCO) in Verona, Missouri. In the process of purifying its hexachlorophene, NEPACCO had amassed a huge quantity of a viscous substance they called "still bottom." This still bottom contained 300 parts per million (ppm) of dioxin, about 150 times the amount in Agent Orange. They paid a St. Louis firm, Independent Petrochemical, to get rid of the foul-smelling goo, and Independent subcontracted the job to a self-employed disposal man, Russell Bliss. Bliss, despite being warned of the toxicity of the still bottom, mixed it with used crankcase oil and used it on his second job, which was tarring dirt roads and stables. He ended up spraying 40,000 gallons of this homemade blacktop on almost every street in the far-flung St. Louis suburb of Times Beach.

The first indication that something was wrong came from a stable that Bliss had tarred in nearby Moscow Mills. Horses, cats, dogs, and birds in and around the stable began dropping dead within a matter of days. The people living on the property became severely ill with diarrhea, headaches, and muscle and joint pains; one girl nearly died from a severely inflamed and bleeding bladder. It came out that Bliss, neglecting to add the fuel oil, had pumped pure still bottom into the stable. In 1974, the CDC identified the toxic agent as dioxin, but it took several more years before the EPA identified all 41 Missouri sites that had been contaminated. Feuds developed within the EPA concerning how to get rid of the dioxin, which was not decomposing nearly as fast as the chemical companies had always claimed it would. Eventually that controversy centered on Times Beach, a town of 2,400 residents, where a flood in late 1982 had spread dioxin throughout the area. Some of the soil in Times Beach registered as high in dioxin as in the death-chamber Moscow Mills stable.

As the EPA struggled to decontaminate the town with workers in white plastic "moon suits," rubber gloves, and respirators, the fiasco provoked bitter disputes in Congress, dominated political campaigns, and splashed across the nation's newspapers. Jack McCloskey, speaking on Agent Orange at the "Vietnam Reconsidered" conference at USC in February 1983, expressed the outrage Times Beach engendered in Vietnam veterans: "I have read about this one town in Missouri, what's happening there, what the government's been doing about it. I've been following that very closely since I first heard about it. But not once have I either seen on television or read in a paper about dioxin and veterans. Not once has that linkage been made by the press. The government is telling people to leave this town because of that dioxin. Not once have they also said in the press, 'This is the same thing used in Vietnam on the Vietnam veterans and the Vietnamese people.'"

The story took an even more astounding turn on February 22, 1983, when the EPA announced that the federal government together with the state of Missouri would buy out each and every resident of Times Beach, for an estimated cost of $33 million. The collective outcry of Vietnam veterans was almost as great as after the welcome home for the hostages from Iran two years earlier. They gasped not only at the sudden largesse of the federal government, but even more at its stony-faced hypocrisy in demanding Vietnam veterans prove that Agent Orange had been injurious to their health. "Could it be that dioxin is poisonous only when it is used within the continental . . . United States?" wrote Vietnam veteran Edward Manear in a letter to the *Washington Post*. "Perhaps dioxin is poisonous only when in proximity to civilians but harmless to men and women in uniform."[186]

VVA's John Terzano, testifying before the Senate Veterans' Affairs Committee on June 22, 1983, concerning the bill to compensate Vietnam veterans for Agent Orange–related illnesses, made Times Beach the centerpiece of his argument. "How can the same federal government that buys out Times Beach, Missouri, for over $30 million continue to turn its back on a group of individuals who have given so much of themselves for their country?" he asked. "When will the Congress, the Executive Branch, and the VA acknowledge and deal responsibly with the existing data, which were deemed sufficient for addressing the situation in Times Beach and other communities in the United States exposed to these chemicals?"

The VFW had supported H.R. 1961 from the start. The major veterans' organizations, heavily populated with aging World War II vets, were starting to realize that their survival depended upon bringing in younger members, which meant being responsive to Vietnam veterans' issues. As soon as the Times Beach buyout hit the news, the American Legion jumped on the Agent Orange bandwagon too. That fall, Daschle's compensation bill was passed by the House. It subsequently died in the Senate, largely due to continuing opposition from the VA and the Reagan administration. Glenn A. Sinclair, an Agent Orange advisor to the state of Ohio, wrote a piece in the VVA *Veteran* describing the hostility of many VA workers to Agent Orange claims. According to Sinclair, one VA employee in Cleveland had said: "We're not worried about you Vietnam veterans, you'll all be dead in ten years anyway." Another, at the nearby Brecksville facility, had declared the Agent Orange screening examination "a waste of time."

Certainly the release of preliminary results from the Ranch Hand study in July 1983 also hurt the Agent Orange bill. The Air Force's Deputy Surgeon General, Major General Murphy Chesney, announced no significant variation in mortality rates between Ranch Handers and the control group, and a slightly higher death rate from liver disorders in the Ranch Handers that he deemed "statistically insignificant." Many flaws in the study would later be exposed—including the fact that many of the participating scientists had begun with the premise that Agent Orange was a "very unlikely" cause of disease. In addition, the Air Force scientists juggled their data so as to change their conclusions almost from month to month.

In February 1984, for example, the Air Force admitted finding significantly higher rates of skin cancers, liver ailments, and circulatory problems in the Ranch Handers, as well as more numerous birth defects and infant deaths among their children. But somehow General Chesney managed (by manipulating the data) to interpret these findings as "reassuring"; and the VA, taking its cue from him, called them "good news." Once that first Ranch Hand release had been made public, however, the credibility of Agent Orange claims had been permanently damaged in the view of many congressmen; and each succeeding report, especially those that seemed to challenge the herbicide's innocence, just seemed to muddy the waters further, so that many legislators stopped looking for scientific answers altogether.

There was an even bigger ogre than either the Defense Department or the VA, or even the whole scientific establishment, menacing any Congress that would vote for Agent Orange compensation. Looming huge, but virtually unmentionable by the U.S. government, was the specter of the thousands, maybe millions, of Vietnamese who might claim that they and their children had also been damaged by Agent Orange—once the slim but ineluctable thread of causation had been acknowledged. By that slim thread an empire could hang itself, a whole nation be held liable for universally recognized war crimes, and consequently be compelled to pay reparations. As Ron Bitzer told the California Assembly: "Clearly, if we get action for American victims, the Vietnamese will be raising their claims, and that constitutes a serious obstacle for governmental officials working on this problem, which is international in scope." Bitzer also thought it significant that one of the co-designers of the Ranch Hand study, and a principal advisor to the VA on the Agent Orange controversy, was Air Force Major Alvin Young, who had previously served as an assistant to the Pentagon's chemical warfare chief, Thomas Dashiell.

Indeed the Vietnamese Communists had decried the Americans' use of Agent Orange against them as a form of chemical warfare, and hence a violation of international law, since the late 1960s. It was Ho Chi Minh's personal physician, Dr. Ton That Tung, who first began investigating the high numbers of North Vietnamese soldiers who returned from the south with severe health problems. Many of these soldiers, besides suffering digestive ailments and certain normally rare cancers, were troubled by a chronic rash that appeared to be chloracne. Their wives had a much higher than normal rate of miscarriages, and too many of their children were born with birth defects to be explained by chance. Although Dr. Tung did not have access to data from the American Bionetics Research Laboratories' study of 2,4,5-T and 2,4-D (which, running from 1964 to 1969, first established the carcinogenic and teratogenic effects of these chemicals on rats and mice), he independently concluded that Agent Orange was sickening his country's soldiers and harming their children.

The Americans dismissed Dr. Tung's warnings as propaganda and scare tactics. Nevertheless, they certainly understood the gravity of his charges. The United States had helped draft and was a signatory to the 1925 Geneva Protocol banning chemical and bacteriological weapons. Though technically not bound to the agreement because the U.S. Senate had never ratified it, the American government had relied upon such documents of international law as the basis for its prosecution of Nazi war criminals at Nuremberg, and it has always pointed an incriminating finger at any other nation that as much as hints at using chemical weapons. In the case of Agent Orange, the United States hoped to deflect such criticism by announcing that the use of herbicides and defoliants somehow didn't count as warfare—even though they were used at least partly to destroy food crops, i.e., to starve the Communists out. Very few nations who weren't close allies of the United States bought that argument, and the World Health Organization (WHO) specifically denounced the United States for its use of chemical agents, including defoliants, in Southeast Asia.

Small wonder, then, that when Dr. Tung came to Washington in 1979, and met with VA doctors and scientists, they declined his invitation to take part in an Agent Orange study using the Vietnamese as subjects. Were political questions not involved, one would be hard-pressed to explain the VA's refusal. The kinds of cancers and birth defects he spoke of in his countrymen were almost exactly what American and Australian Vietnam veterans kept reporting. While claiming it lacked the resources for such an effort, the VA went so far as to outline a possible study of Vietnamese vets, and they even designed a questionnaire for Tung to get started with, which he translated into Vietnamese.

In one year, with very little money, and squeezed by the American embargo of Vietnam (as well as American pressure on other countries not to cooperate with, sell technology to, or financially aid the Communist Vietnamese), Dr. Tung completed his study of several thousand former North Vietnamese soldiers. Half of his subjects were troops that had remained in North Vietnam during the war; the other half had penetrated into areas of South Vietnam sprayed with Agent Orange. Among those troops who had come south, there was a striking increase in the percentage whose wives subsequently miscarried and/or bore children with congenital anomalies. The most striking increase was in the incidence of neural crest anomalies—children born with tiny brains or no brain at all, known medically as microcephaly or anencephaly. Dr. Tung also found that among veterans who had returned from the south there was a significantly higher incidence of hepatic cancer. Such a link was not unexpected, as teratogenic agents are often carcinogenic as well.

In 1980, Dr. Tung gave his results to Dr. Jack Kemp, a former VA physician who had opposed the war and who had come to Vietnam to learn firsthand about its postwar problems. Kemp was astounded that Tung's findings paralleled so exactly the complaints that VA doctors were hearing from American Vietnam veterans—even though the VA never officially recognized such a pattern, and, for that matter, was not legally empowered to treat veterans' wives or children as patients. Back in the States, Dr. Kemp immediately brought Tung's study to the VA, which had been crying to see evidence that dioxin was dangerous to human beings, not just mice, rats, and monkeys. Here was a study that suggested dioxin *was* toxic to humans, and, to Kemp's astonishment, the VA showed not the slightest interest in it.

Kemp then took Tung's study to three prestigious American publications: *Science*, the *New England Journal of Medicine*, and *Mutation Research*. Kemp considered the study "very critical . . . the most serious effort" anyone had yet made to investigate the health effects of herbicides on ground troops in Vietnam. It was rejected out of hand at both *Science* and the *NEJM*. *Mutation Research* tentatively accepted it for publication, although the editor complained that it wasn't "wrapped up absolutely tight." Publication was made contingent on Kemp providing additional data to satisfy the magazine's scientific advisors. Kemp recalls that for three years he and his associate, Dr. Judy Ladinsky, "bent over backwards to meet all of the suggestions and criticisms of the reviewers," which included a voluminous exchange of letters with Tung and his researchers and even, on occasion, the dispatch of a personal courier. They "went down to the wire," but at the last minute the editor yanked the piece. He told her: "It's just a little bit too hot. And since it's not a hundred percent, we're reluctant to take it on." Kemp was outraged, feeling that information "crucial" to Vietnam veterans was being "suppressed" for political reasons. Even should American scientists get the green light and the funding to do a really "tight" study, he postulated, another ten or fifteen years would likely go by before it was considered publishable, and by then it would certainly be "too late" for many veterans and their families.[187]

The issue had grown even hotter in January 1982, when Richard Severo broke a story in the *New York Times* about the secret use of Agent Orange in Laos. According to Severo, who had seen an unpublished Air Force history, the American government had smuggled thousands of gallons of defoliant into South Vietnam in the early 1960s, to keep from being criticized by other nations "for conducting chemical warfare." The history recounted the Pentagon's original plans to spray Agent Orange from unmarked planes flown by Air Force pilots in civilian clothes, who, if caught, would be disavowed by their own government. The covert spraying in Laos, begun in 1965, only three years after herbicide was first used in South Vietnam, was supposedly done with the agreement of the Laotian government; yet the U.S. ambassador to Laos, William H. Sullivan, had strongly objected to it on the grounds that, if known, it would alienate other friendly nations in the area. Sullivan was overridden by the insistence of General William Westmoreland that Communist troops moving down the Ho Chi Minh Trail through Laos be denied hiding places as well as local food crops.

By June of 1966, Severo reported, 200 sorties had been flown over Laos, and 200,000 gallons of Agent Orange dumped on roads and trails north of the 17th parallel. Twenty pages of the Air Force history that were withheld from Severo for national security reasons supposedly dealt with the Pentagon's plans to use Agent Orange "to destroy war-making potential" in still other countries in the region. If a violation of international law were established, the liability to the United States would be astronomical. Robert McNamara, who was secretary of defense when the Laotian spraying began, told Severo he was "unable to recall the details of defoliation, or who ordered or approved it." Former Secretary of State Dean Rusk pled a similar amnesia.

Considering how much was at stake, Congress naturally wanted to evade responsibility for opening the Pandora's box of Agent Orange as much as the VA. Despite the increasing number of Agent Orange hearings held before various committees, it soon became clear to most veteran activists that legislation was not going to be the route to truth, treatment, or compensation. By 1988, in fact, several Agent Orange bills had been passed, and yet only five Vietnam veterans had been recognized by the VA as suffering from chloracne. None of them had received compensation. No other Agent Orange–related diseases had been diagnosed. Out of 150,000 total Agent Orange disability claims, not one had been approved. Thomas Daschle, who was elected to the Senate from South Dakota in 1986, continued to author many of those Agent Orange bills, but by then even he had lost faith in a legislative solution. "There's a big difference between theory and practice," he admitted in 1988. "Legally and technically Agent Orange is compensatable. Practically, you really don't have an Agent Orange compensation program today."

Frank McCarthy was even more vehement in denouncing the folly of the legislative song and dance. "We were naive enough to believe that there was a political solution to the Agent Orange dilemma," he recalled that same year. "So for ten years we struggled and sacrificed. A lot of good men's lives were wasted in giving testimonies and advocacy and organizing veterans. There was a big financial burden on those people. Most of them were Agent Orange victims, and many of them have died off now. We've been guinea pigs for ten years. The congressmen told us, 'Well, this is the first step.' They told us that a decade ago. We have gone the full extent of what it takes to get legislation passed in this country—all the advocacy, all the numbers, proving our cases. And what we come up with are watered-down bills that have absolutely no effect on the veterans suffering in the streets. And nothing pertaining to the children anywhere. . . . Those four or five bills have meant absolutely nothing to veterans needing help. All we did is build political careers for people like Senator [John] Kerry and Dave Bonior and the rest of the gang. I used to think, *They're sincere, they're fighting to end the suffering.* Well, fighting to end the suffering does not end with legislation. It ends with programs and services that directly affect the lives of the people suffering."

The Brookings Institution, a liberal think tank, issued a report on Agent Orange in 1981, warning Vietnam veterans that "what Congress and the Administration are saying is don't expect anything more from the federal government for the next decade—in fact, expect less."

The VA had been a stumbling block to Vietnam veterans from the start; and except for a few kinder years under Carter, the entire executive branch (to which the VA belongs) was equally hostile or indifferent to their needs. Congress, which could compel the VA to change its policies, seemed to prefer the status quo. That left the judiciary, where veterans were, for the most part, legally ineligible to seek relief. The *Feres* Doctrine barred servicemen from suing the government for injuries sustained during military duty, and federal law shielded VA decisions from judicial review by any court other than the VA's own Board of Veterans' Appeals. Even before the BVA, veterans were hamstrung by the nineteenth-century law that forbade them to spend more than $10 for representation by an attorney.

Victor Yannacone was not just the best hope Agent Orange victims had; in the first few years of the 1980s, he was pretty much the only hope. Whether or not Tod Ensign was right that Yannacone was "so far behind the eight ball that there was no possibility of trying that case [the product liability litigation against the chemical companies]," the iconoclastic loner from Patchogue was the only person in America still holding the door open to truth on the Agent Orange issue. The attorney with the father-and-son shingle still hung proudly on his door, with his wife for an assistant, cats sleeping in his file boxes and home-taped jazz blaring from the office in his small gray house, may have been as much a colossal egotist as "a knight on a white charger for more than 40,000 veterans"—as he described himself to a local newspaper. But he truly was, as Frank McCarthy called him, the "general" of over a thousand troops, who were his clients. They took orders from him, as real troops do, not to make money but (in his words) "to get something done." That mission, as he saw it, was to make sure "that this should never happen again."[188]

7. "Keeping the Door to the Courthouse Open": Yannacone & Associates Win Several Victories

Yannacone was no fool. He knew he could not conduct the Agent Orange litigation by himself. He counted on the massive media attention to the case to bring him not only more clients, but also more attorneys to share the workload and, even more importantly, financial backers. He baited the hook with an article called "Battling an Agent of Tragedy," which appeared in *Newsday*'s Sunday magazine in late April 1979. In that article, Yannacone described the Agent Orange case as "the largest class-action suit ever filed in this country's federal courts." He also emphasized that it was a cause for lawyers "with a social conscience" who shared the growing "concern of the American people toward the destruction of the environment through chemicals or radiation." Most tempting of all, he hinted that the case would result in "one of the landmark decisions of American environmental law." Few attorneys, idealistic or not, could turn their back on that kind of publicity. By nightfall, Yannacone's phone was ringing off the hook again.

A lawyer Yannacone had known from the civil rights movement, Hy Herman, called to apologize for his failure to support Yannacone in the DDT litigation. He offered to make up for it now by bringing several lawyers to Yannacone's aid in the Agent Orange case. A few days later, Yannacone presided at a meeting with Herman and twenty of the leading personal-injury law firms on Long Island. Many of the attorneys were World War II vets with a sympathetic interest in the issue. Yannacone began by putting a glass of "very expensive booze" in front of each man, but accounts of what followed differ considerably.

According to Yannacone, he briefly described the nature of the case, then proposed that the attorneys there join him in something called the Long Island Consortium or Yannacone & Associates. He explained, he says, that each law firm would help with the workload of the case, as well as contributing an equal share of the $20,000 a month he estimated it would cost to sustain its prosecution. Yannacone would not have to put in any money himself, but would bring to them his 1,000-plus clients and "state-of-the-art computer technology," devote full time to the case, and serve as unsalaried executive director. He promised them he could bring the case to trial for a flat million dollars; and when they won, each of them would receive a share of the fees equal to his.

The "key question," he recalls, was asked by the scion of a very large firm with a strong interest in "law firm economics": "Yannacone, what happens if they make the usual motion to dismiss?" As reconstructed by Yannacone, their dialogue ran as follows:

"I'll oppose it," Yannacone replied.

"What happens if you lose?"

"Well, we'll take an appeal to the Second Circuit Court of Appeals."

"What happens if you lose there?"

"Well, we'll go to the Supreme Court of the United States."

"How are you going to argue in the Supreme Court?"

"Very simple. We'll say, 'Your Honor, Mister Justices, a hundred years ago, this court was asked to make a decision in another case of great significance for this republic. A hundred years ago, you decided the *Dred Scott* case wrong. For God's sake, don't do it again!' And then I'll sit down."

"What happens a month later, when they throw you out of court?"

"I'll be in Washington for the decision, as will half a million veterans. And as the decision comes out, I'll simply stand on the steps of the courthouse and take my little bullhorn and tell them: 'While you were humping through the jungle, and your comrades were dying in that jungle, I was going from campus to campus throughout this country following [after] Kunstler and his *Burn, baby, burn!* and his riots, saying: "As long as the door to the courthouse is open, the door to the streets should be closed." I guess I was wrong.' And then I will take the shuttle home to New York and watch the six o'clock news as they tear down the courthouse."

At that point, says Yannacone, the representatives of half the firms walked out. The other ten signed on as part of the "consortium." Many of them, however, later claimed that Yannacone had only asked them to chip in $2,000 apiece as an entry fee, and that the only other financial obligation they assumed was to reimburse expenses that they had approved in advance.

By agreement of both Yannacone and Leonard Rivkin, the attorney for Dow, all the Agent Orange lawsuits that had already been filed around the country were consolidated into one case in the Federal Court for the Eastern District of New York. It would be heard in the court's "Long Island annex" in Uniondale, and Yannacone would remain the lead counsel for plaintiffs. The judge assigned to the case was George C. Pratt.

Pratt, a Republican and Ford appointee, was described by journalist Robert W. Greene as "a thoughtful jurist with a keen mind . . . a rising star on the Federal bench." He had soared through Yale Law School with top honors, and would distinguish himself in the summer of 1980 (a year after getting the Agent Orange litigation) as the presiding judge in the first Abscam trial. He would steer the bribery case against Camden Mayor Angelo Errichetti through numerous shoals of political intrigue and media sensationalism to a sound verdict, and he showed every sign of being able to cut through to the essence of the Agent Orange case as well.

Pratt's first important ruling, late in 1979, was that *In re Agent Orange Product Liability Litigation* belonged in a federal rather than state court, and that it would be decided according to federal common law. On May 19, 1979, the chemical companies had made a motion to have the case dismissed on several grounds. Since they objected that Yannacone's 186-page complaint was prolix, he had sat down at his computer with a small group of veterans and their wives, including Mike and Maureen Ryan, and condensed it on the spot. The judge had barely digested his revision when Yannacone filed yet a third amended pleading, irritating even patient Pratt. But the real substance of the motion to dismiss was the defendants' argument that state law, not federal law, should be applied to a case in which private parties were suing other private parties. If state law applied, veterans in many states would already be barred from suing by local statutes of limitation. In addition, many states already had product liability laws that actually shielded manufacturers from excessive damage claims. Since federal common law was a good deal looser on such questions, the chemical companies stood to lose in a much bigger way if a judge used that latitude to shape his own liberal interpretation of the veterans' rights.

Pratt reasoned that there were substantial federal interests in the case not only because it involved millions of veterans and their families and some of the biggest war contractors; but also because under state laws, people "identically situated in all relevant aspects" would be dealt highly different forms of justice, and so deprived of the "equal protection" guaranteed them by the Constitution. The chemical companies, sensing that public opinion would soon begin to snowball against them in a big national case, immediately appealed Pratt's decision.

Indeed news that all Vietnam veterans would have their Agent Orange claims heard in one place, at one time, played into Yannacone's hands in terms of helping him gather more clients. Frank McCarthy began touring the country essentially as Yannacone's ambassador, speaking to every veterans' group he could find, and encouraging anyone who suspected dioxin injury to join the class-action suit. Yannacone soon had major competition, however, from two Houston attorneys, Benton Musslewhite and Newton Schwartz, who were signing up hundreds of their own veteran clients in Texas. Musslewhite gained credibility by associating himself with Tod Ensign and Citizen Soldier, much the same as Yannacone had associated himself with McCarthy and AOVI. Unfortunately, the vast ideological differences between the radical Citizen Soldier and the right-leaning AOVI would only exacerbate the growing rivalries between individual attorneys. The fact that Musslewhite and the Washington, D.C., firm of Ashcraft & Gerel (which also had a substantial number of veteran clients) wanted to sue the U.S. government too—which Yannacone still adamantly opposed—just created further divisions for the chemical companies to exploit.

Yannacone had his own plans for exploiting the chemical companies. He knew that not all of the Vietnam veterans who showed signs of chemical poisoning had been hurt by Agent Orange. The American military had sprayed a variety of other chemicals in Vietnam. Agent Blue was another defoliant, used extensively against rice lands; it contained a form of arsenic. Several other herbicides—Agents White, Pink, and Green—were contaminated with dioxin. Insecticides were ubiquitous. Then there was the widely used, experimental antimalarial drug, dapsone, held responsible for the death of eight servicemen in 1970 and later proven carcinogenic. Yannacone had chosen to focus his lawsuit on Agent Orange not only because the phenoxy herbicides (2,4-D and 2,4,5-T) were so widely used in Vietnam but because they were manufactured by the biggest companies, with the most to lose.

In order to exculpate themselves, those companies would doubtless use some of their immense resources to investigate the toxic potential of rival poisons, which might be made to take the blame instead. Not only would the giants like Dow put their research departments to work to indict all the other possible causes of Vietnam veteran illness, they would in time also likely spill all they knew about Agent Orange, in order to prove that the government knew just as much as they did. And even if the chemical companies then got off the hook by virtue of the "government contract" defense, it would mean that veterans could demand their Title 38 disability benefits from the VA. Under Title 38, if there is any reasonable evidence that a veteran might have gotten sick or died as a result of military service, the VA must give him the benefit of the doubt and presume that his disability or death was service-connected. If Yannacone's strategy worked, the chemical companies would hand him that "reasonable evidence" on a silver platter.[189]

There was still the matter of winning the lawsuit, however, which required a much more rigorous proof. Tort suits normally demanded the clear demonstration of cause and effect. The plaintiff not only had to point at the instrument of his injury, but also to prove that that instrument was capable of so injuring someone. Just as the VA had seen causation as the weak link in the veterans' Agent Orange disability claims, the chemical companies were sure to make causation their last stand, if they failed with the government contract defense. Yannacone rightfully distrusted all the government studies then in progress, especially since they were many years away from completion, but he impetuously decided that the answer was for Yannacone & Associates to conduct their own study. The consortium's list of clients was growing every day, and would eventually number about 8,300 veterans, which seemed like a more-than-adequate base of subjects from which to gather health data. He assured the Associates that he could complete a study within three years at the cost of no more than a million dollars. But the Associates balked at putting up money for something as complex as an epidemiological study, for which Yannacone had neither credentials nor experience. Yannacone decided that he and his wife, Carol, would carry it on anyway, provoking the first serious financial arguments between him and his backers.

Initially, Judge Pratt faced a crucial decision—one which also carried the potential of putting the veterans out of business. He had to decide whether to certify the case as a class action, and if certified, to decide what categories of plaintiffs to admit. There were actually a number of good reasons for Pratt to refuse to certify the case as a class action. Most mass tort cases—including those based on asbestos and the pregnancy drug DES—had been denied certification. Courts had especially shied from certifying class actions in cases where causation was in doubt—as it clearly was in the Agent Orange lawsuit. The Agent Orange case added yet another complication, in that the class would have to include "indeterminate plaintiffs": those veterans who did not yet know that they had been harmed by the herbicide, or for whom that harm had not yet fully manifested. Another major obstacle was the requirement that class actions be brought by "representative plaintiffs" who can "fairly and adequately protect the interests of the class." Their attorneys must be similarly qualified to speak for the entire class, without stirring up any internal conflicts or antagonisms. In the Agent Orange case, of course, the veterans and their lawyers were at one another's throats almost from the day the suit was filed—a fact which Yannacone tried desperately to keep from Judge Pratt. That dissemblance required a kind of high-wire act, in which he had to walk the edge between his money-minded investors and his truth-seeking veterans without provoking the wrath of either, and with the knowledge that most of the time there was nothing holding him up but his own show of confidence.

On November 24, 1980, before Pratt had a chance to rule on any of these critical issues, the veterans were dealt a severe blow by the Second Circuit Court of Appeals. A panel of judges voted two to one that there was no "identifiable federal policy at stake in the litigation" and hence that the case must be decided by state law. (The case would still be heard in federal court only because suits had been filed in so many different states that the so-called diversity jurisdiction applied.) In a stinging dissent, Chief Judge Wilfred Feinberg recalled that the Second Circuit Court had earlier asserted a strong federal interest in assuring uniform treatment of prisoners. It was tragically ironic, Feinberg felt, that the court should deem prisoners more worthy of federal protection than Vietnam veterans. "If the laws of thirty or forty state jurisdictions are separately applied," wrote Feinberg, "veterans' recoveries for Agent Orange injuries will vary widely—despite the fact that these soldiers fought shoulder to shoulder, without regard to state citizenship, in a national endeavor abroad." Yannacone immediately appealed the decision to the Supreme Court, which, at the urging of the U.S. Solicitor General, declined to hear the case.

Despite the blow, Yannacone remained confident, he says, because of Judge Pratt's "tremendous feeling of respect for the veterans." In late December 1980 Pratt issued a series of decisions that showed that respect, putting the veterans' rights back at the center of the case. First, basing his decision on the *Feres* Doctrine, he released the government from all liability in the case. Second, though he approved of the government contract defense (which could get the chemical companies off the hook by saying they merely responded to the precise demands of the government for particular herbicides), he specified that the chemical companies must still prove its relevance to their sale of Agent Orange. In effect, he threw the ball back into the defendants' court, forcing the chemical companies to show—even though the government was out of the case—that the government knew at least as much about the dangers of dioxin contamination as the companies themselves knew.

With individual cases still pouring in from all over the country and even New Zealand and Australia, much of the damage from Agent Orange was obviously still latent. The technical issues related to "proof" were compounding daily—especially now that so many different standards would be invoked—and the collection of data to resolve them would probably never catch up. In such a race between science and the law, the losers were bound to be those who could not afford to keep running forever: the veterans. Pratt contrasted the plaintiffs, "who have limited resources with which to press their claims and whose plight becomes more desperate and depressing as time goes on," with the super-rich chemical companies, "who have ample resources for counsel and expert witnesses to defend them, and who probably gain significantly . . . from every delay they can produce."

To resolve this dilemma, Pratt came up with a four-point "case management plan." First, he announced his tentative decision to certify the case as a (b)(3) class action. He did not address a number of the issues on which (b)(3) certification depends, however, such as how counsel (in this case, Yannacone &

Associates) can adequately represent the whole class, and how everyone in the class (potentially millions of veterans and their families) will be notified. Perhaps it was to forestall such criticism from the defendants, or as a hedge against his own possible error, that Pratt did not immediately issue the formal certification order—an omission that would later have profound consequences.

Second, Pratt announced that he would immediately deal with the problem of conflicting statutes of limitation in the different states. Third, he consented to the plaintiffs' request for a series of trials, in which critical issues would be examined separately. This strategy would ensure that the case could not be lost all in one blow, and it would force the chemical companies—as the case moved from stage to stage—to gradually unfold their secrets, giving the veterans plenty of time to use the information against them. Fourth, Pratt declared that he was lifting his earlier restraint on discovery. In "Phase I Discovery," beginning January 1, 1981, lawyers on both sides could now seek evidence pertaining to the government contract defense.

A gauge of the defendants' panic is the swiftness with which they retaliated. Since the start of the case, Yannacone had had what he calls a "gentlemen's agreement" with the chemical companies that neither side would speak to the media "without cluing their adversary that things had been said." Late one night in January 1981, he got a call from a *Newsday* reporter, just as the next day's paper was being put to bed. The reporter told him that a Dow spokesman had called *Newsday* about six o'clock with a stunning press release. Dow had just filed an answer to Yannacone's complaint, claiming that the U.S. government had full knowledge both of the dioxin contamination in Agent Orange and of dioxin's possible toxicity. Without admitting that American troops had been injured, Dow's attorneys—with typical attorney double-talk—were saying that *if* injury had been done, the United States military was to blame. Still half-asleep, Yannacone snapped: "Oh! That's the Nuremberg defense—you know, the 'good Nazi' defense . . . 'I was only following orders.'" The next day, *Newsday* proclaimed: "Dow raises Nuremberg defense." Furious at Yannacone's inflammatory one-liners, the chemical companies stepped up their own propaganda campaign to convince both federal and state governments that the phenoxy herbicides and even dioxin itself were relatively harmless. They also pressed to have Judge Pratt's class-action decision reviewed by the Second Circuit Court of Appeals.

Yannacone's remark about Nazis turned out more prescient than he realized. One of the main pieces of evidence that the chemical companies had cited to try to establish the U.S. government's complicity was a hitherto top-secret military document known as the *Hoffman Trip Report*. It was authored by a scientist named Hoffman, who had formerly worked for the chemical/biological warfare unit of Hitler's Third Reich. At the end of World War II, the Americans and the Russians had both sought desperately to lay hands on these toxicologic experts. The story was that a clever American colonel had used a paper clip to add the names of several of them to the bottom of a list of Jews who had been accepted for immigration to America. A drunken Russian colonel had thus failed to notice that he was signing the passenger manifest for these scientists, whom the Soviet Union had planned to extradite and enlist in their own military endeavors. The "paper-clip Nazis," as Yannacone dubbed them, happily ended up at Fort Detrick, Maryland, where they formed the core of America's chemical/biological warfare group, working as so-called commodity supervisors of lethal agents beginning with nerve gas and bacterials and ending only God knew where.

In 1959, Hoffman had returned to Germany to meet with some of his former colleagues, to see if any interesting new toxins had turned up since the war. He was told there was "startling information" on a chemical by-product in the manufacture of 2,4,5-T. Exposure to a very small quantity of this substance (dioxin, though as yet unnamed) had reputedly killed several workers in a German plant. Hoffman returned to Fort Detrick with news of his latest "candidate agent"—a substance whose lethality had yet to be verified. Extensive tests were run; and it was decided that although this particular chlorinated hydrocarbon was more toxic than anything ever seen before, it was useless as a lethal agent. The reason for its rejection was that it took fourteen days to kill a victim, and so it was not practical even for assassination. As another of the German "commodity supervisors" told Yannacone: "Too many things can happen in fourteen days."

When the specialists at Fort Detrick dismissed dioxin as a potential military weapon, they buried their findings about it in a classified file. Dow and the other Agent Orange defendants would claim that even discarded lethal agents were cross-referenced in a number of places, and that the Pentagon could not possibly have missed such a powerful warning when it decided to employ 2,4,5-T extensively in Vietnam.

In fact, rather than just passing the buck to the U.S. government, the chemical companies may well have been understating their case to shield the United States from charges of having knowingly waged chemical warfare. It would later come out that the U.S. military not only knew a great deal about the toxicity of the dioxin in Agent Orange from the very beginning, but had actually considered it as a useful weapon against the Viet Cong. One of the more astounding revelations to come out of the Agent Orange litigation was the admission of Dr. James R. Clary, a former government scientist with the Chemical Weapons Branch, Biological Warfare/Chemical Weapons Division, Air Force Armament Development Laboratory, at Eglin Air Force Base in Florida. Dr. Clary, who also prepared the final report on Operation Ranch Hand, wrote to Senator Tom Daschle on September 9, 1988:

> When we (military scientists) initiated the herbicide program in the 1960s, we were aware of the potential for damage due to dioxin contamination in the herbicide. We were even aware that the "military" for-

mulation had a higher dioxin concentration than the "civilian" version due to the lower cost and speed of manufacture. However, because the material was to be used on the "enemy," none of us were overly concerned. We never considered a scenario in which our own personnel would become contaminated with the herbicide. And, if we had, we would have expected our own government to give assistance to veterans so contaminated.[190]

8. The "Smoking Gun" Is Found, and Vietnam Vets Get an Image Upgrade

Throughout 1981 and into the first few months of 1982, things looked increasingly rosy for the chemical companies. They continued to produce more and more documentation of the government's awareness concerning herbicide toxicity, including a 1963 report from the President's Science Advisory Committee (PSAC) to the Joint Chiefs of Staff that warned against the health risks of defoliation in Vietnam. Even more disconcerting to the veterans was the fact that Judge Pratt had apparently bogged down in a number of areas where he had promised quick action. He had never settled the statute of limitations question, and he had never formally certified the class, which prevented notice from being sent out. Thus the veterans' attorneys still had no idea how many plaintiffs they represented. Part of the delay came from Pratt's role as presiding judge in Abscam, which had expanded into a series of six consecutive trials. Another factor was the squabbling that continually worsened among the veterans' attorneys.

Pratt had designated Yannacone as lead counsel in the case, but together Ashcraft & Gerel (who had become linked to VVA) and Musslewhite and Schwartz (drawing clients from Citizen Soldier) now represented almost half of the 3,400 named plaintiffs. In late 1981, VVA began swinging radically to the left, when Bobby Muller and several of his associates made a trip to Hanoi, in what appeared to be an effort at reconciliation with the Communists. That turn of events engendered in Yannacone, McCarthy, and the AOVI vets a profound sense of distrust, which was aggravated by the joint announcement of Ashcraft & Gerel and Musslewhite and Schwartz that all of their veteran clients would be opting out of the class action. For their part, Ashcraft & Gerel, Musslewhite, Schwartz, and a number of other attorneys who had filed Agent Orange cases complained to the judge that Yannacone was not supplying them with copies of discovery documents or other pertinent information, as the court had ordered that he do. They felt that much of the time he deliberately obstructed their path.

In what Yannacone felt was pure spite, these other attorneys suggested that he and his consortium were not competent to handle so many clients and such a complex case. They asked that Pratt create a steering committee composed of Yannacone's consortium, Ashcraft & Gerel, and the Musslewhite-Schwartz group. The steering committee would take charge of the responsibilities Yannacone now tried (and often failed) to manage single-handedly. Most importantly, they asked Pratt to put Ashcraft & Gerel in charge of distributing notices and documents, to keep Yannacone from sitting on them indefinitely, as they claimed he was doing with 10,000 pages the government had provided him.

Yannacone accused his rivals of a "power play." He and McCarthy hinted that many of the other attorneys were paying $50 a head for Agent Orange clients, and that they were betraying their clients by trying to sabotage the consortium's carefully laid-out strategy of serial trials. Yannacone would later claim that both Ensign and Musslewhite were his "bitter enemies in this litigation from day one," that they "were in the litigation to make money" and "to embarrass the American public image internationally." Rather than trying to help veterans, Yannacone asserted, "whenever there was a chance to interfere with the Agent Orange litigation, they did." When Pratt denied the request for an attorneys' steering committee, and reaffirmed his confidence in Yannacone & Associates, he only deepened the paranoia in these others, as well as their resentment of Yannacone's domineering leadership.

Though Yannacone harbored his own suspicions of being conspired against, Tod Ensign, at least, always defended Yannacone as "coming from a sincere place." "He felt moved by what he saw, to his credit," Ensign later explained, "but that, unfortunately, was not enough. It was not even close to being enough." Ensign felt Yannacone's blunders came neither from egotism nor malice but simply because "he had no idea what he was doing." It might be fairer, however, to say that Yannacone always had too many ideas at once, and so became his own worst enemy by continually going off on new tangents.

With the case already freighted with too many issues, Pratt virtually immobilized, and the plaintiffs themselves losing critical momentum like a plane about to stall and nosedive, Yannacone made another of his ambitious moves and filed a second suit on behalf of his veteran clients, this time against the VA. The cause was certainly a good one. Though Congress had passed a law in 1981 requiring the VA to give high priority to the treatment of Vietnam veterans claiming Agent Orange injury, the law was in fact being used to justify the VA's continuing refusal to pay such veterans disability benefits. Public Law 97-72, while offering Vietnam veterans their first prospect of health care for dioxin-related problems, stated that the VA would offer such care "notwithstanding that there is insufficient medical evidence to conclude that such disability may be associated with exposure." The VA thus had a ready-made loophole to continue denying disability claims, since the law clearly stated that Vietnam veterans did not really deserve even the little bit they were about to get.

By the fall of 1982, 14,236 Agent Orange disability claims had been filed, and none had been approved. Yannacone asked the U.S. District Court to compel the VA to reconsider all those claims in light of each veteran's history of herbicide exposure—a criterion that had never been used. But current law still shielded the VA from any form of judicial review other than constitutional challenges to its decisions. Judge Pratt threw the suit out, ruling that Yannacone had failed to prove that constitutional issues were at stake. He chastised Yannacone for attempting to use his court to legitimize "a political struggle between veterans and the VA."

That Yannacone had slowed in prosecuting the main suit against the chemical companies was due not only to the lagging of Judge Pratt. Though he dared not admit it, Yannacone was almost out of money. The problem was that the Associates weren't holding up their end. One of the ten investing firms had dropped out early, but Yannacone still expected a total subsidy of $18,000 a month from the other nine. Instead, only one attorney, Donald Russo, paid the promised $2,000 a month. The others, Yannacone says, gave nothing after the first month, except when they were forced to pay for a court transcript or other materials that would otherwise be withheld. Yannacone claims he got no more than $160,000 from them over the forty months of the consortium's existence, and that when Yannacone & Associates finally dissolved, he had spent almost a million dollars out of his own pocket, much of which he still owed to creditors.

There was reason for the Associates to lose confidence in Yannacone. It became obvious after a while that he was taking shots in the dark. Besides his half-baked epidemiological study and his aborted assault against the VA, he had also tried and failed to get Pratt to ban the spraying of 2,4,5-T throughout the United States. Pratt had ruled that he could not do the work of the EPA.[191] But then no one really knew where to look for answers to what was surely one of the hardest legal riddles of the century, filled with technological twists that had never existed before. Scarcely anyone imagined that the Sphinx itself, Dow Chemical, would indirectly provide the biggest key yet.

Consortium member David Dean was given access to some of Diamond Shamrock's files early in 1982. One day he happened upon a report of a meeting that Dow had held with several of its competitors in March 1965 concerning the manufacture of 2,4,5-T. Besides Diamond Shamrock, representatives of Hercules and several smaller companies were present. Dow had decided to break its secrecy agreement with Boehringer about the health hazards of 2,4,5-T, because the situation was threatening to explode in all of their faces.

In late 1964, workers in Dow's 2,4,5-T plant in Midland, Michigan, had begun falling seriously ill once again. When the government had started purchasing large quantities of the herbicide for use in Vietnam, Dow had had trouble meeting the increased demand. To improve the yield, a Dow engineer, ignorant of past problems, had raised the temperature during production. Dow realized that it had stumbled into the same trap as before, but this time it determined to find out exactly what the hazard consisted of. Workers in white plastic suits went into the plant and brought out samples of the contaminated product, to be examined by Dow's own world-class analytical laboratory. By now, they were able to identify the contaminant as dioxin. Determining that it would be impossible to decontaminate the plant, Dow simply buried the building and made it into a toboggan slide. At that point, it occurred to Dow that if their competitors were making the same mistake in trying to boost production, a worldwide catastrophe might be in the making.

Dow proceeded to analyze all of its competitors' products, and the results were more horrifying than anyone had anticipated. Diamond Shamrock's 2,4,5-T turned out to be contaminated with dioxin at between 90 and 100 parts per million. Monsanto's came in at 60 ppm. Dow's had been contaminated with *only one part per million* when the outbreak of sicknesses occurred among its workers. Their "good" 2,4,5-T had contained one-tenth ppm. Hercules' product also showed only one-tenth ppm, meaning it was relatively clean. Unbeknownst to Dow, Hercules had already learned the lower-temperature trick from its German sister company, Badischer Anilin & Soda-Fabrik (BASF).

Even though the dioxin was diluted by half when 2,4,5-T was mixed with 2,4-D to produce Agent Orange, it was clear to Dow that Agent Orange coming from either Diamond Shamrock or Monsanto would be extremely dangerous to anyone who handled it. What made matters worse for Dow and those companies with a relatively clean product was that Agent Orange was treated as a fungible commodity by the government. Shipments of Agent Orange from many different sources were all mixed together at a central storage facility in Mobile, Alabama, then poured into 55-gallon drums for shipment to Vietnam.

At the March 1965 meeting, Dow warned its competitors that they would all end up getting investigated if the high dioxin content of Agent Orange became public knowledge. Dow admitted that repeated contact with herbicide contaminated at even one ppm could cause health problems. So Dow offered details of its low-temperature technique for free to the other manufacturers, to ensure that none of them triggered a toxic disaster for which they would all be held responsible.

Exultant, Dean rushed to tell the other Associates that he had found "the smoking gun." In the next few months, even more incriminating documents turned up. The most shocking was the memorandum made by a Hercules official on July 12, 1965, after a phone conversation with someone at Dow. Wrote the Hercules official: "Dow was extremely frightened that the situation might explode. They are aware that their competitors are marketing 2,4,5-T acid which contains alarming amounts of [a chloracne-causing substance] and if the government learns of this, the whole industry will suffer. They are particularly fearful of a Congressional investigation and excessive restrictive legislation on manufacture of pesticides which might result."

The plaintiffs now had in hand evidence suggesting that Dow had deliberately kept the truth about the dangerously high dioxin content of Agent Orange from the government. If indeed it could be proved that the manufacturers knew more than the government about the hazards of their product, the government contract defense would be wiped out. The manufacturers might even be liable for punitive damages in the billions of dollars, based on their act of concealment. The knowledge that some of the Agent Orange manufacturers had sold a far more "dirty" product than others made it possible for the plaintiffs to attack the companies one by one, according to their degree of culpability. With the companies split, it would be easier to strike deals, and the firms with the most "guilt" would be likely to push for a settlement.

1982 was the turnaround year for the lawsuit for many reasons. Not only was dioxin almost constantly in the news, due to scandals like Times Beach, but juries were now ready to award substantial damages for even minimal exposure. A case that must have shaken the chemical companies like a major earthquake went to trial in Edwardsville, Illinois, in April 1982. The Norfolk & Western Railway was sued in circuit court by 47 of its employees, who had taken part in the cleanup after a tank car ruptured near Sturgeon, Missouri. The tank car had spilled 30,000 gallons of orthochlorophenol manufactured by Monsanto. The chemical was shown to be contaminated with dioxin at 22 parts *per billion*, which was over four times as "clean" as the cleanest Agent Orange sprayed in Vietnam. But one of the cleanup workers had developed testicular and skin cancer, and several others complained of liver damage, neurological problems, loss of sex drive, dizziness, and difficulty breathing—virtually the same list of symptoms reported by Vietnam veterans.

In trial testimony, Harvard professor Matthew Meselson established that dioxin in concentrations as low as 5 parts *per trillion* caused cancer in some laboratory animals. Monsanto and the manufacturers of the tank car and the car's broken coupling chose to settle out of court for a reputed $8 million. Norfolk & Western waited out a jury verdict, and got hit with $58 million in damages. The majority of workers were awarded over a million dollars apiece. At that rate, using AOVI's estimate of 150,000 Vietnam veterans with valid Agent Orange claims, the chemical companies could be facing a total liability of $150 billion!

If a conservative, small-town midwestern jury was that sympathetic toward railroad workers, it was natural to assume that a similar (if better educated) one on Long Island would be even kinder to the nation's own combat veterans and their families. It was the chemical companies' worst nightmare to contemplate the virtually endless supply of sweet, lovable, deformed and disabled children that the veterans could parade before a jury. As Frank McCarthy put it succinctly: "What jury in the world is not gonna award Kerry Ryan a tremendous amount of money?" One of Yannacone's brilliant moves was to videotape the depositions of some of the veterans with terminal cancer, so that their testimony would not be lost if they died before the case came to trial.[192]

The strongest factor in the plaintiffs' favor, though, was the powerful resurgence of the Vietnam veterans' movement in 1982. For more than a decade, Vietnam veteran activists had been beaten back, ignored, undermined, and co-opted by the right, the left, and their own government. Many had burned out, given up, or gone into hiding outside or inside the country. It would be easy enough to attribute this rebirth to the change in political climate when an enormously popular, war-glorifying hawk, Ronald Reagan, assumed the presidency—except that during his eight years in office, not one advance for Vietnam veterans could be attributed solely to his effort or influence, while he had certainly helped put more than a few obstacles in their path. By contrast, Hollywood, the arts, and the media had all taken up the veterans' cause with increasingly sophisticated and sympathetic portraits.

By 1982, the deranged killer Vietnam vet had been supplanted by the sexy, charismatic figure of Tom Selleck starring in *Magnum P.I.* That TV show, a consistent winner in the ratings, had as its hero a big, tough, handsome, and good-hearted Hawaiian private investigator named Thomas Magnum. As columnist Bob Greene observed: "It is never stated aloud that the reason he is so cool and self-reliant is that he was a Vietnam soldier—but the implication is there." The fact that Magnum's Vietnam service was underplayed served to reinforce the positive sense that he was "integrated into society again." Greene went so far as to claim that Selleck's graceful performance had led to Vietnam veterans being "considered the manliest, gutsiest, most courageous folks in America."

Despite the shift in America's myth making, Vietnam veterans themselves deserved most of the credit for what was the biggest image upgrade since Dee Brown and Marlon Brando humanized the Indians, and since the Japanese went from being demon kamikazes to America's chosen electronics and automobile manufacturers.

Vietnam veterans had shown unbelievable perseverance, especially in the political arena, where—despite the support of a handful of their brothers, the Vietnam Veterans in Congress (VVIC)—they had almost never been welcomed. By 1982, pulled up by their own bootstraps, they had become a political force to reckon with. Muller's VVA was already being torn between liberal and conservative factions; but the fact that it even existed, and that a national Vietnam veterans' organization had taken its place beside the VFW and the American Legion—if not in membership, at least in media and congressional presence—was a minor miracle.[193]

9. VVA Returns to Take On Agent Orange, Negotiations Falter, and a Plot Takes Root to Unseat Yannacone

VVAW, the first national Vietnam veterans' organization, short on diplomacy and long on confrontation, with a gift for making enemies and getting betrayed by its friends, had been left for dead by the side of the road. On that same road Bob Avakian and the Revolutionary Communist Party (RCP, successor to the RU) had gone from hopes of mass revolution to exile in France and a few dwindling, still fanatic cells buried in three or four American cities. But in 1982, a veritable Lazarus, VVAW was thriving again, and active on a whole host of issues. In 1978, a few of the still-credible leaders—including some, like Barry Romo, who had had to renounce a former RU affiliation—forcibly drove the RCP from the organization, and even sued their former Communist comrades to get the VVAW name back free and clear. By court order, the RCP faction was henceforth forced to identify themselves as "VVAW-AI": Vietnam Veterans Against the War Anti-Imperialist.

The new VVAW had taken up the Agent Orange cause with a vengeance. When the Agent Orange story broke in Chicago in early 1978 with Bill Kurtis's "Deadly Fog" TV special, the issue helped the organization restore its focus on veterans' issues. Still headquartered in Chicago, VVAW immediately contacted Maude DeVictor, conferred life membership upon her, and made her their principal speaker for the next half-dozen years. They also became the mainstay of her existence after she was pressured to leave the VA. She recalls how the local vets would drop off boxes of food outside her door in the middle of the night, and how chapters around the country would hold benefit suppers to pay her rent. VVAW took the lead among veterans' organizations in putting out Agent Orange introductory pamphlets and self-help guides, as well as covering the developing story in almost every issue of its newspaper, *The Veteran* (successor to *Winter Soldier*). Even after VVA created its hotline, VVAW was still the best source of detailed, up-to-the-minute reports on dioxin studies, changes in VA policy, and legislative action at all levels.

In December 1979, VVAW held its Winter Soldier Investigation of Agent Orange in Chicago. The testimony from numerous vets exposed to the herbicide was then made public at press conferences and sent to state and national legislators. VVAW initiated a boycott of Dow products, and it helped pressure the Air Force into releasing its so-called HERBS tapes, which were the computerized records of exactly where and when Agent Orange was sprayed in Vietnam. The HERBS tapes, which the government resisted making public, were a tremendous aid to veterans in documenting their dioxin-exposure disability claims. The information therein was eventually published in *The Vietnam Map Book* by Berkeley professor and former GI movement leader Clark Smith. The *Map Book* became even more useful after Big Red One veteran George Ewalt Jr., an Agent Orange victim himself, forced the government to begin releasing the "operational reports" and "after-action reports" that showed where individual units were stationed at any given time.

VVAW educated veterans about how to deal with the VA's cursory Agent Orange exam, what questions to ask of VA doctors, and what other options were open to them. It also encouraged and assisted veterans everywhere to file disability claims. VVAW reasoned that the VA's continued denial of thousands of claims would eventually trigger a congressional reaction in behalf of Vietnam veterans. And even if it didn't, the veteran who filed a claim would at least establish a record of his health concerns, which could be trotted out later, should VA policy ever change to favor service connection for Agent Orange–related ailments. Amassing paperwork, they knew, was the first step in beating the VA at its own game, and it would also aid vets in getting a share of the booty if Yannacone prevailed in the class-action lawsuit. Beyond that, VVAW wanted to prove it had "exhausted all bureaucratic remedies" in order to justify, if necessary, "forcing the government and VA to do something with more militant methods."

Indeed, as the 1980s wore on and the VA continued to deny VVAW's three principal goals—"testing, treatment, and compensation"—VVAW resorted to what some members liked to call "direct actions," including hospital sit-ins, camp-outs on state capitol lawns, and takeovers of politicians' offices. At assembly hearings and on picket lines they often chanted Paul Reutershan's putative last words: "They killed me in Vietnam and I didn't even know it!" Madison VVAW member Jim Wachtendonk, who not only suffered himself from dioxin-related complaints but had fathered two children with serious birth defects, wrote numerous outrageous protest songs that he sang at hundreds of Agent Orange demonstrations. His most famous, "The Claymore Polka," warned toxic-chemical manufacturers as well as unresponsive legislators: "I'd like to blow you away with a claymore / put a booby-trap inside your briefcase / set some punji sticks around your mansion / add some Agent Orange to your tea. . . ."

When the class-action lawsuit came along, VVAW worked long and hard getting word out to potential Agent Orange victims and helping them to sign on as plaintiffs. Though Yannacone was leery of VVAW as an organization, he developed a close relationship with many of the chapters, especially those with a less-pronounced leftist slant. "The Madison group, the Milwaukee group, one in Iowa, and groups in a number of other states all cooperated and did a tremendous amount of work for us during the course of the litigation," he recalled. "They created the network that both distributed information and acted as group support."

VVAW also felt the need to return to the nation's capital. They collaborated with the National Veterans Task Force on Agent Orange in St. Louis to sponsor the first national conference on Agent Orange in Washington, D.C., May 22–24, 1981. While in Washington, VVAW picketed the VA Central Office and attempted to bring a wreath of orange flowers into Arlington Cemetery. Just as in 1971, the gates of Arlington were locked in their faces. They laid the wreath outside and left quietly. This time, they could not so easily be dismissed as a bunch of pseudo-veterans and dope-smoking Communists. Some, like Milwaukee's John Lindquist, still wore the long hair, beard, and jungle fatigues of their six-ties identity; but most now had families and good-paying jobs, and even in appearance had pretty well assimilated into mainstream society. It was clear that they were no longer touting violent revolution, but were there simply to honor their dead comrades, to comfort those who might still be dying, and to seek offi-cial recognition of their ongoing ordeal. Many congressmen were outraged at the spectacle of Vietnam veterans, some of them seriously ill from what their own country had done to them, being denied entrance to the nation's most sacred place of mourning and contemplation, on the eve of Memorial Day. Congressman Robert Kastenmeier (D-Wis.), among others, offered to help them finally gain admission there the following year.

VVAW spent a year building up to yet another Dewey Canyon operation. This one would logically be Dewey Canyon V, but the organization chose to for-get the RU-dominated nightmare called Dewey Canyon IV in 1974. The call for vets to come to Washington May 10–16, 1982, referred to the event as Dewey Canyon IV. This second DC IV focused chiefly on Agent Orange, though other demands such as "No More Vietnams" reaffirmed the organiza-tion's continuing political involvement. Only 200 vets came to camp out on the Mall, a tenth of the showing eleven years earlier, but they represented 23 states and 40 cities. Moreover, many now had wives and children in tow. Their week of demonstrations and lobbying were extraordinarily successful. "They're learn-ing what it takes to effect change," commented an aide to Wisconsin's Republican Senator, Robert Kasten. "We know we have to listen." Once again, Reagan had sent Congress a budget that gave the VA half a billion dollars less than it needed. VVAW argued, less combatively and more persuasively than in 1974, that the United States would do better spending money to deal with its troubled Vietnam veterans than on an inflated defense budget, as the Pentagon readied a new generation of soldiers for a possible war in Central America.

The day VVAW arrived in Washington, *Newsday* ran an unprecedented edi-torial powerfully supporting the organization. It contended that VVAW's polit-ical agenda "shouldn't disqualify them from honoring their dead comrades" at Arlington, and that no veteran should be "denied this opportunity for reconcil-iation." Representative Robert Kastenmeier read the editorial into the *Congressional Record,* along with his own plea that the United States govern-ment stop waging its "cruel and unconscionable" war against Vietnam veterans. For the first time in Congress, someone dared speak a truth whose conceal-ment was wounding and killing a whole generation of American warriors. Vietnam veterans, Kastenmeier declared, "are no different from those who fought and died in any of the other wars in our history. . . . The Government has transferred the black mark of the war to those who fought that war as, in fact, did the American people, seemingly trying to forget the tragedy of our involvement in Vietnam by also forgetting those who fought there."

Kastenmeier proceeded to introduce House Resolution 464, which recommended the Department of the Army immediately grant VVAW the permit it sought for a public ceremony at Arlington Cemetery on May 15, 1982. His resolution also suggested it was time the U.S. government "help honor the veterans of a war whose services have largely gone unrecognized to date." Typically, the resolution was dumped into the black hole of the Veterans' Affairs Committee. But, finally, the Army did relent and allow VVAW to assemble in Arlington. That Saturday, 200 vets wearing orange armbands placed a red-and-yellow wreath just inside the cemetery gates. Red and yellow were the colors of the flag of the Republic of Vietnam, in whose defense they had risked their lives, and they were also the colors of the Vietnam Campaign Ribbon. Mixed together, of course, they produced the color orange.

Meanwhile, in Constitution Gardens, not far from the VVAW encampment, Maya Ying Lin's Vietnam Memorial Wall was already under construction. In November 1982, VVAW would be back in Washington, along with thousands of other veterans, families, friends, and well-wishers, for the dedication of the Wall. VVAW, like many of their comrades, did not approach the Wall with unmixed enthusiasm. As one VVAW spokesman put it: "Better VA care or a realistic jobs program will help vets far more than another monument." VVAW, in fact, used the week of ceremonies marking the Wall's completion to disseminate Agent Orange information to many more veterans, as well as to continue signing up plaintiffs for the lawsuit. Their motto that week was "Honor the Dead, Fight for the Living." But the Wall, once it was unveiled to America, would somehow sweep all partisan concerns aside, and carry the nation forward with an unstoppable momentum of healing that took both its supporters and opponents by complete surprise. A large part of that healing would comprise a greatly enhanced respect for the dignity and the sacrifice of Vietnam veterans.[194]

By the end of 1982, the chemical companies would have had to be deaf and blind to not realize that the wind of public opinion was blowing hard against them. By all accounts, they were actually spending large sums of money to learn as much as they could about the veterans and their legal strategy. McCarthy recalls that investigators from Dow constantly followed him and other AOVI leaders, until Yannacone sought a court order to make them stop. Tod Ensign at Citizen Soldier protested Dow's "surveillance tactics" and "corporate espionage," after he discovered that Dow had sent a spy to his office posing as a journalist. The individual in question brought Dow privileged attorney-client information relating to Musslewhite's Agent Orange cases in Texas. Ensign also complained that Dow's agents were hobnobbing with members of the VA's

Agent Orange Advisory Panel, evidently fishing for useful information there, as well as trying to win allies. Wisconsin VVAW coordinator Dennis Kroll learned of illegal wiretaps on some of the prominent Agent Orange activists in Madison, though it was never proven who initiated them. The Agent Orange lawsuit was certainly one of the targets; among those tapped were plaintiffs in the case.

One thing that was not kept secret was how much the plaintiffs expected to win in damages. Some Vietnam veterans' groups were predicting the defendants would have to pay at least $40 billion into a trust fund for Agent Orange victims. With that large a threat over their heads, it was no wonder that some of the companies were leaning toward an out-of-court settlement. In December 1982, two of Yannacone's Associates, Ed Gorman and Eugene O'Brien, met secretly with Dow's attorney Leonard Rivkin to try to come to terms. A World War II veteran, Rivkin had won a Silver Star in the Battle of the Bulge; and he was, according to Yannacone, "the only lawyer on the other side who treated the veterans with respect." Rivkin's willingness to strike a bargain was not purely selfless, however. Dow had produced almost 30 percent of the Agent Orange used in Vietnam, but, because of its special process, had contributed only 1.3 percent of the total dioxin to which veterans were exposed. Theoretically, Dow was far less guilty of poisoning American troops than most of the other thirteen companies now cited as defendants. But if Judge Pratt ruled that Dow had acted "in concert" with the other companies, they would all be held "jointly and separately liable"—which meant that if the others could not pay their equal share of the judgment, Dow might be held responsible for the entire amount. Rivkin proposed a "structured settlement" to Gorman and O'Brien. After paying $10 million up front, Dow would contribute to an investment fund guaranteed to pay out $90 million to veterans over the next twenty years.

David Dean, another of the Associates, tried to push Rivkin's offer up to $175 million; then Yannacone reputedly tried to cut a separate deal with Dow's in-house claims manager, Charlie Carey, for at least $300 million. At the same time, consortium member Al Fiorella was off trying to use the leverage of a Dow offer to bring Hercules (whose Agent Orange was even cleaner than Dow's) to a similar agreement. Dow evidently decided there were too many balls in the air, and backed out of the negotiations on February 22, 1983. Taking their cue from Dow, Hercules also broke off settlement talks. One of Dow's biggest concerns was that the consortium still had not specified how many veterans it represented, or, for that matter, how many veterans and veterans' children were thought to be Agent Orange victims. With the number of potential plaintiffs still a big question mark, Dow was leery of buying off one group of veterans only to have another group led by different attorneys suddenly take their place.

For the plaintiffs, the biggest horror of the aborted settlement bid was the discovery that Yannacone was bluffing with a mostly empty hand. As soon as the first settlement talks had begun in July 1982, the defendants had requested a detailed list of the purported Agent Orange injuries, as well as a reasonably accurate accounting of the numbers of victims in each category—cancer, liver disease, birth defects, etc. They also asked for a disease profile on 36 representative plaintiffs. For months, Yannacone had been bragging about how he had entered all the Agent Orange evidence and case histories in his "very sophisticated computer system," and how his computerized database would make legal history. The Associates turned to Yannacone, expecting him to deliver a dazzling series of spreadsheets that would bring the chemical companies to their knees. Instead, they found that Yannacone's wife, overwhelmed with thousands of documents, had merely stuffed most of them in boxes for the time being. Nevertheless, Yannacone provided an estimate of 20,000 "hard" injuries—disabling illnesses and birth defects—and 30,000 lesser injuries. He also promised to deliver the representative disease profiles in time for a November meeting with the chemical companies.

When, shortly before the meeting, Yannacone again came up empty-handed, several of the Associates went to his office to procure the requisite data themselves. According to Wayne Wilson, head of New Jersey's Agent Orange Commission, who spoke with some of those Associates afterward, what they found was boxes of general information on toxic chemicals, virtually useless to the case. As for Yannacone's "epidemiological study," it reputedly contained mostly sketchy notes made by veterans and their wives on various health problems. Moreover, most of the material still had not been entered into Yannacone's computers. The Associates were hard put to boil it down into ten profiles. For the remaining 26, they were forced to turn to other attorneys with a large number of Agent Orange clients—notably Yannacone's archrival, Steven Schlegel in Chicago, whose cool efficiency came from a self-admitted quest for fame and fortune. According to Tod Ensign, the Associates were shocked to learn that Yannacone had not even prepared an index of discovery—one of the most basic tasks of any trial lawyer. Says Ensign: "We didn't even have the basis to go into a computer and find out what we knew. That's incredible! For all Yannacone's talk about 'computer this' and 'computer that,' he was a total failure."

Yannacone insists he did have an index and "database management system," which he had developed himself. "I didn't handle four-and-a-half million documents out of my memory and my fingers," he scoffs, although he admits he was waiting for enough money to scan all of them onto laser disk. He also boasts that he successfully sued the Justice Department for its entire Agent Orange file, two-and-a-half million documents, on microfilm—which only cost the consortium $17 a roll, rather than 10 cents a page. The problem, he says, was not that he didn't have adequate and accessible enough information to win the case, but that none of the other Associates knew how to interpret what he had. Indeed Judge Pratt's special master (a sort of assistant judge), Sol Schreiber, would later testify that Yannacone was the only veterans' attorney who was thoroughly grounded in the scientific and medical aspects of the litigation. The Associates, however, claimed that they had tried to familiarize themselves with what Yannacone called "the biochemical molecular biology" underlying the case, but that he had denied their every request to meet with his scientific experts. Yannacone had promised that the testimony of his scientists would resolve the causation issue in the veterans' favor. But as the months passed and he steadfastly refused to even name these experts, many of the Associates began to suspect that they did not exist outside of Yannacone's head.

The chemical companies sniffed the weakness of Yannacone's case. Yannacone must have had his own doubts, since he warned the Associates that the defendants were likely to file another motion for summary judgment soon. It came about 4 P.M. one Friday afternoon in March 1983, in the form of 72 pounds of documents dumped on his doorstep by UPS. Yannacone was asked to respond the following Thursday, but he was able to talk Pratt into giving him a month. During that period, he got five more 70-pound packages from each of the other major defendants. Once he had sifted through them, Yannacone proclaimed that the plaintiffs had nothing to worry about. Although the chemical companies had amassed a number of sources that suggested the U.S. government had "actual knowledge" of the contamination of herbicides with dioxin, and that dioxin was toxic, the only really damning evidence was a single sentence from the deposition of a scientist named Gordon J. MacDonald. MacDonald, a member of the President's Science Advisory Committee (PSAC) under Lyndon Johnson, stated that he had informally discussed the dangers of 2,4,5-T's dioxin content with fellow PSAC members between April and June 1965. The chemical companies claimed MacDonald's statement proved that the government knew essentially as much as they did, and that they should therefore be shielded from further prosecution by the government contract defense.

The chemical companies convinced Judge Pratt that they had produced Agent Orange according to the government's specifications. Pratt also accepted the chemical companies' proof "that the government and the military possessed rather extensive knowledge tending to show that its use of Agent Orange in Vietnam created significant, though undetermined, risks of harm to our military personnel." But Yannacone still beat back the summary judgment motion. What did the trick was his fantastic store of knowledge about the history of several of the chemical companies, especially Dow—the very material that he had all along seen as the core of the case. Yet he never dreamed that his response to the defendants' motion for dismissal would completely transform Pratt's vision of the case, which is exactly what happened.

On May 20, 1983, ruling against the defendants, Pratt undid almost all his previous efforts to structure the litigation. Yannacone had buried him in piles of evidence that illustrated how complex and sophisticated were both Dow's knowledge of dioxin and the company's ability to detect its presence. Dow, Yannacone showed, had learned how to measure dioxin in concentrations as low as one part per million because it knew that higher levels could cause chloracne and liver damage. The U.S. government had never had such specific knowledge, nor the technology to attain it, and Dow had not offered to share either with them. There was thus no real "parity of knowledge" between one of the principal manufacturers of Agent Orange and its chief consumer. Even if the other chemical companies could establish that Dow had kept its trade secrets from them too, they might still be forced to pay damages under the theory of "enterprise liability." That theory held that companies whose products are mixed together are equally responsible for injuries caused by a faulty or dangerous product from any one of them.

Pratt was clearly confused on the issue of enterprise liability. He dismissed the complaints against three of the companies, including Thompson Hayward, because he felt they had no knowledge of their product's health hazards. He dismissed Hercules, however, on the basis of the very low dioxin content of its Agent Orange, even though Hercules had been represented at the now infamous March 1965 meeting convened by Dow, which had produced the "smoking gun" memorandum. Dow was rightfully upset, then, to be kept in the suit by Pratt principally on the basis of its dioxin knowledge, despite its relatively clean product.

What neither defendants nor plaintiffs had expected was that Pratt would proceed to discount the government contract defense—not on its own merits, which he still respected, but because he now saw it as a far too simplistic approach to the problem of Agent Orange culpability. Stunning everyone, he reversed his earlier decision to hold a series of trials, each one focused on a particular aspect of the case, and instead ruled that all the issues must be tried together in one huge, make-it-or-break-it showdown in court. The government contract defense, he concluded, could not be considered apart from other theories of liability, from data concerning dioxin's toxicity at varying levels, or from the thorniest issue of all for the plaintiffs: causation. The previous fall, Pratt had ordered that the two sides should begin arguing the government contract defense on June 27, 1983. Now that trial date was clearly off, and Pratt did not attempt to set a new one, though he hinted that it would certainly be at least a year away.

Yannacone was jubilant, comparing himself to the much-maligned Nisei troops who had pushed back the Nazis in the Battle of the Bulge. He also accurately predicted that his victory would soon be forgotten, for there was already a conspiracy afoot to unseat him as chief spokesman for the consortium. Like

it or not, the name of the game had become money. Lead plaintiff Michael
Ryan, who was closer to Yannacone than any veteran, including McCarthy,
never criticized him for fumbling with the case; though they later fell out, he
believed Yannacone had done the very best he could. It was becoming painfully
evident to everyone, Yannacone included, that he did not have the resources to
marshal the evidence and the experts that would be needed to win such a case.
What Yannacone and many of the vets who believed in him saw as betrayal was
not the fact that new financial arrangements had to be made. The betrayal, they
felt, came from those attorneys—both his own Associates and those who
wanted to get a bigger part of the class action, like Musslewhite and Schlegel—
who used Yannacone's failings as a pretext for dumping him from the case.
Their justification for the mutiny was that Yannacone was difficult to deal with,
but many veterans soon came to believe that a different motivation was at work.
The other lawyers had to get rid of Yannacone, Frank McCarthy later claimed,
because he was the only advocate who "would stand up there and tell the
truth."[195]

10. Yannacone Goes Out, Judge Weinstein Comes In, and the Race to Trial Begins

The deal went down around Memorial Day 1983 at the law offices of Associate
Irving Like. The eight remaining members of the original consortium met with
nine new law firms from around the country. Word was out from the Travelers
Insurance Company, which represented one of the corporate defendants, that
they were ready to settle the case out of court. These new would-be investors
were, in the words of Michael Ryan, "vultures who were on the lookout for mass
tragedies." Several of them had previous experience with mass tort litigation,
including Pittsburgh attorney Tom Henderson and Philadelphia attorney Gene
Locks, who had both prosecuted asbestos-injury cases. Five of the firms gladly
offered a quarter-million dollars apiece to buy into the Agent Orange lawsuit.
A sixth, Henderson's, offered $200,000. Three other attorneys—David Dean,
Musslewhite, and Schlegel—simply offered their time. They were drawn,
Yannacone claims, not by generosity or concern for veterans, but by a fee award
they imagined would be at least $40 million. Tod Ensign, a bit less righteously
indignant than Yannacone, concurs that "none of these lawyers were men on
white horses, but that just isn't the nature of those kind of people."

Yannacone claims that Musslewhite was one of the "packagers of the deal."
He also claims to have seen a memo from Musslewhite to Newton Schwartz,
one of two Houston attorneys who bought quarter-million-dollar shares of the
pie, indicating that Schwartz was supposed to kick back some of the eventual
fee award to him in exchange for Musslewhite's "getting rid of Yannacone." In

fact, Yannacone asserts, all the new investors planned to withhold their money until after he was out of the driver's seat.

In June, Al Fiorella, by now Yannacone's fiercest enemy in the consortium, spoke with the court's special master Sol Schreiber about their need for a new spokesman; and as soon as Schreiber signaled his approval, the consortium voted to replace Yannacone with David Dean. Yannacone, predictably, refused to step aside, and continued acting as spokesman whenever he could get away with it. That summer, his Associates locked him in a financial stranglehold. Without their money or services, Yannacone was powerless to move the case forward. On September 19, 1983, the remaining members of Yannacone's consortium petitioned the court to be removed as lead counsel, pleading insufficient resources. Refusing to participate in the motion, Yannacone told the court he was "ready for trial anyway." Schreiber, who knew better, recommended to Pratt that he replace Yannacone with a Plaintiffs' Management Committee consisting of Schlegel, Musslewhite, and Henderson.

Before these other attorneys could take the helm, the bomb was dropped. On October 14, 1983, Pratt himself resigned from the case. A year earlier, Pratt had been promoted to the Court of Appeals, but thus far he had been allowed to keep the Agent Orange case on his docket. Suddenly his superiors had decided he could not handle both jobs, and he had been pressured to devote full time to the Second Circuit Court. Pratt, in the eyes of Michael Ryan, was "an honorable man you felt you could trust," who "ran the case aboveboard." The vets suspected political treachery, especially since, as Yannacone phrased it, "the case was too close to damaging some very tight industrial-governmental relationships." The judge was also putting heat on the VA because of the credibility he had given the veterans' allegations. There were rumors that Pratt had been ousted by Reagan's controversial, finagling Attorney General Edwin Meese. That rumor was not so improbable, when one considered that Meese was Reagan's closest pal in the cabinet, and that Reagan himself had already sided publicly against the veterans on the Agent Orange issue. In line with Dow's $3 million campaign to counter the "hysteria over dioxin," Reagan had declared: "News reports about dioxin have frightened a good number of people unnecessarily."

A few days later, Pratt's successor was announced. It was Judge Jack B. Weinstein, a Columbia law professor, World War II veteran, and notoriously unconventional jurist. Although his credentials as liberal Democrat might seem to have favored the veterans, he was also known as a "no-nonsense judge," who forced attorneys to work extraordinarily hard in proving their cases. Weinstein's typical demand that only solid facts be presented as evidence might well demolish the veterans' tenuous web of causation, which depended more on anecdotal histories and common sense than on scientific studies or statistical surveys—much of which didn't exist yet, and might never exist. From the start, he enumerated three tough questions it would fall to the veterans to answer: 1) do the chemicals in Agent Orange cause damage to human beings?; 2) did the chemical companies act negligently?; and 3) if these companies did knowingly harm Vietnam veterans, how extensive was that harm, and how could damages be fairly awarded without hopelessly overburdening the legal system?

Weinstein announced that all the attorneys in the case should meet with him in chambers as a kind of judicial icebreaker, at 2 P.M. on Friday, October 21, 1983. Early that morning, Yannacone met with David Dean, who for a long time had been his sole ally in the consortium. Yannacone asked Dean if they could direct the case together. Dean's reply, as quoted in the *American Lawyer,* was: "No fucking way!" Somehow Yannacone got Dean to appoint him "acting executive director"; though Yannacone confessed to Frank McCarthy, waiting outside, that the title was "meaningless," and that the truth was he had been "dealt out." Later, around 11 A.M., Yannacone met with Weinstein, while McCarthy again remained in the hall. The two men, both commanding personalities, took an immediate dislike to each other. Weinstein, Yannacone recalled, exhibited "a kind of paternal disrespect to Vietnam veterans that I have seen at so many VFW halls"; he seemed to "blame the Vietnam veterans for embarrassing their country." He also made it clear he thought "there was no medical or scientific evidence in support of the case." Lastly, Weinstein informed Yannacone that he and his Associates were about to be replaced as lead counsel by a Plaintiffs' Management Committee (PMC) of nine new law firms. Yannacone, of course, protested; he was sent back out of the judge's chambers; and then, he says, he began to feel as if he had slipped into the script of the movie *Mr. Roberts*—which is about a naval officer who is forced to keep quiet, to his own discredit, to protect the men under him.

According to Yannacone, one of Weinstein's law clerks approached him and delivered an ultimatum from the judge. If Yannacone fought to retain control of the case, said the clerk, Weinstein would retaliate by "dismissing the case out-of-hand," ensuring that "the veterans will get nothing." Yannacone was well aware that, in such a scenario, he stood to get nothing too. At that point, by his own reckoning, he had spent over a million dollars for litigation costs, exclusive of his time, and was deeply in debt. Yannacone seethed, feeling he had been "screwed legal"—but also knowing that unless he "kept his mouth shut" from here on out, he would get stuck with the whole loss and, worse, be blamed for the veterans' defeat.

Yet, whether the veterans won or lost, he feared the case had already been fatally derailed. The nine attorneys to whom the case had been handed—the "masters of disaster," as Yannacone scornfully referred to them—intended to sidestep completely the scientific and technical merits of the case. According to Yannacone: "These nine lawyers collectively could not even pronounce

2,3,7,8-tetrachlorodibenzo-para-dioxin without stumbling. . . . What they wanted to do was parade a dozen children like Kerry Ryan in front of a Brooklyn jury [where Weinstein sat], get a hundred million dollars apiece, and then negotiate a settlement out of that." Although Yannacone too had always told the vets that they would eventually settle the case, he had wanted to bring it to trial not just to get a better offer from the chemical companies, but to give the veterans their "day in court," to get the facts out in the open, and to insure that dioxin-containing chemicals were forever banned in the United States.

In McCarthy's view, Yannacone was hated by lawyers on both sides because he was uncompromising on those last three issues. Michael Ryan described even more starkly what he saw as the disaster of Yannacone's removal. "Yannacone was *our* attorney," he says. "They [the nine new law firms] never represented the veterans. They represented their own interests . . . [which were] 'let's get in, let's get as much as we can, let's recoup our investment, and let's get out.'" What was lost in the deal, Ryan says, were the very things he and many other vets wanted most. In two words he names them: "truth" and "justice."

Although Michael Ryan was clearly a very bitter man with his own personal grudge against the government, he made a point that had escaped Judge Weinstein, however renowned for his "blinding brilliance" (according to Peter Schuck). The Vietnam veterans in the class-action suit had somehow forfeited the right to counsel of their own choice. In *The Veteran* a few months later, John Lindquist described the judge's action and its consequences: "We had no say in the matter . . . we no longer have any say in the case . . . we have no control over what happens."[196]

The biggest shocks were yet to come. That afternoon, at the little wine-and-cheese social in his chambers, Judge Weinstein announced that he had a few changes to make in the way Pratt had structured the litigation. In fact, he hurled a "thunderbolt," wrote historian Wilbur Scott; he "completely changed the substance and ground rules in the case." To begin with, Weinstein declared that the lawsuit, now in its fifth year, had dragged on long enough. Intending to see it "promptly disposed of," he announced that jury selection would start on May 7, 1984—a little over six months away! Next, he said he was was temporarily shelving the government contract defense, on which attorneys for both sides had worked for years taking depositions and doing discovery. The first trial would decide the issue of causation instead. Telegraphing his bias, he said he thought the plaintiffs would have a difficult time proving that Agent Orange had harmed specific veterans, and therefore he considered the defendants' liability "highly doubtful." He was aware, he indicated, that he was putting a heavy burden on the plaintiffs, because "some of the statistical material on carcinogens takes many years to develop." But he felt the chemical companies had a right to ask that the veterans substantiate their charges within a reasonable period of time. Fairness dictated that they not be kept dangling for perhaps decades awaiting some phantom proof.

Certainly the PMC attorneys were put off balance to have the ball thrown into their court so abruptly, and to be given such an unbelievably brief time to prepare arguments on an issue, causation, that they had scarcely yet looked into. But at least one of them, Benton Musslewhite, was not totally displeased with the initial strokes of Weinstein's approach. He would later praise Weinstein for "giving it [the case] a firm direction by setting it for trial on the merits." Despite the veterans' trepidation about losing Pratt, Musslewhite felt Weinstein's "toughness and detachment" would be a greater asset for the plaintiffs than for the chemical companies, who would rather not put all their cards on the table. The veterans, after all, could honestly speak of the "unswerving love for their country" that had led them to be sprayed with Agent Orange in Vietnam; while even in the best light, the motivation of the chemical companies looked suspiciously like corporate greed.

Indeed, a number of Weinstein's decisions could not but help the plaintiffs. His removal of the case from suburban Uniondale, Long Island, to Brooklyn would provide the veterans with a more ethnically diversified and probably working-class jury—whose members would be more truly their peers in terms of probably having served, or having known someone who served, in Vietnam. Even more to the veterans' advantage, he brought back into the case all of the chemical companies, including Hercules, that Pratt had informally dismissed (without ever signing a formal judgment to that effect). The more companies that could be held responsible, the greater the damages the plaintiffs could expect to receive. Weinstein added that even the United States government would have to remain in the case a while longer—which, at the time, seemed just a bid to reinforce his impartiality, but would later reveal itself an integral part of the judge's hidden strategy.

Weinstein reaffirmed his belief in the value of jury trials, and assured the veterans that he would allow "the community . . . to be heard" in the final reckoning on Agent Orange. More ambiguously, he spoke of the veterans' need to produce half a dozen "representative plaintiffs"—their "best cases"— that could be tried first, "to see if there is anything to the case" and to give the chemical companies a realistic idea of what the total judgment against them (if there was one) might amount to. Although such a move seemed a welcome simplification to lawyers on both sides, it was, in the end, badly stacked against the veterans. The whole notion of representative plaintiffs was, says McCarthy, "a lot of crap . . . it showed his ignorance of Agent Orange." In reality, he continues, "everybody is different, and nobody's got one problem. Everybody's got a multitude of problems. They got rashes *and* cancer, [or] cancer *and* birth defects, or neurological *and* immunosuppressive disorders *and* cancer *and* birth defects. How're you gonna be representative? You have a million categories."

Weinstein would insist, however, that veterans be found who manifested a single outstanding problem, and he further skewed the concept of sample cases by denying attorney Tom Henderson's request to include three dead veterans, although he did accept one who was dying of soft-tissue sarcoma, Danny Lee Ford. The judge eventually came up with five categories: chloracne, systemic dysfunctions, neurological disorders, cancers, and birth defects. Children were originally to be included among the representative plaintiffs, but were later dropped when the sample cases were limited to five. Michael Ryan, who suffered from both chloracne and peripheral neuropathy, was thus reduced to merely representing his daughter, Kerry, in the category of birth defects. Not one woman—from among a pool of 11,000 servicewomen (7,800 nurses and 3,200 support personnel) and far more affected wives—was selected to represent a category of injury.

The lineaments of the trap were not all clear on October 21, 1983, but some of Weinstein's other innovations were equally disturbing. He announced that he would not only certify the class, as Pratt had planned, but would, if possible, enlarge it so that all veterans and their families were bound by the verdict. He also liked the idea of a class from which vets could not "opt out," though he later did open the door briefly for those who wished to leave—in order to bring suit individually instead. The transformation of the case into a large cage was all the more menacing to veterans because it was clear that he wanted to push a settlement on them—with a heavy hand, if necessary. The case would be "better settled than tried," he said, and then he indicated that he already had a settlement plan in mind, which included "the other two pieces": the VA and Congress.

The government's responsibility in the matter of Agent Orange was one of Weinstein's principal themes that day. He wanted the government's active participation in the case, and also suggested that veterans would be better off looking to the VA for medical help than trying to wrest a lifetime financial cushion from the chemical companies. He somehow imagined that the big corporations might be coaxed to "make a lump sum donation to help defray" the VA's costs in treating Agent Orange health problems. He even hinted that he might allow civilians—such as the veterans' wives and children—to sue the government and to have their claims heard before a jury, even though the Federal Tort Claims Act prohibited jury trials of the government. Later in the proceedings, Weinstein would reverse himself, and declare, as Pratt had, that the claims of the women and children were "derivative" from those of veterans and so equally forbidden by the *Feres* Doctrine.

Taken aback by so many major "rulings" at what was to have been an informal get-together (it was also the judge's wedding anniversary), the lawyers by and large failed to see what Weinstein was driving at. They were doubtless also horrified at the prospect of having to get to trial in half a year, and preoccupied that afternoon thinking of their next dozen moves. But anyone listening between the lines would have caught on to the fact that Weinstein himself had already dismissed the idea that the Agent Orange controversy could be settled by any trial whatsoever. Moreover, he was apparently shaping the litigation in such a way that—by his calculation—the government would be impelled to do the duty it had thus far shirked. To Weinstein, it was self-evident that the government, not the chemical companies, should be taking care of Vietnam veterans. But he was taking an enormous and ill-advised gamble—one that, if lost, others and not he would have to pay for—in depending on the government, and specifically the VA, to voluntarily assume a huge burden just because it was (in his words) "the intelligent way to handle" the Agent Orange crisis. On the other hand, perhaps he alone saw how truly limited is any court's ability to solve a problem of such magnitude, involving the entire society, the military-industrial complex, and a wide range of conflicting values, both political and ethical. And to be completely fair, the evidence of causation between dioxin exposure and an array of illnesses and genetic, hormonal, and immune-system disturbances was nowhere near as well established as it would be a scant fifteen years later.

Whether he realized it or not, however, Weinstein was biting off more than he could chew in attempting to stir the government into action. The dilemma for Weinstein was that he too was a government worker, and a large part of his responsibility was to protect the government by upholding its laws. He acted as if, Samson-like, he could single-handedly pull the government into the Agent Orange issue. In Peter Schuck's phrase, Weinstein hoped "to hold the government hostage." But the United States was far too redoubtable, and far too inertia-bound, to become tractable to a judge of even Weinstein's resourcefulness. He thus risked either failing like Samson, pulling the whole mess onto his own head, or else being forced to defer to the government's incontrovertible right to say no and/or to change the rules of the game any time it liked. In the end, he and his hidden agenda would fall victim to both humiliations.

Weinstein's relentless push to go to trial, and his threat to stick the government with liability, had inadvertently given hope to the defendants. The chemical companies, while refusing to fund a health study of Vietnam veterans, had already spent $20 million on their own defense against the class-action suit. They estimated that it might cost them $100 million just to get to the May 7 court date, and that once the case came to trial, their expenses could easily reach a million dollars a day. If hitherto they had been weakening at the prospect of bankruptcy from possible years of litigation even before they could be found innocent or guilty, the chemical companies now had reason to celebrate. For no matter how taxing financially or otherwise, the short sprint to judgment Weinstein had set for them would clearly take a heavier toll on the challengers, who never knew where their next dollar was coming from, than on the best-paid army of lawyers in the country.[197]

10

Decade of Betrayal: The Vet Centers in the Eighties

1. Horses Get Traded, and the Readjustment Counseling Program Gets Up and Running

Only four months after the first six Vet Centers had opened in October 1979, several dozen more were in operation or about to be so. At the end of January 1980, nearly 100 Vet Center counselors, clinicians, and team leaders met at a ski resort in Park City, Utah, to participate in a training conference. Present were many of the pioneers of post-traumatic stress disorder theory, including Dr. Chaim Shatan, now fifty-five years old. The mood was celebratory, and some of the participants even treated it as a long-deserved vacation. Shatan recalls the immense satisfaction he felt when both professionals and those still in training—ten, twenty, or even thirty years younger than he—came up to say they had done a dissertation on his writings or that they were running a rap group based on his theories. At the end of the final session, a veteran took the microphone to announce, as a complete surprise to Shatan, that they all wanted to give him a special vote of thanks, as the one person "without whose work over the previous ten years, none of this would have come to pass." He felt as if he were being voted Most Valuable Player. Then four vets jumped out of their seats, lifted the diminutive doctor's chair onto their shoulders, and carried Shatan all around the room to thunderous applause.

On the surface, at least, it seemed a great struggle had finally been won— that the American public, the government, and especially the VA, had gained an awareness of the special needs of Vietnam veterans, and more importantly, a willingness to meet those needs. Thousands of people had already contributed to the herculean effort of making both that consciousness and that responsiveness a reality. And virtually none of them had any doubt about the importance of their accomplishment. "It was ultimately about saving lives," said Vet Center cocreator Bill Mahedy. His collaborator, Shad Meshad, wrote later: "It was red sails in the sunset, we thought, for the greatest mental health delivery program in the country." Few, if any, yet realized how illusory their victory was—and how great a distance they had yet to go.

Public Law 96-22, the Vietnam Veterans' Psychological Readjustment Act, which authorized the Vet Centers, had been signed into law by Jimmy Carter on July 13, 1979—with VA administrator Max Cleland beaming over his shoulder. Cleland's general counsel, Guy McMichael III, claimed that the program could not have been implemented much sooner because "the VA could [only] render services . . . for very definable illnesses"—and of course the official definition of post-traumatic stress disorder had not even been published yet in the APA's *Diagnostic and Statistical Manual of Mental Disorders, Third Edition,* due out in January 1980. The Senate had actually passed three different versions of Alan Cranston's Readjustment Act in 1971, 1973, and 1975, but each time the bill had been killed in the House Veterans' Affairs Committee. McMichael claimed it was Carter's election, more than anything else, that "turned around" the House leaders' negative attitude and secured the bill's passage. He also credited the powerful advocacy of Cleland, who confronted the "show me" attitude of VA officials with hard evidence of "what they [Vietnam veterans] needed and didn't have." As far as he was aware, McMichael said, there was none of the usual congressional dirty-dealing, none of the usual "quid pro quos." The Outreach Program, he implied, was an example of Congress— after sufficient education—finally doing right by a deserving constituency.

Nothing was further from the truth.

In 1975, Congressman Ray Roberts (D-Tex.) took over as chairman of the House Veterans' Affairs Committee, though Olin "Tiger" Teague remained on the committee for the next four years. Another hard-bitten World War II vet, Roberts was as adamantly opposed to the Readjustment Counseling Program as Teague; and the congressman in charge of the health care subcommittee, David Satterfield (D-Va.), spoke like a ventriloquist's dummy for both of them. Their position, according to Cranston's chief counsel, Jonathan Steinberg, was that "veterans of all wars had problems, and Vietnam veterans were no different. The VA ought to help them through the regular mental health programs, but not set up special programs." That was also the standard rhetoric of the traditional veterans' organizations. Both the VFW and the American Legion had expressed their opposition to the Vet Center program, based on their fear that the money used to fund it ($12 million out of a total budget of $25 billion) would have an "[adverse] impact on other health services"—i.e., would cut into the health care and pensions for their World War II veteran members. They had conveniently forgotten that in 1946 a special readjustment counseling effort had been established for World War II veterans using fee-basis psychologists.

In 1977, as Roberts' committee prepared to kill the Vet Center legislation for the fourth time, a TV newsman remarked to him: "Of course, the Vietnam veteran is really a minority with veterans' organizations." Roberts responded

with undisguised sarcasm: "Well, he's a minority—period. In five million veterans that were called during Vietnam, a million of them went over there and
saw some [sic]—maybe in a combat zone—as against seventeen million in
World War II. So, he is a minority." As for Roberts' accuracy, there were *nine*
million Vietnam-era vets, and *three* million served in Vietnam; there were
twelve million World War II vets. More to the point, the percentage of World
War II vets who saw combat was as small as the percentage who saw combat in
Vietnam. According to Congressman Dave Bonior, who organized the Vietnam
Veterans in Congress (VVIC) caucus a year later, Roberts' phony numbers were
just a way of saying: "Vietnam veterans had no clout. They just did not count."
For the next two years, until he resigned as chairman in 1980, Roberts stead-
fastly refused to meet with any of the VVIC leaders; and his committee never
held a single day of hearings on the plenitude of legislation introduced by
Bonior and his colleagues.

In fact, to get anything done for Vietnam veterans, the VVIC found they had
to sneak behind the back of the House Veterans' Affairs Committee. To obtain
hearings on Agent Orange, they went to the House Committee on Interstate
and Foreign Commerce. To get a veterans' employment program passed they
went to the House Ways and Means Committee. And to push through the bill
authorizing Vietnam Veterans Week in 1979, they used the Committee on Post
Office and Civil Service.

In 1978, after Cranston again got his Vet Center bill passed in the Senate,
Roberts and Satterfield at last signaled a willingness to negotiate. But it wasn't
because they had developed a kinder attitude toward Vietnam veterans.
Congress controlled the appropriation process for VA hospital construction, but
up till that time the selection of hospital sites was usually done by the House
and Senate Appropriations Committees in consultation with the Office of
Management and Budget (OMB), part of the executive branch. Roberts and
Satterfield argued (according to Guy McMichael) that it was too confusing and
disruptive for them to have the administration throwing new hospital sites at
them like fastballs out of the dark, which they were totally unprepared to deal
with. They wanted, they said, "a five-year plan," in which the White House and
OMB would agree to a long-term program of hospital construction in cities that
the House Veterans' Affairs Committee had helped designate. Their argument
sounded reasonable enough, but everyone knew what the issue was really
about. New VA hospitals were economic plums, and Roberts and Satterfield
wanted some of those plums taken from the president and the Appropriations
committees and put in their own basket.

Roberts and Satterfield were ready to play swap. They offered to stop opposing the Outreach centers if the Carter Administration conceded to them the
right to initiate hospital construction. According to Steinberg, the most immediate obstacle to their grasp on the hospital sites was Alan Cranston, currently

the Senate's majority whip as well as chair of the Senate Veterans' Affairs Committee. The House had already passed legislation which gave the Veterans' Affairs Committees the power to authorize VA hospital construction, but Cranston blocked passage of the bill in the Senate. He felt it was shameless "pork-barrel politics" and, worse, would vastly complicate the selection of hospital sites, because the Appropriations Committees would end up wrangling with the Veterans Affairs' Committees.

In the fall of 1978, Satterfield met with Cranston and Steinberg for three hours in the Whip's office in the Capitol. Satterfield offered Cranston House approval for the three veterans' programs he wanted most: the Vet Centers; a contract program for drug and alcohol treatment outside the VA hospitals; and a program for preventive health services. What he wanted in return was Cranston's support for the hospital-site legislation in the Senate, as well as Cranston's agreement to a three-year time limit on the Vet Centers, since Cranston's original bill had called for the Readjustment Counseling program to be open-ended. Cranston agreed, and the deal was struck.

Max Cleland called it "a standard political trade . . . horsetrading!" But according to Bobby Muller, whose horses got traded were not Satterfield's and Cranston's but rather Satterfield's and Jimmy Carter's. And it was Carter, not Cranston, who had to be talked into making the trade. "The concession didn't come from Steinberg," Muller says. "He was on the legislative side, and they got the fucking benny [benefit]. The concession came from the agency [the VA], or from the executive branch, the presidency's side of the ledger." "What turned the trick," Muller claims, was a closed-door meeting between Carter and most of the VVIC members in mid-November 1978. Carter had been moved by the plight of Vietnam veterans as it had been revealed in the Presidential Review Memorandum issued by his office the month before; but what really made that meeting happen was the advocacy of Carter's domestic policy advisor, Stuart Eizenstat, who had allowed the VVIC caucus to meet regularly with Carter's Domestic Policy Council. Muller claims he handled some of "the mouthpiece aspects of the game," getting the press attention that made both Eizenstat and Carter recognize the validity of their cause. Muller also met directly with Carter a couple of times, but he was forced to sit outside the door during Carter's key meeting with the VVIC. After the meeting broke up, Senator John Heinz (R-Penn.) bolted out the door to break the good news to the press of Carter's support for special Vietnam veteran legislation, only to find that the entire White House press pool had already begun their interviews with Muller, who was not shy about taking credit for the coup himself.[198]

As it turned out, however, nobody had accomplished anything. The whole deal went down the tubes when Senator Warren Magnuson (D-Wash.), chairman of the Senate Appropriations Committee, refused to share construction authorization with the Veterans' Affairs Committees. Rather than make adjustments in their bill that would satisfy Magnuson, Roberts and Satterfield opted to shelve the whole package of VA health care legislation, thus postponing not only the Vet Centers but a whole range of veterans' benefits for yet another year.

In 1979, Cranston and Magnuson (who would soon be retiring) agreed on a modification of the site-selection amendment, giving the House Veterans' Affairs Committee veto power over all future medical-facility construction. The new veterans' health care bill, which established the Vet Center program, was finally passed at the start of June, appropriately enough in the middle of Vietnam Veterans Week. But the money-grubbing hustles and power-grabbing machinations that had paved the way for it had not gone unnoticed. Wrote *Washington Post* columnist David Broder: "Next to tipping over a wheelchair, it is hard to imagine a shabbier way for Congress to mark Vietnam Veterans Week."

Regretful of the long delay, Max Cleland rushed to get the Vet Centers operating as quickly as possible. He desperately wanted Shad Meshad to serve as the program's national director, but Meshad refused. The director had to oversee 91 Vet Centers from Puerto Rico to Hawaii, and the job demanded a five-year commitment in Washington. "I would have killed myself," Shad explains. "My instincts told me that." Though his sunglasses, tank top, cutoff jeans, and ski-boot roller skates were something of an affected costume that he wore down at the Venice boardwalk when he went cruising for disaffected Vietnam vets, the truth was that Meshad was most comfortable "working the streets," and his spirit was nourished by one-on-one interaction with other hurting guys, who placed their trust in him as a brother vet and a friend.

Carter pressured Cleland to appoint a director. Bill Mahedy and Charles Figley had also turned down the job, preferring like Meshad to work in their home base. Cleland quickly chose a Ph.D. psychologist and Navy Vietnam veteran named Don Crawford, who headed a VA rehab unit in West Haven, Connecticut, apparently because he seemed like a "Meshad clone"—although Crawford spent most of his time doing research on biofeedback rather than working directly with veterans.

Crawford, however, turned out to be a better man for the job than anyone expected. He had gone into the Navy right out of high school, in 1957, intending to make it his career. Gung-ho and in love with adventure, he volunteered for every hot spot, and got his first taste of blood and destruction during the Cypriot revolution in 1959, when twelve guys from his unit were killed in the Israeli attack on the *Liberty*. He himself almost got blown away that year in the guerrilla bombing of a civilian bar. From the start, the Navy had funneled him into intelligence, and he got more of an insider's view when he monitored the tragic Bay of Pigs invasion (1961) and then took part in Kennedy's blockade of Cuba (1962). Increasingly he felt cynical about the way his government seemed to expend and abandon the men and women who had committed themselves to serve America, but it was Vietnam that permanently altered his life.

From Japan he watched the war unfold. By the time he got orders for Vietnam, in early 1967, he had grave doubts about the rightness of the cause. He served on the USS *Oxford,* an intelligence-gathering platform that traveled up and down the coast, and often went ashore to do "close tactical support," which meant going into combat areas to provide classified information and briefings and sometimes to interrogate prisoners. Although he never pounded ground with the grunts, he was in Da Nang and Saigon for some of the terrible firefights of Tet 1968, saw guys in his hotel killed by snipers, and watched the parade of bodies being carried into hospitals. By the end of his year-long tour, he felt that the American military was "just throwing away lives here" while at the same time "trashing a nation . . . wasting people [on both sides] for political expediency." Worse, such problems with American foreign policy now seemed the rule, not the exception; and he could not bear to spend the rest of his career participating in similar mockeries of just intervention (or "mistakes," as Robert S. McNamara would later dub America's actions in Vietnam) around the globe.

In early 1968 he was in line for a commission and a transfer, but instead, he says, he told the Navy to "shove it," and they agreed to let him out of his contract as long as he served another six months in Vietnam. That fall, Crawford began his college studies at the University of Nebraska, and he plunged fully into the antiwar and countercultural movements, taking part in protests (sit-ins at the administrative offices and blockades of the ROTC building), growing his hair long, doing his share of drugs, and, most importantly, speaking out as a veteran—educating both teachers and fellow students about what the war was really like. He stayed on at Nebraska through his doctorate in clinical psychology, though his final year (1976–1977) he was sent to do an internship at Yale, whose psychology department was affiliated with the West Haven VA. Once he had his degree, West Haven offered him a permanent job in the just-emerging field of health psychology—investigating and treating the physical ailments that interact with, and sometimes develop alongside, mental illness.

At West Haven he crossed paths with another longhaired, bluejeaned, apparently rebellious Vietnam veteran, Yale psychiatrist Arthur S. Blank Jr. In personality, however, Crawford was much the antithesis of Blank. Where Blank was ultra-cool, tight-lipped, and played his cards close to his vest—so that no one could guess how he was really feeling—Crawford freely expressed the anger he still felt toward the war and for the human damage it had wrought. As a health psychologist he frequently saw multiple amputees and others whose bodies were severely damaged in Vietnam, and he gained a reputation around the hospital as one of the few doctors who would give Vietnam vets a sympathetic ear when they needed to really open up. When Max Cleland sent out a Request for Proposal (RFP) in 1978, the year before the Vet Center program was finally approved, asking for ideas about how to do outreach to stressed-out Vietnam vets, Crawford was the only person in the VA to bother responding with a 20-page, detailed paper. Crawford's response was also by far the most creative. He proposed having Vet Center trailers or vans, which could travel from community to community, perhaps stopping at shopping centers or other crossroads like the mobile units that test blood pressure. He also proposed telephone networking, getting in touch with ministers and other community workers, and going to jails.

When Cleland's first three choices—all prominent Vietnam veteran PTSD pioneers—declined the directorship of the Vet Centers, he turned to his stack of RFP responses, and of course Crawford's jumped out at him. But before Crawford was approved for the job, he had to undergo a grueling interrogation by Meshad, Jack McCloskey, Charles Figley, and several other hard-core combat vets. They "sweated him out in a hotel room," he recalls, demanding he prove his firsthand knowledge of war and show that he could "talk the lingo." That day remains "one of the most uncomfortable memories" of Crawford's professional life; and their final judgment on him—"He's not great, but he'll do"—was only the first of the many deep wounds that job would bring him.

That day a tragic rivalry was born. At forty, Crawford felt superior to the younger vets (in their early to mid-thirties) who were deprecating him. "Arrogant as hell," by his own admission, he felt he could "run the world," let alone save a few million Vietnam vets. Shad Meshad, however, figured *he* had already saved them by inventing the Vet Centers. Bill Brew, deputy general counsel for the Senate Veterans' Affairs Committee, saw trouble coming, and hoped Meshad would "button up and go away," leaving Crawford to take charge of the program in his own manner. Meshad, however, offered (and was immediately hired by Crawford) to act as regional manager for the West, Region 6, which comprised ten states ranging from Hawaii to Texas. Meshad's domain spanned three time zones and rated 44 Vet Centers—almost half the total in the program. The job allowed Meshad to remain in Los Angeles, which, though a boon for him, immediately created a serious administrative problem. It was as if the Vet Centers had two national directors, one on each coast.[199]

From the start, Meshad imagined that Crawford must be "working in his shadow," but nothing was further from the truth. Crawford claims he "didn't know he had a shadow" till much later, after it became apparent that Meshad "had Cleland's ear" whenever he wanted it. At first Crawford knew Meshad merely as "a social worker from California," and by failing to recognize his stature he offended him deeply. But there were far bigger problems for Crawford to worry about that first year in D.C. than Shad Meshad's ego.

Crawford recalls leaving his family in Connecticut and driving down to Washington, his car filled with clothes and personal belongings, only to find himself manager of a program that did not yet exist. No one had bothered to provide him with a staff, a secretary, or even an office to work in! And yet Cleland demanded that by October 1, 1979 (scarcely three months away), Crawford have twelve centers open and running.

Ignorant in the ways of Washington, "dumb and proud" in his belief that he could satisfy everyone's demands on him, the only thing Crawford had going for him was that he really cared about veterans and that he wanted "to do something for these people." He soon discovered that there was a tight-knit group of about twenty veteran activists who had been working the Hill for almost a decade—among them Dean Phillips, Tim Craig, and double amputee Jim Mayer, the first president of NACV—who, like Meshad, had direct access to Cleland. In fact, they may well have had more real influence on Cleland than Meshad, since, according to Craig, they'd frequently meet after hours with Cleland, VA general counsel Guy McMichael, and deputy counsel Bob Coy for drinks and bull sessions. This was the "brain trust" that former NACV vice president Bill Lawson had spoken of; and Lawson soon formalized their meetings by hosting a luncheon for the group once a month in his offices at the American Association of Community and Junior Colleges, where he was director of Veterans' Affairs. Crawford was quickly pulled in as well, and benefited greatly from such informal, behind-the-scenes communication.

Although Lawson liked to style himself "the only black Vietnam veterans' advocate in Washington" (not egotistically, but just to point out the relative isolation of his position), a number of black activist vets participated in this chat group. They pushed Crawford to appoint a black deputy director of the Vet Center program. The man they picked out for him turned out to be one of his biggest assets: Lee Crump, an era vet with a doctorate in clinical psychology from the University of Tennessee.

Hundreds of congressmen, most of whom had for years been either indifferent or outright hostile to the Readjustment Counseling Program, were now appealing directly to Cleland to have a Vet Center placed in their district. Vet Centers were suddenly seen as trophies, to be brandished before one's constituency and later cashed in for votes. Lee Crump's job was to identify Vet Center sites, and to deal with the clamor of claims and counterclaims. He and Crawford had a map mounted on corkboard into which they stuck fresh pins every day, and sometimes the political pressure was such that they were forced to place a Vet Center in an area almost devoid of Vietnam veterans—which led, says Crump, to some "very creative explanations" on his part. Most of the time, fortunately, they were able to avoid congressional interference and use demographics to choose Vet Center locales.

The Vet Center program was very nearly sabotaged from within the VA before it even saw its first client. One of the first steps Crawford had to take was to lease space for his Vet Centers to operate in. He was told that all leasing was done through the VA's Engineering Division. The chief of engineering and his deputy, it turned out, did not like Vietnam vets. They told Crawford that "it takes on the average two years to lease space in the Veterans Administration." Since the Outreach program had originally been granted a life of only two years, that meant the centers might not open their doors (or have any physical existence whatsoever) until the very month they were federally mandated to close. Crawford had hit a stone wall that, he says, almost drove him insane. When he was about to give up, and turn the whole program over to the private sector, he received a confidential phone call from the engineering chief's secretary, Ada Whitt. "What they should have told you, Dr. Crawford," said Whitt, "is that the leasing officer in any VA hospital can go out and lease up to five thousand square feet and sign the lease on the spot." With that one tip, Mrs. Whitt saved the entire Vet Center program from foundering. It turned out her son had died in Vietnam. Afterward, any time Crawford needed a lease signed, and if there was no hospital leasing officer available, he would put Mrs. Whitt on a plane and she would complete the lease herself.

According to Crawford, over and over again the program was saved by the unsought—and sometimes secret—support of people within the VA who (if not veterans themselves) knew something about Vietnam veterans' problems because their husband or son or other relative or even "the neighborhood kid" had gone there. "For every time I can talk about somebody [in the VA] who really screwed us," says Crawford, "I can tell you another story of somebody who gave me tremendous help, who went above and beyond, who worked late, put in tremendous hours. . . . There was a kid named Gary May, a bilateral amputee from Illinois. He would leave his wife and kids for six or eight weeks at a time, flying to training sessions with me. We lived in airplanes. His stumps would be so sore we'd have to carry him on the airplane, and he'd go to the next training program."

Crawford was blindsided repeatedly in those early days. At his first hearing before the Senate Veterans' Affairs Committee, Crawford spent an hour and a half sketching out his dream of what he would like the Outreach program to become. Then Cranston thanked him for coming, but Crawford couldn't resist asking: "Senator, if I can implement this for the Veterans Administration, can I count on you giving us more money next year?" Faces all around him scowled and paled; a few hours later, Crawford found a letter from Senator Cranston on his desk, asking for his resignation. Crawford had violated the Hatch Act, which forbids federal employees from politicking for their own program; and even worse, he had done so in the *Congressional Record*. After fiercely reprimanding him, Cleland shielded Crawford from being fired, but he warned: "Boy, we're going to have to teach you how to do an interview and teach you about the politics of this program."[200]

2. "A Conflicted Program": Crawford and Meshad Go Head to Head

The biggest problem for Crawford, according to Tim Craig, was that he had to wear at least six different hats. He was supposed to build a brand-new program from the ground up, to be a good psychologist, to manage a complex budget, to successfully work Capitol Hill, to keep up good relations with the traditional veterans' service organizations (VSOs), and to be a good bureaucrat in terms of both administering the program and fighting the battles within the VA to ensure the program's survival. "Don was a good clinical person," Craig says, "but he was not a good schmoozer, and not a politician. He was also not the greatest administrator." Crawford's own weaknesses were compounded by his lack of staff. Besides Crump, he had only an assistant named Tom Corbett, who worked on the budget, and his secretary Susan; though he also got help from a guy named Dick Olson in the Domiciliary program. Four or five people to administer a national program, Craig felt, was ludicrous, as well as a sad commentary on how low a priority the program had in the VA, despite Cleland's backing. In fact, Cleland did try to help by creating new administrative slots for Crawford to fill; but Crawford, in his altruistic dedication to the program, would invariably send each new manager out to the field, where he felt they could more directly help veteran clients, rather than keeping them in Central Office to offload some of his own tasks.

Crawford made Cleland's deadline of October 1, 1979, though he opened only six centers that day, which was remarkable enough. The centers ranged from Burlington, Vermont, to Orange County, California; but the first dedication of a center was put off till January and done in Van Nuys, California, to honor Alan Cranston. Crawford was consumed with his mission. "I knew Vietnam veterans were underserved," he says. "I knew these guys had gotten screwed and that they needed a lot of help. I couldn't pass up this opportunity. It was my Jedi crusade." According to Lee Crump, "The Vet Centers were his life . . . he was never not at work"—even when at home, which was taking a heavy toll on his marriage. In fact, Crump and Crawford began having their first arguments when Crawford expected him to put in the same long hours, and Crump refused, determined to save time for his family.

That first year, Crawford spent 85 percent of his time on the road, visiting Vet Centers and attending trainings. There were endless brush fires for him to put out. This was the first and only VA program in the country being run directly from Central Office, with an "earmarked budget" that no one else in the VA could tap into. From the start, recalls Bill Brew, VA hospital directors and chiefs of staff were bitching to their superiors and to Congress: "Why does this thing need this separate line of funding?" They also resented the fact that Vet Center workers "did not report to the [nearest] hospital in any way, shape or form," but instead spoke directly to Crawford, who had a power nearly as great as that of the Chief Medical Director. "There were lots of people [bureaucrats] both in the field and in Central Office," Brew recalls, "who wanted the Vet Centers to come under the hospitals." Crawford often encountered resistance from VA mental health professionals in the field, too, since he sought to make Vet Centers as different as possible from the standard VA health care delivery system.

For starters, Crawford wanted the Vet Centers staffed largely by Vietnam veterans. It didn't matter to him if his workers had a prestigious mental health credential, or any degree at all, so long as they shared (in Crump's words) "the brotherhood and instantaneous rapport between combat vets." By the end of the second year, 80 percent of the Vet Center workers were Vietnam vets, and 50 percent were minorities. He also sought to make every Vet Center different from every other, to individualize them based on area and the type of vets they served—whether farmers, ghetto inhabitants, or, as in San Francisco, bikers, street people, and hippies. But at the same time, the power of the Vet Centers to reach so many different people meant that it was, in Crawford's words, "a conflicted program." "What worked in Boston wouldn't work in San Diego," he elaborates. "Everybody wanted to do their own thing. We had a regional coordinator that actually used my home as a drop-place for dope, and I didn't know it. Turns out, they caught him and he did hard time in the joint for transporting drugs. We had guys who turned Vet Centers into places for peddling dope. I mean, we did some wonderful work. But we made some horrendous mistakes."

Richard Fuller, a Vietnam veteran who worked on the staff of the House Veterans' Affairs Committee, felt that Crawford "accomplished an amazing amount" during the first two years of the program. "He put the program together under tremendous animosity," Fuller recalls. "Guerrilla wars were going on all around him. The people he brought into the program were not used to being regimented, in fact hated the government. He had to try to keep them in line, to make them learn how not to violate federal law or regulation in getting things done."

The problem was far bigger than just Crawford's renegade employees—"the wild and crazy folks," Bill Brew called them. The problem went to the heart of giving psychological and spiritual help to a population as diverse as Vietnam-era veterans—nine million individuals, each with different ideas and theories and his or her own political point of view. No single paradigm of healthy readjustment could be set for all of them. Moreover, the vast majority of those who had served in Vietnam (three million) were resistant and antagonistic toward being led by anyone. Yet Crawford felt the program was workable despite its internal conflicts so long as he held to his model of maximum diversity: "Don't use a cookie-cutter."

That Crawford practiced what he preached was evident just from his selection of the first six regional coordinators, who included a black, Husher Harris; a woman, Heather Brandon; a Jew, Steve Levenburg; a Hispanic, Eloy Flores; a midwestern German, Bill Vondahar; and a Lebanese southerner, Shad Meshad.

The result of trying to please everyone, however, was enormous stress on the boss. Lee Crump recalls that Crawford was often irritable and grumpy, "not an easy man to work for." Though a rebel himself, Crawford had a hard time tolerating waywardness in others, and sometimes his overly straightforward criticism was perceived as insensitivity by his subordinates. It was inevitable that Shad Meshad, outspoken and headstrong himself, would become Crawford's biggest "pain in the ass." Still, according to Tim Craig, both Crawford and Meshad were wrong in not trying harder to get along with each other. Their falling-out and the resentment each held toward the other, Craig feels, struck a crippling blow to the program they ironically both cared so much about.

Whenever trouble arose, Vet Center workers would invariably ask (as would Cleland himself): "What does Shad think?" "Playing second fiddle" to Meshad after having been Cleland's "second choice" was bound to irk Crawford. There were profound personal differences between the two men besides. Both were in effect "married to their job," but in very different ways. Meshad was a self-described "maniac," whose intensity never let down. For him, working seven days a week meant talking nonstop for hours, his phone always ringing, vets always knocking on his door. Moreover, he was a fighter, happiest when he was going against the grain of the system. Crawford preferred to play by the rules and to avoid ruffling anybody's feathers. His emotions were as deep as Meshad's, but he kept them private. Crawford would sometimes isolate himself, feeling the need to "turn it off and numb it out," or else kick back with a few close friends, and occasionally he drank too much. Meshad, by contrast, never drank and stayed "wired" for action round the clock. Crawford tried to make peace with Congress and the VA bureaucracy, and in large part he succeeded because he showed respect for the system and never moved to threaten it. Even the crusty old World War II vets on the House Veterans' Affairs Committee thought highly of him, according to committee counsel Mack Fleming, because he tried to satisfy their demands, at least in terms of accountability. Much to Meshad's disgust, Crawford gave the impression of being a letter-of-the-law man, who sought to preserve VA regulations and protocol as if they were the behemoth agency's lifeblood, which indeed they were.[201]

Of course, many VA bureaucrats worried that the Vet Centers were a lesion capable of bleeding them to death. The truth, according to Meshad, was that the Vet Center program had been "jammed down the VA's throat." It was "an insult and an embarrassment to the VA," he says—an insult because its very existence proved the VA hadn't been doing its job, and an embarrassment because it showed that on $20 million a year an "outside program" could pretty well take care of all the Vietnam vets in the country, only a few thousand of whom had been helped by the VA's $24 *billion*-a-year array of medical facilities. The VA was initially so reluctant to provide logistical support to the Vet Centers, according to Meshad, that one congressman (on their side) actually talked of moving the program to the Forestry Service under the Department of Agriculture, where there was more sympathy for Vietnam vets.

The Vet Center program was given a measure of independence from the VA in terms of "professional autonomy"—meaning the director and the regional managers could do their own hiring—but the money to pay rents, salaries, and every other cost came from the VA's own account. Through its grip on the purse strings, the VA began at once to scale down the Outreach program. Meshad and Mahedy's original plan had called for each Vet Center to have a ten-person team. Of those ten, three would handle employment and education counseling, working especially with the chronically unemployable. They would channel vets into training programs and hold special motivating sessions. Another three members would work chiefly in job placement. Since stress counseling would be done both individually and in rap groups, and since group work was exceptionally draining, there would be three counselors to share that load. The tenth staff member was the team leader, who coordinated the others' activities. In addition, the whole team was to participate in community outreach—contacting vets who needed help wherever they might be found, whether on the street, at a nine-to-five job, or in prison. The original sketch did not call for any mental health professionals, though Meshad envisioned some expansion in that direction, with the centers eventually adding one or more psychologists or degreed clinicians to aid in psychiatric evaluation, individual therapy, and medical referral. Degrees, however, were not an issue initially; the primary goal was to provide the full "circle of treatment."

Right at the start, the VA claimed it could not fund such an elaborate operation, and it forced Crawford to reduce the Vet Center module to a four-man team—a team leader and one person to handle each of the three original components: educational and vocational rehab; job placement; and readjustment counseling. In practice, however, it was impossible to maintain all three components with just four workers. Hence, career rehab and job placement were dropped almost immediately, as was, ironically enough, any substantial effort at outreach. The Vet Centers were left with just one function: "peer counseling."

The Outreach program was originally designed to include stress research and a contract program, linking Vet Centers with private providers of counseling and therapy for Vietnam veterans. Meshad and many others saw the contract program as an especially vital part of the whole endeavor. Even with 91 Vet Centers servicing a constellation of the most important and populous cities in the United States, there were still hundreds of thousands of Vietnam vets living in rural areas or "hiding out in the hills" (as Meshad put it) who would be unable to avail themselves of help at one of the VA storefronts. Meshad had personally spent five years meeting with a group of about 150 combat vets who had set up a "fire base" in the Santa Monica Mountains near Malibu, protected by barbed wire, tripwires, and a huge arsenal of lethal weapons. These men were so bitter and angry over their society's betrayal of them that they avoided as much as possible ordinary human intercourse, fearing most of all that they would lose their precarious remnants of self-control and explode like the "time bombs" they were accused of being, explode as Jim Hopkins finally did, or even worse than Hopkins, go out and start murdering the first human beings that came in sight. So they came into "civilization"—meaning usually the Venice boardwalk or funky little town square—only long enough to make a drug deal or otherwise score some cash, and buy another month's supplies. Then they'd hightail it back to their safe zone, where they didn't have to deal with the "absurdity," as Marine veteran George Swiers wrote, of "fellow Americans" going about "business as usual." Ironically, the place they felt safest was the closest possible replica they could create of wartime Vietnam—perhaps because America had come to seem (in Ron Kovic's phrase) the most "dangerous country" of all to them.

As Meshad knew, no Vet Center in the world was going to reach those guys, at least till somebody—most likely a fellow vet—went to them and broke the ice, and earned enough of their trust to coax them in. And even then, many of these guys were out in the wilds of Wyoming or New Mexico or Washington State, with no city of any size nearby. Besides, many of them would never enter a city again, no matter who coaxed them. It was imperative that the VA hire people in private practice to create surrogate Vet Centers in those outlying places. And in fact, the original legislation, Public Law 96-22, had called for the VA to set aside additional funding for just such a contract program.

For the first two years of the Outreach program, the Carter administration's OMB had allotted $13 million, on paper, for contracts and fees for services from private providers. The VA, however, had no intention of spending any extra dollars on a program the bureaucrats were already planning to phase down almost from the day it started gearing up. In plain language, money that had been given to build the Vet Center program was never actually in Crawford's grasp, never available for him to write checks against, to pay bills with. By Meshad's account, such money was simply absorbed back into the general VA exchequer for "computer systems, nursing scholarships, building funds, and allowance and vacation money." Such abuse would culminate in an exposé on CBS national news, in early 1983, which revealed that during the first three years of the Vet Center program, $40.3 million had been hocus-pocused away in such a manner.

Part of the story was that Crawford was initially too busy just bringing readjustment counseling into existence to even think about starting a contract and fees for services program. He also felt that hiring private providers would be an inefficient way to spend Operation Outreach's limited funds, because, by his calculation, 70 cents on every dollar would go to overhead. But a lot more was going on behind the scenes. Both Senator Alan Cranston and the honchos in the VA Central Office were encouraging Crawford to put the contract program into deep freeze. Crawford "had a very clear, though tacit, understanding," from the people above him, says Bill Brew, that "he needed to expend his energies [solely] on getting the [storefront] program up and running." Of course, even more tacit but just as powerfully felt, was the VA's desire to put the brakes on this new oddball program, to build tight fences around it and shut down its growth before it overran the agency's whole health care system, with God knew what radical results.

Crawford let the VA take back the entire $13 million that had been earmarked for contracts and fees for services under the Outreach program. Meshad was outraged. His position was that the centers had already "come ten years too late." Eighteen of his former counseling clients had committed suicide; and at least some of them, he felt, could have been saved by a Vet Center or a sympathetic professional paid by the VA to listen to their grief and give them a sense of "coming home." To take an iota from the help now available was a high crime in Meshad's eyes, but Crawford told Meshad, "We need to be friends with the VA." Crawford explained that he was trying "to develop a relationship with Central Office," which was the very last thing Meshad and his anti-VA followers wanted him to do.

In truth, it made sense for Crawford to try to mend fences, since his program had powerful enemies in both the VA and Congress. Committee counsel Mack Fleming recalls that many House Veterans' Affairs Committee members were perennially troubled over the apparent lack of "order within the centers themselves" and the fact that only the sloppiest of records, if indeed any records at all, were kept of "the people seen and what they [the staff] were doing [to help them] and the final outcome of the case." According to Fleming, the very existence of the centers continually provoked controversy at the committee hearings—especially when some new "shocking" fact would turn up, such as the discovery that Vet Centers (in their attempt to be user-friendly) did not ask Vietnam veteran clients for a Social Security number before proffering them help. Moreover, says Fleming, there was a strong suspicion that the centers were just seeing the same handful of "bad-apple vets" over and over again; and so the House committee, as well as its sister Senate committee, soon began pressuring the Vet Center program to justify its existence by "identifying the people that came into the system" each month.

This pressure "to bring up the numbers" of new clients became known derisively within the Vet Center program as the quest for "body count"—the same superficial standard of success vets had been forced to answer to in Vietnam. But the House Veterans' Affairs Committee, like the Senate committee, could not be shrugged off lightly, even though they never openly threatened Don Crawford or any other VA official. "We could let the authorization expire," Fleming explains. "That was the hammer we always had." At the time Crawford became director of Operation Outreach, there was a Democratic majority in both House and Senate; and, of course, a Democratic administration, Carter and Cleland, who backed the Vet Center program. When Republican President Ronald Reagan took office in January 1981, he brought with him a Republican Senate, which in turn led to a Republican-chaired Senate Veterans' Affairs Committee; from that point on, Crawford would encounter ever greater opposition to the program, as well as growing pressure to change in the direction of traditional accountability.[202]

Just as with the doomed contract program, Crawford attempted to satisfy the demands of both Congress and Central Office—this time by increasing each center's record-keeping requirements and upping the program's overall client numbers. He tasked Lee Crump with developing "productivity standards" for the whole Vet Center system, which Crump did in a very humane fashion, by meeting with a cross-section of the program's leadership to determine reasonable goals based on a variety of variables. His productivity formula was used to evaluate all Vet Centers, but took into account regional differences, the size of the local veteran population, and so forth. Above all, it was meant to be applied flexibly, and did not set hard-and-fast quotas for each Vet Center; rather, Crump's goal was to provide a "realistic yardstick" against which their use of resources could be measured. Like Crawford, Crump felt that such a yardstick was essential because they were trying to build a case for the *expansion* of the Vet Center program, based on the large number of untreated and, for the most part, still unidentified veterans who needed their services.

For Meshad, however, this was just one more example of Crawford's willingness to "compromise the mission of the program" in order to protect his own job. The two of them began (in Meshad's words) "going at each other's throat." Unluckily for Meshad, he made a far better target than the new director. Meshad operated mainly on his instincts, often with striking success, but he also made many whopping mistakes: he spent money extravagantly, racking up huge phone bills and spending far more than was allotted for training sessions; he kept abysmally poor financial records (he had no time for them with endless human crises thrust under his nose); he never hesitated to break VA rules when it seemed necessary to help someone; and he sometimes acted autocratically, allowing only sporadic input from his own employees and keeping his sprawling operation in line "by terror and retribution" (according to Cranston's chief counsel Jonathan Steinberg). Nevertheless, Meshad's own employees had a far more charitable view of him than the Washington pundits.

Mike Maxwell, a Vietnam-era veteran who became the team leader of the Portland Vet Center, believed Meshad had been set up for failure. At first, Meshad had not even been given an assistant, Maxwell says, and yet the VA expected him "to go around and visit forty teams that were spread across California, Oregon, Washington, Idaho, Nevada, Texas, Arizona, [New Mexico,] Alaska, and Hawaii." At the same time, Meshad was supposed to keep his own L.A. office running smoothly. "It [Operation Outreach] was not meant to be an efficient, functioning program," Maxwell asserts. "It was more or less just to throw some money at Vietnam veterans, make them happy, and then we can say, 'This is what we did for them. Now why are they complaining?'" The VA referred to the Vet Centers as their "bastard program," he says, "and so it was treated like a little bastard, in the sense that when you wanted to get things done, you couldn't." Maxwell credits Meshad with being "a great cheerleader," who accepted the odds against him but pressed on enthusiastically anyway, figuring "that if we got the program going good enough, that they're not going to shut us down."

By late 1980, Meshad's life had already become hell on earth. He "was leading a terrible existence," he says, "of putting out fires and dodging bullets." Many of the "bullets" were coming from Crawford and higher-ups in the VA in the form of warning letters and memos, instructing him to change his ways and stop making waves—all of which he defiantly ignored. In Crawford's defense, he was continually getting complaints about Meshad from Meshad's peers. Explains Crawford: "He [Meshad] got further and further away from the day-to-day aspects of this program. Shad always loved the glamour. We're starting to make phone calls to his office, where Shad isn't there. We actually sent a field investigator out there to monitor his activities. He wasn't going to work." Meshad claimed that work, for him, included going up and down the boardwalk and giving interviews to the media, but that didn't wash with Crawford. "He was in a key position," Crawford continues. "He had office hours, and we could never find him. He had a staff, but he was not available to them. He was not providing them with leadership." Most problematical for Crawford was the fact that Shad rebelled against "counting beans"; he refused to "keep track of how many veterans he saw for how many visits."

Crawford flew out to Los Angeles to confront Meshad with these many charges. Meshad fought back by charging Crawford with collaborating in the theft of millions of dollars from the Vet Centers. Tempers flared, and harsh words were spoken. Crawford called him "a crazy, fucked-up Vietnam vet." Meshad "flipped out on him" (in his words), and they almost came to blows.

The embattled director was pushed to ask for Meshad's resignation. Meshad responded in a fury: "Shove it! Try and take me out! . . . But I'm comin' after ya." The Vietnam War was playing itself out all over again between Washington, D.C., and Southern California.[203]

3. The Push Toward Medical Credentials: Crawford Gets Shot Down, and Art Blank Steps into His Shoes

The growing brush fire in the Vet Center program was fed by a lot more than just the personal animosity between Crawford and Meshad. In Ron Bitzer's view, readjustment counseling had "become not only a bone in the VA's throat, but a thorn in their side." By providing "a place for vets to surface" with their problems and concerns—"a space where people could talk perhaps for the first time about their feelings"—the Vet Centers allowed for the airing of more than a decade's worth of the VA's dirty laundry. Worse, in the VA's eyes, they were places where angry and alienated veterans could connect and dialogue with one another, and such meetings might well lead them to organize in protest of their mutual grievances. The VA's fears in that regard were borne out in the 1981 Wadsworth demonstration, when many of the participants turned out to have been Vet Center clients or patients from the Brentwood Hospital's Resocialization Unit, whose passions had been stirred up in rap groups. There was also a deep distrust, and often antipathy, in VA administrators toward any so-called treatment that took place away from official government premises and hence not under their watchful eye and not subject to their direct control.

According to Mike Maxwell, the hospital directors often fought the Vet Center team leaders "tooth and nail on every item" they wanted to buy. Behind much of their resistance and obstructionism was the fact that despite post-traumatic stress disorder having been legitimized with a definition in the *DSM-III*, most VA doctors and clinicians in 1980 still did not accept it as real, and they refused to employ it as a diagnosis. "For years," says Maxwell, "the argument was: 'Ah, it's bullshit. There are predisposing factors that are causing that [the typical collection of delayed-stress symptoms].'" And of course, with the education and employment components removed, the Vet Centers had become synonymous with treating delayed stress.

There were plenty of real flaws in the Vet Center program those first couple of years—most of which had little to do with either the regional managers or the people running the storefronts. To begin with, the lack of cooperation from hospital administrators meant that many of the centers took a long time moving into their own building and getting their operation established. Many guys heard of the centers before there was actually a place to go to; and by the time most centers opened, they already had a sizable waiting list. The pressure of this backlog only grew worse with time, as positive word-of-mouth continually multiplied the influx of clients.

The situation seemed ripe for disaster, but the VA showed little concern. For the first couple of years, there was little hands-on supervision. As pressure mounted to kill (or at least rein in) the program, Crawford got pinned down by internecine battles within the Beltway, forcing him to drastically curtail his travels. The regional managers, meanwhile, were usually too overloaded to meet with the people they were managing. And although the team leaders were mostly capable individuals, they lacked practical guidelines.

Mike Maxwell, for example, found there was no one and no literature available to tell him "how can you tell when you're done [with a client]?" That problem was especially critical because PTSD tends to be a chronic illness, whose symptoms do not all manifest at the same time. "Answers were being developed as the program went along," Maxwell concedes. He also admits that when the program began, they hadn't even codified "the step-by-step process" of stress treatment. They often did not adequately prepare vets before placing them into group counseling. They also had not yet learned the necessary screening techniques, so that they might inadvertently put someone whose basic problem was substance abuse, or someone with a personality disorder, into a PTSD group. Substance abusers usually need to "get clean" before group therapy works for them, and those with personality disorders usually need a different type of therapy completely. In fact, a sociopath or psychopath thrown by error into a PTSD group could undo months of good work with true stress victims. The latter problem was especially vexing, because PTSD symptomatology sometimes resembles that of personality disorders quite closely. According to Maxwell, it often took counselors years of intense work with hundreds of troubled veterans to learn to tell the difference. It also took considerable practice just to run any group well, especially if that group comprised vets from vastly differing backgrounds, as often happened—those in suit-and-tie mixed with guys who'd been living on the street.

Even with the best information (which they seldom had), much of what the Vet Centers did depended on "judgment calls." Maxwell recalls that the first year or two, team members tended to be overconfident, often rushing out on crisis calls without any backup or police support. As a result, there were many counselors held hostage with a gun or a knife—situations which the press loved to play up, often to the detriment of the program's image. Since most of the counselors were Vietnam vets, their own PTSD would often kick up after such violent encounters. Add to this the fact that many of the counselors worked 60 or 70 hours a week, trying to do all the things—especially the much-needed outreach—that had been stripped from the program by Congress and the VA, and it is obvious why so many of the Vet Center workers were perpetually frazzled during those first few years, and why they often made (as Maxwell says) "stupid mistakes."

A lot of good also came out of the Vet Centers' struggle for a foothold. "Living kind of hard at the time," Maxwell says, the team members learned "to take care of each other, and bonded real closely together." The workers were underpaid, doing much of their work on their own time, but morale was probably never higher than when the program had just begun. A tremendous high came from seeing those first few troubled vets leave with a happy look on their face (even if everyone knew it was only temporary, and years of follow-up work lay ahead). Or as Meshad put it: "It feels so good when you score for these people—it's like a touchdown."

Meshad admits he was not sophisticated in the ways of Washington politics and "hidden agendas," and that he screwed up plenty of times himself. "I was just trying to do my job and trying to do it better than anybody," he says, "and everybody was telling me to get fucked, starting with the VA . . . but I told the truth [about the money that had vanished from the Vet Center budget]." In the spring of 1981, prior to the confirmation of a new VA administrator, the Reagan administration had created a "transition team" to handle the changeover from Democratic to Republican appointees at the VA. At the same time, a congressional oversight committee was convened to investigate the many charges and countercharges that grew out of the Jim Hopkins affair and subsequent Wadsworth strike. This oversight fell to the Subcommittee on Government Information of the House Government Operations Committee, chaired by Glenn English of Oklahoma. Crawford thought he saw his chance to rid himself of Meshad once and for all, and so he dumped his entire dossier on Shad's alleged malfeasance into the laps of both the transition team and the oversight committee.

Meshad was visited by the oversight committee's chief counsel Bill Lawrence and staff investigator Ted Mehl, a recently retired two-tour Vietnam veteran. "They came out to execute me," he says, "and ended up falling in love with me." Although Shad saw it as "cowboys and Indians," recalls Lawrence, he and Mehl were chiefly interested in assessing the economy and efficiency of the Outreach program. Meshad took them on a tour of several Vet Centers, which impressed them favorably, especially in the way the program had won acceptance from, and even *attracted,* a population of veterans characterized by "cockiness, scruffy clothes, pony tails, speaking street lingo," who had heretofore avoided the VA. Initially, however, Mehl and Lawrence were skeptical of Meshad's countercharges concerning the rifling of Vet Center funds; but the tide turned when former Carter aide Dean Phillips, now working at the Disability Review Board, confirmed that the program had gotten a "raw deal" from the VA. Once they started looking, it did not take long to turn up documentary evidence of the $13 million Crawford had given up. In secret, Mehl and Lawrence turned the focus of the investigation from Meshad to Crawford.[204]

The timing could not have been worse. Crawford had finally gotten over the initial hurdles, and the program was already growing beyond everyone's wildest dreams. They had, in fact, broken nearly every VA record for how quickly they had recruited and hired personnel, secured office space and furniture, and so forth. Crawford considered it a major victory that he had won so much cooperation from VA directors around the country, without whom such a swift setup would have been impossible. In their first year of operation, the Vet Centers served a quarter-million clients. But Crawford had even bigger plans. He foresaw that, with a little pushing, his successful outreach strategies could be expanded to the whole VA; so that eventually, instead of this giant agency depending on a puny Readjustment Counseling Service to reach into the community for veterans in need of help, the VA itself would become one big outreach program, and the Vet Centers could simply concentrate on helping Vietnam vets to readjust and heal.

Crawford, however, had more enemies than just Shad Meshad. Ironically, as he started to move the program more in the direction of Meshad's original plan, he antagonized the very people he needed to protect his job and to shield him from Meshad's political assaults. As Bill Brew describes it, "Crawford brought the field model into Central Office, and it didn't play well." Rather than being praised for his accomplishments or his vision, Crawford soon found himself being grilled mercilessly by a House subcommittee, and publicly made to look like a bumbling fool. By the end of 1981, the disclosure of the "missing funds" had brought down both Crawford and his boss, the VA's chief medical director Donald L. Custis.

At the start of 1982, after Congress had extended the life of the Vet Centers, VA administrator Robert Nimmo cast about for a new head of the Outreach program. Once again Meshad was offered the job, and once again he declined. A couple of years earlier, Meshad had created a Vet Center advisory committee, composed of many of the pioneers of stress theory. The committee also included some Vietnam vets who had promoted the need for stress counseling, such as grass-roots activist Jack McCloskey and Yale psychiatrist Art Blank. Blank now offered himself as a candidate for the job of Director of Readjustment Counseling. His candidacy was shot down twice by the Republican administration, but he tried for the job yet a third time, calling upon Meshad to support him.

Though Meshad had never really gotten to know Blank, he liked his resumé and his reputation. By the summer of 1967, only a few months after his return from Vietnam, where he'd served as chief psychiatrist at the 93rd Evacuation Hospital at Bien Hoa and also at the Third Field Hospital in Saigon, Blank had spoken out publicly against the war. At a Hiroshima Day rally in New York, Blank defended antiwar servicemen such as Dr. Howard Levy, who had openly called the Green Berets "murderers of women and children." Blank declared that "Dr. Levy has been convicted for saying in an Army hospital in South Carolina, what can be said without fear of reprisal in an Army hospital in Saigon"; and Blank intimated that he felt much the same as Levy on these issues. As a military doctor himself, and an American citizen, Blank said he too bore responsibility for a war "which produces little else but death, destruction, and misery in a nation of already poor and miserable people."

It took tremendous courage for a high-profile medical professional to say such a thing in 1967, but Blank went even further, signing his name to VVAW's first ad to stop the war, which ran in the *New York Times* on November 19, 1967, and subsequently in many other major newspapers as well. He gave numerous interviews to the media, was the subject of newspaper and magazine articles, and was even quoted in the *Congressional Record* (January 22, 1968), airing his views about the folly and futility of America's continuing military intervention in a Vietnamese civil war. On Veterans Day 1967, he gave a tremendously moving speech at a veterans' antiwar demonstration in New York City, in which he described a whole spectrum of the physical casualties he had witnessed from that war. In his speech, Blank asserted that Vietnam veterans had "a special duty to tell the American people what our country is doing to the people of Viet Nam [*sic*] and to our own soldiers there." Blank organized a Connecticut chapter of VVAW, and he and another Vietnam psychiatrist, Dr. Peter Bourne, helped Jan Barry recruit other Vietnam veteran doctors into the organization. Barry felt that Blank was one of the key early figures in establishing VVAW's credibility.

In 1972, Blank, while continuing to teach at the Yale Psychiatric Institute, had begun working at the West Haven VA Medical Center. His job was to evaluate Vietnam veterans for what was then called "traumatic war neurosis." Blank also did group therapy with Vietnam vets there during those years. Between 1975 and 1982, Blank initiated and supervised a PTSD treatment program at the West Haven VA. Since his return to Yale in 1967, he had conferred with his distinguished older colleague there, Robert J. Lifton; and through Lifton he had begun to meet the other pioneers of traumatic stress theory, such as Chaim Shatan and Sarah Haley. Although he had not been a part of the Vietnam Veterans' Working Group (VVWG), which prepared the first definition of post-traumatic stress disorder, Blank participated in a number of early training sessions for Vet Center teams. He also had written and published a number of respected papers on PTSD.

Meshad decided to push for Blank's appointment as head of the Outreach program. During the negotiations that had ended the Wadsworth protest, Meshad had gained a lot of respect from the VA administrators in Washington, especially the deputy general counsel, Robert Coy. Coy, as it turned out, was one of the strongest opponents of Blank's candidacy. Coy had also rejected other qualified Vietnam veterans, like Brentwood's psychiatric social worker Ray Scurfield and Denver psychologist Tom Williams, who had both had extensive experience counseling veterans. Coy wanted someone with stronger medical credentials, and Meshad pointed out that he could scarcely find someone more authoritative than a Yale psychiatrist.

On the third go-round at Central Office, Coy and Donald Custis asked for guidance from Alan Cranston's office, since Cranston was now the only legislator still fighting to protect the Vet Center program. One of Cranston's staffers responded that Art Blank "knew a bunch of people" and would be a good man to help them fill the post. Somehow, when the message reached Coy, it had been translated into a recommendation from Cranston to hire Blank. Coy immediately settled on Blank as a compromise choice for director of the Vet Centers—a position Blank assumed in April 1982. Meshad was delighted. He felt the program was finally being headed by someone who was "empathetic with Vietnam vets."[205]

4. The Vet Centers in Crisis: Body Count, Fleeing Counselors, and a Silent Director

The Reagan era marked the re-ascendancy of a hard-line conservatism in America, the likes of which hadn't been seen since the early 1950s. Reagan served up his reheated Cold War politics with a dazzling Hollywood smile, but he and his administration had little use—and scarcely more tolerance—for anyone who did not fit into the white, middle-class, hardworking, law-abiding, flag-waving, Communist-hating, Protestant mold. In Reagan's world, the kind of guys who began showing up at Vet Centers—and oftentimes the guys who *ran* them—fell mostly into one big category that, if he were being generous, he might call *degenerate.*

There were, of course, some Vietnam veterans who made a career of outraging, ripping off, and getting back at the American government, and the Vet Centers were just another weapon for them to wield against the Washington fat cats, who had already stripped them—or so they believed—of faith, hope, honor, and decency. For the first year or two of the Outreach program, Vet Center scandals abounded. The team leader of the San Diego Vet Center was caught using his government van to import cocaine from Mexico. In Fort Lauderdale, a group of armed Vietnam vets took over a Vet Center and held it for several days. But the government also was not above manufacturing a few scandals of its own.

The two Alabama Vet Centers, in Birmingham and Mobile, were headed by notoriously antiwar veterans, a fact that drew fierce criticism from Alabama's Republican Senator, Jeremiah Denton, himself a highly decorated Vietnam POW. Having recently discovered a black nationalist, terrorist group running guns and drugs out of Mobile, Denton was convinced that activist Vietnam vets were behind it, and that Alabama's Vet Centers were being used to recruit bodyguards and assassins to protect these criminal operations. A whole slew of law enforcement agencies, from the FBI down to the Alabama Bureau of Investigation (ABI), were only too happy to formulate an entrapment scheme that could shut down such a vile conspiracy, perhaps the whole Vet Center program, and put an end to this horrendous misuse of government funding. One government agent even claimed, later in court, that "delayed-stress syndrome" had been concocted merely as an alibi in case the veterans were ever caught. The worst part was that the VA gladly cooperated in what was later dubbed "Vetscam" (after another famous FBI entrapment plot of the time, Abscam). In a press release afterward, VA administrator Robert Nimmo claimed he had merely been helping "cleanse" the Vet Center program of those who threatened its "integrity."

The primary target of Vetscam was a peer counselor in the Birmingham Vet Center and former First Cav combat artilleryman named Tom Ashby. Not only had Ashby founded the first Alabama chapter of VVAW, but he had subsequently made enemies in the conservative white establishment by his prominent civil rights and prison-reform work. He was especially concerned with the plight of Vietnam vets in prison and founded Alabama Veterans' Services in large part to do prison outreach as well as discharge upgrading. Ron Bitzer of the Center for Veterans' Rights called Ashby "one of the outstanding organizers of veterans" and praised his "credible track record."

Additional targets were the Birmingham team leader Don Reed, a former three-tour Army combat helicopter pilot who had also been a leader in VVAW, and the Mobile team leader Dave Curry, an exceedingly bright man whom the Army had sent to counterintelligence and language schools and who had worked undercover in Vietnam as part of the Phoenix (later renamed Phung Hoang) program. Enraged and disgusted by the political assassinations he had helped arrange, Curry asked and was permitted to resign from active duty in 1971. He proceeded to get his M.A. in sociology from Ole Miss, writing his thesis on hallucinogen users, and his Ph.D. at the University of Chicago, writing a brilliant, book-length thesis (later published under the title *Sunshine Patriots*) on those men in his generation, vets and nonvets alike, who had "run afoul of the military." In fact, despite his academic success, Curry's own life and his marriage went to pieces as he tried to shut out his immense guilt from the war with too many hours of work and vast quantities of booze and drugs. It was only through the intervention of Tom Ashby and the sympathetic camaraderie in VVAW, he would later say, that he survived at all. Like Ashby, he also committed himself to the cause of numerous oppressed minorities, including southern blacks, gay people, and incarcerated veterans. The prospect of helping other vets at the Mobile Vet Center seemed a further means of recovering the sense of purpose he had lost in Vietnam and that he'd spent many self-destructive years in search of.

Unfortunately, the Mobile Vet Center, months in being readied, was shut down before the first veteran client could enter. It was seized on opening day, February 17, 1982, by government agents, and the Birmingham Vet Center was closed the same day. Ashby, Reed, and Curry were all charged with distributing (not selling) a few grams of cocaine to another Vet Center employee, a Marine combat veteran named Grady Gibson. Reed, a highly decorated war hero, was soon released on a three-year probation, but Ashby and Curry went to trial before a notoriously reactionary, anti–civil libertarian judge (a Reagan appointee), W. Brevard Hand, and a poorly educated rural jury. The prosecutor Jeffrey Beauregard Sessions III had previously indicted sixteen black NAACP members for "conspiracy to commit vote fraud" because of their work registering black voters—a case that was thrown out. During the trial, Sessions attacked Ashby for his civil rights work and Curry for his graduate thesis on "drug use." The lifestyle of both men was used to discredit them—such as the fact that they admitted smoking pot with veteran friends or occasionally doing a few lines of cocaine after a softball game. Found guilty, Curry was sentenced to 34 years in prison and fined $80,000, while Ashby got 30 years and a $59,000 fine. Though the sentences were later reduced somewhat, both men's careers were permanently destroyed and their personal lives shattered for more than a decade.

In a period when rich white businessmen like auto designer John Z. DeLorean often got off scot-free on cocaine-trafficking charges far more substantial than those brought against Ashby and Curry, the country clearly had a different standard of justice for Vietnam veterans. Reed, Ashby, and Curry were hardly criminals by any stretch of the imagination. They were Vietnam combat vets who, like tens of thousands of their peers, had little use for regulations or spit-shine propriety. They had been taught to get a job done and to take care of their comrades, and they had thought of Grady Gibson as one of their own.

It came out at the trial that Grady Gibson was a government agent who had been sent to the Birmingham Vet Center to inveigle Ashby and the others into a criminal conspiracy. In fact, he had told Reed, Ashby, and Curry that he had a bad cocaine addiction and had pleaded with them to get him a little cocaine to keep him from going into withdrawal; at the same time, Gibson told them he was about to come into a big inheritance which he would donate to Alabama Veterans' Services. Although Gibson claimed to be a bemedaled war hero like Reed, the truth was he had deserted the Marines just after his return from Vietnam, had been court-martialed and given a bad discharge, and had subsequently gotten in trouble because of his own heavy drug use. The easiest way out for him was to become an informer for the ABI, and eventually he became one of their chief drug agents. In 1987, he and another ABI informer, Eddie Hart, were convicted of murdering Hart's teenage wife to collect on an insurance policy worth $300,000. Gibson was sentenced to life in prison without parole.

Among the more outrageous aspects of the entrapment was the fact that Gibson had worn a body mike and secretly tape-recorded supposedly confidential Vet Center counseling sessions, and then these tapes were played before the judge. Confidentiality was further breached when client files were confiscated by the prosecution and inspected for months. But despite such legal and ethical violations, and despite the fact that many newspapers, like the Mobile *Press-Register,* used Vetscam to denounce the entire Vet Center program as a "nonessential drain on the federal treasury," Operation Outreach's new director, Art Blank, refused to speak up in Ashby and Curry's defense; in fact, he announced publicly that he was "cutting them loose." Blank had already come under fire because more than 10 percent of the staff in his program were former VVAW members, and so he hastened to distance himself from Ashby and Curry's "irresponsible actions," even to the point of denying he had ever been a VVAW member himself. Likewise, Senator Cranston, according to his deputy general counsel Bill Brew, tried to do "damage control" by disowning Ashby and Curry and letting them "take the fall," in order to insure that the Vet Center program survived.

Clearly, one couldn't expect prominent government officials to countenance lawbreaking, but one could have expected someone to speak up for the years of dedicated civil rights, prison, and veterans' work Ashby and Curry had both performed, and to see that the punishment meted out to them was not so far out of proportion to the technically illegal but relatively harmless acts they had done out of friendship—not for profit or with criminal intent. Besides, a great many other veterans were unfairly made to pay the price as well, like the majority of their coworkers, who were also fired or suspended. The Birmingham and Mobile Vet Centers, with their long list of waiting clients, did not reopen for many months. When they did, they were no longer the vet-friendly places they had been under Reed and Ashby, and there were many subsequent staff resignations to protest the new bureaucratic rigidity.[206]

*   *   *

Robert P. Nimmo remained VA administrator till November 1982, and during his tenure his hostility toward Vietnam vets hurt the Vet Centers a great deal. Although he waged no open attack against them, all those who hated the Vet Centers—from David Stockman at OMB to the various medical directors at Central Office and in VA hospitals around the country—knew they would encounter no opposition from Nimmo if they attempted to rein in the Outreach program (oxymoron though that was). Sometimes this reining in was accomplished by holding back money that had been allotted to the program—like the $40.3 million for research and the fee-contract program, which just disappeared—and sometimes it was done by forcing Vet Center employees to follow the protocols set by Central Office and/or the local medical facility to which they were subordinate: i.e., to act less like freewheeling, down-home, street-corner vets and more like typical bureaucrats.

By late 1982, according to a journalist for VVAW's *The Veteran,* the VA had "brought [Operation Outreach] under control with an iron fist." Committed Vet Center employees, who were usually combat vets, were "being driven out wholesale," he wrote, and were consistently replaced with others who would "toe the VA line." The new VA administrator was forty-six-year-old Harry N. Walters, a 1959 West Point graduate who had spent most of his life as a corporate marketing executive. Walters gave tacit consent, just as his predecessor had, to the VA's continuing attempt to transform the Vet Centers into traditional mental-hygiene clinics. Soon the VA medical directors began talking of an even more extreme strategy to eviscerate the Vet Centers. They suggested moving them onto VA hospital grounds or, better yet, absorbing them completely within existing psychiatric units in VA medical centers.

According to one observer, Vet Center workers were subjected not only to the pressure from Washington to homogenize the program, but also to the whims of their "parent facilities"—VA hospitals, regional offices, and outpatient clinics—whose directors wished to "tailor the program to their personal models." Where there wasn't outright coercion used against the centers, there was often neglect or incompetence in meeting the centers' needs; and sometimes it was hard to tell mere bumbling from actual malice. The only sure thing was that the Vet Center teams didn't need any more stress in their lives. Meshad thought it unconscionable for the VA "to play those kind of games, when we were already dealing with Vietnam veterans with severe readjustment problems—when lives were at stake. . . . Our own personnel were burning out left and right just doing the work."

Almost no one thought to blame Art Blank. There was a community of opinion among Vietnam veteran activists, and the word among them was that Blank was "a good guy." VVAW, having thrown out the RCP in 1978 and returned to nonpolitical, though still relentless, veterans' advocacy, announced in its paper that Blank was "on the side of the Vietnam veteran and above the political crap that has marked the VA during this and past administrations." Still, Blank's silence on the Vet Center situation was troubling. When questioned by a Vietnam veteran reporter as to his own plans for ensuring the longevity of the Outreach program, Blank replied, somewhat unsettlingly: "The future of the Vet Centers are [*sic*] in the hands of Congress and top VA administrators."

Although the reporter could have pointed out that Blank himself was a "top VA administrator," no one jumped on him yet, nor for a couple more years. Vietnam vets will cut a fellow vet a good deal of slack—sometimes too much. Blank had already won the trust of most of the Vet Center teams by his initial warmth and gutsiness in the face of VA callousness and rigidity. Mike Maxwell recalls meeting Blank for the first time at a Vet Center planning session on Long Island in October 1979. The motto of the Vet Centers was supposed to be "Help Without Hassles," but no sooner had the meeting begun than a couple of VA heavyweights pulled out a huge stack of forms that they insisted each veteran would have to fill out before being admitted at a Vet Center. Blank grabbed the forms and ripped them to shreds. "This is bullshit!" Blank declared. "We're trying to do an effective program for vets. They won't respond to this paperwork. They shouldn't have to do this." *Wow! This guy's gonna be really good!* Maxwell thought, and later spent some time in conversation with him, looking up to Blank as a mentor.

It was puzzling, then, to find that a year after Blank had taken over directorship of the Outreach program, the Vet Centers were in a huge mess—which opponents in Congress were using as evidence that the program should be killed. Even more puzzling was Blank's apparent indifference to what some had termed "a federal assault on Vietnam veterans' programs and leadership." Despite team leaders across the country crying out for help, Blank, like Nimmo and the rest of the VA mandarins, had never bothered to come out of Central Office to see what was actually going on in the centers.

Three years after the inauguration of Operation Outreach, the VA still had not provided any written standards of performance or program guidelines. The relationship between the centers and their "parent facilities" was not yet clearly defined. Money was still disappearing from Vet Center accounts, and employees were being fired, but no one could say exactly who had the operational decision-making power over the Vet Centers. Because of resignations and terminations, many of the centers were badly understaffed. And it was almost always the combat vets who were going and being let go, replaced usually by nonveteran degreed professionals. Some of the centers were physically deteriorating. The one on Capitol Hill reported that it had no working bathroom, no ramp for wheelchairs, unsafe and erratic electrical wiring, and no routine maintenance, which the VA had promised but never done. Others were being forced to take office space in slum neighborhoods, where even combat vets feared to walk the street.

The question kept coming up: *What's Art Blank say about all this?* But Blank, like the practiced psychiatrist that he was, said almost nothing. Although no one seemed to realize it at the time, that retreat from controversy had been a pattern in Blank's life. The same thing had happened in his brief career with VVAW. After a debut as antiwar activist almost as striking as John Kerry's (whom he preceded by more than two years), Blank quickly began begging off from Jan Barry's increasing requests for him to speak or to participate in demonstrations. He blamed his large workload at the Yale Psychiatric Institute for consuming all his free time, so that all he could continue to lend was "moral and financial support." By early 1968, Blank had dropped out of the Vietnam veterans' movement, never to return, even though the New Haven chapter, led by firebrands like Jack Smith, would soon become one of the most active in the country.

By early 1983, the Vet Centers were in crisis. Though Blank refused to speak up, Vet Center cocreator Bill Mahedy accused the VA administrators of attempting "to administer the Outreach program out of existence." The authorization for the program was set to expire in September 1984. If a new law was not passed, the program would have to begin phasing out in October 1983, and soon all 136 Vet Centers would have to shut their doors for good. Of the 567 employees in the program, 325 had been hired as "Schedule A" personnel, which meant they were considered merely temporary help and could be laid off at any time. With zero job security, a large number of them began quitting as the summer of 1983 approached, in a desperate rush to line up new employment before the whole Vet Center ship went down with them on board.

Blank, apparently fearful of having to play the captain of that ship, began doing his best to placate the VA higher-ups. He began pushing what he called the "professionalization" of the Vet Centers, the replacement of more and more of the streetwise peer counselors with clinicians who had received university training (preferably at a graduate-school level) in psychology, social work, or psychotherapy. Few of the new hirees were Vietnam veterans. Despite this trend toward making the Vet Centers more compatible with traditional VA health care, the Reagan administration once again declared its opposition to extending the program beyond 1984. Seeing the handwriting on the wall, Blank decided that even more drastic changes were called for.

With a Republican president and a Republican Congress, one of the government's biggest gripes with the Vet Centers was the way they were being used to promote left-wing political causes, especially attacks on the government itself. So Blank sent out a directive to his regional managers that placed severe restrictions on what subject matter could be discussed at the centers. Talk of Agent Orange problems was strictly taboo. Another thing that rubbed the Republicans the wrong way was the outreach many of the centers were doing to vets in prison. Prison outreach had in fact been one of Shad Meshad's pet projects. Using his VVRU at Brentwood as a base, he and a combat veteran counselor named Bruce Pentland had started seeing veteran prisoners and running rap groups with them at the federal prison in Tehachapi, in 1971. Aligning himself with the VA's wishes, Blank announced that forthwith the Vet Centers had to sever all connections with prisons; even simple visits on VA time or in

VA vehicles was prohibited. Worst of all in the eyes of Meshad, Maxwell, and many other dedicated Vet Center personnel, Blank began to play "the body count game."

Reagan wanted to earn political capital for every tax dollar spent; and so the very least the Vet Centers could do was to provide him with impressive client statistics that he could show to voters, as evidence of how well his administration was serving freedom's defenders. Blank sent out directives that advised Vet Center counselors to spend no more than 45 minutes in session with each client. Instead of gabbing with only two clients a day (and thereby, perhaps, building the start of solid, comfortable, trusting relationships), counselors were to try to cram in ten a day. This "game of numbers" had Meshad tearing out his wayward hair. He screamed at Blank that the Vet Center program would soon "go down the tubes" just like the VA hospital system had, "because the way they count bodies and services, they can never just deliver good-quality services." Meshad also warned that this new directive would lead to counselors lying about how many vets they had helped, just as soldiers had been coaxed to inflate the number of VC they had killed in Vietnam. Blank replied with official "Article 15–type" (one step below court-martial) letters of reprimand.

Meantime, according to Meshad, the "really good leadership, the dynamic, flexible, community-based counselors," continued "leaving the program like Americans fleeing the fall of Saigon."[207]

5. Blank Starts Bringing in the Centers, and Meshad and Blank Go to War

In the spring of 1983, just as in 1981, a miracle occurred to save the Vet Center program. This time its guardian angels were two young congressmen, Bob Edgar (D-Penn.) and Lane Evans (D-Ill.), and a Navy Vietnam vet named John Terzano. The Senate Veterans' Affairs Committee had approved a bill authorizing only a one-year extension of readjustment counseling services, and there was considerable doubt about even that getting through the House. But Edgar and Evans introduced a bill, H.R. 1443, which called for a *three-year* extension of the Vet Center program, plus a VA-sponsored "comprehensive nationwide study of the readjustment of Vietnam era veterans to civilian life, including information on the prevalence of post-traumatic stress disorder and other health problems."

Edgar, who sat on the House Veterans' Affairs Committee, and chaired the subcommittee on Hospitals and Health Care, was in a position to demand hearings on the bill. Although not a vet himself, the forty-year-old Edgar was of the Vietnam generation. He had spent the war years in divinity school; but unlike David Stockman, he had actually been ordained a minister; and even more unlike Stockman, he had emerged a champion of those who had risked their lives in his place, in Vietnam. Thirty-two-year-old Lane Evans, a Marine veteran who had been stationed in Okinawa while his brother fought in Vietnam, was one of the newest and youngest members of the Vietnam Veterans in Congress. Boyish and energetic, he stirred up enthusiasm for his and Edgar's Vietnam veteran legislation not only among the VVIC but throughout the Republican House. The trick was turned, however, by the testimony delivered before Edgar's subcommittee on March 24 by VVA's legislative director, John Terzano. Tall, dark, and handsome, with a warm, convincing voice, Terzano was God's gift to Bobby Muller. When he had shown up at the Council of Vietnam Veterans' tiny office in 1978, after reading about it in the *Washington Post,* Muller had immediately put him to work at licking envelopes and anything else to keep him around. Muller sized up the twenty-seven-year-old George Washington University undergraduate as the perfect "front man" for his organization; and indeed, later, as VVA's spokesman to Congress, Terzano would overcome much of the antagonism to VVA that had been generated there by Muller's own acerbic, domineering personality.

Terzano laid out in great detail the reasons why the Vet Center program needed to be both expanded and extended for three years. To begin with, he said that to extend funding beyond the next presidential election "would take the program totally out of the political process." Then he pointed out that though the centers had already seen 240,000 vets, another half million who hadn't come in (by the best available estimates) still suffered serious readjustment problems; so that the program had "not even peaked yet on the number of veterans who could use [its] services." He also argued cogently in favor of a comprehensive readjustment study. "We have been saddled for years by the assumption that a veteran is a veteran is a veteran," he said, echoing former House Veterans' Affairs Committee chairman Ray Roberts, "and we must recognize and address the fact that a Vietnam veteran is not a Vietnam veteran is not a Vietnam veteran. It would be important to learn from such a study what might be the differences in these populations."

To everyone's astonishment, Edgar and Evans' legislation sailed through the House as "Veterans Administration Health Programs Amendments" to the latest VA omnibus bill, and became law in November 1983. Public Law 98-160 required that the VA administrator submit a series of close-out reports to the House and Senate Veterans' Affairs committees on the effectiveness of the Vet Center program by mid-1987, but it permitted counselors to continue seeing clients, if necessary, till September 30, 1988. The Vet Centers had a new lease on life.

And then, to everyone's astonishment, the persecution of the Vet Center program continued even worse than before. Blank and his deputy, Gus Martinez, a former team leader from California hired by Meshad, began circulating "hit lists" to the regional managers of Vet Center employees they wanted out of the program. Most of those marked for dismissal were the non-degreed combat vets and community organizers. Terzano may have succeeded too well in selling the program to Congress as a more "cost-effective" means of delivering traditional health care services, which were a lot more expensive when provided by VA medical facilities. Blank seemed to take to heart Terzano's praise for the program's "more clinically, professionally oriented" approach, and he heeded Terzano's call to hire more "high quality clinicians." Unfortunately, Blank seemed to miss altogether Terzano's equally strong call for the Vet Centers to retain their "advocacy role" on behalf of Vietnam veterans, and for them to diversify, rather than limit, their services. Using the analogy of a car with three flat tires, Terzano had said: "If you put air in the counseling tire and none in the educational, employment, and discharge upgrading tires, the car will not go anywhere."

Blank, in fact, acted as if he had been given a mandate to change over the entire Vet Center program, which he hadn't. The regional managers and others who suddenly found themselves under the gun of Central Office began to suspect that the problem was Gus Martinez, who seemed to enjoy the dictatorial exercise of power over others' jobs and to use that power in a vengeful manner against his real or imagined enemies. Originally Martinez was supposed to have been one of Blank's three assistants, along with Ray Scurfield and Ed Lord; but somehow Martinez carved out the new position of deputy manager for himself.

It was Martinez who came up with the idea of running the Vet Centers as a Management By Objective enterprise. The 104 "MBO" circulars he and Blank sent out emphasized collecting showy statistics—the "numbers games" Meshad detested—and forcing employees to spend hours filling out mostly useless paperwork—the kind of "bullshit" (to use Mike Maxwell's word) that the program had been created to circumvent. Martinez created a Hispanic Working Group within the Outreach program, but gave short shrift to women and other minorities. The 42-page report of a special Working Group on Women Vietnam Veterans, produced in 1982 by nine women, most of them Vietnam combat nurses, suggesting a whole range of reforms to make the Vet Centers more helpful and congenial to women, was handed to Blank and Martinez and never seen again.

Sometimes Meshad thought the problem was as simple as the fact that Blank "just wasn't a leader"—that he had never worked with vets at the street level, and had visited only two centers in his first three years as director of the program. Bill Brew felt that Blank sought to isolate himself from the anger and complaints of counselors in the field—that he did not deal well with others' distress—and so he made the bad move of using Martinez as a buffer against the very real failings of the program. In any case, those at the VA with power over Blank all seemed to like what he was doing; and those suffering under him were mostly compelled to watch in frustration as—to quote Meshad—"he and his cohort did serious damage to people in the Vet Centers."

Ray Scurfield, who worked beside Blank in Central Office for over two years, felt that the situation could have been turned around if more people had stood up to Blank. "Very few people were willing to put their names down in writing or do anything formal," Scurfield said. "I don't remember anyone going above Art Blank's head and coming up with a position paper or anything. A lot of people wanted to bitch and moan, but when push came to shove, there weren't many people there." On the other hand, Blank, who wore his balding hair combed forward like Julius Caesar, and had the piercing eyes to match, could be extremely overbearing and intimidating; and those who did go up against him usually lived to regret it.[208]

In 1985, Meshad "took Blank on head-on." Shad (as he tells it) was "ready to take the Vet Center program to its pinnacle." They had now opened 189 centers, and Congress had given them another extension, guaranteeing their funding until 1989. Meshad felt this was the time for them to expand their vision and reach out to the entire population of Vietnam veterans. "The Vet Center program wasn't just for PTSD clean and pure," claims Meshad. "Every Vietnam vet had some type of delayed-stress syndrome, whether classified PTSD in a clinical sense or not." Vietnam vets were now hitting their forties, going through a whole new range of midlife crises, which PTSD only intensified; and Meshad thus felt they needed more services than ever. He wanted to reach out in a much bigger way to the homeless, to vets in prison (Blank's anathema), and even to the apparently successful vets who had stuffed down their anger for decades and who, if not given a chance to "leak it out" somewhere, might someday hit the tripwire that would let it all out at once, blowing their comfortable life and their relationships with those around them to smithereens.

At that moment, when Meshad was filled with joy at what they had achieved, and energized to embark on this new phase, feeling that he had "just the world to do," Blank told him, "No, we're dismantling the program and bringing it in." Blank said he was committed to getting the Vet Centers out of their funky little storefronts and relocating them within the VA hospital system. In a matter of months, Blank brought nine Vet Centers onto hospital grounds. Meshad was aghast. It seemed as if Blank were on a mission to undo fifteen years of hard work by thousands of PTSD pioneers. Blank maintained that they "weren't getting body count like we did in the early eighties," and that this proved that they had done "all the outreach there was to do," that "all those who had PTSD have already come in." As Meshad relates the story, Blank told him, "We've already peaked." He claims Blank tried to get him to see that it was now their job to cut down the Vet Center program, to turn it into "a mental-hygiene program," and to cut costs by operating inside existing facilities, so that money could be returned to the federal treasury, and they could prove what responsible civil servants they were.

Meshad told Blank that he "just one hundred percent professionally totally disagreed." His view was that if new vets weren't arriving in throngs, it was because the Vet Centers were so badly understaffed and buried so deep in daily crises that no one had time to do real outreach. He argued that "the Outreach program is the cheapest, most efficient delivery system in mental health there is," and that it's always better to provide health care "out there where people can get to it, in the community." Moreover, Meshad felt that Vietnam vets had been denied so much basic care for the first fifteen or twenty years since they'd come home that they deserved a few bonuses now. He told Blank, "Even if it's true [that the Vet Centers had outlived their mission to treat delayed stress], it's still worth thirty-two million dollars a year to ensure that two hundred thousand vets get good services."

In typical fashion, Blank told him, "If you don't like it [his plan to dismantle the Vet Centers], think about leaving."

That was a war cry to Meshad, and he went after Blank as he had gone after Crawford. The fighting got unbelievably dirty, with the VA accusing Shad of using the Vet Center program for his own profit—claiming he forced Vet Centers to market his self-published memoir *Captain for Dark Mornings*—and Shad in turn contributed to a *60 Minutes* television exposé by Dan Rather that made Blank look like some rigid Nazi tyrant, who was willing to betray the entire generation of Vietnam veterans because of his blind allegiance to his superiors. Meshad also claimed that Blank had "cut a deal" to save his own job while sacrificing just about everybody else's.

In Blank's behalf, it should be said that he felt he was saving the Vet Center program from its opponents in Congress the only way he could. Many of the key Republicans on the Veterans' Affairs committees felt the program was wildly out of control, and that millions of federal dollars were going down the drain with no accountability whatsoever. Either Blank instituted accountability, which could be achieved a lot easier within VA walls, or they would close it down for good. In retrospect, says Bill Brew, Blank did effectively protect the program—even if it became a good deal less "field-friendly"—so that it grew substantially during his ten-year tenure and reached an ever increasing number of veterans. On Shad's side, the attention he got for the issue resulted in a court order, and later new legislation, that at least temporarily held the line against the VA closing further storefront centers. But the battle to keep the Vet Center program from being absorbed into "regular" VA health care would continue into the next century—even after Art Blank himself, who ended up holding the director's job until 1993, was himself history.

Shad Meshad, however, was one of the first casualties of this latest internecine war. Art Blank was not the easy target Crawford had been. Blank, who could play the bureaucratic game with the best of them, had made powerful allies both in Congress and in the highest echelons of the VA. Under threat of a major investigation by the Inspector General into his many irregular practices, Meshad was forced to resign in May 1986, though he was allowed to take a medical retirement. Shad tried to put the best face on matters, saying he had made a "bad decision" in recommending Blank for the director's job, and would have to live with the results. But the truth was, Meshad was as shattered by his abrupt removal from the program as Crawford had been. Meshad's health deteriorated, his seemingly boundless ability to help other vets evaporated, at least temporarily, and his contributions to the field of stress treatment went into eclipse. Worst of all, the style of concern for his workers that he had implemented—frequent rap sessions among the counselors and administrators, for instance, to allow for the airing of grievances and to prevent "burnout"—fell by the wayside and never came back to what became an increasingly sterile and employee-unfriendly program.

"It took me a year to readjust myself," Meshad says; but even after he "readjusted," he found a lot of his old enthusiasm had vanished forever. He would never work for the VA again.[209]

6. The Waller Street Vet Center: "They Just Didn't Know How Far We'd Take It"

Of all those who worked for the Vet Center program, none was more uncompromising than Jack McCloskey. A pioneer of PTSD theory, a member of the Vet Center Advisory Board, and the team leader of San Francisco's Waller Street center, McCloskey was at the top of every VA hit list, and respectably high on quite a few other government hit lists besides. Yet if ever there was a veterans' advocate who was not in the game for money, fame, or power, but really and simply just to help his fellow veterans, to be there for them day and night, whenever they were in need, it was Jack McCloskey. Said Ron Bitzer, who helped McCloskey found Swords to Ploughshares, one of the nation's first Vietnam veterans' self-help groups: "McCloskey represented the purest feeling we had that we got raped, we signed up once too often, and we were not gonna compromise again. . . . He served to keep many of us honest because he reflected the Vietnam experience as a combat medic, he reflected the early organizing effort against the war and for veterans' rights, and he reflected a consistency in speaking out for over twenty years." In McCloskey's obituary, in 1996, Bitzer said it even more succinctly: "Jack was our beacon of what was needed to help disaffected and disadvantaged Vietnam veterans."

Born in 1942, raised in a Catholic orphanage in an Italian and Irish ghetto of Philadelphia, McCloskey joined the Navy at twenty-one, asking to be trained as a corpsman in emulation of his older brother. Since the Marines use Navy medics (called *corpsmen*), McCloskey ended up wearing a Marine uniform for five years. He first served under hostile fire when the Marines invaded the Dominican Republic in 1965. In 1966, he got out, returned to Philly to tend bar across from the University of Pennsylvania, where he audited classes, and started living with a young Quaker woman named Lydia. On July 4, 1967, he received a government telegram announcing that he had been reactivated because of the Marine Corps's need for corpsmen in Vietnam. Despite Lydia's pacifist objections, and despite his own moral feelings against the war, McCloskey returned to Camp Lejeune, and accepted his orders to serve at a firebase north of Da Nang. He arrived in-country in September 1967.

His unit, Second Battalion of the Seventh Marines, patrolled around the Haiphong Pass on Highway 1, taking heavy casualties almost every day. He never forgot the first kid he treated, an eighteen-year-old Marine who'd stepped on a land mine. He asked, "Doc, Doc, I'm going to live, ain't I?" McCloskey had replied, "Sure, babe," and then the kid died in his arms. McCloskey cried like a baby. And he cried daily until the losses so overwhelmed him that he was forced to "totally shut down" his emotions, he said, "for survival." But he was still "being torn up inside." Forging his own kind of protest, as he was to do all his life, he soon refused to carry a weapon, even on combat missions.

His work counseling veterans began in Vietnam. He was twenty-five years old, and many of the guys, who were a good deal younger, came to him to talk about Dear John letters or their buddies getting hurt. Then the Tet Offensive blew up, and he went down to Hue, where he was overwhelmed with casualties, both physical and psychological. In early March, he met Lydia in Hawaii on his R & R, and they had a huge fight. She tried to get him to desert, saying her upper-middle-class family could help him escape to Sweden, France, or Canada, and would support their life together in exile. McCloskey felt he "had to go back to Nam," because a lot of young Marines depended on him to keep them alive.

He was hit twice himself later in March, by mortars, and the second time took a lot of shrapnel in his knee. Because he risked his life to treat the wounded, while wounded himself and under heavy fire, he was awarded both the Bronze Star and Silver Star. Sometimes, when he needed to calm himself, he would recall images of the Summer of Love on Haight Street, where he'd walked in amazement only hours before shipping out for Vietnam. But he also fell into the habit of using marijuana, as well as the morphine syrettes he carried, to deal with his own physical and mental pain, after a battle was over.

When he returned stateside in October 1968, he was still suffering from his wounds (he walked with a cane all his life), and was given light duty at the Hunters Point Naval Base in San Francisco. He still wore his Marine uniform, because his seabag with all his belongings had been blown up by a mortar. They threatened to punish him unless he bought a new Navy uniform, but he refused. He let his hair grow long too. "What are you gonna do," he asked, "send me back to Nam?"

Lydia had already moved to San Francisco; and after his discharge in June 1969, they married and went to live in a cheap two-bedroom flat on 26th and Castro in a poor, racially mixed neighborhood, adjoining the gay Castro district and just up the hill from the street action, bars, and drug connections in the Mission. McCloskey started drinking a lot, and continued smoking pot, though he quickly got off the morphine. He went to City College, but isolated himself, stayed drunk in the evenings, and never talked about Vietnam. Lydia had tried to drag him into the peace movement, but he was turned off immediately when he heard peaceniks calling Vietnam vets "killers" and cheering at film clips of American planes being shot down. Then Kent State happened; and like so many Vietnam vets, he was outraged that "the guns were being turned around on us now."

In response to the nationwide protests, an "experimental college" was set up on campus, and it was there that McCloskey met his lifelong mentor, a Mexican-American named Carlos Melendrez. In the early 1960s, Melendrez had been in the Army Security Agency, running spy operations against the Communist government in Cuba. With a little pushing from Melendrez, McCloskey found himself speaking to an audience of 5,000 students at City College. And like so many other Vietnam vets, he found that when he talked about his pain and guilt and anger, his own healing began. Within a few days, he started organizing other Vietnam vets on campus into a group called Vets for Peace, and soon he linked up with a similar group organized in Berkeley and Oakland by Lee Thorn. By the end of the year, they had affiliated with VVAW. Then Lee Thorn went to New York and brought back Mike Oliver, to form the nucleus of one of VVAW's most dynamic chapters.

McCloskey served as president of VVAW-San Francisco, as California state and regional coordinator, and even as president of the national organization for two months, in the interim after John Kerry resigned. He was quickly becoming, as Bitzer said, "almost a mythical figure, a walking classic representation of that era." There was, to begin with, McCloskey's unforgettable appearance. A short but sturdy man, who always stood with military erectness, McCloskey's most striking feature was his large, brown, almond-shaped eyes—at times, extraordinarily sad, frank, and wistful; at other times, sparkling with merriment. His slow walk and slight limp added to his dignity. Then there was the flattened boxer's nose, the walrus moustache, and the near–shoulder length wavy hair (worn long till the day he died), which was all silver by the time he reached forty, and white in his fifties. His hands were always covered with a mix of psoriasis and chloracne blisters, shedding white scabs; and his whole body aged so rapidly (another possible Agent Orange effect) that his vet friends used to have fun in bars introducing him as their father. None of this was as striking as the McCloskey voice. Loud, resonant, and distinctly lower-class Philly, it rasped, barked, and trembled with emotion. But the most outstanding thing about him was his heart. Any vet who needed a place to sleep could claim a section of his living room or kitchen floor, and at one time in the early seventies he had a dozen such guests in his cramped apartment—putting more than a little strain on his already shaky marriage.[210]

He started leading rap groups in VVAW. Then in 1973, the RCP drove him away from VVAW and politics; and under the influence of a psychologist, Dr. Steve Pennington, he turned seriously to counseling. Together with a Dutchman named Rob Boudewijn (who had joined the American Army to become a veterinarian and ended up a medic in Vietnam instead) and draft resister David Harris, he founded Twice Born Men, which extended the rap groups to ex-prisoners. The idea for Twice Born Men came from antiwar priest Daniel Berrigan, who had been imprisoned and later forced underground for both real civil disobedience and imagined conspiracies against the government. In a letter later published, Berrigan had equated people who had gone through the prison system with people who had gone through the military, saying both groups had had to face their fears and learn to work through them, and that both were thereby "twice born"—not in a religious sense, but existentially, in the sense of having come through a harrowing crucible.

By this time, McCloskey had his own degree in psychology from Antioch College's San Francisco branch, but his approach to counseling was anything but academic. Using his apartment as "storefront," and Harris's Fresno farm as a retreat, Twice Born Men did outreach to the Tenderloin, the Mission, and other places where the down-and-out roamed the streets or congregated in bars. Many times they would get a 2 A.M. call from some vet or ex-con who had nowhere to go when the bars closed, and usually McCloskey would go down in person to counsel the guy. Besides the rap groups, Twice Born Men provided individual and family counseling. Then, when five VISTA workers—three of them Vietnam combat vets, one a Korean combat vet, and Vietnam-era vet Ron Bitzer—complained about the botched outreach program they had been assigned to at the Fort Miley VA, McCloskey was paid to come in and "retrain" them. In the end, they agreed with McCloskey that the VA program was unfixable; and all of them, together with the core group of Twice Born Men, incorporated as a multiservice veterans' organization called Swords to Ploughshares. Ironically, McCloskey, who claimed his Catholic faith "had gone out the window" in Vietnam, had again chosen to operate under a religious slogan.

Swords got a free office in the YMCA building on the Embarcadero, just off Market, in a part of town that was then close to Skid Row; and almost immediately, McCloskey began reaching vets that had fallen through every other social net. Swords became a model for almost every other self-help group that followed it. Meshad, who'd met McCloskey at the first major delayed-stress conference in St. Louis in 1973, was influenced by Swords' example in shaping his Vietnam Veterans' Resocialization Unit—and many of McCloskey's innovations eventually found their way into the Vet Center prototype, based on the VVRU. The 1970s were hardly a good time for McCloskey himself, however. The more active and visible he became, the more determined grew the government (or so he felt) to persecute and punish him. In early 1973, San Francisco police broke into his apartment, carrying a warrant to search for a fugitive. They opened McCloskey's nightstand and seized his diarrhea medication, and also claimed they found a lid of marijuana—which Jack, though he smoked, was never stupid enough to keep in his home.

By the mid-1970s, McCloskey had become deeply involved with the National Council of Churches' Vietnam Generation Ministries, not only pushing the recognition of PTSD but helping to found the NCC's Incarcerated Veterans Project and beginning to explore Vietnam veteran health problems due to chemical exposure (even before Maude DeVictor's revelations in Chicago). His phone bill was sometimes $900 a month—from calling doctors, lawyers, and psychologists around the country—at a time when his rent was $200. His work with Swords was bringing him national prominence too, as he laid the groundwork for filing the first post-Vietnam syndrome claims against the VA. In San Francisco, in May 1976, he was about to expose a bogus alcohol-treatment program at the Fort Miley VA—a ward which was set up on paper only, funneling VA funds into someone's pocket, but treating absolutely no one.

McCloskey had just finished counseling a vet and was standing at the bus stop on 29th and Mission, when a white guy, about forty, in a suit and tie, crossed the street and made a funny quick step as if to get behind him. Wondering what he was up to, McCloskey started to turn, just as the guy fired a .44-caliber pistol at his mid-back. Because of the move, the bullet just missed his heart and went through his stomach and liver instead. Most crazies talk to their victims, but the shooter had said nothing, nor did he try reaching for McCloskey's wallet; he vanished almost instantly. McCloskey was hospitalized for three months, during which time several loyal Vietnam vets watched over him day and night. He suspected that "somebody in a federal agency tried to do me in." The police came up with nothing.

For a long time after that, McCloskey couldn't fall asleep till the sun came up. Like Scott Camil, who had recently been shot in the back and nearly killed by a DEA agent, in what he (Camil) claimed was an assassination attempt, McCloskey felt himself a prime target in the government's "war on Vietnam veterans." Increasingly, that war began to seem as real as the one they'd fought in Vietnam. But once out of the hospital, McCloskey never slowed a beat in his activist work. In part, that was from the soldier's fatalistic sense that you can't hide from hurt; but it also came from McCloskey's contempt for his own suffering, a dedicated medic's attitude that it would be "selfish" to worry about his own wounds when so many other wounded people needed his help. Not that his own wounds weren't significant and daily growing worse. Despite the birth of two daughters, whom he dearly loved, his marriage continued to fall apart. He admitted the truth of his wife's accusation: "You know, Jack, it's easier for you to love a Vietnam veteran than it is to love me." Like a lot of vets who'd seen friends die in front of them, McCloskey had trouble "accepting love without feeling that people are going to be hurt." The only allowable intimacy in such perilous circumstances was the shared bravado of a soldier's manhood. McCloskey liked to quote a vet who had been in one of his rap groups: "I learned about sex without love through a prostitute, and I learned love without sex through my squad."

Not surprisingly, with so much stress piling up on him, McCloskey's health deteriorated. His skin infections worsened, and he developed liver and heart problems. It didn't help that he chain-smoked almost every waking minute—a habit he'd picked up with the Marines—wolfed down an endless diet of Philly cheese steaks, French fries, and other junk foods, and drank like a fish. He was, as Bitzer said, the quintessential Vietnam vet, fighting to get through one day at a time, scornful of fleshly infirmities and broken rules that "don't mean nothin'," and refusing to look beyond his immediate circle of companions for the values that defined his life.

There was no way that people like Shad Meshad or Max Cleland could ignore McCloskey when it came time to implement the Vet Center program. But while Meshad and Cleland knew how to at least affect the appearance of a truce with the government, whose resources were essential to healing Vietnam veterans, McCloskey's anger and resentment were always right at the surface; and quite naturally, the government looked on his willingness to help with a good deal of trepidation. In 1979, Swords to Ploughshares, powered by McCloskey's determination, had won the first suit against the VA concerning a Vietnam veteran's disability claim for delayed stress. The VA, which had stalled the case for years while the APA fiddled with a definition for combat stress disorder, was forced to cough up $20,000 in retroactive compensation. As if that weren't enough to make the government leery of McCloskey, there was his reputation for being "radical," which many in Washington interpreted as a propensity for violence—so much so that once, while in the capital, he was half-jokingly accused of being behind a bomb threat at the VA's Central Office.

Tim Craig, one of Cleland's special assistants, recalls his sense of impending danger as he walked to the White House with McCloskey for Carter's afternoon reception during Vietnam Veterans Week in 1979. Craig was somewhat reassured by the fact that the fundamentalist president was serving only pink lemonade—not McCloskey's chosen drink—and he kept his eyes trained on more likely hecklers like Ron Kovic and Rusty Lindley. But no sooner had Frank McCarthy finished springing his Agent Orange ambush on Carter than McCloskey too jumped up into Carter's face. Using less abrasive language than McCarthy, McCloskey warned the preachy Georgian that all the kind words and postage stamps in the world couldn't substitute for a range of tough programs, which dealt directly with the problems that were killing and demoralizing Vietnam vets every day.

No one could have been more surprised than McCloskey himself when he was hired a week later as a consultant to the Vet Center program, especially since he had just finished leading an Agent Orange demonstration at the Fort Miley VA. But if the VA distrusted McCloskey, the feeling was mutual. For years, with a few bucks from the National Council of Churches, McCloskey had crisscrossed the country on Greyhound buses, sometimes sharing a cheap hotel room with a dozen other vets, to help found a network of hundreds of self-help groups. Now the VA had him doing essentially the same thing, but this time he was a "jet-setter," flying from city to city to help set up Vet Centers. McCloskey profoundly distrusted the influx of big dollars and especially the heavy hand of government sponsorship. "Here you've got a bastard program that in a way became legitimized," he explained, "and for them to legitimize it they had to have more control over it."

He jumped at the chance to quit his gig as traveling bureaucrat, and to serve instead as team leader of San Francisco's first Vet Center. He chose as its location a small stucco office building on the corner of Shrader and Waller streets, a block from Golden Gate Park and only a few blocks from the corner of Haight and Ashbury—the scene of his most cherished, beatific visions of peace and love in the summer of 1967. The Haight area in 1980 was a strange mix of kitsch merchants, teenage runaways, punks and pseudo-punks, aging hippies, poets and rock musicians, Hare Krishna dancers, drug dealers and junkies, homeless people, bikers, and Vietnam vets. McCloskey was already well known in the neighborhood. Within the Haight Ashbury Free Clinic he had helped create a division called Rock Medicine, whose staff (many of them former Vietnam medics) dealt with medical emergencies at rock concerts. Early on, McCloskey had also realized that many of the people coming in for drug detox were Vietnam vets, and he had set up a liaison between the Free Clinic and Swords to Ploughshares, so that referrals went in both directions. McCloskey's Waller Street Vet Center became, not surprisingly, the most unique storefront in the entire program.[211]

Most Vet Centers said "Vet Center" in standard VA lettering; McCloskey's announced itself in Oriental calligraphy, beside a map of Vietnam painted in GI camouflage. At most Vet Centers, a person seeking help was immediately asked to show proof that he was a Vietnam veteran—usually his discharge form, his

DD-214. At Waller Street, anyone coming in off the street was given a cup of coffee and a day-old doughnut—the doughnuts donated by a shop down the street, the coffee paid for by McCloskey. McCloskey figured it was a big step for a lot of vets just to walk in the door of a place even marginally associated with the VA, and he wasn't about to scare them off by demanding their military papers or throwing a bunch of forms at them to fill out. The motto of the program, after all, was supposed to be "Help Without Hassles." At some point, paperwork was inevitable, especially in claiming benefits, and McCloskey knew that such administrative tasks were his weakest suit. But he solved that problem only a few weeks after the Waller Street center opened by hiring as his office manager a former counselor from the Free Clinic, Mary Sue Planck, an absolute genius at organization and record keeping and as loyal a supporter as McCloskey ever had.

Planck recalls the first few months of 1980 as a halcyon period at Waller Street. It seemed the people in charge of the Vet Center program applauded their unconventional methods and their philosophy of putting veterans' welfare above all else. "Maybe they just talked a good talk or just didn't know how far we'd take it," she recalled years later. There was no question that McCloskey intended to push the limits as far as he could. Despite his collecting a federal paycheck, he still harbored the belief that a true veterans' advocate needed to remain adversarial toward the government.

Yet McCloskey, who'd helped write the initial descriptions of the Vet Centers, believed he was just doing his job by "going to vets where they were"—which often enough was on a park bench or in a bar. The problems began when he tried to bill the VA for his hours out of the office or to request "comp time" for evening and weekend hours he had spent talking to and helping vets. In response, the VA repeatedly reprimanded McCloskey for seeing vets at "unauthorized times and places." McCloskey countered that vets often had their crises outside the nine-to-five time slot; and that when vets called him at 3 A.M. threatening suicide, they often declined to come down to the Vet Center to discuss the matter. In fact, McCloskey kept doing what he'd always done best, giving personal reassurance to veterans whenever and wherever they needed it. But the VA refused to pay him a cent even for an all-night vigil in the hotel room of a vet with a gun to his head, which happened more times than McCloskey cared to count. As a result, he'd either have to come in to work the next day totally exhausted, or else get penalized by the VA for not working enough hours.

McCloskey got in even deeper trouble for drinking with his clients in bars. As Planck said, it would probably have been impossible for McCloskey to spend six hours in a bar (as he was often forced to do by an emergency call) without taking a drink, but it is also true that McCloskey regularly led a group of his clients to a local bar for extended rapping after the Vet Center closed. He also

often took clients to a restaurant and bought them dinner. He had a good rationale for such actions, pointing out that while hardly "professional," it was an
effective way of building trust in veterans who trusted no one. And if the Vet
Centers had one preeminent mission, he believed it was "to embrace the most
disaffected people." According to Planck: "It worked. . . . [After a night in the
bar] people would then come and keep their appointment with the therapist.
Or they would maybe get down to the DAV and finally get their application in
for the disability benefits they had, or get signed for school or something." And
more than one client who made the rounds "getting loaded" with McCloskey
after hours has concurred with Marine corpsman Eric Schwartz that "that was
where the real healing took place."

McCloskey himself realized that he was stretching the definition of "counselor" in ways that might have catered more to his own pathology than that of
his clients. "I never became objective," he confessed. "I never could cross that
professional boundary." He admitted to seeking his own "catharsis." "For a long
time," he said, "I would go down to the Tenderloin, two or three in the morning, not looking for trouble, but to get that edge again." The problem was a profound one, which went way beyond the specific needs of Vietnam veterans and
touched upon a universal dilemma: that of the unhealed healer. That concept
was something the Vet Center program had not yet even begun to deal with;
and in fact—under Art Blank's influence—it would try to avoid ever dealing
with, by getting vets like McCloskey out of the system altogether. But what the
program needed most from the start, according to Melendrez (who served on
the Vet Center Advisory Board), was a special concern for counselors like
McCloskey, whose sensitivity and hurt made them extremely vulnerable to
burnout. Melendrez claims that support for the counselors was almost completely lacking. As a result, when they asked *him* to become a counselor, he
refused, saying he'd probably jump off the Golden Gate Bridge after a week of
listening to the kind of sad stories McCloskey dealt with round the clock.

When Blank took over the Vet Center program, the Waller Street crew
rejoiced that at last "a good guy" was in charge; and for a time the harassment
from Central Office subsided. McCloskey felt free to try out numerous innovations: a women's rap group, the first in the country, composed mainly of veterans' wives and girlfriends, but a couple of Vietnam veteran nurses too; a
group that dealt with detox and PTSD at the same time; a gay combat veterans'
group; and a medics' group, which McCloskey took part in himself. He also
prided himself on the fact that all of his rap groups were racially mixed, as was
his counseling staff. Vets were coming into the Waller Street center "in droves";
and for a time, though it was against the rules laid out in Public Law 96-22, he
allowed in only combat vets. His counselors, too, were all combat vets.

While the center had a broad range of clients, including a bank vice president and the founder of a real estate agency, McCloskey's top priority was those

vets at the bottom of the social ladder, the ones who had nowhere else to go. He told Mike Blecker, a VVAW friend who later became director of Swords, that most of the vets seen by Vet Centers and self-help groups "had their shit half together," but he wanted to provide a haven for "the others—those who don't have it together at all."[212]

7. "Promises to Dead Men": The Power to Heal

Waller Street was a home for these lost vets. Many of them, fearing that the VA (like the rest of the straight world) would just kick them out, had never even tried to find help before. Guys who had no place else to sleep could crash there, and a destitute one-legged vet was a regular camper on the sofa—despite warnings from the landlady, who opposed such use of the space as vehemently as the VA. Sometimes, to forestall eviction as well as VA censure, McCloskey and the other counselors would offer their own homes to the homeless vets. Those who preferred sleeping in the park were allowed to stash their sleeping bag at the Vet Center during the day; and those who needed a mailing address for a government check, or any other good reason, could list their residence as 1480 Waller Street. Many times a vet living on the street needed to give a phone number when he applied for a job, and Mary Sue—with Jack's blessing—was always ready to answer as their "secretary."

Taking on the vets that everyone else had given up on had its dangers, disappointments, and at times, overwhelming psychic cost. McCloskey was stabbed in the arm by a client during a counseling session. Many times he had to take weapons from suicidal vets. Once, in a Tenderloin hotel, he reached for a vet's .38, but the vet blew his brains out into a pillow before Jack could get to him. What hit him even harder were the guys he rescued, who were apparently getting on with their life, and then months or even years later he'd get a call that they were found dead—of suicide, an overdose, maybe just a heart attack from the stress of nightmares and insomnia night after night. In his first few years at Waller Street, he lost twenty clients, and every one of them took something out of him he couldn't replace. Besides, they were never really "clients" to him; he preferred to call them "brothers."

The staff at Waller Street routinely put in 50 or more hours a week, though they were getting paid for only 40. For survival, if nothing else, they needed to find ways to lighten the load, and the answer was holiday parties. On Memorial Day, the Fourth of July, Thanksgiving, and Christmas, the Waller Street Vet Center put on a bash to which all vets and their families were invited. Thanksgiving and Christmas dinners were always held in the center itself. Planck recalls how the "2237s"—supply-request forms they had to submit to the VA—always came back with big black letters scrawled across the top: "Not entitled to food." So McCloskey and the staff chipped in each time to buy the turkeys and other groceries. But they got in trouble for their summer picnics, even though the VA wasn't being charged for the food or staff time, because they would use the Vet Center car to chauffeur people to the park.

Waller Street was soon beset with reprimands from both Central Office and the regional manager in L.A.—Shad Meshad, whom McCloskey had counted on as an ally. But Meshad was already under serious attack himself from Art Blank, and he feared the Waller Street center as his Achilles' heel. As Planck explained, the VA wanted model centers it could showcase to Congress, where "pretty vets" gratefully accepted their nation's help and left saluting the American flag. Neither Waller Street—with a bunch of dirty, scruffy vets, many having just come from sleeping in a doorway, a stretch in jail, or having ridden in on an outlaw motorcycle—or McCloskey himself—with his lumberjack shirt, long, scraggly hair, stubbly face, and likely enough cigarette butts, beer cans, and old newspapers stowed under his desk—filled that bill. McCloskey, in fact, was doing a lot of outreach at San Quentin Prison, till the VA forbade him to go there on Vet Center time or in the Vet Center car. The favorite salute of both crew and clients at Waller Street was: "Screw the government—that's what it did to me!" Moreover, McCloskey insisted on wearing his VVAW and War Resisters League buttons to work, though the VA repeatedly warned that he was breaking federal law by expressing political sentiments while serving as a government employee.

McCloskey was an "embarrassment" to both Blank and Meshad, according to Mary Sue Planck, but she feels in the end it was Jack's politics that brought him down. At the most basic level, it was his antigovernment politics, his anger at the VA for having failed his comrades time and again, and his refusal to say that now the VA was doing its best to take care of Vietnam veterans—because he didn't believe that was true. What he said in public flatly contradicted the government's claims. He lambasted the VA for failing "to get up and cop to what Agent Orange had done." He felt it still did not treat post-traumatic stress disorder as a serious illness, and he pointed out how the victims of both PTSD and Agent Orange faced almost insurmountable obstacles in trying to obtain compensation. The families of the victims got nothing at all. The Vet Centers, he scoffed, were probably going to "wimp out and become another little piece of the VA." Agent Orange was an especially sore topic with him, not only because of his own apparently related ailments, but because his second daughter, Susan, had been born with a defect in her hip—which kept him from trying again for the son he wanted. He absolutely refused to abide by Blank's new regulation that Agent Orange could not be discussed in the Vet Centers. In fact, he thought it an essential subject. "One of the hardest persons to counsel," he said, "is that Vietnam vet that's dealt with his delayed stress, that's finally got his life back together, he has a job, feels good about himself, wants to get married and have kids, and is afraid to [because of Agent Orange]. What do you say to him?"

McCloskey's politics did not stop at the VA, however. He would sometimes throw a bunch of people in the Vet Center car and head for a demonstration against American military aid to the dictatorship in El Salvador, or one in support of the Communist Sandinista government in Nicaragua, which the Reagan administration was desperately trying to overthrow. Even Jack's friends warned him that he faced instant dismissal if caught using government resources to promote a left-wing political agenda. But McCloskey backed down not a whit. To friends and critics alike he had the same response, which sounded stock, but which could not have been more deeply felt: "I made promises to dead men that I'll never let this happen again."

McCloskey's antimilitarist politics extended even to the parties. Christmas at Waller Street was perhaps the most sacred time there, with a tree donated every year by the prisoner-support group Delancey Street, and McCloskey never failing to appear in his Santa suit with a big bag of toys for the veterans' children. But even Christmas parties were, as Melendez described them, "learning experiences for the not-timid." Doctors and lawyers would mingle with rabid revolutionaries, many of whom arrived "armed to the teeth." As in the old-time Western saloon, McCloskey politely asked them to leave their weapons at the door. There was also the annual Christmas play, usually a political satire, like "Santa Wants a Jump Jet," which they put on the year (1982) Britain unleashed its military might against the Falkland Islands—with elves carrying guns and Santa fighting the unionizing of his workers. The VA did not consider the play "appropriate," but vets who heard about it came in to the center because they appreciated the black humor. According to Planck, most vets liked it that the folks at Waller Street were "cool and funny"; it made them feel they could sit down there and talk frankly about anything that might be bothering them.

The VA groused about all of this, including the technically illegal solicitation of free donuts and Christmas trees, but the really heavy artillery Blank brought against them had to do with their lack of "body count." Waller Street would sometimes deal with a vet for two or three months before even asking for his DD-214. If a vet said he'd lost it, Planck would then spend several weeks going through the military bureaucracy trying to get him a new one. And sometimes, of course, it turned out their client had never been in the military at all. Again and again, the VA thundered in outrage that McCloskey's Vet Center had been caught helping civilians. But McCloskey felt it was better to occasionally help a few nonvets than to frighten one real vet away.

The VA was desperate to get something ironclad against him. Waller Street received a visit from the Inspector General's office, but McCloskey had advance warning. Planck was able to tidy up the mess in Jack's office, and they took down some of the Leftist posters and hung a cloth over the Ronald Reagan dartboard. Planck recalls that the IG team seemed to regard McCloskey as a dangerous terrorist, and almost seemed puzzled when they didn't find any bomb-making equipment, firearms, or illegal drugs. Furthermore, Planck had Waller Street's files in such perfect order that they were actually forced to praise the Vet Center's smooth operation.

McCloskey had developed enemies closer to home. During the Vet Center program's expansion under Nimmo, two more Vet Centers were added to San Francisco—a fully staffed one on Mission and Army streets, and a two-person "satellite" nearby. The Mission Street center and its satellite were dominated by team leader Ray Madrid, an overweight and noncharismatic Vietnam-era vet, whose super-straight ethics were in sharp contrast to McCloskey's. Madrid's chief goal seemed to be to please Central Office, though some people also suspected him of feeling jealous toward McCloskey, who was always treated as a star at any veterans' gathering in the Bay Area. In any case, Madrid soon began feeding a steady stream of negative gossip about McCloskey to Meshad in L.A.

Locked in what seemed like a fight to the death with Art Blank, over control of the Vet Centers' destiny, Meshad was already on the verge of a nervous breakdown. The last thing he needed to hear was that the leader of perhaps the most prominent Vet Center on the West Coast had a "severe drinking problem." Madrid reported that McCloskey was consistently coming to work drunk, and drinking all day with his alcoholic clients, who were going down fast with him. Waller Street was no longer a Vet Center, said Madrid; it had become a "clubhouse." Meshad was hearing other tales as well: of pot smoking and drug dealing on the Vet Center premises, of people finding Jack passed out, completely "wasted," on the floor of his office when the center opened in the morning. For Meshad, Waller Street was a "horrendous" nightmare come true. He expected at any moment to hear of a major bust there that would make Birmingham and Mobile look like schoolboy infractions. McCloskey, he figured, was a ticking mega-bomb, one that could take out not only himself but much of the program he'd worked years to build.

McCloskey, meanwhile, was feeling his own outrage against the VA. When the Wadsworth protest erupted in 1981, he wanted to go down and help mediate between the vets and the VA, which he felt especially qualified to do, since Agent Orange treatment was one of the issues in dispute. But the VA ordered him to keep away from the strike; and in the end, he went down on his own, using his vacation time. The following year, when McCloskey was invited to speak on Agent Orange at an international conference called "Vietnam Reconsidered" at the University of Southern California, the VA again refused to consider such time away from the Vet Center as legitimate work—i.e., they refused to pay for his hours there—and once again he did it on his "vacation."

It seemed to McCloskey that the more success he had in helping vets, the more the VA hated him, because he was "showing up their other programs." He had no intention of letting Art Blank turn him into a professional paper-pusher. But every time he thought about quitting, he would get pulled back into his work by his sense of obligation to the thousands of Vietnam vets even more troubled than he.

Thanksgiving of 1983, McCloskey planned to host his biggest dinner yet. With a total of fifty people to feed, they ordered six large turkeys, a couple of sacks of potatoes, many pounds of frozen vegetables, and twelve pumpkin pies. At the last minute, McCloskey showed up with a few bottles of wine, enough for all the adults to have a small glass each. Planck tried to get rid of it, especially since she knew that Ray Madrid and the crews from the other Vet Centers were invited, but McCloskey insisted that it was better for a lot of these guys to have one drink with a good dinner and friends around them, than to end up drinking a whole bottle on a street corner by themselves.

That Thanksgiving dinner turned out to be McCloskey's "Last Supper." The Mission Street people immediately reported to Meshad that they had witnessed McCloskey distributing "controlled substances" at the Vet Center. They also told him that they had seen McCloskey get "ripped" there; that he "was over the line—bad!"; and that a number of the dinner guests had not even been veterans. Meshad felt he finally had the goods on McCloskey, the means to dump his worst liability, a person who until now had been too "sacred" to the veterans' community to touch. Meshad tried to get Jack to admit that he was "crumbling," and that he had a responsibility to his clients to step down before he damaged their lives, as well as the credibility of the whole program. Feeling betrayed, McCloskey responded with furious accusations against Meshad and Blank together: that they were "out for themselves," that they had "built nice careers as veterans' representatives" while they had "sold out" the people they were supposed to be helping, that they were afraid of his shoot-from-the-hip politics, that they had used him to develop their program and now viewed him as "expendable." Increasingly anxious, Meshad charged Jack with paranoia and warned that he wasn't going to wait till Waller Street "blew up," taking Shad's "ass" along with it.

Meshad felt betrayed too. He had trusted McCloskey to preserve the integrity of the Vet Center program, to serve as a kind of "Ron Kovic inside the system," a compelling voice of experience and understanding that even heartless bureaucrats would have to acknowledge. But such a voice had to be sober. McCloskey, instead, had allowed himself to get hooked like a junkie on crisis intervention, to forever chase the adrenaline high of a substitute war zone, to burn out completely in the torch of his own anger. He'd become a souse, a quarterback who couldn't throw the ball anymore, and yet he expected Coach Meshad to send him into the championship game as if he were still a hero.[213]

Meshad gave McCloskey two options: resign, or be fired. Meshad says it was the hardest thing he had to do in his seven years with the program, harder even than his own resignation two years later.

For McCloskey, the choice was really between resigning and contesting his dismissal in court. He knew that he could create a sensational trial, calling out the veteran troops in support of his cause, and making a national media event of it that could well become bigger than the Wadsworth strike. But such a fight might also deal a critical blow to the Vet Center program, bury it for good. The alternative was to walk away from those thousands of vets who needed his help—to fail to be there for the next guy holed up with a gun in a cheap hotel room, for whom Jack alone might have the right words (not to mention the guts) to keep him from becoming yet another postwar casualty. For McCloskey, too, this was the hardest decision of his life.

McCloskey resigned, but he threatened to do everything in his power to keep his dream at Waller Street alive. The staff threw a huge farewell party for him in early March 1984. Then, ever loyal to Jack, they wrote letters to Meshad and other VA administrators demanding that a new team leader be promoted from within the center. They said that no one from outside could understand the special needs of their client population; and they suggested that a black veteran counselor named George Gibbs, who'd lost an arm in Vietnam, be appointed to replace McCloskey. Rejecting Gibbs, Meshad appointed Ray Madrid as Waller Street's temporary team leader, until someone more suitable could be found.

Meshad suddenly found that he had a "revolution" on his hands. McCloskey "declared war" on him, and the staff and clients of Waller Street began picketing their own Vet Center every day—even shutting it down for a few hours, forcing the police to come out to reopen it and making a big splash in the papers. One after the other, McCloskey's hand-picked employees resigned. Meshad came up to San Francisco to talk some sense into the people there. Instead, he met with complete hostility, was treated as an enemy, and made no headway at all. He concluded that the Waller Street Vet Center was "infected with Jack" and would have to be closed.

It was a "horrible time" in Meshad's life. He was trying to "be a good guy" and instead felt as if he had been "turned into a bastard." He was now battling on both coasts at once to save his life's work. On March 16, 1984, while addressing a joint meeting of all three San Francisco Vet Centers, he was struck completely blind. Rushed to the hospital, he underwent three surgeries in three days, which returned a bit of vision to one eye. Three weeks later, he began to see in both eyes again. The doctors had no explanation for his blindness, other than to observe that his optic nerves had appeared swollen. Looking back on it years later, he was certain that the cause had been the enormous weight that had fallen on him as he stood alone, like Atlas, trying to shore up the collapsing Outreach program.

McCloskey fared even worse. The first six months after his resignation, he went through a period of terrible guilt. He had let down the dead, he felt, because he had let down the survivors and the children of his generation—the only people he could really make amends to for the tragedy of Vietnam. He drank all day and night, wept frequently, and fought to survive the heaviest depression of his life. His wife filed for divorce, and he returned to Philadelphia, where he suffered his first heart attack. He was brought into the hospital "clinically dead"—just as he had been after taking the mystery assassin's .44 slug in his back. Revived with defibrillation, he lived to cheat death another nine years, until a second heart attack cut short his life at age fifty-three in February 1996. He had just started treatment in a combined detox and PTSD program at the Fort Miley VA, similar to the one he had pioneered at Waller Street fifteen years earlier.

More and more, the continuing casualties of the Vietnam War were not just those with unhealed wounds from combat or from a thinly veiled chemical warfare. They were also the veterans whom their government had turned one against the other. Blank against Meshad, Meshad against McCloskey, on and on and on. But while the hurt proliferated, a healing proceeded too—a tribute to the perseverance of many of those who had suffered most.

Four hundred people crowded into the largest room at Reilly Funeral Home in San Francisco's Mission District for the memorial to Jack McCloskey. It was held, at his widow Lydia's request, as a "Quaker style meeting," in which people came up by turns to tell a story or give their thoughts about McCloskey's passing. Veteran after veteran came forward to speak of how Jack had helped them through a tough period; many spoke of the Waller Street Vet Center, how the counseling there had saved their life.

One of the most moving speakers stood in a black suit and tie, looking a lot more formal than the others. He talked of an angry McCloskey once whacking him with his cane, and of their not speaking for years. But the speaker had known that "his energy and power and spirit were always there," and he knew for a fact that "Jack McCloskey played as big a part as anyone in making it possible for Vietnam veterans to heal from the war." They had talked again as friends shortly before McCloskey's fatal heart attack.

The speaker was Shad Meshad.[214]

11

The Price of War: Settlement of the Class Action Lawsuit and "One Small Step Toward Resolution"

1. Relentless Persuasion and the Biggest Fizzle-Out in the History of Tort Law

The reality of dioxin poisoning, like the reality of post-traumatic stress disorder, came to be understood much better as the 1980s passed into the 1990s, research techniques were refined, and a body of reliable literature began to accumulate on both. The problem for veterans in the matter of Agent Orange was that both the VA and the federal justice system pushed for a too hasty resolution of the crisis, perhaps because it loomed so terrifyingly large. Certainly many people inside and outside of government had a stake in slaying the Agent Orange dragon as quickly as possible—though, to be fair, some doubtless saw it not as a dragon, but as a foolish bugbear that needed to be laid to rest. The great tragedy of the Agent Orange lawsuit, and in some respects the great mystery, was that the person who seemingly should have fought hardest for justice, Judge Jack Weinstein, was the one most responsible for handing Vietnam veterans an empty bag of answers, and a mostly empty bag of compensation.

From the day Weinstein met the opposing attorneys to the day jury selection was to begin, May 7, 1984, the judge did everything in his power to encourage—and some would say coerce—an out-of-court settlement. His feelings, which he later made public, were that the veterans' claims were "without merit." The deliberately distorted conclusions of the Ranch Hand study, released in February 1984, may well have influenced his judgment on that point. According to Tod Ensign, Weinstein also felt that the veterans could never have overcome the government contract defense, and he thus sought to rescue them from an embarrassing defeat. Yannacone believed that the problem went much deeper, that it had to do with both Weinstein's legal philosophy and his personal temperament.

"Weinstein felt that once the court granted class-action status, the people became superfluous and only the lawyers counted," Yannacone explains. "This way you have management—nice, tidy group of people, all went to the same schools, all spoke the same language, and you didn't have any of these undue influences, like individual veterans who were concerned about being sick." Yannacone felt that Weinstein had a difficult time dealing with the emotional outbursts and the heart-wrenching appeals of deformed children and dying veterans; that he wanted, as much as possible, to keep them out of his courtroom and to deal instead with "sterile legal briefs."

Whatever was going on inside Weinstein, he acted, says Ensign, like a "maniac" by refusing to grant any postponements or to acknowledge that there might be any just cause for delay in getting to the May 7 trial date. One federal magistrate opined privately that Weinstein "would not have delayed that trial even if his mother died." Weinstein even put a huge calendar behind his desk with May 7 circled, and would point to it whenever the lawyers began to argue with him. Ensign says the judge "placed incredible pressure" on the attorneys from both sides. For the veterans' counsel, there was the fear of ultimate loss, of seeing their years of herculean effort "poured out totally." Ensign goes so far as to claim that the way Weinstein structured the case, "it was almost preordained that it would be settled out."

Weinstein had wanted the U.S. government brought back into the case, but the Plaintiffs Management Committee (PMC) could not begin to think of suing the government (a very difficult proposition) when it had to tie up all its resources trying to amass causation evidence for the lawsuit against the chemical companies. According to Peter Schuck, Weinstein fostered a sense of uncertainty and impending calamity in both sides as "a powerful inducement to settle." The irony was that, while Weinstein tried to make the veterans' counsel confess to a hopeless case, the evidence against Agent Orange and dioxin— in the form of scientific studies and court decisions—was growing stronger every day.

Early in 1984, it came out that the VA had not only failed to use the data from its Agent Orange registry, as it had promised, to detect unusual health trends in Vietnam veterans, but that the agency had even manipulated the statistics on soft-tissue sarcoma to make Vietnam veterans appear healthier than they actually were. In truth, the VA was reeling under a huge influx of veterans with Agent Orange–related complaints; by the end of 1983 its registry had swelled to over 130,000 names. Not unmindful of what was going on at the VA, the EPA buckled in October 1983 and agreed to ban almost all domestic sales of 2,4,5-T and Silvex (a related herbicide). Surprising everyone, Dow announced that it would not continue to fight the ban.

Not giving these developments a chance to unfold, Weinstein appointed a new special master, Shira Scheindlin, in January 1984, and instructed her to put the lawyers on "a forced march" to trial. The chemical companies rejoiced, knowing the PMC attorneys, hampered by their internal disunity, could not keep up the pace. Weinstein himself could hardly respond with sufficient care to all the issues demanding his attention. For example, he ruled that, besides sending letters to everyone on the VA's Agent Orange registry, sufficient notice to the entire class of Vietnam veterans could be achieved by national radio and TV announcements and an 800 telephone number. That unorthodox decision did not clear the appeals process until mid-March 1984, which is when notices finally went out. But the veterans had only till May 1 to decide whether or not to opt out of the class Weinstein had certified.

By the end of April, the PMC was nowhere near ready for trial. They still had no computerized index of discovery. In fact, much of the discovery was still incomplete; but Weinstein, in yet another unprecedented ruling, authorized them to continue discovery during the trial. He also ignored the many letters sent to him by veterans in a desperate campaign to persuade him to move up the trial date. As the PMC fumbled with various incomplete theories of causation, the chemical companies explored the medical histories of the representative plaintiffs, finding plausible evidence that many of the cited health problems could have been due to other causes besides Agent Orange exposure. In Weinstein's view, the veterans' case was growing weaker by the day, and might not even merit being heard before a jury.

In February, Weinstein had hired a special master for settlement, a post he more or less invented, since it had never existed before. To fill this unusual role he chose Kenneth Feinberg, formerly chief of staff for Senator Edward Kennedy. Proving as aggressive as Weinstein, Feinberg presented the attorneys with a settlement plan in mid-March. On April 20, Good Friday, Weinstein convened a meeting in his chambers, which included the PMC, the chemical companies' lawyers, Feinberg, and a second special master for settlement, a well-known antitrust lawyer named David Shapiro, whose job (in his own words) was to "get a deal done." Weinstein had wanted a third special master there, an attorney named Leonard Garment, who had worked for both Senator Daniel Patrick Moynihan and soon-to-be Attorney General Edwin Meese. Weinstein was counting on Garment to be able to bring the U.S. government into the settlement; but Garment could not make the meeting, and, besides, it would soon become clear that the government intended to avoid being party to any Agent Orange negotiations, no matter who asked.

At the April 20 meeting and at several more meetings over the next two weeks, Feinberg and Shapiro met separately with the attorneys from each side. Originally the two sides were impossibly far apart in their demands. The PMC had said it would not settle for less than $700 million, and the defendants insisted they would not pay more than $25 million. But Monsanto, which was one of the most vulnerable because of its exceedingly "dirty" product, broke the deadlock by raising their ceiling to $100 million, but only if the government kicked in an equal amount. With the holes in their case becoming more and more apparent, the PMC lowered their demand to $360 million. It began to look like both sides could be coaxed into the same ballpark, and Weinstein instructed his special masters to continue their relentless persuasion by whatever means necessary.[215]

Although Weinstein may have had the best of intentions, there were serious flaws in his method of proceeding. The worst flaw was that all the plaintiffs themselves—the veterans and their families, including the five representative plaintiffs—were completely ignorant of what was happening, and how close their case was verging toward the brink of total dissolution. The hundreds of local lawyers around the country handling Agent Orange claims were equally in the dark about the settlement negotiations. Most of these local lawyers had a far different agenda than the nine PMC lead attorneys.

As western regional coordinator for the class-action lawsuit, Dorothy Thompson represented over a hundred veterans in California and nearby states. Thompson assured her clients that a pretrial settlement did not have high priority. For one thing, Thompson and some other attorneys had filed their own class-action lawsuit against the VA and the Department of Defense, attempting to force the government to care for and compensate Vietnam veterans and their families for both physical and psychological ailments resulting from exposure to herbicides in Vietnam. That lawsuit had been conditionally dismissed by the court because there was still no judicial review of the VA. But the judge had indicated that if the veterans were unsuccessful in their class-action suit against the chemical companies, he would reconsider letting them proceed against the government for the same claims. A full-blown trial would at least have the virtue of letting the veterans assert the logic of their cause, which might benefit Thompson's suit against the government; while a settlement by the PMC, even if woefully inadequate, might let the government off the hook for good.

Furthermore, Thompson assured veterans that, whether by settlement or judicial verdict, she would only consider the PMC's lawsuit successful if it led to a complete ban on the manufacture of phenoxy herbicides in the United States. 2,4-D was still in wide use domestically; and even after the EPA extended its ban on 2,4,5-T in the fall of 1983, virtually removing it from the U.S. market, the chemical companies continued to produce large quantities of it for sale abroad, especially to Third World countries (whose food crops often were marketed in the United States). Thompson was especially concerned about the bootleg return of dioxin to America because it had already been shown that the toxin was bioaccumulative. Since many Vietnam veterans already had significant amounts of dioxin stored in their body fat, ingesting even infinitesimal amounts of it from foreign food sources could be enough to tip the balance toward cancer or birth defects in their children.

The second thing Thompson promised the veterans was a trust fund in perpetuity. The main issue, she told them, was that no one knew how long it might take for dioxin-related health problems to manifest. It was clear that some diseases, such as cancers, often remained latent for many years. Moreover, male veterans could continue to father children for several more decades; and there was still the question as to whether the children of exposed veterans could pass along the genetic damage from dioxin to their children and succeeding generations. The trust fund, as Thompson envisioned it, would not only compensate veterans for their medical bills and their time lost from work, but would also pay for the special costs of caring for children with birth defects, as well as paying the health care costs of their spouses who suffered miscarriages. There would need to be a fund available to all these people, and to children not yet born, far into the future.

Yannacone too had always said that the trust fund was an essential part of the solution; that he would never have settled for anything less. He had also promised the vets that he would never settle until after the trial had begun, so that they would have their "day in court" to address the larger court of world opinion. Only a trial, he felt, could force into the open the secret documents that would damn both the American chemical industry and "McNamara and his accountants," who had repeatedly ignored reports from the field that there was "something seriously wrong with this herbicide." Though money was never Yannacone's top priority, making sure the veterans and their families were all properly taken care of was part of his goal of restoring their dignity, as well as what he called "their vindication as soldiers." To achieve that vindication, he felt the veterans needed to participate in settlement negotiations, and that part of the settlement must also be the public distribution of all documents relating to the case.

Judge Weinstein clearly had something else in mind when he ordered attorneys from both sides locked up, along with the two special masters for settlement, on one whole floor of the federal courthouse on Saturday and Sunday, May 5 and 6. The judge required them to engage in round-the-clock negotiations, with the aim of arriving at a settlement before jury selection began at 9 A.M. on May 7. He apparently not only figured to weaken them with sleep deprivation, but both sides had a tremendous number of last-minute preparations for the trial which could not get done while they were tied up in Weinstein's horse-trading marathon. In effect, Weinstein was giving them the option of settling or else appearing unprepared in court on Monday morning—and by so doing, added anxiety to all the other forces pushing for an out-of-court resolution.

The veterans and their families had no notion of what was going on. Four of the five representative plaintiffs, and their wives and children, had all been moved to a cheap motel near La Guardia Airport earlier that week. Each day they were ferried in chauffeur-driven limousines, with bodyguards, to a newly rented Brooklyn Heights townhouse, where the lawyers themselves were staying. (Danny Lee Ford, the fifth representative plaintiff, was already too sick from soft-tissue sarcoma to leave his home in Michigan; he would die the following year.) Their attorneys told them that they wanted to keep them all near the courthouse, so that they could be shielded from the press and coached about their potential testimony. A working-class Irish cop, Michael Ryan was suspicious of this show of luxury (especially since it seemed more for the enjoyment of the lawyers than for the families); and he wondered who was paying for the lavish brownstone with a view of the harbor and Manhattan skyline. He later came to believe they were deliberately isolated to keep them from being privy to the settlement negotiations. Both Michael and his wife, Maureen, had been promised that (as she recalls) "no settlement is going to happen without the authorization of the veterans." Maureen also remembers the lawyers assuring them that they would be informed as soon as settlement meetings were scheduled, and that the lawyers would actively seek their "input."

While the veterans and their families ate catered food and looked out their million-dollar prison windows by day, and slept in strange, sleazy beds by night, Weinstein's two special masters were browbeating and cajoling the attorneys into submission. Weinstein himself met with both sides together and then each side separately Saturday morning, May 5. The plaintiffs' attorneys had come down to $250 million, and Weinstein and his special masters were trying to edge them toward $200 million. The defendants were putting up a stiffer resistance. Dow's Leonard Rivkin presented Weinstein with a list of ten demands that would have to be met before the chemical companies would settle. Because Weinstein had certified the plaintiffs as a (b)(3) class, any number of veterans could opt out of the settlement and bring their own separate suits against the defendants. The chemical companies wanted to make sure they could "walk away" from the settlement if too many vets opted out. Weinstein agreed to leave the exit open for them.

The chemical companies also worried about making themselves vulnerable to the claims of civilians (including Vietnamese) and an infinity of unborn children; Weinstein again promised them whatever protection he could give. They wanted a low fee award to the PMC, to discourage other attorneys from filing such suits in the future; Weinstein said it would be "reasonable." Perhaps most insulting to the veterans, the companies insisted on their right to claim that Agent Orange had harmed no one; and they also demanded that the plaintiffs return all discovery documents and never reveal their contents. Weinstein, sensing that a deal was in sight, agreed to the "no blame" clause; but he said both parties would have to negotiate a separate solution to the problem of how much information the public had a right to know.

Weinstein also assured the defendants that he would not award punitive damages, and that he would allow a certain amount of the settlement fund to be held back, to indemnify the companies for judgments that might later be brought against them in state courts. In essence, the companies wanted to be able to cut their losses and walk away clean and safe from future damage claims. Weinstein indicated that he would do everything possible to help them attain that kind of closure to this distressing episode. But in case they might still balk at a settlement, he reminded them of how difficult he could make their situation. He warned that he was considering ruling in the plaintiffs' favor on a motion to have all the defendants considered equally liable for dioxin-caused health injuries, no matter how great or small the actual contamination of their product.

Weinstein told the PMC that even if he ruled in their favor, he did not think their case would hold up on appeal, since they still had no hard evidence of causation. His biggest bombshell, however, was to warn the plaintiffs' attorneys that, should they turn down a reasonable settlement offer, and should the case go to trial and the veterans lose, he would hold them personally responsible for the money the veterans had been deprived of. By 4 P.M. on Sunday afternoon, the defendants had raised their offer to $180 million plus interest beginning that day, but said they would not budge a dollar further since they might still be exposed to claims from civilians, Vietnamese, and after-born children. The PMC were inclined to hold out for at least $200 million, but Weinstein's warning about malpractice chilled them considerably. The veterans' lawyers knew that even if they won in court, Weinstein could devastate them with a miniscule fee award. They also knew that if they lost, he could compel them to continue litigating appeals for years under pain of his approving a huge malpractice judgment against them. And even if they litigated the case all the way to the Supreme Court, and lost a final time, he might still find them guilty of malpractice for having let that $180 million slip through their clients' hands.

Shortly after midnight on May 7, 1984, only a few hours before commencement of the trial, the plaintiff's lawyers caved in—all except Yannacone's former sidekick, David Dean, who registered his opposition and then left in tears (though he would later give his grudging assent). The others agreed to $180 million plus most of the defendants' now 14 demands. Weinstein then went to sell the deal to the defendants' attorneys. They sought to drop the provision of "interest beginning this morning," but Weinstein warned them that a long trial, the likely judgment against them by a Brooklyn jury, and the damage to their reputations would cost them a lot more.

The companies feared that the settlement would encourage future mass tort claims against them. Weinstein supposedly allayed this fear by hinting that he would award only modest fees to the veterans' lawyers. The chemical companies finally agreed, and Weinstein hastened back to his office to draft the preliminary settlement document. Many of its 14 points clearly favored the veterans. The class would include those who had not yet manifested injury. The veterans (along with the chemical companies) retained the right to sue the government. Any class member who had opted out would have the opportunity to opt back in. But there were also a few points that would come to stick in the veterans' throats like poisoned hooks. The worst was Point 8, consisting of four words that virtually cancelled out the 50,000 words of Yannacone's original complaint: "Defendants deny any liability." Point 6 said that all of the defendants' documents had to be returned within one year, insuring that their contents would remain private. And point 13 excluded after-born claimants from the class, though Weinstein pledged that "arrangements will be made from the fund to assist afterborns."

At three in the morning, Weinstein and a bunch of slap-happy lawyers broke open several bottles of champagne to celebrate the biggest fizzle-out in the history of personal injury tort law. Nevertheless, the defendants' lawyers had good cause to celebrate. According to *Newsweek*'s report of the settlement, the chemical companies felt they had gotten off by paying "only ten cents on the dollar," since they had privately estimated their liability in a series of jury trials to be at least $400 million, and possibly several times that much. Of course, none of the companies actually paid even that hypothetical dime, since all of them were fully covered by their insurance.[216]

2. Weinstein's Fairness Hearings:
"I Believe You're Naive, Your Honor"

Early May was not an auspicious time for most American Vietnam veterans. Nine years earlier, they had just finished watching Cambodia, Vietnam, and Laos fall like three sequential dominoes to Communist forces, consigning the sweat and blood and truncated lives of so many to an "expense of spirit in a waste of shame" (to borrow from Shakespeare). Many who had labored to bring the Agent Orange case to trial would feel much the same about their exhausting, tension-filled years on the legal and political front lines in what Maureen Ryan called "a David-and-Goliath type of fight for morality and justice."

The Ryans, along with the three other representative plaintiffs and their families, were kept incommunicado in the Brooklyn townhouse for a couple of hours the morning of May 7. While they were thus sequestered, dressed in their best clothes and waiting patiently to be taken to the courthouse, the PMC attorneys were announcing the settlement to the press. Maureen Ryan recalls their lawyers suddenly bursting in, at midmorning, dancing about "like Hare Krishnas" and shouting their joyful news: "My God, it's over! We won! You don't even have to go to court! You're getting the money and you're getting the settlement!" At first, she remembers, there was a feeling of great relief, that their ordeal was finally over; but it was quickly followed by a feeling of disquiet. It was as if they had come to assist at the birth of a baby, she says, but before they ever got to the delivery room they were told "it's a boy," congratulated, and given their tickets home.

Actually the attorneys still had one prime use for them. According to Maureen Ryan, the representative plaintiffs were told that each of them would get at least $100,000 from the settlement, and that they and other "core people" would get an additional $20,000 each to reimburse them for the thousands of hours they had already put into the case, as well as their many incidental expenses. For years, Maureen and Mike had been flying around the country at a moment's notice, every time the lawyers requested they speak at a hearing or to a veterans' group. Often Mike had to take time off from work without pay to keep up his heavy activist schedule, and there was the additional cost of a caretaker for Kerry. Moreover, one or the other was always available to answer calls that the lawyers directed their way. Most of the callers were vets with painful stories of illness and/or crippled children, and to listen and commiserate required not only a sacrifice of time but also to give deeply of themselves. Eventually that emotional drain became well-nigh intolerable, but they never turned away from it—bound by a sense of duty to others who had suffered like themselves. Now they were told they would be paid back handsomely for their "investment" in the case; that the first big chunk of money would be coming to them within a month. They were also assured that all the disabled children would be cared for out of the settlement. When they seemed sufficiently happy, Maureen says, they were told to come outside, where the reporters and photographers were waiting for them.

She recalls she, Michael, and Kerry standing on the front steps of the townhouse and staring skeptically into the cameras. "Your gut level, you didn't trust it," she explains. "A patrolman and his wife get a different kind of an instinct." For Michael, it was more than intuition. "I did the math in my head," he says, "and it didn't take a genius to figure out the numbers were off. They told us, 'Oh, no-no-no. Don't go by the math. That's just the amount for each of the *lead cases*, and the interest will grow. Besides, it's really not as many veterans out there as we originally thought.'" The Ryans' sense of being manipulated grew even stronger when the lawyers spirited them off to Manhattan and ensconced them in the Helmsley Tower, so that they could continue to give interviews for the next couple of days.

According to Michael Ryan, the plaintiffs were "closely watched and supervised" and not permitted to speak to the press unless accompanied by one or more attorneys. At some point, Michael told his wife in disgust: "Let's get out

VVAW marches on the Capitol in the climax of Dewey Canyon IV, July 3, 1974. The march soon erupted in violence as the Washington, D.C., Park Police began driving their scooters into the column of marchers. *Photo courtesy of the VVAW Archive.*

Paul Reutershan in Norwalk Hospital, Norwalk, Connecticut, December 1978, shortly before his death from abdominal cancer, which he believed was due to his exposure to Agent Orange in Vietnam. *Photo courtesy of Jimmy Sparrow.*

Danny Friedman after being beaten up by police at Dewey Canyon IV in Washington, D.C., July 3, 1974. *Photo courtesy of the VVAW Archive.*

Marine veteran James Roger Hopkins, who drove his red Willys jeep through the glass doors of the Wadsworth VA Hospital in Westwood, California, on March 14, 1981, leading to the three-week-long takeover and hunger strike there. *Photo © 1981 Los Angeles Times (from the UCLA collection).*

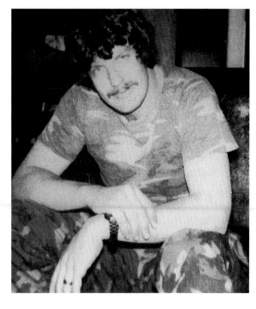

Australian-American cartoonist Pat Oliphant, along with his fellow political satirist Paul Conrad, provided a running commentary on the Vietnam veterans' war with their own government throughout the 1970s and 1980s. *Top: OLIPHANT © 1974 PAT OLIPHANT. Reprinted with permission of the creator. All rights reserved. Bottom: OLIPHANT © 1982 UNIVERSAL PRESS SYNDICATE. Reprinted with permission. All rights reserved.*

Bobby Waddell pushes Ron Kovic out of the Westwood Federal Building in Los Angeles, California, March 2, 1974, after AVM's seventeen-day hunger strike in Senator Alan Cranston's office won significant concessions from the VA concerning health care for Vietnam veterans. Directly behind Waddell is paraplegic veteran Max Inglett. *Photo by Cal Montney © 1974 Los Angeles Times (from the UCLA Collection).*

Senator Alan Cranston (*top of the file cabinet*) and the VA's Chief Medical Director Marc J. Musser (*standing below him*) meet with members of the American Veterans Movement during their seventeen-day hunger strike in Cranston's office in February 1974. Max Inglett is in wheelchair at left; Bob Waddell stands at the window with arm around his wife, Shannon; and Bill Unger sits below Shannon. *Photo by John Malmin © 1974 Los Angeles Times (from the UCLA Collection)*

A Vietnam veteran camps on the lawn of the Wadsworth VA Hospital in Los Angeles during the "inside/outside" strike. *Photo by Ron Bitzer.*

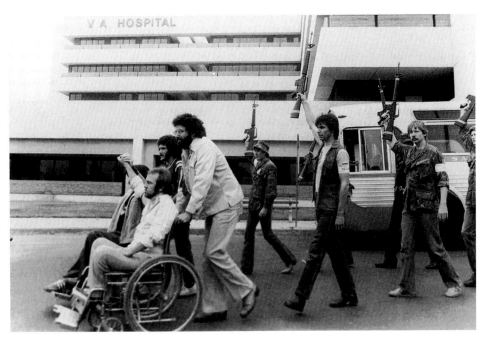

Ron Kovic (*face obscured*) holds up the arm of his fellow wheelchair vet Max Inglett as they lead the funeral march past the Wadsworth VA Hospital for their fallen comrade, James Roger Hopkins, on Memorial Day, May 25, 1981. They are followed by an honor guard of Vietnam veteran actors from the play *Tracers*, directed by John DiFusco (*wearing vest over T-shirt*). *Photo © 1981 Los Angeles Times (from the UCLA Collection).*

Vietnam War hero David Christian upstages President Jimmy Carter on the steps of the amphitheater at Arlington National Cemetery on Veterans Day, 1978. Instead of leading the Pledge of Allegiance as he had been asked, he delivered a speech on the needs of Vietnam veterans. *Photo courtesy of David Christian.*

Maude DeVictor, who "blew the whistle" on Agent Orange–related health problems in Vietnam veterans while working for the VA's regional office in Chicago in 1979. She's seen here at the dedication of the Paul Reutershan Health Care Center for Agent Orange victims on Long Island, New York, 1981. *Photo © Jeff Blechman.*

Frank McCarthy in his office at Agent Orange Victims International in Stamford, Connecticut, circa 1980. *Photo © Jeff Blechman.*

Victor Yannacone Jr., the original lead attorney in the Agent Orange class-action lawsuit, seen here in the Federal courthouse in Uniondale, New York, 1979. *Photo © Jeff Blechman.*

Rear Admiral Elmo R. Zumwalt, Jr., and his son Ensign Elmo R. Zumwalt III, on the day of Elmo III's college graduation and NROTC commission at the University of North Carolina, June 1964. The younger Zumwalt would later attribute his fatal combination of non-Hodgkin's lymphoma and Hodgkin's disease to his exposure to Agent Orange as a swift-boat commander in Vietnam. *Photo courtesy of James Zumwalt.*

Vietnam veteran Jan Scruggs lectures to a group of visitors at the Vietnam Veterans Memorial Wall, Washington, D.C., mid-1980s. More than any other person, it was Scruggs' vision and relentless effort that made the Wall a reality. *Photo © Ankers Imaging, Washington, D.C.*

Agent Orange victim Kerry Ryan asks paraplegic Vietnam veteran Bobby Muller to teach her to "pop a wheelie" in the U.S. House of Representatives, June 21, 1979. *Photo © Jeff Blechman.*

of here!" They went home, he says, "washed their hands of the whole process," and never heard from the PMC attorneys again. For a brief time, however, they remained Yannacone's clients and sought to help him recover his years of lost wages. Yannacone and his wife would eventually get paid at an hourly rate for their work on the case. But both Michael Ryan, whose peripheral neuropathy and skin infections grew progressively worse, and Kerry, in whom the doctors would continue to discover "new" birth defects for years to come, "got zero," he says, from the Agent Orange settlement and the promised (nonexistent) retroactive expense account. "One day you're Miss America," Michael summed it up years later, "and the next day you're the troll under the bridge. It doesn't take a genius to figure out that you've been used and discarded."

Opposition to the settlement sprang up almost immediately. While the chemical companies basked in the glow of their rising stock, veterans across the country denounced it as a "sellout." Even Yannacone, who risked angering the court and possibly forfeiting his own compensation, told the press that it provided "nowhere near enough money to take care of the veterans who are now sick" and especially their "catastrophically damaged" children. Yannacone even pleaded before Weinstein in court to find a way to broaden the settlement, so that the federal government would have to provide "a uniform system of complete medical care for the Agent Orange–injured veterans and their children."

When Yannacone introduced a new suit against the government by the veterans, Weinstein immediately granted the government's motion to dismiss it—though he had promised to preserve their right of action against the government as part of the settlement. What upset Yannacone most, though, was the fact that the defendants "disclaimed any wrongdoing whatsoever." That was tantamount to saying that dioxin was harmless. Yannacone accused several government agencies, including the EPA and the Public Health Service, of having made a "devil's bargain" with the chemical companies to engage in a "systematic cover-up." What was at stake was the profitable manufacture of a whole array of toxic products by American industry, Yannacone asserted. As he saw it, both the PMC and Weinstein's court had shown their loyalty to the system—to the "irresponsible and immoral promotion and sale" of dangerous merchandise—rather than to "the conscience of America." For the next few years, Yannacone would fight in vain to have all documents and testimony in the Agent Orange case become public record.

The "take-the-money-and-run" implications of the settlement frightened many of those whose lives were dedicated to halting or, at the very least, tightly controlling the manufacture of toxic chemicals. Dr. Samuel Epstein of the University of Illinois Medical Center, author of the landmark book *The Politics of Cancer,* called the Agent Orange settlement "disastrous." He saw it as vindicating a morality based on "vast personal fortunes" rather than the necessary "commitments" of a civilized society. James Sparrow, the new executive director of Agent Orange Victims International (AOVI), said the main value of the case had been "to put the chemical companies on the hot seat," so that "the people [would] know what they've been doing"—and without a trial, he felt, that truth would never come out. Other Vietnam veteran organizations, including VVAW, Citizen Soldier, and the New Jersey Agent Orange Commission, lobbied Judge Weinstein to undo the settlement before it became law.

The New Jersey AOC, the best-funded and most active such organization in the nation, was headed by a gutsy and abrasive former noncom named Wayne Wilson. A high school dropout from Camden, Wilson had joined the Army in 1960, intending to make it his career. He rose quickly to platoon sergeant, and served two tours in Vietnam, the first with an assault helicopter company, the second in an infantry unit of the Americal Division, and both times in areas of I Corps that saw sustained heavy fighting. On his first tour, his helicopter was shot down doing a resupply run to a surrounded unit. On his second tour in 1971, he became "disheartened" to see American soldiers dying to recapture the same ground they had fought over when he had been in-country in 1968–1969; and in protest he went AWOL big-time, like Tim O'Brien's Cacciato, all the way back to San Francisco. When the Army caught up with him, he was threatened with court-martial, but he returned voluntarily to Vietnam "to ensure the survival of my people." Ironically, he was almost killed himself a second time when the M-48 tank he was riding on struck a booby-trapped artillery shell. A year later, in 1973, he was medically retired.

It was then, as an older, angry, alienated Vietnam vet student at Rutgers, that Wilson's real ordeal began. The VA lost and otherwise delayed his paperwork; his checks never came on time. After receiving the cold shoulder at the VFW and the American Legion, he began organizing the Vietnam vets on campus himself; and thus began his lifelong career in veterans' activism. In 1977, his own PTSD kicked in heavily; and, fresh out of college, he quit his job as a college veterans' counselor to vagabond around the country. But no matter where he went, he could not keep clear of veterans' issues. He hung out with Bobby Muller when Muller was just starting to organize the Council of Vietnam Veterans—when they were both "naive" enough, he says, to "trust that the system would respond to the suffering and hardship of Vietnam veterans" as soon as the wrongs were pointed out. He took part in veterans' counseling groups in Portland, Maine, and Portland, Oregon, and was banished from the one in Oregon in 1980 for fomenting "political activities."

Eventually Wilson moved on to California and Hawaii, where he organized veterans and campaigned to revitalize Vietnam veteran civic councils. Originally such civic councils had been established around the country by federal law, to critique the effectiveness of regional VA facilities in terms of their service to Vietnam veterans, and to send reports and recommendations directly to the administrator in Central Office. Most of the councils, however, had been subverted by the VA to various nonthreatening social and public relations functions, like the one in Honolulu whose efforts were directed toward selecting "NCO of the Year" at Hickam Air Force Base. Wherever he went, Wilson complained loudly about the status quo. He got the reputation of a "troublemaker" and "hell-raiser," but he also brought about a great deal of change in the way government dealt with Vietnam veterans, including the rehabilitation of numerous civic councils from Hawaii to New Jersey.

If there was anyone both fearless and credible enough to go up against Judge Weinstein, it was Wayne Wilson. Under the Federal Rules of Civil Procedure, Weinstein was obligated to let members of the class give their views about the settlement before he approved it; and in light of their testimony, he was charged to approve the settlement only if it still seemed "fair, reasonable and adequate." The Second Circuit Court had already given trial judges a great deal of latitude in making such decisions, however. Going out of his way to prove his impartiality, Weinstein authorized a series of "fairness hearings" on the settlement, to take place in Brooklyn, Chicago, Houston, Atlanta, and San Francisco. Wayne Wilson went before Weinstein at one of the very first hearings in Brooklyn, in August 1984.

Wilson stated that the New Jersey Agent Orange Commission not only opposed the settlement, but that it would take no money from the settlement even if approved. The settlement would, he said, "provide little or no remedy to Vietnam veterans," and he claimed that those who were promoting it had "sold Vietnam veterans down the river." In his view, the terms of the settlement were "a disgrace," and he even suggested that those who had framed it had cause to "be ashamed of themselves."

Wilson said the main flaw in the settlement was that the Agent Orange problem was of a far greater magnitude than the court or any of the lawyers, even Yannacone, had ever imagined. He estimated that before the claims period ended, at least 250,000 veterans would file, and that another quarter-million potential claims would never find their way to the court. Weinstein, says Wilson, looked at him in utter disbelief, and indicated that he had been assured the total number of claims would fall between 20,000 and 30,000. Wilson countered that even if the numbers did not reach 250,000, they would surely exceed 30,000; and that as time passed, veterans who were now only mildly ill would likely grow sicker and need more help from the fund. Weinstein said he had been taken aback by some of the horror stories about the VA, but he was still convinced that the agency would come through and do its part in treating and compensating sick veterans. He suggested Wilson should regard the settlement as "only part of the pie." The settlement, Weinstein felt, would stimulate Congress to respond legislatively, and provoke other political responses to assist Vietnam veterans.

"I believe you're naive, Your Honor," replied Wilson, who left the courtroom with a sinking heart, certain that Weinstein was charting the same tragic course already taken by many other well-meaning government officials. It was Representative Thomas Daschle (D-S.Dak.), leader of the VVIC, who had come up with the idea that once Congress passed the first piece of legislation recognizing Agent Orange–related health problems, Vietnam veterans would have "one foot in the door," and it would become progressively easier for a succession of other, more all-embracing Agent Orange compensation bills to get passed. That logic had fallen flat on its face. The first Agent Orange bill had been passed in 1981, and in the next three years Congress had approved nothing more than compensation for chloracne. Granting limited compensation, Wilson explains, "works against us. People that don't know any better say, 'Well, they got what they need. Why are they still crying?' That's what congressmen hear in briefings by the Veterans Administration and by the traditional veterans' organizations. The congressman gets home and has a town meeting, and about three-quarters of the way through, some guy stands up and says, 'What about the Agent Orange issue?' The congressman says, 'I voted for compensation two years ago. . . . See my aide in the back when we're done.'"[217]

Weinstein never doubted the wisdom of his scheme. When the fairness hearings concluded in San Francisco, he went even further, assuring the veterans that the VA would eventually pay their "daily medical bills, which will run into the billions of dollars, while you use [the settlement fund] to give you leverage to make sure you get what you're entitled to."

Over 400 of the 480 people who testified at the fairness hearings opposed the settlement—despite the fact that the PMC had made every effort to stack the witness docket with vets and their families who approved the deal. There was also manipulation in the order of witnesses, with those who were pro-settlement always speaking first. The most virulent critics of the settlement were almost always held back for the second day, when media coverage had waned, and often were forced to speak "off the record." Despite these attempts at censorship, a consensus began to emerge. Veterans talked over and over about their right to know the truth of what had been done to them, and their right to put those who had hurt them—the chemical company fat cats, and, if applicable, those in their own government who had lied to and betrayed them—before a jury of common people. They also wanted the defendants' documents unsealed. Some talked about the impossibility of ever stanching the production of toxic chemicals unless the big companies were branded with a criminal verdict. (Weinstein, who sometimes ordered high-powered lawyers about like schoolchildren, objected that he had no injunctive power over the chemical industry.) Another universal complaint was that, though money was not the object, they still did not expect to be shortchanged; and almost all agreed that, judging by past performance, the VA would probably never provide adequate care for Agent Orange victims.

The most disturbing development for many veterans, though, was the more and more insistent rumor that the birth-defective children were going to be cut from the list of beneficiaries. From the moment that the settlement was announced, new claims began pouring in. It was becoming apparent to those who had fashioned the settlement that it would be hard enough to stretch the $180 million, plus interest but minus lawyers' fees, over just the increasing crowd of veterans demanding help. If the fund also had to be divided among the tens of thousands of disabled children who required extensive medical care and expensive corrective operations, it would be exhausted before the majority of claimants ever saw dollar one.

In every city, mothers with their crippled children came to testify before Weinstein, to plead with him that no settlement should be approved that did not adequately care for the needs of those innocent victims. For the mothers, the settlement was worthless if it could not buy back at least part of their children's futures. In Chicago, Suky Wachtendonk (wife of the Madison VVAW songwriter Jim) broke into tears as she spoke, and Weinstein sharply reprimanded her that such emotion was out of place in court. She pleaded in vain that she was not crying or making her voice shake "for effect," but because those feelings were real for her and inescapable. "I'm talking about *my babies, my babies*," she said. It was Maureen Ryan in San Francisco, however, who finally put Weinstein in his place.

Maureen stood at the microphone, with Kerry by her side, while a courtroom crowded with vets and media people hung on her every word. Speaking without notes, she said the veterans had been "financially raped" by the settlement. "After this circus finishes its tour," she went on, "the attorneys will collect their fees, capitalize on their brief moment of glory, and write their books, while we will continue to bury our dead." She then spoke eloquently about the need to use whatever money was available to help the injured children first. Weinstein tried to point out that he intended to set aside about $40 million for genetic research, to help veterans plan their future families, but this only made Maureen angrier. Her husband and most of the vets she knew were done having children, she said, and so that $40 million would be "a gift certificate to an empty store." She suggested that another black granite wall as long as the original could be erected in Washington, listing the names of the children already born with birth defects. As she talked, she recalls, Weinstein began to look uncomfortable, and soon grew very agitated. At one point he jumped up from his bench and started pacing back and forth, with his "black robes flapping." Finally, as she explained how the representative plaintiffs had been "duped," Weinstein angrily interrupted her. According to her, he "screamed" that she had no right to be making such accusations in his courtroom. He instructed her to leave the podium and sit down. Maureen Ryan, however, had never backed down from anyone, authority figure or no. "Your Honor," she replied calmly, "I guess that's where we differ, because as an American citizen I thought this was *my* courtroom."

Weinstein's face went beet red, and the courtroom exploded in applause. Even the reporters were yelling: "Right on!" Maureen then encouraged Kerry, who was thirteen years old, to tell her side of the story. This was more than Weinstein could stomach, and he tried to have them both removed. But Maureen shouted down the judge, insisting that Kerry had a right to speak, and Weinstein finally took his seat again and let them finish.

As they left the podium, there was another round of thunderous applause. One journalist remarked, loud enough for everyone to hear: "If Weinstein had the set of balls that woman has, the veterans would have gotten a fair shake."

Not long afterward, in Los Angeles, Senator Alan Cranston held his own hearings on the settlement. This time, Maureen Ryan prefaced her remarks with the story of how Michael's father had fought with MacArthur in the Philippines, and how her own father had fought in the invasion of Normandy and the Battle of the Bulge, winning a Bronze Star with two oak leaf clusters. Cranston, she recalls, paid no attention, and actually read some transcripts of previous testimony as she talked. He only looked up when the vets in the room began clapping and cheering at her condemnation of the settlement. Then, like Weinstein, he tried to shut them up; but, she says, his heart was not even in that. Later, when it became apparent that Cranston had no interest in affecting the course of the settlement, she wondered why he had even bothered with the hearings in Los Angeles, unless it was to get his picture in the paper again as "the veterans' friend."

A man she had a lot more respect for was Admiral Elmo Zumwalt Jr. In command of Vietnam's "brown-water navy," Zumwalt had ordered the spraying of Agent Orange to clear riverbanks and coastal regions of potential ambush sites. Zumwalt's son, Elmo III, who commanded a swift-boat in the Mekong Delta, in a heavily sprayed area, would father a son with a learning disability; and Elmo III would himself later die of cancer. Maureen met Zumwalt at a christening party for the first child of her brother Danny, who was with the CIA and had studied under the admiral. Having sought her out, Zumwalt took her hand and told her he was "so sorry" for what he had done. Hugging him, she forgave him. "You worked with the information that you had," she said. "By virtue of you asking to meet me, I can see the moral courage in you."

Had Weinstein had the same kind of moral courage, she felt, he would have admitted his miscalculations and nullified the settlement agreement. Instead, on September 25, 1984, Weinstein issued his "fairness opinion," approving the settlement he had essentially fashioned himself. Even Schuck, whose opinion of the judge at times borders on worshipful, admitted that Weinstein "should have left the evaluation of the settlement to another, more detached judge. His failure to do so was a serious error in judgment." By that time, well over 100,000 claims had come in, and the number of applicants was increasing daily. Faced with such a deluge, Weinstein was forced to extend the deadline for submission of claims from October 24, 1984, to January 2, 1985. (A little later, he would extend it a third time to January 15.) But he addressed neither the question of how so many additional applicants might lessen the value of the settlement, nor how a great many vets might have been cheated of the chance to apply because of lack of notice. Written notice had been sent out to less than 10 percent of Vietnam veterans, and a third of the letters had come back because of out-of-date addresses. Moreover, few radio and TV stations had actually broadcast the public service announcements they had been sent. Ironically, Weinstein tried to make capital off the fact that so few Vietnam veterans knew about the settlement by emphasizing what a small percentage of them had chosen to opt out.

Once again, in his fairness opinion, Weinstein stressed his belief that the veterans could never have proved either their own or their children's injuries attributable to Agent Orange exposure. He also declared that the plaintiffs had no cause for punitive damages, since (in his opinion) they could not show the "evil motive or reckless indifference" deemed necessary for such damages. He claimed that his judgment was based on the fact that the chemical companies had merely failed to "pass on to the government information they did have." Somehow he had managed to forget Dow's famous "smoking gun memorandum," which by his earlier admission showed "an understanding among the manufacturers to keep the government 'in the dark' about the dangers [of Agent Orange]." Such a "conspiracy of silence" would have qualified in most courts as sufficient grounds for punitive damages.

Weinstein indicated that his approval of the settlement hinged in part on his sense that the plaintiffs' attorneys would soon have to abandon the case for lack of financing. Most curiously, he claimed that he was sparing the veterans the negative impact of a legal defeat, which he felt would deter the president and Congress from ever offering them VA care and compensation. He somehow did not see that the converse of his argument could be used to oppose the settlement—the fact that, by his own logic, a victory in court would thus have influenced the president and Congress to honor Agent Orange claims. Of course an even more basic flaw in the judge's argument was his failure to address the question of why the government had consistently denied Agent Orange claims, and the Congress had voted down Agent Orange bills, during the five years that the Agent Orange case had gained steadily in credibility.

Even before the settlement was approved, Weinstein had set Special Master Feinberg the task of drafting a tentative distribution plan. By the time Weinstein issued his fairness opinion, the basic outline of the plan was known. It called for dropping at least three categories of victims from consideration: 1) children with birth defects; 2) civilians exposed in Vietnam; 3) military personnel sprayed anyplace other than Vietnam. Even with those exclusions, it soon became evident that the settlement fund was severely inadequate. By the time the third closing date had arrived, almost a quarter-million vets and family members had filed for compensation from the settlement fund—just as Wayne Wilson had predicted. Many thousands had rushed to submit their application during the first two weeks of 1985, when news stories about the end of the filing period had awakened them to their eligibility. Many more could not get through on jammed-up toll-free telephone lines. Clearly a much greater number would have applied had they too learned of the deadline in time. The reaction of many vets to this travesty was summed up by one New York veteran who told Judge Weinstein: "We were told when Saigon fell that the war was over; when the Vets Outreach Centers were started, we were told the war was over; when the vets were welcomed home and the Wall was built, the war was over. Now with this settlement we are once again told, 'The war is over.' Well, it is not over; this is not the end, but only one more chapter."

Although Weinstein never showed the slightest doubt about the wisdom of the settlement, and certainly never wavered in asserting its validity, one member of the PMC broke ranks to turn against it once the final tallies were in. On January 16, 1985, Benton Musslewhite filed a motion in federal court in Brooklyn on behalf of Citizen Soldier, asking that Weinstein rescind his final order of January 7 approving the settlement. "The outpouring of claims is so great," he explained, "that no claimant stands to receive more than a pittance from it." He also reasoned that for the court to approve a settlement before the distribution plan had been revealed gave veterans no chance to decide intelligently whether to opt out of the class. At the very least, fairness dictated that the judge grant potential claimants a second opt-out period after the compensation scheme was announced.

On February 27, 1985, Feinberg's suggested criteria for distribution were made public, and they were even more detrimental to the majority of claimants than Musslewhite and others had feared. To date, the claims of 67,000 disabled children had been submitted, none of whom would be eligible for compensation under Feinberg's plan. The claims of 40,000 veterans' wives who had suffered miscarriages or stillbirths would likewise be dismissed. Feinberg removed $60 million from the total fund, to be set aside for various endowments: $30 million to go to organizations helping children with birth defects and their families, and the other $30 million to be expended in grants to Vietnam veteran service organizations. The remainder of the money, which he estimated (after lawyers' fees) to be about $130 million, would provide cash payments directly to eligible veterans and their families. To maximize those payments, Feinberg came up with an ingenious, and stunningly unfair, method of screening out potential applicants. Recipients would have to be 100 percent disabled—as certified by the VA—as of December 31, 1984, or else the family of a veteran already dead.[218]

3. Everyone Gets Paid, Except for Most of the Veterans

Musslewhite argued his motion to nullify the settlement before Weinstein on March 18, 1985. "I'm willing to admit my mistake," he said. "I now urge the Court to likewise admit the error of its ways." Throughout his plea, Musslewhite sought to avoid impugning Weinstein, and instead to persuade the judge to join him in helping to "avert the greatest catastrophe in the history of our jurisprudence." He also appealed to Weinstein's patriotism, reminding the judge that the people he was about to deny both a trial by jury and, in most cases, any right to compensation for their injuries were those with the most "unshakable belief in our system of justice." These people whose fate Weinstein was about to decide, Musslewhite reminded him, had not only risked their lives for the government that employed him, but they had also remarkably retained "their unswerving love" for a country that had in numerous ways already "let them down."

Musslewhite's appeal was far from just emotional. He confronted Weinstein with a series of stark, jolting facts. With the parameters set by Feinberg, only 1 out of 21 claimants would receive any compensation—less than 5 percent of the total. Even that 5 percent would end up with only a few thousand dollars each. Of the 2,000 veterans he personally represented, an "overwhelming majority," he attested, "are opposed to this settlement and would prefer, win or lose, to have their day in court." Then he challenged Weinstein's assertion that the veterans would never have been able to go before a jury on the issues of causation and punitive damages. He pointed out that the defendants had not even attempted to make a motion for summary judgment on the causation issue. They had motioned for dismissal of punitive damages, but the judge had never ruled on that request. Meanwhile, the plaintiffs had submitted prima facie evidence concerning both issues. To have refused the veterans a jury trial under those circumstances, he asserted, would have been a denial of due process. Moreover, he pointed out that with 235,000 individual claimants, each with his or her own unique medical history, it would be impossible to declare in advance that *none* of them could prove causation. Finally, he attacked Weinstein's assertion that, in the absence of a definitive epidemiological or statistical study, the veterans would have no case to put before a jury. Musslewhite pointed out that many similar claims for damages were won simply "on the opinion of a legitimate expert or experts . . . if the opinion is based upon sufficient clinical linkage."

Most legal experts, including Schuck, felt that Musslewhite had made a solid case for setting aside the settlement. Another such motion, equally strong, had been filed by Robert Taylor of Ashcraft & Gerel. Nevertheless, Weinstein denied both motions from the bench on March 18. Musslewhite and Citizen Soldier immediately appealed his decision to the Second Circuit Court.

Speculation ran rampant about the source of Weinstein's adamancy. Suky Wachtendonk and some of the other plaintiffs believed that the judge sought to avoid bankrupting these six multinational chemical corporations, which would lead to a major economic crisis. Maureen Ryan, by contrast, felt Weinstein was protecting the VA and the national treasury. The judge, she maintains, never lost sight of the fact that every turn of events in his courtroom had a potentially enormous impact on the perceived obligations of the federal government. If Weinstein had let the case go to trial, and it had been established that "in essence, the children were totally disabled Vietnam veterans," she speculates, "the government would have owed the children back to the day of their birth. It would have cost hundreds of thousands of dollars in back VA benefits [for each one], plus the VA would have had to send them benefits for the rest of their lives."

Appeals filed against the settlement dragged through the courts until the summer of 1988, when the U.S. Supreme Court refused to hear the last outstanding challenges. But for all intents and purposes, the case against the chemical companies had ended with Weinstein's final order of approval on January 7, 1985. Although VVAW and other veteran lobbying groups fought valiantly to keep the cause alive, the only organization with enough weight to have made a difference was VVA. But VVA chose to step aside, with several of its leaders referring to the settlement as a "sideshow." Wayne Wilson broke with VVA over what he saw as their cowardice in refusing to denounce the injustice of the settlement. Far from insignificant, Wilson felt the settlement would affect Vietnam veteran politics, mostly for the worse, for years to come.

Despite hundreds of pages of rhetoric, VVA did not show much actual commitment to the Agent Orange issue till well into the 1990s. Though VVA initially created standing and special committees to deal with almost every major issue, including POW/MIAs, it took more than a decade before a VVA Agent Orange Committee was formed. Throughout the 1980s, Agent Orange remained buried in VVA's vastly overextended Veterans Affairs' Committee; and VVA leaders, according to Wilson, would repeatedly have to be "dragged kicking and screaming to the issue." The key to that paradox, Wilson felt, lay in the strange personal ambiguity of Bobby Muller himself. In one disturbing private conversation, Muller told him that he felt vets who blamed Agent Orange for their problems were "crybabies," just as the VA said. And though Muller was removed from leadership in the organization in 1987, says Wilson, he had already imprinted on many of his loyal followers the belief that "there really is no Agent Orange issue."

Whether or not there was an Agent Orange issue, there was indeed not much in the way of financial compensation, even for the few successful claimants. By the time payout began, in March 1989, the settlement fund had grown to $240 million. It sounded impressive, but what that actually meant for each 100 percent disabled Vietnam veteran who had entered a valid claim was a check in his mailbox for $1,280. Such checks would be sent out yearly for the next nine years, to a maximum benefit of $12,800. The total benefit for a family who had lost a husband and/or father was $3,400. Families of children with birth defects received nothing. Michael Ryan received nothing because he was not 100 percent disabled. His fellow representative plaintiff Danny Lee Ford had already died, at age thirty-seven, in 1985. Another of the five, David Lambiotte, was close to death from non-Hodgkin's lymphoma, which he had fought off for nine years. Lambiotte was currently collecting $308 a month from Social Security and another $180 a month from the VA for a "nonservice-connected" illness—but his $100 a month from the settlement would have to be subtracted from his VA compensation.

Elmo Zumwalt III, who suffered from a rare and invariably terminal combination of Hodgkin's disease and non-Hodgkin's lymphoma, had also been asked to be a representative plaintiff. Fearing that the class-action suit would drag on for years, and thus deprive him of what little time he had left with his family, he had declined to participate. When Zumwalt learned how little each vet would get from the settlement, he deeply regretted not having used his honored military name to represent his comrades. In his memoir, published two years before his death (at age forty-two, in September 1988), Zumwalt wrote: "I am a lawyer and I do not think I could prove in court, by the weight of existing scientific evidence, that Agent Orange is the cause of all these medical problems. But I am convinced that it is. I believe Agent Orange is responsible for my cancers, for Russell's [his son's] learning disorder, and for illnesses suffered by many Vietnam veterans."

The usual arrangement for fee recovery on contingency in tort cases gave attorneys one-third of the award—generally reduced somewhat if there was a pretrial settlement. Initially, the PMC attorneys had asked for $40 million in fees and expenses, a figure Harvard law professor Arthur Miller (a friend of Weinstein's) judged equitable. Nevertheless, the PMC soon lowered their request to $26 million. One of the "masters of disaster," Stan Chesley, had suggested the judge ought to award a substantial "multiplier," doubling or tripling their actual hours of work, to reward them for their "monumental" achievement on behalf of Vietnam veterans. Weinstein rebuffed him by discounting the work of the PMC entirely. The settlement had resulted, the judge claimed, not from any of their work but from the fact that the defendants "had . . . to get rid of" the case. Had they gone to trial, Weinstein speculated, the PMC "would have gotten nothing." Moreover, he admitted his desire to discourage "cases like this" in the future by keeping plaintiffs' lawyers' fees as low as possible. Weinstein awarded only $10.7 million in fees and expenses to the nine firms of the PMC. Because of poor record keeping, Yannacone was paid only $100,000 for his expenses, but the judge allowed him to apply a 1.25 multiplier for his hours. Together, Yannacone and his nine Associates added another $3 million to the total legal bill.

Only two PMC attorneys received over a million dollars for their services. Yet, considering that a dead veteran was worth only $3,400, many vets were enraged that their lawyers seemed to be walking away with the lion's share of the settlement. Frank McCarthy showed up at Weinstein's fee hearings calling the lawyers "pieces of shit, pieces of garbage," and protesting that they should be paid nothing. (McCarthy had approved of the settlement, because he felt the veterans had waited long enough already—"how many years can you watch people die unnecessarily, and kids with birth defects go unattended, before you don't care about winning anymore?"—and because he thought $180 million would be sufficient if it were all put into a trust fund, to be used mainly for the disabled children.) He rationalized that the lawyers "were all wealthy men" and that they should have been glad to be of service to Vietnam veterans; moreover, he suggested they would "all make more money because of their involvement with this case." Yannacone, though certainly voting that he get paid himself, likewise thought it obscene that the nine PMC firms got back $10 million on an investment (he claims) of slightly over $2 million. He also claimed the PMC lawyers had indulged in huge amounts of expense padding; he pointed to frequent dinner tabs of $300 or $400 and one attorney who had run up $80,000 in cab fares from midtown Manhattan to Brooklyn. The *New York Times* concurred with such criticisms, referring to the PMC's fees in a harsh editorial as "orangemail."

Nevertheless, the veterans' attorneys had earned far less than those firms employed by the chemical companies, who had been raking in $2 million a week at the height of the settlement negotiations. Their total fees have been estimated at $100 million. Two of Weinberg's special masters earned over a million dollars for their work in helping fashion the settlement. In view of all that, at least some attorneys have argued convincingly that the PMC members were underpaid—especially considering the apparently hopeless, quixotic fight they undertook. "Legal fees of five percent are terrible for this reason," explains Tod Ensign. "That when you or I or anyone else has to go out and take on Monsanto or Dow, we need people on our side who are able to put the bucks into it and commit the resources it takes. What Weinstein did sent a very clear message to the plaintiffs' bar. And that is this: 'You want to get involved in big, high-risk, very visible tort liability cases, you better be prepared to pay the price.' Weinstein was slapping the lawyers down. That message registered throughout this country, and you can already see the effect in product liability law, the difficulty of finding people to represent these kinds of speculative cases."[219]

4. Dennis Rhoades Puts On His Blue Jeans, and More Than 100,000 Families Get Help

Between the time of Judge Weinstein's final approval order in 1985 and the start of disbursement of the settlement fund four years later, the judge met regularly with his special masters and a number of Vietnam veteran advisors. Further hearings were held around the country, to permit Vietnam veterans' groups and affected individuals to offer suggestions and criticism concerning the final distribution plan. The plan stirred up some of the worst civil wars yet within the veterans' community.

Originally, Weinstein had intended to set aside $60 million from the settlement to create two foundations, one for birth defects and the other for social services. Thirty million dollars was earmarked to reimburse veterans for "catastrophic expenses incurred for health-related needs of children with birth defects"; and any amount left over, according to McCarthy, would have been used to research and develop treatment for the whole spectrum of Agent Orange–related diseases. In early 1988, the Second Circuit Court ruled that a lawsuit cannot be brought to establish a foundation; it can only yield monetary compensation to victims. In McCarthy's words: "Again, the legal system reached down and kicked our teeth in." The Second Circuit Court reduced the amount of money Weinstein had held back from direct compensation to $30 million, and specified that it must be used for the benefit of the entire class of Vietnam veterans. Weinstein was thus forced to transform the projected foundations into an Agent Orange Class Assistance Program (AOCAP).

In June 1988, the Supreme Court refused to hear a challenge to the Second Circuit Court's decision. Following the Supreme Court's dismissal of some three hundred other appeals, the settlement became law. The judge then formalized his Board of Veteran Advisors, composed of 10 vets and 1 nonvet from around the country, and handed them the tough question of how best to spend the class-assistance money—which by 1988 had grown with interest to $42 million. Furthermore, since the opt-out suits had apparently reached a dead end, the $10 million reserved to pay back the chemical companies for any losses they might incur in state courts would have to be returned to the general settlement fund; and Weinstein directed that it should eventually be added to AOCAP's account, for a grand total of $52 million. (The last such opt-out suit, the Ivy Case brought by Citizen Soldier in Texas, was returned to federal jurisdiction— and the insurmountable wall of the government contractor's defense—in 1991. Though legally able to withhold that $10 million for fifteen years, Dow voluntarily turned it over to AOCAP in 1994.)

The advisory board became a source of controversy in itself. The people Weinstein appointed were of the "smooth," professional demeanor—a judge, a social worker, a minister, two attorneys, including VVA cofounder and former assistant secretary of the Air Force, Joe Zengerle, and former deputy director of the VA, Chuck Hagel (later a Republican senator from Nebraska)—as opposed to streetwise agitators, the Jack McCloskey type of vet. The only board member who had actually worked with Agent Orange victims was Frank McCarthy. AOCAP was slated to run for seven to ten years, with grants to be made quarterly over that whole period. In August 1988, the board sent out a formal "Request for Proposal" to 1,000 organizations that served Vietnam veterans, many of whom had already been banging on their door for months; and by the end of November they had received 147 concept papers from prospective grantees. It soon became apparent that the board tended to prefer proposals from well-established organizations to fund projects dealing with (as McCarthy put it) "noncontroversial issues."

For the most part, these projects fell into the category of social services. The Vietnam Veterans of America Foundation asked for money to reprint and promote its *Viet Vet Survival Guide*. The Vietnam Veterans Leadership Program (VVLP) in St. Louis sought a grant to fund small business loans. Other favored proposals dealt with homeless veterans, adult education programs, and job training for unemployed vets—"Everything under the sun," McCarthy recalls, "except nothing for Agent Orange victims." Filled with anger and bitterness, McCarthy felt his many years of work on the Agent Orange case would be a complete waste if it resulted in no help for the ones who deserved it most: the children.

Taking his cue from his hero Reutershan, McCarthy decided maybe it was time for another vet (himself) to single-handedly grapple with the problem, which continued to befuddle the VA, Congress, and the federal court system. For several years, McCarthy had been helping a friend, Hank Schieb, one of the most highly decorated Vietnam veterans in Connecticut, get medical care for both his own ailments (of stomach and kidneys) and the birth defects of his daughter Brandie. Born in 1979, Brandie had no eyelids, cheekbones, or ear canals (which caused partial deafness); her face was further deformed by an unusually high palate and a stunted, barely visible jawbone.

In March 1988, after Vietnam Veterans Agent Orange Victims, Inc. (VVAOVI), the successor to Agent Orange Victims International, received a $20,000 grant from Shad Meshad's Vietnam Veterans Aid Foundation, McCarthy used the money to bolster his own ad hoc rescue agency: the Brandie Schieb Children's Fund. McCarthy had originally begun raising money to pay for reconstructive surgery on Brandie's face, but he suddenly decided to aim at a more ambitious goal: "helping all children who may be suffering as a result of their father's exposure to Agent Orange." It seemed to some a grandiose gesture born of McCarthy's dramatic flair, but there was sound logic behind it. At that time, there was not one group in the country dedicated to helping the second generation of Agent Orange victims. Moreover, on January 11, 1988, the Supreme Court had refused to hear most of the remaining appeals of the so-called opt-out veterans, who were suing the chemical companies on their own. The court essentially agreed with the correctness of lower-court rulings, which had released the chemical companies from all damage claims by military personnel on the basis of the government contractor's defense. The dismissal of those appeals by the Supreme

Court made hardly a news ripple; but it was a cataclysmic event for the families with disabled children. What it meant was that if help was not forthcoming from the settlement fund, they would probably be left to their own misery forever.

McCarthy and VVAOVI's executive director, James Sparrow, lobbied to have the entire $42 million that was already accessible set aside to help the children. They submitted their own grant proposal to AOCAP, suggesting that a preponderance of the first year's grant money go directly to the Brandie Schieb Children's Fund. Once again, McCarthy's critics, such as Tod Ensign, thought him "on another planet." McCarthy nonetheless began plying Weinstein, the special masters, the advisory board, and the press with his unique brand of relentless, self-lacerating persuasion. "Now I can't be beaten," he declared, "even though I'm at the bottom of the fund-raising ring. If I don't get any of this money, I'm gonna do the job anyway. It's just a matter of getting enough money to set that apparatus in motion to process these kids: enough people to make the calls to the doctors, to get them to defer their fees; to go to corporations for matching donations; to set up the operations; to coordinate with the families—to do all that."

McCarthy did not win any friends with his letter to Judge Weinstein on July 5, 1988. In it, he took aim at every other claimant vying for a share of the class assistance fund. He described VVA as "fat with funds" and their request for a publishing subsidy as "ludicrous." To use settlement money for counseling programs he called "redundant over-kill and a waste of funds"; and to use it for a "small business incubator service," he asserted, was as much an "insult" to Agent Orange victims as sinking it into rehabilitation programs for "dope addicts, alcoholics, the unemployed, and the homeless." As McCarthy's anger and intransigence increased, he unavoidably isolated himself from the rest of the advisory board and the court. But Weinstein's selection of an executive director for AOCAP in December 1988 went in McCarthy's favor, more than he could ever have hoped.[220]

The man who would wield a power over the grant selection process second only to the judge's, and do so for the entire life of the program, was forty-four-year-old Dennis Rhoades, recruited from his post as economics director of the American Legion. Rhoades was a Vietnam vet, but had nothing in common with the average grunt. After getting his degree in English from UCLA, he'd joined the Army to avoid getting a lousy draft assignment and had ended up with the prestigious Communications Engineering Installation Agency, working all over Southeast Asia for two years. In Vietnam, he confesses, he was "a REMF [rear-echelon motherfucker] pulling cable for the crypto equipment." Before getting called to AOCAP, by his own laughing admission, he'd "had no connection with Agent Orange"—a self-deprecation not exactly true. After graduate work in American Studies at the University of Wyoming, he became a self-described "career employee" of various government veterans' agencies; he also served as a founding member of the Vietnam Veterans' Leadership Program (VVLP) and, later, as executive director of VVA. Tall, reserved, with a preference for well-cut, three-piece charcoal suits, he was, on the surface, about the least likely person in the universe to find common ground with Frank McCarthy.

But Rhoades had had his eyes opened to the limitations of public agencies in one of his first jobs, as a veterans' employment representative for the Department of Labor in San Francisco. There he met Peter Cameron, founder of the community-based veterans' self-help organization, Flower of the Dragon, in neighboring Santa Rosa. Cameron quickly became one of his mentors. At the same time, he also interfaced with McCloskey's Swords to Ploughshares, and helped both groups obtain CETA funding. It was immediately clear to him that a few unsalaried, highly motivated individual veterans working at a grass-roots level, no matter how crazed or off-the-wall they might appear, were doing far more to get their fellow vets into good jobs and educational programs, and doing it a lot faster, than armies of well-paid, strait-laced bureaucrats. When Rhoades was later brought to Washington to work for the DOL's Veterans Employment Service, he funded a program in which Cameron and other Flower of the Dragon workers met with Vietnam veterans throughout California, with the aim of organizing a statewide network of such community-based organizations (CBOs).

Hired as director of the Veterans' Federal Coordinating Committee in the Carter White House, Rhoades expanded his CBO-building project into twelve cities nationwide, filling a void with important new entities such as the Philadelphia Veterans' Multiservice Center and giving new life to faltering older groups like SEAVAC in Seattle. He then took the project back to the DOL, expanded it again into the Targeted Technical Assistance Program, and was about to send several teams of CBO advisors into forty cities, when Reagan took office and yanked their entire budget. The main reason he got involved with the "national Republican Vietnam veterans' club" (as he later called the VVLP) was to find a new source of funding for his orphaned CBOs—an only partly successful venture. And although for several more years he remained at DOL, as just another docile government functionary, Rhoades had not lost his sensitivity to the down-and-out and those on the wrong side of respectability—a sensitivity that was heightened by his other mentor in government work, Agent Orange activist and victim Dean Phillips. Given the chance at AOCAP, Rhoades would prove to be a man of extraordinary compassion.

The Brandie Schieb Children's Fund did not receive one of the first eight AOCAP grants, although four of them went to organizations serving children with developmental disabilities and chronic illnesses—and providing help to their families. Three others went to stress-counseling programs, including one that dealt with wives and children of vets. And one went to attorneys David Addlestone and Bart Stichman, who had just created the National Veterans

Legal Services Program (NVLSP), in large part to argue VA claims before the new Court of Veterans Appeals (CVA), which had just been signed into law by outgoing President Reagan. The CVA would give veterans a right to judicial review, however limited, for the first time in U.S. history—which had been the late Dean Phillips' dream.

Seeing that work in all these areas would need to be carried on long past the exhaustion of the settlement money, Rhoades sought to teach his grantees how to obtain their own funding and "leverage" other government money. He came up with the idea of creating a partnership between three different kinds of service organizations that did not normally deal with one another: veterans' services, family services, and services for children with developmental disabilities. This partnership became formalized in 1994 as the National Alliance of Veteran Family Service Organizations (NAVFSO), which briefly outlived the termination of AOCAP as the Veterans' Families of America (VFA). Despite a 1996 grant from President Clinton's Americorps, which kept it going for another year or so, VFA failed to find new sources of endowment to continue its work. As veteran activists like McCarthy and Wayne Wilson had foreseen years earlier, getting the chemical companies to pay in full for the damage of Agent Orange had been worth holding out for, because there just aren't enough other rich people, corporations, or foundations in America that even "have veterans on their radar screen."

AOCAP's first eight grants were relatively small and dispersed by design throughout the country. McCarthy had asked for half a million dollars just to get his program started, which seemed out of line to Rhoades. But it wasn't just the sizable financial risk of McCarthy's project that upset AOCAP's director; it was McCarthy's style. McCarthy, Rhoades recalls, would come to each meeting "hostile and mistrustful," and the two of them would invariably end up in a "screaming contest." More to get him off his back than anything else, Rhoades finally gave VVAOVI and its Schieb Fund a hundred-thousand-dollar grant in late 1989—without naming McCarthy as a recipient, since it seemed like a possible conflict of interest with Frank being on the advisory board. McCarthy, who had moved his base to Oviedo, Florida, took the ball and ran with it literally across the United States.

With his salary funded by the State of Connecticut, McCarthy spent three and a half weeks of every month on the road, locating children who were victims of Agent Orange, as well as doctors and financial sponsors to help them. By the end of the first year, Rhoades was impressed enough by the success of McCarthy's hands-on approach to nearly double VVAOVI's funding; and the third year, AOCAP endowed the Schieb Fund with almost a quarter-million dollars. From then on, McCarthy's project would receive only slightly decreasing grants each year till AOCAP terminated in June 1996—with Rhoades happily breaking his original plan not to fund any organization for more than three years. Over a six-year period, VVAOVI would help almost 300 children in 38 states. In the end, it was only the AOCAP money that kept McCarthy's organization going, as a new gubernatorial administration in Connecticut tried to kill them by completely cutting off their right to receive donations and then subjecting the organization to investigation by two powerful state agencies. Though they were eventually cleared of having mishandled funds, the stigma of the charges devastated their fund-raising. In the midst of that hell, McCarthy also had to ride out a painful split with Paul Reutershan's sister, Jane Dziedzic, who had been his chief assistant. Dziedzic accused McCarthy of neglecting his role as veterans' advocate in his seemingly frantic obsession to help every Agent Orange–injured child in the country.

McCarthy's tenacity was, in fact, his greatest strength. Despite the satisfaction, that first year, of helping give dozens of kids a more normal life, one thing still troubled him greatly: the memory of those 67,000 claims for disabled children that had been filed with the court after the settlement of the Agent Orange lawsuit. With the stroke of Weinstein's pen in finalizing the settlement plan, every last one of those claims had been denied. McCarthy continually pressed Rhoades to reopen those claims; but Rhoades thought it a hopeless task, since most of the addresses were five to ten years old and veterans, especially those who were poor and struggling, tended to move frequently.

Still, Rhoades was leaning toward the view that services to disabled children should be the chief priority of the Class Assistance Program. Weinstein, in his haste to get money out the door (to make up for the many years of delay), seemed to be pushing him to make grants "willy-nilly." "I was worried," Rhoades recalls, "that this program didn't really have a center that I could identify with." Unsure how to find those needy kids, Rhoades went down to the University of South Carolina, where former U.S. Surgeon General C. Everett Koop had set up a Center for Developmental Disabilities a few years earlier. One of the center's most outstanding features was a computer database for tracking disabled children, the National Information System (NIS), what Rhoades called "a big birth-defect clearinghouse." Out of his visit there came a plan for a national birth-defect referral service for Vietnam veterans, which would be operated by NIS with funding from AOCAP. NIS's 800 number for Vietnam veterans went into service in the fall of 1989.

Rhoades had come to concur with McCarthy about there being a large number of parents and children who were "really hurting," and that action to help them was needed immediately. But at that point, he says, the knowledge was still theoretical with him. Meanwhile, McCarthy kept at him like a bulldog to investigate that huge file of dead applications, which had begun accumulating from the time Yannacone came on board. One day in mid-1990, Rhoades finally agreed "to get a handle on the situation." That meant changing into jeans and

T-shirt and taking a couple of assistants down to the courthouse in Uniondale, Long Island, where the original 240,000 Agent Orange claims were stored in dusty boxes in the basement. Rhoades and his helpers spent several days down there, sifting through several thousand claims in search of those that dealt with "reproductive effects"; and what they found, he says, "astonished" them.

Rhoades read through one life story after another, and he was moved to the depth of his being. It was one thing to hear terms like *spina bifida, cerebral palsy,* or *sensory integration dysfunction* and to have some idea of the impairment they represented. It was quite another, he recalls, to get a sense of the years of suffering these families had endured, and were still enduring, by reading their own words, written in their own hand. Quite suddenly, they had all become real people to him. He was also struck by how Agent Orange illnesses and birth defects, PTSD, guilt, and anger often converged in a single family to wreak havoc in every aspect of their daily life. The number of families in which physical and psychological ailments intertwined and fed one another was also astoundingly large. That week in the courthouse basement, he says, "really changed my mind." One of the first things Rhoades did was to apologize to McCarthy. He admitted that McCarthy had been right in demanding they spare no expense to find and help every damaged family.

Rhoades' staff pulled out about a thousand claims that had to do with birth defects and miscarriages, to do a trial mailing. Because of confidentiality requirements, each claim bore only a sequential number; but Aetna Insurance, which had handled the actuarial work for the individual payment program, was able to provide the original addresses for each family. NIS at the University of South Carolina sent out letters to each one. Once again, Rhoades was surprised out of his socks by the high number of families that answered. A little digging revealed that families with a disabled child generally avoid relocating, since they're often wedded to a particular school that offers special education, or to a job whose insurance benefits pay their astronomical medical bills. Based on that knowledge, Rhoades hired a whole team of law students from nearby Touro University, who needed summer work. After a couple of months of sorting, they had accumulated over 60,000 claims that spoke of developmental disabilities, and over 10,000 that dealt with failed pregnancies. A few months later, NIS began the process (which would take a full three years) of mailing a personal letter from Rhoades to the entire 70,000.

The response from the families was overwhelming. The birth-defect referral service at NIS then began taking case histories and referring each family to one or more of the programs funded by AOCAP. Immediately it became apparent that there were not enough programs to handle them all. As a consequence, Rhoades began to fund more and more programs having to do with birth defects and family services. Technically, Rhoades could only make recommendations to Weinstein, who had final approval over every grant; and there was some concern as to whether Weinstein would accept this radical transformation of AOCAP. Plenty of veterans' groups were demanding that AOCAP money be used primarily for other things, especially research and treatment for PTSD. At the time when the money first became available, the VA was shutting a number of Vet Centers, and many of the proposals sent to Rhoades asked for AOCAP money to keep these centers open or to create new centers. Weinstein vetoed any such use of the money, warning that if the settlement were used to fund programs the VA should be paying for, a dangerous precedent would be set, and the government would likely dump a whole lot more of its veterans' expenses in AOCAP's lap. But to everyone's amazement, and the great relief of Rhoades and many others, the usually thorny judge made not one demur to the decision to focus on children and family services.

McCarthy, who had once hated Weinstein, claimed the judge was "the one person of power in this country who did not turn his back on Agent Orange victims and their kids." According to McCarthy, the judge defied the Second Circuit Court's restrictions on how the settlement money could be used, in allowing something very near a foundation to be created. The judge's courage, he says, gave him something he thought he'd lost forever: *hope*—and in so doing, wrought an enormous change in his own life, "turning him around" from the raging bull of the veterans' movement to a cross between Mother Cabrini and Mr. Rogers.

In his seven and a half years at AOCAP, Rhoades had a lot of his preconceptions changed as well. He had formerly imagined that the only way to help children with birth defects was through expensive operations. He and most of the advisory board had the misperception, he says, "that a kid with a birth defect was like a broken transmission—you take him to AAMCO and you get it fixed and you drive on." But he soon learned that there is no way to correct the majority of birth defects, that they are indeed lifelong afflictions. Early on, he and his staff sought tutoring from the University Affiliated Programs for Persons with Developmental Disabilities, to learn what these individuals need, how they function, and where they can go for help. It turned out there were at least a modicum of services available already, but the problem was that most families did not know where to find them. As Rhoades puts it, "Vietnam veterans are resistant to institutions anyway," and most of them would rather return to their worst firefight than undergo the hassle and humiliation of applying for SSI or Medicaid.

Rhoades decided the largest number of vets could be helped through a case management system. For the remaining duration of the program, one of AOCAP's biggest yearly grants went to Bazelon (formerly the Mental Health Law Project), for a counseling group specifically geared to helping Vietnam veteran families apply for Medicaid and SSI for their children. Rhoades also looked for programs that would make life easier or pleasanter for these children on a daily basis. One of his surprises was to learn that this was the first generation of spina bifida children who were living into adulthood, because of a recent medical innovation called a brain shunt, that drained the accumulation of cerebrospinal fluid that usually proved fatal to sufferers. In addition to funding agencies that would help raise the "$100,000 a pop" necessary for straightening these victim's spines, so that their bodies could fully mature, AOCAP sponsored much more modest but equally necessary social projects, like the first summer camp for spina bifida kids.

By the time AOCAP shut down, in 1996, Rhoades figured that 220,000 vets and their wives had been "served," as well as about 75,000 children. Moreover, virtually every program in the last few years, he asserts, "had a component for children." The numbers are impressive; and Rhoades, who did a herculean job with relatively limited resources, need never apologize for the things he failed to accomplish, but one must be aware that to "serve" in this context does not necessarily mean to heal or even to alleviate suffering. It might mean as little as a brief, supportive phone conversation. The $72 million Rhoades expended ($52 million principal plus eight years of interest) had to be spread exceedingly thin over a network of 70 grant programs in all 50 states, Puerto Rico, and the District of Columbia. The one to two hundred thousand dollars a year that went to the Brandie Schieb Fund, for example, paid the salaries of just a handful of counselors and negotiators, each of whom had a caseload of 200 families.

One of the problems was that Vietnam vets did not stop having kids in their thirties; but many have continued doing so well into their fifties; so that for every year that passes, the average age of the entire pool of Vietnam veterans' children increases only a few months. In 1989, when AOCAP began, the average child's age was 12; in 1996, it had risen only to 15. The next problem, an exceedingly frightening one, was that before AOCAP ceased to exist, agencies like the Brandie Schieb Fund had begun to get calls for help from the children of Vietnam veterans *for their children.* According to McCarthy, there have already been over a thousand cases reported of Vietnam veterans' children, apparently healthy themselves, having children with birth defects almost identical to those attributed to dioxin exposure. NAVFSO made the decision to help this next generation of Agent Orange victims whenever possible. Likewise, with the advent of Gulf War Syndrome in the early 1990s, the children of Gulf War vets also began appearing with birth defects very similar to those in the children of Agent Orange victims. Some scientists believe the burning of Kuwaiti oil wells may have filled the air with dioxin-laden smoke; and if so, this time there was often no need to explain so-called "male-mediated" birth defects, since a large number of women troops were directly exposed.

Even lacking proof of dioxin exposure, McCarthy argued that the U.S. government ought to take responsibility for these children, since "one and one is still two," and birth defects of a certain type are readily identifiable as chemically induced. He and other AOCAP advisors felt these children should not have to wait, as did the progeny of Vietnam vets, for a decade of studies to be completed before receiving assistance. Since Gulf War vets and their families appeared to be suffering many of the same medical, financial, and social problems as Vietnam vets, NAVFSO determined that no Gulf War vet asking for help would be turned away from any of their programs.

If nothing else, the Vietnam veteran Agent Orange victims had blazed a trail for others to follow, and could pass their hard-won wisdom along to the next generation of veterans. "The problems the Gulf War vets are dealing with, the VA and the government," says McCarthy, "it's almost a mirror of the way they treated us. First thing they do is tell them it's all in their head. Then they tell them it's all stress. Then they create a registry. Then they do studies. It's following the same damn poor rulebook that they did with Agent Orange." The rub, of course, was the inevitable dwindling of money spread over a wider and wider expanse of victims.

The same problem had afflicted AOCAP's individual payment program. The original deadline for veterans to apply for disability compensation (and families to apply for death benefits) was December 31, 1994. The amount to be paid to each applicant had been figured by Aetna Insurance, based on their actuarial tables and the court's estimate of eligible claimants. In late December 1994, media around the country ran sensational stories about how much money waited to be claimed by injured veterans. At that point, about 29,000 claims had been honored. But during the last two weeks of the year, phone lines were clogged with thousands of calls daily, and the payment program received an unprecedented surge of 200,000 applications! Although many who responded were not even Vietnam veterans, and many more lacked the 100 percent disability qualification, so many of the claims were valid that Weinstein extended the deadline to January 17, 1995. Some people interpreted the response as just natural greed; but it also showed that, unfortunately, many veterans and families had never known of their eligibility for settlement money.

By the end of the application period, the large number of successful claimants had drastically reduced the size of benefit checks. The family of a dead veteran, applying just before the program expired, wound up with only $350, an amount McCarthy deemed "insulting and a disgrace." There have also been even more disheartening stories about people who wrote in during that period with a valid claim—like Joanne Calkins, widow of Vietnam veteran James Chapman, who died of lymphoma—who were never contacted back by the court, and simply "slipped through the cracks."[221]

5. New Studies Incriminate Agent Orange,
and the Reagan White House Undertakes Damage Control

The most convincing argument of the ultimate inadequacy of both the payment program and the Agent Orange Class Assistance Program itself—even the well-meaning but overworked Brandie Schieb Fund—comes from Michael Ryan. Not only did his family never catch a glimpse of the settlement money, but they ended up, by his own account, $100,000 in the hole from lost sick time and vacation, unpaid leaves of absence, expenses on the road, and day-care costs for Kerry as he and his wife promoted the case from coast to coast. "Kerry had twenty-two birth defects. She is blind and in a wheelchair. Kerry was the lead child from the beginning," he recounts. "Nobody [including McCarthy's group] has ever called Kerry and offered a single penny of help." Of course, as McCarthy readily admits, the Brandie Schieb Fund only rarely paid for current medical costs (with the exception of anesthesia, which could seldom be gotten for free or reduced charge). Neither he nor any other AOCAP program had sufficient funds to reimburse veterans for the tens or hundreds of thousands of dollars they might already have spent on their children's surgeries and ongoing daily care.

In May of 1994, as AOCAP began its wind-down phase, it sponsored a symposium to discuss the lessons its participants had learned. Out of that symposium came a tremendously valuable tome on the subject of veteran readjustment, *The Legacy of Vietnam Veterans and Their Families,* with a preface by none other than Jack Weinstein. It is to Weinstein's credit that he avoids thumping his own chest in the piece, and in fact finally acknowledges the huge reality of Vietnam veteran and veteran family casualties that he once scoffed at when Wayne Wilson tried (perhaps too brusquely) to thrust it in his face. "The programs funded through the Agent Orange Class Assistance Program," he writes, will never "reach all of those who are in need of help." And what he was once so sure would happen he now expresses in the form of a plea: "The federal government must reconsider its obligation to veterans' families." The man who had tried to shout down Maureen Ryan finally admits that "the VA has often failed to consider veterans' families relevant to services or benefits"; and most tellingly, he himself describes the bitter circle so many of those families were sent in: "human service agencies . . . reduce[d] caseloads by making referrals back to the VA, even though there was no reason to believe help would be available from that agency to address the needs of the veteran's family." In an astonishing aside, the iron-fisted judge confesses that what gratified him most about the outcome of the Agent Orange case was that "such a large share of the funds available through the settlement" was "used to help the children of Vietnam veterans. . . ."

Even the ever-ebullient McCarthy suspected that NAVFSO would fall apart before it had a chance to gather sufficient new funding. By 1996, his organization already shrunken and himself without salary, he felt he "couldn't do it anymore"; and he was stuck with the bitter knowledge that there were still 40,000 kids who would probably never be helped by him or anyone else. His old anger resurfaced when he thought of the "horror" of the $200 million given out under the payment program. "Now, at a time when we're going out of business, we should be kicking into high gear helping people," he complained. "If it wasn't for those nasty bastards who call themselves judges in the Supreme Court and the Second Circuit Court of Appeals, we would be helping a lot more people and we'd be helping a hell of a lot of Desert Storm folks now as well. I'm still hateful of the people who did that deed."

With the remaining money in the Agent Orange Class Assistance Fund, Dennis Rhoades made three large terminal grants: to the National Veterans Legal Services Program, to the National Information System, and to the Brandie Schieb Children's Fund. That money carried McCarthy's organization through 1997. But just as Frank feared, when AOCAP support dried up, their "budget was decimated." As with NAVFSO, no eager veterans' patrons stepped in to mend their shortfall. On the contrary, he says, everywhere they went to solicit donations, they got the same rebuff. "There are already plenty of charities that help children," the folks with money told them. As a result, Agent Orange Victims, Inc. (transformed into the National Veterans Services Fund) went from nine offices nationwide back to one office and one paid counselor in Connecticut—only a few miles from where Frank had started out. This time it wasn't McCarthy who did the work, however. He retired to Florida, hoping to find some tranquility after two decades of activism. The next thing he knew, he fell ill with lung cancer himself. In a final irony, since his diagnosis occurred slightly more than thirty years after his return from Vietnam (the official cut-off limit), the VA told him he was ineligible for compensation.

*   *   *

Concurrent with AOCAP's international symposium, in May 1994, Congressman Lane Evans chaired a subcommittee hearing of the House Veterans' Affairs Committee, which looked not only at what the settlement fund had accomplished but also "what remains to be done"—especially "the VA's inability to establish enough appropriate programs to meet the overwhelming demand for services." Evans sought to introduce a bill that would compel the VA to continue funding NAVFSO programs once the AOCAP money was shut off. With the 103rd Congress on its way out, legislators nervous about reelection were looking for juicy budget cuts to show their constituents, not fresh programs to soak up more tax dollars. In support of Evans' bill, AOCAP produced a whole series of veterans and family members who had been helped by

NAVFSO programs. But the government followed with its own expert witnesses, who claimed the VA already had enough of its own programs in place to take over the job of helping Agent Orange victims and veterans' families. McCarthy, hearing a VA spokesman claim the Vet Center program already adequately handled disabled children (based on a single program at a Connecticut Vet Center), accused the government of "outright lying."

Rhoades, amused to see McCarthy ferociously defending AOCAP, boasted that "Frank would kill for us!"; but it was clear to everyone that he was speaking metaphorically, and that McCarthy, like everyone else in this long struggle, had grown far beyond his earlier limitations, his temper tantrums and unpredictability. One totally surprising development for both men was that they had become friends. Somehow this horrible thing, this 2,3,7,8 tetrachlorodibenzo-para-dioxin, and the millionfold terrible things it had done to human physiology, had led to a powerful healing—if not always in the victims themselves, then unquestionably in those who had tried to act as healers. "We're all part of the *process*," Rhoades says somewhat reverently of that mysterious transformation of hurt into kindness and beauty, of antagonism into peace and reconciliation.

Lane Evans' bill to provide a federal endowment for NAVFSO never got out of his subcommittee. That fall, Republicans swept control of the House—creating a "hostile climate," he recalls, for such legislation. The new Republican leaders, in line with their Speaker Newt Gingrich, saw the support of Vietnam veterans' families as more "wasteful spending" by the Democrats and made a concerted effort to kill it.

One final irony was that the first U.S. president to announce compensation for at least a few hundred of the Agent Orange–disabled children was William Jefferson Clinton. On May 28, 1996, Clinton announced that two more diseases in Vietnam veterans, prostate cancer and peripheral neuropathy, would be treated as service-connected disabilities, even without proof of exposure to Agent Orange. Then, setting a new precedent, he announced that the VA would compensate children of Vietnam veterans who suffered from spina bifida, as soon as Congress authorized the agency to do so. A few months earlier, the Institute of Medicine had found a statistical link between exposure of Vietnam veterans to Agent Orange and an increased risk of spina bifida in their children. But as the law was then written, the VA could treat or compensate only veterans themselves, not their family members. Under Clinton's urging, VA officials worked with congressmen Tom Daschle and Lane Evans, as well as with Rhoades and others at AOCAP, to write a bill that would extend the VA's domain, mandating the agency to care for at least some children of veterans. The bill specifically provided that benefits for these children were to be provided regardless of the character (Honorable or Dishonorable) of the veteran's military discharge. With the president's force behind it, it passed quickly, and was signed into law on September 26, 1996. Beside Bill Clinton in the Rose Garden for this historic occasion were Frank McCarthy and many other Vietnam veteran activists, as well as a number of dioxin-disabled children.

There were many who criticized Clinton for opportunism in using the announcement to improve his relations with the veterans' community, which had hit an all-time low a few days earlier. The defendant in a sexual harassment suit, Clinton (in his role as commander in chief) had sought to avoid going to trial under a 1940 law that shielded active-duty servicemen from such damage actions. Veterans' groups had complained angrily that someone who admitted evading the Vietnam War draft—as Clinton had done by studying abroad— should not seek legal protection as a "soldier." But in the view of Michael Ryan, Clinton's past made his decision only that much more courageous.

"Clinton did more in two days for Agent Orange victims, especially by throwing kids into the mix for the first time," Ryan says, "than all the veterans who were president did in two decades. Jimmy Carter, who was in the Navy, did nothing. Ronald Reagan, the great 'let's rattle the sword' conservative, did nothing. Bush, the pilot shot down and rescued by a submarine, did next to nothing. And then we've got old Rhodes Scholar Bill, who never inhaled. He's done more than all these veterans for their brother veterans!" "Clinton the draft-dodger," adds Ryan, "owned up to a mistake . . . he's admitting that we have drafted the unborn and the unborn are now going to war with their fathers and mothers."

Agent Orange, miraculously, had healed—at least for the moment—the biggest rift of all: the seemingly unbridgeable chasm between those who fought and those who stayed home.[222]

· · ·

Wayne Wilson was right in his belief that the class-action settlement would put a damper on legislative efforts to compensate Agent Orange disabilities. After the congressional defeat of H.R. 1961 in late 1983, Tom Daschle continued to author and fight for Agent Orange legislation. He was instrumental in the passage of the Veterans' Dioxin and Radiation Exposure Compensation Standards Act in 1984. The so-called Dioxin Act required the VA to create an advisory committee of non-VA scientists, to set formal guidelines for Agent Orange compensation. When Daschle moved up to a Senate seat in 1986, he drafted another Agent Orange compensation bill with former VVAW leader John Kerry, who had been elected to the Senate from Massachusetts two years earlier. The Veterans' Agent Orange Disabilities Act of 1987, S. 1787, called for the VA to presume as service-connected the occurrence in Vietnam veterans of non-Hodgkin's lymphoma, lung cancer, and any disease caused by the immunosuppressive effects of dioxin exposure. Known as the Kerry-Daschle bill, it required the VA to begin compensating the first two diseases immediately; and it also mandated the VA to consult with the National Academy of Sciences (NAS) in order to determine what other diseases "are reasonably associated with damage to or suppression of the human immune system resulting from exposure" to Agent Orange. The VA would then have to add any diseases listed in the NAS's report to the list of compensable illnesses within 90 days. The Kerry-Daschle bill passed in the Senate twice, only to be killed each time in the House.

House opposition to the Kerry-Daschle bill was led by the same old Mississippi warhorse (with thirty-five years in the military and medals from both WWII and Korea) who had been slighting Vietnam veterans for years: Veterans' Affairs Committee chairman Sonny Montgomery. In October 1988, explaining his rejection of S. 1787, Montgomery asserted that "further studies were needed to prove a connection between various diseases and Agent Orange before the government should be held liable for disability benefits." Somehow Montgomery managed to ignore several such studies that had been made public during the previous two years, including studies by the National Cancer Institute and the VA (of Marines) and one by the New Jersey Agent Orange Commission, whose results had been published in the prestigious *Journal of the American Medical Association (JAMA)* in March 1988.

March 1988 also saw the release of the Air Force's revised Ranch Hand study, which revealed that the original study (supposedly exonerating Agent Orange) had been seriously flawed. The Air Force scientists concluded that personnel who had sprayed Agent Orange suffered from serious cancers more frequently than they had originally thought; and that more of their children had serious birth defects than had initially been reported. Finally, in the May 1988 issue of *JAMA*, just a few months before Montgomery's complaint about the dearth of scientific evidence, the CDC had announced the findings of Stage Two of its Vietnam Experience Study (VES): the last piece of research completed before the CDC, asking to be let off the Agent Orange hook, had canned VES completely. Stage Two, a morbidity study of 18,000 veterans, showed that those who had gone to Vietnam were more likely to suffer hearing loss, liver disease, and blood in their stools than their peers who had served elsewhere; the Vietnam vets were also more likely to have a low sperm count and a higher percentage of abnormal sperm cells.

Congressman Montgomery, ironically, encouraged passage of a bill that called for a stronger "medical outreach" program to inform Vietnam veterans about "the possibility of illnesses related to Agent Orange"—as if what they needed most, twenty years after coming home from the war, was just more people telling them that Vietnam was bad news.

In fact, the bad news kept coming of its own accord. In November 1988, a month after Montgomery's House speech on Agent Orange, the American

Legion released their own study of the herbicide's toxic effects. The two principal researchers, a married couple named Steven and Jeanne Stellman, had
top credentials. Formerly vice president of epidemiology at the American
Cancer Society, Dr. Steven Stellman now worked as assistant commissioner for
biostatistics in the New York City Health Department. Dr. Jeanne Stellman, an
associate professor at Columbia University's School of Public Health, had
started the Foundation for Worker, Veteran, and Environmental Health.
Furthermore, the study had been based on almost 3,000 Vietnam vets and a
control group of almost 4,000 era veterans, chosen randomly from the
American Legion membership rolls—a sampling considerably broader than
the one used in the Ranch Hand study, and comparable to that of the mammoth CDC study, which had consumed $65 million in taxpayers' money. Like
the CDC scientists, the Stellmans had observed their subjects over a period of
five years.

The American Legion study, made public on Veterans Day, November 11,
1988, shook the veterans' community from coast to coast. Not only did it
emanate from that former bastion of conservatism, one of the charter members
of the iron triangle of veterans' service organizations, but it challenged the government's failed CDC study head-on. The CDC had relied on the so-called
"hits method"—using the intersection of spraying records (the HERBS tapes)
and troop-movement records to determine how often certain companies were
in the immediate vicinity of an herbicide mission. Each time a company inter-
sected with a spray mission, each man in the company would be credited with
having received a "hit" of Agent Orange. One of the main justifications given
by the CDC for abandoning its study, in 1987, was the supposed inaccuracy of
the government records, and the concomitant lack of veterans who could show
proof of exposure to Agent Orange. The Stellmans, by contrast, allowed veterans to "self-report" the times they were exposed to defoliant. By comparing
what the veterans said they experienced with the spraying and unit-location
records, the Stellmans determined that the military's daily journals were in fact
highly reliable.

The Stellmans concluded that, at the very least, tens of thousands of Vietnam
veterans were "heavily exposed" to Agent Orange. After examining 35 combat
battalions (units of about 1,000 men), they found that half of them had been in
areas near Saigon sprayed with Agent Orange in 1967–1968. Several of those
units, they ascertained, had been "right in the midst of very heavy spraying."
The CDC, having tested the blood of 646 veterans who had served in such
areas, had reported (in an article in *JAMA* the previous September) that only
two of the men showed elevated dioxin levels; and thus they concluded that the
vast majority of the men had not come in contact with Agent Orange at all. The
Stellmans, forced to use a Freedom of Information Act request to get around

the CDC's secrecy, exposed the government agency's flawed methodology—especially the bogus blood tests, which were incapable of measuring significant differences in dioxin level after a lapse of twenty years.

Jeanne Stellman publicly accused the CDC of using such medical hocus-pocus to "belittle and obscure" the "extremely important material" they had received from the Pentagon on troop exposure to Agent Orange. Interestingly, the Stellmans claimed that many of the CDC study's preliminary results—though largely discounted by the government scientists—had actually conformed with their own findings. Before it was aborted, the CDC study had already shown, for example, that Vietnam veterans were dying at a rate 45 percent higher than veterans of the era who had served elsewhere; that Vietnam veterans had a 72 percent higher suicide rate than era vets; and that they more frequently suffered other violent and unnatural deaths, including homicides, motor vehicle accidents, poisonings, and drug overdoses.

What gave teeth to the Stellmans' charges were the stunning findings of the American Legion study. It showed, for starters, a strong correlation between exposure to Agent Orange and a range of benign tumors and skin diseases. Veterans who had been exposed also showed a greater disposition to faintness, fatigue, body aches, and colds. Wives of such veterans were more likely to miscarry; their miscarriage rate matched that of women who smoke during pregnancy. The study also showed, in a larger context, that Vietnam veterans were more likely than other veterans of the era to suffer from an array of physical and psychological problems. A bigger percentage of Vietnam veterans had high blood pressure, heart disease, ulcers, venereal disease, and nervous system disorders than veterans who had served outside of Vietnam. Among "high combat" veterans (20 percent of their sample) there was an even greater incidence of these ailments. The "high combat" vets were also four times more likely to have been separated from their spouses or divorced than all other veterans of the era. Vietnam vets were more likely than era vets to have a "serious drinking problem"; "high combat" vets were twice as likely as era vets to be addicted to alcohol and cigarettes. The likelihood of a veteran developing post-traumatic stress disorder also increased with his amount of combat experience. Although combat alone was a sufficient stressor to account for many of these physical and psychological problems, there was the added correlation that vets in high combat areas were also the most likely to have been in contact with Agent Orange.

"This study clearly establishes the serious health problems caused by Agent Orange and the mental anguish [of PTSD] that exists among Vietnam veterans," declared H. F. "Sparky" Gierke, the American Legion's national commander.

Right on the heels of the American Legion study came the results of an extensive Vietnamese government study on the health effects of Agent Orange.

Speaking to the American Public Health Association in Boston on November 17, 1988, Dr. Le Cao Dai reported that infant mortality in villages located near heavily defoliated forests was more than twice that of villages far removed from herbicide use. Moreover, the risks of liver cancer and birth defects were three to four times greater among exposed villagers, Dr. Dai said. Even more tellingly, his researchers had found the infant mortality rate in exposed villages falling steadily since the spraying had stopped in 1970. Preeminent Agent Orange researcher Dr. Arnold Schecter of the medical school at the State University of New York, Binghamton, confirmed the reliability of Dai's study. At the same conference, the Massachusetts Department of Public Health reported the results of its own study, which showed that the state's Vietnam veterans were three times as likely to suffer from soft-tissue cancers as other vets of the era.

Meanwhile, in Ho Chi Minh City, Dr. Nguyen Thi Ngoc Phuong, who had collected (and embalmed in jars) several hundred deformed fetuses, had established a significant correlation between mothers exposed to Agent Orange and these monstrous products of their spontaneous abortions. Dr. Phuong also found that many women exposed to the herbicide developed uterine cancer and other pelvic tumors in their early twenties. A parallel study by the Vietnamese National Committee for Investigation of the Consequences of Chemicals Used in the Vietnam War (like the earlier study by Dr. Ton That Tung) found that NVA soldiers who had gone south had fathered a higher percentage of children with major birth defects than soldiers who had remained in the north.

In the fall of 1988, the U.S. District Court in New York unsealed the documents from the class-action lawsuit. Among those documents was evidence that the U.S. military knew at least some of the health hazards of Agent Orange as early as 1962, three years before it began widespread use of the defoliant in Vietnam. The documents also showed that the Pentagon had deliberately misled the public concerning the herbicide's alleged harmlessness.

In the face of so much incriminating material, one might have expected the U.S. government to finally acknowledge responsibility for the illnesses of Vietnam veterans and their families. On the contrary, the government went on the attack once again. Dr. Vernon C. Houk, who had directed the CDC's Agent Orange study, impugned the American Legion study as the work of "pretty lousy scientists" who had "turned logic on its head." Houk stood behind his belief in a high blood-level of dioxin as the "gold standard validation" of Agent Orange exposure, even though other reputable scientists, such as Rutgers University's Dr. Peter Kahn, had found evidence of dioxin having been "excreted from the body after already causing biochemical havoc in its victim." Dr. Houk went so far as to condemn the editor of *Environmental Research*, the journal that had published the American Legion study. The White House Agent

Orange Working Group, of which Dr. Houk was a leading member, sent denunciations of the American Legion study to both Congress and the press.

In testimony to Congress, the Stellmans expressed great astonishment that the CDC should have launched such vicious personal attacks against them, in many cases misstating the Legion study's goals, design, and methodology—apparently to avoid the same conclusion which the CDC's own study had tended toward: that "the men who fought for their country [in Vietnam] . . . might now, as a direct consequence, be suffering emotional stress, have psychological problems, [and] have combat-related illnesses. . . ."

As for the charges lodged by the Vietnamese, they required no such complex discrediting. The U.S. government wrote them off, according to the *St. Louis Post-Dispatch,* as "a possible wedge by which Vietnam would seek to claim reparations from the United States for damages to the population."

Despite all the new evidence from both sides of the Pacific, by 1989 the VA still had not set up a category of disability for Agent Orange exposure. On August 3, 1989, riding the momentum of the American Legion study, the Kerry-Daschle bill passed the Senate a second time, then bogged down as usual in the House. In many respects, the congressional attitude that the class-action settlement had ended the need for government involvement in the Agent Orange issue was just a smoke screen. Had there been strong support in the White House during those years for Agent Orange compensation, the congressmen would have been singing a far different tune.

The Reagan White House, at least, was doing everything possible to sabotage such compensation. Whenever some worrisome scientific study came along, it was quickly discredited by Dr. Alvin Young, a former Air Force captain who had helped design the nozzles on the C-123 planes that sprayed Agent Orange, and who was eventually appointed to head the Agent Orange group at the White House Office of Science and Technology. There were many who believed Young had been assigned by Reagan to do "damage control." When the VA came out with its study showing that Marine Vietnam veterans were dying of lung and lymph-system cancers at an abnormally high rate, for example, Young announced from the White House that "the numbers are small; it just doesn't add up" and that the findings were "a statistical fluke." And when the Stellmans were doing their study, they encountered White House obstructionism at every turn. Richard Christian, the retired Army colonel who had been hired by the CDC to study military records of Agent Orange spraying, was forbidden by Reagan's Justice Department to even speak with them.

It later came out, in congressional hearings chaired by Representative Ted Weiss (D-N.Y.) in July 1989 that there had been considerable dissension inside the CDC over the issue of abandoning the Vietnam Experience Study (VES), and that many scientists there felt that good progress had been made toward establishing a correlation between exposure to Agent Orange and veterans' illness. The Weiss hearings revealed that many of the key decisions in framing the study came not from the study's supposed director at the CDC, Dr. Vernon Houk, but from the Agent Orange Working Group (AOWG) at the White House. The biggest bombshell, however, was the disclosure that the decision to cancel the study came directly from the White House, in the form of political pressure on Dr. Houk from both the Agent Orange Working Group and the Surgeon General's office. Although Dr. Houk denied such influence, documentary evidence was produced showing that the director of the CDC, Dr. James Mason, who was also the Assistant Surgeon General, had been "instructed" by AOWG in October 1987 "to begin the process of cancelling the contracts and closing out all activities to the Agent Orange Exposure Study."

Reagan's betrayal seems all the more craven when one reads the position papers that helped him get elected in 1980. Acting as champion of the armed forces, Reagan had gone so far, while running against Carter, as to promise immediate "temporary" medical care as well as "adequate compensation [in the long term] for veterans who were harmed" by Agent Orange. Through the uncovering of private memos, Richard Severo and Lewis Milford have traced Reagan's covert reversal on the Agent Orange issue. Reagan was first pressured by the VA's Agent Orange Advisory Committee to cancel a planned TV appearance inviting Vietnam veterans to get an Agent Orange exam at their local VA medical center. The VA feared national TV spots with that message would create "excessive workloads." What subsequently caused Reagan to cave in on the issue was a "directive" from the Office of Management and Budget (OMB). This memo (which was subsequently seen by Admiral Elmo Zumwalt as well) warned Reagan that the "incipient movement towards federally financed toxic substances compensation" posed "political difficulties of the highest order . . ." and threatened some of the nation's biggest corporations with potentially devastating tort liability.

However popular a cause, compensating Vietnam veterans for Agent Orange illnesses, OMB cautioned, would set a dangerous precedent that might end up bankrupting the government as future toxic claims continued to pour in. OMB's director, David Stockman, further warned Reagan that toxic substances compensation would derail the delicate balance the president sought to strike between tax cuts and large-scale defense spending—forcing the sacrifice of one or the other. OMB suggested Reagan create a secret cabinet-level working group to hinder Agent Orange compensation, and Severo and Milford find significant, if circumstantial, evidence that such a group did exist.

Numerous other instances would surface of pressure from the Reagan White House to shut the mouth of any individual or group that sought to question the official government position of Agent Orange's alleged harmlessness. Yet Ronald Reagan would be credited by former chairman of the Joint Chiefs of

Staff, General Colin Powell, at the 1996 Republican National Convention, with having "restored the dignity of the American soldier."[223]

6. "The Curses of Witches and Warlocks": The VA Tips the Scales, Then Admiral Zumwalt Cuts the Knot

For many veterans in the 1980s, it seemed that every avenue to Agent Orange compensation was effectively blocked by their own government. But there was one chink in the government's armor: Public Law 98-542, known as the Veterans' Dioxin and Radiation Exposure Compensation Act, which had been driven through Congress by the zeal of Tom Daschle in October 1984. The Dioxin Act required the VA to create an advisory committee of eleven scientists to review the entire body of literature on the health effects of phenoxyacetic acid herbicides (such as 2,4-D and 2,4,5-T) and their associated contaminants, the chlorinated dioxins. The advisory committee was also charged with drafting new rules to govern the VA's handling of Agent Orange compensation claims. These guidelines, along with the literature report, were to be delivered to Congress no later than July 1, 1985. The whole purpose of the act was to end the VA's blanket denial of Agent Orange claims and to compel the VA to use a more reasonable standard in adjudicating those claims. Up to that point, the VA had demanded veterans seeking compensation prove that Agent Orange had *caused* their illness. That strict standard, used in tort litigation to determine liability, was impossible for any veteran to meet. Moreover, it was far stricter than the standard used by the VA to decide any other service-connected disability claims.

The Dioxin Act instructed the VA to use its normal standard in deciding Agent Orange cases, which was to ask only that a "preponderance of the evidence" show a "statistically significant association" between the illness in question and the purported cause (exposure to dioxin). In practice the standard was usually even looser; in most cases, the VA simply required proof that a veteran's disability was incurred or aggravated while in the military, regardless of causation. Moreover, the Dioxin Law reaffirmed that an attitude of trust should prevail regarding veterans' claims, so that "when, after consideration of all evidence and material of record, there is an approximate balance of positive and negative evidence . . . the benefit of the doubt in resolving each such issue shall be given to the claimant." Giving Agent Orange victims the "benefit of the doubt" was about as far as possible from demanding they come into their local VA with a massive dossier establishing "cause and effect."

The problem, however, was that the VA chose to largely ignore Public Law 98-542. For its new Agent Orange Advisory Committee, the VA hand-picked only scientists who believed in the relative harmlessness of dioxin exposure. They were, in addition, all VA employees, though Congress had instructed the VA to use non-VA scientists for the literature review. The reports they read were selected by Dr. Lawrence Hobson, head of the VA's own Agent Orange Office. Hobson had spent years trying to convince people that the supposed dangers of Agent Orange were no more real than (in his words) "black magic . . . [the curses of] witches and warlocks." Then the VA all but guaranteed that Hobson's crew would fail to produce a comprehensive analysis of the dangers of Agent Orange, by limiting their *yearly* budget to $45,000 (about the cost of one good executive secretary)! Finally, flouting the plain intention of the Dioxin Act, the VA instructed its Veterans' Advisory Committee on Environmental Hazards (as it was officially titled) that the only diseases warranting service-connection were those for which dioxin exposure was already a scientifically proven cause.

Not surprisingly, the Advisory Committee considered a mere seven reports on the toxicity of dioxin (from over 1,000 available) before delivering its report to Congress the following July (1985). Also predictably, the committee determined that the only disease with any demonstrable connection to Agent Orange exposure was chloracne. Hence they recommended that only Vietnam veterans with chloracne be compensated under the new, formal Agent Orange disability guidelines (which differed not a whit from the old informal ones). Moreover, the VA would continue to insist that to be rated eligible for compensation, a veteran must have developed chloracne within three months of his exposure to Agent Orange in Vietnam—a condition which thus far had been met by only five veterans.

The two attorneys who had founded the National Veterans Law Center at American University as well as (a few years later) VVA's Legal Services, David Addlestone and Barton Stichman, decided they had a possible legal shot at the VA for outright breaking the law. They knew that since 1933 Congress had prohibited the courts from reviewing VA claims decisions; but they were also aware that federal courts in a few jurisdictions had recognized a narrow exception to that rule. The loophole was simple but usable: while the federal judiciary clearly could not dispute individual benefit decisions, some jurisdictions held that it was allowable to review the legality of VA regulations. On October 31, 1986, VVA Legal Services filed suit against the VA, on behalf of thirteen Vietnam veterans and their heirs, in the Northern District of California, one of the venues that recognized the loophole. The suit, known as *Nehmer et al. v. U.S. Veterans Administration,* challenged the VA's denial of tens of thousands of Agent Orange claims, alleging that the VA had disregarded both its own traditional principles of adjudication as well as the requirements set down in the Dioxin Act. The plaintiffs asked that the court strike down the VA's latest regulations, and thus void all the decisions that had been made in a wrongful manner; and they sought to compel the VA to abide by the wishes of Congress, which meant starting over and seeking recommendations from a truly independent and well-funded advisory committee.

The VA immediately tried to get the lawsuit transferred to the federal district court in Washington, D.C., which had always granted the VA complete judicial immunity. But the suit remained in California; and in December 1987 a liberal black judge, Thelton E. Henderson, certified the case as a class action. Henderson ruled that the suit would define the rights not only of all those who had already sought compensation for an Agent Orange–related illness, but also the rights of all those who might ever file a claim in the future.

The case came to trial in January 1989 in San Francisco. The lawyers for VVA Legal Services, as well as private attorney Linda Peterson who worked with them, lambasted the VA's Agent Orange policy from start to finish. They pointed out that the VA's Advisory Committee, mandated to make its deliberations public, had acted almost exclusively in secret. They also accused the VA of having relied on the results of seven studies, while ignoring a thousand others, without ever having determined what variables made one study more valuable than another. Perhaps most damning, the plaintiffs' attorneys revealed that of the roughly 20,000 veterans who had filed Agent Orange claims since 1985, when the VA's new regulations were put in place, not one had been granted compensation. The VA's Advisory Committee meetings were a "sham," Peterson told Judge Henderson: "The government had a pre-ordained result. . . . the committee was used as a rubber stamp."

Judge Henderson agreed with her completely in his ruling on May 3, 1989. In his 48-page decision, he accused the VA of having "sharply tipped the scales against veteran claimants." Not only had the VA imposed "an impermissibly demanding test for granting service-connection" for Agent Orange illnesses, wrote the judge, but it had "refused to give veterans the benefit of the doubt in meeting that demanding standard"; so that the two errors "compounded one another, as they increased both the *type* and the *level* of proof needed for veterans to prevail. . . ." Without going so far as to charge the VA with deliberate criminal action, Henderson reprimanded the agency for its clearly biased "misinterpretation" of the 1984 Dioxin Act. Anyone with sense, he implied, knew it was "very unlikely that Congress would legislate a system in which veterans would actually be made worse through the rule-making process."

Henderson ordered the VA to reconsider some 31,000 Agent Orange cases—a veritable logistical nightmare—but only after it went back and developed a new set of rules consistent with the intentions of the Dioxin Act. He directed the VA's Advisory Committee to peruse a broader range of the literature on dioxin, and he insisted that the VA's new guidelines must refer to all the diseases—not just chloracne—that were found to be associated with Agent Orange. The veterans' community braced for another big legal battle; but

Secretary Ed Derwinski of the newly created, cabinet-level Department of Veterans Affairs (DVA) repudiated the advice of a slew of die-hard VA bureaucrats who felt the VA should appeal. Eight days after the *Nehmer* decision, Derwinski announced that the VA was ready to comply with the law. President George Bush had only recently taken office, promising to create "a kinder, gentler America," and Derwinski said he could do no less for the nation's veterans.

Among those who appreciated his courtesy was Beverly Nehmer of Santa Cruz, the lead plaintiff in the case, whose Vietnam veteran husband, Daniel, had died of leukemia in 1978, leaving her to support a family on her own. Although a veteran's pension would ease her life, it would not bring back her childhood sweetheart, she said, nor erase the memories of how "real awful" life had been for her during his sickness and after his death, just as it still was, in many cases, for the hundreds of veterans and their families who had contacted her—to express their gratitude—after the lawsuit was filed.

Just prior to the *Nehmer* decision, Addlestone and Stichman terminated their role as VVA's in-house lawyers—largely because of political difficulties with the rightward-shifting organization—though they continued to do contract work for VVA until 1994. They began operating independently under the title of National Veterans Legal Services Project (NVLSP). NVLSP immediately applied to AOCAP for funding. From the time of the class-action settlement, Judge Weinstein had said one of his top priorities was to see some of the money used to create a "national legal center" for Vietnam veterans, which could help promote and defend their interests in the courts and with Congress and the VA. Headed by Addlestone and Stichman, who between them had several decades of experience practicing veterans' law, NVLSP seemed the perfect answer to the judge's wish. It received one of the first AOCAP grants in 1989, for just under a million dollars, and continued to receive yearly funding at nearly that level throughout the life of the program. NVLSP quickly took over the role of "watchdog" over the VA's Agent Orange rule-making process, and Rhoades would later credit the Legal Services Project with having become the "center piece" of AOCAP's support network.[224]

The *Nehmer* decision had opened a whole new vista of possibilities for Vietnam veterans to be helped by the VA, and NVLSP tried to push that advantage as far as possible. Their biggest fear was that the VA would conduct its re-review of the dioxin literature in much the same fashion as before, and come to exactly the same conclusions. In the four years since it had issued its preliminary guidelines, the Veterans' Advisory Committee on Environmental Hazards had plodded through only 67 more dioxin studies. By comparison, the Environmental Protection Agency had already reviewed over 700 such studies, and subjected their analysis to peer review by 34 prominent scientists from all walks of life. Members of the VA's Advisory Committee had already complained about the hopelessness of doing their job with the inadequate resources allotted them.

Derwinski, for all his goodwill, refused to change the membership of the Advisory Committee, although in August (1989) he did bring in one fresh viewpoint by hiring Admiral Elmo R. Zumwalt Jr. as a special consultant. Little did he know that his "special consultant" would change the entire dialectic of the Agent Orange issue well into the next century.

Zumwalt was chosen doubtless because he had appeal to both sides of the debate. Although he had opposed American ground involvement in the Vietnam War, he was held in the highest regard by professional military men and the old warhorses in Congress. An Annapolis graduate, he had served on the staff of Navy Secretary Paul Nitze, one of the key figures in Vietnam War policymaking in the days of LBJ; and with Nitze's backing, Zumwalt (the youngest admiral in Naval history) was appointed Commander of U.S. Navy Forces Vietnam in 1968. Two years later, he was called to serve in an even more prestigious post, as Chief of Naval Operations, from which he retired with honors in 1974—though he had already begun speaking out against Nixon and Kissinger. Zumwalt was a straight arrow. He had undying allegiance to his country, was a steadfast husband and father, and held himself to the strictest imaginable work ethic. Furthermore, his apparently limitless energy left other career officers feeling like laggards; his ability to go round the clock for weeks on end was equaled perhaps only by the legendary Colonel John Paul Vann. He had been credited with single-handedly modernizing the U.S. Navy—ending the discrimination against blacks and women in the higher command levels, for example, as well as eliminating a host of "demeaning and abrasive regulations" (as he called them) for sailors.

But Zumwalt's fate was also inextricably intertwined with that of Agent Orange. In Vietnam, Zumwalt had used U.S. Navy swift-boats in the many small rivers to effectively cut enemy supply lines from Cambodia. The biggest problem those boats had was getting ambushed from the thickly overgrown riverbanks, and so Zumwalt had eagerly ordered the spraying of Agent Orange to defoliate almost every area that was penetrated by his "brown-water navy." Zumwalt's son, Navy Lieutenant Elmo Zumwalt III, volunteered for duty in Vietnam, and commanded a swift-boat in the Coastal Surveillance Force. As such, the young Zumwalt was heavily exposed to Agent Orange, whose use had been ordered by his own father. In 1977, seven years after returning from Vietnam, Elmo III fathered a boy, Elmo Russell Zumwalt IV (called Russell), who soon manifested severe learning disabilities. Then in 1983 Elmo III developed a combination of non-Hodgkin's lymphoma and Hodgkin's disease that was so incredibly rare—like winning the biggest cancer lottery in the world— that his doctors believed it must have been caused by exposure to the dioxin in Agent Orange.

One can only imagine the horrific sense of irony both father and son must have felt. Both of them were convinced that Agent Orange was indeed responsible for this formerly athletic young man's sudden critical illness, as well as for young Russell's developmental problems; but during the five years that Elmo III fought for life, neither father nor son made any public denunciation of Agent Orange or the U.S. government's use of it. Not only did they wish to avoid appearing unpatriotic, but they also felt that there was not yet enough scientific evidence to make such an indictment. Moreover, Admiral Zumwalt always said he had four allegiances, to "duty, honor, intelligence, and compassion." As much as he felt compassion toward his own son, he also felt that he had had to act as he did—ordering the spraying of defoliant—out of duty to insure the safety of all the men he commanded. Even after the scientific evidence did arrive establishing Agent Orange as a virulent human toxin, Admiral Zumwalt did not repent of his use of it. To the very end, he affirmed that he "would order the spraying of Agent Orange again under similar circumstances, because in my judgment it kept thousands of American servicemen from being killed and maimed."

Nevertheless, Zumwalt's willingness to speak out about the dangers of herbicide use made him seem like a good ally to the Agent Orange activists, the Frank McCarthys and Wayne Wilsons. Derwinski must have thought he had the ideal figurehead to restore credibility to his much-maligned Veterans' Advisory Committee on Environmental Hazards. The only problem with that scenario was that Admiral Zumwalt took his new job seriously, as seriously as he had taken his earlier jobs of preventing a Communist takeover of South Vietnam and keeping his own men alive and well.

Yale law professor Peter Schuck had once imagined Jack Weinstein to be the only genius able to cut the Gordian knot of Agent Orange, but in truth that superior mind belonged not to Weinstein but to Elmo Zumwalt Jr. For nine months, Zumwalt did nothing but read thousands of pages of Agent Orange studies and reports, and confer about them daily with his own hand-picked team of assistants: an Air Force doctor from the Ranch Hand study; a Navy doctor; and three epidemiologists from the Fred Hutchinson Cancer Research Center in Seattle. For starters, the Air Force doctor showed him how the Ranch Hand conclusions were "inaccurate" and how they had been "changed for political reasons."

The scientists in charge of Ranch Hand had originally found that Ranch Handers (the Air Force personnel who flew the defoliant missions) were five times more likely to suffer serious health problems than non–Ranch Hand veterans in the control group. They also found that major birth defects among Ranch Hand children were double those of children in the control group, and that the children Ranch Handers sired after returning from Vietnam showed a significantly higher rate of birth defects than those sired before their tour overseas. But after the White House Agent Orange Working Group (WHAOWG) got its hands on the initial draft of their report, much of the evidence had been omitted and their conclusions were altered substantially (the birth defects were construed as "minor," for example) so that the Ranch Hand study could then be used to exonerate, rather than condemn, Agent Orange as the culprit that was sickening Vietnam veterans. Hence the Air Force's Deputy Surgeon General, Murphy Chesney, had called the report "reassuring" to veterans, and the chemical manufacturers had even cited it to Judge Weinstein as "irrefutable proof" of their innocence.

The chemical companies were not above cooking their own reports, to bolster the ones the government had cooked for them. Zumwalt was shocked to find that several of the studies that were cited most often by the government to prove dioxin's nontoxicity had been "fraudulently" concocted by none other than one of the world's greatest dioxin producers, the Monsanto Corporation. While the Admiral condemned such "deception and fraud," he also condemned the more insidious "political interference" that managed to alter the conclusions of even aboveboard studies. The problem was that every government committee or scientific panel always seemed to contain one or more members who received some financial benefit from the chemical industry. Zumwalt explains: "I found that as you went through the documents [of the Veterans' Advisory Committee], you could find case after case where a group of scientists, the members, would come close to deciding that a study showed a positive correlation between exposure to Agent Orange or dioxin and disease—and that then the three doctors who were associated with corporations in one way or another would maneuver the consensus away from a positive finding to an indeterminate finding. Or if the study were coming out indeterminate, they would maneuver that to a negative finding. The scientists who went through the documents with me strongly agreed and came out infuriated at the pseudoscience that that represented."

Zumwalt continues: "It's right in the transcript of the [EPA] hearings, one of the corporate doctors says words to this effect: 'Those of us who find bread being put on our table by corporations should be forgiven if sometimes our professional judgments seem not to correlate with those of others.' It's just that blatant as to what goes on with the corporate hiring of scientists and the reports that those scientists come out with!"

The true data from the Ranch Hand study only came to light ten years later when Tom Daschle, now a senator from South Dakota, forced the Air Force to release it. No one could tell how far up the line this criminal lying actually went; but, good American that he still considered himself, Zumwalt was determined to put an end to it. On May 5, 1990, the admiral issued a report that blasted the U.S. government's "systematic effort to suppress critical data or alter results to meet preconceived notions of what alleged scientific studies were meant to find." Zumwalt posited that if you "threw out all the fraudulent studies and looked just at the legitimate studies, you would conclude that there are twenty-eight diseases for which it is as likely as not that there is a correlation [with exposure to Agent Orange]." He asked the Secretary of Veterans Affairs to "resolve doubts in favor of the Vietnam veteran" in service-connecting those twenty-eight diseases. Zumwalt further recommended that the Veterans' Advisory Committee on Environmental Hazards be disestablished as "fraudulent," that its current members be dismissed for their "disturbing bias," and that a new system (with new people) be set up to review further veteran Agent Orange claims. He even asked the secretary to cancel his [Derwinski's] upcoming meeting with the Advisory Committee, scheduled for May 16 and 17. Finally, the admiral advised Derwinski that he alone should make his own "independent evaluation of the existing scientific and medical evidence on the health effects of exposure to dioxins," to avoid once again being swayed by biased so-called experts.

In his conclusion, Zumwalt urged Derwinski to act decisively to end "the embarrassingly prolonged Agent Orange controversy." He urged the secretary to seize "the opportunity finally to right a significant national wrong committed against our Vietnam veterans."

A decade after its release, Zumwalt would still be waiting for the full implementation of the recommendations in his report. But its effects were tremendous nonetheless. It has remained like a dagger pointed at each successive VA chief who might otherwise try to ignore the injuries and suffering wrought by Agent Orange.

In an April 1999 lecture, Zumwalt demonstrated that science was still bending to the will of the chemical industry. In October 1998, for example, the Toxicology Committee that advises the National Institute of Environmental Health voted to make dioxin a "known carcinogen." But in December, lobbying pressure on the members of the Toxicology Committee forced another vote, and dioxin's status was changed from a "known" to a "probable carcinogen." In another case that Zumwalt cited, the EPA's dioxin reassessment committee had recently come out with a draft report declaring dioxin a "known carcinogen," but, he said, "we can't get the report published because the lobbying continues." He thus dedicated the remainder of his own life to make the truth known, through his own corporation—which, among other things, funded dioxin research in Vietnam—and the Agent Orange Coordinating Council he chaired. But this last battle was his toughest, he admitted, because "there is a powerful corporate interest group fighting our veterans on this, [spending] hundreds of millions of dollars. . . ."

"We now have thirteen diseases compensated," Zumwalt said, weary but undaunted at almost eighty years old, "and if I live, we'll get very close to that twenty-eight."

Unfortunately, the admiral fell suddenly ill in October 1999 and was diagnosed with mesothelioma, a cancerous tumor in his chest cavity that forced the removal of one lung. His doctors felt it might have been caused by exposure to asbestos in his early years in the Navy. On January 2, 2000, Elmo R. Zumwalt Jr. died of complications following surgery, leaving much of his work still unfinished.[225]

7. A New Standard for Veterans Is Created . . . by a New War

During those nine months that Admiral Zumwalt was doing his homework on dioxin, the VA inched ever so slowly toward helping chemically afflicted Vietnam veterans. On October 2, 1989, obeying the *Nehmer* ruling, the VA issued new criteria for service-connecting Agent Orange–related maladies based on a "significant statistical association" between those maladies and exposure to dioxin. But that alone hardly seemed enough to develop a whole new Agent Orange policy, given the entrenched skepticism of so many VA officials and scientists regarding Vietnam veteran health claims.

The National Veterans Legal Services Project (NVLSP) went to both VVA and the American Legion for help in creating an independent Agent Orange Scientific Task Force. Seven non-VA scientists agreed to donate their work on the project. They reviewed many more reports than the ninety being looked at by the VA Advisory Committee, and they evaluated the VA committee's methodology, finding it severely wanting. The Advisory Committee was simply classifying studies as "positive" or "negative"—i.e., showing an association between dioxin exposure and disease, or failing to show such an association— or else "invalid" or "inconclusive." The independent Task Force attempted to "synthesize all available data," so that each study contributed (some more, some less) to an "aggregate meaning."

While the Task Force deliberated, the official Advisory Committee met on October 31, 1989, to revise its opinion on the first disease under consideration: non-Hodgkin's lymphoma (the one that had killed Zumwalt's son, though they had not bothered to ask for his input). The meeting was a disaster. Dr. Colton protested that there was no way they could balance ninety different studies by arguing for half a day. Another member suggested they "go with their gut reactions." Various words and phrases were bandied about: "nonassociational," "can't rule out an association," "maybe . . . an association," "not convinced," etc. Of the nine members who had showed up, only five voted; two voted for the existence of an association, three against. But one absent member, Dr. James Neel, had sent a note saying he'd found an association "as likely as not." The vote was thus tied, but the committee was too nervous to put its neck on the line by giving veterans "the benefit of the doubt," as the judge had told them to. Instead they chalked a few words about insufficient evidence on the room's blackboard, then had someone copy that fragmentary assessment onto paper and xerox it as their official pronouncement.

As noncommittal as Pilate, the Advisory Committee neither found a significant statistical association nor ruled one out. A month later, they told Derwinski they could not recommend for service-connecting non-Hodgkin's lymphoma, though neither were they certain that service-connection should be denied— leaving him as confused as before about what to do.

In March 1990, as Derwinski continued to procrastinate his decision, NVLSP's Task Force issued its own report. They concluded that there was unquestionably a significant statistical association between exposure to dioxin and five illnesses: 1) non-Hodgkin's lymphoma; 2) soft-tissue sarcoma; 3) chloracne and related skin disorders; 4) certain "subclinical" liver problems; and 5) porphyria cutanea tarda. Furthermore, they found that there was at least as much evidence for as against a significant statistical association concerning three more categories of illness: 1) Hodgkin's disease; 2) neurologic effects; and 3) reproductive and developmental effects (in veterans' children). "For each of these [latter three] health effects," they wrote, "there are sound scientific studies showing statistical significance and strong scientific evidence of an association between exposure and effect." By the standards laid down by Judge Henderson, all eight of those disorders qualified for disability compensation and should have been service-connected.

The Task Force added yet another category. It found that there was "sound scientific evidence" which did not yet "reach the level of formal statistical significance" of an association between dioxin exposure and an even larger range of diseases, which included leukemias; cancers of the kidney, testes, pancreas, stomach, prostate, colon, hepatobiliary tract, and brain; psychological disorders; immunological abnormalities; gastrointestinal ulcer; and altered lipid metabolism. The Task Force not only recommended more research in these areas; it also suggested that if veterans were indeed to be given the benefit of the doubt, the VA ought to go the whole way and compensate all of these health effects, until further evidence should indicate otherwise.

The Vietnam Veterans in Congress, together with leaders of VVA and the American Legion, recommended Secretary Derwinski act on the Task Force's conclusions. Late in the month, while Derwinski pondered what to do, the CDC released its own Selected Cancers Study, which had been part of the original cluster of studies pertaining to the health effects of military service in Vietnam. Although all the studies based on exposure to Agent Orange had been dropped, the CDC had still felt it possible to assess whether Vietnam veterans were at greater risk of contracting various cancers than other veterans. The latest CDC results showed that the rate of non-Hodgkin's lymphoma among Vietnam veterans was 50 percent higher than among their Vietnam-era veteran peers. Although the CDC made no claim that the disease's increase among Vietnam veterans was due to herbicide exposure, Derwinski decided it was time for the nation to stop fighting its own warriors. Rejecting the recommendations of his Advisory Committee, he announced that death and disability compensation for non-Hodgkin's lymphoma would be granted to all Vietnam veterans, regardless of when they contracted the disease.

A watershed had finally been crossed, twelve years after Paul Reutershan had pointed his finger back at Uncle Sam's chemical-stained hands. The government had finally admitted that it had harmed the health of at least some veterans by sending them to Vietnam. The numbers were relatively small. Eighteen hundred Vietnam veterans currently suffered from non-Hodgkin's lymphoma; and about 450 new cases manifested each year. But the impact of having finally won a major battle gave many veterans, especially the longtime activists, a desperately needed psychological boost. It made it possible to carry on in spite of the many remaining, painful realities. One such reality was Derwinski's refusal to even comment about the possibility that these veterans had been sickened by Agent Orange. Another such reality were the tens of thousands of Vietnam veterans dead or dying from all those other cancers and dioxin-related diseases still uncompensated.

The VA's Advisory Committee, apparently sobered by the sudden turn of events (and perhaps by Zumwalt's report as well), reported to Derwinski in May 1990 that there was a significant statistical association between exposure to dioxin and soft-tissue sarcomas—a group of about twenty-five malignancies of muscle, fat, blood vessels, and connective tissue. A landmark in its own right, that decision was the committee's first admission of any dioxin-caused disease besides chloracne. Derwinski acted the next day to service-connect soft-tissue sarcomas for all Vietnam veterans. This meant another 1,100 veterans and their heirs would begin collecting compensation immediately; and all new claimants, about fifty a year, would be eligible as well.

The U.S. government finally began to assume a little of the cost of the loss and pain of its Vietnam veterans—to the tune of $104 million in the first two years of compensation for non-Hodgkin's lymphoma and soft-tissue sarcoma.

The Vietnam Veterans in Congress now had substantial ammunition to get a new Agent Orange bill passed. Among their latest weaponry was a report released by the House Committee on Government Operations on August 9, 1990. That report, written largely by Subcommittee on Human Resources Chair Ted Weiss (D-N.Y.), documented a high-level conspiracy within the Reagan administration to kill the possibility of Agent Orange compensation. The report quoted various memos of Mike Horowitz of the Office of Management and Budget to his boss, OMB director David Stockman, and to Attorney General Edwin Meese.

In those memos, just as in the "directive" that Zumwalt had seen, Horowitz warned of "the enormous fiscal implications" of compensating Agent Orange victims. To compensate Vietnam veterans for chemical poisoning, he felt, would set a precedent that might well lead to government compensation for all such toxic victims—from the so-called "atomic vets" of the forties (the troops intentionally exposed by the military to radiation from nuclear weapons' fallout) to civilians inadvertently poisoned by government carelessness, like the citizens of Times Beach, Missouri. Envisioning "hundreds of billions of dollars" pouring from the U.S. Treasury for such purposes, Horowitz advised Stockman and Meese to organize a covert opposition to Tom Daschle's Agent Orange compensation bill of 1984. That opposition took the form of the White House Agent Orange Working Group (AOWG) pushing to stop the CDC's Vietnam Experience Study (VES) and otherwise plotting to cover up the truth about Agent Orange—which it was the Working Group's ostensible job to uncover! White House paranoia about Vietnam veteran claims ran so high that—in another exchange of memos quoted in Weiss's report—one OMB staffer cautioned against testing the dioxin level in veterans' blood because of the "legal risks" of incurring lawsuits from those veterans whose blood tested unnaturally high in the toxin.

When a government had come to fear the very people it existed to serve—in this case, people who had gambled their own lives to preserve its existence—things had clearly gone too far. Nor could Congress ignore the insult of an executive branch trying to bias its judgment by consciously feeding it false, or at best incomplete, information. By 1990, moreover, Congress's record of failing Vietnam veterans was being assailed by the most respectable of sources. In March, VVA's new president, Mary Stout, who had taken over from Bobby Muller, complained that it had taken a 50 percent increase in the incidence of non-Hodgkin's lymphoma for Vietnam veterans to win compensation. At the rate of one disease compensated in a dozen years, she pointed out, most sick Vietnam veterans would not live to see their particular illness added to the list. The National Commander of the American Legion, Miles S. Epling, likewise chided DAV Secretary Derwinski (and by implication, Congress) to pick up the pace, lamenting that after more than a decade they had only taken "one small step toward resolution of this problem." In a rare outburst of anger, Epling also blasted the CDC's conclusion, which Derwinski had parroted to the press, that there was still "not . . . any evidence that the increased risk [of non-Hodgkin's lymphoma] might be due to Agent Orange exposure."

Throughout 1990, Senator Thomas Daschle (D-S.Dak.) and Representative Lane Evans (D-Ill.), current chairman of the VVIC, worked on new Agent Orange legislation. To start, they sought to disband the VA's own Advisory Committee, as Zumwalt had recommended, and to provide congressional funding for the National Academy of Sciences to review the whole body of scientific literature on dioxin. Though the NAS had been established by an act of Congress, to serve as a scientific advisor to the U.S. government, its members could not draw a government salary and were thus independent of government control. Once the NAS had announced its findings, the Secretary of Veterans

Affairs would be required to draft a new set of Agent Orange compensation rules. In addition, Daschle and Evans' bill codified Derwinski's decisions on non-Hodgkin's lymphoma and soft-tissue sarcoma, so that a subsequent DVA secretary could not reverse his compensation policy for those diseases. It also codified the requirement that the VA "apply the benefit of the doubt principle" when deciding veterans' claims.

Most innovatively, Daschle and Evans sought to change the scientific standard by which veterans' claims were adjudged. The Agent Orange Scientific Task Force's report had argued that the VA's former requirement, "significant statistical association," was virtually meaningless when dealing with dioxin and other rare but potent, man-made toxins. To find such associations between exposure and health effects, studies had to be capable of measuring almost impossibly small amounts of these chemicals, and they also had to have access to large populations known to have been exposed to them. In the case of dioxin, such large populations had yet to be identified, and the procedures for detecting potentially harmful doses were prohibitively expensive. Therefore, the Task Force had recommended that a new standard be employed for Agent Orange complaints: "positive association," which it defined as an amount of "credible evidence . . . equal to or outweigh[ing] the credible evidence against the association." That was the standard Daschle and Evans mandated the VA to use in their new Agent Orange Act.

The situation was ripe for this new legislation, but Congress faltered again on the one-yard line. In July 1990, the Senate Veterans' Affairs Committee reported on an early version of the bill, but it never came to a vote before the outgoing 101st Congress. In October, the House passed a different version, which then stalled in the Senate. Daschle and Evans' bill did not pass both houses of Congress until the end of January 1991. On February 7, George Bush's signature turned it into Public Law 102-4. But the sudden prompt attention given the bill by the incoming 102nd Congress, and the now settled-in 41st president, did *not* represent a governmental change of heart toward Vietnam veterans.[226]

8. A New Generation of Veterans Learns from the Unfinished Business of the Last One

On August 2, 1990, Mideast politics had been profoundly altered by Iraq's invasion and occupation of its small but wealthy neighbor, Kuwait. After years of economic and military support to Iraq's dictator, Saddam Hussein, the United States government now targeted him as its foremost enemy—a dire threat to its supply of Mideast oil. George Bush, who had yet to forge a strong presidential image, gained prestige as the nation's tough-talking commander in chief. He backed up this "bare-knuckled" posture (as the *Christian Science Monitor* termed it) with a rapid, impressive military response, which included the dispatch of 200,000 American troops to the Persian Gulf as part of Operation Desert Shield. For the next five months, the so-called "Gulf crisis" took a precipitous slide toward outright war.

Bush had one big problem, however, in convincing the nation to take up arms against Iraq: the "Vietnam syndrome." That phrase, apparently coined by jingoist Republican politicos, referred to a widespread antipathy to military ventures on foreign shores, along with a fear that American troops, if fighting for anything but the nation's own protection, would surely get bogged down in another quagmire of internal divisiveness, turncoat allies, and fatally hemorrhaging morale.

Indeed, a movement to stop the Gulf War sprang up before the war even began, and many of its leaders were Vietnam veterans. One of the first to speak out was writer Ron Kovic, who was riding the crest of worldwide fame after the huge splash of Oliver Stone's movie about him, *Born on the Fourth of July*. On August 22, 1990, Kovic read his "Open Letter to the President" in a Santa Monica church. In it, he explicitly called on Bush to remember the lessons of Vietnam, saying: "My life is a living example of the devastation and loss that can result from a miscalculated, deceptive and secret foreign policy." He also demanded that Bush consider the unfinished business of America's last war, the veterans, like himself, who still had not fully healed, before putting a new generation through the same experience. The Vietnam War, asserted Kovic, "left countless [veterans] . . . wandering the streets of this country, stunned and distressed with no one to help them, to care for their needs, or show concern for the savage wounds inflicted upon them by our foreign policy. . . . They were neglected and abandoned by the very government and people that sent them to Vietnam."

Moreover, it wasn't just radical antiwar activist vets like Kovic who spoke out against the coming Gulf War. Retired Army Colonel David Hackworth, who had earned 110 medals during twenty-five years of military service and two wars, and whom the *Washington Post* called a "soldier's soldier," warned in *Newsweek* that "wars like the Gulf, like Vietnam, like Korea, are damned easy to get into, hard to get out of, and the pain and the hurt never go away." West Pointer and former general staff officer at MACV, John Wheeler, who as chairman of the Vietnam Veterans Memorial Fund had done more to make the Wall a reality than anyone except Jan Scruggs, told Congress it could not afford to pay the price of another major war like Vietnam, especially when one counted in the coming decades of "medical care for the wounded." Perhaps the most surprising voice of conscience was Eugene "Red" McDaniel, a highly respected Vietnam POW who'd spent six years in the "Hanoi Hilton," and who'd later founded the conservative American Defense Institute. McDaniel felt it criminal for the U.S. government to embark upon another war when it had not yet accounted for all the men it had lost in the last one. "All the servicemen preparing for war in the Gulf," he told *USA Today* in November, "know the government might abandon them."

On January 16, 1991, Desert Shield became Desert Storm, as Bush unleashed the full terror of America's high-tech weaponry (everything from smart bombs to M1-A1 tanks clad with depleted uranium) against the out-of-date Iraqi forces. Despite tremendous early American successes in routing and slaughtering the enemy, the antiwar movement in the United States grew by leaps and bounds—largely because more and more prominent leaders of the Vietnam peace movement, like Daniel Ellsberg, Noam Chomsky, and Ramsey Clark, came forward to condemn the Gulf War, and to situate that condemnation on the moral high ground they had won in the sixties. Even more remarkable was that the Gulf War triggered powerful emotional reactions in many Vietnam veterans who had never yet communicated their war experiences to anyone; and many of these veterans were moved to speak out publicly about the horrors of war for the first time in their life, joining their voices with more typical left-wing activists in organizations like the Bay Area's Committee Against a Vietnam War in the Middle East (CAVME).

What surely worried the Gulf War's commanders and government supporters most of all was the potential for a massive troop revolt, based on the kind of GI resistance that had developed slowly during the Vietnam War. That revolt was now springing up with a lightning speed because of the encouragement of those who had paid the dues (and survived the odium) of such dissent decades earlier. Among the leaders of the anti–Gulf War movement were three articulate young Marines who had refused to be sent to the Persian Gulf (as had dozens more of their comrades): two of them tall, all-American-looking white youths, Jeff Paterson and Erik Larsen, and one (clearly even more dangerous) an African-American from Oakland named Tahan Jones. Like a cooler and more cynical rap version of Al Hubbard, Jones calmly ticked off the horrific facts. "Black soldiers died in disproportionate numbers in Vietnam," he said, and now during the Gulf War they were still viewed as the military's most likely "cannon fodder"—while black people at home were "victimized [once again] by police brutality, disproportionate unemployment, high infant mortality, lack of decent and affordable housing, decreasing life expectancy, escalating incarceration rates, high drop-out rates, and [most recently] AIDS." The government threw its full prosecutorial weight against such young men, but could not dissuade them from spreading their message that "blood is more precious than oil."

Moreover, not only were there soldiers refusing to fight, but this time—for the first time in American history—there was a nationwide organization of families advocating to keep their children out of combat. That organization was the Military Families Support Network (MFSN), founded by Alex Molnar in

Milwaukee, whose Marine son Chris served honorably in the Gulf War. Molnar had published a letter to President Bush in the *New York Times* in August 1990, in which he excoriated Bush for continuing to play golf in Kennebunkport (his retreat in Maine) after having ordered a whole new generation of working-class kids to Saudi Arabia to defend "the American way of life." Molnar received back thousands of letters in response, and enough financial support to give his organization a powerful presence on Capitol Hill throughout the war, and for many months afterward. In fact, it was the Military Families Support Network, in their quarterly newsletter, that first broke the story of what came to be called Gulf War syndrome, and it was the MFSN that first lobbied Congress to create a registry of Gulf War syndrome victims, similar to the Agent Orange registry.

A lot of the criticism of the Gulf War was directed against Congress, which once again had allowed a president to take America into an undeclared war. There was enormous pressure for congressmen to show their patriotism and support for "men and women in uniform," especially when it was revealed that our Gulf troops might be subjected to the horrifying chemical weapons in Iraq's arsenal. Daschle and Evans, seeing their opponents' vulnerability, struck quickly. How could congressmen oppose compensation for Agent Orange illnesses, they asked, when they might now be responsible for servicemen in the Gulf suffering similar toxic injuries? One of the chief arguments used to get the Agent Orange Act passed was that it "would establish a process for deciding claims pressed by American military personnel exposed to possible chemical or biological substances used against U.S.-led forces by Iraqi President Saddam Hussein." For the first time ever, the House and Senate voted unanimously (on January 29 and 30 respectively) to guarantee compensation for veterans who were victims of Agent Orange. Representative Sonny Montgomery (D-Miss.), who had staunchly opposed similar legislation only a year earlier, stood behind George Bush (for the benefit of cameramen) when he signed the bill into law on February 6, 1991. In voting for the Agent Orange Act, Montgomery said he hoped to "salve the bitterness, anxiety, and disappointment which have engulfed both this issue and the earnest attempts to respond to our Vietnam veterans' concerns in a fair and rational manner." He did not appear aware of the pun.[227]

The irony compounded even further when servicepeople back from the Gulf did indeed begin to manifest mysterious health problems similar to those caused by Agent Orange, and the U.S. government immediately denied (just as it had with Vietnam vets) that such problems were real. Nine years later, dozens of causes have been proposed—low levels of sarin or other nerve gases released when enemy bunkers were destroyed; radioactive smoke and dust from the explosion of depleted-uranium (DU) munitions; dioxin from burning oil wells; a precautionary nerve gas pill, pyridostigmine bromide, given to all American troops in combat zones. As with Vietnam vets, the only thing for sure is that tens of thousands of vets are sick; everything else is still being argued.

And while the argument goes on, people's lives deteriorate to a ghost of what they once were: jobs are lost, marriages break up, joy and hope are drowned in endless misery and complaint, and even friends turn away. The aftermath of Vietnam has been mirrored down to the smallest details, including the panels of experts who at this point have spent over $100 million contradicting one another.

On November 13, 1996, President Clinton's Advisory Committee on Gulf War Veterans' Illnesses released a draft of its final report. After fifteen months of study, the so-called "White House panel" found no evidence that Gulf War veterans were dying or falling seriously ill in unusual numbers, and declared (shades of the old White House Agent Orange Working Group) that "psychological stress is likely a major contributing factor to the broad range of illnesses"—i.e., the sicknesses vets reported were either in, or caused by, their heads. Furthermore, the White House Panel ruled out Iraqi chemical or biological weapons as a cause of most of the illnesses. A week later, however, the Department of Veterans Affairs' Persian Gulf Expert Scientific Committee concluded that the White House panel had been irresponsible in writing off "the widespread exposure [of American troops] to chemicals during the war" as a health hazard. The White House panel, accused the DVA's experts, "had rushed to judgment in singling out the physical ailments resulting from battlefield stress as the explanation for many of the ailments experienced by Gulf War veterans." Then the following week, the CDC and the Navy announced the results of their own studies. The CDC study, based on the health records of 4,000 Gulf War vets, and the Navy study of 1,500 sailors both determined that Gulf War vets were falling sick at a much higher rate than their peers who did not go to war, and that their illnesses were often disabling, though usually not fatal or even of a severity to require hospitalization.

Just as in the Agent Orange scenario, the U.S. government (according to one journalist) trembled at the possible "financial repercussions" of these new findings—and with good reason. By the end of 1996, over 80,000 Gulf War veterans (out of a total of 700,000) had sought medical examinations from the VA because of unexplained health problems. By the end of 1999, that figure had risen to over 100,000. A totally disabled veteran whose disability is service-connected now receives about $26,000 yearly in tax-free government compensation. Should all 100,000 of those Gulf War vets become 100 percent disabled—and should their disability be recognized as service-connected—the cost to the government would be over $2.5 billion a year! Though odds are against all 100,000 winning such entitlement, the cost of compensating Gulf War veterans may still become an enormous burden as time goes on, justifying the warning of John Wheeler—scoffed at by most congressmen in the fall of 1990—that a war in the Gulf might easily cost the United States three times as much as the $300 billion it spent on Vietnam.

Early on, the Gulf War vets realized that the government was not going to give ground without a fight. They turned to Vietnam veteran activists for support and guidance, especially those in VVA. Inspired by the organizational models forged by Vietnam veterans, several hundred Gulf War vets met in Dallas in February 1995. Out of that conference, the National Gulf War Resource Center (NGWRS) was founded a few months later in Washington, D.C. "There's no doubt," said NGWRS President Chris Kornkven in 2000, "if it weren't for the Vietnam veterans we wouldn't be nearly as far as we are now."

In 1998, a second presidential commission (the Presidential Special Oversight Board) was established, chaired by former New Hampshire senator and Korean War veteran Warren Rudman, to look objectively at the new evidence of "chemical and biological incidents" in the Gulf War. But when the interim report of Rudman's commission, released in August 1999, appeared to discount many of the most likely causes of Gulf War veterans' illness, veteran activists again felt they were getting sandbagged and some claimed that "money had a lot to do" with the commission's conclusions.

Meantime, in a familiar refrain, Deputy Defense Secretary John White called for the National Academy of Sciences (NAS) to resolve this latest controversy over sick veterans. In 1998, thanks again to the work of Illinois Representative Lane Evans, Congress passed the Persian Gulf War Veterans Act. This law mandated the Department of Veterans Affairs once more to seek guidance from the NAS in terms of possible causative agents for what is loosely called Gulf War syndrome. A previous (1996) law had provided for the DVA to treat and compensate "undiagnosed illness" in Gulf War veterans, but the DVA got around it much of the time, says Chris Kornkven, by giving Gulf War vets "frivolous diagnoses" that had little to do with their actual health problems. As it was instructed, the DVA asked the NAS's Institute of Medicine to begin a study of all available literature on the various biologic and chemical agents to which Gulf War vets were exposed; and after some prodding, the DVA actually began granting compensation to a small percentage of sick Gulf War vets. But this process was again hindered, says Kornkven, by DVA Secretary Togo West's failure to seat a Gulf War Advisory Committee, which was also mandated by the 1998 law, and which was supposed to include Gulf War vets, who at this point are still "locked out" of the decision-making. A new law before Congress, introduced by Wisconsin congresswoman Tammy Baldwin, would establish a "National Post-Deployment Health Research Center," which would provide an avenue for the nation's veterans to have direct input into the study and determination of their own health problems.

Gulf War veteran and activist Dan Fahey explains the need for such measures: "With depleted uranium, this is a weapon that we're not only increasing the use of it [ourselves], but we're selling it, mostly to Middle East countries, and we don't want to admit that there could be any negative effects from using it. . . . There was a combination of toxic exposures in the Gulf, but it all points toward: *this is modern warfare.* And we need to understand this, because we're going to be fighting wars like this again in this [the twenty-first] century, and we need to understand, when we expose people to these types of substances, what kind of problems are going to result, and then be there to take care of people. . . . Many of these substances affect civilians too."

But Fahey also warns that, just as with Agent Orange, there has been a continuing effort by the Department of Defense to "stonewall" the whole issue—to deny its very existence, to fiddle with the numbers of exposed vets, and, in the case of depleted uranium, even to rewrite its own reports and regulations to downplay the potential toxic dangers that had been warned against *before* the war. According to Fahey, the head of the Pentagon's Gulf War Illnesses Office, Bernard Rostker, keeps insisting "We don't need more [scientific] research" even as Congress, the DVA, numerous veterans' groups, and even the military's own investigators are crying out for such research. Fahey has also been busy writing to the United Nations Human Rights Commission in Geneva and other entities that oversee international law, to lobby for the establishment of a global code of conduct in the use of such new, quasi-chemical weapons as depleted uranium. Because such weapons may well result in "superfluous injury or unnecessary suffering" to civilian populations, Fahey believes they are possibly already in violation of earlier Geneva Convention protocols. "In Iraq and most recently in Kosovo," he points out, "the Department of Defense has failed to warn civilian populations and relief agencies about the presence and hazards of depleted-uranium contamination. To the best of my knowledge, the Pentagon has denied any responsibility for identifying areas of DU contamination or conducting any post-conflict clean up."

Even with regard to our own Gulf War veterans, Fahey feels a lot of wrongs still have not been righted. He speaks of the latency period associated with many chemically induced illnesses, especially the cancers, and points out that while the DVA can now compensate a Gulf War veteran's "undiagnosed illness" it still cannot compensate any specific illness he or she came down with after the war. Nor is there likely to be a specific category for Gulf War illnesses added to the DVA's medical lexicon any time soon. As the National Academy of Sciences' Institute of Medicine warned Fahey in a recent letter (January 11, 2000): "The committee [on health effects of the Gulf War] has not been constituted to determine an etiology (cause) for Gulf War Illnesses or to determine whether or not there is a unique Gulf War Syndrome." In the case of Gulf War vets, NAS's study of peer-reviewed literature may not lead directly to a compensation program, as it has with Vietnam veterans exposed to Agent Orange, simply because there is still no agreement even as to which toxic agents Gulf War vets were exposed to.

*   *   *

The National Academy of Sciences has certainly made a big difference in terms of compensation for Agent Orange victims. The Agent Orange Act of 1991 established a new mechanism for adding (or deleting) presumptions of service connection for herbicide-related illnesses, based on the findings of the new sixteen-member Agent Orange panel of NAS's Institute of Medicine. If the NAS found a positive association between exposure to dioxin and a particular disease, the secretary of the DVA was required to award compensation to sufferers of that disease within 60 days of the finding, or else justify his refusal to do so.

Attorneys for the National Veterans Legal Service Project (NVLSP) had made that provision in the new law even more lucrative for affected veterans, by forcing the DVA to agree (in a consent decree) to pay such benefits retroactively to the date on which a claim had initially been filed or the date of disability or death, whichever was later. But the DVA tried to get around that provision also, says NVLSP codirector Bart Stichman, by only honoring claims in which Vietnam veterans had themselves used "the magic word *Agent Orange.*" In fact, NVLSP had originally advised Vietnam veterans *not* to refer to Agent Orange in their claims because mention of the defoliant often prejudiced VA staff against a veteran's case. Hence most of the original claims did not cite Agent Orange as a cause of illness, giving the DVA an easy rationale for denying retroactive compensation. Addlestone and Stichman had to go back to court again to get the DVA to adhere to the consent decree—which said nothing about a veteran having to identify Agent Orange as the cause of his health problems—and once again (in February 1999) they got a favorable ruling from Judge Henderson, in a decision referred to as *Nehmer 2*.

With a million-dollar budget, the NAS Agent Orange panel spent eighteen months reviewing 6,400 abstracts of scientific and medical articles and analyzing 230 epidemiological studies. Their findings, released in July 1993, differed significantly from conclusions of the VA's own (underfunded and now disbanded) Agent Orange committee. In addition to non-Hodgkin's lymphoma and soft-tissue sarcoma, the NAS panel found a positive association between dioxin exposure and both Hodgkin's disease and porphyria cutanea tarda (PCT), a liver dysfunction. DVA secretary Jesse Brown, himself a disabled black Marine Vietnam veteran, announced that Vietnam veterans would immediately be eligible for compensation for Hodgkin's disease and PCT. Brown, who had come up through the Disabled American Veterans' excellent leadership program, declared that he was "committed to taking a fresh look at the issue and to doing the right thing"; but it took another nudge from the NVLSP—in the form of a legal brief suggesting the DVA was about to violate Public Law 102-4—for

Brown to go another step further, in October, and add bone-marrow cancer and the three most common respiratory cancers to the list of compensable illnesses, based on other recent NAS findings.

Another victory NVLSP won was a court order requiring the VA to send notices to the 200,000-plus veterans on its Agent Orange registry, apprising those individuals that they might benefit from the recent changes in compensation rules. In late 1993, the DVA projected that these changes alone would cost the government in excess of $450 million over a five-year period. Partly due to the urging of the NAS, several new studies to assess the health effects of Agent Orange were undertaken, at a cost of over $60 million. As the 1990s progressed, the NAS expanded its Agent Orange committee, which continued to collect and review the ever-growing body of literature on dioxin.

Gaining less than a rung a year, Vietnam veterans slowly climbed the ladder of service connection for Agent Orange illnesses. Nevertheless, when Clinton granted compensation for prostate cancer and peripheral neuropathy, in mid-1996, many veterans, including Admiral Elmo Zumwalt Jr., openly expressed their gratitude. Secretary Jesse Brown calmly acknowledged the DVA was biting off an obligation to pay Vietnam veterans at least another $350 million over the next five years; and that obligation would probably increase greatly over time, since most vets were just approaching fifty years old, while prostate cancer, one of the commonest male diseases, occurs most frequently a decade or more later. There was still more gratitude, even among the most skeptical, when Clinton encouraged Congress to pass legislation compensating veterans' children who suffered from spina bifida.

Many Vietnam veterans were ready to declare that they had won on Agent Orange—that they had accomplished far more than anyone could have imagined just a few years earlier. But Vietnam veterans continued to suffer and die in large numbers from many of the still-uncompensated diseases, such as leukemia, heart disease, and diabetes. A 1995 update of the Ranch Hand study, in fact, showed a definite increase in the number of heart disease deaths among the Ranch Hand ground crews, the subgroup with the highest blood levels of dioxin. It also disclosed a relationship between dioxin and glucose metabolism (including the production of insulin) that could well induce, or at least exacerbate the tendency to develop, diabetes. In March 2000, yet another Ranch Hand report yielded "particularly strong evidence" of a link between Agent Orange exposure and adult-onset diabetes in veterans, but still the DVA offered no compensation for it. And despite the well-merited hoopla over VA benefits for spina bifida kids, Clinton's decision spelled relief for only 3,000 of the over 100,000 disabled children born to Vietnam veterans. The termination of AOCAP in 1996, and the ensuing collapse of NAVFSO, hit many of those children even harder because of the Republican Congress's welfare reform bill, signed into law on August 22, 1996. The new law ordered the case review of

260,000 disabled children on the welfare rolls. Under the law's much stricter definition of disability for children, it was estimated that up to 200,000 physically and mentally impaired youngsters would lose their cash benefits (averaging a paltry $424 a month) and, in some cases, also their Medicaid coverage. Many of those kids, whose support was cut in the name of reducing the national debt (which the Vietnam War had helped build), were arguably Agent Orange victims.

Then there was the matter of women's cancers and other female disorders that may well have been caused by Agent Orange. None of these had loomed large enough to the men in Congress and in the DVA to merit being considered for compensation. Though there appear to be no accurate statistics on women Agent Orange victims, stories of serious health problems abound among the 7,500 military nurses who served in Vietnam. Former Army nurse Lily Adams, who has spent most of her life since her return from the Vietnam War caring for its veterans, and who has organized extensively for women veterans' causes, lost too many female veteran friends to breast cancer and cervical cancer not to suspect Agent Orange as the cause. Adams herself, having served in a heavily sprayed area, suffered toxemia during her first pregnancy; she gave birth prematurely to twins, both dead. Her second live child, son Daniel, was born without nerve cells in half of his large intestine—a defect known as Hirschsprung's disease—for which he had to undergo two surgeries, and from which he nearly died. During the decade following her return, she also developed a breast tumor, immune problems, and chronic fatigue. On top of all this, she suffered from terrible, causeless depressions and chronic insomnia—which, though clearly symptoms of PTSD, tend to be worsened by dioxin poisoning. Others, like Vietnam veteran Lynda Van Devanter, have suffered for years with debilitating neurological and autoimmune ailments that no doctor can explain.

Vietnamese women who lived in defoliated areas have experienced many similar health (especially reproductive) problems both during and since the war. Author and former war resister David Harris reports that many of the female casualties are "young women who were breast-fed after their mothers were exposed," and who later developed cancer of the placenta when carrying their own children.

Of course, a lot *had* been won. By the start of the 1990s, Vietnam veterans no longer had to get defensive—or make themselves look foolish by "protesting too much"—in order to assert a claim of having been harmed by Agent Orange; just as they could now honorably recount their wounds from posttraumatic stress. But, as Lane Evans said in a backhanded compliment to Secretary Derwinski's "kinder and gentler bureaucracy," it was "regrettable" that veterans had "had to go to the federal courts to get the Veterans Administration to live up to the law of the land."

Agent Orange poisoning and delayed stress had left America with a permanent disgrace—not because its veterans suffered from them, though they had certainly been made to feel that way, but because the nation itself had abandoned its wounded. The American government had had to be forced, arm twisted and head to the mat, to do right by its veterans; and even then it had stopped short of doing all that was needed. The great mystery of those maladies turned out to be not what had caused them, but why it was taking so long for people to acknowledge and fix them. Deafness and delay had been so favorable to the government that many had suspected it to be a conscious strategy. But even conscious strategies play out after a time, after their rationale is unmasked.

Mindful of a new generation of veterans who looked to them for answers to the same painful questions, Vietnam veterans at the start of a new millennium, those who were still alive, found themselves stuck in the same tough place as those Biblical prophets whose only wisdom, only hope, consisted in asking: "How long . . . O Lord?"[228]

The Long View of History: An Epilogue

In the clash of egos that inevitably accompanies the struggle for human rights and justice, it is often tempting to label heroes and villains, but it is usually a mistake to do so. There are always larger forces at play. In the case of the Vietnam veterans' movement, the conflicts between numerous individuals were acted out amidst the contest between much greater issues—foremost among these, the sovereign power of government versus the responsibility of government to serve the people it governs. On an even more inclusive level, one can look upon every government as having an additional responsibility to humanity itself—a responsibility even more subject to abuse than the former. Thus, in a real sense, the fights within the veterans' movement sprang from that much greater war between government and the people upon whom power is exercised—a war that is never lost or won, but just goes on in a kind of seesawing of victories and defeats as long as there is a mankind to wage it.

An example of this ongoing battle is the fact that none of the fierce disputes between Vietnam veterans and the U.S. government—disputes that were literally tearing lives apart in the 1970s and 1980s—had even been remotely resolved as the twentieth century turned to the twenty-first. Many of the original combatants—Jan Barry, Al Hubbard, Ron Kovic, Jack Smith, Don Crawford, Shad Meshad, Art Blank, Frank McCarthy, Victor Yannacone, the Ryan family, and scores of others—had receded far into the background of their own private lives. Others—like Dean Phillips, Sheldon Ramsdell, Sarah Haley, Max Inglett, Jack McCloskey, Mary Sue Planck, Elmo Zumwalt III, Elmo Zumwalt Jr., Agent Orange activist Dennis Kroll; Robert Laufer, father of the Legacies Study; Tony Diamond of BRAVO; Gainesville Eight attorney Morton Stavis; Agent Orange attorney Dorothy Thompson; William Corson, the first high-ranking United States Marine Corps officer to dissent against the Vietnam War; and Lewis Puller Jr., author of *Fortunate Son*—had died too young. Yet the struggle itself had grown even more critical.

To begin with, a strange phenomenon began to be observed as Vietnam veterans moved into their forties and fifties. At the VVA convention in 1999, someone pointed out that most of the vets—balding, gray- or white-haired, deeply wrinkled, with huge potbellies or else emaciated, many walking slowly with canes—looked as though they were in their sixties or seventies, when in fact they were actually twenty years younger. Premature aging has been universally observed among Vietnam veterans, and in some respects it has already been medically verified. Rick Weidman, one of VVA's founders, began tracking this problem after he himself, in his late forties, almost went blind in his right eye from retinal bleeding—a disease called central serous retinopathy, which ordinarily he shouldn't have developed till at least his sixties.

Vietnam vets, according to Weidman, were exposed to a "toxic battlefield," just as people in industry refer to a "toxic workplace." "It wasn't just Agent Orange," he explains. "It was all kinds of other chemicals and foreign substances that were ingested as a result of branch of service, dates of service, duty stations, MOS [job description], and what actually happened to you. And in addition to that, you have all of the normal stressors of combat that lead to post-traumatic stress disorder and other neuropsychiatric wounds of war, which change your electrical/chemical reactions in your body and have physiological manifestations, which are only now starting to be understood." A DVA-sponsored study in Atlanta, which he cites, shows that the brain of a veteran with chronic acute PTSD actually looks different than a normal brain. "For many years, we said, 'God! We're just different!'" Weidman says. "Well, we didn't realize how true that was. We *are* different. We are physiologically different from prolonged exposure to extreme stress." One of the causes of this difference is something called "cortisol flooding," which refers to a hormone released in human bodies under stress. Cortisol flooding has been tied to heart problems, congestive heart failure in particular, and to other ways in which a body ages. While the chemical language may seem remote and abstract, it is manifesting daily in a hard reality. In 1995, VVA's newspaper *The Veteran* began a section called "Taps": a record of its member veterans who had died. Within five years, the author, Reverend Phil Salois, had compiled over a thousand names, most of them men in their late forties or early fifties.

In the best of all possible worlds, the Department of Veterans Affairs would have tracked these same issues and problems and developed strategies and programs to adequately deal with them. But the 1990s saw Congress struggling to reduce the national debt, cut taxes, preserve vital programs like Social Security, and at the same time beef up national defense; as a result, the DVA, like many other agencies and programs, was hit with major budget cuts. In 1996, as a way to help the DVA make do with less money—at a time when the medical needs of an aging veteran population were actually increasing—Congress decentralized the Veterans Health Administration (VHA) and divided it into twenty-two Veterans Integrated Service Network (VISN) regions. Each VISN was given a certain percentage of the total DVA budget and told (in Weidman's words): "You figure out how to use it best." Meantime, the Under Secretary for Veterans Health Administration, Kenneth Kizer, had his marching orders from the White House to get the entire veterans' health care system to "make do with less." The actual reductions for many of the "specialized services" were devastatingly large. For example, from 1997 to 1998, there was a 17 percent budget cut for all mental health and behavioral science programs, including treatment of PTSD. Blind and Visually Impaired Services were also cut by 17 percent. Spinal Cord Injury services were cut 15 percent. Most veterans' advocates feel that these specialized services are actually at the heart of the VHA's mission— providing medical help for those who were hurt in defense of their country, and providing services it would be hard (and often prohibitively expensive) for these people to get elsewhere. Worst of all, the VHA bureaucrats in Washington had no way of knowing how the budget cuts were actually being implemented by the various hospital directors and VISN directors across the country. In Weidman's words, the administrators in Central Office "flat didn't know what was going on at the service delivery point."

The results were disastrous. At a practical level, most VISN and medical center directors instituted a rationing of health care services as a way of doing what they thought was their duty to conserve limited financial resources. Amputees who had gotten used to a particular brand of prosthetic limb, for example, were suddenly told they had to use a different, cheaper brand. Paraplegic vets were being told they could no longer use the wheelchair they were most comfortable in, but had to make do with the economy model from whichever manufacturer had submitted the lowest bid. Two VISNs completely curtailed inpatient PTSD treatment. In the late 1990s, hepatitis C suddenly loomed as one of the most critical health care issues for Vietnam veterans. It appeared that tens of thousands of veterans had been exposed to this virulent liver disease in Vietnam; but because of the long latency period (up to thirty years), only now were significant numbers of veterans starting to manifest the symptoms. It was imperative for all Vietnam veterans to get tested for this disease as soon as possible, since the quicker it is treated, the better the chance of preventing or reducing permanent liver damage. But because of VHA budget cuts, many individual hospitals and medical centers simply refused to test for hepatitis C; in some cases, they even declined to treat it after it had been diagnosed. In the worst instance of denying care, VISN 1 (New England) slashed services across the board in order to proudly return $138 million to the VHA coffers, and the VISN director was rewarded with a $10,000 bonus for his excellent work in saving the government money.

Not surprisingly, in a report released in December 1999, a team of the DVA's own investigators documented "3,000 medical mistakes" and over 700 patients who died because of them in veterans' hospitals during the previous two years. But because of even greater budget cuts looming on the congressional horizon, the DVA had no answer for such horrendous conditions other than to project the closing of even more health care facilities.

Vietnam Veterans of America led the charge into Congress to decry the diminishment and deterioration of health care services for those citizens who arguably deserved them most. Rick Weidman, VVA's new director of government relations, read the riot act to both the congressmen who kept voting for such budget cuts and the VHA administrators who so carelessly implemented them. He accused them of having ignored two of the most important basic military principles: "One is that you can delegate authority, but you may not delegate responsibility. And a concomitant axiom is that a unit does well that which the commander checks well." No one, he reprimanded, had bothered to check what was happening to the nation's veterans. And so at the very end of the century, VVA launched into a major crusade to demand accountability from every veterans' health care facility—a crusade that had actually been attempted many times before, not least of all by Ron Bitzer and his two-man-staffed Center for Veterans' Rights in Los Angeles, two decades earlier, when he had besieged the VA with letters demanding the apparently nonexistent "quality-assurance studies" the agency had already been legally obligated to provide.

But even in the face of so much wrong done to this nation's veterans of every color and stripe, one would err to assume that there is some depravity or malice at the heart of our government, which leads to such unconscionable acts. Inherent in government is a paradox, in that what is created to serve men often takes on a life of its own, and ends up serving only itself. Every government—like every person—has a dark or shadow self, which resists the *shoulds* and *musts* of reason and conscience, and which often turns on its own better self in the most self-destructive, insane twists of common sense.

Not only do governments sometimes make mistakes, but they sometimes stubbornly pursue actions they know to be wrong. There could not be a better case in point than the Vietnam War, followed close after by this government's shabby treatment of the veterans of that war. Not till the inevitable dark side of government is fully recognized will the role of activists and dissenters be sufficiently honored. Activists and dissenters are not a nuisance and necessary evil of democracy, as they are often regarded. They are in truth the one and only self-regulating mechanism that can save democracy as a form of government.

Arthur Wilson had won two Purple Hearts in the Pacific before commanding a company that was decimated in the Korean War, from which he returned with permanently crippled hands and feet from fighting in 30-below-zero weather. Suffering for the rest of his life with severe PTSD, he perhaps summed up better than anyone the gap between individuals and governments when it comes to war. "The more you talk about it, the more you get rid of it," he told a reporter, explaining that once a soldier is discharged, he is essentially cast upon his own resources, expected to deal in a private, nondisruptive way with whatever public tragedies he has experienced. "The attitude was, only babies cry," he continued, "but the older I get, the more I cry—and I'm not ashamed of it now."

If there is a time for talking, there is also a time for silence. In October 1999, Scott Camil attended a reunion of his unit in Vietnam, the First of the First— First Battalion, First Marine Division. "It was a different kind of veteran there," he recalls. "It wasn't the antiwar veterans; it was the other veterans." He was "chastised," he says, by a captain who was wounded along with him on Operation Stone in February 1967. While Camil had merely taken shrapnel in his leg from a Bouncing Betty land mine, the captain had lost both his legs, and was in a wheelchair ever since. On that operation, the Marines had killed 292 Vietnamese, of whom 13 were children. The captain was aware of the fact that Camil had publicly denounced the Marines for their indiscriminate slaughter of civilians. At the reunion he told Camil: "I lost ten percent of my men [that day]. All of those fuckin' people [the Vietnamese] deserved to die, and you did us a disservice." Although Camil has been speaking out and lecturing on the war quite articulately—especially in classrooms—for nearly thirty years, he was not able to reply. It was not for lack of answers. "I couldn't argue with him," Camil explains, "because I felt so bad for him. All that time he's been in a wheelchair, he can't get laid. I'm gonna give him a fuckin' hard time? He wants to feel good about what he did. It's not my place to put him in his place."

Camil saw his silence as a chance to further the healing of a man that all his years of talking had not helped at all. And in that instant he clearly saw the difference between governments and men: a man can show another man respect; a government cannot.

There may be no two Vietnam veterans who dislike each other more than Rick Weidman and Bobby Muller. They dislike each other as only two men who once worked closely together on the same project can—after each has gone a different way, each feeling the other betrayed their original vision. Bobby Muller conceived VVA, but Rick Weidman made it a reality by getting him millions of dollars in funding—specifically, by helping to make VVA eligible for donations from the Combined Federal Campaign (CFC), to which millions of federal workers contribute. But when Muller first conceived VVA, he did not intend for it to go on indefinitely like the VFW or the American Legion. Instead, he determined that it would have to be killed at a certain point, after it had "done its job";

and that job was to serve as his forum and to fulfill his own agenda. "Bob's attitude," says Weidman, "was, 'This is my organization, and I can do whatever I want with it.'" Weidman, by contrast, worked so hard for VVA—and still does—because he felt it belonged to all Vietnam veterans; that it was the one thing, besides their service in Vietnam, that they could all be proud of.

Muller was forced out of the leadership of VVA in 1987. Three years later, he broke off completely from the organization. When he took the VVA Foundation and the millions of dollars from the CFC with him, Weidman was horrified. He felt it was a betrayal for Muller to begin using money that had been donated to help Vietnam veterans for a host of international social justice causes—even though many of them were good causes, like banning land mines, for which a Nobel Prize was awarded that should have gone to Muller but was snatched out from under him by a woman whose work he had funded. Perhaps the worst betrayal, though, in Weidman's eyes, was the fact that Muller spent the next decade "trashing" VVA every chance he got. Although Muller hardly talks to him anymore, Weidman has been wanting for a long time to tell him: "You don't have that right. Too many people have devoted too much of their lives, time, and energy and countless hours above and beyond the call of duty and in many cases the baby's milk money to make this thing go, for it to be solely yours."

Despite all that, Weidman concedes that Muller is a "great man." And not the least of that greatness, he says, is that Muller may have pulled off the biggest con of all time. There was a running joke at the VVA office that Bobby had learned his technique from the great scene in Mel Brooks' comedy *Blazing Saddles,* where actor Cleavon Little plays a black sheriff who's about to be killed by a town full of white bigots. They've all got their guns trained on him; but before they can fire, he whips out his six-shooter and sticks the barrel against his own neck. As Weidman narrates the story: "He yells, 'Look out! The nigger's got a gun!' And walks himself to the jail. Everybody says, 'Make way! He might shoot!' He gets into the jail and says, 'Whew! These people are so dumb!' And that's Muller's act: 'Look out! The vet's got a gun!'"

If one looks for a common denominator in the Vietnam veterans' movement, it might well be Weidman's image of Muller with his gun to his own head. The whole Vietnam veterans' movement was a kind of high bluffing in the face of history. And it proved, once and for all, that history is made by individuals who can convince the world they have more power than they actually do.

In the end, it was also about being able to laugh in the face of a lost cause. "Fuck 'em if they can't take a joke, and joke 'em if they can't take a fuck," Ron Kovic used to say so often with his trademark sarcastic smile. It's the same smile that was surely on Angel Almedina's face when he wrote from Ward 14AB of Franklin Delano Roosevelt Hospital in New York a few years before his death:

Gerry,

I am at Montrose VA in a psychiatric ward. It is a locked ward but I am OK, I think. I've met Patton and MacArthur. They are black. There is a Marine who's spaced out on crack who says he is Spock (Star Trek). I am taking no medication. Talk to you soon. The Asylum is in good hands.

Angel[229]

Sources

For brevity, the following abbreviations are employed in the notes. The dates following people's names are of interviews that I conducted with them in person or on the telephone. Please note that where several interviews were conducted with the same individual, I have given consecutive numbers to each interview. For example, the third interview with Robert O. Muller would be cited in a note as "ROM, 3." Where I am involved in a citation—for example, in the capacity of receiving a letter—I use my initials, GN.

Archival material came from a wide variety of sources, including the large collection of antiwar and veterans' papers at the Wisconsin State Historical Society in Madison, as well as the Center for Veterans' Rights archive, which is still seeking a permanent home. Often the source was veterans themselves, with clippings stashed in an attic or basement. Citations are as full as possible, given the enormous body of original stories, which could not always be traced back to their publishing source. When dates or page numbers were not available their lack is noted with n.d. or n.p., respectively.

Abbreviations for the names of interviewees (also used for letter writers and recipients):

AA	Angel Almedina, Oct. 31, 1988
AB	Arthur S. Blank Jr., April 5, 1988
AC	Alfredo Cabrera, Dec. 15, 1988
ACR	Alan Cranston, July 10, 2000
AE	Arthur Egendorf, Nov. 3, 1988
AH	Al Hubbard, Dec. 17, 1992
AL	Annie Luginbill, Jan. 10, 1988
ANH	Anne Hirschman, April 17, 1988
AS	Arnold Schecter, No. 1: April 17, 1999; No. 2: Aug. 4, 2000
AV	Anthony Velez, Nov. 5, 1988
BA	Brian Adams, Oct. 13, 1988
BB	Bill Branson, March 11, 1988
BBR	Bill Brew, No. 1: Oct. 20, 1988; No. 2: Dec. 17, 1996; No. 3: Aug. 1, 2000
BD	Bill Davis, Jan. 16, 1988
BJ	Butch Joeckel, Jan. 30, 1989
BL	Bill Lawson, June 28, 2000
BP	Bruce Pentland, Dec. 12, 1988

BR   Barry Romo, No. 1: Dec. 30, 1987; No. 2: March 11, 1988; No. 3: March 13, 1988; No. 4: July 3, 2000

BS   Barton F. Stichman, No. 1: Sept. 20, 1996; No. 2: Aug. 3, 2000

BU   Bill Unger, No. 1: Dec. 12, 1988; No. 2: Dec. 13, 1988; No. 3: Jan. 13, 1989

BW   Bob Waddell, No. 1: March 21, 1987; No. 2: July 11, 1988; No. 3: July 20, 2000

CF   Charles Figley, March 28, 1988

CK   Chris Kornkven, July 12, 2000

CM   Carlos Melendrez, March 25, 1996

CR   Carl Rogers, Dec. 9, 1988

CS   Chaim Shatan, No. 1: April 14, 1988; No. 2: February 12, 1996

CSM   Clark Smith, Feb. 10, 1988

DA   Dave Addlestone, No. 1: April 12, 1988; No. 2: Sept. 20, 1996

DB   Dennis Boyer, Oct. 6, 1988

DBO   Dave Bonior, April 12, 1988

DC   Dave Curry, March 12, 1988

DCH   Dave Christian, Oct. 24, 1988

DCO   Dean Contover, Nov. 17, 1988

DCR   Don Crawford, Dec. 18, 1996

DF   Dan Friedman, Nov. 8, 1988

DFA   Dan Fahey, Jan. 19, 2000

DH   David Harris, Jan. 10, 1996

DK   Dennis Kroll, Oct. 5, 1988

DM   David McReynolds, Nov. 4, 1988

DR   Dennis Rhoades, No. 1: Feb. 13, 1989; No. 2: Aug. 4, 1989; No. 3: Aug. 7, 1996; No. 4: June 21, 2000

DS   Donald Sproenhle, April 2, 1988

DT   David Thorne, July 24, 2000

ED   Ed Damato, April 22, 1988

EL   Ed Lord, Jan. 31, 1997

ERZ   Elmo R. Zumwalt Jr., April 17, 1999

ES   Eric Schwartz, Feb. 18, 1996

FC   Frank Cavestani, Jan. 28, 1988

FM   Frank McCarthy, No. 1: Nov. 10, 1988; No. 2: April 4, 1996; No. 3: July 18, 2000

FRL   Forest "Rusty" Lindley, April 5, 1988

FSM   Floyd "Shad" Meshad, No. 1: Jan. 27, 1988; No. 2: Dec. 12, 1988; No. 3: Feb. 7, 1996; No. 4: Feb. 15, 1996; No. 5: March 10, 1996

GM   Guy McMichael III, Feb. 7, 1989

GRN   Graham Nash, Oct. 19, 1992

HH   Husher Harris, March 13, 1997

HLB   Horace Leon Bracy, Dec. 19, 1996

JAT   John A. Talbott, Oct. 21, 1988

JB   Joe Bangert, No. 1: April 26, 1988; No. 2: April 27, 1988; No. 3: April 28, 1988; No. 4: Oct. 15, 1988

JBC   Jan Barry Crumb, No. 1: Jan. 30, 1988; No. 2: April 18, 1988; No. 3: April 19, 1988; No. 4: Nov. 1, 1992

JBE   John Beitzel, April 1, 1988

JC   Jim Credle, April 16, 1988

JCA   John Catterson, Nov. 2, 1988

JCS   Jan C. Scruggs, Oct. 22, 1988

JFK   John Forbes Kerry, No. 1: Nov. 15, 1988; No. 2: Jan. 31, 1989

JL   John Lindquist, Oct. 4, 1988

JM   Jack McCloskey, Feb. 14, 1988

JME   Jerry Melnyk, No. 1: Jan. 29, 1988; No. 2: Dec. 20, 1996

JMU   John Musgrave, July 4, 1988

JS   Jack Smith, No. 1: March 30, 1988; No. 2: May 2, 1988

JST   Jonathan Steinberg, Oct. 20, 1988

JT   John Terzano, April 13, 1988

JTH   James "Thor" Halassa, April 1, 1988

JU   Joe Urgo, No. 1: Feb. 1, 1988; No. 2: Nov. 6, 1988

JUP   John Upton, July 3, 1988

JW   John Wilson, No. 1: May 2, 1988; No. 2: Oct. 25, 1988

JWA   Jim Wachtendonk, Oct. 6, 1988

JWE   James Webb, Dec. 28, 1988

JWH   John Wheeler, Feb. 13, 1989

JZ   Joseph Zengerle, Feb. 6, 1989

KB   Ken Berez, Feb. 11, 1989

KC   Ken Campbell, April 2, 1988

LA   Lily Adams, March 3, 1996

LC   Lee Crump, March 4, 1997

LE   Lane Evans, No. 1: April 13, 1988; No. 2: March 23, 2000

LH   Larry Heinemann, No. 1: Aug. 17, 1988; No. 2: Feb. 1, 1989

LR   Larry Rottmann, No. 1: July 2, 1988; No. 2: Nov. 3, 1999

LT   Lee Thorn, Feb. 12, 1988

LVD   Lynda Van Devanter, Dec. 16, 1996

LW   Leroi Wolins, March 28, 1988

MAS   Marla Schorr, July 1, 1988

MAR   Maureen Ryan, July 8, 1996

MB   Michael Blecker, Feb. 9, 1988

MDV   Maude DeVictor, Feb. 16, 1988

MF   Mack Fleming, Feb. 21, 1997

MI   Max Inglett, No. 1: Dec. 29, 1988; No. 2: Jan. 18, 1989

MM   Mike Maxwell, June 20, 1988

MO   Michael Oliver, No. 1: March 21, 1989; No. 2: Jan. 11, 1990

MR	Michael Ryan, May 30, 1996
MS	Morton Stavis, Oct. 28, 1988
MSP	Mary Sue Planck, Feb. 25, 1996
NS	Nancy Stearns, Oct. 31, 1988
PAM	Pat Marinello (numerous conversations, pertaining to Ron Kovic, David Harris, and her many other friends in the veterans' and antiwar movements)
PG	Philip Gioia, Oct. 30, 1999
PM	Peter Mahoney, Jan. 31, 1988
RB	Randy Barnes, No. 1: July 3, 1988; No. 2: Aug. 14, 1999
RBI	Ron Bitzer, No. 1: Jan. 21, 1988; No. 2: Feb. 3, 1988; No. 3: Feb. 4, 1988; No. 4: Jan. 21, 1996
RBO	Richard Boyle, Jan. 26, 1988
RF	Ron Ferrizzi, April 2, 1988
RFU	Richard Fuller, March 10, 1997
RJL	Robert Jay Lifton, April 20, 1988
RK	Ron Kovic, No. 1: Jan. 21, 1988; No. 2: May 2, 1989; No. 3: May 9, 1990 (Note: I only conducted three formal interviews with Ron Kovic; but over the course of a two-decades-long friendship, which also involved joint peace activism and collaborative literary projects, Ron and I had literally hundreds of conversations on Vietnam, veterans, and the veterans' movement. Material from these conversations is simply noted "conv.")
RL	Robert Laufer, Oct. 25, 1988
ROK	Robert Klein, July 7, 1988
ROM	Robert O. "Bobby" Muller, No. 1: April 21, 1988; No. 2: Oct. 17, 1988; No. 3: Oct. 21, 1988; No. 4: Feb. 8, 1989; No. 5: Feb. 9, 1989; No. 6: Feb. 10, 1989; No. 7: July 11, 2000
RP	Ron Podlaski, Oct. 20, 1988
RS	Ray Scurfield, No. 1: Oct. 25, 1988; No. 2: Jan. 20, 1997; No. 3: Feb. 20, 1997; No. 4: Feb. 25, 1997
RSA	Rose Sandecki, Dec. 18, 1996
RW	Rick Weidman, No. 1: April 30, 1988; No. 2: Aug. 14, 1999
SA	Steve Androff, Dec. 12, 1988
SC	Scott Camil, No. 1: April 8, 1988; No. 2: April 9, 1988; No. 3: Oct. 22, 1999; No. 4: Jan. 18, 2000; No. 5: July 24, 2000
SF	Stuart Feldman, No. 1: Feb. 8, 1989; No. 2: June 30, 2000
SH	Sarah Haley, April 28, 1988
SM	Craig Scott Moore, March 31, 1988
SMH	Seymour M. Hersh, April 12, 1992
SR	Sheldon Ramsdell, Aug. 30, 1991
SRO	Skip Roberts, March 17, 1988
SS	Sam Schorr, Jan. 23, 1988
STC	Steve Champlin, Feb. 12, 1989
SW	Sukie Wachtendonk, Oct. 6, 1988
TA	Tom Ashby, April 3, 1996
TC	Tim Craig, No. 1: Feb. 5, 1989; No. 2: Feb. 12, 1989; No. 3: Feb. 1, 1995; No. 4: March 5, 1996; No. 5: Jan. 20, 1997; No. 6: Feb. 25, 1997; No. 7: June 30, 2000

TD	Tony Diamond, No. 1: Feb. 2, 1988; No. 2: Nov. 1, 1995
TDA	Thomas Daschle, April 12, 1988
TE	Tod Ensign, No. 1: April 20, 1988; No. 2: Oct. 31, 1988
TH	Tom Hayden, Nov. 9, 1990
THA	Tom Harvey, Feb. 24, 1997
TP	Tony Principi, Feb. 24, 1997
TZ	Tom Zangrilli, Oct. 12, 1988
VY	Victor Yannacone Jr., Nov. 6, 1988
WFC	William F. Crandell, April 30, 1988
WPM	William P. Mahedy, Dec. 8, 1988
WS	Wilson Sproenhle, April 2, 1988
WSC	William Sloane Coffin, April 7, 1988
WW	Wayne Wilson, Oct. 27, 1988
YM	Yael Margolin, April 16, 1988

Abbreviations for newspapers and magazines frequently cited:

BG	*Boston Globe*
CCT	*Contra Costa Times*
CO	*Charlotte Observer*
CS	*Citizen Soldier*
CSM	*Christian Science Monitor*
CST	*Chicago Sun-Times*
CT	*Chicago Tribune*
DFP	*Detroit Free Press*
DP	*Denver Post*
GS	*Gainesville Sun*
HIP	*Harrisburg Independent Press*
HP	*Houston Post*
JAMA	*Journal of the American Medical Association*
LADN	*Los Angeles Daily News*
LAFP	*Los Angeles Free Press*
LAHE	*Los Angeles Herald-Examiner*
LAR	*Los Angeles Reader*
LAT	*Los Angeles Times*
LBI	*Long Beach Independent*
LIP	*Long Island Press*
LT	*Louisville Times*
MH	*Miami Herald*
NO	*National Observer*
ND	*Newsday*
NW	*Newsweek*
NYDN	New York *Daily News*

NYHT	*New York Herald Tribune*
NYP	*New York Post*
NYT	*New York Times*
PI	*Philadelphia Inquirer*
SAS	*The Stars and Stripes—The National Tribune* (a private newspaper published for U.S. veterans)
SFC	*San Francisco Chronicle*
SFE	*San Francisco Examiner*
SLPD	*St. Louis Post-Dispatch*
SMEO	*Santa Monica Evening Outlook*
SPT	*St. Petersburg Times*
SRPD	*Santa Rosa Press Democrat*
TMP	*The Mobile Register*
TN	*The Nation*
TV	*The Veteran* (VVAW's second and current newspaper)
USAT	*USA Today*
VV	*Village Voice*
VVAV	*The VVA Veteran* (VVA's newspaper)
WDN	*Washington Daily News*
WES	*Washington Evening Star*
WSN	*Washington Star-News*
WP	*Washington Post*
WS	*Winter Soldier* (VVAW's first newspaper)
WST	*Washington Star*

Abbreviations of books frequently cited:

AAO	Charles De Benedetti and Charles Chatfield, *An American Ordeal: The Antiwar Movement of the Vietnam Era* (Syracuse: Syracuse Univ. Press, 1990)
AAV	Joan Baez, *And a Voice to Sing With: A Memoir* (NY: New American Library, 1987)
ABSL	Neil Sheehan: *A Bright Shining Lie: John Paul Vann and America in Vietnam* (NY: Random House, 1988)
AF	David Hackworth with Julie Sherman, *About Face* (NY: Simon and Schuster, 1989)
AOOT	Peter H. Schuck, *Agent Orange on Trial: Mass Toxic Disasters in the Courts* (Cambridge: Harvard Univ. Press, 1986)
APMH	*A Piece of My Heart: The Stories of Twenty-Six American Women Who Served in Vietnam,* ed. Keith Walker (NY: Ballantine, 1985)
ATW	Ron Kovic and Gerald Nicosia, *After the War* (unpublished manuscript, 1992)
BL	*Blacklisted News: Secret Histories from Chicago to 1984* (NY: Bleecker Publishing, 1988)
BOTF	Ron Kovic, *Born on the Fourth of July* (NY: Pocket Books, 1977)

CAC   Lawrence Baskir and William A. Strauss, *Chance and Circumstance: The Draft, the War, and the Vietnam Generation* (NY: Vintage, 1978)

CFDM   Shad Meshad, *Captain for Dark Mornings* (Playa del Rey, Cal.: Creative Image Associates, 1982)

COW   *Crimes of War,* ed. Richard A. Falk, Gabriel Kolko, and Robert Jay Lifton (NY: Random House, 1971)

DAO   Michael Gough, *Dioxin, Agent Orange: The Facts* (NY: Plenum Press, 1986)

DC   Cril Payne, *Deep Cover: An FBI Agent Infiltrates the Radical Underground* (NY: Newsday Books, 1979)

FAL   Hunter S. Thompson, *Fear and Loathing on the Campaign Trail '72* (NY: Warner, 1973)

FOD   Richard Boyle, *Flower of the Dragon: The Breakdown of the U.S. Army in Vietnam* (San Francisco: Ramparts, 1972)

GIGP   Michael Uhl and Tod Ensign, *GI Guinea Pigs: How the Pentagon Exposed Our Troops to Dangers More Deadly Than War* (NY: Wideview Books, 1980)

HEAL   Arthur Egendorf, *Healing from the War: Trauma and Transformation After Vietnam* (Boston: Houghton Mifflin, 1985)

HFTW   Robert Jay Lifton, *Home from the War: Vietnam Veterans Neither Victims Nor Executioners* (NY: Basic Books, 1985)

IIC   John P. Wilson, *Identity, Ideology and Crisis: The Vietnam Veteran in Transition: Report Submitted to the Disabled American Veterans on the Forgotten Warrior Project* (Cleveland: Cleveland State Univ., 1977–1978), 2 vols.

KAO   Clifford Linedecker with Michael and Maureen Ryan, *Kerry: Agent Orange and an American Family* (NY: St. Martin's Press, 1982)

LOV   Arthur Egendorf, Charles Kadushin, Robert S. Laufer, George Rothbart, and Lee Sloan, *Legacies of Vietnam: Comparative Adjustment of Veterans and Peers: A Study Prepared for the Veterans' Administration, Submitted to the Committee on Veterans' Affairs, U.S. House of Representatives* (Wash., D.C.: U.S. Government Printing Office, 1981), 5 vols.

LTP   Myra MacPherson, *Long Time Passing: Vietnam & the Haunted Generation* (Garden City, NY: Doubleday, 1984)

LVV   *The Legacy of Vietnam Veterans and Their Families: Survivors of War: Catalysts for Change: Papers from the 1994 National Symposium,* ed. Dennis K. Rhoades, Michael R. Leaveck, James C. Hudson (Wash., D.C.: Agent Orange Class Assistance Program, 1995)

MFMS   Admiral Elmo Zumwalt Jr. and Lieutenant Elmo Zumwalt III with John Pekkanen, *My Father, My Son* (NY: Macmillan, 1986)

NAV   Telford Taylor, *Nuremberg and Vietnam: An American Tragedy* (Chicago: Quadrangle, 1970)

NOWK   John Schultz, *No One Was Killed* (Chicago: Big Table, 1969)

NS   John Kerry and Vietnam Veterans Against the War, *The New Soldier,* ed. David Thorne and George Butler (NY: Collier, 1971)

ONA   Fred Halstead, *Out Now!: A Participant's Account of the American Movement Against the Vietnam War* (NY: Monad, 1978)

OTN   William P. Mahedy, *Out of the Night: The Spiritual Journey of Vietnam Vets* (NY: Ballantine, 1988)

OW   Elmo R. Zumwalt Jr., *On Watch: A Memoir* (Arlington, Va.: Admiral Zumwalt and Associates, 1976)

RKAHT   Arthur M. Schlesinger Jr., *Robert Kennedy and His Times* (Boston: Houghton Mifflin, 1978), 2 vols.

SAH   *Strangers at Home: Vietnam Veterans Since the War,* ed. Charles R. Figley and Seymour Leventman (NY: Praeger, 1980)

SDAV   *Stress Disorders Among Vietnam Veterans: Theory, Research and Treatment,* ed. Charles Figley (NY: Brunner/Mazel, 1978)

SIR   David Cortright, *Soldiers in Revolt: The American Military Today* (Garden City, NY: Anchor Press/Doubleday, 1975)

SV   B. G. Burkett and Glenna Whitley, *Stolen Valor: How the Vietnam Generation Was Robbed of Its Heroes and Its History* (Dallas: Verity Press, 1998)

TAIW   *Trauma and Its Wake,* ed. Charles R. Figley (NY: Brunner/Mazel), volume 1: *The Study of Post-Traumatic Stress Disorder* (1985); volume 2: *Traumatic Stress Theory, Research, and Intervention* (1986)

THAN   Jan C. Scruggs and Joel L. Swerdlow, *To Heal a Nation* (NY: Harper & Row, 1985)

TPOP   Seymour M. Hersh, *The Price of Power: Kissinger in the Nixon White House* (NY: Summit Books, 1983)

TPR   Wilbur J. Scott, *The Politics of Readjustment: Vietnam Veterans Since the War* (Hawthorne, NY: Aldine De Gruyter, 1993)

TWG   *The Wounded Generation: America After Vietnam,* ed. A. D. Horne (Englewood Cliffs, NJ: Prentice-Hall, 1981)

TVV   David Bonior, Steven M. Champlin, and Timothy S. Kolly, *The Vietnam Veteran: A History of Neglect* (NY: Praeger, 1986)

TWSI   Vietnam Veterans Against the War, *The Winter Soldier Investigation* (Boston: Beacon Press, 1972)

TWW   Tom Wells, *The War Within: America's Battle Over Vietnam* (Berkeley: Univ. of California Press, 1994)

VR   *Vietnam Reconsidered: Lessons from a War,* ed. Harrison E. Salisbury (NY: Harper & Row, 1984)

VWA   Harry G. Summers Jr., *Vietnam War Almanac* (NY and Oxford, Eng.: Facts on File, 1985)

WAL   Gloria Emerson, *Winners and Losers* (NY: Random House, 1976)

WFAA   Fred A. Wilcox, *Waiting for an Army to Die: The Tragedy of Agent Orange* (NY: Vintage, 1983)

WMBP   Robert Klein, *Wounded Men, Broken Promises: How the Veterans Administration Betrays Yesterday's Heroes* (NY: Macmillan, 1981)

WSU   Nancy Zaroulis and Gerald Sullivan, *Who Spoke Up?: American Protest Against the War in Vietnam 1963–1975* (Garden City, NY: Doubleday, 1984)

WOW   Richard Severo and Lewis Milford, *The Wages of War: When America's Soldiers Came Home—From Valley Forge to Vietnam* (NY: Simon and Schuster, 1989)

Abbreviations of organizations and demonstrations frequently cited:

AVM   American Veterans Movement

CVR   Center for Veterans' Rights (Los Angeles)

DCIII   Dewey Canyon III

NCUUA   National Council for Universal and Unconditional Amnesty

VVA   Vietnam Veterans of America

VVAW   Vietnam Veterans Against the War

VVOP   Vietnam Veterans Outreach Program (also known as Vet Center Program or Operation Outreach)

WSI   Winter Soldier Investigation

Notes

Chapter 1. Coming Up with a Politics: Vietnam Veterans Against the War

1. SIX VETS AND A BANNER

1. Interviews: JBC, 1,2,3; MS. Documents: FBI files on VVAW, 1968–1977, received through Freedom of Information Act.
2. Interviews: JBC, 1; BR, 1.
3. Interviews: JBC, 1; BR, 1; LW.
4. Interviews: JBC, 1. Letters: Ira Glasser to JBC, Aug. 21, 1967.
5. Interviews: CR. Articles: Norman M. Lobsenz, "What Can I Do, One Unimportant Person?" *Redbook,* March 1968, 81–160. Books: WAL, p. 366 (including supplemental manuscript material cut from the printed book, provided by Carl Rogers).
6. Interviews: CR. Articles: *Redbook,* March 1968, op. cit., 147, 155; Lee Rodgers, "Battle Zone," *The Times Leader* (Chardon, Ohio), Feb. 4, 1967, n.p. The malfunctioning of the early M-16 is discussed in many books such as W. D. Ehrhart, *Vietnam-Perkasie: A Combat Marine Memoir* (Jefferson, N.C.: McFarland, 1983) and David Hackworth, *About Face* (New York: Simon and Schuster, 1989).
7. Interviews: CR. Documents: Carl Rogers, unpublished policy paper written for the McCarthy presidential campaign, summer, 1968; several Negotiation Now! brochures provided by Rogers. Letters: American Van Lines to Negotiation Now!, n.d. (circa 1967). Dr. Levy's case is described in S. Brian Willson, *A Beginning Outline of Resistance to the Viet Nam War* (San Francisco: self-published, 1989), 15.
8. Interviews: JBC, 1; CR. Documents: VVAW broadside describing the MACV patch and their own logo, 1968. Books: *AF,* 463, 481–83.
9. Interviews: JBC, 1. Articles: *Redbook,* March 1968, op. cit., and several articles mentioned without citation in JBC's letter cited in this note. Documents: VVAW Steering Committee policy paper, Oct. 12, 1967; VVAW advertisement, *NYT,* Nov. 19, 1967. Letters: JBC to supporters of VVAW, n.d., circa Nov.–Dec. 1967.

2. TEAR GAS, CLUBS, AND CONFETTI: THE CHICAGO BLUES

10. Articles: Peter Grose, "War of Attrition Called Effective by Westmoreland," *NYT,* Nov. 20, 1967. n.p. Books: *VWA,* 334–35; *RKAHT,* vol. 2, 881–88; *WAL,* 917–19.
11. Interviews: SR. Documents: "Proposal for the Expansion of the VVAW" submitted by Carl Rogers to the Executive Committee, Feb. 3, 1968; Vietnam Veterans for McCarthy newsletter, n.d.; advertisement mock-up entitled "Viet-Nam Veterans Speak Out," n.d. Books: *NOWK,* passim.
12. Interviews: JBC, 1; CR; LR, 1. Documents: Robert F. Kennedy's speech on the Vietnam War, Feb. 8, 1968, quoted in the *Congressional Record,* vol. 114, no. 19.
13. Interviews: CR; RK, conv. Books: *RKAHT,* vol. 2, 906 ff.; *ATW,* passim.
14. Interviews: JBC, 1; CR. Letters: John A. Talbott to "Concerned Americans," n.d.; letter of William Rodder Jr., to the delegates to the Democratic National Convention in Chicago, July 21, 1968; letter of Richard T. Roth to the delegates, Aug. 8, 1968. The letter from the young veteran in Arkansas has been lost but was recalled by Rogers.
15. Interviews: JAT; LR, 1; CR. Documents: press release from Dr. John A. Talbott and Viet-Nam Veterans for McCarthy, Aug. 23, 1968. Books: *NOWK,* 133–35.

3. CHANGING DIRECTIONS

16. Interviews: SR.
17. Interviews: LR; JBC, 1. Books: *Winning Hearts and Minds: War Poems by Vietnam Veterans,* ed. Larry Rottmann, Jan Barry, and Basil T. Pacquet (New York: First Casualty Press, 1972); *Free Fire Zone: Short Stories by Vietnam Veterans,* ed. Wayne Karlin, Basil T. Pacquet, and Larry Rottmann (Coventry, Conn.: First Casualty Press, 1973).

4. THE GI MOVEMENT

18. Interviews: JBC, 1; Keith Mather, May 26, 1989; Susan Schnall, Nov. 5, 1988. Articles: Carl Rogers, "The Beginning of a New Day: Reflections on Chicago," unpublished, circa 1968; Robert Sherrill, "Must the Citizen Give Up His Civil Liberties When He Joins the Army?" *NYT Magazine,* May 18, 1969 (reprint by the Committee for the Presidio 27), 3; Alan Lewis, "First Amendment on Trial," *Argus* (student magazine at the University of Maryland), vol. 5, no. 2, circa 1969 (reprint by LINK), 2–3; William N. Curry, "Admiral Ordered to Answer Allegations in Antiwar Case," *WP,* Dec. 20, 1969, n.p.; Roger Priest, "1st Amendment: 'It's Crap,'" and numerous other articles in *OM—The Servicemen's Newsletter* (Priest's underground GI newspaper), Oct. 1969, 2–4 passim; Roger Priest, "Stop the Trial!" and numerous other articles in *OM—The Servicemen's Newsletter,* Jan. 1970, 2 passim. Documents: "Biographical Facts on Roger Lee Priest" (broadside from LINK NEWS), circa fall 1971. Letters: Ira Glasser to JBC, Aug. 21, 1967. Books: Fred Gardner, *The Unlawful Concert: An Account of the Presidio Mutiny Case* (NY: Viking, 1970), passim.
19. Interviews: AL. Documents: "National GI Week: A Message to GIs," broadside put out by the National Mobilization Committee to End the War in Vietnam, Nov. 1968. Letters: JBC and CR to VVAW membership, Oct. 14, 1968. Books: *WSU,* 135–42 passim.
20. Interviews: JBC, 1. Articles: Robert Sherrill, "Must the Citizen Give Up His Civil Liberties When He Joins the Army?" op. cit., 3, 6; Richard Nixon quoted in Alan Lewis, "First Amendment on Trial," op. cit., 1. Documents: Carl Rogers, internal memo of LINK, Nov. 3, 1968; Nguyen Dinh Uoc, speech at Third Triennial Vietnam Symposium, Vietnam Center, Lubbock, Tex., April 15, 1999; LINK (The Serviceman's Link to Peace) newsletter, circa fall 1969. Books: *ABSL; AF;* David Cortright, *Soldiers in Revolt: The American Military Today* (Garden City, NY: Doubleday, 1975); Haynes Johnson, *Army in Anguish: The Washington Post National Report* (NY: Pocket Books, 1972); Richard Boyle, *Flower of the Dragon: The Breakdown of the U.S. Army in Vietnam* (San Francisco: Ramparts, 1972).
21. Documents: LINK newsletter, circa fall 1969; S. Brian Willson, "A Beginning Outline for Study of the Vietnam War" (circulated privately), circa 1988. Books: *CAC,* 3–5, 153–58.

5. ENTER AL HUBBARD

22. Interviews: CR. Documents: LINK newsletter, circa fall 1969. Books: *WSU,* 257, 269–71, 277–79, 267, 286, 296; *TPOP,* 120.
23. Interviews: CR; SR; JBC, 1.
24. Interviews: AH; SR; MO, 2; ANH. Articles: Art Goldberg, "Vietnam Vets: The Anti-War Army," *Ramparts,* n.d., 16–17. Documents: VVAW newsletter, March 1971, 3.
25. Documents: Al Hubbard, untitled policy paper written for VVAW's Executive Committee, circa summer 1970.
26. Books: W. D. Ehrhart, *Marking Time* (NY: Avon, 1986), 93–94.
27. Interviews: AH; SR; MO, 2. Numerous Vietnam veterans, including Ron Kovic, have told me they became active against the war because of Kent State. I have also heard from numerous veterans who told me their campus veterans' clubs turned into VVAW chapters after Kent State. Articles: Martin Luther King Jr., "A Time to Break Silence" (also known as "Declaration of Independence from the War in Vietnam"), in *A Testament of Hope: The Essential Writings and Speeches of Martin Luther King, Jr.,* ed. James Melvin Washington (San Francisco: HarperCollins, 1991), 231–44. Documents: Al Hubbard, untitled policy paper, op. cit.; "Opening Statement—VVAW Regional Coordinators' Conference," misdated Feb. 19, 1970 (actually 1971), probably authored by Mike Oliver.
28. Interviews: SR.

Chapter 2: Shared Nightmares: From Operation RAW to the Winter Soldier Investigation

1. ON THE ROAD TO VALLEY FORGE

29. Interviews: RK in conversation pointed out to me that the enemy in guerrilla theater was ignorance. Documents: "Operation R.A.W.: Viet Vet March Stirs Thought," a press release issued by VVAW, Sept. 7, 1970.
30. Interviews: SM; MO, 1.
31. Interviews: MO, 2; SM; JU, 2. Books: *Facing My Lai: Moving Beyond the Massacre,* ed. David L. Anderson (Lawrence: University Press of Kansas, 1998), passim.
32. Interviews: JU, 2; SM. Articles: William F. Crandell, "They Moved the Town: Organizing Vietnam Veterans Against the War in Ohio 1968–1975," unpublished, circa 1988. Documents: certificate of incorporation of Vietnam Veterans Against the War, Inc., approved Aug. 12, 1970, Albany, NY; "Opening Statement—VVAW Regional Coordinators' Conference," Feb. 19, 1971, op. cit.; "Ambushes Maim or Kill G.I.s in Vietnam Everyday," VVAW flyer printed up for Operation RAW, Sept. 1970; "A U.S. Infantry Company Just Came Through Here," VVAW flyer printed up for Operation RAW, Sept. 1970.
33. Interviews: TE, 1,2. Articles: Charles Childs, "Our Forgotten Wounded: Assignment to Neglect," illustrated by Co Rentmeester, *Life,* May 22, 1970 (vol. 68, no. 19), 3, 28. Documents: list of 7 goals of RAW, composed by Al Hubbard and issued to all veterans participating in the march, as part of a "fact sheet," circa August 1970.
34. Interviews: WFC; SM. Articles: Al Haas, "War Brought Home to Middle America," *PI,* Sept. 8, 1970, n.p. William F. Crandell, "They Moved the Town," op. cit., 6–8; Gloria Negri, "Retired General Hester Raps U.S. Global Grab for Power," *BG,* May 13, 1970, n.p. Documents: "Statement for Press Conference with Vietnam Veterans Against the War" by Brigadier General Hugh B. Hester, U.S. Army (ret.), presented at the U.S. House of Representatives, March 16, 1971; "Operation RAW Report Number 3," memorandum to participants in the march, Aug. 18, 1970; "Operation RAW Interim Report Number 2," July 31, 1970; the FBI files on VVAW, 1968–1977. Films: *Different Sons,* a documentary of Operation RAW made by Bowling Green Films, Inc., 1971.
35. Interviews: WFC. Articles: Sheldon Ramsdell, "Soldiers of Peace at Valley Forge," *The World Magazine (Daily World),* Sept. 19, 1970. Films: Al Hubbard and William F. Crandell quoted in *Different Sons.*

2. A SPOKESMAN EMERGES: "LINCOLN AND KENNEDY COMBINED"

36. Interviews: MO, 2; JU, 1, 2. Articles: Al Haas, "War Brought Home to Middle America," op. cit., 33; "Anti-War Vets End 86-Mile March," AP wire story, Sept. 8, 1970. The phrase "international racism" comes from an unsigned interview with Al Hubbard called "Vet Doves Hear from Jane Fonda, Karen Burstein" in the *Long Island Free Press,* Sept. 9, 1970. Documents: "Objectives of VVAW," first draft and official draft, fall 1970; "VVAW Report on Operation RAW," authored largely by Al Hubbard, Sept. 23, 1970; "Summary Report on the Winter Soldier Investigation," March 1971. General Creighton Abrams had succeeded General William Westmoreland as commander of MACV and all field forces in South Vietnam. Films: *Different Sons.*
37. Articles: "Disruptives Chased Away from Antiwar Rally," Combined Services wire story, Sept. 8, 1970; "Anti-War Vets End 86-Mile March," Sept. 8, 1970 (source unknown); Hoag Levins, "Veterans Stage Rally at Valley Forge," *PI,* Sept. 8, 1970, n.p.; "Vet Doves Hear Jane Fonda, Karen Burstein," *Long Island Free Press,* op. cit.; Sandy Grady, "Jane Fonda Tells Why She Protests," *PI,* Sept. 8, 1970, 3.
38. Interviews: JFK, 1. Articles: "Angry War Veteran: John Forbes Kerry," *WP,* April 22, 1971, n.p. Books: A succinct history of John Kerry's political campaigns can be found in *Politics in America: Members of Congress in Washington and at Home,* ed. Alan Ehrenhalt (Wash., D.C.: Congress Quarterly Press, 1985), 695–96.
39. Interviews: JFK, 1; SR; MO, 2. Articles: "Angry War Veteran: John Forbes Kerry," op. cit.; John Kerry quoted in Hoag Levins, "Veterans Stage Rally at Valley Forge," op. cit.; Sandy Grady, "Jane Fonda Tells Why She Protests," op. cit., 4; "Vet Doves Hear Jane Fonda, Karen Burstein," *Long Island Free Press,* op. cit. John Kerry has quoted from his Valley Forge speech—which in its final form he delivered before the Senate Foreign Relations Committee in April 1971—throughout his

political career. Its most famous line—"How do you ask a man to be the last man to die for a mistake?"—was even used by Senator Kerry as the opening of a fund-raising letter he sent out nationally when campaigning for reelection in 1990. Films: *Different Sons.*

3. WAR CRIMES TESTIMONY: FONDA, LANE, AND "BRANDS OF SWISS CHEESE"

40. Interviews: JBC, 2, 3; TE, 1; SMH. Articles: Jan Barry, "For They Are All Honorable Men," *WIN,* March 15, 1971, 10–11; Edward Tivnin, "Jeremy Rifkin Just Says No," *NYT Magazine,* Oct. 16, 1988, 38–46. Books: *TPOP,* 135, 175; Jeremy Rifkin, *Beyond Beef: The Rise and Fall of the Cattle Culture* (NY: Dutton, 1992).

41. Interviews: TE, 1. Noam Chomsky's words and other details of the Town Hall meeting are reported from memory by Ensign. Books: Bertrand Russell, letter to Lyndon B. Johnson, Aug. 25, 1966, printed in *Against the Crime of Silence: Proceedings of the Russell International War Crimes Tribunal,* ed. John Duffett (NY and London: Bertrand Russell Foundation/O'Hare Books, 1968), 18.

42. Interviews: TE, 1. Articles: Neil Sheehan, review of Mark Lane's *Conversations with Americans, New York Times Book Review,* Dec. 27, 1970, 5. Books: James Simon Kunen, *Standard Operating Procedure: Notes of a Draft-Age American* (NY: Avon, 1971), 23; Mark Lane, *Conversations with Americans* (NY: Simon and Schuster, 1970), 16. In his review of *Conversations with Americans,* Sheehan cautioned: "Mr. Lane succeeds . . . in making it impossible to reach any factual judgment."

43. Interviews: TE, 1; SM; Chris Moore, March 31, 1988. Articles: William F. Crandell, "They Moved the Town," op. cit., 10. Documents: Thomas Paine quoted in "Opening Statement" for the Winter Soldier Investigation, delivered by William Crandell at the first session, Jan. 31, 1971. Books: *The Winter Soldier Investigation* (pamphlet), printed and distributed by VVAW and signed by Timothy C. Butz, William F. Crandell, Craig Scott Moore, and Michael Oliver; *TWSI,* 1–4.

44. Interviews: TE, 1. Mark Lane, *Conversations with Americans,* op cit, passim; *Crimes of War,* ed. Richard A Falk, Gabriel Kolko, and Robert Jay Lifton (NY: Random House, 1971); James Simon Kunen, *Standard Operating Procedure,* op. cit., 24–25.

45. Interviews: TE, 1; JBE; KC. Books: James Simon Kunen, *Standard Operating Procedure,* op. cit., 25–27.

4. BREAKING DOWN IN DETROIT: "I DIDN'T KNOW WHAT WAS GOING ON"

46. Interviews: MO, 2. Films: *Winter Soldier,* a documentary by the Winterfilm Collective and Vietnam Veterans Against the War, 1972.

47. Interviews: TH; SC, 1; JU, 2. Articles: William F. Crandell, "They Moved the Town," op. cit., 12. Films: *Winter Soldier.*

48. Interviews: JFK, 1; JU, 1; SM; Ken Cloke, Dec. 13, 1988. Articles: Jan Barry, "For They Are All Honorable Men," op. cit., 11; William F. Crandell, "They Moved the Town," op. cit., 12; William L. Claiborne, "Protest Planned Near Capitol," *WP,* March 17, 1971, A13; William Schmidt, "Five Ex-Marines Tell of 1969 Invasion of Laos," *DFP,* Feb. 1, 1971, 1A, 5A;. Documents: VVAW circular put out in preparation for WSI, Jan. 16, 1971; VVAW newsletter, 1971, no. 1; "The Winter Soldier Investigation" (official report of VVAW), March 1971; "Say It for Willie," handout prepared in advance for DC III; "Opening Statement—VVAW Regional Coordinators Conference," Feb. 17, 1971, op. cit. Books: Kunen, *Standard Operating Procedure,* op. cit., 27; *TWSI,* xiii–xiv.

49. Interviews: JFK, 1; SM; JU, 1; JB, 1, 2. Articles: Mark Lane and William Crandell quoted in Chris Singer, "Winter Soldier," *The Fifth Estate* (Detroit, Mich.), Jan. 21–Feb. 3, 1971 (vol. 5, no. 19), 1; "Dewey Canyon Three," *WS,* April 1, 1971 (vol. 1, no. 1), 2; Gerald Meyer, "Three Ex-Pilots Report Secret Raids in Laos by U.S. Soldiers," *BG,* Nov. 2, 1972, 16. Documents: "Call to the Winter Soldier Investigation," a policy paper put out by VVAW, circa Sept. 1970; ad for VVAW in *Playboy,* Feb. 1971, 65; VVAW newsletter, 1971, no. 1. Scott Moore spoke of using his father's influence to get one of the more brilliant young executives at Hicks and Greist to take on the assignment of designing the *Playboy* ad.

50. Ken Cloke, Dec. 13, 1988; M.O., 2. The suppression factor in PTSD has been well documented by many of the experts in this field, including Dr. Chaim Shatan, Dr. Robert Jay Lifton, Dr. Charles Figley, Arthur Egendorf, and Jack Smith, among others.

5. THE WORLD BEGINS TO LISTEN

51. Interviews: GRN; SC, 1. Music: "Oh! Camil (the Winter Soldier)," by Graham Nash on his *Wild Tales* album, 1973.

52. Articles: "Dewey Canyon Three," *WS*, April 1, 1971 (vol. 1, no. 1), 1–3. Documents: "The Winter Soldier Investigation" (official report of VVAW), March 1971.

53. Interviews: MO, 2; JK, 1. Documents: "Women's Statement" read at WSI by Barbara Dane (typescript kept privately as part of the WSI archive by Madeleine Moore).

Chapter 3: A Limited Incursion into the Country of Congress: Dewey Canyon III

1. PREPARING FOR THE ASSAULT

54. Interviews: JK, 1; MO, 2. Documents: "Operation Dewey Canyon III" flyer issued by VVAW, circa March 1971; "Opening Statement—VVAW Regional Coordinators' Conference," Feb. 17, 1971, op. cit. Books: *NS*, 26;; *WSU*, 345–46.

55. Interviews: MO, 2; JK, 1. Articles: William L. Claiborne, "Protest Planned Near Capitol," op. cit., A-13; Mary McGrory, "Peace Offensive Crushes Nixon," *WST*, April 23, 1971, n.p.; William F. Crandell, "They Moved the Town," op. cit., 14; "Veterans Plan a War Protest in Capitol," *NYT*, March 17, 1971, n.p.

56. Interviews: BR, 1, 2; JB, 1, 2. Books: John Kerry, "Statement for the Vietnam Veterans Against the War before the Senate Foreign Relations Committee," April 22, 1971, quoted in *NS*, 24. (Note: a slightly fuller version was printed in a pamphlet by Another Mother For Peace.) The lack of combat readiness of the Army of the Republic of Vietnam (ARVN) even in 1971, and the private awareness of this catastrophe-in-the-making by American military brass in the field, have been discussed at length in such works as *About Face* and *A Bright Shining Lie.*

57. Interviews: SS; RK, 1. Articles: "Veterans Plan a War Protest in the Capitol," *NYT*, op. cit.; Jerry T. Baulch, "Jobless Rate Climbs Among Disabled Vets," *LIP*, April 21, 1971, n.p.; James Wieghart, "Capitol Stuff," *NYDN*, April 23, 1971; n.p.; Myron S. Waldman, "Peace Activities Open in Washington," *ND*, April 19, 1971, 6. Documents: "Dewey Canyon III," executive memo circulated to leaders of VVAW, circa March 1971; VVAW Regional Coordinator's Weekly Report No. 2, circa March 1971, authored probably by Jan Barry; John Kerry, "Statement Before the Senate Foreign Relations Committee," op. cit.; Brig. Gen. Hugh B. Hester, "Statement for Press Conference with Vietnam Veterans Against the War," U.S. House of Representatives, March 16, 1971.

58. Interviews: JFK, 1; SM; SS. Articles: Frank Von Riper, "Vietnam Veterans Win Camp-in at Foot of Capitol Hill," *NYDN*, April 23, 1971, 6; Carl Bernstein, "Vietnam Veterans Camped on Mall Resemble Basic Training Outfit," *WP*, April 20, 1971, n.p.; Documents: VVAW Regional Coordinators' Weekly Report No. 2, op. cit.; "Dewey Canyon III," executive memo, op. cit. Although many of the tactics enumerated here are spelled out in detail in this executive memo of VVAW, I have also relied on the testimony of numerous participants to flesh out the master plan of Dewey Canyon III.

2. SHUT OUT AT ARLINGTON: THE CRAZY AND THE DEAD

59. Interviews: SM; SRO. Articles: "Justice Department Admits Misjudgment on Veterans' Camp-Out," *WP*, April 24, 1971, A-12; Mary McGrory, "Veterans Versus War," *BG*, March 26, 1971 (reprint by VVAW-Mass. Pax office), n.p.; Mary McGrory, "Peace Offensive Crushes Nixon," op. cit.; Myron S. Waldman, "Anti-War Vets Protest with Feet," *ND*, April 20, 1971, 3, 11; "Veterans Defy Court Order Against Camp on Mall, *LAT*, April 23, 1971, 1; Frank Van Riper, "Arlington Bars Vet Protest," *NYDN*, April 20, 1971, 6. Books: *NS*, passim.

60. Interviews: JS, 1; SS. Articles: Myron S. Waldman, "Anti-War Vets Protest with Feet," op. cit., 3; Paul W. Valentine, "Vets March Hill, Protest Their War," *WP*, April 20, 1971, A-1; Mary McGrory, "The Funky New 'Legionnaires,' " *WST*, April 25, 1971, n.p.; "1,200 Vietnam War Veterans Stage Opening Protest Here," *WP*, April 20, 1971, n.p.; "Nam Vets State Guerrilla Theater," *The Purdue Exponent,* April 21, 1971, 4. Books: *NS*, 104.

61. Interviews: JS, 1; SS; JFK, 2. The idea that the war would inevitably end within weeks, if not days, of the veterans' arrival in Washington was held by numerous veterans on Operation DCIII—at

least as they have testified in retrospect during the course of my interviews. Articles: Don McLeod, "[Vietnam Veterans Take] Protests to Capitol," *NYP*, April 20, 1971, n.p.; Myron S. Waldman, "Anti-War Vets Protest with Feet," op. cit., 11.

62. Interviews: MO, 2; JK, 2; JS, 1. Articles: Sanford J. Ungar and William L. Claiborne, "Vets' Camp on Mall Banned by Burger," *WP*, April 21, 1971, 12; John W. Finney, "Senators Open Hearing on Ending War," *NYT*, April 21, 1971; n.p.; James McCartney, "Senate Doves: Set Pullout Date," *NYHT*, April 21, 1971, n.p.; "Nam Vets State Guerrilla Theater," *The Purdue Exponent*, op. cit., 4.

63. Interviews: JS, 1; SS.

3. OUTLAWS ON THE MALL

64. Interviews: JS, 1; BR, 1, 2; SS; SR. Audio: Barry Romo speech at an anti–Contra Aid rally at Washington Irving H.S., NYC, Jan. 20, 1988. Articles: Sanford J. Ungar and William L. Claiborne, "Vets' Camp on Mall Banned by Burger," op. cit., A-12; Tim Ferraro and Michael Bernstein, "Veterans Vow to Stay on the Mall, *WDN*, April 21, 1971, n.p.; Judy Luce, "Viet Vets Try Cemetery March Again," *WDN*, April 20, 1971, n.p.; "1,200 Vietnam War Veterans Stage Opening Protest Here," *WP*, op. cit.; George C. Wilson, "Hearing Applauds War Denouncer," *WP*, April 24, 1971, n.p. Documents: Barry Romo's Bronze Star citation, Department of the Army, Headquarters Americal Division, Feb. 27, 1968. Books: *NS*, 42. Sam Schorr quotes, *NS*, 20–23.

65. Interviews: JUP; JS, 1; JFK, 1; SR. Books: John Upton quoted in *NS*, 88.

66. Interviews: MO, 2. Articles: Tom Ferraro and Michael Bernstein, "Veterans Vow to Stay on the Mall," op. cit.; "Nam Vets Refuse to Leave Capitol," AP wire story, April 22, 1971; Henry Aubin, "Weary Vets Quietly Await Police Move," *WP*, April 22, 1971, n.p.; Sanford J. Ungar and Carl Bernstein, "Veterans Turn Minor Prelude into a Major Anti-War Event," *WP*, April 24, 1971, n.p.; Stuart H. Loory, "Veterans Defy Court's Order Against Camp on Capitol Mall," *LAT*, April 22, 1971, A-1, A-17; Frank Van Riper, "Viet Vets Defy Court, Hold Mall," *NYDN*, April 22, 1971, 2; Sanford J. Ungar and William L. Claiborne, "Vets' Camp on Mall Banned by Burger," op. cit, A-1, A-12; "Vets Overrule Supreme Court," *WDN*, April 22, 1971, 1. Books: *WSU*, xiii.

4. DEMOCRACY IN ACTION: PLAYING IT FOR THE MEDIA

67. Interviews: SS. Articles: "Demonstrators Seized at Supreme Court," *Washington Evening Star*, April 22, 1971, A-8; Sanford J. Ungar and William Claiborne, "Vets Disobey Order, Sleep on Mall," *WP*, April 22, 1971, A-1, A-14; "Veterans Staying in Camp on Mall," *WST*, April 22, 1971, 1; Stuart H. Loory, "Veterans Defy Court's Order Against Camp on Mall," op. cit., 17.

68. Interviews: JS, 1; JFK, 2; MO, 2. Articles: "Nam Vets Refuse to Leave Campout," AP wire story, April 22, 1971; Lance Gay and Lyle Denniston, "Vets on Mall Defy Court Order on Camping," *WST*, April 22, 1971, A-1; Frank Van Riper, "Viet Vets Defy Court, Hold Mall," op. cit., 2; "Veterans Defy Court's Order Against Camp on Mall," LAT, op. cit, A-1, A-17.

69. Interviews: MO, 2; SS; JBC, 4; Madeleine Moore, April 1, 1988; JTH. Articles: Stuart H. Loory, "Veterans Defy Court's Order Against Camp on Mall," op. cit., 1, 17; "Nam Vets Refuse to Leave Campout," AP wire story, April 22, 1971, op. cit.; Mary McGrory, "Peace Offensive Crushes Nixon," op. cit. Books: *NS*, 29, 86.

70. Interviews: JTH; MO, 2; JS, 1; AV (on Kennedy smoking joint). Photos: AP wire photo syndicated for publication on April 22, 1971. Articles: "Vets Disobey Order, Sleep on Mall," *WP*, April 22, 1971, 1; Henry Aubin, "Weary Vets Quietly Await Police Move," *WP*, April 22, 1971, n.p.; Nicholas Von Hoffman, "Keep 'Em Down on the Mall," *WP*, Thurs. April 22, 1971, editorial page. Books: *NS*, 29, 68–75. I. F. Stone quoted in *NS*, 76.

71. Interviews: JFK, 1, 2; JS, 1. Articles: "Demonstrators Seized at Supreme Court," *WES*, April 22, 1971, A-8; Henry Aubin, "Weary Vets Quietly Await Police Move," *WP*, April 22, 1971, n.p. Books: *AAO*, 94, 142, 345; *WSU*, 23, 266.

5. THE RETURN OF MEDALS: FORGIVING THE LIVING
AND MAKING PEACE WITH THE DEAD

72. Articles: "Vets Overrule Supreme Court," *WDN*, op. cit, 1; Lance Gay, "Protesters Defy Order of Justices," *WS*, April 22, 1971, A-1, A-8; "Medals Are Tossed Onto Capitol Steps," *WES*, April 23,

1971, A-6; Ken. W. Clawson, "Justice Department Admits Misjudgment on Veterans' Camp-Out," *WP*, April 24, 1971, A-12; Frank Van Riper, "Viet Vets Win Camp-In at Foot of Capitol Hill," *NYDN*, April 23, 1971, 6; Sanford J. Ungar and Carl Bernstein, "Veterans Turn Minor Prelude into a Major Antiwar Event," *WP*, April 24, 1971, n.p.; James M. Naughton, "Judge Lets Veterans Sleep on Mall, Rebukes U.S. Aides," *NYT*, April 23, 1971, 1, 4; "Vets Dump Medals at Capitol," *WDN*, April 23, 1971, n.p.; William L. Claiborne and Sanford J. Ungar, "Judge Lifts Ban on Vets, Scolds U.S.," *WP*, April 23, 1971, A-1.

73. Interviews: SS. Photos: Some of my description of the arrests at the Supreme Court comes from several UPI and AP wire photos of the event. Articles: Frank Van Riper, "Viet Vets Win Camp-In at Foot of Capitol Hill," op. cit., 6; Maurine Beasley, "Trial Clears 4 Veterans, 102 Freed," *WP*, Aug 24, 1971, A-9; "Vietnam Veterans Arrested on Court Steps," *The Purdue Exponent*, April 23, 1971, 1; "Police Move Quickly, Gently in Arresting Protesting Vets," *WP*, April 23, 1971, n.p. Books: *NS*, 30.

74. Interviews: JS, 1; JFK, 1. Articles: "Veterans' Leader Before Senate Panel," *NYT*, April 23, 1971, n.p.; "Vet Says U.S. 'Created a Monster,'" *Washington Daily News*, April 22, 1971, n.p. Documents: "The Testimony of Lieutenant John Kerry for the Vietnam Veterans Against the War Before the Senate Foreign Relations Committee, Washington, D.C., April 22, 1971," reprinted as a booklet by Another Mother for Peace (Beverly Hills, Cal.: 1971). The phrase "a devastating Communist attack on rear guard American troops heading for home" is actually a newsman's paraphrase of Senator Clifford P. Hansen (R-Wyo.) printed in an unsigned UPI story.

75. Interviews: WSC; JS, 1. Articles: An anonymous "parade marshal" quoted in "Medals Are Tossed Onto Capitol Steps," *WES*, April 23, 1971, A-1, A-6; "Vets Dump Medals at Capitol," *WDN*, op. cit.; William L. Claiborne and Sanford J. Ungar, "Judge Lifts Ban on Vets, Scolds U.S.," op. cit.; "Cathedral Eulogy: 'Our War Is Not Yet Over,'" *WES*, April 24, 1971, n.p.; Sanford J. Ungar and Carl Bernstein, "Veterans Turn Minor Prelude in a Major Antiwar Event," op. cit.; Paul W. Valentine and William L. Claiborne, "Vets Leave; Mass March Slated Today," *WP*, April 24, 1971, A-1. Books: *NS*, 23.

76. Interviews: JS, 1; RF. Articles: Art Goldberg, "Vietnam Vets: the Anti-War Army," *Ramparts*, n.d., 14; Paul W. Valentine and William L. Claiborne, "Vets Leave; Mass March Slated Today," op. cit., A-1; Ron Ferrizzi quoted by William L. Claiborne in "Yesterday's Hero Now Feels Clean," *WP*, April 24, 1971, A-9; an anonymous vet quoted by Patrick Owens in "A Garbage Heap of Honor," *ND*, April 24, 1971, n.p.; Frank Van Riper, "The Vets Throw Away Their Vietnam Medals," *NYDN*, April 24, 1971, n.p. Books: Rusty Sachs quoted in *NS*, 138.

77. Interviews: JS, 1; JFK, 1; PG; LR, 2. Articles: Patrick Owens, "A Garbage Heap of Honor," op. cit; Frank Van Riper, "The Vets Throw Away Their Vietnam Medals," op. cit. The words "duty bound" are Kerry's own, spoken in our interview.

78. Articles: "Medals Are Tossed Onto Capitol Steps," *WES*, op. cit., A-1; Sanford J. Ungar and Carl Bernstein, "Veterans Turn Minor Prelude into a Major Antiwar Event," op. cit.; "Veterans Discard Medals to Protest Vietnam War," *WP*, April 24, 1971, A-6. Books: *NS*, 31. Although there is probably no causal connection with the tree planting on the Mall, some veterans were aware of the fact that a graft of the American elm under which George Washington took command of the Continental Army grows in Golden Gate Park, San Francisco.

6. AFTERSHOCKS

79. Interviews: ROM, 1; DT. Books: Bobby Muller quoted in *NS*, 100–102. David Thorne, John Kerry's brother-in-law and the initiator of the book *The New Soldier*, is another veteran who recalls Muller's presence at Dewey Canyon III—and like Hubbard, he also recalls him off to the side of the main action.

80. Interviews: ROM, 1; AH. Articles: Charles Childs, "Our Forgotten Wounded: Assignment to Neglect," with photographs by Co Rentmeester, *Life*, May 22, 1970, 24D–33. Documents: VVAW executive committee memo listing all the regional coordinators, circa 1970–1971; it lists Bob Muller as the "Long Island coordinator." Books: Muller recalls both his military experience in Vietnam and his difficult homecoming in *NS*, 102, 104.

81. Interviews: RP; AH; ROM, 7. Audio: taped speech of Bobby Muller at Bergen County Community

College, April 21, 1988. Articles: "Veterans Discard Medals to Protest Vietnam War," *WP*, April 24, 1971, A-6. Books: *NS*, 96–104.

82. AH; JBE; SRO. Articles: Maurine Beasley, "Trial Clears 4 Veterans, 102 Freed," op. cit., A-9; Joseph Volz, "Vets Tell of 'Killing Everybody,'" *WDN*, April 24, 1971, n.p.; "Fulbright Panel Hears Antiwar Vet," *WP*, April 23, 1971, A-4; Nicholas Von Hoffman, "Army of Peace," *American Report*, May 21, 1971 (vol. 1, no. 32), n.p.; Jan Barry quoted by Art Goldberg in "Vietnam Vets: The Anti-War Army," *Ramparts*, May, 1971, 12. Books: *WSU*, 362. The poster "Girls Say Yes" featured a cheesecake photo of the three Baez sisters—Joan, Pauline, and Mimi.

83. Interviews: RK, 1 and in conv.; ROM, 1; Tony Russo and Daniel Ellsberg in separate conversations with GN. Articles: Donald Jackson, "Confessions of 'The Winter Soldiers,'" *Life*, July 9, 1971 (vol. 71, no. 2), 22–27. Books: *WSU*, 365–69; *BOTF*, 146.

7. NIXON HITS BACK, AND THE POW MOVEMENT IS BORN

84. Interviews: RJL; ROM, 1; DT. Books: *HFTW*, 185–86.

85. Interviews: RJL; DT; FRL. Books: *WSU*, 407–9; *TPOP*, 390–91; *Facts on File* (1973), 683. Today, in fact, used copies of *The New Soldier* are exceedingly rare.

86. Books: Kissinger's view of soldiers as "dumb, stupid animals to be used as pawns for foreign policy" is reported in Bob Woodward and Carl Bernstein, *The Final Days* (NY: Simon and Schuster, 1976), 194–95. Quotes and interpretations of Richard Nixon's press conferences (March 4, 1971 and April 16, 1971) are from H. Bruce Franklin in *M.I.A. or Mythmaking in America* (Brooklyn: Lawrence Hill Books, 1992), 49–52, 63, 71, 74, 200. "Bring our Daddy home safe, sound and soon" was a slogan used in advertisements run by Texas billionaire H. Ross Perot's United We Stand organization. Perot at that time was a director of the Richard M. Nixon Foundation. See H. Bruce Franklin, op. cit., 50.

Chapter 4: Invisible Wounds: Post-Traumatic Stress Disorder

1. THE RAP GROUPS: AN INTUITIVE SORT OF TRUST

87. Interviews: RJL. Articles: Robert Jay Lifton, "Beyond Atrocity," and "Victims and Executioners" in *COW*, 23–25, 419–25. Books: *HFTW*, 75; *COW*, xi–xiii; *Oversight of Medical Care of Veterans Wounded in Vietnam* (Government Printing Office, 1970), 419–510.

88. JBC, 1, 2; RJL; CS, 1. Max Cleland's testimony to the Cranston Committee is quoted in *COW*, 424. Articles: Chaim F. Shatan, "Bogus Manhood, Bogus Honor: Surrender and Transfiguration in the United States Marine Corps," in *Psychoanalytic Perspectives on Aggression*, ed. George D. Goldman and Donald S. Milman (Dubuque, Ia.: Kendall Hunt Publishing, 1978), 77–100. Books: *HFTW*, 420.

89. Interviews: RJL; CS, 1; SS; JS, 1. Articles: RJL, "Beyond Atrocity," in *COW*, 18. Books: *HFTW*, 75–79, 80–81, 87–88, 145–47, 191–92. I am indebted to Larry Heinemann for the insight, during one of our conversations, that "Vietnam veterans get a joke that nobody else gets, and Marines get a joke that even other veterans don't get."

90. Interviews: RJL; AE. Books: *HEAL*, 2–3, 22–23, 27–29, 32–39, 55–57, 61, 65–67, 79–80, 85, 89–93.

2. A CRISIS OF IDENTITY: LIFTON AND SHATAN "JOIN THE VETERANS' CLUB"

91. Interviews: JW, 1. Articles: Chaim F. Shatan, "Post-Vietnam Syndrome," *NYT*, May 6, 1972, op-ed page; Chaim F. Shatan, "The Grief of Soldiers: Vietnam Combat Veterans' Self-Help Movement," the text of a paper presented at the 1972 annual meeting of the American Orthopsychiatric Association in Detroit, printed as a Special Report of the *American Journal of Orthopsychiatry*, July 1973 (vol. 43, no. 4), 640–73. Dr. Shatan was so kind as to present me with his original uncut text of this seminal essay. Books: Erik Erikson, *Identity: Youth and Crisis* (NY: W. W. Norton, 1968), passim; Erik Erikson, *Young Man Luther: A Study in Psychoanalysis and History* (NY: W. W. Norton, 1962), passim; *HFTW*, 28, 33–36, 86–88; Robert J. Lifton's "Testimony before Subcommittee on Veterans Affairs, U.S. Senate, January 27, 1970," reprinted in *The Vietnam Veteran in Contem-*

porary Society: Collected Materials Pertaining to Young Veterans (Wash, D.C.: Veterans Administration, 1972), part 4, n.p.

92. Interviews: RJL; AE; CS, 1. Articles: Chaim Shatan, "The Grief of Soldiers," op. cit. 648–53.
Books: *HFTW,* 69, 426.

3. SARAH HALEY STARTS A REVOLUTION IN BOSTON: "WHEN THE PATIENT REPORTS ATROCITIES"

93. Interviews: LH, 1. Larry Heinemann was only one of many Vietnam veterans who recounted being
treated by the VA in this cavalier fashion. Articles: Douglas R. Bey Jr., and Walter E. Smith, "Organizational Consultation in a Combat Unit," *American Journal of Psychiatry,* Oct., 1971 (vol.
128), 401–6, quoted in *HFTW,* 416–17; General William C. Westmoreland, "Mental Health—An
Aspect of Command" (no citation available). Documents: Dr. Chaim F. Shatan, "Memo: The Vietnam Veteran and the Psychoanalytic Community," Feb. 2, 1971, circulated to the New York psychoanalytic community from the Post-Doctoral Psychoanalytic Office at NYU. Letters: LH to GN,
Dec. 2, 1999. Books: *HFTW,* 337–39, 419–22; *WAL,* 20–21.

94. Interviews: CH, 1.

95. Interviews: SH. Articles: Sarah Haley, "When the Patient Reports Atrocities: Specific Treatment
Considerations of the Vietnam Veteran," *Archives of General Psychiatry,* Feb. 1974 (vol. 30),
192–93.

96. Interviews: SH; CH, 1. Articles: Sarah Haley, "When the Patient Reports Atrocities," op. cit.,
193–96; Henry S. Rouss, "Yale Psychiatrist: It's on the War in Vietnam," *Congressional Record,*
Jan. 22, 1968, E106. Letters: Arthur S. Blank Jr. to JBC, circa Jan. 1968.

4. A COMMUNITY OF HEALING FORMS: THE FIRST NATIONAL CONFERENCE IN ST. LOUIS, 1973

97. Interviews: SH; CH, 1; FSM, 1. Leonard Neff died before I began my work on *Home to War,* but
I learned much about him and his eminent influence in the field of PTSD studies from Haley, Me-
shad, and other of his colleagues. Articles: Leonard Neff, "Traumatic Neurosis," paper presented
at the annual meeting of the American Psychological Association, California, May 1975, quoted in
Sarah A. Haley, "Treatment Implications of Post-Combat Stress Response Syndromes for Mental
Health Professionals," in *SDAV,* 258. Books: *CFDM,* vi–vii, 166–67.

98. Interviews: CS, 1; SM, 1; JS, 2; WPM; JM; RJL; YM. The quotes from Lifton are obviously as
Shatan remembers them. Books: *CFDM,* 238.

5. TURNING THE PSYCHIATRIC GUNS AROUND: POST-TRAUMATIC STRESS DISORDER GETS RECOGNIZED

99. Interviews: CS, 1; FRL; JST. Articles: Forest Lindley Jr., "The History of Vietnam Veterans: Initial
Policy Decisions: Who Would Live and Who Would Die," *The Stars and Stripes—The National
Tribune,* Nov. 11, 1982 (vol. 105, no. 45), 17; Forest Lindley Jr., "The History of Vietnam Veterans: Fear and Loathing in the White House and the VA," *The Stars and Stripes—The National Tribune,* Nov. 18, 1982 (vol. 105, no. 46), 5.

100. Interviews: FRL; CS, 1; SH. Articles: Sarah Haley, "The Vietnam Veteran and His Pre-School
Child: Child Rearing as a Delayed Stress in Combat Veterans," *Journal of Contemporary Psychotherapy,* Spring–Summer 1984 (vol. 14, no. 1), 114–21. Books: *A Study of the Problems Facing
Vietnam Era Veterans in Their Readjustment to Civilian Life,* 92nd Congress, 2nd Session, Senate
Committee Print No. 7 (Wash., D.C.: U.S. Government Printing Office, Jan 31, 1972), v–vii, 1–11,
178–81, 236–37. Many Vietnam veterans I interviewed spoke of having gone to a VA hospital but
having left in anger or frustration (or sometimes even terror) before they were even seen by any
professional on staff there.

101. Interviews: SH; CS, 1. Dr. Spitzer's words were recalled by Sarah Haley, and admittedly the whole
slant of this first meeting between Chaim Shatan's Vietnam Veterans' Working Group and Dr.
Spitzer's *DSM-III* task force is presented from the PTSD advocates' point of view. I assume that
"the St. Louis group," as Shatan calls them, would probably have a very different view of the challengers' case. Articles: Bonnie L. Green, John P. Wilson, and Jacob D. Lindy, "Conceptualizing

Post-Traumatic Stress Disorder: A Psychosocial Framework," in *TAIW*, vol. 1, 62–63; E. L. Quarantelli, "An Assortment of Conflicting Views on Mental Health: The Consequences of Traumatic Events," in *TAIW*, vol. I, 180, 189–93; Jeffrey C. Savitsky and Donald M. Hartsough, "Use of the Environment and the Legal Impact of Resulting Emotional Harm," in *TAIW*, vol. 1, 383–84; James L. Titchener, "Post-Traumatic Decline: A Consequence of Unresolved Destructive Drives," in *TAIW*, vol. 2, 17; Susan D. Solomon, "Mobilizing Social Support Networks in Times of Disaster," *TAIW*, vol. 2, 236.

102. Interviews: CS, 1; SH. The terms "Ice Princess" and "devil's advocate" come from Sarah Haley, as well as the phrases "just go away quietly" and "bombarded us with methodology." Articles: R. Grinker, "The Medical, Psychiatric and Social Problems of War Neurosis," *Cincinnati Journal of Medicine*, 1945, vol. 26, 241–59. Books: John Russell ("Jack") Smith, *A Review of One Hundred and Twenty Years of the Psychological Literature on Reactions to Combat from the Civil War through the Vietnam War: 1860–1980*, thesis submitted in partial fulfillment of the requirements for the degree of Doctor of Philosophy in the Department of Psychology of the Graduate School of Arts and Sciences, Duke University, Durham, N.C., Feb. 1981, 122–25.

Chapter 5: Trampling on the Bill of Rights: The Gainesville Conspiracy

1. WINNING BATTLES AND LOSING THE WAR: FROM OPERATION HEART OF AMERICA TO OPERATION PEACE ON EARTH

103. Interviews: JU; AH; MO, 2; JMU. Books: *WSU*, 367–68 passim.

104. Interviews: JU; SRO; MO, 2; DM; AH. Articles: Leonard Boscarine, "Cairo Newspaper—House Organ for Whites," *Focus Midwest/71* (St. Louis: 1971), vol. 8, no. 54, 8–9; William R. Brinton, "The Story of Confrontation," *Focus Midwest/71*, op. cit., 10–12; Gelvin Stevenson, "The Economic Basis of the Cairo Conflict," *Focus Midwest/71*, op. cit., 19–20; Betty Shiflett, "Cairo, U.S.A.," *Evergreen Review*, June, 1971 (vol. 15, no. 90), 21–31, 57–64. Books: Tom Wicker, *A Time to Die* (NY: Times Books, 1975), 311–17 passim.

105. Interviews: AH; SRO; RB, 1; SM. Articles: John McHugh, "Vets Mark Day with Protest," *Chicago Today*, Oct. 26, 1971, n.p.; James Campbell, "Vietnam Vets Parade for Peace," *CST*, Oct. 26, 1971, n.p. Documents: VVAW memo to regional and state coordinators from Mike Oliver, Executive Committee, Aug. 10, 1971; New York VVAW schedule of events, Aug. 1971; "Staff Meeting Minutes," VVAW Executive Committee, Sept. 22, 1971 (presumably written by Secretary Joe Urgo); "Vietnam Veterans Against the War Invites You to Attend an Evening to Reflect with Daniel Ellsberg—William DeKooning—Peter Yarrow," VVAW flyer for event Oct. 25, 1971; "A Report to the Executive Committee of VVAW concerning a month's trip to the field and other observations," uncorrected draft by Craig Scott Moore, circa Nov. 1971; memo to VVAW regional coordinators from Mike Oliver, Nov. 18, 1971; Ed Damato, memo to membership from VVAW, New York State Regional Office, Aug. 13, 1971. Letters: Randy Barnes to GN, circa 1988; Joseph M. Taussig (counsel of the American Legion) to Bart Savage, Chicago Regional Coordinator of VVAW, July 20, 1971.

106. Interviews: SRO; ED; JB, 2; DB; AH; DS; WS; KC. Articles: John Kyper, "Vietnam Vets Get It On!!!" *WIN*, Feb. 1972 (vol. 8, no. 2), 6–9; "The Reason We Chose," *NYT*, Dec. 29, 1971, n.p.; Jan Barry, "The Spirit of '71," *WIN*, Feb. 1972 (vol. 8, no. 2), 10–12. Documents: Testimony of Joseph Bangert in *TWSI*, 72–74; VVAW National Office memo giving nationwide chronology of operations, Jan.–Dec. 1971. Letters: Jon Birch and the VVAW National Office to Scott Camil, Dec. 2, 1971. Books: *WSU*, 372–75; *TWW*, 531–32.

2. CAUGHT BETWEEN THE MAOISTS AND THE POLICE: THE WINTER SOLDIER ORGANIZATION

107. Interviews: SC, 1, 2; RB, 1; JU; AH; RBO; MO, 2. Articles: Jan Barry, "The Spirit of '71," op. cit., 10–11; Ward Just, "Introduction" to *AF*, 16–17 (from which I quote Just's summary of the *Issues and Answers* interview); Scott Camil quoted in Fred J. Cook, "Justice in Gainesville: The Real Conspiracy Exposed," *TN*, Oct. 1, 1973, 298; Scott Camil, "Undercover Agents' War on Vietnam Veterans," in *It Did Happen Here: Recollections of Political Repression in America*, ed. Bud Schultz and Ruth Schultz (Berkeley: Univ. of California Press, 1989), 318–33. Letters: Jon Birch

and the VVAW National Office to Scott Camil, Dec. 2, 1971. Books: *FOD,* 222–56 passim; *AF,* 784, 790–91. Almost every VVAW vet I interviewed had a Scott Camil story and strong feelings about the man, one way or the other. The phrases "totally committed" and "a good person to have covering your backside," as well as many other details about Camil, come from Mike Oliver in our second interview.

108. RB, 1; SC, 1, 2. Documents: FBI Director J. Edgar Hoover's memo to the Jacksonville Director, Dec. 22, 1971, is quoted in Scott Camil's "Undercover Agents' War on Vietnam Veterans," op. cit., 325. Scott Camil let me read his FBI file (such of it as was not blacked out) obtained through the Freedom of Information Act. The second memo I quote from is undated; it begins simply: "Teletype to Jacksonville et al./RE: Scott Camil/ 100-463962."

109. Interviews: AH; DF; ANH; PM. Pete Mahoney offered the quote from his FBI files during our interview. Documents: Memo from VVAW National Office to regional chapters, Jan. 21, 1972. Books: *WSU,* 377–93; *WAL,* 334.

110. Interviews: SC, 1. Articles: "Florida Antiwar Leaders Plan Renewed Rallies" (AP wire story), *Gainesville Sun,* April 17, 1972, 33; Arnold Bucholtz, "YD, VVAW condemn YR resolution," *The Florida Alligator,* April 24, 1972, 5; Elli Moss, "War Demonstrators asked to leave Reitz Union," *The Florida Alligator,* May 1, 1972 (vol. 64, no. 128), 1. Books: *WSU,* 372, 377–78, 389; *DC,* 77, 80–81.

111. Interviews: TH; JU, 1; TZ. Articles: William F. Crandell, "They Moved the Town," op. cit., 20–21. Documents: Brian Adams, "Thoughts on the Future," in VVAW Report on the Sept. 29, 1972, National Steering Committee Meeting in Palo Alto, Calif., report dated Oct. 18, 1972, n.p.; VVAW/ Winter Soldier Organization, a statement of purpose reprinted in *WS,* June 1973 (vol. 3, no. 4), 3. Letters: Brian Adams to Jan Barry, Sept. 6, 1974. Books: Tom Hayden quoted in *WSU,* 393.

3. THE GOVERNMENT INDICTS THE VETERANS' MOVEMENT

112. Interviews: Skip Morgan, Jan. 25, 1988; BR, 2. Articles: Steven E. Conliff, "The Dreaded Yippie Curse: Campaigns, Conventions, Confrontations and Other Madness," in *BL,* 350–97. The details of Muskie's crying episode are reported in Conliff. Documents: VVAW Chicago Office, "Dateline Chicago," internal news bulletin, circa May–June 1972. Books: *WSU,* 390–92; *SIR,* 115; S. Brian Willson, *A Beginning Outline of Resistance,* op. cit., 11; Jeb Stuart Magruder, Watergate testimony to U.S. Congress, June 14, 1973, quoted in *BL,* 350; *DC,* 60. Films: *The Last Patrol,* documentary produced and directed by Frank Cavestani, 1973.

113. Interviews: NS; MS. Articles: Scott Camil, "Undercover Agents' War on Vietnam Veterans," op. cit., 326. Documents: The Gainesville 8 Collective, "Free the Gainesville 8 and All Political Prisoners," handout included in *WS,* April, 1973 (vol. 3, no. 2), 8–9; "Tallahassee Proposal," part of the notes from the VVAW National Steering Committee meeting in Milwaukee, July 21, 1972.

4. KOVIC CONFRONTS THE FLORIDA NATIONAL GUARD: A CALL TO REVOLUTION

114. Interviews: JM; SC, 1, 2, 5; TZ; FC; RBO; BR, 2; BD; RBI, 1; ANH; PM. Articles: Steven Conliff, "The Dreaded Yippie Curse," op. cit., 354; Donald M. Rothberg, "Disabled Vets Are Up Front in Anti-War March," AP wire story, July 22, 1972. Documents: "Free the Gainesville 8 and all political prisoners, handout, op. cit. Books: *BOTF,* 14–21 passim; *DC,* 84–85 passim. Films: *The Last Patrol,* documentary produced and directed by Frank Cavestani, 1973.

115. Interviews: RK, 1; BD; TZ, SC, 1; RBO; BR, 2. Photographs: There is a striking series of photographs of Kovic, Muller, and Wyman, their three wheelchairs abreast, often linked arm in arm, by Per-Olof Odman, a Swedish-American Vietnam veteran, two of which were published in *25 Years Fighting for Veterans, Peace & Justice,* a 25th anniversary souvenir publication of VVAW (NY: 1992). Articles: Abe Weisburd, "New and Forceful Role for Vietnam Vets," *The Guardian,* May 1972 (VVAW reprint). Books: *FAL,* 387; *ATW,* 1, passim. Films: *The Last Patrol,* Frank Cavestani, 1973.

5. THE BATTLE OF MIAMI BEACH

116. Interviews: BR, 2; RBO; MO, 2. Articles: Steven Conliff, "The Dreaded Yippie Curse," op. cit., 337, 354–58 passim. Books: *DC,* 74, 83–86, 97–98, 104–7; *FAL,* 386–92.

117. Interviews: FC; RBO; BR, 2. Books: *BOTF*, 176–84. Films: *The Last Patrol*, Frank Cavestani, 1973; *Born on the Fourth of July*, feature film directed by Oliver Stone and produced by Universal Studios, 1989.

6. ONE STRESSED-OUT AGENT PROVOCATEUR AND A ROOMFUL OF MACHO VETS

118. Interviews: BR, 2; PM; RK, conv.; SC, 1; DB; JS, 1. Articles: "Gainesville 8 Trial Set/Demos Planned!—July 17," *WS*, June 1973 (vol. 1, no. 4), 12; Rob Elder, "What Led Anti-War Vets to Gainesville?", *MH*, Aug. 13, 1972 (vol. 62, no. 258), 24; John Kifner, "Informer Appears Key to U.S. Case Against 6 Antiwar Veterans," *NYT*, Aug. 14, 1972, n.p.; "Anti-War Veterans' Case Resembles Berrigan Trial," editorial in *CO*, Aug. 29, 1972, n.p.; Shawn D. Muller, "War Hero of 1967 Now Finds He's Become 'Political Criminal,'" *Wilmington Evening Journal* (Delaware), Jan. 5, 1973, n.p.; Frank Donner, "The Confession of an FBI Informer" (no citation available); Scott Camil, "Undercover Agents' War on Vietnam Veterans," op. cit., 329. Documents: *The United States of America v. John K. Briggs, Scott Camil, Alton C. Foss, John W. Kniffin, Peter Mahoney, Stanley K. Michelsen, Jr., William J. Patterson, and Donald P. Perdue*, indictment filed in the U.S. District Court for the Northern District of Florida, Gainesville Division, Oct. 1973. Books: *ATW*, 15.

119. Interviews: NS; SC, 1. Articles: "Conspiracy's Sorry Record," editorial in *SPT*, Aug. 10, 1972, n.p.; "Anti-War Veterans' Case Resembles Berrigan Trial," op. cit.; Lucien K. Truscott IV, "Watergate & the VVAW: To Discredit the Vets," *VV*, May 31, 1973, n.p.; Nicholas Von Hoffman, "My God! Is This America?" *SPT*, Aug. 23, 1972, n.p.; John Kifner, "Informer Appears Key to U.S. Case Against 6 Antiwar Veterans," op. cit.; Fred J. Cook, "Justice in Gainesville: The Real Conspiracy Exposed," op. cit., 300–1; Frank Donner, "The Confession of an FBI Informer," op. cit. Books: *WSU*, 378–80.

7. PEACE WITH HONOR; HEROES DISHONORED

120. Interviews: BR, 2; SC, 1; PM. Articles: "Vietnam Veterans Plead Innocent," *MH*, Nov. 7, 1972, 1B–2B; Rob Elder, "Convention Spy Data Called Garbage," *MH*, June 10, 1973, n.p.; William Patterson quoted by Shawn D. Mullen, "War Hero of 1967 Now Finds He's Become 'Political Criminal,'" op. cit. Letters: Jan Barry to Herbert Mitgang of the *NYT*, Dec. 28, 1972. Books: *FAL*, 392; *WSU*, 390–99; *TPOP*, 563–635; *TWI*, 553–63; *AAO*, 343; *ONA*, 692; *NAV*, 168–82; *AAV*, 193–225.

121. Interviews: NS; RBO; SC, 1; TZ; BR, 1; PM. Articles: Rob Elder, "What Led Anti-War Vets to Gainesville," op. cit., 1-A, 24-A; Shawn D. Mullen, "War Hero of 1967 Now Finds He's Become a Political Prisoner," op. cit.; Fred J. Cook, "Justice in Gainesville: The Real Conspiracy Exposed," op. cit., 298–99; Rob Elder, "VVAW Rejected Offer of Guns, Police Say," *MH*, May 26, 1973, n.p.; Rob Elder, "The Gainesville Eight: Dirty Tricks on Trial," *Ramparts*, Aug.–Sept. 1973, 27, 51; "Support of VVAW by Sale of Drugs Is Investigated" (AP wire story), July 20, 1972. Documents: *The United States of America v. John K. Briggs . . .* , op. cit. Letters: Jan Barry to Herbert Mitgang, Dec. 28, 1972.

8. "INNUENDO AND SUPPOSITION," AND FBI AGENTS WITH EARPHONES

122. Interviews: NS; MS. Articles: Trudy Rubin, "Antiwar Vets' Trial May Yield Watergate Data," *CSM*, June 14, 1973, n.p.; Rob Elder, "The Gainesville Eight: Dirty Tricks on Trial," op. cit., 27; Jack Anderson, "Vets Suspect Watergate Antics," *GS*, July 5, 1973, n.p.; Fred J. Cook, "Justice in Gainesville: The Real Conspiracy Exposed," op. cit., 296–98; Mike Henderson, "Gainesville 8 Charge Trial Is a Cover-Up," *GS*, May 30, 1973, n.p.; "Vets Trial: One Carton of Slingshots," *HIP*, March 9–16, 1973, n.p.; Jere Moore, "Mitchell Denies Gainesville 8 Bugging," *TMR*, April 26, 1973, n.p.; John Mueller, "Judge Blocks Watergate Link to Trial of Vets," *LT*, June 21, 1973, n.p. Letters: Jan Barry to Herbert Mitgang, Dec. 28, 1972. Books: *TWW*, 555; *WSU*, 222–23, 385, 389, 409; *TPOP*, 572–73, 576, 590.

123. Interviews: MS; NS; PM. Articles: "Vets Trial: One Carton of Slingshots," op. cit.; "Gag Rule Clamped on Gainesville 8 Trial Here," *GS*, July 14, 1973, n.p.; "Saga of Taintsville," editorial in *GS*,

July 17, 1973, n.p.; John Mueller, "Judge Blocks Watergate Link to Trial of Vets," op. cit.; Jan Barry, "Vietnam Veterans' 'Conspiracy' Trial," unpublished draft of a newspaper story, circa 1973; "Antiwar Veterans Group Urges that Data on It Be Made Public," *NYT,* May 22, 1973, n.p.; "Vets Trial: One Carton of Slingshots," op. cit.; Fred J. Cook, "Justice in Gainesville: The Real Conspiracy Exposed," op. cit., 296–97, 299; Rob Elder, "The Gainesville Eight: Dirty Tricks on Trial," op. cit., 27, 52.

9. "IS PERJURY PART OF A PROSECUTOR'S DUTY?"

124. Interviews: DB; NS; PM; Ron Kovic, conv. Novelist James Park Sloan, who had been a paratrooper in Vietnam, was one of the people who expressed the conviction (in 1973) that the 82nd Airborne would soon be called in to stop an impeachment trial. Articles: "What Peace?" *WS,* April 1973 (vol. 3, no. 2), 2; Documents: "Information for Participants from VVAW: 'Sign the Treaty' March, January 20, 1973," VVAW/WSO flyer reprinted in *WS,* June 1973 (vol. 3, no. 4), 3; "Amilcar Cabral Assassinated," *WS,* April 1973 (vol. 3, no. 2), 5; "Pat Chenoweth Framed," *WS,* April 1973 (vol. 3, no. 2), 6; "Operation County Fair," *WS,* April 1973 (vol. 3, no. 2), 7; "Acquittal and Retrial: Gary Lawton," *WS,* April 1973 (vol. 3, no. 2), 12; "Wounded Knee," *WS,* June 1973 (vol. 3, no. 4), 7; Tom Zangrilli, "VVAW Attacked Again," *WS,* April 1973 (vol. 3, no. 2) 10; Fred J. Cook, "Justice in Gainesville: The Real Conspiracy Exposed," op. cit., 299;. Letters: Randy Barnes to GN, 1988. Personal Journals: Journal of GN, entry Jan. 28, 1973. Books: *TPOP,* 633–35; *WSU,* 402–3; *TWW,* 564–65; Donald Freed, *Agony in New Haven: The Trial of Bobby Seale, Ericka Huggins and the Black Panther Party* (NY: Simon and Schuster, 1973), 329.

125. Interviews: MS; PM; RBO. Articles: Fred J. Cook, "Justice in Gainesville: The Real Conspiracy Exposed," op. cit. 299–301; "Vets Trial: One Carton of Slingshots," *HIP,* op. cit.; Scott Camil, "Undercover Agents' War on Vietnam Veterans," op. cit., 328.

10. WINNERS WITH A BROKEN BACK

126. Interviews: RBO; CS, 1; SC, 1; PM; NS; MS. Articles: "The Panther Acquittal," *NYT,* May 14, 1971, quoted in Donald Freed, *Agony in New Haven,* 298; Fred J. Cook, "Justice in Gainesville: The Real Conspiracy Exposed," op. cit., 300–1; "Used by U.S. as Decoy, VVAW Informer Claims," AP wire story in *MH,* Aug. 5, 1974, n.p. Documents: "Scott Camil's Closing Statement: Pro Se," Aug. 1973. Letters: Doris Peterson to Dr. Jon B. Bjornson, Oct. 13, 1972. Books: *Scott Camil's Legal History,* 1975, a pamphlet prepared by Camil's attorney Larry Turner to raise money for yet another government prosecution of Camil on trumped-up charges of selling cocaine and assaulting federal officers, of which he was again acquitted.

Chapter 6: Unfinished Business: The War Against the VA

1. JOHN MUSGRAVE AND THE WALKING DEAD, USMC

127. Interviews: MAS. Articles: "A Lost War," *Time,* April 24, 1995 (vol. 145, no. 17), 22–48. *WSU,* 380–85; *AAO,* 381.

128. Interviews: MAS; JMU; BJ. Documents: "Viet Vets 'Distrust' VA," AP wire story, reprinted in Charles A. Stenger and Lidi Verdi, "Vietnam Era Veteran: Entitlement and Utilization of VA Health Care Benefits," in-house document prepared for the VA Central Office, March 1978.

2. THE MEN WHO GOT LEFT BEHIND

129. Interviews: JMU; JW, 1. Books: *VWA,* 40–42; John P. Wilson, *Identity, Ideology and Crisis: The Vietnam Veteran in Transition,* Parts 1 and 2 (Cleveland: Cleveland State Univ., 1977–1978); *TPR,* 55–57.

3. "BAD PAPER" AND "A FRIEND IN THE WHITE HOUSE"

130. Interviews: SRO; FRL; LH in conv. Audio: Tape of Michael Leaveck, lecture at the "Vietnam Legacies: Twenty Years Later" conference, University of California, Davis, April 28, 1995. Articles: Charles Childs, "Our Forgotten Wounded: Assignment to Neglect," illustrated by Co Rentmeester, *Life,* May 22, 1970 (vol. 68, no. 19), 24D–33; "VA Takeover," *WS,* Dec. 1973 (vol. 3, no.

9), 7. Documents: "Guidelines for the Rehabilitation of Military and Veteran Heroin Addicts," VVAW policy paper prepared by the Veterans Action Group for the National Office in New York, summer 1971; "Proposals for Improving VA Facilities and Suggestions for Improving the Care Which Its Patients Receive," VVAW policy paper prepared by the Veterans Action Group for the National Office, New York, summer 1971. Books: *CAC*, 122–31, 153–58, passim. The Daniel P. Moynihan quote is from *CAC*, 125.

131. Interviews: JL. Articles: "Secret Discharge Codes," *WS*, April 1974 (vol. 4, no. 4), 7; "No Help Here!: V.A. vs. Vets," *WS*, April 1974 (vol. 4, no. 4), 6; "Discharge Review Boards," *WS*, March 1974 (vol. 4, no. 3), 5; "VVAW/WSO: Discharge Upgrading," *WS*, Feb. 1974 (vol. 4, no. 2), 6; "Veterans Benefits?" *WS*, Oct. 1973 (vol. 3, no. 8), 6; "Vietnam Vets Day," *WS*, May 1974 (vol. 4, no. 5), 14; Tim O'Brien, "The Vietnam Veteran: Prisoner of Peace," *Penthouse*, March 1974, 114; William Greider, "Viet Vets Press for Jobs, Tuition Aid," *WP*, March 29, 1974, A-26. Donald Johnson's secret warning to his regional directors concerning the Vietnam Veterans Day demonstrations at VA sites was reported by nationally syndicated columnist Jack Anderson, March 29, 1974, and excerpted in "Vietnam Vets Day," *WS*, May 1974, op. cit., 14; "Milwaukee Takes V.A. Office Again!" *WS*, Jan. 1974 (vol. 4, no. 1), 7. Books: *TVV*, 180–82.

4. VIETNAM VETERANS DAY WITHOUT THE VETERANS, AND A VA CHIEF TOO BUSY FOR HIS CLIENTS

132. Articles: William Greider, "Viet Vets: A Sad Reminder," *WP*, March 30, 1974, n.p.; Joseph Volz, "Outflanked on $: Viet Vets," *NYDN*, March 30, 1974, 1; "Nixon Hails Veterans' Efforts in Vietnam," *NYT*, March 29, 1974, n.p.; Ned Scharff, "A Veteran Battles to Readjust," *WSN*, March 29, 1974, A-1, A-4; Mary McGrory, "Nixon: Ungiving to Warriors, Unforgiving to Dodgers," *WSN*, March 29, 1974, n.p.; William H. Greider, "The Vietnam Veteran: Losing the Paper War," *Penthouse*, Sept., 1974, 125–29; Joseph Volz, "Viet Vets & Cops Clash Atop Monument in D.C.," *NYDN*, March 29, 1974, n.p.; Lee Stillwell, "All-Out Attacks Hurled at Johnson," *Scripps-Howard* newspapers, April 19, 1974, n.p.; "Head of Veterans Agency Says He Will Not Quit," UPI news dispatch circa mid-April 1974, n.p.; Richard Harwood, "VA Chief Johnson to Resign," *WP*, April 23, 1974, A-1, A-12; "Nixon," UPI news dispatch from Key Biscayne, Fla., April 1, 1974. Books: *TPR*, 7–8, 54, 68.

133. Interviews: AH. Articles: "Free Gary Lawton and All Political Prisoners," *WS*, Feb, 1975 (vol. 5, no. 2), 8–9; "Ashby Leach Campaign: Lessons Learned: Armed for the Future," *TV*, June 1977 (vol. 7, no. 3), 8–9, 15; "National Campaign Builds to Free Ashby Leach," *TV*, Nov/Dec., 1976 (vol. 6, no. 6), 1–2; "Free Ashby Leach: Vets Battle for Better Life," TV, Oct. 1976 (vol. 6, no. 5), 2; "A New Opportunity for the VA," editorial in *WP*, April 24, 1974; n.p.; "US-Saigon Ignore Peace Agreement: Vietnam," *WS*, Aug. 1974 (vol. 4, no. 7), 2; "Demonstrate: July 1–4 in Washington, D.C.," *WS*, June/July 1974 (vol. 4, no. 6), 8–9; "Editorial: The Vets' Movement," *WS*, Aug., 1974 (vol. 4, no. 7), 10; Books: *The Case of Gary Lawton and Zurebu Gardner,* pamphlet published by VVAW/WSO, circa Feb. 1974; *CAC*, 122–31; 153–58; *TVV*, 180–82; *TPR*, 7–8, 54, 68.

5. DEWEY CANYON IV: DEFEAT IN WASHINGTON

134. Interviews: DF; BB; DC; DCO; FRL. Articles: "Zumwalt Says He Turned Down VA Post, Cites Domestic Politics," UPI story, *WP*, July 1, 1974, n.p. Documents: FBI Milwaukee Office internal document, analyzing the attempt of the RU to take over VVAW, dated March 9, 1976. Books: *WSU*, 413; *TPOP*, 568–70, 626, 634; *WAL*, 332–35.

135. Interviews: DF; DCO. Articles: "Veterans Clubbed in Capitol Protest," UPI nationally syndicated story, July 4, 1974; "VVAW-WSO Demo Builds Unity!" *WS*, Aug. 1974 (vol. 4, no. 7), 7. Books: *WAL*, 332–35.

6. KOVIC MEETS UNGER: THE PATIENTS'/WORKERS' RIGHTS COMMITTEE IN LONG BEACH

136. Interviews: SS; BU, 1, 2; RK, 1, conv. Books: *ATW*, 68–86.

137. Interviews: RK, conv.; RBO; DH; MI, 1, 2; JMU. Articles: Richard Boyle, "Paralyzed Vets Spur Investigation of Hospital Terror," *LAFP*, July 20, 1973, 1, 5; Richard Boyle, "Intimidation & Surveil-

lance at VA Hospital," *LAFP,* July 27, 1973, 5; Myra Forsberg, "VVAW Campsite—Discussion, Reflection" and "VVAW Spokesman Attacks Arnow," *The Independent Florida Alligator,* Aug. 2, 1973, 12–13; David Harris, "Ask a Marine," *Rolling Stone,* July 19, 1973 (no. 139), reprinted in *Rolling Stone: A Twenty-Fifth Anniversary Special,* June 11, 1992 (no. 632), 77–81. Books: *ATW,* 68–86.

138. RK, conv.; PAM, conv.; DH; BW, 1, 3; TZ. The terrible breakup of Southern California's VVAW has been recounted to me several times by Bob Waddell, on whom it left a lasting imprint. Tom Zangrilli has also recounted the pain that that final falling out with Kovic caused him. Many of the people in that room, like Kovic and Zangrilli, have not seen each other again for going on three decades.

7. THE AMERICAN VETERANS MOVEMENT

139. Interviews: RK, 1, conv; BU, 1; BW, 1, 2; AC; RBO. Books: *ATW,* 87–98.

140. Interviews: RK, 1, conv.; BU, 1; MI, 1, 2; BW, 1, 2; RBO; Leonard Weinglass, Feb. 18, 2000; Holly Near in conversation. Songs: Holly Near, "Hang in There," produced by Holly Near and Hereford Music. Books: *ATW,* 87–98. The vets also sang a few choruses of "Hang in There" for the news cameras upon their triumphant exit from the Federal Building after the fast had ended.

141. Interviews: RK, 1, conv.; BU, 1; RBO; MI; BW, 1, 2; TD, 2; RBI, 2, 3. Ron Bitzer recalls seeing on television the Nixon press conference in which Sarah McClendon confronted the president about the hunger-striking veterans in Cranston's office. Articles: "Vet Sit-In Wins V.A. Hearing," *Indochina Focal Point,* March 1–15, 1974, 1, 4 (includes Sarah McClendon quote from *NYT,* Feb. 26, 1974); Jon Nordheimer, "Veterans in Sit-In Meet Head of V.A.," *NYT,* March 3, 1974, n.p.; "VA Director Decides to Meet Protesting Vets," *WSN,* March 2, 1974, A-3; Molly Burrell, "U.S. Encampments to Protest VA Care," *LBI,* March 26, 1974 (vol. 32, no. 322), A-1, A-10; Mary Neiswender, "Vets Assail 'Abuses' at L.B. VA Hospital," *LBI,* Feb. 14, 1974 (vol. 32, no. 294), A-1, A-5; Lou Godfrey, "Vets Seize Cranston's Office," *LBI,* Feb. 13, 1974 (vol. 32; no. 293), A-1, A-3; "Veterans Occupy Cranston Office," *SMEO,* Feb. 1974; n.p.; S. J. Nadler, "Veterans Hunger Strike, Sit-In Continues," *UCLA Daily Bruin,* Feb. 20, 1974 (vol. 91, no. 31), n.p.; Jack Anderson, "The Forgotten Americans: Vietnam Veterans," United Features Syndicate column, n.d., circa March 1974. Documents: AVM bulletin from 24½ Hurricane St., Marina Del Rey, Calif., mimeographed, circa April 1974; transcribed notes to meeting between AVM and Donald E. Johnson, March 25, 1974, in possession of Bill Unger; "Meeting Changed," AVM flyer, mimeographed, distributed to the press, March 25, 1974. Letters: Barbara Avedon open letter to U.S. Congress, Feb. 27, 1974; Donald E. Johnson to Ron Kovic, March 22, 1974; Tony Diamond form letter to BRAVO members, n.d., circa late 1970s. Some of the congratulatory telegrams after the ending of AVM's hunger strike—like one from the Veterans Association at the University of California, Santa Barbara—were shown to me by Bill Unger. Books: *ATW,* 87–98.

8. TWO "MOTHERFUCKERS," TWO "GODFATHERS," AND THE DREAM OF "A FAIR SHAKE" FOR VETERANS

142. Interviews: RK, 1, conv.; BU, 1, 2; MI; AC. Articles: "VA, Nixon Under Fire from Angry Veterans," *Indochina Focal Point,* April 1–15, 1974, 6; John Sherwood, "Crippled Vets Protest: Police Clear Monument," *WSN,* March 29, 1974, 1; "Veterans' Protest Broken Up," *WP,* March 29, 1974, A-1, A-27; Joseph Volz, "Viet Vets & Cops Clash Atop Monument," *NYDN,* March 29, 1974, n.p.; "L.B. Vets in D.C. Scuffle," LBI, March 29, 1974, n.p. Letters: telegram from Steve Allen to AVM, April 1, 1974; telegram from Mr. and Mrs. Jerry Lewis to AVM, April 12, 1974; unsigned draft of letter from AVM headquarters, 24½ Hurricane St., Marina Del Rey, Calif., May, 1974, describing plans for the Second American Bonus March. Books: *ATW,* 116–26.

143. Interviews: RK, 1, conv.; BU; AA; JM; LT. Documents: "The Veterans Crisis; Broken Bodies. Broken Hearts. Broken Promises," policy paper issued jointly by AVM, the National American G.I. Forum, and the National Association for Puerto Rican Civil Rights, July 1974 (includes the results of the recent Daniel Yankelovich study of Vietnam veterans). Books: *The American Veterans Movement: A History* (self-published by AVM, May 1974); *ATW,* 116–26.

144. Interviews: BU, 1, 2; JM; MI, 1, 2; AC; Rick Kuhlmey, Dec. 6, 1995. Letters: Mary Bartsas to GN, Jan. 5, 1996.

9. THE SECOND AMERICAN VETERANS' BONUS MARCH

145. RK, 1, conv.; BU; AA; LT; JM; ANH; BB; BR, 3; MI; BW, 1, 2. Articles: Wesley Pruden, "Veterans Make Plans for a 'Nixonville,'" *NO,* June 22, 1974, 7; "Wheelchair Brigade," editorial in *GS,* June 25, 1974, 3A; "Editorial: The Vets' Movement," *WS,* Aug., 1974 (vol. 4, no. 7), 10. Documents: "The Veterans Crisis: Broken Bodies. Broken Hearts. Broken Promises," flyer for the Second American Veterans' Bonus March, distributed by the National American G.I. Forum, circa June 1974; Bill Unger, draft of petition from the Bonus March Coalition to the U.S. Supreme Court, circa late June 1974; congressional petition in support of the Bonus March Coalition's right to use Lafayette Park, circa late June 1974; VVAW, "Press Information and Tentative Schedule of Events," handout for Dewey Canyon IV, June 1994. Letters: Bill Unger, draft of letter to the American Federation of Government Employees, circa late July, 1974. Books: *ATW,* 116–26.

10. A TUTORIAL IN THE VA ADMINISTRATOR'S OFFICE— COMPLETE WITH HAMMER AND NAILS

146. Interviews: JS, 2; FRL; JC; RL; TC, 3. Articles: "Veterans Administration Running Scared: 'War on the VA' Grows," *WS,* Feb. 1975 (vol. 5, no. 2), 3; "War on VA Grows," *WS,* Oct. 1975 (vol. 5, no. 6), 1, 8–9; Sarah McClendon, "The VA: Nothing Ever Changes," *Penthouse,* Feb. 1975, 63–66, 96; "Roudebush, Richard Lowell," entry in Current Biography Yearbook, 1976, vol. 37 (NY: H. W. Wilson Co., 1977), 352–55. Documents: "Proposed Budget for Cross Generational Study of Impact of Vietnam War," submitted to various foundations by Jack Smith, early 1974. Books: *LOV.*

147. Interviews: JS, 2.

148. Interviews: JS, 2; CS, 1; FSM, 1, 2; GM. Articles: "Veterans Administration Expands Services as Rolls Grow," in *The World Almanac & Book of Facts: 1976,* ed. George E. Delury (NY: Newspaper Enterprise Association, 1975), 359; "Veterans Administration Keeps Pace with Change," in *The World Almanac & Book of Facts: 1978,* ed. George E. Delury (NY: Newspaper Enterprises Association, 1978), 330–31.

11. UNIVERSAL AND HYPOCRITICAL AMNESTY

149. Interviews: CF; TC, 1, 2; Gerry Condon, Feb. 16, 1988; Jack Colhoun, Oct. 19, 1988; Louise Ransom, Nov. 11, 1988; Fritz Efaw, May 29, 1992. Articles: Jack Colhoun, "What It Took to Desert," *TN,* Jan. 15, 1977, 45–46, 50–51; Jack Colhoun, "The Exiles' Role in War Resistance," *Monthly Review,* March 1979, 27–42; "Gold Star Mother Directs National Amnesty Campaign," news clip in possession of Louise Ransom, no citation, circa 1975; Louise Ransom, Ron Kovic, and Fritz Efaw, "Transcript of Speeches: Democratic National Convention: July 15, 1976," in *Amnesty Update* (publication of the National Council for Universal and Unconditional Amnesty), Dec., 1976, 3; "Who Needs Amnesty: 1961–1975," NCUUA publication, Oct. 29, 1976; Betty Segal, "Real Amnesty on Ice," *Berkeley Barb,* April 23–29, 1976 (no. 558), n.p. Documents: "Jimmy Carter on Vietnam Pardon," a Jimmy Carter presidential campaign flyer, circa early 1976; "AMEX Interview with Stuart Eizenstat," issued as a handout by AMEX/Canada, dated June 18, 1976; Fritz Efaw, "Statement of NCUUA," presented at press conference, Statler Hilton, Nov. 19, 1976; Ron Bitzer, "Bad Discharge," unpublished paper, circa 1976. Books: *CAC,* 210–26 passim; *Presidential Clemency Board: Report to the President* (Wash., D.C.: U.S. Government Printing Office, 1975); *LTP,* 398–401.

150. Interviews: Jack Colhoun, Oct. 19, 1988. Articles: Colhoun, "The Exiles' Role in War Resistance," op. cit., 41. Books: *CAC,* 226–35, passim; *LTP,* 398–401; *TVV,* 108.

Chapter 7: Too Little Too Late: Operation Outreach

1. TWO NEW CHAMPIONS ENTER THE FRAY: MAX CLELAND AND STUART FELDMAN

151. Interviews: ACR; RBI, 2, 3; GM; FRL; JS, 2. Articles: Charles R. Figley, "A Postscript: Welcoming Home the Strangers," in *Strangers at Home: Vietnam Veterans Since the War,* ed. Charles R. Figley and Seymour Leventman (New York: Praeger, 1980), 363–67. Letters: Stuart Feldman to GN, Feb. 22, 1989; Guy H. McMichael III to James R. Hoffman, July 18, 1978. Books: Max Cle-

land, *Strong at the Broken Places (A Personal Story)* (Atlanta: Cherokee Publishing, 1989), 38–39, 146–49, 152–55, passim.

152. Interviews: GM; TC, 1, 2; JST; CF; WPM; FRL; FSM; BL. Books: *TPR*, 64–66, passim; *LTP*, 58–59; *OTN*, 55–68, passim.

153. Interviews: SF, 1; GM. Articles: Juan Cameron, "Carter Takes on Budget Monster," *Fortune*, Jan. 1977, n.p.; Stuart Feldman, "Sunbelt States Reap G.I. Bill Bonanza," National League of Cities/U.S. Conference of Mayors publication, Wash., D.C., Dec. 8, 1976. Documents: Stuart Feldman, "An Examination of the Lobbying Process—Why Unrepresented Groups Like Vietnam Veterans Need a Lobby," staff paper for the Committee for Public Advocacy, Wash., D.C., March 3, 1976.

2. A NEW GI BILL OVER DANISHES AND COFFEE, AND MULLER AND KOVIC PART COMPANY

154. Interviews: SF, 1; Douglas Brinkley, Dec. 13, 1995. Articles: Jimmy Carter, "Remarks by President Carter at the Veterans' Day Ceremony, Arlington National Cemetery: Oct 24, 1977," in *WP*, Nov. 2, 1977, n.p.; Colman McCarthy, "A Special Debt," editorial, *WP*, Oct. 30, 1977, n.p.; Colman Mc-Carthy, "HIRE, Promises and Jobs," editorial, *WP*, March 25, 1978, n.p.; Ray Marshall, "HIRE *Is* Helping the Jobless Vietnam Vet," *WP*, March 25, 1978; n.p.; Colman McCarthy, "Veterans' Un-employment," editorial, *WP*, March 6, 1978, n.p.; William Greider, "Promises of Jobs Unfulfilled, Vietnam Veterans Assert," *WP*, April 28, 1977, n.p.; Austin Scott, "Labor Department Asks Jobs for 200,000 Viet Veterans," *WP*, Jan. 28, 1977, n.p.; Colman McCarthy, "The President and the GI Bill," editorial *WP*, Nov. 12, 1977, n.p.; Colman McCarthy, "'Tiger' Teague and the Veterans Com-promise," *WP*, Nov. 21, 1977, n.p.; Colman McCarthy, "A Full Debate for the GI Bill," editorial, *WP*, Nov. 2, 1977, n.p.; "Evening Up Veterans' Benefits," editorial, *BG*, Sept. 21, 1977, n.p.; Stu-art Feldman, "Introduction: Those Who Served," preface to the privately compiled *WP* editorials on veterans, 1977–1978; Colman McCarthy, "Vietnam Veterans in Congress," editorial, *WP*, May 8, 1978, n.p.; Stuart F. Feldman, "Our Failure to Discuss Vietnam Vets," editorial, *BG*, Sept. 15, 1978, n.p. Books: *TVV*, 179–89.

155. Interviews: SF, 1; TC, 3; ROK; RK, conv.; ROM, 1. Articles: Haynes Johnson, "The Odyssey of Max Cleland, Symbol of Vietnam's Price," *WP*, Aug. 7, 1977, n.p.; Don Winter, "Cleland—The Vietnam Vet in the World War II Vet Mold," *National Journal*, Dec. 10, 1977, 1915–1917 (this ar-ticle includes quotations from the VA health-care study released by the National Research Coun-cil of the National Academy of Sciences in June 1977); Jan Craig Scruggs, "Forgotten Veterans of 'That Peculiar War,'" *WP*, May 25, 1977, n.p.; Frank Greve, "A Legacy of 'Lost' Veterans, *WP*, Nov. 18, 1977, n.p.; Colman McCarthy, "The Class That Went to War," editorial, *WP*, Dec. 2, 1977, n.p.; Colman McCarthy, "An Advocate for Vietnam Veterans," *WP*, Feb. 10, 1978, n.p.; "Rethink-ing Veterans' Pensions," editorial, *BG*, Nov. 4, 1978, n.p. Books: *WMBP*, 184–86, 190, passim.

3. FIGHTING BACK: MULLER TAKES ON THE WHOLE GOVERNMENT, AND DAVE CHRISTIAN TAKES ON JIMMY CARTER

156. Interviews: SF; DBO; ROK; GM; ROM, 2, 3. Articles: Colman McCarthy, "Vietnam Veterans in Congress," editorial, *WP*, May 8, 1978, n.p.; "Vietnam Era Vets in Congress," *The American Legion Magazine*, April, 1978, 7, 42. Books: *TVV*, 153–56, 179–89; *TPR*: 86, 11–114; *WMBP*, 182–94, 203–9. The claim that Rusty Lindley and other veteran leaders gave some degree of credence to Cleland having been fragged is made in Robert Klein's book *Wounded Men, Broken Promises*, 184–89.

157. Interviews: RK, conv.; JS; DCH; SF, 2; FRL; JCS; JWH. Articles: Jeffrey Jay, "After Vietnam: In Pursuit of Scapegoats," *Harper's*, July 1978 (vol. 257, no. 1538), n.p.; William Greider, "The Old, Unhealed Wounds of Vietnam," *WP*, Jan. 23, 1977, n.p.; Jan Craig Scruggs, "Forgotten Veterans of 'That Peculiar War,'" *WP*, May 25, 1977, n.p.; Bernard Weinraub, "Removal of a Decorated Vet-eran Brings Controversy," *NYT*, Jan. 25, 1979, 1; Mary McGrory, "Hero's Firing a Symbol of Atti-tude Toward Vietnam Veterans," *WST*, Jan. 26, 1979; n.p.; "No Heroes Need Apply," *BG*, Jan. 27, 1979, 19; "Mr. Christian Volunteers for a Second Tour of Duty," editorial, *Bucks County Courier Times*, March 6, 1979, n.p.; Jim Reid, "GI Preference Plan Hit," *Daily Oklahoman*, May 25, 1978,

n.p. Books: *THAN,* xiii–xv; 7–25. It was Stuart Feldman who pointed out to me that Scruggs had been influenced by a number of others who had raised the issue of a monument to Vietnam warriors. In fact, in "The Old, Unhealed Wounds of Vietnam," Greider profiled Scruggs side by side with Giovanni "Gino" Pacheco, so Scruggs could not have missed Pacheco's lament over the lack of a Vietnam memorial. Feldman also recalls Scruggs proposing a Vietnam memorial to the U.S. Conference of Mayors, and everyone in the room except for attorney Bob Doubek rejecting the idea as impractical.

4. FRANK MCCARTHY SPRINGS A SERIES OF AMBUSHES, AND ANOTHER VIETNAM VETERAN LEADER GOES DOWN

158. Interviews: MDV; FM, 1; GM. Books: *WFAA,* 80–85; *AOOT,* 24, 37–38, 78. During our interview, Guy McMichael was at pains to defend Max Cleland's slowness in responding to the Agent Orange issue and to put the best possible face on what many veterans still feel was his unwarranted resistance to dealing squarely with dioxin-related health problems. "We were in a difficult position at the time," he recalled, "of being placed in a position of demonstrating that Agent Orange doesn't hurt people, as opposed to evaluating the evidence of where it does harm people. That's just the way the debate was structured. It was a terribly emotional issue. It was very difficult to take a rational, scientific approach to it. . . . When it first started to break, [people at the VA asked,] 'What is this? Are these people having all kinds of problems?' One of the things that we found out were the kinds of symptoms that people were complaining about were the kinds of symptoms that people complain about generally when they go in to see a physician: 'I have some numbness in my fingers. I have this malaise.' Kind of standard types of complaints. Some doctors suggested that these kinds of complaints aren't necessarily related to dioxin, but may very well reflect very real psychological problems that veterans have."

159. Interviews: DBO; SF, 1; FM; JM; TC, 3; MR; MAR; SC; ROM, 2, 3; RW, 1. Books: *WMBP,* 190 (Cleland's remark about veterans' organizations being "in the business of advocating"); *KAO,* 166–71. Many of Bob Muller's closest original advisors, including Steve Champlin and Rick Weidman, spoke of his initial reluctance to take up the Agent Orange issue. Video: "Vet," episode 8511 of the television show *Lou Grant,* starring Ed Asner, first aired Jan. 15, 1979. The show is amazingly accurate, due to the host of Vietnam veteran advocates such as Shad Meshad who served as advisors.

160. Interviews: FM, 1; SF, 1. Articles: "VA Chief Marks Holiday with Plea for Viet Veterans," *LAT,* May 29, 1979, part 1, 4; Evelyn Short, "The Bitter Taste of Agent Orange," *Gannett Westchester Newspapers,* May 27, 1979, n.p. Documents: press release dated Jan. 24, 1980, from Center for Veterans' Rights; "To Anyone Who Will Listen," flyer put out by a Vietnam veterans' group at the dedication of one of the first Vet Centers, in Van Nuys, Calif., Jan. 26, 1980. The story of an Agent Orange activist veteran challenging Cleland's masculinity—"Did you lose your balls in Vietnam, too?"—is told in both Robert Klein's *Wounded Men, Broken Promises,* 162–63, and in Peter Schuck's *Agent Orange on Trial,* 78.

Chapter 8: An Indictment of the System: The Wadsworth Strike

1. THE HOSTAGES ARE WELCOMED BACK, AND RONALD REAGAN TAKES AIM AT THE VET CENTERS

161. Interviews: RK, conv.; RBI, 2, 3; FSM, 1. Articles: Melvin Sheya, "A Terrible Ordeal as Japanese Prisoners," and J. R. Champion, "Don't Adulate Former Hostages," in "Reader Opinions: The Open Forum," *DP,* circa early Feb. 1981, n.p.; Lance Morrow, "Bringing the Viet Nam Vets Home," *Time,* June 1, 1981, 41–45; "Heroes' Welcome Angers Viet Veterans," *The Australian,* Feb. 2, 1981, 5. Letters: "Message from Senator Alan Cranston to Green Ribbon Unity Day Rally," March 8, 1981; "An Open Letter to Friends and Supporters of the Center for Veterans Rights," CVR document, Feb. 1981; "Open Letter from Michael Burt McCarthy to Friends and Supporters," CVR document, Feb. 1981; telegram of Alan Cranston to Ronald Reagan, May 27, 1981; letter of Alan Cranston to "All Vet Center Teams," May 13, 1981. Documents: Ron Kovic, speech on *Nightline,* Feb. 3, 1981, included in press release of the CVR, March 8, 1981; "Status Report on Is-

sues of Special Interest," internal document of the VVOP, circa Feb. 1981; CVR press release, Feb. 17, 1981; Ron Bitzer, analysis of David Stockman's budget cuts, prepared for CVR, Feb., 1981. Books: *TPR*, 132–35; *ATW*, 904–14. The quotes from David Stockman and material on his background are from *LTP*, 187, 265–66.

162. Interviews: RBI, 2, 3; DCH; JZ. Articles: "Still in the Running," *Bucks County Courier Times*, Feb. 26, 1981, n.p.; "VA Candidate Cannot Accept Cuts," *SAS*, April 23, 1981, 1; Bruce Beans, "About Face on VA," *Philadelphia Journal*, April 16, 1981 (vol. 4, no. 110) n.p.; "Disabled Vietnam War Veteran to Head VA," *SRPD*, Feb. 20, 1981, n.p.; Carla Marinucci, "Concord's Viet Vets Get Belated Welcome," *CCT*, March 3, 1981. Books: William S. Cohen and George J. Mitchell, *Men of Zeal: A Candid Inside Story of the Iran-Contra Hearings* (NY: Viking, 1988), 221, 327–30; *TVV*, 187.

163. Interviews: RK, conv.; RBI, 2, 3. Articles: "Military Affairs" (profile of Bill Corson), *Penthouse*, Nov. 1995, 87; Tom Morgenthau, "The Troubled Vietnam Vet," *NW*, March 30, 1981, n.p.; Lance Morrow, "Bringing the Vietnam Vets Home," op. cit.; Lance Morrow, "The Forgotten Warriors," *Time*, July 13, 1981, 18–25; Richard Turner, "An 'Army of the Unusual,' Anti-War Rally," *LAHE*, March 9, 1981, n.p. Documents: press release of CVR, March 20, 1981; memo from CVR organizers to organizers of Green Ribbon Unity Day (March 8, 1981) activities, dated March 4, 1981; Ron Bitzer, "Delayed Re-Entry Program," CVR document, circa Feb. 1981. Letters: Ron Bitzer, "Open Letter to Vietnam Vets," CVR document, circa July 1981. Books: *WAL*; *LOV*; *ATW*, 914–26.

2. JIM HOPKINS: A MARINE TWICE BETRAYED

164. Interviews: RBI; FSA; CS, 1; YM. Articles: Dave McNary, "Agent Orange Comes Home," *LAR*, Feb. 20, 1981, 1, 4–6; Ron Smith and Richard Warren Lewis, "Jim Hopkins: How Many More Vets Will Agent Orange Kill?" *Hustler*, Oct. 1981, 36–41, 52, 56, 135; Ronald Soble, "Viet Veterans' Martyr—A Fantasy Hero?" *LAT*, June 20, 1981, 26–28; John Kendall, "Brewing Anger Led to Attack on VA," *LAT*, March 16, 1981, part 1, 3; John Kendall, "Vietnam Vet Who Raided Hospital Is Found Dead," *LAT*, May 18, 1981, part 1, 3; "The VA Runaround," *Penthouse*, Feb. 1975, 65; Frank McAdams, "'Crybabies' No More—Except in Mourning," circa early June 1981, n.p. Documents: James R. Hopkins, "Statement from V.A. Facility, Brentwood," March 19, 1981; Suzanne Hopkins, untitled statement, March 20, 1981. Letters: Ron Bitzer open letter to Dr. Donald L. Custis, March 16, 1981; Books: *WMBP*, 200–209.

165. Interviews: RBI, 2, 3; FSA; John Keaveny, July 13, 2000. Articles: "7 Vets on Hunger Strike," *LADN*, May 25, 1981, sec. 1, 7; Dana Ward, "Vietnam: Special Report," *Topanga Messenger*, June 18–July 2, 1981. Arnie Friedman, "Probe Sought in Veteran's Death," *LADN*, May 19, 1981, n.p.; Arnie Friedman, "VA to Act on Complaints of Vietnam Vets," *LADN*, May 29, 1981, 1, 16; Daniel Winkel, "Viet Veterans: 'Whipping Boys' in Rage," *Press Telegram* (Long Beach), May 31, 1981, A-1, A-8; "Vets on Hunger Strike Seek Reagan Response," AP wire story, May 26, 1981; Leonard Greenwood, "Service Honors Troubled Veteran," LAT, May 26, 1981, 1,3; Lennie Le Guire, "'Inside Six' Protest Continues as Service Held for James Hopkins," *LAHE*, May 26, 1981, n.p. Letters: Ron Bitzer telegram to Ronald Reagan, May 20, 1981, 10.

3. FROM PROTEST TO CIRCUS: MESHAD AND MULLER BATTLE KOVIC AND BITZER

166. Interviews: RBI, 2, 3, 4; RK, conv.; FSM, 1; SA; ROM, 5. Muller's exchanges with Ron Kovic and Ron Bitzer from their televised debate were recalled by Kovic and Bitzer; I was unable to locate a tape of the program.

167. Interviews: RBI, 2, 3, 4; RK, conv.; FSM, 1; SA; ROM, 5. Articles: "Fasting Vet Hospitalized," AP wire story, May 27, 1981; "President Flies Back to Capital," *Los Angeles News Press*, May 26, 1981, A-1; William Corson, "The Vietnam Veterans Adviser," *Penthouse*, circa late 1981, 114; "'Helplessness' remains as Vietnam Veteran Ends Hunger Strike, *HP*, May 28, 1981, n.p.; "Fasting Vet Hospitalized," AP wire story, May 27, 1981; Arnie Friedman, "Vietnam Veterans on Hunger Strike in West L.A. Over Treatment by VA," *LADN*, May 27, 1981, 1, 22; "From the Media: To Heal the Nation, Help Vets," an editorial from *CO* reprinted in "Opinion and Commentary," *CSM*, July 21, 1981, 23; Hayden Perry, "Vietnam Vets Hold Firm in VA Demands," *The Militant*, June 10, 1981, n.p.; Sandy Dennison, "Viet Vets End Elsmere VA Sit-In," (Wilmington, Del.) *News-Journal*,

June 4, 1981; Richard Turner, untitled piece, *LAHE,* June 8, 1981, n.p. Documents: Ron Bitzer, "Veteran's [*sic*] Coalition Statement," early July 1981; Paul Conrad editorial cartoon, *LAT,* circa early June 1981. Letters: Alan Cranston telegram to Ronald Reagan, May 27, 1981. The letters and telegrams of support sent to the veterans' encampment from which I quote are part of the CVR archive kept by Ron Bitzer.

168. Interviews: RBI, 2, 3, 4; RK, conv.; SA. Articles: "5 Quit Fast after White House Message," source unknown, May 29, 1981, n.p.; Arnie Friedman, "VA to Act on Complaints of Vietnam Vets," *LADN,* May 29, 1981, 1, 16; "Still Living With the War," in "Nation," *Time,* June 8, 1981, 24. Documents: CVR press release, May 29, 1981. Letters: Dr. Donald Custis to Ron Bitzer, May 28, 1981; Robert O. Muller to Ron Bitzer and Ron Kovic, n.d., circa May 29, 1981; open letter of Ron Bitzer to Vietnam veterans in the Wadsworth protest, June 1981.

4. TENTS IN LAFAYETTE PARK: THE HUNGER STRIKE MOVES TO WASHINGTON

169. Interviews: RBI, 2, 3, 4; RK, conv.; PAM; MI; SA; RS, 1. Articles: Frank McAdams, "'Crybabies' No More—Except in Mourning," *LAT,* circa early June, 1981, n.p.; Robert Coy quoted in Patt Morrison and Eric Malnic, "VA Protest: 20-Day Demonstration Ended," *LAT,* June 10, 1981, 3, 21; Patt Morrison, "Vets, VA Report 'Serious, Delicate' Talks on Strike, *LAT,* June 6, 1981, 1, 12; Richard Turner, untitled piece, *LAHE,* June 8, 1981, n.p.; David Holley and Tendayi Kumbula, "Talks Collapse, Vets May Take Fight to Capital," *LAT,* June 8, 1981, 1, 5; Patt Morrison, "Protesting Vets Won't Fight Hospital Eviction," *LAT,* June 9, 1981, n.p.; "VA Police Evict 35 Veterans," *HP,* June 10, 1981, 2A. Documents: Ron Bitzer, public statement from the CVR on the content of Dr. Custis's June 5, 1981, letter, dated June 6, 1981. Letters: Dr. Donald Custis to Ron Bitzer, June 5, 1981.

170. Interviews: RBI, 2, 3, 4; SA. Articles: Allan Parachini, "The Focus Changes in Protest of Vietnam War Veterans," *LAT,* "View," June 18, 1981, part 5, 1, 10–13; "Are They Listening?" editorial in *LAT,* June 26, 1981, n.p.; Ronald L. Soble, "Viet Veterans' Martyr—A Fantasy Hero?" *LAT,* June 20, 1981, 26–27; "Dead Calabasas Veteran Not a Hero," *Ventura County Star-Free Press,* June 21, 1981, B-10. Documents: Ron Bitzer, "Consequences of Pressure on the V.A. Concerning the Outreach Centers to Mentally Troubled Vietnam Veterans," CVR document, circa June 25, 1981; Ron Bitzer, "Consequences of Pressure on the V.A. for Independent Evaluation of V.A. Hospitals," CVR document, circa June 25, 1981; Paul Conrad editorial cartoon (of veterans' tombstones) in *LAT,* June 12, 1981 (another Conrad cartoon around this time showed the neat rows of white veterans' tombstones with the caption: "For Best Supporting Actors . . ."); Ron Bitzer, "Conclusions of the Political Consequences of the 1981 Wadsworth VA [Strike]," CVR document, circa mid-June 1981 (probably co-authored by Michael McCarthy); "Veteran's [*sic*] Coalition Policy Statement," late June (probably authored by Michael McCarthy); Veteran's [*sic*] Coalition Hunger Strikers [*sic*] Statement," June 30, 1981; "Veteran's [*sic*] Coalition Statement," n.d., circa early July 1981; statement of the Veterans' Coalition, July 10, 1981.

5. THE COST OF A 10-SECOND JEEP RIDE: "THIS PROTEST ISN'T OVER"

171. Interviews: SA; MI; RBI, 2; TDA. Articles: Peter Kihss, "U.S. Adding 42 Centers for Veterans of Vietnam," *NYT,* July 20, 1981, A-6; "New V.A. Chief Says Veterans of Vietnam Aren't Neglected," *NYT,* July 16, 1981, n.p.; Documents: account of the hearing of the Select Subcommittee of the House Veterans' Affairs Committee, 334 Cannon, in *Congressional Record: House of Representatives,* July 16, 1981, n.p.; press release of CVR, Aug. 14, 1981; "VA Memorandum to Chief Medical Director, Subject: Site Visit—VA Medical Centers Wadsworth and Brentwood, June 2–5, 1981," dated June 22, 1981; "VA Memorandum to Chief Medical Director, Subject: Consolidated Report on the Three California Site Visits," dated Aug. 7, 1981. Letters: Ron Bitzer to Robert P. Nimmo, July 17, 1981; Robert P. Nimmo to Ron Bitzer, Sept. 10, 1981. Books: *LTP,* 675; Ron Bitzer quoted in *The Effects of Agent Orange and Related Herbicides on Returning Vietnam Veterans: Transcript of Proceedings* (Lawndale, Calif.: Assembly Select Committee on Veterans' Affairs, July 21, 1981), 12.

172. Interviews: SA. Articles: "Vietnam Vet Held on Assault Charge," (no source), late Aug., 1981, n.p.; Carol A. Crotta, "Last Desperate Days of a Vietnam Vet," *LAHE,* Sept. 16, 1981, n.p.; Eric Malnic

and Patt Morrison, "Veteran Who Took Part in Protest Leaps to Death at L.A. Hotel," *LAT,* Sept. 16, 1981, part 2, 1, 8; Patt Morrison, "Vietnam Vets Flay VA Over Suicide of Activist," *LAT,* "Metro," Sept. 18, 1981, 1, 5; John L. Mitchell, "Protest Heeded, Veterans Declare," *LAT,* June 19, 1982, n.p.; Ronald L. Soble, "Drugs Blamed in Veteran's Death," *LAT,* Nov. 11, 1981, part 1, 22; Emily Karnes, "Clarence Stickler," *The Topanga Messenger,* June 18–July 2, 1981, 11.

Chapter 9: The Specter of Chemical Warfare: Agent Orange

1. VICTOR YANNACONE TAKES ON "A WALKING WOUNDED, SICK, AND DYING ARMY"

173. Interviews: VY; FM, 1. Articles: Evelyn Short, "The Bitter Taste of Agent Orange," *Gannett Westchester Newspapers,* May 27, 1979, n.p.; Moira K. Griffin, "Poisoned Patriotism," *Student Lawyer,* March 1982 (vol. 10, no. 7), 22–25, 51–53; Gilbert Rogin, "All He Wants to Save Is the World," *Sports Illustrated,* Feb. 3, 1969, n.p.; Mary Tynan Weber, "Suffolk Profile: Victor Yannacone vs. the World of Chemistry," *Suffolk,* vol. 1, no. 1, 1979, 58–73; JoAnn McGrath, "Yannacone: On the Side of the Angels?" Patchogue newspaper (unidentified), n.d., circa 1979, 1, 14; John Pascal, "Battling an Agent of Tragedy," *Long Island* magazine, *Newsday,* April 29, 1979, n.p.; Whitney Gould, "DDT on Trial: The Wisconsin Chapter," *Isthmus,* Jan. 9, 1987, 9. Documents: Victor John Yannacone Jr., resume, 1986. Books: Rachel Carson, *Silent Spring* (Boston: Houghton Mifflin, 1962).
174. Interviews: VY; FM, 1. Articles: Mary Tynan Weber, "Suffolk Profile," op. cit., 63; JoAnn McGrath, "Yannacone: On the Side of the Angels?" op. cit., n.p. Documents: "In re 'Agent Orange' Produce Liability Litigation: Petition for a Writ of Mandamus/Prohibition on Behalf of Viet Nam Veterans and Their Families," submitted to the United States Court of Appeals for the Second Circuit, Sept. 4, 1986.
175. Interviews: VY; FM, 1; RBI, 1, 2. Articles: Karen J. Payne, "Beyond Vietnam, Beyond Politics, Beyond Causes . . . ," *Barrister,* spring 1979 (vol. 6, no. 2), 11–14; Karl Grossman, "Suffolk Close-Up: Victor Yannacone: A Case Makes a Lawyer a Star and a Vocal Critic Too," Suffolk County newspaper (unidentified source), circa June 1984. Books: *AOOT,* 58–60; *DAO,* 157–71; quotes from Dr. Matthew Meselson and Dr. Wilbur McNulty to the effect that dioxin "is the most toxic small man-made molecule we know of" are in *WFAA,* 128.

2. "BREAKING BALLOONS": THE FILING OF THE CLASS ACTION LAWSUIT AND THE BIRTH OF "THE CAUSE"

176. Interviews: VY; RBI, 2; TE, 3. Documents: "In re: 'Agent Orange' Product Liability Litigation," op. cit. Letters: Ron Bitzer to GN, Jan. 13, 1988. Books: Judge Weinstein's quote about *Hamlet* is in *AOOT,* 58; *GIGP,* xiv–xv.
177. VY; FM, 1; STC; JWE; ERZ. James Webb's remark about not being worried about Agent Orange comes from my interview with Admiral Elmo R. Zumwalt Jr. Articles: David Bonior, "The AO Evidence Continues to Mount," *VVAV,* May 1983 (vol. 3, no. 1), 1–2; Karen Payne, "A Killer Comes Home," *Illinois Times,* April 13–19, 1979, n.p.; Eileen Keerdoja, Rick Rutz, and Carolyn Friday, "Fears Still Cloud Italy's Toxic Town," *Brotherhood of Vietnam Veterans, Inc. Newsletter* (Austin, Tex.), March 1982, 4. Audio: tape of Dr. Arnold Schecter's lecture on Agent Orange at the Triennial Vietnam Symposium, Vietnam Center, Lubbock, Tex., April 17, 1999. Books: *KAO,* 139–51. Bobby Muller's conflicts with the right wing of the veterans' movement as he began organizing VVA are discussed in "A Symposium with Philip Caputo, James Fallows, Robert Muller, Dean K. Phillips, Lucian Truscott IV, James Webb and John P. Wheeler III" in *TWG* (pp. 95–154), which includes a few early shots traded between Muller and Webb. At one point Webb tells Muller, "Vietnam Veterans Against the War . . . that's a symbolic organization," 120. Dr. Jacqueline Verrett is quoted on the teratogenic potency of dioxin in *WFAA,* xi; *WFAA,* 138–42; *SV,* passim. Dr. John Bederka is quoted on the toxicity of Agent Orange in Karen Payne's "A Killer Comes Home."

Much of Yannacone's early theorizing about the damage inflicted on the human immune system by dioxin has been confirmed by Dr. Arnold Schecter, who has been studying the health effects of Agent Orange and dioxin both in the United States and Vietnam for the past two decades. Dr. Schecter is currently Professor of Environmental Sciences at the Health Science Center of the University of Texas in Houston. In the 1980s, he was the lead researcher on two major studies of

TCDD levels in the blood of Vietnam veterans, one in Massachusetts and one in Michigan. He has also been studying TCDD blood levels in the Vietnamese since 1984. Peter Kahn did a similar study of TCDD blood levels in New Jersey Vietnam veterans. All three American studies, Dr. Schecter points out, show that some American Vietnam veterans have elevated levels of TCDD (which is the specific type of dioxin in Agent Orange) in their blood. "These studies prove that dioxin really, really gets into people," he says, "and stays there for a long time." He found American veterans with as high a TCDD blood level as 660 parts/trillion, when 2 parts/trillion is normal. Correspondingly, he has found only normal levels of TCDD in North Vietnamese but as high as 1,850 parts/trillion in South Vietnamese. (AS, 2).

178. Interviews: VY; STC; JZ; FM, 1; ROM, 3; JCA. The near universal outrage within VVA over Bobby Muller's trip to Hanoi (where he offended the entire right wing and most of the center of the veterans' movement by laying a wreath at the tomb of North Vietnamese Premier Ho Chi Minh) has been recounted to me in vivid detail by numerous VVA members, including Joseph Zengerle, John Catterson, and Rick Weidman. In 1981, the Socialist Republic of Vietnam was still considered an enemy nation by the U.S. government, and any kind of trade or travel there was strictly forbidden.

3. AN EIGHT-YEAR-OLD STICK OF DYNAMITE CRACKS THE GOVERNMENT'S ARMOR

179. Interviews: STC; FM, 1; ROM, 3; MR; MAR. Articles: John Terzano, "VVA Supports H.R. 1961," statement before the Subcommittee on Compensation, Pension and Insurance of the House Veterans Affairs Committee, April 26, 1983, in *VVAV*, May 1983 (vol. 3, no. 2), 5–6; Margot Hornblower, "A Sinister Drama of Agent Orange Opens in Congress," *WP*, June 27, 1983, 27. Books: *TVV*, 140–41; *KAO*, 23–37, 77 (Michael and Maureen Ryan's testimony before Congress), 166–72; *WFAA*, 55; *TPR*, 110, 126. The latest results (2000) from the ongoing Ranch Hand study show a significant correlation between exposure to Agent Orange and adult-onset diabetes.

180. Interviews: RBI, 2; FM, 1; TE, 1. Articles: "Agent Orange: Is It to Blame?" interview with Tony Messner and Phil Thompson by Steve Cosser, July 9, 1981, transcript made available by the Parliamentary Library of the Commonwealth of Australia. Documents: Ron Bitzer, "Testimony Before the California State Assembly," July 31, 1981, in *The Effects of Agent Orange and Related Herbicides on Returning Vietnam Veterans* (transcript of proceedings) (Sacramento: Assembly Publications Office, 1981), 6–16. Books: *TVV*, 140–41; *WFAA*, 126–30.

4. THE VA'S AGENT ORANGE EXAM AND OTHER SMOKE SCREENS

181. Documents: Dr. Barclay M. Shepard, "Statement Before the California Assembly Select Committee on Veterans Affairs," July 30, 1981; "Agent Orange Update," Veterans Administration news release, Aug. 17, 1981; Center for Veterans' Rights press release, Aug. 17, 1981. Books: *AOOT*, 49; *TPR*, 181; Joe Cole, *What's Evidence* (Olympia, Wash.: self-published, 1988), 53; the VA's claims about its Agent Orange registry and screening examinations are in *WFAA*, 49–50, 87, passim.

182. Interviews: RBO, 2. Articles: Susan Kirvin, "Southland News: Agent Orange Poll Yields Results," *LADN*, Nov. 22, 1981, n.p.; "Our Money, Your Life," editorial, *Brotherhood of Vietnam Veterans, Inc. Newsletter*, Austin, Tex., Dec.. 1981, 3; Scott Brown, "Five Years Later, Troubles Go On for Camarillo Vietnam War Veteran," (source unidentified), Jan. 27, 1981, n.p. Brown's story about Alan Wynn includes quotes by Robert Nimmo about his fears concerning the cost of potential Agent Orange compensation. Documents: Larry Don Shaw, "Testimony Before the California State Assembly Select Committee on Veterans' Affairs," July 24, 1981, in *The Effects of Agent Orange and Related Herbicides on Returning Vietnam Veterans*, 23–45; Ron Bitzer, "Testimony Before the California State Assembly," July 31, 1981, 5; Dr. Barclay Shepard, "Statement Before the California State Assembly," July 31, 1981, 3; Center for Veterans' Rights press release, Aug. 17, 1981. Books: Muller's testimony about the veteran's suicide is in *WFAA*, 142–243.

5. THE CALIFORNIA STATE HEARINGS: THE POLITICS OF SCIENCE AND THE MANIPULATION OF CERTAINTY

183. Interviews: JB, 1; WW. Articles: Marlene Cimons, "Wider Exposure of U.S. Troops to Agent Orange Told," *LAT*, Sept. 24, 1981, 1, 14; Gary DuFour, "16,000 Vets Ask for AO Comp," article reprinted from *The Stars and Stripes*, Wash., D.C., Jan. 1983, (source unidentified), n.p.; Karen

Payne, "A Killer Comes Home," *Illinois Times,* April 13–19, 1979, n.p. Documents: "Testimony of John G. Cano," in *The Effects of Agent Orange and Related Herbicides on Returning Vietnam; Veterans,* op. cit., 1–6; "Testimony of Larry Don Shaw," op. cit., 23–35; transcript of Dorothy Thompson's speech at Agent Orange Seminar, "Vietnam Reconsidered" conference, University of Southern California, Los Angeles, Feb. 6–9, 1983. Letters: Patricia Devitt to Senator Alan Cranston, n.d., circa Jan. 1980.

184. Interviews: RBI, 2; KB; TDA; SA. Articles: Richard Severo, "House Study Assails Herbicide Actions," *NYT,* March 29, 1981, n.p.; Patt Morrison and Marika Gerrard, "VA Lacks Data to Diagnose Delayed Stress, Panel Finds," *LAT,* Aug. 18, 1981, 1, 3; Eileen Keerdoja, Rick Rutz, and Carolyn Friday, "Fears Still Cloud Italy's Toxic Town," *Brotherhood of Vietnam Veterans, Inc. Newsletter,* Austin, Tex., March 1982, 4; "Self-Help Guide: Defoliant Agent Orange," a special issue of *TV,* Nov. 1981; Penny Pagano, "Report Assails VA Policy on Agent Orange," *LAT,* Oct. 26, 1982, part 1, 4. Documents: Larry Don Shaw, "Testimony Before the California State Assembly," op. cit., 23; Ron Bitzer, "Testimony Before the California State Assembly," op. cit., 8–9; Dr. Gary Spivey, "Testimony Before the California State Assembly" along with responses of chairman Richard E. Floyd, in *The Effects of Agent Orange and Related Herbicides on Return Vietnam Veterans,* op. cit., 93–108. Letters: Thomas Daschle and Leon Panetta to Dr. Donald Custis, July 29, 1981. The story of Tim Boyajian assaulting Dr. Spivey was related by Steve Androff during his interview.

185. Interviews: SA. Articles: "Agent Orange Linked to Birth Flaw," *NYT* story reprinted in *Orlando Sentinel,* March 15, 1996, n.p.; Evelyn Short, "The Bitter Taste of Agent Orange," op. cit., 3. Documents: "Testimony of Dr. Gary Spivey," op. cit., 96–100; Alan Cranston, Senate speech, Jan. 24, 1980, quoted in *The Effects of Agent Orange and Related Herbicides on Returning Vietnam Veterans,* op. cit., p. 24; Jeff Godoy, "Testimony to California State Assembly," in *The Effects of Agent Orange,* op. cit., 108–9; "Testimony of Ron Bitzer," op. cit., 9; "Testimony of Larry Don Shaw," op. cit., 29. Books: *TPR,* 195–96, 202; *WOW,* 403. Bob Muller's testimony before the House Veterans' Affairs Subcommittee is quoted in *WFAA,* 142–43.

6. THE RANCH HAND STUDY AND THE WORK OF DR. TON THAT TUNG

186. Interviews: TDA. Audio: Jack McCloskey's speech from Agent Orange panel, "Vietnam Reconsidered" conference, USC, Feb. 6–9, 1983. Articles: "Agent Orange Bill Passed," *VVAV,* Sept. 1983 (vol. 3, no. 4), 1; Edward Manear, "Poison or Not?", *WP* Jan. 14, 1983, A14. Documents: Major Jack Spey, USAF, ret., testimony to Congress, May 3, 1988, quoted in Joe Cole, *What's Evidence* (Olympia, Wash.: self-published, 1988), 53. Books: *WOW,* 396, 409 ("Vietnam veterans . . . should not be paid"); *TPR,* 170–77 (the relationship between Times Beach, Vietnam veterans, and H.R. 1961), 191 ("Somebody's gonna have to take him on"), 202.

187. Audio: The story of Dr. Ton That Tung's work and Dr. Kemp's quotes are from a recording of the Agent Orange panel, "Vietnam Reconsidered" conference, USC, Feb. 6–9, 1983. Articles: Glenn A. Sinclair, "Agent Orange—The Fight Continues," *VVAV,* June 1983 (vol. 3, no. 3), 1, 5. Documents: John F. Terzano, "VVA Testifies," statement before the Committee on Veterans Affairs, U.S. Senate, June 22, 1983, reprinted in *VVAV,* June 1983 (vol. 3, no. 3), 6; "Testimony of Ron Bitzer" in *The Effects of Agent Orange and Related Herbicides,* op. cit., 7; CVR press release, Aug. 17, 1981. For a recent appraisal of the continuing health effects of Agent Orange on the Vietnamese people, see Robert Dreyfuss, "Apocalypse Still," *Mother Jones,* Jan.–Feb. 2000, 42–51, 90. Books: *TPR,* 176–77, 181–84; *KAO,* 63–64.

188. Interviews: FM, 1; VY; TDA; TE, 1. Articles: Richard Severo, "Air Force Report on Vietnam War Says Laos Was Secretly Sprayed," *NYT,* Jan. 25, 1982, 1, 14; JoAnn McGrath, "Yannacone: On the Side of the Angels?" op. cit., 1, 14; Moira K. Griffin, "Poisoned Patriotism," op. cit., 23; Karen J. Payne, "Beyond Vietnam, Beyond Politics, Beyond Causes," op. cit., 52. Documents: CVR press release, Aug. 17, 1981.

7. "KEEPING THE DOOR TO THE COURTHOUSE OPEN": YANNACONE & ASSOCIATES WIN SEVERAL VICTORIES

189. Interviews: VY; FM, 1; TE, 1. Articles: John Pascal, "Battling an Agent of Tragedy," op. cit.; Phillip M. Bofey, "Agent Orange: Despite Spate of Studies, Slim Hope for Answers," *NYT,* Nov. 30, 1982,

n.p. Documents: CVR press release, Aug. 17, 1981. Books: *AOOT,* 16–17, 49–51, 54–57, 62–63, 70; *WFAA,* 39, 63, 78. The description of Judge Pratt comes from Robert W. Greene, *The Sting Man: Inside Abscam* (NY: E. P. Dutton, 1981), 261.

190. Interviews: VY. The story of the *Hoffman Trip Report* comes from my interview with Yannacone. Documents: Michael Leaveck, statement of lobbying strategy for California Assembly Bill 14, issued by office of Calif. Assemblyman Richard Floyd, Aug. 1981. Letters: Dr. James R. Clary to Senator Thomas Daschle, Sept. 9, 1988, quoted in Elmo R. Zumwalt Jr., *Report to the Secretary of Veterans Affairs The Honorable Edward J. Derwinski: First Report* (Wash., D.C.: self-published by Admiral Zumwalt, May 5, 1990), 5–6. Books: *AOOT,* 9, 66 (Judge Feinberg's dissent), 60–65, 67–71 (Pratt's 4-part scheme), 80.

8. THE "SMOKING GUN" IS FOUND, AND VIETNAM VETS GET AN IMAGE UPGRADE

191. Interviews: VY; FM, 1; TE, 1. Books: *AOOT,* 17, 74, 79–81, 99; *GIGP,* 210.

192. Interviews: VY; FM, 1. Articles: Richard Severo, "Workers Exposed to Dioxin Win $58 Million Damages," *NYT,* Aug. 27, 1982, n.p. Books: *AOOT,* 85–87 (the discovery of the "smoking gun"); *KAO,* 186. The Hercules official's memorandum, July 12, 1965, is quoted in *AOOT,* 87.

193. Interviews: RW, 1; ROM, 3, 4. Articles: Bob Greene, "Teens See Different Vietnam," *CT* column reprinted in the *Brotherhood of Vietnam Veterans, Inc. Newsletter,* March, 1982, 3–5. Bobby Muller spoke about the sea change in attitude toward Vietnam veterans beginning in 1981. Rick Weidman and many other VVA members spoke of the fierce war that began quite early in VVA between conservative and liberal factions. Muller, of course, was perceived even by the liberal members of the organization as an off-the-chart radical.

9. VVA RETURNS TO TAKE ON AGENT ORANGE, NEGOTIATIONS FALTER, AND A PLOT TAKES ROOT TO UNSEAT YANNACONE

194. Interviews: MDV; BR, 3; JL; JWA; CSM; DK. Audio: "The Claymore Polka," written and performed by Jim Wachtendonk, from *Incoming* tape, self-distributed, 1985; George Ewalt Jr., quoted on tape of Agent Orange panel, "Vietnam Reconsidered" conference, USC, Feb. 6–9, 1983. Articles: George Ewalt Jr., "Agent Orange and the Effects of the Herbicide Program," in *VR,* 191–95; Daniel Miles Kehoe, "The Long Road to Washington," *Milwaukee Magazine,* July 1982, n.p.; Daniel Miles Kehoe, "In D.C., 200 Veterans Relive War at House," *In These Times,* May 26–June 1, 1982, n.p.; "An Occasion for Reconciliation," *ND* editorial quoted in full by the Hon. Robert W. Kastenmeier in "Let the Vietnam Veterans in Arlington Cemetery," *Congressional Record,* May 11, 1982, n.p. Documents: Robert W. Kastenmeier, House Resolution 464, 97th Congress, 2nd Session, submitted May 11, 1982; "We Want You to Join!!: Point Man of the Vets' Movement," VVAW flyer, 1986; "National Salute to Vietnam Veterans," VVAW flyer, Nov. 1982. Books: *Agent Orange Dossier* (Chicago: VVAW, 1983), passim; Clark Smith, *The Vietnam Map Book: A Self-Help Guide to Herbicide Exposure* (Berkeley: Winter Soldier Archive, 1980).

195. Interviews: VY; WW; TE, 1; DK; MR; FM, 1. Books: *Agent Orange Dossier,* op. cit., 16; *AOOT,* 88–89, 95, 97–98, 99 (Pratt's ruling against the defendants), 100–101, 104–5 (Yannacone quoted on "molecular biology"). Dow's "surveillance tactics" are reported in *GIGP,* 219–20.

10. YANNACONE GOES OUT, JUDGE WEINSTEIN COMES IN, AND THE RACE TO TRIAL BEGINS

196. Interviews: VY; FM, 1; MR; TE, 2. Articles: Karl Grossman, "Suffolk Close-Up: A Case Makes a Lawyer a Star," op. cit.; "Agent Orange Case Settled, $250 Million Awarded Victims," *CS,* June 1984 (vol. 1, no. 7), 1, 7; Fred A. Wilcox, "Agent Orange: the Deadly Fog," *TV,* Feb.–March 1984 (vol. 14., no. 1) 12–13; John Lindquist, "Trial Set for Agent Orange," *TV,* Feb.–March 1984 (vol. 14, no. 1), 1–5. Books: *AOOT,* 51, 106, 111–12, 115–16, 121. Schuck's reference to Weinstein's "blinding brilliance" is in *AOOT,* 112.

197. Interviews: MR; FM, 1; LA; RW, 2. Articles: Benton Musslewhite, "Argument to the Court, March 18, 1986," in "Agent Orange Update," *Citizen Soldier,* April 1985 (vol. 1, no. 8), 4; George Dewan, "The People vs. Agent Orange," in "Punch," *SFC,* Oct. 2, 1988, 3; "Agent Orange Case Settled,"

op. cit., 1; Fred Wilcox, "Agent Orange: The Deadly Fog," op. cit., 12–13; Agnes Feak, "Report on Women Veterans: Enlisted Women in Vietnam," *VVAV,* June 1996 (vol. 16, no. 6), 11. Books: *TPR,* 178–79; *AOOT,* 59–60, 112, 113 (Weinstein quoted on the defendants' "highly doubtful liability"), 114–15, 118; *APMH,* 2. Rick Weidman pointed out to me (in our second interview) the close proximity in time between the initial release of Ranch Hand study results in early 1983 and Weinstein's subsequent decision that the plaintiffs had no evidence of causation to support their case. Weidman feels the initial Ranch Hand results, which were clearly presented in a way to favor the harmlessness of Agent Orange, were deliberately slanted to hurt the veterans' chances of winning the lawsuit.

Chapter 10: Decade of Betrayal: The Vet Centers in the Eighties

1. HORSES GET TRADED, AND THE READJUSTMENT COUNSELING PROGRAM GETS UP AND RUNNING

198. Interviews: CS, 1, 2; FSM, 1, 2; WPM; GM; JST; ROM, 3. Video: William Mahedy quoted in National Veterans Foundation promotional video, Los Angeles, 1992. Books: *CFDM,* 238; *TPR,* 68–71; *TVV,* 130–34. Cleland's description of the passage of the Vet Center bill as "horse trading" is in *TPR,* 69.

199. Interviews: FSM, 1, 2; DCR; BBR, 2; BP, MM. Articles: David Broder, "The Pork Barrel Price for Helping Vets," *WP,* June 3, 1979, n.p.; Charles R. Figley, "A Postscript: Welcoming Home the Strangers," in *SAH,* 363–67. Books: *TVV,* 133–34; *CFDM,* x; Robert S. McNamara with Brian VanDeMark, *In Retrospect: The Tragedy and Lessons of Vietnam* (NY: Times Books, 1995), xv, passim.

200. Interviews: FSM, 1, 2; DCR; TC, 4; BL; LC; MM.

2. "A CONFLICTED PROGRAM": CRAWFORD AND MESHAD GO HEAD TO HEAD

201. Interviews: TC, 4, 5; DCR; LC; BBR, 2; RFU; MF.

202. Interviews: FSM, 2; DCR; RK, conv.; BBR, 2; MF. Video: Dan Rather, 2-part series for *60 Minutes* examining the current state of the Vet Center program, 1985. Articles: George Swiers, "'Demented Vets' and Other Myths," in *VR,* 196–97.

203. Interviews: DCR; LC; FSM, 3; JST; MM; RS, 1.

3. THE PUSH TOWARD MEDICAL CREDENTIALS: CRAWFORD GETS SHOT DOWN, AND ART BLANK STEPS INTO HIS SHOES

204. Interviews: RBI, 2; MM; FSM, 3; Glenn English, March 27, 1997; Ted Mehl, March 25, 1997; Bill Lawrence, March 21, 1997.

205. Interviews: DCR; FSM, 2, 3; BBR, 2, 3; TC, 7. The story of Cranston's misunderstood "recommendation" of Blank for director of the Vet Center program was recounted by both Tim Craig and Bill Brew. The description of Blank as someone who "knew a bunch of people" comes from Brew. Articles: Arthur S. Blank Jr., "The Army, Dr. Levy, and Viet Nam," unpublished paper delivered at Hiroshima Day Rally, NYC, Aug. 5, 1967, 2–3; Arthur S. Blank Jr., "Veterans Day Speech," NYC, Nov. 11, 1967; "Viet-Nam Veterans Speak Out," VVAW's advertisement in the *NYT,* Nov. 19, 1967, read into the *Congressional Record* by Senator Ernest Gruening, Nov. 20, 1967, S16771; Henry S. Reuss, "Yale Psychologist: It's on the War in Vietnam," *Congressional Record,* Jan. 22, 1968; "Vet Centers: Contracting Effort Begins," *U.S. Medicine,* April 1, 1982 (vol. 18, no. 7), 1, 14. Documents: Arthur S. Blank Jr., "Background Questionnaire" for VVAW, early 1968; transcript of "Hearing Before a Subcommittee of the Committee on Government Operations, House of Representatives, Ninety-Seventh Congress, First Session, Oct. 21, 1981" (Wash., D.C.: Government Printing Office, 1981), 124–26; Vietnam Veterans Outreach Centers, "Eighteenth Report by the Committee on Government Operations," Dec. 11, 1981 (Wash., D.C.: Government Printing Office, 1981). Letters: Arthur S. Blank Jr. to Jan Crumb, n.d., circa early 1968.

4. THE VET CENTERS IN CRISIS: BODY COUNT, FLEEING COUNSELORS, AND A SILENT DIRECTOR

206. Interviews: DC; TA; RBI, 2; Bruce Rehmer, April 11, 1988; JC; BBR, 2; AB. During the course of my interview with Blank, he categorically denied having belonged to VVAW. Articles: Alabama Veteran

Services newsletter quoted in "Vet Centers Under Attack: Exclusive Report," *TV*, Nov.–Dec., 1982 (vol. 12, no. 4), 2; Thomas Hargrove, "Vietnam Vets Center Officials Indicted in Drug Conspiracy," *Birmingham Post-Herald*, June 5, 1982, B-12; John Sellars, "Sweet Scam," (source unidentified), circa early 1982; Sidney Bedingfield, "VA Probing Vietnam Vet Counselor Misconduct," *Birmingham Post-Herald*, Feb. 20, 1982, A6; "Files Seized, Meetings Wired: Vet Center Ambushed," *TV*, summer 1982 (vol. 12, no. 3), 13; Sidney Bedingfield, "Suspended Counselors to Continue Work," *Birmingham Post-Herald*, Feb. 24, 1982, F3; "Curry, Ashby Given Stiff Prison Sentences," *Mobile Register*, Nov. 23, 1982, B1; Alvin Benn, "Defendant Acknowledges Having an Affair with Key Prosecution Witness," *Montgomery Advertiser*, Sept. 13, 1987, 1A, 20A; Alvin Benn, "Husband, Ex-Agent Charged in Slaying," *Montgomery Advertiser*, May 15, 1987, 1A; Alvin Benn, "Ex-ABI Agent Sentenced to Life," *Montgomery Advertiser*, Sept. 16, 1987, 1A, 2A; Alvin Benn, "State Murder Trial Hot Enough for Hollywood," *Montgomery Advertiser and Alabama Journal*, Sept. 20, 1987, n.p.; "Ex-ABI Agent, Drug Informant Lose Appeal," *Mobile Press Register*, Dec. 1, 1990, 4-C. Letters: Tom Ashby to Bill Edwards, May 10, 1984; Tom Ashby to GN, March 8, 1996; Tom Ashby to GN, April 29, 1996. Books: G. David Curry, *Sunshine Patriots: Punishment and the Vietnam Offender* (Notre Dame, Ind.: Univ. of Notre Dame Press, 1985); *LTP*, 267–72, 333. For a comparison with Abscam, see Robert W. Greene, *The Sting Man: Inside Abscam* (NY: E. P. Dutton, 1981).

207. Interviews: AB; FSM, 3; MM; BBR, 2; BP. Articles: The exchanges between Blank and the veteran reporter, as well as the William Mahedy quote, are from "Vet Centers Under Attack: Exclusive Report," *TV*, Nov.–Dec. 1982 (vol. 12, no. 4), 2; John Terzano, "VVA Testifies . . . ," testimony before the U.S. House of Representatives Committee on Veterans' Affairs, March 24, 1983, reprinted in *VVAV*, May, 1983 (vol. 3, no. 2), 4–5.

5. BLANK STARTS BRINGING IN THE CENTERS, AND MESHAD AND BLANK GO TO WAR

208. Interviews: JT; LE; BBR, 2, 3; RS, 1, 2, 3; EL; HH; HLB; FSM, 3; LA; RSA. Articles: "John Terzano Testifies . . . ," *VVAV*, op. cit., 4–5; "Evans Bill to Extend Vet Center Program Approved by House," *VVAV*, June 1983 (vol. 3, no. 2), 1, 3. Documents: "Report of a Working Group on Women Vietnam Veterans and the Operation Outreach Vietnam Vet Center Program," prepared by Jane Thomson, Rose Sandecki, Lillian Barajas-Gallego, Elaine Alvarez, Claire Garcia, Myrna Solganick, Jane Ott, Lily Adams, and Lynda Van Devanter, submitted Dec. 15, 1982.

209. Interviews: AB; FSM, 3, 4, 5; BBR, 2, 3; JME; TP; THA. Video: Dan Rather, 2-part series for *60 Minutes* examining the current state of the Vet Center program, 1985. Articles: David Carver, "Father of the 'Vet Center' Program Resigns," *The Veterans Observer*, March/April 1985 (vol. 7, no. 9), 1, 4; "The Vietnam Veterans Adviser," *Penthouse*, Jan. 1988, n.p.; Mark Allen Peterson, "The Long Fight for the Vet Centers," *SAS*, Oct. 24–30, 1994, 16. Republican congressional counsel Tom Harvey and Tony Principi both spoke of urging and at times warning Blank that he had to "professionalize" the Vet Center program. Said Principi of the Vet Centers he visited: "I wouldn't trust my family to these people."

6. THE WALLER STREET VET CENTER: "THEY JUST DIDN'T KNOW HOW FAR WE'D TAKE IT"

210. Interviews: RBI, 2; JM; MO, 1; CM; LT. Articles: Larry D. Hatfield, "Veterans' Activist Dies at 53," *SFE*, Feb. 18, 1996, B-9. I was able to gather a wealth of biographical material on McCloskey by listening to the more than 100 speakers at his wake at Reilly's Funeral Home in San Francisco, Feb. 19, 1996.

211. Interviews: JM; DH; FSM, 1; SC, 1; TC, 4; FM, 3; MB; Rob Boudewijn, Dec. 10, 1988. Again, much of this material was gathered at McCloskey's wake, such as Al Rivera talking about McCloskey's 1973 arrest and his widow Lydia talking about the challenges of being married to Jack. It should be noted that Vietnam veteran Peter Cameron founded an innovative veterans' self-help group called Flower of the Dragon in Santa Rosa, California, two years before McCloskey helped to found Swords to Ploughshares. Flower of the Dragon also served as a model for the Vet Center Program as well as for many later self-help groups. McCloskey and Cameron knew each other and shared ideas but, for the most part, worked independently.

212. Interviews: JM; MSP; ES; MB; CM; FSM, 3.

7. "PROMISES TO DEAD MEN": THE POWER TO HEAL

213. Interviews: JM; MSP; FSM, 2, 3 4. Audio: tape of JM speaking on Agent Orange panel at "Vietnam Reconsidered" conference, USC, Feb. 6–9, 1983.

214. Interviews: JM; MSP; ES; FSM, 2, 3; AL. The outpouring of love for McCloskey at his wake on Feb. 19, 1996, was an astounding thing to behold. It came not just from his wife and two daughters, or coworkers like Meshad, but from hundreds of veterans whose lives he had touched. I lost count of how many veterans began their reminiscence with the words (or some variation thereof): "If it wasn't for Jack McCloskey, I wouldn't be alive today. . . ."

Chapter 11: The Price of War: Settlement of the Class Action Lawsuit and "One Small Step Toward Resolution"

1. RELENTLESS PERSUASION AND THE BIGGEST FIZZLE-OUT IN THE HISTORY OF TORT LAW

215. Interviews: TE, 2; VY; RW, 2. Articles: "Vietnam Vet Leads Court Fight Against Domestic Spray," *CS*, June 1984 (vol. 1, no. 7), 4; "Agent Orange Registry," *CS*, June 1984 (vol. 1, no. 7), 4; "Loose Threads: The Cancellation of 2,4,5-T," *CS*, June 1984 (vol. 1, no. 7), 3. Books: *AOOT*, 118–19, 122 ("forced march" to trial), 123–27, 142–48.

216. Interviews: MR; MAR; VY. Audio: tape of Dorothy Thompson speaking on Agent Orange panel, "Vietnam Reconsidered" conference, USC, Feb. 6–9, 1983; George Dewan, "The People vs. Agent Orange," in "Sunday Punch," *SFC*, Oct. 2, 1988, 3. Articles: "Loose Threads," *CS*, op. cit., 3; "Stipulation of Settlement," *CS*, June 1984 (vol. 1, no. 7), 1; Ari Press, "A Fast Deal on Agent Orange," *NW*, May 21, 1984, 56. Letters: Ron Bitzer to GN, Jan. 13, 1988. Books: *AOOT*, 150–65.

2. WEINSTEIN'S FAIRNESS HEARINGS: "I BELIEVE YOU'RE NAIVE, YOUR HONOR"

217. Interviews: MR; MAR; RBI, 2; VY; WW; TDA. Articles: George Dewan, "The People vs. Agent Orange," op. cit., 3; Karl Grossman, "Suffolk Close-Up: Victor Yannacone," op. cit.; "New $1.8 Billion Lawsuit Filed Against Uncle Sam," *CS*, April 1985 (vol. 1, no. 8), 6; "Agent Orange Settlement," *TV*, fall 1984 (vol. 14, no. 4), 8–9. Books: *AOOT*, 166–67, 173.

218. Interviews: MR; MAR; SW; JWA; BR, 3, 4; JL; Annie Bailey, Oct. 4, 1988; John Zutz, Oct. 4, 1988; ERZ. Articles: the New York veteran's remarks to Judge Weinstein ("the war is not over") are quoted in Elton Manzione, "Vets Speak Against Agent Orange," *TV*, fall 1984 (vol. 14, no. 4), 8–9; Maureen Ryan quoted in "New $1.8 Billion Lawsuit Filed Against Uncle Sam," *CS*, op. cit., 6; "Agent Orange Settlement," *TV*, op. cit., 1; "The People vs. Agent Orange," *SFC*, op. cit., 3; "Citizen Soldier Sues to Stop Agent Orange Settlement," *CS*, April 1985 (vol. 1, no. 8), 1, 6; "The Agent Orange Settlement: A Bad Deal," *CS*, April 1985 (vol. 1, no. 8) 1, 6; "Summary of Proposed Distribution Plan," *CS*, April 1985 (vol. 1, no. 8), 4; "Agent Orange Update: Benton Musslewhite Argues in Support of Motion to Set Aside Settlement (Excerpted from Argument to the Court, March 18, 1985)," *CS*, April 1985 (vol. 1., no. 8), 4. Books: *MFMS*, passim; *AOOT*, 174–77, 179–80, 189–90, 206.

3. EVERYONE GETS PAID, EXCEPT FOR MOST OF THE VETERANS

219. Interviews: TE, 2; SW; JWA; VY; WW; FM, 2; ERZ. Articles: "Agent Orange Update: Benton Musslewhite Argues in Support of Motion," *CS*, op. cit., 5; "The Agent Orange Lawsuit: A Bad Deal," *CS*, op. cit., 1, 6; "New $1.8 Billion Lawsuit Filed Against Uncle Sam," *CS*, op. cit., 6; "Summary of Proposed Distribution Plan," *CS*, op. cit., 6; George Dewan, "The People vs. Agent Orange," *SFC*, op. cit., 3; "Orangemail: Why It Got Paid," *NYT*, March 8, 1985, A34. Books: *MFMS*, 145, 154, 156, 158, 159 ("I am convinced that Agent Orange is responsible for my cancers"); *AOOT*, 194–95, 200–205; *TPR*, 187.

4. DENNIS RHOADES PUTS ON HIS BLUE JEANS, AND MORE THAN 100,000 FAMILIES GET HELP

220. Interviews: FM, 2; DR, 2, 3, 4; TE, 2. Articles: Kenneth T. Dixon, "High Court Clears Agent Orange Settlement," *The Telegram* (Bridgeport, Conn.), July 1, 1988, 1–2; Tom Condon, "For

Brandie, Vietnam May Never Be Over," *Hartford Courant,* March 9, 1985, n.p.; "Veterans Expand Agent Orange Fund," *Hartford Courant,* March 26, 1988, n.p.; Laura Palmer, "Welcome Home: Suffer the Little Ones," *NYDN,* July 10, 1988, n.p.; Linda Stowell, "Veterans Group Aids Agent Orange Victims," *Waterbury (Conn.) Republican,* March 11, 1988, n.p.; Linda Stowell, "Money Raised to Help Children of Vets Exposed to Agent Orange," *Bridgeport (Conn.) Post,* March 28, 1988, n.p. Letters: Frank McCarthy to Judge Jack Weinstein, July 5, 1988; Michele and Hank Schieb to Judge Jack Weinstein, July 11, 1988. Books: *Backgrounder: The Agent Orange Class Assistance Program* (pamphlet) (Wash., D.C.: AOCAP, 1989), 1–4; *AOOT,* 165.

221. DR, 1, 2, 3; Peter Cameron, June 20, 2000; DR, 4; BS, 2; FM, 2; Joanne Calkins, April 6, 1997. Audio: tape of Dennis Rhoades' speech at VVA National Convention, Chicago, Aug. 4, 1989. Articles: Phillip R. Kraft, "The Children of Vietnam Veterans: Complex Concerns and Innovative Solutions," in *LVV,* 428–35. Books: *Backgrounder,* op. cit., 3; *MFMS,* 153. The phrase "not even on their radar screen" was actually given to me by Bart Stichman (in our second interview), referring to the low priority veterans' causes have with the majority of humanitarian funding sources.

5. NEW STUDIES INCRIMINATE AGENT ORANGE, AND THE REAGAN WHITE HOUSE UNDERTAKES DAMAGE CONTROL

222. Interviews: MR; FM, 2, 3; DR, 1, 2; LE, 1, 2. Articles: Jack Weinstein, "Preface," in *LVV,* xi–xii; Lane Evans, "Forward," in *LVV,* ix–x; "Agent Orange Linked to Birth Flaw," *Orlando Sentinel,* March 15, 1996, n.p.; "Clinton Expands Aid for Agent Orange Victims," *SFC,* May 29, 1996, A-3. Letters: Steve Vetzner to GN, March 22, 2000. Compensation for children of Vietnam veterans with spina bifida is mandated by Public Law 104-204.

223. Interviews: TDA. Audio: tape of Mary Stout's speech at VVA's National Convention in Chicago, Aug. 4, 1989; tape of Elmo R. Zumwalt's speech on Agent Orange panel at Third Triennial Vietnam Symposium, Vietnam Center, Lubbock, Tex., April 17, 1999. Articles: "House Rejects Benefits for Agent Orange," *PI,* Oct. 20, 1988, n.p.; Peter C. Kahn, Michael Gochfeld, Martin Nygren, Marianne Hansson, Christoffer Rapp, Henry Velez, Therese Ghent-Guenther, and Wayne P. Wilson, "Dioxins and Dibenzofurans in Blood and Adipose Tissue of Agent Orange–Exposed Vietnam Veterans and Matched Controls," *JAMA,* March 18, 1988 (vol. 259, no. 11), 1661–67; Phillip Boffey, "Cancer Deaths High for Some Veterans," *NYT,* Sept. 4, 1987, A-10; Tom Daschle, "New Air Force Report Raises Questions About Health Effects of Agent Orange Exposure," news circular issued from the South Dakota Senator's office, March 21, 1988; H. F. "Sparky" Gierke quoted in "Agent Orange Linked to Tumors," *Bridgeport (Conn.) Telegram,* Nov. 11, 1988, n.p.; Michael Weisskopf, "Scientists Say Vietnam Troops Heavily Exposed to Defoliant," *WP,* Jan. 25, 1989, n.p.; David Arnold, "Infant Mortality Found Much Higher in Areas Sprayed with Agent Orange," *BG,* Nov. 17, 1988, 17 (includes quotes from Dr. Le Cao Dai and Dr. Arnold Schecter); Repps Hudson, "Sad Aftermath of War: Jars Filled with Fetuses," *SLPD,* Jan. 5, 1989 (description of Dr. Nguyen Thi Ngoc Phuong's work); Barton F. Stichman, "Between the Courts and Congress: Leveraging VA Benefits or the Agent Orange Plaintiff Class," in *LVV,* 300–316; Bob Egelko, "Judge Hears Vets Protest VA's Agent Orange Benefits," *Daily Journal,* Jan. 1, 1989, n.p. Books: *TPR,* 193–208, 214–18; *WOW,* 365, 385–87, 407–12. The work of the Stellmans and the hostile reactions to it are reported in *TPR,* 203–6, and in *WOW,* 411–12. The testimony from Congressman Ted Weiss's oversight hearing in which Dr. Houk concedes that it was pressure from the White House Agent Orange Working Group that caused the CDC to begin "closing out all activities to the Agent Orange Exposure Study" is reproduced in *TPR,* 215–16. A portion of the secret OMB directive that led Ronald Reagan to oppose Agent Orange compensation (and which Admiral Zumwalt claimed to have read in full) is quoted in *WOW,* 387. Colin Powell's remarks about Ronald Reagan were made at the Republican National Convention and nationally televised on Aug. 12, 1996.

6. "THE CURSES OF WITCHES AND WARLOCKS": THE VA TIPS THE SCALES, THEN ADMIRAL ZUMWALT CUTS THE KNOT

224. Interviews: DA, 2; BS, 1. Articles: Barton F. Stichman, "Between the Courts and Congress," op. cit., 6–7, 14; Ken Jedermann, "VA Agent Orange Regulations Challenged in Lawsuit," *SAS,* Jan. 16, 1989, 1, 12; "VVA Sues Over AO Rules," in *VVA on Agent Orange,* pamphlet (Wash., D.C.:

Vietnam Veterans of America, 1988), 10–11; "Viet Vets Try New Tactic on Agent Orange Claims," *SFC*, Jan. 10, 1989; Norman Melnick, "Agent Orange Cases Ordered Reevaluated," *SFE*, May 9, 1989, A1, A24; Harriet Chiang, "New Ruling Revives Agent Orange Suits," *SFC*, May 9, 1989, A5; "VA Issues Regulations for Evaluation of Dioxin Studies" in *The Agent Orange Review*, May, 1990 (Vol. 7, No. 2), 2. Documents: "Fifth Annual Report," Agent Orange Class Assistance Program, Wash., D.C., Nov. 1993, 10. Letters: Mary Stout, open letter to "Friends of VVA," n.d., in *VVA on Agent Orange*, 1. Documents: Public Law 98-542, "Veterans' Dioxin and Radiation Exposure Act," 98th Congress, passed into law Oct. 24, 1984. Books: *TPR*, 208. Dr. Lawrence Hobson's remarks about the alleged harmful effects of dioxin being like "black magic . . . the result of ill-intentioned witches and warlocks" are quoted in Stichman, "Between the Courts and Congress," op. cit., 9.

225. Interviews: ERZ; AS, 1; LE, 2. Audio: tape of Elmo Zumwalt Jr.'s talk on the Agent Orange panel at the Third Triennial Vietnam Symposium, Vietnam Center, Lubbock, Tex., April 17, 1999 (contains many of the quotes in this section, including "duty, honor, intelligence, and compassion"; Monsanto "fraudulently concocting" studies on the harmlessness of Agent Orange; accusations of "deception and fraud" and "political interference"; and "If I live, we'll get close to that 28"); tape of Arnold Schecter's talk on Agent Orange panel at Third Triennial Vietnam Symposium, April 17, 1999. Dr. Schecter corroborated almost all of Admiral Zumwalt's charges about major scientific organizations, such as the Toxicology Committee, repeatedly softening their initial assessments of dioxin's toxicity. Articles: "Secretary Names Zumwalt as Advisor on Agent Orange," *The Agent Orange Review*, May 1990 (vol. 7, no. 2), 3; Barton F. Stichman, "Between the Courts and Congress," op. cit., 14–16; Arnold Schecter, "Agent Orange and Dioxin," handout at Third Triennial Vietnam Symposium, Vietnam Center, Lubbock, Tex., April 17, 1999; Jim Reckner, "Admiral Elmo R. Zumwalt Ill," *Friends of the Vietnam Center*, Nov. 1999 (vol. 6, no. 3), 1-2; Richard Goldstein, "Elmo R. Zumwalt Jr., Admiral Who Modernized the Navy, Is Dead at 79," *NYT*, Jan. 3, 2000, A17; "Admiral Who Ordered Use of Agent Orange Dies," *SFC*, Jan. 3, 2000, A5. Documents: Admiral Elmo R. Zumwalt Jr., "Report to the Secretary of Veterans Affairs the Honorable Edward J. Derwinski from the Special Assistant Agent Orange Issues, First Report," May 5, 1990 (Wash., D.C., self-published by Elmo R. Zumwalt). Books: *OW*, passim; *MFMS*, passim. The Navy recently honored Admiral Zumwalt's enormous contributions to the American military and to the medical care of the nation's veterans by naming a new class of destroyers (DD-21) after him.

7. A NEW STANDARD FOR VETERANS IS CREATED . . . BY A NEW WAR

226. Interviews: ERZ; LE, 2. Articles: John M. Broder, "VA to Pay Some Agent Orange Cancer Claims," *LAT*, March 30, 1990, A1, A24 (contains Miles S. Epling's quote about "one small step"); "Derwinski Approves Compensation for Soft Tissue Sarcoma; Secretary Acts in Response to Advisory Group Finding," *The Agent Orange Review*, Aug. 1990 (vol. 7, no. 3), 1; Barton F. Stichman, "Between the Courts and Congress," op. cit. 16–18; "Veterans Sue Over Agent Orange Study," *LAT*, Aug. 3, 1990, A20; "Veterans Study" in "Nation Line" in *USAT*, Nov. 13, 1990, 3A; "President Bush Signs Agent Orange Act of 1991," *The Agent Orange Review*, April 1991 (vol. 8, no. 2), 1–2. Documents: House Committee on Government Operations, *The Agent Orange Cover-up: A Case of Flawed Science and Political Manipulation, Twelfth Report, Together with Dissenting Views*, Aug. 9, 1990 (Wash., D.C.: Government Printing Office), passim. Books: *TPR*, 223–24.

8. A NEW GENERATION OF VETERANS LEARNS FROM THE UNFINISHED BUSINESS OF THE LAST ONE

227. Interviews: RK, 3; DFA; Erik Larsen, March 10, 1996; LE, 2. Articles: Edward W. Said, "Behind Saddam Hussein's Moves," *CSM*, Aug. 13, 1990, n.p.; Josh Meyer, "Ron Kovic Calls for Pullout from Gulf," in "Metro News," *LAT*, Aug. 23, 1990, B12; Col. David Hackworth, "Americans Take Sides," *NW*, Nov. 26, 1990, 31–32; "Ex-POW: Gulf Troops Are Uneasy," *USAT*, Nov. 13, 1990, 2A; William J. Eaton, "Ex-Admiral Projects 10,000 U.S. Deaths in a 6-Month Iraq War," *LAT*, Nov. 28, 1990, A8; Ronald L. Soble, "1,500 Attend Teach-In Against Gulf Presence," *LAT*, Dec. 17, 1990, n.p.; Tahan K. Jones, "Marine Corporal Tahan K. Jones Speaks," in *Bring the Troops Home Now!* (newsletter published by Committee Against a Vietnam War in the Middle East), Jan. 1991 (vol. 2, no. 1), 3; "No More Vietnams," an unpublished essay circulated by an anonymous Vietnam veteran

at anti–Gulf War rallies in the San Francisco Bay Area, circa Jan. 1991; Amy Wallace, "Marine in Growing List of Enlisted Objectors," *LAT,* Nov. 27, 1990, A3, A26; "Statement of Unity" in *Support Jeff Paterson,* a pamphlet distributed by U.S. Out of the Persian Gulf, Dec. 14, 1991, 5; J. E. Geovanis, "When John M. Came Marching Home," *Chicago Reader,* Jan. 17, 1992 (vol. 21, no. 15), 1–22; Alex Molnar, "If My Marine Son Is Killed," *NYT,* Aug. 23, 1990, n.p.; William Matthews, "Relatives Unite to Oppose Offensive Action," *Navy Times,* Oct. 29, 1990, 18; William J. Eaton, "House Passes Agent Orange Claims Funding," *LAT,* Jan. 30, 1991, A1, A21; Sonny Montgomery quoted in "President Bush Signs Agent Orange Act of 1991," *The Agent Orange Review,* April 1991 (vol. 8, no. 2), 2. Documents: *Newswire,* newsletter of the Military Families Support Network, fall 1991 (vol. 1, no. 3). Letters: Ron Kovic, open letter to President George Bush, Aug. 22, 1990.

228. Interviews: DFA; LE, 2; FM, 3; DR, CK; LA; LVD. Articles: Mark Allen Peterson, "'Stress' Likely Cause of Gulf Illnesses," *SAS,* Nov. 18–24, 1996 (vol. 119, no. 47), 1, 15; David Brown and Bill McAllister, "'Gulf War Syndrome' Not Found," *SFC,* Nov. 4, 1996, A-3; "Dispute Over 'Stress' Diagnosis for Gulf War Vets' Ailments," *SFC,* Nov. 21, 1996, A8; "President Bush Signs Agent Orange Act of 1991," *The Agent Orange Review,* op. cit., 1; Philip Shenon, "2 Studies Confirm Gulf War Syndrome," *SFC,* Nov. 26, 1996, A5; Barton F. Stichman, "Between the Courts and Congress," op. cit., 18, 20, 23–24; John Wheeler quoted in William J. Eaton, "Ex-Admiral Projects 10,000 U.S. Deaths in a 6-Month Iraq War," op. cit., A8; William J. Eaton, "House Passes Agent Orange Claims Funding," op. cit., A1, A21; "Vietnam Veterans Win Agent Orange Battle," *Orlando Sentinel,* July 28, 1993, A11; Christine Gorman, "Agent Orange Redux," *Time,* Aug. 9, 1993, 51; "Agent Orange Compensation," *Time,* Oct. 11, 1993, 20; "Agent Orange Special Treatment Authority Extended" and "NAS Review Ongoing," in *The Agent Orange Review,* May, 1995 (vol. 11, no. 2), 1; "Clinton Expands Aid for Agent Orange Victims," *SFC,* May 29, 1996, A3; "President Clinton Announces New Benefits; VA Will Recognize Prostate Cancer, Nerve Disorder, Propose Birth Defect Legislation" and "Secretary of Veterans Affairs Jesse Brown on President Clinton's Agent Orange Announcement" in *The Agent Orange Review,* Aug. 1996 (vol. 12, no. 1), 1; Robert Pear, "Parents of 260,000 Children Told Disability Checks May End," *SFC,* Nov. 28, 1996, A-11; Lane Evans ("kinder and gentler bureaucracy") quoted in "Opening Rounds: Victory: VVA Wins A/O Judgment," *VVAV,* June 1989 (vol. 9, no. 6), 6, 11, 22–23, 28; Steven Lee Myers, "Survey Links Gulf War Syndrome to Nerve-Gas Antidote," *NYT,* Oct. 19, 1999, n.p.; Sabin Russell, "Nerve Gas Pill Was Called Suspicious 2 Years Ago," *SFC,* Oct. 20, 1995, A2; "Veterans Organization to Push Gulf War Syndrome Bill," Armed Forces Newswire Service, Nov. 10, 1999; "Gulf War Syndrome Tied to Brain Damage," *Marin Independent Journal,* Dec. 1, 1999, A3. Documents: Dan Fahey, *Policy Paper on the Use of Depleted Uranium in Ammunition,* prepared for the Military Toxics Project, Wash., D.C., Dec. 15, 1999. Letters: Carolyn Fulco and Cathy Liverman, NAS, IOM, to Dan Fahey, Jan. 11, 2000; Dan Fahey to Steve Fox, GAO, Jan. 22, 2000; Dan Fahey to Lane Evans, Jan. 22, 2000; Steve Vetzner to GN, March 22, 2000. Books: David Harris, *Our War: What We Did in Vietnam and What It Did to Us* (NY: Times Books, 1996), 166. The "money had a lot to do" quote is from Dan Fahey. The final question, of course, comes from the Psalms of David, 13:1.

THE LONG VIEW OF HISTORY: AN EPILOGUE

229. Interviews: RW, 2; SC, 4. Articles: "Taps," a recurring feature in *VVAV* since 1995, in which former Army chaplain Reverend Phil Salois compiles obituaries of Vietnam veterans from around the nation; Bill McAllister, "Future of VA Hospitals Tied to Ft. Lyon Ruling," *DP,* Aug. 31, 1999, 1A, 15A; Bob Maras and Rick Weidman, "Interview: Dr. Thomas Garthwaite, Acting Under Secretary for Veterans Health Administration," *VVAV,* Oct.–Nov. 1999 (vol. 19, no. 10–11), 20–21, 44; "Valley Voices: Vets Bemoan Diminished Facilities," *LAT,* Nov. 7, 1999, B-21; Robert Pear, "VA Medical Mistakes: 700 Dead in 2 Years," *SFE,* Dec. 19, 1999, A1, A18. Larry Margasak, "'Chaos,' Mismanagement at Veterans Agency," *SFC,* Jan. 19, 2000, A10. Arthur Wilson's quotes are from Richard T. Cooper, "Vets Still Conflicted Over Korea," *LAT,* Jan. 19, 2000, A1, A10; Jordan Lite, "VA Must Review Agent Orange Cases," AP wire story, Feb. 12, 1999; Philip Shenon, "Air Force Report Links Agent Orange to Diabetes," *NYT,* March 29, 2000, A23. Documents: press release from the National Veterans Legal Services Program, Feb. 11, 1999. Letters: Angel Almedina to

GN, April 24, 1989. Books: *Vietnam Veterans of America Foundation Annual Report* (Wash., D.C.: VVAF, 1999). Rick Weidman was the source of most of the VA statistics in this section. There is now an Angel Almedina Veteran Service Award given yearly at the "Still Hidden Client" conference held each May at Hunter College in New York City. The conference is sponsored by a coalition of VA and regional veterans' service organizations, and the recipient can be "anyone whose work in the community or with individuals has significantly assisted those who suffer from the trauma of war." It is "presented in the spirit of Mr. Angel Almedina, whose service to survivors of the Vietnam War made a significant difference in the lives of many."

Acknowledgments

Looking back on this extraordinary twelve-year journey, it is hard to know where to start in making acknowledgments—or to be plain about it, giving thanks. Well over a thousand people have contributed significantly toward making this book a reality, and the sad prospect is that, with the best of intentions and a fifty-year-old's failing memory, I am sure to miss many dozens of them here. To those who should be included in my list of debts but aren't, my deepest apologies, and a round of drinks (alcoholic or otherwise) next time we meet.

At the top of my list of helpers I must put Ron Kovic, Ron Bitzer, Bobby Muller, Barry Romo, Shad Meshad, and Tim Craig. All of them are born networkers, and all of them put me in touch with scores of other people critical to my project. Bill Ehrhart gave me entrée to the Philadelphia area activists, as John Lindquist did in Wisconsin and Jack McCloskey in the San Francisco Bay Area. Other people provided vast resources of paper archives: Jan Barry and Carl Rogers, who still have much GI movement and early VVAW paperwork; Scott Camil, who retains perhaps the most complete file on the Gainesville Eight; Bill Unger, who loaned me the American Veterans Movement archive; Ron Bitzer, who loaned me the Center for Veterans' Rights archive; Barry Romo and John Lindquist, who made a great deal of later VVAW material available to me; Stuart Feldman, who collected all of the important press on the Vietnam veterans' movement from the 1970s; Shad Meshad and Chaim Shatan, who offered a wealth of material on the evolution of a post-traumatic stress definition and the founding of the Vet Centers; Jonathan Steinberg, who copied a wealth of congressional documents for me; Joe Bangert, Wayne Wilson, Joe Cole, and Frank McCarthy, who provided volumes of material on Agent Orange; and Bobby Muller, who opened his Vietnam Veterans of America files to me.

Special thanks to John Kerry, David Addlestone, and a number of pro bono lawyers who banged on the door of the FBI (with letters and phone calls) for ten years, till it finally coughed up the ten-foot stack of surveillance files on Vietnam Veterans Against the War, which I had applied for in 1988 through the Freedom of Information Act.

Others loaned or gave me access to archives that I had intended to use for this book, but when the book grew beyond my naive expectations into a 2,000-page manuscript—with numerous publishers, editors, and two different agents all pulling out their hair in distress at what to do with me and "it"—several key areas had to be abandoned to a later book or books—notably, the GI movement, the POW/MIA movement, healing through art (the enormous range of books, films, and graphic art that have come out of Vietnam), and the international veterans' movement, which has led Vietnam veterans to Central America, the Soviet Union, and back to Southeast Asia in droves to continue their healing and the work they have undertaken to heal others with similar pain and needs. Even though those sections did not make it into *Home to War,* I owe thanks especially to Dave Cline and Keith Mather for GI movement materials; to Earl Hopper and Jimmie Butler for POW/MIA materials; to a whole range of Vietnam veteran writers and artists who shared their work process with me, especially Larry Rottmann, Steve Hassna, and Wayne Karlin, none of whose names is as well known as they deserve to be; and to Brian Willson, Asa Baber, Larry Heinemann, Freddy Champagne, Steven Stratford, Scott Rutherford, Steve Brooks, the Bill Motto Post of the Veterans of Foreign Wars, and Boston's Smedley Butler Brigade, all of whom have contributed materials concerning the international movement.

A few brave souls served as my Beatrice through the dark wood and fiercely burning fires of the veterans' movement. To them goes a deeply personal thanks for sustaining my spirit (and occasionally my body) through some very difficult periods: Ron Kovic, Larry Heinemann, Asa Baber, Ron Bitzer, and Tim Craig.

There were also numerous non-veterans who helped me on my many pilgrimages crisscrossing the country in search of research materials and interviews—folks who put me up, gave me a work space and a telephone, and the camaraderie I needed to keep going. Foremost among these people are Brad Parker in Boston, Dr. John Zielinski and Dr. Jack Kowalski in Chicago, and Suzanne Shelhart in Marin County, California. Perhaps the most generous of all was Hollywood historian Lee Harris. When my first wife, Marcy, and I were temporarily homeless in Southern California, I was reduced to carrying the entire Vietnam veterans' movement (or should I say, a facsimile of it, preserved in dozens of boxes of papers and over 500 audiotapes) in the backseat and trunk of our two cars. Fearing we would be broken into and years of research lost forever, Lee offered to store the materials in his home till we found a place of our own.

This book would not exist at all if not for the diligent work of an army of tape-transcriptionists. I ended up with over 1,000 hours of audiotaped interviews; and since it can often take eight hours to carefully transcribe one hour of audiotape, the job of making sound readable on paper or, later, diskette was vast. For the first year, I was fortunate to have a virtual full-time volunteer: Mark Frazel. Over the next nine years, by far the biggest part of the job was done by Carol Tingle—with phenomenal accuracy.

Money was always a major problem. There were three small advances from the first three publishers (although the third publisher asked for their money back when they cancelled the book); but *Home to War* would not have been finished without grants from the William Joiner Center for the Study of War and Social Consequences at the University of Massachusetts, Boston, the Link Foundation, and the Vietnam Veterans of America Foundation (VVAF). In addition, VVAF provided a hotel room and free telephone on several occasions when I was working in Washington, D.C. I also need to thank Jeff Mackler for hosting a benefit for the book in Oakland, and Country Joe McDonald and Maxine Hong Kingston for volunteering as the star attractions. There were scores of individual donors—from homeless vets to rich rock stars—to whom this book, and myself, are deeply indebted.

And, of course, endless gratitude to the librarians throughout the country who have helped me find needed materials, most especially those who manage the huge collection of Vietnam-related documents at the State Historical Society in Madison, Wisconsin.

Finally, I wish to thank all those individuals who allowed me to interview them, who gave not only of their precious time but also shared a precious part of their lives as well. They are the real heroes of this book: Brian Adams, Lily Adams, David Addlestone, Linda Alband, Angel Almedina, Tom Amirante, Tim Andrews, Steve Androff, Tim Andruss, Ron Armistead, Trisha Arms, Tom Ashby, Ed Asner, Asa Baber, Annie Bailey, Joe Bangert, Randy Barnes, Yosh Barnes, James Barnett, Jan Barry, Mike Beanan, Norma Becker, John Beitzel, Roy Benavidez, Ben Benet, Bill Bennett, Steve Bentley, Ken Berez, Tom Bird, Carl Bissinger, Ron Bitzer, Jon Bjornson, Arthur S. Blank Jr., Mike Blecker, Linda Block, Don Bodey, Dave Bonior, Robert Borden, Rob Boudewijn, Father Roy Bourgeois, Kevin Bowen, Dennis Boyer, Richard Boyle, Horace Leon Bracy, James Bradshaw, Bill Branson, Bill Brew, John Briggs, Douglas Brinkley, Steve Brooks, Joseph Bruch, Thomas Burch, Terry Burke, Jim Bush, George Butler, Jimmie Butler, Jan Butterfield, Alfredo Cabrera, Ray Cage, Joanne Calkins, Rich Camacho, Peter Cameron, Sally Camil, Scott Camil, Sherry Camil, Ken Campbell, Walter Capps, John Catterson, Frank Cavestani, Fred Champagne, Steve Champlin, Sam Cherry, Noam Chomsky, David Christian, Maryann Clark, Nancy Clarke, Tom Cleaver, Charles Clements, Dave Cline, Ken Cloke, Jill Cochran, Reverend William Sloane Coffin, Jim Colaneri, Joe Cole, Jack Colhoun, Gerry Condon, Dean Contover, Tom Corey, David Cortright, Bruce Coslor, Paul Cox, Tim Craig, Joan Craigwell, Bestor Cram, Bill Crandell, Alan Cranston, Jeffrey Crafts, Don Crawford, Jim Credle, Lee Crump, Dave Culmer, Dave Curry, Ed Damato, Thomas Daschle, Michael Daily, Bill Davis, Ed Deaton, Louis De Benedette, Skip Delano, David Dellinger, Maude DeVictor, Tony Diamond, John Dickerson, Fred Downs, Frank Dufner, Donald Duncan, Rick Duvall, Lee Edel, Fritz Efaw, Paul Egan,

Arthur Egendorf, W. D. Ehrhart, Daniel Ellsberg, Gloria Emerson, Glenn English, Tod Ensign, Pam Escarcega, Dave Evans, Lane Evans, Dan Fahey, John Fairbank, Stuart Feldman, Leslie Feldstein, Mike Felker, Ron Ferrizzi, Charles R. Figley, John M. Finn, Mike Fischman, Tom Fischer, Larry Fisher, Mack Fleming, Ron Flesch, Louis Font, Steve Fournier, Danny Friedman, Marvin Friedman, Matthew Friedman, Richard Fuller, Joan Furey, Bob Galbraith, David Gallup, Gerry Genesio, Judy Genesio, Philip Gioia, Diana Glasgow, Walt Glocke, Mike Gold, Ruben Gomez, Dave Grady, Joel Greenberg, Chris Gregory, P. J. Griffin, Anthony Guarisco, Tim Hagelin, Jim Halassa, Sarah Haley, Robert Hall, Elizabeth Hallett, Larry Halpern, Gib Halverson, Bob Hansen, Tim Hansen, Juanita Harrington, David Harris, Husher Harris, John Hart, Tom Harvey, Steve Hassna, Tom Hayden, Le Ly Hayslip, Larry Heinemann, Seymour Hersh, Joe Hertel, Ted Heselton, Anne Hirschman, Mary Holub, Earl Hopper, Al Hubbard, Jeff Huch, Tom Hurwitz, Dick Ihlenfeld, Max Inglett, Jim Janko, Stoney Jeffries, Butch Joeckel, George Johnson, Norman Johnson, Greg Kane, Wayne Karlin, Tom Katenay, Bill Kaye, John Keaveny, Tom Keeney, Michael Kelley, John Keogh, John Forbes Kerry, Mark Kissella, Robert Klein, Bob Koenig, Bessel Van der Kolk, Chris Kornkven, Ron Kovic, Dennis Kroll, Richard Kulka, Olga Kvasova, Gordie Lane, Erik Larsen, Robert Laufer, Bill Lawrence, Bill Lawson, Bob Leong, Michael Leaveck, Bill Lewis, Robert Jay Lifton, Forest Rusty Lindley, John Lindquist, Charles Liteky, Bob Livesy, Meg Livesy, Danny Lliteras, Jim Long, Chavel Lopez, Ed Lord, Mike Lowry, Lee Lubinski, Edna Lucano, Annie Luginbill, John Luvender, Jack Lynch, David Lynn, Din Magomed-Eminov, William Mahedy, Peter Mahoney, Yael Margolin, Job Mashariki, Patience Mason, Robert Mason, Keith Mather, Mike Maxwell, Jim Maye, Jim Mayer, Dennis McBride, Carl McCardin, Frank McCarthy, Pat McClellan, Jack McCloskey, Country Joe McDonald, Gordie McKay, Guy McMichael III, David McReynolds, Ted Mehl, Carlos Melendrez, Jerry Melnyk, Roger Melton, Louanne Merkle, Harry Meserve, Floyd "Shad" Meshad, John Messmore, Marvin Meyers, Craig Scott Moore, Madeleine Moore, Skip Morgan, Bob Mulholland, Robert O. Muller, John Mulligan, David Munro, Duncan Murphy, Ed Murphy, John Musgrave, Hal Muskat, Graham Nash, Holly Near, Vince Nobile, Jim Noonan, Don North, Bill O'Brien, Dennis O'Brien, Tim O'Brien, Per-Olof Odman, Rick O'Dell, Bill O'Hara, Michael Oliver, Peter Orris, Jim Packer, Mike Pahios, Danaan Parri, Ray Parrish, Greg Payton, Jim Pechin, Bruce Pentland, Don Perdue, Lucy Phenix, Foster Phillips, Ron Phillips, Douglas Pike, Mary Sue Planck, Ron Podlaski, Ray Pozzi, John Clark Pratt, Tony Principi, Bryan Quinlan, Sheldon Ramsdell, Louise Ransom, Bruce Rehmer, Jane Reutershan, Dennis Rhoades, Pete Rivas, Skip Roberts, Richard Rocco, Carl Rogers, Ed Rogers, Barry Romo, Lenny Rotman, Larry Rottmann, Sam Russo, Tony Russo, Scott Rutherford, Maureen Ryan, Michael Ryan, Ron Sable, Rusty Sachs, Rose Sandecki, Al

Santoli, Arnold Schecter, Robert Scheer, William Schlenger, Ralph Schoenman, Rick Schoos, John Schuchardt, Marla Schorr, Sam Schorr, Jeff Schutts, Eric Schwartz, Jan Scruggs, Ray Scurfield, Tony Seldin, Ted Sexauer, Chaim Shatan, Steve Sherlock, Tom Sherwood, Bill Shunas, Ellie Shunas, Dave Silk, Patty Skelly, Lee Sloan, Clark Smith, Gordon Smith, Jack Smith, Loretta Smith, Winnie Smith, Wayne Smith, Jim Snelling, Jimmy Sparrow, Don Sproehnle, Wilson Sproehnle, Jerry Starr, Morton Stavis, Nancy Stearns, Barbara Stec, Jonathan Steinberg, Barton F. Stichman, Gene Stimmel, Ian Stirton, Mary Stout, Steven Stratford, Phil Straw, Steve Suwalsky, Robert Swanson, John Swensson, John Talbott, Susan Talbott, Vlad Tamarov, Craig Taylor, Wallace Terry, John Terzano, Paul Thompson, Lee Thorn, David Thorne, Rick Tingling-Clemmons, Dave Trucello, Bill Unger, Nguyen Dinh Uoc, John Upton, Joe Urgo, Larry Vaughn, Lynda Van Devanter, Tom Vallely, Tony Velez, Jim Wachtendonk, Sukie Wachtendonk, Bob Waddell, Winston Warfield, James Webb, Bruce Webster, Rick Weidman, John Wheeler, Bill White, June Willenz, Tom Williams, Brian Willson, John Wilson, Wayne Wilson, Lynn Witt, Wayne Wittmann, Leroi Wolins, Mike Woloshin, Michael Wong, Dennis R. Wyant, Tom Wynn, Victor Yannacone Jr., Igor Zakhrov, Tom Zangrilli, Johanna Zangrilli, Pete Zastrow, Joseph Zengerle, Elmo R. Zumwalt Jr., and John Zutz.

This book owes its final form to the work of many editors. Among the more notable, Walt Bode, Bryan Oettel, and Allan Peacock all saw the book through some of its early stages. It was Philip Turner's vision that brought *Home to War* to Random House, and it was Chris Jackson who did the last, intensive, line-by-line march through the book, fighting his own war with a dauntingly large text to help clarify facts and sharpen meaning wherever possible and to keep the story focused always on the soldiers who fought in Vietnam, rather than let it get lost in politics and passion, which it is still so easy to do with that war.

Thanks to my agent Deborah Schneider for sticking with this project through thick and thin.

Finally, more thanks than I can ever say to my wife, Ellen, and our two children, Amy (Wu Ji) and Peter, who have helped in untold ways and who have shown an unbelievable patience with the thousands of hours I have had to be away from them to complete this book. This is also the place to remember my mother, Sylvia Anna Fremer Nicosia, who died just as this book was being finished, and who had supported it in every possible way, including financially, until she was incapacitated by a stroke in 1995.

Thanks, above all, to God, through whose grace come all good things and, prayerfully, an end to the pain of war.

GERALD NICOSIA
Corte Madera, California
July 31, 2000

Index

About the Author

GERALD NICOSIA's *Memory Babe: A Critical Biography of Jack Kerouac* won the Distinguished Young Writer Award from the National Society of Arts and Letters and is still regarded as definitive almost two decades after its publication. His poetry and literary criticism have been widely published, and he frequently lectures and gives readings of his own work. He also taught writing and literature at both the University of Illinois in Chicago and UCLA. In addition, he helped collect, edit, and publish the work of other, lesser-known Beat Generation writers, such as Bob Kaufman and Jack Micheline. Having grown up and begun his career in Chicago, he currently lives in the San Francisco Bay Area with his wife and two children.